COLLECTED WORKS OF JOHN STUART MILL

VOLUME VI

The Collected Edition of the works of John Stuart Mill has been planned and is being directed by an editorial committee appointed from the Faculty of Arts and Science of the University of Toronto, and from the University of Toronto Press. The primary aim of the edition is to present fully collated texts of those works which exist in a number of versions, both printed and manuscript, and to provide accurate texts of works previously unpublished or which have become relatively inaccessible.

Editorial Committee

J. M. ROBSON, *General Editor*

V. W. BLADEN, HARALD BOHNE, ALEXANDER BRADY,
J. C. CAIRNS, J. B. CONACHER, D. P. DRYER,
FRANCESS HALPENNY, SAMUEL HOLLANDER, JEAN HOUSTON,
MARSH JEANNERET, R. F. MCRAE, F. E. L. PRIESTLEY

Essays on England, Ireland, and the Empire

by JOHN STUART MILL

Editor of the Text
JOHN M. ROBSON
Professor of English,
Victoria College, University of Toronto

Introduction by
JOSEPH HAMBURGER
Professor of Political Science,
Yale University

UNIVERSITY OF TORONTO PRESS
ROUTLEDGE & KEGAN PAUL

82102924

© *University of Toronto Press* 1982
Toronto and Buffalo
Printed in Canada

ISBN 0-8020-5572-9

London: Routledge & Kegan Paul
ISBN 0-7100-9277-6

Canadian Cataloguing in Publication Data
Mill, John Stuart, 1806–1873.
Collected works
Includes bibliographies.
Contents: v. 6. Essays on England, Ireland, and the empire / editor of the text John M. Robson; introduction by Joseph Hamburger.
ISBN 0–8020–5572–9
1. Philosophy – Collected works. 2. Political science – Collected works. 3. Economics – Collected works. I. Robson, John M., 1927–
B1602.A2 1963   192   C64-188-2 rev.

This volume has been published
with the assistance of a grant
from the Social Sciences
and Humanities Research Council
of Canada

Contents

INTRODUCTION, by Joseph Hamburger	vii
TEXTUAL INTRODUCTION, by J. M. Robson	liv
Brodie's History of the British Empire (1824)	1
Ireland (1825)	59
The Game Laws (1826)	99
Intercourse between the United States and the British Colonies in the West Indies (1828)	121
Notes on the Newspapers (1834)	149
The Close of the Session (1834)	281
Postscript to the London Review, No. 1 (1835)	289
Parliamentary Proceedings of the Session (1835)	295
Postscript: The Close of the Session (1835)	309
State of Politics in 1836 (1836)	319
Walsh's Contemporary History (1836)	329
Fonblanque's England under Seven Administrations (1837)	349
Parties and the Ministry (1837)	381
Radical Party and Canada: Lord Durham and the Canadians (1838)	405
Lord Durham and His Assailants (1838)	437
Lord Durham's Return (1838)	445
Reorganization of the Reform Party (1839)	465
What Is to Be Done with Ireland? (1848?)	497
England and Ireland (1868)	505

APPENDICES

Appendix A. England and Ireland: First Draft (1867–68)	535
Appendix B. List of Titles of "Notes on the Newspapers" (1834)	544
Appendix C. Textual Emendations	546
Appendix D. Bibliographic Index of Persons and Works Cited, with Variants and Notes	550

INDEX 669

FACSIMILES

Folio 1r of "What Is to Be Done with Ireland?" MS The King's School, Canterbury	500
Folio 3r of draft of *England and Ireland* MS Houghton Library, Harvard University	510

Introduction

JOSEPH HAMBURGER

MILL THE PHILOSOPHER, the economist, the general essayist and critic appears here in yet another capacity—as a radical journalist and party politician. Most of the articles in this volume were written to define the purpose of, and give direction to, the Radical party in Parliament during the 1830s; and even the articles on Ireland and the early articles on other subjects provide evidence of Mill's radical inclinations at other times, though, of course, Mill's discussion of Ireland is also important in the history of English controversy about that island. Most of these essays were written for journals that Mill helped to establish: the *Westminster Review*, the *Parliamentary History and Review*, the *London Review*, and the *London and Westminster Review*. The only exceptions were the independently published pamphlet *England and Ireland*, and his contributions to the *Monthly Repository*, which was edited by his friend, the Radical and Unitarian, William Johnson Fox. His successive contributions to each of these journals is closely related to the history of Benthamite radicalism; and, especially when combined with his correspondence, they show that Mill's radicalism during the 1820s and 1830s defined a distinct and important episode in his life, and that he participated in events significant in parliamentary history. This introduction, except for the last part on Ireland, describes Mill's radicalism during this early period, including his rationale for a Radical party, and his activities on behalf of that party during the 1830s. It also, in describing the relation of the mental crisis to his radicalism, shows that his resolution of the crisis allowed him to continue working and writing for the radical cause despite the changes in outlook and political philosophy that accompanied it.

Since most of the articles in this volume deal with party programmes and tactics, they emphatically belong in the realm of practice, and they are markedly different from the theoretical writings on politics that we usually associate with Mill.[1] Practically oriented as these articles were, however, they also had a theoretical

---

[1]See *Essays on Politics and Society, Collected Works* [*CW*], XVIII-XIX (Toronto: University of Toronto Press, 1977).

dimension, for he promoted a political enterprise with arguments that originated in Benthamite political philosophy. Mill's radicalism, as an extension of the Benthamite position, is readily distinguished from other radical doctrines. Its principled basis allowed him to claim that it was uniquely philosophic, and thus it justified his invention and use of the phrase "Philosophic Radicalism."

A RADICAL EDUCATION

MILL'S CAREER as a radical reformer began with his early education. When he was only six his father thought of him as the one to carry on the work begun by Bentham and himself. James Mill, during a period of illness, told Bentham of his hope that, in the event of his own death, his son would be brought up to be "a successor worthy of both of us."[2] James Mill, however, lived to carry out his educational mission himself, and he accomplished it with great effectiveness. John Stuart Mill later recalls having had "juvenile aspirations to the character of a democratic champion"; and, he continues, "the most transcendant glory I was capable of conceiving, was that of figuring, successful or unsuccessful, as a Girondist in an English Convention."[3]

Mill's wish to be a reformer was given additional impetus in 1821 (at age fifteen) when he read *Traités de législation*, Dumont's redaction of Bentham. His education up to this time "had been, in a certain sense, already a course of Benthamism": but the impact of this book was dramatic—it was "an epoch in my life; one of the turning points in my mental history." All he had previously learned seemed to fall into place; Mill now felt he had direction and purpose as a reformer. Bentham's book opened "a clearer and broader conception of what human opinions and institutions ought to be, how they might be made what they ought to be, and how far removed from it they now are." Consequently Mill "now had opinions; a creed, a doctrine, a philosophy; in one among the best senses of the word, a religion; the inculcation and diffusion of which could be made the principal outward purpose of a life." This new understanding was the initiation of Mill into radical politics, for he now had a "vista of improvement" which lit up his life and gave "a definite shape" to his aspirations.[4]

Mill's early assimilation of radicalism was evident in "Brodie's History of the British Empire" (3-58 below),[5] an article written at age eighteen. He used Bentham's ideas to analyze seventeenth-century constitutional conflicts and to

[2]Letter from James Mill to Jeremy Bentham, 28 July, 1812, in *The Works of Jeremy Bentham*, ed. John Bowring, 11 vols. (Edinburgh: Tait; London: Simpkin, Marshall; Dublin: Cumming, 1843), X, 473.
[3]John Stuart Mill, *Autobiography, CW*, I, ed. J. M. Robson and Jack Stillinger (Toronto: University of Toronto Press, 1981), 65-7.
[4]*Ibid.*, 67-71.
[5]Page references to material printed in this volume are given in the text.

criticize Hume's defence of Charles I. Hume wrote a "romance," Mill said, which generally "allies itself with the sinister interests of the few" while being indifferent to the "sufferings of the many," and he failed to consider "the only true end of morality, the greatest happiness of the greatest number" (3-4). Mill savagely criticized Hume as a defender of Stuart despotism, a dissembler, a perjuror (49), who involved himself in a "labyrinth of falsehood" (43). Indulgent to Stuart persecution (17), Hume became "the open and avowed advocate of despotism" (16). When Mill turned his attention to the parliamentary opposition, he tried to cast the Independents as seventeenth-century versions of nineteenth-century Radicals. They were republicans who upheld "the religion of the enlightened, and the enlightened are necessarily enemies to aristocracy" (47).[6]

Bentham's views on sinister and universal interests and the need for democratic reforms, and his belief that the most important conflict was between the aristocracy (represented by Whigs and Tories) and the people (represented by Radicals), were passed from Bentham to James Mill and subsequently to John Stuart Mill and the Philosophic Radicals. Bentham was critical of all institutions sanctioned by traditional authority, especially the common law and the British constitution. He regarded all law-making and administration of public affairs as disfigured by the aristocratic (and monarchical) monopoly of power. This monopoly created sinister interests which had many undesirable consequences, including unnecessary wars and unjustifiable empire building, but Bentham especially emphasized domestic corruption. The monarch and the aristocracy obtained benefits, such as sinecures and pensions, denied to others. The government, supposedly acting as trustees for the people, instead adopted the principle that "the substance of the people was a fund, out of which . . . *fortunes* . . . ought to be—*made.*" Such predatory activity and the improper distribution of "power, money, [and] factitious dignity" were made possible by "*separate,* and consequently with reference to the public service, . . . *sinister* interests."[7] This concept of sinister interests was central to Bentham's radical political analysis.

Bentham's remedy was "democratic ascendancy." Under it, office-holders would be restrained from seeking corrupt benefits. Universal suffrage, secret ballot, and annual parliaments would subject office-holders to scrutiny by those who stood to lose from the existence of sinister interests; thus these democratic practices would promote "the *universal interest* . . . of the whole people." Democratic ascendancy was recommended as the best means to the desired goal, the greatest happiness of the greatest number.[8]

---

[6]Mill had to acknowledge, however, that among the Independents there was a willingness to persecute (47) and that they participated in the regicide, which was an "act of a nest of despots, [who were] removing a rival despot out of their way" (53).

[7]*Plan of Parliamentary Reform, in the Form of a Catechism, with Reasons for Each Article: With an Introduction, Showing the Necessity of Radical, and the Inadequacy of Moderate, Reform* (London: Hunter, 1817), xi-xii, ccxxiii.

[8]*Ibid.*, xxxvi-xxxvii, cclxix-cclxx, cccvi.

Any persons or groups, whatever their social class or economic condition, could, according to Bentham, have sinister interests, but in the circumstances of the early nineteenth century the aristocracy was the most obvious and compelling example of a class that enjoyed such corrupt interests. His analysis pointed to fundamental conflict, under existing constitutional arrangements, between the aristocracy and the remainder of the populace. In this dispute the aristocracy was represented by the Whigs and the Tories, and the populace by Radicals, whom he also called "People's-men."[9] This conflict superseded the contest of parties familiar to most observers, and although it was invisible to many, to Bentham it was the more significant contest. Whigs and Tories, far from being enemies, were not significantly different. "Both parties . . . acting under the dominion of the same seductive and corruptive influence—will be seen to possess the same separate and sinister interest:—an interest completely and unchangeably opposite to that of the whole uncorrupt portion of the people."[10] Despite their superficial quarrels, the two aristocractic parties shared a class interest: "That which the Tories have in *possession* . . . the Whigs have before them in *prospect* and *expectancy*."[11]

Bentham laid the foundation of the Mills' radicalism, but James Mill generated most of the argument and rhetoric that John Stuart Mill adopted in his early years. Young Mill read his father's works, usually if not always in manuscript, conversed about them at length with him, and proof-read some as well. Among these works was the *History of British India*, which, James Mill said, "will make no bad introduction to the study of civil society in general. The subject afforded an opportunity of laying open the principles and laws of the social order. . . ."[12] There were also James Mill's *Encyclopaedia Britannica* articles, which diagnosed problems and outlined remedies on such matters as government, colonies, education, law, the press, prisons, and poor relief.[13] And a few years later there were his articles in the *Westminster Review* on the main Whig and Tory quarterlies and the parties they represented.[14]

Parliamentary reform was regarded by Bentham and James Mill as supremely important, for they assumed that all other reforms, those of tariffs, education, and law, for example, would be achieved without difficulty once the popular or universal interest was represented in Parliament. An early statement of James Mill's arguments for radical reform of Parliament may be found in his essay "Government," although John Stuart Mill probably was familiar with them from

---

[9]*Ibid.*, cccvi.

[10]*Ibid.*, cccvi-cccvii.

[11]*Ibid.*, cccvii.

[12]Letter to David Ricardo, 19 Oct., 1817, *The Works and Correspondence of David Ricardo*, ed. Piero Sraffa (Cambridge: Cambridge University Press, 1952), VII, 195-6.

[13]Reprinted in *Essays* (London: printed Innes, n.d. [1825]).

[14]"Periodical Literature: *Edinburgh Review*," *Westminster Review*, I (Jan., 1824), 206-49; "Periodical Literature: *Quarterly Review*," *Westminster Review*, II (Oct., 1824), 463-503.

his father's unpublished dialogue on government composed on the Platonic model.[15] Written in an austere style for the *Encyclopaedia Britannica*, "Government" in fact was a polemical statement, as both Ricardo and John Stuart Mill recognized.[16]

The essay, far more extreme than was apparent, was influential in shaping the political thought of Philosophic Radicalism. Frequently it has been suggested that because it was a defence of the middle class, it was not an argument for complete democracy. This interpretation, however, ignores the fact that it was in its main features consistent with Bentham's *Plan of Parliamentary Reform*, a fully democratic work. Certainly John Stuart Mill regarded his father as a democrat. James Mill, he said, "thought that when the legislature no longer represented a class interest, it would aim at the general interest," and therefore "a democratic suffrage [was] the principal article of his political creed."[17] James Mill's severest and most discerning critic, Thomas Babington Macaulay, also recognized that Mill was "in favour of pure democracy."[18]

James Mill's rationale for a democratic suffrage was an important link between Bentham's advocacy of universal suffrage and John Stuart Mill's radicalism during the 1830s. "Government," which was more widely read than any of his other political writings, had a powerful impact on the young Radicals, becoming

---

[15]*Autobiography*, *CW*, I, 67. See John M. Robson, *The Improvement of Mankind: The Social and Political Thought of John Stuart Mill* (Toronto: University of Toronto Press, 1968), 17, n42, for the suggestion that "Government" may have been based on this dialogue. "Government" was written for the *Supplement to the Fourth, Fifth, and Sixth Editions of the Encyclopaedia Britannica* (Edinburgh: Constable, 1824), IV, 491-505. Parts (in half-volumes) were issued separately between 1815 and 1824; the part containing this article appeared in September, 1820.

[16]Ricardo thought Mill was right to avoid discussion of the secret ballot, as "it would have given the article too much the appearance of an essay on Reform of Parliament which it was perhaps desirable to avoid" (letter to James Mill, 27 July, 1820, *Works and Correspondence of David Ricardo*, VIII, 211); John Stuart Mill thought his father should have acknowledged that he was "writing an argument for parliamentary reform" (*Autobiography*, *CW*, I, 165).

[17]*Autobiography*, *CW*, I, 109. James Mill's belief in democracy was deliberately obscured in "Government" as a matter of prudence and rhetoric. His well-known eulogy of the middle class, far from indicating a wish to restrict the suffrage to the middle class, served to show that the suffrage could be safely entrusted to the classes with lesser rank because they would be guided by the exemplary middle class. For a fuller discussion of Mill's essay as a defence of universal suffrage and of the middle-class theme, see Joseph Hamburger, *Intellectuals in Politics: John Stuart Mill and the Philosophic Radicals* (New Haven: Yale University Press, 1965), 36-8, 49-52; and Joseph Hamburger, "James Mill on Universal Suffrage and the Middle Class," *Journal of Politics*, XXIV (1962), 172-83. Although Mill pointed to an electorate without pecuniary or property qualifications, he suggested the exclusion of men under forty and of women. Women's interests, he argued, were involved in their father's and husband's; and men under forty were protected by virtue of older men's not distinguishing between their sons' interests and their own ("Government," *Utilitarian Logic and Politics: James Mill's "Essay on Government," Macaulay's Critique and the Ensuing Debate*, ed. Jack Lively and John Rees [Oxford: Clarendon Press, 1978], 79-80). Unlike class and property qualifications, age and gender were not regarded as relevant to definitions of democracy.

[18]Speech of 10 July, 1833, *Speeches by Lord Macaulay*, ed. George Malcolm Young (London: Oxford University Press, 1952), 126.

"almost a text-book to many of those who may be termed the Philosophic Radicals."[19] James Mill's influence was greatly reinforced by his conversation with the notable, even if not large, group of disciples that gathered around him during the 1820s and early 1830s, including some that John Stuart Mill brought into the fold: Charles Austin, Edward Strutt, John Romilly, William Ellis, and John Arthur Roebuck. James Mill's impact was enhanced by the distance between these disciples and the aging Bentham (now in his seventies), who at this time was more interested in law reform and codification than in parliamentary politics. Bentham's distance from the Radicals close to the Mills was accentuated by his intimacy with John Bowring, who was disliked and distrusted by James Mill. In 1825 some of these tensions surfaced when the Mills and their followers reduced their contributions to the *Westminster Review* and began publication of the *Parliamentary History and Review*, a journal in which they proclaimed Bentham's principles without Bowring's editorial interference.

Many, in addition to his son, have testified to James Mill's strengths as a political teacher. George Grote, who began his parliamentary career as a Radical in 1833, recalled James Mill's "powerful intellectual ascendency over younger minds."[20] Roebuck, despite an early quarrel with James Mill, called him his political and philosophical teacher and said, "To him I owe greater obligations than to any other man. If I know any thing, from him I learned it."[21] Another of John Stuart Mill's young friends, William Ellis, said of his early encounter with James Mill, "'he *worked a complete change* in me. He taught me how to think and what to live for.'" Indeed, Mill supplied him "with all those emotions and impulses which deserve the name of religious."[22] Harriet Grote, the historian's wife, also observed that under James Mill's influence "the young disciples, becoming fired with patriotic ardour on the one hand and with bitter antipathies on the other, respectively braced themselves up, prepared to wage battle when the day should come, in behalf of 'the true faith,' according to Mill's 'programme' and preaching."[23] Such strong influence allowed John Stuart Mill to say that his father "was quite as much the head and leader of the intellectual radicals in England, as Voltaire was of the *philosophes* of France."[24]

---

[19]John Stuart Mill, "Mr. Mill," *CW*, I, 594.

[20]*The Minor Works of George Grote* (London: Murray, 1873), 284.

[21]Letter to Henry Brougham, 29 June, 1836, Brougham Papers, University College, London.

[22]Florence Fenwick Miller, "William Ellis and His Work as an Educationist," *Fraser's Magazine*, n.s., XXV (Feb., 1882), 236. John Black, editor of the *Morning Chronicle*, remembered "the force of [James Mill's] personal character. . . . Young men were particularly fond of his society; and it was always to him a source of great delight to have an opportunity of contributing to form their minds and exalt their character." ("Death of Mr. James Mill," *Morning Chronicle*, 25 June, 1836, 3.)

[23]Harriet Grote, *The Personal Life of George Grote* (London: Murray, 1873), 23. Joseph Parkes said of Henry Warburton that James Mill had been "his chief political instructor" (Obituary, *The Times*, 21 Sept., 1858, 7; evidence of Parkes's authorship: letter from Parkes to Brougham, 23 Sept., 1858, Brougham Papers, University College, London).

[24]*Autobiography*, *CW*, I, 213. For their activities, see the Introduction to *CW*, I, xii-xiii.

This comparison with the *philosophes*, made by John Stuart Mill more than once, identifies the spirit in which he and the other Philosophic Radicals approached politics. His father's opinions, he said,

> were seized on with youthful fanaticism by the little knot of young men of whom I was one: and we put into them a sectarian spirit, from which, in intention at least, my father was wholly free. What we (or rather a phantom substituted in the place of us) were sometimes, by a ridiculous exaggeration, called by others, namely a "school," some of us for a time really hoped and aspired to be. The French philosophes of the eighteenth century were the example we sought to imitate, and we hoped to accomplish no less results.[25]

The Philosophic Radicals' sectarian spirit was evident in their use of a distinctive jargon irritating to others. John Stuart Mill's adopting the utilitarian label as a "sectarian appellation,"[26] for example, led Macaulay to ridicule "the project of mending a bad world by teaching people to give new names to old things." The utilitarians, Macaulay added, invented "a new sleight of tongue."[27] Mill also confessed that "to *outrer* whatever was by anybody considered offensive in the doctrines and maxims of Benthamism, became at one time the badge of a small coterie of youths."[28]

Mill and others in his coterie displayed this sectarian spirit in the London Debating Society where they preferred to engage in political debate with ideological opposites whose principles were as clear and explicit as their own. Mill's group, not the liberal moderates or trimming Whigs (such as Macaulay), provided the opposition to the Tories in the Society, and almost every debate, Mill recalled, "was a *bataille rangée* between the 'philosophic radicals' and the Tory lawyers." The debates, he said, were unusual for being philosophically extreme, so that the opponents were "thrown often into close and *serré* confutations of one another."[29] In noting that the Society was the only arena in which such conflict was to be found, Mill was making an allusion to the defects of Parliament itself as well as giving a hint of the worldly ambitions which were linked to his and the other Philosophic Radicals' political speculations.

Their conduct and opinions did not go uncriticized. Henry Taylor, an official in the Colonial Office and later author of *The Statesman*, regarded John Stuart Mill's views in the 1820s as being "at heart something in the nature of political fanaticism," and in the London Debating Society Taylor spoke against the same

---

[25]*Ibid.*, 111.
[26]*Ibid.*, 83.
[27]Macaulay, "Bentham's Defence of Mill: Utilitarian System of Philosophy," *Edinburgh Review*, XLIX (June, 1829), 296.
[28]*Autobiography*, *CW*, I, 81. Whereas his father avoided using terms like democracy and universal suffrage, John Stuart Mill showed no such restraint (for example, "Speech on the British Constitution," 19 May, 1826, in James McCrimmon, "Studies toward a Biography of John Stuart Mill," Ph.D. thesis, Northwestern University, 1937, 358).
[29]*Autobiography*, *CW*, I, 133. On economic issues the opposition came from the Owenites.

facet of radicalism that provoked Macaulay's famous critique of James Mill.[30] William Empson also complained about "the most peremptory and proselytizing seminary of *ipse dixitists*, (to use one of their own beautiful words,) which has ever existed." The Benthamite Radicals reminded Empson of "those abstract and dogmatical times when men were principally distinguished by the theory of morals that they might happen to profess."[31] Macaulay, at this time a prolific publicist but not yet in the House of Commons, suggested that the disciples of James Mill (whom he called a "zealot of a sect")[32] were potentially dangerous.

Even now [1827], it is impossible to disguise, that there is arising in the bosom of [the middle class] a Republican sect, as audacious, as paradoxical, as little inclined to respect antiquity, as enthusiastically attached to its ends, as unscrupulous in the choice of its means, as the French Jacobins themselves,—but far superior to the French Jacobins in acuteness and information—in caution, in patience, and in resolution. They are men whose minds have been put into training for violent exertion. . . . They profess to derive their opinions from demonstrations alone. . . . Metaphysical and political science engage their whole attention. Philosophical pride has done for them what spiritual pride did for the Puritans in a former age; it has generated in them an aversion for the fine arts, for elegant literature, and for the sentiments of chivalry. It has made them arrogant, intolerant, and impatient of all superiority. These qualities will, in spite of their real claims to respect, render them unpopular, as long as the people are satisfied with their rulers. But under an ignorant and tyrannical ministry, obstinately opposed to the most moderate and judicious innovations, their principles would spread as rapidly as those of the Puritans formerly spread, in spite of their offensive peculiarities. The public, disgusted with the blind adherence of its rulers to ancient abuses, would be reconciled to the most startling novelties. A strong democratic party would be formed in the educated class.[33]

Such criticism was not likely to undermine the confidence of John Stuart Mill and his fellow enthusiasts. The Philosophic Radicals were distinguished, Mill said, for writing with an "air of strong conviction . . . when scarcely any one else seemed to have an equally strong faith in as definite a creed. . . ." Thus the public eye was attracted by "the regular appearance in controversy of what seemed a new school of writers, claiming to be the legislators and theorists of this new [reformist] tendency."[34]

---

[30]*Autobiography of Henry Taylor* (London: Longmans, 1885), I, 78-9, 90-5; Macaulay, "Mill's Essay on Government: Utilitarian Logic and Politics," *Edinburgh Review*, XLIX (Mar., 1829), 159-89. See also Robson, *Improvement of Mankind*, 24, n6.

[31]"Bentham's Rationale of Evidence," *Edinburgh Review*, XLVIII (Dec., 1828), 463. The phrase *ipse dixitism* derives from Bentham. See, e.g., *Rationale of Judicial Evidence*, ed. J. S. Mill, 5 vols. (London: Hunt and Clarke, 1827), I, 127. For Mill's use of the term, see *ibid.*, 126n, and "Speech on the British Constitution," in McCrimmon, "Studies," 346.

[32]"Utilitarian Theory of Government, and the 'Greatest Happiness Principle,'" *Edinburgh Review*, L (Oct., 1829), 124.

[33]"The Present Administration," *Edinburgh Review*, XLVI (June, 1827), 260-1. Whereas Macaulay's analysis in 1827 indicates that the Philosophic Radicals are dangerous, in the better known 1829-30 articles he leans more to the view that they are ridiculous.

[34]*Autobiography, CW*, I, 103.

RADICALISM INTERRUPTED: THE MENTAL CRISIS

DURING THE MIDDLE AND LATE 1820s John Stuart Mill might have felt confidence in his future as a leading member of an influential coterie, but his commitment to radicalism was shaken by his mental crisis and related events, particularly, at the end of the decade, by Macaulay's critique of James Mill's "Government," John Austin's arguments in his course of lectures on jurisprudence at the University of London in 1829-30, and the early writings of Auguste Comte and the St. Simonians.

The mental crisis, which beset him in the autumn of 1826, made Mill indifferent to reform. Having been converted, as he reported, to a political creed with religious dimensions, and having seen himself as "a reformer of the world," he now asked himself if the complete reform of the world would bring him happiness and, realizing it would not, he felt that the foundations of his life had collapsed. "I was thus, as I said to myself, left stranded at the commencement of my voyage, with a well equipped ship and a rudder, but no sail; . . . ambition seemed to have dried up within me. . . ."[35] Mill for a time lost his political calling.

This crisis was responsible, as Mill acknowledged, for an "important transformation" in his "opinions and character."[36] So far as opinions were concerned, the change came, not directly from the crisis, but from certain subsequent events. These events occurred after the period of his greatest dejection had ended but before his recovery of purpose and confidence. In fact, by undermining his old beliefs, the crisis opened the way for a commitment to new ideas. Part of the process was the undercurrent of negative feelings about James Mill that are evident in his record of the crisis.

The first of these events, the publication in 1829 of Macaulay's critiques of James Mill's "Government," did much to shake John Mill's beliefs. Macaulay charged James Mill with using *a priori* reasoning inappropriate to political analysis, and argued that Mill compounded this error by making deductions from inadequate premises. James Mill's democratic prescription, Macaulay argued, would not necessarily promote policies reflecting the universal interest.[37] This attack, John Stuart Mill confessed, "gave me much to think about." Though, he says,

the tone was unbecoming . . . there was truth in several of his strictures on my father's treatment of the subject; that my father's premises were really too narrow, and included but a small number of the general truths, on which, in politics, the important consequences depend. Identity of interest between the governing body and the community at large, is not,

---

[35]*Ibid.*, 137, 139, 143.
[36]*Ibid.*, 137.
[37]"Mill's *Essay on Government*," 161-2, 168-9, 176-7, 181-2. For discussion of the Mill-Macaulay controversy, see the introduction by Lively and Rees to *Utilitarian Logic and Politics*, 1-51; and Joseph Hamburger, *Macaulay and the Whig Tradition* (Chicago: University of Chicago Press, 1976), 49-62.

in any practical sense which can be attached to it, the only thing on which good government depends; neither can this identity of interest be secured by the mere conditions of election. I was not at all satisfied with the mode in which my father met the criticisms of Macaulay.[38]

Mill now thought there was something "fundamentally erroneous" in his father's "conception of philosophical Method."[39]

Also contributing to the change in Mill's beliefs were John Austin's lectures (which Mill attended during the session that began in November, 1829) and his exposure to St. Simonianism. Whereas Macaulay's attack undermined his confidence in the soundness of "Government," and by extension much else, without providing anything to put in its place, John Austin and the St. Simonians suggested to Mill political principles that were alternatives to his old radicalism and that, at least to their authors, seemed incompatible with Benthamite radicalism. Mill's adoption of several ideas from Austin and the St. Simonians for a while prevented him from resuming his former role as a champion of the older radicalism. Only after an intellectual struggle was he able to accommodate the new ideas to the old.

The most important of these new ideas concerned political authority. In 1829 he began to develop the view that it ought to be exercised by those with special knowledge of public matters, and began speaking about the "authority of the instructed."[40] Since this notion circumscribed the political role of ordinary citizens, he also advocated the multitude's deference to knowledgeable authority. These opinions, markedly alien to Benthamite radicalism and his father's political principles, had their origin in writings of the St. Simonians and in John Austin's lectures on jurisprudence (which is not to say that Austin's political thought and St. Simonianism were the same).[41]

Austin's advocacy of vesting authority in those with knowledge was closely tied to his complete confidence that the method of science could be applied to most fields of knowledge. He was so impressed by the achievements of natural science and the progress of political economy that he looked forward to a parallel emergence of political and moral science. By using the principle of utility, these sciences would discover the sources of improvement, and the result would be a science of ethics, including the sciences of law, morality, and political science.

---

[38]*Autobiography*, *CW*, I, 165.

[39]*Ibid.*, 167.

[40]Letter to Gustave d'Eichthal, 7 Nov., 1829, *Earlier Letters* [*EL*], ed. Francis E. Mineka, *CW*, XII-XIII (Toronto: University of Toronto Press, 1963), XII, 40.

[41]For a different estimate of the connection between Mill's views in 1831 and his father's, see William Thomas, *The Philosophic Radicals: Nine Studies in Theory and Practice, 1817-1841* (Oxford: Clarendon Press, 1979), 176. See Richard B. Friedman, "An Introduction to Mill's Theory of Authority," in *Mill: A Collection of Critical Essays*, ed. Jerome B. Schneewind (New York: Anchor, 1968), 379-425, for the illuminating suggestion that Austin's views on authority influenced Mill. The questions as to whether Mill was exposed earlier to Austinian or St. Simonian ideas on this subject and as to which had the greater influence remain unanswered.

Since such scientific knowledge was accessible only to comparatively few, however, authority could be properly exercised only by them, and most persons were expected to accept their conclusions "*on authority, testimony, or trust.*"[42]

These ideas made Austin anything but a radical. He had been an orthodox Benthamite until, in 1827, he began a year-and-a-half stay in Germany, but his new attitudes to authority and trust were incompatible with the democratic arrangements proposed by Bentham. Austin unmistakably rejected radicalism in his denying that "the power of the sovereign flows from the people, or [that] the people is the fountain of sovereign power."[43] He also complained about "the stupid and infuriate majority," and condemned Radical leaders, saying that "the guides of the multitude [were] moved by sinister interests, or by prejudices which are the offspring of such interests."[44] John Mill noted Austin's move away from radicalism, reporting that in Germany Austin "acquired an indifference, bordering on contempt, for the progress of popular institutions. . . ."[45] Austin's relations with Bentham became somewhat strained at this time, and Sarah Austin (whose views were very close to her husband's) said she "excite[d] horror among [her] Radical friends for not believing that all salvation comes of certain organic forms of government."[46]

Another alternative to Benthamism was St. Simonianism. Mill became acquainted with the sect in 1829 and 1830, and he claimed to have read everything they wrote, though, of course, he did not share all their beliefs.[47] Among other things, he found in St. Simonian writings a theory of history that asserted that society progressed through alternating stages, called organic and critical. Organic epochs are characterized by widely shared beliefs and clearly defined, shared goals. In such periods society is arranged hierarchically, with the truly superior having the power to direct moral, scientific, and industrial activity. Although there is gross inequality, there is no discontent and no conflict. For the St. Simonians, organic eras existed when Greek and Roman polytheism were in full vigour (ending, respectively, with Pericles and Augustus), and when Catholicism and feudalism were at their height.[48] Critical epochs, in contrast, are characterized by deep scepticism about the values and beliefs of the preceding organic era and finally by rejection of them. All forces join to destroy the values and institutions of the preceding era, and when this destruction is accomplished, one finds irreligion, lack of morality, and egoism, as particular interests prevail over the general

---

[42]*The Province of Jurisprudence Determined* (London: Murray, 1832), 61-4.
[43]*Ibid.*, 323. For evidence of Austin's orthodox Benthamite radicalism before 1827, see his "Disposition of Property by Will—Primogeniture," *Westminster Review*, II (Oct., 1824), 503-53.
[44]*Province of Jurisprudence*, 59, 86.
[45]*Autobiography, CW*, I, 185.
[46]Letter to Jane Welsh Carlyle, 25 Dec., [1832], National Library of Scotland.
[47]*Autobiography, CW*, I, 171, 173-5.
[48]*The Doctrine of Saint-Simon: An Exposition*, ed. and trans. Georg G. Iggers (Boston: Beacon Press, 1958), 52-3, 93, 198, 206-7.

interest. In the resultant anarchy, there is conflict between ruler and ruled, and men of ability are ignored. The St. Simonians found examples in the periods between polytheism and Christianity and from Luther to the present.[49]

St. Simonian ideas, like Austin's, were far removed from Benthamite radicalism, implying, as they did, that organic were superior to critical periods, and approving cultural and religious unity and hierarchy. All that Benthamite radicalism aimed to achieve assumed the continued existence of a critical epoch, and radicalism's highest achievement would have involved the most extreme development of the distinguishing characteristics of critical eras. The Radicals' blindness to the necessary supercession of critical periods by organic ones was, for the St. Simonians, a disqualifying limitation.

These ideas—both Austin's and the St. Simonians'—had a powerful impact on Mill. He came to believe that those most instructed in moral and political subjects might "carry the multitude with them by their united authority."[50] His assumption that most persons "must and do believe on authority" was an implicit rejection of Benthamite views on the role of a sceptical electorate always alert to the operation of sinister interests.[51] The full extent of his commitment to these new ideas was evident in his "The Spirit of the Age," which appeared in 1831, but even earlier his changed ideas were reflected in changed activities. Unlike his father, Mill for a few years thought there was little point in stimulating public opinion; he dropped out of the London Debating Society in 1829 and wrote little for publication.[52] Although he claimed to have "entered warmly"[53] into the political discussions of the time when he returned from Paris in September, 1830, his manuscript bibliography records few publications on domestic politics during the reform period, and during the height of the Reform Bill agitation he was "often surprised, how little" he really cared about extra-parliamentary politics. "The time is not yet come," he wrote, "when a calm and impartial person can intermeddle with advantage in the questions and contests of the day."[54]

---

[49]*Ibid.*, 52, 54-5, 206-7.

[50]"Rejected Leaves of the Early Draft of the *Autobiography*," CW, I, 616.

[51]Letter to d'Eichthal, 9 Feb., 1830, EL, CW, XII, 48.

[52]Mill thought it was "utterly hopeless and chimerical to suppose that the regeneration of mankind can ever be wrought by means of working on their opinions" (*ibid.*, 47; *Autobiography*, CW, I, 137, 163). This opinion influenced the argument in *On Liberty*, CW, XVIII, 257. Henry Cole said the London Debating Society was "in a bad way, doubtless owing to the secession of Mill and his friends" (entry of 19 Feb., 1830); after Goldsmid introduced the question, "that the utilitarian system of philosophy is pernicious and absurd," Cole said there was no debate, but only "a satyrical [sic] reply from C. Buller he being the only disciple of that system present" (entry of 8 Jan., 1830; Cole's Diary, 1827-1834, Victoria and Albert Museum).

[53]*Autobiography*, CW, I, 179.

[54]Letter to John Sterling, 20 to 22 Oct., 1831, EL, CW, XII, 78. This letter was written less than two weeks after the riots at Derby and Nottingham. Mill was not completely indifferent, however; he wrote an article recommending several friends as parliamentary candidates (*Examiner*, 2 Sept., 1832, 569); he contributed £1 to the National Political Union (British Library, Place Collection of Newscuttings, Set 63, Vol. 1, f. 276); and he attended the meeting to organize the Parliamentary Candidates Society on 14 Mar., 1831 and contributed £1 (letter from Francis Place to Bentham, 18 Mar., 1831, Bentham Papers, University College, London).

Mill recovered his sense of calling as a reformer and his radical beliefs, but only after he accommodated his new ideas about the authority of the instructed to Benthamite radicalism. He felt compelled to make the accommodation:

I found the fabric of my old and taught opinions giving way in many fresh places, and I never allowed it to fall to pieces, but was incessantly occupied in weaving it anew. I never, in the course of my transition, was content to remain, for ever so short a time, confused and unsettled. When I had taken in any new idea, I could not rest till I had adjusted its relation to my old opinions, and ascertained exactly how far its effect ought to extend in modifying or superseding them.[55]

The process of weaving anew, which involved influences coming from Coleridge, Carlyle, and Harriet Taylor, as well as from John Austin and the St. Simonians, continued for much of his life, but it was a major occupation for him during the 1830s.

If Mill's metaphor of weaving suggests a harmonious intertwining, it is somewhat misleading, for initially his old and new ideas were not so much woven together as simply combined. Rather than choose between them, Mill now regarded both the old ideas, which emphasized popular control, and the new, which emphasized instructed leadership, as equally necessary: "the grand difficulty in politics will for a long time be, how best to conciliate the two great elements on which good government depends; to combine the greatest amount of the advantage derived from the independent judgment of a specially instructed Few, with the greatest degree of the security for rectitude of pupose derived from rendering those Few responsible to the Many."[56] This combination was necessary because each of its main ingredients was by itself insufficient. Benthamite radicalism provided a popular check on authority but made no provision for instructed authority. By attempting to combine these two approaches, Mill was hoping to provide for "the two great elements on which good government depends."[57]

This wish to combine two diverse outlooks led Mill to use the language of eclecticism. He described the truth as "many sided,"[58] and advocated "a catholic

---

[55]*Autobiography*, *CW*, I, 163-5. "The decade 1830 to 1840 was that in which he put together the strands of the past with the filaments of the present, and it ended with the assertion of his independent position" (Robson, *Improvement of Mankind*, 32).

[56]"Rationale of Representation" (July, 1835), *CW*, XVIII, 24.

[57]Mill also said, "what was good in the influences of aristocracy, is compatible, if we really wish to find it so, with a well-regulated democracy" ("De Tocqueville on Democracy in America [I]," [1835], *CW*, XVIII, 54). Mill's wish to combine the two outlooks was also evident in his consideration of the "three great questions in government." Bentham provided an answer to only one of them, "By what means are the abuses of . . . authority to be checked?" Bentham's proposal of democratic checks was accepted by Mill, but he was worried that these checks might restrict public functionaries too much. To the other questions, however, Bentham gave no answer whatsoever: "To what authority is it for the good of the people that they should be subject?" and "How are they to be induced to obey that authority?" ("Bentham," *Essays on Ethics, Religion, and Society*, *CW*, X, ed. J. M. Robson [Toronto: University of Toronto Press, 1969], 106.) Consideration of these questions and possible answers to them arose from the work of Austin, the St. Simonians, and Coleridge.

[58]*Autobiography*, *CW*, I, 169-71.

spirit in philosophy."[59] Trying to combine fragments of the truth and to reconcile persons who represented different "half truths,"[60] he sought "practical eclecticism,"[61] and he tried to keep "as firm hold of one side of the truth as [he] took of the other."[62]

At this time Mill thought of his political speculations as taking place on a higher plane than they had occupied earlier. Whereas previously he (like Bentham and his father) had regarded certain model institutions as the end result of speculation, now, without rejecting his old conclusions about model (i.e., democratic) institutions, he went further. In his words, "If I am asked what system of political philosophy I substituted for that which, as a philosophy, I had abandoned, I answer, no system: only a conviction, that the true system was something much more complex and many sided than I had previously had any idea of, and that its office was to supply, not a set of model institutions, but principles from which the institutions suitable to any given circumstances might be deduced."[63] Of course, viewed from this higher plane, James Mill's contribution to political philosophy was greatly diminished. Thus John Mill became "aware of many things which [his father's] doctrine, professing to be a theory of government in general, ought to have made room for, and did not."[64] He no longer accepted "Government" as embodying scientific theory, and thought his father should have answered Macaulay by acknowledging that the essay was not a scientific treatise but only a tract in support of parliamentary reform.[65] Although he did not use the phrase in reference to his father, clearly he thought James Mill had grasped only a "half-truth."

Mill's search for ways of combining the diverse understandings of Bentham and his father, on the one hand, and of Austin and the St. Simonians, on the other, was revealed most clearly in his articles on Bailey, Tocqueville, Bentham, and Coleridge (and much later, of course, in *Considerations on Representative Government*). Whereas he castigated as false democracy the simple majoritarianism which he associated with the recommendations of Bentham and James Mill, he saw true or rational democracy as the kind that, in allowing for representation of minorities, including the minority of the educated, facilitated leadership by the instructed few in combination with a democratic suffrage that provided popular control. This line of thinking was also evident in his belief that the main thrust of eighteenth-century political philosophy, represented by the *philosophes* on the Continent and in England by Bentham (and, by implication, his father), had to be combined with the main theme of nineteenth-century thought as represented by the

---

[59]Letter to Sterling, 4 Nov., 1839, *EL, CW*, XIII, 411.
[60]*Autobiography, CW*, I, 171.
[61]Letter to d'Eichthal, 7 Nov., 1829, *EL, CW*, XII, 42.
[62]*Autobiography, CW*, I, 169.
[63]*Ibid.*
[64]*Ibid.*, 165.
[65]*Ibid.*, 165, 177.

German romantics and in England by Coleridge. Whereas Bentham taught the need for popular control, Coleridge, with his notion of a clerisy, promoted the idea of enlightened authority that commanded deference from the populace. "Whoever could master the premises and combine the methods of both [Bentham and Coleridge], would possess the entire English philosophy of their age,"[66] Mill said, and described his wish to synthesize Bentham and Coleridge as a "scheme of conciliation between the old and the new 'philosophic radicalism.'"[67]

In combining the new ideas with the old radicalism, Mill was greatly helped by a theory of history that allowed him to visualize the progressive development of society. He was exposed to such a theory in St. Simonianism, which provided him with a "connected view . . . of the natural order of human progress."[68] This permitted him to assume that the combination of enlightened leadership and democratic control would be viable; that is, true democracy as he understood it could come to exist.

After Mill had persuaded himself that the old radicalism was reconcilable with his new ideas, he could co-operate with the other Radicals in practical politics. While he had some goals that were not theirs, he shared their wish for an extended suffrage, shorter parliaments, and the secret ballot. The "change in the premises of my political philosophy," he says, "did not alter my practical political creed as to the requirements of my own time and country. I was as much as ever a radical and democrat, for Europe, and especially for England."[69] Democracy, however, would have put into practice only some of Mill's political principles, whereas for the other Radicals it would have been closer to complete fulfilment of their hopes.

In the absence of complete agreement, relations between Mill and the other Philosophic Radicals were somewhat strained. Since they were willing to apply only some of his political principles, he regarded them as narrow. They saw "*clearly* what they did see, though it was but little." As they were narrow, he regarded them as incomplete, "half-men."[70] All the same, he was "able to cooperate with them in their own field of usefulness, though perhaps they would not always join [him] in [his]."[71] Mill also subjected his father to two standards of judgment, approving his ideas at one level but not the other. There was oblique criticism of him in an appendix to Edward Lytton Bulwer's *England and the English* (London, 1833) and in references to spokesmen for the philosophy of the eighteenth century in the essay on Bentham; also in the *Autobiography* Mill confessed to feeling quite distant from James Mill's "tone of thought and feeling," and said his father probably considered him "a deserter from his standard,"

---

[66]"Coleridge," *CW*, X, 121.
[67]*Autobiography*, *CW*, I, 209. Also the *London Review* "ought to represent not radicalism but neoradicalism" (letter to Edward Lytton Bulwer, 23 Nov., 1836, *EL*, *CW*, XII, 312).
[68]*Autobiography*, *CW*, I, 171.
[69]*Ibid.*, 177.
[70]Letter to Thomas Carlyle, 22 Oct., 1832, *EL*, *CW*, XII, 126-8.
[71]Letter to Carlyle, 17 Sept., 1832, *ibid.*, 117.

although at the same time "we were almost always in strong agreement on the political questions of the day."[72]

Although Mill was willing to co-operate with the other Philosophic Radicals, their feelings about him were affected by suspicions that his new ideas undermined his status as a Radical. Roebuck complained about Mill's belief "in the advantages to be derived from an Aristocracy of intellect."[73] Mrs. Grote referred to that "wayward intellectual deity John Mill,"[74] and after the publication of the article on Bentham, Francis Place expressed the view "that [since] John Mill has made great progress in becoming a German Metaphysical Mystic, excentricity [sic] and absurdity must occasionally be the result."[75]

During the 1830s Mill advocated both parts of his political philosophy. On some occasions he explained the need for allowing the "instructed few" a large measure of authority; at other times he emphasized the more restricted vision of Benthamite radicalism, and sought to be the guide and tactician for the parliamentary Radicals. In the latter mood, he looked for fairly quick results, whereas in the former he was trying to prepare the ground for the acceptance of new principles to be realized in the more distant future. Although his explanations of the new ideas mainly appeared in essays published in other volumes of the *Collected Works*, occasionally these ideas are found in articles in this volume. A notable example is his anticipation of his proposal in *Considerations on Representative Government* (1861) for a Legislative Commission in an article of 1834 in the *Monthly Repository* (160).[76]

THE RATIONALE FOR A RADICAL PARTY

MILL BECAME A POLITICAL JOURNALIST to implement his radical creed. He often wished to be in Parliament with other Philosophic Radicals, and only his official

---

[72]*Autobiography, CW*, I, 189.

[73]*Pamphlets for the People* (London: Ely, 1835) (no. 20, 22 Oct., 1835), 3. All the same, Roebuck in his *Pamphlets for the People* reprinted extracts from the *London Review* and approved Mill's Review for its "general tendency . . . [and] most of the leading doctrines"; all contributors (and Roebuck was one of them) shared "a common purpose, and agree[d] in the general principles of their moral and their political system" ("Democracy in America"; "The London Review and the Irish Church Question," *ibid.*, 1-4, 7). Political co-operation continued, despite their personal quarrel, so that Mill said his differences with Roebuck "became so strongly pronounced that we ceased to be allies either in opinion or in action except as to the immediate objects of radicalism" ("Early Draft," *CW*, I, 154).

[74]Letter to Place, 16 Aug., 1837, British Library, Add. MSS 35150, f. 279.

[75]Letter to Thomas Falconer, 2 Sept., 1838, British Library, Add. MSS 35151, f. 86.

[76]Among other examples, see 164 for an allusion to Coleridge's conversation about clergy and clerisy; and 227-8 for a theoretical defence of state responsibility for religious instruction on the ground that religion is closely connected with conscience and duty (the editor, W. J. Fox, in a footnote—227n—took exception to this suggestion that the state might legislate in matters of religion).

position at India House prevented his going to the hustings.[77] Consequently he turned to journalism with the belief—or the hope—that "words are deeds, and the cause of deeds."[78] He looked enviously at France where "editors of daily journals may be considered as individually the head, or at lowest the right hand, of a political party."[79] There was the example of Armand Carrel, who "made himself, without a seat in the legislature or any public station beyond the editorship of his journal, the most powerful political leader of his age and country" (380). With ambition to play such a role, Mill, in co-operation with his father and Sir William Molesworth, set up a new quarterly journal in 1835 (initially the *London Review* and, after a merger in 1836, the *London and Westminster*). It was to be "a periodical organ of philosophic radicalism, to take the place which the *Westminster Review* had been intended to fill." One of its principal purposes "was to stir up the educated Radicals, in and out of Parliament, to exertion, and induce them to make themselves, what I thought by using the proper means they might become—a powerful party capable of taking the government of the country, or at least of dictating the terms on which they should share it with the Whigs."[80] Mill was the real though not the nominal editor, and after Molesworth withdrew in 1837 he became the proprietor as well.

Mill in his journalism frequently discussed Radical party goals, explaining that constitutional change, that is, organic reform, was essential, but that it was only a means to the real end, improvement. Thus he said that Radicals wanted codification of the laws, cheap legal procedures, access to the courts for the poor, abolition of the corn laws and of restrictions on industry, elimination of useless expenditures, improvement of conditions in Ireland, and a rational administration (348, 397). Thinking the Reform Act of 1832 "wholly insufficient" (186), he did not expect much improvement from the post-Reform Bill parliaments, and therefore advocated organic reform, that is, a more democratic constitution. Of course, if improvements could have been achieved without such fundamental changes, Mill would have been satisfied, but he assumed that the aristocratic classes were unwilling to make more than trivial concessions to liberal opinion. Thus, although constitutional changes were only the means to general improve-

---

[77]"I often wish I were among them [the Radical party in the House of Commons]; now would be the time for knitting together a powerful party, and nobody holds the scattered threads of it in his hands except me. But that cannot be while I am in the India House. I should not at all mind leaving it if I had £300 a year free from anxiety and literary labour, but I have at most £100." (Letter to John Pringle Nichol, 29 Jan., 1837, *EL, CW*, XII, 324.) "For the first time these ten years I have no wish to be in Parliament" (letter to John Robertson, 6 Aug., 1837, *ibid.*, 345).

[78]"Armand Carrel," *London and Westminster Review [L&WR]*, XXVIII (Oct., 1837), 69.

[79]"Letter from an Englishman to a Frenchman, on a Recent Apology in the 'Journal des Débats,' for the Faults of the English National Character," *Monthly Repository*, VIII (June, 1834), 393-4.

[80]*Autobiography, CW*, I, 207, 221. "The principal radicals in parliament and many of those out of it have a scheme for starting a new quarterly review.... The first promoters of it were Roebuck, Buller, and I...." (Letter to Carlyle, 22 Dec., 1833, *EL, CW*, XII, 201.)

ment, Mill said, "necessary means we believe them to be" (348).[81] Consequently, the demand for organic reforms became the hallmark of Philosophic Radicalism.

Although Radicals might differ about how far to go in shifting power away from the aristocracy, they agreed about the kind of change required: "it must be by diminishing the power of those who are unjustly favoured, and giving more to those who are unjustly depressed: it must be by adding weight in the scale to the two elements of Numbers and Intelligence, and taking it from that of Privilege" (479). The traditional Radical programme for achieving this change emphasized universal suffrage, secret ballot, and frequent elections. Mill said little about annual parliaments but appears to have wanted shorter, perhaps triennial, ones. He was outspoken in calling for the ballot, not only because it would reduce bribery and intimidation of electors, but because it would help shift the balance of power: once it became a cabinet measure, "reform will have finally triumphed: the aristocratic principle will be completely annihilated, and we shall enter into a new era of government."[82] As to the franchise, he wanted to see it greatly extended at this time, but he did not press for universal suffrage, although he regarded it as ultimately necessary and desirable. By arguing that it could be put off for a time, he was not doubting its importance and value but was recognizing that it was unlikely that a broadly based radical movement could be formed if extremists within it insisted on universal suffrage. He therefore called for its gradual introduction and was evidently pleased when its not being a pressing issue allowed him to avoid an unequivocal statement of his opinion (482, 488-9).[83] When he could not avoid stating his view, however, Mill, although hesitantly, showed his hand, as when he said of the parliamentary Radicals:

They are the only party who do not in their hearts condemn the whole of their operative fellow-citizens to perpetual helotage, to a state of exclusion from all direct influence on national affairs.... They look forward to a time, most of them think it is not yet come, when the whole adult population shall be qualified to give an equal voice in the election of members of Parliament. Others believe this and tremble; *they* believe it, and rejoice; and instead of wishing to retard, they anxiously desire ... to hasten this progress. (397.)

Of course, this description of the parliamentary Radicals was a description of Mill himself.

Mill's wish to promote a Radical party with a programme of organic reform rested on the assumption that a fundamental conflict was taking place between the aristocratic and non-aristocratic classes over control of government. This notion was adopted from Bentham and his father, but the language Mill used to describe

---

[81]See also 401; and compare 61.

[82]Letter to Alexis de Tocqueville, 7 Jan., 1837, *EL, CW,* XII, 317. For an account of Mill's view on the secret ballot at this time in relation to his later opposition to it, see Bruce Kinzer, "J.S. Mill and the Secret Ballot," *Historical Reflections / Réflections Historiques,* V (Summer, 1978), 19-39.

[83]In 1839 he favoured household suffrage (467). "Happily there is no necessity for a speedy decision of the question" ("Rationale of Representation" [July, 1835], *CW,* XVIII, 32).

the conflict was more varied than theirs: the Disqualified vs. the Privileged; Natural Radicals vs. Natural Opponents of Radicalism; Numbers and Intelligence vs. Privilege; the Aggrieved vs. the Satisfied; the Many vs. the Few. Whatever the labels, Mill, like Bentham and his father, had in mind a conflict between Radicals, as spokesmen for the universal or general interest and representing the "People," and Conservatives, as spokesmen for particular or sinister interests and representing the Aristocracy. Mill's analysis was evident in much of what he wrote during the 1830s, but it was presented most elaborately in the remarkable essay, "Reorganization of the Reform Party," where he described the conflict as arising out of social structure. Political views, he explained, were a matter of social position, interest, and class (465-95 *passim*, esp. 469).[84]

Mill's view of the aristocratic classes was not very different from his father's. They were, generally, the landed and monied classes, especially the former, and they controlled the legislature, the House of Commons as well as the House of Lords (101-2 and 184). They made laws in their own interest, most notably the monopolistic Corn Laws which made bread unnecessarily expensive for the poor (170, 470), and also in defence of their amusements, as Mill explained in his early article on the Game Laws, which had important consequences for a great part of the agricultural population (101-3, 107). They also biassed justice by administering the laws in their own class interest (471, 483). Furthermore, they administered the Poor Laws; and the army, navy, and civil patronage belonged to them exclusively (170). Altogether the government was "a selfish oligarchy, carried on for the personal benefit of the ruling classes" (479). The Church, too, was but a branch of the aristocracy (471).[85] In short, the aristocracy had vast unjust power; it was exploitive, selfish, and indifferent to the interests of others. Clearly its members, the bulwark of what Mill called the Privileged, Conservative, Satisfied Classes, exploited their sinister interest at the expense of the people (469-70).

In opposition to the aristocratic classes, Mill portrayed the combination of groups that made up the Numbers and Intelligence and who, in their struggle against Privilege, became "natural Radicals" (468, 470). All who suffered deprivation as a result of aristocratic exclusions—whether through legislation or custom—were the Disqualified, and therefore by definition opposed to the Privileged.

All who feel oppressed, or unjustly dealt with, by any of the institutions of the country; who are taxed more heavily than other people, or for other people's benefit; who have, or consider themselves to have, the field of employment for their pecuniary means or their bodily or mental faculties unjustly narrowed; who are denied the importance in society, or the influence in public affairs, which they consider due to them as a class, or who feel debarred as individuals from a fair chance of rising in the world; especially if others, in whom they do not recognize any superiority of merit, are artificially exalted above their

---

[84]The argument in this article was anticipated in "Parties and the Ministry" (395-6, 401-3).
[85]See also 287, 262-3, 270-1.

heads: these compose the natural Radicals; to whom must be added a large proportion of those who, from whatever cause, are habitually ill at ease in their pecuniary circumstances; the sufferers from low wages, low profits, or want of employment.... (470.)

Such was Mill's attempt to define the comprehensive coalition of the discontented.

Turning to the sources of such discontents, Mill looked to amount of property and to occupational and financial circumstances—in other words, to class. First, there were the middle classes, the majority of whom, including the bulk of the manufacturing and mercantile classes (except those in protected trades), were on the side of change. In addition, there were the ten-pound electors in the towns, who belonged to the "uneasy classes," for they lived a life of struggle and had no sense of fellow feeling with the aristocracy (476). In part these were Dissenters, who had their own grievances against the Church to supplement those they experienced as members of the middle class. "Between them and the aristocracy, there is a deeper gulph fixed than can be said of any other portion of the middle class; and when men's consciences, and their interests, draw in the same direction, no wonder that they are irresistible" (476).[86]

There was another aspect of middle-class discontent about which Mill was perceptive, perhaps because he personally experienced it. It arose less from inequities leading to material deprivation than from resentments about social status, and it was experienced by "the men of active and aspiring talent" who had skilled employments "which require talent and education but confer no rank,—what may be called the non-aristocratic professions...." Such persons were natural Radicals, for, Mill asked, "what is Radicalism, but the claim of pre-eminence for personal qualities above conventional or accidental advantages" (477)? As examples Mill mentioned stewards and attorneys, but one recalls his claims for "the most virtuous and best-instructed" in "The Spirit of the Age,"[87] and his observation that journalists and editors, who were influential but regarded as ungentlemanly, did not enjoy public recognition of their real power (163-4). All such persons together might be called the intelligentsia. Of course, the word was not used in England in Mill's time, but there can be little doubt that he had in mind the phenomenon to which it refers when he discussed the political outlook of such persons.[88]

There is a class, now greatly multiplying in this country, and generally overlooked by politicians in their calculations; those men of talent and instruction, who are just below the rank in society which would of itself entitle them to associate with gentlemen. Persons of

---

[86]The Scots and Irish were also included (472-3, 477-8).

[87]"The Spirit of the Age. No. 5," *Examiner*, 29 May, 1831, 340. "Society may be said to be in its *natural* state, when worldly power, and moral influence, are habitually and undisputedly exercised by the fittest persons whom the existing state of society affords.... Society may be said to be in its *transitional* state, when it contains other persons fitter for worldly power and moral influence than those who have hitherto enjoyed them." ("The Spirit of the Age. No. 3," *ibid.*, 6 Feb., 1831, 82.)

[88]For scepticism about the use of the term "intellectuals," see Thomas, *Philosophic Radicals*, 449-50.

this class have the activity and energy which the higher classes in our state of civilization and education almost universally want. . . . They are, as it is natural they should be, Radicals to a man, and Radicals generally of a deep shade. They are the natural enemies of an order of things in which they are not in their proper place. (402-3.)

In this statement, which suggests his resentment at exclusion from a deserved political station in society, Mill (despite his position in the East India Company) identified with the class of which he said, "We are felt to be the growing power . . ." (403). His identification with such persons may explain the bitterness that is evident in some of his observations about the aristocracy (162).

Mill gave equal prominence to the working class as the other main constituent part of the opposition to the aristocracy. This was not only a matter of taking note of Chartism during the late 1830s, for before then Mill complained about the injuries done to "the people of no property, viz. those whose principal property consists in their bodily faculties." Like the middle class and those with small property, "the most numerous and poorest class has also an interest in reducing the exorbitant power which is conferred by large property" (218, 219). So Mill included in the large, naturally radical body "the whole effective political strength of the working classes: classes deeply and increasingly discontented, and whose discontent now [1839] speaks out in a voice which will not be unheard" (478).

In discussing both middle and working classes as the opposition to the aristocracy, Mill was not unaware of conflicts of interest that divided the working from the middle classes. He took note of disagreements about universal suffrage; of quarrels between supporters of the Church and Dissenters; and above all, of "an opposition of interest, which gives birth, it would seem, to the most deep-rooted distrusts and aversions which exist in society—the opposition between capitalists and labourers" (479). When the Chartists were providing evidence of class conflict between proletariat and bourgeoisie, Mill proposed that such antagonism be subordinated to the other kind of class conflict—between the aristocracy and the non-aristocratic classes—that was required by his political position. He appealed to the middle and working classes to co-operate in taking the next step, which was opposition to the aristocracy by a parliamentary Radical party (480-1). Since many middle-class radicals would not agree to universal suffrage, such co-operation required postponement of that demand, which was what the Chartists most wanted. The wish to postpone universal suffrage was also supported by Mill's belief that education ought to precede full democracy. Meanwhile it was necessary to redress the practical grievances of the working classes without yet allowing them full participation. "The motto of a Radical politician should be, Government *by means of* the middle for the working classes" (483).[89] Despite this concession to middle-class fear of the working class, Mill went far in asking that there should be "some members returned chiefly by the working classes. We think it of importance

---

[89] Also, "the Radicals may claim to themselves, as their peculiar office, a function in politics which stands more in need of them than any other: this is, the protection of the poor" (396).

that Mr. Lovett and Mr. Vincent [both Chartists] should make themselves heard in St. Stephen's as well as in Palace yard [i.e., in the House of Commons as well as in public meetings], and that the legislature should not have to learn the sentiments of the working classes at second-hand." (489.)

Mill's supportive words for the middle class, like his father's, were not intended to promote the interest of that class to the exclusion of the working class, nor was he particularly sympathetic to the middle class. He criticized the shopocracy (162) and, in urging that the working classes have some representation, said, "We would give [them] power, but not all power. We wish them to be strong enough to keep the middle classes in that salutary awe, without which, no doubt, those classes would be just like any other oligarchy. . . ." (489.) It is evident that Mill was far from being comfortable with middle-class rule:

The people of property are the stronger now, and will be for many years. All the danger of injustice lies from them, and not towards them. Nothing but the progressive increase of the power of the working classes, and a progressive conviction of that increase on the part of their superiors, can be a sufficient inducement to the proprietary class to cultivate a good understanding with the working people; to take them more and more into their councils; to treat them more and more as people who deserve to be listened to, whose condition and feelings must be considered, and are best learned from their own mouths; finally, to fit them for a share in their own government, by accustoming them to be governed, not like brute animals, but beings capable of rationality, and accessible to social feelings. (219-20.)

Mill's view of party politics during the 1830s was shaped by his belief that party conflict ought to reflect the class conflict between the aristocracy and its opponents. A Radical party should represent the anti-aristocratic interest of the diverse groups which Bentham and James Mill called the numerous classes or the People. Their party was to rest "on the *whole body* of radical opinion, from the whig-radicals at one extreme, to the more reasonable and practical of the working classes, and the Benthamites, on the other."[90] Far from excluding the working classes, Mill said, "A Radical party which does not rest upon the masses, is no better than a nonentity" (396). The labels he used for this party varied—it was the Radical party, popular party, Reform party, liberal party, Movement party—but whatever the label, "the small knot of philosophic radicals," as he called them, to whom Mill offered guidance throughout the decade, was to be the most advanced part of it, and he hoped it would provide the party with leadership.

On the other side of the great conflict Mill looked for an aristocratic party made up of both Whigs and Tories. The Whigs were included despite their use of a liberal and reformist rhetoric that superficially distinguished them from the Tories. They were attached to the existing distribution of power as much as the Tories and

---

[90]Letter to Bulwer, 3 Mar., 1838, *EL*, *CW*, XIII, 380. In another formulation Mill described "a phalanx, stretching from the Whig-Radicals at one extremity (if we may so term those among the persons calling themselves Whigs who are real Liberals) to the Ultra-Radicals and the Working Classes on the other" (467).

were equally "terrified at the remedies" (297). In response to popular pressure the Whigs occasionally made concessions, and at these times Mill allowed a place for the most liberal of them in a comprehensively defined Radical or Reform party, but his wish and expectation was that they would combine with the Tories in an aristocratic party. This would be the party of "the English oligarchy, Whig and Tory," and its organ (Mill said in 1834) was Lord Grey (262).

Since Radicals and Conservatives had clearly defined views on the large issue of democracy and aristocracy, they deserved to survive, but the Whigs, because of their half-hearted equivocations, did not. Thus he regarded the Whigs as "a coterie, not a party" (342), and rather optimistically noted that Conservatives and Radicals were gaining strength "at the expense not of each other, but of the Indifferents and the *juste milieu*," and, he added, "there will soon be no middle party, as indeed what seemed such had long been rather an appearance than a reality" (341).[91] The realignment of parties Mill wanted would remove the equivocating Whigs and make political conflict an accurate representation of the underlying class conflict. He did not use the word "realignment," but the phenomenon to which it refers was in his mind, as it was in Bentham's and James Mill's. Forcing the Whigs (other than the most liberal of them) to acknowledge their shared aristocratic interest with the Tories would create a place for a Radical party that was not a subordinate partner in an uneasy alliance with the Whigs. The proper alignment would come, he said, "when the present equivocal position of parties is ended, and the question is distinctly put between Radicalism and Conservatism" (477).[92]

Mill's view on party realignment illuminates his use of the phrase "Philosophic Radical." His fairly precise notion of the meaning of the term—which he himself coined—sharply contrasts with the loose usage among historians, for whom it has referred to such things as Benthamism, utilitarianism, liberalism, laissez-faire doctrine, and radicalism so loosely defined as to include the mixture of economic and political ideas of Adam Smith, Bentham, the Mills, Nassau Senior, and Cobden.[93] Mill invented the phrase to identify a small group among the many radicals who existed during the 1820s and 1830s. This group was deeply influenced by James Mill and most had associated with John Stuart Mill in the London Debating Society and in the production of the *Parliamentary History and Review*. Among them were George Grote, who later distinguished himself as an historian of Greece and of Greek philosophy; John Roebuck, who had a long and prominent career as a member of Parliament; and Charles Austin, who had a

---

[91]Also, "it deserves notice as one of the signs of the times, that the Whig *coterie* is not renewed. There are no young Whigs." (344-5.)

[92]For an account that attempts to explain Mill's politics without reference to the quest for realignment, see Thomas, *Philosophic Radicals, passim*.

[93]Mill said in 1851, "'Philosophic Reformers' is a worn-out and gone by expression; it had a meaning twenty years ago" (letter to John Chapman, 9 June, 1851, in *Later Letters* [*LL*], ed. Francis E. Mineka and Dwight N. Lindley, *CW*, XIV-XVII [Toronto: University of Toronto Press, 1972], XIV, 68).

dazzling success at the bar. Older than most of the others, Joseph Parkes, a successful attorney and political agent, played a part in their deliberations; although less an enthusiast than the others, he shared some of their convictions. Francis Place, the legendary Radical tailor, must be included, although his age and his participation in the Radical movement from the 1790s gave him a special position. It also would be difficult to exclude Harriet Grote, whose lively political interests and aggressive temperament made her an active participant. Others became associated with the Philosophic Radicals during the 1830s—Henry Warburton, Charles Buller, and Sir William Molesworth being most noteworthy. What characterized the group was their association with the Mills and a belief—held by some with greater enthusiasm than by others—that by means of party realignment the Radicals could replace the Whigs. This belief was promoted by several of these Philosophic Radicals in their journalism and their parliamentary careers.

Mill used the adjective "philosophic" in describing the Radicals with whom he felt a close affinity because they took a principled—a philosophic—position on politics. Mill's political philosophy—or perhaps one should say half of it, the part derived from Bentham and James Mill—was mainly occupied with justifying democracy against aristocratic government. He contrasted the Philosophic Radicals with historical Radicals who demanded popular institutions as an inheritance from the distant past; with metaphysical Radicals whose belief in democracy was based on a notion of abstract natural rights; with Radicals marked by irritation with a particular policy of government; and with "radicals of position, who are radicals . . . because they are not lords" (353).[94] Mill's favoured Radicals deserved to be called philosophic because they traced practical evils back to their cause, which was the aristocratic principle. Thus their motto was "enmity to the Aristocratical principle" (353).[95]

This justification for the adjective "philosophic" makes the label appropriate not only for Radicals, for there was an opposing position which was also philosophic. There was a type of Tory "who gives to Toryism (what can be given to it, though not to Whiggism) something like a philosophic basis; who finds for [his] opinions the soundest, the most ingenious, or the most moral arguments by which they can be supported" (335). This was "speculative Toryism," such as Coleridge's:

As whatever is noble or disinterested in Toryism is founded upon a recognition of the moral duty of submission to rightful authority, so the moral basis of Radicalism is the refusal to pay that submission to an authority which is usurped, or to which the accidents of birth or

---

[94]Mill also classified Radicals, other than Philosophic Radicals, as "demagogic radicals, such as Wakley, and . . . the historical radicals of the Cartwright school, and . . . the division of property radicals if there be any" (letter to Albany Fonblanque, 30 Jan., 1838, *EL, CW,* XIII, 370).

[95]Mill also used the adjective "educated," but the adjective "philosophic" was not merely a synonym for "educated."

fortune are the only title. The Tory acknowledges, along with the right to obedience, a correlative obligation to govern for the good of the ruled. . . . (478-9.)[96]

In the House of Commons, however, Toryism was quite different; it acted on behalf of the aristocratic "selfish oligarchy" (479); it was the Toryism for which Sir John Walsh "gets up and vents . . . shattered and worn-out absurdities," including a defence of Tory policy in Ireland (335). Even Peel was disdained by Mill (403-4). Yet because Toryism could address the large question of aristocracy and democracy it was capable of having philosophic status. The Whigs, in contrast, although "a portion of the privileged class," and "hostile to any thorough reform," pretended to favour reform on behalf of the people, and consequently could be seen to be unprincipled. "Since the questions arising out of the Hanoverian succession had been set at rest, the term Whig had never been the symbol of any principles" (342).

A consequence of Mill's "philosophic" approach to politics was a preference for conflict between extreme parties, a preference which placed the highest priority on the issue of aristocracy versus democracy. Mill, in describing how the Philosophic Radicals and the Tories gained domination of the London Debating Society, said, "our doctrines were fairly pitted against their opposites," and with evident pride he reported that these debates "habitually consisted of the strongest arguments and most philosophic principles which either side was able to produce."[97] Later he encouraged such conflict in the House of Commons because it would be a contest "between the representatives of the two great principles,—not between two men whose policies differ from one another only by the shadow of a shade" (495). In such a contest the Whigs would be set aside and "the question [would be] distinctly put between Radicalism and Conservatism" (477).

Mill's confidence that the Whigs could be set aside, to be replaced by a Radical party led by the Philosophic Radicals, may seem surprising in retrospect. Yet he clearly believed that if the Philosophic Radicals played their cards correctly, that is, aggressively, the Radicals would become an independent party and might ultimately gain office. As unrealistic as this view appeared to many contemporar-

---

[96]Speculative Toryism, it may be noted, although opposed to Philosophic Radicalism in the realm of practical politics, somewhat resembled the position associated with Austin and the St. Simonians and Coleridge, which, according to Mill, complemented Benthamite radicalism in the realm of philosophy. See also 402 on men of speculative ability who were "theoretically Tories."

[97]"Early Draft," *CW*, I, 132. Extreme Tories sometimes had a reciprocal perception. Disraeli said, "A Tory and a Radical, I understand; a Whig—a democratic aristocrat, I cannot comprehend" (*Whigs and Whiggism: Political Writings*, ed. William Hutcheon [London: Murray, 1913], 19). Also, the Radical or Utilitarian party was called "a more shrewd, intelligent, and philosophical class of men than the Whigs, accustomed to a closer method of reasoning" (James B. Bernard, *Theory of the Constitution* [London: Ridgway, 1834], 5). For an illuminating account of the sources of Mill's beliefs about conflict, see Robson, *Improvement of Mankind*, 191-9.

ies,[98] it did not seem impossible to Mill (or to his father or to the other Philosophic Radicals).[99] That he seriously entertained this possibility is an indication of his doctrinairism and his high political ambition during the 1830s. Sophisticated and careful as Mill was, his words show that he thought the Philosophic Radicals eligible for the highest offices. There were Radicals in and out of Parliament, he said, with the talent and energy which in time would qualify them to play a distinguished part in either a government or an opposition (386).[100] He also spoke about the prospective party of moderate radicals as "*our* party,"[101] and discussed what would happen "the moment a Ministry of Moderate Radicals comes into power." "All things," he said, "are ripe for it," and its leader "is sure of everything, to the Premiership inclusive" (494, 495).[102] A similar speculation in the *Spectator* did not exclude Mill; in describing a possible Radical cabinet, in addition to Durham (as Prime Minister), Grote (Exchequer), Hume (Home Secretary), Buller (Colonies), Warburton (Board of Trade), Molesworth (Board of Control), John Romilly (Solicitor General), it mentioned, without suggesting offices, Roebuck, Charles Austin, and Mr. John Mill.[103]

Since Mill denied the Whigs their usual position as a major party, they regarded his views on parliamentary politics as doctrinaire. His arguments indeed had many doctrinaire features (which were present despite his reaction against his own early Benthamite sectarianism): he looked for large-scale change, and he depreciated reforms that did not contribute to the redistribution of power;[104] he was uncomfortable with compromise, and he criticized compromisers and trimmers as

---

[98]Palmerston, in asking whether Molesworth thought of coming into office with his own followers, advised "if he meant to be a leader of a party, to improve his knowledge of Parliamentary strategy" (*Hansard's Parliamentary Debates* [*PD*], 3rd ser., Vol. 41, cols. 489, 521-3 [6 Mar., 1838]). Lord John Russell taunted the Radicals with the problems they and the country would have if Grote were Chancellor of the Exchequer and leader of the House, and he asked whether Molesworth's administration could command a majority (*Letters to the Electors of Stroud, on the Principles of the Reform Act*, 6th ed. [London: Ridgway, 1839], 32, 35).

[99]Roebuck looked forward to the time when "we . . . shall take up our position at the *head* of the opposition" and when "*we* shall govern" (letter to Brougham, 7 Sept., 1836, Brougham Papers, University College, London). James Mill foresaw the time when the "powers of government will be put in [the Philosophic Radicals'] hands" ("State of the Nation," *London Review*, I [Apr., 1835], 18).

[100]Also, "If Radicalism had its Sir Robert Peel, he would be at the head of an administration within two years . . ." (404). Here Mill alludes to Peel's skills in parliamentary management; for his estimate of Peel's politics, see 403-4.

[101]Letter to Robertson, 30 Jan. or early Feb., 1838, *EL, CW*, XIII, 371.

[102]Mill later recognized that he "had expected too much" and that he had had "an exaggerated sense of the possibilities" (*Autobiography, CW*, I, 203, 205).

[103]*Spectator*, 9 Dec., 1837, 1164, 1166; see also *ibid.*, 16 Dec., 1837, 1192.

[104]For example, in 1826 Mill did not think Catholic Emancipation very significant, as it would not improve conditions in Ireland; it was hotly debated by both aristocratic parties because it would not remove the "great abuses" which benefited the class represented by both those parties (66-7). For Mill's view on the abolition of slavery, see 180 below. In "these days of Movement, the place which any session, any single event, will occupy in history, depends not upon the intrinsic importance of the event, or value of the Acts of Parliament which have passed during the session; but upon the far greater consideration, how much it has helped forward the Movement, or contributed to hold it back" (284).

unprincipled;[105] he assumed that considerable changes could be achieved easily;[106] and, as mentioned, he regarded conflict with an ideological opposite as the worthiest kind, and so was critical of moderates who stood for gradual change. This last feature of the Philosophic Radicals' approach was identified by the Whig publicist Francis Jeffrey as early as 1826, when he responded to James Mill's castigation of Whigs as insincere reformers and moderates: "The real reason of the animosity with which we [Whigs] are honoured by the more eager of the two extreme parties, is, that we . . . impede the assault they are impatient mutually to make on each other, and take away from them the means of that direct onset, by which the sanguine in both hosts imagine they might at once achieve a decisive victory."[107] Although other moderate critics of the Philosophic Radicals did not match Jeffrey's incisive rhetoric, they recognized the doctrinairism. Fonblanque, once a Radical himself, late in the 1830s called them (and especially John Mill) Ultras, fanatical Radicals, pseudo-Liberals, Detrimentals, Wrongheads, and, since their tactics would have led to a Tory government, Tory Radicals.[108]

Mill was aware of the "philosophic" origin of the ambition he entertained for radicalism. And he was also aware of British uneasiness with anything theoretical. "There is no passion in England for forms of government, considered in themselves. Nothing could be more inconsistent with the exclusively practical spirit of the English people." (339.) Indeed, England was "a nation *practical* even to ridiculousness; . . . a nation given to distrust and dislike all that there is in principles . . ., and whose first movement would be to fight against, rather than for, any one who has nothing but a principle to hold out" (392-3). In this uncongenial environment, Mill tried—though hardly with success—to conceal the theoretical aspect of his political enterprise. He used the phrase "Philosophic(al) Radical" rather infrequently (165, 191, 212, 353),[109] and he tried to divert attention from the "philosophic" side of his radicalism by using equivalent

---

[105]Mill referred to the "middle course which so often unites the evils of both extremes with the advantages of neither" (216).

[106]For example, "The approaching session will be next to that of 1830/1831, the most important since 1688—and parties will stand quite differently at the commencement and at the close of it" (letter to Tocqueville, 7 Jan., 1837, *EL, CW,* XII, 317). Mill also spoke of "the practicability of Utopianism" ("Rationale of Representation" [1835], *CW,* XVIII, 42).

[107]"Moore's *Life of Sheridan,*" *Edinburgh Review,* XLV (Dec., 1826), 35.

[108]*Examiner,* 6 Aug., 1837, 497; 27 Aug., 1837, 545; 3, 10, and 17 Sept., 1837, 563, 581, 595; 28 Jan., 1838, 49; 4 Feb., 1838, 65-6; letter to Lord Durham, 2 Jan., 1837, Lambton Papers, in the Lambton Estate Office, Chester-le-Street, County Durham. Fonblanque regarded the reasoning of Mill and his associates as bizarre but purposeful; he characterized it in the following way: "With a Whig Ministry we play second or third parts, but with a Tory Ministry we should fill the first ranks in opposition. Therefore, as what is best for the exhibition of ourselves is best for the public, it is best for the public that there should be a Tory Ministry." (*Examiner,* 4 Feb., 1838, 66.)

[109]See also "Mr. Mill," in *CW,* I, 594; letter to Fonblanque, 30 Jan., 1838, *EL, CW,* XIII, 370. For use of the phrase by others, see *Spectator,* IX, 1051 (Nov., 1836); 1251 (31 Dec., 1836); XII, 34 (12 Jan., 1839); *Examiner,* 23 Jan., 1838, 808; *Morning Chronicle,* 29 Jan., 1838, 3; William James, in *PD,* 3rd ser., Vol. 40, col. 1169 (15 Feb., 1838).

phrases, these too used sparingly. They included "thorough Reformers" (292, 322, 378, 380), "complete reformers" (301, 307), "enlightened" Radicals (378), "decided Radicals" (389), "real reformers" (326), and "more vigorous Reformers" (322). Mill explained that "because this designation [Philosophic Radicals] too often repeated gave a *coterie* air which it was felt to be objectionable, the phrase was varied."[110] Despite such attempts to evade criticism, the Philosophic Radicals, including Mill as their self-appointed spokesman, attracted increasing attention as the size of the Whig majority in Parliament diminished and Radical votes became more important.

RADICAL PARTY TACTICS

SINCE MILL WISHED to promote Radical leadership of the reform party in Parliament, the tactics he recommended to the other Philosophic Radicals focused on their relations with the Whigs. Much of what he suggested depended on his estimate of Whig policy on reform. Those in the Whig government, like their supporters, varied greatly in their reformist zeal, but they were sufficiently favourable to reform for Lord Grey's government to cultivate a liberal image by calling itself the Reform Ministry.

This image, when combined with pressures for additional reform from the press and the liberal wing of their own party, created a dilemma for the Whig leadership, according to Mill. In the face of demand for reform, the Whigs had to choose either to make concessions and become more reformist than Whig, or they could refuse concessions and become hardly distinguishable from the Tories. They "must either join with the Tories in resisting, or with the Radicals in carrying, improvements of a more fundamental kind than any but the latter have yet ventured to identify themselves with" (326). Whichever choice they made, the reform cause would be promoted. If they chose concession, considerable improvements would be made: "there is hardly any limit to what may now be carried *through* the Ministry" (192). On the other hand, if the Whigs resisted and were forced to coalesce with the Tories, much good would result even if the government was then openly opposed to additional reform. For then the Radical party would be invigorated and the country would be "delivered from the anomalous state, in which we have neither the benefits of a liberal government, nor those of a liberal opposition; in which we can carry nothing through the two Houses, but what would be given by a Tory ministry, and yet are not able to make that vigorous appeal to the people out of doors, which under the Tories could be made and would be eagerly responded to" (385). If this situation occurred, of course, the realignment strategy would have

---

[110]Letter to Fonblanque, 30 Jan., 1838, *EL, CW*, XIII, 370. This letter arose out of disagreements about Mill's attribution of Philosophic Radical opinions to Fonblanque and criticism of Philosophic Radicals by Fonblanque.

been implemented; that is, the Radicals would have ceased to be a mere appendage to the Whigs and the Radical party would have achieved independent existence.[111]

The Whigs may have faced a dilemma, but Mill was not without one of his own, for he wanted both additional reform *and* the establishment of an independent Radical party, and Whig policy that promoted one of these goals made the other harder to attain. If the Whigs made concessions to the pressures for additional reform, Radicals, even extreme Radicals, became more generous in the support of the government, and thus the achievement of independence for the Radical party became more difficult. On the other hand, the gaining of such independence would be facilitated by Whig resistance to further reform. For Mill's former goal to be achieved, the Whig leadership would have had to move to the left; for the latter, they would have had to move to the right. Since Mill wanted both results, he was inevitably dissatisfied, no matter what the Whigs did. His response to the dilemma changed as the decade unfolded. During the first four years or so following the Reform Bill, Mill thought the Whigs could be persuaded to make concessions, and therefore he recommended conditional support of their governments. Increasingly during these years, however, he became disappointed with them, despite the abolition of slavery and the passing of the New Poor Law. A turning-point came later in the decade when the Whigs' unequivocal refusal to consider reform of the constitution put an end to Mill's expectations that Radicals and Whigs might co-operate. Thereafter he urged the Philosophic Radicals to adopt a more independent line of conduct, and he experienced exhilaration at the prospect of a separate Radical party. Yet, even in this mood, he complained about the lack of movement towards the implementation of the Radical programme.

Either of Mill's goals, however, could be promoted by pressure on the Whig government, and therefore throughout the decade he called on the Philosophic Radicals to "attempt much" (395). They were supposed to "put forward, on every fitting occasion, with boldness and perseverance, the best political ideas which the country affords" (191). Despite their small numbers, the strong public support for radicalism would allow a few to accomplish great things: "there is a vitality in the principles, there is that in them both of absolute truth and of adaptation to the particular wants of the time, which will not suffer that in Parliament two or three shall be gathered together in their name, proclaiming the purpose to stand or fall by them, and to go to what lengths soever they may lead, and that those two or three shall not soon wield a force before which ministries and aristocracies shall quail" (397-8).[112] Despite what Mill saw as their great opportunity, however, some of the Philosophic Radicals were unaggressive. Grote, from whom so much was

---

[111]Mill referred to the Radicals as needing "to shake off the character of a *tail*" (letter to Bulwer, 3 Mar., 1838, *EL*, *CW*, XIII, 380); and he asked, "why have they sunk into a mere section of the supporters of the Whig Ministry" (344-5)?

[112]Also, "what a power they [the complete reformers] might wield, if they . . . were not, unhappily, (with some meritorious exceptions,) the least enterprising and energetic" (301).

expected, deeply disappointed Mill. "Why does not Mr. Grote exert himself" (314n)?[113] The Radicals, Mill said, were without policy, a leader, or organization, and therefore they failed to call forth their strength in the country (467). Mill sometimes called them torpid (327) and ciphers (165) and accused them of lacking courage (212), though there were exceptions, notably Roebuck, whom Mill generally praised.[114]

Putting pressure on the Whig government should have been easy, Mill thought, for he assumed that the great burst of reform agitation that forced aristocratic acceptance of the Reform Act manifested a fundamental change, making public opinion permanently favourable to further reform. Therefore he thought opinion would support either a Whig-led reform party or a genuine Radical party in opposition to both Whigs and Tories. The events of 1831-32 revealed a public angry and outspoken enough to be capable of intimidating the governing classes (430).[115] These events changed the understanding of the constitution, "which [since the Reform Bill] enables the people to carry all before them when driven by any violent excitement" (299). Mill thought the governing classes knew it could happen again: "where the public voice is strong and unanimous, the Ministry must now go along with it" (317). Although public opinion became much less agitated after the Reform Bill passed into law, Mill assumed that "there [was] a great deal of passive radicalism in the electoral body,"[116] and he confidently announced that "England is moderate Radical" (389).[117] He also thought this latent opinion could be reawakened at any time, and therefore that the "progress of reform appears . . . certain" (292).[118]

The period immediately following the Reform Bill understandably began with high Radical hopes. The aristocracy apparently had suffered a severe defeat, and the Whigs, despite their sponsorship of the Reform Bill and their hopes for party advantage from it, were worried about its long-term consequences. In May 1832

---

[113]"Nobody disappointed my father and me more than Grote. . . . We had long known him to be fainthearted. . . . If his courage and energy had been equal to the circumstances, or to his knowledge and abilities, the history of those ten years of relapse into Toryism might have been very different." ("Early Draft," *CW*, I, 155.) This passage was left out of the *Autobiography*, where Mill wrote, "I can perceive that the men were less in fault than we supposed, and that we had expected too much from them" (*CW*, I, 117).

[114]On Roebuck, see 191, 200-1, 202, 307n, 385-6, 389, 452n-3n. On Buller, see 324. On Hume, see 326.

[115]He says, "we now know that they [the Ministers] will yield to gentle violence" (285); "did any political body . . . ever reform itself, until it trembled for its existence" (491)?

[116]Letter to Fonblanque, 3 Feb., 1838, *EL, CW*, XIII, 374.

[117]"To the people . . . let them hold themselves in readiness. No one knows what times may be coming. . . . Let England and Scotland be prepared at the first summons to start into Political Unions. Let the House of Commons be inundated with petitions. . . ." (*Ibid.*, 26.) It hardly need be said that Mill's estimates were exaggerated and even unrealistic. This was a feature of the doctrinairism mentioned above, xxxii-xxxiii. Another example: "If any ministry would now bring forward the ballot, they would excite greater enthusiasm than even that which was excited for the Reform Bill" (letter to Tocqueville, 7 Jan., 1837, *EL, CW*, XII, 317).

[118]"Radicalism is a thing which must prevail" (407).

Mill thought there was "nothing definite and determinate in politics except radicalism; and we shall have nothing but radicals and whigs for a long time to come."[119] It is not known what Mill thought when his Radical friends in Parliament sat on the opposition benches,[120] but it should have gratified him, for it set them off from the Whigs as the nucleus of a new party. He also must have been pleased by Grote's motion on the ballot, which was supported by 106 votes and threw Whigs and Tories together to defeat it by a majority of 105.[121] After his initial enthusiasm, however, the first session of the Reform Parliament was, on the whole, disappointing to Mill. Although the Whigs adopted the reform label and introduced some measures of reform, he depreciated most of the proposed legislation because it was so far removed from the organic reform sought by genuine Radicals. Slavery was abolished; the Bank Charter was renewed; and free competition in the China tea trade was established as part of the renewed East India Company charter. Mill was not opposed to these things, but they fell far short of what he wanted. When the government defended its record in the first session with its pamphlet *The Reform Ministry and the Reformed Parliament*, Mill, in his review of it, complained that it "passes over three-fourths of the essentials of the case." The Whigs must be judged, he wrote, not only by what they had done, but by considering "what they have opposed, and so *prevented* from being done."[122]

In these circumstances—the Whigs were the only agency through which reform could be achieved, yet they proposed only changes that Mill regarded as insufficient—it was difficult to withhold support, and yet it was also difficult to be enthusiastic. So Mill acceded to the Philosophic Radicals' voting in support of the government, but he called on them to be demanding, and he held out the threat of renewed agitation of public opinion and a return to the nervous days prior to the Reform Bill.

Three events in 1834 reduced Mill's uneasiness about Philosophic Radical support of the Whig government. First, the resignation of Stanley and Graham in May signalled a reduction of conservatism in the cabinet (252, 285). Next, the government sponsored the Poor Law Amendment Act. Although not an organic reform, it was far-reaching and dear to all whose views on administration and poor relief had been shaped by Bentham and the political economists. This was the one achievement of the session, Mill said; he had not expected such a development, especially as there was no public clamour for it; consequently "we give them [the Whigs] due honour" (285). Finally, Lord Grey retired and was replaced by Melbourne. The retirement of Grey, a man of the 1790s, would allow the Whigs to be more responsive to the needs of a new age (263-5). As this period of

---

[119]Letter to Carlyle, 29 May, 1832, *EL, CW*, XII, 107.
[120]For evidence that the Radicals sat on the opposition benches, see Hamburger, *Intellectuals in Politics*, 122-3.
[121]*PD*, 3rd ser., Vol. 17, col. 667 (26 Apr., 1833).
[122]"The Ministerial Manifesto," *Examiner*, 22 Sept., 1833, 593.

Whig-Radical relations ended, Mill thought that the Whigs might regain the popularity they enjoyed in 1832, and that their errors of omission would be forgiven. "From us, and we believe from all the enlightened reformers, they may expect, until they shall have had a fair trial, not only no hostility, but the most friendly encouragement and support. They must now throw themselves upon the people." (243.)

Such a trial had to be postponed, for in November, 1834, the Whigs were turned out and replaced by a Tory government under Peel. Mill and the Philosophic Radicals were jubilant, for they correctly assumed that this would be a brief interlude, and they were delighted to witness the Whigs in defeat. The Whigs now joined the Philosophic Radicals on the opposition benches, and the Radicals—about seventy of them—co-operated with the Whigs to expel Peel from office.[123] When the Whigs under Melbourne returned to the government benches in April, 1835, the Philosophic Radicals' old problem—of defining their relation to the Whigs—returned in an acute form, for they had to adopt a position that took into account both their recent co-operation with the Whigs in opposition and their long-standing enmity to them.

Mill now offered guidance to the Philosophic Radicals from the pages of the *London Review*, which began publication just as the change in government took place (297). In a brief comment which was a postscript to his father's political article, Mill said he did "not call upon the thorough Reformers to declare enmity against [the Whig Ministry], or to seek their downfall, because their measures will be half-measures . . . nor even because they will join with the Tories in crying down all complete reforms . . ." (292). At the same time, Mill suggested that the Philosophic Radicals refuse any offers of office. This he called "qualified and distrustful" support, and in the next issue he warned that such co-operation might not last very long (297).[124] In keeping with this advice, the Philosophic Radicals sat on the government side, to indicate their support of the Whig Ministry, but below the gangway, to demonstrate their distance and independence from it.[125]

A crisis in this arrangement occurred as the Municipal Corporations Bill passed through Parliament, for this legislation and the way it was amended raised fundamental questions for the Radicals. The Bill provided for the elimination of the "little oligarchies," as the Webbs later called them, that ruled in towns, and replaced them with town councils elected by household suffrage.[126] Although not fully democratic, the Bill went rather far in that direction. It pleased the Radicals,

---

[123]Estimates of the size of the Radical group varied: Parkes said there were seventy or eighty; Richard Potter said there were more than fifty; Thomas Young put the number at seventy-eight (letter from Parkes to Durham, 26 Jan., 1835, Lambton Papers; letter from Young to Edward Ellice, 3 Mar., 1835, Ellice Papers, National Library of Scotland; Potter's Parliamentary Diaries, Vol. 8, f. 2 [entry of 18 Feb., 1835], London School of Economics and Political Science).

[124]See also a letter from Mill to Aristide Guilbert, 8 May, 1835, *EL, CW*, XII, 261. James Mill made similar recommendations ("State of the Nation," *London Review*, I [Apr., 1835], 16-18).

[125]Henry Reeve, "Personal Memoir of Mr. Grote," *Edinburgh Review* (July, 1873), 138, 232.

[126]Sidney and Beatrice Webb, *English Local Government* (1908), 11 vols. (Hamden: Archon, 1963), III, 748-9.

even delighted some of them, including Mill, who said "the destructive part . . . is of signal excellence," and he acknowledged that, despite deficiencies in its constructive part, there was much merit, particularly the extension of the suffrage to householders, for which the Ministers were "entitled to great praise" (303). Overall, Mill said, it was "one of the greatest steps in improvement ever made by peaceable legislation in the internal government of a country" (308). The features of the Bill that elicited such praise were not altered by several amendments made in the House of Lords.

Yet the Philosophic Radicals were so eager to assert their fundamental principles that several of them, including Mill, responded angrily to the Lords' amendments. It was the Lords' tampering that caused the difficulty, because the Radicals, recalling the submission by the House of Lords in 1832, interpreted the post-Reform Act constitution as tolerating an upper house only so long as it remained quiescent. The suggestion that the House of Lords had a veto indicated that the Lords, as Roebuck said, "have not yet acquiesced in this arrangement," as they did not comprehend their "real position."[127] For Mill the Bill was "a challenge of the House of Lords to mortal combat" (302); and to allow the Lords' amendments to stand would be "to abandon all the ends to which the Reform Bill was intended as a means" (343). Roebuck, Place, Molesworth, and even Grote were extremely angered, even more, it seems, than Mill.[128] Their anger was so great that they criticized the House of Lords as a second chamber, and in the end, Mill joined them. "An entire change in its constitution is cried out for from the remotest corner of the three kingdoms; and few would be satisfied with any change short of abolishing the hereditary principle" (313). He proposed an upper house chosen by the lower. The choice was to be made from the existing peerage supplemented with qualified persons not in the Commons who were to be given peerages. This was not the best design he could make, but only the result of his attempt to "remodel" the existing House of Lords. Its purpose was a second chamber "unlikely to set itself in opposition to what is good in the acts and purposes of the First."[129] As well as attacks on the Lords, this episode produced complaints about the "truckling" by the Whig government and its moderate radical supporters (317).

Mill continued, however, to recommend cautious and selective support of the government, despite his disapproval of its yielding to the Lords on the Municipal Corporations Bill. Although he complained about the appearance of a tacit compromise between the government and the thorough reformers, he said, in October, 1835: "We do not wish the Radicals to attack the Ministry; we are

---

[127]Roebuck, "The Crisis: What Ought the Ministers to Do?", *Pamphlets for the People* (no. 12, 27 Aug., 1835), 8; "The Conduct of Ministers Respecting the Amendments of the House of Lords," *ibid.* (no. 14, 10 Sept., 1835), 1.

[128]*PD*, 3rd ser., Vol. 30, cols. 1162-8, 1435-6. Mill criticized the Philosophic Radicals for not forcing more divisions, "not to carry their propositions, but to force public attention to the subject" (308n; evidently written and published in September at the earliest).

[129]"The House of Lords," *Globe and Traveller*, 16 Oct., 1835, 2.

anxious that they should co-operate with them. But we think they might co-operate without yoking themselves to the ministerial car, abdicating all independent action, and leaving nothing to distinguish them from the mere Whig coterie. . . ." (316.) In April, 1836, Mill continued to argue that the Whigs deserved support from the thorough reformers, for they introduced or at least promised a marriage bill that removed certain grievances of dissenters; a bill for the registration of births and deaths; a bill to consolidate turnpike trusts; an Irish Corporation reform bill; and a measure of church reform (322-5). A far cry from organic reform, these proposals were yet enough to justify his call for support of the government. Despite his distrust of Whigs, he was reluctant to call for an attempt to turn out the government (344). At the same time, however, he asserted Radical independence and looked forward to the realignment of parties (326-7).

Mill's mixed view reflected certain difficulties which he and the other Philosophic Radicals faced. Their principles made co-operation with the Whigs disagreeable and directed them to an independent course of action. The political situation in 1836 also might have encouraged them to adopt aggressive tactics, for Melbourne's majority, including Irish and moderate radicals, was perhaps fifty or sixty, and Mill thought Melbourne dependent on the small group of Philosophic Radicals for support.[130] Other circumstances, however, called for restraint, for it became evident that the large number of moderate radicals, whose support was required for the implementation of the Philosophic Radicals' realignment strategy, might not go along with an attempt to turn out the Whig government. These so-called "200 ballot men," the "nominal" Whigs, supported Grote's ballot motion and were more reformist than the Whig leadership, but probably would keep the Whigs in office rather than risk a Tory government.

Among the small group of Philosophic Radicals there was disagreement. Aggressive, anti-Whig tactics were advocated by Molesworth and Roebuck, strongly supported by Francis Place and Harriet Grote. Molesworth's "Terms of Alliance between Radicals and Whigs" (January, 1837) was a clear and forthright statement of their position.[131] Others were more cautious, though not without sympathy for the extremists; these included Grote, Buller, Warburton, and Hume. Both Joseph Parkes and Fonblanque were vigorously opposed. The issue was hotly debated (as Harriet Grote put it) "as to the true play of the Rads."[132]

Mill, like the Philosophic Radical group as a whole, was of two minds. He took note of "the plan which [Molesworth] and several other of the radical members

---

[130]"Without the systematic support of the Radicals, [the Ministry] could not exist for a day" (345).

[131]*L&WR*, XXVI, 279-318. Mill, who corrected and altered this article, called it "a *coup de parti*, a manifesto as we say of the radicals (or rather *for* the radicals) on the subject of the Whigs" (letter to Tocqueville, 7 Jan., 1837, *EL, CW*, XII, 316). Harriet Grote called Molesworth "the Mirabeau of the day. . . . His [article] has given him a high reputation among our Philosophical Radicals." (Letter to Frances Eliza von Koch, 7 Feb., 1837, *The Lewin Letters: A Selection from the Correspondence and Diaries of an English Family, 1756-1884*, ed. Thomas Herbert Lewin [London: Constable, 1909], I, 353.)

[132]Letter to Place, 28 Jan. [1837], British Library, Add. MSS 35150, f. 235.

have formed and are executing. I think them quite right."[133] He also said, "As for me I am with the extreme party; though I would not always go so far as Roebuck, I entirely agree with those who say that the whole conduct of the Whigs tends to *amortir l'esprit public*, and that it would be a good thing for invigorati[ng] and consolidating the reform party if the Tories were to come in."[134] In this spirit he lamented Fonblanque's desertion, evident in his effective criticism of the Philosophic Radicals and in his appeal to moderate radicals for support of the Melbourne government. Mill said it was only Fonblanque's "past reputation for radicalism which prevents him from being mistaken for a ministerialist with radical inclinations" (380). He also complained that since 1835 Fonblanque had "acted as if his first object was to support and glorify the ministers, and the assertion of his own political doctrines only the second" (379).[135] Yet in the same letter in which he identified himself with the extreme party, Mill also noted, "the country does not go with us in [the extreme tactics] and therefore it will not do for the radicals to aid in turning out the ministry; by doing so they would create so much hostility in their own party, that there would be no hope of a real united reform party with the country at its back, for many years. So we must linger on. . . ."[136] Doctrine called for one line of conduct; circumstances pointed to another: as Mill said, they were in a "false position."[137]

In late 1837 Mill suddenly broke loose from the "false position" by declaring open hostility to the Whig government. He was provoked to do so by Lord John Russell's "Finality" speech, and he was joined in this move by other Philosophic Radicals, who recently had been deeply disappointed by the thinning of their ranks in the elections of August, 1837.[138] In response to Radical amendments to the Address urging consideration of an extended suffrage, ballot, and shorter

[133]Letter to Tocqueville, 7 Jan., 1837, *EL, CW*, XII, 316-17.

[134]Letter to Guilbert, 19 June, 1837, *ibid.*, 338.

[135]Fonblanque had financial difficulties in maintaining the *Examiner*, and money for the paper was raised by Ellice and Durham. "The rescue completed the conversion of the *Examiner* from radicalism to moderate Whiggism. . . . The *Examiner* had by 1838 become an organ of the ministry," according to Thomas, who argues that "It would be over-simple to conclude that Fonblanque had been bought. . . . But he had compromised his independence, and if his critics like Roebuck and Mill had known of the scheme to pay his debts, they would have been more indignant than they were." (*Philosophic Radicals*, 328-9.)

[136]Letter to Guilbert, 19 June, 1837, *EL, CW*, XII, 338.

[137]Letter to Tocqueville, 7 Jan., 1837, *ibid.*, 317. Greville said the Radicals found their "hands tied," and therefore they "lingered on," but they were "very irate and sulky." Yet, "as they still think that there is a better chance of their views being promoted by the Whigs remaining in, they continue to vote with them in cases of need" (*The Greville Memoirs, 1814-1860*, 8 vols. [London: Macmillan, 1838], III, 401; entry of 25 June, 1837).

[138]Roebuck, Hume, Ewart, and Thompson were defeated, and Grote ranked last among the four successful candidates in the City of London; he won by a margin of six votes (he had led the poll in 1832). Hume was soon returned for Kilkenny. Fonblanque said the election marked "the wide chasm that now separates the main body of the Radicals from the extreme section" (*Examiner*, 4 Mar., 1838, 130). Unlike his fellow-Radicals, Mill managed to find comfort in the election results: "The Radicals *seem* to have lost most only because they have lost some of their most leading men, but those will come in again for some other place very soon; and a great number of the new members are very decided Radicals . . ." (letter to Robertson, 6 Aug., 1837, *EL, CW*, XII, 345). See also 388-9.

parliaments,[139] Russell said the amendments would repeal the Reform Act, whereas he regarded that Act as a final measure and not one he was willing to repeal or reconstruct.[140] Not only did Russell declare his opposition to further constitutional reform, but he carried with him a majority of the moderate radicals, who refused to vote for the Radical amendments.[141] Most of the Philosophic Radicals, both in and out of Parliament, were depressed by this development, but Mill was angry. He attended a meeting at Molesworth's house in order to rouse the others. He argued that "the time is come when all temporizing—all delicacy towards the Whigs—all fear of disuniting Reformers or of embarrassing Ministers by pressing forward reforms, must be at an end."[142] Now outspoken in advocating complete separation from the Whigs, he urged the Philosophic Radicals to "assume the precise position towards Lord Melbourne which they occupied in the first Reformed Parliament towards Lord Grey. Let them separate from the Ministry and go into declared opposition." (412.)

Events arising out of the Canadian rebellion of 1837-38 were to be the occasion for Mill's last call for the organization of a Radical party in opposition to Whigs and Tories. Initially, Canadian events clouded his hopes for renewed Radical activity, for the Philosophic Radicals' response contributed to their isolation from the moderate radicals. When in January, 1838, the government proposed the suspension of the Canadian constitution for four years and the creation of a high commissioner, the Philosophic Radicals were opposed, but failed to gain support from liberal reformers and moderate radicals.[143] Edward Lytton Bulwer taunted them about their disagreements with other reformers:

Those who were called philosophical Radicals, . . . were . . . the same small and isolated knot of Gentlemen, who, on the first day of this session declared so much contempt of the

---

[139]Amendments were moved by Wakley, seconded by Molesworth, and supported in speeches by Hume and Grote. Grote said, "Conservative principle was really predominant in Parliament, and when he said Conservative he meant the negation of all substantial reform" (*PD*, 3rd ser., Vol. 39, cols. 37-48, 58-60 [20 Nov., 1837]). Molesworth said the Whig Ministry "adopts Tory principles in order to retain office" (*ibid.*, Vol. 41, cols 488-9, 577 [6, 7 Mar., 1838]). Hume said, "Little now remains either in principle or in act between the Tories and the Whigs" (letter to Place, 1 Jan., 1838, British Library, Add. MSS 35151, f. 48). And Grote added, it was "not at all worth while to undergo the fatigue of a nightly attendance in Parliament for the simple purpose of sustaining *Whig* conservatism against *Tory* conservatism" (letter to John Austin, Feb., 1838, in Harriet Grote, *Life of George Grote*, 127).

[140]*PD*, 3rd ser., Vol. 39, cols. 46, 69-70 (20 Nov., 1837).

[141]Wakley's first amendment, for an extension of the suffrage, received twenty votes; among the twenty were Grote, Hume, and Leader (Wakley and Molesworth were tellers) (*ibid.*, col. 81 [20 Nov., 1837]). In view of this result, Wakley did not bother to divide the House on his two other amendments.

[142]"To the Electors of Leeds," *Morning Chronicle*, 4 Dec., 1837, 1 (advertisements), and *Spectator*, 2 Dec., 1837, 1149. Although the article was nominally by Molesworth, Mill wrote all but a few words at the beginning and the end (*Bibliography of the Published Writings of John Stuart Mill*, ed. Ney MacMinn, J. R. Hainds, and James McNab McCrimmon [Evanston: Northwestern University Press, 1945], 49-50). For Mill's account of the meeting at Molesworth's house, see *EL*, *CW*, XII, 365.

[143]*PD*, 3rd ser., Vol. 37, cols. 37, 137-44; Vol. 38, cols. 211, 216-48. Roebuck lost his seat in 1837, but he spoke at the bar of the House as agent for the Canadian legislature.

Reform Bill, and so much hostility to the Government [in response to Russell's Finality speech], who now differed also from the whole people of England in their sympathy for a guilty and absurd revolt. Whether those Gentlemen called themselves Radicals or not, the great body of Liberal politicians neither agreed with them in their policy for Canada nor their principles for England.[144]

The small size of the Philosophic Radical vote (six to thirty-nine at this juncture) demonstrated their isolation.

Mill defended the Philosophic Radicals in the *London and Westminster* for January, 1838, but Fonblanque in the *Examiner*, like Bulwer in the House of Commons, criticized the "Grote conclave" for sympathizing with colonial rebellion. "The London Reviewer," he wrote, "asserts that the alliance between the Ministry and the Radicals is at an end; but how many members out of the Radical minority of little less than 200 have spoken or acted as if the alliance was at an end, or as if they desired it to be at an end . . . ?"[145] Fonblanque's observations must have had a ring of truth, for Mill was acutely aware of the cleavage between the Philosophic Radicals and the other, more moderate radicals in the House of Commons. He had already complained that the Canadian question "suspends all united action among Radicals, . . . sets one portion of the friends of popular institutions at variance with another, and . . . interrupts for the time all movements and all discussions tending to the great objects of domestic policy" (408). He was so dismayed by this development that the next two numbers of the *London and Westminster Review* appeared without his usual political article (though he did publish the essays on Vigny and Bentham, as well as shorter articles), and the number for October, 1838, did not appear at all.[146] Mill could well say that the Canadian question "in an evil hour crossed the path of radicalism."[147]

Mill's outlook changed suddenly in October, 1838, when he learned of Durham's resignation as Governor General in Canada, consequent on the Whig government's failure to sanction the ordinances by which he granted amnesty to most of the captured rebels but transported a few of their leaders to Bermuda. In view of Durham's anger towards the Melbourne Ministry, Mill thought Durham might be prepared to lead the liberal reformers and moderate radicals in a challenge to the Whig government, especially as he had always been much more a reformer than his Whig colleagues—indeed, so much so, that in 1834 he had called for the ballot, triennial parliaments, and household suffrage.[148] The opportunity to turn

---

[144]*Ibid.*, Vol. 40, cols. 398-9 (23 Jan., 1838).

[145]*Examiner*, 4 Feb., 1838, 66, 65. Fonblanque referred to the "***** conclave," but he left no doubt that the asterisks stood for Grote.

[146]Mill did include a brief article in the second edition of the July number, which was published in August: "Lord Durham and His Assailants" (437-43 below). The second edition was probably made necessary by demand for Mill's article "Bentham."

[147]Letter to Bulwer, 5 Mar., 1838, *EL, CW*, XIII, 382.

[148]Mill said that generally, though rich landowners would support one of the aristocratic parties, there were exceptions. "In all privileged classes there are individuals whom some circumstance of a

this event to Radical party advantage was greatly facilitated by the presence of Buller and Wakefield on Durham's staff in Canada. They sent Mill information about Durham's outlook and tried to direct Durham's attention to the possibility of turning the Canadian affair to domestic political advantage. Wakefield reported to Molesworth that Durham "is mortally but coolly and immovably offended at everything Whig,"[149] and Buller, having read Mill's recent political articles, wrote, "You will see what attitude the Radicals ought to assume with respect to his returning now at open defiance with Whigs and Tories.... Circumstances seem to be approaching, in which it will be perfectly possible for us to force him into power. The cue of all Radicals then is to receive him not as having failed, but as having done great things.... But you know best what is to be done."[150] Durham was to be cast as the popular leader who could bring together the coalition of moderate radicals, liberal reformers, and Philosophic Radicals that Mill wished to establish as the party of the "natural Radicals."

Mill's depressed mood now quickly evaporated. Durham's resignation, he said, "has awakened me out of a period of torpor about politics." With obvious enthusiasm he wrote to Molesworth: "The present turn in Canada affairs brings Lord Durham home, incensed to the utmost (as Buller writes to me) with both Whigs and Tories—Whigs especially, and in the best possible mood for setting up for himself; and if so, the formation of an efficient party of moderate Radicals, of which our Review will be the organ, is certain—the Whigs will be kicked out never more to rise, and Lord D. will be head of the Liberal party, and ultimately Prime Minister."[151] Even in his *Autobiography*, years later, Mill observed that "any one who had the most elementary notions of party tactics, must have attempted to make something of such an opportunity."[152]

Durham sailed for England on November 1st and was due to arrive a month later. Mill thought there was "a great game" to play in the next session of Parliament. He realized Durham's course of action was uncertain, but he believed the result "will wholly depend upon whether Wakefield, we ourselves, and probably Buller and his own resentment," on the one hand, "or Bulwer, Fonblanque, Edward Ellice, the herd of professing Liberals, and the indecision and cowardice indigenous to English noblemen," on the other, "have the greatest

---

personal nature has alienated from their class, while there are others sufficiently generous and enlightened to see the interest of their class in the promotion of the general interest.... Lord Durham is such a man." (473.) For an account of Durham's opinions and his reputation among Radicals, see Thomas, *Philosophic Radicals*, 338-71.

[149]Letter of 29 Sept., 1838, in Millicent Fawcett, *Life of the Right Hon. Sir William Molesworth* (London: Macmillan, 1901), 201.

[150]Letter to Mill, 13 Oct., 1838, *Report of the Public Archives for the Year 1928*, ed. Arthur G. Doughty (Ottawa, 1929), 74-6.

[151]Letter of 19 Oct., 1838, *EL, CW*, XIII, 390.

[152]*Autobiography, CW*, I, 223.

influence in his councils." Mill added, "Give us access to him *early* and I will be d....d if we do not make a hard fight for it."[153]

Mill's article "Lord Durham's Return" (December, 1838)—quickly published in an unscheduled issue of the *London and Westminster*—carefully followed Buller's advice to show Durham not as having failed, but as having done great things. Although most of the article was a defence of Durham's conduct and policy in Canada, Mill carefully combined with the Canadian matter an account of the significance of Durham's resignation for domestic politics. When he told Molesworth that Durham was returning prepared to set up for himself, Mill explained that "for the purpose of acting at once upon him and upon the country in that *sens* I have written an elaborate defence of him."[154] Durham's mission to Canada, he wrote, could become "the turning point of English politics for years to come," because it involved "the prospects of the popular cause in England . . . [and] the possibility of an effective popular party" (447). He held out the hope that this could become a major party and "break the power of the aristocratic faction" (448). Here he saw an opportunity finally to achieve the party realignment to which his Philosophic Radical doctrine was directed.

A meeting was held to co-ordinate the efforts of those working with Mill. Rintoul, editor of the *Spectator*, agreed to publish extracts of Mill's article before it could appear in the *London and Westminster Review*.[155] Wakefield, who returned from Canada ahead of Durham, went with Molesworth to Plymouth to meet Durham, apparently in hope of persuading him to act on his resentment and of stage-managing an enthusiastic popular reception.[156] On the Whig side, Edward Ellice, a former Whig whip and owner of vast tracts of land in Canada, tried to blunt Radical efforts. To his son, who had accompanied Durham as a private secretary, Ellice wrote that the public "are not prepared for a Durham, Wakefield, and Buller Cabinet, and mark my words, that if they come home with that expectation, they will be laughed at."[157] He warned Durham against the "recommendations of the writer in the Westmr. Review!"[158] He also saw danger in

---

[153]Letter to Robertson, [Nov., 1838,] *EL, CW*, XIII, 391-2.

[154]Letter of 14 Nov., 1838, *ibid.*, 391. Mill closely followed Buller's agenda for such an article and he even used some of Buller's language.

[155]*Spectator*, 24 Nov., 1838, 1108-9. This was probably how Durham became acquainted with Mill's defence of his conduct.

[156]Some of the Philosophic Radicals did not approve of Mill's defence of Durham's ordinance; indeed Roebuck said it justified "an act of undisguised tyranny" (letter to Brougham, 31 Aug., 1838, Brougham Papers, University College, London). Roebuck's views were probably dictated by his personal sentiments (he was born in Canada) and his service as agent of the Canadian legislature which put him in close touch with Papineau, the leader of the rebellion. Mill defended Durham's ordinance against the criticism of it in Parliament by John Temple Leader, who cooperated with Roebuck, especially after Roebuck's loss of his seat (440-3).

[157]Letter of 23 Oct., 1838, Ellice Papers, National Library of Scotland.

[158]Letter to Durham, 29 Nov., 1838, in Chester New, *Lord Durham* (Oxford: Clarendon Press, 1929), 479.

Buller, who, though "an intelligent, handy, and most amiable fellow . . . has neither experience, or prudence, and is in the hands of the younger Mill (I wish it were the elder one) a person very much of his own character—with considerable learning, and critical talent—but also a 'denisen of Utopia.'"[159]

Mill's efforts went for nought. Durham refused to play the part for which he was cast by Mill. Although he felt personal animosity towards his former colleagues and remained moderately radical in opinion, he was unwilling to attempt a party rebellion, especially in view of the disagreements among reformers. He also was reported to have called the Radicals "great fools."[160] Mill at last recognized that his goals for a Radical party were impracticable. Durham's conduct, he said,

> cannot lead to the organization of a radical party, or the placing of the radicals at the head of the movement,—it leaves them as they are already, a mere appendage of the Whigs; and if there is to be no radical party there need be no Westminster Review, for there is no position for it to take, distinguishing it from the Edinburgh. . . . In short, it is one thing to support Lord Durham in *forming* a party; another to follow him when he is only joining one, and that one which I have so long been crying out against.

He also said, "if the time is come when a radical review should support the Whigs, the time is come when I should withdraw from politics."[161] And this he now proceeded to do.

DEMISE OF THE PHILOSOPHIC RADICAL PARTY

WHEN HIS ARTICLE "Reorganization of the Reform Party," which had been planned for publication in January, 1838, finally appeared in April, 1839, it could serve only as an epitaph to Radical hopes, and Mill regretted its appearance "in a posture of affairs so unsuitable to it."[162] He published two more numbers and then ended his connection with the review, deciding that it was "no part" of his "vocation to be a party leader."[163]

Now in 1839, little more than a decade after the dream of establishing a powerful parliamentary party first took shape, John Stuart Mill began to share a sense of failure with the other Philosophic Radicals. The moderate reformers continued to oppose the aggressive tactics designed to force the Whigs to coalesce with their "natural" aristocratic allies, the Tories. The Melbourne government's existence became increasingly tenuous, and moderate reformers and Whigs alike became more and more critical of those on their left who threatened it. The

---

[159]Letter from Ellice, sr., to Durham, n.d. [*c*. Dec., 1838], Lambton Papers.
[160]Letter from E. J. Stanley to Parkes, 20 Jan., 1837, typescript, University College, London. Durham's observation was made before the controversies about Canada.
[161]Letter to Robertson, 6 Apr., 1839, *EL*, *CW*, XIII, 396-7.
[162]*Ibid.*, 397.
[163]Letter to Sterling, 28 Sept., 1839, *ibid.*, 406.

Edinburgh Review described the extreme Radicals as "a small, conceited, and headstrong party" that should be called "the sect of the *Impracticables*."[164] The cleavage between the Radicals and the moderate reformers remained, and the expected merger of Whigs and Tories into an aristocratic party did not take place. On the contrary, the Whigs continued to look upon the Tories as their strongest opponents, whereas the Philosophic Radicals were regarded as merely an annoying faction. Both in public opinion and in electoral organization, the Tories throughout the decade increased their strength. In 1839, far from having merged into an aristocratic party, the Whigs and Tories were poised against one another in a fairly even struggle; the aristocratic factions that Mill had been opposing for more than a decade continued to dominate the political scene.

The Philosophic Radicals were too disheartened by 1839 to celebrate their part in provoking the resignation of the Whig government, an event which two years earlier would have brought them to a high pitch of excitement.[165] Nor were they much moved by the increase in conversions to the ballot. When the Whig Macaulay defended Grote's motion in 1839, Mill said the ballot "is passing from a radical doctrine into a Whig one."[166] As Chartism rose to prominence the Philosophic Radicals also lost their sense of leadership in the democratic movement. Although they might have welcomed it—after all, the Philosophic Radicals could agree in principle with the six points of the Charter—they were made uneasy by some of the violent Chartist rhetoric and by the Chartists' criticism of private property and opposition to repeal of the Corn Laws. They also disapproved of the Chartists' use of the language of class, which rested on assumptions that challenged Philosophic Radical doctrine about universal and sinister interests.[167] The Philosophic Radicals were also depressed by the attrition of reform sentiment after the passing of the Reform Bill; as Mill said, "Their lot was cast in the ten years of inevitable reaction, when the Reform excitement being over . . . the public mind desired rest."[168]

Mill and his associates recognized that they had so dwindled as to become insignificant. They could no longer regard themselves as the nucleus from which a great party would soon grow. Macaulay said in 1839 that the Radical party was

---

[164]Thomas Spring-Rice, "Present State and Conduct of Parties," *Edinburgh Review*, LXXI (Apr., 1840), 282-3.

[165]The Government resigned in May, 1839, after it carried a bill for the suspension of the Jamaican constitution by only five votes. Ten Radicals (including Grote, Hume, Leader, and Molesworth) voted with the Tories, and ten others stayed away. The Whigs continued in office, however. For Mill's reaction, see *EL*, *CW*, XIII, 400.

[166]Letter to John Mitchell Kemble, 14 Oct., 1839, *ibid.*, 410.

[167]Even Mill referred to "brutish ignorance" and to "the barbarians" who would gain influence through universal suffrage; he did not condemn all Chartists, however, for whereas the "Oastlers and Stephenses represent only the worst portion of the Operative Radicals," the intelligent leaders of the Working Men's Association in London, who framed the Charter, "represent the best and most enlightened aspect of working-class Radicalism" (485).

[168]*Autobiography*, *CW*, I, 203-5.

xlviii   INTRODUCTION

reduced to Grote and his wife; and Grote himself was depressed by the diminution, saying he "felt indisposed to remain as one of so very small a number as now constituted the Radical cluster."[169] Mill was poignantly aware that hopes for the party, both as it existed and as he had imagined it, had dissolved. "Even I," he said, "who have been for some years attempting it must be owned with very little success, to induce the Radicals to maintain an independent position, am compelled to acknowledge that there is not room for a fourth political party in this country—reckoning the Conservatives, the Whig-Radicals, and the Chartists as the other three."[170] As Mill put it in his *Autobiography*, "the instructed Radicals sank into a mere *côté gauche* of the Whig party."[171]

The bitterness turned several of the Philosophic Radicals against active politics. Harriet Grote, for example, confessed feeling "sick and weary of the name of politics"; at times, she said, "I sigh over those ten years of infructuous devotion to the public service; unrequited even by [Grote's] constituents . . . and only compensated by the esteem and admiration of some dozen high-minded men."[172] Mill's feelings, as Caroline Fox reported, were similar: "'No one,' he said with deep feeling, 'should attempt anything intended to benefit his age, without at first making a stern resolution to take up his cross and to bear it. If he does not begin by counting the cost, all his schemes must end in disappointment.'"[173] He also confessed being "out of heart about public affairs—as much as I ever suffer myself to be," and soon he had "almost given up thinking on the subject."[174]

Of course the Philosophic Radicals did not cease to have political opinions, but now that they acknowledged the disappointment of their ambition for radicalism,

---

[169]Harriet Grote, *The Philosophical Radicals of 1832: Comprising the Life of Sir William Molesworth, and Some Incidents Connected with the Reform Movement from 1832 to 1842* (London: Savill and Edwards, 1866), 63; *Greville Memoirs*, IV, 176.

[170]Letter to Macvey Napier, 22 Apr., 1840, *EL, CW,* XIII, 430.

[171]*Autobiography, CW,* I, 205.

[172]Letter to Leon Faucher, 27 Aug., 1839, in Lady Eastlake, *Mrs. Grote* (London: Murray, 1880), 75; letter to Raikes Currie, Nov., 1842, in George Grote, *Posthumous Papers: Comprising Selections from Familiar Correspondence during Half a Century,* ed. Harriet Grote (London: Clowes, 1874), 70-1.

[173]Caroline Fox, *Memories of Old Friends,* ed. Horace N. Pym, 3rd ed. (London: Smith, Elder, 1882), I, 138 (entry of 20 Mar., 1840). She added, "This was evidently a process through which he (Mill) had passed, as is sufficiently attested by his careworn and anxious, though most beautiful and refined, countenance." She also described a walk with Mill and Sterling: "They talked on politics. I asked if they would really wish for a Radical Government. . . . John Mill sighed out, 'I have long done what I could to prepare them for it, but in vain; so I have given them up, and in fact they have given me up.'" (*Ibid.,* 151, entry of 27 Mar., 1840.) And in 1833 he had written, "every honest and considerate man, before he engages in the career of a political reformer, will inquire whether the moral state and intellectual culture of the people are such as to render any great improvement in the management of public affairs possible. But he will inquire too, whether the people are likely ever to be made better, morally or intellectually, without a *previous* change in the government. If not, it may still be his duty to strive for such a change at whatever risks." ("Alison's History of the French Revolution," *Monthly Repository,* 2nd ser., VII [Aug., 1833], 514-15.)

[174]Letter to d'Eichthal, 25 Dec., 1840; and letter to Robert Barclay Fox, 9 Sept., 1842, in *EL, CW,* XIII, 456, 543.

their attitude to the Whigs softened considerably. Mill, Buller, and even Roebuck began contributing to the *Edinburgh Review*, and Mill appears to have been the intermediary between Napier, the editor, and some of the former contributors to the *London and Westminster*.[175] Harriet Grote made peace with the Whigs by accepting an invitation to Holland House, and George Grote, who ten years earlier avoided aristocratic company as a matter of principle, now accompanied her "without any twinges of conscience."[176] Mill's views had altered sufficiently for him to tell Fonblanque in 1841 that "there is nothing of any importance in practical politics on which we now differ for I am quite as warm a supporter of the present [Whig] government as you are."[177]

Since parliamentary politics ceased to be a preoccupation, several of the Philosophic Radicals turned to authorship. Molesworth worked on his edition of Hobbes, and Grote on his *History of Greece*. Even Place and Roebuck took to writing history. And Mill too began his series of essays on French historians, though his main preoccupation was with his *System of Logic*, on which he had been working at intervals throughout the previous decade. Now that his plan for a parliamentary party devoted to fundamental constitutional changes had failed, his interest in politics, with its emphasis on institutions, diminished, and he turned to the realm of thought. Having been disappointed as a politician, he downgraded political activity and looked to philosophy for improvement. He consoled himself with the belief that he was entering an era when "the progress of liberal opinions will again, as formerly, depend upon what is *said* and *written*, and no longer upon what is *done*. . . ."[178]

IRELAND

THAT MILL'S DISILLUSIONMENT, which put an end to his hopes for a Radical party, did not conclude his radicalism, is nowhere so evident as in what he said and wrote about Ireland. In his journalism just after the famine, the *Principles of Political Economy* (1848), and speeches, mainly in the House of Commons from 1866 to 1868, he poured forth a powerful condemnation of the social system and economy in Ireland and of the way that country was governed by England. His essay on Irish affairs in the *Parliamentary History and Review* perhaps is partially an exception, for it focusses mainly on Ireland as an issue in British domestic politics. The 1848 speech and the pamphlet *England and Ireland* (1868), however, demonstrate Mill's radical rejection of old ways and his search for far-reaching remedies.

The extent of Mill's radicalism was evident in his sympathetic understanding of

---

[175]Letters to Napier, 27 Apr., 1840, 21 Sept., 1840, *ibid.*, 431, 444.
[176]Harriet Grote, *Life of George Grote*, 132.
[177]Letter of 17 June, 1841, *EL, CW*, XIII, 478.
[178]Letter to George Henry Lewes, [30 July, 1841,] *ibid.*, 483.

Irish rebelliousness. He even suggested a moral basis for outrages against the landlord; the Whiteboys and Rockites, he said, "fought for, not against, the sacredness of what was property in their eyes; for it is not the right of the rent-receiver, but the right of the cultivator, with which the idea of property is connected in the Irish popular mind" (513). Mill also claimed that the more a person emphasizes obstacles to reform, "the further he goes towards excusing, at least as to intention, the Irish revolutionary party" (503). Moreover, there was the example of the French Revolution. Before 1789 the peasantry in France was more destitute and miserable than Irish cottiers, but the revolution led to a great shift in peasant ownership: "the result was the greatest change for the better in their condition, both physical and moral, of which, within a single generation, there is any record." Who was to say, Mill asked, that Irish anticipations of similar benefits from an Irish revolution were wrong? (503.)

Mill's sympathetic understanding was not directed only to material circumstances in Ireland, for he was also sensitive to the stirrings of Irish nationalism. He knew that conditions had improved since the famine, especially because of emigration, and that many old grievances had been removed. Yet to be complacent—for gentlemen "to soothe themselves with statistics"[179]—was to bask in a fool's paradise and to misunderstand Fenianism, which was "a rebellion for an idea—the idea of nationality" (510).[180] The rulers of Ireland "have allowed what once was indignation against particular wrongs, to harden into a passionate determination to be no longer ruled on any terms by those to whom they ascribe all their evils. Rebellions are never really unconquerable," Mill added, "until they have become rebellions for an idea." (510.)

Disaffection was so great that only a remedy of revolutionary proportions would have a chance of relieving it. Thus in 1868 Mill asserted that "revolutionary measures are the thing now required," and he added, "In the completeness of the revolution will lie its safety" (518-19). He also said, "Great and obstinate evils require great remedies."[181]

Mill's analysis in this case emphasized economic considerations, both in the identification of abuses and in the prescription of remedies, but since he focussed on the conflict of interest between landlord and tenant, it is reminiscent of his Philosophic Radical assumption that the class conflict between aristocracy and the people took precedence over all other issues. His analysis in 1868, which is similar to what he wrote about Ireland in his *Principles of Political Economy*, recognized a variety of causes for Irish rebelliousness, but the land question, he said, outweighed all others.[182] Irish wretchedness was the result of "a radically wrong

---

[179]Speech of 12 Mar., 1868, *PD*, 3rd ser., Vol. 190, col. 1518.

[180]Also, "So deadly is the hatred, that it will run all risks merely to do us harm, with little or no prospect of any consequent good to itself" (509).

[181]Speech of 12 Mar., 1868, cols. 1517-18.

[182]*Ibid.*, col. 1516. See also *Principles of Political Economy*, *CW*, II-III, ed. J. M. Robson (Toronto: University of Toronto Press, 1965), II, 316-19, 324-8.

state of the most important social relation which exists in the country, that between the cultivators of the soil and the owners of it" (502). Against the background of overpopulation and underemployment (84-5), the specific problem was vulnerability to arbitrary eviction and arbitrary increases of rent of tenants who worked the land (516-17). Consequently, the bulk of the population "cannot look forward with confidence to a single year's occupation of [the land]: while the sole outlet for the dispossessed cultivators, or for those whose competition raises the rents against the cultivators, is expatriation" (515). As a result, improvements were not made, and poverty was added to insecurity: "these farm-labourers are entirely without a permanent interest in the soil" (514).[183]

Mill's remedy was to alter the system of land tenure by changing the relationship between landlord and tenant. He proposed making "every farm not farmed by the proprietor . . . the permanent holding of the existing tenant" (527). The rent would be fixed by an official tribunal; the state would guarantee that the landlord received the rent and that rents were not arbitrarily increased.[184] In this way Mill proposed to eliminate exploitation by landlords and, by making tenants secure, give them incentives to make improvements.

The genuinely radical character of this proposal arose from its implications for the doctrine of private property. Mill argued, as he had already done in the *Principles of Political Economy*, that land has characteristics that distinguish it from property created by labour and skill.[185] In contrast, land is "a thing which no man made, which exists in limited quantity, which was the original inheritance of all mankind, and which whoever appropriates, keeps others out of its possession. Such appropriation," he goes on, "when there is not enough left for all, is at the first aspect, an usurpation on the rights of other people." (512.) Using ideas and language from Locke's famous chapter on property, Mill changed Locke's

---

[183]Scepticism about the argument that the land tenure system was the main cause of Ireland's economic difficulties can be found in Barbara Lewis Solow, *The Land Question and the Irish Economy, 1870-1903* (Cambridge: Harvard University Press, 1971), 12-13, 195. "From the premise that the land law contained investment disincentives, we can draw no conclusions about actual historical development without an examination of the concrete economic situation. Such an examination for post-Famine Ireland will reveal a pattern of tenure customs in which eviction was rare, rents were moderate, and tenant investment incentives were established." (13.)

[184]See also speech of 12 Mar., 1868, cols. 1523-4, 1527-8, 1532; *Autobiography*, CW, I, 280.

[185]See *Principles of Political Economy*, CW, II, 208, 228-32, 326. A hint of this doctrine appeared as early as 1826; see 108. Steele has argued that Mill's extreme and emotional position in the 1868 pamphlet sharply contrasted with cautious, moderate judgments on the same issues in his *Principles of Political Economy*, even as revised in 1865. He acknowledges that Mill in the *Principles* challenged belief in absolute private property in land at an abstract level; and that there was plenty in the *Principles* to inspire hostility to landlordism. But he also holds that Mill was reluctant to alter laws of property; that "he substantially withdrew the harsh criticism of Irish landlords and retracted the endorsement of fixity of tenure." Steele concludes that the 1868 pamphlet "unsaid—though it did not refer to—virtually everything about Irish land in the latest editions of the *Principles*." (E. D. Steele, *Irish Land and British Politics: Tenant-Right and Nationality, 1865-1870* [London: Cambridge University Press, 1974], 49-50, 53, 55; E. D. Steele, "J. S. Mill and the Irish Question: The *Principles of Political Economy*, 1848-1865," *Historical Journal*, XIII [1970], 216, 226-8, 232-3, 236.)

argument as it applied to land,[186] asserting that the idea of "absolute property in land," especially when the land is "engrossed by a comparatively small number of families," is an obstacle to justice and tranquillity (512). Vicious conditions in Ireland were "protected and perpetuated by a wrong and superstitious English notion of property in land" (502). Indeed, there was a contradiction between English law and Irish moral feelings (512-13).[187]

The pamphlet *England and Ireland*, in which, as Mill said, he spoke his "whole mind,"[188] was written late in 1867 against the background of intense Fenian activity in England as well as in Ireland, marked by the killing of a policeman during the rescue of captured Fenians in Manchester and the trial and execution of the rescuers.[189] Mill's pamphlet, which was "probably the most influential single contribution to the extended debate on Irish land problems which was carried on in England between 1865 and 1870,"[190] caused a great furore, largely because it aggravated fears about the security of property in England where landlords were apprehensive that radical Liberals and spokesmen for the working classes would use Mill's observations about property in Ireland as authority for an attack on the landed classes generally.[191] There were many who were surprised that Mill cast doubts on the doctrine of private property, among them former Philosophic Radicals such as Joseph Hume and John Arthur Roebuck.[192] Mill explained that he put forth extreme views to startle his readers and prepare them at least to accept other measures. He subsequently said his proposals "had the effect of making other proposals, up to that time considered extreme, be considered comparatively moderate and practicable."[193]

---

[186]Another modification of Locke's argument occurs in the speech of 12 May, 1866, *PD*, 3rd ser., Vol. 183, col. 1095; Mill alludes to Locke's argument (in *The Second Treatise of Government* [1690], Chap. v) that private property in land had its origin in improvements and says that "unless we recognise on the same ground a kindred claim in the temporary occupier [i.e., the tenant], we give up the moral basis on which landed property rests. . . ."

[187]This argument was akin to Mill's characterization of political economy as a science that requires flexible application in light of particular circumstances (speech of 12 Mar., 1868, cols. 1525-6). See also his spirited defence of political economy at 91-2.

[188]*Autobiography*, *CW*, I, 280.

[189]E. D. Steele, "J.S. Mill and the Irish Question: Reform, and the Integrity of the Empire, 1865-1870," *Historical Journal*, XIII (1970), 419, 425.

[190]R. D. Collison Black, *Economic Thought and the Irish Question, 1817-1870* (Cambridge: Cambridge University Press, 1960), 53. See also 60-2 on the parliamentary debate concerning Ireland, in which Mill's pamphlet was discussed by, among others, Mill himself (on 12 Mar., 1868). See also 34, 51, 53-7, 70 on Mill's views on Irish land tenure in relation to classical economic theory and contemporary pamphlet literature.

[191]Steele, "Mill . . . *Principles of Political Economy*," 216; Steele, "Mill . . . Integrity of the Empire," 420, 437. For an account of the press reaction to Mill's pamphlet, see the latter, 438-42.

[192]Steele, "Mill . . . Integrity of the Empire," 438. On Hume and Roebuck, see Steele, "Mill . . . *Principles of Political Economy*," 218, 220. In 1837 Mill said the people of property ought to consider "that even *their* interests, so far as conformable and not contrary to the ends for which society and government exist, are safer in the keeping of the Radicals than anywhere else" (398). Thus "the Radicals are the only true Conservatives" (399).

[193]Letter to Philip Henry Rathbone, 9 Jan., 1869, *LL*, *CW*, XVII, 1545. See also letter to John Elliot Cairnes, 10 Mar., 1868, *ibid.*, XVI, 1373; *Autobiography*, *CW*, I, 280.

Radical as Mill's views were on land tenure and landed property in Ireland, he rejected the most radical political solution, that of separation. He understood that the Fenians wanted independence and that, regardless of concessions, it might be impossible to divert them from this nationalist goal.[194] Yet he had recently written in *Representative Government* that the Irish and Anglo-Saxon races were "perhaps the most fitted of any two in the world to be the completing counterpart of one another."[195] When in 1868 he considered the relation between the two countries, he concluded that Irish independence would be bad for Ireland and dishonourable to England (520-1, 523-4, 526).[196] Therefore he ended the pamphlet with a statement of hope that reconciliation was still possible (531-2).[197]

In his discussions of Ireland Mill revealed an intense moral concern as an aspect of his radicalism that was much less evident in what he wrote as a Philosophic Radical, where he generally argued on grounds of consequences and utility. That Ireland engaged his moral feelings is evident in his eloquent statements of sympathy for the Irish—they were the "poorest and the most oppressed people in Europe" (66)—and in his outrage with the causes of this condition: "The social condition of Ireland . . . cannot be tolerated; it is an abomination in the sight of mankind" (503). Mill made it clear that within the rationalist and utilitarian there was indignation, sympathy, and moral passion.

[194]Speech of 12 Mar., 1868, col. 1518.
[195]*Considerations on Representative Government*, *CW*, XIX, 551.
[196]See also 214-18; *LL*, *CW*, XVI, 1328. Steele suggests that Mill was moved by concern for the security of England against invasion as well as a combination of complacency about English institutions, patriotism, and imperialist sentiments which prevented him from seriously considering independence ("Mill . . . Integrity of the Empire," 430, 432-3, 435, 450).
[197]Thus he said, "I maintain that there is no country under heaven which it is not possible to govern, and to govern in such a way that it shall be contented" (speech of 12 Mar., 1868, col. 1523).

Textual Introduction

JOHN M. ROBSON

ONE OF JOHN STUART MILL'S strongest claims on our attention derives from his political writings. His lifelong concern with the problems of good government produced durable analysis, description, and advice. Best known for their range and perception are his writings on political theory: *Considerations on Representative Government*, *On Liberty*, and the other major essays in Volumes XVIII and XIX of this edition, and sections of his *Principles of Political Economy* and *System of Logic*; also important are his speeches and newspaper writings, which have a preponderant political bias. A further essential source, however, for an appreciation of Mill's political thinking is the body of material contained in this volume. These essays make clear, especially when compared with the other works, that the main tenor and focus of his writings altered about 1840. He began and remained a Radical—his speeches in the 1860s match in fervour his articles of the 1830s, and his anger over the condition of Ireland is as evident in 1868 as in 1825—but there are differences in what may simply be called breadth of approach, of subject matter, of polemic, of form, and even of provenance. In general, his approach became more theoretical, his subjects less immediate, his polemic (with marked exceptions) less evident and (almost always) less one-sided, and the form and provenance of his writings more varied. The standard—the Millian—view (which I share) would assess these changes as gains, but the earlier work is not mere apprentice labour; these essays have their place in the study of the development of a powerful and committed thinker, as well as in any history of British radicalism. Most of these matters are dealt with more fully by Joseph Hamburger in his Introduction above; of them, only the form and provenance of the writings properly occupy a textual editor—though in some places my comments, out of necessity (or wilfulness), overlap his.

All but the last two items in this volume (an unpublished manuscript and a monograph) appeared in periodicals: two in the *Westminster Review* during its first period, two in the short-lived *Parliamentary History and Review*, two (one of them the extensive series of "Notes on the Newspapers") in the *Monthly Repository*, and the other eleven in the periodical Mill himself edited, the *London Review* (renamed the *London and Westminster Review* after its amalgamation with the *Westminster*). The first four periodical articles date from what Mill calls in the *Autobiography* his period of "Youthful Propagandism" in the 1820s; the first was written when he was eighteen years of age, the fourth when he was twenty-one. The others are all from the years 1834 to 1839; he was twenty-eight when he wrote the first of these, and thirty-three when he wrote the last. None of these articles—few of them are truly "reviews"—was republished by Mill, and consequently they are less known than many other of his periodical writings. Of those in the *Parliamentary History and Review* he says:

These writings were no longer mere reproductions and applications of the doctrines I had been taught; they were original thinking, as far as that name can be applied to old ideas in new forms and connexions: and I do not exceed the truth in saying that there was a maturity, and a well-digested character about them, which there had not been in any of my previous performances. In execution, therefore, they were not at all juvenile; but their subjects have either gone by, or have been so much better treated since, that they are entirely superseded, and should remain buried in the same oblivion with my contributions to the first dynasty of the *Westminster Review*.[1]

The concluding judgment is expanded and broadened in his Preface to *Dissertations and Discussions*, where he justifies his criteria in choosing essays for republication. The papers excluded, he says, "were either of too little value at any time, or what value they might have was too exclusively temporary, or the thoughts they contained were inextricably mixed up with comments, now totally uninteresting, on passing events, or on some book not generally known; or lastly, any utility they may have possessed has since been superseded by other and more mature writings of the author."[2] Whatever propriety this policy had at that time and for Mill's purposes, reasons can easily be found for now disregarding it. Only a few disparate examples need here be cited to support the case implicit in Joseph Hamburger's analysis. For instance, one gets a very partial view of Mill's passionate and abiding concern over Irish affairs without looking at the pieces he chose not to republish: *England and Ireland* gives us his considered opinion late in life, but cannot show his responses to the recurrent manifestations of the "Irish Question." Similarly, the strength of his objection to brutality against women is seen not to be spasmodic when one reads the passage from "Notes on the Newspapers" at 267 below. Light—ironically shaded—is thrown also on changes in Mill's views by such passages as that at 159 when he heaps scorn on the notion that a "representative of the people" need "be always at his post" in the House of Commons; thirty years later he prided himself on the regularity of his own attendance.

Textual assessment of the essays is facilitated when they are considered in three

---

[1]*Autobiography*, *CW*, I, 121-3.
[2]Appendix A, *CW*, X, 493.

groups: those of the early propagandistic period in the 1820s, those of his activism in the 1830s, and the two later pieces on Ireland.

ESSAYS OF THE 1820s

LITTLE IS KNOWN of the composition of the first four essays, the subjects of which may well have been offered to Mill, or chosen by him in editorial sessions when topics were assigned to contributors to the *Westminster Review* and the *Parliamentary History and Review*. The goals, spirit, and to some extent the planning of these radical reviews are described by Mill in his *Autobiography* in illuminating passages, unfortunately too long to be quoted here (see *CW*, I, 93-103, and 119-23). To the *Westminster* Mill contributed thirteen articles between 1824, when the review was founded, and 1828, when he withdrew from it. The tone and content of at least the earliest of these are well illustrated in "Brodie's History of the British Empire" (published in the issue for Oct., 1824), the first essay in this volume. It shows the strengths and weaknesses of the exacting training school of the older Philosophic Radicals. The most obvious of its sectarian marks is, in Alexander Bain's words, "the exposure of Hume's disingenuous artifices" in his *History of England*, justified in Mill's mind because Hume's "resplendent" reputation as a metaphysician was disguising "his moral obliquity as a historian."[3] Indeed the abuse of the Tory Hume outruns the praise of the Whig Brodie; but both abuse and praise are, as one would expect in a Radical review, attuned to the theme that the follies of the past as well as the biases of historians can be used to enlighten the present. Echoes of James Mill, whose educational experiment with his eldest child was now bearing fruit, are evident: for example, his "Government" lies behind such remarks as "If [these statesmen] had possessed undue power, they would probably, like other men, have abused it . . ." (28-9), and "That the king had no intention of resigning any power which he could safely keep, is sufficiently certain from the principles of human nature . . ." (36). As to rhetorical form, the accomplished ease of his later essays is but scantily adumbrated in his saying, for instance, that his objects in the review "may best be united by such a concise sketch of the events of the period as is compatible with the narrow limits of an article [56 pages in the present edition!]; and to this, after requesting the indulgence of the reader to the very general view which it is in our power to afford, we shall proceed" (9). The awkwardness having been admitted, however, one might well ask what grade is appropriate for such an essay by an eighteen-year-old part-time student (he had joined the East India Company as a clerk in 1823). While a comparison of the essay with Brodie's book reveals that

---

[3]Alexander Bain, *John Stuart Mill* (London: Longmans, 1882), 34. For a later attack on Hume by Mill see "Bentham," *CW*, X, 80^{q-q}; this attack, penned in 1838, was deleted by Mill in the reprinted version of 1859.

much of the material for which no references are given derives from Brodie, as do some of the references to other sources, there is no plagiarism here, and Mill includes matters and sources that show him going beyond Brodie and Hume: he almost certainly read Catharine Macaulay (see 23), Burnet's *Memoires* (26), Laing's *History of Scotland* (37), and Perrinchief (7 and 55); also, looking to other sources used in the article, James Mill's Commonplace Books include passages from Clarendon's *History* and *Life*, and Rushworth's *Historical Collections*, as well as from Hume (in the 8-vol. London ed. of 1778)—such texts almost certainly were shared by father and son.

The second essay here included, "Ireland," presumably written in 1825,[4] though it appeared in the *Parliamentary History and Review* in 1826, shows the same marks, though it is more typical of the essays in this volume in dealing with recent parliamentary events. The Radical attack is strongly pressed, and in a manner proper to a periodical designed to exploit the weapons of Bentham's *Book of Fallacies* (see, e.g., 78-9). In further echoes of James Mill's language, we are told that the "*few*, in every country, are remarkable for being easily alarmed" (70), and that a "principle of human nature" is "well established" (and therefore needs no demonstration) (80). Again the *exordium*, with an explicit *divisio*, is stiff and almost graceless. But apart from the interest in the matter, the powers of organization and analysis, and again even the sheer bulk (38 pages in this edition) are impressive, especially when one realizes that in addition to his work at the India Office he was engaged then in the massive task of editing Bentham's *Rationale of Judicial Evidence*, and doing much else.[5]

The other two early essays, "The Game Laws" and "Intercourse between the United States and the British Colonies in the West Indies," merit similar comments. "The Game Laws," like "Ireland," centres on an immediate issue in the parliamentary session of 1825 (though much of its material derives from that of 1824, as Mill explains at 113), and undoubtedly it was written in that year. The same guiding judgments are present (see the antithesis between "the Many" and "the Few" at 102, as well as the continued attack on landowners), but with more ease than in "Ireland," presumably because the issues were clearer and the need to comment on all verbal follies less pressing, as Bentham's *Book of Fallacies* was not an explicit benchmark. Indeed the quiet wit that has been little discerned in Mill's writings begins to show itself (perhaps because, as some of the references reveal, he had been reading Sydney Smith). The article on trade between the United States and the West Indies, written in December, 1827 (see 147n) for the *Parliamentary Review* of 1828, is more mature than "Ireland" in analysis and polemic; he was then more comfortable, one may infer, with general economic

---

[4]The parliamentary events covered occurred in the first half of 1825, and in Mill's list of his own writings the article is mentioned before "The Game Laws," which appeared in the *Westminster* for January, 1826.

[5]For a summary, see *CW*, I, xii-xiii.

than with concrete political issues. The target, outlined more sharply by the use of Ricardo's ideas, is that of his mentors, but there is evident an individuality, as he said, "a maturity, and a well-digested character." The conclusion, for example, shows the balance and precision for which he became known:

That strength of intellect which comprehends readily the consequences of a false step, and what is a still rarer endowment, that strength of character which dares to retrace it, are not qualities which have often belonged to a British ministry. That the present ministers possess these attributes, it still remains for them to prove. For us, if we can contribute in any degree to give the right direction to the opinions of any portion of the *public* on this question, we shall have effected all that we aim at, and all that is in our power. (147.)

Only a little tolerance—and that little lessened by reference to his other writings of 1827-29—is needed to accept Mill's judgment about the effect of his editing of Bentham: "Through these influences my writing lost the jejuneness of my early compositions; the bones and cartilages began to clothe themselves with flesh, and the style became, at times, lively and almost light."[6]

ESSAYS OF THE 1830s

MILL'S CONCLUSION to the essay on British-American trade, quoted above—"For us, if we can contribute in any degree to give the right direction to the opinions of any portion of the *public* on this question, we shall have effected all that we aim at, and all that is in our power"—might be taken as the theme of his political writings from 1834 to 1839. During the Reform crisis, he was, curiously, almost silent about British politics, though he wrote extensively in the *Examiner* about French affairs after the Revolution of 1830. But the post-Reform parliaments called forth his most sustained burst of commentary on current domestic issues.

W.J. Fox having begun in his *Monthly Repository* a series of short comments on topics of the day, under the title of "Notes on the Newspapers," Mill contributed an extensive and continuous commentary from March through September, 1834—that is, covering the sitting of parliament in that year, but mentioning some non-parliamentary subjects. Francis E. Mineka says that these notes "constitute a kind of political diary, and are perhaps the best extant record of Mill's day-to-day application of his political philosophy."[7] The "perhaps" can be removed, and the last clause should conclude "his political philosophy at the time," but the comment is cogent. Mill states his attitude to the "Notes" in a letter of 2 March, 1834, to Thomas Carlyle: he wishes "to present for once at least a picture of our 'statesmen'

---

[6]*Autobiography, CW,* I, 119.

[7]*The Dissidence of Dissent: The Monthly Repository, 1806-1838* (Chapel Hill: University of North Carolina Press, 1944), 280. For ease of reference, the titles of the "Notes" are listed in Appendix B below. The Note for 1 Mar., 1834, appeared in the *Monthly Repository,* as it does in our text, after that for 5 Mar. (see 181-3, and 178-81).

and of their doings, taken from the point of view of a radical to whom yet radicalism in itself is but a small thing."[8] And, writing to Fox on 26 June, he says that William Adams (who also contributed to the series as "Junius Redivivus") "will like my notes this time. . . . There is much of 'the devil' in them."[9] The devil, it is said, is a radical, and one with a strong bent for reform.

"The Close of the Session," which appeared in the *Monthly Repository* coincident with the last of the "Notes," was a summary of the progress of reform and a forecast, using the language of the "Movement" to induce acceptance of inevitable change. The trope is most evident at the close:

More slowly, but as certainly, the Church Establishment of England will share the fate which awaits all bodies who pretend to be what they are not, and to accomplish what they do not even attempt. And the fall of the Church will be the downfal of the English aristocracy, as depositaries of political power. When all the privileged orders insist upon embarking in the same vessel, all must naturally expect to perish in the same wreck. (286-7.)

Mill thought at this time of founding a new review to represent what he saw as a new radicalism, more attuned to the times and to the aspirations of the younger group. His goal was achieved when the *London Review* appeared in April, 1835, with Mill as the real, though not the ostensible, editor; in April of the next year it amalgamated with the *Westminster*, and continued as the *London and Westminster* under Mill's editorship and eventual proprietorship until 1840. Here Mill had an organ responsive to his will—though subject to the variable tides of popularity and the gusty winds of contributors and sub-editors—and used it to the full, supplying all or part of over thirty articles, including eleven of those reprinted in this volume. The themes are fully covered in the Introduction above, the texts present no major problems,[10] and so little need here be said about these important articles. It is excusable to mention, however, the continuing pattern of fluctuating hope and frustration in them, leading finally to an abandonment of this road to reform. Mill evidently wished to remain behind the scenes as an *éminence grise*, but there was no one to play Richelieu to his Père Joseph: he tried to arouse Grote[11] and then to lead a rally round Durham,[12] but no one rose to the occasion. The Radicals in Parliament quarrelled and scattered, and Mill became a contributor to the *Edinburgh Review*, the old Whig instrument so excoriated by him in his first

---

[8]*EL, CW,* XII, 218. Again the last clause needs qualification: it is true that Mill had begun to re-assess his radicalism, but the sentiment and the language are designed to please the letter's recipient.

[9]*Ibid.*, 227. For other references to the "Notes on the Newspapers," see *ibid.*, 213, 215.

[10]It should be noted that "Radical Party and Canada: Lord Durham and the Canadians" is sometimes referred to by critics as "Radical Party in Canada," an evident misnomer arising from a typographical error in the running titles of some copies; the second part of the title here used derives from the running titles of the conclusion of the article and the table of contents of the bound volume. "Lord Durham's Return" has proved elusive for many students because it appeared only in the second edition of the *London and Westminster* for August, 1838.

[11]See 314n below.

[12]See 405-64 below.

periodical article in the *Westminster*.[13] His last political essay in the *London and Westminster*, "Reorganization of the Reform Party," is curiously anticlimactic.[14] Its running titles (see 466) provided a programme for the Radicals just as their strength was fading, and its thesis might well have expressed Mill's aspirations at the founding of the review rather than just before he withdrew: "Radicalism has done enough in speculation; its business now is to make itself practical. Most reformers are tolerably well aware of their ends; let them turn to what they have hitherto far less attended to—how to attain them." (468.)

LATER WORKS ON IRELAND

THE PATTERN OF MILL'S LIFE, at least as author, changed markedly after his disposing of his interest in the *London and Westminster* in 1840 and the completion of his *System of Logic* (published in 1843, but virtually finished two years earlier). Henceforth he took for the most part to a broader canvas and a more abstract style, and also chose his "sitters" less frequently from the Houses of Parliament. He did not, however, abandon immediate issues, though this volume contains only two examples of his continued political interest. That interest found its outlet in the abundance of specific illustrations in his theoretical works, in newspaper writings, in speeches, and in a few essays on subjects not immediately political: all these will be found in other volumes of the *Collected Works*.

The final two items in this volume both deal with Ireland, and in similar terms, but formally they are very different. "What Is to Be Done with Ireland?" is an undated manuscript, apparently unpublished, which may have been designed as a speech or a newspaper article, or perhaps as part of a longer work (the title is used in *England and Ireland*, 507); given Mill's ready access to different media, there is no evident reason for its remaining unused. The manuscript, now in the Hugh Walpole Collection, the King's School, Canterbury, was sold as part of lot 669 on 27 July, 1927, by Sothebys to Maggs for £1, at the second sale of the effects of Mary Taylor (Mill's step-grand-daughter).[15] The text, in Mill's hand, is written recto and verso on the first four and one-quarter sides of three folios, c. 21 cm. x 34 cm., watermarked without date, now bound in green morocco. Throughout there are pencilled revisions in the hand of Harriet Taylor, who became Mill's wife in 1851, but who assisted him with revisions at least as early as 1848, when his *Principles* first appeared.[16] The manuscript then most certainly was written before

---

[13]"Periodical Literature: *Edinburgh Review*," *CW*, I, 291-325.

[14]This was his only contribution in 1839; his last essay before handing over the periodical in 1840 was his valedictory "Coleridge."

[15]The lot (subsequently sold, evidently intact, to the bookseller James Tregaskis) included Mill's twenty-five pages of notes sent to George Grote concerning his *Plato and the Other Companions of Sokrates*, the manuscripts of his speech to the Education League and of his main election speech of 1865, six letters, and portraits.

[16]Her revisions are recorded in our text, according to principles described on lxiii below.

1858, when she died, and since discussion of it is not found in the extensive (though incomplete) correspondence between them in the mid-1850s, it is at least likely that it predates those years. No external evidence has been found, but the reference internally to the "military operations of Mr. Smith O'Brien" (499-501), which are discussed as though recent, makes a date of late 1848 very likely, as does the mention of the large and liberal English gifts of "less than two years ago" (501).

Nearly twenty years passed before, in 1867, Mill thought that the time had come "to speak out [his] whole mind" on Ireland;[17] he did so in *England and Ireland*, published in 1868. This is the only item in this volume to have been republished by Mill; though he says it "was not popular, except in Ireland,"[18] it went through four editions in 1868, and into a fifth in 1869, and was translated into French for the *Journal des Economistes* for the issue of March, 1868.[19] In fact, the "editions" are just new impressions (one change—"these" for "those"—was made in the 2nd ed.), except for the 3rd, which incorporates a few changes, the most important of which is a footnote (516n-17n) added in reply to criticisms.

Most of what is almost certainly the first draft of *England and Ireland* exists in manuscript. Many of Mill's papers and books remained after his death in his Avignon home, where he had spent about one-half of each year following his wife's death there in 1858. When Helen Taylor, his step-daughter, who had taken over the house, returned finally to England in 1905, the papers were sorted by Mary Taylor, her niece, and a friend of hers; some were sent (or taken back) to England by Mary Taylor, and the rest were either burnt or given for sale to the Avignon bookseller, Roumanille. The manuscript of *England and Ireland* must have been mistakenly divided at that time, the larger portion remaining in Avignon, where it was bought as part of a parcel by Professor G.H. Palmer, who gave the collection to Harvard (catalogued in the Houghton Library as MS Eng 1105). A smaller fragment appears to have been returned to England, where it was sold at Sothebys in the first sale of Mary Taylor's effects on 29 March, 1822, as part of lot 730 ("With various unfinished MSS. in the hand of J.S. Mill") to Maggs for £2. 8s. (On the verso of the second folio, in what appears to be Helen Taylor's hand, is "Unimp.") The rest of the manuscript seems not to be extant, perhaps having been burnt at Avignon or (since the missing sheets contained the beginning and conclusion) given away to friends. The manuscript is written in ink on unwatermarked blue French paper, c. 40 cm. x 26 cm., folded to make 20 cm. x 26 cm. folios, which are inscribed recto. Mill numbered only the first folio of each

---

[17]*Autobiography, CW*, I, 280. He had, of course, been expressing his opinions forcibly for two years in the House of Commons. Indeed his first speech in the Commons, which has generally been thought to have been disappointing because of its delivery, offended more because of its apparent extremism on the Irish question.

[18]*Ibid*. The first two editions appeared in February, 1868 (each 1500 copies), the third in April (250 copies), the fourth in May (250 copies), and the fifth in October, 1869 (250 copies). The fifth was reissued in April, 1870 (again 250 copies). (Information from the Longman Archive, Reading University.) A sixth edition appeared in 1881.

[19]Vol. IX (15 Mar., 1868), 421-49. See *LL, CW*, XVI, 1384-5.

pair: the Harvard portion consists of the sheets numbered by Mill as 3, and 6 through 11; the Yale portion (following directly on) is sheet number 12 (the draft almost certainly concluded with a few lines on sheet number 13). The text of the draft is printed as Appendix A below, keyed to that of the 5th ed. (the copy-text for this edition). The revisions, typical of Mill, show an attempt to attain precision and force. The polemic, *ars artium*, is less evident than in the apprentice essays in this volume, but is still very strong, as Mill justifies radical action by criticizing weak policy.

In sum, these essays from all three periods add detail to our picture of one whose life, in his own as in our estimation, centred on public issues: we see here more of his strong immediate reaction to politics than we do in his more theoretical writings. We also have material for an enriched assessment of nineteenth-century political questions in these reactions of an acute and engaged mind. Since Mill was in his earlier years a member of a distinct group, indeed one of its spokesmen (sometimes self-appointed), and that group reveals many characteristics of young radical sectarians, there is matter here useful for analysis of the development, cohesion, and dissolution of such groups. The main interest, however, lies in the revelation of a powerful theoretic intellect struggling with the rhetoric of practical politics, analyzing, accusing, prodding, proclaiming, persuading, not always with success or balance by the standards of his time or ours, but never with stupidity or dullness.

TEXTUAL PRINCIPLES AND METHODS

AS THROUGHOUT the *Collected Works*, the copy-text for each item is that of the final version supervised by Mill;[20] in this volume, however, there is but a single version for all of the essays except *England and Ireland*, where the fifth edition provides the copy-text. In one case, "What Is to Be Done with Ireland?", never before published, the copy-text is the MS, described above. Details concerning each text, including the descriptions in Mill's own list of his published writings,[21]

---

[20]The argument for this practice is given in my "Principles and Methods in the Collected Edition of John Stuart Mill," in *Editing Nineteenth-Century Texts*, ed. John M. Robson (Toronto: University of Toronto Press, 1967), 96-122.

[21]Ed. Ney MacMinn, J.R. Hainds, and J.M. McCrimmon, *Bibliography of the Published Writings of J.S. Mill* (Evanston: Northwestern University Press, 1945). Entries from this work, based on the MS, which is a scribal copy, are given in the headnotes to each item, with the following emendations (scribal reading, followed by the emended reading in square brackets):
60.4   Parlamentary [Parliamentary]
282.2 "the ['The]
320.4 entituled [entitled]
320.4 1836, [1836,']
320.5 —Progress [—'Progress]

TEXTUAL INTRODUCTION   lxiii

are given in the headnotes to each item. Running titles from the periodical articles have, when necessary, been used as titles.[22]

Textual notes. The method of indicating substantive variants in the *Collected Works*, though designed for more elaborate revisions, is used in *England and Ireland* for the few changes Mill made, only one of which is extensive. Five of the lesser ones involve the substitution of a word or words; in these cases the final words in the copy-text are enclosed in superscript italic letters, and a footnote gives the editions in which the earlier version appeared, with its wording. E.g., at 516 the text gives "^{b}interfere^b" and the note reads "$^{b-b}68^1,68^2$ prevent"; the interpretation is that in 68^1 (1st ed., 1868) and 68^2 (2nd ed., 1868) "prevent" appears where "interfere" appears in the 3rd, 4th, and 5th eds. In one case (516^{c-c}) the footnote reads "$^{c-c}+68^3,68^4,69$"; this means that "of", the word in the text bracketed by $^{c-c}$, was added in 68^3 (3rd ed., 1868), and retained in 68^4 (4th ed., 1868) and 69 (5th ed., 1869). The most significant change is the addition of a long footnote (516n-17n); this is signalled by the insertion, at the beginning of the note, in square brackets, of "[68^3]", indicating that the footnote first appeared in the 3rd ed.

The MS of "What Is to Be Done with Ireland?" shows only current revisions by Mill, with the cancellations and interlineations indicating minor syntactic and semantic second thoughts. The MS makes evident, however, as mentioned above, that Harriet Taylor, as was normal practice for them, read the MS and suggested changes. These are recorded in footnotes, using the system of superscripts described above, with one further kind to indicate an addition: see 499^k, where the single superscript in the text, centred between "would" and "be" indicates that an additional word or words (in this case, as the footnote shows, "perhaps") had been proposed.

The other MS represented in this volume, the early draft of *England and Ireland*, shows signs only of current revisions by Mill. (It was written after his wife's death.) Although (as the discussion above indicates) there was little time between the writing of this draft and the publication of the 1st ed., the extensive differences between the two suggest that Mill, as usual, wrote another complete version, which probably served as press-copy. The nature as well as the extent of

---

350.5   Administrators [Administrations]
382.11   entituled [entitled]
382.11   Review" [Review]
466.12   Reorganization ['Reorganization]

One possible emendation has not been made, because the wording may reflect Mill's indecision: "Reorganization of the Reform Party" (the left-hand running title) is given in the bibliography as "Reorganization of the Radical Party."

[22]To avoid confusion with either "The Close of the Session" (*Monthly Repository*, Sept., 1834) and "Postscript" (*London Review*, Apr., 1835), the article for October, 1835, in the *London Review*, which is identified simply as "Close of the Session" in Mill's bibliography and in the running titles, has been given as title the full heading, "Postscript: The Close of the Session." For simplicity, the heading, "State of Politics in 1836" (also used in Mill's bibliography), is used as title for the article of April, 1836. The title "Radical Party and Canada: Lord Durham and the Canadians" is explained at lix n above.

lxiv TEXTUAL INTRODUCTION

the changes makes it impracticable to employ our usual method of indicating substantive variants in footnotes; therefore the MS has been printed in full as Appendix A, keyed to show parallel passages, additions, omissions, and reordering, by using superscript Greek letters (to avoid confusing these with the variants among the printed texts), with editorial explanations in square brackets. Non-substantive variants, such as changes in spelling, hyphenation, and punctuation, are not indicated.

Textual liberties. In editing the MSS, end-of-line punctuation has been silently added when the sense requires, and (except in Appendix A) the ampersand has been printed as "and". In both printed texts and MSS, superscripts in abbreviations have been lowered, and (for consistency) periods supplied after such abbreviations as "Mr." References to monarchs have been altered to the standard form (e.g., from "Charles the first" to "Charles I"). In the two early essays from the *Westminster* initial capitals have been added to titles of position and status, and to institutional and party names, for consistency (neither Mill nor the *Westminster* later used the lower-case forms) and to avoid confusion. Dashes are deleted when combined with other punctuation before quotations and references, and italic punctuation closing italic passages has been made roman. Indications of ellipsis have been normalized to three dots plus, if needed, terminal punctuation. One authorial headnote has been made into a footnote (168), and one editorial footnote in the *Monthly Repository* deleted.[23] The positioning of footnote indicators has been normalized so that they appear after adjacent punctuation marks; in some cases, for consistency, references or footnote indicators have been moved to the end of passages. All long quotations are given in reduced type and (when necessary) the quotation marks have been removed; consequently, square brackets have occasionally been added around Mill's words in those quotations, but there is little reason for confusion, as there are no editorial insertions except added references. Double quotation marks are used throughout, and titles of works originally published separately are given in italics. For consistency, in one place (10) round brackets have been substituted for square to enclose a reference; in another (261), square for round, to enclose an authorial intervention. The nineteenth-century practice of printing names of signators in small capitals has not been followed.

Typographical errors and some anomalies have been emended; Appendix C lists them. Mill's references to sources, and additional editorial references, are normalized. When necessary, his references have been emended; a list of the alterations is given in the note below.[24]

Appendix D is a Bibliographic Index, listing the persons and works cited and

---

[23]The "Notes on the Newspapers" for April, 1834, were divided into two sections; the first concluded (at the end of the note, "The Trades' Unions," 191) with a note, "For the remainder of the Notes on the Newspapers, see page 309." This reference is, of course, unnecessary in the present edition.

[24]The reference in the copy-text is followed by the emended reference in square brackets. Not indicated are changes from commas to hyphens joining adjacent pages, the replacement of "P." or

TEXTUAL INTRODUCTION lxv

referred to by Mill. These references are consequently omitted in the analytic Index, which has been prepared by Dr. Maureen Clarke.

ACKNOWLEDGMENTS

FOR PERMISSION TO PUBLISH MANUSCRIPT MATERIAL, we are indebted to the King's School, Canterbury, to the Houghton Library, the Yale University Library, and the National Provincial Bank (literary executors and residual legatees

---

"Pp." by "p." or "pp." (or the reverse), or the addition or deletion of the volume number from the reference.
6.32-3   110 [110n-14n], 263 [263n-4n], 265 [265n], 306 [306n-8n], 316 [136n], 334 [334n-5n], 336 [336n], 389 [389n], 552 [551n-4n]
14n.2-3   90 [77-8, 90-1]
45n.2   310 [310n]
73n.6   104 [104-5]
81n.2   170 [169]
88n.7   435-6 [436-7]
88n.11   290 [280]
93n.4   233 [733] [*here and in the next nine places listed, JSM was using a version with different pagination*]
96.35   54, 55 [554-5]
96.35   79 [579]
96.36   109 [609]
96.36   [131, 132], 159, 163, [165], 179 [[631-2], 659, 663, [665], 679]
96.37   134, [137], 139 [634, [637], 639]
97.1   204 [704]
97.1   219 [719]
97.2   228, 229, 230, 231 [728-31]
97.2   [233, 234] [[733-4]]
97n.9   270 [270-1]
103n.1   22 [22-3] [*reference moved in this ed.*]
103n.2   6 [6-7] [*reference moved in this ed.*]
104.41   26 [26-7] [*reference moved in this ed.*]
110n.1   7 [7-8] [*reference moved in this ed.*]
110n.5   14 [14-15] [*reference moved in this ed.*]
112n.2   26 [26-7] [*reference moved in this ed.*]
123n.3   867 [21-51] [*here and in the next two places listed, JSM was using versions with different pagination*]
126n.1   7 [31]
129.23   27 [51]
140n.3   287-8 [288-9]
339.10   33 [33-4]
341.8   78 [78-9]
346.16   56 [56-7]
357.5   237-239 [237-41]
361.34   vol. 1. pp. 168, 169, 171 [Vol. II, pp. 168-71.]
361.42   234 [234-5]
361n.2   265 [265-72]
361.44   299 [299-308]
370.4   147, 148 [146-8]
372.20   182-186 [182-5]

of Mary Taylor, Mill's step-grand-daughter). Their librarians have been most gracious to us, as have those of the Archives Nationales du Québec, the British Library, the New York Public Library, Somerville College, the University of London, the University of Toronto, and Victoria University. The unfailing competence, zeal, and co-operation of the staff of the University of Toronto Press, and especially of our copy-editor, Rosemary Shipton, earn as always our unstinted thanks. Individuals who have generously aided include the members of the Editorial Committee, and Robert Adolph, William Baker, John Beattie, Joan Bigwood, J.M.S. Careless, Martin Davies, M.L. Friedland, F.D. Hoeniger, J.R. de J. Jackson, Bennett Kovrig, W.E. McLeod, Peter Munsche, Peter J. Parsons, Alan Ryan, H.G. Schogt, C.A. Silber, James Steintrager, William Thomas, D.F.S. Thomson, and Elizabeth Zyman.

Our greatest benefactor is the Social Sciences and Humanities Research Council, whose generous Major Editorial Project Grant supports both publication and the work of our talented and dedicated editorial team. For this volume, most of the credit goes to Marion Filipiuk, Bruce Kinzer (now, alas, lost to us by translation to the Department of History at McMaster University), Maureen Clarke, Rea Wilmshurst, Mary O'Connor, Allison Taylor, and Mark Johnson. My wife, the historian, has as ever lessened my still manifold sins of omission and commission by developing my understanding and appreciation of the English and the past.

BRODIE'S HISTORY OF THE BRITISH EMPIRE

1824

EDITOR'S NOTE

Westminster Review, II (Oct., 1824), 346–402. Headed: "Art. V. *A History of the British Empire, from the Accession of Charles I, to the Restoration; with an introduction, tracing the Progress of Society, and the Constitution, from the Feudal Times, to the Opening of the History; and including a particular Examination of Mr. Hume's Statements, relative to the Character of the English Government.* By George Brodie, Esq., Advocate. In Four Volumes, 8vo. Edinburgh. Bell & Bradfute. London. Longman & Co. 1822." Running titles: "Brodie's History of the British Empire." Unsigned; not republished. Identified in Mill's bibliography as "A review of Brodie's history of Charles I and the Commonwealth, in the fourth number of the Westminster Review" (MacMinn, 6). Vol. II of the *Westminster* in the Somerville College Library has no corrections or alterations. For comment on the review, see viii–ix and lvi–lvii above.

Brodie's History of the British Empire

MR. BRODIE has rendered no mean service to his country by these volumes. We allude, not so much to the merits of his work as a history, though these are considerable, as to the unexampled exposure which he has furnished of the demerits of former writers, and particularly of Hume.[*] In no portion of our history has mis-representation more extensively prevailed, because in no portion of it have the motives, which lead to mis-representation, been more strong.

Hume possessed powers of a very high order; but regard for truth formed no part of his character. He reasoned with surprising acuteness; but the object of his reasonings was, not to attain truth, but to shew that it is unattainable. His mind, too, was completely enslaved by a taste for literature; not those kinds of literature which teach mankind to know the causes of their happiness and misery, that they may seek the one and avoid the other; but that literature which without regard for truth or utility, seeks only to excite emotion. With the earlier part of his work, we at present have no concern. The latter part has no title to be considered as a history. Called a history, it is really a romance; and bears nearly the same degree of resemblance to any thing which really happened, as *Old Mortality*, or *Ivanhoe*,[†] while it is far more calculated to mislead. As every romance must have a hero, in his romance of the Stuarts, the hero is Charles I: and in making a pathetic story about Charles I, the thing he gave himself least concern about was, whether it was true.

Romance is always dangerous, but when romance assumes the garb of history, it is doubly pernicious. To say nothing of its other evils, on which this is no place to expatiate, it infallibly allies itself with the sinister interests[‡] of the few. When events come to be looked at, not as they affect the great interests of mankind, but as they bear upon the pleasures and pains of an individual; a habit is engendered of

[*David Hume, *The History of England from the Invasion of Julius Caesar to the Revolution in 1688*, 8 vols. (London: Cadell, Rivington, *et al.*, 1823). Hereafter cited as Hume, with volume and page references.]

[†Walter Scott, *Old Mortality*, in *Tales of My Landlord*, 4 vols. (Edinburgh: Blackwood; London: Murray, 1816), Vols. II–IV; and *Ivanhoe: A Romance* (Edinburgh: Constable, 1820).]

[‡The phrase derives from Bentham; see, e.g., *Plan of Parliamentary Reform*, in *Works*, ed. John Bowring, 11 vols. (Edinburgh: Tait; London: Simpkin, Marshall; Dublin: Cumming, 1843), Vol. III, pp. 440, 446.]

considering the pleasures and pains of an individual as of more importance than the great interests of mankind. That this is one of the most pernicious of all habits, is proved by merely telling what it is; that it is one which the prevailing system of education carefully fosters, is too true; that it is a habit into which the mind has of itself too strong a tendency to fall, is matter of universal experience. The pleasures and pains most interesting to an ill-cultivated mind, are those of the one and of the few; of the men in exalted stations, whose lot is most conspicuous, whose felicity, to the ignorant, appears something almost divine, and whose misfortunes, from their previous elevation, most powerfully affect the imagination. The sufferings of the many, though multiplied almost beyond calculation from their indefinite extent, are thought nothing of: they seem born to suffer; their fall is from a less height; their miseries lie hidden, and do not meet the eye. Who is there that would not admit, that it is better one should suffer than a million? Yet among those who can feel and cannot reason, nothing is so rare as to sympathize with the million. The one, with them, is every thing, the million, nothing; merely because the one is higher in rank, and perhaps suffers rather more, than any one assignable individual among the million. They would rather that a thousand individuals should suffer one degree each, than that one individual should suffer two degrees.

This propensity is so thoroughly incompatible with the pursuit of the only true end of morality, the greatest happiness of the greatest number, that genuine and enlarged morality cannot exist till it be destroyed; and to this object, he who writes to benefit his species will bend his most strenuous efforts: but he who writes for effect, without caring whether good or evil is the consequence, must address himself to the prevalent feeling, and to this, one of the strongest of prevalent feelings. He must select a hero; if possible a monarch, or a warrior; and to excite a strong interest in this hero, every thing must be sacrificed. If he be an historian, he will probably have to relate, among the actions of his hero, some by which the many are made to suffer; these it is necessary for him to justify or excuse. He may have to relate attempts on the part of the many, to guard themselves against those actions of his hero by which they are made to suffer; these attempts he must represent as extremely wicked, and the many as villains for engaging in such attempts. In short, whenever the interests of mankind, and of his hero, are at variance, he must endeavour to make the reader take part with his hero against mankind.

Such was the object of Hume; and the object to which he deliberately sacrificed truth, honesty, and candour. When, in order to attain the most mischievous of ends, a man does not scruple to employ the most mischievous of means, it makes very little difference in the degree of his immorality, whether he be himself the dupe of his own artifices or not. To that extent, Hume may very possibly have been sincere. He may, perhaps, have been weak enough to believe, that the pleasures and pains of one individual are of unspeakable importance, those of the many of no importance at all. But though it be possible to defend Charles I, and be an honest man, it is not possible to be an honest man, and defend him as Hume has done.

A skilful advocate will never tell a lie, when suppressing the truth will answer his purpose; and if a lie must be told, he will rather, if he can, lie by insinuation than by direct assertion. In all the arts of a rhetorician, Hume was a master: and it would be a vain attempt to describe the systematic suppression of the truth which is exemplified in this portion of his history; and which, within the sphere of our reading, we have scarcely, if ever, seen matched. Particular instances of this species of mendacity, Mr. Brodie has brought to light in abundance;[*] of the degree in which it pervades the whole, he has not given, nor would it be possible to give, an adequate conception, unless by printing Mr. Brodie's narrative and Hume's in opposite columns. Many of the most material facts, facts upon which the most important of the subsequent transactions hinged, and which even the party writers of the day never attempted to deny, Hume totally omits to mention; others, which are so notorious that they cannot safely be passed over in silence, he either affects to disbelieve, or mentioning no evidence, indirectly gives it to be understood that there was none. The direct lies are not a few; the lies insinuated are innumerable. We do not mean that he originated any lies; for all those which he could possibly need were ready made to his hand. But if it be criminal to be the original inventor of a lie, the crime is scarcely less of him who knowingly repeats it.

The authorities from which the history of those times is to be collected are various. There are royalist writers, and republican writers; and there are original documents, letters, and others, from which the facts may be gathered, free from that colouring which is put upon them in the apologetical writings of either party. There are, in particular, a variety of letters, written, some of them by Charles himself, others by Strafford, and other eminent persons in the royal party, where they unfold to one another designs which were carefully concealed from the public, and which, when imputed to them by their opponents, they repelled as the vilest of calumnies.[†] Almost the whole of these documents Hume passes over, as

[*See, e.g., Brodie, *A History of the British Empire*, Vol. II, pp. 292n, 314–15; Vol. III, pp. 311n–12n, 553n. Hereafter cited as Brodie, with volume and page references.]

[†Mill has in mind letters printed in William Bray, ed., "Private Correspondence between King Charles I and His Secretary of State, Sir Edward Nicholas," in *Memoirs, Illustrative of the Life and Writings of John Evelyn, Esq., F.R.S.*, 2 vols. (London: Colburn, 1818), Vol. II; Gilbert Burnet, *The Memoires of the Lives and Actions of James and William Dukes of Hamilton and Castleherald* (London: Royston, 1677); Thomas Carte, *An History of the Life of James, Duke of Ormonde*, 3 vols. (London: Knapton, Strahan, et al., 1735–36); Arthur Collins, ed., *Letters and Memorials of State*, 2 vols. (London: Osborne, 1746); Thomas Wagstaffe, *A Vindication of King Charles the Martyr*, 3rd ed. (London: Wilkin, 1711); and Thomas Wentworth, *The Earl of Strafforde's Letters and Despatches*, ed. William Knowler, 2 vols. (London: Bowyer, 1739). For specific references, see, e.g., pp. 40, 26, 52, 32, 31 below.]

if they did not exist: because they prove his hero, not only to have been an adept in dissimulation and perfidy, but to have been in the constant habit of making asseverations, and corroborating them by the most solemn appeals to Heaven, which asseverations, when he uttered them, he perfectly well knew to be totally false. And as this fact, if known, would have spoiled him for a hero, Hume makes a point, not only of concealing, but of constantly and unblushingly denying it.[*]

Exclusively of these documents, the authorities which remain are the publications of the two parties at the time, and those of their partisans afterwards. If compelled to draw his whole information from these questionable sources, a fair historian would at least take nothing upon trust from either party; would compare their statements with one another, reject the exaggerations of both sides, and while he would repose tolerable confidence in their admissions against their own cause, would attach little weight to their assertions, when tending to asperse an adversary, or vindicate themselves. As for Hume, had he never looked into any but the royalist publications, the spirit in which he has written his history might have been pardoned, as the effect of blind credulity and partiality. But the names of Whitelocke, Ludlow, Rushworth, May,[†] appear so often at the bottom of the page, as to leave no doubt that, with regard to many of the events which he relates, he knew the truth, and wilfully concealed it. The republican writers are believed—when they bear testimony in favour of the royalists; while the royalists are never disbelieved, except when, by any chance, they make admissions against themselves.

If we consider who these royalists were, we shall be able to form some estimate of the credibility of a history, nearly the whole of which is copied from them.

The first, and, on the whole, the most respectable, is Clarendon;[‡] whom, though he was himself an actor in the scenes which he describes, and was not the more likely to be impartial, that he was a renegade, it has been usual to regard as a man of unimpeachable veracity, for no other reason that we can discover, but because Hume says so;[§] for it surely is no proof that a man will tell truth, because, like every man of sense and prudence, he is sparing of foul language. The question, however, concerning the veracity of Clarendon, may now be considered as settled; see Brodie, Vol. III, pp. 110n–14n, 263n–4n, 265n, 306n–8n, 316n, 334n–5n, 336n, 389n, 551n–4n, *et passim*, for various instances of his dishonesty and bad faith. It is too much to require that we should believe what Hume says of

[*See, e.g., Hume, Vol. VII, pp. 147–8. See also p. 34n below.]

[†Bulstrode Whitelocke, *Memorials of the English Affairs* (London: Ponder, 1682); Edmund Ludlow, *Memoirs*, 3 vols. (Vivay: n.p., 1698–99); John Rushworth, *Historical Collections*, 7 vols. (London: Thomason, Wright and Chiswell, *et al.*, 1659–1701); and Thomas May, *The History of the Parliament of England Which Began Nov. the Third, 1640* (London: Thomason, 1647).]

[‡Edward Hyde (Earl of Clarendon), *The History of the Rebellion and Civil Wars in England*, 3 vols. (Oxford: printed at the Theater, 1702–04).]

[§See, e.g., Hume, Vol. VII, p. 348.]

Clarendon rather than what Clarendon says of himself. A writer who makes a boast of the dexterity with which he fabricated speeches, and published them in the names of some of the parliamentary leaders,[*] was not likely to be over scrupulous, when he sat down to write an express vindication of himself and of his party.

If such be the character of the most candid of the royalist writers, it may be judged what credit is due to the more furious partisans. Even Clarendon, indeed, is too honest for Hume; for he occasionally lets out facts which it suits Hume to conceal.[†] His other authorities were less scrupulous. The chief of these are Carte, Clement Walker, and Perinchief;[‡] particularly the former, whom he seems almost to have taken as his text book, but whom he rarely ventures to quote; and he frequently commits the dishonesty of referring to Whitelocke or Rushworth for a story, of which the important features are to be found only in Carte. It is chiefly towards the latter end of the story that Perinchief and Walker come into play. Of these three, it is difficult to say which is least deserving of credit. Carte was a vulgar fanatic on the side of royalty, who believed every thing in favour of Charles, and nothing against him; and it is some presumption in favour of his sincerity, that, by the documents published in his Appendix, he furnished, in a great measure, the materials of his own refutation. Of Walker we shall say more hereafter. Of Perinchief we need say nothing, because we are quite sure that no man who has ever read a page of his work, will pay the least regard to any thing that he asserts.

The arts by which Hume has succeeded in obtaining belief for a period so much exceeding the ordinary duration of party lies, are various, and well worthy of examination.

In the first place, he avoids the appearance of violence, and yields some points, in order to make a show of moderation; knowing well that a writer, if he acknowledges only a tenth part of what is true, obtains a reputation for candour which frequently causes people to overlook the mis-statement of the other nine-tenths. Such points, therefore, as are wholly untenable, he gives up with a good grace. He allows some merit to the popular leaders, and acknowledges that they had some reason to complain. Yet, though the people may sometimes have been in the right, he will not allow that Charles can ever have been in the wrong; and if he allows that the people can have been right, it is only to a trifling extent.[§] To extenuate the abuses of the government, there is no sort of concealment which

[*See Edward Hyde, *The Life of Edward, Earl of Clarendon* (Oxford: Clarendon Printing House, 1759), Pt. II, pp. 69–71.]
[†See Brodie, Vol. III, pp. 315–16.]
[‡Clement Walker, *The History of Independency*, 2 pts. (London: n.p., 1648–49); Richard Perrinchief, *The Royal Martyr; or, The Life and Death of King Charles I* (London: Royston, 1676).]
[§Hume, Vol. VI, pp. 203–4, 220.]

he does not practise: for those which cannot be concealed, while, by an ordinary artifice, he represents them as solitary instances, and exceptions to the general rule, he industriously supplies every palliation which the most refined ingenuity can devise. In the first place, however bad the government might be, it was milder under Charles than under his predecessors;[*] as if that were true; or any thing to the purpose if it were. In the next place, we are told, in at least twenty places, that he was driven to these abuses by an appearance of necessity;[†] when Charles himself never pretended to be moved by necessity, but asserted that he had a right to do all that he did. The religious grievances are expressly declared to be of no consequence;[‡] as if it were of no consequence when a king attempts to force his own religion down the throats of the people; as if this were not of itself one of the most tyrannical of all acts of power; and as if a king who would do this, would not do any thing. If it be fanaticism to resist the introduction of a superstitious observance, how much greater is the fanaticism of upholding that observance, by cutting off men's ears and imprisoning them for life? Or, if Charles was himself conscious of the frivolity of the ceremonies which he imposed, what more charitable supposition remains, than that he supported Laud's religion, that Laud might support his power?

Another of the artifices of Hume consists in attempting to prepossess the reader for or against a particular person, while he is still in ignorance of those actions of that person, from which, and not from the assertions of his partisans, or of his enemies, his character ought to be inferred. Thus, every opportunity is taken of holding up King Charles as a person distinguished by every moral excellence: many of his actions indicate the reverse; but as the character has the advantage of coming first, it is hoped that the reader will credit the character rather than the actions. The parliamentary leaders, on the other hand, he represents as hypocrites or fanatics, and (when he dares) as uneducated, coarse, and brutal in their manners and in their character.[§] All this, as Mr. Brodie has shown, is untrue;[¶] but it answers the purpose; and the reasoning amounts to this: Vane, Ireton, and Harrison were fanatics, therefore King Charles's government was good: a specimen of argumentation which, if not strictly logical, is, at any rate, extremely convenient, since it is hard if a partisan, however weak his cause, cannot contrive to pick a hole either in the intellectual or moral character of some one or more of his opponents.

We might fill a whole article with an analysis of the artifices of Hume; but a few specimens are necessary, to convince the reader that we have not brought charges which it is not in our power to prove; imperfect as the conception is which can be

[*Ibid., Vol. VII, p. 526.]
[†See, e.g., ibid., Vol. VI, pp. 199, 204, 206, 212, 213, 214, 227–39.]
[‡Ibid., pp. 203, 210–11.]
[§Ibid., Vol. VII, pp. 109–10, 145, 314, 383.]
[¶See Brodie, Vol. III, pp. 19n, 22n–4n, 499n–508n.]

given by specimens, of a work of which almost every sentence contains in it more or less of misrepresentation. And as it is also incumbent on us to give some idea of what Mr. Brodie has done to throw light upon this portion of history, it seems to us that these two objects may best be united by such a concise sketch of the events of the period as is compatible with the narrow limits of an article; and to this, after requesting the indulgence of the reader to the very general view which it is in our power to afford, we shall proceed.

It is first, however, necessary to say something on the nature of the government before the time of the Stuarts. Mr. Brodie has written a long, and, he will forgive us for saying, a dull, introductory volume, to prove that it was by no means so arbitrary as is generally imagined. Though this volume contains much valuable information concerning the practical workings of the government, and the condition of the people, we wish he had placed it at the end rather than at the beginning; for it looks formidable, and its bulk may alarm the reader, while it contributes little to the main object of the history. The agitation, indeed, of such a question is of little use for any purpose, and, assuredly, of no use whatever for the purpose of enabling us to form a correct judgment on the events which ensued. It is of little consequence whether misgovernment was of an ancient or of a modern date in Great Britain; in either case, resistance to it was equally a duty; the opposition to that resistance, equally a crime; and it is a strange doctrine, that we are not entitled to good government, unless we can prove, that our ancestors enjoyed it: although, as mankind, educated as they have hitherto been, are governed by custom and precedent much more than by reason, it was perfectly natural that each party at the time should endeavour to throw the reproach of innovation upon its opponents.

The truth, in as far as it can be elicited from the facts which have been handed down to us, seems perfectly to coincide with what the experience of all nations, similarly situated, would have led us to infer. There was no distinct line of demarcation between what was permitted to the king, and what was forbidden. He was not nominally recognized as absolute; at the same time, he was practically so, as often as he was a man of talents, and circumstances favoured his power. When, on the other hand, a weak prince filled the throne, the nobles were every thing, and the king nothing. Precedents, therefore, may be found (if by precedents the question is to be decided), both for and against the claim of absolute power. If it be true, as Mr. Brodie asserts, that Elizabeth and Henry VIII rarely attempted to raise money without consent of parliament,[*] what does this prove, except that the parliament was always willing to grant, if not as much as those monarchs desired, so much that, dependant as they were on public opinion from their peculiar situation, they did not care to provoke the people by exacting more? In like manner, if it be true that the Tudors did not imprison and fine men in the

[**Ibid.*, Vol. I, pp. 47-8, 250.]

star-chamber to so great an extent as is supposed,[*] so neither, it should be remembered, did Charles, unless when some one resisted his authority; and under the Tudors there was no resistance to authority, or none capable of exciting any uneasiness in the breast of the sovereign. But, at length, resistance came; and with resistance came cruelty, for the purpose of its suppression.

The great deficiency in Mr. Brodie's work, is, that he has not explained why resistance began so soon; how it happened, that sentiments and ideas, in almost every other country then utterly unknown, were at this early period so widely diffused in Great Britain. It is scarcely fair, indeed, to blame Mr. Brodie for a deficiency which he shares with all former English historians. Our present concern, however, is not with the causes of the resistance, but with the resistance itself.

There is sufficient evidence to prove, that James I had a strong leaning to popery;* moved, it may be supposed, in part, by respect to the memory of his mother,[†] but chiefly by the readiness with which that religion allies itself with arbitrary power. In proportion to his inclination for popery, was his hatred of all the protestant sectaries. Where he had, as in England, archbishoprics and bishoprics to give away, he had a tolerable security that the conduct of a majority in the church would be sufficiently conformable to his wishes, whatever they might be. In Scotland, where he had no such precious gifts at his disposal, he found the clergy by no means equally compliant. To the presbyterian church government, therefore, he professed an inveterate dislike; "declaring that, under it, Jack, and Tom, and Dick, and Will, presumed to instruct him in affairs of state." (Brodie, Vol. I, p. 333.)[‡] His aversion extended to the Puritans in England, who were Presbyterians, and hostile, if not at first to episcopacy, at least to the intermeddling of bishops in secular affairs. And throughout the reign of James they were severely visited with the penalties of the law. Nor was the civil government of James less despotic than the ecclesiastical. In profession, indeed, his claim of arbitrary power

[*_Ibid._, pp. 158ff., 192–4, 244.]

*In his very first speech to parliament he acknowledged the Romish church to be his mother church, though defiled with some deformities and impurities; he declared that he would indulge their clergy, if they would but renounce the pope's supremacy, and his pretended power to grant dispensation for the murder of kings; if they would but abandon their late corruptions, he would meet them half way; but he did not specify what these corruptions were. [Mill is indirectly quoting Brodie, Vol. I, p. 336n, who is referring to James I's First Speech to Parliament (1603): see _The Parliamentary History of England_, ed. William Cobbett and John Wright, 36 vols. (London: Bagshaw, Longmans, 1806–20), Vol. I, cols. 982–4 (hereafter cited as Cobbett, with volume and column references).]

[†Mary (of Scotland).]

[‡See James I's speech (14 Jan., 1604) in "Proceedings in a Conference at Hampton Court," in _A Complete Collection of State Trials_, ed. Thomas Bayly Howell, 34 vols. (London: Longman, _et al._, 1809–28), Vol. II, col. 35 (hereafter cited as _State Trials_, with volume and column references).]

went far beyond that of his most tyrannical predecessors. "The power of kings," he told the parliament, "was like the divine power; for, as God can create and destroy, make and unmake at his pleasure, so kings can give life and death, judge all and be judged by none. As it was blasphemy," he added, "to dispute what God might do, so it was sedition in subjects to dispute what a king might do, in the height of his power."[*] Nor did his practice fall short of his professions.

In ecclesiastical matters he assumed supreme power, and struck at the very vitals of the constitution by issuing illegal proclamations with penalties, which were enforced by the court of star-chamber, while, by levying taxes without an act of parliament, he prepared the way for the disuse of that assembly. He, of his own accord, imposed new duties at the ports, and arrogated the right of doing so at pleasure, a pretension in which he was supported by venal statesmen and corrupt lawyers, who concurred in fabricating precedents to deceive the people; nay, his judges solemnly decided so monstrous a principle in his favour. Innumerable projects and monopolies were devised for raising money, but he was latterly obliged to pass an act against them: forced loans, without the pressing emergencies which were used as an apology for them in the preceding reign, were resorted to; and the hateful measure of benevolence, which had been so much reprobated, and so opposed even in Henry VIII, and so long discontinued, was revived. (*Ibid.*, pp. 351–2.)[†]

All offices were filled by creatures of the unworthy favourite, Buckingham; selected, not for their fitness, but for subservience to his will. We except, of course, such offices as were sold (which was the case with many) for the benefit of the king or of his favourite.

Let us suppose that Charles I, when he ascended the throne, had expressed the strongest determination to redress these abuses; is there any one who will have the folly to say that he ought to have been trusted? That, because he found it convenient to make promises, in contradiction to his obvious interest, he should have been left at full liberty to perform them, or not, as he pleased? But when there was not only no reason to anticipate a reform, but every reason to anticipate the contrary; when, in defiance of public opinion, he had just married an avowed Catholic,[‡] and issued warrants to forbear all proceedings against recusants; when he not only pursued the same measures as his predecessor; but the same men, and especially Buckingham, so deservedly the object of popular odium, still maintained a boundless ascendancy over his counsels; this surely was not the time to show unlimited confidence, but rather the time to push for beneficial concessions, before the king should have advanced so far as to be unable, without humiliation, to recede.

We may be excused for dwelling at so much length upon the state of affairs at the commencement of Charles's reign, when it is considered what reproaches have been cast upon his first parliament by Hume, because, instead of granting

[*Brodie, Vol. I, pp. 350–1; for James I's speech, see the preceding note.]
[†See, e.g., *State Trials*, Vol. II, cols. 371ff., 899ff.; for the Act against monopolies, see 21 James I, c. 3 (1623).]
[‡Henrietta Maria (of France).]

immediately all the money which he required, they gave him, at first, but little, that they might still retain some control over his actions. Hume, however, declares that, at this period, "an unbounded power was exercised by the crown," and that "it was necessary to fix a choice, either to abandon entirely the privileges of the people, or to secure them by firmer and more precise barriers than the constitution had hitherto provided for them."[*] What, then, in his opinion, ought they to have done? To have submitted to despotism? If not, what means had they to resist it, other than by withholding supplies? They are further accused of having acted an ungenerous part, by forcing the king upon a war, and then refusing him the means of carrying it on.[†] True, as usual, in sound, and false in substance. It was well known by Hume to have been one main cause of the war, that Charles and Buckingham, on their return from Spain, had told (or, at least, the one had looked on while the other told) some few lies to the parliament, concerning the transactions in which they had been engaged.[‡] And the other motive by which the parliament were swayed, when they urged the king to a war, was the hope of, by that means, preventing him from marrying a Catholic, which, notwithstanding, he immediately did; their quarrel was not with Spain, but with popery and slavery: it was Charles and his favourite who now pressed the war, and from motives of purely personal pique.

The last subsidies had been granted under an express condition that their expenditure should be controlled by commissioners appointed by parliament;[§] this condition had never been fulfilled, and it was now complained, surely not without reason, that an account of the expenditure, though promised, did not make its appearance. Great complaints, too, were heard against an oppressive imposition which the late king had imposed, by his own authority, upon wines.[¶] It was evident, that by summoning the parliament to the metropolis during one of the most dreadful pestilences ever known in England, it had been hoped to obtain an immediate supply, without leaving time to enter upon the consideration of grievances. The Commons, therefore, wisely granted two subsidies, and no more.[‖]

At this time, Montague, one of the king's chaplains, published a work,[**] called, by Hume, "a moderate book, which, to their great disgust, saved virtuous Catholics, as well as other Christians, from eternal torments:"[††] but he does not

[*Hume, Vol. VI, p. 204.]
[†*Ibid.*, pp. 200–7.]
[‡See Villiers' address of 24 Feb., 1624, to both Houses of Parliament, in *Journals of the House of Lords*, Vol. III, p. 220.]
[§21 James I, c. 34 (1623).]
[¶See Cobbett, Vol. II, cols. 45–6.]
[‖1 Charles I, c. 6 (1625).]
[**Richard Montagu, *Appello Caesarem* (London: Lownes, 1625).]
[††Hume, Vol. VI, p. 210.]

state that this moderate book was a tissue of the most furious invective against the Puritans; that it openly vindicated many of the popish tenets, and more covertly, though not less really, defended that religion as a whole. A committee of the Commons was appointed to report upon this work, and Montague was bound, under recognizances, to answer for it at the bar of the House. From this transaction Hume takes occasion to accuse the Commons of illiberality, forgetting, that in the age in which they lived, some degree of intolerance towards popery was necessary for self-defence; that those dangers which are now chimerical, were then real and alarming; that those disabilities, which can now serve no purpose, except that of oppression, were necessary then to hinder Protestants from being blown up, or, once more, burnt in Smithfield. Such a book, too, from a chaplain of the king, and that chaplain retaining his place, proved surely that the king himself could not be very hostile to the sentiments which it contained. The Commons had no claim upon Charles for the punishment of Montague, but they had a claim for his dismissal. Proceedings, however, were stopped by a message from the king, declaring that he meant to take the matter under his own consideration.[*] So well did he keep his word, that, ere long, Montague was made a bishop.

It is for acts like this that we read so often in Hume's history of Charles's mild and tolerant disposition.[†] As if any man in his senses could believe that the persecutor of Leighton and Prynne was an enemy to persecution; as if it were any proof of a mild and tolerant disposition, to bestow rewards upon one religion and inflict punishments upon another. We had always thought that this was the very essence of intolerance; what else, we take leave to ask, does intolerance mean?

Before the parliament was re-assembled, an incident had occurred, which, alone, would have sufficed to justify all its subsequent proceedings. The French king[‡] was then at war with his protestant subjects at Rochelle: to aid him in subduing them, Charles lent him a fleet; and, but for the manly resistance of the sailors, a fleet, equipped with the very money granted for the defence of the Protestants in Germany, would have been employed for the suppression of the protestant religion in France, and the support of popery and arbitrary power. As an excuse for Charles, Hume observes, that he was probably deceived by the French government; which is more than was asserted by Buckingham himself, in the long speech which he made in parliament on the occasion.[§] But Hume is not ashamed to defend the transaction itself; and because the English resented it, he thence infers, that of all European nations they were at that time the most bigotted.[¶] If this be bigotry, may they always continue bigots.

Had the parliament been previously inclined to add any thing to their former

[*See Cobbett, Vol. II, cols. 6–7.]
[†E.g., Hume, Vol. VI, pp. 206, 210, 223, 293.]
[‡Louis XIII.]
[§Cobbett, Vol. II, cols. 26–31.]
[¶Hume, Vol. VI, pp. 209–10.]

grant, they would scarcely have done so after this experience of the use to which they might expect it to be applied. The king's complaint of poverty[*] was met by remonstrances against extravagant expenditure;* and he was petitioned against the sale of offices, against monopolies and illegal impositions: yet Hume does not scruple to say, that the growth of popery was ever the chief of their grievances, and now their only one; though he had said, a few pages before, that an unbounded power was exercised by the crown; but this, in his opinion, was no grievance.[†] Charles dissolved the parliament, and supplied his present wants by a compulsory loan, the produce of which being dissipated in an unsuccessful expedition against Cadiz, he was compelled to summon another parliament. By pricking several of the popular leaders[‡] sheriffs of counties, he incapacitated them from being returned to parliament. This paltry artifice, by which he hoped to secure compliance with his desires, only exposed his weakness, without repressing the spirit of resistance to mis-rule.

The Commons immediately voted three subsidies and three fifteenths, and, soon after, one subsidy more; but deferred passing their vote into a law, until after the public grievances should have been considered.[§] Situated as they were, it is difficult to see how they should have adopted a wiser, or a more moderate course.

A condition, [says Hume,] was thus made, in a very undisguised manner, with their sovereign. Under colour of redressing grievances, which, during this short reign could not be very numerous, they were to proceed in regulating and controlling every part of government which displeased them; and if the king either cut them short in this undertaking, or refused compliance with their demands, he must not expect any supply from the Commons. Great dissatisfaction was expressed by Charles, at a treatment which he deemed so harsh and undutiful.[¶]

This is the way in which the people of England are spoken of, for exercising their legal and acknowledged privilege of withholding supplies. For what purpose was that privilege given to them, but to enable them to "make conditions with their sovereign?" for what purpose, but that they might avail themselves of his necessities to curtail his mischievous power? To hold up the making "conditions" with their sovereign in this manner *ad invidiam*, as if to make conditions with their sovereign were a crime, is to insinuate a doctrine which Hume himself does not dare to acknowledge as his own, and which, therefore, he artfully puts into the mouth of another.[‖] Their grievances, too, "during this short reign, could not be

[*See Cobbett, Vol. II, cols. 11–16.]
*How well founded these remonstrances were, may be seen in Brodie, Vol. II, pp. 77–8, 90–1. [See also Cobbett, Vol. II, cols. 11–12.]
[†Hume, Vol. VI, pp. 210, 204.]
[‡Including Edward Coke, Robert Phelips, Francis Seymour, and Thomas Wentworth.]
[§Cobbett, Vol. II, cols. 56, 101.]
[¶Hume, Vol. VI, pp. 213–14; see also Cobbett, Vol. II, cols. 47–50.]
[‖Hume, Vol. VI, p. 226.]

very numerous." As if a grievance ever consisted in a single oppressive act; as if the continual liability to such acts—the system, the state of things, which renders them possible, were of no consequence whatever. The individual act, however tyrannical, is past, and cannot be recalled. What is sought is, security against its renewal; and it is for this aiming at security, that the people of England, throughout this portion of Hume's history, are held up to scorn and detestation.

The sale of offices, and the exorbitant gifts lavished upon Buckingham and his creatures, being warmly complained of, and some members not sparing their censures upon the favorite himself, Charles summoned both houses to Whitehall, where he told them, that to reflect upon the duke was to reflect upon himself, and threatened them, if they persevered, with a dissolution. The Commons, however, were not to be discouraged by menaces; and they soon shewed their resolution, by preferring an impeachment against the duke.[*]

None of their proceedings has been more grossly misrepresented than this. They have been reproached for voting, that common fame was a sufficient ground for accusation.[†] Common fame is not, certainly, a sufficient ground for punishment; but punishment is one thing, and accusation another. It may not only be justifiable, but an imperative duty, to proceed against an individual, even upon a slight suspicion, that so his guilt or innocence may be fully ascertained. If a charge were never brought until it were known with certainty that it could be proved, where, we ask, would be the use of trial?

All the charges, Hume goes on to say, appear, from comparing the accusation and reply, to be either frivolous, or false, or both.[‡] How their truth or falsehood can be established, by hearing the accusers affirm, and the accused deny, Hume, with his usual accuracy, omits to inform us. If embezzlement, extortion, neglect of duty as admiral, the purchase and sale of offices, the loan of ships to suppress the Protestants in France, and the poisoning of the late king, be frivolous accusations, then, indeed, the charges against Buckingham were frivolous—that they were false, remained to be proved by trial: that trial which the Commons sought, and which Charles and Buckingham avoided. The principal managers[§] of the impeachments were sent to the Tower, and soon after the parliament was dissolved.

After a breach with the parliament, [says Hume,] which seemed so difficult to repair, the only rational counsel which Charles could pursue was, immediately to conclude a peace with Spain, and to render himself, as far as possible, independent of his people, who discovered so little inclination to support him, or rather, who seem to have formed a

---

[*See Cobbett, Vol. II, cols. 46, 50–1. For the King's Speech to Parliament of 28 Mar., 1626, see *ibid.*, col. 60. See also "Articles of Impeachment Exhibited by the Commons against the Duke of Buckingham," *ibid.*, cols. 106–19.]
[†Hume, Vol. VI, pp. 215–16; Cobbett, Vol. II, col. 55.]
[‡Hume, Vol. VI, p. 216.]
[§Dudley Digges and John Eliot.]

determined resolution to abridge his authority. Nothing could be easier in the execution than this measure, nor more *agreeable to his own and to national interest.*[*]

The same man, who thus stands forward, the open and avowed advocate of despotism, can nevertheless lavish hypocritical praises upon the popular leaders, for resisting designs, so "agreeable to national interest."

Despotism in the design, hypocrisy in the outside, he here acknowledges to have characterized the conduct of his hero. "Had he possessed any military force, on which he could rely, it is not improbable that he had at once taken off the mask, and governed without any regard to parliamentary privileges."[†] To some it may appear, that he could not well have taken off the mask more completely than he did. Ship-money, benevolences, and a general forced loan, were the expedients resorted to for obtaining money: for resisting these illegal exactions, seventy-six gentlemen were imprisoned, five of whom appealed to the law for redress. Sir Randolph Carew, chief justice, not being found a ready-enough tool, was displaced to make room for Sir Nicholas Hyde, who readily pronounced the power of arbitrary imprisonment to be legal.[‡] Billetting of soldiers was another instrument of extortion. Manwaring, the king's chaplain, published two sermons,[§] maintaining broadly the doctrine of active and passive obedience, and particularly the right of levying taxes without consent of parliament. For refusing to licence these sermons (which were printed by the king's special command), the primate Abbot was suspended from his office, and confined to his country house. The employment of popish recusants was continued, notwithstanding a solemn promise to the parliament.[¶]

One of the grand objects of Hume's *History* is, to prove, that Charles's conduct, throughout, was open and sincere. "Some historians have rashly questioned the good faith of this prince: but, for this reproach, the most malignant scrutiny of his conduct, which in every circumstance is now thoroughly known, affords not any reasonable foundation. Probity and honor ought justly to be numbered among his most shining qualities."[‖] It is difficult to understand, what Hume meant by probity and honor. The instances of Charles's bad faith are far too numerous to be named; some of the more remarkable of them will be noticed as we go on: but, in this instance, Hume admits him to have violated a solemn pledge; and mark the attempt to palliate this breach of faith: "he was apt, in imitation of his father, to

[*Hume, Vol. VI, p. 223.]

[†*Ibid.*, p. 224.]

[‡See "Proceedings on the Habeas Corpus, Brought by Sir Thomas Darnel, Sir John Corbet, Sir Walter Earl, Sir John Heveningham, and Sir Edward Hampden, . . . 1627," in *State Trials*, Vol. III, cols. 51–9.]

[§Roger Maynwaring, *Religion and Allegiance: In Two Sermons* (London: Badger, 1627).]

[¶See Cobbett, Vol. II, cols. 248–53.]

[‖Hume, Vol. VII, p. 147.]

imagine that the parliament, when they failed of supplying his necessities, had, on their part, freed him from the obligation of a strict performance."[*] Apt to do what? Only to lie; an offence which, in Hume's estimation, seems to be very venial.

Fortunately the king was mad enough to plunge himself into a war with France; which compelled him, once more, to summon a parliament. Resolved to leave him no just ground of complaint, the Commons voted five subsidies, the largest supply, according to Mr. Brodie, ever before granted in parliament.[†] They withheld, however, for a time, the bill of supply, and proceeded to frame a law, called the Petition of Right, which should secure them in time to come from the oppression under which they had suffered.[‡] By this enactment (which inquirers of all parties are, to an extraordinary degree, unanimous in applauding), "forced loans, benevolences, taxes without consent of parliament, arbitrary imprisonments, the billetting of soldiers, martial law"* were declared illegal.

The king, by an ambiguous answer,[§] evaded giving his assent to the petition of right. Meanwhile, the Commons sent up an impeachment against Manwaring,[¶] for the two sermons to which we before referred. It is very easy to cry out against intolerance; but, if they had not met their opponents with their own weapons, they could not have met them at all. It was surely excusable to punish adversaries, whom they were not permitted to refute. No one is so great an enemy to intolerance as Hume, when it is the intolerance of the Puritans; but, he is very indulgent to the bitterest persecution, when Charles is the persecutor. It is better to avoid persecution, as it is better in war to refrain from the massacre of prisoners; but, if your enemy obstinately refuses to give quarter, it would be very false humanity on your part, to abstain from retaliation.—Manwaring was sentenced to imprisonment, deprivation, and fine. No sooner did the session terminate, than he was pardoned, received a living, and some years after was promoted to a bishopric.

The Commons proceeded to inquire into a commission which had been granted to levy troops in Germany, and transport them into England. As the number mentioned was only a thousand horse, Hume insinuates a doubt that they were intended for a mischievous purpose:[||] omitting to state, that arms were likewise ordered for ten thousand foot.

At length the king, being hard pressed for money, gave his assent to the petition

[*_Ibid._, Vol. VI, p. 220.]
[†Brodie, Vol. II, pp. 174–5. For the five subsidies, see 3 Charles I, c. 7 (1627).]
[‡For the debate on Supply, see Cobbett, Vol. II, cols. 253–6; the "Petition of Right" was enacted as 3 Charles I, c. 1 (1627).]
*Hume [Vol. VI, p. 246].
[§Cobbett, Vol. II, col. 377.]
[¶"The Declaration of the Commons against Roger Manwaring," in Cobbett, Vol. II, cols. 388–90; for the sentence mentioned below (1628), see _State Trials_, Vol. III, col. 356.]
[||Hume, Vol. VI, pp. 257–8.]

of right, and the subsidy bill passed immediately after.[*] The Commons then framed a Remonstrance, recapitulating their grievances, and ascribing them wholly to the counsels of Buckingham.[†] "As this," says Hume, "was the first return which he (Charles) met with for his late beneficial concessions, and for his sacrifices of prerogative, the greatest by far ever made by an English sovereign, nothing could be more the object of great and natural indignation."[‡]

A grosser falsehood than is insinuated here, it is scarcely possible to conceive. The remonstrance was the "first return" for his concessions! when Hume has just before told us, that the "first return" was the grant of money. In the next place, Charles had made no concessions which had not been forced upon him, and which he did not, as we shall presently see, intend to revoke, as soon as it should be in his power.

Soon after, the king, hearing that they were preparing a remonstrance against the levying of tonnage and poundage, in open infringement of the petition of right, without consent of parliament, came suddenly to the house of Lords, and ended the session by a prorogation.[§]

The petition of right was no sooner passed, than it was violated: duties were levied, and merchants imprisoned for refusing to pay them, as before. Charles likewise gave a striking proof of the insincerity of his concessions, by suppressing the copies of the petition of right which the parliament had ordered to be printed, and circulating others with his former evasive answer annexed: "an expedient," says Hume, "by which Charles endeavoured to persuade the people, that he had nowise receded from his former claims and pretensions."[¶] Yet this writer has the effrontery to say of Charles, in another place, "In every treaty, those concessions which he thought he could not in conscience maintain, he never could, by any motive or persuasion, be induced to make."[‖]

No sooner was the parliament re-assembled, than the Commons proceeded to inquire into this pitiful evasion: they took notice of the recent violations of the petition of right; complained of the popish ceremonies which the prelates had already begun to introduce, and resumed the consideration of the question of tonnage and poundage. When, at length, at the motion of Sir John Elliot, and after a discussion of more than usual violence, a remonstrance was passed against levying that impost without parliamentary authority, Charles was so enraged that he at once dissolved the parliament,[**] and committed Elliot, Hollis, and other

[*3 Charles I, c. 7 (1627).]
[†"Remonstrance of the Commons against the D. of Bucks, as Being the Cause of All Grievances," in Cobbett, Vol. II, cols. 420–7.]
[‡Hume, Vol. VI, p. 259.]
[§See Cobbett, Vol. II, cols. 431–4.]
[¶Hume, Vol. VI, p. 265; Cobbett, Vol. II, cols. 410, 430, 442.]
[‖Hume, Vol. VI, p. 147.]
[**Cobbett, Vol. II, cols. 435–7, 443–53, 466; for the Remonstrance and the King's Declaration, see cols. 488–504.]

leading members,[*] to prison; where Elliot soon after died, a victim to his exertions to free his country from the yoke of despotism.

For twelve years after this period, no more parliaments were summoned: and here Mr. Brodie pauses to pass under review the individuals who at this time swayed the counsels of Charles.[†] In this we shall follow his example, confining, however, our attention to the principal figures in the picture—Strafforde and Laud.

The tragical close of Strafforde's life has enabled his partisans to throw a theatrical glare over his character, which has long concealed its deformity from the public eye. In private life he was haughty, vindictive, and cruel; in public, he had no principle, other than the aggrandizement of himself: from his first entry into public life, he put himself up to auction, and only when the court refused to buy him, threw himself into the popular party: when bought, he turned round, and at once became not only the unblushing advocate, but the active instrument, of that system of tyranny which he had been the loudest to condemn.

With equal tyranny, and equal servility, were joined in Laud the most furious bigotry and the most puerile superstition. Himself a papist, in every thing except the supremacy of the pope, he caused the popish tenets and the popish ceremonies to be adopted by the Church of England: and so general was the expectation, that through his means Great Britain would again be brought within the catholic pale, that he actually had the offer of a cardinal's hat, which, however, he did not venture to accept. In lending himself, body and soul, to the service of despotism, he only did what almost any man would have done in a similar situation. His other vices were peculiarly his own; cringing and adulation in order to rise, insolence after he had risen; the basest ingratitude towards his benefactors, and the most inveterate hatred towards all whom he believed to be, in any way, obstacles to the increase of his power.*

But how shall we attempt to describe the atrocities perpetrated during the twelve years' intermission of parliament, under the government of Charles and of these worthy instruments? In the space to which we are confined, it would be the height of absurdity to make the attempt. Mr. Brodie has dedicated a long chapter to the purpose, and to him, therefore, the reader must refer.[‡] Suffice it to say, that ship-money, benevolences, loans, were now the least oppressive modes of extortion. Obsolete forest laws, statutes concerning tillage, and an old law against

[*Including William Coryton, Peter Heyman, Miles Hobart, Walter Long, John Seldon, William Strode, and Benjamin Valentine.]

[†Brodie, Vol. II, pp. 236ff.]

*If Hume is to be believed, Laud was perfectly sincere and disinterested. "All his enemies were also imagined by him the declared enemies to loyalty and true piety, and every exercise of his anger, by that means, became in his eyes a merit and a virtue." [Vol. VI, p. 285.] How Hume knew all this he has not thought it proper to inform us.

[‡Brodie, Vol. II, pp. 274-403.]

the increase of the metropolis, were revived;[*] and under pretence of these laws, fines were levied upon hundreds. Every person who possessed £20 a year in land was compelled to receive the honour of knighthood, which involved the payment of exorbitant fees. On the pretext of remedying defective titles to land, those who would not pay largely for a new title were threatened with the loss of their estates. Monopolies were carried to an extent before unknown; and the severest penalties were inflicted on all who infringed them. Chambers, a merchant of London, for refusing to pay tonnage and poundage without parliamentary authority, was summoned before the council, where having remarked that the merchants of England were as much screwed up as in Turkey, he was fined £2,000 in the star-chamber;[†] and lay twelve years in prison, because he would not degrade himself by submission. One Hillyard was fined £5,000 for selling salt-petre, contrary to proclamation: Rea, £2,000 for exporting fuller's earth;[‡] and so in hundreds of instances which it would be tedious to mention. "Such severities," says Hume, "were afterwards magnified into the greatest enormities."[§] They really were not, then, in his opinion, enormities!

In respect to religion, Hume labours to the utmost of his power to excite contempt and scorn for the great mass of the people, because they thought there was reason to apprehend the re-establishment of popery; and he says that "the groundless charge" of popery against Laud, "was belied by his whole life and conduct."[¶] We would willingly ask Hume, or any who share his sentiments, what there is in popery which renders it so great a curse to mankind? Its intolerance? But if in this respect there was any difference between the Church of England and the Church of Rome, it was only that the one employed one sort of torture, and the other another; that the one persecuted by burning, the other by protracted torments, exceeding in magnitude a hundred burnings. But they differed, perhaps, in tenets. Scarcely so; when image-worship, prayer to the dead, adoration at the altar, worship of saints, the real presence, confession, and absolution, were part of the established religion.* In ceremonials? But the formalities of the catholic church,

---

[*Respectively, the "Assize of the Forest" of Henry II (in *Select Charters*, ed. William Stubbs [Oxford: Clarendon Press, 1870], pp. 150–2); 4 Henry VII, c. 19 (1487); 35 Elizabeth, c. 6 (1593).]

[†Brodie, Vol. II, p. 275; see also "Proceedings against Mr. Richard Chambers, in the Star-Chamber, for Seditious Speeches before the Privy-Council, 1629," in *State Trials*, Vol. III, cols. 373–5.]

[‡See Rushworth, *Historical Collections*, Vol. III, pp. 68–9, and Vol. II, pp. 348–9.]

[§Hume, Vol. VI, p. 306.]

[¶*Ibid.*, Vol. VII, p. 38.]

*Hume, with his usual candour, constantly represents the disputes about religion as involving nothing but mere ceremonies: "the surplice, the rails placed about the altar, the bows exacted on approaching it, the liturgy, the breach of the sabbath, embroidered capes, lawn sleeves, the use of the ring in marriage, and of the cross in baptism. On account of these," says he, "were the popular leaders content to throw the government into such violent convulsions." [*Ibid.*, Vol. VI, p. 388.] Can disingenuousness go beyond this?

whether with respect to worship, or to days, meats, and vestments, were scrupulously exacted. Nor was this all: even the supremacy of the king was denied; and the divine authority of bishops, and their superiority to the civil power, became fundamental articles of the high-church creed. Nay, an open defence of popery itself, published by one Chowney,[*] was dedicated to, and patronized by, Laud. The assertion, therefore, that there was no danger of popery, if it be true in sound, is in substance one of the grossest falsehoods ever palmed upon the credulity of the world.

Of the punishments inflicted upon all who vindicated the doctrines of the reformed, in opposition to popery and to the Church of England, we shall present the reader with a few examples.

Leighton, a doctor of divinity, for writing against the hierarchy, and the new ceremonies,[†] was seized by the officers of the high-commission, and after the most brutal treatment, was adjudged by the star-chamber to pay 10,000 pounds; in addition to which, it was ordained that,

after degradation, he should be whipped at Westminster, and set in the pillory there during the sitting of the court; have one ear cut off, one side of his nose slit, and one cheek branded with s. s. for sower of sedition: that he should then be carried back to prison, and, at a future convenient time, be brought to Cheapside, on a market-day, and be there whipt again, and set in the pillory, and have his other ear cut off, his other cheek branded, and the other side of his nose slit: after which was only to follow imprisonment for life.*

The whole of this sentence was executed to the letter. What an unfeeling slave must he be, who can talk in the following strain of these atrocious cruelties:

Leighton who had written libels against the king, the queen, the bishops, and the whole administration, was condemned by a very severe, if not a cruel sentence; but the execution of it was suspended for some time, in expectation of his submission.† All the severities, indeed, of this reign were exercised against those who triumphed in their sufferings, who courted persecution, and braved authority; and, on that account their punishment may be deemed the more just, but the less prudent.‡

A king, then, may justly be guilty of any cruelties which he pleases, provided he practises them only upon those who resist his power; only upon those on whom alone he can have any motive to practise them. The robber, who murders you to obtain your purse, would find this doctrine extremely convenient: had you quietly consented to give up your money you might possibly have escaped with your life; for which reason he is perfectly justified in depriving you of both.

[*Thomas Chouneus, *Collectiones theologicarum quarundam conclusionum, ex diversis authorum sententiis . . . excerptae* (London: Seyle, 1635).]

[†Alexander Leighton, *An Appeal to the Parliament* (Amsterdam: successors of G. Thorp, 1629).]

*Brodie, Vol. II, p. 313 [based on "Proceedings in the Star-Chamber against Dr. Alexander Leighton, for a Libel, 1630," in *State Trials*, Vol. III, col. 385].

†This assertion by the way is proved by Mr. Brodie to be false. [Vol. II, pp. 313–14.]

‡Hume [Vol. VI, p. 295].

Prynne, declared by Lord Clifford in the House of Lords (10th May, 1809) to have been one of the most eminent lawyers whom England ever produced, had written a book to prove the unlawfulness of stage-plays.[*] Bastwick, a physician, in a work against popery and prelacy, had asserted the supremacy of the king.[†] For these crimes, Prynne was condemned to lose his ears, to stand twice in the pillory, to be degraded from the bar, and at the university, to pay a fine of £5,000, and to be imprisoned for life. Bastwick, to pay £1,000; to be debarred his practice of physic, to be excommunicated, and imprisoned till he made a recantation.

These two individuals published vindications of themselves;[‡] not without considerable warmth of expression (and no wonder): for this they were adjudged to lose their ears (Prynne's having, on the former occasion, been imperfectly cut off), and to be closely imprisoned for life in the isles of Jersey, Guernsey and Scilly, without access of kindred or friends, and without books, pens, ink, or paper.[§] In this situation they continued until released by the long parliament. Burton, a divine, for two sermons which he had published, suffered the same punishment. This "severity" (such is the mild expression of Hume), he is pleased to acknowledge as having been "perhaps, in itself, somewhat blameable."[¶]

Persecution was not confined to the opponents of the established religion; it was extended to all who resisted arbitrary power, and to all against whom Laud and Strafforde had any personal pique.

Sir David Foulis, a member of the council of York, was, upon a charge of speaking irreverently of his office, opposing the commission of knighthood, and throwing out some remarks against Wentworth, which he denied, fined by the star-chamber, 5,000$l.$; assessed in damages to Wentworth, 3,000$l.$; and ordained to make an acknowledgment of his offences, both to his majesty and to Wentworth, not only in the star-chamber, but in the court of York, and at the assizes, and condemned to imprisonment during the king's pleasure, and to be deprived of his various offices as member of the council of York, deputy-lieutenant, and justice of peace; his son, Henry, was likewise fined 500$l.$*

Williams, bishop of Lincoln, who had raised Laud to his present power, and whom, as a formidable rival, Laud was resolved to crush, was, on frivolous

[*William Prynne, *Histrio-Mastix* (London: Sparke, 1633); the sentence is given in "Proceedings against Wm. Prynn, Esq. in the Star-Chamber, . . . 1632–33," in *State Trials*, Vol. III, col. 576.]

[†John Bastwick, *Flagellum pontificis* ([Holland:] n.p., 1633).]

[‡Prynne, *Newes from Ipswich* (Ipswich [Edinburgh: Anderson], 1636); Bastwick, Πράξεις τὸν ἐπισκόπων, *sive Apologeticus* ([London:] n.p., 1636), and *The Letany of John Bastwick* ([London:] n.p., 1637).]

[§For the sentences, see "Proceedings in the Star-Chamber against Dr. John Bastwick, Mr. Henry Burton, and William Prynne, Esq. for Several Libels, 1637," in *State Trials*, Vol. III, cols. 725 and 755.]

[¶Hume, Vol. VI, p. 307; Henry Burton, *For God and King: The Summe of Two Sermons* ([London:] n.p., 1636).]

*Brodie, Vol. II, p. 319 [based on "Proceedings in the Star-Chamber against David Fowlis, . . . 1633," in *State Trials*, Vol. III, cols. 585–92].

pretences, suspended from his office, fined 10,000*l.*, and imprisoned during the king's pleasure; and further, on a charge of having *received* letters, in which contemptuous allusions were made to some one, *supposed* to be Laud, he was fined 8,000*l.* more, and again imprisoned.*

These are a few of the acts of that administration, under which Hume can say that the people enjoyed "every blessing of government except liberty"[*] (*quære*, what does he mean by liberty). These are some of the grievances which, in his opinion, were "neither burthensome on the people's properties, nor anyway shocking to the natural humanity of mankind."[†] And when Hampden, Pym, and others, resolved to seek refuge in another hemisphere from the tyranny which oppressed them at home, Hume can assert, that they fled in order to "enjoy lectures and discourses of any length or form which pleased them!"[‡]

But we are now drawing near to a period when these horrors were to be at an end; and the first blow was struck from a quarter from which it was least to be expected—from the aristocracy.

While in England the accumulation of property, and the rise of the commercial towns, had raised up a wealthy mercantile class, which trimmed the balance between the king and the nobility; the neighbouring country of Scotland had continued poor, and like the other poor countries of Europe, to a great degree feudal and aristocratic. Hence an important difference in the character of the struggle which ensued. In England, the people were strong enough to overcome the united force of the king and of the nobility. In Scotland, the quarrel was substantially nothing more than that struggle for power between the aristocracy and the king, which had existed in one shape or another from the earliest period of its history. The people followed, as usual, the banner of their superiors, with only the additional stimulus of religious zeal.

The king had never been so powerful in Scotland as in England, because the nobility had been more so. By the addition which he obtained to his power from his accession to another throne, he was enabled to carry various measures into effect, which, though hurtful to the aristocracy, were beneficial to the people. The greater part of the church-lands had, at the Reformation, been granted out to the nobility.

---

*[See Brodie, Vol. II, p. 367; and "Proceedings in the Star-Chamber against Dr. John Williams, Bishop of Lincoln, . . . 1637," in *State Trials*, Vol. III, cols. 769–804.] A curious rule of evidence was laid down on this occasion. Whatever might be brought in evidence against the accused, he was not allowed to rebut it by counter-evidence, because this would be to impeach the credit of the king's witnesses, who, deposing *pro domino rege*, must be reputed holy, and incapable of falsehood. This rule was afterwards found very convenient by Charles II, and his judges. [See Catharine Macaulay, *The History of England, from the Accession of James I to That of the Brunswick Line*, 8 vols. (London: Nourse, 1763–83), Vol. II, p. 236n.]

[*Hume, Vol. VI, p. 320.]
[†*Ibid.*, p. 319.]
[‡*Ibid.*, p. 309.]

A general revocation[*] was now published; it was never executed, but suspended, *in terrorem*, over their heads. The tithes, which had been transferred to them at the same period, and which they had exacted from the smaller proprietors, or heritors, with much greater rigour than ever the church had done, they were now ordered to dispose of to the heritors at a fixed rate.[†]

It was by the extraordinary institution of the Lords of Articles that the passing of these acts had been obtained. The lords of articles were a committee of thirty-two (eight barons, eight prelates, and sixteen commoners), appointed originally to prepare bills for the parliament, but who had by custom obtained the initiative of the laws. In this committee the spiritual lords chose the temporal, and the temporal the spiritual; but the commons had hitherto chosen deputies for themselves.[‡] By giving the choice of the sixteen commoners to the sixteen lords, James had given absolute power over the committee, and consequently over the parliament, to the prelates, that is, to himself, the parliament retaining only a veto, which they were usually afraid to exercise.[§]

Even this power Charles might have retained, could he have refrained from insulting the religious feelings of the people. But, whether from bigotry or love of power, or, as is most probable, from both combined, he cherished an inveterate hatred against the presbyterian religion.

For the overthrow of this sect, James had already done much; he had re-established episcopacy, as the religion of the state; he had obtained in a packed general assembly the ratification of the five articles of Perth, by which, ceremonies borrowed from the English church, and savouring of popery, were introduced; he had further, without any colour of law, established the high-commission court, which assumed the power of summoning persons before it, interrogating them on their religious opinions, and if their answers were not deemed satisfactory, inflicting the most arbitrary punishments.[¶] All this the people had borne; but this was not enough for Charles: not content with having established the episcopal church government, he must needs impose upon them the episcopal tenets also.

He visited Scotland in person, and summoned a parliament, which gratified him by passing, among other obnoxious acts, one which gave him the power of regulating the habits of the clergy.[||] It was generally believed that this and other

[*See Charles I, 1633, c. 9, "The Kings Generall Revocatione," in *The Acts of the Parliaments of Scotland, 1124–1707*, ed. T. Thomson and C. Innes, 12 vols. (Edinburgh: "By Command," 1814–75), Vol. V, p. 23. The revocation, of Oct., 1625, was confirmed in 1633.]

[†See Charles I (1628–29), "Submissions and Surrenders of Teinds, &c. with His Majestie's Decreets Following Thereupon," and Charles I (1630), "Ratification of the King's Decreets upon the Submissions," *ibid.*, pp. 189–207, and 209–26.]

[‡See Charles I (1633), "Domini electi ad articulos," *ibid.*, pp. 9–10.]

[§See Charles I (1639), "Domini electi ad articulos," *ibid.*, pp. 253–4.]

[¶See James I, 1621, c. 1, *ibid.*, Vol. IV, pp. 596–7.]

[||See Charles I, 1633, c. 3, *ibid.*, Vol. V, pp. 20–1.]

acts were obtained by making a false return of the votes. A petition which had been prepared against them, but which had never been presented nor published, was, nevertheless, made use of to crush Balmerino, one of the refractory lords. The only crime which could be laid to his charge, was that of possessing a copy of the petition, and showing it confidentially to a friend. For this he was tried by a packed jury, condemned to death, and only not executed from apprehension of popular resentment.[*]

The accurate, the candid Hume, who so often asserts that a groundless dread of popery was the sole cause of the Scottish troubles—what says he of this? Not a word. Of an event so notorious, he gives no intimation whatever; because it is alone sufficient to stamp with falsehood the whole of his assertions concerning the mildness of Charles, and the inoffensiveness of his measures.

Having thus struck terror, as he thought, into the Scottish aristocracy, Charles next proceeded to introduce a new liturgy and canons, resembling closely, in most respects, the religion of the Church of England, but in some points more nearly approaching to popery than their model.[†] A despot never knows when his safety requires him to stop short. At the introduction of the new service-book, the tumult was so great that it could not be read, and the bishop[‡] who attempted to read it was compelled to fly for his life. Charles still persisted in his design, and by his imprudent measures, the ferment was still further increased. The nobles improved the opportunity: petitions without number were poured in against the service-book; a great proportion of the gentry, and twenty peers, openly protested against it; the people thronged to Edinburgh, and the council, alarmed at their numbers, consented to the appointment of representatives to manage the concerns of the whole body. The popular party was thus regularly organized, and the four tables, so the deputies were called, gave unity to all their proceedings.

The king, as is usual with weak persons when their will is unexpectedly resisted, first bullied, and then became alarmed. A furious proclamation was put forth, bestowing praise on the liturgy, and abuse on the petitioners, and commanding them, under the penalties of high treason, to disperse.[§] This proclamation was protested against as soon as issued, and led to the famous Covenant, which was now drawn up and signed by a great majority of the Scottish population.[¶] The

[*See "Trial of John Lord Balmerino, in Scotland, for a Libel, 1634," in *State Trials*, Vol. III, cols. 604–8, 593, 712; the friend was John Dunmore (or Dunmure).]

[†*The Booke of Common Prayer and Administration of the Sacraments* (Edinburgh: printed by Young, 1637), and *Canons and Constitutions Ecclesiastical Gathered and Put in Form for the Government of the Church of Scotland* (Aberdeen: printed by Raban, 1636).]

[‡David Lindsay, Bishop of Edinburgh.]

[§See Rushworth, *Historical Collections*, Vol. II, pp. 830–3.]

[¶See Charles I, 1640, c. 18, in *Acts of the Parliaments of Scotland*, Vol. V, pp. 270–6; the Covenant, or Confession of Faith (drawn up and signed in 1638) is on pp. 272–6.]

king at length took the alarm, and determined to temporize. He sent the Marquis of Hamilton into Scotland, with authority to treat; and "he thought," says Hume, "that on his part he had made very satisfactory concessions, when he offered to suspend the canons and the liturgy, till, in a fair and legal way, they could be received, and so to model the high-commission that it should no longer give offence to his subjects."[*] The Covenanters, however, were not to be so easily duped; and it was as impossible to disunite, as to deceive or overcome them. The commissioner wrote to the king, saying, that he must either prepare for war, or recal the canons, the liturgy, and the five articles of Perth, summon a parliament, and convoke a general assembly of the church.[†] Charles soon took his resolution; but directed Hamilton to temporize till his preparations for war should be completed. In Burnet's *Memoirs of the Hamiltons*, a work to which Hume continually refers, several of Charles's letters are preserved, in which he permits the commissioner to *flatter the covenanters with what hopes he pleases*, provided he does not commit the king himself; and tells him, that *his chief end is, to win time* till the royal fleet shall have set sail.* Yet, Hume can say, that Charles "was candid, sincere, upright, as much as any man whom we meet with in history;" that "it would be difficult to find another character so unexceptionable in this particular;" and that, "even his enemies, though they loaded him with many calumnies, did not insist on this accusation."[‡]

Hamilton returned to London and, finding the king's preparations less advanced than he had expected, convinced him that, to gain time, great concessions must be made. While the king, therefore, was maturing his preparations, Hamilton was sent back into Scotland with power to recal the canons and liturgy, to abolish the high-commission, to suspend the five articles of Perth, and to summon a parliament and a general assembly. He carried down with him a counter-covenant,[§] containing a bond to maintain the established religion as at present professed, a phrase applicable alike to both the contending sects. So palpable an evasion had no effect, but still further to disgust the opposite party. The general assembly met: and before any thing had been done, the commissioner, *by the king's direction* (see his own letters), found a pretext for dissolving it.[¶] (Yet the king was ever "candid, upright, sincere.") Matters were now at a crisis. The alternative was, to disobey, or to give up all that had been gained. Having proved

[*Hume, Vol. VI, p. 330.]
[†See Burnet, *Memoires*, pp. 53–4.]
*[Letter to Hamilton of 11 June, 1638, *ibid.*, p. 55.] A more remarkable picture than is exhibited in these letters, of a mind so thoroughly depraved by undue power as to lose all concern for the rest of mankind, is scarcely anywhere to be found. The king deliberately weighs his own grandeur against the prosperity of millions, and coolly gives the preference to the former.
[‡Hume, Vol. VII, pp. 526, 526, 523.]
[§See Burnet, *Memoires*, pp. 72–8.]
[¶E.g., *ibid.*, letters of 29 Oct. and 17 Nov., 1638, pp. 88, 99–100.]

by precedents their right of sitting, notwithstanding any injunction to the contrary, the assembly proceeded to abolish episcopacy, and abrogate the articles of Perth.[*]

It was impossible any longer to avoid a war. The king appears to have anticipated an easy conquest: so ill was he prepared for the resistance which he experienced, that without a single battle, or almost a single skirmish, he was compelled to patch up a peace, and convoke an assembly and a parliament.

Without mentioning the former assembly, that which was now convened proceeded to confirm its acts; and the new commissioner, Traquair, was authorized by the king to ratify these regulations, but not without captious distinctions. Even Hume is here compelled to admit, that the king secretly "retained an intention of seizing favourable opportunities, in order to recover the ground which he had lost:"[†] and yet, "in every treaty, those concessions which he thought he could not in conscience maintain, he never could, by any motive or persuasion, be induced to make."[‡]

A piece of casuistry, therefore, was provided. The bishops protested against the acts of the assembly; that the non-concurrence of what they deemed an essential part, might afford a pretext for disregarding the proceedings of the whole. Traquair was also directed to put in, at the close of the session, a reservation, that anything done in the king's absence might be challenged afterwards, if prejudicial to his interest.

Episcopacy having been abolished, the institution of Lords of Articles, as formerly constituted, could no longer exist; and the parliament proceeded to place it on a different footing. It was now enacted, that each estate should choose its own deputies to sit on the articles, and that they should no longer possess a veto on debate, but merely the powers of a committee.[§] A bill was also prepared for triennial parliaments,[¶] and several other important measures were in progress, when Traquair, by the king's direction, prorogued the parliament, a power hitherto exercised solely by the parliament itself. Cautious not to give any hold against them, they obeyed the order, and in the mean time, sent commissioners to London to protest against the prorogation.

Charles, however, now determined to take off the mask. Scarcely had the commissioners reached London, when they were thrown into prison. "The earl of Traquaire," says Hume, "had intercepted a letter written to the king of France by the Scottish malcontents."[||] The insinuation contained in this phrase is false. The

---

[*See "Minutes Done in the Articles," and Charles I, 1640, c. 19, in *Acts of the Parliaments of Scotland*, Vol. V, pp. 599, and 276–7.]

[†Hume, Vol. VI, p. 343.]

[‡*Ibid.*, Vol. VII, p. 147.]

[§Charles I, 1640, c. 21, in *Acts of the Parliaments of Scotland*, Vol. V, pp. 278–9.]

[¶Charles I, 1640, c. 12, *ibid.*, p. 268.]

[||Hume, Vol. VI, p. 345; for the letter, see Cobbett, Vol. II, col. 534.]

letter had never been intercepted, for it had never been sent. It had only been written: and besides, there was nothing in it which did not fairly bear an innocent interpretation. This, however, was the pretence on which the commissioners, Loudon and Dunfermline, were imprisoned.

When, to the ordinary charges of government, was to be added the expense of a war, the illegal resources, which were adequate to all common occasions, could no longer suffice. Charles called a parliament at Westminster, but the Commons, as before, refused to give supply the precedence over grievances.[*] He saw, or thought he saw, that if they continued to sit, they would pass a vote declaring ship-money to be illegal. This he prevented by a hasty dissolution,[†] before they had granted a supply, and committed three of their leading members to the Tower.[‡] To obtain money, new extortions were practised; the East India company (on pretence of a purchase on credit) were robbed of all their pepper, which was sold at a great discount for ready money. A grant from the convocation, and three subsidies which had been obtained from the Irish parliament, did something;[§] voluntary contributions from the royalist party supplied the rest.

The second Scottish campaign was still more unsuccessful than the first. No sooner had the king's army advanced to Newcastle, than the Scots passed the Tweed, routed Lord Conway, and forced the king to retreat. Newcastle then fell into their hands. With an army disaffected, and a people more disposed to join with the Scots than to attack them, Charles did not venture to fight. A negotiation was opened, and during its continuance he had to maintain the Scottish army as well as his own. The money which, for this purpose, he was compelled to borrow from the city, could only be obtained on condition of summoning a parliament.

It was under new and favourable auspices that the long parliament was convened. Secured against dissolution by the necessities of the king, and by the presence of the Scottish army in England, they had only to improve the opportunity, and tyranny might yet be overthrown.

The same historian, who has laboured to disguise the selfishness of Charles under the mask of conscience and of principle, has endeavoured, by malicious insinuations, to discredit the motives of the popular leaders.[¶] With their motives, however, we have nothing to do; nor, if we had, is it possible that their motives should ever be, with any certainty, ascertained. During their lives these statesmen enjoyed a high reputation for integrity; nor do they appear, by any thing which they did, to have deserved to forfeit that character. If they had possessed undue power,

[*Cobbett, Vol. II, cols. 561–71.]
[†For the King's Declaration, see *ibid.*, cols. 572–9.]
[‡Henry Bellasis, John Crew, and John Hotham.]
[§See John Nalson, *An Impartial Collection*, 2 vols. (London: Mearne, *et al.*, 1682–83), Vol. I, p. 362; see also a letter from the Council of Ireland to Secretary Windebank of 19 Mar., 1639, in *Earl of Strafforde's Letters*, Vol. II, pp. 394–5.]
[¶Hume, Vol. VI, pp. 364, 372, 375.]

they would probably, like other men, have abused it; not having such power, they are to be judged by what they did, and not by what, under other circumstances, they might have done.

Among the first and best of their acts was the impeachment of Strafforde.[*] His general support of despotism, and specific acts of misgovernment, as lord lieutenant of Ireland, and president of the council of York, were the principal charges. Finch and Laud were likewise impeached.[†] The former in his successive capacities of Speaker of the House of Commons, chief-justice and lord-keeper, had been the instrument of some of the worst acts of the government of Charles. He fled, and it is a striking proof of the moderation of the popular leaders, if, as was suspected, they connived at his escape. Some judges, ecclesiastics and others, the subordinate instruments, shared the fate of their superiors.[‡] Prynne, Bastwick, Burton, and other victims of judicial tyranny, were liberated from confinement. Ship-money, and other extortions, were declared to be illegal.[§] The levying of tonnage and poundage, without consent of parliament, was forbidden.[¶] Petitions against episcopacy, and complaints against the lives of the clergy, were received from all parts of the kingdom.[||] To inquire into this last grievance, a committee was appointed, which Hume stigmatizes with the strongest epithets of reproach.[**] That in some cases undue severity may have been used, or venial trespasses exaggerated, is probable enough; we will add, that it is not to be wondered at: for when was it known that, in a dispute of such magnitude, either party confined itself scrupulously within the bounds of moderation? The only question which deserves the slightest consideration is, which party was substantially in the right. To lay undue stress upon a trifling irregularity, is among the strongest of all presumptions against the goodness of a cause.*

To prevent that disuse of parliaments, which had been the fruitful cause of so

---

[*"Articles of the Commons, Assembled in Parliament, against Thomas Earl of Strafford," in Cobbett, Vol. II, cols. 737–9.]

[†See "The Accusation and Impeachment of John Lord Finch, 1641," and "Articles of the Commons Assembled in Parliament, in Maintenance of Their Accusation against William Laud, Archbishop of Canterbury, . . . 1641," in *State Trials*, Vol. IV, cols. 11–14, and 326–30.]

[‡Including, among the judges, Robert Berkeley, John Bramston, Francis Crawley, and Humphrey Davenport; among the ecclesiastics, John Cosin, William Piers, and Matthew Wren; and among "others," Francis Windebanke.]

[§16 Charles I, c. 14 and c. 20 (1640).]

[¶See the preambles to 16 Charles I, c. 8 (1640), and subsequent grants in that year.]

[||See, e.g., Cobbett, Vol. II, cols. 673–8.]

[**Hume, Vol. VI, pp. 386–7.]

*Even Hume admits, that throughout the whole of the troubles (such was the moderation of the Commons), Juxon, Lord-Treasurer and Bishop of London, notwithstanding those obnoxious offices, was preserved by his "mild and prudent virtues" from molestation. [*Ibid.*, p. 395.]

many evils, the triennial act was passed,[*] that one meeting of parliament, at least, in three years might be secured. It was not without great reluctance that Charles assented to this important bill.

At this period, however, if Hume is to be believed, he "resolved to alter his whole conduct, and to regain the confidence of his people by pliableness, by concessions, and by a total conformity to their inclinations and prejudices."[†] This is one of those bold assertions by which Hume has generally succeeded in deceiving his readers, merely because they cannot believe, that a historian of eminence would hazard an assertion which he must necessarily have known to be false. But the insincerity of Charles is a subject on which, as yet, we cannot enter. The trial of Strafforde first demands our attention, as well from its importance, as from the utter want of candour which Hume's account of it displays.

A committee had been appointed to prepare the articles of charge, "with authority," says Hume, "to examine all witnesses, to call for every paper, and to use any means of scrutiny, with regard to any part of the earl's behaviour and conduct."[‡] This he calls an inquisition. In the first place, his account of it is false. They were not authorized to employ the torture: they could not therefore be authorized to use "any means of scrutiny." What is probably true is, that their powers were not defined; nor, indeed, in English law, is any thing defined: but it does not appear that they went, in any respect, beyond the bounds of justice. In the next place, nothing is easier than to call any kind of investigatorial procedure an *inquisition*. "No man can be expected to oppose arguments to epithets."* The question is simply this: Shall, or shall not, the accusers be compelled to bring charges, without knowing what charges there is evidence to support? Is it meant, that to examine witnesses, and to call for papers, is an inquisition? If so, it is an inquisition which ought always to exist.

What, above all, excites the indignation of Hume, is, that the committee was permitted to examine privy counsellors with regard to opinions delivered at the board; which banished, he says, all confidence from the deliberations in council.[§] One thing is clear—either the king who acts, or the ministers who advise, must be responsible: but whether the one or the other be punished, Hume's indignation is the same.

He then deliberately asserts, that the impeachment of Sir George Ratcliffe had no other purpose than to deprive Strafforde of the assistance of his best friend. And where is the proof? the charge, it seems, was not prosecuted against him.[¶] As if

[*16 Charles I, c. 1 (1640).]
[†Hume, Vol. VI, p. 391.]
[‡*Ibid.*, p. 396.]
*[James Mackintosh,] *Vindiciae Gallicae*, [2nd ed. (London: Robinson, 1791),] p. 95.
[§Hume, Vol. VI, p. 397.]
[¶See "Proceedings against Sir George Ratcliffe, Knt. on an Impeachment for High Treason: 1640," and "Impeachment of . . . Sir George Ratcliffe, Knt. before the House of Lords in Ireland, 1641," in *State Trials*, Vol. IV, cols. 47–52, and 51–8.]

Hume did not know, that not Ratcliffe only, but numbers of the tools of power were now impeached, and never afterwards molested. Ratcliffe was the principal accomplice in all the atrocities of Strafforde's government in Ireland; all the evidence against Strafforde, was evidence against him; and he might with perfect justice have been put to the bar with Strafforde, tried, condemned, and executed along with him. The Commons were satisfied with one sacrifice to public justice; they spared the rest: and their moderation and forbearance are to be construed into a proof of intentional injustice!

In commenting upon the articles of charge, Hume has, if possible, been still more disingenuous. The odium which Strafforde had drawn upon himself in Ireland, Hume coolly ascribes to his virtues; and the general character of his administration Hume asserts to have been "innocent, and even laudable."[*] We cannot convey a better idea of the character of Hume, than by advising the reader to look into Mr. Brodie,[†] nay, into the letters and despatches of Strafforde himself, and see what was Hume's idea of innocent and laudable conduct in public men. Would space permit, we might enlarge upon the despotism, the rapacity, the cruelty, which characterized this "laudable" administration, and leave the reader to judge of the feelings of the man who can assert, that his conduct was "equally promotive of his master's interests, and that of the subjects committed to his care."[‡] But we willingly stake our case upon one single act: and that act we will quote in the words of Hume himself.

It had been reported at the table of Lord Chancellor Loftus, that Annesley, one of the deputy's attendants, in moving a stool, had sorely hurt his master's foot, who was at that time afflicted with the gout. *Perhaps*, said Mountnorris, who was present at table, *it was done in revenge of that public affront which my lord deputy formerly put upon him*: BUT HE HAS A BROTHER, WHO WOULD NOT HAVE TAKEN SUCH A REVENGE. This casual, and seemingly innocent, at least ambiguous, expression, was reported to Strafforde, who, on pretence that such a suggestion might prompt Annesley to avenge himself in another manner, ordered Mountnorris, who was an officer, to be tried by a court-martial for mutiny and sedition against his general. The court, which consisted of the chief officers of the army, found the crime to be capital, and condemned that nobleman to lose his head.[§]

A pretty stretch of authority, and a tolerable proof what must have been the spirit of Strafforde's administration. But mark what follows:

In vain did Strafforde plead in his own defence, against this article of impeachment, that the sentence of Mountnorris was the deed, and that, too, unanimous, of the court, not the act of the deputy; that he spake not to a member of the court, nor voted in the cause, but sat uncovered as a party, and then immediately withdrew, to leave them to their freedom; that sensible of the iniquity of the sentence, he procured his majesty's free pardon to

[*Hume, Vol. VI, p. 399.]
[†Brodie, Vol. III, pp. 47–75.]
[‡Hume, Vol. VI, p. 399; see letters from Strafford to the Lord Treasurer and Secretary Coke of 31 Jan., 1633, and to King Charles I of 16 July, 1633, in *Earl of Strafforde's Letters*, Vol. I, pp. 193–4, 201, and 93.]
[§Hume, Vol. VI, p. 401.]

Mountnorris; and that he did not even keep that nobleman a moment in suspense with regard to his fate, but instantly told him, that he himself would rather lose his right hand than execute such a sentence, nor was his lordship's life in any danger.[*]

If ever the truth was so told, as to have the effect of a lie, it is here. What is true, is, that Strafforde did make these assertions, as is represented: what is not true is, that Hume believed them. When Strafforde, and his panegyrist, asserted that the sentence was the act of the court, and that he procured the king's pardon, because he was sensible of the iniquity of the sentence, they forgot to state, that it was at the persuasion of Strafforde himself, and not without great difficulty, that the court was persuaded to pass sentence, and that they did not at length comply, without previously stipulating for Mountnorris's life; in consequence of which stipulation, he was only dismissed the army, imprisoned for three years, and deprived of his estate. It may be pardonable in a man, whose life is at stake, to endeavour to save himself by a falsehood;* but what shall we say of a historian, who, with the facts before him, repeats and countenances a story which he must have known to be false?

Being unable to extenuate the conduct of the council of York, which, if possible, exceeded even that of the star-chamber in atrocity, Hume does his best to exculpate Strafforde, by asserting that he never in person presided in the court.[†] But what is to become of official responsibility, if a public functionary is not responsible for the conduct of a deputy, removeable at his pleasure, and sure, therefore, to act in the way which he knows to be agreeable to his superior?

With regard to the evidence of the illegal advice which Strafforde was accused of having given as a privy counsellor, Hume has a number of cavils, which have been fully exposed by Mr. Brodie,[‡] but which, in fact, were scarcely deserving of notice. To prove the words, was rather necessary on technical, than on rational, grounds. If the tyranny of the government was notorious, and if, of that government, Strafforde was a member, he was surely responsible for its tyranny, in justice, and even in law, unless he could prove that he had actually done whatever he could to prevent it.

The most plausible part of Strafforde's defence, was that in which he endeavoured to make it appear, that, whatever might be his guilt, he was not a

---

[*Ibid., pp. 401–2. See also Strafford's letters to Mountnorris of 19 Aug., 1632, to Secretary Coke of 7 Apr., 1635, and 14 Dec., 1635, and to Lord Conway of 6 Jan., 1637, in *Earl of Strafforde's Letters*, Vol. I, pp. 73–4, 402–3, 497–8; Vol. II, p. 145. The sentence is recorded *ibid.*, Vol. I, pp. 499–501.]

*Not Strafforde merely, but Charles, were sufficiently disposed, on this occasion, to carry their point by falsehood. "On the 10th of September 1640, Northumberland writes, *in cypher*, to the Earl of Leicester, that he doubts the king is not very well satisfied with him— *because he will not perjure himself for Lord Lieutenant Strafforde.*" (Brodie, Vol. III, p. 83.) [Brodie is quoting from *Letters and Memorials of State*, Vol. II, pp. 664–5.]

[†Hume, Vol. VI, p. 399.]

[‡Ibid., pp. 397, 402–3; Brodie, Vol. III, pp. 76ff.]

traitor, the legal definition of treason not including his offence.[*] Nothing, indeed, can be more conclusive than his arguments against the practice of inflicting punishment for undefined offences; and it would be well if our lawyers, and lawyer-ridden legislators, would bestow somewhat more of attention upon them than has hitherto been usual. Unless, however, there be punishment for undefined offences, under English law there can be no punishment at all. Judge Hale long ago confessed, that he knew not what theft was;[†] yet we see men, every day, hanged for theft. It may be replied, moreover, that Strafforde, if he had not violated any one law, more than any other, had violated all the laws, by setting the royal authority above them: that if he was not tried under any particular law, so neither was he tried before a court of law, but before a tribunal expressly created to take cognizance of those offences, to the treatment of which the ordinary law was considered inadequate.

The legal argument, however, after considerable discussion, had so much weight with the Commons, that they dropped the impeachment and brought in a bill of attainder; a course which, though strictly legal, and a striking proof of their regard for the forms, as well as for the substance, of justice, is represented by Hume as a proof of their consciousness that grounds had not been shewn for a conviction.[‡] The impeachment, he says, was against law; and yet, to drop the impeachment, and proceed according to law, was, it seems, a proof of injustice.*

When the bill of attainder had passed both houses,[§] and awaited the royal

---

[*See Hume, Vol. VI, pp. 404–5.]

[†See Matthew Hale, *Historia placitorum coronae*, ed. Sollom Emlyn, 2 vols. (London: Gyles, *et al.*, 1736), Vol. I, p. 509.]

[‡Hume, Vol. VI, pp. 406–7.]

*This mode of procedure (by bill of attainder) which, in the case of Strafforde, is represented as so irregular and iniquitous, is the same which was adopted on the trial of Sir John Fenwick [see 8 William III, c. 4 (1696)], at a period subsequent to the "glorious revolution," and under the government of William III of "immortal memory." [For these phrases, see *Whig Club, Instituted in May, 1784, by John Bellamy, to Be Composed of Gentlemen, Who Solemnly Pledge Themselves to Support the Constitution of This Country, according to the Principles Established at the Glorious Revolution* ([London: n.p., 1786]), which gives the first "Standing Toast": "The glorious and immortal memory of King William the Third" (p. 15).]

It is curious to mark the inconsistency of the pleas set up by Hume in favour of Strafforde. Compare the following passages: "Such were the capacity, genius, and presence of mind, displayed by this magnanimous statesman, that while argument and reason and *law* had any place, he obtained an undisputed victory." [Vol. VI, pp. 398–9.] And in the very next page comes the following admission. "While the managers of the Commons demanded every moment that the deputy's conduct should be examined by the line of *rigid law* and severe principles, he appealed still to the practice of all former deputies, and the uncontrollable *necessity* of his situation." [*Ibid.*, p. 400.] Necessity! well characterized by William Pitt, on a memorable occasion, as the *tyrant's plea*. [See Pitt's speech in the House of Commons (18 Nov., 1783), in Cobbett, Vol. XXIII, col. 1209; Pitt is quoting John Milton, *Paradise Lost*, in *The Poetical Works of Mr. John Milton* (London: Tonson, 1695), p. 97 (IV, 394).]

[§16 Charles I, Private Acts, c. 1 (1640).]

assent, information was received of a conspiracy among the officers, instigated by Charles, to bring the army to London, rescue Strafforde, and dissolve the parliament. It is impossible to exceed the disingenuousness with which this incident is spoken of by Hume.[*] His object is, to make it appear that there was no plot, and to insinuate, that the whole story was a forgery of the popular leaders. He cannot deny that there was a secret association among the officers, in close correspondence with some of the king's servants; that a petition was sent to Charles, countersigned by him, and sent back, to be signed by the army; and that in this petition they offered to come up to London.[†] He asserts, however, first, that the project had been laid aside, two months before it was disclosed to the parliament. In this he follows Clarendon:[‡] that the assertion is false, has been proved by Mr. Brodie from Clarendon himself, as well as by giving at length the evidence taken by the Commons on the occasion.[§] In the next place, he also copies from Clarendon in his account of the petition itself; although, as Mr. Brodie well observes, the gross anachronisms in Clarendon's petition prove it conclusively to be a forgery. But, thirdly, he suppresses part, even of what Clarendon admits; viz. the recommendation to *punish the ring-leaders* in certain alleged tumults, for the *suppression of which* the army offered its services. But the plan, he says,[¶] was an absurd one, while the Scots were in England; yet the king is admitted to have countersigned the petition; folly, indeed, characterized his counsels throughout: and in calculating upon the probable conduct of a despot, we must never proceed upon the supposition that he possesses common sense.*

The king now finding it no longer safe to withhold his assent from the bill of attainder, the bill passed, and Strafforde was executed. The perfection of history, like the perfection of a novel, has usually been considered to be a strong dramatic effect. So fine an opportunity for pathos was not to be lost; of the last meeting of Strafforde with Laud, Hume has attempted to make a most affecting scene, and to call forth all the sympathies of mankind in favour of these great criminals, after turning the sufferings of their hundreds of victims into a jest.[||] But this practice is

[*Hume, Vol. VI, pp. 410–11.]

[†"The True Copy of the Petition Prepared by the Officers of the Late Army, and Subscribed by His Majesty, with C.R.," in *An Exact Collection of All Remonstrances, Declarations, Votes, Orders, Ordinances, Proclamations, Petitions, Messages, Answers, and Other Remarkable Passages* ("Husbands' Collection") (London: Husbands, Warren, and Best, 1643), pp. 563–4.]

[‡See Hyde, *History*, Vol. I, pp. 192–5, for this and the next two references.]

[§See Brodie, Vol. III, pp. 109n–14n, and "Note to Volume III," pp. 583–607, for the references in this paragraph.]

[¶Hume, Vol. VI, p. 419.]

*The king solemnly called God to witness, that he never *knew* of such a design as that of bringing up the army. [Brodie, Vol. III, pp. 323–4.] Now, whether he encouraged it or not, he certainly knew of it, since it is admitted that he countersigned the petition. What trust, then, could be reposed in the assertions of a man, who could swear to so gross a falsehood?

[||Hume, Vol. VI, pp. 417–18.]

universal with Hume; the many, and their sufferings, he laughs to scorn: are the one and the few affected? then is the time to whine.

Another bill, which received the royal assent conjointly with the bill of attainder, was, in its consequences, most fatal, and has never yet received due attention. We mean, the bill by which the parliament was made indissoluble, except by its own consent,[*] and was thus erected into a perpetual aristocracy. The professed object of this act was, to prevent the king from dissolving the parliament. But this might have been done, without rendering it indissoluble. The people, on those few occasions on which they have risen against misgovernment, have seldom, unhappily, been wise enough, while they overthrew one tyranny, to provide securities against the establishment of another.

The Commons might reasonably be expected still to continue faithful to their duty so long as they were weak; but no sooner was Charles overcome, and the powers of government thrown wholly into their hands, than the public interest was sure to be postponed to theirs, and their subsequent proceedings to degenerate into a mere struggle for power.

This bill gives Hume another opportunity for pathos; and he endows his hero, for the occasion, with an appropriate quantum of sentimentality.

> Charles, in the agony of grief, shame, and remorse, for Strafforde's doom, perceived not that this other bill was of still more fatal consequence to his authority, and rendered the power of his enemies perpetual, as it was already uncontrollable. In comparison with the bill of attainder, by which he deemed himself an accomplice in his friend's murder, this concession made no figure in his eyes.[†]

Very pathetic truly; but history is not to be written like a tragedy. The truth is, that, without an abuse of terms, such a thing as friendship, between a king and his subject, cannot be said to exist; still less between a despot and his tool. As well might that name be applied to the connexion between a debauchee and the pimp who ministers to his pleasures. Charles knew, that by employing and protecting Strafforde, he was promoting his own interest; Strafforde knew, that, in serving Charles, he was promoting his. The real truth is, that Charles gave his assent to the bill, not out of grief for Strafforde, but as a means of getting money; a Lancashire knight having offered to procure him a loan of 650,000*l.* upon that condition. For the hero, however, of a romance, who could do so very unromantic a thing as to abandon his friend, it was absolutely necessary to find some palliation, and it was a very obvious thought to endow him with a remorse, which there is no sufficient reason to believe that he actually felt.

During the course of the above proceedings, bills had been prepared for the abolition of the council of York, the star-chamber, the high-commission, and other arbitrary and oppressive jurisdictions.[‡] After some hesitation, Charles passed the

---

[*See Cobbett, Vol. II, cols. 786–7; the bill was enacted as 16 Charles I, c. 7 (1640).]
[†Hume, Vol. VI, p. 416.]
[‡See 16 Charles I, c. 10 and c. 11 (1640).]

bills; and, though with great difficulty, was prevailed upon to disband the Irish army, which having been raised solely for the subjugation of Scotland, was now no longer required. The Scots immediately returned to their homes, and the English army was dismissed.

The king now determined to visit Scotland, where he had already begun to intrigue with a powerful party. "He arrived," says Hume, "in Scotland with an intention of abdicating almost entirely the small share of power which there remained to him, and of giving full satisfaction, if possible, to his restless subjects in that kingdom."[*] Hume's language always imports, that he can dive into the hearts of all his characters. It is difficult to understand how that which he here asserts could have been known to him, even had it been true. In reality, however, he knew that it was not true; he must have learned as much even from Clarendon, who, for these transactions, is his chief authority.[†] That the king had no intention of resigning any power which he could safely keep, is sufficiently certain from the principles of human nature; but the perfidy which he meditated was of a still more atrocious kind; and the entire suppression of the evidence of it by Hume, had he been guilty of no other violation of truth, would alone suffice to cover him with eternal infamy.

Argyle and Hamilton, being seized with an apprehension, real or pretended, that the Earl of Crawford and others meant to assassinate them, left the parliament suddenly, and retired into the country; but, upon invitation and assurances, returned in a few days. This event, which had neither cause nor effect, that was visible, nor purpose, nor consequence, was commonly denominated the *incident*.[‡]

Would it be believed, that the event which is thus slurred over was a plot to seize, if not to assassinate the most distinguished of the popular leaders?

There were three parties at this time in Scotland; the royalists, the covenanters, and the trimmers. Of the covenanters, the acknowledged head was Argyle. The royalists had recently acquired a leader in Montrose, a man of no principle, who had begun his career as a covenanter, but finding himself supplanted in the field by Leslie, and in counsels by Argyle, went over to the court, and entered into a treaty to betray his late associates. Among those who by trimming and compromise endeavoured to keep well with both parties, Hamilton and his brother Laneric were the chief. As is usual with trimmers, they had no credit with either party; and were abhorred as rivals by Montrose, scarcely less than Argyle himself. A conspiracy was formed to seize the Hamiltons and Argyle, who were to be detained on board a frigate in Leith roads, and assassinated on the slightest resistance. Thus much is proved beyond the possibility of dispute, and confirmed, in the most material circumstances, by the evidence of the actors themselves. Such a project would

[*Hume, Vol. VI, p. 426.]
[†See *ibid.*, pp. 425–9.]
[‡*Ibid.*, p. 428.]

never have been formed, without some ulterior design. The immediate renewal of the war is the very least which can have been contemplated. At the time, it was believed that the royalists were to rise in arms and possess themselves of Edinburgh, before the other party could recover from its surprise. We learn from Clarendon,[*] that Montrose had before offered to assassinate the three lords; but that the king had recommended as a preferable measure, that proofs should be prepared for a parliamentary impeachment. As it is evident by what sort of a parliament the impeachment would have been tried, if the conspiracy had succeeded, the atrocity would have been much the same whether perpetrated with or without the forms of law.

In a subsequent note,[†] Hume endeavours to prove, that Clarendon must have been mistaken in ascribing such an offer to Montrose; since, during the whole of Charles's continuance in Scotland, Montrose was in prison; having been detected, during the expedition into England, in a secret correspondence with the court. But even men who are in prison may, notwithstanding, have ways and means of communicating with those who are without; no very recondite truth, one would suppose, but a truth of which Hume seems to have been ignorant. It is proved that three letters were conveyed to the king from Montrose, and that Cochrane, who carried the letters, and who was one of the chief actors in the conspiracy, had a secret interview with the king. We do not learn this from Hume, but we learn it from Murray,* groom of the chamber, through whose intervention Cochrane was introduced to a private audience.

The failure of this conspiracy did not deter Charles from engaging in new projects of a similar nature. And it was at this period that he resolved upon the violent proceedings, which almost immediately followed his return to Whitehall.

When he returned, he found the parliament already re-assembled, and the celebrated remonstrance already passed.[‡] In this document, the Commons recapitulated the principal of the grievances which had been complained of since Charles ascended the throne, ascribing them to the influence of evil counsels, which the king showed no inclination to discard. Nothing can be more undeserved than the reproaches thrown out by Hume upon this part of their conduct; nor any thing more unfair, than his whole representation of the posture of affairs at this crisis. "All these grievances had been already redressed, and even laws enacted for future security against their return."[§] In the first place, it is not true, that *all* the grievances had been redressed. But secondly, in strictness of speech, none of them

[*Hyde, *History*, Vol. I, p. 236.]
[†Hume, Vol. VII, p. 44n.]
*See the evidence taken before a secret committee of the parliament, and published by Mr. [Malcolm] Laing, in his *History of Scotland* [2 vols. (London: Cadell and Davies, 1800), Vol. I, pp. 501–7].
[‡"The Remonstrance of the State of the Kingdom," in Cobbett, Vol. II, cols. 946–64.]
[§Hume, Vol. VI, p. 449.]

had been redressed at all. What, in fact, had been done? They had been declared illegal: was this an adequate "security against their return?" As much as this had been done by the petition of right; and with what advantage, the years of tyranny that followed abundantly testify. But further, Hume has entirely misrepresented the very nature and object of this celebrated state paper, in as far, at least, as it is possible to gather from his statements any conception of its nature and object at all. What the Commons complained of was, not the grievances, which had been removed, but the counsels which had occasioned them, and the want of securities against their revival.[*] Their object was, to obtain a real and effectual security, by making the appointment of public officers dependent upon the approbation of parliament. This, among many other beneficial regulations, had already been enacted in Scotland;[†] and a bill to the same effect had been introduced into the English House of Commons.[‡] The object of the remonstrance was, to prepare the way for this bill; and had the majority which passed the remonstrance been a large one, the bill would have been pressed with almost a certainty of success; the majority, however, being small, it was permitted for the present to drop.

The first act of Charles, on his return to the capital, was to dismiss a guard, which the parliament, in their alarm at the *incident*, had appointed under the Earl of Essex for their own protection. Hume plainly insinuates that their alarm was feigned,[§] which is exactly of a piece with all the rest of the story, as he tells it. The guard was no more than what is allowed to every petty court of justice; and when an attempt was made to circumvent the principal leaders of the popular party in Scotland, the leaders of that party in England had surely some reason for alarm. In lieu of the guard which he dismissed, the king offered them another; but they chose rather to dispense with a guard altogether, than to accept one under a commander of his appointment.[¶]

Various circumstances now contributed to hasten a breach. By the power of impressing any of his subjects at pleasure, the king could inflict a severe punishment upon any one who might be obnoxious to him for any reason. The bill which was before the House, for pressing soldiers to serve against the Irish rebels, seemed to offer a favourable opportunity for redressing this grievance; and a clause, directed against the power of arbitrary imprisonment, was inserted in the bill, and sent up to the Lords along with it.[‖] That Charles should willingly acquiesce in this invasion of his power, was certainly not to be expected; and in violation of parliamentary privilege, he came to the upper House, while the bill

[*See the Petition accompanying the Remonstrance, in Cobbett, Vol. II, cols. 943–6.]
[†Charles I, 1641, c. 21, in *Acts of the Parliaments of Scotland*, Vol. V, pp. 354–5.]
[‡See clause ii of the Petition accompanying the Remonstrance, in Cobbett, Vol. II, col. 945.]
[§Hume, Vol. VI, pp. 428–9, 462–3.]
[¶For the Commons' Petition and the King's Answer, see Cobbett, Vol. II, cols. 1001–2, 1004–5.]
[‖See 16 Charles I, c. 28 (1640); for the clause, see *Statutes of the Realm*, Vol. V, p. 139 (clause iii).]

was there depending, and declared that he would not pass the bill if it contained any such clause.[*] The growing strength of the popular party had already begun to alarm the aristocracy; and the Lords endeavoured to delay the bill, not daring openly to reject it.

Although the designs of Charles were, as yet, by no means matured, he had the imprudence to act as if they had already been successful. Sir Henry Vane was dismissed from his office, for no apparent cause except the evidence he had given against Strafforde. A frivolous accusation was brought by Charles himself against Lord Newport, another material witness on the same great occasion. And he unaccountably chose this time to publish a proclamation, for conformity to the established church and worship;[†] thus clearly manifesting a determination to refuse all the demands of the Commons with respect to religion. At the same time, he gave fresh cause for alarm, by dismissing Sir William Balfour, Lieutenant of the Tower, and appointing in his stead one Colonel Lunsford, who was actually under outlawry for an attempt at assassination. Meanwhile, the king had collected round him a number of discharged officers and soldiers who, together with some royalist gentlemen, and students of the inns of court, formed, under the command of Lunsford and others, a sort of irregular guard, ready to act as circumstances might require.

Against the appointment of Lunsford as Lieutenant of the Tower, petitions were presented, and resolutions passed:[‡] when these were found ineffectual, Lord Newport, Constable of the Tower, was ordered by the parliament to reside within it, as a check upon Lunsford; but was immediately dismissed from his office. And when at length the king felt himself under the necessity of dismissing Lunsford, he appointed Sir John Byron, who was almost equally obnoxious.

The alarm of the Commons was still further heightened, when twelve of the bishops, alleging that their access to the House of Peers was obstructed by the mob, protested against any thing which might be done in their absence. This, it will be remembered, was the very artifice which had already been employed to invalidate the proceedings of the general assembly of the Scottish church. The bishops were impeached and thrown into confinement.[§] Their conduct, though in itself merely

[*Cobbett, Vol. II, cols. 968–9.]

[†"A Proclamation for Obedience to the Lawes Ordained for Establishing of the True Religion in This Kingdom of England," in *An Exact Collection*, pp. 2–3.]

[‡See Cobbett, Vol. II, cols. 982–4.]

[§"The Humble Petition and Protestation of All the Bishops and Prelates Now Called by His Majesties Writs to Attend the Parliament," *ibid.*, cols. 993–5; see also "Proceedings against the Twelve Bishops; namely, Dr. John Williams Archbishop of York, Dr. Thomas Moreton Bishop of Durham, Dr. Robert Wright Bishop of Coventry and Litchfield, Dr. Joseph Hall Bishop of Norwich, Dr. John Owen Bishop of St. Asaph, Dr. Robert Skinner Bishop of Oxford, Dr. William Piers Bishop of Bath and Wells, Dr. George Coke Bishop of Hereford, Dr. Matthew Wren Bishop of Ely, Dr. Godfrey Goodman Bishop of Glocester, Dr. John Warner Bishop of Peterborough, and Dr. Morgan Owen Bishop of Llandaff, . . . 1641," in *State Trials*, Vol. IV, cols. 63–82.]

contemptible, and utterly unworthy of notice, was calculated, from the accompanying circumstances, to give serious reason for alarm. The protestation, before it was presented to parliament, had been communicated to the king, and approved by him. This even Hume calls an "egregious imprudence."[*] But was it no more? A declaration of the king (for having received his approbation it was his), that whatever the parliament might hereafter do, was by him considered to be invalid, and, therefore, not binding upon him, however he might find it convenient to give it his nominal assent—was this no more than an imprudence? To the impartial reader, it may perhaps appear to be treachery, and treachery of the basest, because of the most pernicious, kind.

"A few days after," says Hume, "the king was betrayed into another indiscretion, still more fatal; an indiscretion, to which all the ensuing disorders and civil wars ought immediately and directly to be ascribed. This was the impeachment of Lord Kimbolton and the five members."[†]

Even this admission from Hume is important. The measure, however, to which, as he truly says, the war which ensued is directly to be ascribed; the measure by which the king declared open war against his parliament, and demonstrated that his ever cordially acquiescing in the just and necessary diminution of his power was hopeless; this measure, which, in a most artful and plausible manner, Hume labours to represent as the effect of passion and precipitation,[‡] had actually been resolved upon before the king left Scotland.

In justice to Hume, it is necessary to state, that the correspondence between Charles and Secretary Nicholas, by which this important fact is completely and indisputably established, had not, at the time when he wrote, been given to the world.[§] Enough, however, was even then known to render it almost certain, that this violent measure had been long premeditated, and was by no means adopted, as he represents, in a moment of haste. The whole conduct of the king, from his arrival at Whitehall; the dismissal of the guard under Essex; the appointment of Lunsford and Byron to the command of the Tower; the large number of reformed officers whom he had assembled round him, and the threatening language which they held; all these are important articles of circumstantial evidence, and the exact similarity of the project to the Scottish *incident*, renders it probable that both were part of the same preconcerted plan of operations.

[*Hume, Vol. VI, p. 465.]
[†*Ibid.* See also "Articles of High Treason, and Other High Misdemeanours, against the Lord Kimbolton, Mr. Denzill Hollis, Sir Arthur Haslerig, Mr. John Pym, Mr. John Hampden, and Mr. William Strode [1642]," in *State Trials*, Vol. IV, col. 85.]
[‡Hume, Vol. VI, pp. 466–7.]
[§Bray's edition of the "Private Correspondence between King Charles I and His Secretary of State, Sir Edward Nicholas," in *Memoirs of Evelyn*, Vol. II, did not appear until 1818; see, e.g., letters from Nicholas to the King, with the latter's marginal notes, of 27 and 29 Sept., 1641, pp. 25, 27–8.]

The charges against the six members, Kimbolton, Hampden, Hollis, Pym, Hazlerig, and Strode, were, that they had attempted to subvert the fundamental laws, to alienate the people from the king, and deprive him of his authority, that they had endeavoured to draw the king's army into disobedience, had encouraged a foreign power to invade the kingdom, had countenanced tumults, and lastly, had conspired to levy, and actually had levied, war against the king.

With the exception of the latter charge, which we do not understand, there was none of these accusations which was not equally applicable to a great majority of the parliament: if the leaders were guilty of high treason, so also were all those who had followed in their steps. Resistance was now an act of self-defence. In a period of peace and order, when a fair trial can be rationally hoped for, if the accused does not submit to it, he may fairly be presumed to be guilty; but such rules are not applicable to a crisis like the present; deprived of their leaders, the parliament would have been an easy prey to their infuriated enemy: war might now be regarded as openly declared, the king was plainly the aggressor, and on his head were all the consequences which might ensue.

A party was sent, by the sole authority of the king, to seal up the trunks and doors of the impeached members. This conduct the Commons declared to be a breach of privilege;[*] meanwhile, a serjeant at arms came to the lower house, and demanded the five members. The Commons hereupon appointed a committee to acquaint the king, that his message was so important as to require a serious consideration, but that they would return an answer as speedily as possible, and in the meantime would take care that the members should be ready to answer to the accusation. Without replying to this message, Charles came in person, the next day, to the lower house, "accompanied," says Hume, "by his ordinary retinue to the number of above two hundred, armed as usual, some with halberds, some with walking staves."[†] Thus much could not be concealed; but the fact was, that, in addition to his ordinary retinue, he was accompanied by the lately-enlisted guards, and that the whole number of his attendants was not less than five hundred; in addition to which, the gentlemen from the inns of court, who had recently been gained over, were ordered to be ready at an hour's notice. The king's followers used the most insulting and threatening language towards the Commons, and some of them asked, "When comes the word?" Being questioned afterwards by a committee of the House of Commons, what they meant by that expression, they answered that "questionless, in the posture they were set, if the word had been given, they should have fallen upon the House of Commons, and cut all their throats."[‡] It was further proved, that a hundred stand of arms, and two barrels of gunpowder, with match and shot in proportion, were sent, on this very day, from

[*See their statement of 3 Jan., 1641, in *An Exact Collection*, p. 35.]
[†Hume, Vol. VI, p. 469. See also "His Majesties Speech in the House of Commons, 4 Jan., 1641," in *An Exact Collection*, p. 36.]
[‡Brodie, Vol. III, p. 268.]

the Tower to Whitehall, with the knowledge of the lieutenant.[*] All these facts, which Hume prudently conceals, render it manifest that the employment of force, if any resistance should be offered, had been fully determined on beforehand. The five members, however, having received timely notice of the king's intention, had already left the house.

The same evening, they removed for protection into the city, whither Lord Digby proposed to follow them, "with a select company of gentlemen," says Clarendon, "*whereof Sir Thomas Lunsford was one*, to seize upon them and bring them away alive, or leave them dead in the place, which," he continues, "must have had a wonderful effect."[†] The king chose rather to go in person into the city and demand them; but, though he was received without disrespect, he obtained no encouragement.* A petition against his late proceedings was presented, two days afterwards, from the city, but received an evasive answer.[‡] The total failure of the intended arrest had, for the present, disconcerted Charles's plans; he issued a proclamation for the apprehension of the impeached members, and immediately retired from the capital.

Here was another fine opportunity for pathos:

the king, [says Hume,] apprehensive of danger from the enraged multitude, had retired to Hampton Court, deserted by all the world, and overwhelmed with grief, shame, and remorse, for the fatal measures into which he had been hurried. His distressed situation he could no longer ascribe to the rigours of destiny, or the malignity of enemies. His own precipitancy and indiscretion must bear the blame of whatever disasters should henceforth befal him.[§]

This may, for aught we know, be very pathetic; but it is wholly untrue. We pass over the insinuation of danger from the multitude, where there is no appearance that there was, and great appearance that there was not, any danger whatever. There is falsehood at the very root of the whole. The king, who is described as having left London thus overwhelmed by remorse, left it with a determination immediately to make war upon his people.

[*Ibid., pp. 269–70.]

[†Hyde, *History*, Vol. I, p. 283, and "Lord Digby," in Supplement to Vol. III of *State Papers*, 3 vols. (Oxford: Clarendon Printing House, 1767–86), pp. lv–lvi; but Mill takes the quotation from Brodie, Vol. III, pp. 263n–4n.]

*"One of the populace," says Hume, "drew nigh to his coach, and called out with a loud voice, 'To your tents, O Israel;' the words employed by the mutinous Israelites, when they abandoned Rehoboam, their rash and ill-counselled sovereign." [Hume, Vol. VI, p. 471. See I Kings, 12:16, for the Biblical passage. The person who, Hume says, called out was Henry Walker.] This story is in itself insignificant; but it throws light upon the veracity of Clarendon (from whom it is taken [*History*, Vol. I, p. 283]), as well as upon the accuracy of Hume. The person alluded to did not cry out, but threw a paper into the king's coach, on which paper the words in question were inscribed. He was committed, and proceeded against at the sessions. [See Brodie, Vol. III, p. 265n.]

[‡"The Humble Petition of the Major, Aldermen, and Common Councell, of the City of London, and His Majesties Answer," in *An Exact Collection*, pp. 45–8.]

[§Hume, Vol. VI, p. 472.]

The labyrinth of falsehood in which Hume found it necessary to involve himself, in order to exonerate Charles from the criminality of the ensuing war, is in itself no trifling presumptive evidence of that monarch's guilt. In the first place, it was necessary to make it appear that the parliament were the aggressors; that they were encroaching upon him, not he upon them; that he was upholding that ancient constitution which they were endeavouring to destroy. For this purpose it was necessary to dwell minutely upon the most trifling instances of discretionary power in former reigns, and to make it appear that there was systematic despotism, where there was really nothing systematic at all; that there was a regular and definite constitution, when even the forms of public business had nothing settled or defined, and the substance still less than the forms.[*] In the next place, supposing this to have been established, what does it prove? It might have been retorted, that although the Commons had aimed at subverting the ancient constitution, yet, if the ancient constitution was a bad one, to subvert it was not only excusable, but meritorious. That it *was* a bad one, Hume admits; since he says it was a despotism; and no one but a supporter of despotism would blame those who resisted it. All this might have been said, Hume himself felt how justly; it being impossible, therefore, to blame the resistance itself, there still, however, remained two things to blame, the *time* and *manner* of the resistance, and the *extent* to which they pushed it. The manner, he represents as insidious, harsh, and cruel;[†] and the insinuations, for they are insinuations rather than reasons, by which he supports this representation, leave no other inference, than that he disapproved of the resistance itself: on no ground can resistance at that period be condemned, which would not be an equally good ground for condemning resistance at any period; on no ground can resistance by the means which they adopted, and which were the only means that they could adopt, be disapproved of, unless upon the supposition that they ought not to have resisted at all. So much for the means. Next, as to the extent of the resistance, it is Hume's indefatigable endeavour, to prove that, after having obtained the temporary cessation of immediate oppression, they should have stopt short and left Charles with full possession to re-establish it: that so long as they resisted present tyranny, they were right; so soon as they attempted to obtain future security, they were wrong; an inference which the experience of every age and nation laughs to scorn; but which it was only for that reason the more necessary to support by falsehood and concealment. For this it is, that all the pretended perils of the king are magnified into the most serious dangers, while the well-grounded fears of the popular party are derided as visionary, or exclaimed against as feigned alarms—feigned for the mere purpose of stimulating the passions of the populace. For this, did Hume, with the evidence before him, ridicule the army-plot as an unfounded and calumnious imputation, and slur over the royalist conspiracy in Scotland, without even adverting to it as a subject of

[*See, e.g., *ibid.*, pp. 549–51, 551–2, 560–3, 578–80, 582–5.]
[†*Ibid.*, p. 477.]

controversy. For this, finally, does he represent the project of resorting to arms, as having originated with the parliament; and as having been adopted by Charles, only in consequence of the attempt to wrest from him the power of the sword:[*] though Clarendon admits that Charles, before he left Whitehall, despatched the Earl of Newcastle to seize and garrison Hull; and that at the same time it was resolved, that the queen should proceed to Portsmouth, which Goring, the governor, had already engaged to surrender.[†] Not a trace of this is to be found in Hume, who abandons even the royalist historians, when by any accident they deviate into sincerity and candour.

In the same spirit, when Charles's band of discarded officers, with Lunsford at their head, retired to Kingston-upon-Thames, and when Digby, having gone to them by the king's command, accepted of their service in the king's name, arms and ammunition being at that very time actually on their passage to the same place; the following is Hume's version of this transaction: "Lord Digby having entered Kingston in a coach and six, attended by a few livery servants, the intelligence was conveyed to London, and it was immediately voted that he had appeared in a hostile manner, to the terror and affright of his majesty's subjects, and had levied war against the king and kingdom."[‡] Would it be believed, that Digby himself, in his apologetical defence of his conduct, admits that "*many soldiers and commanders*" were assembled at Kingston, and that he was sent there to convey his majesty's good acceptance of their service?[§]

There can be little doubt that the purpose of Charles, at this juncture, was to assemble troops and march upon London, where a sure person was already in command of the Tower. This design, however, was frustrated by the vigilance of the Commons. The arms and ammunition which were on their passage to Kingston were stopped, and any attempt in that quarter was guarded against, by raising the four neighbouring counties. Goring was enjoined to obey no orders but such as came from the king and parliament: Sir John Hotham was sent as governor, with similar orders, to Hull. Hume, while he dwells invidiously upon these precautionary measures, omits to state the motives by which they were occasioned, and leaves it to be inferred, that they were acts of unprovoked aggression. Sir John Byron, Governor of the Tower, was ordered to attend the parliament and give an account of certain suspicious proceedings: on his refusal, he was voted a delinquent, a guard was placed round the Tower, and the king was petitioned for his removal, which was at length granted, now when he could be of no further use.[¶]

The immediate designs of Charles being thus defeated, the queen, under

[**Ibid.*, pp. 484–6, 474, 481, 419, 478–9; Vol. VII, p. 44.]
[†Hyde, *History*, Vol. I, pp. 304, 326.]
[‡Hume, Vol. VI, p. 484.]
[§George Digby, *The Lord Digby's Apology*, in Nalson, *An Impartial Collection*, Vol. II, p. 865.]
[¶Hume, Vol. VI, pp. 478–9; see also Cobbett, Vol. II, cols. 1029, 1031.]

pretence of conveying her daughter, the Princess Mary, to her husband in Holland, went abroad to solicit assistance from foreign states, and raise money on the security of the crown jewels.* Meanwhile, the king resolved to temporize till he could reach a place of security, where he might organize an army.

A bill for removing the bishops from parliament had already passed both houses; and now, together with the bill for impressment,[*] received the royal assent. These bills, which he found it necessary to pass, when he feared lest the queen should be detained in England by the parliament, he never intended to observe; and we are told by Clarendon that he satisfied his conscience with the wretched subterfuge, that in their passage through the houses there had been something like constraint. Hume, though compelled to acknowledge this piece of jesuitry in a note, has the boldness to say, "neither Clarendon, nor any other of the royalists, ever justify him from insincerity, as not supposing that he had ever been accused of it."[†] He asserts, moreover, that this scruple of the king affected only the two bills in question;[‡] directly in the teeth of Clarendon (an unquestionable authority), who says, "I doubt this logic had an influence upon other acts, of no less moment than these."†

The bill for vesting the command of the militia in officers appointed by parliament, was the pretext, rather than the cause of the final breach.[§] By this bill,

---

*Hume has been convicted by Mr. Brodie of the most paltry misrepresentation, concerning the conduct of the parliament towards the queen, (Brodie, Vol. III, p. 310n [Hume, Vol. VI, pp. 477–8,]) suppressing the evidence of her sinister designs, and ascribing to bigotry and malice, measures which were adopted merely for the sake of security.

The petitions, which in such numbers were poured in against the proceedings of Charles, and upon which Hume endeavours at this juncture to throw ridicule, are equally misrepresented. One, said to be from the porters, is obviously a forgery of Clarendon. Mr. Brodie could not trace it, as he did the others, in the journals of the Commons. Another, which Hume calls a petition from "several poor people, or *beggars*," never had any existence; the petition to which he alludes being admitted, even by Dugdale and Clarendon, whom he quotes, to be professedly from "poor artificers and tradesmen." To such petty arts of misrepresentation is he reduced. [See Hume, Vol. VI, p. 475; Hyde, *History*, Vol. I, pp. 322–3; Brodie, Vol. III, p. 306n; *Journals of the House of Commons*, Vol. II, pp. 33–5, and William Dugdale, *A Short View of the Late Troubles in England* (Oxford: printed at the Theater, 1681), p. 87. Mill takes the phrasing of the second quotation from Brodie.]

[*16 Charles I, c. 27 and c. 28 (1640).]

[†Hume, Vol. VII, p. 523.]

[‡*Ibid.*, p. 525.]

†[Hyde, *History*, Vol. I, pp. 335–6.] Not content with denying the insincerity of Charles, Hume [Vol. VII, p. 523] has the effrontery to say, that the imputation was of a later growth than his own age, and that Ludlow is the only parliamentary writer who ever lays it to his charge! [Ludlow, *Memoirs*, Vol. I, pp. 15–17, 153–6.] Had Hume never read Milton's *Eikonoclastes*? [In *The Prose Works of John Milton*, ed. Charles Symmons, 7 vols. (London: Johnson, *et al.*, 1806), Vol. II, pp. 383–472.] Had he never read any of the manifestoes of the long parliament? [E.g., Cobbett, Vol. II, Cols. 1114–20, 1155–62, 1454–6.]

[§See Cobbett, Vol. III, cols. 1071–2, 1077–80, 1083–5, 1091, 1106–11.]

the parliament did not arrogate to themselves a greater power than the parliament of the present day constantly exercises by means of the annual mutiny-bill. In the posture of affairs at that time, it is not too much to say that it was absolutely necessary. The king still continued to temporize. Hume wishes it to be understood, that he had even yet no intention of war;[*] though even Clarendon does not attempt to conceal that, before the queen left England, not only had he resolved upon war, but had even promised never to make peace without her consent. Yet, even now, and long after, he continued to declare with the most solemn asseverations before God, that he had no thought of making war. Even after a supply of arms had been received from Holland, and when his warlike preparations were already far advanced, he issued a declaration, expressing in the strongest terms his abhorrence of such a design; and this declaration was signed by all the lords and counsellors present, not excepting the virtuous Lord Falkland;[†] of all which, not a word in Hume. At length, after some acrimonious correspondence between the king and parliament, and a fruitless attempt on the part of Charles to obtain admittance into Hull, he erected his standard at Nottingham, and hostilities commenced.

Thus, for the gratification of his own appetite for power, did Charles voluntarily plunge his country into all the horrors of a civil war. Next in immorality to the monarch, who could perpetrate, with his eyes open, this greatest of all crimes, may justly be reckoned the historian who could praise it, and who could hold up such detestable selfishness to the applause of the world, under the high-sounding names of conscience and of principle.

Had Charles succeeded in his guilty undertaking, we have it on unquestionable authority, that of the more moderate men in his own party, that all appearance of moderation would have been discarded from his counsels, and that he would have been wholly governed by the most furious of the royalists, particularly by his Catholic queen, and her Catholic faction. Such was the opinion of Lord Savile, afterwards Earl of Sussex; such was known to be the opinion of Lord Falkland; and such, from the letters of Lord Spencer, another distinguished royalist, Mr. Brodie proves to have been his opinion also.[‡] These men, who had not utterly discarded all regard for their afflicted country, dreaded almost as much the success of their own, as that of the opposite party.

More than once during the war, negotiations were opened for a treaty; and Hume, as often as he can, endeavours to throw the blame of their failure upon the parliament;[§] but Clarendon informs us, that the king's overtures were feigned, and that from the beginning he was resolved against peace, upon any other terms

[*See, e.g., Hume, Vol. VI, pp. 481, 484, 485.]
[†The text of the declaration is in Hyde, *History*, Vol. I, pp. 508–13.]
[‡Brodie, Vol. III, pp. 344n–5n, quoting from "Letters of Lord Spencer to His Lady, Dorothy" (21 Sept., and 13 Oct., 1642), in *Letters and Memorials of State*, ed. Collins, Vol. II, pp. 667–8.]
[§E.g., Hume, Vol. VI, pp. 510–11, Vol. VII, pp. 30–8.]

than absolute submission; "the promise to the queen having shut out all opposite consultations."[*]

As it is not our intention to write a history of the civil wars, we shall content ourselves with sketching the rise and progress of the dissentions in the popular party itself; a portion of history which even Mr. Brodie seems not fully to comprehend, though his conception of it is more correct than that of any former historian.

Of the two sets of men into which the popular party was divided, because one set called themselves Presbyterians, and the other set Independents, it has been supposed that the contest between them was mainly a religious dispute. In reality, it was essentially a struggle for power. The parliament, we have already observed, was an aristocracy, and, like every other aristocracy, it split into factions. It would have done the same thing had there been no religious disputes; though, as there were, the two parties naturally fell in with the two sects. Religion merely constituted that bond of union, which otherwise would certainly have been supplied by something else.

These calamitous dissentions were heightened by the death of the two men of highest character in the party, Hampden and Pym, which threw the government into the hands of such men as St. John, Hollis, Hazlerig, and Vane; men, for the most part, either unprincipled, or weak; and enabled one man of superior talents, to subdue one party, overreach the other, and raise himself to sovereignty upon the ruins of both.

Various circumstances combined to make the Presbyterian party, and the aristocratic, coincide. In the first place, the Independent tenets were nearly akin to republicanism. In the next place, the Scottish covenanters were bigotted Presbyterians. Further, the military leaders, being *novi homines*, were the great opponents of the aristocracy; but the military leaders were naturally of that religion which enabled them, in the capacity of preachers, to secure to themselves an undivided ascendancy over the soldiers, whose obedience they must otherwise have been content to share with the ministers of religion. Add to this, that Independency, excluding persecution, was the religion of the enlightened, and the enlightened are necessarily enemies to aristocracy. The leaders of the Independents were Vane and Cromwell; of the Presbyterians, Hollis, who was driven, we are told, into that party, principally by jealousy of those eminent men.[†]

Though weak, and in numbers insignificant in the commencement, the Independent party gained strength with the continuance of the war, by the gradual rise to power of the military leaders. But the epoch of their decisive victory was the self-denying ordinance,[‡] which, by excluding all members of either house from

---

[*Brodie, Vol. III, p. 316, quoting Hyde, *Life*, Pt. II, pp. 57–8.]
[†Brodie, Vol. III, p. 515.]
[‡See Cobbett, Vol. III, cols. 355–7.]

civil and military employments, threw the command of the army into the hands of Fairfax and Skippon, both of whom belonged to the Independent party.

Of the mode in which the Independents effected the passing of this act, Hume has borrowed from Clarendon a long account, which it is scarcely possible to believe that he did not know to be false.[*] The story is, that they caused a general fast to be proclaimed the day before, and procured the preachers at all the churches in the metropolis to exert themselves strenuously on that day in favour of the measure; of which concurrence they afterwards availed themselves, as a declaration from heaven in its favour. Now, Rushworth, who is also quoted by Hume, gives a circumstantial account of the whole proceedings, with dates and speeches, proving, says Mr. Brodie, "that the new model was resolved upon before a fast was even voted, and that the ordinance itself had undergone the fullest discussion before the fast was held:"[†] that the fast, moreover, when it did take place, was kept only by the two Houses, and not by the public, so that there could not possibly be that concurrence in the language of the different preachers on that day, which is pretended.

The self-denying ordinance was unquestionably a stroke of party, but it does not follow that it was a bad measure. Essex, Manchester, and the other aristocratic commanders, were destitute of military skill; and, as it was not their interest that the king should be entirely subdued, they did not exert to the utmost even the talents which they possessed. The new model placed the command of the army in abler and more efficient hands, and was so far good. In what respect it was bad we are yet to learn. If it be said that the new commanders would abuse their power, so also, we answer, would the old ones, or any others, under an equal absence of control. Power, without responsibility, can no more be trusted in the hands of one man, than in those of another.*

At length the decisive defeat of Naseby compelled Charles to throw himself upon the mercy of the Scots. Had this infatuated prince even then been capable of common honesty and fair dealing, he might have retained his throne, and with it a considerable share of power. But while in public he professed a resolution to put an end to the war, and wrote to Ormonde, Lord Lieutenant of Ireland, to suspend the negotiations which he had been directed to open with the Irish rebels,[‡] he at the same time, sent privately to him, commanding him to disobey; and the result of his

---

[*Hume, Vol. VII, pp. 23–6; Hyde, *History*, Vol. II, pp. 434–7.]

[†Brodie, Vol. III, p. 552n; Rushworth, *Historical Collections*, Vol. VI, pp. 3ff.; Hume, Vol. VII, pp. 27–8.]

*It has been supposed that the self-denying ordinance was passed for the mere purpose of giving power to Cromwell [Hume, Vol. VII, pp. 28–9]; because that officer had a dispensation granted to him for the period of forty days. Mr. Brodie, however, renders it highly probable, that this was the mere effect of accident. [Vol. III, pp. 560–2.] The question, indeed, is of little consequence.

[‡See Charles's letter of 11 June, 1646, in Carte, *History*, Vol. III, p. 474.]

intrigues was, the conclusion of a treaty, by which the Irish agreed to pour an army of 20,000 men into Scotland. Even this, however, was not enough. Like most cunning persons, he laid so many trains that they interfered with one another. We shall not here enter into the history of the commission to Glamorgan; that transaction, which was so strenuously denied by the royalist party at the time, and the evidence of which has been so craftily, and, at the same time, so impudently evaded by Hume, who has not scrupled, for that purpose, to make assertions which even the royalists did not venture to hazard in their own vindication. The reader who has drawn his conception of Charles's character from Hume, if he peruse the evidence as adduced by Mr. Brodie,[*] will be filled with astonishment at finding this paragon of candour to have been as finished a dissembler, and even perjurer, as the page of history can supply; false to his word, nay, false to his oath, and a traitor even to Ormonde, the most devoted of his adherents. "It is impossible," says Hume, alluding to a letter in which the king tells Ormonde that he never meant Glamorgan to act independently of his control, "it is impossible that any man of honour, however he might dissemble with his enemies, would assert a falsehood in so solemn a manner to his best friend."[†] Suffice it, then, to say, that Mr. Brodie has shown, that he actually did assert such a falsehood; and has laid open a scene of complicated treachery, which nothing can equal but the disingenuous arts of the historian, who, to pander to the vulgar appetite for an affecting story, has condescended to erect such a man into a hero!

Meanwhile, the struggle between the two parties was rapidly drawing to a crisis: the Presbyterian party still retained a majority in parliament, which was considerably increased since the close of the war: for when, at length, the western counties, so long the seat of military operations, began again to send members to parliament, these members, who were mostly royalists, joined with the Presbyterian party, as the best inclined to monarchy of the two. The grand object of Hollis, and the Presbyterian leaders now was, to rid themselves of the army: but while they were anxious to disband the troops, or send them to fight against the rebels in Ireland, they were by no means equally anxious to pay them their arrears, for which, indeed, they had not the means. The discontents in the army, which this had a tendency to excite, were the grand resource of the Independent party for raising themselves to power. They exerted themselves, not only to stimulate but to organize the malcontents. A council was formed of deputies from every troop, called adjutators, a word afterwards corrupted into agitators: Ireton, son-in-law of Cromwell, a staunch republican, took the lead in their proceedings. Deputies were appointed to negociate with the parliamentary commissioners. Encouraged by their growing strength, they were not content with demanding payment of their

[*Brodie, Vol. IV, pp. 36–9; Hume, Vol. VII, pp. 66–8.]
[†Hume, Vol. VII, p. 517; for the letter of 31 Jan., 1645, see Carte, *History*, Vol. III, pp. 445–6.]

arrears. They soon preferred other complaints; they did not object to the Presbyterian church-government, but they objected to its intolerance; and complained that the parliament, notwithstanding the self-denying ordinance, shared all offices among their own body, and appropriated the public money to themselves.

Alarmed at the rising spirit of the army, and sensible that the probability of its quietly disbanding grew every day less and less, the Presbyterian leaders took measures for raising another. The army were guided at this time by men of talents. They acted with promptitude and decision; they possessed themselves of the king's person (of importance now, when parties were so nearly balanced), and marched, without loss of time, against the parliament. Their professed object was to obtain a speedy dissolution, with a biennial law to secure a frequent change;[*] and, the seclusion, in the mean time, of eleven obnoxious members, including Hollis, Stapleton, Waller, Massey, Maynard,[†] and the other leaders of the Presbyterian party. The two Speakers,[‡] and a great proportion of both Houses, seceded, and joined with the army: after some unavailing attempts at resistance, the parliament was compelled to yield, the eleven members were expelled, and the Independent party became for the present supreme.

Their power, however, was still far from being firmly established. They had yet to conquer the whole Scottish nation; all of whom, whether Royalists or Presbyterians, were their irreconcileable enemies. Even in England, both Presbyterians and Cavaliers were still far from being entirely subdued. Thus situated, the Independent leaders were naturally anxious to obtain the king's support and sanction to their undertakings, and so far were they, at this time, from meditating the abolition of monarchy, that they offered him better terms than had been proposed before the commencement of the war.

That unhappy prince, however, instead of hearkening to accommodation, only meditated a fresh war upon his people. Courted now by all parties, he was intoxicated by hope, and vainly believed that he had it in his power to hold the balance between them. Without relaxing in his exertions to obtain the aid of the Irish rebels, he was now intriguing with the Scottish commissioners, Laneric and Lauderdale: and at this time was laid, according to Clarendon, the foundation of the famous *engagement*.[§] So elated was he with the prospect of success in these various intrigues, that he not only rejected the overtures of the Independent leaders, but had the imprudence to give them personal offence. Not long after, finding that his secret plottings began to get wind, he determined upon flight, but

[*Cobbett, Vol. III, cols. 619–23.]
[†The other six were John Clotworthy, John Glynne, Edward Harley, William Lewis, Walter Long, and Anthony Nichols; *ibid.*, Vol. III, cols. 664–78.]
[‡William Lenthall and Edward Montagu.]
[§Hyde, *History*, Vol. III, p. 77.]

managed his enterprise so ill as to fall into the hands of Hammond, Governor of the Isle of Wight, and a faithful adherent of the parliament.

Without one particle of evidence, Hume takes upon himself to assert, that the Independent leaders rejoiced at Charles's flight because it gave them a pretext for keeping him in close confinement.[*] But why should we suppose them insincere in their wish for an accommodation? It was obviously for their interest; that they thought so, is proved by the mildness of their terms. They were not now so insane as to have any confidence in his sincerity; yet it is not true that they treated him with any degree of severity, beyond what the security of his person absolutely required; and they offered him, even now, better terms than had been proposed by the Presbyterians when he was in the Scottish camp. But Charles had now completed his negotiations with the Scottish commissioners. A clandestine treaty had been concluded, in which he engaged to confirm the covenant, to establish presbytery for three years, and to join in extirpating the sectaries, that is, the Independents. This treaty, which was never intended to be kept, but only to purchase the aid of a Scottish army, and enable Charles to recover the power of the sword, was inclosed in a sheet of lead, and buried in a garden, as it was suspected that the Scottish commissioners might be searched on leaving the Isle of Wight. It was afterwards, however, transmitted to them in London. The warmest advocates of Charles are unable to justify this new attempt to plunge his country into a war. It is in fact so difficult, even of palliation, that Hume found it the shortest course to say nothing about it. His silence, however, is in this case nearly as expressive as his words. Could any thing, even plausible, have been urged, either to justify the treaty, or to invalidate its authenticity, the historian who has ventured to deny the commission to Glamorgan, would not have allowed the "engagement" to pass unnoticed.

Not content with suppressing the truth, he tells a direct falsehood, or rather two: first, he asserts that the vote of the Commons to send no more addresses to the king, and the precautionary measures which they took to prevent his escape, were occasioned solely by his rejecting their terms,[†] when in reality they were occasioned by the detection of his intrigues with the Scots. Secondly, he has described those precautionary measures themselves, as being much more severe than they really were: as may be seen by comparing his statement with that of Herbert, a keen royalist, who, at this time, was in actual attendance upon the king.[‡] Herbert, however, was too honest a man to assert what he knew to be false. From what source Hume drew his statements, or whether from any source, except his own invention, we cannot pretend to determine.

Meanwhile, the effects of the *engagement*, so the secret treaty was called, began

[*Hume, Vol. VII, p. 108.]
[†*Ibid.*, pp. 111–15; for the vote, see Cobbett, Vol. III, cols. 831–2.]
[‡Thomas Herbert, *Memoirs of the Two Last Years of the Reign of . . . King Charles I* (London: Clavell, 1702), pp. 39–40.]

to manifest themselves. The royalists rose in all parts of the kingdom. On the return of Laneric and Lauderdale to their own country, an invasion of England was resolved on by the Scottish parliament,[*] notwithstanding the vehement opposition of Argyle, and the rigid Presbyterians, who, however attached to presbytery, and averse to a republic, would not trust Charles, nor unite themselves to the royalist party.

The renewal of the war, by removing from the English parliament such of its members as held commands in the army, restored a temporary preponderance to the Presbyterian party. The eleven secluded members resumed their seats, and in their turn opened a negotiation with Charles; who, even now, had he agreed to their terms, might have regained considerable authority. But he confidently expected that the success of the insurrection would restore him to absolute power. "Of all the demands of the parliament," says Hume, "Charles refused only two. Though he relinquished almost every power of the crown, he would neither give up his friends to punishment, nor desert what he esteemed his religious duty."[†] And upon this foundation, Hume proceeds to ascribe to him a high sense of principle and moral duty, as if he had been in reality a martyr to his friendship and to his religion. It happens rather unfortunately for Hume, that during these negotiations Charles himself writes to Sir William Hopkins, "To deal fairly with you, the great concession I made to-day was merely in order to my escape, of which, if I had not hopes, I had not done."[‡] And from this and other evidence, which proves him to have been at this time meditating an escape, it is obvious that there was no sincerity in his concessions, that he was only temporizing, and that he made a stand upon the two points of religion and of his friends, merely because he thought them to be the most popular grounds he could choose.*

[*See Charles I, 1648, c. 94, in *Acts of the Parliaments of Scotland*, Vol. VI, Pt. ii, pp. 53–6.]

[†Hume, Vol. VII, p. 124.]

[‡Brodie, Vol. IV, p. 144, quoting a letter of 9 Oct., 1648, in Wagstaffe, *A Vindication*, p. 161.]

*He continued, during the whole of this negotiation, to write to Ormonde, desiring him to disregard whatever he might hear of a treaty near to be concluded, and to disobey any commands which Charles might send him, until he should have sent him word that he was free from restraint. *See the documents in the Appendix to Carte's Ormonde*. [Vol. II, p. 17, letters of 10 and 28 Oct., 1648.]

We may notice, *en passant*, another falsehood into which Hume is betrayed by a desire to extol his hero. "The parliamentary commissioners," [Earls of Northumberland, Pembroke, and Salisbury, and Messrs. Holles and Crew, among others,] says he, "would allow none of his council to be present, and refused to enter into reasoning with any but himself. He alone, during the transactions of two months, was obliged to maintain the argument against fifteen men of the greatest parts and capacity in both houses; and no advantage was ever obtained over him." [Hume, Vol. VII, p. 122.] Yet Mr. Brodie has proved, from Herbert and Warwick, who were present, that he had with him many of the ablest lawyers and divines, and that although nominally they were not permitted to speak, he had their assistance,

This letter of Charles is in direct contradiction, by the way, to another also of Hume's assertions: "Having given his word to the parliament, not to attempt the recovery of his liberty during the treaty, and three weeks after, he would not, by any persuasion, be induced to hazard the reproach of violating that promise."[*] A very different story, we see, is told by the unhappy monarch himself.

While Charles was thus endeavouring to gain time, with a view to escape, the opportunity passed away. The royalist insurrection was suppressed; the Scottish army was defeated; Hamilton was taken prisoner, and Argyle and his party restored to undisputed sway. Triumphant now in every other quarter, the Independents had only to regain the ascendancy in the legislature. The army marched to London, and purged the parliament of almost all the Presbyterian members, thus finally crushing that party, which never recovered from the blow.

It was now manifest that the king was not to be trusted. No engagement which he might enter into would be held valid one moment longer than while he had not power to set it aside. While he survived, a hundred accidents might restore him to power. The dominant party consulted their own safety by bringing him to the scaffold.

That Charles deserved punishment, it has been our object, throughout this article, to prove. Whether, under a good government, he ought to have been put to death, would have been a question of policy, not a question of justice. He was sacrificed, however, not to the good of the many, but to that of the few, who then happened to possess power. His execution was the act of a nest of despots, removing a rival despot out of their way.

But Hume, whose grand object is, to render his hero interesting, and the enemies of his hero odious, seems to have picked up indiscriminately all the old woman's stories which he could find, about the prodigious sufferings of Charles, and the unheard of enormities of those by whom he was put to death; to such of them, indeed, as are not of themselves sufficiently pathetic, he adds copiously from his own stores.

It is lamentable to find a writer like Hume, who cannot easily be suspected of credulity, retailing with an air of sincerity, the puerile tales of Clement Walker and Perinchief. The former of these he represents as a writer of vast authority; and why? because he is a parliamentarian.[†] Now we can inform the reader, that there were two sets of parliamentarians—Presbyterians and Independents; each of

---

whenever he pleased, in framing his replies. [Brodie, Vol. IV, pp. 144n–5n; Herbert, *Memoirs*, pp. 69–71, mentions as counsellors the Duke of Richmond, the Marquis of Hertford, and the Earls of Southhampton and Lindsey, and, as chaplains, Drs. Juxton and Sanderson, among others; Philip Warwick, *Memoires of the Reigne of King Charles I with a Continuation to the Happy Restauration of King Charles II* (London: Chiswell, 1701), pp. 321–2.]

[*Hume, Vol. VII, p. 130.]
[†*Ibid.*, p. 92n.]

which hated the other with at least as much bitterness as either hated the royalists: and that Clement Walker happened to belong to that set by whom the regicides were considered to be little better than demons. As for Perinchief, from whom, without acknowledgment, Hume copies whole paragraphs almost word for word, he does not even dare to make a reference to him more than once;[*] well aware that any thing known to rest upon such authority, would never obtain so much as a moment's belief.

Notwithstanding the length to which this article has extended, there are some of these stories, addressed either *ad misericordiam* or *ad invidiam*, which we cannot pass unnoticed. He puts a speech into the mouth of Cromwell, in which he makes him assert, that, when offering up prayers for the king, he felt his tongue cleave to the roof of his mouth. The first part of this speech is taken, without acknowledgment, from Walker; where he found the latter part we know not, except that there is something a little like it in Perinchief, which it is probable that Hume manufactured, to suit his purpose. (See Brodie, Vol. IV, p. 183.)[†]

He next makes up a good story concerning a prophesying woman of Herefordshire, out of a passage in Whitelocke.[‡] The passage, to be sure, does not bear him out in more than one half of the story; but this was nothing to a writer of Hume's ingenuity; he could easily fill up the outline.

For the same purpose of making a good story, he affirms that Charles, when in the Isle of Wight, allowed his beard to grow as if estranged from the world; when, in reality, he was wholly intent upon the renewal of the war.[§] Now the fact is, that Charles was in the habit of wearing his beard. And what is the foundation of this story? A passage in Perinchief, stating that Charles neglected during that period to have his beard so neatly picked as was his custom![¶] Had not these artifices formed part of a system, we should be ashamed to insist upon things so little worthy of the notice of an historian. But Hume seizes hold of every thing that can be adapted to his purpose, from the gaining of a battle down to the combing of a man's beard.

"The soldiers, instigated by their superiors, were brought, though with difficulty, to cry aloud for justice. '*Poor souls*,' said the king to one of his attendants, '*for a little money they would do as much against their commanders.*' Some of them were permitted to go the utmost length of brutal insolence, and to spit in his face as he was conducted along the passage to the court."[‖] Now, is it possible to believe that, if this story of the spitting had been true, Herbert, the

[*See Brodie, Vol. IV, pp. 183n–4n; for the single reference, see Hume, Vol. VII, p. 141.]

[†Hume, Vol. VII, pp. 134–5; Walker, *History of Independency*, Pt. ii, p. 54; Perrinchief, *The Royal Martyr*, pp. 153–4.]

[‡Hume, Vol. VII, p. 135; Whitelocke, *Memorials*, p. 360.]

[§Hume, Vol. VII, p. 121.]

[¶Perrinchief, *The Royal Martyr*, p. 262.]

[‖Hume, Vol. VII, p. 140.]

king's most faithful attendant, and who was present at the time, would have omitted to mention it? Yet not only does he omit the spitting, but tells a very different story concerning the cry for justice.[*] Hume was not, however, without authority, for Mr. Brodie saw his pencil marks opposite to this story, in the copy of Perinchief belonging to the Advocate's library.[†]

The silly story of the four lords who offered themselves to suffer instead of Charles, Hume himself quotes from Perinchief, and Lloyde, another writer of equal authority.[‡] The story about the conversation between Charles and the young Duke of Glocester, is taken, without acknowledgment, from Lloyde.[§] Both these tales, if true, must have been known to Herbert, yet he seems not to have been acquainted with them.

From the same Perinchief, Hume drew the ridiculous stories which he gravely relates, concerning women who miscarried, and men who died of grief, at the news of Charles's execution. There is only one important part of the story which he has omitted to mention; an omission the more surprising, as it is very fully related by Perinchief. We allude to the miracles which were worked by handkerchiefs dipped in the royal martyr's blood.[¶]

Hume likewise asserts, that, every night during the interval between his trial and his execution, "the king slept sound as usual, though the noise of workmen, employed in forming the scaffold and other preparations for his execution, continually resounded in his ears."[||] This, we presume, is meant to be a fine dramatic incident: it is taken from Walker. Not only is it false, but Hume knew it to be such; for Mr. Brodie found his pencil marks in Herbert's *Memoirs*, opposite to the very passage in which we are informed that Charles slept at St. James's, and therefore could not possibly hear the noise of the scaffolding at Whitehall.[**] Even Walker himself unguardedly admits, that he came from St. James's to Whitehall on the morning of his execution.

But the instance of misrepresentation and misquoting which we have now to mention, is probably unmatched in the pages of any historian of reputation.

A fresh instance of hypocrisy was displayed the very day of the king's death. The generous Fairfax, not content with being absent from the trial, had used all the interest which he yet retained to prevent the execution of the fatal sentence; and had even employed

[*Herbert, *Memoirs*, pp. 113–14.]
[†Brodie, Vol. IV, p. 200n; Perinchief, *The Royal Martyr*, pp. 194–5.]
[‡Hume, Vol. VII, p. 141, citing Perinchief, *The Royal Martyr*, pp. 188–9, and David Lloyd, *Memoires* (London: Speed, 1668), p. 319. The four lords were Bertie Montague, Earl of Lindsey; William Seymour, Marquis of Hertford; James Stuart, Duke of Richmond; and Thomas Wriothesley, Earl of Southampton. Mill, here and in the next sentence, is relying on Brodie, Vol. IV, p. 207n.]
[§Hume, Vol. VII, p. 142; Lloyd, *Memoires*, pp. 215–16.]
[¶Hume, Vol. VII, pp. 144–5; Perinchief, *The Royal Martyr*, pp. 211, 205–6.]
[||Hume, Vol. VII, p. 143, based on Walker, *History of Independency*, Pt. ii, p. 110.]
[**Brodie, Vol. IV, p. 206n; Herbert, *Memoirs*, p. 117.]

persuasion with his own regiment, though none else would follow him, to rescue the king from his disloyal murderers. Cromwell and Ireton, informed of this intention, endeavoured to convince him that the Lord had rejected the king; and they exhorted him to seek by prayer some direction from heaven on this important occasion: but they concealed from him that they had already signed the warrant for the execution. Harrison was the person appointed to join in prayer with the unwary general. By agreement, he prolonged his doleful cant until intelligence arrived that the fatal blow was struck; he then rose from his knees, and insisted with Fairfax, that this event was a miraculous and providential answer, which heaven had sent to their devout supplications.[*]

This is another of Perinchief's stories, though Hume has the assurance to quote Herbert for it. Mr. Brodie has given the very passage of Herbert which Hume had marked in the copy belonging to the Advocate's library.[†] And what does this passage prove? Merely that Herbert met Fairfax, who had been at prayer with other officers in Harrison's room, and that from a question which Fairfax casually asked, Herbert *inferred* that he was ignorant of the king's execution!

The truth is, that Fairfax was among the foremost in all the measures of the Independent party to a late period: at the Restoration, however, he *ratted*, and became a courtier, for which reason, as well as his high character, the royalists are eager to exculpate him from all these transactions, and to throw the blame upon any one rather than upon him.

But we have already far exceeded our ordinary limits, and we must refer our readers for further information to Mr. Brodie. One word, however, is required in justice to the memory of that unfortunate and traduced body, the Long Parliament.

They were despots, no doubt: but compare them with other despots—compare them with any English parliament before or since. What British legislature, subsequent to our boasted Revolution, has dared to execute the plans which they devised? Had their authority continued, landed property would have been made liable for simple contract debts; the absurd fictions of fine and recovery would have been abolished; a system of universal registration would have been established for contracts in land; and the whole body of law would have been digested into a code. Bills for all these reforms had been introduced into the Long Parliament,[‡] and were broken off only by its abrupt dissolution. So much for what they would have done. What they did was, perhaps, the most important step to a reform in the law, which in this country has ever been taken, down to the present day. The legal proceedings, which, till that time, had been carried on in Norman-French, were

[*Hume, Vol. VII, p. 145.]

[†Perrinchief, *The Royal Martyr*, p. 203; Herbert, *Memoirs*, pp. 135–6; Brodie, Vol. IV, p. 213n.]

[‡See, e.g., An Act for the More Speedy and Effectual Relief of Creditors (23 June, 1649); An Act for the Taking Away of Common Recoveries, and the Unnecessary Charge of Fines; and to Pass and Charge Lands, Intailed, as Lands in Fee (15 Apr., 1652); and An Act Touching Recording Conveyances and Incumbrances (7 Aug., 1649), in *Journals of the House of Commons*, Vol. VI, p. 242; Vol. VII, p. 121; and Vol. VI, p. 275. There was interest in, but no act concerning, codification.]

ordered to be henceforth transacted in the vulgar tongue.[*] The abolition, at the same time, of monopolies, and other exclusive privileges, gave a new stimulus to industry and accumulation, and caused wealth to increase with a rapidity before unknown.[†]

The Independent leaders have been as disgracefully calumniated by Hume, in their private, as in their public capacity. He has, indeed, made it his business to hold them up, individually and collectively, to sovereign contempt; yet they were men of the best education which their age and country could afford; men, for the most part, of approved integrity, and many of them of distinguished talent. The reader who wishes for specimens of the inaccuracy and disingenuousness which he has here displayed, may refer, in particular, to his characters of Cromwell, Harrison, Ireton, and Vane, with Mr. Brodie's remarks.*

We shall not now relate the subjugation of the Presbyterian or monarchical party in Scotland; the forcible dissolution of the Long Parliament, and the elevation of one man to unbounded power; the struggles of that man to maintain himself against the two parties, the royalists on the one hand, and the republicans on the other; the impotent attempt of the Long Parliament to recover their authority at his death, and their renewed dissolution by the army; when the contest degenerated into a struggle between two rival generals,[‡] and he who was victorious found it more for his interest to restore the exiled king, than to take his chance of maintaining himself in that seat which Cromwell himself had scarcely been able to hold. Even

[*An Act for Turning the Books of the Law, and All Proces and Proceedings in Courts of Justice, into English (22 Nov., 1650), in *Acts and Ordinances of the Interregnum, 1642–1660*, ed. Charles Harding Firth and Robert Sangster Rait, 3 vols. (London: HMSO, 1911), Vol. II, pp. 455–6.]

[†An Act for Abolishing the House of Peers (19 Mar., 1649), and An Act for Advancing and Regulating of the Trade of the Commonwealth (1 Aug., 1650), *ibid.*, Vol. II, pp. 24, 403–6.]

*[See, e.g., on Cromwell, Hume, Vol. VII, pp. 221–5, 284–91, and Brodie, Vol. III, pp. 499n–508n; on Harrison, Hume, Vol. VII, pp. 135, 145, and Brodie, Vol. IV, pp. 179n–80n; on Ireton, Hume, Vol. VII, pp. 109–10, and Brodie, Vol. IV, pp. 164n–8n; and on Vane, Hume, Vol. VI, p. 540, Vol. VII, pp. 314, 383, and Brodie, Vol. III, pp. 22n–3n, Vol. IV, p. 460n.] With Hume's artful calumnies of the Independent leaders, we may contrast the theatrical glare which he has endeavoured to throw over Montrose. [Hume, Vol. VII, pp. 43–50, 179–83, 315, 318–19.]

What he could find to admire in this man it is difficult to discover. Originally a violent covenanter, Montrose apostatized, and, as we have already seen, offered to assassinate the friends whom he had betrayed; he then took arms and butchered friend and enemy, man, woman, and child. When expelled from Scotland, he actually perpetrated the crime which he had promised before, by assassinating Dorislaus, the English minister at the Hague. Yet this man has been painted in the most glowing colours, as a man of high principles and exalted heroism. He had not even generalship, bating the two qualities of courage and activity. He owed his brilliant successes merely to the weakness of his opponents, who had sent the far greater part of their force to the assistance of the Parliament in England.

[‡George Monk, who was victorious, and John Lambert.]

Monk, of whose character the lowness and meanness has long been universally acknowledged, is not too contemptible to be made a hero by Hume.[*] But we may now leave this writer, after the specimens we have given, to the fair judgment of the impartial reader.

It is necessary to say something, though our limits preclude us from saying so much as we would wish, on the character of Mr. Brodie as a historian. From what we have said, it will readily be understood, that his principal merits are diligence, accuracy, and perseverance. He displays, too, considerable skill in evolving the facts from a number of scattered, and seemingly unconnected, articles of circumstantial evidence. In the higher qualities of an historian, in aquaintance with the great principles of legislative philosophy, and in that comprehensiveness of intellect, which traces up effects to their causes, and teaches the reader to take in by a *coup d'œil* the mutual connexion of all the great events of the age, Mr. Brodie has not evinced any extraordinary degree of excellence. His style, though not strikingly deficient, has no peculiar merit. He has produced, nevertheless, one of the most important historical works of which modern English literature has to boast; and although something had already been done by Mr. Laing and Mrs. Macauley, he has added so many new facts, and confirmed by so much new evidence the facts which they had adduced, that we cannot but express a hope that we do not now part with him for ever. We trust that he will persevere in his useful undertaking; that he will carry on his labours to the period immediately following the Restoration, and will render the same service to the history of the second Charles, which he has already rendered to that of the first.

[*Hume, Vol. VII, pp. 307–11.]

IRELAND

1825

EDITOR'S NOTE

Parliamentary History and Review; Containing Reports of the Proceedings of the Two Houses of Parliament during the Session of 1825:—6 Geo. IV. With Critical Remarks on the Principal Measures of the Session. 2 vols. London: Longman, Rees, Orme, Brown, and Green, 1826, II (*Review*), 603–26. Headed: "Ireland./*The ADDRESS—Catholic Association—Catholic Claims—Elective Franchise—Provision for Catholic Clergy—Church Establishment, &c.*" Running titles as title. Unsigned; not republished. Identified in Mill's bibliography as "An article on the Catholic Question which appeared in the Parliamentary Review for 1825" (MacMinn, 7). For comment on the article, see xlix and lvii above.

Ireland

IT IS NOW our duty, conformably with the plan of this work, to pass judgment upon that portion of the proceedings of Parliament, a report of which is contained under the general head of *Ireland*.[*]

These proceedings divide themselves into two parts; the one consisting of acts, the other of discussions: the one comprising what was *done*, by one or other House, as a body; the other, what was *said*, by individual members.

In our examination of what was *done*, it will be necessary to state our own opinions on the great public questions which occupied the attention of Parliament; to assign the grounds of those opinions, without which neither our opinions, nor those of any one, are worth regarding; and, lastly, to examine how far what *was* done, did or did not accord with what, in our estimation, ought to have been done.

In our examination of what was *said*, it will be our duty to scrutinize rigidly the arguments advanced on both sides of every question; to expose the shifts and pretences of a bad cause, and rid a good one of those bad arguments by which its real merits are often so materially obscured.

When a ground shall thus have been laid for passing a deliberate judgment upon the conduct, both of the legislature as a whole, and of every member of it individually; something more will be necessary, to give to this part of our work all the utility of which it is susceptible.

Though many proceedings in Parliament are very important in their effects, few of them are so important in their effects, as they are in their causes. When an event, in addition to whatever good or evil may result immediately from itself, gives indication of the existence of a cause, from which an indefinite number of events of like tendency may be expected to flow; an estimate of its importance would be very imperfect, in which this indication should not be included.

The actions of public, like those of private, men, are governed by their interests. Their interests result directly from the institutions under which they live: if these be good, public men have no interest that is not in unison with the interest of the community: under bad institutions, their interest is frequently different from, and even opposite to, that of the community. Accordingly, the working of good or bad institutions may always be traced in the conduct of public men. If the institutions

[**Parliamentary History* (hereafter cited as *PH*), 1825, pp. 46–282.]

be good, their conduct is directed towards the advantage of the community, which in that case is also their own. If the institutions be bad, they pursue either their individual interest, or that of the class, or party, to which they belong: and the interest of the community is sacrificed.

In our comments, therefore, upon the proceedings in Parliament, we shall endeavour, in each instance, to bring to view, not only the events themselves, but their causes; viz.—the interests, generated by political institutions, and variously modified by those numerous and diversified circumstances which compose what is termed the spirit of the age.[*]

In all these points of view, few events will demand a greater share of our attention, than the proceedings of the last session in regard to the Catholics of Ireland. The range of these proceedings took in, not one only, but several great questions: the Catholic Association; the Catholic Claims; and the two measures, called the wings.[†] On each of these, rooted prejudices exist: the merits, therefore, of the different questions must be entered into, at least sufficiently to place every conclusion upon evidence sufficient to support it. The multiplicity of arguments, or what passed under that name, which were brought forward by all parties, render a proportional number of words necessary for making a due estimate of their validity: and finally, discussions, in which almost every prominent person in both Houses took a part, bore unusually strong marks of that general character which is impressed upon British statesmen by British institutions, and by the particular stage of intellectual and moral improvement at which the British nation has arrived.

The main question—that of Catholic emancipation—is, in our opinion, by no means a difficult one: and that any person capable of reasoning should feel a moment's doubt upon the subject, would surprise us, if we did not know that the strongest reasoning powers desert their possessor, when he is frightened. With all opponents of the Catholic Claims, in whose instance private interest is out of the question, the contest is simply, as it seems to us, between the great principles of justice on the one hand, and vague apprehensions on the other.

The public mind, in this country, is now so far advanced, that we may affirm, without hazard of being openly contradicted, even by those who would contradict

[*The term (later used by Mill as the title of a series of articles) seems to derive from Ernst Moritz Arndt's *Der Geist der Zeit* (1805, part trans. into English, 1808), which was abused by William Hazlitt in the *Examiner*, 1 Dec., 1816. Hazlitt used the term in 1820, and then published *The Spirit of the Age* (London: Colburn, 1825), which is probably Mill's immediate source.]

[†These appear in *PH*, 1825, as sections of "Ireland": "Catholic Association," pp. 47–148; "Catholic Claims," pp. 148–88, 208–12, and 215–62; and the two "wings," "Elective Franchise," pp. 188–204 and 212–15; and "Catholic Clergy," pp. 204–8. The statutes objected to by the Irish Catholics included 13 Charles II, second session, c. 1 (1661), 25 Charles II, c. 2 (1672), 30 Charles II, second session, c. 1 (1677 [1678]), and 7 & 8 William III, c. 27 (1696).]

us if they dared, that to subject any person to temporal inconvenience in any shape, on the ground of his religious opinions, is, *primâ facie*, injustice and oppression: that it cannot be justified on any such ground as that his religion is bad, or unacceptable in the sight of God: nor by any thing but the certainty, or at least a preponderant probability, that some great temporal calamity will befal the rest of the community, unless averted by imposing restraints, disabilities, or penalties, upon persons of some particular faith. It will also be allowed, that, if there be a danger, and if security against that danger require the imposition of disabilities on account of religious opinions; at least no disability should exist which does not, in some way or another, conduce to the end in view; that end being, security. We might join issue on both points, and maintain, not only the non-existence of danger, but the existence of disabilities, which, with whatever view they were *imposed*, can under no conceivable supposition (except that of extreme mental imbecillity) be now *maintained*, with any such view as that of guarding against danger. But as we have not space to argue both these questions, we will confine ourselves to the first and most important.

Before we can be called upon to say, what the danger is *not*, we are entitled to expect that the opponents of Catholic emancipation will declare what it *is*. This, however, the greater number of them would find an embarrassing question: accordingly few of them have ever attempted to answer it. So vague and indefinite are those fears, on the ground of which they are willing to degrade five or six millions of their countrymen to the condition of an inferior caste, that if they were asked *what* great calamity it is which they apprehend from the concession of the Catholic claims, we doubt whether one in ten of them could tell. What they have in their minds is an indistinct feeling that the Catholics are dangerous persons: and this being assumed, it never occurs to them to consider, whether the Catholics *not emancipated* are not fully as dangerous as the Catholics *emancipated* would be.

We will concede one point, about which there has been much unprofitable discussion: that no confidence is to be reposed in the professions of the Catholics; that, whatever they may *now* say, or think, they would not be satisfied with equality, if they could obtain superiority. We know of no body of men who would. We have no doubt—it would be absurd to doubt—that the Catholic clergy would willingly possess themselves of the temporalities of the Protestant Church; that the Catholic nobility and gentry, in destroying Protestant ascendancy, would willingly supply its place by the ascendancy of their own creed; and that the great body of the Catholics would gladly embrace any opportunity, and any means, of making their own religion the dominant religion of the state. We will even allow that they would aim at the suppression of all other religions, by persecution: for this is no more than *has* been done by Catholics; and not by Catholics only, but, in every age and country, by that sect of religionists who have been uppermost, as far as they have dared.

That the Catholic aristocracy and clergy should desire a monopoly of political power, and of the wealth which that power affords, is no more than natural. The propensity to pursue their own interests, is not peculiar to *Catholic* human beings. To persecute, indeed, is not the interest of any sect: and this the majority of every sect would see, if they were wise. But the majority of every sect has hitherto been unwise: accordingly no sect (with at most but one or two exceptions) which has had the power to persecute, has ever failed to make use of it. The Romish Church persecuted, and does persecute, wherever it is strong enough: so did the Church of England, as long as it was strong enough; so did the Greek Church; so did the Presbyterian.

Now, therefore, when we have made every concession against the Catholics which the most unreasonable opponent could demand, we require of our antagonists, in our turn, that they will find some better ground for imposing disabilities upon millions of human beings, than the mischief which it is feared they would do, if it were but in their power.

If the Catholic disabilities were upheld as a measure of hostility, it would be fit to consider whether the Catholics were proper objects of hostility. But as they are professedly measures, not of hostility, but of security; the question, and the only question, is, not what the Catholics would be willing, but what they would be able, to do.

It is hard to guess what precise evil the fears of most of the Anti-Catholic orators point to. Some of them talk of a *divided allegiance.* "The Protestant," says Lord Liverpool, "gives an entire allegiance to his sovereign; the Catholic, a divided one. The service of the first is complete, of the last only qualified."*

Now, if by the sovereign be meant the king, we should be sorry to think that every, or any, Protestant gave to his sovereign an unqualified allegiance. If allegiance mean obedience, and what else it can mean we know not, an entire allegiance is suitable only to a despotic government. What there is of meaning in this accusation, must be, that the Catholics acknowledge a foreigner as the head of their church, to whose interests, it is imagined, they are disposed to sacrifice the interests of their country. That there is a party of persons, professing the Catholic faith, who are so disposed, is true: that this party is any thing but a small minority, is not true: for, if it were, what must be the situation, we do not say of Protestant states in which Catholics lie under no disqualifications, but of countries in which a vast majority of the people are Catholics, as France, Austria, and Spain? If the authority of the Pope be *there* paramount to that of the temporal sovereign; if the Pope be there suffered to depose kings; the danger apprehended is real: if not, it is imaginary.

The few Anti-Catholics who can tell what they are afraid of, seem chiefly to fear that the Catholics would attempt to subvert the established church; and this is the only tangible ground which they have assigned for their alarm.

*[Robert Banks Jenkinson, Speech on Roman Catholic Relief (17 May, 1825),] *PH* [1825], p. 244.

In the first place, then, we think we may lay it down as an indisputable axiom, that the re-establishment of Catholicism, as the dominant religion in this country, is an event quite beyond the range of human probability. That six millions of persons, not having the powers of government in their hands, should either convert or conquer twelve millions, does not seem a very probable contingency. If probable at all, however, it is more probable before emancipation than after: since the power, whether of converting or of conquering, is the same, and the motive incomparably greater. They are six millions now, they would be but six millions then: their clergy would hardly be more eager to convert, nor their laity more able to rebel.

But though they might not be able, in opposition to the whole body of Protestants, to make their own religion the religion of the state; they might still, it is perhaps supposed, in concert with the sectarians, and with those other Protestants who are hostile to a church establishment, bring about the downfal of the existing church, and make all religions equal in the eye of the law.

This is to suppose, that, persons of all persuasions being included, a decided majority of the population of the two islands either is, or is likely to become, hostile to the continuance of the present church establishment. For, under any other supposition, it is difficult to see what danger there could be in throwing an additional weight into a scale, which would continue, notwithstanding, to be the lighter. Now, if this be true; without giving any opinion on the question, how far good government, good order, or religion itself, would suffer, if all religions *were* made equal in the eye of the law; we may be permitted to doubt whether the minority should be allowed to establish *their* religion, against the will of the majority; and whether the few might not, with as much justice, tax the many to build palaces for them as churches, and to pay their physicians and their lawyers as their clergy. But we do not wish to argue the question on a ground which would provoke so much opposition.

If the church were to be subverted, it would be in one of two ways: by means of the legislature, or in opposition to it; that is, by rebellion. If, then, after emancipation, it would be in the power of the Catholics, aided or not by the dissenters, to effect, in either of these two ways, the subversion of the church; what hinders them from doing it at this moment? Is it to be done by physical force? But if they are not strong enough now, emancipation would not make them so. Is it to be done by commanding a majority in Parliament? A few Catholic peers would take their seats in the Upper House; but in the Lower, beyond those whom they command at present, they would not be able to command a single vote. There would not be one Catholic elector—the Catholic aristocracy would not possess one borough—more than at present. They would indeed be enabled to return Catholics to Parliament; and, if nobody could be found but Catholics to assail the church, the disabilities would be some security: but it would be affectation in the most zealous churchman to pretend to doubt that the number of Protestants who are hostile to the church, is at least sufficient to fill the few seats which are at the disposal of the Catholic party. How happens it then that the church is not destroyed? The question is absurd. With almost every liberal Protestant on their side, the Catholics cannot command votes enough to carry their own emancipation; and it is supposed that with the great body of the Protestants against them they could command enough to overthrow the Protestant church!—But their influence in Parliament may increase. The Catholic electors may grow more numerous; more Catholics may become borough proprietors.—They may: and so they may, while their disabilities continue, and to the full as easily.

For the above reasons, and many others which we have not room to mention, we dismiss the idea of danger from Catholic emancipation. On the other hand, we are inclined to abate much from the current estimate of its advantages. An importance has been attached to it, both in respect of good and of evil, for which we are at a loss to find any adequate ground. We do not think that of itself it would do much for Ireland; the evils by which that country is afflicted, are not to be so summarily cured: and though Catholic emancipation might be a useful preparative to other and more important ameliorations, we do not think that it is by any means a necessary one.

Catholic emancipation would do nothing for the body of the people. Eligibility to office would be to them but a nominal privilege: excluded in *fact* by their situation in life, it is scarcely an additional evil to be excluded in *law* too. If they really feel as strongly on the subject of emancipation, as the friends of that measure wish it to be believed,—a belief which we find it difficult to entertain,—they must expect much more from it than the removal of disabilities; they must expect something which cannot be realized: to them, therefore, the effect of emancipation would be disappointment; and disappointment is seldom followed by tranquillity.

It is idle to expect tranquillity in Ireland so long as its inhabitants are the poorest and the most oppressed people in Europe. That they are the poorest, appears from the testimony of all who know them: that they are the most oppressed, no unprejudiced person can doubt, who will read the evidence taken before the Committees of the two Houses in the sessions of 1824 and 1825.[*] He will there find, that whatever the end of government in Ireland may *be*, it at any rate is *not* the protection of the weak against the strong: that government and law exist in that country solely for the benefit of the strong: that, while the Negro slave is at least protected against the encroachments of all masters except his own, the Irish peasant is at the mercy, not only of a whole series of landlords, from the proprietor of the soil down to the lowest middleman, but moreover of the tithe-owner and the tithe-farmer or proctor, to say nothing of vestries and grand juries: that against

[*See "Minutes of Evidence" (Commons), *Parliamentary Papers* (hereafter cited as *PP*), 1825, VII, 1–499; "Minutes of Evidence" (Lords), pp. 501–802; first, second, third, and fourth Reports from the Select Committee on Ireland (Commons), *ibid.*, VIII, 4–855; and "Minutes of Evidence" (Lords), *ibid.*, IX, 1–675.]

undue demands on the part of all these persons he has no remedy: that there is no law, no administration of justice for *him*; the superior courts being at all times inaccessible to him, and those of the country magistrates who do not take bribes, being for the most part leagued together to deny him redress; which is in general the less difficult, as the defects of the law are such, that he who would oppress under color of the law must be exceedingly unskilful if he cannot accomplish his object without incurring the penalties of the law.

All these causes of misery, and of that discontent which does, and, we hope, ever will, accompany all remediable evils, are perfectly independent of the Catholic disabilities, and would in no respect be affected by their removal. And why should we deem it impossible to apply remedies to these evils, leaving the Catholic disabilities as they are? That "purer administration of justice," which even the bishop of Chester* admits to be necessary, would of itself suffice, and without it nothing will suffice, to tranquillize Ireland. It is not the power of the Protestant over the Catholic, which has made Ireland what she is: it is the power of the rich over the poor.

A superficial observer might perhaps infer, from the active demonstrations of hostility between the two sects, that it is the Catholics who are oppressed as Catholics, not the poor as poor, and that the body of the people, if they were not oppressed as Catholics, would not be oppressed at all. But if, in removing the Catholic disabilities, the power of landlords over tenants, of the tithe-owner over the tithe-payer, and of magistrates over the great body of the people, were left untouched, we cannot perceive that the condition of the Irish peasantry would be in any respect altered for the better. There is no evidence that a Catholic landlord treats his tenants better than a Protestant landlord. Catholic emancipation would not affect the mode of collecting tithe; and the few Catholic magistrates that there are, have now an interest in protecting the poor against their brother magistrates, which, in the event of emancipation, it is possible they might not retain.

That the Protestant aristocracy, who are now in possession of a monopoly of political power and of its attendant profit, should be averse to sharing that power and profit with the Catholic aristocracy, is quite natural. It is quite natural also that the Catholic aristocracy should feel uneasy under this forced exclusion: and as the aristocracy are much better able to make their complaints heard, than the people are, it is also natural that their grievances should be more thought of, than those of the people; but we are not therefore to suppose them of more importance.

There still remains another question to be answered, before we proceed with our comment upon the debates. If the Catholic disabilities be not in reality the grand evil of Ireland, how happens it that, in the two Houses of Parliament, they are so often spoken of as if they were?

---

*[Charles James Blomfield, Speech on Roman Catholic Relief (17 May, 1825),] *PH* [1825], p. 239.

Questions of this sort are what, in the sequel of this work, we shall very frequently have occasion to put.

In reviewing the proceedings of Parliament, it may in general be remarked, that the great abuses almost always escape its notice. The composition of the Parliament affords a key to this, as it does to so many of its other peculiarities.

The truth is, that there is scarcely an individual in either House whose interest it is that the great abuses should be reformed. The members of both Houses belong, almost all of them, to those classes for the benefit of which all great abuses exist; and not being accountable to, nor in any other way under the influence of, that much larger class, who suffer by the abuses, they have abundant motives to uphold, and no sufficient motive to redress them.

This interest being common to both parties in the two Houses of Parliament, the great abuses are, in Parliamentary discussions, by a sort of tacit consent kept out of view. The Opposition party, however, must have something to attack; or they could shew no ground for finding fault with the party in power. Nothing, therefore, remains for them to do, except to fall might and main upon the small abuses, and do every thing in their power to cause them to be taken for great ones.

To apply these principles to the case now in hand. Here is a country, the most miserable, and at the same time the most turbulent, of all countries pretending to civilization; and that, under a set of institutions, which all—that is, all who derive either money or power from them—unite in designating as the best institutions that wisdom ever devised for the government of mankind. Here then is an anomaly to be explained; a cause must be found for it, and that too without imputing blame to these admirable institutions. The Catholic Question, appearing well adapted to the purpose, is eagerly laid hold of by the Whigs, and a part of the Tories, and exalted into a sovereign remedy for the ills of Ireland. It answers the purposes of the Whigs, by affording a handle for attacking the ministry, who, having such a *panacea* in their hands, neglect to apply it. It serves the purposes of both sections of the Tories, by diverting the public attention, from much more important grievances. All parties being thus interested in making as much noise about this question as possible, it is not wonderful that so much noise has been made.

* * * * *

The subject which chiefly engaged the attention of Parliament, on the day of its meeting, and for some time afterwards, was the Catholic Association. We need not inform our readers what this Association was: it may, however, be of some use to put them in mind of its objects. It held meetings—and it raised money. At the meetings, certain persons, mostly Catholics, and of the higher ranks, were in the habit of expressing, in strong language, their dissatisfaction at the existing state of things in Ireland, chiefly as it regarded the Catholic disabilities. To what purposes the money was applied, has never been fully made known: the offer of the

Association to produce their books not having been accepted by Parliament.[*] Part of it, however, is known to have been laid out in defraying the law expenses of such persons as had been, or were supposed to have been, injured, and were too poor to seek redress for themselves. The Association, moreover, put forth at least one address to their Catholic countrymen, earnestly exhorting them to remain peaceable and obedient to the laws.

Bodies of men very seldom act wisely: and it was little to be expected that a body of Irishmen should form an exception to the rule.

All men love power: most men love it better than any other thing, human or divine. There are times when, by joining in sufficient numbers, and acting in a body, men are enabled to exercise very considerable power. In this power, every man among them is eager to participate, by giving himself up heart and soul to the prosecution of the common design. The only part, however, of their joint operations which displays power, is the *acting* part; and this, accordingly, is the only part in which every man is eager to take a share. But to wise conduct, *thinking* is necessary, as well as acting. Thinking, however, is trouble: to the mass of mankind it is the most insupportable of all kinds of trouble: and trouble being pain, and pain being a thing which every body avoids as much as he can, we find that, as a general rule, a man will never do any thing requiring trouble, which he thinks he can, without too great a sacrifice, prevail upon another person to do for him. While every individual, therefore, is eager to *act*, the business of *thinking* for the whole body generally falls into the hands of a few: and these few will naturally be those who are known to the greatest numbers; the noisiest talkers, who, even when they have no private interest of their own to serve, are very seldom the best thinkers. As, moreover, people are naturally guided, other things being the same, by those who profess the greatest zeal to serve them; and as one very obvious mode of shewing zeal in a man's service, is to rail vehemently against those whom he considers to be his enemies; the leaders will, in addition to their other attributes, be in general among the most intemperate of the set.

These considerations would have prepared us to expect much intemperance of language in the speeches of the Association, and no very great measure of wisdom in their acts. The most foolish of their acts, however, as far as they are known (and let it be remembered by whose fault they are not all known) were not of a nature to do much harm to any body except to themselves. Considering the number of persons interested in bringing whatever was exceptionable either in their purposes or in their measures to light, it is astonishing how little has appeared but what was allowable, if not laudable. The purpose of tranquillizing the Irish people was undoubtedly a laudable purpose; the purpose of exciting attention to their own claims, cannot well be said to be a blameable one. The purpose of giving the poor man access to that justice which the expensiveness of the law has put out of the

[*See *ibid.*, pp. 120–1 (18 Feb., 1825).]

reach of every man who does not come with a full purse in his hand,—this surely was among the most laudable of all purposes. And suppose that occasionally a party in the wrong were by their assistance enabled to come into court, and be told publicly, by judge and jury, that he was in the wrong—for that was the only privilege which their assistance conferred upon him—was this a thing to be complained of? There would be little use in a public trial, if no one were to have the benefit of it until it had first been ascertained that the right was on his side. Until *malâ fide* suitors shall wear their characters stamped in large letters upon their foreheads, a public investigation is, and ought to be, the privilege of every one, whether an honest man or a knave.

Such, however, as they were, these proceedings of the Association gave great alarm to the Protestant aristocracy of Ireland. The *few*, in every country, are remarkable for being easily alarmed; more especially when any one takes upon himself to censure their acts. So easily are they frightened at censure, that they never seem to feel secure until they imagine that they have put a stop to it entirely; and whenever they have been able, they have treated such censure as a crime which could never be punished too severely. It is no wonder, therefore, that they should have taken alarm at the Catholic Association. They did take alarm at it a year before. Even then, as Mr. Canning said, the ministers were "goaded" to put it down;* and, as the Association went on, the alarm increased, and ministers were "goaded" more and more, till at last they were goaded into compliance.[*] That which a large portion of their parliamentary supporters really and earnestly demand, the ministers, if they would continue ministers, cannot long persist in refusing.

At the opening of Parliament, it was stated from the throne, that there existed associations in Ireland, which had "adopted proceedings irreconcileable with the spirit of the constitution," and were "calculated, by exciting alarm and exasperating animosities, to endanger the peace of society, and to retard the course of national improvement."[†]

What is called a King's speech enjoys a prescriptive right to be unmeaning, and we are not disposed to find fault with it for being so in the present instance. We cannot refrain, however, from representing to the framers of the speech, that a *sic volo sic jubeo* would have been more decent than the mere pretence of a reason. Such vague phrases as "irreconcileable with the spirit of the constitution," "endanger the peace of society," and the like, deserve no better name. They are not reasons; they are mere expressions of dislike. When a cause affords no better reason, there is little to be said for it: when it does, these phrases are useless, and can serve at best no higher purpose than that of swelling a period.

*[George Canning, Speech on the Address from the Throne (3 Feb., 1825),] *ibid.*, p. 38.
[*See 6 George IV, c. 4 (1825).]
[†Speech from the Throne ("King's Speech"; 3 Feb., 1825), *PH*, 1825, p. 29.]

If the King's speech afforded few reasons, and those few of little worth, the subsequent speeches made ample amends, in quantity of reasons, if not in quality. We will lay before our readers the whole catalogue. We imagine that the more rational and sober among the Anti-Catholics will view it with as little complacency as we ourselves.

It was alleged, then, of the Catholic Association, 1st, that its tendency was to overthrow the constitution; 2nd, that the language of some of its members was inflammatory; 3d, that it imposed taxes, issued proclamations, made laws, and in fact, exercised all the powers of government; 4th, that its business was to evade and nullify the laws; 5th, that it was a convention; 6th, that it was an *imperium in imperio*; 7th, that it frustrated the effect of beneficial measures of government; 8th, that it diverted the attention of the people from honest industry; 9th, that its subscriptions were collected by Catholic priests; 10th, that it retarded emancipation; 11th, that it adjured the Catholics "by the hatred they bore to Orangemen";[*] 12th, that it was a second Parliament, and used parliamentary forms; 13th, that it employed coercion in levying the Catholic rent; 14th, that it prevented capital from flowing into Ireland; 15th, that it pandered to the prejudices and passions of the multitude; 16th, that it interfered with the administration of justice; 17th, that even in cautioning the people to be quiet, it libelled the law; 18th, that its members, in their speeches, made attacks on private character; 19th, that it named those who should and should not be returned as members of Parliament; 20th, that it had not its freedom of speech from the crown, nor could the crown suspend it; 21st, that if it had power to quell disturbances, it had power to raise them; 22nd, that it could sit whenever it pleased; 23rd, that if it continued, it would demand the Church property; 24th, that it was the machinery of a rebellion, for the time when an occasion might arrive.

Of these twenty-four *reasons*, we abandon twenty-one to the justice and mercy of the reader. The remaining three we reserve in our own hands: viz. the inflammatory speeches; the levying of the rent, and the interference of the Association in the administration of justice.

By inflammatory language is, of course, meant, language calculated to excite hostility. Now whether hostility, and the language of hostility, be blameable or not, depends upon the occasion, and the manner. Both the occasion and the manner were in this case very peculiar.

Here is a country of which it has been said by a Lord Chancellor—Lord Redesdale—who will not be suspected of aspiring to that character which another Lord Chancellor says, he has lived too long to have much respect for, the character of a *reformer*:*—Here is a country, we say, in which a Lord Chancellor says, that there is one law for the rich, and another for the poor. Here is a people, who,

[*See p. 74n below.]
*[John Scott, Speech on Roman Catholic Relief (17 May, 1825),] *PH* [1825], p. 249.

having but the smallest pittance beyond what is barely sufficient to sustain life, are compelled to give up nearly the whole of that pittance to build churches and pay clergymen for about one-fourteenth part of their number: in return for which, that fourteenth part take every opportunity of expressing their hatred and contempt for those who furnish them with money for these purposes, and their firm determination to extort as much more money from them, for other purposes of all sorts, as they can. Now then comes the Catholic Association, and, addressing itself to the thirteen-fourteenths, tells them that all this misery and degradation is not the work of nature, but of men; powerful men, who produce it for their own advantage, who for their own advantage will continue it as long as they have power, and who therefore, as a first step to effecting any improvement, must be deprived of power. This may be called exasperating animosities; in a certain sense, it is exasperating animosities: to tell the many in what way the few have treated them, certainly has no tendency to make them love the few: and if the Catholic Association are to be tried by this standard, their cause, we fear, must be given up: as must also that of all other reformers, ancient or modern. If it be always a crime to excite animosities, it must be always a crime to expose abuses. If the exposure is to be deferred until it can be made in such language as will excite sentiments of affection and good-will towards the authors of the abuses, it would be as reasonable, and more honest, to say, that it is not to be made at all.

The language of the weaker party is ever inflammatory; that of the stronger, never: because it is the stronger who is the judge. A man may rail as much as he pleases at the party which is undermost, and the language which he makes use of will not be very nicely scanned: he may inflame the passions of the powerful; he may incite those to tyrannize, who have it in their power to tyrannize; and "every thing is as it should be."[*] But let him address himself to the weak; let him attempt to stir them up, not to tyrannize, for that is not in their power, but to use their efforts to take from the strong *their* power of tyrannizing—and the state is going to wreck: sedition, insurrection are abroad: and one would imagine that heaven and earth were coming together.

It is a mockery to tell a man that he is wronged, and to bid him at the same time feel no hostility against those who have wronged him. The proper exhortation is, not to let his feelings of hostility overcome his reason, and drive him to acts of useless and wicked violence: not to wreak his vengeance upon the hay-stacks and barns of those who have acted so ill a part towards him, nor to set fire to their houses, and burn them and their families alive; but to direct all his energies to one great object, the ridding them of their mischievous power. Now all this, the Catholic Association did. It not only exhorted the people to be peaceable, but many of its enemies acknowledge, that it actually made them so.

[*William Blackstone's phrase, undoubtedly taken by Mill from Jeremy Bentham; see *A Fragment on Government*, in *Works*, Vol. I, p. 230.]

When a man has resolved to do a thing, and has it in his power, any reason will in general suffice. If the Association had not pacified the Irish, that would have been a reason for putting it down: but it did pacify the Irish: and this also was a reason for putting it down. It was discovered, that, as it had power, to quell disturbances, it probably had power to raise them: and as it was probable that it had the power, it could not but appear certain that it had the will. Upon this principle, we should be justified in throwing a man into prison, for helping a drowning person out of a river. If he had power to drag him out, he has power to push him in: so dangerous a man must not be suffered to go at large: no time must be lost in depriving him of the means of doing mischief.

It seems, however, that they had a way of pacifying the people, which made it much worse than if they had bid them go and cut throats: they adjured them to be peaceable, "by the hatred they bore to Orangemen:" it being deemed preferable by certain members of Parliament, that they should slaughter and burn the Orangemen, probably out of love, than live with them, out of hatred, in the peace of God and of the king. We will not now go over Dr. Lushington's argument, which instead of answering, Mr. Canning sneered at, and put to flight a whole army of syllogisms with a volley of jokes.[*] But we do think that the Orangemen, who so rigidly act up to the Christian principle of returning good for evil, should make some allowance for the frailty of those inferior natures which fail of reaching that standard of perfection. They should bear in mind that all men cannot, like *them*, love their enemies, turn the left cheek to those that smite them on the right, and do good to those that hate them, and despitefully use them.[†] Pure as they are themselves from all malignant passions, Christianity does not surely enjoin so much severity, towards those who aim at no more than to make those passions subservient to virtue. We have no great objection to a species of hatred, which inspires men to obey the laws, and be good citizens and peaceable subjects.

We pass to the accusation of levying money, by improper means, from the people.

The Catholic Association was not the only association which was in the habit of levying money from the people. To say nothing of any others, the Methodist Conference is accustomed to levy money to a much greater amount, and for purposes much more strictly sectarian.* As therefore the receiving of the money could not, without too gross a violation of decency, be adduced as the heinous part of the offence; a vigorous attempt was made to get up a case which should shew that the subscriptions were obtained by coercion. It was first said, that the priests

[*Stephen Lushington, Speech on Unlawful Societies in Ireland (14 Feb., 1825), *PH*, 1825, pp. 88–9; Canning, Speech on Unlawful Societies in Ireland (15 Feb., 1825), *ibid.*, p. 98.]

[†Luke, 6: 27–9.]

*See Mr. [Henry Peter] Brougham's speech [on Unlawful Societies in Ireland (15 Feb., 1825)], *PH* [1825], pp. 104–5.

were in the habit of encouraging and collecting the rent: which not being denied, it was next insinuated, that they extorted subscriptions by refusing the sacraments to those who did not subscribe. We say insinuated, because it was only spoken of as a possibility; and upon this possibility the House was called upon to legislate. It was not shewn that the priests *did* as was represented, it being sufficient that they *could* do so, without violating their religion: this last was, indeed, denied by the Catholic prelates; but then it was affirmed by Mr. Goulburn,* and the Solicitor General.†

Without cavilling at this logic; which, however, if nicely looked into, might probably be found to be not quite formal; we will content ourselves with asking one question. Since after all no *physical* coercion was used, what definition is it possible to give of *moral* coercion? Or how are we to distinguish that legitimate influence, by which the Rev. Mr. Wilson persuades his parishioner to give, through the fear of God, his guinea to the Bible Society, from that improper influence, that coercion (since that is the word) by which the Catholic priest persuades *his* parishioners to give, through a similar fear, their several pennies to the Catholic rent? We might also ask, if the peasant can be persuaded to give money, in order to purchase absolution, how it is expected, that this sort of traffic should be put a stop to by an Act of Parliament? But we have not space to follow out this question as we could wish.

Another sort of coercion, it was positively affirmed, was practised, not by the priests, but by the Association itself. This consisted in making entries in a book, which was called the black book, of the names of all those who refused to subscribe.‡ Without repeating the question, which we put just now, or asking how a pretence can ever be wanting to the strong man, if such a proceeding as this is to be called coercion; we will content ourselves with one fact. It was publicly stated by Mr. Brougham,§ in behalf of the Association, that the names of those who refused to subscribe were *not* entered in *any* book: proof of this assertion was offered to be presented at the bar of the House; and the House would not hear it: the fact speaks for itself.¶

The only remaining charge against the Association, which we intend to notice,

---

*[Henry Goulburn, Speech on Unlawful Societies in Ireland (10 Feb., 1825),] *ibid.*, p. 52. [In this speech Goulburn quotes (p. 53) from the Catholic Association the words about hatred to Orangemen cited by Mill at pp. 71 and 73 above.]

†[Charles Wetherell, Speech on Unlawful Societies in Ireland (18 Feb., 1825),] *ibid.*, p. 112.

‡See the speeches [on Unlawful Societies in Ireland (18 Feb., 1825)] of Mr. [Robert] Peel (*ibid.*, p. 115), and of the Solicitor General [Wetherell] (*ibid.*, p. 112).

§[Henry Brougham, Speech on Unlawful Societies in Ireland (18 Feb., 1825),] *ibid.*, p. 120.

¶Another assertion made by the enemies of the Association (see Lord Liverpool's speech [on Unlawful Societies in Ireland (3 Mar., 1825)], *ibid.*, p. 140), that a peasant had been distrained upon, for non-payment of the Catholic rent, was summarily contradicted by Lord Kingston upon the spot [*ibid.*, p. 143].

is one to which we have already made some allusion: the charge of interference with the administration of justice. We do not know very well how to meet this charge; having some difficulty in discerning through the vague and misty language of the accusers, what sort of improper conduct it is, that was really imputed to the Association. One of them, indeed, Mr. W. Lamb, has not left *his* sentiments on the subject uncertain.

> There was already too much disposition, [said he,] about the lower orders, even in England, to litigation. Every body knew, that if half the indictments and causes which were tried in courts were entirely omitted, it would be for the benefit of all the parties concerned in them. Then, if people would go to law, and prosecute each other needlessly, at their own expense, and even to their own ruin, where would be the end of petty ill-blood and dissension, when they were enabled to do that free of cost!*

It having been made quite clear, by these shrewd observations, that the great fault of the judicial administration of both countries is, that justice is too accessible; that the only use of an administration of justice is to create "petty ill-blood and dissension," and that it is a great crime to have been wronged; it is no wonder that Mr. Lamb should condemn the Catholic Association: who, instead of lamenting, with him, that people should apply for justice, were perverse enough to tell them that it was their due; and even gave them money to assist them in obtaining it.

Others said, that the Association, by putting forth *ex parte* statements, biassed the minds of the jury, and deprived those whom they prosecuted of their fair chance for justice. And this, we believe, is what the charge of "interfering with the administration of justice"[*] amounts to. In proof of this, two instances were given, and no more, of what were considered to have been improper prosecutions by the Association. In both these instances, Mr. Brougham succeeded in rendering the impropriety of the prosecution at least a matter of doubt.[†] But let us see what it is that is to be proved, and what it is that is given in evidence to prove it. The assertion is, that the minds of juries were prejudiced against the persons whom the Association selected for prosecution; and the proof is, two prosecutions in both of which the prisoners were *acquitted.*

One word on the subject of prejudging, and *ex parte* statements: a subject which we thought had long ago been set at rest for ever. What notion can these gentlemen have of trial by jury, if they imagine that jurymen, who have sworn to decide according to the *evidence*, will suffer themselves to be biassed by the vague rumours, the extrajudicial and unsupported *opinions*, which they have heard out of doors? If this be a true character of an Irish jury, either an Irish jury must be a very different thing from an English one, or jury trial is altogether a very different thing from what it is supposed to be.

*[William Lamb, Speech on Unlawful Societies in Ireland (15 Feb., 1825),] *ibid.*, p. 93.
[*Goulburn, speech of 10 Feb., 1825, *ibid.*, p. 52.]
[†Henry Brougham, speech of 15 Feb., 1825, *ibid.*, pp. 102–3.]

When it has been determined that a thing is at all events to be found fault with, it is usual, in making an account of its effects, to strike out all the good items, and leave the bad ones standing alone: to hold up to view the possible evils which may arise from it, and to say nothing of the necessarily accompanying good. When publicity was given, by the Catholic Association, to the whole story of the supposed offence, the minds of the jury, say these gentlemen, might possibly be biassed against the prisoner: well—we grant them this; let them make what they can of it. But may not this very publication raise up persons, to bear witness in his favour? Is it nothing that the public eye has been attracted to the case, and fixed anxiously upon the behaviour of the judge and the jury? And is it no advantage, to the prisoner himself, to know the prosecutor's case,—the assertions which he intends to make, and the evidence by which he expects to prove them? What could be of more use to the defendant in a cause, than that the counsel for the prosecution should allow him to inspect his brief? Surely then it is no injury to him, that all which is contained in that brief should be made, before the trial, a subject of public discussion.

* * * * *

The petition of the Catholics of Ireland for emancipation was presented to the House of Commons on the first of March by Sir Francis Burdett, who, on the same evening, moved a string of resolutions setting forth the expediency of granting the Catholic claims.[*] The motion was introduced by what is termed a conciliatory speech; that is to say, a speech in which every body found himself praised, who had any reason for expecting that he would be blamed. "A more enlightened and liberal body of men" than the clergy of the Church of England, "did not do honour to this or any other country. The Church of England was, of all others, the faith he would rather adopt," and no wonder, if we consider the excellent reason he had for adopting it: he had been "bred up" in it, "as ample a reason as any man could be called on to give for his religion."* The Orangemen, too, were nearly perfect. "There did not exist more honourable or more liberal men." They had, to be sure, one small failing, an "unfortunate propensity to domination;" an "unwillingness to be deprived of the power they had been accustomed to exercise;" a "right which they fancied they had by birth, to trample upon their Catholic fellow-subjects."†
They had no fault, in short, but a desire to *get* and *keep*, at all costs, as great a quantity of undue power as they could. We would ask, in what other habit of mind the worst acts of the worst tyrants have taken their rise? What else was it that

---

[*Leading to "A Bill to Provide for the Removal of the Disqualifications under Which His Majesty's Roman Catholic Subjects Now Labour," 6 George IV (23 Mar., 1825), *PP*, 1825, III, 441–50 (not enacted).]

*[Francis Burdett, Speech in Presenting a Petition (1 Mar., 1825),] *PH* [1825], p. 151.
†*Ibid.*, p. 152.

prompted the crimes of an Augustus or an Aurungzebe? What else made an Alexander or a Napoleon the scourges of mankind?

There is no mistake which seems to be more universal among public men, not to speak of other men of all descriptions, than that of imagining it to be of no consequence what they do with their praise. In most other matters it seems to be pretty generally understood that the gift which is meant to be valued must be sparingly bestowed: but no measure, no temperance, is thought necessary in the distribution of praise; people seem in general to be ready to throw it at the first dog they meet. After what fashion men bepraise their *friends*, the proceedings at any public dinner will testify. At such entertainments (next to eating and drinking), the principal purpose for which the guests are assembled, seems in general to be that of receiving assurances from one another that they are patterns of every human virtue. Most men, too, are glad of any decent opportunity for bestowing laudation upon their *opponents*. It has so candid an appearance, and men are so naturally, and even so properly, eager to shew that they have no private hatred of those to whom they are politically hostile, that, even in bringing accusations against their opponents, which, if true, import the very essence of imbecillity and wickedness, they frequently clothe them in language expressive of the most profound veneration.

If Sir Francis Burdett,—after representing the state of things in Ireland as uniting a flagrant breach of faith with the most odious tyranny—after characterizing the Orangemen as the upholders of this state of things, and imputing to them as motives, a "propensity to domination" and a fancied right to "trample upon their Catholic fellow-subjects,"—can yet affirm, in the same breath, that "there did not exist more honourable or more liberal men" than these same Orangemen; how is it possible, henceforth, to set any value on any praise which *he* can bestow? We are not blaming the disposition to conciliate opponents; and we have the strongest objections to vague and general vituperation: but excessive praise, much more that which is totally unmerited, is equally mischievous, and almost equally offensive.

Bating this one fault, which, however much to be regretted, is too common not to be quite venial, and which we are far from imputing to any but the most creditable motives; the tone of Sir F. Burdett's speech was highly commendable. In some of his reasonings we are not quite sure that we concur; in particular where he partly founds the claims of the Catholics upon the treaty of Limerick. We are favourable to those claims, because we are unfavourable, on general principles, to all religious distinctions; unless when there is strong ground for them in point of expediency, which, in the case of the British Catholics, we think that there is not: but if there were,—if it were really dangerous to admit the Catholics into a participation of political power,—we are by no means prepared to say that we should be bound to incur this danger, because certain persons, none of whom are now in existence, promised something about a hundred and thirty years ago, to certain other persons, none of whom are now in existence. Every man is bound to keep his promise—agreed: that is, he ought not to make the promise, unless he is sure that he can keep it. But that the Government of *that* day should be at liberty to make promises which should be binding under all circumstances upon the Government of *this*, or that we should be pledged to do for one set of men, whatever our ancestors promised to do for another, is a maxim of much wider extent, and we will add, of much more dubious propriety. Granting, for the sake of the argument, that the Catholics of that day, though all of them partisans of the exiled family, were wronged by the non-fulfilment of the pledge which was given to them at Limerick: nothing which can be done *now*, will be any reparation to *them*. The question at present is, what is to be done with *another* set of men professing the same religion, but in no other conceivable sense the same, and who, whatever claims they may have upon our justice, or our humanity, can have none upon our good faith, since our faith has never been plighted to them. The fallacy of *irrevocable laws* is alike absurd, in every one of its shapes.

Mr. Leslie Foster, Mr. Peel, and the Solicitor General, followed in the debate,[*] on the side opposed to the Catholics, and set forth, at considerable length, the badness of the Catholic religion, the intolerance of Catholics in other countries, &c. &c., all which being very little to the purpose, unless it could be shewn that they would derive an increase of power for bad purposes, from the concession of their claims, the following arguments were thrown as a makeweight into the scale: 1. Grant this, and they will ask for more:* (fallacy of *distrust*). 2. "This concession to the Catholics would involve a violation of the Constitution: Was not the principle of the Protestant religion in church and *state*, made a fundamental and inviolable part of the compact with King William III after the expulsion of James II?[†] and would they abandon that indispensable principle of the Bill of Rights?"† (fallacies of *irrevocable laws*, and *vague generalities*, cloaking a *petitio principii*).[‡] 3. The House ought not to yield to menace and intimidation:‡ or, in other words, having driven the Catholics to exasperation by denying them justice, they were to make that exasperation a reason for denying it to them still longer. 4. The great men, who framed the Act of Union with Scotland,[§] introduced into that measure the principle of excluding Catholics from office:§ (fallacies of

[*John Leslie Foster, Robert Peel, and Wetherell, Speeches on Roman Catholic Claims (1 Mar., 1825), *ibid.*, pp. 154, 160–3, and 155–6, respectively.]

*Solicitor General [Wetherell], *ibid.*, p. 155. Mr. Peel, *ibid.*, p. 162. [For the fallacy of distrust, see Peregrine Bingham, "Prefatory Treatise on Political Fallacies," *Parliamentary Review* (hereafter cited as *PR*), 1825, pp. 12–13.]

[†1 William and Mary, second session, c. 2 (1688).]
†Solicitor General, [speech of 1 Mar., 1825,] *PH* [1825], p. 156.
[‡See Bingham, "Prefatory Treatise," pp. 8–10 and 20–1.]
‡Solicitor General, [speech of 1 Mar., 1825,] *PH* [1825], p. 155.
[§6 Anne, c. 6 (1707).]
§Mr. Peel, [speech of 1 Mar., 1825,] *PH* [1825], p. 161.

irrevocable laws, and *wisdom of ancestors*).[*] 5. Retaining the religion of the minority as the religion of the state, would it be safe to allow the majority to come into an equal participation with them of rights and power?*—A mere assumption, in the first place; and in the next place, it looks a little too much like the argument of the highwayman who ties your hands in order that he may more safely rob you.

Mr. Plunkett and Mr. Brougham, without grappling with the question, pointedly exposed some of the fallacies of their opponents, and addressed themselves to the House in the manner which alone has much influence with an interested audience, by appealing to their fears.[†] In the present case, it was not possible to act upon this passion but through the medium of a fallacy. The two assumptions, upon which these gentlemen proceeded, were that Catholic emancipation *would,* and that, without that measure, any thing else would *not,* tranquillize the Irish people.† The unconscious action of those interests, to which we have before pointed as the secret springs of the conduct both of Whigs and Tories on this question, will sufficiently account for the course pursued by both these gentlemen. But to those who desire the passing of this question on its own account, and on its own account solely, we recommend a much more effectual mode of frightening its opponents into concession. Let them drag forth and hold up to view the real evils of Ireland: let them assail the abuses of the Church, the Law, and the Magistracy: and the alarmed participators in the profits of these abuses will soon consent to forego the small interest, which they have in the exclusion of Catholics from office, in hopes of disarming some portion of the opposition to those much greater evils, to which they are indebted for so much of *their* wealth, and *their* power, the power of the few over the many.

In the interval between this first debate on the Catholic question in the Commons, and its final rejection in the Lords,[‡] much of the time of both Houses was occupied by angry discussions, arising out of the petitions which were presented for and against the bill. This, which would have required no notice if it had occurred only once, having been repeated so often as to become a marked feature in the history of the Session, we will not omit those observations which appear to us to be applicable to it.

[*See Bingham, "Prefatory Treatise," pp. 8–10 and 6–7.]
*Mr. Peel, [speech of 1 Mar., 1825,] *PH* [1825], p. 162.
[†William Conyngham Plunket and Henry Brougham, Speeches on Roman Catholic Claims (1 Mar., 1825), *ibid.,* pp. 157–60 and 163–5, respectively.]
†Mr. Brougham went so far, not long after, as to say of Catholic emancipation—"Grant that to the people of Ireland, and it would allay all dissensions and disturbances—it would give us their hearts, and in giving us their hearts, it would secure our dominion over them, so that a world in arms should not be able to wrest it from us." See [Speech on the Catholic Clergy of Ireland (29 Apr., 1825),] *ibid.,* p. 208.
[‡I.e., between 1 Mar. and 17 May, 1825. See *ibid.,* pp. 150 and 250.]

The grand object, with both parties, in these discussions, was to make it appear that public opinion was in their favour. When a petition was presented, either from the friends or the opponents, but particularly from the opponents of the bill, up started somebody on the contrary side to prove that the petition did *not*, followed by somebody on the same side with the petitioners, to prove that it *did*, represent the true state of public opinion on the question. All this solicitude about public opinion clearly shewed how nicely the two parties were balanced. When either of them is sure of a majority, right or wrong, it seldom troubles itself much about public opinion.

The meaning (if it had any meaning) of all this talk, must have been either, 1st. That, if the public were with them, they must necessarily be in the right, (*vox populi, vox Dei*);[*] or, 2nd. That public opinion had declared itself so strongly on one side, that for Parliament to take the opposite side, however right at other times, would at this time be unsafe, and therefore wrong. The first supposition (the fallacy of *authority*, in its least delusive shape)[†] is too obviously absurd, to be imputed to any body: and the very fact, that there could be any dispute upon the subject, proves the falsity of the second. Those who felt sufficient interest in the question to put their names to a petition being in number no more than a minute fraction of the public, and these being nearly equally divided, things were exactly in that state in which it was quite certain that Parliament might take either course without one atom of risk from public opinion. To what end, then, all these acrimonious discussions?

If we disapprove of the end, we disapprove equally of the means; we see as much to blame in the tone and spirit which characterized the discussions, as we do in the discussions themselves.

It is a principle of human nature, as well established as any principle can be, that, taking men as they are (that is, ninety-nine out of every hundred of them), a man's opinion, as such, is of no value, on any matter in which his interest is concerned. Not only the assertion of the knave, but the unfeigned opinion of the honest man, if he be not a man of an unusually powerful mind, is sure to follow any strong interest, or fancied interest. On this principle nobody attaches any weight to the opinion of a Catholic, in favour of Catholic emancipation: and, on the same principle, no weight ought to be attached to the opinion of a clergyman of the Church of England, against that measure.

It admits of no question that the clergy of the Established Church in general apprehend great danger to the Church, from the concession of the Catholic claims. The clergy of an establishment, and dissenters from the establishment, are seldom on very good terms with one another; and the clergy, knowing that no Catholic can possibly approve of a Protestant church establishment, imagine that the establish-

[*Alcuin, Letter to Charlemagne, in *Opera omnia*, Vols. C–CI of Jacques Paul Migne, ed., *Patrologiae cursus completus, series latina* (Paris: Migne, 1851), Vol. C, col. 438.]
[†Cf. Bingham, "Prefatory Treatise," p. 5.]

ment would go to pieces immediately if a single Catholic were admitted into power. The correctness or incorrectness of this notion, is not now in question; its existence is all that we are arguing for; and while it exists, every body must perceive that the clergy are as incompetent witnesses on Catholic emancipation, as they would be on the expediency of the Church Establishment itself.

When, therefore, petitions were presented from clergymen of the Church of England against the bill; supposing Lord King, or any other supporter of the Catholic claims, to have said any thing, what would it have been proper for him to say? Simply this:—that the petitions came from a body of men, who, as to this question, were an interested body: that if their only object were to shew that the opinions of the petitioners were unfavourable to Catholic emancipation, this was scarcely worth proving, since it was hardly to be expected that they would be favourable; but that if the object of the petitioners were to prove that the measure ought not to pass, they deserved not one particle of regard beyond what might be due to their reasons, if they gave any; and that these were no more than a repetition of what had been said and answered a hundred times in that House.

This would have been common sense, and would have had its effect, both in Parliament and out of it, without the aid of declamation or invective.—The advocates of the Bill took, however, a different course. Instead of shewing that the *opinions* of the clergy, on this question, were worth nothing, they did what was utterly useless as well as irrelevant, they vituperated the *men*. They told them, that they were intolerant, that they were illiberal, that they were deficient in Christian charity; all which language, besides that it assumed the very point at issue, namely, that the sentiments of the petitioners were wrong,—really meant nothing, except that those who used the terms were very much dissatisfied with those to whom they applied them; and moreover had all the appearance of that disposition which is itself the very essence of intolerance, a disposition to apply bad names to others for having a different opinion from ourselves.

The handle which was so injudiciously given by the one party was eagerly laid hold of by the other. They retorted the charge of intolerance upon the impugners of the clergy; they called the clergy a *proscribed* body.* As the other side had begged the question *against* the clergy, they, not content with begging it in their favour, proceeded to something like a threat, saying, that "the petitioners belonged to a body of men whom their lordships would find out one day, as their ancestors had found before them, that they ought to treat with respect, and not with contumely."†

The debate on the second reading of the Catholic bill opened with an exhibition of honesty and courage not often exemplified in public men. Mr. Brownlow, a leading Orangeman, abjured his old opinions, and declared himself a convert to

---

*Bishop of Exeter [William Carey, Speech on Catholic Claims (13 Apr., 1825)], *PH*, 1825, p. 169.

†Bishop of Chester [Charles James Blomfield, Speech on Roman Catholic Claims (29 Mar., 1825)], *ibid.*, p. 168.

the cause of Catholic emancipation.[*] Such things rarely happen in the sphere of party morality, where consistency in right or wrong usurps the praise of honesty, and where the merit of having chosen and for half a century rigidly adhered to that path which is the shortest cut to honour, wealth, and power, is accepted as an equivalent for every quality which goes to make a good minister or an honest statesman.* Where the interests of rival parties have succeeded in rendering almost infamous the highest act of virtue perhaps which a public man can perform, we hail with joy the dawn of a better morality in the public recantation of Mr. Brownlow. The manner in which that recantation was received is among the most striking marks of the improving spirit of the age.

At the same time, we must be permitted to remark, sorry as we are to say any thing which may seem indicative of a wish to tarnish the credit which Mr. Brownlow has so justly earned,—that his new opinions, upon his own shewing, have scarcely more foundation in reason than his old ones; and we should not be surprised if some of the late proceedings of the New Catholic Association were to shake his recently acquired liberality, and re-incline him to his former prejudices.

The evidence before the Committees had wrought, he said, his conversion. Dr. Doyle had declared that two doctrines, the power of the Pope to exercise temporal authority over the subjects of other sovereigns, and his power to grant dispensations for crimes, were not doctrines of the Catholic church. Dr. Doyle certainly did say so.[†] He also said (what Mr. Brownlow did not mention) that these doctrines *never had been* doctrines of that church; by which latter assertion he took away the whole value of the former. If, according to Dr. Doyle, the temporal authority of the Pope is as much a doctrine of the Catholic church as it was when a Gregory or a Boniface fulminated their excommunications and sentences of deposition against kings and emperors; if the power of dispensation is as much a doctrine of the church as it was when indulgences were openly sold from one end of Europe to the other; of what consequence is it that, in the opinion of one man, or of two men (Dr. Doyle and Dr. Murray), these powers were not authorized? Their not being authorized did not prevent their being acted upon then, nor could it prevent them, if an opportunity offered, from being acted upon now. If individual opinions were wanted, we had opinions already; opinions of foreign universities, at least as high authority as Dr. Doyle. As for the Pope, we can hardly conceive any thing more ridiculous than to talk of danger from *him*. The real danger is from the power of the priests, whether concentrated in one man, or

---

[*Charles Brownlow, Speech on Catholic Relief (19 Apr., 1825), *ibid.*, p. 174.]

*Mr. Peel [Speech on the Address from the Throne (4 Feb., 1825)], *ibid.*, p. 43: "Of the Lord Chancellor, he could not speak in terms of adequate praise; but he believed he would go down to posterity as a man of exalted merits, and as the most *consistent politician* who had ever held the great seal."

[†James Warren Doyle, "Evidence Taken before the Select Committee Appointed to Inquire into the State of Ireland," *PP*, 1825, VIII, 190–2 and 195.]

diffused through a great number. If they place the supreme direction in his hands, it is for their own purposes: and if they do not, it is for the same reason. His power is only their power: and does Mr. Brownlow really think that either priests or any other sort of men ever give up any power which they can possibly keep; or are withheld from resuming it by any other reason than because they cannot?

We shall pass slightly over the remainder of the debate. Mr. Dawson brought forward several arguments against emancipation, the chief of which were, that Mr. O'Connell and Dr. Doyle were temperate before the committee but turbulent in Ireland: that the Catholics, in 1824, petitioned parliament for a reform in the temporalities of the Irish church, and that a Catholic parliament treated the Protestants in 1687 pretty much as Protestant parliaments have treated the Catholics ever since.[*] Sufficient answers having been given to these objections, either by the speakers who followed, or in the former part of this article, we shall not waste our readers' time and our own by going over them again.

Mr. Goulburn and Mr. Peel again insisted upon danger to the Constitution, the Church, and the State,[†] but without proving, any more than their predecessors had done, that whatever danger there might be would be in any wise increased by Catholic emancipation. Mr. Peel illustrated his general argument by a particular example; he put the case of a Catholic king, who, by the bill before the House, would have it in his power to appoint a Catholic ministry.[‡] The contingency is somewhat distant, as well as somewhat improbable: but suppose it certain and near at hand; unless a majority in Parliament were Catholics too, what harm could be done by a Catholic king, though backed by a Catholic ministry? If such chimerical terrors are to be listened to, what dangers are we not exposed to already! What is there to hinder the King from turning Presbyterian, and filling every office in the ministry with Presbyterians? yet is this very likely to happen? or where would be the harm if it did? Has the King, with or without a ministry of his choice, the power to change the established religion, against the will of his people? If so, he can as well change the constitution itself; whatever advantages we owe to it, exist only by his sufferance, and the government of this country is in reality despotic. But if not, what becomes of the imaginary danger?

We must now need say something (much we need not) on the celebrated speech of the Duke of York.[§] What there was objectionable in it has been sufficiently exposed by others; and the station of the royal speaker has drawn down animadversions more severe than the speech, if delivered from other lips, would

[*George Dawson, Speech on Roman Catholic Relief (19 Apr., 1825), *PH*, 1825, pp. 175–6.]

[†Goulburn and Peel, Speeches on Roman Catholic Relief (19 and 21 Apr., and 21 Apr., 1825), *ibid.*, pp. 178–80 and 184–6.]

[‡Peel, *ibid.*, p. 185.]

[§Frederick Augustus, Duke of York, Speech on Roman Catholic Claims (25 Apr., 1825), *ibid.*, pp. 187–8.]

probably have called forth. As a piece of argument, it cannot be spoken of seriously; indeed it scarcely laid claim to that character. With the exception of what Mr. Canning called "the idle objection of the coronation oath,"* it only offered one reason, which turned upon the oddest of all *équivoques.* No clergyman can sit in the House of Commons; therefore (said his Royal Highness), the Protestant church, meaning the *clergy,* is not represented; *ergo,* the Catholic church, meaning the *laity,* ought not to be represented either. Considered merely as a declaration of opinion, we have not much to say against this speech: his Royal Highness was as well entitled, as any other person, to choose his side. It may be questioned, however, whether it would have been in any way discreditable to his Royal Highness, if, in testifying his attachment to the opinion he had chosen, he had remembered that even the Heir to the Throne is not infallible, and that it was just possible, that the opinion, to which he was thus solemnly vowing an eternal adherence, might be *wrong.*

In the interval between the second and third reading of the Catholic bill, two auxiliary measures were introduced into the Lower House, which have excited much discussion, and occasioned much difference of opinion, both among the supporters and among the opponents of the Catholic claims.[*]

The question of a state provision for the Catholic clergy does not seem to us encumbered with many difficulties. Such a provision certainly is not *per se* desirable. To a Protestant, it must of course appear desirable that there should be none but Protestants, in which case there would be no Catholic clergy, and consequently no need of paying them.—There are, however, Catholic clergy, and they exercise great influence over the people. We should be very glad to see that influence weakened: but, in the meantime, the question is, whether every thing which can be done ought not to be done, towards rendering it as little noxious as possible.

By the admission of all who know any thing of Ireland, one of the greatest evils of that country is, a deficiency of employment compared with the numbers of the people, or, what is the same thing, an excess of numbers, compared with the means of employment. As the best established general principles forbid us to expect that any measures, having for their object to provide employment for the people, can afford any thing more than a temporary palliation to the evil, whilst their numbers continue to increase at the present rate—there is nothing to be done without correcting the prevailing habit of early marriages and heedless increase of families. But to the introduction of any change in this respect, no state of things can

---

*[Canning, Speech on the State of Ireland (26 May, 1825),] *ibid.,* p. 261. See also [Peregrine Bingham, "Prefatory Treatise"] , *PR,* 1825, p. 9: Fallacy of *Vows.*

[*For the first, a Resolution concerning state provision for a Catholic clergy (29 Apr., 1825), see *PD,* n.s., Vol. 13, cols. 308–36; for the second, "A Bill to Regulate the Exercise of the Elective Franchise in Counties at Large, in Ireland," 6 George IV (22 Apr., 1825), *PP,* 1825, III, 85–6 (not enacted).]

be more adverse than one in which the priests derive their chief emoluments from marriages, baptisms, and funerals.* We make no invidious insinuations; we will not ask, whether the priests have given direct encouragement to those early marriages, which have co-operated with bad government to make the Irish people what they are;† but we say that nothing can be more impolitic, nor can shew a greater ignorance of human nature, than to admit of the continuance of a state of things in which it is their interest to do so.

Whenever, therefore, a public provision shall be granted to the Catholic clergy of Ireland, we hope that the act conferring it will contain a clause, providing, not for the discontinuance of the fees on marriages and baptisms, but for their being regularly handed over to some officer, for the benefit of the public revenue. To reconcile the priests themselves to this transfer, we would suggest that a portion of their stipends should be in name as well as in reality a commutation for their fees. Under this arrangement they would no longer have an interest in encouraging improvident marriages, while the money received on account of fees would in part contribute to defray the expense of the stipends.

Another reason for paying the Catholic clergy, is to diminish the interest they now have in proselytism. Believing, as we do, the Catholic religion to be a bad one, we of course think it undesirable that proselytes should be made to it. The motives to proselytism will be but too strong, without the aid of pecuniary interest: but when the priest's emoluments entirely depend upon the number of his flock, those motives are at the highest pitch. Surely all Protestants should wish this to be at an end.

It deserves notice, that of all those who advocated this measure in the House of

---

*Mr. Dennis Browne says in his Evidence before the Commons' Committee, that the priests have not, at an average, in his part of the country, 100*l*. a-year, and that they get for a marriage sometimes half-a-guinea, sometimes 15*s*., never less than half-a-guinea; independently of the collections made at the wedding among the visitors, which, according to Dr. Doyle, have been known to amount to 40*l*. [For Browne, see *PP*, 1825, VIII, 30; for Doyle, *ibid.*, p. 185.] The Rev. Malachi Duggan, parish priest of Moyferta and Killballyowen, who stated his annual income to be about 200*l*., declared himself to have celebrated in the preceding year about fifty marriages; whereof about thirty produced pounds or guineas each; thirteen produced various sums from 2*l*. 10*s*. to 6*l*.; four produced various sums from 5*s*. to 10*s*.; and three, to the best of his recollection, were gratuitous. Out of an income, therefore, of 200*l*., nearly 90*l*. were derived from the fees on marriages alone. (Rev. M. Duggan's Evidence before the Commons' Committee of 1824 [*ibid.*, pp. 211, 217].)

†See, however, the evidence of Mr. [Thomas] Frankland Lewis, before the Lords' Committee of 1825, who says, "I believe it is known that the priests avow that they do recommend early marriages" ([*ibid.*, IX,] 41); and the evidence of Mr. Leslie Foster, "I believe it is a matter pretty well ascertained, that the Roman Catholic clergy are in the habit of suggesting marriages to young persons, and not merely recommending, but enjoining them." ([*Ibid.*,] p. 66.) See also the evidence of Mr. Justice [Robert] Day (*ibid.*, p. 534,) to the same effect.

Commons, there was not one who placed the expediency of it upon the right grounds. One reason assigned was, that the Catholic clergy were a meritorious body.[*] Another, that it was desirable they should be connected with the state;[†] a proposition in which, if, by connexion with the state, is meant dependence upon the government, we are so far from agreeing, that if the stipends were to be put upon such a footing as to create any such dependence, it would shake our confidence in the expediency of the measure itself. Another reason was, that it was desirable that a portion of the higher classes should form a part of the Catholic clergy.[‡] We do not exactly see why; or how the higher classes could be drawn into it by changing the source of its emoluments; unless at the same time an increase were made in the amount, which would be objectionable on another score.

If the reasons given *for* the measure were bad, the reasons against it were still worse.

The first was, that no provision is made for the clergy of any of the dissenting sects. But there is no other sect, for the payment of whose clergy there are the same reasons.[§]

The second was, that the Catholic clergy, if paid at all, ought to be paid out of the superfluous property of the Established Church: and if the payment could not be made in that way, it ought not, however desirable, to be made at all.[¶]

The third was, that the measure tended to undermine the Established Church. Of this tendency no proof was so much as pretended to be given. But danger to the church is that sort of thing which persons of a certain stamp are accustomed to see in every thing which they do not like.[‖]

The fourth was, that the House ought not to establish a Papal Church, armed with all the jurisdiction belonging to Papacy.* Who would not have supposed that the question before the House was whether there should be a Catholic church in Ireland, or not?

The fifth was, that it would diminish the influence of the Catholic clergy over their flocks. This objection was brought forward in the House by nobody but Mr.

[*See Francis Leveson Gower, Speech on the Roman Catholic Clergy (29 Apr., 1825), *PH*, 1825, p. 204.]

[†*Ibid.*]

[‡*Ibid.*]

[§See William John Bankes, Goulburn, Joseph Hume, and Robert Peel, Speeches on the Roman Catholic Clergy (all on 29 Apr., 1825), *ibid.*, pp. 205, 207, 205, and 206, respectively.]

[¶See Thomas Creevey, Speech on the Roman Catholic Clergy (29 Apr., 1825), *ibid.*, p. 207.]

[‖See Thomas Peregrine Courtenay, Speech on the Roman Catholic Clergy (29 Apr., 1825), *ibid.*, p. 205.]

*Solicitor General [Wetherell, Speech on Roman Catholic Relief (10 May, 1825)], *ibid.*, p. 223.

Goulburn;[*] in whose mouth it seems to be any thing but appropriate: but it is the objection which we have heard oftenest urged in other places. It has not, however, been proved by any sufficient evidence, that the Catholics would like their priests the less for being no longer a burden on them; that they feel the burden most severely, is well known: that the priests' fees were a subject of complaint with the discontented, almost equally with tithes and rents, has been given in evidence by several witnesses before the Committees.* Further, if it were made out, that the influence of the priests would be diminished by a public provision, we should not consider this an evil, but a good; it appearing to us to be any thing but beneficial, either to religion or morality, that a body of priests should exercise any such influence over the people, as is exercised by the Catholic clergy: and the influence of the priests having besides afforded to the enemies of emancipation their most plausible topic of alarm.

The proposed alteration of the elective franchise in Ireland appears at first sight a measure of greater delicacy. To those, however, who look to things rather than names, there is no great difficulty in the question.

The forms of liberty, are one thing; the substance another. These two things are often confounded; and the consequence is, that the substance is very often sacrificed to the forms. There is a certain set of politicians, who maintain it as an established principle, that the substance always *ought* to be sacrificed to the forms; the form being in their estimation every thing, the substance nothing. It is, according to them, not only useful, but essential to good government, that the body of the people should, at every election, go to the poll, and vote for somebody; because this contributes exceedingly to the generation of public spirit: but once there, it is not of the slightest consequence whom they vote for; at least, it is not necessary that they should exercise any choice; or rather, it would be of the most fatal consequence if they did. Elections, according to them, are on the best footing, when there are but two or three real choosers; the two or three thousand, who are the nominal choosers, discharging no other functions, in regard to the favoured candidate, than that of committing to memory his name, and repeating it at the hustings, to a person stationed there to hear it.

This class of politicians find in Ireland a system of election management to their heart's content. Droves of electors, driven to the poll often without knowing, till they reach the spot, the name of the candidate whom they are to vote for; themselves the property of their landlord, a sort of live stock upon the estate, whom nobody thinks of canvassing, and who would probably stare on being told that the franchise (as it is ironically called) was regarded as a privilege to

[**Ibid.*, p. 207.]
*See the evidence of Mr. [Anthony Richard] Blake (p. 40); of Dr. [Daniel] Murray (p. 237); of Dr. [Oliver] Kelly (p. 259), before the Commons' Committee of 1825 [*PP*, 1825, VIII]; and the evidence of Major [Richard] Willcocks (p. 118), before that of 1824 [*ibid.*, VII].

themselves. In one or two instances of late years, when the state of misery to which they were already reduced rendered ejectment from their wretched tenancies an event scarcely to be dreaded, they did, in considerable numbers, break through their subjection, and from being the tools of their landlords, became the tools of their priests: in consequence of which defection they had to endure all the sufferings which the rage of their thwarted taskmasters could inflict upon them.*

It is moreover well established, though in the lamentable ignorance which prevails in this country with respect to Ireland, it seems not to be generally known, that, of those who are called, and give their votes as, forty-shilling freeholders, it is a very small proportion indeed who are really so; the remainder consisting of persons who not only have not an interest to the value of forty shillings in the land, but who pay to their landlords a full, and more than a full rent; and are registered as freeholders by the grossest perjury on their own part, and the grossest subornation or rather compulsion of perjury on that of the Irish gentlemen, their landlords.†

It is true, as was justly observed by Col. Johnson, that the proper remedy for these evils is not disfranchisement, but vote by ballot.[*] Vote by ballot, however, there was no chance of obtaining. Disfranchisement there was a chance of obtaining: it could do no harm, and might do good; by taking away from a few lords of the soil the power of bringing their thousands and tens of thousands to the poll, it would tend to give at least *somewhat* more importance to the small number of electors who can choose for themselves, without drawing down upon their heads inevitable ruin. It is no mark of wisdom to reject what is good, because you cannot have what is better.

On the other hand, we agree with Lord Milton,‡ that the good effects of this measure have been much exaggerated. It has been assumed, as it appears to us on scarcely any evidence, that the desire of making freeholds for electioneering purposes, has been a great cause of the minute subdivision of lands. That it may have been so in one or two instances we do not deny; indeed it is sufficiently proved

---

*See particularly the evidence of Mr. Leslie Foster before the Lords' Committee of 1825, "There have fallen, within my own knowledge, frequent instances of the tenants having been destroyed in consequence of their having voted with their clergy." ([*PP*, 1825, IX,] p. 79.)

†See the evidence of Mr. Blake (p. 43); of Dr. [Oliver] Kelly (p. 252); of Col. [William Samuel] Currey (pp. 303–4); of the Rev. Henry Cooke (p. 372); of the Rev. Thomas Costello (p. 416); of Mr. [John Staunton] Rochfort (pp. 436–7); of Mr. [Matthew] Barrington (pp. 577–8); and of Dr. [William] O'Brien (p. 588), before the Commons' Committee of 1825 [*PP*, 1825, VIII]; the evidence of Mr. Justice [Robert] Day (p. 263), before the Commons' Committee of 1824 [*ibid.*, VII]; of Mr. Leslie Foster (p. 78); Mr. Blake (p. 106); [William Knox,] the Bishop of Derry (p. 280); Mr. [Arthur Irwin] Kelly (p. 492); Mr. Justice Day (p. 534); and Mr. Dominick Browne (pp. 586–7), before the Lords' Committee of 1825 [*ibid.*, IX], &c.

[*William Augustus Johnson, Speech on the Elective Franchise in Ireland (9 May, 1825), *PH*, 1825, p. 213.]

‡[Charles William Wentworth Fitzwilliam, Speech on the Elective Franchise in Ireland (9 May, 1825),] *ibid.*, p. 214.

that it has. But, that, as a general rule, such political influence as the landlords of the predominant party might acquire by splitting farms, over and above what they might have had without it, could act upon them with sufficient force to counterbalance the direct and obvious interest which they have in the good cultivation of their estates, is a conclusion not to be founded on one or two, or even on ten or twenty, instances. That the lands should be parcelled out in small farms, was no more than is natural in a country where, till of late, scarcely any tenants had capital enough to occupy large ones. *Now*, when capital is flowing into the country, the landlords are rapidly clearing their estates of the wretched cottier tenantry; uniting numbers of small farms into one, and introducing a better system of cultivation. Observe that the church lands, on which no freeholds can be created, are just as minutely divided as the rest;* while in England, where political influence is fully as much valued as in Ireland, the land is generally let in large farms: why? because there are farmers possessed of sufficient capital to occupy them; and because it is in general of much more importance to a landlord that his lands should be cultivated by persons of capital and intelligence, than that he should gain a few votes, by means which are equally open to the opposite party, if they are willing to make the same sacrifice.

We, therefore, do not claim for the proposed bill, the merit of giving to Ireland a "sturdy and independent yeomanry;"† we bound its pretensions to those of diminishing, in some small degree, the power of the aristocracy, and putting an end to a great amount of perjury. Though, even for these purposes, we are much inclined, with Mr. Leslie Foster and Mr. Vesey Fitzgerald,[*] to think that it did not take a range sufficiently wide, and that to produce any very sensible improvement, the disfranchisement ought to have extended to freeholders in fee, as well as to freeholders for lives.

In the debates on this question, it may be remarked, that the extremes both of Toryism and of Whiggism were found on one side, and the more moderate of both parties on the other. This anomaly appears to us to have naturally arisen out of the circumstances of the case. The thorough-goers on both sides, in their opposition to this measure, will be found to have been perfectly consistent with themselves; while the more moderate have on this occasion made a sacrifice of party principles, from an honest desire to promote the public good.

*See the evidence of Col. Currey (p. 304); of Major-Gen. [Richard] Bourke (p. 318); and of Mr. Rochfort (p. 437), before the Commons' Committee of 1825 [*PP*, 1825, VIII]; the evidence of Mr. [Maxwell] Blacker (p. 78); of Justice Day (p. 264); of Mr. [Justin] Macarty (p. 320); of Mr. [Richard] Simpson (p. 406); of Mr. [James] Lawler (p. 442); and of Dr. [John] Church (p. 450), before the Commons' Committee of 1824 [*ibid.*, VII]. Mr. Leslie Foster, indeed, is of a different opinion: see his evidence before the Lords' Committee of 1825, [*ibid.*, IX,] p. 81.

†Mr. [William Conyngham] Plunkett, [Speech on the Elective Franchise in Ireland (26 Apr., 1825),] *PH*, 1825, p. 200.

[*Foster and William Vesey Fitzgerald, Speeches on the Elective Franchise in Ireland (9 May, 1825), *ibid.*, pp. 213 and 212–13, respectively.]

Every Englishman who knows any thing of the manner in which the legislature of his own country is formed, knows perfectly well that the great mass of the electors, though they have somewhat more of the *form*, have as little of the *reality* of a free choice, as their degraded brethren, the forty shilling freeholders of Ireland. If all the English electors were disfranchised, who dare not vote but according to the bidding of their landlords, or customers, so few would be left that there would be no semblance of a popular choice, and the real amount of the aristocratic power would be made universally apparent. This would not suit either section of the aristocracy: neither the stronger section, who are now the absolute masters of the government, nor the weaker section, who hope to become the stronger, and by that means to become the masters of the government in their turn.

In confirmation of the above remark, so far as it affects the Whig party, it may be observed that the various plans which have been proposed by that party for putting the election of Members of Parliament upon a different footing, have been of a nature to add to the aristocratic power, not to diminish it: and to add to it, too, in the very manner to which the principle of the Irish freeholders' bill is most directly hostile, viz. by giving the franchise to a set of electors who are irresistibly under aristocratic controul. One of these plans is to take away the franchise from the electors of the rotten boroughs who do exercise a free choice, though from their small number they are interested in making a bad one, and to give an additional representation to the county electors, who are almost all of them under the absolute command of their landlords, and who are the very same class of electors whom the Irish freeholders' bill would disfranchise.[*] Another of their plans, is to extend the elective franchise to copyholders; who would be every where under exactly the same influence as the freeholders.[†]

The more consistent, therefore, and clear-sighted among the Whigs, perceived that it was impossible for them to give their support to this measure, without departing from the principles on which they had constantly acted, and to which they were determined to adhere. Mr. Lambton's declaration, then, that he would oppose Catholic emancipation in order to frustrate this measure, appears to us perfectly consistent, and, on his own principles, proper.[‡]

The consistent Tories had exactly the same interest in opposing the measure, as the consistent Whigs: they were also actuated by the general hostility to change; and several (Mr. Goulburn for instance)[§] who approved of the measure, opposed it with the view of thwarting Catholic emancipation. Some persons have wondered that such men as Mr. Bankes should stand forward on this occasion as the champions of popular rights: but to us it appears nothing surprising, that a man

[*See *PD*, n.s., Vol. 5, cols. 604–22 (9 May, 1821).]

[†*Ibid.*, Vol. 7, cols. 51–88 (25 Apr., 1822).]

[‡John George Lambton, Speech on the Elective Franchise in Ireland (9 May, 1825), *PH*, 1825, p. 214.]

[§Goulburn, Speech on the Elective Franchise in Ireland (26 Apr., 1825), *ibid.*, p. 202.]

who has been all his life a determined opponent of all innovation, should oppose it on this occasion as on any other.[*]

If we have succeeded in laying open the springs of action which impelled both classes of opponents to say and do what they said and did against the bill, the reader will be able to make the application to the different speeches without our assistance, and we should have quitted the subject had there not been one passage in the speech of Mr. Brougham, which appears to us to call for particular animadversion.[†]

We do not allude to the bitter complaint which he made [pp. 192–3], oddly enough, of the want of information, when there is probably no subject relative to Ireland, in respect to which the information was equally complete; nor to the still odder reason that he gave for suffering the Irish freeholders to continue perjuring themselves, because officers in the army, members of parliament, and bishops, perjured themselves too [pp. 194–5]; nor even to the excellent definition which he gave of the "natural influence of property," when he defined it to consist in driving Englishmen by threats to go to the poll and utter a deliberate falsehood, enforcing that falsehood by the ceremony of an oath, to put a candidate into parliament of whom they knew nothing; of which influence he added that he did not complain, and that it must exist every where.* The only part of his speech which we have it in view to touch upon, is the unprovoked attack, which he went out of his way to make, upon "the political economists."

> They were told by a class of men, who had carried their dogmatical notions almost as far, and with a spirit similar to the religious persecutions of other times—he meant the political economists, who had held up a valued friend of his, Mr. Malthus, to public ridicule, only because he differed from Mr. Ricardo on a mere metaphysical, not a practical point—that they ought to pass this measure, &c. &c. (*Ibid.*, p. 193.)

We cannot see in what manner a knowledge of the circumstance, that the political economists were intolerant, or had dogmatical notions, conduced to the forming a right decision on the subject of Irish freeholds; but the irrelevancy of this accusation is the least of the faults, with which it is justly chargeable.

If, by the term "political economists," Mr. Brougham intended to designate any particular individuals, we would recommend him,—before he again vituperates the cultivators of a science, the first principles of which it would do him no harm to study,—to consult Lindley Murray's *English Grammar*,[‡] from which he will learn the difference between nouns *proper* and *appellative*, and will be taught to avoid confounding *classes* with *individuals*. But if he include under the expression

---

[*Henry Bankes, Speech on the Elective Franchise in Ireland (26 Apr., 1825), *ibid.*, p. 200.]

[†Henry Brougham, Speech on the Elective Franchise in Ireland (26 Apr., 1825), *ibid.*, pp. 192–8.]

*Ibid., p. 193.

[‡York: Wilson, Spence, and Mawman, 1795.]

"political economists," all or most of those who have made the cultivation of that science their particular pursuit, we have not heard of any act which has emanated from these persons as a body; and we imagine that Mr. Malthus must have been somewhat surprised to find himself represented by his "valued friend" as having been "held up to public ridicule," by a class of philosophers, among whom he probably esteems himself to be not one of the least considerable. It strikes us, too, as rather odd, that the act of "holding a man up to public ridicule" should be regarded as proof of "a spirit similar to the religious persecutions of other times." Religious persecutors have been wont to resort to tortures of a keener description than public ridicule: and is Mr. Malthus the first person who has been held up to ridicule for a "merely speculative" opinion?

To be serious, it is astonishing, that a man like Mr. Brougham should either be ignorant himself, or should count upon so extraordinary a degree of ignorance on the part of his audience, as to impute intolerance to the political economists: a class of men who are by nothing more distinguished, than by the mildness and urbanity with which their warmest discussions have been carried on: a mildness till then unknown in the history of controversy; and forming a most striking contrast with the bitterness and animosity which have characterized the disputes not merely of politicians and theologians, contending for power over the bodies or souls of mankind, but even of the professors of purely abstract science, for example the mathematicians: who in their controversies with one another, or with those who have impugned any of their doctrines, have on several occasions displayed even more than ordinary arrogance, petulance, and ill-temper. He who was ignorant of all this, or knowing it could charge the political economists with dogmatism and intolerance, must have merely taken up the first bad name which occurred to him, and without for a moment considering whether it was applicable or not, flung it at the heads of those whom he had a mind to assail.

We have not left ourselves space to comment at much length upon the two remaining discussions on the Catholic question.[*] The subject was much more thoroughly sifted in these two debates than in the foregoing: we allude particularly to the speeches of Mr. Horace Twiss and Lord Harrowby, by both of whom the only argument was put forward which really goes to the bottom of the question, namely, that, for any mischievous purpose, the Catholics would not gain one particle of power by emancipation.[†] Mr. Charles Grant was, as usual, honest and manly.[‡] The opponents of the Catholics begged the question against them, in all the old, and a variety of new ways: but their speeches were in every material feature so like those of their predecessors, that we need not waste any words upon

[*Debate on the Roman Catholic Relief Bill (10 May, 1825, Commons, and 17 May, 1825, Lords), *PH*, 1825, pp. 215–27, 232–56.]

[†Horace Twiss and Dudley Ryder, Speeches on Roman Catholic Relief (10 and 17 May, 1825), *ibid.*, pp. 216–21 and 247–8, respectively.]

[‡Charles Grant, Speech on Roman Catholic Relief (10 May, 1825), *ibid.*, pp. 221–2.]

them. The only speech deserving of notice on that side of the question was the speech of the Bishop of Chester: and this not so much from the merits or demerits of its arguments as from the lengths to which the right reverend prelate was hurried by the clerical *esprit de corps*, and the cavalier manner in which he treated all classes in Ireland, except the priesthood of the church, "a priesthood," (including, we suppose, the Honorable and Venerable Archdeacon Trench, and the Rev. Mr. Morrett of Skibbereen)* "which, in the moral desolation of Ireland, remained the Oasis of the desert, and gave to the eye some points on which it could rest with pleasure."† It was ludicrous enough too, to hear a man who is pocketing thousands a year by his opinions, and who has nothing to fear from a strict adherence to them but removal from a lower grade of emolument and grandeur to a higher, spout mock-heroics, and talk of *martyrdom*.

* * * * *

Hitherto what we have been mainly considering, in the different speeches, has been their arguments. The occasion now calls for another sort of remark.

In private life, no maxim, that has human conduct for its subject, is more universally assented to than the paramount importance of an inviolable adherence to truth. To charge a man with a disregard to truth is justly considered as the most flagrant insult which can be put upon him: and the state of mind which characterizes an habitual liar, as one with which no good or great quality can easily coexist.

It has however been long ago observed by Addison, that party lies are in a great measure exempt from this stigma; and that men who would sooner die than be guilty of the slightest violation of truth for their individual advantage, are ready, for the benefit of their party, to put forth assertions which they not only know to be false, but which they know cannot, in the common course of things, be believed by any body for more than a few days.[*]

Whether matters have altered in this respect, since the days of Addison, is what we do not pretend to determine. Thus much, however, will, it is believed, be found to be borne out by a considerable body of modern experience: that what would be a falsehood anywhere else, is a justifiable piece of rhetorical artifice in the House of Commons; and that gentlemen, in all other respects of the most unblemished

---

*See the evidence of [John Evans-Freke,] Lord Carbery (p. 603) before the Commons' Committee of 1825 [*PP*, 1825, VIII]; of Mr. Blacker (pp. 60–1), and the Rev. Michael Collins (pp. 375–7), before the Commons' Committee of 1824 [*ibid.*, VII]; and of Mr. [John] O'Driscol (p. 733) before the Lords' Committee of 1824 [*ibid.*]. See more particularly the evidence of Mr. [Randle Patrick] Macdonell, before the Commons' Committee of 1825 ([*ibid.*, VIII,] pp. 759–60), and the whole. For further information concerning the Oasis, see the evidence of Major [George] Warburton (p. 147) before the Commons' Committee of 1824 [*ibid.*, VII].

†[Blomfield, speech of 17 May, 1825,] *PH*, 1825, p. 240.

[*Joseph Addison, *Spectator*, No. 507 (11 Oct., 1712), in *The Spectator*, 8 vols. (London: Buckley, and Tonson, 1712–15), Vol. VII, pp. 179–82.]

honour, and quite incapable of saying or doing any thing which is generally regarded as dishonorable, are in the daily habit of making assertions in Parliament, which would infallibly lead an indifferent auditor to suppose that the *convenience* of an assertion for their purposes was a circumstance much more regarded by them than its *truth*.

It will be for the reader to judge, whether the assertions which we are now about to quote, belong to the class of assertions which we have just mentioned, or not. We will deal fairly by *him* and *them*; we will lay before him,—together with the assertions,—if not the proofs, at least an indication of the proofs, which lead us without hesitation to pronounce them unfounded. It is possible that the gentlemen to whom they are ascribed, may have been misrepresented by the reporters; if so, they are bound in justice to the public and to themselves, to disavow them. It is also, in the case of some of these gentlemen, just possible, that they may not have known positively that the assertions were unfounded, but only, not known them to be true. We shall be extremely glad to find that the gentlemen have been misrepresented. We bear them no ill will; on the contrary, we have for some of them individually great respect. In the code of party ethics, the stain may not be a very black one; but we confess it is one from which we would gladly see them freed.

Mr. Doherty:

Frequent allusions had been made to the partial administration of justice in Ireland. Now he would say, and the experience of some years entitled him to say it, that the Catholics of Ireland enjoyed the fullest and fairest administration of justice. He affirmed, without fear of contradiction from any Irish member, that THE COURTS OF JUSTICE WERE EQUALLY OPEN TO THE RICH AND THE POOR, without distinction of religious sentiments.*

The same gentleman:

As far as the experience of seventeen years' attendance on the Irish circuit enabled him to judge, THE ADMINISTRATION OF JUSTICE IN IRELAND WAS PERFECTLY PURE. He repeated that the administration of justice in Ireland was perfectly pure, that THE RIGHTS OF THE POOR MAN WERE EQUALLY RESPECTED WITH THOSE OF THE RICH, and that no distinction whatever was made between Catholic and Protestant.†

---

*[John Doherty, Speech on Unlawful Societies in Ireland (11 Feb., 1825),] *PH*, 1825, p. 67.

†[Doherty, Speech on Unlawful Societies in Ireland (25 Feb., 1825),] *ibid.*, p. 127. Contrast this with Mr. Doherty's own words to the jury in the case of *Lawrence* v. *Dempster*. "This case will shew the manner in which the insurrection act has been administered in a part of this county. I rejoice that the cases of oppression which have been developed at these assizes were not earlier made public, lest the sturdy guardians of our rights and privileges, who yielded lately such a reluctant assent to this harsh, but, I believe, necessary law, should have been confirmed in their opposition, from seeing the vile, selfish, and tyrannical purposes to which it has been made subservient in the hands of arrogant and oppressive magistrates; and lest they should have formed their opinions from the abuse

Mr. North:

Mr. Cobbett, who within the last two months had become the oracle of the Catholics, had desired them to make out a list of the cases in which justice had been denied, or in which oppression and violence had received a sanction from the law. The Catholics, however, had drawn out no such list, BECAUSE THEY COULD NOT; NO SUCH CASES OF SUCCESSFUL INJUSTICE EXISTING except in the heated imaginations of those who had fabricated them.*

Mr. Goulburn:

It had been said that there was one law for the rich and another for the poor in Ireland. *If that meant that there was a denial of justice to the poor man,* HE BEGGED TO DENY THE FACT. With respect to magistrates, he would assert, and he defied contradiction, that THERE WAS NO SUCH THING AS A DISPOSITION AMONG THEM TO TAKE BRIBES for the administration of justice to the poor.†

To the above list, it is with great pain we add the following passage; which, however, is so vague and intangible that it can hardly be said to contain an assertion at all, consequently not a false assertion.

Mr. Brownlow:

The Protestant gentlemen of Ireland, in the relations of parents, landlords, and magistrates, FOLLOWED THE PRECEPTS OF THEIR RELIGION, BY STUDYING THE GOOD OF ALL COMMITTED TO THEIR CHARGE, in a manner not to be surpassed by a similar body of men in any country.‡

The following assertion belongs to the same class:

The Earl of Roden:

The situation of the peasantry of Ireland had, he conceived, been very much misrepresented. NO SET OF PEOPLE ENJOYED MORE AMPLY THE BENEFITS OF THE BRITISH CONSTITUTION THAN THE PEASANTRY OF IRELAND.§

We shall not attempt to do what volumes would not do effectually, to present the

---

rather than the use of this salutary law. Teach him, if he continue in the commission of the peace, that he must learn to administer the law in its true meaning, and not, as in the present case, torture it into an instrument of caprice or malevolence." [See *The Times*, 8 Aug., 1823, p. 3. The law referred to is 3 George IV, c. 1 (1822), continued by 4 George IV, c. 58 (1823), and further continued (and amended) by 5 George IV, c. 105 (1824).]

We quote from the speech of Mr. Spring Rice [on Unlawful Societies in Ireland (25 Feb., 1825)], *PH*, 1825, p. 127. See also, in the same speech, the energetic language of Chief Justice Bushe; language imputing to the Irish magistracy as a body, a degree of wickedness, beyond what any person in a lower station would have dared to lay to their charge. [For Charles Kendall Bushe's views, cited by Spring Rice, see *The Times*, 2 Aug., 1823, p. 3, and 5 Aug., 1823, p. 2.]

*[John North, Speech on Unlawful Societies in Ireland (14 Feb., 1825),] *PH*, 1825, p. 87.

†[Goulburn, Speech on Unlawful Societies in Ireland (25 Feb., 1825),] *ibid.*, p. 128.

‡[Brownlow, Speech on Unlawful Societies in Ireland (14 Feb., 1825),] *ibid.*, p. 81.

§[Robert Jocelyn, Speech on Unlawful Societies in Ireland (7 Mar., 1825),] *ibid.*, p. 147.

reader with the original of this delightful picture: but we can at least tell him what to *read*. If he will peruse those passages in the Evidence before the Committees to which we are about to refer him, he will form some conception of the purity of the administration of justice in Ireland (we are not speaking of the superior courts), both in other respects, and in regard to the taking of bribes; of the benefits which no set of people enjoy more amply than the peasantry of Ireland, to wit, those of the British constitution; and of the manner in which the Protestant gentlemen of Ireland follow the precepts of their religion, by studying, in the character of landlords and magistrates, and we will add, *grand jurors*, the good of all committed to their charge. We have inclosed our references to the most important passages within brackets. The authority of any *one* of these witnesses may be cavilled at; but we recommend to the reader to *count* them.

Before the Commons' Committee of 1825.

Mr. [Daniel] O'Connell, pp. 51, 55–6, [60, 61]. Col. Currey, 297, [312]. Major Gen. Bourke, 324, [325], 326–7, 330, [336], 339, [340]. Rev. John Keily, 397. Rev. Thomas Costello, [417], 418. Mr. Rochfort, 446, 448, [449]. Mr. [Arthur] Kelly, 521, [522, 526]. Mr. Barrington, 578. Lord Carbery, [603]. Mr. [John] Currie, [634]. Mr. [John] Godley, 741. [*Parliamentary Papers*, 1825, VIII.]

Before the Commons' Committee of 1824.

Mr. Blacker, pp. [60, 61]. Major Willcocks, 101, [109], 113. Major Warburton, 164. Mr. [William Wrixon] Becher, [183, 184, 185]. Mr. Leslie Foster, 242. Mr. Justice Day, [253, 257–9, 264]. Mr. [William Henry] Newenham, 306. Mr. Macarty, [328–9, 332]. Rev. Michael Collins, 335, 336, [337, 371–7]. Mr. O'Driscol, 381, [383–5, 396]. Dr. [John Richard] Elmore, [417]. Dr. Church, 424, [429–30]. Mr. Lawler, 441, 442–3. [*Ibid.*, Vol. VII.]

Before the Lords' Committee of 1825.

Mr. Leslie Foster, pp. 55, [60], 65. Mr. Doherty, 91, 94, [95]. Mr. O'Connell, [130], 131, 134, [135]. Major Gen. Bourke, 173, 176, [178], 180. Mr. [Joseph] Abbott, [196–8]. Rev. Henry Cooke, 217. Sir John Newport, 288. Mr. Barrington, 305. Earl of Kingston, [437, 439]. Archdeacon Trench, [447]. Mr. Justice Day, [524], 526, 527, [528–9]. Mr. Dominick Browne, 588. [*Ibid.*, Vol. IX.]

Before the Lords' Committee of 1824.

Major Willcocks, pp. 554–5. Major Warburton, [579]. Major [Thomas] Powell, 609. Mr. [Alexander] Nimmo, [631–2], 659, 663, [665], 679. Mr. Becher, 634, [637], 639. The Duke of Leinster, [Augustus Frederick Fitzgerald,]

704. Mr. Macarty, 719. The Marquis of Westmeath, [George Thomas Nugent,] 728–31. Mr. O'Driscol, [733–4]. [*Ibid.*, Vol. VII.]

But, infinitely more than all these, let him read from beginning to end the evidence of Mr. Macdonnell, of Ballinasloe, before the Commons' Committee of 1825: that part of it which relates to *magistrates*, that part of it which relates to *grand juries*, that part of it which relates to *illegal tolls*, and other illegal charges, and that part of it which relates to *tithes*.[*] He will find there—it is not safe to tell him what he will find: let him read for himself.

* * * * *

Among the minor proceedings of the last session relative to Ireland, none are of sufficient importance to require notice, with the exception of Mr. Hume's motion concerning the Irish church, and the debate to which it gave rise.[†]

As this was only a motion for inquiry, we are not called upon to give any opinion on the expediency of a revision of the Church Establishment of Ireland: a large subject, and one upon which we shall have other opportunities of stating our opinions, at greater length than our limits would have enabled us, on the present occasion, to afford. We shall content ourselves, then, with an examination of the grounds, on which the House resolved, that there was no need of inquiry.

The only speaker against the motion (Mr. Peel said but a few words)[‡] was Mr. Canning. His arguments were two. One was, that a revision of the Irish Church Establishment was contrary to the Union.[§] The other consisted in calling the church revenues *property*, in denouncing all interference with them as *spoliation*, and affirming that the House might, with equal right, seize upon the lay tithes, and the property of corporations. To these arguments Mr. Canning added (what is often more effective than argument) vituperation: "he had never heard a principle so base propounded for consideration in that House."*

The first argument is defective in two ways: in the first place, because, as was remarked by Sir Francis Burdett[¶] in his pointed answer to Mr. Canning, the Act of Union is not a law of the Medes and Persians; in the next place, because, supposing it were so, the opponents of the motion failed, on their own shewing, in making it out to be a violation of the Union. It is a mockery to say, that, in merely enacting that the churches of England and Ireland should be united in one Protestant

---

[**PP*, 1825, VIII, 752–8, 760–1 (on magistrates), 761–6 (on grand juries), 746–52 (on illegal tolls and other illegal charges), and 759–60 (on tithes).]

[†Joseph Hume, Speech in Introducing a Motion on the Established Church in Ireland (14 June, 1825), *PH*, pp. 267–70.]

[‡Robert Peel, Speech on the Established Church in Ireland (14 June, 1825), *ibid.*, p. 271.]

[§I.e., the Act of Union, 39 & 40 George III, c. 67 (1800).]

*[Canning, Speech on the Established Church in Ireland (14 June, 1825),] *PH*, 1825, pp. 270–1.

[¶Burdett, Speech on the Established Church in Ireland (14 June, 1825), *ibid.*, p. 271.]

Episcopalian church, to be subject to the same laws, it was ever intended to tie up the hands of the legislature from introducing any reform into either, which might render it more conducive to its object, or to the good of the state. Mr. Peel attempted to bolster up this flimsy argument, by referring to that article of the Union by which it was provided, that the Irish bishops should succeed in a certain order to seats in Parliament:[*] this he called recognizing the number of bishops; and so it was: recognizing the actual number; recognizing it as *being* the actual number: but not surely as a number never to be altered, should any other number be, in the opinion of the legislature, more eligible. Is a law to be construed as giving perpetuity to every thing, the existence of which it takes for granted as a fact, and provides for the consequences of it accordingly? If there had been a provision in the Union to regulate the right of pasturage upon a common, or of cutting turf upon a bog, would it have been a consequence of that provision, that the common should never be ploughed up, the bog never drained? If a man had bound himself by a contract to give his footman a livery, would he by that contract have debarred himself from ever parting with his footman?

The other argument, which turns upon the words *property* and *spoliation*, was completely demolished in the masterly speech of Mr. Brougham,[†] who pointed out the inherent distinctions between the revenues of the Church and private property, and the consequent inapplicability of such a term as spoliation to any measure for regulating their amount. Spoliation,—whatever be meant by spoliation, must at any rate be spoliation of *somebody*. The spoliation in question, if such it is to be called, would not be spoliation of the present incumbents, since it was proposed to leave their incomes untouched: it would not be spoliation of their children, or heirs, since these would not have got the incomes, and therefore cannot lose them. No man, no person, no actually existing being would be deprived by the proposed measure of any thing which he has, nor of any thing which he is entitled to expect. Of whom then would it be spoliation? Of an ideal being; a mere imaginary entity: an abstract idea: a name, a sound. It would, in one word, be spoliation of *nobody*.

Having no better arguments than these, it is no wonder that Mr. Canning should have had recourse to the old expedient of "*flinging dirt.*" It is the characteristic of a bad cause to resort to such helps, as it is of a good one to have no need of them.

[*39 & 40 George III, c. 67, §5.]
[†Henry Brougham, Speech on the Established Church in Ireland (14 June, 1825), *PH*, 1825, pp. 271–3.]

THE GAME LAWS

1826

EDITOR'S NOTE

Westminster Review, V (Jan., 1826), 1-22. Headed: "ART. I. *Report from the Select Committee on the Laws relating to Game.* Ordered by the House of Commons to be printed, 18th April, 1823. [*Parliamentary Papers,* 1823, IV, 107-53.] / [John Weyland.] *A Letter on the Game Laws.* By a Country Gentleman, a Proprietor of Game. [London:] Baldwin, [Cradock, and Joy,] Paternoster Row, and Hatchard, Piccadilly, 1815. / [John Weyland.] *A Second Letter on the Game Laws.* By a Country Gentleman, a Proprietor of Game. [London:] Baldwin, [Cradock, and Joy,] Paternoster Row, and Hatchard, Piccadilly, 1817. / [Edward Harbord.] *Considerations on the Game Laws.* By Edward Lord Suffield. [London:] J. Hatchard and Son. 1825. / *Reconsiderations on certain proposed Alterations in the Game Laws.* By George Bankes, Esq. [London:] J. Hatchard and Son. 1825." Running titles: "*The Game Laws.*" Unsigned; not republished. Identified in Mill's bibliography as "An article on the Game Laws, in the 9th number of the Westminster Review" (MacMinn, 7). For comment on the essay, see lvii above.

The Game Laws

WHEN WE LEARNED from the newspapers, that a bill to reform the Game Laws had been introduced into parliament by the representative of the greatest agricultural county in England, had been supported by a home secretary, and triumphantly carried through the Lower House; we pleased ourselves with the thought that, for once, at least, the aristocracy of Great Britain had shewn that the happiness and virtue of the bulk of the community were not altogether a matter of indifference in their eyes.[*] They have hastened to undeceive us. They have shewn a commendable anxiety that the public may not continue long to think better of them than they deserve. It has pleased our lords the peers to exercise, on the occasion of Mr. Stuart Wortley's bill, that glorious privilege of crushing improvement, which has been vested in them, no doubt, for wise purposes, by our happy constitution. The legislature of this country has once more solemnly declared, that, come what will of the morals, the liberties, and even the lives, of the great mass of the agricultural population, the amusements at least of the aristocracy shall not be invaded. It remains to be seen how this declaration will be received by the public. How it ought to be received is evident enough.

To a superficial observer it might appear, that the wisdom and virtue to which we are thus indebted for the perpetuation of poaching, and (by an infallible consequence) of all other kinds of crime, are those of the House of Lords. More accurate reflection shows, that the root of the evil lies far deeper; that the peers have but borne their share in the triumph of the few over the many; and that to lay the blame upon them would be to throw that responsibility upon a part, which in justice belongs to the whole.

In the examination which we thought it necessary to institute in our first number

[*James Archibald Stuart-Wortley, Speech in Introducing the Game Laws Amendment Bill (17 Feb., 1825), *Parliamentary Debates* (hereafter cited as *PD*), n.s., Vol. 10, cols. 187-9; he brought forward "A Bill to Amend the Laws for the Preservation of Game," 6 George IV (21 Mar., 1825), with the support of Robert Peel, the Home Secretary, in speeches of 17 Feb. and 7 Mar., *PD*, n.s., Vol. 10, cols. 528 and 952-6. The bill sought the repeal of such laws as 22 & 23 Charles II, c. 25 (1670) and 57 George III, c. 90 (1817). On 30 Apr., 1825, p. 5, *The Times* reported the passing of the bill in the Commons; on 10 May, 1825, p. 2, its defeat in the Lords. The authoritative report of the debates not being available to Mill, he uses in this article the debates on the similar bill brought forward by Stuart-Wortley (and supported by Peel) in 1824; see p. 113n.]

into the nature and composition of the British aristocracy, we pointed out the manner in which the governing power is shared between the landed and the monied interests; the landed interest, however, retaining a decided preponderance.[*] Had any new proof been wanted of this preponderance, such a proof would have been afforded by the fate of Mr. Stuart Wortley's bill. It is well known that those members of both branches of the legislature, who voted against the bill, have belonged almost exclusively to the class of landholders. The monied interest have been almost unanimous in its favour. The reason is obvious: the exclusive privilege which it was the object of the bill to take away, was a privilege created not for them, but against them. The whole body of peers are, almost without exception, landholders. Even in the Lower House a large majority are either themselves landholders, or are returned by that class. In that House, however, there were found landholders possessed of common humanity, and of an ordinary share of understanding, in sufficient numbers, when supported by the monied interest, to turn the balance in favour of improvement. That it was otherwise in a House composed almost entirely of landholders, only proves that in the agricultural class, as in every class, the purely selfish always form a large majority.

The fate of the Game bill, therefore, is a pretty conclusive proof, what, in this country, the landholders *can* do: it is also a pretty decisive specimen of what they *will* do, and such a specimen as, antecedently to experience, it would not have been very easy to anticipate.

Let us see what it is which the landholders *get* by these laws. They have a little more game to shoot, and a little more game to eat, than they possibly might have, if the game laws were amended; and they have the privilege of sending such game as they have shot, and do not desire to eat, as a present, to an unqualified friend, under pretence of its being a rarity; though all the world knows that it may be had of any poulterer for a few shillings.

Let us now turn our eyes to the other side of the account; and try to form some conception, though it be but an imperfect one, of the price which the Many pay to secure the Few in the enjoyment of these inestimable advantages.

If we were writing for the "great men," we should descant upon the hardship of denying to the "second son of a man of £20,000 per annum," the liberty of shooting over his father's estate,* and refusing to the merchant or manufacturer the luxury of game, unless he happen to have a qualified friend who is able and willing to keep his table supplied. In the eyes of the said second son, or of the said merchant or manufacturer, these grievances might, for aught we know, be more acceptable subjects of remonstrance than those which we have chosen; and there have been pamphlets enough, and speeches enough, in which these and similar topics have

---

[*James Mill, "Periodical Literature: *Edinburgh Review*," *Westminster Review*, I (Jan., 1824), 206–68.]

*See Mr. Secretary Peel's speech [on the Game Laws Amendment Bill], *PD*, [n.s., Vol. 10, col. 913,] March 11th, 1824.

been dwelt upon *usque ad nauseam*. As, however, the little men happen to outnumber the great men in the proportion of some thousands to one; and as, moreover, in our estimation, to be first tempted to crime, and then transported for it, with a considerable probability of being ultimately hanged, is a greater evil than that of being debarred from the pleasure of shooting, or the pleasure of eating, a partridge; we shall leave these last-mentioned privations to the generous indignation of would-be sportsmen, and of aldermen, with their associate speech-makers and pamphlet-makers. *Our* objection to the Game Laws rests upon a different ground. The class of evils to which we shall direct the attention of our readers, are so immeasurably superior in magnitude, that we cannot think it worth while to insist upon any others.

That among the poorer classes in the game-preserving districts, the crime of poaching is almost universal, and that the habitual poacher almost constantly ends by being a thief, are facts unhappily so notorious, that to adduce any proofs in support of them is a labour which may be spared. It is instructive, however, to mark the acute sense which is entertained of these evils by those who, in their capacity of magistrates, are best able to appreciate their magnitude and extent.

The receipt to make a poacher, [says Lord Suffield,] will be found to contain a very few and simple ingredients, which may be met with in every game county in England. Search out (and you need not go far) a poor man with a large family, or a poor man single, having his natural sense of right and wrong, and as much more as he was taught before he was seven or ten years old; let him absent himself from church, or go to sleep when he is there; give him little more than a natural disinclination to work; let him exist in the midst of lands where the game is preserved; keep him cool in the winter, by allowing him insufficient wages to purchase fuel; let him feel hungry upon the small spare pittance of parish relief; and if he be not a poacher, it will only be by the blessing of God. In the poacher thus easily concocted, my experience justifies me in asserting, that we have at least a fair promise, if not the absolute certainty, of an ultimately accomplished villain.*

The extent and progress of the evil, [says the able author of the letters on the Game Laws,] cannot be conceived by those who are not conversant with the lower ranks in the country villages. From extensive observation and inquiry, I believe in my conscience, that it is not too much to assert, that three fourths of the crimes which bring so many poor men to the gallows, have their first origin in the evil and irregular habits, NECESSARILY introduced by the almost irresistible temptations held out, in consequence of the prohibitions of the Game Laws, to a nightly breach of their enactments. This I can safely declare of my own knowledge—that of the numerous country villages with which I am acquainted, NOT ONE exists in which the profligate and licentious characters may not trace the first and early corruption of their habits to this cause. The experience of every impartial magistrate, of every judge of assize, will fortify this assertion; many, indeed, have openly declared it.†

This state of things, dreadful as it is, the situation in which the country labourer is placed, might of itself have led us to anticipate.

---

*[Harbord, *Considerations on the Game Laws*,] pp. 22–3.
†[Weyland, *A Letter on the Game Laws*,] pp. 6–7.

It is well known that, over a great part of England, the common agricultural labourer, by the most incessant toil, can scarcely earn more than nine-pence or a shilling a day. In comparison with this the gains of the poacher must be enormous. A gang of poachers has been known to take as much as three sacks of game in one night.* At however low a price game may occasionally have been sold, the dividend of each poacher upon a booty like this must have been ample. The pursuit is not only no toil, but a positive pleasure; the risk of detection is little or nothing; for though an habitual poacher probably is in most cases ultimately discovered, the chances are many to one against the detection of any individual act. The same feelings which guard the honesty of the poor man on other occasions, have no existence here; for nothing is more notorious than that the taking of game is regarded as no crime, either by the offenders themselves, or by their neighbours. A little wire and string are the only materials required; and the facilities which exist for the immediate disposal of game can only be appreciated by those who have read the minutes of evidence taken before the committee of the House of Commons. Is it not, then, much more wonderful that any should resist such temptations, than that so many should yield to them?

If, by frequent and undetected repetition, the poor man has acquired a habit of trusting either wholly or in part to the illegal traffic for his subsistence; the first time that by accident or precaution he is prevented from obtaining his usual supply of game, he is averse to return to that life of toil which he has abandoned, and unable, perhaps, if his practices are suspected, to obtain employment were he to seek it. Inured now to the breach of the laws, he no longer regards the violation even of acknowledged property in the same light as before; what little scruple he has, soon yields to the pressure of necessity, and the orchard, the hen-roost, or the sheep-fold becomes the next object of his depredations. His illicit pursuits, too, bring him into contact with other characters of greater experience in crime; with poachers of longer standing than himself, and of more depraved habits; with thieves by profession, who, in the exercise of their calling, do not neglect a line of business at once so easy and so safe.

> The thieves who become poachers, [says Lord Suffield,] united with the poachers who become thieves, are usually those who lead the gangs whose bloody and ferocious deeds are so frequently recorded during the winter months in all the newspapers of the day. These desperadoes provide guns and other instruments, the *materiel* for poaching—they hire (the fact falls within my own immediate knowledge) poor men, generally upon the same wages, or very little more, than are paid by the game-preserver to his night-watchers—they discipline these unhappy mercenaries in the exercise of their calling—they sometimes claim the whole of the booty—offer their mighty protection, and often actually do pay the penalties, if any novice should *get into trouble* by detection in a trivial offence on some other occasion; and finally, they undertake to dispose of the game with safety and profit, whenever it suits the convenience of the young beginner to produce any. (Pp. 26–7.)

*See the evidence of Daniel Bishop, before the Committee of the House of Commons [on the Laws Relating to Game, *PP*, 1823, IV, 136].

Under such tuition it is not necessary to trace the progress of the unhappy novice from crime to crime. He who knows the first steps, can imagine the last.

If, on the other hand, he be detected, he is imprisoned for one, two, or three months, with or without hard labour, as the caprice or revenge of the game-preserving magistrate, who sits in judgment in his own cause, may dictate. If things were so ordered in an English gaol, that imprisonment should have the effect of making a man better, instead of worse, this temporary suspension of his illegal pursuits, and separation from his guilty associates, might be made the means of saving him from destruction. After he had endured, or while he was enduring, his allotted quantum of punishment, pains might be taken to eradicate his mischievous habits, to implant good ones in their stead, and to send him forth an altered man. This is what might be done, if prisons were what they might be made. To all who know what English prisons are, it is unnecessary to say, that their effects are precisely the reverse. There is nothing, even in the best of them, which deserves the name of reformatory discipline. Nothing is done to make the prisoner better; and when there is nothing doing to make him better, it is pretty certain, that there is enough doing to make him worse. Habituated to the society of criminals, he not only becomes prepared for the perpetration of any villainy, but learns from his associates the most skilful modes of committing crime and eluding detection. On leaving prison, he finds himself shut out from all decent means of obtaining a livelihood; those to whom he once looked for employment have learned from experience what sort of characters the discipline of an English gaol turns out upon society; his imprisonment, instead of being the instrument of his reformation, is the badge of his infamy, and an effectual bar to his ever retracing his steps, and quitting the path which leads from crime to crime, from punishment to punishment, and terminates in premature death.

This may suffice for a general sketch of the progress of village criminality. Particular instances, without number, might be selected from the works before us, if particular instances could give any additional certainty to general facts so unhappily notorious.

Daniel Bishop, one of the principal officers of the Bow-street Police Office, said on his examination,

"I think within four months there have been twenty-one transported that I have been at the taking of, and through one man turning evidence in each case, and without that they could not have been identified; the game-keepers could not, or would not, identify them." [*Parliamentary Papers*, 1823, IV, 138.]

"You detected some men in Dorsetshire; how far did they come?—Sixteen miles, the whole of the village from which they were taken were poachers; the constable of the village, and the shoemaker, and other inhabitants of the village." [P. 137.]

"Does not the poacher become frequently, what he does not allow himself in the first instance to be, a thief?—Yes; they go on from step to step; I had a case at Bishop's Stortford, where they began with poaching and went on to thieving; and one was hanged, and there were seven or eight transported for life." [P. 138.]

"Have you ever heard from any of the poachers that they have been concerned in other robberies?—Yes, I have; poaching is the first step to all depredations; if they are disappointed in poaching, they will go on and rob hen-roosts, or break into any farmer's house, or steal a sheep, they have told me that." [P. 136.]

Mr. John Stafford, chief clerk at the Bow-street office, being asked whether he was acquainted with any cases of particular atrocity, answered:

"I think one of the worst cases that I recollect, and that was a pretty early one (in the year 1816), was the case in Gloucestershire, where there was a large gang thoroughly organized, and bound together with secret oaths, that attacked the keepers belonging to the Berkeley estate, near Berkeley castle. Vickery, who was a very intelligent officer, was sent down upon that occasion, and from his exertions and the assistance he met with in the neighbourhood, he was enabled to bring the whole gang, or pretty nearly so, to justice. It consisted of about twenty; there were thirteen or fourteen of them, I think, tried and convicted of the murder. A man of the name of William Ingram, one of the principal keepers, was shot dead upon the spot; another of the keepers had an eye shot out; another was shot through the knee; and several of them were dangerously wounded. A man of the name of Allen, who was a farmer, and also a collector of rates or taxes in the parish, and looked upon as a respectable man, was at the head of that gang; and Allen was executed with a man of the name of Penny, who was a labourer, and was supposed to be the man that actually shot the game-keeper who was killed; the other offenders were all transported for life. And after that a young man, who was a lawyer or a lawyer's clerk in some village adjoining, and who had administered the oath to those people to bind them together, was also tried and transported; it turned out that he swore them upon a Ready Reckoner,[*] but the court took that as sufficient, it having the effect to bind them."

"Was the union of these men solely for the purpose of poaching?—Solely for the purpose of poaching in that instance, and the offence arose in the act of poaching. About the same time, I rather think a little before that, there were two men executed at Chelmsford; their offence was not committed in the act of poaching, but they certainly commenced their career by being poachers. There was a shoemaker of the name of Trigg, who lived at a little village called Berden, in Essex, who was shot . . . . Vickery and Bishop were sent down, and I went afterwards myself to direct them, and after a little time they succeeded in apprehending two men whose names were Turner and Pratt; they were apprehended at Bishop's Stortford, and the number of implements that were found in the possession of these two men, exceeded any thing I ever heard of or saw before. It was astonishing the number of picklock keys they had, also wires, snares, every thing for the carrying on the combined operations of poachers and thieves . . . . Both were convicted and executed for the murder; and one of these men himself told me, that he had all his misfortunes to blame himself for, from originally commencing poacher; that poaching led them out at nights, and into bad company; that when they went out to get game, if they were disappointed in getting game, they would take poultry sometimes, and sheep; and that sometimes, rather than go home without any thing, they would break open houses; and it was in the breaking open of this shoemaker's shop, that the man was shot in coming down to prevent the act; each charged the other with the actual commission of the murder, but they admitted they were both present."

"Were these people at the time connected with poaching, and was poaching one of their occupations?—Certainly."

[*A work such as *The Complete Ready Reckoner, or Trader's Companion; Shewing . . . the Value of Any Quantity of Goods* (London: Tallis, 1822).]

"From the result of your information, has it appeared to you, that thieves and poachers are frequently connected together in the country, and that they are frequently the same persons?—I think that very soon after men become poachers, they either become thieves or are led into connection with them. I think that many men, perhaps, would not have been thieves if they had not previously become poachers." [*Ibid*., pp. 143-4.]

Mr. Page, a Surrey magistrate, whose evidence to this point is particularly valuable, because he is hostile to any alteration in the law, says "I conceive that poachers are all poultry stealers and sheep stealers also." [*Ibid*., p. 149.]

Mr. William Peel, another opponent of the bill, stated in Parliament, that one fourth of all the commitments in England were on account of offences against the game laws.[*]

The return made to the House of Commons shews that the number of persons in prison for such offences, in England and Wales, on the 24th February 1825, amounted to 581.[†]

And lastly, Mr. Secretary Peel, in his place in Parliament, declared, that the commitments for this class of offences, during the last six or seven years, had exceeded 9000; being considerably more than 1200 annually.[‡]

When we consider that, at least, eleven-twelfths of these unfortunate persons, from the loss of character which they suffered by being thrown into gaol, and the habits which they acquired while there, became, by a sort of moral necessity, confirmed and accomplished depredators, and the majority in all probability ended their career in New South Wales, in the hulks, or on the gallows, we may form some faint conception of the amount of evil which is annually inflicted upon the community by the game laws. And for what purpose?

Let us concede to the advocates of these laws, all which they could ask. Let us grant that the end and object for which all this misery is occasioned, is not the mere maintenance of an exclusive privilege. Let us grant that the measures proposed by Mr. Stuart Wortley would altogether extirpate the breed of game. This, at least, is the *maximum* of its mischievousness, the very "head and front of its offending;"[§] and if it did so much, it could not well do more. Now, is there any one, we ask, whose love of partridge is so strong, or his love of his fellow creatures so weak, that if he had to choose between depriving himself of the former, and inflicting all the evils, which we have attempted to delineate, upon the latter, he would feel so much as a moment's hesitation in making his choice? Or if our great landholders be such persons, have *they* any reason to complain of any one for holding them up to hatred and contempt?

[*William Peel, Speech on the Game Laws Amendment Bill (11 Mar., 1824), *PD*, n.s., Vol. 10, col. 906.]

[†"Return of the Number of Persons Confined in the Different Gaols of Great Britain, for Offences against the Game Laws," *PP*, 1825, XXIII, 565.]

[‡Robert Peel, speech of 11 Mar., 1824, cols. 918-19.]

[§Shakespeare, *Othello*, I, iii, 80.]

The end of property, as of all other human institutions, is, or ought to be, no other than the general good. If the existence of any particular kind of property be contrary to the general good, that kind of property ought not to exist. If the existence of game, and the existence of all this crime and misery, be necessarily concomitant, a reward ought to be offered for every head of game till the whole breed be extinct. Nor have there been wanting men who have had honesty enough and courage enough to avow such a doctrine, in the very face of an assembly of landholders. Lord Milton "thought the House had nothing to do with the effect which the bill might have, either as to the increase or the diminution of game. It was not the duty of parliament to provide for the amusement of country gentlemen, but to legislate for the preservation of the morals of the country."* Lord Suffield, whose benevolence and manliness form so striking, and, to him, so honourable a contrast with the cowardice, the bigotry, and the selfishness, which fill the benches around him, declared in the House of Lords (February 20, 1824) that "so enormous were the evils produced by the present system, that he would give his support to the proposed alteration, though its effect were to be, to sweep every head of game from the face of the earth."†

According to Mr. William Peel, indeed, even the extirpation of game would not put an end to those evils, of which the existence of game is positively proved to be the cause. "Because if there were no poachers, there would not cease to be criminals. After a few years, when the occupation of poachers should be destroyed, was it supposed that these men would return to the habits of honest industry?"[*] We never met with any one who supposed that because there were no poachers, there would cease to be criminals; nor did we ever meet with any one who supposed, that if there were no murderers, there would, for that reason, cease to be criminals. As little, however, did we ever meet with any one, who argued from thence, that it was not desirable there should cease to be murderers; or that it was not worth while to make a considerable sacrifice, if by any sacrifice this object could be attained. That they who have grown old in the crimes to which they were first allured by the temptations arising out of the game laws, might not cease to be criminals under any laws, is probable enough. But if the dreadful evils which these laws have produced in time past cannot now be remedied, *even* by the abolition of the laws, does it follow that they should not be prevented from continuing to produce evils equally dreadful in time to come? If it be proved, and the reader can judge for himself whether it be so, that poaching is, to an enormous extent, the *cause* of other crimes, that cause to which they owe their existence, and but for

---

*[Charles William Wentworth Fitzwilliam, Speech on the Game Laws Amendment Bill,] *PD*, [n.s., Vol. 11, col. 958,] May 31st, 1824.

†[Edward Harbord, Speech on the Game Laws (20 Feb., 1824), *ibid.*, Vol. 10, col. 267.] Lord Normanby also said on one occasion, in the House of Commons, that he wished there was not a head of game in England.

[*William Peel, speech of 11 Mar., 1824, col. 906.]

which, they would not have been; the truism, that "because there were no poachers, there would not cease to be criminals," will avail the country gentlemen very little.

Mr. Stuart Wortley's bill is an experiment, and ought to be considered as such. It is an experiment to ascertain, whether it be possible to have the pleasures of game, without the evils of poaching. Granting that its success is doubtful; granting that its promoters have failed of making it perfectly certain that it would really produce all the good which they anticipate; does this exculpate those by whom the bill has been thrown out? No! If they, who have forbidden this experiment, had instituted any other experiment which might afford a better chance of mitigating the evil—if, objecting to this mode, they had pointed out any other mode by which their amusements might be reconciled with the happiness and virtue of their countrymen,—something more might have been said for their benevolence as well as for their wisdom. But if they who have so strenuously resisted this alteration, are as strenuous in their resistance to every alteration in that system which is the cause of such unspeakable evils; if they oppose this plan, only as they oppose every plan by which their exclusive privileges are to be curtailed; then are they accountable for all the misery which is produced, for all the lives which are sacrificed, by the direct or indirect consequences of the system; and whatever appellation is due to the man who, for a paltry gratification, knowingly and wilfully inflicts the greatest conceivable evils upon hundreds and thousands of his countrymen, that appellation properly belongs to them.

The alterations proposed to be made in the existing game laws by Mr. Stuart Wortley's bill are principally three: 1. to legalize the sale of game. 2. to abolish qualifications. 3. to render game the private property of the person on whose land it is killed.

Of the first two of these proposed changes, we unequivocally approve; and of the principle of the third, though we disapprove of some of the details.

It is against the first proposition, to legalize the sale of game, that the enemies of the bill have mainly directed their opposition. Let us hear what can be said for them on this point, by the ablest of their advocates.

I must be allowed, [says Mr. Bankes,] to insert a short extract from Lord Suffield's pamphlet. "Few persons, I am apt to think," says his lordship, "are aware of the sum it costs to rear pheasants. I have seen a very accurate calculation, made upon a series of years, for one of the best stocked estates in the kingdom, and computing at the very lowest rate, it appears that every pheasant killed thereon, has cost the proprietor twenty shillings." I suggest, then, [continues Mr. Bankes,] that if the proprietor attempts to undersell the poacher, supposing game to be sold at the same rate at which it stands at this day, as between poulterer and poacher, viz. for pheasants, sometimes no more than one shilling a head, he, the proprietor, will lose nineteen shillings a head upon every item of his dealings, and this on the very lowest rate of computation: the idea of underselling, therefore, is absurd, and some other principle of excluding poachers from the market must be fixed upon, or the subject will not bear a grave consideration; for, admitting that the profit of the poacher were reduced far below even the low quotation which I have above made, if he gained only one penny a head, and subjected the landed proprietor, his competitor, to a loss of nineteen shillings and eleven pence farthing, still, is it not clear, that he would poach and sell to advantage? the prime cost of the pheasants to the poacher being the expense of a little wire and string; a cheap and durable material! Of the value of his time and trouble, I say nothing, for it is admitted that he is allured by an innate love of the sport, which is the common property of our nature; no wonder, therefore, if he shall unwillingly forego a course of life, which combines profit with amusement; and, in whatever ratio the profit may decrease, the amusement is still the same: he will pursue it, therefore, so long as the produce will barely feed and maintain him.*

Now this, we own, might appear very plausible, did we not happen to possess positive proof directly in the teeth of it. The evidence taken before the committee establishes, that a considerable proportion of the game which is sold in London, is even now received from the rightful owners. One poulterer says, that he draws one third of his supply from that source. Another, that he has had upwards of 400 head of game per week from a qualified person. Another, that he has had two hampers, or three hampers, a day, from noblemen.[*]

> I have heard, [says Lord Suffield,] from a friend, on whose veracity I can place the most perfect reliance, of a nobleman who did send his game to a poulterer. The poulterer returned him in exchange a certain quantity of poultry, for which, without this set-off, he would most unquestionably have been paid in cash. From another friend, equally entitled to credit, I have heard of another nobleman who actually did sell his game to a London dealer, and was annually paid for it in money. From a third friend, whom I believe as implicitly as the two former, I have heard of a country magistrate who now annually pockets from three to five hundred pounds by the sale of his game. . . . An example has fallen within my own knowledge, of a proposal made by a London dealer, to take all the game a gentleman, possessing a large estate well furnished, might choose to send him. And what renders the matter still more singular, and still more illustrative of the fact, that such contracts are common—the party applied to was a gentleman whose character was of a kind to render his entering upon such a traffic utterly improbable, and the dealer had not the slightest knowledge of him, either personally or by intercourse of business. I ask, then—I confidently ask, is it reasonable to suppose that such a proposal as this could be made to a gentleman, unless the professed dealer in game had some reason to think it would be accepted? And what reason could he have for thinking it would be accepted in this instance, but the positive knowledge of similar transactions?[†]

Proprietors, then, in considerable numbers, do sell their game, and find poulterers to buy it, even under the present law, under which it is alike punishable to deal with the lawful proprietor, and with the poacher; notwithstanding, too, that the game which the gentlemen send, being mostly shot, is usually in worse condition than the snared game of the poacher. There could not well be a more

*[Bankes, *Reconsiderations*,] pp. 7–8.
[*The evidence of the three poulterers ("C.D.," "I.K.," and "L.M.") is given in "Evidence Taken before the Select Committee on the Laws Relating to Game," *PP*, 1823, IV, 120, 129, and 139.]
†[Harbord, *Considerations*,] pp. 14–15.

complete practical refutation of Mr. Bankes's nineteen shilling argument. If a proprietor can afford to sell his pheasants* contrary to law, he can afford to sell them according to law.

We have reason to believe, that Lord Suffield's estimate of the cost of rearing pheasants is greatly above the mark.† Be this, however, as it may; game is an article, the price of which is not regulated by its cost of production. It is killed for amusement, and not for profit. If so many landholders are willing to rear pheasants at so enormous a cost, for the mere amusement, when they are not permitted to send them to market at all, it is not very likely that, if the sale were legalized, they would cease to rear them, because, in addition to the amusement, they could *only* obtain five shillings a head for them, and not twenty.

As we are anxious to make every possible concession to our opponents, we will suppose that the object for which game is preserved, is not the pleasure of killing it, but the pleasure of giving it away; a pleasure which would cease, when the game itself ceased to be, or rather to be called, a rarity; and that the game-preserver would no longer incur so great an expense merely for the amusement of shooting. What then? The worst that could happen, is, that there would be no preserves, no feeding, no artificial multiplication of game. Whatever might be the case with the game which is fed and preserved, it cannot be said of the game which flies about and finds subsistence for itself, that the cost of its production is nineteen or twenty shillings. Of such game the cost of production is really nothing; and what Mr. Bankes says of the thief, may be said, with equal truth, of the proprietor, that "even the lowest price must always bring in more than he gave."[*] The sum total, then, of the greatest evil, which, under any possible circumstances, could arise from the measure, is, that there would be no more battues, and that gentlemen would be under the necessity of resigning themselves to the hard fate of killing, like their fathers before them, twenty or thirty birds in a day, instead of four or five hundred. We cannot say that we think them much to be pitied; we have no sensibility to spare for this kind of distress; and even if the worst fears of the country gentlemen were realized, if an end were put, for good and all, to game-preserving, we are inclined to suspect that the sun would continue to rise and set, very much as usual. Such a consummation, perhaps, is rather to be wished than dreaded;[†] for experience has proved, that if there be one passion, more than another, which, when once it takes possession of a man, has a tendency to extinguish in his mind every spark of

---

*See the evidence of L.M., porter at an inn, from which we learn, that even pheasants are sold by the proprietors in the same way as other game. ["Evidence," p. 141.]

†Extract from the evidence of I.K., poultry salesman: "What is the lowest price you ever take for pheasants?—*About a shilling or eighteen-pence a-piece*; it has been so low this season, at times, that gentlemen who send me game have written to me to say, that *the prices were so low, it scarcely paid them for feeding.*" [*Ibid.*, p. 129.]

[*Bankes, *Reconsiderations*, p. 5.]

[†Cf. Shakespeare, *Hamlet*, III, i, 63.]

humanity, and to make him inflict, without remorse, for the sake of a selfish gratification, the most immeasurable evils upon his fellow-creatures, it is the passion of game-preserving; "the very mention," it has been truly said, "of hares and partridges in the country, too often puts an end to common humanity and common sense."[*]

But we are told, that, if game were made saleable, no penalty could be inflicted upon any one for having it in his possession, and the principal means of detecting poachers would thus be sacrificed.

If game is made saleable, [says Mr. Bankes,] it may, by possibility, form part of the provision of the bill which makes it so, that licensed brokers alone shall deal it forth to the public, and that qualified persons alone shall be the first suppliers of it; but, that there should be any qualification or license required for the buyer, is of course out of the question; that which every man may buy, it follows of consequence, every man must have a right to hold in possession, unmolested and uncontrolled; consequently, when the proposed law shall have passed, if the poacher shall succeed in taking his prey from the trap or wire unnoticed, his danger is at an end; if questioned, the law will have furnished him with an answer; nay, how shall the law allow of his being questioned? unless, indeed, under such suspicious circumstances relative to time or place, as would justify the detention of a man under the same circumstances, who might have fowls or any other articles of property about him; but in such cases the detention is solely intended to give opportunity for an owner to come forward, and if no owner shall appear, the suspected party is necessarily discharged. With respect to game, since it cannot be identified, ownership of course cannot be proved; a game-keeper, who should attempt to swear to the bulk or plumage of his master's pheasants, would he not be laughed at by a jury? It will be of no avail, therefore, to commit a man, though you should meet him not far from your own preserves, with part of your patrimony, *ratione soli*, peeping from his pockets; for, unless by his own confession, he never can be convicted. Will it be said—Oh! but a poor man—a pauper—a man who has no means—a man who cannot have bought; we may convict *him*—What? convict him of being poor!*

It is a very trite adage, that prevention is better than cure. If you cannot go to the root of the evil, it is the next best thing, but *only* the next best, to lop off the branches. So far as regards those who poach for gain, it is sufficiently proved that the motive to poaching would be taken away, if the sale of game was legalized, since they would be undersold by the rightful owner. It is of very little consequence, therefore, so far as they are concerned, whether the facilities of detection would be increased or diminished. What it is not a man's interest to do, he will not do, whether the facilities of detection be great or small. It is only with respect to those who poach for sport, that the means of detection need to be attended to. What proportion this class of poachers bears to the whole, it is impossible to guess—it can only be proved by experiment. We may be permitted to doubt, however, whether the penalty against unqualified persons having game in their possession, be the chief, or anything like the chief, security against

[*Sydney Smith, "The Game Laws," *Edinburgh Review*, XXXI (Mar., 1819), 301.]
*[Bankes, *Reconsiderations*,] pp. 26–7.

poaching. "Poachers," says Mr. Secretary Peel, "are much more frequently convicted for being detected in the act of killing game than for having game in their possession. It appeared, from a return of persons convicted for having game in their possession, in Norfolk, Suffolk, Dorsetshire, and Sussex, that they bore no proportion to those convicted for being found out at night in the act of destroying game."* In fact, as we have already observed, and as is fully proved by the Minutes of Evidence, the facilities for the immediate disposal of game are such, that unless from mismanagement, it can very rarely happen to a poacher to be found with game in his possession, unless the game-keepers have the good fortune to catch him immediately after he has shot it, or taken it out of the snare. It would still be punishable, in any but persons legally entitled to game, or their game-keepers, to possess snares, or any other engines for the destruction of game, except a gun. To be found out at night with a gun, unless for sufficient reasons assigned, might also be punishable.

We have hitherto contented ourselves with pointing out the specific evils arising out of the prohibition of the sale of game, and have abstained from insisting upon the general argument, that all laws, which are practically inoperative, should be repealed. Yet this is an argument which the supporters of the existing laws would find it extremely difficult to answer. "If laws," says Mr. Secretary Peel, "stand upon our Statute Book which are practically evaded and violated every day; this is of itself a sufficient reason for their repeal—the constant violation of laws is a bad example. And by whom are these laws violated? In general, by those whose duty it is to enforce the laws of the country. It often happens that a gentleman who is occupied during the morning in enforcing the laws, himself sets the example of violating them in a subsequent part of the day."[*]

The extent to which these laws are violated needs not to be dwelt upon, for it is sufficiently known. Suffice it to say, that one poulterer says, he would undertake to provide every family in London with a dish of game on the same day; another, that he would engage to supply the whole House of Commons, without the least difficulty, twice a week for the whole season; and a third, that he sells on the average 500 head per week for about three months in the season, and has sold upwards of 1200 head in the course of a single week.[†] It appears, indeed, that almost the only person who is ever prevented, by the existing laws, from selling game, is the rightful owner. For the end for which they were designed, no laws can be more completely and notoriously inefficacious. For the end of securing to the

---

**PD*, [n.s., Vol. 10, col. 918,] 11th March, 1824. We quote the debates of 1824, because, when this article was written, those of 1825 had not been published in an authoritative form. [In 1824 the debate centred on Stuart-Wortley's "Bill to Amend the Laws for the Preservation of Game," 5 George IV (23 Feb., 1824), *PP*, 1824, I, 579–92. For the debates of 1825, see p. 101n above.]

[*Speech of 11 Mar., 1824, cols. 914–15.]

[†"Evidence," pp. 126 ("G.H."), 118 ("C.D."), and 127 ("I.K.").]

thief almost a monopoly of the market, they are unfortunately to a great degree effectual.

On the subject of qualifications, but little needs be said; the state of the law under this head is too ridiculous to require any exposure. Let the reader who wishes to know it in all its absurdity, turn to Mr. Secretary Peel's humorous description.[*] For what reason should not the poorest man in the kingdom be at liberty to kill game, if invited by the owner of it? except in so far as it might be expedient to make this privilege a source of revenue, by requiring the payment of a certain tax for a game certificate. There cannot be a more unobjectionable subject of taxation; and the only restriction necessary to be observed (a restriction applicable to all other taxes) is, not to raise the tax so high as to afford an adequate motive for its evasion.

To the general principle of vesting the property of game in the owner of the soil on which it is found, there can, as it appears to us, be no valid objection. It has, indeed, been said, that, inasmuch as the produce of the soil which the game feeds on, belongs to the occupier, and inasmuch as it is just that the game should be the property of him at whose expense it is maintained, therefore, the ownership of game should be vested in the occupier, and not in the landlord; a question, in reality, of mere form, and not of substance, since in whatever way this matter might be regulated, the terms of the lease would be adjusted accordingly. The tenant, of course, would be willing to give a considerable additional rent, for the power of destroying, and the right of appropriating game. On the other hand, if the landlord chose to reserve to himself the exercise of the same privileges, either conjointly with his tenant or exclusively (as he now reserves the right of sporting over the land), he would also, as a matter of course, make a proportional abatement of rent.

So much for the principles of the bill. Details are foreign to our present purpose. We shall not, therefore, take up the time of our readers by examining, whether the subordinate arrangements might or might not be improved. We trust that we have sufficiently established the general expediency of the measure.

There is scarcely any thing so bad, as not to have its use; and however bad a thing may appear on the whole, nevertheless in a fair estimate of its character, such uses as it may have, ought not to be omitted. Even the Game Laws, it must be acknowledged, have their uses; and it is but just that these should be taken for as much as they are worth. Accordingly, near the commencement of this article, we made an enumeration of as many of them as at that time occurred to us; which seemed chiefly to consist in affording to honourable gentlemen a few additional pheasants and partridges, to be consumed at their own tables, or despatched (with compliments) to their friends. We omitted, however, to notice one highly important use, of which, to say the truth, we were not, at the time, apprized; but, having since received information of it, fairness requires that we should afford it a

[*Speech of 11 Mar., 1824, cols. 913–14.]

place in our pages. That our readers may not suppose it to be the work of our invention, we inform them that it rests on no less authority than that of a writer in the *Sporting Magazine*, under the signature of "Nimrod," who, we are told, is regarded as a sort of oracle by the sporting world; and that the person to whom, according to Nimrod, mankind are indebted for the idea, is "a large landed proprietor, a magistrate for two counties, a preserver of game" (this we could have guessed) "and a member of parliament of more than twenty years standing."

> I am one of those, [says this preserver of game,] who think that *evil alone* does not result from poaching. The risk poachers run from the dangers that beset them, added to their occupation being carried on in cold dark nights, begets a hardihood of frame, and contempt of danger, that is not without its value. I never heard or knew of a poacher being a coward. They all make good soldiers, and military men are well aware, that two or three men, in each troop or company, of bold and enterprizing spirits, are not without their effect on their comrades. Keepers are all brave men, and willingly subject themselves to great perils to preserve their employer's property.[*]

What a pity that the good old English practice of highway robbery has of late years so lamentably declined; a misfortune for which we are in some measure indebted to the mistaken policy of our ancestors, who most unwisely laid hold of every highwayman they could catch, and hanged him. Had they been gifted with a tithe of the wisdom which falls to the lot of a modern game-preserver, they would have joyfully embraced the opportunity of recruiting the army with such undaunted spirits; in which case the highway might very probably, to the great advantage of the state, have remained a nursery for soldiers to this day. Bereft of this resource, the squires are now compelled to betake themselves to the poachers; who, if they are not highwaymen, are something very nearly as bad.

Considering the vast importance of an army to Great Britain, it would be squeamishness to find fault with the morality of filling the country with bloodshed and murder, in order to make good soldiers; since, after all, it is not much worse than impressment, which, however, we do not remember to have ever heard so ingeniously defended. But we submit that, if to the training of a good soldier it be indispensably necessary that he be engaged, once a week, or thereabouts, in a nightly affray, means might be found of securing to him this inestimable advantage without the expense of so much crime and so much wretchedness to the community. Instead of fighting against the gamekeepers, these future heroes might be set to fight against one another: a battle-royal might be held, if deemed requisite, every "cold, dark night" in the season; with the assistance of a drill-serjeant, they might be put in the way of destroying one another scientifically, which would at all events be a point gained; and if an adequate motive were found wanting, when pheasants and partridges were no longer to be the reward of their toils, parliament could not decently refuse an annual grant, to

[*Charles James Apperley ("Nimrod"), "Of the Game Laws," *Sporting Magazine*, n.s. XVI (Aug., 1825), 307–8.]

promote so laudable an end. Or if it be the pains and penalties of poaching, rather than the nighly affrays, which beget that "contempt of danger," so highly prized by this sporting philanthropist, we would suggest the sending down commissioners, once a year, into every village, there to call together all the able-bodied men in the neighbourhood, for the purpose of drawing lots, which of them should be hanged or transported. This scheme (besides being fairer than the present system) would have a twofold operation, and, indeed, in every supposable case, could not but prove highly advantageous, since if it failed in producing "hardihood and contempt of danger," it would have the opposite advantage of striking a salutary terror into the lower classes. There is indeed, as we are informed by the same authority, "a certain canting party in the House of Commons, who want to appear better than their neighbours; and, in affectation of finer feelings, would soon, if left to themselves, alter the bold and manly character of this country" (of the poachers, we presume) "but I hope they will never succeed:"[*] these persons who "want to appear better than their neighbours," for which insolent wish they deserve to be hunted out of respectable society, will be apt to state, as an objection to the proposed plan, that it involves the shedding of innocent blood; but if it be necessary that a certain number of our countrymen should be annually hanged, *pour encourager les autres*,[†] we conceive that it is better to take hold of the first man you meet, and hang him out of hand, than to wait till he shoots a gamekeeper, and then hang him for the offence.

The arguments of the landed gentlemen against Mr. Stuart Wortley's bill, are not all of them, it may be supposed, of the force of that last mentioned; several of them, however, are curious, and characteristic. Thus, Mr. William Peel's "great objection to the bill was, that it would destroy the noble amusement of fox-hunting; for when to the other inducements to destroy foxes, the occupier of land had the additional one of preserving his game, the race would soon be extinct."[‡] If this be fox-hunting morality, truly fox-hunters seem to be blessed with an easy conscience.

Mr. Lockhart was of opinion, that "qualifications had their value; they afforded inducements to the acquisition of learning and honour, and to the perseverance necessary to attain the stations which conferred them. They were cheap incentives to exertion."[§] Mr. Lockhart seems to imagine that learning and honour, like waifs and estrays, are perquisites which attach themselves to the lord of the manor.

Mr. Horace Twiss objected to legalizing the sale of game, because "its tendency

[**Ibid.*, p. 308.]
[†François Marie Arouet Voltaire, *Candide, ou l'optimisme*, in *Oeuvres complètes*, 66 vols. (Paris: Renouard, 1817–25), Vol. XXXIX, p. 290.]
[‡Speech of 11 Mar., 1824, col. 906.]
[§John Ingram Lockhart, Speech on the Game Laws Amendment Bill (11 Mar., 1824), *PD*, n.s., Vol. 10, col. 910.]

would be, to degrade the country gentlemen into hucksters."[*] This being said of those who without any scruple sell the consciences of their tenants at every election, either for money or for power, is not a little ridiculous; but it seems that a man then only becomes a huckster, when he sells that which is his own. Yet we never heard that country gentlemen felt any invincible aversion to selling their timber, or any other part of the produce of the land.

Mr. William Peel "was surprised that his honourable friend, the member for Yorkshire, who was so little of a reformer in general, should have disposed in so radical a manner of the Game Laws, by a bill which would annihilate all the Game Laws in the country."[†] It is, indeed, but too plain, that this is the first step towards the subversion of the social fabric; and had Mr. Stuart Wortley succeeded in carrying his bill for the annihilation of the Game Laws, no doubt his next step would have been, to bring in a bill for the annihilation of *all* laws. Mr. Peel, however, did not go far enough, in calling this bill a *radical* measure. Why not call it atheistical? The epithet would have been equally appropriate.

"Had not this country," asked Sir John Shelley, "had not this country risen to its highest pinnacle of glory during the existence of these laws."* We cannot be too thankful to the country gentlemen for their conduct on this occasion. They have ridden all the vulgar fallacies so hard, that one would almost think they had a mind to try how ridiculous they could make them.

But the argument which has been repeated oftenest, and insisted upon most earnestly, is the importance of a resident gentry; a favourite topic in an assembly of landowners, and which was re-echoed from all sides of the House, it is difficult to

[*Speech on the Game Laws Amendment Bill (31 May, 1824), *ibid.*, Vol. 11, col. 957.]
[†Speech of 11 Mar., 1824, col. 905.]
*[Speech on the Game Laws Amendment Bill (11 Mar., 1824), *PD*, n.s., Vol. 10, col. 905.] It was the same Sir John Shelley, who, in the last session, made it a matter of reproach to the Spring Gun Bill, that it "made the preservation of a gooseberry of greater value than the preservation of a pheasant." Had he been wise, (for we will not speak here of justice or humanity), he would have reserved such sentiments for his sporting companions: though even among these (such is now the prevalence of liberality and right feeling) he might have chanced to find some to whom they would have been far from acceptable. We do not affect surprise, that a country gentleman should esteem nothing of any importance, except his own amusements; any more than that a child who has been spoiled at home, should continue when abroad to expect that the interests and inclinations of every body should give way to his whims. That a man should prefer himself to others is natural enough; but a prudent man takes pains to hide this preference, instead of ostentatiously publishing it to the world. We presume that Sir John Shelley (as frequently happens to our agricultural Solons) conscious that he had the sympathies of a majority of the audience whom he was addressing, had forgotten that there is now a *public* in this country: we think he could not else have failed to perceive that such an exhibition of undisguised selfishness was calculated to be any thing rather than creditable to him in their eyes. It might become Sir John Shelley to reflect (if it be not too much to expect reflection from an agricultural pericranium) that if a gooseberry be

say by whom loudest, the supporters or the opponents of the measure.[*] By the latter, it was made the foundation for the following exquisite ratiocination. It is of the greatest importance that there should be a resident gentry—now if there be no game, there will be no resident gentry, it being notorious that the only purpose, for which a country gentleman ever resides on his estate, is that of killing game; but if the law be altered, there will be no game; the law, therefore, ought to remain as it is, and we ought to go on as hitherto, making poachers first, giving them time to ripen into thieves, and hanging them afterwards. This is not bad logic, for a country 'squire, and, but that every one of the premises is false, it would be quite unobjectionable.

Assumption the first: Alter the law, and you destroy game. Destroy game, and there will be no resident gentry; this is assumption the second, and a curious one too. A resident gentry is of vast importance; this is the grand assumption of all. If we were content to refute them out of their own mouths, we might ask what great good can come out of the residence of a country gentleman, whose sole motive for residing upon his estate, is, by their own confession, the killing of game? But we wave this: their authority is not worth having, even against themselves.

We ask, then, *why* it is of such vast importance that country gentlemen should reside on their estates? By what means do they contrive to render their presence so great a blessing to their tenantry? Is it by riding with horses and hounds through the growing corn, destroying for a day's amusement the labours of a year? Is it by carrying with them a whole host of London retainers, to infect the village with the vices of the town, as if the vices of the country were not sufficient? or if not in either of these ways, how is it?

We shall be told, no doubt, of the unwearied exertions of the country gentlemen in administering justice, and preserving the peace of the country. Particular stress will be laid upon the circumstance, that these exertions are unpaid; it being in this country an article of faith, that whatsoever is unpaid is good, and that every thing is unpaid which a man does not actually pocket money for. The real character of that unpaid magistracy, who, if credit is to be given to their own assertions, are the most glorious of all the glories of this happy country, and who are really the cause why, in England, which is called the land of freedom, the mass of the people are

---

not so good a mark as a pheasant, for a country gentleman to shoot at, the consumers of gooseberries, however, are rather more numerous than the consumers of pheasants; and that the fruit and vegetables of a market gardener, on which his subsistence depends, may be as well worthy of protection, and may need it as much, as the hares and partridges of a sporting 'squire. [For the Bill, which was not enacted, see "A Bill, Intitled, An Act to Declare Unlawful the Setting of Spring Guns, and Other Offensive Engines," 6 George IV (28 Mar., 1825), *PP*, 1825, III, 599–601.]

[*See, e.g., William Peel and Shelley, speeches of 11 Mar., 1824, cols. 906 and 905.]

the slaves of a more degrading despotism than they probably are in any other country in Europe, will, on some future occasion, be examined in detail. For the present purpose, a few obvious reflections will suffice: That one-fourth of the annual commitments in England and Wales, and probably, as far as regards the agricultural population, much more than half, are for offences against the Game Laws: That on every one of these occasions, the committing magistrate is at the same time judge and party; that he is deciding in his own cause, just as truly as if he were pronouncing sentence upon a poacher taken on his own estate. The consequences, in a tribunal unchecked by publicity, and subject to no appeal, unless from the magistrates individually to the magistrates collectively, are exactly such as might be expected. But the oppressions practised upon poachers *convict*, are nothing in comparison with the oppressions which are practised upon those who are only *suspected* to be poachers. Every one who has lived in the country knows what we mean, and the memory of every one will supply him with numerous instances; though it is not every one who is aware of the legal traps which it is in the power of a magistrate to lay for any one who has offended him—of the number of sleeping laws which he can revive when he pleases, laws which are not, and cannot be, impartially executed, or common justice and common humanity would be shocked, but which it is left to the discretion of a vindictive or tyrannical magistrate to execute or not as he will. Many a man has been immured, many a man is even now lying in a gaol, whose nominal offence has been that of cutting a twig, or going off a path; his real offence, that of being poor, and being suspected, truly or untruly, of being a poacher.

If the reader wishes to form some conception of the extent of the arbitrary power which magistrates possess, let him look at the late Report of Commitments under the Vagrant Laws.[*] Under these laws it is scarcely too much to say, that there is not a man, certainly there is not a poor man, who is not in the power of any one who will take the trouble of watching him for a short time; there is scarcely an act of human life which, if done in the way in which it often *must* be done by the poor man, is not an act of vagrancy. To convict a man of being a vagrant, little more is necessary than to find him guilty of the crime of being poor.

It is an insult to our understandings to say, that powers like these are not abused. Till lately, indeed, the abuses of magisterial power, like the abuses of almost every other power, were comfortably hidden from the public eye. Of late, however, it has not been in the power of libel law to prevent occasional instances from becoming known. In one instance within our own knowledge an unfortunate man was committed to the treadmill for a month as a "rogue and vagabond" under the Vagrant laws, on no ground whatever but that of being found on a private path.

[*"Return of Persons Committed under the Vagrant Laws," *PP*, 1824, XIX, 215–338. For the law, see 5 George IV, c. 83 (1824).]

This act of magisterial tyranny took place in Yorkshire.* *Ex uno disce alios.* It is not every magistrate who would commit an act of this kind; but every magistrate can do so if he please.

> *The case to which we allude is notorious in the county. The committing magistrate was indicted, and a true bill found against him by the grand jury, but the prosecution was dropped, the affair (it is universally believed) having been compounded by the payment of five hundred pounds to the prosecutor.
>
> As an example of the consequences of being suspected to be a poacher, and of the liberties which country gentlemen take with the "lower orders," we give the following anecdote of "Nimrod," in his own words: "Some years since, a man lived near me who never had been detected as a poacher, but *I had good reason to suspect* he was one. Going out shooting one day, his dog (a common cur) followed me. I saw in less than half an hour, what use he had been applied to, so going up to a labourer who was at work on my farm, I made him dig a grave for him, and *shot him on the spot.*" [Apperley, "Of the Game Laws," p. 306.]

INTERCOURSE BETWEEN THE UNITED STATES AND THE BRITISH COLONIES IN THE WEST INDIES

1828

EDITOR'S NOTE

Parliamentary Review. Session of 1826–7:—7 & 8 Geo. IV. London: Baldwin and Cradock, 1828, 298–335. Headed as title. Running titles: "FOREIGN RELATIONS.—*United States.*" Unsigned; not republished. Identified in Mill's bibliography as "An article on the Commerce between the West-Indies and the United States of America, which app. in the Parliamentary review for the session of 1827" (MacMinn, 9). In the Somerville College copy of this volume an inked note in Mill's hand on the title page identifies this article as his, and, at the equivalent of 133.27–9, there is a pencilled comment (possibly in Mill's hand) that reads (ignoring a cancellation and an incomplete revision): "The Superior skill of Shipbuilders & Seamen is decidedly with the Americans". For comment on the article, see lvii–lviii above.

Intercourse between the United States and the British Colonies in the West Indies

A SHORT CONVERSATION which took place when a late correspondence between the British Government and the Envoy of the United States was laid upon the table of the House of Commons by Mr. Canning,* affords us an opportunity, of which we gladly avail ourselves, to lay before our readers the history of that correspondence, with a few observations on the subject which has produced so much unfriendly feeling between two kindred nations.

It is known that, until within a short period, it was a favourite object of British policy that British shipping should engross as large a share as possible of the commercial intercourse of the world. With this view, foreign vessels resorting to the ports of Great Britain and her dependencies, and goods imported into Great Britain and her dependencies in foreign vessels, were made subject to numerous burthens and restrictions, from which British vessels, and goods imported in British vessels, were exempt.

It is known, also, that by several recent statutes commonly called the Reciprocity Acts, these restrictions were relaxed, and some of them entirely abrogated, in favour of such countries as should relieve British shipping from all similar restrictions, to which, by the laws of those countries, it was subject. Among the Reciprocity Acts, was one called the 6 Geo. IV, c. 114, an Act passed on the 5th of July, 1825, which permitted foreign nations, upon certain conditions of reciprocity, to trade, in their own vessels, with the British colonies.[*]

Among foreign nations, that which, from its situation and productions, is capable of carrying on the most beneficial trade with our colonies, is the United States of America. That country, however, did not comply with the conditions of reciprocity which the act of parliament required, and consequently did not become entitled to the privileges which that act conferred. An order in council was therefore issued, in July 1826, interdicting, after a certain day, all intercourse, in

---

*["Correspondence between Great Britain and the United States, Relative to Commercial Intercourse between America and the British West Indies,"] Presented to both Houses of Parliament by command of his Majesty, March 26, [1827,] *PP*, 1826–27, [XXV,] 21–51. [See also *PD*, n.s., Vol. 17, cols. 44–67 (26 Mar., 1827). The United States Envoy was Albert Gallatin.]

[*Other "Reciprocity Acts" included 4 George IV, c. 77 (1823), and 5 George IV, c. 1 (1824).]

American vessels, between the United States and the British West India colonies;[*] and, consequently, the shipping of the United States not only did not acquire any new privileges under the Act of 1825, but lost those which it already enjoyed by virtue of a partial relaxation of our Navigation Laws which took place in 1822.[†]

On the appearance of the Order in Council, Mr. Gallatin, Envoy Extraordinary of the United States, addressed an official note to Mr. Canning, as Secretary of State for the Foreign Department, remonstrating against it. He observed that, by the laws of the United States, our commerce and navigation stood, in every respect, on the footing required by the Act of 1825, with the exception of certain discriminating duties on British vessels, and on goods imported in British vessels, entering the ports of the United States from the British colonies. That the British government had already retaliated, by the imposition of countervailing duties on American vessels, resorting to our colonies, and on their cargoes. That, the only inequality supposed to exist having been removed by these countervailing duties, there could be no reason for adopting the harsher measure of altogether interdicting the intercourse, in American vessels, between the United States and so important a part of those colonies.[‡]

In answer to this communication from Mr. Gallatin, Mr. Canning addressed a letter to that gentleman,[§] of which we shall next endeavour to explain the purport. It is, however, not easy to present a connected view of Mr. Canning's argument, without *expressing* much of what he himself has rather left to be *understood*. This is no matter of blame to him; it is no fault of his, if what was meant only for purposes of information, is not sufficiently explicit for purposes of argument. But when a proposition is to be discussed, it must be written out at full length. Mr. Canning rather indicated than stated the several points which he sought to establish; and did not so much make out a case, as bring together the materials, out of which, when properly connected together, a case might be made.

He began by complaining that Mr. Gallatin treated the question as if there were no inherent distinction between colonial trade and the trade of independent nations. Mr. Gallatin misconceived the nature of the colonial trade. It was the unquestionable right, and had, till within these few years, been the invariable practice, of countries having colonies, to reserve to themselves the trade with those colonies, and to relax that reservation only under special circumstances, and on particular occasions. The right, therefore, which Great Britain clearly possessed, as against all nations, the United States could not justly complain if she thought fit

[*Order in Council on Colonial Trade, 3 May, 1826, in *London Gazette*, 30 June, 1826, p. 1614.]
[†See 3 George IV, c. 44 (1822), and, for the earlier laws, 12 Charles II, c. 18 (1660), and 15 Charles II, c. 7 (1663).]
[‡Gallatin, "Correspondence," *PP*, 1826–27, XXV, 25–7.]
[§Canning, "Correspondence," *ibid.*, pp. 27–32.]

to exercise against *them*. In 1822, Great Britain conceded to the shipping of the United States, under certain restrictions, the privilege of trading with the British West India colonies; a privilege which she still withheld from all the powers of Europe. It could not, however, be supposed—it was not affirmed by Mr. Gallatin—that, by granting this privilege to one nation, Great Britain came under any implied engagement, not at any future period to extend it to others. As little could be supposed that, because Great Britain submitted, at a moment of necessity, to terms which were inconvenient to her, she bound herself to continue to submit to them when that necessity should have passed away. She had a right to open the ports of her colonies, or to keep them closed, as might suit her own convenience. She had a right to open them either unconditionally or conditionally; and if conditionally, on what conditions she pleased. She had a right—(but this necessary step in Mr. Canning's argument was rather understood than expressed) —she had a right, after her original conditions had been accepted, to revoke them whenever she pleased, and impose others; and though she might profess to take the principle of reciprocity for the guide of her counsels, no other nation had a right to remonstrate, as Mr. Gallatin had done, if the conditions she imposed were at variance with the principle of reciprocity; for Great Britain was not bound to abide by that principle.

Having thus disposed of the general subject of Colonial Trade, Mr. Canning proceeded to explain why the British Government, not satisfied with laying the same burthens upon the trade in American vessels which had been laid upon that in British vessels by the United States, had recourse to the more severe measure of prohibiting the trade in American vessels altogether.

In 1822, when Great Britain permitted the United States, under certain limitations and conditions, to trade in their own vessels with our West India colonies; in accepting these terms Congress at the same time imposed on all British vessels trading between the United States and the West Indies, and on all goods imported in such vessels, an alien duty.[*] This duty was to continue until American vessels, and their cargoes, should be admitted into our colonies on the same terms as British vessels, and as the same description of goods imported from *elsewhere*: meaning by elsewhere, not only all foreign nations, but the other trans-marine possessions of Great Britain, and even the mother country herself.

This unwarrantable pretension on the part of the United States, to an equalization of the duties on their produce with those on our own, was the motive which had induced the British Government, after an interval of three years, to issue the Order in Council now complained of. The delay which had intervened, Mr. Canning thus accounted for: The British Government at first misapprehended the import of the term *elsewhere*, conceiving it to apply to foreign countries alone, and not to the British possessions in North America; and could not, for some time, be

[*See 17th Congress, Sess. II, c. 22 (1823).]

brought to believe, that it was intended to lay claim to the admission of American produce into our colonies, subject to no higher duties than that of the mother country herself, and her other dependencies. When such was at length ascertained to be the true construction of the Act of Congress, our Government, by their own Act of 1822, were entitled to have at once interdicted all intercourse between the United States and the British West India colonies. The milder measure of a retaliatory duty was preferred, because it was not supposed that a claim so extraordinary as that implied in the above-mentioned Act of Congress would be persisted in after explanation. The attempt, however, to obtain the abandonment of it by means of negociation having failed, and Congress having, during the last session, rejected a motion for the repeal of the discriminating duties, Great Britain had now asserted that right, which, as long as there appeared to be any chance of an amicable arrangement, she had forborne to exercise.

But further, Mr. Canning could not admit the assertion that the discriminating duties were our *only* ground of complaint. In making this averment, Mr. Gallatin appeared to overlook the fact, that, by the same enactment which imposed those duties, it was provided that no British ships not coming directly from the West Indies, should be allowed to clear out for the West Indies, from a port of the United States. It was true that something analogous to this regulation had existed on our side. By the Act of 1822, American vessels entering the ports of our colonies, were prohibited from clearing out for any country other than the United States. But such was the peculiar character of colonial trade, that we *were* justified in imposing this restriction; the Americans were *not* justified in retaliating.

To allow a foreign ship to enter colonial ports at all, and upon any terms, is a *boon*; to withhold from the ship of a country having colonies, trading from the mother country to a foreign state, under a regular treaty between the two countries, the right of clearing for another port belonging to that mother country, in another part of the world, is an *injury*.*

Had the restriction, therefore, still existed on our part, this would have formed no justification for its imposition on theirs. But it did not exist on our part. It had been repealed by the Act of 1825; and yet the retaliatory restriction, expressly founded upon it, continued in force.

Since the 5th of January, 1826, an American ship trading to a British West India colony, may clear out from thence to any part of the world, the United Kingdom and its dependencies alone excepted. But the British ship in the American port still remains subject to all the restrictions of the American law of 1823, prohibiting a trade through the United States between the mother country and her West India colonies. (*Ibid.*)

In conclusion, Mr. Canning said, that the British Government could not consent to enter into any further negociation upon the intercourse between the United States and the colonies, so long as the pretension recorded in the Act of 1823 remained part of the law of the United States. But further, after the United States

*[Canning, "Correspondence,"] p. 31.

had declined conditions which other nations had thought worthy of their acceptance, and by so doing had compelled the British Government to apply to them the interdict prescribed (he should have said *allowed*) by the Act of 1825, it could not hold itself bound to remove that interdict, as a matter of course, whenever it might suit the convenience of the United States to reconsider the measures by which the application of that interdict was occasioned.

We have thought it necessary to give this full abstract of Mr. Canning's first letter to Mr. Gallatin, because the views of the British Government concerning the whole matter to which the Order in Council relates, are no where else so clearly and fully set forth. The same minuteness will not be necessary in the account, which it now remains for us to give, of the remainder of the correspondence.

Mr. Gallatin intimated his dissent from the doctrine of Mr. Canning with respect to Colonial Trade.[*] The *right* of Great Britain to reserve to herself the trade with her colonies, or to open it to whatever nations, and upon whatever terms she thought proper, was not denied; but, considered purely as a matter of right, this, which was an attribute of sovereignty, applied to all other territories as well as to colonies. The real distinction between the trade of foreigners with colonies, and that with other territories, did not consist in a greater or less complete right, but in a difference in the usage and practice. Since the late final separation, however, of the greater part of the continent of America from the mother countries, and the more liberal policy adopted towards the remaining colonies, the usage of nations in respect to colonial policy might be considered to have changed, and the Colonial Trade to have been so far assimilated to all other trade as to admit of being discussed on the basis of equal and reciprocal conditions. Indeed, in every negociation which had taken place on this subject between the United States and Great Britain, the principle of reciprocity had been the basis assumed, by the consent of both parties.

Mr. Gallatin next proceeded to vindicate, at some length,[†] the enactments of Congress, to which exceptions had been taken by Mr. Canning: the imposition, or rather revival, of the discriminating duties, and the prohibition of what is called the circuitous intercourse between Great Britain and her colonies, through the United States. But the reasons which induced Congress to adopt these measures will be more conveniently stated in a subsequent part of this article.

Finally, Mr. Gallatin said, that the United States could scarcely be expected to repeal their restrictions upon British vessels, when not only the intercourse was altogether prohibited in American shipping, but when they were with frankness informed, that a removal of that interdict would not, as a matter of course, follow such repeal on their part.[‡] Since Mr. Canning, however, had refused to negociate while the pretension involved in the Act of 1823 continued part of the law of the

[*Gallatin, "Correspondence," pp. 33–6.]
[†*Ibid.*, pp. 36–7.]
[‡*Ibid.*, pp. 37–8.]

United States, Mr. Gallatin informed him, that the Act complained of was already repealed, by virtue of one of its own provisions, which enacted, that it should cease to operate if at any time the British Government should prohibit the intercourse with our colonies in American vessels. That contingency having taken place, the laws of 1818 and 1820 had revived, which prohibited the intercourse in British vessels altogether;[*] and all laws since passed to *regulate* the intercourse, were abrogated by its entire *interdiction*.

The answer of Mr. Canning was brief,[†] and replied only to that part of Mr. Gallatin's letter which denied the peculiar character of the Colonial Trade. It might be true, as stated by Mr. Gallatin,[‡] that every country had a *right* to interdict to foreign nations a trade even with *itself*; but the exercise of that right had been so unusual, that foreign nations might justly complain of such interdiction as a grievance. They had no such ground of complaint, and no other nation than the United States had ever complained, of the interdiction of trade to the colonies; because, in all ages, all nations having colonies had maintained such an interdiction. The assumption that the colonial system was at an end, Great Britain explicitly denied. Whatever relaxation Great Britain might think fit to introduce, for her own sake, and for that of her colonies themselves, into her colonial system, she held her right to maintain that system, as with respect to foreign nations, to be unaltered and entire. Considerations of which she alone was the judge, had induced her to open her trade to other nations, on specified conditions, offered to all nations indiscriminately. Other nations had accepted these conditions; the United States, having declined them, were excluded from our colonies, not by any act of ours, but by their own free and deliberate choice.

After an interval of a few weeks, Mr. Gallatin, having received a despatch from the Secretary of State of the United States, again addressed Mr. Canning[§] with a statement of the reasons which had hitherto prevented the United States from accepting the conditions of the Reciprocity Act of 1825. The first of these reasons was, that they had so much difficulty in comprehending the import of the act, and how much it did or did not repeal of former acts, that they did not venture to legislate on the subject without receiving such previous explanations as could not fail to be obtained in the course of the negociation which Mr. Gallatin came authorized to renew. In the next place, so far as they were able to understand the meaning of the act, the reciprocity which it offered appeared to be a reciprocity in name only, not in fact; and this Mr. Gallatin, at some length, proceeded to demonstrate.

In reply to the above communication, Mr. Canning declined entering into any

[*15th Congress, Sess. I, c. 70 (1818), and 16th Congress, Sess. I, c. 122 (1820).]
[†Canning, "Correspondence," pp. 38–41.]
[‡Gallatin, "Correspondence," pp. 33–6.]
[§*Ibid.*, pp. 42–7.]

discussion with respect to the nature of the reciprocity offered by the act of 1825.[*] He contented himself with justifying the resolution of the British Government, not to enter into any further negociations on a subject on which there had been clearly ascertained to be an incurable difference of opinion; and with adducing evidence to prove that it was not for want of a sufficient understanding of the intent of the act of parliament, that the conditions of it were not accepted by the United States.

We quote some of the concluding paragraphs of Mr. Canning's letter, chiefly because they afford indication of the opinion which our Government entertains concerning the principle of reciprocity, and the nature of trade in general.

> The undersigned trusts that it is unnecessary for him, in concluding this note, to return to Mr. Gallatin's assurances of the friendly disposition of the United States of America—assurances equally sincere, that there is the most cordial desire, on the part of Great Britain, to cultivate the friendship of the United States.
>
> The ties of common origin, laws, and language, must always form strong bonds of national alliance between them. Their respective interests, well understood, harmonize together as much as their feelings.
>
> But it has never yet been held a duty of international amity (any more than of friendship in private life) to submit to unequal compacts; nor has it ever been held an offence against such duty that a nation (any more than an individual) should decline to make uncompensated sacrifices.
>
> The refusal to regulate the trade of our colonies by a commercial treaty, which the British Government may think (even if erroneously) disadvantageous to its interests, cannot give just cause of offence to any power whatever. (*Ibid.*, p. 51.)

Among the many observations suggested by the perusal of this correspondence, none is more obvious than the continual endeavour of Mr. Canning, not, perhaps, sufficiently resisted by Mr. Gallatin, to give a character to the discussion foreign to that which belongs to the nature of the subject. The whole argument is made to turn upon the question of *right*; as if our right to regulate the trade of our colonies were disputed, or as if the conduct either of a nation or an individual, in the exercise of a right, could never be a proper subject for censure or animadversion. The clearness of our right does not justify whatever use we can make of it. One person may injure another almost to any extent, by the exercise of an acknowledged right. A man who quarrels with his friends, turns off his servants, or disinherits his children, merely does what every person will allow to be his right; yet surely any of these things, if done without just cause, is an injury, and the party aggrieved by it might very reasonably complain, without being supposed to dispute the right which every man possesses of cultivating what acquaintances, employing what servants, and appointing what legatees he pleases.

But, in the case before us, there is neither any question of right, nor any complaint of injury, except on our side. No such complaint could be made without absurdity. In the commercial intercourse between two nations, as in

---

[*Canning, "Correspondence," pp. 48–51.]

transactions of the same nature between man and man, the only considerations relevant to the subject are those of *mutual interest*. If each party, instead of seeking or making occasions for crimination where none exist, would put aside all feelings except those which arise from a calm and dispassionate consideration of the interests of the parties,—those interests, in the case of commercial intercourse, never being contrary, but always the same,—there might be reasonable hope that some arrangement would be adopted advantageous to both. But if either country is more anxious to prove to the other that it will not suffer itself to be dictated to, than to establish the commerce of both upon the most desirable basis, and does not choose to concede to foreigners on their asking, what it ought to grant even if unasked, not for their sake, but for its own; then, indeed, neither the commerce nor the friendship between the two nations, rests upon a very secure foundation.

Putting apart any pretended right on either side to prescribe measures to the other, let us consider merely the interests of the two nations, and examine how far each of them appears to understand rightly what those interests require.

It seems, then, in the first place, that the two parties,—who are, so far, perfectly agreed, that both entrench themselves within the principle of reciprocity, but who differ so widely in its application,—are neither of them by any means aware of the serious objections which may be made to the principle of reciprocity itself.

According, indeed, to Mr. Canning's view of the principles of trade, there is no room for doubt or hesitation. The permitting foreign vessels, under any circumstances, to carry goods to any part of our possessions, he considers as an advantage to the foreigner, not only unattended with any benefit to ourselves, but implying a sacrifice on our part, and therefore not to be conceded, unless an equal advantage, either of the same or of some other kind, be granted to us in return.

But this, surely, is a very partial view of the case, and implies an entire misconception of the nature and objects of commerce.

That a measure is injurious to Great Britain because it diminishes the employment for British shipping; that it causes a loss to the country because it causes the loss, or the decay, of some particular branch of manufactures, or some particular branch of trade; this would have been consistent language from the lips of a merchant of the days of Sir Josiah Child, but it is scarcely what we might expect from a ministry who inscribe free trade upon their banners, and claim the merit of being guided, in their commercial legislation, by the principles of Smith and Ricardo.

Bread, we apprehend, does not exist for the sake of the farmer, cloth for the sake of the manufacturer, ships and navigation for the sake of the builder and ship-owner. The numerous and diversified productions which conduce, each in its way, to the relief of human necessities, or the convenience of human life, are not called into existence merely in order that somebody may be paid for producing them. That a large number of productive labourers should be employed and maintained, where a small number would suffice, is no advantage, but the reverse.

The real advantage would be, if the same amount of produce could be obtained by employing, that is to say, expending, less labour and less capital. Whatever was thus saved would constitute an addition to the fund which might be appropriated to further production, and the further increase of the comforts and enjoyments of man. For what reason, then, does the language we hear from all practical statesmen, even from those who make pretensions to political economy, always import that the one grand danger in the production of commodities is, lest we should get them without employing capital enough? The golden age, then, was not, after all, so desirable a state of existence; since all human wants were then supplied, if we are not mistaken, without employing any capital at all.

The proper and only end, both of production and of commerce, is, to supply commodities: nor, with a view to the national wealth, does one employment of capital possess any advantage over another, except that of supplying them at less cost. It is for the interest of the consumer, not for that of the producer or carrier, that production and commerce exist. The interest of the consumer, however, is an element which is usually left out of the calculations of practical statesmen. They generally imagine that it is their business to take care of the producer. The consumer is commonly left to take care of himself.

Now, the direct contrary of this ought to be the case. The late Mr. Ricardo, in replying to those who never ceased to talk of protection to the farmer, and protection to the manufacturer, and protection to every other description of producer, used to say, that it was strange nobody ever called for protection to the consumer, when, in fact, it is the consumer alone who needs protection.[*] The producer can protect himself. If he is not paid for producing he will not produce. *Time*, for disengaging his capital, and allowing that portion to wear out gradually which cannot be disengaged, he may justly claim; the rest is in his own hands. It is to the consumer that protection, protection against too high a price, is indispensable. The only protection that is effectual (but it is always effectual) is liberty to supply his wants wherever they can be supplied at the smallest cost. Our legislators are prodigal of protection to those to whom it is superfluous; they withhold it from those to whom alone it is needful.

When we take this view, which surely is not a visionary, overstrained, or fanciful, but a sound, practical, and experimental view of the nature of trade, we are led to conclusions, on the subject discussed in Mr. Canning's correspondence, widely at variance with his. We conclude, that the opening our ports to foreign vessels is not a boon to foreigners, but a benefit to ourselves, and a much greater benefit to ourselves than to foreigners; that our interest is more promoted by our allowing foreigners to bring goods to *us*, than even by their granting permission to our vessels to carry goods to *them*.

[*Cf. David Ricardo, Speech on a Motion for a Committee on the Agricultural Distress (18 Feb., 1822), *PD*, n.s., Vol. 6, cols. 479-86.]

To those who cannot perceive that commerce yields any benefit to the nation, other than what it yields to its own instruments and agents, overlooking the great body of consumers, for whose sake it really exists, the above thesis may seem a paradox; but to them alone will it appear so.

From the language which our statesmen hold, one would imagine them to suppose, that, by obtaining the privilege of importing into foreign countries in our own ships, we should gain an entire new branch of trade, with the whole of its profits as a neat addition to the national income. Yet, this is only true in the sense in which it might be said that by planting vineyards on the Surrey hills we should gain a new branch of productive industry. The industry and trade of a country are limited by the capital of the country: if a new channel be opened to either, the capital which supplies it must be drawn from the other channels. We cannot raise capital from the ground, as Pompey imagined that he could raise armies, by stamping upon it with our feet.[*] So that the subject of all this contention is merely the difference between one mode of employing capital and another. The new employment may, indeed, be the more profitable one; and in this consists the advantage, when advantage there is, of the opening of a new channel of trade. But the commonest principles of trade shew us, that when the profits in any employment exceed what can be obtained in others, additional capital rushes in, and restores the level. If it were found that our ship-owners, on being permitted to carry for other countries, could gain more than the ordinary profits of British stock, British competition would compel them to go on lowering their freights (by which reduction the foreigner alone would benefit) until, with the exception of the extra profit which they had made for a short time, neither they nor their country would have gained any thing by the privilege they had acquired. So little is a nation benefitted by being a carrier for other countries; except, indeed, so far as it is an advantage, for purposes of national defence, to possess a large commercial marine; an advantage which, as our marine is already so much more than sufficient for that purpose, may be laid out of the question.

But it is impossible to set any limits to the degree in which we might be benefitted, by permitting foreign vessels to carry for *us*. They would not be able to do so, unless they could do it cheaper than our own vessels; and if they could, what would be saved in freight would be gained by the British consumer in the price of the goods. If we consider how much of what all of us consume is imported from abroad,—how much more there is which could not be produced, unless the "appliances and means"[†] of its production were imported from abroad,—as likewise, how much of all this is composed of bulky goods, and how great a proportion of its price is occasioned by cost of carriage,—we shall be enabled to

[*See Plutarch, *Life of Pompey*, in *Lives* (Greek and English), trans. Bernadotte Perrin, 11 vols. (London: Heinemann; Cambridge, Mass.: Harvard University Press, 1914–26), Vol. V, p. 267.]

[†Shakespeare, *Henry IV, Part II*, III, i, 29.]

form a rough estimate of what the country would gain by allowing its trade of importation to take place in foreign vessels, *if* the fact be, that it can be carried on less expensively in that way. If, in consequence, any British shipping were thrown out of employment, the evil to the ship-owners might easily be prevented from being considerable. The foreigner would probably be willing to purchase their ships; and, at the worst, a ship does not last one third part so long as a house, or even so long as a steam-engine; and, if a few years were allowed, those ships which could not find other employment would wear out in the course of nature, as would have happened in any other circumstances. Nor would there be the slightest reason to fear, from such an event, the loss of any useful naval strength. Were we excluded from all other commerce—our fisheries, and the perils of the most difficult coasting navigation in Europe, would keep us supplied with ships and seamen to meet every possible emergency.

The admission, therefore, of American vessels to trade with our colonies, not being any sacrifice, does not require any compensation; and if our colonies are to be considered (which for this purpose they must) as a part of ourselves, it is a moot point by which of the two we should gain most, the compensation, or the sacrifice.

The state of the case is this: so far as concerns the trade *to* the United States, that it should take place in ships of the one country rather than of the other may be of consequence to the people of the United States, who consume the cargoes, but to us it is merely a question whether a certain amount of British capital shall be employed in navigation, or in some other equally profitable business. With respect, however, to the trade *from* the United States, or *from* any third country, *to* our colonies, it is a concern of the colonial consumer, and exclusively so. It is his interest that the goods should be carried by whichever of the two countries, or of all other countries, and carry them cheapest. If the two countries are nearly equal—(which we believe to be the case; for the advantage which America possesses in cheapness of material, we make up by the superior skill of our ship-builders and seamen,) even in this case it is very much the interest of the consumers, who are the inhabitants of our colonies, that the trade should be left open to the competition of both, in order that each may be urged on to the rapid adoption of every species of improvement, by the rivality of the other.

All these things, which are demonstratively true, if such a thing as demonstration be possible in human affairs, clearly show what the principle of reciprocity, in the commerce between two nations, is, and on what grounds it may admit of justification. The only case which offers any difficulty may be stated as follows:

Two nations have carried on, for many years, a war of prohibitions, to the great detriment of both; each of the two perceiving, in the effect of its own interdictions, that part only which is injurious to the other country, and being blind to that part which affects itself. One of these governments subsequently embraces sound and liberal principles of trade, while the other still adheres to antiquated prejudices. As long as the enlightened government maintains its restrictions, it has in its power to offer to the stupid government what that government may consider as an equivalent for the abandonment of the counter-prohibitions. By giving up the restrictions unconditionally, this advantage would be sacrificed. It is a question between the immediate advantage of getting rid of one evil, and the chance of being freed from two by suffering that one a little longer. And we can easily conceive that it may be a very fit problem to propose, though often a very difficult one to solve, whether the enlightened government is justified in maintaining its own restrictive laws, after it has become sensible of their mischievousness, in order to induce the bigotted government to purchase their abrogation by renouncing its own.

But the case before us has none of these difficulties. Perfect reciprocity is here the declared object of both nations: and neither party objected to the conditions proposed by the other, on any ground excepting that they were *not* reciprocal; each country professing complete readiness to take off its restrictions, provided that the other country would do the same. That two nations, meeting one another with these avowed dispositions, should so far misunderstand one another as to terminate their negociations without removing a single restriction, is sufficiently unaccountable: but that the attempts of both parties to render the trade free, should end by interdicting it altogether, argues either a strange obliquity of intellect, or at least a complete misunderstanding of the principle of reciprocity, on one side, or on both. It shall be our endeavour, in the remainder of this dissertation, to shew, by which of the two governments the principle which both profess has been misunderstood, and at whose door the failure of the attempts at an amicable arrangement ought to be laid.

In order that the commercial intercourse between two countries should be on a footing of exact reciprocity, it is necessary that either there should be no discriminating duties in either country, upon the shipping of the other; or that those duties, if any exist, should be equal. On the first of these suppositions there is free trade on both sides, and consequently reciprocity: in the second case, there is reciprocity of restriction, which, though never desirable, may be allowable as a means of arriving at reciprocity of free trade.

It was in conformity with these principles, that the trade between the United States and the Kingdom of Great Britain and Ireland, was regulated by the Convention of 1815.[*] That treaty provides, that no distinction shall be made by either nation, between the ships of the other country coming directly from that country, and its own. Thus far there is reciprocity of free trade. In what follows, there is reciprocity of restriction:—neither country enjoys the privilege of importing into the other the produce of a third country, on any conditions or under any circumstances whatever.

[*"Convention of Commerce, between Great Britain and the United States of America; Signed at London, 3rd July 1815," *PP*, 1816, XVII, 143–6.]

This treaty of commerce extends only to the King's European dominions. The party, at whose instances it was thus limited, was Great Britain. It was the wish of the United States, that the British colonies should, for the purposes of the treaty, be considered as a part of Great Britain, and the trade between America and those colonies laid open, like that of the mother country, to the shipping of both nations, on a footing of perfect equality. This proposition was recommended, not only by its conformity with sound principles, but by what, to the then ministry, might be supposed a more powerful recommendation,—the authority of Mr. Pitt. We believe it is not generally known, that this statesman, shortly after the close of the American war, introduced a bill into Parliament, admitting American vessels, so far as regards the direct trade between the United States and the West Indies, to all the privileges of our own.[*] The bill was lost by the breaking up of the Shelburne Administration; when the vulgar and exploded ideas of commercial policy regained their ascendancy, by the elevation of Mr. Fox. But the Castlereagh ministry, faithful to their custom of borrowing nothing from Mr. Pitt except whatever was bad in his principles or policy, were resolved to keep, so far as it was still in their power, the monopoly of the colonial trade unimpaired. The colonies were therefore excepted from the Convention of 1815; and the intercourse, in American vessels, between the United States and the West Indies, remained interdicted. The United States, becoming impatient under the exclusion, at length interdicted the intercourse in British vessels, until it should be permitted in their own: a measure which Mr. Canning, in his first letter to Mr. Gallatin, allows to have been, under the circumstances above stated, justifiable.[†]

We have mentioned these circumstances, (although they have no immediate bearing upon the matter at issue,) because they shew that it was Great Britain, and not the United States, who commenced the war of prohibitions; and that nothing, except the obstinate refusal of Great Britain, prevented a perfect system of reciprocity from having been established as long ago as 1815. From what cause such a system failed to be established, when a ministry hostile to free trade had been succeeded by one which has given substantial proofs of an inclination to it, remains to be accounted for.

An examination of the provisions of our Act of Reciprocity, will, we think, explain very satisfactorily the causes of this failure.

The privilege conferred by the Act in question upon foreign nations was, in all cases, one and the same. It was that of trading to our colonies in their own vessels, subject to the same duties, and no more, which were imposed upon the same intercourse when carried on in British ships.

[*"A Bill for the Provisional Establishment and Regulation of Trade and Intercourse between the Subjects of Great Britain and Those of the United States of North America," 23 George III (3 Mar., 1783), *House of Commons Sessional Papers of the Eighteenth Century*, XXXV (Bills 1782–84), 71–3.]

[†Canning, "Correspondence," p. 28.]

But while the privilege offered was the same to all nations, there was a great diversity in the conditions by the acceptance of which, that privilege was to be purchased. Even the apparent difference in the terms was very great; but the real difference still greater.

From nations which, having colonies, could repay us in kind, nothing more was required than that they should do so. Their colonies were to be opened to *our* vessels, in the same manner, and on the same footing of equality, on which our colonies had been opened to *theirs*.

If we examine these terms of reciprocity by the principles laid down by Mr. Canning, in his correspondence with Mr. Gallatin, we must pronounce them highly disadvantageous to Great Britain. No other nation now possesses colonies, in any degree to be compared for extent and productiveness with those of Great Britain. If, therefore, the admission of foreigners to share the trade and navigation of our colonies be indeed, as Mr. Canning represents it, a sacrifice, assuredly *our* admission to a like share of the trade and navigation of *theirs*, is by no means an adequate compensation. Sweden, for instance, (as Mr. Gallatin very pertinently observed,)[*] by admitting British vessels to trade, on the same terms as her own, with the single island of St. Bartholomew, would obtain all the privileges which were offered to the United States. All this, in *our* opinion, is no evil; because it is not the carrier nation, but the nation for whose use it carries, that we consider to be mainly, we may almost say solely, benefitted by the existence of the trade. But Mr. Canning's opinion was different, and it was his part to shew, how such opinions and such conduct could be reconciled.

These terms, which were offered to nations having colonies, being in their nature inapplicable to those which had not; other conditions, therefore, had to be thought of for these last, of which class America was one. It was accordingly required, that they should place the commerce and navigation of Great Britain and her dependencies on the footing of the most favoured nation.

It is obvious, without proceeding further, that this was a very different, and might be a much greater concession, than that which was required from nations having colonies. A nation, therefore, which possessed colonies, might act very reasonably in accepting the reciprocity offered to it, while yet the United States might be perfectly right in supposing, that what was required from them was not reciprocity, but something totally different. From the acceptance, therefore, of the conditions of the Act, by any nation having colonies, no just argument can be drawn, in condemnation of the policy of the American government in refusing them.

But further, even to countries in a similar situation with the United States, the terms which the Act offered differ in their nature as widely as the laws of one country differ from those of another. What is required is, that they should admit

[*Gallatin, "Correspondence," pp. 44–5.]

Great Britain to the privileges of the most favoured nation. But the privileges of the most favoured nation are as diversified as the commercial policy of different states. In some countries they may amount to a free trade; in others, to no more than an intercourse loaded with innumerable burthens and restrictions. Nor should we omit to observe, that the concession required from nations without colonies, by what Mr. Canning terms reciprocity, is great in proportion to the general liberality of their policy. And as the policy of the United States, in respect to navigation, is more liberal than that of any other maritime power, Mr. Canning's assertion, that the United States had rejected terms which other nations had accepted, cannot be admitted. From no other nation were concessions required, equal to those which were demanded from the United States.

Mr. Gallatin, however, with great propriety, waived this objection.[*] He made no complaint on account of the more favourable conditions which were offered to other countries: he looked only to the conditions offered to the United States; and we shall follow his example.

By the laws of the two countries, the trade, both in British and in American vessels, between the West Indies and the United States, had been long prohibited, and when permitted, loaded with heavy duties on both sides. For our permitting this trade to be carried on in *American* vessels, the proper equivalent would, it should seem, have been, that America should permit the same trade to be carried on in *British* vessels; to which, equally with those of America, it had, up to that time, been closed. With regard to discriminating duties, if none were imposed on our side, the equivalent would have been, that none should have been imposed on theirs.

Our Reciprocity Act required much more than this; and for what it required beyond this, it offered no equivalent.

It claimed for British vessels freedom of trade between our colonies and the United States; and for this it offered the proper equivalent,—freedom of the same trade to American ships. But it claimed, moreover, certain privileges in the ports of the United States, for the commerce and navigation of the mother country. Now the commerce and navigation of Great Britain, considered as distinct from her colonies, already enjoys every privilege in the American ports, which Great Britain herself grants to the commerce and navigation of the United States. The sole object, therefore, of our pretended reciprocity must have been, to obtain further privileges from the United States, which we ourselves do not grant to that power; or to retain the privileges which our commerce and navigation now enjoy, although we should cease to grant the corresponding privileges to that of the United States.

It has been already mentioned, that, with respect to the direct trade between Great Britain and the United States, British shipping enjoys all the privileges not

[**Ibid.*, pp. 44–6.]

only of the most favoured nation, but all those of American shipping itself. British vessels, however, are not permitted to trade from any third country to the United States. A similar prohibition applies, in this country, to American shipping. But with us this restriction is founded on the exclusive principles of our Navigation Laws;[*] with the United States, it is part of the general system of reciprocity, and therefore extends only to those countries which have adopted a similar regulation. Were we admitted, therefore, to the privileges of the most favoured nation, (merely in return for our admitting American vessels to our colonies,) we should acquire this privilege without giving the equivalent which the most favoured nation has given for it.

If the United States had accepted what we termed reciprocity, British vessels would have been permitted to trade between the United States and all foreign nations without any discriminating duties whatever; while American vessels would still have been entirely prohibited from trading between Great Britain and any foreign country except the United States. Is this reciprocity?

Moreover, Great Britain, after the expiration of the convention of 1815, (which was concluded for a limited period only,) might have imposed whatever restrictions she pleased upon American vessels trading to the mother country, while the United States must have continued to admit British vessels, on an equality with their own, to every branch of their trade except the coasting trade, or have lost that participation in the colonial trade which was extended to them by this Act. Is this reciprocity?

The reciprocity, then, which we offered to the United States, was a sham reciprocity, a reciprocity only in name. Instead of requiring concessions from America only equivalent to those which we offered in return, we demanded privileges for our vessels which we withheld from hers, and which if we ceased to withhold from hers we should by that alone, as her law actually stands, obtain for ourselves without difficulty.

The navigation laws of the United States are founded on perfect reciprocity.[†] No nation which does not impose restrictions on American vessels, has any restrictions imposed upon its own. But Congress did not think it fair reciprocity that our vessels should be relieved from all restrictions, while restrictions continued in this country on the shipping of America; our ministers *did*. *This* was the radical and incurable difference of opinion, which Mr. Canning held it to be beyond the power of negociation to remove.[‡] And certainly any minds which were capable of for a moment *entertaining* such an opinion as that professed by our

---

[*12 Charles II, c. 18 (1660) and 15 Charles II, c. 7 (1663) were repealed by 6 George IV, c. 105 (1825), and replaced by 6 George IV, c. 109 (1825).]

[†See 1st Congress, Sess. II, c. 30 (1790), 14th Congress, Sess. II, c. 31 (1817), as well as 15th Congress, Sess. I, c. 70 (1818), 16th Congress, Sess. I, c. 122 (1820), and 17th Congress, Sess. II, c. 22 (1823).]

[‡Canning, "Correspondence," pp. 50–1.]

ministers on the subject, might be very well presumed capable also of *holding* that opinion, in spite of any arguments which it would be in the power of the ablest negociator to adduce in opposition to it.

Thus far, it will probably be admitted, that the state of the case, as we have represented it, has not tended to place the conduct or policy of ministers in a very advantageous light. But it may perhaps be supposed that although the rejection, by the United States, of the conditions of our act of 1825, might not be a sufficient reason even for withholding from them the privileges of that Act, much less for depriving them of that partial trade with our Colonies which they had enjoyed since 1822; those Acts of Congress which Mr. Canning complains of as unfair and injurious to this country, must be of a character to justify the very strong measures which were adopted in retaliation.

It is proper, therefore, that we should give some account of these Acts of Congress, which unquestionably, on the face of every statement yet laid before the British public, appear highly discreditable to the United States. Yet these Acts were not passed without sufficient cause, although the cause has never been clearly stated in this country; and if it were stated, it is doubtful whether it would be listened to. The people of this country expect little wisdom in the commercial legislation of a nation who can be persuaded to pay 25 per cent for the pleasure of having manufactures of their own. Their preposterous tariff,[*] contrasted with the liberal policy which has been adopted and is still adhered to by our ministers, has prepared the most intelligent Englishmen to consider any thing which can be said or done by the Americans, against such antagonists as our ministers, in the matter of free trade, as worthy of entire disregard. This prejudice, or prejudgment, is a natural, well-grounded, and unavoidable one under the circumstances of the case. If the people of the United States did but know how much injury the tariff has done them, and will continue to do as long as it exists, in the opinion of all instructed and unprejudiced persons in this country, of all who were best able to appreciate their character, institutions, and policy when good, and on whom they might otherwise have confidently relied for doing them justice, and forcing the British public to do them justice, now when they are in the right—this alone ought to make them lose no time in blotting out this absurd law from their statute book, and in consigning the foolish idea of protecting manufactures to the contempt it deserves.* But, be their commercial policy in all other respects what it may, they are entitled to a vindication of it where it is justifiable, as we are prepared to maintain that it has been with respect to the question between our navigation and theirs. And the

---

[*See 18th Congress, Sess. I, c. 136 (1824).]

*In justice, however, to the people of America, we are bound to state, that the direct or virtual exclusion of almost all their staple productions (except cotton) from the mother country, by the general regulations of our customs, together with the impediments on their trade with the colonies, furnished to the advocates of American manufactures their most plausible and most effectual argument.

partial and prejudiced representations which have been made to the British public on the question, by authorities which in other respects rank deservedly high, ought to be, and so far as depends upon us, shall be, fully exposed.

The reader will not have forgotten, that the enactments of Congress, which Mr. Canning resented as acts of injustice at least, if not of special hostility, to this country,[*] were the imposition of an alien duty on British vessels trading between America and our Colonies, and the prohibition of the circuitous intercourse between Great Britain and her colonies, through the United States. We shall consider these questions separately, since they are separate in their nature.

The following extract from Mr. Huskisson's speech in Parliament, on the 21st March, 1825, contains the history of the alien duty, placed in the point of view in which it was convenient to our ministers that it should appear:

> The committee would perceive that, in allowing the countries of America to trade with our colonies in their own vessels, we had, in fact, conceded to the navigation of the United States a privilege which was not granted to any state in Europe; and this privilege, though nominally extended to all the countries of America, was really a boon to the United States alone, as the other countries had as yet scarcely any commercial marine. What had hitherto been the return made by the United States for this indulgence? In the first session of their Congress, which had followed the opening of this trade by our Act of Parliament, they passed a law, imposing alien duties in their ports upon all British ships which might trade between those ports and our colonies, to be levied until the productions of the United States should be admitted into our colonies upon the same terms and duties as the like productions of any other country; meaning thereby, the like productions not of any other foreign country, but of our own country, or of our own provinces in North America. Whatever might have been the arguments used to induce the American Congress to adopt this course, their real reason for making the attempt was an impression, on their part, that we had yielded this intercourse to necessity, and that as our colonies could not subsist without it, they might prescribe the conditions under which it should be carried on.*

The name of Mr. Huskisson has long been so completely identified with liberal and enlightened principles of commercial policy, that his reputation is national property, and we should be most unwilling to prejudice it undeservedly, or to put any other than the most favourable interpretation upon his words or actions. Yet the representation contained in the above passage is so grossly unfair, the facts of the case are so egregiously misstated, and the intentions imputed to the government of the United States are so directly contradicted by the whole tenor of their conduct, that the promulgation of such a statement by Mr. Huskisson seems to argue a degree of blindness which, if involuntary, cannot possibly be too much regretted, nor, if wilful, too severely condemned.

Mr. Huskisson pretends, that Congress requited us for removing restrictions from their ships, by laying restrictions upon ours. Now the direct contrary of this is

[*Canning, "Correspondence," pp. 30–1.]
*[William Huskisson, Speech on Colonial Trade (21 Mar., 1825),] *PH*, 1825, pp. 288–9. [In *PD*, n.s., Vol. 12, col. 1106. The U.S. statute referred to is 17th Congress, Sess. II, c. 22 (1823).]

notoriously the truth. To *lay on* restrictions did not happen to be in the power of the United States; since the intercourse in British ships, being already altogether prohibited, did not admit of being further restricted by any act of theirs. Far from *laying on*, the sole intention and effect of the Act was to *take off* restrictions; and all the complaint is, that it did not, in Mr. Huskisson's opinion, take off *enough*.

Could Mr. Huskisson have forgotten that, previously to the measure of which he complains, the intercourse between the United States and our colonies in British vessels was *prohibited*? And because the act of Congress which took off the prohibition, did not also take off the discriminating duties, which have existed by the American navigation laws ever since 1790, and which have never been rescinded except in favour of those nations which would extend similar privileges to the United States, is it fair in Mr. Huskisson to represent the Act as *imposing* restrictions, when all the effect it was intended to have, or could have, was that of *mitigating* them?

So anxious were Congress to meet all our concessions by corresponding ones with the least possible delay, that they began to legislate even while our Act of 1822 was still pending in parliament. In order not to lose even the interval between two sessions of Congress, they passed a temporary bill, authorizing the President, on receiving satisfactory evidence that the trade had been opened to American vessels, to open it by proclamation to British vessels, on what he should consider fair conditions of reciprocity.[*] The President did so, and what they had authorized him to do by proclamation, was done in the succeeding session of Congress by a permanent law.

It is another question, whether Congress would have done right in taking off the duties as well as the prohibition; whether, when we removed the interdict from American vessels, they were bound in justice, or on the principle of reciprocity, to have taken off all restrictions whatever, and left the trade with our colonies subject only to the general regulations of their customs. Yet if this ground be taken by Mr. Huskisson's partisans, it may very properly be asked in return, had *we* also taken off all special restrictions on our side? By no means. Our Act of 1822 only opened the ports of our colonies to certain enumerated articles, and that under high duties. Among these articles, pot and pearl ashes, dried and pickled fish, beef, pork, bacon, whale oil, spermaceti oil and candles, butter, and cheese, which are articles of considerable importance among the exports from the United States, were not included. All these commodities not only could not be imported in American, but could not even be imported in British vessels.

Did Mr. Huskisson—did our ministry—did these patrons of reciprocity seriously expect, that in return for the partial freedom of trade thus conceded to the United States, entire freedom of trade should be granted by them to Great Britain?

[*17th Congress, Sess. I, c. 56 (1822); this temporary Act was replaced by 17th Congress, Sess. II, c. 22 (1823).]

If instead of opening their ports to all the produce of our colonies, Congress had opened them only to certain enumerated articles, excluding from the number some of the most valuable staple productions of the West Indies, this surely nobody would have thought of denying to be fair reciprocity. And perhaps it is to be regretted that Congress did not take *this* mode of limiting their concessions, to correspond with the limitation of ours. They preferred to open their ports to *all* the produce of our colonies, subject, when imported in British vessels, to a discriminating duty. This restriction was certainly different in *kind* from the restriction which provoked it; but if it was not greater in *degree*, it is no ground of complaint against the United States, that being entitled on the principle of reciprocity to withhold something, they thought proper to be themselves the judges what they would withhold.

Such is the true history of the Alien Duty. It was not, as Mr. Huskisson mistakenly imagined, an attempt to take advantage of our necessities, and engross the whole trade of our colonies to the shipping of the United States. It was adopted in perfect simplicity, as a matter of course, arising naturally out of the system of reciprocity, which they had uniformly and consistently observed towards us. As they had met our interdict by another interdict, so they never dreamed of giving any thing in return for our partial concessions, but partial concessions. In the choice of a limitation, they were guided by their own convenience, and by the ancient established principle of their navigation laws; never suspecting that our government would resent their not giving up the *whole* in return for a *part*, or that, if the nature of the restrictions which they retained did not please us, it would deprive them, in our eyes, of the whole merit of those they gave up.

Our ministers, misunderstanding the object of the discriminating duties, imposed countervailing duties, of equal amount, in the ports of our colonies, upon the shipping of the United States. And that measure, although condemned in the first volume of this publication,[*] would have been proper, if Mr. Huskisson's view of the conduct of the United States had been the true one. It was the interest of our colonies that there should be freedom of competition between the vessels of the two countries; and the Americans having created an artificial inequality in favour of their own ships, our countervailing duty did no more, so far as navigation was concerned, than restore the equality. The error of our ministry consisted in not reflecting, that,—restrictions having been imposed by America, only because restrictions existed in our colonies,—to impose ulterior restrictions would not be to retaliate upon the United States, but to create a new source of inequality, justifying retaliation on the other side.

The following was now the comparative state of the restrictive regulations on both sides. Their duties on our shipping were equivalent to our duties on theirs, and so far there was reciprocity; but, on our side, many productions of the United

[*Anon., "Foreign Dependencies, Colonial Trade Bill," *PR*, 1825, pp. 630–40.]

States were prohibited, while all those of our colonies were admitted into the American ports. The principle of reciprocity would have justified *them* in imposing fresh restrictions; but from this they, with great good sense and moderation, abstained: while *we*, who could neither plead the principle of reciprocity nor any other rational principle for restricting still further an intercourse in which already the excess of restriction was on our side,—*we* chose rather that there should be no trade, than this equal trade—equal as respects navigation, unequal in other respects by our own act, and, as we imagined, in our own favour. We interdicted the trade in American vessels; knowing all the time that when our ports should be closed to their ships, their interdict on ours would revive; so that not even our ship-owners, and our cherished navigation, would gain one jot by this ebullition of national jealousy and pique.

Perhaps, if Congress had simply re-enacted the discriminating duties, and had evinced no disposition to consent to the abandonment of them upon any conditions whatever, they would have produced considerably less irritation in the minds of our government. But by offering to give up the duties on a condition which ministers considered derogatory to our dignity—namely, the admission of their produce into our West India colonies, subject to no higher duties than that of Canada,*—they rendered their case considerably worse than it could have been made by expressing the most fixed resolution to hold fast by the discriminating duties to the end of time.

This stipulation,—(we do not, with Mr. Canning and Mr. Huskisson, call it a *pretension*;[*] for the offer of a benefit, upon conditions however inadmissible, is no pretension; nor does there seem any peculiar propriety in treating it as an affront,)—this stipulation, it must be allowed, was evidently an ill considered one. It is true that what it required from us was no more than what we ought to have had no hesitation in consenting to; the abolition of a most pernicious and indefensible tax, imposed by us on the West Indies, ostensibly for the benefit of Canada, but with no effect save that of diverting the capital of that colony to other than its natural and most beneficial employment. However, on the principle of reciprocity, the United States were bound, if they claimed this, to grant us the corresponding privilege, by admitting our colonial productions into their ports, subject to no higher duties than their own produce carried coastwise.

The United States were not indeed without plausible, and even, to a certain extent, sound reasons, for insisting on this point. The British North American

*We say *Canada*, although we are aware that the mother country herself, as well as her transmarine dependencies, were included in the stipulation of the Act of Congress. But the latter only are really concerned in it, since the exports of Great Britain, being altogether different from those of the United States, can never come into competition with them; whereas those of our North American provinces, and those of the United States, are exactly the same, and do, in fact, meet each other continually in the West India market.

[*Cf. Canning, "Correspondence," pp. 32, 41, and Huskisson, quoted above, p. 140.]

colonies (they urged) have by no means a large surplus produce to dispose of, and cannot export much to the West Indies, without importing, for their own consumption, from the United States. The trade, therefore, between the West Indies and Canada, is in reality a circuitous trade through Canada, between the West Indies and the United States: with this difference, that, being a trade between one part of the British dominions and another, it is confined by our navigation laws exclusively to British vessels. To admit, therefore, the produce of Canada, on more favourable terms than that of the United States, is really to admit the produce of the United States on more favourable terms when imported in British, than when imported in American vessels. This argument, though it does not entirely destroy, must be admitted to weaken considerably, the force of the objection to the supposed pretension involved in the Act of Congress.

But our ministers were destined to lose even the feeble apology which this infringement of reciprocity on the part of the United States might, by very partial judges, have been supposed to afford them. The negociations of 1824, regarding, *inter alia*, the Colonial Trade, had been suspended, with the understanding that they were to be renewed at an early period. The United States had never been informed that the Act of 1825, passed in the interval, was intended to preclude the resumption of these discussions. This our ministers knew; and they knew moreover, that Mr. Gallatin was actually on his way to Europe, specially commissioned to renew this very negociation. What might be his instructions they knew not; and therefore, probably, most persons in their situation, knowing that they had not the ultimatum of the United States, would have thought it expedient to wait for its arrival before they acted upon the presumption that nothing beyond what had been offered previously, would be granted now. Unfortunately for their foresight, two days after the publication of the Order in Council, Mr. Gallatin arrived, with instructions to *give up* the claim to an equality of duties between the produce of the British possessions and that of the United States. Any person may peruse these instructions, by consulting *Niles's Register* for 23d June 1826, which contains the original document signed by Mr. Clay, Secretary of State to the United States.[*] The principal point of difference, and the only one in which the United States were not thoroughly in the right, being thus removed, Mr. Canning chose rather to take refuge in the pretence of an "incurable difference of opinion,"[†] than to retract the uncalled-for interdict, or, by resuming the negociation, to draw forth information which would have shewn his conduct as petulant and precipitate as it was: and up to this day it has never been stated, and is not

[*Henry Clay, "Extract of Instructions to Albert Gallatin" (19 June, 1826), *Niles' Weekly Register*, XXXI, or 3rd ser., VII (23 Dec., 1826), 266–8. Mill would appear to have mistakenly conflated the month when the instructions were given with the month when they were published.]

[†Canning, "Correspondence," p. 51.]

generally known to the British public, that Mr. Gallatin had authority to waive the pretension characterized in Mr. Canning's correspondence as the ground of the interdict, and the one insuperable bar to all further negociation.

The only measure of the United States which still remains unexplained, is the prohibition of what is termed the circuitous intercourse: and Mr. Canning's remonstrances on this point are so vehement,[*] that it must not be passed by without full consideration. We shall therefore explain the motive which induced the United States originally to withhold, from British vessels, the privilege of clearing out from their ports for the British colonies.

To understand the circumstances which dictated, and sufficiently warranted this restriction, it is necessary to remember, that previously to our Act of 1822, all commerce in ships of either country, between our colonies and the United States, was interdicted by the reciprocal prohibitions of the two countries.

The means of enforcing the prohibition on our side, were simple and obvious. We had only to declare that no American vessels should be permitted to unload their cargoes in our colonial ports. But the United States could not, in the same manner, prohibit British vessels from trading to their ports; because the trade, in British vessels, between America and the mother country, was not, nor consistently with the treaty could be, interdicted. Not being at liberty, therefore, nor probably desiring, to prohibit British vessels from coming to them at all; what means had they of excluding such vessels from the prohibited trade, except by requiring bonds that they should not take in cargoes in America and land them in the West Indies? All the attempts of the United States to enforce the prohibition would have been fruitless, if what they might forbid to be done in vessels coming directly from the colonies, they were bound to permit in the same vessels coming from any other part of the British dominions.

It may be asked, why the prohibition of the circuitous intercourse, adopted as being necessary to the due enforcement of the prohibition against the direct intercourse, continued after this latter prohibition was done away by the Act of Congress of 1823.

The reason was, because a similar restriction existed on our side.

In permitting the trade between our colonies and the United States, as well as all other countries of America, in foreign vessels, our Act of 1822 required, that goods *imported* from these countries in other than British ships must be brought and shipped *directly* from the country of which they were the produce; and that goods *exported* to these countries from our colonies in foreign ships must be exported *directly* to the country to which those ships belonged. By this Act, therefore, no trade could take place in vessels of the United States between that country and our colonies, unless such vessels came directly from the United

[**Ibid.*, pp. 29–30.]

States, and returned thither directly. Hence it is obvious that the United States only exercised a fair reciprocity in confining the same trade, when carried on in *British* vessels, to such as came directly from our colonies, and returned directly to them.

Mr. Canning's attempt to shew that the one restriction did not justify the other, because the colonial trade is, by the consent of nations, an exclusive trade, is founded on incorrect reasoning. We may admit his premises, and yet deny his conclusion. However widely the colonial trade may differ from that of independent nations, yet, if we have a right to prescribe the conditions on which we will admit the United States to our colonial trade, they have an equal right to determine for themselves on what conditions they will accept of it.

It is, indeed, made matter of additional complaint by Mr. Canning, that although the prohibition of the indirect intercourse had been removed on the side of Great Britain by the Act of 1825, no steps had yet been taken by Congress to remove theirs.[*] In answer to this, Mr. Gallatin could only say, that he, and (as he conceived) his Government likewise, had been unaware that the Act of 1825 had the effect now ascribed to it.[†] This appears, from documentary evidence, to be perfectly true. Mr. Gallatin's instructions, which may be perused, as we have already observed, in *Niles's Register*, proceeded upon the supposition that the restriction imposed by the Act of 1822 still continued; and any one who will take the trouble to read a despatch from Mr. Gallatin to Mr. Clay, printed in the number for 6th January, 1827, of the same periodical work,[‡] will not wonder that an enactment so confusedly and unskilfully drawn up as our Act of 1825, should not have been understood by those who had no access to any commentary, and to whom no official explanation was afforded.

After all, this Act, even as interpreted by Mr. Canning, takes off only one half of the interdict on the indirect intercourse. Foreign vessels trading to our colonies may now *export* colonial produce to a third country; but they may not *import* into our colonies the produce of any other country than that to which the vessels belong.

These, and all other misapprehensions, would at once have been cleared up, if the negociations which the United States have professed throughout to wait for, in order that they might be guided by the result, had been renewed. But Ministers had determined otherwise; and when Mr. Gallatin arrived on the implied understanding that the discussions were to commence immediately, and bearing instructions in which almost the only disputed claim which was not given up was that which, according to Mr. Canning, *we* have yielded, a participation in the trade between our colonies and foreign countries; he is told that not only now, but hereafter, even if the United States should grant to us every thing which our

---

[**Ibid.*, p. 31.]
[†Gallatin, "Correspondence," p. 33.]
[‡Gallatin, "Extract of Despatch to Henry Clay" (27 Oct., 1826), *Niles' Weekly Register*, XXXI, or 3rd ser., VII (6 Jan., 1827), 300.]

pretended reciprocity system demands, we will not pledge ourselves to suffer any trade in American vessels, between our colonies and America![*]

Could we hope that Mr. Canning's American policy had died with him, it would be no inconsiderable advantage to set off against the evils of a loss otherwise so deeply to be lamented. We are persuaded that no impartial person, who takes for his standard of approval any kind of reciprocity, except that which is jocularly said to be all on one side, will consider that any one has deviated from the principle of reciprocity, except our Government; or that any thing would be necessary to bring America to reason, except to be ourselves reasonable. We wish it were in our power to add, that the present ministers,* by the conduct which they have pursued either before or since they came into office, had afforded much ground for hope that they are the men through whose agency these differences will be accommodated. That strength of intellect which comprehends readily the consequences of a false step, and what is a still rarer endowment, that strength of character which dares to retrace it, are not qualities which have often belonged to a British ministry. That the present ministers possess these attributes, it still remains for them to prove. For us, if we can contribute in any degree to give the right direction to the opinions of any portion of the *public* on this question, we shall have effected all that we aim at, and all that is in our power.

[*Canning, "Correspondence," pp. 31, 41, 49.]
*Written in December, 1827.

NOTES ON THE NEWSPAPERS

1834

EDITOR'S NOTE

Monthly Repository, n.s. VIII (Mar., 1834), 161–76 ; (Apr., 1834), 233–48, 309–12; (May, 1834), 354–75; (June, 1834), 435–56; (July, 1834), 521–8; (Aug., 1834), 589–600; (Sept., 1834), 656–65. Headed as title. Running titles: left-hand, as title; right-hand, as sub-titles for each "Note." Each month's entries signed "A." Not republished. Identified in Mill's bibliography as "Notes on the Newspapers: in the Monthly Rep. for March 1834, April 1834, May 1834, June 1834, July 1834, August 1834, and September 1834" (MacMinn, 38). The numbered headings for each month's entries have been added. In Somerville College there is a proof set of the "Notes" for Mar., 1834, with, on one page, four corrections (which were made): "Divorse" is corrected to "Divorce" (160.8); "when they see a place uncovered," is added in the margin (160.17); "*ume*" is corrected to "*une*" (160.22); and a quotation mark is added after "boue;" (160.22). Also in Somerville College are tear-sheets of all of the "Notes," with four corrections that have been adopted in the present text: "Reformed Ministry" is corrected to "Reform Ministry" (151.17–18); "not" to "but" (213.35); "base" to "lease" (243.26); and "acts" to "arts" (262.17). There are two other corrections marked, perhaps not in Mill's hand, that have been adopted: "Alliance" is altered to "Affiance" (173n.20), and "Pedrillo" to "Pedro Garcias" (224.7). For comment on the "Notes," see lviii–lix above.

Notes on the Newspapers

NO. I, MARCH, 1834

5th February

The King's Speech[*]

The Session now commencing will probably decide, in the minds of the many, who wield the physical force, the question whether anything is to be hoped from the higher classes, and whether the people shall, or shall not, take their affairs into their own hands.

In the first Session of the Reformed Parliament, many allowances were made, which will not be made again: the new legislative body had the full benefit of the reluctance to consider a first trial as final; and the novelty of the situation was such that the public were bewildered, and did not themselves see with sufficient clearness what ought to be done, to render them very severe judges of their representatives for what they left undone. The public had expected much, but did not know exactly what. They felt sure that the Reform Bill[†] must somehow be a great good to them, and they trusted that those who had been sufficiently their friends to give them the Bill, would find the means of making it have its natural effects. The first session taught them that they were not to expect this: the Reform Ministry and the Reformed Parliament would do no good spontaneously. The second will show whether they are capable of doing any when they are forced. If this trial should also fail, we live in times when mankind hurry on rapidly to ultimate consequences; the next question will be, what is the easiest and most expeditious way of getting rid of them.

Were Ministers in their senses, when, in so critical a position, they opened a session, perhaps destined to be the most important in our annals, with a speech, if possible, more unmeaning even than the common run of King's speeches? A speech studiously framed in such language as to promise nothing—to commit the Government to nothing?

Ministers are ignorant of the very first principles of statesmanship. The one

[*William IV, Speech at the Opening of Parliament (4 Feb., 1834), *PD*, 3rd ser., Vol. 21, cols. 1–5.]
[†Enacted as 2 & 3 William IV, c. 45 (1832).]

maxim of a wise policy, in times of trouble and movement, is that which Madame Roland recommended to the Girondists: "Take the initiative!" Be you the first in the field, with whatever purpose. Whatever you do, do it before you are forced to it: do it while you may be supposed to have willed it, and not to have been passive instruments of some other will. If you would not be like dead twigs on an eminence, ready to be swept away by the first gust—if you would be something and not nothing—could you not for once seem to have a purpose, a plan, an idea, of your own! Could you not assume what gives dignity even to wickedness! Do good, do even evil, but let it be from choice. If you cannot show a worthy character, show some character: if you cannot be loved, prithee be hated, but be not despised!

Among modern statesmen, at least in England, the wisdom of the serpent seems even more infinitely rare than the innocence of the dove.[*] The curse of a highly civilized state of society, are the half-honest, the men of feeble purposes. Scarcely any one has character enough to be either good or wicked. Give us rather a "*bold bad man,*"[†] a villain as villains were of old, with a strong intellect and a strong will. Give us for a ruler one who could and would do right whenever it was his interest; who could and would prevent all wrong, but such as he chose to promote: not men who, for want of courage to do either good or harm, fold their hands and let harm come.

If the vessel is merely to scud before the wind, what need of a steersman? We do not support a Government that we may ourselves redress our own grievances. We want rulers who do not wait to be told by us how we wish to be governed; men who can teach us what we should demand, who can at least anticipate our demands, not slowly and grudgingly obey them. We want men from whom it shall not be necessary to extort all they give, men who shall not, instead of gaining, actually lose popularity by every fresh concession.

We want, in short, men who on every great question will act as the present Ministers have acted on the Reform Bill, and on that alone.

The people were anxiously waiting for the propositions of the Ministry on Municipal Corporations, on the Poor Laws, and on the abuses in the Church. The speech says, that the reports of the Commissioners on these several subjects will be laid before Parliament, and will afford them "much useful information," whereby they will be enabled to judge of "the nature and extent of any existing defects and abuses, and in what manner the necessary corrections may in due season be safely and beneficially applied."[‡] Not even a promise to propose anything. They may have something to propose, but their minds are not yet made up. When are such minds ever made up? It is literally true, that the only two things to which the speech

[*Cf. Matthew, 10:16.]
[†Shakespeare, *Henry VIII*, II, ii, 43.]
[‡Speech from the Throne, 4 Feb., 1834, col. 2.]

either directly or by implication pledges the Ministry, are, first to propose a "final adjustment" of Irish tithes, (the *extinction* of which was announced by Mr. Stanley two years ago,)[*] and this "without injury to any institution in Church or State;"[†] secondly, not to consent to a repeal of the Union with Ireland. On this latter point, indeed, the speech is as explicit, and as emphatic, as heart could wish. They will resist Mr. O'Connell even to the death. The collective energy, courage, and determination of the entire Cabinet, have been all thrown into this one act of what they doubtless deem antique heroism and magnanimity.

The debate which ensued, and which, as those say who were present, was as flat and dull as if the Session had already lasted six months, made no further disclosure of the purposes of Ministers: but in the course of the evening it was discovered, that they intended to propose some trifling amendment (it did not appear what) in the marriage law, and that they hoped, but were not sure, that on the subject of English tithes, some measure might be brought to completion in the present Session. It has further transpired that they do not mean to propose a registration of births, marriages, and deaths; that they have not decided whether or not to re-introduce the Local Courts' Bill;* but that there are two things, besides the repeal of the Union, which they are firmly determined to resist: any alteration in the Corn Laws,[‡] and any separation of Church and State.

Is this the way to retain any hold on a people every day becoming more alienated from the higher classes, and every day growing in the capacity and in the habit of organized co-operation among themselves?

On the showing of these very men, a great change has taken place in the structure of society, and has, through their instrumentality, been communicated to our political institutions. Power has passed from the few into the hands of the many. On their own showing too, the many are most imperfectly informed, most liable to error, and likely to make a most dangerous use of their newly-acquired power, unless they somewhere find wiser guidance than their own. Accordingly, the Whigs deliver to them, by word and deed, the following instructions: "We are the wisest and most excellent persons in the world; the only persons who are fit to govern you, as all, except Tories and anarchists, acknowledge. But do not expect

[*Edward George Stanley, Speech on Arrears of Tithes (Ireland) (16 Apr., 1832), *PD*, 3rd ser., Vol. 12, cols. 593–5.]

[†Speech from the Throne, 4 Feb., 1834, col. 4.]

*Since this was written, Ministers have announced that they *have* made up their minds to propose a Local Courts' Bill, and *not* to propose any modification of the Timber Duties. Once beaten on this important measure by a Tory Parliament, they have not the heart to try again. [See John Charles Spencer, Statement on Local Courts—Judges' Rules (11 Feb., 1834), *PD*, 3rd ser., Vol. 21, col. 210, and Speech on Timber Duties (4 Mar., 1834), *ibid.*, col. 1114; and "A Bill Intituled an Act for Establishing Courts of Local Jurisdiction," 3 William IV (28 Mar., 1833), *House of Lords Sessional Papers*, 1833, CCCXIV, 205–38. For the Timber Duties, see 1 & 2 George IV, cc. 37, 84 (1821).]

[‡See 9 George IV, c. 60 (1828).]

from us any thing to improve your condition. If that is your object, you have only yourselves to look to. We, if you would but let us alone, desire no better than to leave every thing as it is. Some things we do not mean to give you, say or do what you will: you shall not have cheap bread, nor be allowed to choose your own parsons. But whatever else you ask for, you may have, by making us sufficiently uncomfortable; for we are a liberal and enlightened Administration, and are always ready to quit any spot as soon as it is made too hot to hold us. Therefore, if you want us to stir, make ready your fuel and light your fire. But as long as we conveniently can, we are your men for upholding existing institutions. We are the pillars of the Constitution, and it cannot be in safety if it rests any where but upon us, because of our yielding nature. If the Tories had it, you would storm and rave, and blow down it and them together; but we, you see, go upon castors, and, you are aware, do not absolutely object to being pushed from under it when we must."

What is this but exhorting the people to incessant agitation? "We will yield nothing to reason," say the Whig ministry, "but every thing to clamour." These are the men who call Radicalism dangerous. It is Radicalism to demand that the people may be ruled by men of their choice; men, therefore, in whom they can confide; in whose hands they may place their affairs, and feel at liberty to be quiet. Whig policy, on the contrary, relies on a perennial conflict between opposite principles of evil: on the one hand, a Government, which, never attempting to originate any good, neither has nor claims public confidence; and on the other, perpetual agitation.

It is policy like this which alone can render the prospects of our country and of the world seriously alarming. The people are always eager to follow good guidance, and the sole danger is of their not finding it. Intelligence abounds among the English democracy; but it is not cultivated intelligence. It is mostly of the self-educated sort; and this is commonly more microscopic than comprehensive: it sees one or a few things strongly, and others not at all; it is the parent of narrowness and fanaticism. The coming changes, for come they must and will, are fraught with hope in any case, but also with peril, unless there be found to lead the van of opinion, to place themselves in the front rank of the popular party, a section of the wisest and most energetic of the instructed classes; men whose education and pursuits have given them a wider range of ideas, and whose leisure has admitted of more systematic study, than will, for a long time to come, be possible, save in occasional rare instances, to those who labour with their hands.

It cannot be but that there are such men in England; but we know not where to look for them in public life. The present Ministers not only are incapable of *being*, but do not even attempt to *seem* such men. They have neither the intellect, the knowledge, the energy, the courage, nor even the wish. They are wanting in the very first of the necessary conditions,—faith in improvement; without which it is impossible to take the lead in a nation which not only believes in, but demands improvement. They have no belief that the very measures which they are instrumental in carrying, will have any beneficial consequences. To their minds the Reform Bill itself was but a prudent and necessary concession to popular opinion. What can be expected from such men, but what we find? that they will never do any thing till they are forced, always do as little as they are permitted, and endeavour that even that little should lead to nothing.

There is a question which a short time must solve, and on its solution the fate of this nation entirely depends:—Can the higher classes, before it is too late, furnish the country with ministers, who, together with strong popular sympathies, have the capacity and the energy to lead, and not wait to be driven?

* * * * *

6th February

Mr. Shiel and Lord Althorp

The House of Commons have availed themselves of this affair to pay largely that peculiar tribute to virtue, which vice, according to the old proverb, loves to render.[*] They have made a truly edifying exhibition of rigid morality. Mr. Shiel's fate is a great moral lesson; he has been made a signal example of the inconveniences of being found out. If Mr. Shiel be guilty of what is laid to his charge,[†] a high-minded man might look down upon him; but how, in reason, is it possible that the present House of Commons should do so? No one does or can despise in another person his own vices: and contemptible as a man's conduct may be in itself, we can never without the sincerest pity see one man singled out from a multitude, and mercilessly immolated for being *proved* to have done what all the others are *known* to do; made the scapegoat of those whose only advantage over him is that of Lady Bellaston in the novel,[‡] that nobody calls them what every body knows they are.

Who, that knows any thing of the sentiments and conversation of public men, is not aware, that there is hardly one of them who has the slightest scruple in doing what is imputed to Mr. Shiel,—voting and speaking contrary to his private opinion, for the sake of retaining his seat? There were many present that evening, who could have pointed at the instant to at least two hundred members, and said to each of them, "On such a day you did so." It is a thing so perfectly understood, that allowances are made for it as for any other *nécessité de position*: men talk of it to each other as they would of the most innocent or laudable act of their lives. There is

[*See Spencer, Statements on the Character of Irish Members (5 Feb., 1834), *PD*, 3rd ser., Vol. 21, cols. 121, 126.]

[†See Matthew Davenport Hill, Speech at Hull (22 Oct., 1833), *Examiner*, 10 Nov., 1833, p. 706.]

[‡In Henry Fielding, *The History of Tom Jones a Foundling* (1749), in *Works*, 12 vols. (London: Richards, 1824), Vols. VII–X.]

indeed a tacit understanding that these things are not to be mentioned in the hearing of the reporters: but when such conduct is spoken of in private to their own circles, the only thing which could excite surprise or offence would be, to pretend to be shocked at it; *that* would be resented, as an attempt to impose upon themselves, to overreach the fraternity. But the public are fair game.

If all who hear and are disgusted at such conversation were as indiscreet as Mr. Hill, how many a curious tale would be revealed! In the last Session it was reported to us, on undoubted authority, that an English county member, of far greater weight in the country and in Parliament than Mr. Shiel, after having voted on an important division decidedly on the wrong side, (which for once happened to be against the Ministry,) said to an acquaintance, "That vote was the dirtiest I ever gave; but my constituents in * * * compelled me to it." We do not believe that this member thought he had done wrong; it was something in his favour, that he was evidently conscious of having done what he would willingly have avoided. We would on no account do the injustice to another which has been done to Mr. Shiel; and we should not give publicity to this anecdote, if we were not well assured that no one, not already acquainted with the facts, will recognize the individual.

Since the above was written a Committee has been appointed, at the instance of Mr. Shiel's friends, to investigate the charges against him, and the inquiry has terminated in his complete and honourable acquittal.[*] His first accuser, Mr. Hill, has made all the reparation in his power,[†] but too late to save his own credit, which has received a shock it will not easily recover. Lord Althorp pleads guilty only of having acted *imprudently* as a man and as a minister; though he confesses, that he had given a false impression of the purport of what his informant told him.[‡] To misunderstand and misstate facts to the injury of another, is that only imprudence? Would it not have been as easy to put the question to Mr. John Wood *before* as *after* uttering the calumny? Lord Althorp will not escape so easily as he probably flatters himself: he is more deeply culpable than he perhaps thinks, and it will require many good deeds to obliterate the memory of this act of criminal recklessness.

The debates on this affair will reveal to the world without, much more, we suspect, than they previously knew, of the state of parliamentary morality. If Mr. Shiel had really done what Lord Althorp imputed to him; if in private society he had declared himself favourable to the Coercion Bill,[§] while in Parliament he was speaking and voting against it; few, very few members of parliament would have been entitled to throw the first stone: but the act itself would have been not the less a disgraceful one, and no electors could, without great folly, have again returned

[*"Report from the Committee of Privileges," *PP*, 1834, XI, 313–16.]
[†In *ibid.*, pp. 315–16; read from the "Report" by the Clerk of the House of Commons (14 Feb., 1834), *PD*, 3rd ser., Vol. 21, col. 398.]
[‡Spencer, Speech on Mr. Sheil (14 Feb., 1834), *ibid.*, cols. 399–400.]
[§3 William IV, c. 4 (1833).]

such a man to Parliament. Yet all those who took part with Mr. Shiel, not content with excusing the man, exculpated the act too: it stands recorded as their opinion, that a man whose private professions are at variance with his public conduct, does no wrong; it was what they were all liable to. That they are almost all liable to it is too true, and they would have felt the confession a most humiliating one, if they were not from habit callous to their own ignominy. Sir Francis Burdett went furthest, and was the most unabashed, in his avowal that in the moral code of Parliament hypocrisy was no vice.[*] This is not the first time that Sir Francis Burdett has made himself conspicuous by uttering sentiments even more scandalously immoral than the House is accustomed to hear: not that he is in reality worse than the rest, but on the contrary better; for he is more unconscious, less of a hypocrite himself, and when he speaks out what they all think, does it in mere naïveté.

The *Examiner* of February 16th has commented upon the whole affair in its best manner; taking a just and discriminating view of the case as it affects Mr. Shiel, and reading a lesson to the members of the House, such as they seldom receive, and still more seldom profit by.[†]

* * * * *

7th February

The Monopoly of the Post Office Clerks

The *Times* announces that this complication of jobbing and vandalism is to be abolished, and that the clerks of the Post Office, instead of enjoying, to the prejudice of rival dealers and of the public, an entire monopoly of the trade in foreign newspapers, and great privileges with regard to English ones, will henceforth be prohibited from dealing in newspapers either English or foreign.[‡]

Who will say after this that exertions for the reform of abuses are lost labour? But six months ago, the French Postmaster General[§] was here on a mission to negociate for the free circulation of newspapers between Great Britain and France: but the private interests concerned in the privileged traffic were too strong both for the influence of the French government, and for the collective wisdom of our Ministers; who, observe, had at the very time two Commissioners in France,[¶] to impress upon the tardy and unenlightened understandings of the French govern-

---

[*Francis Burdett, Speech in the House of Commons (10 Feb., 1834), *The Times*, 11 Feb., 1834, p. 2 (not in *PD*).]

[†Anon., "The Inquisition," and "The Acquittal,"*Examiner*, 16 Feb., 1834, pp. 97-8, and 98-9.]

[‡Leading Article on the Post Office, *The Times*, 5 Feb., 1834, p. 4.]

[§Antoine Conte.]

[¶John Bowring and George William Frederick Villiers.]

ment the benefits of free trade. When the failure of the negociation was announced, the press made some severe remarks, after which the matter dropped, or seemed to drop; and now when nobody expected to hear any thing more about it, the animadversions have produced their effect, the obstacles have given way, and the abuse is to be extirpated. Abel Handy was not so far wrong when, having exhausted all possible means of extinguishing the conflagration, he reflected that "perhaps it would go out of itself."[*] Evils very often go out apparently of themselves, after human exertion seemed to have done its utmost in vain: but the evil would not have been got rid of, if the exertion had not been made.

The *Times* has, in an excellent article, pointed out the further measures which are necessary to render the destruction of the Post Office monopoly of any avail.[†] The French Government must be invited to renew the negociation. The newspapers of either country should circulate in the other post free, as English newspapers do in England, or at a very small postage duty. The arrangement should be extended to any other country whose Government is willing to accede to it. If free trade in silks and broadcloth is important, free interchange of ideas and feelings is still more so, both for the maintenance of peace and friendship among civilized nations, and for the advancement of civilization itself, by the mutual blending and softening of national peculiarities.

* * * * *

12th February

Attendance in the House

Mr. Ward has obtained what it was very proper should be granted,—a Committee to make arrangements for preparing accurate lists of the majorities and minorities;[‡] those which now appear in the newspapers being supplied by individual members, irregularly, and often inaccurately. On this occasion, the *Chronicle* has an article, in the main, excellent; but in which much greater stress is laid than we can see any reason for, upon the importance of mere regularity of attendance.[§] We yield to no one in the rigour with which we would hold a legislator to the discharge of his duty, but we protest against considering the constancy of his bodily presence as a test of it. So long as the people of Great Britain do not see fit to give salaries to their representatives, and so long as talents

[*In Thomas Morton, *Speed the Plough: A Comedy in Five Acts* (London: Longman and Rees, 1800), V, ii, 35 (not paged).]

[†Leading Article on the Post Office, *The Times*, 7 Feb., 1834, p. 2.]

[‡Henry George Ward, Speech in Introducing a Motion on the Record of Divisions in the House of Commons (11 Feb., 1834), *PD*, 3rd ser., Vol. 21, cols. 239–43; see also "Report from the Select Committee on Divisions of the House," *PP*, 1834, XI, 325–8.]

[§Leading Article on Attendance in the House of Commons, *Morning Chronicle*, 12 Feb., 1834, p. 3.]

and energy are of scanty growth among those who are born to riches, the people must either renounce being served by men of talents and energy, or consent to their withholding from Parliamentary business as much of their time as is necessary for gaining their subsistence. A member, indeed, who is in independent circumstances, owes all his time to his constituents; but he does not owe it to them to waste that time in listening to the floods of meaningless, pointless, endless talk, which are poured forth in tenfold profusion under the excitement of a numerous audience. The real business of Parliament is all transacted in thin houses, and could not be got through if the members attended regularly. A representative of the people, it is said, should be always at his post. His post! As well might it be said that a good soldier should be always mounting guard. The *post* of a good and wise legislator is his own study: it is there that all good laws are made, all improvements in human affairs really elaborated. To look at the present practice, one would imagine that the government of a great nation was performed by talking and hearing talk. It is performed by thinking. If (not to mention Committees) seven or eight hours out of the twenty-four, as large a portion of time as what are called the respectable classes usually devote to gaining their livelihood, are to be passed in hearing bad speeches—of all occupations (if occupation it can be called) the most deadening and dispiriting; what time remains for reading, what for meditation, for conversing with persons of appropriate knowledge, for *preparation*, either by studying the great questions, or by carrying on that general mental culture, which renders a person's opinion worth having, even on what he has not studied?

Were there any concert, or mutual understanding, among the faithful delegates of the people, all the objects which it is sought to compass by exacting attendance, would be provided for, without the endless waste that now takes place of valuable time, which, for the interests of constituents, might be far more profitably bestowed. There would always be a certain number of members standing sentinels, to stop any unforeseen mischief, by denouncing it to the public, or, if necessary, by counting out the House. There are some, such as Mr. Hume, to whose tastes and faculties this mode of serving the people is so congenial, that their "post" would really be at the outposts, and they would attend constantly. When occasions arose on which public duty required that all should be present, either at the debate or at the divison, all would attend. But these occasions, though of frequent, are not of daily occurrence; and, at other times, he is good for very little who cannot serve his country to better purpose elsewhere, than by destroying his health and exhausting his spirits in a crowded assembly. The lives of several valuable Members of Parliament, and almost the whole usefulness of many more, have fallen a sacrifice to regularity of attendance. The main question is, not how often has a member attended, but what he has done when he did attend? However irregular his attendance, he should be honourably acquitted if he can appeal to valuable services actually achieved, as a proof that his time on the whole has been well expended for the public benefit.

These remarks will no longer apply, or at least not in an equal degree, when for the first time common sense shall be at length applied to the distribution of public business; when the cumbrous machinery of a multitudinous legislature shall no longer be put in motion for purposes for which it is manifestly unfit, and to which it never would have been applied, but that the simple means which would be efficacious to the end are not in existence. Can there be a spectacle more like Smollett's vast machine for cutting a cabbage,[*] than the two Houses of Parliament engaged in passing a Divorce Bill, or a Turnpike Bill, or a Bill to enable a Joint Stock Company to sue and be sued in the name of an individual? When the numbers of the House of Commons shall not exceed two or at most three hundred—when local representative councils, of twelve or twenty members each, shall be constituted for the transaction of local business—when the necessity of legislating for individual cases shall have been obviated, to the extent it easily might, by well-considered general laws enacted once for all—when statesmen shall arise whose logical habits shall enable them to foresee and provide for large classes of cases at once, instead of merely darning holes in the laws, or laying on, as at present, when they see a place uncovered, a little patch of law just large enough to cover it—and when the preparation of Bills for Parliament shall be the duty of a responsible Minister of Legislation, aided by a standing Commission of the first jurists in the nation; an arrangement without which all the representative Governments of Europe are in danger of making, in the words of General Lamarque, "*une halte dans la boue*;"[†]—then, perhaps, and not till then, the business of Parliament will neither, in quantity or quality, be such as to justify any of the members in withholding constant attendance.

* * * * *

15th February

Lord Althorp's Budget[‡]

The prosperity of the country has better availed the Ministry than their own counsels. Last year they squandered a considerable surplus revenue in remitting, not taxes, but halves and quarters and half-quarters of taxes. They seemed to have found the secret of giving away a large sum of money so that nobody should be even temporarily the better for it. They left themselves with the interest of twenty

---

[*Tobias George Smollett, *The Adventures of Peregrine Pickle*, 4 vols. (London: printed for the Author, 1751), Vol. IV, p. 129 (Chap. ciii).]

[†The statement is reported in Joseph François Michaud and Louis Gabriel Michaud, eds., Biography of Jean Maximilien Lamarque, in *Biographie universelle ancienne et moderne*, 2nd ed., 45 vols. (Paris: Desplaces and Michaud; Leipzig: Brockhaus, 1854–65), Vol. XXIII, p. 18.]

[‡See Spencer, Speech in Introducing a Motion on the Budget (14 Feb., 1834), *PD*, 3rd ser., Vol. 21, cols. 360–8.]

millions of new debt to provide for, and resources not more than equal to the existing expenditure. But an increasing revenue has been to them like a rising tide; by its assistance they have found themselves in deep water where they had reason to expect rocks and shallows. The revenue of the year exceeds last year's estimates by a million and a half; and having effected (for which we give them all reasonable credit) further retrenchments to the amount of half a million, they have two millions to meet the expected charge of 800,000*l.*; leaving a surplus of 1,200,000*l.*; about equal to the produce of the house-tax, which accordingly is to be taken off. The abrogation of this tax will certainly afford relief: this time the remission of taxation will be a benefit to somebody; but to whom? To the most clamorous and troublesome; not to the most overburthened.

Are the "low Radicals," as the *Times* calls them,[*] altogether wrong, when they affirm that the Reform Bill has but created what they term a shopocracy,[†] in the place of, or rather by the side of, the aristocracy; and that the people are still to be sacrificed for the joint benefit of both? The first use which the middle classes have made of their power, is to shake off *their* burthens, leaving those of the working classes as great as ever. The window-tax is objectionable; but a house-tax, honestly assessed, seems to us as unexceptionable an impost as exists, and one of the very last which an enlightened policy would have abandoned. Mr. Byng, indeed, "wishes to see all direct taxes abolished:" this we suppose passes for "good old English feeling:" English liberty has always felt itself seriously aggrieved by the visits of the tax-gatherer: an Englishman, being free born, dislikes extremely, not the burthen, but to see the face of the man who lays it on. If Mr. Byng were mortally wounded by an invisible weapon, he would think he died a natural death. Let but the "keen knife see not the wound it makes," he will never "peep through the dark and cry 'hold, hold.' "[‡]

This is very childish; or rather like, not a child, but a hunted hare, who thinks she escapes her pursuers by hiding her face, and managing not to see them. Direct taxes are the best of taxes, because there is least of juggle about them, and least uncertainty upon whom they really fall. With taxes on commodities there is always so much doubt, or at least such interminable dispute, who pays them, that it is impossible to agree upon a mode of imposing them so as to bear equally on all classes and on all fortunes. Besides, to be productive, they must be laid on articles of general consumption, and of such the poor consume more, in proportion to their incomes, than the rich. A poor family consumes proportionally much more bread, more beer, more tea, more sugar, than a rich family. No tax can be perfectly just, but a direct tax. And, where the rent of land, the best of all sources of revenue, has been permitted to become the property of individuals, of all direct taxes none

[*Leading Article on British Foreign Policy, *The Times*, 17 Jan., 1834, p. 4.]
[†See Leading Article on the Reform Bill, *Poor Man's Guardian*, I (26 May, 1832), 401.]
[‡Shakespeare, *Macbeth*, I, v, 52-4.]

practically speaking is so eligible as a house-tax. It is the best of income-taxes. What a man pays for his habitation measures his income, not perfectly indeed, but better than any tax-gatherer can; and makes all those allowances which an income-tax never makes, perhaps never can make. No income-tax can be precisely graduated according to the precariousness, the variableness, the limited or unlimited duration of incomes: all which circumstances a fair house-tax allows for, because they are all taken into consideration in hiring or buying a house. In short, a house-tax (except that a miser may escape it) realizes far more perfectly than an income-tax, the perfection of an income-tax itself,—that of being proportioned not to what a man has, but to what he can afford to spend.

But it was not by considerations so subtle and refined as those of the comparative justice or policy of different taxes, that this question was destined to be decided. When the Reformed Parliament met, the people of England, that part of them at least who are called the "better classes," commenced a contest, not to reduce the public expenses, but to shift off their burthen each man *from* himself *upon* all the rest. In this ignominious scramble, the shoparchy have carried off the lion's share. The house-tax, though it did not touch the poor, was unpopular, because it fell disproportionately upon the middle classes, and spared the higher: and the aristocracy, having to choose between its equalization and its abolition, made a compromise with the middle classes, and removed the tax, to avoid paying their just share of it. The reconciliations, like the quarrels, of the privileged orders, are always at the people's expense.

We should give Lord Althorp some credit for the manifest reluctance with which he gave up this tax,[*] if we did not remember how perseveringly, last year, he defended those inequalities in its assessment,[†] which so disgusted the public, and which are the real cause of its unpopularity. If instead of defending those inequalities he had remedied them, the clamour against the tax would have been stilled. Now, it is too late.

We observe by the *Chronicle* report, that when Mr. Hume recommended as a substitute for the present tax on wines, what if practicable would be so greatly preferable, an *ad valorem* duty, on the ground that by lightening the pressure of the duty on the cheaper wines, it would enable the poor to drink wine for a shilling a bottle, the House laughed.[‡] The idea of wine at a shilling a bottle, and poor men drinking it, altogether overset what little seriousness nature had bestowed upon them. The House is not aware how much it often betrays by a laugh. Tell me when

---

[*Spencer, speech of 14 Feb., 1834, cols. 366–7.]

[†E.g., Spencer, Speech in Introducing a Motion on Supply (19 Apr., 1833), *PD*, 3rd ser., Vol. 17, cols. 334–5; Speech in Introducing a Motion on House and Window Taxes (30 Apr., 1833), *ibid.*, cols. 769–76; and Speech on the Inhabited House Duty (7 Aug., 1833), *ibid.*, Vol. 20, cols. 421–5.]

[‡Joseph Hume, Speech on the Budget (14 Feb., 1834), *ibid.*, Vol. 21, col. 384, in *Morning Chronicle*, 15 Feb., 1834, p. 3.]

a man laughs, and I will tell you what he is. We make no comment upon the good feeling or the good sense of this exhibition. What we would point attention to is, its inherent vulgarity. There has been some discussion whether the House of Commons has become less *gentlemanly* in its composition since it has been said to be reformed. This we cannot presume to decide: but, gentlemanly or not, a more essentially vulgar assembly than it is and was, both before and since, we sometimes think could scarcely be found in Europe.

* * * * *

17th February

The Leeds Election

The liberal papers are exulting in the success of the liberal candidate, Mr. Baines, yet they all overlook what forms in our view the chief importance of the victory.[*] If Mr. Baines had been a Tory, we should still have hailed as one of the greatest triumphs hitherto achieved by liberal principles, the return to Parliament of a man who has gained all his reputation and his success in life as editor of a newspaper. It is time that the ostensible power should be where the real power is, and that those who have long, by persuasion or by compulsion, dictated to the Legislature what laws it should make, should no longer be thought unfit themselves to take a direct part in making those laws.

The social position of the newspaper press in this country is altogether anomalous. In all the circumstances by which we are surrounded there is no more striking indication of a society in a state of moral revolution. If there be a law in human affairs which seems universal, it is, that the respect of mankind follows power, in whatsoever hands residing. In England, however, the seat of power has changed, and the respect of mankind has not yet found its way to the new disposers of their destiny. Nobody denies that the newspapers govern the country; hitherto (it is true) much more by making themselves the organs of opinion already formed, than by influencing its formation; yet to an immense extent in both modes. To mention a striking example, we affirm without fear of contradiction from any one who has watched the progress of opinion, that Mr. Black, the Editor of the *Morning Chronicle*, has been the great proximate cause of the law reforms now in progress, and of the downfal of that superstition which formerly protected the vices of the courts of law and of the magistracy from the denunciations of opinion and the controlling hand of the legislator. Sir Robert Peel first, and Lord Brougham afterwards, have only reaped the harvest which he had sown.

Allowing, however, that the newspaper press is but an instrument, and not an independent agent, the two Houses of Parliament have for many years renounced

[*See, e.g., Leading Article on the Leeds Election, *Morning Chronicle*, 17 Feb., 1834, p. 2.]

all pretension to being anything but the more or less reluctant instruments of that instrument. Yet, a year or two ago, even Radicals would have turned away from the proposition of returning a newspaper editor to Parliament; because newspaper editors, as a class, have only talents, and have not rank or fortune. Even now, we are convinced that most of Mr. Baines's supporters would have voted in preference for the greatest dolt among the rich manufacturers or bankers of Leeds, if he would have professed as strongly their political opinions. The occupation of a journalist is under the ban of society. An individual here and there, though with difficulty, escapes the stigma, and is placed, by personal qualities or adventitious circumstances, as high in conventional estimation as a barrister is placed by his mere calling. But the profession is decidedly not a gentlemanly one. It stands about on a level with the lower branches of the legal profession. The fact is almost universally admitted, that an editor, and that an attorney, *may* be a gentleman. Nay, many go so far as to say that some *are* so.

Another anomaly is, the very different degree of solicitude which society bestows upon the training up of those who are its real teachers, and of those who only pretend to be its teachers, having long ceased to be so in reality. We once heard the profoundest observer and critic on the spirit of the times whom we ever knew, dilate upon this topic.[*] Observe, he said, what an apparatus is put in motion, what large sums of money are expended, what a world of trouble is taken, to educate a select individual from his infancy upwards, for the ultimate end of placing him in a pulpit,—from whence he discourses to the people, in language which nine-tenths of them scarcely understand, matter which has altogether ceased (it may almost be said) to have a meaning to them; which never reaches their intellect, their imagination, or their affections, and has lost all power over their will. Meantime, there has arisen a new set of instructors, who really do govern the minds and conduct of the people, who have succeeded to the place which the clergy formerly filled, and are, however unworthy in many respects, the sole priesthood of our time; and the rearing up of these men, the work of qualifying them for the highest and most dignified office to which a human being can be called, is abandoned to chance, that is, to all manner of demoralizing influences. The priest of the nineteenth century struggles into existence no one knows how, and having served his apprenticeship in some cellar or garret which society never looks into, sets up his pulpit in a newspaper-office, and there, from the materials which he has picked up, and the faculties which it has pleased heaven, not society, to bestow upon him, preaches to the world how they are to think, feel, and act; and they follow his instructions.

This parallel is well fitted to give rise to reflections, which whoever follows up, will be led much further than he is probably aware of.

[*Probably Thomas Carlyle; cf., e.g., "Signs of the Times," *Edinburgh Review*, XLIX (June, 1829), 455.]

Mr. O'Connell's Bill for the Liberty of the Press[*]

The Radical party in the House of Commons is a rope of sand.[†] It is not only without a head, but without members or a body. It is *not* a party; the Radicals in Parliament are incapable of forming one. No body of men ever accomplished any thing considerable in public life without organized co-operation; and these seem incapable, not merely of organized, but even of casual co-operation. The evil consequences of this incapacity display themselves most of all, in the case of those who aspire to be, and in some measure deserve to be, distinguished as the instructed and philosophical Radicals; for *they* appear to be incapable, not only of acting in concert, but also of acting singly. There is always a lion in the path.[‡] One is too despairing; he thinks no good is ever to be done; another is too fastidious; he will not "mix himself up," or "allow himself to be confounded" with somebody or something: another is too timid, another too indolent, another too unenterprising. With one or two exceptions at most, none of them have sufficient strength (there needs no little) to stand alone: they will never be any thing but ciphers, till they are grouped together with a unit or units at their head; yet they cannot, it would seem, endure the imputation of acting together. Not only there is no principle of attraction among them, there seems a principle of repulsion. They do not even verify the old story of John doing nothing and Tom helping him. They will not be helped to do nothing. Each man is immovably bent upon doing his nothing single-handed.

The consequence is, that the men who will neither lead nor be led, are passed by; and those who do not wait to be led, become the real leaders. We have heard it spoken of in a tone of complaint, that Mr. Hume, or that Mr. O'Connell, hold themselves forth as the parliamentary leaders of the popular party in the nation. For our part, so long as Mr. Hume and Mr. O'Connell are the only persons who are never unprepared to stand up for the cause, in season and out of season, whatever may be thought of them by fine people, and to force discussions on all the great questions, whatever may be the unwillingness of the House, we hold these gentlemen to be the leaders of the Radicals in fact, whatever some who allow themselves to be called Radicals may say or wish to the contrary. And, although they may often execute the office in a manner which compels us to wish that the people had other leaders, or rather that those who are so good were still better, we make an immense distinction in our estimation between those who continually

---

[*See Daniel O'Connell, Speech in Introducing a Bill on Libel Law (18 Feb., 1834), *PD*, 3rd ser., Vol. 21, cols. 468–78; and "A Bill to Secure the Liberty of the Press," 4 William IV (25 Feb., 1834), *PP*, 1834, III, 449–53 (not enacted).]

[†Mill may have adopted this common image from John Locke, *Two Treatises of Government*, in *Works*, new ed., 10 vols. (London: Tegg, Sharpe, Offor, Robinson, and Evans, 1823), Vol. V, p. 212.]

[‡Proverbs, 26:13.]

accomplish far *more* than any one thought there was reason to expect of them, and those who accomplish less.*

Those who do not originate any thing, must consent to act with, and under, those who do, or to be nothing. There are members of the House in whose hands, far rather than in those of Mr. O'Connell, we would gladly have seen such a question as the Liberty of the Press: but we are well assured, from experience, that not one of them would have moved hand or foot in the matter, if a bolder man had not led the way. We give Mr. O'Connell the greatest credit for introducing the subject; and we now trust, that those who have the capacity may have also the will to assist him in rendering the very imperfect measure which he proposes as perfect as possible.

Mr. O'Connell's measure, if we may judge from his opening statement, goes, as it appears to us, too far, and not far enough. He seems to have taken nothing into his view but personal libels. He said not a word of any provision for the free discussion of doctrines, or of institutions, although this is, if possible, still more important than even the liberty of criticising the conduct of public functionaries. On the subject of religion, that on which beyond all others discussion ought not to be restrained by law—being already restrained so much more than is consistent with a wholesome state of the human mind, by mere opinion—Mr. O'Connell avows his intention of not innovating on the existing law; though, greatly to his honour, he has not flinched from declaring, in the strongest terms, that, in his opinion, discussion on the subject of religion ought to be perfectly free. But restrictions of a similar nature exist on the subject of politics also, and Mr. O'Connell has not yet said that he proposes to remove them. We cannot so much as conceive any great improvement in the law of libel, not commencing with a declaration that it shall be lawful to controvert any political doctrine, or attack any law or institution, without exception; in any manner and in any terms not constituting a direct instigation to an act of treason, or to some other specific act to which penalties are attached by the law. Mr. O'Connell has held out no promise of any such provision.

On the other hand, Mr. O'Connell goes farther than we are able to follow him, when he proposes that in all cases of private libel, truth should be a justification. Where, indeed, the imputation is not upon the private, but upon the public character of a public man; or where the act imputed, though belonging to private life, is in its nature public, (for instance, any violation of decency in a public place,) or has already received publicity, (for instance, by the proceedings of a Court of Justice,) we think, with Mr. O'Connell, that the truth of the charge ought to be a sufficient defence; and we would even allow the alleged libeller to clear

---

*This was written before Mr. O'Connell's profligate declaration in favour of the pillage of the widow and the orphan. [Speech on Agricultural Distress (21 Feb., 1834), *PD*, 3rd ser., Vol. 21, cols. 684–6.]

himself, though the charge be false, by showing that he had good grounds for believing it to be true. But we would not permit the press to impute, even truly, acts, however discreditable, which are in their nature private. We would not allow the truth of such imputation to be even pleaded in mitigation. The very attempt to establish the charge by evidence, would often be a gross aggravation of the original injury. We see insuperable objections to allowing the details of a person's private conduct to be made the subject of judicial investigation, at the pleasure of any malignant accuser. We are not insensible to the *prestige* attaching to the word truth, and we go farther than most persons would like, in maintaining that it is good to speak the truth, whatever be the consequences. But it is not the letter of the truth, it is the spirit that is wanted; and, unhappily, the letter is all that admits of being substantiated in a Court of Justice. Every one knows how easy it is, without falsifying a single fact, to give the falsest possible impression of any occurrence; and, in the concerns of private life, the whole morality of a transaction commonly depends upon circumstances which neither a tribunal nor the public can possibly be enabled to judge of. Let any person call to his recollection the particulars of any family quarrel, for example, which has come within his personal knowledge, and think how absolutely impracticable it would be to place before the public any thing approaching to the most distant likeness of the real features of the case! The moral character of the transaction cannot possibly be understood, nor even the evidence on which the facts themselves rest, be properly appreciated, without a minute acquaintance with a thousand particulars of the character, habits, and previous history of the parties, such as must be derived from personal knowledge, and cannot possibly be communicated. Any "truth" which can be told to the public on such matters must almost necessarily be, with respect to some party concerned, a cruel falsehood: and only the more cruel, if what tells against the party can be proved in a Court of Justice, while what would tell in his favour may be in its nature unsusceptible of such proof.

The proper tribunal for the cognizance of private immoralities, in so far as any censorship can be advantageously exercised over them by opinion at all, is the opinion of a person's friends and connexions; who have some knowledge of the person himself, and of the previous circumstances, and therefore something to guide them in estimating both the probabilities of the case and the morality of it. And even their knowledge, how insufficient it generally is! and how doubtingly and hesitatingly a conscientious and modest man will usually draw from such imperfect evidence, conclusions injurious to the moral character of a person of whose position he must necessarily be so insufficient a judge! Is not that the meaning of the Christian precept, "Judge not!"[*] And when the individual who is nearest, and best informed, can scarcely ever be sure that he is informed sufficiently, it is proposed to authorize a general inquisition into private life by the

[*Matthew, 7:1.]

public at large! the public, who *cannot* in the nature of the case be informed but in the loosest and most defective manner, nor can be qualified by previous knowledge to estimate the trustworthiness even of such partial information as is in its nature capable of being laid before them!

* * * * *

NO. II, APRIL, 1834*

21st February

The Ministerial Resolutions on Irish Tithe[*]

It is a common excuse for people who promise little, that what they do promise they perform. Like most other stock excuses, this plea is much oftener made than established: one thing, however, is unquestionable, that they who promise little *ought* to perform all they promise. The King's Speech[†] made but one promise, the settlement of Irish tithes; and Ministers have produced a measure, which, if proposed many years ago, might have really settled the question, at least for a season. But concessions in politics almost always come too late. When reforms are granted, not because they are eligible in themselves, but because it is not considered safe to refuse them, it seems to be in their very nature that they should always lag behind the demand for them. There seldom arises an immediate necessity for conceding anything until the storm has risen so high that it cannot be prevented from ultimately sweeping away everything.

It was right to retain a land-tax equal to the present amount of the tithe. In Ireland, where the intermediate class of farmers scarcely exists, the whole produce of the soil is shared between the labourer and the landlord. But the labourer in Ireland being reduced by competition to the mere necessaries of life, which he is sure to retain as long as he occupies the land; and the residue, whatever its amount, being the landlord's; all imposts charged upon the land subtract so much from what would otherwise be paid to the landlord: it is therefore the landlord who in reality pays them; if they were laid directly upon him, his situation

---

*The following notes were written as the events occurred, and are given to the public in the order in which they were committed to paper. The dates annexed are those of the newspapers which contained the first announcement of the facts taken for the subject of remark. The history of the session is taken up in the present number where it broke off in the last; which accounts for the appearance in our number for April of so early a date as the 21st of February. [Given by Mill as a headnote to the entries for April.]

[*See Edward John Littleton, Speech in Moving a Resolution on Tithes (Ireland) (20 Feb., 1834), *PD*, 3rd ser., Vol. 21, cols. 572–91; and "A Bill to Abolish Compositions for Tithes in Ireland, and to Substitute in Lieu Thereof a Land Tax, and to Provide for the Redemption of the Same," 4 William IV (27 Feb., 1834), *PP*, 1834, IV, 241–303 (not enacted).]

[†Speech from the Throne, 4 Feb., 1834, cols. 1–5.]

would not be altered; if they were abolished without equivalent, he would be the sole gainer.

The course, therefore, would be very clear, if there were no existing contracts between landlord and tenant. A tax payable by the landlord might be substituted for the tithe payable by the tenant, and the landlord left for compensation to the natural course of things. The tenant would then, without any special enactment for the purpose, pay, on account of rent alone, the same amount which he now pays for rent and tithe: the tithe would be blended with rent, collected without a separate process, and would cease to figure as an individual grievance; while all the odium would be saved, of collecting from the bulk of the Catholic population a tax expressly designed for the pockets of the Protestant clergy. The provision for the Church would then be seen to be, what, in Ireland, it really is; not a burthen upon the public, but a certain portion of the rent of land, which the State has not permitted individual landlords to appropriate, but has retained in its own hands for another purpose.

But during the currency of existing leases, the tithe, if exacted at all, cannot justly be levied from any but those who are at present liable to it. If paid by the landlord, it must be recoverable from the tenant; because the landlord cannot, until the expiration of the lease, be indemnified by an augmentation of his rent. On this shoal it requires no prophet to foretell that the measure will be wrecked. During the existing leases, the present grievance will continue; and does any one think that without far more drastic remedies the present constitution of society in Ireland can last as long as the unexpired leases? For the next few years the Bill does not abolish tithe, but, as Mr. O'Connell observed, merely makes the landlord the tithe-proctor;[*] and a few years, in the present condition of Ireland, are an eternity.

Even when the leases expire, the tithe will not merge in the rent by operation of law, but only at the option of the landlord. Unless there be a stipulation to the contrary in the new lease, the tithe (or land-tax, as it is to be called) will still be kept separate from the rent; and any landlord, whose purposes, either political or personal, it may happen to answer, may still force the Catholic peasant to individualize the tithe; to distinguish it from his other payments; to be distinctly conscious on each occasion how much exactly he is paying to a Church which he detests.

Since the above observations were written, the Bill has been printed; and we preceive that it does not even free the tithe from the chief objection which lies against it as tithe—its perpetual increase. By an Act passed in 1832, the tithes of every parish in Ireland are already compounded for;[†] and the land-tax now to be imposed in lieu of tithe, is to be of the same amount as the composition. The

---

[*O'Connell, Speech on Tithes (Ireland) (20 Feb., 1834), *PD*, 3rd ser., Vol. 21, col. 596.]

[†2 & 3 William IV, c. 119 (1832).]

composition, however, under the Act of 1832, is not fixed, but variable every seven years, according to the price of corn. As, in the progress of population and cultivation, the price of corn tends always to a rise, the new land-tax, instead of being a fixed charge, will be augmented every seven years, and the memory of tithe will be kept alive for ever, by the periodical readjustment of the amount. This is an error in principle, of the first magnitude: but its practical consequences will merge in the general failure of the measure; which certainly will not last unaltered for seven years.

* * * * *

22nd February

The Debate on Agricultural Distress[*]

The landowners of England are remarkable for being always in distress. Upon no portion of the sons of men does the common destiny of our race seem to press so heavily. This speaks but ill for their own wisdom; for they have wielded during one hundred and forty-five years previous to 1832, the entire powers of the British Legislature, and still compose the whole of one House of Parliament, and a majority of the other: they have done their best indeed to possess the whole of that too, as they compel every man, before he becomes a member of it, to make oath that he is one of their body. Persons thus circumstanced must be either very unskilful or remarkably conscientious, if they do not contrive to make some other people distressed instead of themselves. If the landlords have not effected this, it has not been for want of trying. All that laws could do they have done to force other people to buy from them every description of the produce of the soil at their own price. All that laws could do they have done to secure to themselves, as borrowers, at the expense of the lenders, the advantage of a low rate of interest. They have exempted their land from several of the taxes. Of their local burthens they have reserved to themselves the entire controul; for the county rates are voted by themselves in quarter sessions, and the administration of the poor laws is entirely in their hands. The army, the navy, and the civil patronage of the State, belong to them almost exclusively. The lay-tithes are theirs for their own use, the ecclesiastical tithes for the use of their younger children. When new land has been inclosed, it has usually been distributed, not among the poor, but among the landlords.

Being thus accustomed to have every thing their own way, it may appear extraordinary that they should be always complaining of distress. But is not that the very reason? A spoiled child is always dissatisfied. No spoiled child has all that it asks for, and the more is bestowed, the more it is indignant that anything should be withheld. If it meet with no resistance from human will, it is angry that the laws of

[*PD, 3rd ser., Vol. 21, cols. 649–94 (21 Feb., 1834).]

nature are not equally compliant; and so are the landlords. Let it not be imagined that we contest the fact of the distress. Distressed they are, for they never have so much money as they would like to have. Most of them have not even so much as they spend. This they feel, quite sincerely, as a grievous hardship and wrong; and consider themselves injured men if something is not done to relieve them from it.

Really, since they compel us to say it, there is no class whom, as a class it would better become to bear patiently any unavoidable diminution of their incomes, since a far smaller proportion of them than of any other class have acquired even the smallest part of those incomes by their own labour. Society is their creditor for every thing, and their debtor for nothing. In return for its protection and guarantee to their great fortunes, few indeed among them ever did any thing for society but what they think they do by being "large consumers," and "spending in the country" the money which they draw from it. Their property must be protected because all property must be protected; those who by the accident of birth obtain the large prizes have a right to enjoy them, but not a right to find fault with the course of nature, because the riches they were born to, have turned out less than they expected; especially if the true and only cause of their distress be their own improvidence.

Because a territorial Aristocracy, a class notorious in all the countries of the world for spending all it has, is always needy—because people whose income is in its very nature subject to fluctuations, greatly increased by laws of their own making, and who invariably live up to the full measure of that income when at the highest, are put to considerable inconvenience when a change comes, and to make their suffering less are often tempted to make it ultimately greater, by obliging their tenants to share it—is that any peculiar affliction, any visitation from heaven upon the unfortunate "agriculturists?" When Ministers, in the speech from the throne, countenanced the cry of "agricultural distress," they gave a virtual sanction not only to unfounded complaints but to unjustifiable claims. Their predecessors would not have committed such a blunder. The Duke of Wellington and Sir Robert Peel, whether they had seen through the delusion or not, would not have expatiated upon an evil when they did not intend to propose any remedy.

Ministers were taunted with this inconsistency, in the debate on Lord Chandos's motion,[*] deservedly; and they met the taunt by a piece of inconceivable *mal-adresse*. They said that the agriculturists must look for relief to a diminution of the poor rates, and that a Bill was about to be brought in, which would have that effect.[†] If this be the tone in which they mean to advocate Poor Law Reform, it were better, grievous as are the evils to be remedied, that the question should sleep

[*Richard Plantagenet Grenville, Speech in Introducing a Motion on Agricultural Distress (21 Feb., 1834), *ibid.*, cols. 649–59.]

[†Spencer, Speech on Agricultural Distress (21 Feb., 1834), *ibid.*, cols. 661, 663. The Bill was eventually enacted as 4 & 5 William IV, c. 76 (1834).]

for a season. To swell their majority by a few votes on a division which decided nothing,[*] they held forth to the world their contemplated poor law amendments as designed for the pecuniary benefit of the rich; which consequently, it will immediately be inferred, must be at the expense of the poor, and must therefore be tyranny, and to be resisted with the utmost force. For a momentary convenience they courted popular odium for their intended measure; they incurred the risk, first of not being able to carry it, and next of not being able to execute it, by representing it, contrary to the fact, as a piece of unfeeling selfishness. We know, and perfectly agree in, what they *meant* to say. The administration of the poor laws, which has produced so much evil to the poor, has produced evil to the rich too; and the amendments which are absolutely required by the interests of the poor themselves, will also alleviate, and wherever they have been tried have alleviated, the burthen of poor rates. But to legislate for the poor with that for the principal object, would be the act of a demon. Neither Ministers nor the Poor Law Commissioners are liable to such an accusation. The exclusive object of all which the Commissioners propose[†] is the good of the working classes themselves; and their recommendations ought to be adopted, even if the effect were to double instead of diminishing the poor rates. Ministers know this, and, we firmly believe, are actuated, in whatever changes they may propose, principally by this motive. But do they forget that the very ground which will be taken against any measure of Poor Law Reform, the great engine of prejudice and calumny against its authors and promoters, will be the assertion that it is a mere contrivance for reducing the poor rates? Whoever chooses to affirm this, may now quote, or affect to quote, their own authority for it. And this mischief is done to stop the mouths of an agriculturist or two for a single night! The agriculturists were present; the public were absent: and it was with Ministers as it is with most persons of infirm character—the small immediate motive prevailed over the greater but more distant one; to be out of sight, was to be out of mind.

Mr. O'Connell's Declaration for the Pillage of the National Creditor[‡]

Mr. O'Connell is almost the only public man now living, who is, in himself, something; who has influence of his own, and is not one of those whose influence is only that of the places they fill, or the class or party of which, for the time, they may happen to be the representatives. Almost alone among his contemporaries, he individually weighs something in the balance of events, and though far inferior to Mirabeau, may yet say with him "*Ma tête est aussi une puissance.*"[§] No man

[*See *PD*, 3rd ser., Vol. 21, cols. 694–5 (21 Feb., 1834).]
[†See "Report from His Majesty's Commissioners for Inquiring into the Administration and Practical Operation of the Poor Laws," *PP*, 1834, XXVII–XXXIX.]
[‡Speech of 21 Feb., 1834, cols. 684–6.]
[§See Joseph Mérilhou, "Essai historique sur la vie et les ouvrages de Mirabeau," in *Oeuvres de Mirabeau*, 9 vols. (Paris: Dupont and Brissot-Thivars, 1825–27), Vol. I, p. ccxi.]

ever exercised a great ascendancy by personal qualities, in whose character there was not much to admire: and in times like these Mr. O'Connell commands a far larger share of our respect than many of whose honesty we think far more highly. It is very true that a perfect character is the same in all ages; but our estimation of imperfect ones must vary exceedingly, according as their good qualities are merely those of their age, or are those which raise them above their age. Mr. O'Connell lives in an age in which to have a character at all is already a considerable distinction, and to have courage to act up to it, an extraordinary one; an age in which the rarest of all men is he "*qui bene est ausus vana contemnere*;"[*] in which even a man of no very scrupulous conscience, who dares to will great things, or at least things on a large scale, and finds in himself and his own qualities the means of accomplishing them, extorts from us more admiration by the contempt which he thus manifests for a thousand paltry respectabilities and responsibilities which chain up the hands of the "weak, the vacillating inconsistent Good,"* than he

[**Livy* (Latin and English), 14 vols., trans. B. O. Foster, *et al.* (London: Heinemann; New York: Putnam's Sons; and Cambridge, Mass.: Harvard University Press, 1919–59), Vol. IV, p. 230 (IX, xvii, 16). The allusion is to Alexander the Great.]

*Wordsworth's *Excursion* [in *Poetical Works*, 5 vols. (London: Longman, Rees, Orme, Brown, and Green, 1827), Vol. V, pp. 143–4 (IV, 295–318)]. We subjoin the entire passage. It will be long ere its moral shall become obsolete; though so much of it as ascribes to the Bad any exemption from the enervating influences of the age, is less true at present than in the times to which the poet refers. The Bad, fortunately for the destinies of the race, have mostly become as spiritless and nerveless as the well-intentioned:

> At this day
> When a Tartarian darkness overspreads
> The groaning nations; when the Impious rule
> By will or by established ordinance,
> Their own dire agents, and constrain the Good
> To acts which they abhor; though I bewail
> This triumph, yet the pity of my heart
> Prevents me not from owning, that the law
> By which Mankind now suffers, is most just.
> For by superior energies; more strict
> Affiance in each other; faith more firm
> In their unhallowed principles; the Bad
> Have fairly earned a victory o'er the weak,
> The vacillating inconsistent Good.
> Therefore, not unconsoled, I wait—in hope
> To see the moment, when the righteous Cause
> Shall gain Defenders zealous and devout
> As They who have opposed her; in which Virtue
> Will, to her efforts, tolerate no bounds
> That are not lofty as her rights; aspiring
> By impulse of her own ethereal zeal.
> That Spirit only can redeem Mankind;
> And when that sacred Spirit shall appear,
> Then shall *our* triumph be complete as theirs.

forfeits by not having sufficient greatness of mind to choose worthier objects or worthier means.

In Mr. O'Connell's case we felt the more inclined to overlook much in the politician which is objectionable in the man, because we deemed it certain from his position (even if to his personal feelings it were a matter of indifference) that the main direction of his exertions would always be on the popular side, and that he would render valuable service to the popular cause. But there are political crimes of so atrocious a character, that whoever is accessary to them, must for the common safety be cast out of the communion of honest men: every politician who thinks, or even would be believed to think that in politics there is a right and a wrong, must endeavour that the line drawn between himself and such men, may be as broad and as conspicuous as possible. We consider the pillage of the fundholder to be a crime of this description; and Mr. O'Connell, having advocated it, ought to be put into political quarantine, until he purge himself by confession and retractation.

Mr. O'Connell is much mistaken if he imagine that, by the course he has adopted, he is serving Radicalism, or recommending himself to the better part of the Radicals. He is playing into the hands of the Aristocracy. The fundholder has more to fear from them than from the Radicals. Accustomed, by their paramount influence over the Legislature, to take, when it suits them, what is not their own; feeling that the country is clamorous for a reduction of its burthens, and not knowing how they should contrive to live, if deprived of the power of taxing the public for their own benefit—the landholders are under constant temptation to appease the anger of the public, not by restoring to them their own, but by plundering somebody else and presenting them with a part of the spoil. The most inveterate enemies of the fundholder are a party among the landlords: and although the majority, we trust, would shrink from any personal participation in the mingled folly and atrocity of a national bankruptcy, we cannot expect from them any strenuous resistance to it. The only tried friends the fundholder has, the only combatants who plant themselves in the breach whenever he is assailed, who are ever ready to peril their influence in his defence, are Radical writers. To whom but to the *Westminster Review*, or *Tait's Magazine*, or the *Examiner*, can the fundholder look, to place the justice of his cause in a striking light before the public? While the *Quarterly Review* was urging Parliament to rob him;[*] while Earl Grey was proclaiming in the House of Lords that the robbery was greatly to be deprecated, but that necessity had no law, and *nemo tenetur ad impossibile*;[†] while Sir James Graham was writing a pamphlet expressly to prove that 30 per cent. ought to be struck off from the national debt and from all private mortgages;[‡]

[*See William Jacob, "Funding System," *Quarterly Review*, XXXI (Mar., 1825), 326.]
[†Charles Grey, Speech on the Corn Laws (1 May, 1826), *PD*, n.s., Vol. 15, col. 757.]
[‡James Robert George Graham, *Corn and Currency; in an Address to the Land Owners* (London: Ridgway, 1826).]

nobody repelled these iniquities with any thing like energy or indignation but the Radical press.

There is much to be said for paying off the national debt by a tax on property; treating the debt of our fathers as a mortgage upon the property which our fathers left, and therefore a charge upon those to whom that property has descended, and not upon unborn generations of those who have nothing but their labour. *This* proposition may become a popular one among the Radicals generally. But, if the landlords attempt to effect a compromise with the profligate portion of the Radicals, and save themselves who contracted the debt from paying their due share of it, by cancelling it either wholly or partially, they must be plainly told, that they may have the power of determining where confiscation shall begin, but not where it shall end. Of all kinds of property, the public funds consist the most peculiarly of the savings of honest industry, and the pittance of the widow and the orphan. These may be the first robbed, but let the robbers rely on it, they shall not be the last. The people consent to bear with a most mischievous and demoralizing inequality of fortunes, for the sake of the security which springs from the general inviolability of property. But let that inviolability be once seriously infringed, that security destroyed, and it will not be, and ought not to be, longer endured that there should be men who have 100,000*l.* a year, while others are starving. Ere long it would be told to the Aristocracy in a voice of thunder, that if the funds are confiscated to the state, the land *shall* follow; and, if necessary, not only the land, but all fortunes exceeding 500*l.* or 1000*l.* a year. Not a tenth part of the fundholders possess any thing approaching to the smaller of these sums.

We subjoin two passages from two Radical writers, each of which contains in a small compass some of the considerations by which the attempts of robbery to give itself a colourable pretext, may best be counteracted. The first is aimed directly against the proposition with which Mr. O'Connell has chosen to identify himself—that a large portion of the debt having been contracted in a depreciated currency, the interest ought not be paid nor the principal liquidated in money of the ancient standard:

The restoration of the ancient standard, and the payment in the restored currency of the interest of a debt contracted in a depreciated one, was no injustice, but the simple performance of a plighted compact. All debts contracted during the Bank restriction, were contracted under as full an assurance as the faith of a nation could give, that cash payments were only *temporarily* suspended. At first, the suspension was to last a few weeks, next a few months, then, at furthest, a few years.[*] Nobody dared even to insinuate a proposition that it should be perpetual, or that, when cash payments were resumed, less than a guinea should be given at the Bank for a pound note and a shilling. And to quiet the doubts and fears which would else have arisen, and which would have rendered it impossible for any Minister to raise another loan, except at the most ruinous interest, it was made the law of the land, solemnly sanctioned by Parliament, that six months after the peace, if not before, cash

[*See 37 George III, cc. 45, 91 (1797).]

payments should be resumed. This, therefore, was distinctly one of the conditions of all the loans made during that period. It is a condition which we have not fulfilled. Instead of six months, more than five years intervened between the peace and the resumption of cash payments.[*] We, therefore, have not kept faith with the fundholder. Instead of having overpaid him, we have cheated him. Instead of making him a present of a per-centage equal to the enhancement of the currency, we continued to pay his interest in depreciated paper five years after we were bound by contract to pay it in cash. And be it remarked, that the depreciation was at its highest during a part of that period. If, therefore, there is to be a great day of national atonement for gone-by wrongs, the fundholders, instead of having anything to refund, must be directed to send in their bill for the principal and interest of what they were defrauded of during those five years. Instead of this, it is proposed, that, having already defrauded them of part of a benefit which was in their bond, and for which they gave an equivalent, we should now force them to make restitution of the remainder!

That they gave an equivalent, is manifest. The depreciation became greatest during the last few years of the war; indeed, it never amounted to anything considerable till then. It was during those years, also, that by far the largest sums were borrowed by the Government. At that time, the effects of the Bank restriction had begun to be well understood. The writings of Mr. Henry Thornton, Lord King, Mr. Ricardo, Mr. Huskisson, Mr. Blake, &c. and the proceedings of the Bullion Committee, had diffused a very general conviction, that the Bank had the power to depreciate the currency without limit, and that the Bank Directors acted on principles of which that evil was the natural consequence.[†] Does anybody imagine that the loans of those years could have been raised, except on terms never before heard of under a civilized government, if there had been no engagement to pay the interest or the principal in money of any fixed standard? but it had been avowed, that to whatever point the arbitrary issues of the Bank might depress the value of the pound sterling,—there it would be suffered to remain.

What avails it, then, to cavil about our paying more than we borrowed? Everybody pays more than he borrows; everybody, at least, who borrows at interest. The question is not, have we paid more than we borrowed? but, have we paid more than we promised to pay? And the answer is,—we have paid *less*. The fundholder, as the weaker party, has pocketed the injury; he only asks to be spared an additional and far greater one. We *covenanted* to pay in a metallic standard; we therefore are bound to do it. To deliberate on such a question, is as if a private person were to deliberate whether he should pick a pocket.*

[*See 59 George III, c. 49 (1819).]

[†Respectively, Henry Thornton, *An Enquiry into the Nature and Effects of the Credit of Great Britain* (London: Hatchard, 1802), and *Substance of Two Speeches . . . on the Report of the Bullion Committee* (London: Hatchard, 1811); Peter King, *Thoughts on the Restriction of Payments in Specie* (London: Cadell and Davies, 1803), and *Speech . . . upon the Second Reading of Earl Stanhope's Bill* (London: Ridgway, 1811); David Ricardo, *The High Price of Bullion* (London: Murray, 1810), *Observations . . . on the Depreciation of Paper Currency* (London: Murray, 1811), *Reply to Mr. Bosanquet's Practical Observations on the Report of the Bullion Committee* (London: Murray, 1811), and *Proposals for an Economical and Secure Currency* (London: Murray, 1816); William Huskisson, *The Question Concerning the Depreciation of Our Currency Stated and Examined* (London: Murray, 1810); William Blake, *Observations on the Principles Which Regulate the Course of Exchange* (London: Lloyd, 1810); and "Report from the Select Committee on the High Price of Gold Bullion," *PP*, 1810, III, 1–232.]

*From an article [by John Stuart Mill] in *Tait's* [*Edinburgh*] *Magazine* [Vol. II] for January 1833 [pp. 463–4], headed "The Currency Juggle." [In *CW*, Vol. IV, pp. 187–9.]

The argument of our second quotation relates less to the morality than to the political economy of the question. It is from the excellent *Catechism on the Corn Laws*, by Colonel Perronet Thompson. We quote from the seventeenth edition:

To rob the fundholders of their interest, after having spent their capital, would, besides all the evils of breach of contract, have the hardship of an *ex post facto* law, with the unique addition of being made in the teeth of the invitation of an existing law. The nation which should do it, would virtually declare itself incapable of contracting any national engagement, or performing any national act. A community must either acknowledge the possibility of being bound to-morrow by its act of to-day, or it must disband; for if it declares its own incompetency, it will be treated with as a community by nobody. And for any thing that could be gained by such a proceeding, it might as well be proposed to gain by robbing all the individuals who had red hair. The individual robbers might gain by it, but the community could not gain; because the red-haired men are themselves part of the community. If the principal expended could be called back again, it would be a different case. But nobody can seriously believe, that by what has been called applying a sponge to the national debt, the community would be one shilling the richer; or that by robbing one individual of five pounds per annum in order to put it into the pocket of another, the smallest progress would be made towards recovering the hundred which was spent thirty years ago. A man might as well try to repair the loss of a leg, by shifting the deficiency from one side to the other. If every individual was a fundholder in the same proportion that he is a tax-payer, it would be clear that the attempt was only shifting the leg. And it is the same when the case is as it is; except that the fundholders are the smaller party, and therefore might possibly be robbed.

And this is not the fallacy of saying that a national debt is no evil. It is a very great evil; and the worst thing about it is, that there is no getting rid of it. When a million is borrowed and spent, the evil is inflicted *then*; and not by the shifting of the interest from one pocket to another afterwards. It is not the evil that is denied, but the possibility of getting rid of it by refusing to pay the interest.

The magnitude of the evil or punishment is the same as if there had been inflicted a judicial necessity for throwing the amount of the interest annually into the Thames. For if the money had never been borrowed, the man who is now the fundholder would have had the principal in his pocket; and the tax-payer would have saved the interest, which is the same thing to him as saving it from the Thames. But there is a special provision of Providence that when money has been thus raised, no possible dishonesty shall get rid of the burden. If the principal had been borrowed from Prester John, the community might possibly gain by cheating him of his interest. But since the interest is owed to a component part of the community, it is in the constitution of things, that the community, however inclined to the practice of larceny, can gain nothing by robbing itself.

To propose that the fundholders should contribute, in their separate character, to any imaginable object of national expenditure, is as unjust as to propose that certain of the creditors in a case of bankruptcy should suffer the average loss of the creditors in general, and have a sum struck out of their original account besides. The fundholders pay all taxes like other men, and to attack the amount of their claims upon the public besides, is precisely the operation supposed in the case of the bankruptcy. They make no objection to paying at the same rate as other people, to a property-tax, or to any other. What they object to, is being taxed and plundered too.

That people have been miserably cheated nobody doubts, but not by the fundholders. The fundholders have lost and not gained, in their character of fundholders; and they have borne, and do bear, their share of the general suffering besides. How the suffering is to be diminished nobody seems able to tell. A gone-by Government indulged itself with an unjust war, of the expense of which it never paid a shilling, and has left the whole for us. The immediate defendants are out of reach; they are where nobody will go to fetch them. All that is left for us in the way of recovery, is the possibility of recovering something from the interests in favour of which the fraud was enacted. And to this, if Corn Laws go on,[*] it will come at last, though probably not till the necessity is such as to be equally convincing to all parties.[†]

* * * * *

5th March

Mr. Buckingham's Motion on Impressment [‡]

It is not astonishing that in an age of barbarism men should commit barbarities. That Lord Chatham, one of a generation of statesmen among whom common humanity seems to have been almost as rare as common honesty, and in an age in which nothing was esteemed wickedness by which nobody suffered but the common people—that Lord Chatham should have seen no harm in impressment, can surprise no one; but it is equally unexpected and unwelcome to find Lord Chatham's authority quoted for it now, as conclusive, by a Reform minister.[§] Necessity! so well described by Milton as "*the tyrant's plea;*"[¶] it is also Sir James Graham's, and no one has yet, in our own day, or in any preceding, carried impudence so far as to pretend that there can be any other. It is difficult not to feel degraded by the very act of replying to so base a pretext. Necessity! yes: to borrow the apt expression of a vigorous writer, "it is exactly the sort of necessity which men are hanged for;" the convenience of taking the property of other people without paying for it, with the aggravation of its being their *sole* property, and the slight additional circumstance that the entire wealth of the nation is yours to purchase it withal, if you must have it. If the whole matter were laid before a community of ignorant savages; if they could be made to conceive the clamour, the indignant uproar, which rises from all the benches of a certain assembly at the bare suggestion of laying a sacrilegious finger upon anything which borders upon a *vested right*, upon anything which by the utmost straining can be construed into *property*, and then could be shown the spectacle of the same men hallooing on their leaders to denounce and insult men for asserting the *vested right* of the labourer to his own bodily powers, and calling it injustice to knock him down and rob him, not of his purse, seeing that he has none, but of all the *property* he has, his labour, in order to save to their own pockets a fractional part of the wages for which he would consent to sell it—would not the assembly of savages deem the assembly of civilized Christians fit objects for a hurricane to sweep

---

[*When Thompson first wrote (1827), the reference would be to 3 George IV, c. 60 (1822).]

[†Thomas Perronet Thompson, *A Catechism on the Corn Laws: With a List of Fallacies and the Answers* (1827), 17th ed. (London: Westminster Review, 1833), pp. 40–1.]

[‡James Silk Buckingham, Speech in Introducing a Motion on Impressment of Seamen (4 Mar., 1834), *PD*, 3rd ser., Vol. 21, cols. 1063–79.]

[§James Robert George Graham, Speech on Impressment (15 Aug., 1833), *ibid.*, Vol. 20, cols. 676–84; in that speech (at col. 684) Graham quotes William Pitt, Speech in the House of Lords (22 Nov., 1770), which is in John Almon, *Anecdotes of the Life of Pitt . . . With His Speeches in Parliament*, 3 vols. (London: Longman, Hurst, Rees, and Orme, 1810), Vol. II, pp. 197–8.]

[¶*Paradise Lost*, in *Poetical Works*, p. 97 (IV, 394).]

from the earth? What would they think if they were then told, that this same assembly had just voted twenty millions for the redemption of negro slaves?[*] These men are not fools, mere absolute fools they cannot be; they cannot think that kidnapping our own countrymen, and keeping them to forced labour for the whole or the better part of their lives, differs from negro slavery: why, every one of the incidents is the same, down to the very cart whip! call it, if you please, the cat. There is identity even in the wretched apologies which are set up; the captains, or masters, are an ill used, calumniated race of men, and free labour, forsooth, would be vastly dearer![†]

This was written last year. This year the exhibition has been repeated,[‡] though with some abatement of the former insolence, and a salvo to some Members of tender consciences, in the form of an amendment,[§] which, as we learn from the newspapers, was not too shallow to answer the purpose of an excuse for voting with the Ministry. Sir James Graham successfully fitted his measures to his men.

The pertinacity with which the power of tyranny is clung to, even by persons of the least tyrannical disposition, is almost incredible. We should forget it, if we were not continually reminded of it by the proceedings of public men.

Any person who defends slavery, is perfectly consistent in defending impressment too. Such a person thinks, with Callicles in the *Gorgias* of Plato, that the weak are by nature the property of the strong, and that if you *can*, with impunity, seize a man by main force, keep him in fetters till his spirit is broken, and compel him by threats and blows to labour for your profit, you have a right to do so.[¶] A man may think this, or at least practise it, without any imputation on his intellect. He only proves himself to be a ferocious animal, who being unrestrained by the ordinary ties of conscience or humanity, must be bound down by cords, or manacled with chains, to prevent him from doing mischief to others.

But the misdoings of the Whigs do not arise from the abuse of reason; they arise from deficiency of it. Like most public men, they are often judged with too much harshness in respect to intentions, because they are presumed to have that qualification which is necessary to the admission of a witness in an English court of justice: "the faculty of distinguishing right from wrong." Of lukewarmness in the performance of some of their most important duties, of the want of a stronger active principle of honesty, we fear they can by no means be acquitted. But we believe them to be wrongfully suspected of positive knavery; because few persons

---

[*3 & 4 William IV, c. 73 (1833).]

[†John Stuart Mill, Review of Harriet Martineau's *A Tale of the Tyne*, *Examiner*, 27 Oct., 1833, p. 678.]

[‡See *PD*, 3rd ser., Vol. 21, cols. 1063–1112 (4 Mar., 1834).]

[§See Graham, Speech in Moving an Amendment on Impressment (4 Mar., 1834), *ibid.*, cols. 1088–90.]

[¶Plato, *Gorgias*, in *Lysis, Symposium, Gorgias* (Greek and English), trans. W. R. M. Lamb (London: Heinemann; Cambridge, Mass.: Harvard University Press, 1953), pp. 384–6 (483^d–484^c); for Mill's own translation of the passage, see *CW*, Vol. XI, pp. 121–2.]

are aware how much in human conduct that looks like knavery, is sufficiently accounted for by defects of the intellect. There is a strong and growing impression in the country, founded upon the conduct of Ministers on this question, and on many others, that their denunciations of slavery, as well as their advocacy of Reform, were tricks to get into place, or to secure themselves in it. But this, in reality, does not follow; and to suppose that it does, argues ignorance of the incapacity of ordinary minds, either to feel or think for themselves. Any one who had really felt the detestableness of slavery; whose imagination had represented to him its horrors, or whose reason had made sensible to him its shocking immorality, could never have thought of impressment without similar detestation. But there are men in abundance, and most of the Whig Ministers seem to be of the number, whose own minds never tell them anything which is not first shouted to them by the voice of a united world. Left to themselves, they would never have found out that there was anything condemnable, either in impressment or in slavery: but when, for thirty years, they had grown accustomed to hear dinned in their ears, by men who *had* found it out for themselves, that negro slavery was a blot upon our national character, an enormity, a crime, a sin, it at last appeared so to them. In thirty years more, by an equally intense expression of national abhorrence, their consciences might, we dare say, be awakened on the subject of impressment too.

But what words can be found to characterise Sir James Graham's amendment? The grievance was, that you seized upon men by force, and robbed them of their only property, their labour:—the remedy proposed is, that instead of going out into the streets, knocking down the first man you meet, and robbing him, you shall for the future draw lots whom you will rob; the power, however, of knocking down in the streets not being given up, but still held in reserve to be used in cases of emergency!

It is hardly worth while to ask the question, how seamen are to be induced to submit to a registry which they will know is intended to facilitate catching them for the purpose of being robbed? Nor need we do more than just allude to the vehement objection at first made on account of the expense, to so important a public institution as a registry of births and marriages,[*] while expense is no objection to registering men for the purpose of robbing them.

Our indignation when we think on the lives which have been filled with bitterness, and the noble hearts which have been broken by the pressgang

[*John Wilks moved on 28 Mar., 1833, that there be a Select Committee on a Parochial Registry for Births, Deaths, and Marriages (*PD*, 3rd ser., Vol. 16, col. 1209); there was, apparently, then no objection on the grounds of expense. On 8 May, 1833 (see *ibid.*, Vol. 17, col. 1043), William Brougham brought in a bill, printed as "A Bill for Establishing a General Register for All Deeds and Instruments Affecting Real Property in England and Wales," 3 William IV (13 May, 1833), *PP*, 1833, III, 489–540; this was criticized as costly (see *PD*, 3rd ser., Vol. 17, cols. 1044–63, and Vol. 18, cols. 1001–10). Mill may be conflating the occasions, as both involved discussion of "Registry bills." See p. 196 below.]

abomination, gives way to astonishment at the quality of the understanding which can think to justify it by such arguments, or to uphold it for a short time longer by such miserable evasions.

* * * * *

1st March

The Dudley Election

On personal grounds we should regret the defeat of Sir John Campbell: there are few persons connected with office for whom we have so real a respect. In his peculiar department he is most valuable; at once an eminent lawyer and a strenuous law-reformer. In his general conduct he manifests this great superiority over almost all other official people, whether Ministers or underlings, that his opinions always seem to be the growth of his own mind; and he therefore is not afraid to commit himself by enunciating them. He is not one of those who, never talking but by rote or from tradition, never know whether they may venture to assent to a proposition which is not in their books. He has what so few men have, reasonable self-reliance: and this quality, along with that preference for truth and reason on all subjects which usually accompanies the capacity for comprehending them, render the Attorney General a most useful Member of the House of Commons, and one whose absence from it would be a public misfortune.

But Sir John Campbell cannot fail to find, in a short time, some door open for his readmission into Parliament; and, meanwhile, it is matter of just rejoicing that the Ministry have received a lesson, of a kind which they can understand. If you seek to make an impression upon a Minister, there is a much surer method than argument; arguments serve well enough to convince him that he is in the right; but to make him conscious of being in the wrong, there is nothing like the loss of votes. The present Ministry are, in this, remarkably like every other Ministry. The way to move them is not to overthrow their syllogisms, but to turn out their candidates. This is the only point where they are always vulnerable; and, fortunately, it is by no means hard to be come at. Here, indeed, lies the chief reason for preferring a Whig to a Tory Ministry. The check operates much sooner. To defeat a Tory candidate, the independent electors must come to the poll; to annihilate a Whig, they have only to stay away from it, and leave the rest to the "natural influence of property." A Tory Ministry is in no danger, except from great positive unpopularity; but mere indifference on the part of the public is fatal to a Whig Ministry.

This ensures on the part of the present Ministers greater deference than would be paid by the Tories to public opinion when actually declared. To foresee, indeed, what will probably be the public opinion a month hence, or what judgment the public will pronounce on any measure not yet laid before it, is what no reasonable man will expect from them. To be capable of this, they must be either philosophers or men of the world; and their misfortune is that they are neither. They are unskilled alike in books and in men. They have neither theory nor experience.

To the world at large, the Dudley election tells only what was known before: to Ministers, it was, we should think, a revelation of something they dreamed not of; namely, that the nation were not perfectly satisfied with their conduct. And, lest they should fail in drawing this inference, their fast friends and supporters, the *Times* and *Chronicle*, have undertaken the kind office of instilling it into their minds, accompanied by suitable admonitions.[*] The *Times* reads them a severe lecture on the folly of half-measures. The *Chronicle* bestows on them a catalogue of their errors of omission and of commission,[†] and tells them they have lost the confidence of the country. On this the *Examiner* remarks:

> Upon any discomfiture of the Ministry, such as the defeat of the Attorney General at Dudley, it is very frankly told its faults by journals which, so long as the tide flowed smoothly, have countenanced and encouraged it in all its errors. The first deviations from the right course are the deviations which should be closely watched and corrected; but the supporters of Government in the daily press are silent, or apologists, or approvers, of such declensions, till they have extended to a broad departure from the just line, and brought Ministers to a position of conspicuous disgrace. Which is the time to tell a man that he is in the wrong path? when he first steps into it; or when, exhausted and bemired, he has wandered miles from the right way? The information may be better late than never, but it would have been better at first than at last. The attempt, however, to correct the first false step has been censured and resisted as an act of hostility. The angry remark has been, "Why point out the little deviation from the right path in which they have advanced so far, and deserve indulgence? Apply yourself to commending their line of movement where it has been well directed, instead of ungraciously dwelling on the present declension of some few degrees." Now we could never understand the kindness of not telling a man when he was going wrong, especially when marching straight into a slough; nor, on the score of his having travelled right up to a certain point, could we admit that he had earned a title to lose his way, and that it was ungrateful to admonish him that he had mistaken his course. But this was for some time fashionable doctrine, and when Ministers were first truckling to the Tories and adopting Tory principles, as upon sinecures and the duration of Parliaments, and falling into divers Tory practices, and putting forth the hacknied Tory pretences for them, our animadversions upon these backslidings were called "attacks upon the Ministry," instead of attacks upon the errors which would ultimately disgrace and ruin them. When these things have advanced to a certain pitch, and public opinion recoils and marks its displeasure with some rebuff to the Ministry, their former flatterers or apologists turn round upon them, and recite the long catalogue of the faults which have been cherished, instead of nipped in the bud. They then say, "It is now time to speak the truth." It was not time to speak the truth when the men were first going wrong, and easily to be better guided; but it is time to speak the truth when, having been cheered on in the wrong direction, they have stuck in the slough.[‡]

There is nothing surprising in this. Ministers are treated by the newspapers as

[*Leading Article on the Dudley Election, *The Times*, 1 Mar., 1834, p. 3; and *Morning Chronicle*, 1 Mar., 1834, p. 4.]
[†For the phrase, see the "General Confession" in *The Book of Common Prayer*.]
[‡Anon., "The Spoiled Cabinet," *Examiner*, 9 Mar., 1834, p. 146.]

they themselves treat the public. They shape their conduct to the convenience of the day, leaving the morrow to shift for itself; and the newspapers praise or blame them by the same rule. The newspapers are a greater power than the Ministry, but are mostly as far as they are from having any lofty conception of the dignity of their mission. They have no particular motive to warn the Ministers, until the evil hour arrives: why should they sail against the stream? when the tide turns, so can they. What Ministers may expect from them is, to be encouraged in their faults, and never forgiven for the consequences; flattered while each blunder is in progress, and reproached with it when it is consummated. This fair-weather friendship answers the purposes of the newspapers very well, but those of the Ministers very ill. A Ministry, however accustomed to the evolution, cannot halt and wheel round with the same rapidity as a newspaper can. Ministers are known men, with the public eye upon them, noting their words and actions; all they say and do is remembered, and helps either to found a reputation or to destroy it. But a newspaper-writer nobody knows; nobody thinks about him, or inquires who he is; nobody remembers to-day what he wrote yesterday, nor will remember to-morrow what he may choose to write to-day. He can afford to praise a Ministry up to the last moment, and then turn round upon them. Few, indeed, are the journalists whose support contains in itself any guarantee of permanency.

Fortunately a journal, like a Ministry, may be very faulty and yet very useful. Judge the *Times* or the *Chronicle* by their faults only, and they would be insufferable; yet, without the *Times* and *Chronicle*, what should we do?

* * * * *

8th March

The Debate on the Corn Laws[*]

It is vain and wearisome to beat the air with never-ending discussion of exhausted questions. Who supposes that the landlords' monopoly is standing at this day for want of arguments to batter it down? All has been said on the Corn Laws: and it is now to be proved by other means than words, who is strongest. If the decision last night[†] does not convince the manufacturers of this, they must be unconvincible. Argument may be overcome by argument, but will must be vanquished by will. The time of calm discussion is gone by, and that of agitation must commence. The people *are* convinced, they are now to be stimulated. Reason is satisfied; the appeal must now be (however little the word may be relished) to passion. Injustice was never hurled from its throne by men who remained cool. The people must show that when they are wronged they can be indignant, and that the deliberate profes-

[*PD, 3rd ser., Vol. 21, cols. 1195–1262 (6 Mar., 1834), cols. 1266–1345 (7 Mar., 1834).]
[†*Ibid.*, cols. 1346–9 (7 Mar., 1834).]

sion of a determined purpose to persevere in wronging them, can only be expiated by the complete loss of political influence.

Sir James Graham—who was selected as spokesman of the Ministry, solely, we presume, because he had written a pamphlet, and published it with his name, in which the landlords' monopoly was condemned;[*]—Sir James Graham placed the maintenance of the monopoly on its true basis.[†] He said openly, that the bread-tax must be endured, because the landlords would be ruined if it were abolished. If rents were to fall twenty per cent., (he said,) the greater part of the landed property of the country must change hands. The landlords, then, are so deeply in debt, that they cannot keep their estates if compelled to live honestly; they must therefore be allowed to plunge their hands into the pocket of every person who lives by bread, in order to keep themselves out of the *Gazette*. They cannot afford to be landholders unless we pay them for it. We must tax ourselves to give them salaries for being a landed Aristocracy. We thank them for nothing. Their creditors will do it gratis.

A bolder language must be held to these people than they have been accustomed to. The landlords have hitherto been the ruling power, and, like all ruling classes, have been estimated at whatever value they chose to put upon themselves. If there were a man to whom nobody dared tell that he was not a god, he would end by believing it. Almost every member of the House of Commons really is, and all have sworn that they are, landlords;[‡] to such Sir James Graham was quite safe in thinking that he had said enough, when he said that without a subsidy from the public the landlords could not remain landlords. But what concern is it (except as a question of humanity) of any but themselves? Are the present landlords so much more precious to us than any other landlords, that when they cannot live upon their own means we should subscribe to enable them to live upon ours? If they are so deeply in debt that they own no more than twenty per cent. of their nominal incomes, and are mere receivers of the other four-fifths for the benefit of their creditors, the sooner they abandon their false position, cease to pretend to a character they have no right to, and let the real owners of the land become the avowed owners, the better. Land is power; and power cannot be more fatally placed than in the hands of spendthrifts by station; of men who have to maintain the externals of a large income with the resources of a small one; of men with the wants and habits of the rich, and the fortunes of the poor.

One word here on the philosophy of Aristocracy. The theoretic foundation both of Toryism and Whiggism; the moral and philosophical basis of all the modern European aristocratical politics; the justification of that paradox in practical ethics, the doctrine that the working bees should be governed by the drones, is the axiom,

[**Corn and Currency* (1826).]
[†Speech on the Corn Laws (6 Mar., 1834), *PD*, 3rd ser., Vol. 21, cols. 1223-46.]
[‡For the oath, see 9 Anne, c. 5 (1710).]

so dear to Aristocracy, that those who have the greatest stake in the country are the fittest to govern it. When the doctrines of Oligarchy are at variance with the interests of Oligarchy, we see which gives way. Who so far from having a stake in the country as needy rich men? people accustomed to profuse expenditure, which they have no longer the means of keeping up; through whose hands large incomes are constantly passing, only to be paid away to other people; to whom great wealth is constantly shown, while nothing of it is theirs except its wants—wants which have become unconquerable, and which they are under the strongest temptations to find the means of supplying at whatever cost? It is false that poor men, as such, are dangerous in a State; but those who are really dangerous are the poor who are miserable if they are not rich. Over such men not only the interest of others, but their own permanent interest has no hold; it is worth their while to be ruined in two years rather than to economize in one; they are dishonest debtors, bad landlords; gamblers themselves, they compel all under them to be so; rather than submit to a diminution of their rents to-day, they would run the risk of losing them altogether to-morrow, by forcing their tenants to exhaust the land; they are dishonest legislators; they must have a bread-tax, and their sons and nephews must have a provision out of the other taxes. In an age of conspiracies such men are conspirators; Catiline was such a man.

If the class to which Sir James Graham belongs, are in the condition which he describes, they may be an Aristocracy, but they are not a landed Aristocracy; they are a debtor Aristocracy: an Oligarchy not of the rich, but of the grasping and dissipated poor. Have they "a stake in the country?"[*] No. But let the land pass from them to the mortgagees, the real owners, *there* would be a landed Aristocracy; the new landlords would have a real, not a pretended stake in the country; we should be governed by the rich, since that is so great an advantage; and at least the land, in which we are all so deeply interested, would be in the hands of men, who, instead of ruining it for posterity in order to have this year a few more pounds to spend, could afford to lay out money without any immediate return for the increase of its productiveness at a distant period. Though there are many reasons for desiring this change, we are not anxious to see it; let the existing race of landlords save themselves if they can; but it must be honestly. We will not help them to pay their debts with a slice off the loaf on every man's table.

We have but one observation to add. Such questions as these are tests of the sufficiency of the Reform Bill; they gauge, if we may be permitted the metaphor, the strength of the popular influences in the House of Commons. When we say, that *all* the people's representatives should be elected by the people, we are told that the influence of the people, is the influence of the numerical majority; that minorities have rights, and that unless particular classes are allowed to have

[*See William Howe Windham, Speech on a New Military Plan (22 July, 1807), *PD*, 1st ser., Vol. 9, col. 897.]

representatives as well as the people, the majority will not be satisfied with justice, but will demand injustice; will not content themselves with security against being plundered by minorities, but will insist upon plundering the minorities in their turn. Be it so. Produce to us then a Parliament which holds the balance even; which obliges each party to be content with justice, and allows neither to plunder the other; and we will acknowledge that the Parliament is reformed enough. At present it is proposed to free the immense majority from the most insupportable of their burthens, the most flagrant of their injuries; this is refused, avowedly for the pecuniary benefit of the present landowners, and the refusal is backed by a majority of 312 to 155.[*] The interest, or supposed interest of the landowners, therefore, is an overmatch for obvious justice and the interest of all the rest of the community together, by more than two to one. Here is a case for a further Parliamentary Reform, which the stupidest can understand. We demand, then, further Reform. We demand it on the ground, not of any preconceived theory, but of the recorded failure of the present experiment. The Reform Bill has been tried, and proved wholly insufficient.

To Mr. Poulett Thomson, Mr. Littleton, Mr. Ellice, Lord Howick, and the other Members of the House connected with the Ministry, who spoke or voted in favour of Mr. Hume's motion,[†] belongs the praise of the seraph Abdiel,[‡]—that of submitting to temporary defeat in a cause certain of ultimate triumph. Lord Althorp did not give his vote to the cause, but he gave it his good word, saying, with much *naïveté*, that he voted against it, but could not speak against his own conviction.[§] Perhaps a time will come, when he will think it as impossible to *vote* against his conviction, as to speak against it.

* * * * *

12th March

Political Oaths[¶]

Mr. O'Connell has had the merit of being the first to speak out, we mean in Parliament, what every rational person thinks, that oaths of office, and oaths taken by Members of Parliament, are worthless formalities, which do no good whatever,

[*The Division on the Corn Law Bill (7 Mar., 1834), *ibid.*, 3rd ser., Vol. 21, cols. 1346–9.]

[†Joseph Hume, Speech in Introducing a Motion on the Corn Laws (6 Mar., 1834), *ibid.*, cols. 1197–1216; Charles Edward Poulett Thompson, Speech on the Corn Laws (7 Mar., 1834), *ibid.*, cols. 1276–1307; Edward John Littleton (vote only); Edward Ellice (vote only); and Henry George Grey, Speech on the Corn Laws (7 Mar., 1834), *ibid.*, col. 1340.]

[‡See Milton, *Paradise Lost*, in *Poetical Works*, pp. 146–7 (V, 872–907).]

[§Spencer, Speech on the Corn Laws (7 Mar., 1834), *PD*, 3rd ser., Vol. 21, cols. 1328–9.]

[¶See 9 George IV, c. 17, clause 2 (1828), and 10 George IV, c. 7 (1829).]

and much harm. His declaration drew forth adhesions from several Members, in particular an animated one from Dr. Lushington, who brought upon himself a sarcastic reply from Mr. Stanley, by the strength of his commendations of bold policy.[*] The lesson to Ministers was good, though the occasion scarcely required it; where would be the boldness of abolishing these frivolous ceremonies? It is not courage that is wanted, but common sense.

When you require a man, before he is admitted into Parliament, or accepts an office, to swear that he will not attempt to change the existing form of government, or to destroy the Church, or some particular institution in the State; is it supposed that you ever in reality prevent the nation from abolishing their Constitution or their Church, if they cease to think them essential to the public well-being? It would be monstrous, if one generation could thus tie up the hands of all succeeding ages, and impose its institutions upon the most remote posterity, against their will. The living will never submit themselves to the tyranny of the dead. Happily, though self-conceited legislators may *say* to their own handiwork *esto perpetua*, it is out of their power to make it so. As soon as it ceases to be thought worth preserving, it will cease to be preserved. But this they may do; they may render it impossible to make the most necessary alteration without perjury: which is much the same thing as to establish perjury by law.

If it be of importance that there should be sacredness in oaths, or in any solemn engagements, legislators should beware of compelling or tempting men to bind themselves not to do, what it may possibly be the dictate of their duty to do. Cases *must* occasionally occur of incompatible obligations; cases in which, whatever course we adopt, we unavoidably violate some moral duty, or we should rather say, some general rule, of which the observance is important to morality. But to all conscientious persons, except those of the strongest intellect or the most decided character, such an alternative is extremely distressing; and it is under cover of these extreme cases, lying exactly on the boundary between guilt and exalted virtue, that laxity of principle most commonly creeps in. It is of the utmost moment to the maintenance of a high standard of moral sentiment among the mass, that such cases of what may be termed justifiable immorality should rarely occur, and when they do occur, should not be forced forward into public notice and discussion. We are persuaded that the applause lavished upon Brutus and Timoleon, whether merited or not, has had a strong tendency to create indulgence for private crimes when supposed to be committed from public motives. Infidelity to engagements is far more likely to propagate itself by example than assassination. How much, then, have those to answer for, who arbitrarily create, in the most extensive sphere of publicity, a conflict of duties, of which this is sure to

[*O'Connell, Stephen Lushington, and Edward George Stanley, Speeches on Oaths of Catholic Members (11 Mar., 1834), *PD*, 3rd ser., Vol. 22, cols. 15–24, 33–5, and 40–6, respectively.]

be the result! who compromise the sanctity of the most binding of promises, by exacting it where its observance may possibly be a breach of obligations still more sacred! For there is no limit to the baneful consequences which an institution may produce, if it be not altered, when all other things are altering around it. And the framers of the oaths have so contrived matters, that be these consequences what they will, there shall be no means of averting them without a previous perjury. Is it a trifle to have made it unavoidable, that, in a contingency which is not improbable, which in a given lapse of time is virtually certain, it shall be the study, not of bad men, but of the best and most pure-minded, to reconcile themselves to the intentional evasion of a solemn promise? to preach to the mass of mankind that oaths are not binding? to invent artful contrivances for slipping their heads out of the yoke of a positive engagement?

Such is the morality inculcated both with precept and example, by the organs of the political Church of England. Sir R. H. Inglis avers, that human society is built upon oaths.[*] It is built upon oaths, and in order to stengthen the foundations, men are to be placed in such a situation, that, in a contingency not unlikely to occur, they must perforce disregard either their oaths or their country's good; and that, in proportion to their attachment to duty and ardour for the public weal, will be their efforts to vanquish their own reluctance to perjury! The real enemies of public morals, and weakeners of the ties which hold mankind together, are such teachers. It is impossible even to conceive the existence of a healthy and vigorous morality, until the reign of such men and of such doctrines is over.*

* * * * *

15th March

The Trades' Unions

The *Times*, this morning, has an article in which it seems to urge the Ministers to what they have by very alarming symptoms evinced themselves to be too much inclined to; the introduction of a measure for the suppression of the Trades' Unions.[†]

Now it would be wise, if, before they commit themselves to a course of policy of

---

[*Robert Harry Inglis, Speech on Oaths of Catholic Members (11 Mar., 1834), *ibid.*, col. 39.]

*Since this was written the Duke of Richmond has obtained a Committee of the House of Lords to inquire what oaths it may be expedient to abolish, with reference especially to promissory oaths. This is rational and commendable. A better commencement could not be made than by expunging all the promissory oaths, which the ministerial Bill relating to Irish Tithes is full of. [Charles Gordon Lennox, Motion on Oaths (20 Mar., 1834), *Journals of the House of Lords*, LXVI, 81, leading to "First Report from the Select Committee of the House of Lords, Appointed to Inquire into the Expediency of Substituting Declarations in Lieu of Oaths," *PP*, 1835, XIV, 399–520.]

[†Leading Article on Trades Unions, *The Times*, 15 Mar., 1834, p. 5.]

which they cannot doubt that the consequences would be most serious, they would consider well the character of the step which they are exhorted to take. It will be received as neither more or less than a declaration to the working people, that is, to about four-fifths of the whole population, that the Government is their enemy; that it is determined to *keep them down*; to keep them for ever poor, dependent, and servile, trampled into the earth under the feet of their employers.

We speak not, of course, in these terms, of anything which may or may not be done or attempted, for the more effectual prevention of violence, threats, or personal annoyance, when employed, as by many of the Unions they are said to be, to deter labourers from working for employers who do not comply with their rules. Against all such infringements by a part of the working population upon the just liberty of the remainder, the most effectual security ought to be taken (if it does not already exist) which is compatible with another liberty not less sacred; the right of the working classes, not only to concert with one another, either for raising wages, or for accomplishing any other end which they are permitted by law to pursue individually, but also to sanction their compact by giving free utterance to the disapprobation which it is natural they should feel towards those whom they consider as traitors to their caste; and the expression of which should be no further restrained by *law*, than the expression of the most just horror at any undoubted crime is restrained by the laws of most civilized countries; namely, by not being permitted to amount to personal insult or serious molestation.

But any attempt to confine the liberty of combination among workmen within narrower limits than these, is systematic tyranny; and the feelings of unconquerable resentment and abhorrence which it would most surely inspire in the whole of the labouring population towards the governing classes and the existing institutions of their country, would be natural and excusable. How *could* they view it, but as a measure of hostility taken against them as enemies by a superior caste, whom they regard, often most unjustly but often too truly, as actuated by the most hardened selfishness, and by all manner of evil feelings towards them; and whose grand object they believe to be, while living sumptuously on their labour, to withhold from them any but the scantiest share of its produce for which they will consent to work?

In vain would the employers, and their organs in the press or in Parliament, put in requisition doctrines of political economy, true indeed, but which they themselves only half understand, to this effect, that combinations never in reality keep up the rate of wages. What then? The working people are entitled to try: unless they try, how are they ever to learn? You, their employers, have not been wont to show either so infallible a wisdom, or so pure and disinterested a zeal for *their* interests, that you should expect them to take the proposition on your word, on the word of the adverse party. And we have yet to learn what you have done to assist the cultivation of their understandings, and the formation of vigorous intellectual faculties which should enable them to discern without trial what modes of bettering their condition are practicable and what are chimerical. And in truth how could you impart what has never yet been imparted to you? Show us an occasion on which the higher classes have ever received, except through the lessons of bitter experience, any political truth opposed to the suggestions of their direct and immediate interest, and we will allow them to complain of the absence of similar perspicacity in the labouring classes.

We cannot conceive any conduct much more discreditable, though unhappily in perfect keeping with the mode in which the world is habitally governed, than this: altogether to neglect the promotion, by such means as are practicable, either of the worldly prosperity or the mental and moral culture of the labouring classes; to use no means for conciliating, but a thousand for alienating, their good will; to allow them, as far as depends upon ourselves, to grow up barbarians in the midst of our civilization; and when they, despairing of help from us, have turned to helping themselves, and are taking the only means we have given them of learning how to better their lot, by mutual consultation and practical experiment, then to bear down upon them with the strong hand of power, and close that door also against them. But it cannot be done: there are passions aroused strong enough to effect it if it were practicable, but it is not.

The hope that experience, when allowed freely to take its course, will be the mother of wisdom to the operative classes as it has been to all mankind, is already justified by an actual result. The mechanics have discovered and recognised that strikes on the old principle, strikes by cessation of working, are always failures. The doctrine of the Trades' Unions now is, that when they resolve upon a strike, their course must not be to cease working, but to work on their own account; and that the common funds, which formerly went to support them in idleness, must now be administered as a capital for their productive employment. Can any thing be at once more unexceptionable and more desirable, than such an experiment as this? Possessing the necessary funds, the labourers mean to become capitalists, and to make actual trial of the difficulties of a joint management. If they succeed, who will not hail as one of the most important fruits of modern civilization, the demonstrated possibility of arrangements of society under which the whole produce of labour would belong exclusively to the labourers? But if, as is infinitely more probable, they fail; is not this the very lesson which their superiors are most anxious, and ought to be most anxious that they should learn? When they perceive that the laws of property, which so revolt their moral sense, by rendering the condition of the idle so often preferable to that of the industrious, are the necessary condition of a large production; when they find that the attempt to realize (otherwise than with the slow progress of human improvement) the cooperative principle as applied to the production of wealth, causes so much waste of labour in the intricate business of management and check, and such a relaxation of the intensity of individual exertion, that under the fairest possible distribution there is a smaller share for each, than falls or might fall to the lot even of the most scantily remunerated, under the present arrangements; then, and not till then will they patiently submit to the necessity of not moving faster than their limbs will carry them; and instead of aiming at impracticable changes in the general order of society, will combine with all other honest and intelligent men, in introducing all the improvements which the existing social system admits of.

* * * * *

19th March

The Solicitor General's Motion on the Law of Libel[*]

Few of the results of the Reform Bill have fallen more short of our hopes, than the conduct of the little band of enlightened and philosophic Radicals, whom that great change introduced into the Legislature. Our expectations of improvement in the general composition of Parliament, were never so sanguine as those of the more enthusiastic reformers. The majority of the House of Commons have not much disappointed us. We believe them to be as honest as men usually are, and in point of intellect and acquirements a fair sample of the higher classes of this country. The circumstances of society, and the prevalent modes of thinking among the people, unite in preventing the electors from seeking their representatives in the classes below the higher: and if they did, although a greater number of conspicuous individuals might be selected from the whole of the community than from a part, it is by no means certain that the general mass would be improved in quality. We doubted before the Reform Bill, we doubt still, whether the general mind of the community is sufficiently advanced in its ideas, or sufficiently vigorous in its tone, to furnish, even under the best system of representaion, any but a very indifferent Legislature. But we did expect that, through the avenues opened by the Reform Bill, individuals would find their way into Parliament, who would put forward, on every fitting occasion, with boldness and perseverance, the best political ideas which the country affords: and we thought we saw, in some of the names composing the Radical minority at the opening of the Reformed Parliament, a guarantee that our hope would be fulfilled. But the promise has not been kept. With one or two exceptions, at the head of which we must place Mr. Roebuck, (who, against innumerable obstacles, some of them of his own creating, is, with signal merit, working himself up into the station in public life to which his talents, energy, and sincerity entitle him,) none of the new Radical members on whom we had founded any hopes, have done enough to keep those hopes alive; and the cause of the Movement still rests exclusively upon its ancient supporters.

We cannot understand how men so conscientious as some of these are, can reconcile this self-annihilation to their notions of worthiness. With the exception

[*John Campbell, Speech in Introducing a Motion on the Law of Libel (18 Mar., 1834), *PD*, 3rd ser., Vol. 22, cols. 410–18.]

of their votes, which have been steadily given on the right side, we can name few things which any of them have done, more than might have been done by adherents of the present Ministry; and it was not for this, nor on the faith of these expectations, that they were sent to that House, in preference to men who, on any footing but that of strenuous advocates of the people's cause, had perhaps equal claims to theirs.

The usual excuse for inaction, that "there is no good to be done," never was so manifestly inapplicable. At all times there is much good to be done, if men will but resolve to do it. But the effects of individual exertion, though sure, are usually slow. Not so in the present state of politics. Every well-directed attempt, even by a solitary individual, to accomplish any worthy object, is sure of a certain measure of immediate success. It may be true that it is impossible to carry anything against the Ministry. But there is hardly any limit to what may now be carried *through* the Ministry. Though Ministers seldom lead, they are willing to be led. To most of the reforms which a vigorous and enlightened Ministry would, in the present state of the public mind, venture to propose, the present Ministers are by no means hostile. Their faults, like those of the Radical Members, are chiefly those of omission. They do not like to involve themselves in new questions. They have already more to think of, more difficulties to surmount and exigencies to provide for, than they feel the strength to cope with. When you have forced a discussion on any subject, and compelled them to turn their minds to it, and make up an opinion one way or another, your business is half done. From having been anxious to stave off the question, they become anxious to settle it, so that the discussion may not be revived. The independent Members should take their measures accordingly. They should insist upon having all the great questions discussed. They should not yield to the representations which are sure to be made, which were made by the Chancellor on the Jewish question,[*] that to be unremitting in exertion is not the way to succeed. It is the sure, and the only way. They should let no question sleep, and should agitate all the more important questions incessantly.

Mr. O'Connell, among whose faults inactivity is not to be numbered, did not think that to force a discussion on the liberty of the press would do no good; and already his motion has compelled the Government to take up the subject, and a part of the necessary reform has a fair chance of being accomplished in the present Session.

Since the publication of our last month's Notes, Mr. O'Connell's Bill for the Reform of the Law of Libel has been printed;[†] and the objections to which it seemed liable, from his own statement, as reported in the newspapers, are

---

[*Henry Brougham, Speech on Jewish Disabilities (3 Mar., 1834), *ibid.*, Vol. 21, col. 991; see also "A Bill for the Relief of His Majesty's Subjects Professing the Jewish Religion," 4 William IV (25 Apr., 1834), *PP*, 1834, II, 587–8 (not enacted).]
[†See pp. 165–8 above.]

applicable to it in a very inferior degree to what we had supposed. It does make provision for freedom of criticism on institutions and doctrines, with the single exception of religion; and, in case of private libel, instead of making truth in all cases a justification, it only allows the truth to be given in evidence, leaving the jury to decide what weight shall be allowed to it as a defence. Even this we continue to think objectionable, but, undoubtedly, in a far less degree.

* * * * *

20th March

Sir Robert Peel on the Corn Laws

In the House of Commons yesterday an incidental discussion of the Corn Laws took place on the presentation of a petition.[*] After a speech from Mr. Roebuck, of the great merits of which we should have remained ignorant if we had not accidentally seen the report of it in the *Morning Post*,[†] Sir Robert Peel rose. Having first accused, by implication, Mr. Roebuck of presumption, in saying that the subject might be disposed of in five minutes, while he, though he had spoken much longer than five minutes, had not disposed of half of it; Sir Robert endeavoured to supply the remaining half by a speech in which all which was not truism was irrelevancy.[‡] Though Mr. Roebuck said, and said truly, that what is relevant to the question might be stated in five minutes,[§] he could not have meant that so short a time would suffice for answering all the fallacies which may be accumulated round this or any other subject by ingenuity or folly. Sir Robert Peel's first argument was that of the peculiar burthens pressing upon the land; a consideration which no one who ever spoke or wrote against the corn laws has overlooked: but which is a reason for equalizing taxation, not for compensating a class supposed to be peculiarly overtaxed, by another and the worst of taxes—a tax on the people's food. The remainder of the speech may be thus summed up:—That the corn laws could not be termed a monopoly, because, if the landlords have a protecting duty, so have all classes of manufacturers. It would take nearly five minutes to enumerate all the mistaken assumptions included in this argument. Whoever agrees with Sir Robert Peel must think the following things:—1. That if there are many monopolies instead of one, they cease to be monopolies. 2. That it

[*PD, 3rd ser., Vol. 22, cols. 433–49 (19 Mar., 1834), initiated by William Ewart, Speech in Presenting a Petition on Free Trade, *ibid.*, cols. 433–6; see Petition from the Inhabitants of Liverpool for Repeal of the Corn Laws (5 Feb., 1834), in "First Report of the Select Committee of the House of Commons on Public Petitions," 1834, p. 4.]

[†John Arthur Roebuck, Speech on Free Trade (19 Mar., 1834), *PD*, 3rd ser., Vol. 22, cols. 439–42, in *Morning Post*, 20 Mar., 1834, p. 1.]

[‡Robert Peel, Speech on Free Trade (19 Mar., 1834), *PD*, 3rd ser., Vol. 22, cols. 442–9.]

[§Roebuck, speech of 19 Mar., 1834, col. 439.]

is a legislative business not to do justice, but to establish an equal balance of injustice. 3. That if A gains sixpence by making B lose a shilling, the way to set all right is for B to treat A in the same manner: while in the meantime C, D, and E are robbed by both. 4. That duties on the importation of manufactures are a benefit to the manufacturer, in the same sense as duties on the importation of corn are a benefit to the landlord; whereas, in truth, the landlord obtains a higher rent, but the manufacturer does not obtain a higher profit, the protected trade being no better off as to profits than those which are not protected. 5. That an equal benefit is conferred on two persons, by protecting the one against a cheaper article than his own, the other against a dearer: that it is the same thing, in fact, to shut the door against the food which *would* come, and against the cottons and hardware that would *not*.

When propositions which contain in a nutshell a whole *Iliad*[*] of error, are put forth with an air of authority, and by a person of authority, as if they were the *dernier mot* of some great question, it is lamentable that there is no one, even of those who understand the subject, ready to start up at the instant and present the simple truth in the point of view in which it most vividly illuminates the fallacy, and makes its character visible. But the union of energy and ardour with knowledge and dialectical skill, is a combination too rare in our days to be soon hoped for.

* * * * *

26th March

The Ministry and the Dissenters

The principal interest of the session, thus far, has been the question of the Church and the Dissenters. Even Church Reform, so prominent a topic for the last two years, has almost ceased to be talked of; and the subject now pressed upon the Legislature is the entire abolition of the Establishment. This is a fearful truth to Conservatives of all denominations; and even to considerate Radicals, there is matter for very serious reflection in so striking an instance of the artificial celerity given to the natural progress of change, by the very conduct which is expected to check it.

If Ministers can profit by experience, they must surely by this time see how utterly the course which they have not adopted, but fallen into, is at variance with their own purposes. Those who most agree with them in their ends, have most cause to complain of their means. It is not as friends of the Movement that we lament the deficiencies of Ministers; in that character we ought much rather to

[*See Cicero's comment, recorded by Pliny, *Natural History* (Latin and English), trans. H. Rackham, 10 vols. (London: Heinemann; Cambridge, Mass.: Harvard University Press, 1938–62), Vol. II, pp. 560–1 (VII, 21, 85).]

rejoice at them; for the tide of change sets in far more violently through this passive resistance to it. But we wish the current to be gentle as well as rapid. We dread lest the violence of the struggle which is so needlessly made the sole means of obtaining reforms, should leave neither the leisure nor the frame of mind for choosing the most considerate mode of accomplishing them. One half the good, moreover, which we expect from the redress of grievances, will be lost, if, being extorted from the unwillingness of the Legislature, they leave behind them the feelings not of reconciliation but of victory and defeat.

What a commentary have the last few weeks afforded on the principles of the King's Speech![*] If Ministers had announced of themselves, the intention of doing for the Dissenters all which in this short period they have been obliged successively to promise, they would have retained the large measure which they formerly possessed of the confidence of that immense body, and we should not have heard, perhaps for a long time to come, of a single petition for the separation of Church and State. The Movement has gained several years upon them in a few weeks; while in the same time they have let half their power of guiding its course slip out of their hands, by teaching their surest friends to hope for nothing from them but through the means which would be taken with enemies.

Ministers made but humble pretensions at the opening of the session, and humble has been their conduct. They gave fair warning; they let all men know that it was no business of theirs to stir a step in improvement unless somebody drove them, and that whoever came with a petition in one hand, must come with a cudgel in the other. But it was absurd to imagine that those who had carried Catholic Emancipation, and the repeal of the Test and Corporation Acts, could have any objection to concede the little which is still withheld of religious liberty; and the Dissenters feeling this, did not use the cudgel, but quietly stated what they thought themselves entitled to demand, deeming that as they were speaking to friends, nothing further was requisite. They waited, and nothing came but the ridiculous Marriage Bill:[†] and they received every intimation short of an express declaration, that this was all they had to expect. Not because what they claimed was considered unfit to be granted; but merely because it *could* be refused. Thus warned, the Dissenters resorted to the cudgel: and now mark with what result. At each application of the weapon, Ministers rose in their offers. First they vaguely told the Dissenters not to conclude that nothing more was to be done for them.[‡] Then they would "call the attention" of the House to the subject of Church Rates, and propose, as was at first given out, a diminution, which afterwards rose into a

[*See p. 151 above.]

[†"A Bill for Granting Relief in Relation to the Celebration of Marriages to Certain Persons Dissenting from the United Church of England and Ireland," 4 William IV (10 Mar., 1834), *PP*, 1834, II, 147–59 (not enacted).]

[‡Charles Grey, Speech on the Dissenters (3 Mar., 1834), *PD*, 3rd ser., Vol. 21, col. 993.]

commutation, and was at last announced, though not officially, as an entire abolition.[*] Next, the Marriage Bill was virtually given up, and several Ministers expressed their private opinion that marriage should be a civil contract.[†] Next came a proposition for a general registry of births, marriages, and deaths; but at first, only from a brother of the Lord Chancellor;[‡] afterwards Lord Althorp hoped that such a registry, by being combined with another measure, might be introduced as a Government question; and possibly some relief might be afforded to the Dissenters on the subject of burials also.[§] Lastly, a petition from Cambridge for the admission of Dissenters to graduate in that University, was presented by the Premier in the Lords, and by the Secretary to the Treasury in the House of Commons,[¶] and warmly supported both by them and by other leading members of the Administration. On this occasion (because it is a small one) they at length spoke as statesmen *should* speak: the tone was not that of reluctant concession, but of earnest advocacy: as if they were not only willing to do justice, but were glad of the opportunity.

How much more highly would they now have stood in reputation and in real power, had they adopted this tone throughout, and from the commencement! How much might they yet retrieve, were they even now to adopt it!

* * * * *

NO. III, MAY, 1834

16th April

The Tithe Bill[‖]

This project appears to us no improvement upon the tithe commutation of last

[*Spencer, speech of 14 Feb., 1834, col. 360, and Speech on Church Rates (18 Mar., 1834), *ibid.*, Vol. 22, col. 389.]

[†John Russell, Speech on Dissenters' Marriages (10 Mar., 1834), *ibid.*, Vol. 21, col. 1400.]

[‡William Brougham gave notice of motion on 7 Mar., 1834, of a registry bill (see *The Times*, 8 Mar., 1834, p. 3; not recorded in *PD*). Finally, in his Speech in Introducing a Bill for Registry of Births, Deaths, and Marriages (13 May, 1834), *PD*, 3rd ser., Vol. 23, cols. 940–9, Brougham introduced "A Bill to Establish a General Register of Births, Deaths and Marriages in England," 4 William IV (14 May, 1834), *PP*, 1834, III, 459–77 (not enacted). See p. 180 above, and p. 231 below.]

[§Spencer, Speech on Church Rates (18 Mar., 1834), *PD*, 3rd ser., Vol. 22, cols. 388–92.]

[¶Charles Grey, Speech in Presenting the Cambridge University Petition (21 Mar., 1834), *ibid.*, cols. 497–508, and Thomas Spring-Rice (24 Mar., 1834), *ibid.*, cols. 569–87, presenting "Petition from Resident Members of the Senate of the University of Cambridge to Open the University to Dissenters" (21 Mar., 1834), *Journals of the House of Lords*, LXVI, 88.]

[‖"A Bill for the Commutation and Redemption of Tithes in England and Wales," 4 William IV (17 Apr., 1834), *PP*, 1834, IV, 193–234 (not enacted).]

year.[*] Both schemes have many of the requisites of a good measure, but the present one is open to objections far more weighty than those which have induced Ministers to abandon their original proposition.

We fully concur in the principle laid down by Lord Althorp, that no portion of the tithe must be given away to the landlords.[†] The amount must remain undiminished, not indeed for the reason he assigns, that it is all required for the maintenance of the Church Establishment; but to preserve what the *Examiner* very properly calls the reversionary interest of the State.[‡]

Both measures, that of last year and the present, leave the aggregate tithe of the whole country unaltered in amount. But the former left also to every individual tithe owner, the very sum which he had been accustomed to receive; while, by the present bill, there will hardly be a receiver of tithe in all England who will not either gain or lose by the commutation. It is obvious that the poorer the land is, the less rent it will yield in proportion to the produce. On poor lands the gross produce may be ten times, or any number of times the rent: on some rich lands it cannot be more than double. The tithe being proportioned to the gross produce, must bear an infinitely varying proportion to the rent. Yet the commutation is to be a per-centage uniform for a whole county. If the average tithe of the county is one-fourth, or one-third of the rent, though it may not be exactly so in any particular instance, it is to be fixed at that proportion everywhere.

In one half the parishes of England, therefore, the tithe owner will obtain an increase of his income, and a spoliation of property will take place to the prejudice of the landlord. In the other half, the life interests of the clergy will be impaired, the lay impropriators robbed of a portion of their property, and the landowners gratuitously presented with an addition to their rent. So extensive an invasion of vested rights is scarcely consistent with the unbounded respect for them professed by all English ministers.

In attempting to avoid one evil, Ministers have fallen into a worse. Against the scheme of last year, which fixed the tithe everywhere at its present amount, it was urged that an incumbent who had rigidly exacted his utmost dues, would be confirmed in the possession of them, while one who had been lenient would forfeit the right which he had forborne to enforce. We do not think there was much in this argument, since no injury would have been done to the more liberal incumbent by giving him no more than he had himself adjudged to be sufficient; while the condition of those who were under the more rigid taskmaster, would be left no worse than it was before. However, these last would certainly lose the chance of being more indulgently treated by a future incumbent. There was therefore some, though but little, force in the objection. To meet it, what have the Ministry done?

[*"A Bill to Effect a Commutation of Tithes in England and Wales," 3 William IV (17 May, 1833), *ibid.*, 1833, IV, 431–73 (not enacted).]

[†Spencer, Speech in Introducing a Motion on Commutation of Tithes (England) (15 Apr., 1834), *PD*, 3rd ser., Vol. 22, cols. 818–19.]

[‡Anon., "Tithe Commutation," *Examiner*, 20 Apr., 1834, p. 242.]

That they may not, by leaving matters just as they are, give the rapacious man an advantage over the more moderate, they strike a medium between the two, giving to the one more than he asks for, to the other less: forgetting, in this clumsy attempt to make legislation the agent of distributive justice, that if there are inequalities in the rigour with which the tithe is exacted, there are also inequalities, and greater ones, in the tithe itself; all which are to be stretched and clipped to the Procrustes-bed of a uniform proportion.

In most other respects the bill is deserving of praise. It removes all complication and annoyance in the collection of tithes, by making the demand no longer from the tenant, but from the proprietor; and allowing him the option of redeeming it, on terms sufficiently easy to induce all who have the means, to avail themselves of the permission. It also takes the tithe off the consumer, and lays it upon the landlord. Tithe will no longer operate as any discouragement to cultivation. It will no longer be one of the expenses of production, which the price must be sufficient to repay; but a fixed proportion of the rent, that is, of the surplus after the expenses are paid. It will be liable indeed to increase, but only as the rent increases, and can never, under any circumstances, be any thing but a deduction from the rent.

This, however, opens a view of the subject in some other of its bearings, which have not yet attracted the attention of those most interested. We see the landowners apparently taking a burthen off the shoulders of their customers the bread-eaters, and placing it on their own. What is the meaning of so unlandlordly a proceeding? It is, that they reckon upon being able to maintain the Corn Laws. While those laws subsist, the landlords will escape the consequences of the measure to which they are about to give their consent. This will appear from a very brief explanation.

If all the food consumed in England were grown on our own soil, the effect of abolishing tithe would be a fall of price. The consumer and not the landlord would reap the benefit; and if a charge in commutation of tithe were laid upon the rent, the landlord would be out of pocket by the entire amount. But this fall of price cannot take place while the Corn Laws last. As long as we are an importing country, the price must depend upon the cost of production abroad, not upon the cost of production here; and nothing which can be done here will lower it, while we continue to derive any portion of our food from abroad. Unless, therefore, the stimulus given to cultivation at home by taking off the tithe, be sufficient to render us entirely independent of foreign supply, the sole effect of relieving the agriculturist from the burthen is, that we shall grow more corn, and import less. The landlord, therefore, will pocket the whole amount of the tithe; and by laying an equivalent burthen upon him in the form of a rent-charge, he will be left, while the Corn Laws continue, in the exact position in which he is now.

This suggests one most serious objection to the present measure, and to any commutation of tithes not accompanied by a corresponding reduction of the duties on foreign corn. It adds to the injustice of the Corn Laws. It increases the artificial premium upon raising food from the soil instead of importing it. We are perpetually told, and it is true, that if we tax our own corn, we must lay an equal duty on that which comes from abroad. Equally true is it, and for precisely the same reason, that if we tax foreign corn we must levy an equal duty on that which is grown at home. If tithes are a reason for retaining corn laws, corn laws are a reason for retaining tithes. If we relieve English corn from tithes without relieving foreign corn from corn laws, we create a new factitious inequality; we hold out a fresh motive to a disadvantageous employment of labour and capital; and besides, we encourage the breaking up of lands which will be thrown out of culture, and the expenditure of capital which will become useless, as soon as the Corn Laws shall be repealed.

Happily that period is near at hand; and happily, too, this is so obvious, that although the landlords, as a body, will, by fair means or foul, do all they can to avert it, neither landlord nor farmer will like to risk much of their own money upon the chance. We do not believe, therefore, that much extension of cultivation will take place. The uncertainty of the Corn Law has long paralysed all such speculations, and will continue to paralyse them as long as any bread-tax exists.

* * * * *

17th April

National Education

The declarations of Mr. Spring Rice on Monday, and of the Lord Chancellor yesterday,[*] amount to a promise of the very greatest benefit which could be bestowed upon any country at so small an expense—the establishment of Normal Schools. Ministers will atone for a thousand faults by this admirable measure, if the care and pains devoted to superintending its execution, correspond to the good intentions which dictate its adoption.

Doubtless it is important, that additional schools should be established, a greater number of children taught. The diffusion even of merely nominal education has been greatly exaggerated; few persons are aware how large a portion of our people are still destitute of any means of instruction whatever. But the mere *quantity* of teaching is a secondary consideration to the *quality*; and that we believe to be, for the most part, more thoroughly bad, than any one without facts before him would dare to conjecture. We believe this to be true of all ranks, and all branches of education alike. The youths who attend the London University, must be at least a fair selection from the grammar schools, public and private, in the country; and we have heard from teachers in that institution, things which have perfectly amazed us of the ignorance in which the great majority come to them, of all things which are professed to be taught in the schools at which they have been brought up. The

[*Spring-Rice, Speech on Supply (14 Apr., 1834), *PD*, 3rd ser., Vol. 22, col. 761; Henry Brougham, Speech on the Progress of Education (16 Apr., 1834), *ibid.*, cols. 848–9.]

elementary schools for the children of the working classes, are still worse. They scarcely even profess to aim at anything more than teaching words; and words out of a book. No attempt is made to communicate ideas, or call forth the mental faculties. The mind of the teacher is never once brought into contact with the mind of the child. An automaton could do all that is done by such teachers, and all that they are qualified to do. Among the enthusiastic promoters of education who direct the two great School Societies, there are doubtless many who are more or less sensible of the deficiencies of their system, and would gladly amend them; but the material is wanting: teachers, who even know what it is to teach, are not to be had. School-houses may be had, or money to build them; all the "properties," the mere instruments of teaching, may be complete; even books, though of them there is a sad deficiency, may be provided: if one good book is written, copies may be multiplied without limit. But it is not brick walls, nor instruments, nor books, nor dead matter that is wanting; mind must be taught by mind. Most true is the maxim of the Prussian system, "what the teacher is, that will the school be." Even if we were to think with the vulgar, that any one who knows a thing can teach it—even so the bulk of the existing schoolmasters could teach nothing, for they know nothing; no *thing*, no *words* even, except the very words set down in their books. They cannot make their scholars, what they themselves are not. Ask *them* any question, in geography or history for instance, out of the narrow round of questions they are accustomed to put, and you will find them as ignorant as the most untaught of their scholars. Is this doubted? Put it to the proof.

Is it not extraordinary that Lord Brougham, in his speech of yesterday, and in that other speech which he delivered last session *against* a National Education,[*] should have built up what seemed to him a conclusive argument, out of a mere numerical statement of the increase of schools, and proved to us the sufficiency of individual and undirected exertions, by mere arithmetic? Are all schools alike, then? Is it enough that there are places *called* schools, that there is something *called* teaching? Is it of no consequence what is taught, and how? We know not why education should be so highly lauded if this be education. What, in itself, is it, to be merely able to read? But the children do not at present even learn to read. What proportion of those who have been taught reading can read *fluently*? or have had the meaning of half the words they laboriously spell out, explained to them? Put a book into their hands, and see how many of them will answer that they can only read in the book they are accustomed to. And is this the teaching, the multiplication of which has rendered a national education unnecessary?

Mr. Roebuck, whose advocacy of education, as of every thing else, is that of a person really in earnest about it, has announced for next week, a motion similar to that by which he did so much good last year.[†] But a more important motion still,

[*Henry Brougham, speech of 16 Apr., 1834, cols. 845–6, and Speech in Introducing a Motion on Education (14 Mar., 1833), *ibid.*, Vol. 16, cols. 632–8.]

[†Roebuck, Speeches in Introducing Motions on National Education (30 July, 1833, and 3 June, 1834), *ibid.*, Vol. 20, cols. 139–66, and Vol. 24, cols. 127–30.]

and one which we trust we shall see him introduce—for of any other of the professing friends of education we have small hope—would be one for an address to the crown, to appoint a commission for ascertaining and reporting upon the quality of the instruction at the various existing schools. Anything less than a public investigation, embracing the whole country, would not suffice. Cases resting on private authority will not do; they will be denied, or represented as exceptions selected to make out a case. The abuses of the Poor Laws would have been so represented, if there had been no Poor Law Commission. But when an inquiry was set on foot, with a real desire to make it an effectual one, the evils which we had heard of as occasional, perhaps even frequent, were found to pervade the whole country; and what proved to be the rare and scattered exceptions, were the cases of good, not those of bad administration. An inquiry is wanted into the state of education, as searching and as comprehensive as that into the administration of the Poor Laws. Until there has been such an inquiry nothing will be done, nor will the public feel the necessity of doing anything, to bring the education of the people generally, under a more active and intelligent superintendence.

Meanwhile the Ministers will deserve high praise, if they are serious in their purpose of establishing Normal Schools. This is at once the most important step towards a national system, and a good in itself of inestimable value. If a scheme for the education of the whole people had already received the sanction of the Legislature, its execution must have waited until an improved race of schoolmasters could be raised up; but if even without founding any schools of our own, we educate teachers for the existing schools to a standard greatly exceeding the present average, we shall, by this single measure, change the whole character of the education of the country. The great school societies would, it is to be hoped, supply themselves with schoolmasters from the Normal Schools; and private teachers not trained at these institutions, could only stand their ground by showing qualifications equal to that high standard which the public would learn to exact.

Normal Schools, sufficient for all the wants of the country, might be founded and carried on at a very moderate expense; and the Chancellor's objection to a national provision for education, that it would put a stop to private subscriptions,[*] would not apply. If the contribution of 20,000*l.* towards building school-houses, has called forth individual subscriptions to more than double the amount, a still greater stimulus would be given to private beneficence if the State were to supply, what is so much greater a desideratum than a place to teach in, masters fit to teach.

Lord Malmesbury, good man, objects to Normal Schools, because "the founders of charity schools always take care to supply them with proper masters."[†] We admire the noble Lord's unsuspecting innocence, and are curious to

---

[*Henry Brougham, speech of 16 Apr., 1834, cols. 843–4.]
[†James Edward Harris, Speech on the Progress on Education (16 Apr., 1834), *The Times*, 17 Apr., 1834, p. 3 (cf. *PD*, 3rd ser., Vol. 22, col. 852).]

know where he has lived. A suspicion never crossed his ingenuous mind that an inadequate teacher is to be found in the whole country. Any one probably is fit for a schoolmaster according to his ideas, who is able to read. We imagine most of them could stand that test. Meanwhile Lord Malmesbury's *dictum* should stand upon record, that posterity may know what the House of Lords was like. We hope historians will not forget to inform them that he was by no means its most ignorant member. There cannot be fewer than two hundred of their Lordships who are decidedly more ignorant still.

* * * * *

18th April

Mr. Roebuck and The Times

The *Times*,—which of all newspapers is the most swayed by personal enmity, and which looks upon every one as an enemy to whom it has ever behaved ill, especially every public man who has the impertinence to be successful after it has attempted to ruin him,—has a snarling article this morning upon Mr. Roebuck's motion, which, like all the rest of its conduct towards him, will be remembered as an example of its malice, but not of its power.[*] No one who compares the present position of Mr. Roebuck in the House of Commons, with that which he occupied a year ago—or who can appreciate the complete victory which, by a good use of the advantages of a better cause and a superior knowledge of his subject, he has just obtained over the most redoubted debater in the House[†]—will imagine for a moment that his upward career can now be retarded by a hostility, obviously arising from personal ill-will. A young, and till then obscure individual, coming into Parliament with neither money, rank, connexion, nor previous reputation, allying himself with no party, neither compromising a single opinion, nor courting the favour of one human being, but often injuring himself by giving needless offence—he already occupies a station of honour and importance, both in the House and in the country; he has defied alike Whigs, Tories, and demagogues, yet has extorted respect from them all, and he alone of the young members is rapidly rising in estimation. Having conquered so many obstacles, and achieved the first and most difficult part of a successful career, without aid from any newspaper (most of his speeches are scarcely reported,) and against the undisguised enmity of so powerful a journal as the *Times*, he can well afford to disregard that enmity, until it ceases of its own accord; that is, until the *Times* thinks him of sufficient consequence to be worth courting. It is of excellent example, that he should continue to afford a demonstration of the sufficiency of energy and courage to

---

[*Leading Article on the Canadas, *The Times*, 19 Apr., 1834, p. 5, concerning Roebuck, Speech in Introducing a Motion on the Canadas (15 Apr., 1834), *PD*, 3rd ser., Vol. 22, cols. 767–90.]

[†Stanley; see his Speech on the Canadas (15 Apr., 1834), *ibid.*, cols. 790–811.]

command success in that House, against the opposition of the press, as well as against every other possible disadvantage.

The Proposed Reform of the Poor Laws

It is creditable to Ministers that the measure which Lord Althorp yesterday introduced into the House of Commons,[*] departs so little from the recommendations of the Poor Law Commissioners. Wherever it does deviate from them the change is for the worse; nor do we believe that any change would be for the better. The proceedings of that Commission are an example, unique in our history, of sagacity and skill in investigating the innumerable details of a most extensive and complicated subject, and wisdom in devising, for evils which seemed insuperable, remedies which promise the most unhoped-for success.

Lord Althorp's statement, as we are informed by persons who were present, was unusually clear and cogent. Little or no opposition was made in any quarter; and from the reception which the House gave to the proposition, there is little doubt that it will pass without material alteration. A considerable part of the press has, however, declared hostility to its leading provisions, and in particular the *Times*; which has more than once touched upon the subject, in a tone calculated to do much mischief, and which has probably had a large share in deterring the Ministry from adopting the recommendations of the Commissioners in their full extent.[†]

The foundation of the Poor Law Report, is the principle upon which all good government, and all justly-constituted society rest; that no person who is able to work, is entitled to be maintained in idleness; or to be put into a better condition, at the expense of the public, than those who contrive to support themselves by their unaided exertions. Any infringement of this principle, whether by rich or poor, is not only immoral, but nine-tenths of the immorality in the world are founded on it. The desire to live upon the labour of others, is at the root of almost all misgovernment, and of most private dishonesty. The inquiries of the Poor Law Commission have afforded melancholy evidence of the extent to which this desire, and the facilities afforded for gratifying it by the administration of the Poor Laws, are demoralizing our rural, and a large portion of our town population; accustoming them to rely for support, not on their own efforts, but on assistance to be afforded them by the administrators of a common stock, from which they endeavour by all sorts of fraudulent contrivances to draw as much, and to contribute to it by their labour as little, as their ingenuity and good luck enable them.

To arrest this demoralization, before the labouring population shall be entirely corrupted, and the whole produce of the country swallowed up by the poor rates, is

[*Spencer, Speech in Introducing a Motion on the Poor Laws (17 Apr., 1834), *ibid.*, cols. 874–89.]

[†E.g., Leading Article on the Poor Law Report, *The Times*, 25 Feb., 1834, p. 2, and Leading Article on the Poor Laws, *ibid.*, 19 Apr., 1834, p. 5.]

the object of the Commissioners; and they have been able to imagine no means but one; nor (as must be evident) are any others possible. The condition of a pauper must cease to be, as it has been made, an object of desire and envy to the independent labourer. Relief must be given; no one must be allowed to starve; the necessaries of life and health must be tendered to all who apply for them; but to all who are capable of work they must be tendered on such terms, as shall make the necessity of accepting them be regarded as a misfortune; and shall induce the labourer to apply for them only when he cannot help it, and to take the first opportunity of again shifting for himself. To this end, relief must be given only in exchange for labour, and labour at least as irksome and severe as that of the least fortunate among the independent labourers: relief, moreover, must be confined to necessaries. Indulgences, even those which happily the very poorest class of labourers, when in full employment, are able occasionally to allow themselves, must be rigidly withheld.

These objects the Commissioners seek to accomplish, by granting relief to the able-bodied (as a general rule) only within the workhouse; relief at their own houses being an exception, never to be made but upon special grounds. The reason assigned for this, and borne out by the evidence, is, that anywhere but in a workhouse it is quite impossible to make pauper labour efficient. Parish work, as at present conducted, is notoriously, universally, and by the necessity of the case, very much the same thing as total idleness. Even when set to work on the roads, a kind of labour susceptible of more easy and efficient superintendence than most others, it is found impracticable to exact from the paupers much more than nominal work. In the workhouse alone can the life of a pauper, consistently with an ample supply of necessaries, be rendered other than enviable, as compared with the hard labour and poor fare of those who find their own subsistence. Yet against this fundamental principle of all Poor Law Reform have the *Times* and other papers raised the cry of inhumanity. They call it treating poverty as a crime. It is but making pauperism no longer a piece of good fortune.

The spirit manifested by the newspapers is exactly similar to that which the Commissioners say they have met with in almost all the parties to whom they addressed their printed queries. They found every where the bitterest complaints of the present system, the most alarming predictions of universal ruin if it be persevered in, and the most vehement objections to the adoption of any remedy. People seemed to expect that evils, which were threatening the subversion of society, should be extirpated without causing the most trifling, the most momentary inconvenience to anybody. The newspapers expect the same thing. They look for ends, and will consent to no means. Thus, the *Times* assents to the principle that the independent labourer must be better off than the pauper; and yet accuses the Commissioners of making proverty a crime, for proposing simply this very thing. How, we beg to know, is the independent labourer to be better off than the pauper, and yet the pauper no worse off than the independent labourer? If pauperism is to be made undesirable, that may always be called treating it as a crime. Not one hint does the writer in the *Times* give, of any other means of making pauperism undesirable, but those which the Commissioners suggest. He must have known that they did not make the suggestion lightly. When men of rare acquirements and talents, with unlimited access to information, have employed more than two years in the most diligent examination and study of the subject in all its bearings—one who does not pretend to know more of the subject than we all know, is at least bound, if he disputes their conclusion, to be prepared to answer their case.

The Ministry, however, have been so far influenced by these unreasonable objections, as to depart in some degree from the propositions of the Poor Law Report. The Commissioners proposed, that, after a certain time, say two years, relief to the able-bodied, anywhere but in the workhouse, should, as a general rule, be unlawful;[*] and, in the mean time, the Central Board were invested with the power of erecting workhouses, to receive such persons as from choice or necessity should remain paupers after that period. Lord Althorp's Bill fixes no time after which out-door relief is to be prohibited: it gives indeed to the Central Board, the power of prohibiting, or regulating the conditions of, such relief, but not the power to erect workhouses, except with the consent of the parish. On the other hand, the Bill provides (which the plan of the Commissioners did not) that the allowance system, *i.e.* relief in aid of wages, shall cease on the 1st of June, 1835. On that day, therefore, a very large proportion of the labouring population will have to make choice, either to go off the parish entirely, or to become, not inmates of a workhouse, for there will perhaps be neither workhouses to receive them nor power to send them thither, but paupers receiving out-door relief. Very few would have made their voluntary election for the former kind of pauperism; very many, it is to be feared, will have no objection to the latter. The reform which it is hoped to accomplish in the habits of the rural population, will thus be indefinitely retarded; the difficulty of subsequently abolishing out-door relief, probably much augmented; and the measure exposed to much local unpopularity, by producing, as it will at first, an increase, perhaps, instead of a diminution of the poor-rates.

Against these evils, our sole reliance is on the extent of discretionary power still confided to the Central Board; even pared down as that power has been, in deference to a short-sighted clamour against what is really the hinge upon which the whole measure turns. Would not one imagine that it had been proposed to invest some body of functionaries with new and unheard-of powers? instead of merely placing under the controul of a few conspicuous, responsible, and carefully selected officers, free from local interests, and inaccessible to local intimidation, the very powers which are now exercised without controul by several thousands of petty jobbing local bodies, under every temptation to abuse which the case admits

[*See "Report," *PP*, 1834, XXVII, 146.]

of, without any acquaintance with the principles of the subject, and virtually irresponsible even to an effective public opinion? Without a Central Board, the framing and administering of a new system would be left, to whom? To the very authorities whose mismanagement has rendered a new system necessary. The very people who did the mischief would be the chosen instruments for administering, and in part devising, the remedy! But this is the spirit of that liberty, which, being different from that of any other people, is called "English liberty." An English patriot of the old school reserves all his jealousy of power, for power in hands of the general government: he is terrified at the thought of confiding to them, or to persons appointed by them, functions, of which he sees every day, without indignation, the most wanton and flagrant abuse by some paltry knot of incapable or interested persons in his own neighbourhood. A jobbing corporation, or a jobbing vestry, may systematically plunder the public to give lucrative contracts to their own members; and when it is proposed to place any check upon these malversations, we are gravely told, that English liberty requires the people to manage their own affairs; management by the people meaning management by a little section of the people; and management of their own affairs being management of the affairs of some thousands of other persons. Happily, these prejudices, which but lately were nearly universal, are rapidly wearing away: and we may soon hope to see acknowledged, what it is wonderful should ever be denied; that if France errs by too much centralization, we err as grossly by having too little; and that no country can be well governed, unless every branch of its local administration, by whomsoever carried on, is closely and vigilantly looked after by the central government, itself duly responsible to the nation at large. Because in England it is no part of the business of the central government to keep any functionaries to their duty, except those appointed by itself; and because it does not appoint those by whom the far greatest part of the real government of the country is performed; therefore are we, in proportion to our degree of civilisation, the very worst administered country in Europe. Where there is a free press, and a well-constituted representative body, the danger is not in giving too much, but too little controul, to the functionaries who are under the eye of the general public, over those who are not. If there is a principle in politics which all experience confirms, it is this—that popular controul never acts purely, intelligently, or vigorously, except on a large scale.

* * * *

19th April

Government by Brute Force

This country is threatened at present with almost the only danger by which its safety and tranquillity can, in the existing aspect of the times, be seriously compromised—an absurd interference with Trades' Unions. The newspapers, with their usual recklessness, have laboured to create an excitement on the subject; and though the Government have not announced any definite intentions, a hundred little symptoms have shown the *animus* by which they are possessed, and which needs only last a little longer to prepare them for any folly. There are a kind of persons who, when once they begin inflaming one another, will go any length, and talk themselves up to any pitch of irrationality.

The uncalled-for interference of the Admiralty, on the occasion of the coopers' strike, was of little importance in itself, but of much from the spirit which dictated it. If, in a country where the poor and the rich never know each other but either in the relation of charity or in that of hostility, any government could possess the confidence of the working people, that confidence would have been justly forfeited by this single act. When different sections of the community have clashing interests, and are ranged under hostile banners, the proper place of a government is not in the ranks of either body, but between them. A government which abdicates its legitimate office of a mediator and peace-maker, and assumes that of an auxiliary on either side, no matter in how innocent a manner or in how limited a degree, not only steps out of its province, but unfits itself for its proper duty; precludes itself from being listened to as an impartial and unprejudiced friend; and can no longer interfere with effect at all, unless by throwing its sword into the scale of one or other party.

Immediately after this unthinking proceeding, and Sir James Graham's defence of it,[*] came the sentence of seven years' transportation upon six Dorsetshire labourers, under a sleeping statute,[†] which nobody dreamed of, and which was not known to be applicable to the case. The attempt to prevent any demonstration of public opinion in behalf of these poor men, by hurrying them out of the country, has signally failed. Petition succeeds petition, and meeting succeeds meeting, in their behalf. Their case has become the popular question, the inflammatory topic of the day.

And now, in defence of the conduct of Ministers in not remitting the sentence, comes a speech from Lord Howick, in a more reprehensible and a more dangerous spirit than all that went before.[‡]

Report characterizes Lord Howick as an intelligent and a well-meaning man: we should not have inferred him to be either from this specimen of his statesmanship. His speech amounts to a declaration of open hostilities. A member having alluded to the melancholy conflict at Lyons, as an example of the consequences of

[*Graham, Speech on the Trade of Coopers (13 Mar., 1834), *PD*, 3rd ser., Vol. 22, cols. 161–6.]

[†57 George III, c. 19 (1817). The labourers were James Brine, James Hammet, George and James Lovelace, and John and Thomas Stanfield.]

[‡Henry George Grey, Speech on the Dorsetshire Labourers (18 Apr., 1834), *PD*, 3rd ser., Vol. 22, cols. 940–4.]

attempting to coerce Trades' Unions,[*] Lord Howick said that he derived from those occurrences a directly opposite lesson; that he saw in them the fatal consequences, not of interference, but of being too tardy and backward in interference.[†]

Lord Howick may have any private theory he pleases about the events of Lyons. No person's individual absurdities are any concern to the public. But if a government, which, like that of France, absolutely prohibits *all* combinations among workmen; which but the other day made a law to put down all societies whatever, not licensed by its own police;[‡] which had just before condemned some Paris operatives to three years' imprisonment for belonging to a Trades' Union; and which has now brought upon the second city in the empire the horrors of a five days struggle of life and death, by attempting to punish the leaders of a strike, after the strike was terminated;—if the government which did this, did not, in the opinion of our Ministers, interfere enough; if they erred by not taking their measures earlier, or more vigorously; if our Ministers have taken warning from them, and are resolved not to be guilty of a like error;—why then it is time for every Englishman, who has the means, to provide himself with a musket: for there is no knowing how soon the consequences of such a policy may leave him destitute of any other protection.

Whoever is to blame for the Lyons' catastrophe, it most deeply concerns the Ministry that no similar one should take place here. Government by the sword will not succeed in this country. England, like France, may, by the imperiousness of power, or the desperation of cowardice, be plunged into civil war, but not, as in France, with impunity.

Our Ministers never, surely, had their equals in the art of converting a small difficulty into a great one. They had only to let the Trades' Unions alone. It was well worth the partial stoppage of two or three branches of trade, to let the experiment be tried fairly, what Unions can do. They have at present no ulterior designs; and if they had, would be utterly powerless for carrying those designs into effect. But, give them a grievance; let them have cause to believe themselves injured; let them be bound together by a sense of wrongs, and taught to regard the overthrow of existing institutions as the means of obtaining a fair field for pursuing a just end by just means—and they will be formidable indeed.

We do not pretend that they ought to be tolerated in using compulsion, either against employers or fellow-workmen. If, as we believe often happens when outrages are committed, the reluctance of the operatives to inform against each other renders it impossible to bring the perpetrators to justice, this is a valid ground

---

[*Aubrey William Beauclerk, Speech in Presentation of a Petition on the Dorsetshire Labourers (18 Apr., 1834), *ibid.*, col. 938.]

[†Henry Grey, speech of 18 Apr., 1834, col. 943.]

[‡Loi No. 261 (10 avril, 1834), in *Bulletin des lois du royaume de France*, 9me sér., 1re partie, Tome IV, Bulletin 115, pp. 25–6.]

for enforcing such restraints, of the nature of police regulations, as may render the commission of such offences more difficult, or detection more easy.

Anything more would be wholly unjustifiable. There has been much cant about tyrannizing over masters, because the workmen chose to annex conditions to the contract by which they agreed to labour for the profit of others. The conditions might be foolish, or they might be wise; but, whatever they were, the men had a perfect right to insist upon them, as long as they neither had nor sought any means of enforcing the requisition but by exercising their undoubted right of refusing to work. If they had said they would not work for less than five hundred a year each, it would have been silly enough, but surely no tyranny. The language in which the demands of the Unions were made, is said to have been, at times, overbearing. This is neither more nor less foolish or reprehensible, than an equally offensive style when used by employers. From vulgar minds in either rank, we must expect vulgar pretensions. But until, in the progress of cultivation, insolence shall become an unfrequent accompaniment of power, we ought to rejoice that one side has no longer the monopoly of it. Any relation is preferable to that in which one party may inflict, and the other must bear. When both can presume, both are near to feeling the good of forbearance.

To suggest the proper precautions against the offences liable to arise from Trades' Unions, local experience is requisite. One regulation which could not fail to be useful, would be the enforcement of publicity. We see no reason why all associations should not be declared illegal, whose statutes are not registered in some public office. The enactment under which the Dorsetshire labourers were convicted, was, we think, a salutary one. The hardship was in not remitting their sentence, when the trial had given the requisite publicity to the law. Promissory oaths are bad enough when imposed for state purposes, and by the authority of the Legislature. It is out of the question that individuals should be permitted to impose upon others, even with their consent, a religious obligation to persevere in conduct of which their consciences may cease to approve. But the Unions are not wedded to these mischievous ceremonies. It was enough to promulgate the fact that they were illegal. The trial at Dorchester has acted as a promulgation, and the word has gone forth throughout the country to discontinue the oaths. The only rational object of the sentence has been attained; yet the cry of the people for a remission of the sentence is unheeded.

Lord Howick argues that though the labourers may not have known of the particular statute, or of the penalty, they knew that they were doing wrong; else why did they take an oath of secrecy?[*] If it is upon such logic as this that unoffending peasants have been torn from their homes, and doomed to the punishment and to the fellowship of the refuse of gaols, those who sent them richly deserve to take their place. Is Lord Howick so ignorant of the rudiments of the

---

[*Henry Grey, speech of 18 Apr., 1834, cols. 941–2.]

subject on which he presumes to talk, as not to know that, although the Trades' Unions were never before brought under one general organization, the Unions themselves existed, and their regulations were adopted, at a time when the very fact of belonging to a Union, or being concerned in a strike, was an offence by statute?[*] Need we ask a member of the British Legislature if laws are always abrogated the moment the reason for them has ceased? Yet, a man who could not make this obvious reflection, sets up a shallow conceit of his own against the general belief of the whole country that the members of Trades' Unions did not know, did not believe the oaths to be illegal. Illegal or not, that they believed them to be wrong, a person's mind must be in a curious state who can surmise: and even if they did, are you to pounce upon men unawares with legal penalties, on the assumption that they know they are doing wrong? Then all *ex post facto* penal laws are justified; for no one dared ever propose such a law, unless he thought, or affected to think, that the nature of the offence itself was a sufficient warning of its criminality.

We cannot quit the subject without adverting to a flagrant misrepresentation in the *Times*, respecting the strike now taking place at Derby; on which there has been some controversy between that paper and Mr. Robert Owen.[†] It is generally known to those who have attended to the subject, though not perhaps to the public, that, in the present instance, the suspension of work was not the act of the workmen, but of the manufacturers; a numerous body of whom, on learning that a Trades' Union had been established, agreed to refuse employment to all who were members of it. The *Times*, however, in direct contradiction to the fact, represents the strike as having originated with the men. "A considerable body," says that journal, (14th April,) "of the workmen of Derby *struck for wages* which their masters could not grant. They were accordingly discharged, as belonging to the hostile Union, and other persons were found willing to occupy their places at the wages which they *refused to take*." This being denied by Mr. Owen, the *Times* reiterated the assertion, and affirmed that, on inquiry, he would find that before the masters resolved upon discharging all men belonging to the Union, an attempt had been made by that body to impose conditions on the masters. We found it difficult to believe that such an assertion would have been made without some foundation in fact, and we therefore applied for information to a Derby manufacturer,[‡] who is not a party to the combination of the masters, and whose workmen, though they belong to the Union, have not ceased to work. He states positively that no advance

[*See 39 & 40 George III, c. 106 (1800).]
[†Leading Article on the Strike at Derby, *The Times*, 14 Apr., 1834, p. 4; Robert Owen, Letter to the Editor (14 Apr., 1834), *ibid.*, 15 Apr., 1834, p. 3; Owen, Letter to the Editor (15 Apr., 1834), *ibid.*, 18 Apr., 1834, p. 7; Leading Article on the Strike at Derby, *ibid.*, p. 5.]
[‡Mill may be referring to Edward Strutt (Lord Belper), with whom he was closely acquainted.]

of wages has been demanded; that the turn-out was solely by the masters; and that the "printed tariff of wages, and list of other conditions," which the *Times* speaks of, never existed as an act of the Union, nor, to his knowledge, at all. He also (though this is of less importance) contradicts another assertion of the *Times*, that the masters "gave their workmen a considerable time to consider the steps which they were taking, before they invited other hands from the country to supply their place."[*] The new hands were invited immediately, though, of course, some time elapsed before they could arrive.

We do not attempt to account for this perversion of the truth. It is difficult to imagine any sufficient motive in the case, for being guilty of it wilfully. The assertion was probably made at first rashly and in ignorance, and the writer afterwards had not candour to own that he had been in the wrong.

* * * * *

22nd April

The Church-Rate Abortion

During the first week after the reassembling of parliament, Ministers were beginning to regain some of their lost reputation; but they have not known how to keep it long: yesterday has swept it away. In spite of many good deeds, their character is always bankrupt. The moment they see a balance accumulating in their favour, they make such large draughts upon it, that they have soon overdrawn their account. Lord Althorp's astonishment at the ill reception of this emanation of his legislative wisdom by the organs of the Dissenters in the House, was curious enough.[†] Could a person live in England, and look round him, and expect any thing else? But when Lord Althorp looks round him, he sees only a few Whig families, and his officials in Downing-street. In every other street in London it would be considered self-evident, that when a government waits and does nothing until the whole country is preparing to refuse a tax, taking off only half the tax will no longer do.

This is no fiscal question: it is not pecuniary relief that is demanded. The Dissenters object to being taxed at all, for the support of a favoured sect: they do not complain of paying too much, but of paying any thing. Was it likely, then, that because a part of the tax, which was expended, it seems, on mere superfluities, is to be remitted, they would submit, not only to paying the remainder, but to having it fixed upon them for ever, and losing the power of controuling it by their votes in the vestry, or even by a vote of the House of Commons? Mr. Stanley says, if there

[**The Times*, 18 Apr., 1834, p. 5.]
[†Spencer, Speech on Church Rates (21 Apr., 1834), *PD*, 3rd ser., Vol. 22, col. 1057. The measure was "A Bill for the Abolition of Church Rates," 4 William IV (19 June, 1834), *PP*, 1834, I, 615–26 (not enacted).]

is to be a Church Establishment, the churches must be kept in repair by the State; for (he actually said it) keeping the churches in repair, is the meaning of having a Church Establishment.[*] If that be true, it will be no injury to the Church Establishment not to pay the clergy; who we hope will give up their revenues, and in return we will engage to vote as much for repairing the churches as will give Mr. Stanley full satisfaction. But while the Church retains those national endowments, the possession of which is every day more and more strongly contested against her, the least which the people will be content with, even as a temporary compromise, is that she shall not ask from them any thing out of their own pockets besides. She must pay her expenses out of her own funds, which are amply sufficient to afford it; or, if that be contested, it is a poor compliment to the Church, if, while the Dissenting sects willingly maintain without any compulsion each of them its own Church Establishment, the sect to which almost all the richest families in the country belong cannot raise by voluntary offerings even a small supplementary contribution towards the support of theirs. If such be the fact, the established sect must be the feeblest and least numerous of the sects; and is convicted of only making up its account of numbers, by crediting itself with the great multitude of those who care for no religion at all.

The minority against the Ministerial project was 141; and the debate was one of the most spirited of the session. Mr. Whittle Harvey's denunciation of the trimming policy of Ministers was highly effective.[†] Mr. Gisborne, one of the most consistent and earnest refomers in the House, and one who is not, like many of the liberal members, afraid to utter a word which may be unpalatable to the enemies of his opinions, made a simple, straightforward, and unpretending declaration of hostility to the principle of a Church Establishment.[‡] We wonder when any of the little knot of philosophic radicals, those of them we mean who really are of Mr. Gisborne's opinion, will have the courage to say as much. We believe they will be nearly the last men in parliament to avow publicly the opinion which they were perhaps the first to adopt.

* * * * *

24th April

The Beer-Houses

We have not been sparing of animadversions upon a speech of Lord Howick, in a former page of these notes:[§] it is the more imperative on us to acknowledge that he

[*Stanley, Speech on Church Rates (21 Apr., 1834), *PD*, 3rd ser., Vol. 22, cols. 1034–9; the remark is in col. 1035.]
[†Daniel Whittle Harvey, Speech on Church Rates (21 Apr., 1834), *ibid.*, cols. 1039–48.]
[‡Thomas Gisborne, Speech on Church Rates (21 Apr., 1834), *ibid.*, cols. 1022–4.]
[§Pp. 207–9 above.]

yesterday spoke the first few words of common sense which have been uttered this year, upon a subject on which, during the whole session, Whigs, Tories, and professed Reformers, have vied with one another in loathsome cant, and truckling to interested clamour. Most truly did Lord Howick say that if there is a real wish to raise the morality of the labouring classes, the way to do it is to retrace that course of bad legislation and bad administration, by which, for the last thirty years, we have systematically demoralized them; and of which the prime authors and agents have been the unpaid magistracy, who now, because the beer-houses are not under their arbitrary power, have raised a hue and cry against their pretended immorality.[*] When we have surrounded a whole people with circumstances which, unless they were angels, *must* render them immoral; when, by the administration of the Poor Laws, we have placed them in a position in which none of the ordinary motives to good conduct can act upon them; when we have deprived them of almost every innocent amusement; when, by stopping up foot-paths and inclosing commons, we are every year excluding them more and more even from the beauties of nature; when, by our savage punishments for killing the game we tempt them with for our amusement, we have made our gaols little better than what the bitter patrician sarcasm of Appius Claudius termed the Roman prisons, the *domicilium plebis*;[†] when, by whatever we have attempted, for them or against them, well meant or ill meant, we have been constantly labouring to alienate them from us, it is with a good grace, is it not, that, after letting loose the torrent, we attempt to dam it up with a straw? Make the people dishonest, make them disaffected, and then fancy that dishonesty and disaffection will be at fault for want of a place to meet in! With one hand turn virtue out of doors, and with the other try to refuse an entrance to vice!

We admit no title in a government like ours, or in higher classes such as ours, to legislate for the morals of the people. They do not know enough of the people. They do not feel enough with the people. Nobody is qualified to be a censor over the morals of persons whose ways of thinking, whose feelings, whose position, whose very means of living and daily occupations, he does not understand. All the judgments of our higher classes respecting the working people, are made in ignorance of the essential circumstances. Nine out of ten of those judgments, though clothed, even to the parties themselves, with the disguise of morality and conscience, originate in some interest or some fear relating not to those whom they persuade themselves that they are concerned for, but to the higher classes themselves. Their attempts to exercise a guardianship over public morals by acts of parliament, always end in some curtailment of the people's liberty, never in any improvement of their morality. Does not even the Chancellor propose, and think

---

[*Henry Grey, Speech on Sale of Beer (23 Apr., 1834), *PD*, 3rd ser., Vol. 22, cols. 1159–61; the remark is in col. 1160.]

[†*Livy*, Vol. II, p. 192 (III, lvii, 4).]

himself extremely moderate for proposing no more, that the poor shall be excluded from the pleasures of social enjoyment, by being prevented from drinking their beer in the only place where they can ever meet for social purposes, the place where they buy it?[*] We can conceive few regulations more exasperating, to any population not accustomed to be trampled on and treated like dirt, than that which Lord Brougham recommends, and claims credit for having always advocated.

We object altogether to these attempts to be religious and moral at the expense of the working people. Let us first mend our own ways. Let us enable ourselves to stand erect without shame in the presence of the immorality which we complain of, by washing our hands of all participation in producing it. Let us cease to make vice by wholesale, and we may leave off this silly skirmishing with it in detail. Make it the labourer's interest to be frugal and temperate, and you will not need to make his cottage his prison, in order to keep him from wasting his wages and getting drunk. Accustom him to look to himself and not to you for his means of subsistence, and he will not go out at night, either from his cottage or from the beer-house, to fire your stacks because you do not give him enough. But continue to sow tares and you need not expect to reap wheat. Go on teaching the labourer that his wages are to be regulated by his wants, not by the market value of his labour, and he will consider you a robber and an oppressor if your wants are better cared for than his. Let him know that if he spends all you will give him more, if he saves anything you will give him nothing, and he must be a fool, on any worldly calculation, if he denies himself any indulgence within his reach. We do not say, reform all your dealings with the poor; we are not such visionaries as to expect it: we say, reform the Poor Laws alone; try the effect of that for two or three years, and, in heaven's name, a truce with the beer-house purism for that period.

* * * * *

25th April

Repeal of the Union

The first person who drove a coach with six horses, was thought a wonderful man; and so was the first person who spoke for six hours. But after him of the coach-and-six, came he of the coach-and-eight; and coaches and six became very ordinary phenomena. So true is it, that man has never yet done that which man may not hope to surpass! No one has yet tried the daring experiment of an eight hours' speech, and it is still a problem whether mortal ears can stay and listen for so long. But Lord Brougham's achievement has been now proved to be nothing extraordinary.[†] He has met with his equals in Mr. O'Connell and Mr. Spring

[*Henry Brougham, Speech on the Sale of Beer Bill (1834) (15 Apr., 1834), *PD*, 3rd ser., Vol. 22, col. 762.]

[†The reference is to Henry Brougham's six-hour Speech on the State of the Courts of Common Law (7 Feb., 1828), *ibid.*, n.s., Vol. 18, cols. 127–247.]

Rice, and no unworthy rival even in Mr. Emerson Tennent.[*] The two former gentlemen spoke each an entire night, the latter two-thirds of one. We know not if all the rest of the debate is to be upon this scale, or if the remaining 103 Irish members intend to bestow an equally large share of their wisdom and eloquence upon the House. If so, we shall not have to trouble our readers with any more Notes for several months to come. In the mean time, we will venture on a few words, which we are certain will not be said by any one who will vote either for Mr. O'Connell's motion, or for Mr. Spring Rice's amendment; and which, although they can be said in less than six hours, are, we think, more to the point than any part of what it took each of the above gentlemen all night to say.

The object of those who call for a repeal of the Legislative Union is, to have all the advantages of being united with England and Scotland without paying any part of the price. They wish to be defended by British money and British troops; to have their produce admitted duty free into the British market, while that of all other nations is excluded; to have all the rights of citizenship throughout the British dominions; to have all offices and honours open to them in the more powerful country; to have their indigent population subsisted, and found in money to pay their rents, with the bread which they take out of the mouths of British labourers; all this they want to have, and along with it the power to vote no more taxes than they please, and govern themselves as they please, without our having any right to be consulted. Now, these are not terms which will suit us: we must decline bearing all the burthens of the connexion, and leaving to Mr. O'Connell and his associates all the benefits. We are ready for either extreme, only this unhappy medium will not do for us. Great Britain and Ireland shall either be one country or they shall be two countries; only they shall not be the one or the other according as it suits Mr. O'Connell. They must be one people, united under one legislature and one executive, or all connexion must cease, and England and Ireland become as foreign to one another as England and France. If we were wise, we should prefer the latter side of the alternative for our own sake; if we were honest, we should choose the former side of it for the sake of Ireland.

We have never been able to understand the vast benefits which Great Britain is supposed to derive from her connexion with Ireland. Her commerce we should have, if the two countries were separated; the interests of the Irish landlords would not allow them to deprive themselves of the principal vent for their produce. Financially we not only gain nothing by the connexion, but it is the heaviest of the burthens we have to bear; half our army is kept up solely on account of Ireland; a full third of it is constantly stationed in the country. If it be as a military post that the possession of Ireland is deemed important, it would cost us less to conquer the

[*O'Connell, Speech in Introducing a Motion on Repeal of the Union (22 Apr., 1834), *ibid.*, 3rd ser., Vol. 22, cols. 1092–1158; Spring-Rice, Speech in Moving an Amendment on Repeal of the Union (23 Apr., 1834), *ibid.*, cols. 1164–1283; and James Emerson Tennent, Speech on Repeal of the Union (24 Apr., 1834), *ibid.*, cols. 1288–1333.]

island at the beginning of every war, than it costs us in a very few years to govern it in time of peace.

But we have no right to keep a nation in leading-strings till she has a giant's strength, teach her by our perverse treatment all quarrelsome and rebellious and ungovernable propensities, and then let her loose to do herself a mischief. We have been far too guilty in our treatment of Ireland, to be entitled to shake her off, and let her alone abide the consequences of our misconduct. We are bound not to renounce the government of Ireland, but to govern her well; if indeed we are too weak or too base for that, rather than continue to govern her as we have done, we ought to leave her to herself. And perhaps we have let the time slip away. By governing Ireland ill for so many centuries, we have made it so difficult to govern her well, that we *may* be compelled to renounce the attempt.

When one country, and, as the case implies, a less civilized one, falls under the power of another, there are but two courses which can rationally be taken with her. She is either fit to be incorporated with the more powerful country, to be placed in a state of perfect equality with her, and treated as part of herself, or it is best for her to be governed despotically, as a mere province. Either Ireland was sufficiently advanced in civilisation to be fit for the same kind of government for which we were fit, and if so she ought to have been treated exactly like Scotland or Yorkshire; or she was in that stage of advancement at which absolute subjection to a more civilized and a more energetic people, is a state more favourable to improvement than any government which can be framed out of domestic materials; and if so, she ought to have been governed like India, by English functionaries, under responsibility to the English Parliament. She would then have been habituated to government on fixed principles, not by arbitrary will; would at an early period have obtained security to person and property; would have rapidly advanced in all the arts of life; would have known the protection of law, and learned to value it. She would have become civilized, would have acquired all those qualifications for self-government she now has not, and would long ere this have either achieved her independence by a successful contest like the United States, or been admitted to real, not nominal, equality, as an integral part of the kingdom of Great Britain.

But we, as usual, took that middle course which so often unites the evils of both extremes with the advantages of neither. We did *not* govern Ireland as a province of England, but we *did* put the military force of England at the disposal of an indigenous oligarchy, and delivered to their tender mercies, bound hand and foot, the rest of the people. We did not give the people, in lieu of their savage independence, the despotism of a more cultivated people; we left them their own barbarous rulers, but lent to those barbarians the strength of our civilisation to keep the many in subjection. In this one pervading error, not to call it crime, lies the philosophy of Irish history. A country may be improved by freedom; or it may be improved by being brought under the power of a superior people: the greater part of the Roman empire was raised from a comparatively savage state by being brought under Roman dominion. But there is not an instance in history of a native government supported by foreign force, which did not become a curse to its subjects. The best government which the mind of the nation can produce, may be a very bad one; but if it be relieved from the only check upon a bad government, the dread of its subjects; if it be propped up by the military strength of a more powerful people, who allow it to govern as it pleases, and only step in to shield it from the consequences, there is generated a prodigy of odious tyranny, such as in no other combination of circumstances could possibly exist. It is so found in the native states of India, a country in many respects bearing no slight resemblance to Ireland; and that it has been so found in Ireland, the whole of Irish history, and the habits of the whole Irish people, high and low together, bear witness.

By persisting in this wretched system from century to century, we have lost the opportunity of preparing the Irish nation for self-government. They have not acquired that experience of lawful rule, and that reverence for law, without which no people can be any thing but, according to their physical temperament, savages or slaves. In England, notwithstanding the defects of our laws and of their administration, the law, if thought of at all, is always thought of as the shield of the oppressed. In Ireland it has never been known but as an additional engine in the hands of the oppressor. This is not declamation or exaggeration, but a matter-of-fact statement of the feeling which is in the people's minds. What they want is, what they have never yet had, protection for the weak against the strong. When they have had this for a sufficient time, they will be ripe for every other political benefit; but that is the condition which must precede all others. That benefit they would even now most readily obtain, if they were treated as an English province; if all the powers of government in the island were in the hands of functionaries responsible to England alone, and not one of whom should be an Irishman.

But this cannot be. Though the habits of civilisation, and its powers, are far from always propagating themselves by proximity, its aspirations do. We have managed to prevent Ireland from being ripe for self-government; we have not been able to prevent her from demanding it. Communication with England has stimulated the democratic spirit to a premature growth, before the country had reached the point of advancement at which that spirit grows up spontaneously. And we, instead of employing our opportunities to hasten forward the civilisation of Ireland, have, by our deplorable misgovernment, left her far more destitute of the feelings, ideas, and modes of conduct of a civilized people, than she probably would have been if we had managed her avowedly as an estate for our own benefit. We now find her in that unhappy state, *quâ nec mala nec remedia ferre potest*;[*] unfit for freedom, yet resolved to be no longer enslaved. And in that state we seem

[*Livy, Vol. I, p. 6 (I, Praef., 9).]

likely to leave her; for as there appears no prospect, for a long time to come, of our finding statesmen who can apply intellects above those of babies to the government of a country which, like ours, could go on almost without any government at all—it is vain to hope for such as shall redeem a people for whom every thing is still to be done, for whom every thing has first to be undone; among whom opinion and conscience and habit, instead of doing, as with us, much more for the ends of government than government itself, are more obstacles than helps; a people whose national character has run wild, and in many of its most important elements has yet to be created; and, to crown all, who have (and no wonder if they have) the strongest prejudices against the only rulers from whom any kind of good government, of which in their present state they are susceptible, can easily come.

It will be far rather the good fortune of Ireland than our merit, if a connexion, hitherto so unprofitable to both countries, shall be able to subsist until a new wisdom shall arise in the councils of England, and the means of rendering our influence in Ireland a blessing to the Irish people shall be sought with sincerity, and with a determined purpose that when found they shall be employed.

* * * * *

NO. IV, JUNE, 1834

1st May

The Press and the Trades' Unions

Whatever may be the case in other matters, in politics we believe that mankind are oftener led into danger by being afraid of it, than by being careless about it: to escape the tiger, they fly into the tiger's mouth. Most empires have been lost through over-anxiety to keep them: most revolutions have been provoked, by conduct dictated by the fear of revolution. But bodies of men seldom learn wisdom from the errors of their predecessors: the same blunders are repeated, whenever the same circumstances recur. The middle classes of this country, whose opinions and sentiments are represented by the daily press, are repeating the very same series of errors by which almost all governing bodies have been ruined.

By the present institutions of England, the powers of government reside in the people of property, to the exclusion of those who are said to have no property; being dependent for the whole or the chief part of their subsistence on bodily labour. Of this power, which is shared among the people of property, the people of large property had formerly engrossed nearly the whole, and have still much more than their just portion; whereby they are enabled to keep up for their own benefit, many bad institutions and bad practices, injurious both to the people of small property and to the excluded class, the people of no property, viz. those whose principal property consists in their bodily faculties. The liberals among the people of small property, are those who think, not that property, but that large property, should not confer so much power as it does at present. Now, as the most numerous and poorest class has also an interest in reducing the exorbitant power which is conferred by large property, since by doing so they would get rid of the abuses, such as Corn Laws and the like, with which they are oppressed, not for the benefit of the owners of property generally, but of a small minority of that number; this constitutes a common object, for which all classes, not directly interested in these abuses, might advantageously co-operate, adjourning the settlement of their own separate differences until after the victory.

It is very natural, however, that the working classes, even at this early stage in the developement of their collective intellect, should feel that their real position in society depends upon something far deeper than the redress of any of the grievances which the majority of their superiors have in common with them. It depends upon the relation which may be established between them and the people of property generally. It depends, not upon the manner in which their superiors share the powers of government, they being excluded; but upon whether they themselves have power enough, by political institutions or otherwise, to secure due consideration for their interests on the part of those, be they great proprietors or small proprietors, who make the laws and appoint officers for their administration.

A person must be a poor judge of human affairs, who can fancy that this point has been attained now; that the labouring multitude have now more than sufficient weight in the commonwealth to secure a just attention to their grievances; and sufficient to warrant a fear that their supposed interests or their opinions, will be allowed unjustly to prevail over those of any other part of the nation. On the contrary, they have notoriously but just emerged from a state in which they had no power of claiming attention from any one; in which laws were made, avowedly to prevent them from taking the commonest means of improving their condition; in which their education was reputed dangerous to church and state; in which they were actually kept at home, like cattle belonging to a master, for their very emigration was illegal;[*] in which no legislative measure ever passed merely for the good of the working classes, when no powerful section of their superiors had an interest in it; in which their opinions were never appealed to but when some party of the aristocracy wanted a popular cry. We are not so far from this state yet. The shadow of it is still upon us. When we see indications that the working classes are beginning to be counted for too much in the calculations of politicians, we shall think it time to take precautions against that danger. At present we should as soon think of looking out for a substitute against the time when the coal fields shall be exhausted. The people of property are the stronger now, and will be for many years. All the danger of injustice lies from them, and not towards them. Nothing

[*See 5 George I, c. 27 (1718).]

but the progressive increase of the power of the working classes, and a progressive conviction of that increase on the part of their superiors, can be a sufficient inducement to the proprietary class to cultivate a good understanding with the working people; to take them more and more into their councils; to treat them more and more as people who deserve to be listened to, whose condition and feelings must be considered, and are best learned from their own mouths; finally, to fit them for a share in their own government, by accustoming them to be governed, not like brute animals, but beings capable of rationality, and accessible to social feelings.

But this is a mode of treatment which ruling classes never yet could reconcile themselves to adopting voluntarily, with those who are subject to them. When they see a power growing up, which is not wholly under their control, their first impulse always is, fear; their second, anger. The middle classes of London, through their organs the London newspapers, are now manifesting both these feelings, on the subject of the Trades' Unions.

The Trades' Unions attempt to raise wages; and must fail in the attempt. What then? Surely it is highly desirable to raise wages. If it cannot be done by the means they adopt, teach them better means. But when were persons who had committed no crime, ever remonstrated with by any one who meant them well, in the manner which the *Times* has adopted, for instance, on the Tailors' Strike?[*] Is that a tone in which to point out to people who are pursuing a desirable end, that the means by which they are pursuing it, cannot succeed? It is obvious that the writer of the article in this morning's paper, is not roused to such excess of indignation because the means which the people are trying cannot succeed; he would be ten times more angry if they *could* succeed. He actually compares the Unions to the landlords' monopoly, and complains that the rise of wages, if they could obtain it, would be a tax on the consumer! Why, so much the better. Let there be no force or fraud, but, within the limits of an honest bargain, we are altogether for the bees against the drones. If a person who has a commodity to sell, can, without shutting out competitors, by mere voluntary agreement with those competitors, fix his own price, why should he not? certainly it is no reason, that the sellers in this case are nine-tenths of the community in number, are (to say no more) the least favoured part of it in the present distribution of the produce, and are those who, by their labour, produce all commodities whatever. But the misfortune is, that they cannot, by any such contrivances, raise the price of their commodity. No combination can keep up the value of an article, when the supply exceeds the demand. But instead of teaching them on what their condition depends, those who ought to be their instructors rail at them for attempting to better it. They say, indeed, that it is only for using wrong means; but so, from slave-traders upwards, those who wish to keep their fellow-creatures in a degraded condition, *always* say.

The tone which we condemn, may be in a great measure the result of thoughtlessness, but it is not the less the index to a habitual feeling. This feeling

[*Leading Article on the Tailors' Strike, *The Times*, 1 May, 1834, p. 3.]

must be got rid of, or the next generation, perhaps the present, will severely suffer for it.

* * * * *

2nd May

Sir Robert Heron's Motion, and Mr. Bulwer's Amendment[*]

The proposition of Sir Robert Heron, for giving to the King the nomination of a certain number of members of the Legislature, by annexing seats to various offices, outrages the first principle of a Representative Government; it is *pro tanto* a return to the system of nomination boroughs, though without its fraudulent pretences; and is both really and ostensibly a mere contrivance to save Ministers from one of the immediate inconveniences of unpopularity. The disfavour naturally attaching to such a proposition, has undeservedly extended itself to Mr. Bulwer's Amendment, which is no infringement of the representative principle, but an important auxiliary to it, and only errs by not going far enough. That any but the representatives of the people should have votes in the legislature, should help to make up a majority for enacting a law, or voting away the public money, is totally inadmissible: but the *presence* of all the great officers of state in both Houses, to answer for their measures, to be called to account for their conduct, and to give promptly the information which Parliament may require, and which can be given on the spot by no persons but those practically conversant with the public business, would be not an encroachment upon the privileges of Parliament, but an extension of them; and would add to the securities for good government, by ensuring a more thorough probing of the measures and acts of the government, and by making the struggle which may decide the fate of a ministry a conflict of principals, not subordinates.

In France, where the framers of the constitution, having an altogether new system to construct, were not restricted to the choice of means already sanctioned by usage, all cabinet ministers, whether peers or commoners, are entitled to be present and to speak in both Houses, though not to vote in either unless they are regularly members. It is not found that this regulation diminishes the desire of members of the ministry to obtain the suffrages of electors; every minister who is not a peer, always presents himself to some constituency, and succeeds sooner or later in becoming a member of the representative Chamber. But the manner in which the rule works is this: The real head of each department is enabled to be present in whichever House his conduct is under discussion; to answer questions, and defend his own measures. Lord Grey himself would be obliged to undergo the "badgering" of a popular assembly in person, and not merely by deputy. In every

[*Robert Heron, Speech in Introducing a Motion on Vacation of Seats on Acceptance of Office, *PD*, 3rd ser., Vol. 23, cols. 382–6; Edward Lytton Bulwer, Speech in Moving an Amendment on Vacation of Seats on Acceptance of Office, *ibid.*, cols. 386–91 (both 1 May, 1834).]

branch of the public service the principal would have to make his own defence, instead of having it made for him (worse, or perhaps better, than he could make it) by a comparatively irresponsible subordinate.

There is another peculiarity in the practice of the French Parliament, which has a beneficial effect. Whenever any measure is brought forward by the Government collectively, the Government may, for the purposes of that one measure, be represented by whomsoever it pleases. Any number of persons may be named King's Commissioners for the debate on that particular bill, and if so named, may be present during its discussion, along with the Ministers, and with the same privilege of speaking but not voting. What is gained by this is, that the real framers of the measure, those officers of Government who are most conversant with the details of the subject, and to whose suggestion every part of the bill except its leading principles was probably due, are present to give their own reasons for their own propositions; not as with us where those reasons come before Parliament and the public at second hand, through a minister, probably altogether ignorant of the *minutiae* of the question, until *crammed* by that very subordinate, who is not present to state the considerations which influenced him with the freshness and the clear convincing decisiveness belonging to one who knows the subject by his own knowledge. It is pitiable to see how, for want of some such regulation, the discussion of great public questions is often mismanaged in our Parliament, from the imperfect manner in which heads of departments understand or are able to state the grounds of their own measures. This is perhaps inevitable, overburdened as they are with variety of business. If so, there is the greater reason to allow them every attainable help for stating their case fully and with effect.

The subject however is of no pressing exigency. It is sufficient that the suggestion has been put forth. The degree of attention it has met with, will help to familiarize the popular mind with the novelty; on a second discussion it will be no longer strange to the public; and when the reasonableness of a proposition, without any pressing demand from without, shall be a sufficient motive to a legislative assembly for adopting it, this principle will be introduced into our parliamentary law. A subject of so little importance compared with a hundred others, can afford to wait.

* * * * *

8th May

Loss of the Registration Bills[*]

The defeat of these important improvements in the law, now for the second time

[*"A Bill for the Public Registering of All Deeds, Conveyances, Wills and Other Incumbrances," 4 William IV (13 Mar., 1834), *PP*, 1834, III, 563–88; and "A Bill for Establishing a General Register for All Deeds and Instruments Affecting Real Property," 4 William IV (14 Mar., 1834), *ibid.*, pp. 591–639; both were defeated on the same day on second reading (*PD*, 3rd ser., Vol. 23, cols. 740, 741 [7 May, 1834]).]

repeated, is one of the most lamentable proofs yet afforded of the spirit of our legislature, when left to itself, and not taken out of itself by the force of a strong popular feeling. If there ever was a proposition recommended by the most obvious expediency, and to which it was difficult for imagination to conjure up even the shadow of objection, it is a measure which goes simply and exclusively to giving publicity to all future contracts affecting land; so that when, in the course of a generation or two, the change shall have come into full effect, every one may know before buying land, whether the land really belongs to the person who sells it, and every one may ascertain before lending money on the security of land, that the land is not already mortgaged beyond its value. The publicity which would be given by registration, is of the same kind and degree, which is already given to wills by the registry in Doctors' Commons; and any one but those who are personally interested, and therefore entitled to correct information, would be as little likely to gratify idle curiosity by prying into the records of the one registry office, as of the other. From the greater certainty which would be given to all conveyances, the saving to the landowners, in annual law expenses, would be greater than any one can conceive, who is unaware how great a percentage every landlord now pays out of his annual rental for the vices of the law. And hence, as well as from the increased security to purchasers, the market price of all land would be most materially increased. Yet the landlords, the very class who are principally, who alone are directly interested in supplying this strange *hiatus* in our legislation, are the persons who (with the aid of that large class of members who depend for the management of their elections upon provincial attornies) have twice rejected by a large majority, not the details of any particular bill, but the very principle of Registration.

On the part of the landowners there are but two motives possible for this dereliction of one of the first duties and strongest interests of honest men. The worst of these motives is, a desire for the power of making fraudulent sales, and fraudulent mortgages: the best is, the pitiable weakness of not liking that other people should know the extent of their incumbrances. Most fortunate would it have been for hundreds of families now inextricably involved, if they had not been able to conceal the early stages of their embarrassments. It was the puerile desire to go on deceiving their neighbours, and keeping up the appearance of an income they no longer possessed, which prevented them from retrenching when retrenchment would have come in time to save them; and which has brought the whole class into a state, in which their champion, Sir James Graham, avers that the subtraction of twenty per cent. from their incomes, would be their absolute ruin.[*]

On the part of the provincial attornies, who thrive by the litigation caused by defective titles to land, and who derive all their consequence from the management, which they now hold in their hands, of the pecuniary affairs of the whole landed aristocracy, the motives to oppose the publicity as well as the

[*Graham, speech of 6 Mar., 1834, col. 1245.]

simplification of titles, are more obvious, and we have no doubt, far more consciously dishonest. The attorney, who under good laws and a good system of judicature would be nobody, is now the most influential personage in every small place: and the landowner, whose secrets he knows, and whose affairs (of which the landowner himself is tremblingly ignorant) he alone is competent to manage, is held by him in a state of the most slavish dependence. As the soul of the licentiate Pedro Garcias was interred with his money bags,[*] that of an English landowner, intellect, conscience, and all, is folded up in his title deeds, and kept in a box at his attorney's office. He dares not call his soul his own, for he dares not call his estate his own, without the leave of his attorney.

It is by the influence of this pernicious class, the only one, perhaps, whose interest as a class is radically irreconcilable with the public good, (being indissolubly linked, not with the perfection but with the imperfection of all the institutions for the protection of property)—it is by this class that all the well-intended measures of the present ministry, for straightening the crookednesses of the law, and bringing justice home to the people's doors, are, and will continue to be, thwarted. In the particular instance before us, their baneful spell has enslaved the mind of the minister to whom we owe the Reform Bill. It is well understood that Sir John Campbell, when he became connected with the ministry, yielded to a higher authority in giving up the Registration Bill, while he retained and carried through all the other law reforms which he had originated as the organ of the Real Property Commission.[†] Earl Grey is understood to be a fanatical opponent of Registration; as well as a fanatical adherent of the Corn Laws and of the Usury Laws.[‡]

We cannot leave the subject of Registration, without giving due honour to the *Times* for the service which it has rendered to that important principle by its powerful advocacy.[§] That advocacy, it would be injustice not to admit, is, on almost all questions of *immediate* interest, usually given to the cause of rational improvement; and when given, never without rendering a service to that cause, such as no other of the periodical commentators on public affairs have it in their power to render. The hostility of the *Times* to the Poor Law Bill, is an exception to its usual soundness of practical judgment, and will be found, we doubt not, as injurious to its own as to the public interest. Whatever may be the merits and

[*Alain René Lesage, "Gil Blas au lecteur," *Histoire de Gil Blas de Santillane*, 4 vols. (Paris: Ribou, 1715–35), Vol. I, pp. [ix–x].]

[†"Copy of the First Report Made to His Majesty by the Commissioners Appointed to Inquire into the Law of England Respecting Real Property," *PP*, 1829, X, 1–671; "Copy of Second Report," ibid., 1830, XI, 1–627; "Copy of Third Report," ibid., 1831–32, XXIII, 321–450; "Copy of Fourth Report," ibid., 1833, XXII, 1–194. The resulting acts include 3 & 4 William IV, cc. 27, 42, 74, 104, 105, and 106 (1833).]

[‡For the Usury Laws, see 12 Anne, second session, c. 16 (1713).]

[§Leading Article on Registration of Instruments Affecting Land, *The Times*, 2 Apr., 1834, p. 4.]

demerits of the *Times*, there can be no question of its being by far the most potent organ of the Movement; which, at the same time, it does not blindly hurry on, but is incessantly pointing out to Ministers, and to the influential classes, the means by which, while yielding to the tide of change, they may rationally hope to temper its violence. The *Times* is without doubt one of the great powers in the State. It would not be so, if either Ministers or Opposition had the energy, the strength of will, or the knowledge of the world, by which that journal has acquired the ascendancy naturally given by those qualities in an age which, without much of the exaggeration of a satirist, may be termed the age of cowards and fribbles.

* * * * *

13th May

Lord Brougham's Defence of the Church Establishment

The Lord Chancellor is curiously destitute of consistency. We do not mean by consistency, the Tory virtue of being always wrong because you have been once wrong; we mean that quality of the intellect and of the moral perceptions, which prevents a person from holding two conflicting opinions at once. It was but the other day that Lord Brougham declared himself against a National Education, because it would put an end to voluntary contributions.[*] And now, without owning any change of opinion, he maintains that voluntary contributions are good for nothing, and that the State must do all.

There were some wants which the animal instincts of nature left safely to encumber us, since they were sure of being provided for; because hunger and thirst and other purely animal necessities, would of themselves compel us to take means to relieve ourselves of their pressure, and the more we felt them the more sure we were to endeavour to provide for them; but it was not so with wants of a more refined, and he might say nobler kind,—it was not so with respect to education; he did not mean religious, but common secular education. On the contrary, the more ignorant we were, the less we knew of the use of learning, and the less we should bestir ourselves and take means to ensure the advantages to be derived from its acquirement.[†]

This was to prove that the State ought to provide an endowed ecclesiastical establishment: and of course, we presume, ought to furnish common secular education also.

We subscribe to Lord Brougham's premises, and strongly recommend them to his own consideration. He shall hear of them again if he ever repeat his declaration against a national provision for elementary instruction. But adopting his principles, we differ altogether from the conclusion he draws from them, in favour

---

[*Henry Brougham, speech of 16 Apr., 1834, cols. 843–4.]

[†Henry Brougham, Speech on Dissenters (12 May, 1834), *PD*, 3rd ser., Vol. 23, cols. 845–6; in *Morning Chronicle* (from which Mill is probably quoting), 13 May, 1834, p. 1.]

of a Church Establishment, taking that term in its received meaning. What he said last year in favour of the voluntary principle,[*] and what he says this year against the voluntary principle, are at complete variance, and we hold him to be most felicitously wrong in both.

We hold, with Lord Brougham and all other rational persons, that the only objects fit to be undertaken by the State, which derives the principal part of its pecuniary resources from compulsory taxation, are those which either cannot be accomplished at all, or not so well, by the voluntary principle. Instruction, meaning by that term the systematic culture of the intellectual faculties, we hold to be one of these; and to be a most proper subject for a State provision. We do not except religious instruction; though we consider it as, of all branches of a general course of instruction, that which least requires such a provision, and in which the influence of Government is least likely to be of a salutary kind. The extension of secular education thousands are anxious to impede, and few comparatively are willing to give themselves any trouble to promote it; but all are abundantly eager to inculcate religion, and we may count by millions those who either by purse or person are actively engaged in propagating their religious opinions through all channels. On other subjects almost any teaching which could emanate from the State, would be an improvement on what exists: on that one subject the voluntary principle already provides, in ample measure, instruction quite equal to any which our present statesmen seem to have the capacity to conceive.

As to Church Establishments, such as exist in Europe, and even such as are conceived in the abstract, by all mankind except a few closet philosophers; we deny their claim to the title of institutions for religious instruction. Their objects we conceive to be of a quite distinct character, and such as not only may safely be left to the voluntary principle, but cannot justly be provided for in any other manner.

The Clergy, indeed, are, in a certain measure, teachers of religion, and it is easy to conceive a clergy of whom that might be the sole office. But the leading feature in the conception of a clergyman, in the minds of the majority of believers in Christianity, is that of a person appointed, not to teach them, but to go through certain ceremonies with them; in the Catholic church to perform for them, in Protestant churches to assist them in the performance of, the religious observances which they consider as means of obtaining the favour of the Supreme Being. Now this is, if anything ever was, an individual and personal concern. If any one deems a particular kind of observances to be conducive to salvation, and the assistance of any other person to be necessary for the performance of them, it is for him, or those who share his persuasion, to defray the expense. If aid be afforded by the State, it ought to be afforded impartially; each should be assisted to support the worship he voluntarily prefers. But in principle, this is not one of those wants of individuals

[*Henry Brougham, speech of 14 Mar., 1834, cols. 632–8.]

which the State is called upon either to awaken or to relieve. It is not a matter in which society is concerned, either by its interests or by any call of duty; though doubtless, in the choice of a mode of worship, individuals are determined by the general state of their intellectual and moral nature, and in that, society has the deepest interest. Let society then go to the fountain-head, and address itself to the cause, not to the symptom. Let it provide adequate means, and adequate encouragement, for the mental culture of all classes of the people, leaving it to them to provide themselves with all helps necessary for their individual devotions. Let it *instruct* the people: we do not say *educate*; that task must necessarily devolve upon the family; a State never educates, except by the general spirit of its institutions. But it can instruct; and by instruction it can not only form the intellect, but develope the moral perceptions.

We know of no branch of the general culture of the mental faculties, which is not a fit subject for a State provision. People may be trusted to themselves to learn whatever is necessary for gaining their daily bread. The instruction which is intended to form, not human beings, but tradesmen and housewives, need not, except to the very poor, be afforded by a State establishment. Professional instruction may be left to the competition of the market; if we except a few professions, such as physicians, and schoolmasters, in which the purchaser is not a competent judge of the quality of the article. But all instruction which is given, not that we may live, but that we may live well; all which aims at making us wise and good, calls for the care of Government: for the very reason given by the Lord Chancellor; that the majority have neither the desire, nor any sufficient notion of the means, of becoming much wiser or better than they are.

*When we say that instruction of all kinds, connected with the great interests of man and society, ought to be provided by the State, we by no means (as we have already observed) except religious instruction. We see, indeed, in the present state of the public mind, formidable obstacles to including in any course of public teaching, such religious instruction as shall not be worse than none. But difficulties arising not from the nature of the case, but from the literal and dogmatic character and sectarian spirit of English religion, must not hinder us from asserting in speculation, if we cannot realize in practice, a great principle. An important, if not the most important part of every course of public instruction, is that which is intended to awaken and to enlighten the conscience, or principle of duty. This essential part of national instruction must either be omitted entirely, or it must be such as does not clash with the moral convictions of the majority of the educated classes. A country must be in a wretched state, in which the best moral instruction

---

*Very rarely does the editor differ from the correspondent to whom our readers are indebted for these notes, and for other contributions to our pages. It is, however, necessary to say, that he must not be held responsible for any speculation, or expression, in the present note, which may be construed into an allowance of the right of political authorities to legislate in matters of religion. [Note by W. J. Fox.]

which can be afforded consistently with this condition, is not better than none at all. But in all Christian countries, the prevalent moral convictions, the best conceptions popularly entertained of the rule of life, are thoroughly interwoven with, and in great part founded upon, religion. To exclude religious instruction, is therefore to exclude moral instruction, or to garble it, and deprive it of all systematic consistency, or to make it of a kind decidedly objectionable to the majority of the educated classes.

It is true mankind differ widely on religion; so widely that is impossible for them to agree in recommending any set of opinions. But they also differ on moral philosophy, metaphysics, politics, political economy, and even medicine; all of which are admitted to be as proper subjects as any others for a national course of instruction. The falsest ideas have been, and still are, prevalent on these subjects, as well as on religion. But it is the portion of us all, to imbibe the received opinions first, and start from these to acquire better ones. All that is necessary to render religion as unexceptionable a subject of national teaching as any of the other subjects which we have enumerated, is, that it should be taught in the manner in which all rational persons are agreed that every other subject should be taught—in an inquiring, not a dogmatic spirit—so as to call forth, not so as to supersede, the freedom of the individual mind. We should most strongly object to giving instruction on any disputed subject, in schools or universities, if it were done by inculcating any particular set of opinions. But we do not conceive it to be the object of instruction to inculcate opinions. It is the grossest abuse of the powers of an instructor, to employ them in *principling* a pupil, (as Locke calls it in his *Essay on the Conduct of the Understanding,*)[*] a process which tends to nothing but enslaving and (by necessary consequence) paralyzing the human mind. An enlightened instructor limits his operations in this respect to apprizing the learners what are the opinions actually entertained; and by strengthening their intellects, storing their minds with ideas, and directing their attention to the sources of evidence not only on every doubtful, but on every undisputed point, at once qualifies and stimulates them to find the truth for themselves. Let the teaching be in this spirit, and it scarcely matters what are the opinions of the teacher: and it is for their capacity to teach thus, and not for the opinions they hold, that teachers ought to be chosen. The most enlightened pupils have often been formed by the most mistaken teachers. We repeat, it is a total misunderstanding of all the objects of teaching to suppose that it has anything to do with impressing the teacher's opinions. These may be all true, and yet not only may be, but if the inculcation of them be what the teacher considers his duty, probably *will* be, so taught as to have no effect upon the understanding but to contract and fetter it; while, on the

---

[*John Locke, *Essay Concerning Human Understanding*, Vols. I–III of *Works*, Vol. I, p. 53 (I, iii).]

contrary, we are so far from apprehending any bad effect from teaching even the falsest religion, in an open, free spirit, that we should hardly object, under a good method of teaching, to a professorship of astrology.

All this, we grieve to say, is (not we trust) useless, but, with respect to any hope of immediate application, wholly unpractical. We hold it utterly unavailing, in the present state of the national mind, to hope for any national religious instruction, not calculated, in a most eminent degree, to narrow and pervert the intellect and feelings. In Prussia, such things may be; for not only does the spirit of free inquiry pervade both the institutions of that people, and the popular mind, but there is no exclusiveness, because there is no literalness in their religion; no German values dogmas for their own sake, nor cares for any thing in a religious sytem but its spirit. In Prussia,—will an Englishman believe it?—the two great divisions of the Reformed Church, the Lutheran and the Calvinistic, in the year 1817, by a voluntary agreement, actually united themselves into one church.* This most astonishing fact speaks of a state of religion, to which that which is almost universal in our own country, presents, unhappily, a diametrical contrast.

To speak no longer of Prussia, or Utopia, or any other purely ideal model, but of England; looking at the English Ecclesiastical Establishment as an existing fact, as part of the present machinery of society, which must either be made available for the purposes of society, or swept away; and considering, not whether we would establish such an institution if we had to begin *de novo*, but in what manner we would deal with it now when it exists; we should not press for its abolition, if either in its own councils or in those of the State we saw the faintest glimpse of a capacity to perceive and understand the real religious wants of the country. That moral influence of the State over the clergy, which has been used solely to purchase the sanction of religion for existing political institutions, and even for existing Ministries might, by an enlightened Government, be made largely available to improve the spirit of the popular religion. By bringing forward into stations of dignity and influence those among the clergy in whom religion assumed the most generous and the most intellectual form, a Government in whom the people had confidence, might do much to unsectarianize the British nation. But this is supposing a Government far wiser than the people, and it is much if we can hope that ours will not be inferior to them. The Establishment, in its present state, is no corrective, but the great promoter of sectarianism; being itself, both in the exclusiveness of its tenets, and in the spirit of the immense majority of its clergy, a thoroughly sectarian institution. Its very essence is subscription to articles, and the bond of union by which it holds its members together is a dead creed, not a living

---

*See one of the notes (p. xxxii) to Mrs. Austin's admirable translation of one of the most important public documents ever printed—M. Cousin's *Report on the State of Primary Instruction in Prussia* [London: Wilson, 1834].

spirit. We would rather *not* have any changes which left this unchanged; and any change in this we shall not see. Generations would be required to reform the principles of the Church; to destroy it will only be the work of years.

We have wandered far from our original topic, the Lord Chancellor's speech. That speech is itself the strongest of confirmations of the hopelessness of any improvement in the Church through the influence of the State. Here is a man, confessedly of mental endowments far superior to any other of the ministry, perhaps to any one who is likely to be in the ministry; and he, in a discussion involving the very existence of the Church Establishment, a discussion so naturally suggesting every topic connected with the religious condition of the country, the tendencies of the age in respect to religion, and what is to be desired, or may be done, in respect to any of those tendencies—what does he find to say? Nothing but the veriest common places, familiar to every schoolboy, on the advantages of *some* Establishment or other. Not a word either of general and comprehensive theory, applicable to all times, or of statesman-like estimation of the exigencies of the present time. Neither the philosophy of the question, nor its immediate practical policy.

The Primate followed, with a speech of which *naïveté* was the most prominent characteristic. He wondered how it was that "while Churchmen entertained the most friendly feeling towards Dissenters, and addressed them in a friendly spirit, the Dissenters should manifest such personal hostility to Churchmen." It was true that Churchmen thwarted the Dissenters in all their wishes, but then it was entirely for their good. He, for instance, and most of the other bishops, had resisted the repeal of the Test and Corporation Acts: "not," however, "from any feeling of hostility towards Dissenters, but because they conceived the measure would be productive of injury as regarded the general policy of the country."[*] The Dissenters, however, dislike being trampled upon, even when it is from such laudable and disinterested motives. As to the question, which side feels most resentment, we see no proof that the most hostile feeling is on the side of the Dissenters, but we should feel neither surprised nor indignant if it were so. The Archbishop is probably the first who ever thought it wonderful that the party in possession should be in the better temper. When one brother has given to the other the outside of their father's house, and taken to himself the inside, it is amusing to see him look out of his warm place upon the other who is shivering with cold, and profess to be astonished at so much unbrotherly feeling.

* * * * *

[*William Howley, Speech on Dissenters (12 May, 1834), *PD*, 3rd ser., Vol. 23, cols. 853, 854; in *Morning Chronicle*, 13 May, 1834, p. 2.]

14th May

Mr. William Brougham's Bills for a Registry of Births, Deaths, and Marriages[*]

There are people who would have all aggrieved persons and classes measure their demands, not by what they are entitled to, but by what it suits the convenience of Ministers to give. The course of events is now affording a series of most signal discomfitures to such counsellors. The Dissenters had scarcely a chance for the removal of their minor grievances, until they commenced agitating against the greatest grievance of all. *Now*, most of the little boons to which they were advised to limit their pretensions, are flung to them *en masse* in a sort of panic, and they are most rapidly hastening on their final object, the equalization of all sects by the abolition of a Sectarian Establishment. Yet there are people, and Dissenters too, who still call upon them, for their own sake, to be "moderate," and to ask for no more than is "attainable;" forgetting that what is attainable, altogether depends upon what is demanded; that the Tories and high Churchmen will not be "moderate" if the Dissenters are so; that Ministers are between two contrary impulses, and are sure to yield to the stronger pressure. The Dissenters are wise enough to know, that to a compromise there must be two parties, and that he must be a poor dupe who asks for an inch while his adversary takes an ell.

The Registry which will be provided by Mr. Brougham's Bill, will supply a grievous defect in our institutions, and one which concerns the whole community as well as the Dissenters, though, as in most cases, if no powerful class had been especially aggrieved by the evil, we might have waited long enough for a remedy.

The Registers, it seems, are to be kept by the collectors of taxes. We do not foresee any inconvenience from this arrangement, except a slight tendency to render the Registry unpopular. But the fact is strikingly illustrative of the total absence of machinery for the conduct of administrative business. In France the *registres de l'état civil*, as they are called, are kept by the mayor of every commune, an unpaid officer, usually one of the principal inhabitants, who is selected by the Crown from a Municipal Council chosen by the people. These officers, and the *préfets*, who are the more direct delegates of Government, are an agency ready prepared for collecting any information, for executing any law, or for transacting any local business which the Legislature may impose upon them. They are also a fit agency to look after the performance of all duties, which the Legislature may delegate to any other class of functionaries. But in England, when

[*On 13 May, 1834 (see p. 196 above), William Brougham introduced "A Bill to Establish a General Register of Births, Deaths, and Marriages in England," 4 William IV (14 May, 1834), *PP*, 1834, III, 459–77. In doing so, he announced that, if this measure passed, he would introduce a marriage bill. As the Registry Bill failed, he did not bring the other forward in the session.]

local inquiries are to be conducted, or local business done, which the Legislature are in earnest about, they are forced to create special officers and grant separate salaries. Even a Factory Bill cannot be executed without appointing Inspectors:[*] and the registration of voters under the Reform Bill, was turned over to illiterate overseers; revising barristers being afterwards appointed at considerable expense, to rectify their blunders. For want again of local authorities to whom the immediate control of all these temporary or special officers could be confided, they make their reports directly to the Home Office; which is thus overburdened with business of the most multifarious and distracting kind, is unable both from the quantity and variety to give reasonable attention to any part of it, and a "centralization" is created of a different, but scarcely a better kind, than that which Napoleon established in France.

Mr. Brougham's Marriage Bill will, we presume, supersede the unfortunate abortion produced by Lord John Russell. It is an improvement upon its predecessor, but it goes a very little way towards placing that important contract on its true foundation. The validity of the civil engagement is still to depend upon the performance of a religious ceremony, by a recognised Minister of some, though it may now be a Dissenting, sect. The Bill merely provides for registering the performance of the religious ceremony.

This imperfect measure may satisfy the consciences and stay the clamour of a large portion of the Dissenters; but it is impossible that such a settlement can be final. The following intelligence, which we extract from a Nottingham paper, and which is not the first of its kind, is an example of the opinions and feelings which are growing up in the country on this subject:

At Laurence-street chapel, Birmingham, on Sunday last, after the service was over, the congregation was desired to stay, when four Dissenters took the marriage affair into their own hands, in a very short manner. Charles Bradley rose up and read the following document:

"Before this congregation, I, Charles Bradley, jun. give you, Emma Harris, this ring to wear as a memorial of our marriage, and this written pledge stamped with the impressions of the United Rights of Man and Woman, declaring I will be your faithful husband from this time forward.
(Signed)   CHARLES BRADLEY, jun."

Emma Harris then in turn read as follows:
"Before this congregation I, Emma Harris, receive this ring to wear as a memorial of our marriage, and give you, Charles Bradley, jun., this written pledge, stamped with the impressions of the United Rights of Man and Woman, declaring I will be your faithful wife from this time henceforward.
(Signed)   EMMA HARRIS."

The same ceremony was gone through by Roger Hollinsworth and Mary Louisa Bradley, after which the papers were signed by several witnesses, and thus the marriage contract was made without the intervention of either priest or clerk. It should never be forgotten that two

[*See 3 & 4 William IV, c. 103, §§17 and 18 (1833).]

sisters, who married without a priest at Calverton, were incarcerated in the county jail of Nottingham, by the unrelenting severity of the ecclesiastical court, for more than twelve years. They were in released in 1798. We opine, that the ecclesiastical court will not serve Mrs. Bradley and Mrs. Hollinsworth in the same way.[*]

* * * * *

17th May

Sir Edward Knatchbull's Beer Bill[†]

It is scarcely credible that in the second year after Parliamentary Reform, the reformed Parliament should, by an immense majority,[‡] be actually setting itself to undo what a Tory Parliament had done towards the enfranchisement of the working classes;[§] reimposing that censorship over the social enjoyments of the rural population, which public indignation at the purposes to which it was perverted, had wrung out of the hands of the county magistracy, to whom it is now again proposed to be confided under another name and with a different machinery.

Sir Edward Knatchbull's proposal is to make the opening of a beer-house depend upon the production of certificates from six ten-pound householders, in favour of the petitioner; which certificates must be renewed annually. These certificates are not attestations to character, which may be demanded in the manner of subpœnaing a witness; but may be given or withheld at pleasure; and though in populous towns any person of creditable character would probably have little difficulty in obtaining them, in a rural district the small number of ten-pound householders, together with the known sentiments of the landed gentry, render the exaction of such a condition tantamount to the entire suppression of beer-houses. We regret to see Lord Howick chiming in with the prevailing false sentiment; though the amendment he proposes would be far less mischievous than the original proposition.[¶] His plan is, not to interfere with the opening of beer-houses, but to empower the vestry to close them, by a majority of two-thirds, on a representation from a certain number of householders that any particular beer-house is a nuisance. This is perhaps the least exceptionable form in which the discretionary power of interference, proposed to be created, could exist; and if by a clause in the Bill, the keeper of the criminated place of entertainment were secured a public hearing in his defence, and the right of cross-examining his accusers, with the benefit of an appeal to the judge of assize, or to the local court when such shall be established, Lord Howick's proposition might not be seriously objectionable.

[*Anon., "The Marriage Ceremony," *Nottingham Review*, 16 May, 1834, p. 4.]
[†Enacted as 4 & 5 William IV, c. 85 (1834).]
[‡See *PD*, 3rd ser., Vol. 23, col. 1135 (16 May, 1834).]
[§See 1 William IV, c. 64 (1830), amended by 4 & 5 William IV, c. 85 (1834).]
[¶Henry Grey, Speech in Moving an Amendment to the Sale of Beer Act (16 May, 1834), *PD*, 3rd ser., Vol. 23, cols. 1115–20.]

But there is in the Bill, even if it were thus amended, one fatal provision, with which Lord Howick does not propose to interfere, and which brands the whole measure with the double stamp of tyranny and hypocrisy. We allude to the clauses which prohibit the houses from selling beer to be drank on the premises.[*] The debate on this subject was replete with cant; for the expression even of just feelings deserves the name of cant, when the party expressing them would be confounded by being merely taken at his word. Mr. Buckingham said that if beer is a necessary of life, the labourer might surely fetch it home and drink it there, for he ought not to wish to have his enjoyments separately from his wife and from his children.[†] Very fine certainly; but we detest fine sentiments which are never meant to be acted upon. Do we find Mr. Buckingham, or any other supporter of the Bill, proposing to prevent *all* houses from taking in labourers to drink with one another, apart from their families? No; the object is to permit one set of houses and to forbid others; to let the houses licensed by the magistrates retain this obnoxious privilege, and to take it away from the remainder; to create a monopoly of the evil they complain of, in favour of the landlords' houses. The obvious effect, doubtless by many of the promoters of the bill clearly foreseen and calculated upon, is to confine the sale of beer to the landlords' houses. The labourer, as every person of common sense must foresee, will generally prefer the place where he can obtain rest as well as refreshment, and where alone he can have the excitements and the pleasures of society. Scarcely a member opened his lips in favour of the measures who did not think it decent to disavow any wish of restoring the former monopoly: is it possible that any one of all who made the disavowal, should not see, that whether this be the purpose or not, it will certainly be the effect?

We, too, detest, probably as much as these careful guardians of other people's morality, the selfishness with which the demoralized and brutal part of the working population squander their earnings on their own separate debaucheries, leaving their families in want. But if to provide against this evil were the real object, it could be effected, not by restraining the just liberty of the one party, but by giving a remedy to the other. Upon proof that too much of a labourer's earnings was spent from home, his wife ought to have the power of demanding that a suitable proportion of his wages should be paid, not to him, but to her, for the support of herself and of her children. Supposing this done, we know not why the legislature should enact, either directly or indirectly, that a husband should have no society except that of his wife: the misfortune is, that the privilege is not reciprocal; and it is another misfortune that mere defects of physical arrangements prevent the married poor from having their social as well as their domestic life in common. A time will come, when the more general application of the co-operative principle in

[*Clause 1.]
[†James Silk Buckingham, Speech on the Sale of Beer Act (16 May, 1834), *PD*, 3rd ser., Vol. 23, col. 1124.]

household economy, will enable the poor to command, without the equivocal instrumentality of public houses, many of those facilities for social enjoyment, even in a refined form, which have hitherto been the exclusive portion of the opulent classes. The attention of all real wellwishers of the poorer classes should be turned to this most important topic. But in the mean time, we protest utterly against making the labourer's cottage a place of confinement, by refusing him shelter or harbour elsewhere.

* * * * *

19th May

My Grandmother's Journal

We seldom see the *Morning Herald*; but the number for this day accidentally fell into our hands; and of six articles printed in large type, the following was the purport of five. One was a twaddling defence of the pretensions of the Church to superiority of numbers over the Dissenters; this was the least ridiculous of the five; another was a defence of Lord Wynford's Sabbath-day Bill;[*] another of Sir Edward Knatchbull's Beer Bill. A fourth was a philippic against the Poor Law Bill, and its "bashaws;" the fifth, a philippic against omnibuses, with a demand that they be prohibited east of Temple Bar.[†] All this in a single number. Any one of these opinions, except, perhaps, the last, might singly be held by a person not absolutely destitute of reason; each is among the extravagancies of some particular creed, when pushed to its utmost; but no one except "My Grandmother," could have united them. That personage has made up her budget of opinions out of the separate anilities of the sillier part of every existing party or persuasion.

* * * * *

22nd May

Death of Lafayette

There would, in any circumstances, have been something solemn and affecting in the separation of the last link which connected us with the dawn of American Independence and the youthful enthusiasm of French liberty; in the extinction of the sole survivor among the great names of the last age. But this feeling must assume a deeper character when he who has departed from us, was the one man who stood before our eyes, and might, it so seemed, have stood for many years

---

[*"A Bill Intituled an Act for the Better Observance of the Lord's Day, and for the More Effectual Prevention of Drunkenness," 4 William IV (6 May, 1834), *House of Lords Sessional Papers*, 1834, [n.s.] I, Pt. 1, 227–32.]

[†For these anonymous leading articles, see *Morning Herald*, 19 May, 1834, p. 2.]

longer, the living representative of whatever was best and purest in the spirit, and truest in the traditions of his age. Lafayette not only had lived for mankind, but every year of his existence was precious to them, and grievously will he be missed. His was not the influence of genius, nor even of talents; it was the influence of a heroic character: it was the influence of one who, in every situation, and throughout a long life, had done and suffered every thing which opportunity had presented itself of doing and suffering for the right, and who was ready to repeat the same course of doing and suffering, or a severer one, whenever called upon by duty. Such an example, in so conspicuous a station, is ever most valuable, seldom more needful than now.

If a life made up of the most extraordinary vicissitudes, and a soul on which prosperity and adversity vainly exerted all their most corrupting influences, be the materials of an inspiring biography, the life of Lafayette would be one of the noblest subjects for a writer of genius. Even in the simplest narrative, it is in itself a heroic poem. The different epochs of his existence would afford the finest scope to a biographer. There would be, first, the opening period, when, at twenty years of age, he left the attractive and brilliant life of the French Court, to serve as a volunteer in the apparently desperate cause of the revolted colonies of America; and when, having seen the efforts of the noble constellation of patriots, with whom he had associated himself, successful, almost against all hope, and not without having materially contributed to that success, he returned, and we see him first the idol of the people, heading the enfranchisement of his own countrymen, but strenuously, and at all personal hazard, opposing himself to every excess; and three years later deliberately staking life, liberty, fortune, and the love of his countrymen, and losing all except the first, to arrest the precipitate course of the revolution. We next follow him to the dungeon of Olmutz, where for five years the vengeance of an infuriated despot[*] retained him in secret captivity, without communication by word or writing with any who loved him, or tidings from that external world where so tremendous a drama was then enacting. Here he remained, and remained with spirit unbroken, until, by the treaty of Leoben, his release was made by his country part of the price of her mercy to his unrelenting oppressor. But his country then fell upon evil days: he could in nothing serve her, and he retired into the obscurest private life. He reappeared at the restoration, stood once more at the head of the friends of liberty, and was revered as their patriarch. He saw America once more, on the fiftieth Anniversary of her liberation, and his presence was, from one end of the Union to the other, a national jubilee. He saw the infant people which he had nursed in the cradle, grown into one of the mightiest empires of the earth: he lived to taste all the enjoyment which the heartfelt gratitude and love of ten millions of human beings could bestow. He returned to preside at another revolution; gave a king[†] to his own country; withdrew from that king

[*Frederick William II of Prussia.]
[†Louis Philippe.]

when he abandoned the principles which had raised him to the throne; bore up, even against the bitterness of disappointment; and died with his hopes deferred, but not extinguished.

Honour be to his name, while the records of human worth shall be preserved among us! It will be long ere we see his equal, long ere there shall arise such a union of character and circumstances as shall enable any other human being to live such a life.

* * * * *

23rd May

Lord Althorp and the Taxes on Knowledge

Lord Althorp's defence for voting against his recorded opinion on the subject of the Newspaper stamps, is truly characteristic, both of the man and of the ministry.[*] Mr. Bulwer and Mr. Roebuck, the proposer and seconder of the motion,[†] introduced it to the House as a question of the highest public policy, or rather above all policy, since it concerns the ends to which government itself is but a means. They referred the question to the interests of civilization. Lord Althorp refers it to the interests of the revenue. The tax yielded £500,000 (or some such sum) a year. That was his first averment. His second was, that the House did not force him to abolish the tax, and therefore he would not. This is a favourite argument with the leader of the House of Commons. That the House does not force him to do his duty, is always with him a sufficient plea against the propriety of doing it. The other day, on the subject of the Danish claims, a question of simple pecuniary honesty, a judicial question whether the claimants were or were not entitled to certain monies, did not Lord Althorp tell the House, that since, contrary to his expectation, he saw they were desirous to be honest, he was willing to be so too?[‡] He will most uprightly do justice between man and man, provided he is compelled.

This predicament of finding their honesty lagging behind that of the House, is one in which Ministers are now well accustomed to find themselves. An example of it was their ignominious defeat on Mr. Lyall's motion respecting the sixpences taken from the wages of merchant seamen to support Greenwich Hospital.[§] It is scarcely credible that so despicable a motive as dislike of the trouble of finding so small a sum as £22,000 elsewhere, should induce men of creditable character to volunteer, in defence of so gross an iniquity, excuses of even a grosser iniquity

[*Spencer, Speech on Stamps on Newspapers (22 May, 1834), *PD*, 3rd ser., Vol. 23, cols. 1210–13.]

[†Edward Bulwer, Speech in Introducing a Motion on Stamps on Newspapers, *ibid.*, cols. 1193–1206; Roebuck, Speech on Stamps on Newspapers, *ibid.*, cols. 1206–10 (both 22 May, 1834).]

[‡Spencer, Speech on Danish Claims (16 May, 1834), *ibid.*, cols. 1138–9.]

[§George Lyall, Speech in Introducing a Motion on the Merchant Seamen's Widows' Bill (1834) (21 May, 1834), *ibid.*, cols. 1146–8; for the defeat, see *ibid.*, cols. 1157–8.]

than the abuse itself. The merchant seaman may enjoy the benefit of Greenwich Hospital! Yes, if you rob him; yes, if you kidnap him; make him a slave, and keep him in your service by force, for wages below the honest price of his labour, until he is lamed and made useless, and an object of charity: and, in anticipation of this injury which you intend to inflict upon him, you make him pay beforehand (whether or no he be the unfortunate person on whom the misfortune will fall) a tax out of his earnings, to pay for his maintenance when you shall have disabled him, and rendered him unfit to gain a livelihood. The House was not base enough to let itself be influenced by such arguments: they left Ministers in a miserable minority; and Ministers, no longer finding themselves in the position in which Lord Althorp was on the Danish claims, before he was forced to be honest, have found it necessary to give way.

* * * * *

24th May

Progress of the Poor Law Bill

The Ministry have held out, with a firmness little usual with them, against the prejudiced hostility to Poor Law Reform. They have compromised none of the essential principles of their measure, and their concessions as to the details have till now been either entirely unimportant, or positive improvements. Among the latter we must rank the discretion given to the Commissioners of suspending the operation of the clause by which the payment of wages out of rates is prohibited after the 1st of June 1835.[*] The success of the whole measure might in many places be greatly endangered, if the alternative were offered to the pauperized population of coming entirely upon the parish, before the introduction or improvement of the workhouse system shall have given them adequate motives to prefer to the life of a pauper the condition of an independent labourer.

We however observe, in the debate of last night, a tendency to a concession of a decidedly mischievous character: we allude to the willingness expressed by Lord Althorp, to limit the duration of the Central Board to five years.[†] The effect of this limitation would be to encourage all who are either prejudiced or interested in favour of the old system, to thwart the operation of the measure; since it affords them a hope, that if they can contrive, during the five years, to make out a plausible case of failure against the Bill, they will be permitted to revert to the old system, and mismanage the poor as before. There is nothing whatever gained by the limitation; it will not buy off a single opponent; and in principle it is absurd for

[*Spencer, Speech on Poor Laws Amendment (14 May, 1834), *ibid.*, cols. 972–3; clause 46 of the Bill, here referred to, became section 52 of the Act.]

[†Spencer, Statement in the House of Commons (23 May, 1834), in *The Times*, 24 May, 1834, p. 4.]

Parliament to enact that something shall terminate in five years, which Parliament may put an end to in one month if it see cause. The proviso will only operate in one way; as a declaration to the country, that Ministers and Parliament are not sure they are doing right; that they are preparing for a possible change of opinion, which is tantamount to a warning to the friends of Ministers, not to confide in them, not to suppose that they have duly considered the subject; and an invitation to the enemies of the measure, by no means to relax their opposition.

The idea of limiting the duration of the Central Board is, we conceive, erroneous in principle. The expression, "a temporary dictatorship," unguardedly used by some of the advocates of the Bill, was singularly infelicitous in its application. In the first place, (as the *Chronicle*, we think, observed,) who ever heard of a dictatorship under the control of Parliament? But the Central Board may be and ought to be defended, not as an expedient for a temporary purpose, but as in itself the best and only proper principle of administration for a system of Poor Laws. Assume that the Board will continue until the existing evils are remedied, and the management of the poor thoroughly reformed: what, except the prolongation of the same superintendence, is to prevent affairs from relapsing by degrees into as bad a state as before? Acts of Parliament? Declarations of the Legislature that the abuses shall hereafter be illegal? But they have always been illegal. They have crept in gradually in spite of the law, because the local functionaries had strong immediate motives to introduce them, none of which motives an Act of Parliament will or can take away; and because there was no authority to which they were forced to submit their proceedings, and whose duty it was to keep them within the law. And this very state of things will be restored from the first moment that the Central Board shall be discontinued; and will be attended of course with the same consequences. The diffusion of sound principles, which will be the natural effect of the present temporary reform, will retard, no doubt, this inevitable progression, but the inroads of abuse, if more slow, will not be less sure.

The opposition to the Bill has been feeble beyond example. We never remember a public measure in the discussion of which every rational argument was so completely confined to one side. We may add, that we remember none in which the party in the wrong has been more strangely reckless of its own reputation, both in its arguments or in its facts. Who, for instance, would have expected to be told (as in the *Times* of the 14th of May) that this Bill renders fruitless the "protracted struggle from which the British people never ceased, until they had succeeded in making it part and parcel of their constitution, that the meanest subject in the realm should neither be subjected to any taxes, nor amenable to any rules of conduct, except such as should be imposed by the joint consent of King, Lords, and Commons in Parliament assembled."[*] Does the *Times* mean that the Poor Rates are now voted by King, Lords, and Commons in Parliament assembled? or that the

---

[*Leading Article on the Poor Law Bill, *The Times*, 14 May, 1834, p. 5.]

rules which regulate relief are made by Parliament, and not by the Magistrates and Vestries? Is it credible that any person, not drunk with anger or intoxicating liquors, could have penned such an assertion? It is valuable however, in one respect, as bringing into a strong light the truth and value of constitutional clap-traps. It is not, it never was, nor ought it to be, part and parcel of the Constitution of any people out of Bedlam, nor was it ever dreamt of in England, that no one should be empowered to raise money from the people, or make rules to bind them, except Parliament. What is part of the Constitution, is that no one can do these things except in the manner and to the extent which Parliament may authorize; which is only saying what we all know, that Parliament is the Sovereign.

The *Times* finds it very absurd to argue that the Commissioners will be responsible, and asks, where is their responsibility if a civil action lie not against them for injury to individuals?[*] We ask, where is the responsibility of Ministers, or any other constituted authorities? In the certainty of their losing their offices at the discretion of Parliament; and the probability, if public opinion, through the customary channels, calls for their removal. What must be the good faith, or the discernment of a writer, who deems this no responsibility, and who at the same time considers the magistrates responsible, because about once a year or less, for some very gross abuse of authority, some magistrate is called to account in the King's Bench, and let off (for the most part) entirely unharmed?

The *Times* has discovered that republicans are the principal supporters of the Poor Law Bill, and that they support it as a means of disorganizing society, and getting rid of King, Lords, and Commons.[†] The present Poor Law Bill is undoubtedly approved by most of those who judge of public measures from a consideration of means and ends, and not from blind traditions: and if such are generally republicans, that is no compliment to King, Lords, and Commons. But as far as we know anything of English republicans, and there are few who have had more extensive opportunities of knowing their sentiments, it is far truer of them that they are republicans for the sake of such measures as this, than that they wish for such measures because they are republicans. We have hardly ever conversed with any English republican, who was not almost indifferent to *forms* of Government, provided the interests of the mass of the people were substantially cared for, in the degree which he considered adequate; and if among the educated and philosophical reformers, to whom the *Times* seems more particularly to allude, there be any who desire extensive alterations in the Constitution, we believe we may say with some confidence, that there is not one in whom that wish does not originate in despair of seeing an effectual reform in the inward structure of society, except by a previous bursting asunder of its external framework. Any

[*Ibid., 23 May, 1834, p. 5.]
[†Ibid., 20 May, 1834, p. 2.]

Ministry which should deal with all our social evils, as the present Ministers are dealing with one of the principal of them, by probing the evil to the very bottom, and cutting away, cautiously but unsparingly, all that is pernicious, would convert all the philosophical republicans: by practically demonstrating the possibility of carrying the same practical measures in the same efficiency, under a monarchy as in a republic, the basis of their republicanism would be taken from under them; for the *Times*, and most of those who have written against these people, utterly mistake their character and spirit. Instead of wishing that the present system should work ill, in order that they may obtain one, founded, as they think, on better speculative principles, their habit is to disregard even to excess, the nominal principle and spirit of a nation's institutions, provided the immediate and definite practical interests of society are provided for by such laws, and such organs of administration, as are conformable to their views.

* * * * *

25th May

Honours to Science!

The *Examiner*, in its number of this day, (the best which has appeared for several weeks,) denounces with a proper feeling the slavish spirit of a correspondent of the *Times*, who, after a long preamble on the importance of showing honour to science, sets forth as a distinguished instance of it, that the King spoke to Dr. Dalton at the levee.[*] There is something, to our minds, unspeakably degrading to the literary and scientific men of this country, in the eager avidity with which they are laying themselves out for the paltriest marks of court notice: those, even, which have become ridiculous to all men of the world, and for which they are competitors, not with the aristocracy, but with those whom the aristocracy laugh at and despise. Think of the pitiable vanity with which so many of these people have allowed themselves to be dubbed Guelphic Knights. With this abject spirit in our intellectual men, who can wonder if honour is not shown to intellect? They have put their own value upon themselves, and have rated it at the smallest coin current in the market.

It is a vain and frivolous notion, that of *showing* honour: the honour which is worth showing is that which is felt; and *that* shows itself, not by some one premeditated demonstration, but as a pervading spirit, through the whole conduct of those who feel it. Who says it is not important that those who are at the head of the State should have reverence for intellect? But will they ever have that reverence until intellect shall be the source of their own elevation? The consideration, which is gained by nobleness of character, men of science and letters have the same

[*See anon., "Men of Science and Letters," *The Times*, 22 May, 1834, p. 3; and anon., "Much Ado about Nothing," *Examiner*, 25 May, 1834, pp. 323–4.]

opportunities of acquiring as other people,—the only other source of consideration is power. Do what we will, where in any state of society the power is, there also will the honour be. Society, with regard to the source of power, may exist in two different states: in the one, what confers power is intellect; in the other, wealth and station; the former state has never yet been realized, though some societies have approached nearer to it than others, and all are tending towards it, in proportion as they improve; the latter, exists in England, and in most countries in Europe. Now, is it a rational expectation that while power shall still accompany wealth and station exclusively, the honour which always goes with power, can be diverted from it, and become an appendage of intellect? And is it not a mean ambition in persons of intellect to desire a merely reflected honour, derived from the passing notice of people of wealth and station? Precisely the same kind of honour which poets enjoyed when they were domestics in the household of great men.

There are but two stations in the affairs of the world, which can, without dishonour, be taken up by those who follow the pursuits of intellect. Either intellect is the first of all human possessions, that which in its own nature is fitted to rule, and which for the good, not of its possessors, but of the world, ought to be exalted over the heads of all, and to have the sole guidance of human affairs, all persons being ranked and estimated according to the share they possess of it; either this, or it is a mere instrument of the convenience and pleasure of those to whom, by some totally different title, the direction of the world's affairs happens to belong, and is to be rated at the value which they put upon it, in proportion to the use it is of to them, and to its relative importance among the other things which conduce to their gratification. Whoever deems more highly of wisdom than he deems of rope-dancing, or at most of cotton-spinning, cannot think less of it than that it ought to rule the world; and, knowing that to be its proper station, he will, on the one hand, by the conscientious use of such power as it gives him, do the utmost which an individual can do to place it there; and, on the other, he will never, by any act of his, acknowledge the title of any competitor; far less put up a petition that a nod or a civil word from the usurper may be occasionally vouchsafed to the rightful prince. The State ought to yield obedience to intellect, not to sit in judgment upon it, and affect to determine on its pretensions.

So long as no conventional distinctions are conferred upon intellect, the State abstains from putting any value upon it, and leaves it to assume its proper place, without deciding what that place is: but when it affects to confer a distinction, and confers the very lowest in the conventional scale, it does set a value on intellect, and rates the highest honour which is due to intellectual attainments exactly on a par with the lowest which can be claimed from any adventitious circumstance. Is this the "honour to science" which scientific men should be desirous of?

There is but one thing which Government, as at present constituted, can do for scientific men, and that is the one thing which is not thought of. It is absurd in the

State to confer upon them what it calls honours; but it may afford them the means of subsistence, not as a reward, but to enable them to devote themselves to their scientific pursuits, without hinderance from those petty occupations which they are mostly obliged to follow for their daily bread. Every person of scientific eminence, whose genius and acquirements, destined at the best to perish so soon out of the world, are in a great measure lost to it while he is living, for want of some small provision which would keep him independent of mechanical drudgery: every person of distinguished intellectual powers, whom society has not sense enough to place in the situation in which he can be of the greatest use to it, is a reproach to society, and to the age in which he lives. It is here, if any where, that improvement may be hoped for; and we hope it is here that we shall, in time, see it contended for.

* * * * *

28th May

The Change in the Ministry

We have had little faith hitherto in the impression which generally prevailed, of divisions in the Ministry, amounting to a decided difference of principle between two sections of it. We had been so much accustomed to find members of the Cabinet who were reputed the most liberal, making themselves the organs of whatever was most illiberal in its practical policy, that the present schism in the Cabinet has taken us almost by surprise. We confess ourselves mistaken. When a body breaks to pieces, and the parts fly off in contrary directions, there must have been a previous tendency of each part to move in the direction in which it is impelled the moment it is set at liberty. It is evident that one portion of the Ministry must have been worse, and another portion must have been better, than their collective conduct.

The Ministry will now have a new lease of popularity. If they so please, all past errors will be considered as cancelled, and in two months from this time they may have acquired a new character. If their future conduct show vigour of purpose and a strong spirit of improvement, all that they have done ill, will be imputed to Mr. Stanley and Sir James Graham; all that they have done well, to themselves. From us, and we believe from all the enlightened reformers, they may expect, until they shall have had a fair trial, not only no hostility, but the most friendly encouragement and support. They must now throw themselves upon the people. All their strength is there; and it will not fail them.

The names which are talked of to replace the retiring Members of the Cabinet, are of good augury. In Lord Durham and Sir Henry Parnell, the ministry will have two men more devoted to popular objects, than almost any other public men not decidedly numbered among radicals; and in Mr. Abercromby, one of the most upright, strong-minded, and unprejudiced of the members of the old opposition, and one who is thoroughly alive to the spirit of the times.

The change is a decided progress of the Movement, and will carry all the great public questions several steps in advance. But what is more important perhaps than even the change itself, is the immediate cause of it; the general expectation that Mr. Ward's resolution for reducing the Temporalities of the Irish Church,[*] would have passed the House of Commons, even in opposition to the Ministry. It is well understood that this was what determined the retirement of the more Conservative section of the Ministry.

* * * * *

NO. V, JULY, 1834

2nd June

Abolition of Patronage in the Church of Scotland

Alone among all Protestant churches, the Church of Scotland for some time was the people's church; not the church of the aristocracy, kept for them at the people's expense. This privilege the Scottish people possessed themselves of, not without a battle of several generations, against their own aristocracy first, and next against their own and our aristocracy combined. In the conflict, as much heroism, both of action and endurance, was displayed, as has probably signalized any cause since the beginning of the eternal war between right and wrong. For a century this battle lasted, and for a century more the fruits of it were enjoyed. The prize was kept, for about as long as it took to acquire. But corruption crept in; the Church of Scotland proved no exception from the evil tendencies of human affairs in general, and of the age in particular; the tendency of power to concentrate itself in few hands, and of what originally was sufferance, to convert itself into a right, and the tendency of the institutions of this country, since the Revolution, to become more and more aristocratic. The appointment of the ministers of religion gradually became private property; the Church of Scotland followed, though at a considerable distance, the steps of the Church of England, and progressively (for degeneracy as well as improvement is gradual) became the laird's church, no longer the church of the people.

Dissent from the Church of Scotland took its rise with this departure from the voluntary principle. The Seceders seceded from the abuses of the Church, not from its tenets: when the ministry of religion became a place for a great man to give away, it ceased to be a ministry for them. But dissatisfaction spread much further than avowed dissent; and now at length, aided by the spirit of the times, it has prevailed over the evil influences opposed to it, and enforced a reform.

It is the good fortune of the Scottish Church, that its government is not a

[*Henry George Ward, Speech in Introducing a Motion on the Church of Ireland (27 May, 1834), *PD*, 3rd ser., Vol. 23, cols. 1368-96.]

monarchy or an aristocracy, but a democracy; it depends not upon a bench of bishops, but upon a representative assembly; and one, moreover, in which the laity as well as the clergy have a voice. In the Scottish Church, the power to root out evils resides in the sufferers from them, not in those who are the creatures of the evils, and who profit by them. Accordingly, no sooner was the evil generally recognized as an evil, than it has been forthwith remedied. By the regulation just adopted by the General Assembly, no patron will hereafter have the power of presenting any clergyman to a living, whose appointment is disapproved of by a majority of the heads of families in the parish.[*]

It is thus that a Church is to be saved, if any of the Churches can be saved from the storm which is now, and not prematurely, rising against them. A national endowment for the support of teachers of religion might still be preserved, if the people, for whom the Church exists, the people, who *are* the Church, were allowed even a negative voice in determining by what body of persons, and by what member of that body, religious instruction should be imparted to them. But the people will no longer receive their religion from a corporation of priests, imposed upon them as teachers by their political superiors. And, as the ruling powers in the Church of England are incapable of opening their eyes to this truth, that Church, as a national institution, is tottering to its fall.

* * * * *

4th June

Mr. Rawlinson and the Man of No Religion

In the *Chronicle* of to-day we read the following paragraph:

Yesterday, at Marylebone office, a poor man, far advanced in life, suffering under the dreadful affliction of a paralytic affection, which has deprived him of the use of one side, applied to the sitting magistrates, Messrs. Rawlinson and Hoskins, for an order to be admitted into Marylebone poor-house. The old man stated that he had lived in Marylebone parish upwards of thirty-one years; and that, during the greater portion of that period, he had been master of a flourishing business, and spent thousands of pounds in bringing up his family. His trade, however, went gradually to decay; and, to crown his misfortunes, he had, in his old days, been seized with paralysis, which deprived him wholly of the means of obtaining a livelihood, and he was now in a state of great destitution. In this extremity he had applied to the parochial authorities to be admitted into the workhouse, which had been refused. Mr. Rawlinson asked Mr. King, (one of the parish officers in attendance,) why the man had been refused admittance. Mr. King replied, that it was in consequence of his having refused to say where his wife was; as the Board had decided that they could not receive one without the other. The old man said that she had run away from him, and that he did not know where to find her. Mr. Rawlinson directed that he should be sworn to that fact. The old man accordingly took the book in his hand. *Mr. King.* "Are you a Catholic?" *Old Man.* "I was bred in that persuasion, but have abjured it." *Mr. Rawlinson.* "What are you?"

[*The regulation resulted in 4 & 5 William IV, c. 41 (1834).]

Old Man. "That is best known to my Maker: I am of no religion at all." *Mr. Rawlinson.* "Then I shall not compel the officers to relieve a man of no religion. Go about your business." He accordingly quitted the office, sighing as he limped away.[*]

From long experience, we expect nothing from the London magistrates but subservience to the worst feelings and lowest prejudices of the vulgarest part of the community: and never was there a more signal instance in point than this of Mr. Rawlinson.

If the man had been a convicted felon—an outcast from society; if his life had been spent between the hulks and the house of correction,—if he had been convicted at the Old Bailey, of every crime short of such as could bring him to the gallows; and, after suffering his sentence, had come before Mr. Rawlinson in a destitute state, claiming to be supported by his parish, Mr. Rawlinson would not have dared refuse an order for relief: he would have known that a magistrate is appointed to sit in judgment, not on men's moral characters, but on their legal rights; that there is no statute empowering him to dispense with the laws, when they award something to a person of bad character; and he would have resented the very attempt to raise the question, as an irrelevancy, a cruelty towards the unfortunate, and an insult to the understanding of the magistrate. Such would have been his conduct if this poor man had been a convicted criminal; but against a "man of no religion," all is fair. An unbeliever has no rights: the whole vicious part of the community may be let loose with impunity to injure *him*: the law promises him its protection; but the law can only act through those who administer it; and, in *his* favour, it shall not be administered.

If Mr. Rawlinson thinks at all, (it is an undeserved compliment to one who can thus act in such times as ours, to suppose him capable of thinking,) he would most likely defend himself by saying that "a man of no religion" must be a man of no virtue; for he will scarcely, we should think, plead guilty to what is probably the fact, that he had no motive but a wretched antipathy to a person who disbelieves something which *he* flatters himself he believes. Here, then, on the most favourable statement which can be made, a poor man has been treated, on a mere presumption of immorality, in a manner which would not have been tolerated if his guilt, instead of being presumed, were proved, and were of the blackest kind which a person could commit, and be suffered to live.

Let us go one step further, and notice the profound ignorance of the world, (the most fatal kind of ignorance to a person in Mr. Rawlinson's situation,) which is manifested by those vehement presumptions so readily made by vulgar minds, of all sorts of immorality, from the absence of religious belief. We will not be so uncharitable as to surmise that such people as this police magistrate, judge of others from themselves; and finding that their own natural inclinations are towards all kinds of evil, or what they regard as such, cannot believe that any person could

[*Leading Article on Mr. Rawlinson, *Morning Chronicle*, 4 June, 1834, p. 3.]

be prevented from being a scoundrel, except by the slavish and selfish terror of hell-fire. We will not press this. But we will appeal to facts. Does Mr. Rawlinson know anything whatever of the state of opinion among the lettered, or as they are called, educated classes? If so, he knows, that not less than one-fourth or one-third (at a moderate computation) of all the persons whom he meets at dinner, are either actual unbelievers, or have only the faintest and most doubtful belief; though they do not chuse, by avowing their sentiments, to expose themselves to martyrdom. Now, is there any perceptible difference between the conduct, in every relation of life, of this portion of Mr. Rawlinson's acquaintance, and the remaining three-fourths or two-thirds? Would he himself, on any occasion requiring confidence, place one particle less of it in them, than in the average of the remainder? Certainly not; nor is it possible for religion to exercise less influence over the lives and characters of actual unbelievers, than it does over the vast majority of professing Christians. If there be any difference, it is not in favour of those who call themselves Christians; for the speculative homage paid to a rule of life which they never for one half-hour sincerely endeavour to act up to, has rather a perverting than an elevating effect upon the character. Unbelievers, if they have not the direct influences of Christianity, have reason and natural feeling, and by those aids may, and generally have, worked out for themselves some moral convictions, by which they may really govern their conduct; but Christians who live in the world, and do as the world does, that is to say, who lead a life the main objects of which are such as Christianity either makes light of, or actually condemns, and in which nothing, except a certain small number of acts and abstinences, either flows from religion, or reminds them of it; such persons have perpetually to reconcile conduct of one kind, with a creed of a quite opposite kind; they cannot with any satisfaction to themselves, reflect on morality, or question themselves on their own moral state; all their moral perceptions become dim and confused; they acquire the habit of sophisticating with themselves, and paltering with their notions of duty: Christianity is practically disregarded, except on new or peculiar exigencies; and they live, if of a cautious character, according to respectability, and the breath of men; if incautious, by mere impulse.

Compared with such Christians, he who has the manliness to speak out, with simplicity and without ostentation, the fact of his unbelief, is a religious man. And he is turned out to starve—while they, possibly, are on the very bench which condemns him.

* * * * *

6th June

Business of the House of Commons

It is just now beginning to be found out that the House of Commons has too much to do, and does it in a clumsy manner. The schoolmaster is certainly abroad;[*] intellect is on the march; it will soon be discovered, after due investigation by a commission or a committee, that two and two make four, and that the sun is the cause of day. The Business Committee of the House of Commons has passed the following resolutions:

1. Resolved, that it is the opinion of this Committee, that with a view to promote the convenience of members, and to facilitate the dispatch of private business, it is expedient that certain measures which, under the existing laws, must be brought separately under the consideration of Parliament, should be provided for by general enactments, enabling parties interested therein to proceed to their accomplishment without having constant reference to the special sanction of the Legislature.

2. Resolved, that it is the opinion of this Committee, that if possible, a General Inclosure Act should be passed, which may enable parties having an interest therein, to enclose lands, subject to such provisions as may secure the rights of all concerned, without subjecting themselves to the heavy expenses which are now incurred.

3. Resolved, that it is the opinion of this Committee, that powers of providing for paving, macadamizing, watering, draining, and otherwise improving cities, towns, and places, should be vested (under certain conditions and regulations) in the inhabitants, to be carried into effect without the necessity of appealing to Parliament.[†]

Why stop here? Does the self-evident general principle involved in the first resolution, include no cases but those of inclosure bills, and bills for local improvements? Are these even the fittest cases to begin with? Is it not absurd, that from the clumsiness of the law of partnership, every numerous association for commercial purposes requires a special act to entitle it to one of the simplest of the privileges which ought to belong to all joint-stock associations, that of being treated in all legal proceedings as a single person?* Why should a turnpike bill, more than a bill for paving and watering, occupy the time of the Legislature? Would not *all*, or almost all local matters, be best provided for by "parties having an interest therein;" the Legislature interfering only where national as well as local interests are concerned, and are in danger of being compromised by the supineness of the local authorities? To ascend to higher matters: what can be more monstrous than that there should be such things as divorce bills? Is it not self-evident, that what is good for a small number of the higher classes, must be good for the whole community; that the grant of a divorce ought to depend upon something else than length of purse; that there ought either to be (as is, to us, obvious) a general law of divorce, or else no divorces at all?

In regard to the particular points for which the Business Committee recommends that provision may be made, there is another recommendation which should

[*See Henry Brougham, Speech on the Address on the King's Speech (29 Jan., 1828), *PD*, n.s., Vol. 18, col. 58.]

[†"Second Report from the Select Committee on the Business of the House," *PP*, 1834, XI, 321.]

*The Attorney General, we are glad to observe, has since obtained leave to bring in a bill for remedying this grievous and mischievous defect in our institutions. [Enacted as 4 & 5 William IV, c. 94 (1834).]

have preceded. They should have recommended that the House do immediately commence the organization of an efficient representative system of local government. Till then, we should be afraid to trust the local authorities with any new powers; especially any powers of encroaching on the rights of the poor. Who would tolerate, that the men who have stopped up, literally, every path in some of the most populous counties of England, should have the power, without passing the ordeal of Parliament and the public, to confiscate remorselessly the vested interest of the poor labourer in the free air and the pasturage, and the vested interest of the whole people in the enjoyment of the beauties of nature?

It is something that the House of Commons will now no longer pass Bucklebury and Kingsclere Inclosure Bills.[*] These were considered as cases of *pecuniary* injustice to the poor. But there are other kinds of injustice, besides pecuniary; injustice to the whole nation, as well as to the poor. Is it too much to expect from those who vote away 11,000*l*. of the people's money for two Correggios,[†] that they should show some value for the people's tastes and enjoyments, as well as for what are called their *interests*? Hampstead Heath, it is said, is now on the point of being enclosed; the Sir Thomas Maryon Wilson, whose cupidity is the motive to this sacrilege, has already enclosed Charlton Wood, and stopped up every, or almost every, foot-path between Blackheath and the Thames. The writer of this, who has been a pedestrian in the neighbourhood of London for about ten years, has, during that time, had to lament the loss of the two finest pieces of natural scenery within twelve miles of the capital,—Penge-wood, between Dulwich and Beckenham; and the Addington hills, near Croydon. The first, an inclosure bill[‡] having been obtained by a man named Cator, who has a house in the neighbourhood, is now in preparation for being cut up into citizens' boxes and bits of garden ground. The Addington hills, one of the most remarkable pieces of heath and forest scenery in the south of England, have been usurped by the Most Reverend Father in God, Doctor Howley, Archbishop of Canterbury, the author of the famous "prostration of the understanding and will,"[§] and of the doctrine, that the King, not in legal fiction merely, but in fact, can "do no wrong."[¶] When Dr. Howley was appointed to the archbishopric, to which a house and park adjoining these beautiful hills are unfortunately appended, one of his first acts was to obtain an order of two magistrates, for stopping a public road which ran along the summit of the hills; and, this being effected, he immediately enclosed nearly

---

[*See, for Bucklebury, *PD*, 3rd ser., Vol. 23, cols. 748–53 (8 May, 1834); and, for Kingsclere, *ibid.*, Vol. 24, cols. 174–80 (5 June, 1834).]

[†By 4 & 5 William IV, c. 84, §17 (1834).]

[‡7 & 8 George IV, Private Acts, c. 35 (1827).]

[§William Howley, *A Charge Delivered to the Clergy of the Diocese of London* (London: Payne and Foss, and Hatchard, 1814), p. 16.]

[¶Howley, Speech on the Bill of Pains and Penalties against Her Majesty (7 Nov., 1820), *PD*, n.s., Vol. 3, col. 1711.]

the whole tract with a paling seven or eight feet in height. By this the people of Croydon have lost their most frequented walk, and the people of London and the neighbourhood, the most beautiful scenery to which they had ready access. It is some comfort to think, that the ground which has thus been added to the primate's domain, will in a few years, with the rest of the church property, be at the disposal of the State. When the time comes, and it will come, when we shall see the people of Croydon sally out with axe in hand, and level the fences which have been set up to exclude them from what was morally as much their birthright as any man's estate is his—then, and not till then, we shall feel that the Reform Bill has done its work, and that the many are no longer sacrificed to the few.

* * * * *

14th June

The Tom-foolery at Oxford

We know not if the sow ever mistakes the squeaking of her own pigs for the voice of the whirlwind; but the Tory aristocracy certainly mistake the voices of their sons and their sons' toadeaters for the "spirit of the age."[*] The present exhibition wonderfully exemplifies that great fact in human nature, the importance of a man to himself. From Doctor the Duke of Wellington down to poor Lord Encombe, every character in the farce felt so solemnly persuaded that he was, or at least looked like, a hero or a martyr! while in reality he only looked like a fool. It is really too simple of the Tories to fancy that any one except themselves cares for, or so much as thinks about, what Oxford says or does. We all knew already that it is the hot-bed of Toryism, and that the clergy of the Church of England and the youths whom they educate are sure to be Tories. We know no more now. Tories they are, and Tories let them be. As they were the last Jacobites in the country, so will they be the last Tories. The only remark (beyond an occasional interjection of contempt) which we have heard from the lips of any Radical on the affair, was an expression of regret that a place pretending to be the fountain-head of morality and religion, should teach its youth to cheer a Lyndhurst and a Wynford; as if the youth of the London University should toss up their hats for Mr. Wakley or Mr. Whittle Harvey.

Oxford was powerful once; but even the *prestige* of its power has passed away; it is as effete as the Pope, also an important enough personage in his day. But what has once been powerful, usually lives on until it becomes ridiculous; and that evil day has arrived for Oxford. Peace be with it! for it can now do no harm.

* * * * *

[*See p. 62 above.]

17th June

Parliamentary Monstrosities

Lord Bacon recommends that in studying the nature and laws of any principle or element of the universe, we should observe it where it exists in the greatest abundance and strength, and is least counteracted by the presence of any adverse element.[*] We think this a good rule; and in obedience to it, we shall exhibit from time to time such specimens as offer themselves, of the characteristic vices of some institution or some state of mind, carried to the monstrous. Two such have presented themselves within the last few days.

1. What a Bishop is:—In the House of Lords, on a petition for removing the civil disabilities of the Jews,[†] some one remarked, that as they tolerated Socinians, they might as well tolerate Jews, who were not one whit greater blasphemers, (such at least seemed to be the spirit of the noble lord's remark.)[‡] Dr. Grey, bishop of Hereford, and brother of the Prime Minister, hereupon observed, "The Socinians were a set of persons whom he held in utter abhorrence—as a Christian he could not do otherwise;" but yet he must say that the Socinians, though they rejected the divinity of our Saviour, believed him to be the Messiah, while the Jews affirmed the Lord Jesus Christ to be an impostor.[§]

Pious soul! As a Christian he could not do otherwise than hold a large body of his fellow-creatures "in utter abhorrence," because, though they acknowledge the same revelation with himself, they differ as to some few points of its interpretation; yet, even these people whom he utterly abhors, he thinks it but just to protect from being confounded with those who acknowledge only a part of the same revelation: for these last, "utter abhorrence" is not enough; we know not what words he has reserved to express the bitterness of his feelings towards them.

Protect us from such Christianity! If this be the figure under which Christianity is to continue to be exhibited by its recognized teachers, there needs no prophet to predict, that, as the religion of the people of this country, it will not last two more generations. The religion which men shall ever again reverence, and shape their lives by, will be, Dr. Grey may depend on it, another kind of religion than *this*.

2. What a Landlord is.—In a debate, a highly important one, raised on the

---

[*See Francis Bacon, *Novum organum*, in *Works*, ed. James Spedding, Robert Leslie Ellis, and Douglas Denon Heath, 14 vols. (London: Longman, *et al.*, 1857–74), Vol. I, pp. 271–2 (II, xxiv).]

[†"Petition of Persons of Christian Faith Resident in Edinburgh for Removal of Jewish Disabilities" (12 June, 1834), *Journals of the House of Lords*, LXVI, 580.]

[‡Richard Grosvenor (Marquis of Westminster), Speech on Jewish Civil Disabilities (9 June, 1834), in *The Times*, 10 June, 1834, p. 3.]

[§Edward Grey, Speech on Jewish Civil Disabilities (9 June, 1834), *ibid.*]

Emigration clause of the Poor Law Bill by Mr. Whitmore,[*] who took that opportunity of pressing upon the House those enlightened views of colonization, which are about to be, for the first time, realized in the formation of a new colony, Major Handley called upon all supporters of the corn laws to oppose emigration, saying that the principle was exactly the same, for the people "ought to stop at home and eat the corn grown in this country."[†]

The principle *is* exactly the same, being no other than that the whole people of England are the live-stock of the English corn-growers. And we, in imitation of Major Handley's *naïveté*, but reversing the terms of his proposition, call upon all who do *not* think it the duty of all English people to "stop at home and eat the corn" grown for them by Major Handley, to vote for the repeal of the corn laws: for it is mere twaddling to affect to see any difference between the two pieces of tyranny.

The Ministry

In common with the remainder of the liberal press,[‡] we augured no good from Lord Grey's filling up his cabinet with mere stop-gaps, promoted from the lower ranks; the resistance of the modified cabinet to Mr. Ward's motion;[§] and that unfortunate letter to Lord Ebrington, deprecating what constitutes the sole strength of a reforming ministry, a "constant and active pressure from without."[¶] But our anticipations have been materially changed by Mr. Abercromby's accession to the cabinet, and by Lord Grey's noble speech on the Irish Church.[||] How the *Times* and the *Examiner* could possibly see in that speech a truckling to the Lords,[**] passes our comprehension: we see nothing in it but a defiance to the Lords; and the Lords, we are fully persuaded, see it in no other light.

To say that the Tories had the majority in that House, was merely to say what Lord Grey could not possibly be supposed to be ignorant of. To say that he knew it, and that knowing it, he should steadily pursue his own course, and that they, not

---

[*William Wolryche Whitmore, Speech in Introducing a Motion on Poor Laws' Amendment (16 June, 1834), *PD*, 3rd ser., Vol. 24, cols. 451–6. For the Emigration Clause, see "Report from His Majesty's Commissioners for Inquiring into . . . the Poor Laws," *PP*, 1834, XXVII, 199–202.]

[†Benjamin Handley, Speech on Poor Laws' Amendment (16 June, 1834), *PD*, 3rd ser., Vol. 24, col. 475; in *Morning Chronicle*, 17 June, 1834, p. 2, from which Mill is presumably quoting.]

[‡See *Examiner*, 1 June, 1834, p. 338; cf. *The Times*, 5 June, 1834, p. 5.]

[§Ward, Speech in Introducing a Motion on the Church of Ireland (27 May, 1834), *PD*, 3rd ser., Vol. 23, cols. 1368–96; for the Cabinet's resistance, see *ibid.*, Vol. 24, cols. 11–84 (2 June, 1834).]

[¶Charles Grey, Letter to Lord Ebrington (31 May, 1834), *Examiner*, 8 June, 1834, p. 355.]

[||Charles Grey, Speech on the Church of Ireland (6 June, 1834), *PD*, 3rd ser., Vol. 24, cols. 250–60; in *Morning Chronicle*, 7 June, 1834, p. 2.]

[**Leading Article on the Ministry, *The Times*, 9 June, 1834, p. 2; anon., "The Government and the Peers," *Examiner*, 15 June, 1834, p. 369.]

he, had anything to dread from a collision, was not only no cowardice, but the most triumphant refutation of the charge of cowardice; the distinctest proclamation that, let them do their worst, he feared them not. Lord Grey's speech was the bravest act of his ministerial life, next to the framing of the Reform Bill. He said everything which could have been wished or asked for—everything which it had been the reproach of the ministry that it had not dared to say. We were not to expect that he would declare himself an enemy to Church Establishments; there is no reason to doubt that he is a sincere friend to them. Short of this, what did he not say that could have been said on the occasion by the most determined reformer? He avowed principles which went to the root of the whole subject. He declared, that if the endowments of the Protestant Establishment exceed the wants of the Protestant population, it is the right and duty of the State to apply the surplus to the general purposes of moral and religious instruction. He declared that if, when those purposes were fully provided for, a further surplus remained, it was the right of the State to take that further surplus, and apply it to any purpose which it deemed most advisable. He declared it as his deliberate conviction, that, in the case of the Protestant Church of Ireland, after the religious wants of the Protestant population were fully supplied, there would remain, not only a surplus, but a large surplus. And he distinctly affirmed, that upon these principles, he, as a minister, was prepared to act. Nor did he, as is the practice of some of his colleagues, say bold things so timidly, that the impression left is of spiritlessness, and not of boldness. The *tone* of his speech was wholly in accordance with its substance: the style was that of a dignified determinedness of purpose, and by no means, as it has strangely appeared to some of our contemporaries, querulous and dejected.

What matters it, if Lord Lansdowne or Lord Brougham used language[*] which did not come up to the mark of Lord Grey's speech? The principles of a ministry are the principles of the minister who is at its head. Lord Grey is a man who weighs his words: every word with him means all it seems to mean. Lord Brougham's words are thrown out at random; he never speaks twice of the same thing in the same tone.

Few things could have been more solemn and impressive than the warning addressed by Lord Grey to the assembly—addressed to them on an authority so imposing to them as that of Napoleon—that he, the conqueror of Europe, had fallen, not by the strength of his enemies, not by his wars or his imprudences, but because he had opposed the spirit of the age—that the Bourbons who succeeded him, and all the old governments of Europe, would perish from the same cause—and that every government, and the order to which Lord Grey belonged, and which he was as desirous as any one to maintain, unless they profited by the example, would share the same fate.[†] That such truths should be spoken to that

[*Henry Petty-Fitzmaurice and Henry Brougham, Speeches on the Church of Ireland (6 June, 1834), *PD*, 3rd ser., Vol. 24, cols. 290–3 and 298–306.]
[†Charles Grey, speech of 6 June, 1834, *ibid.*, col. 259.]

assembly, by an English prime minister, was what, very few years ago, would have been deemed impossible. The Lords have never received such a lesson; they will never forget it, though they will never profit by it; it will ring in their ears till the day of their fall.

After Lord Grey's speech, we were not surprised at Mr. Abercromby's acceptance of a cabinet office; and we do not doubt that he had grounds for what he is represented to have said to the electors of Edinburgh, that "he has become a member of the administration, because he believes it now to entertain views more consonant to his own, and because he has a strong hope that its measures will henceforth more decidedly attack, and more completely remove abuses; and that thus our institutions, being thoroughly renovated, will more surely tend to accomplish the good of the whole community."[*]

Almost all that we have hitherto observed of the conduct and declarations of Ministers, since the debate on Mr. Ward's motion, has been of a kind to justify our hopes. We must particularly commend the feeling which they manifested, and which, it must in justice be said, was manifested by the whole House, on the subject of national education, when brought before them by Mr. Roebuck.[†] An excellent committee has been appointed, and there is now reason to hope that on that grand subject something not inconsiderable will be done.

The only bad symptom which we have yet discerned is, their declared purpose of renewing the Irish Coercion Bill.[‡] On this subject we suspend our final judgment until the bill is brought in. The military tribunals, which Mr. Abercromby, before he was in office, steadily and uncompromisingly opposed, were the principal blemish in that bill; and we would fain hope that his influence may now induce his colleagues to provide a substitute for that odious jurisdiction. It is not in the least necessary to the efficiency of the bill; and is the great cause of its well-merited unpopularity. To deliver men to be tried for their lives to-day, into the hands of the very men who were fighting against them yesterday, and who come fresh from the excited passions of a life-and-death struggle, to judge people who have been attempting to kill them—is so dreadful a principle, that no person of common justice or common feeling should on any human consideration vote for a bill containing such a provision.

* * * * *

[*James Abercromby, Speech on the Edinburgh City Election (16 June, 1834), *Morning Chronicle*, 17 June, 1834, p. 2.]

[†Roebuck, Speech in Introducing a Motion on National Education (3 June, 1834), *PD*, 3rd ser., Vol. 24, cols. 127–30; for the reception of the Motion, see *ibid.*, cols. 130–9. See also "Report from the Select Committee on the State of Education," *PP*, 1834, IX, 1–261.]

[‡3 William IV, c. 4 (1833), continued by 4 & 5 William IV, c. 38 (1834).]

20th June

The Beer Bill

This odious measure has passed through the committee: and the meritorious efforts of Mr. Warburton[*] to obtain the omission of one of its worst clauses, that which prohibits beer from being sold to be drunk on the premises, have been unsuccessful. It is some satisfaction to think that the tyrannical purpose will be easily frustrated, as the beer will be sold in one house, and drank in another. The Act, however, will remain a memorable example of the spirit of our legislature; which, with all its pretended regard for vested interests, when they are the interests of persons who have an interest in those two houses, will have deliberately sanctioned a more extensive confiscation of vested interests than has almost ever, within our recollection, been deliberately and undisguisedly propounded in a bill introduced into Parliament.*

* * * * *

NO. VI, AUG., 1834[†]

21st June

The Alleged Increase of Crime[‡]

It is recorded that King Charles the Second, in one of his merry moods, requested the Royal Society to explain the fact that a fish has no weight when weighed in its own element. The philosophers laid their heads together, and

---

[*Henry Warburton, Speech on the Repeal of the Malt Duty (27 Feb., 1834), *PD*, 3rd ser., Vol. 21, cols. 889–90.]

*Two other notes on subjects not of temporary interest are postponed to next month. [See the Notes for 21 June below.]

†In the Notes for last month, during the course of some observations on the display of Tory feeling at the Oxford Commemoration, occurred the following passage: "The only remark (beyond an occasional interjection of contempt) which we have heard from the lips of any Radical on the affair, was an expression of regret that a place pretending to be the fountain-head of morality and religion, should teach its youth to cheer a Lyndhurst and a Wynford; as if the youth of the London University should toss up their hats for Mr. Wakley or Mr. Whittle Harvey." [See p. 250 above.] The writer of the Notes is anxious to state, that, from an unlucky concurrence of circumstances, the above passage went through the press without having been seen by the editor; and the writer himself, on subsequent consideration, feels that he had no right, even when repeating what was actually said by another person, to introduce into a printed discourse the names of individuals in connexion with implied reflections upon their moral characters. On the subject of the imputations, great or small, merited or unmerited, current against any of the four persons mentioned, the writer does not pretend to know any thing but what the public knows: that the imputations existed was all that his argument required, and their existence is so universally notorious, that he did not conceive himself to be adding to their notoriety by his allusion. But no one has a right to

thought of a variety of explanations, but forgot to verify the fact itself, which was a mere invention of the jocular monarch.[*] A similar blunder appears to us to have been fallen into by the House of Lords last night, and by many others among those who occupy themselves with public affairs. They are all quarrelling over conflicting theories as to the causes of the increase of crime, and actually debating whether the increase is caused by education! forgetting, meanwhile, to ascertain whether crime *has* increased. We have never seen or heard of any evidence of increase which appeared to us deserving of the slightest regard. It is astonishing, not only how little pains mankind will take to get at the truth, on matters which are every body's concern, and not theirs peculiarly, but also how little evidence contents them, in such a case, as ground for believing assertions the most deeply implicating the highest interests of their country and of their kind. A somewhat greater numerical account of commitments or convictions during two or three years, will prove to them, beyond a doubt, that the labouring classes are becoming fearfully demoralized; and if you presume to suspend your judgment, and desiderate further proof, you are reputed a disregarder of "facts." Facts! no: it is not facts we disregard, it is unfounded *inferences* from them. Grant that convictions have increased,—grant, even, that the increase is permanent and not temporary, arising from general and not local causes; does it follow that more crimes are *committed*? May it not be merely that a greater number are *detected*, or that a greater number are *prosecuted*? Though, perhaps, most *criminals* at some period of their career undergo punishment, the immense majority of *crimes* go unpunished. It has been calculated by solicitors, the best authorities on such a subject, that in London a youth who begins business as a thief may reckon upon not less than six years of impunity before he is removed by legal process. Here is

---

presume that his words are of no consequence, when they contribute, in however slight a degree, to swell a hostile cry against any of his fellow-creatures; and the present writer, who, on principle, denies that private life is a fit subject to be made amenable through the press to the jurisdiction of the general public, ought not to have lent himself to the execution of the verdict pronounced by so incompetent a tribunal, even had that verdict been (what in some of these cases it certainly is not, and in none of them does he know it to be) decided and unanimous. In fact, it is when the charges against any person become the subject of incidental and cursory allusion—it is then, and not before, that the bulk of mankind, who have given little or no attention to the evidence for the charges, conclude them to be proved. A writer who permits himself such allusions, incurs, therefore, a most serious moral responsibility; and no one ought to do so who has not formed his judgment on the case with the care, deliberateness, and solemnity of a judicial act. [Given by Mill as a headnote to the entries for August.]

‡This and the following note are those alluded to in *The Repository* of last month as postponed for want of room. [See the footnote to the Note for 20 June above.]

[*See Isaac Disraeli, "The Royal Society," in *Quarrels of Authors*, 3 vols. (London: Murray, 1814), Vol. II, pp. 19n–21n.]

"ample room and verge enough"[*] for a large increase of convictions without any increase of crime.

Some years ago a worthy city-magistrate distinguished himself by extraordinary activity in the performance of the duties of his mayoralty. He gave, at the same time, a corresponding energy to the police of the city, and the consequence was that a greater number of cases by several hundreds were brought before him than was ever known to have been investigated by any other chief magistrate. Such is the habit of looking to these returns alone [the returns of commitments and convictions] as showing the state of crime in any given district, that we have seen it charged in print, and heard it mentioned by public men, as a reproach to this magistrate, that more crime had been committed in the city during his mayoralty than during any other.*

Again, have there been no circumstances to diminish the reluctance of injured persons to prosecute? Has not the severity of punishments within the last few years been greatly mitigated? Is it not by an innovation introduced within the last few years, that prosecutors are allowed their expenses? Many increased facilities of other kinds have also of late years been afforded to prosecutors and witnesses. Has not a notion grown up within a few years, (we believe a very false one,) that the increased mildness of prison-discipline has made our gaols not only no longer the dens of horror they were, but places where the prisoner is actually too comfortable, and too well off? and has this opinion no tendency to weaken the scruples which good men felt about sending a fellow creature thither! One principal chapter of the criminal calender,—juvenile delinquency,—has grown up almost entirely of late years; not because boys did not formerly steal apples, but because formerly when they stole them they were whipped and sent home, while now they are prosecuted and sent to gaol. This change is probably owing to increased mildness of manners; men can no longer bear to convert themselves into executioners; yet, if there *have* been any increase of crime, here is as likely a cause of it as any other: for the child, whom a brief though severe punishment immediately following the offence might have deterred from a repetition of it, usually comes out of gaol irreclaimably corrupted.

But though there is no sufficient reason to believe that crime *has* increased, nobody in his senses can doubt that it *will* increase, if we do not carefully watch and promptly remove everything in our institutions which operates as an incentive to it. Persevere in the present administration of the Poor Laws, and the whole of the agricultural population will, in a few years, be converted into criminals. What else can you look for, when you shall have completely succeeded in obliterating from

[*Thomas Gray, "The Bard," in *Works*, ed. Thomas James Mathias, 2 vols. (London: Porter, 1814), Vol. I, p. 27 (II, 1).]

*From an admirable article on Police, by Mr. Chadwick, printed in 1829, in a periodical (*The London Review*) which only reached a second number. [Edwin Chadwick, "Preventive Police," *London Review*, I (1829), 252–308; the passage is quoted from p. 260. The words in square brackets are Mill's.] We much wish to see this paper reprinted in a separate form.

the minds of the agricultural labourers, all traces of any line of demarcation between what is theirs, and what is other people's; and persuaded them that they have a right to whatever their wants require—they being the best judges of their own wants? Whether crime have increased or not, the administration of the Poor Laws is a grand source of future increase which must be removed. Another, is the inadequacy of our police-arrangements; which have not kept pace with the growth of wealth and population, but afford less protection to property than any police-system in Europe, and that too in the country where there is most to protect. What wonder, again, if crime should be found to increase, when, after gradually ceasing to inflict, we have at last ceased even to threaten, capital punishment, except for a few of the most odious offences; while, by the admission of every competent witness, from Lord Liverpool formerly to Earl Grey now,[*] we have no secondary punishments but what are almost worse than none at all. Lord Liverpool admitted the evil and let it alone; perhaps feeling as Louis XV did, when he talked of the fine things he would do if he were Minister. An English Minister seldom considers himself as Minister for the purpose of doing any useful thing which he is not obliged to do. Something better might have been hoped from the present Ministers; but they are (we say it without presumption) too ignorant; they have neither read enough, nor reflected enough. The most accomplished man among them, without question, is Lord Brougham; and is it not truly deplorable, after all that has been given in evidence, and argued, and written on the subject, to find Lord Brougham still advocating the maintenance of transportation as a punishment, and Lord Denman supporting him?[†] Both these law-lords pledge their professional experience that transportation *is* dreaded. Yes; but by whom? Transportation is like death: a terrible punishment to the innocent, a most severe one even to the *almost* innocent; but to the criminal by profession, an object of almost entire disregard.

If the Lord Chancellor will not read Mr. Bentham, or Archbishop Whately, or any of the philosophical writers on the theory of punishment, he can surely find time to read a work of less pretensions, Mr. Wakefield's *Letter from Jack Ketch to Mr. Justice Alderson*, a pamphlet which may be purchased for threepence of Mr. Effingham Wilson, and which all who have threepence to spare ought to read.[‡]

[*See Robert Banks Jenkinson, Speech on Criminal Law (18 July, 1820), *PD*, n.s., Vol. 2, col. 526; and Charles Grey, "Secondary Punishments—Transportation," *Edinburgh Review*, LVIII (Jan., 1834), 336–62.]

[†Henry Brougham and Thomas Denman, Speeches on Prison Discipline (20 June, 1834), *PD*, 3rd ser., Vol. 24, cols. 623–4 and 630–1.]

[‡Jeremy Bentham, *The Rationale of Punishment* (London: Heward, 1830); Richard Whately, *Thoughts on Secondary Punishments in a Letter to Earl Grey* (London: Fellowes, 1832); and Edward Gibbon Wakefield, *The Hangman and the Judge; or, A Letter from Jack Ketch to Mr. Justice Alderson* (London: Wilson, 1833).]

Debate on the Universities Admission Bill[*]

It is not a favourable symptom of the state of the public mind, when a great noise is made about little things. What is it that the Dissenters want? Is it education? or is it that their sons should herd with lords' sons? If the former, they ought to know, and by taking the proper means they may know, that Cambridge and Oxford are among the last places where any person wishing for education, and knowing what it is, would go to seek it. No one goes to Cambridge or Oxford for the education he expects to find there. The sons of the aristocracy go because their fathers went, and because it is gentlemanly to have been there. Those who are to be clergymen go, because it is very difficult otherwise to get into orders. Those who are to be barristers go, because they save two years of their apprenticeship by it, and because a fellowship is a considerable help at the outset of their career. No one else goes at all.

One of the most important objects, certainly, with which Parliament or a Ministry could occupy itself, would be to make the Universities really places of education; to clean out those sinks of the narrowest and most grovelling Church-of-Englandism, and convert them into reservoirs of sound learning and genuine spiritual culture. But is this what the Dissenters are striving for? Nothing of the sort. The place remaining as it is, all they solicit is, permission to subject their children to its pernicious influences.

Unless we would become a nation of mere tradesmen, endowed institutions of education must exist. There must be places where the teachers can afford to teach other things than those which parents (who in nine cases out of ten, think only of qualifying their children to *get on* in life) spontaneously call for. There must be places where those kinds of knowledge and culture, which have no obvious tendency to better the fortunes of the possessor, but solely to enlarge and exalt his moral and intellectual nature, shall be, as Dr. Chalmers expresses it, *obtruded* upon the public.[†] And these places must be so constituted, that they shall be looked up to by the public; that parents who are too narrow-minded to see of themselves what is good, shall believe it to be good because it is there taught. In order that benefits which we estimate so highly may not be lost; in order that the means may still be preserved of maintaining places of education, which shall not be the subservient slaves of the opinions and desires of the vulgar—we would have those means rescued from the hands of men who render the very idea of resisting the spirit of the age at once odious and contemptible—men who differ from their

---

[*"A Bill to Remove Certain Disabilities Which Prevent Some Classes of His Majesty's Subjects from Resorting to the Universities of England, and Proceeding to Degrees Therein," 4 William IV (21 Apr., 1834), *PP*, 1834, IV, 515-17 (not enacted).]

[†Thomas Chalmers, *Considerations on the System of Parochial Schools in Scotland* (Glasgow: Hedderwick, 1819), p. 6.]

age chiefly by wanting its good points; who combine the worldly spirit of the present times with the indolence of monks, and the bigotry and sectarianism of two centuries ago. The first scholar in Great Britain, and the only clergyman of the Church of England who has acquired a European reputation, has just been ejected from his lectureship in the most liberal college of the most liberal of the two Universities, for asserting in a printed pamphlet, that the University does not give religious education;[*] an assertion which every member of the University knows to be true. And Dissenters would send their sons to be educated by these men! Rather, if their sons had been already there, they ought to have indignantly withdrawn them.

But the degrees of the Universities are of importance for professional purposes. Be it so: there, then, lies the evil; there apply your remedy. Abolish the monopoly of the Universities. Until public opinion shall have ripened for a reform in the places themselves, the law which should be enacted by Parliament is not one for admitting Dissenters to degrees, but one for rendering degrees no longer necessary for the enjoyment of any civil privileges. The title for exercising a profession should be a good education, wheresoever acquired: not the fact of having been educated at a certain place, least of all at a bad place. The certificates of Oxford and Cambridge should pass current only at their intrinsic value; and those of every other place of education should do the same.

In the debate last night, Mr. Ewart, of Liverpool, an active and valuable Member of Parliament, had the courage to say that the education of our higher ranks is below that of some other countries.[†] This notorious truth having excited a murmur, Mr. Ewart defended himself by the instance of Germany, and by rather an unfortunate one, that of the United States. We have always understood that in America there is still less of sound literary and philosophical instruction than even here, and that the superiority of that country consists in the superior education of the poorer classes, not of the richer. Mr. Ewart might have said "Germany and France."

If Mr. Ewart exhibited one kind of courage, two members for Universities exhibited another kind. Mr. Estcourt held up Oxford and Cambridge as the two great causes of the prevalence of Christianity in this kingdom. "He would say, Do not disturb us; allow us to go on as we have done, launching into the world young men perfectly capable of carrying that religion into every relation of life."[‡] Mr. Goulburn adjured every parent, who had sent his son to a University, to "reflect

---

[*Connop Thirlwall; see his *A Letter to Thomas Turton on the Admission of Dissenters to Academical Degrees* (Cambridge: Deighton, 1834).]

[†William Ewart, Speech on Admission of the Dissenters to the Universities (20 June, 1834), *PD*, 3rd ser., Vol. 24, cols. 651–3.]

[‡Thomas Grimston Bucknall Estcourt, Speech on Admission of the Dissenters to the Universities (20 June, 1834), *ibid*., cols. 632–40; in *Morning Chronicle*, 21 June, 1834, p. 2.]

what he [the son] might have been, had not his passions been subdued by daily and regular devotion."[*] This is rather a bold offer to let the tree be judged by its fruits. Will Mr. Estcourt's and Mr. Goulburn's constituents bear out their representatives in this challenge? Will *they* allow judgment to pass upon the Universities according to the practical regard paid by the majority of the pupils to Christianity, considered as enjoining them to subdue what Mr. Goulburn is complimentary enough to call their "passions?" *Solvuntur risu tabulæ.*[†] We admit that those venerable places succeed in inspiring the young men with highly friendly feelings towards religion, in common with the other institutions of the State, and a very proper respect for the Deity, as one of the constituted authorities.

* * * * *

4th July

The Chancellor's Declaration against the Taxes on Political Information

A good aim (how often it has been remarked) is seldom lost; if the good object aimed at be not furthered, some other of perhaps equal value is so. Mr. O'Connell's motion for the reform of the law of libel[‡] will be the destruction of the taxes on knowledge.[§] That question, after being discussed and apparently lost for the session, was referred to the Committee on the Law of Libel. Lord Brougham attended that Committee as a witness, and said and unsaid all manner of liberal and ultra-liberal things on the libel question; but when interrogated as to the taxes on newspapers and political tracts, he delivered a firm, steady, and well-reasoned opinion in condemnation of them.[¶] Last night he repeated this opinion in the House of Lords, and intimated his intention of bringing the subject before Parliament.[‖] There is little doubt that these taxes will be taken off at the beginning of the next session; for this is one of the subjects on which there is reason

---

[*Henry Goulburn, Speech on Admission of the Dissenters to the Universities (20 June, 1834), *PD*, 3rd ser., Vol. 24, cols. 670–82; in *Morning Chronicle*, 21 June, 1834, p. 3.]

[†Horace, *Satires*, in *Satires, Epistles, and Ars poetica* (Latin and English), trans. H. Rushton Fairclough (London: Heinemann; New York: Putnam's Sons, 1926), p. 132 (II, i, 86).]

[‡See O'Connell, Speech in Introducing a Bill on Libel Law (18 Feb., 1834), *PD*, 3rd ser., Vol. 21, cols. 468–78.]

[§See 10 Anne, c. 19 (1711).]

[¶For Henry Brougham's testimony, see "Report from the Select Committee of the House of Lords Appointed to Consider the Law of Defamation and Libel," *PP*, 1843, V, App. A, 277–96, esp. 282–6; the Committee of 1834 met and took evidence, but did not issue a report. Mill is presumably basing his remarks on the summary that appeared in the *Spectator*, 5 July, 1834, p. 633 (reprinted in *The Times*, 7 July, 1834, p. 6).]

[‖Henry Brougham, Speech in Introducing a Petition on Stamp Duties (3 July, 1834), in *Morning Chronicle*, 4 July, 1834, p. 2.]

to believe the Chancellor to be really in earnest; and we see that he now considers the time to be come for carrying his opinion into effect.

There will now, therefore, be vastly greater facilities than were ever before known for the diffusion of important truth among the people, and also of mischievous error. But up to this time error has had the field to itself. Truth will now, for the first time, have its natural chances of superiority. In the immensely increased number of readers which will be the effect of the cheapness of newspapers and political tracts, any writers of talent may hope, whatever be their sentiments, to find the quantity of support necessary for a moderate degree of success, without prostituting themselves to the hired advocacy of the opinions in vogue.

* * * * *

5th July

The Irish Tithe Bill[*]

This will not do. Sir Robert Peel last night uttered a sentiment which is the bitterest censure upon many of the acts of the present Ministry: "Of all the vulgar arts of government to which a Ministry can resort, the solving of political difficulties by putting their hands into the public purse is the most vulgar."[†] That is the art by which the Ministry are attempting to solve the difficulty of Irish tithe.

For centuries the English oligarchy have billetted their own priesthood upon a hostile nation, until that nation positively will not bear the insult and injury one hour longer. No appeal to reason, justice, or even the fear of ultimate consequences, has been hearkened to. The Irish have, therefore, taken the only means which were left them; they refuse to pay. The English oligarchy, Whig and Tory, through their organ Lord Grey,[‡] and through all their other organs, proclaim that this is all the fault of agitators; that the Irish would have gone on paying the hostile priesthood for ever, if it had not been for O'Connell; and that O'Connell is a demon, for having, on their own showing, accomplished what no person recorded in history ever did without being reputed by posterity a hero. After having thus exhaled unavailing resentment against O'Connell, the Ministry proceed to give up to him the object he contends for. The tithe is no longer to be appropriated exclusively to the use of the un-Irish Church. But it is not convenient to make up their minds this year, to what purpose it shall be appropriated. For the sake of six months' ease to Ministers, two-fifths of the tithe are to be flung away. If the landlords will only be so good as to collect it for us, they may keep forty per cent.,

[*See p. 168 above.]
[†Robert Peel, Speech on Church Temporalities and Tithes (4 July, 1834), in *Morning Chronicle*, 5 July, 1834, p. 3.]
[‡See Charles Grey, Speech on Suppression of Disturbances (Ireland) (4 July, 1834), *PD*, 3rd ser., Vol. 24, cols. 1127–30.]

and we will only ask them for the remaining sixty. This is rather a large discount to give for present payment.

Why so eager to save all we can this year, as if next year the whole would have evaporated, or fallen into the sea? The entire produce of the land will be there next year as well as this year, and may be laid hold of by taxation then as well as now, for any purpose to which the sentiments of the people are not violently opposed. If the new appropriation meditated for next year be of a kind not obnoxious to the people, the whole tithe will be as readily paid by them as three-fifths of it. If the contrary be the case, it will be as impossible to levy three-fifths, or even one-fifth, as the whole. It is not to the tithe, as tithe, that the Irish people object, but to the payment of it to a hostile priesthood. Let that cease, and you may secure the whole fund with ease. Let that continue, even one year longer, and you will never, during the currency of existing leases, realize another farthing. In any sense it is absurd, permanently, and under the pledge of the national faith, to abandon to the landlords two-fifths of what they will gain in their rents, on the expiration of the present leases, by the abolition of tithe. What harm if no tithe at all is paid this year? Wait till the next. To support the incumbents for one year, there will be no difficulty in raising a sum by loan on the security of the future fund.

* * * * *

18th July

The Ministerial Changes

The ministry has lost its chief, and is about to go on with little other alteration. The change, however, is not a trifling one. The occasion seems insignificant, compared with the magnitude of the result; but so seemed the division on the Civil List, which turned out the Wellington Ministry.[*] In both cases, what seemed the cause was but the pebble in the road, which shook to pieces the already crazy vehicle.

Lord Grey could not long remain Minister after the Reform Bill. He was the man to carry through a Reform Bill, not the man to execute it. We say this not in disparagement, but, on the contrary, with the most unfeigned respect. Lord Grey is a far braver man, a loftier man, a man of greater dignity of character, with more of the heroic in his composition, than any member of what is now the Ministry, or than all of them put together. But he is of the old school; they are willing to be of the new. Lord Grey has principles, they are men of shifts and circumstances; but his principles are unfit for these times, and he cannot change them. He is the very man he was in 1789. Age has neither corrupted him nor brought him wisdom.

When Lord Grey, in early youth, adopted Reform principles, the people of England were mostly satisfied with the main features of their institutions, and

[*See *ibid.*, Vol. 1, cols. 429–71 (12 Nov., 1830), and cols. 525–56 (15 Nov., 1830).]

complained only of extravagant expenditure and a few superficial abuses. If Reform had been carried at that time, these would have been remedied, and the social machine generally would have remained untouched. The people would not have had their eyes opened to the great and rapidly-increasing vices of their social polity in general. Government would have been cheap and bad, and so it would have remained until the mere progress of philosophy, unaided by any previous alienation of the people from the ruling classes, had convinced them of its defects. This might have required centuries. Times are altered now; but Lord Grey is still of the same mind. He still sees no evils in our social condition, but those which the people then saw; and if he had his way, Reform would now lead to no consequences but those to which it would then have led. But fifty years of public discontent, though they have made no changes in Lord Grey's opinions, have made a wonderful revolution in those of mankind. The people are now possessed with an opinion that their institutions, *en masse*, are in many respects bad, and a cause of evil to them. Lord Grey partly perceives and recognises as a fact, the prevalence of this new opinion, but without any perception of its justice; and his object—his conscientious object—is to prevent the new opinion from having its way; to stem the current which has set in towards change. A man who thus resists the just and necessary tendencies of his times is not fit to be Minister. It may be very fit that those tendencies should be moderated, but by their friends, not by their enemies.

Lord Grey has recently, in a most forcible manner, expressed his sense of the folly of those who resist "the spirit of the age;"[*] nor would he have opposed any obstinate or rash resistance to that spirit; but being at heart its foe, he would have done his utmost to discountenance it, and would have embroiled himself with it in his own despite; as this very affair of the Irish Coercion Bill, which has broken up the Ministry, exemplifies.

It was believed, even before the late disclosures, that the renewal of the Coercion Bill had been forced upon the other Members of the Cabinet by Lord Grey. It is well known that to Lord Grey are to be attributed all the foolish ebullitions of the Ministry, in King's Speeches[†] and otherwise, against Mr. O'Connell. This could not but be. Irish agitation and Mr. O'Connell, *must* appear in a quite other light to Lord Grey than to Reformers of a less antiquated school. To others they may seem the exceptionable, and even dangerous, but most efficacious, instruments of the accomplishment of a great public good: to him they cannot but appear as noxious influences, which, by bringing a country to the verge of anarchy, force upon Parliament the adoption of measures, which, although justifiably conceded to necessity, are in themselves wholly to be deprecated. Let Mr. O'Connell be what he will, to us he is the enemy of evil, to Lord Grey he is the

---

[*Charles Grey, speech of 6 June, 1834, *ibid.*, Vol. 24, col. 259; in *Morning Chronicle*, 7 June, 1834, p. 2 (see pp. 62 and 250 above).]

[†See pp. 153 and 168–70 above.]

enemy of good. Lord Grey therefore regards him with aversion, and would pass Coercion Bills to restrain his operations. The other Ministers perhaps think no better of the man, but they probably think quite as much good as evil of the effects of his influence.

In losing Lord Grey the Cabinet has lost the greater part of such weight of personal reputation as it possessed; it will now have little strength, save that which it may derive from its measures. We fear it has lost most of its real strength of character also; it will now be a mere straw on the surface of the waters; it will drift forward with the current, or backward with the eddy; it will be more afraid of the people, but also more afraid of the Peers. In Lord Grey, what seemed fear of the Peers was, we believe sincerely, fear *for* the Peers; he could not bear that their obstinacy should ruin them; he threw himself between them and the people, and spared them the shock of a conflict with public opinion, by bearing the brunt of it himself. The present Ministers will do nothing of this sort. Truckle to the Lords they may, if the people will let them; but (except Lord Lansdowne and perhaps one other at most) we doubt if there is a man among them who, if he thought circumstances required it, would not turn the whole order out of doors without a pang.

The people, therefore, have their cause in their own hands. Let them make it less trouble to quarrel with the Lords than with them, and their object, whatever it be, will quite surely be gained.

* * * * *

23rd July

Lord Brougham's Speech on the Poor Law Amendment Bill[*]

We have never studied to direct the reader's attention to the infirmities of individuals; and we are least of all inclined to dwell upon those of the Lord Chancellor; because, with many weaknesses, and even some littlenesses, we believe him to have higher and better aspirations, and a more genuine sympathy with mankind, than any other man in power, or who has held power in England for many years. We shall therefore, of all his recent exhibitions in the House of Lords (by which he little knows how grievously he has lost ground in public estimation,) confine ourselves to the most recent, that on the Poor Law Bill; and to this we shall advert solely for the purpose of disconnecting that Bill from the speculative opinions in disapprobation of Poor Laws in general, with which Lord Brougham, on his own showing most unneccessarily, and as we conceive most mischievously, thought proper to encumber it. As might have been expected, the advantage thus

[*Henry Brougham, Speech on Poor Laws' Amendment (21 July, 1834), *PD*, 3rd ser., Vol. 25, cols. 211–51.]

given has been eagerly seized by the enemies of the Bill. *The Times* exclaims, that the truth has come out at last, and that the real object of the Poor Law reformers is now visible.[*] Whether *The Times* asserts this factiously or ignorantly, it is probable that many, who have no opportunity of being better informed, will share the impression.

Now, if there be any thing which may be predicated with certainty of the Poor Law Bill it is this, that if carried into effect in the spirit in which it is conceived, it will leave no excuse whatever for attempting to abolish Poor Laws. It affords the means by which society may guarantee a subsistence to every one of its members, without producing any of the fatal consequences to their industry and prudence, which though arising only from the manner in which the law has been administered, have been erroneously supposed to be inseparable from its principle.

We hold a public provision for the poor to be an indispensable part of the institutions of every civilized country. To put the least dignified consideration first, it is necessary even as part of a system of police; for where such a provision does not exist, there must be unbounded toleration of mendicity, the very worst species of pauperism next to that which now exists in the southern counties of England. Besides, it is impossible to refuse to an innocent person in want, that subsistence which you will be obliged to afford to him as soon as he becomes a criminal. Let mere poverty be attended with consequences equal to the most terrible of your punishments, and the chances of crime will be preferred to the certainty of starvation.—Secondly, Poor Laws are necessary on still higher grounds of public policy; as the only means by which an alliance can be established between the pecuniary interest of the rich and the comfort and independence of the poor.—Lastly, Poor Laws are required by the plainest dictates of justice; since it is monstrous that human creatures, who exercised no choice in being born, should be starved for the fault of their progenitors. There is food enough on the earth for all who are alive, and society has motives, short of capital punishment, by which it can enforce, when enforce it must, any necessary restraint upon the increase of the numbers of mankind.

The anti-poor-law doctrine is now almost universally exploded among political economists, though political economy still continues to be most unjustly burthened with the discredit of it, and though Lord Brougham doubtless thought he proved himself a master in the science by professing one of its discarded errors. Of the prudence of perking in the faces of mankind opinions abhorrent to them, on an occasion when those opinions were perfectly irrelevant, we say nothing, as we think with *The Chronicle*, that statesmen are not to be very severely reproached for sincerity;[†] and we are well pleased to find that Lord Brougham, after so many years of public life, has at last, for once, lain under that reproach.

[*Leading Article on the Poor Law Bill, *The Times*, 23 July, 1834, p. 4.]
[†Leading Article on Lord Brougham and Poor Laws, *Morning Chronicle*, 25 July, 1834, pp. 2–3.]

The Rich and the Poor

A certain Major Pitman, a magistrate of the county of Devon, having been convicted before a bench of magistrates in Petty Sessions, of a series of most brutal assaults, committed, with scarcely any provocation, upon his maid-servant,[*] accompanied with the grossest and most disgusting abuse, and continued through two days; the following was the decision of the Bench:

From the very difficult situation in which we are placed with a brother magistrate, we could have wished that we had not had the case to decide. The Court, however, is unanimously of opinion that *this case is not of sufficient importance to be sent to the Sessions; they do consider the assault proved*, and do adjudicate the full penalty of *five pounds* to be paid by the defendant.[†]

Assuredly all persons in England, of whatever sex or age, who happen to be weak of body, have abundant reason to be grateful for the mildness and humanity of modern manners; for it is now proclaimed to the world that any person of property and station, who is sufficiently a brute in his own nature, and is not ashamed of being considered so by others, may beat and kick his female servants to any pitch, short of danger to life or limb, and may insult them with any degree of contumely, without incurring from the justice of his country the slightest inconvenience. Suppose that this girl had a brother, or a lover, who had resented the injury to her, let us say only by knocking down the wretch who committed it; was there a man on that Bench who would not have thought him most leniently dealt with by being sent for only a month to the tread-mill? And these dastardly creatures would be the foremost, probably, to inveigh against the insubordination and against the immorality of the poor. Why, if the English people, being a brave people, were not also a most obedient, peaceable, and moral people, these men would not have dared show themselves in the streets without an escort of soldiers after delivering such a judgment.

The *Chronicle* says it cannot doubt that the matter will be investigated, and that if the facts stated are correct, Major Pitman will be dismissed from the magistracy.[‡] Alas! no. Who ever heard of a magistrate dismissed for oppressing the poor, or tyrannizing over the weak? It is not for such trifles, that Chancellors and Home Secretaries will be uncivil to a gentlemanly man. If Major Pitman had even done any thing *really* ungentlemanly; if he had refused to pay a gaming debt, or shown the white feather in an affair of honour; even then, though a minister might cut him, no minister would think of turning him out of the Commission of the Peace. He would retain the power of imprisoning and transporting his fellow creatures until he happened to be hanged or transported himself.

But these things will not last much longer. Every such occurrence is but another

[*Mary Stamp.]
[†"An Old Tory Magistrate an Oppressor of the Poor," *Morning Chronicle*, 23 July, 1834, p. 4.]
[‡Leading Article on the Case of Major Pitman, *ibid.*, 24 July, 1834, p. 4.]

kick to the ball which is rushing down hill with perpetually increasing velocity. The magistracy of England, with the rest of our aristocratic institutions, will, in a few years, have ceased to be.

* * * * *

27th July

Flogging in the Army

The late disgusting exhibition at Charing Cross Barracks has excited a feeling in the public, which has compelled the Secretary of War to promise that a commission shall be issued to revise the whole of our military system. In the speech in which he made this announcement, Mr. Ellice declared that since public opinion has so greatly restricted the punishment of flogging, military discipline has greatly relaxed; that acts of insubordination have become much more frequent than before, and that in the last year one-fifth of the whole army have been subjected to charges of different kinds.[*] *The Examiner* hints that there has been another cause of the relaxation of discipline; that a spirit of hatred between the soldiers and the people has been sedulously cultivated by their officers:

We suspect that the truculent spirit boastfully manifested by the officers towards the people has had some effect on the actions of the men. Military outrages against the people have been looked upon by the officers with an indulgent eye, and hence, doubtless, an increase of such offences; and misconduct in one direction begets misconduct in another, and the solider who has spurned the civil law, under a superior provoking the transgression which he seems to chide, soon ventures to trespass also against the military law. We could mention cases in which there has been mixed a violation of military and civil law, and in which the wrong against the people seems to have redeemed, in the eyes of the military judges, the infraction of military rule, for the punishment allotted in consideration of both offences has been far short of what it would in all probability have been had the military offence been unmingled with the other. We have put a question thus to military men: What would be the punishment of a party drunk on their march, who used their troop-horses for the sport of women picked up on the road side?—And the sentence supposed in the answer has far exceeded the punishment which was actually awarded in such a case—with this (excusing) addition, that the sword was drawn upon people who manifested their disgust at the most indecent and brutal conduct. The remark which will not want examples in various quarters in this—that offences against the discipline of the army, which would be severely punished if solely offences against discipline, are more leniently dealt with if mixed up with offences against the laws of the land. The people of the lower part of Westminster will bear testimony to the truth of this observation. But there is not only an indulgence for military riot at the expense of the public peace, but a direct defiance of the civil law is occasionally taught to the soldiery; thus a commanding officer lately ordered the barrack-gates to be closed against a constable with a warrant for the apprehension of one of the privates. Whatever insubordination there now is in the army, is the natural effect of the spirit and

[*Edward Ellice, Speech on Military Flogging (21 July, 1834), *PD*, 3rd ser., Vol. 25, cols. 279-83, esp. 281-2.]

countenance of its officers since the agitation of the Reform Bill. The license of the soldiery has extended, as license always will do, beyond the intention of those who were pleased to relax discipline for a particular object.[*]

We fear there is much truth in these remarks. But we conceive that the root of the matter lies still deeper. It is a vice inherent in an army or a navy exclusively officered by gentlemen, that the soldiers and sailors must be treated like brutes. If indeed the commanding officer be a man to whom those under him can look up with reverence, that reverence renders his mere displeasure so severe a punishment, that he is able to dispense with corporal torture. Nelson needed it not, nor Collingwood, nor Sir Alexander Ball; and never were ships' crews so admirably disciplined as theirs. Whether in a regiment, a ship, or a school, those only govern by torture who have not the virtue necessary for governing by personal influence. When the scourge is needed, it is always the fault and often the crime of the superior. But from almost all superiors, faults, and from many, crimes, are to be expected. No army or navy is officered with Nelsons and Collingwoods. These were rare men. The discipline of an army or navy cannot be left dependent upon the qualities of individual men; it must be provided for by the general system of military and naval rewards and punishments.

Now rewards, in the English army, there are none; for no soldier can rise beyond the rank of a sergeant. As for punishments, for the greater military offences only three are possible: 1st, The offender must be shot; or, 2dly, Flogged; or, 3dly, Dismissed from the service. Now this last, which in almost all other armies is a punishment of extreme severity, with us is a reward. The soldier is but too happy to get his discharge, and would commit offences purposely for a very slight chance of obtaining it. Until this is remedied, discipline in the army never can by possibility be kept up but by shooting or flogging. The men will be either shot, flogged, or undisciplined, until dismissal from the army shall be a punishment and not a privilege: and a privilege it will be until the pay of the common soldier be raised beyond what any taxes which the British people will pay afford the means of, or until, as in France or Prussia, every common soldier shall have the possibility before him of rising to be colonel of his regiment.

Now, as the people of England have neither the passion of equality which distinguishes the French, nor the passion of justice which has hitherto distinguished no nation, this most desirable result will only be brought about through the passion of humanity; which, by not allowing soldiers to be either shot or flogged, will compel recourse to the only means of government fit for rational beings; and will secure, at length, for that important portion of the people the privileges of men, by not tolerating that they should any longer be treated like brutes. We therefore rejoice from our souls that the public loathing at the practice of flogging is becoming too intense to be resisted, and we most earnestly hope that every word

[*"Military Misrule," *Examiner*, 27 July, 1834, p. 467.]

which fell from Mr. Ellice on the insubordination of the army is literally true. We trust that the army is, and will progressively become more and more undisciplined, until the time comes when from sheer necessity, on the failure of all other means of keeping the soldiers in subjection, the oligarchy must perforce loose their hold of what will be the last and most cherished of their monopolies. They will part with it as with their life's blood, but ere many years shall have passed over their heads, they may rely upon it, it will be theirs no longer.

* * * * *

NO. VII, SEPT., 1834

2nd August

Lord Melbourne's Reason for His Religion

In the debate of last night on the admission of Dissenters to the Universities, Lord Melbourne took the trouble of stating to the assembly of which he is an hereditary member, that he is an adherent of the Church of England.[*] We could have guessed as much of any Prime Minister, without his assurances: who expects him to profess any thing else while it is yet only the eleventh hour, and one entire revolution of the minute-hand is yet wanting to the final doom? However, it has for some years past been customary for Prime Ministers to take occasional opportunities of protesting that their devotion, their reverence, their respect, their fidelity, &c., (we are not masters of the whole vocabulary,) continue unimpaired towards that venerable establishment, &c., to which, under God, &c., pure form of Christianity, &c., bulwark of the Constitution, &c., barrier against sectarianism, &c., and infidelity, &c.; in all which they are probably as sincere as in any other of their speculative opinions; and as much so as they are capable of being, in any creed, or world-theory, or abstract principle. In spite of which, what, philosophically considered, do all these assurances, so perpetually repeated, mean, except that by the reckoning of him who keeps the ship's log, it still wants some minutes to the dreaded hour?

Lord Melbourne, however, did not merely say that he was an adherent of the Church of England: he even said why. In the first place, he did not pretend to understand all the doctrines of the Church of England, but so far as he did understand them he thought them true. This, however, was not all:

> He would say further, though he was well aware that he should expose himself to the censure of some persons by making the declaration—he would say further, that he was attached to the Church of England, and would support it to the best of his power, because it was the religion of his forefathers, and because it was the religion of his country.—(Loud cheers from the Opposition benches.)

[*William Lamb, Speech on Admission of Dissenters to the Universities (1 Aug., 1834), in *Morning Chronicle*, 2 Aug., 1834, p. 2.]

We consider this declaration as quite invaluable. It is a *naïve* statement of what an average English gentleman really feels. They believe in their religion, not as any thing involving truth or falsehood, or in which their own eternal welfare, or that of mankind, are concerned; but as part of the duty they owe to their country, as English gentlemen, to uphold what they find in existence. That the sentiment found a ready echo in aristocratic breasts, was testified, not only by the "loud cheers" already alluded to, but by the speech of the succeeding orator, Lord Caernarvon, (better known as Lord Porchester the poet,) who expressed his warm approbation of the reason which the noble lord had given for being of the Church of England, and his regret that a sentiment in every respect so worthy of that (the Tory) side of the house, should not have been delivered from it.[*]

What a reason for being of a religion! It was the religion of his forefathers, meaning his father and grandmother, (omitting the forty generations of Catholics, and the forty times forty of pagans;) and it was the religion of his country, meaning about half, or less than half of the people of his country. Are these such reasons as any one would assign for believing any thing which he cared about the truth of? Would he believe in geometry because it was the geometry of his forefathers, or in history because it was the history of his country? If a religion were to be believed because of its truth, who would ground his belief of it upon a consideration which militates so much more strongly in favour of Brahma or of Fo? But when belief is made a matter of family affection, or social obligation, the case is altered. Then, as the Englishman or the Chinese are required by patriotism to serve different countries, so they may be bound by religion to worship different gods. Lord Melbourne's religion is an affair between him and his family, or between him and his country, nowise between him and his God; the Deity alone not being a party concerned in the religious belief or observances of his creatures. But this is a genuine representation of the feeling really entertained. In an ordinary conservative gentleman's scheme of religion, the part assigned to the Deity is by no means a dignified one. He is to be believed in, for his existence is implied in several of the thirty-nine articles;[†] and such honours are to be paid him as the Church has been accustomed to render: but as for believing their religion because it comes from Him, that is out of the question in their case: as the "religion by law established,"[‡] it comes to them, with the rest of their social obligations, from Parliament; though doubtless they would admit that it comes from God too. But the truth is, that to them God comes from it.

Lord Althorp and the Beer Bill

To their indelible disgrace, the Ministry have adopted Sir Edward Knatchbull's

[*Henry John George Herbert, Speech on Admission to the Universities (1 Aug., 1834), *PD*, 3rd ser., Vol. 25, cols. 845–6.]
[†See *The Book of Common Prayer*.]
[‡See, e.g., 5 & 6 Anne, c. 5, "An Act for Securing the Church of England as by Law Established" (1706).]

Beer Bill as a Government measure; and this act of real insult and injury to the industrious poor will pass into the statute-book under their auspices,* as a companion to the Poor Law Bill, and an index, as too many will be apt to think, to the real *animus* of this last.

We have so often, in these Notes, exposed the pretences of the beer-house suppressors, that we return to the subject only to notice, in a speech of Lord Althorp, an observation of almost miraculous shallowness. The bill, it seems, gives an appeal to the Quarter-Sessions against the decisions of individual magistrates: and this not being deemed by some persons a sufficient remedy, Lord Althorp declared that he "looked upon an appeal in open Court to be as sure a protection to justice as trial by jury; at all events, in cases such as occurred under the present bill. The magistrates who tried appeal cases came from distant and various parts of the country, unfettered by previous pledges, and devoid of any local prejudices."[*] Very true; but sheepstealers also "come from different parts of the country," yet if we merely set one gang of them to watch another, it will fare but ill with the flock. As a chairman of Quarter-Sessions, Lord Althorp ought to have known better what his brother justices are made of. What if they be "devoid of *local* prejudices?" Are they not all magistrates, and country gentlemen? and among what class, not excepting even the clergy, exists there so intense an *esprit de corps* as among these? "Ask my brother if I am a thief," says the proverb; but Lord Althorp would think the brother an unexceptionable referee if he were only a *half*-brother. Of what avail has been the power of appeal to the Quarter-Sessions against the stopping up of paths? Even between man and man there is notoriously not a tribunal in the country, exposed to the public eye, where grosser injustice is constantly committed than at the Quarter-Sessions. There are exceptions, where a man of weight in the country, who happens to be laborious, and a lover of impartial justice, fills the chair. But these are exceptions. The contrary is the general rule.

* * * * *

9th August

Major Pitman's Dismissal

In our comments on this discreditable case in last month's Notes, we expressed our persuasion that the Ministry would not remove Major Pitman from the Commission of the Peace.[†] It is, therefore, doubly incumbent upon us to make our acknowledgments on behalf of the public, to the Lord Chancellor, for an act of

---

*It has since passed, [4 & 5 William IV, c. 85 (1834),] and stands with the Poor Law Bill, as the only notable legislative enactment of the session.

[*Spencer, Speech on the Beer-House Bill (1 Aug., 1834), in *Morning Chronicle*, 2 Aug., 1834, p. 3.]

[†See p. 267 above.]

justice which, obvious as it is, no former Chancellor would have thought it incumbent upon him to perform.

We cannot, however, bestow the merited commendation on this proceeding of Lord Brougham's, without at the same time remarking, that if justice has been done, it is no thanks (to use a familiar expression) to the *Morning Chronicle*. Our worthy cotemporary, who, though his paper has become a regular Ministerial organ, will always have our best wishes and our most perfect respect, inserted an article on the 5th of this month, which fully prepared us for a whitewashing of Major Pitman.[*] Though he might be a brute in his family, that did not, the *Chronicle* argued, prove him unfit for the bench; since he might be able to command his temper there, though not elsewhere. Yes, doubtless; and to read moral lectures from the bench on command of temper and pass sentence, most imperturbably upon poor and ragged people, for offences not grosser than his own, and infinitely more excusable. We are sure that the excellent editor of the *Chronicle* had no hand in this miserable sophistry. It was not in this spirit that he conceived those memorable articles, which made the country ring with the offences and follies of the country magistracy, and did more than has perhaps been done by any single individual to bring down the oligarchy of England.

* * * * *

10th August

The Government of Departments

There are facts occurring, we might say constantly occurring, which necessitate one to believe, not only that the Whig Ministry is altogether a government of departments,—that the collective will, or the collective understanding of the Cabinet, is hardly ever brought to bear upon anything,—that any single Minister commits the Ministry to the most important acts, without consulting with his colleagues,—but even more than this: we must believe that their ignorance of each other's proceedings is systematic and designed, and has for its object, that when one of them does an exceptionable thing, and the question is put to another, he may wash his hands of it. What a disclosure has just taken place in the affair of the *Brighton Guardian*!

The participation of Government, in that most censurable prosecution, by a previous engagement to pay its expenses, (a fact studiously withheld from the public when the affair was undergoing discussion in Parliament,)[†] was blurted out by Mr. Sergeant Doyley, at a meeting of the Sussex magistrates, on some day in

---

[*Leading Article on the Case of Major Pitman, *Morning Chronicle*, 5 Aug., 1834, p. 3.]
[†See *PD*, 3rd ser., Vol. 25, cols. 929–30 (4 Aug., 1834), cols. 993–4 (5 Aug.), and col. 1003 (6 Aug.).]

the week ending July 19th; for, on Sunday, the 20th, the *Examiner* founded upon the sergeant's statement, the following just and forcible remarks:

> In the course of the discussion, a fact transpired, most disgraceful to the Government. . . . Who can be safe, if the public purse may be secretly applied to attempts to crush him? The prosecutors in this case (their expenses being guaranteed) have nothing to lose; while the prosecuted party, supposing him to escape a verdict under the unjust libel law, may be ruined by the costs. We look upon this transaction as a conspiracy between certain gentlemen and the Home Office, for the ruin of Mr. Cohen. "If you will stand forward and prosecute, we will pay," was the disgraceful bargain of the Government. But the Minister for the Home Department did not choose, in his gentle mercies, to overwhelm the defendant by employing the Attorney-general. The employment of the Attorney-general is apt to recoil, and not always to overwhelm the party whose destruction is aimed at. Governments have suffered as much by Attornies-general as defendants; and, doubtless, Lord Melbourne remembered that the Grey Ministry, at its onset, had not overwhelmed Mr. Cobbett. There are more reasons than reasons of mercy for the forbearance of Government from prosecutions for libel; but it is for the interest of the public, that whatever Government does in prosecutions, it should do openly, and by responsible functionaries. There should be no underhand maintenance of prosecutions,—no secret subsidy for a war against the Press,—no encouragement of the vindictive feelings of individuals, by the promise to pay privately the price of their gratification. Such practices are most malignant and most dangerous; and it is the duty of the public to take care that the powers of its purse shall not have so vicious an application. Willing as we have been to think well of Lord Melbourne, it is with no common regret that we find so foul a blot in his administration of the Home Office.[*]

The public money was thus prostituted to support a proceeding, by which, as some newspaper has forcibly remarked, Mr. Cohen was tried for a libel on the magistrates, before a bench of magistrates, and a jury of magistrates. And it has since transpired, from a letter published by Sir Charles Blount, (who has retired from the magistracy, disgusted with this transaction,) that "the magistrates were all of opinion that no opportunity should be lost to suppress the *Guardian* newspaper."*

Now, here is an act of Government, of so much importance at least, not to say of so questionable a character, published to the world in the middle of July, by one of the parties concerned,[†] and made the subject of severe strictures by the Press immediately afterwards; and of this act, Lord Althorp, (by whose department it

---

[*"Public Money Applied to Private Prosecution," *Examiner*, 20 July, 1834, p. 452. Levy Emanuel Cohen was editor of the *Brighton Guardian*.]

*Sir Charles Blount adds, with honest indignation, "I will not trust myself to make any comment upon this hitherto hidden object. It at once dispels the cloud that has rendered the course pursued by the committee so indistinct and so unusual; it accounts for the rejection of Mr. Cohen's offered atonement, and well accords with that part of the sentence which imprisoned the defendant in a jail of a distant county, and far removed from the office of his paper." [Letter to the Editor of the *Sussex Advertiser* (30 July, 1834, in *The Times*, 7 Aug., 1834, p. 1).]

[†In the letter cited in the footnote immediately preceding.]

must have been sanctioned,) on August the 4th, the question being put to him by Mr. Hume, denied that he had any knowledge.[*] Mr. Francis Baring, the Secretary to the Treasury, added that, neither had *he* any knowledge of it; and Mr. Spring Rice volunteered his testimony, that he had been Secretary to the Treasury at the time of the prosecution, and that, to the best of his knowledge, no such act had taken place.[†] The very day after, Lord Althorp returned to the subject, admitted the fact, and justified it![‡]

Now, mark the singularity of these facts. An act of so much importance as a prosecution for libel, is authorized, and the public money drawn upon for the purpose, by the Home Minister, and of course through the Treasury. All the Sussex magistrates knew this; but two Cabinet Ministers, whose peculiar department is the expenditure of the public money, and one of them the organ of Government in the House of Commons, have never heard of it. A motion, in condemnation of the prosecution, is made and discussed in the House of Commons,[¶] and still these Ministers have never heard that the Government are concerned in it. But at length, when they must have heard of it,—when the other parties concerned have published the fact,—when it has been carried through all England by the newspapers, and made the subject of severe censures upon the Ministry by their political opponents for three whole weeks—not even curiosity prompts these singular specimens of rulers of the nation to step across Downing-street and ask their colleague whether the assertion is true. Is it possible not to believe that they voluntarily refrained from asking the question, in order that, when it was put to them, they might be unable to answer it? They *did*, however, answer it,—answered it with a virtual denial; which they were forced to change the next day into an admission and vindication.

As to the vindication, we shall leave the *Examiner* to deal with it:

In admitting the fact, Lord Althorp coolly observed, that the circumstance was not new, and that several instances were on record. No doubt; it would be difficult to strike out anything new in misgovernment or abuse of powers, after the long course of Tory sway; but we were promised, under the Reform Ministry, a renouncement of these old ways. If the present Ministers are to justify acts of oppression, simply by saying that the Tories did the same before them, we should like to know in what respect they are better than the Tories, in whose steps they follow; and why their government should be preferred? Mr. Warburton expressed his conviction that the noble lord would not, on principle, defend such a case.

[*Hume, Question on Criminal Prosecutions (4 Aug., 1834), *PD*, 3rd ser., Vol. 25, col. 929; Spencer, Statement on Criminal Prosecutions (4 Aug., 1834), *ibid.*]

[†Francis Thornhill Baring, and Spring-Rice, Statements on Criminal Prosecutions (4 Aug., 1834), *ibid.*]

[‡Spencer, Statement on Supply, &c. (5 Aug., 1834), *ibid.*, col. 993.]

[§See Isaac Newton Wigney, Speech in Introducing a Motion on the Case of the *Brighton Guardian* (4 Mar., 1834), *ibid.*, Vol. 21, cols. 1115–17; for the debate, see *ibid.*, cols. 1117–43.]

What matters it, if he pleads practice as a sufficient justification? The plain fact is, that the Home Office conspired with the Sussex magistrates to ruin Mr. Cohen.[*]

* * * * *

12th August

Defeat of the Irish Tithe Bill

The Lords have been most felicitous this year, in the occasions which they have chosen for opposing themselves to the opinion and will of the popular House. They have played into the hands of their enemies most dexterously, though not exactly in the manner which the Ministerial prints ascribe to them.

It would be very absurd to aim at the abolition of the House of Lords, merely because (as the phrase goes) it is bad in the abstract—because it is not such an institution as a wise man would establish if he were framing a constitution for a new country. We have it, and such are the inconveniences of constitutional changes, that if we could get on passably well with it we ought to keep it. But it is impossible, in an age of Movement, to get on with a legislative body which will never move except upon compulsion; and as we knew that this would be the case with the House of Lords, we, from the first, felt that they would render it necessary to thrust them aside. With this conviction, then, we know not what other or better political boon we could have prayed for, than that they should so steer their course as to make the most offensive display before the nation of the *animus* which actuates them, with the least possible retardation of important measures. We know not by what other means they could have contrived to accumulate so great a heap of obloquy on their own heads with so little harm to the country, as by throwing out the Jew Bill, the Universities' Admission Bill, and the Irish Tithe Bill.[†] The first two measures would not, if passed, have effected one atom of practical good, while, being rejected, they involve the House which rejected them in the whole odium of setting itself against civil equality and religious liberty; and the loss of the Universities' Bill, by so immense a majority, throws the whole of the vast and powerful Dissenting body into the arms of the popular party. The rejection of the Irish Tithe Bill is a positive good; but it has been rejected on grounds which place

---

[*Leading Article on the Prosecution of the *Brighton Guardian*, *Examiner*, 10 Aug., 1834, p. 505. The references are to Spencer's Statement on Supply on 5 Aug., cited above, and to Warburton, Speech on Supply, &c. (5 Aug., 1834), *PD*, 3rd ser., Vol. 25, cols. 993–4.]

[†"A Bill for the Relief of His Majesty's Subjects Professing the Jewish Religion" (*PP*, 1834, II, 587–8), defeated on 23 June, 1834; "A Bill to Remove Certain Disabilities Which Prevent Some Classes of His Majesty's Subjects from Resorting to the Universities" (*PP*, 1834, IV, 515–17), defeated on 1 Aug.; and "A Bill to Abolish Compositions for Tithes in Ireland" (*PP*, 1834, IV, 241–303), defeated on 11 Aug. See *PD*, 3rd ser., Vol. 24, cols. 720–31; Vol. 25, cols. 886–8; and *ibid.*, cols. 1204–7, respectively.]

the Lords in direct hostility to the great principle to which the Ministers have newly been forced to commit themselves; the alienability of ecclesiastical property.

We feel for the Irish clergy, whom this act of their pretended friends consigns to something like starvation. Most of them, however, are relations or hangers-on of the Aristocracy, and these must be supported by their families or their patrons. For the remainder, we trust that those who have doomed them to indigence are prepared to subscribe liberally. In every other point of view we rejoice that the Bill, which gave away for ever to a class of the most useless, selfish, and unfeeling drones in human shape who live and kill game on the surface of the earth, two-fifths of the collective estate of the Irish nation called Tithe, has met the fate it deserved.

This act of prodigality and folly will not, we trust, be repeated. The question will have altered its shape before the next session. Nobody, we should think, indulges the fond hope that a single shilling of tithe will ever again be collected in Ireland. Thus, on the one hand, the great problem of rooting out the Irish Church will be brought to a speedier solution, while, on the other, the tithe, being no longer paid to the Church, will fall into the hands of the landlords by the mere force of circumstances, without any interference of the legislature. The whole tithe being thus added to the rent, and the hands of Parliament not being tied, as they would have been if the Bill had passed, by a bargain with the landlord, Parliament may step in when it pleases, and impose upon the landlords at its pleasure, without their having any right to complain, a land-tax equal to the whole tithe.

* * * * *

15th August

The Chancellor's Doctrine of Appeals

It is a practice of Lord Brougham to bring in some Bill on an important subject at the very end of a session, whereby he goes off the stage with *éclat*, and retains the power of silently dropping the measure if it should not suit his convenience to proceed with it in the year following. There are some advantages, even of a public kind, in this mode of proceeding, and we by no means hold it up as in all cases to be condemned. The Bill which he laid on the table of the House, on the last day but one of the session, is laudable in its object, which is to supersede that mockery of the administration of justice, the appellate judicature of the House of Lords.[*] The Chancellor took great pains to impress upon their Lordships that the Bill does not interfere with their privileges; nor does it, any more than a King's privileges are interfered with, by the appointment, with his consent, of a Regent: but the measure

[*Henry Brougham, Speech on Appellate Jurisdiction (14 Aug., 1834), *ibid.*, cols. 1255–60; introducing "A Bill Intituled an Act to Alter and Amend the Appellate Jurisdiction of the House of Lords, and for Certain Other Purposes," 4 William IV (14 Aug., 1834), *House of Lords Sessional Papers*, 1834, [n.s.] I, Pt. 2, 1265–70 (not enacted).]

is simply to appoint another court of appeal, to whom the House shall hand over the causes as they arise, to be by them decided; and this is a pretty effectual supersession, though not an infringement of their judicial authority.

Lord Brougham's notions of appeal, however, which have always appeared to us to be very imperfect, have manifested themselves with all their imperfections in this Bill, and in the speech by which it was prefaced. He laid down two principles: one, that an appeal should never lie to one judge, but always to several; the other, that a judge of appeal should always be, at the very same time, acting as a judge in an inferior court. What should *he* be worth, he asked, as an appeal judge, were it not for the forensic *strepitus* in which he is constantly involved?

Now, both these principles we hold to be fundamentally and absolutely erroneous. We consider it to be of the first importance in all judicature, whether supreme or subordinate, that the judge should be *one*. It is a rule which holds true in all affairs, public or private, that what is one person's business is better done than what is the joint business of several. One judge relies only upon himself, several rely upon each other. One judge feels that the whole merit and the whole responsibility will lie with him; one of several knows that he had only his aliquot part, and "responsibility which is divided is destroyed."[*] When four judges are set to try one cause, (as in the Common Law Courts, and in Lord Brougham's proposed Court of Appeal,) the best that happens is, that one judge really decides, using the others as screens, and occasionally as drudges: while it too often happens that not even one of the four gives his whole mind to the subject; and, perhaps, from the carelessness in making appointments, which is likely to prevail in nominating not a judge but a fourth part of a judge, not one of the four has a mind which he *can* apply, with any prospect of advantage, to a difficult cause.

A good judicial establishment would consist only of local courts, and one great Court of Appeal, in the metropolis, composed of a sufficient number of the most experienced and skilful judges. Each judge should sit separately to hear causes, but when a point of law has to be settled, then, to secure uniformity of decision, all the judges of the Court of Appeal should sit together.

And then, touching the forensic *strepitus* which Lord Brougham thinks of so much importance;[†] is there any meaning in this loosest of all terms, and what is it? Surely not, that noise and bustle conduce to excellence, in the operation which, of all others performed by human beings, most demands that the mind be in a cool and collected state. If it be meant that, in the present state of English law, the judge cannot pick out the law applicable to the case without learned lawyers on both sides of the cause to suggest it to him, we grant it; but of such *strepitus* there will be as much, indeed more, in the highest court, the court of last resort, than in the inferior ones. What is wanted in a judge, besides knowledge of the law, is skill in

---

[*Cf. Jeremy Bentham, *Rationale of Judicial Evidence*, in *Works*, ed. Bowring, Vol. VI, pp. 556n, 557–8.]

[†See Henry Brougham, speech of 14 Aug., 1834, col. 1258.]

judging of evidence. As this skill can only be the result of experience, it is most important that a judge in the supreme tribunal should *have been* a judge in one of the courts below, but nowise that he should *be* so. If he be fit for the higher duty, it is a mere waste of capacity to set him to work in a narrower field, and under correction from a superior. The judges who can be trusted without a superior over them, are not so numerous that the nation can spare any part of their time for acting under other people.

We abstain from comment on the very unexpected eulogium, (as we think it must have been to those who were the objects of it) which Lord Brougham pronounced upon the House of Lords, as the amenders of the absurd legislation of the House of Commons.[*] We have not been observers of Henry Brougham for fifteen years, to learn *now*, that when once his lips are unsealed he never knows where to stop. When his cue was to assail the Lords, he could not restrain within the bounds of dignity his fatal facility of sarcastic language; this time, that they might not be alarmed at his meditated encroachment on their judicial functions, his cue was to cajole them, and neither in this, when he once began, could he stop short of the bounds of truth or of discretion. He is a slave to his own flux of words. His tongue governs him, not he his tongue.

* * * * *

16th August

The Prorogation

At length the session has closed, and closed with a most characteristic speech from the throne. Not a word was said in it of Ireland, or Church Reform, or the claims of the Dissenters, subjects on which even any allusion to the past, much more any suggestion concerning the future, might have been inconvenient. In lieu of such, the whole glories of the session were passed in review: and these did not require a long enumeration. Silence was observed on the subject of the Beer Bill. They had passed the Poor Law Bill; and—they had enlarged the jurisdiction of the Old Bailey![†] *Macte virtute, generose puer; sic itur ad astra.*[‡]

With a lurking consciousness, possibly, that the expiring session, with the exception of the Poor Law Bill, makes but a sorry figure in the way of legislative amendments, Ministers have drawn upon the session to come for anticipated renown, and have exhorted Parliament to apply itself to the consideration of "our jurisprudence," and "our municipal corporations."[§] If we may augur from this that Ministers will themselves do what they bid others do, and will meet

[**Ibid.*, cols. 1259-60.]

[†By 4 & 5 William IV, c. 36 (1834).]

[‡Virgil, *Aeneid*, in *Works*, trans. H. Rushton Fairclough, 2 vols. (London: Heinemann; New York: Putnam's Sons, 1916), Vol. II, p. 156 (IX, 641).]

[§William IV, Prorogation of Parliament (15 Aug., 1834), *PD*, 3rd ser., Vol. 25, col. 1268.]

Parliament next February with their minds made up, and their measures already matured, though it be only on those two subjects, we shall hail such a change in their practice as one of the most laudable symptoms they can evince of minds at length alive to the exigencies of the times, and to the serious nature of their duties. We trust that the proposed amendments in "our jurisprudence," will be not merely some trumpery consolidation of statutes, or mitigation of penalties, but that at least a bill for local courts, and local registration in all departments, will accompany the bill for a well organised local administration, which would be the fulfilment of the pledge for a reform of the municipal corporations.

THE CLOSE OF THE SESSION

1834

EDITOR'S NOTE

Monthly Repository, n.s. VIII (Sept., 1834), 605–9. Heading and running titles as title. Unsigned; not republished. Identified in Mill's bibliography as "An article headed 'The Close of the Session' in the Monthly Repository for Sept. 1834" (MacMinn, 42). There are no corrections or emendations in the copy (tear-sheets) in Somerville College. For comment on the essay, see lix above.

The Close of the Session

AT THE TERMINATION of the first session of the Reformed Parliament, a radical reformer, hearing some one make the complaint, so often made at that period, that the session had accomplished nothing, made answer, "Do you call it nothing to have completely discredited the Reform Ministry? Could this, in the course of nature, have been accomplished in a shorter time than one session?"

Subsequent events have proved that this reformer did not err in his estimate of the great step which was achieved in the session of 1833. Another session has now concluded; and the cry is even stronger than before, that in this session also, nothing has been accomplished. We hold that in every session something is accomplished; and in this one in particular, more than in any other since the Revolution, save only that which witnessed the birth of the Reform Bill.

In measures of actual legislation the present year has not been fruitful. If reforms were not to be weighed but counted,[*] the first session of the Reformed Parliament was a prodigy of activity compared with the second; for during it the Parliament did a greater number of things ill, than have been done well by all the Parliaments of the present century. The present session has realized no more than one measure of any note, the Poor Law Bill: that, however, is of far greater practical importance than all the Slave Bills and East India Bills of the preceding session,[†] and was, moreover, distinguished from them all in this, that what was intended to be done, was done; there was no bungling, no botching; the subject was not trifled with: the whole of what was needful to be done, and not a part only, was aimed at, and the means chosen were really adapted to the end. Even if the value of a session consisted solely in its positive enactments, the session which has produced only this great measure has not been ill spent. We had no such expectation from the Reform Bill, even in our most sanguine moments, as that in two years from its passing into a law, one of the greatest social reforms which this country needed, or for which any country could be indebted to its government,—one, too, which was not clamorously demanded by public opinion—would be, so far as depends on legislative enactments, completed.*

[*Cf. Samuel Taylor Coleridge, *Second Lay Sermon* (1817), 2nd ed., in *On the Constitution of Church and State, and Lay Sermons* (London: Pickering, 1839), p. 409.]

[†3 & 4 William IV, cc. 73, 85 (1833).]

*We say this not without considerable misgivings as to the Bastardy Clauses. [4 & 5 William IV, c. 76, §§ 69–76.] The more we reflect on this part of the subject, the more we

But in these days of Movement, the place which any session, or any single event, will occupy in history, depends not upon the intrinsic importance of the event, or value of the Acts of Parliament which have passed during the session; but upon the far greater consideration, how much it has helped forward the Movement, or contributed to hold it back. The question is not what village, castle, or city is our halting-place for the night, but how much lower down the stream, our day's journey has landed us. Look back, then; measure the interval between the point we started from and that which we have reached, and see if we have not made as much way in a given time, as might satisfy any rational person's most impatient desires.

By the passing of the Reform Bill, the instrument seemed to be obtained, by which all the evils of our political condition could be remedied, and all who had grievances could, or thought they could, get them redressed. But an instrument is nothing without somebody to work it. The new instrument of government could be worked either by Ministers or by the people. Those who made the machine, seemed the likeliest persons to be able to work it; at least, it seemed fair that they should have a trial. They had their trial; and after handling their tools as never workmen did before, and turning out such pieces of work as would disgrace a boy in the second year of his apprenticeship, they threw up the task, and said to the nation, You must work the machinery yourselves, we are only fit to oil the wheels. The nation have taken them at their word. During the first year of the Reformed Parliament the people were passive; they stood by, that Ministers might act: this year the people have acted. Last year was spent in showing what Ministers could do; and the result seems to have satisfied both themselves and the public that they could do little or nothing. This year has shown what the people could do.

In the Notes on the Newspapers, for last March, we said,

The session now commencing, will probably decide, in the minds of the many, who wield the physical force, the question whether anything is to be hoped from the higher classes, and whether the people shall, or shall not, take their affairs into their own hands.—The public had expected much, but did not know exactly what. They felt sure that the Reform Bill must somehow be a great good to them, and they trusted that those who had been sufficiently their friends to give them the Bill, would find the means of making it have its natural effects. The first session taught them that they were not to expect this: the Reform Ministry and the Reformed Parliament would do no good spontaneously. The second will show whether they are capable of doing any when they are forced. If this trial should also fail, we live in times when mankind hurry on rapidly to ultimate consequences; the next question will be, what is the easiest and most expeditious way of getting rid of them.[*]

As we expected, so has it proved. The people have taken their affairs into their

---

regret that the experiment was not first tried of merely postponing the inquiry into paternity until *after* birth, and limiting the demand upon the putative father, to the *actual maintenance* of the child.

[*John Stuart Mill, "Notes on the Newspapers," *Monthly Repository*, n.s. VIII (Mar., 1834), 161; p. 151 above.]

own hands. Ministers and Parliament, who, in being expected to think for themselves, had been put upon a task they were nowise equal to, have had a new trial upon an easier tenure, and have got through it much better. The second session has, as we anticipated, decided the question whether they are capable of doing good when compelled by the public voice. They *can* do good when they are forced. They have even proved, that when not opposed by the interests or prejudices of any powerful class, they can, as in the case of the Poor Law Bill, do good spontaneously. For this we give them due honour: we thank them for it as for a great service past and done. But there are no services of like importance remaining to be rendered, at no cost to the peers, or the clergy, or the landlords, or the lawyers, or the manufacturers, or the shipowners, or any other kind of persons who are accustomed to be kept at the public expense, and who are able to fight hard for the privilege. We have, therefore, little expectation of further unforced service from Ministers and their adherents. But we now know that they will yield to gentle violence. What wishes they have, are now on the people's side. When the Movement left off waiting for them to lead the van, its onward pressure bore down all those among them who would not move, or who would only move at their own pace. None remain but those who always go with the stream, and those whose preference is for the cause of improvement, although they were wanting in courage to head the contest for it. Not only are these the men now in place, but until a better and nobler race of public men shall arise, none but such as these, it is now evident, *can* be in place.

With these the people will carry by peaceable means, whatever they are bent upon carrying. The pike and the bayonet will not be wanted in this country. What the ten days of May, 1832, rendered probable, the session of 1834 has made certain; that the English revolution will be a revolution of law, and not of violence. The resistance will give way before the moral force of opinion. The experiment was fairly tried on Lord Grey's resignation. That two years ago the Tories were not allowed to step in between the people and the great constitutional change which they so ardently desired, cannot so much be wondered at: but after the Reform was safe, and no measure which the people cared about was in any immediate jeopardy, the Ministry broke down by its own imbecility; the Conservatives had such a chance as they can never again have; yet even then, Tories and Conservative Whigs were alike rejected; and even out of the ruins of the same shattered Cabinet, a still feebler one was patched up, because the only Ministry which *could* exist, was a Movement Ministry, and because, just at that time, no better Movement Ministry could be formed. And until the phrase shall cease to have a meaning, and Reformer and Conservative shall be a distinction in history alone, a Movement Ministry and no other will govern England; or rather, will be governed by her.

If we be asked, then, what has been gained? our answer is, *Circumspice*. Is not the general aspect of politics quite altered since the opening of the session? Is not the very air we breathe of another quality? The contest, whether the Reform Bill was to have its consequences, or another and a more drastic Reform Bill was necessary to our deriving any benefits from the first—this contest had not commenced when the session opened: the battle has now been fought, and the good cause has triumphed. Then, there was a dead calm; now, the wind has risen. We breathe an atmosphere of movement; and it is speeding us forward on our course.

It is no abatement from what has been gained, that the seal has not yet been put upon any part of it by an Act of Parliament. When the ministerial manifesto, last year,[*] boasted of the great things which the Ministry had *done*, the *Examiner* said—What care we for what you have done? It is the *spirit* of what you have done, that we care for. All you can *do*, until the public mind is more matured, would amount, if you were the wisest statesmen in the world, to a very trifle.[†] What we want to know is, what a Minister *says*.—And the Ministers had *said* nothing. They had put forth nothing which either committed themselves, or prepared the public mind: they had not announced a single *principle*. This year the case is reversed. They have *done* for the popular cause, on their own showing, nothing: but their *sayings* have been most valuable *doings*. They have made themselves the heralds of the victory which the national voice has now finally achieved over the combined strength of the supporters of bad institutions. They have proclaimed, and with impressive solemnity, that the power, be it what it may, which sets itself against the spirit of the age, must fall. And they have identified themselves with that spirit, on the great question which, first of the many which are impending, will be brought to a practical issue. They have declared the indefeasible right of the State, if the Church property exceeds what can usefully be applied to ecclesiastical purposes, to apply the residue to other purposes; and on this principle they have announced that it is their resolution to act.

This satisfies us. They who will do thus much, will do more when the time comes. One question at a time is as much as the public mind can be occupied with; and the enemy's country can be equally conquered whether we invade it on one point or on several. We now know that he cannot keep the field against us, and it matters little which of his fortresses we first besiege. But there is none which more invites an assailant than the Church Establishment; for it is the most vulnerable point in the whole line of defence, and yet, as the whole force of the enemy will be collected in it, and as it will hold out to the death, its fall will throw the whole country into our hands.

The curtailment of the Irish Church will be the Reform Bill of the next session: to be fought for by a union of the Ministry, the House of Commons, and the people, against the House of Lords. More slowly, but as certainly, the Church

---

[*Denis Le Marchant, ed., *The Reform Ministry, and the Reformed Parliament* (London: Ridgway, 1833).]

[†John Stuart Mill, "The Ministerial Manifesto," *Examiner*, 22 Sept., 1833, p. 593.]

Establishment of England will share the fate which awaits all bodies who pretend to be what they are not, and to accomplish what they do not even attempt. And the fall of the Church will be the downfal of the English aristocracy, as depositaries of political power. When all the privileged orders insist upon embarking in the same vessel, all must naturally expect to perish in the same wreck.

POSTSCRIPT TO THE LONDON REVIEW, NO. 1.

1835

EDITOR'S NOTE

London Review, I (equivalent to *London and Westminster*, XXX) (Apr., 1835), 254–6. Heading and running titles as title. Signed "A." Not republished. Identified in Mill's bibliography as "The Postscript to No. 1 of the London Review" (MacMinn, 44). There are no corrections or emendations in the copy (tear-sheets) in Somerville College.

Postscript to the London Review, No. 1

SINCE OUR ARTICLE on the political state of the country was sent to press,[*] the experiment which, when that Article was written, was but in an early stage of its progress, has been completed. By the result of that experiment, it is ascertained, first, that even with all the defects still inherent in our representative system, the crown and the aristocracy can no longer force upon the nation a ministry against its will; and, secondly, that the nation will not endure a conservative ministry. The time, indeed, is not come for a ministry of thorough Reformers; and the Tories, as little as the Whigs, now profess themselves thorough anti-reformers. Tories may grant reforms; and Whigs, as the people well know, will often refuse them, or pare them down into insignificance. But there is this difference between the two parties: the Whigs at least profess to *love* reform; the spirit of examination and change which is abroad is no subject of lamentation to them; they declare themselves gratified by it, and take credit to themselves for having helped to produce it. The Tories, on the contrary, look upon that spirit with avowed suspicion, most of them with absolute terror; they make no pretence of sympathizing with it; and whatever concessions they are willing to make to it are made avowedly to necessity.

By such persons the nation has now declared, in a manner not to be misunderstood, and which has carried conviction to the minds even of those to whom such a fact is least palatable, that it will not be governed. It will not have for ministers men who confess that their hearts are not in the cause of reform—who lay claim to support, not for what they will, but for what they will not, do, to forward the amendment of our institutions. Men who would govern this country from henceforward must not be men who thought our institutions perfect five years ago, and who declare that their opinions have not changed. They must either have the sincere belief, or the decent pretence of a belief, that those institutions were and are imperfect—that there are changes, which are not merely necessary evils which the people unthinkingly demand, but a good in themselves.

This is a lesson, not without its value to those who still needed it. In all other respects, the prospects of the nation appear to us, after this change, exactly as they

[*James Mill, "The State of the Nation," *London Review*, I (*L&WR*, XXX) (Apr., 1835), 1–24.]

appeared three months ago. The progress of reform appears to us certain; and we know full well that it will be slow. Any ministry which can be formed out of the scanty and inefficient materials afforded by the present houses of parliament will leave much to be desired—much to be criticised—much to be pardoned. We do not call upon the thorough Reformers to declare enmity against them, or to seek their downfall, because their measures will be half-measures, often not more than quarter-measures; nor even because they will join with the Tories in crying down all complete reforms, and will fight the battle of half-reform with anti-reform artillery. This the thorough Reformers are prepared for, and we believe they will disregard it. But we do implore them not to implicate themselves in the responsibility of a half-reform policy. They may support a ministry, where it deserves support, with far greater effect out of office; and they will retain the inestimable advantage of being at liberty to advocate what, as members of a cabinet, they would not have it in their power to carry into effect. Let them not allow themselves to be circumvented by the time-serving doctrine, that it is imprudent to propose anything which has no chance of immediate success. All great things which have ever been accomplished in the world, since Opinion became the ruler of it, have been accomplished by attempting things which for years, or generations, or ages after the first attempt, had not the remotest chance of success. Whoever, as a statesman, acts upon any other maxim, aims not at the glory of himself exercising any influence over the fortunes of his country or of mankind, and aspires only to register decrees, in the framing of which he voluntarily declares himself unworthy to have any voice.

If the ambition of the thorough Reformers be not limited to this paltry object, they will penetrate themselves with the conviction, that it is for others to consider what can be carried through the House of Commons; but that *they* are there to stand up for what is good in itself, let who will be minister, and however small a portion of the House may go along with them.

From the ministry we neither expect nor demand all this; nor has the time yet come when so manly a course would be consistent with their remaining a ministry. But there is one thing which is not too much to require of them. We cannot expect that they will propose measures which are in advance of the House of Commons; but, unless they would be utterly contemptible, let them not, this time, confine themselves to such as they trust will be agreeable to the House of Lords. That this was the principle, the systematic principle, of Earl Grey's ministry, we have the public testimony of Lord John Russell, in a speech to his constituents in Devonshire; and Lord Melbourne's answer to the Derby address was in the same spirit.[*] If the new ministers act upon a similar principle; if, as often as they believe that the House of Lords would throw out a measure of improvement, they

---

[*John Russell, Speech at Totnes (2 Dec., 1834), *The Times*, 8 Dec., 1834, p. 1; William Lamb, Speech at Derby (1 Dec., 1834), *ibid.*, 5 Dec., 1834, p. 3.]

mutilate it, or refuse absolutely to introduce it, and perhaps even assail it when introduced by others; if they again place themselves as a barrier between the Lords and public odium, and, to shield the real culprits, take upon themselves the responsibility of withholding from the nation its just demands,—their administration will assuredly not last one twelvemonth. Recent events are proof more than sufficient, if proof had been wanting, that it is impossible to please the Tories and the people both. The people will not have the Tories, even on a promise to act like Whigs; and ridiculous indeed would the expectation be, that they would tolerate Whigs who should again make it their avowed principle to act like Tories.

PARLIAMENTARY PROCEEDINGS OF THE SESSION

1835

EDITOR'S NOTE

London Review, I (July, 1835), 512–24 (equivalent to *London and Westminster*, XXX). Headed as title. Running titles: 512–18, as title; 519–24, "Municipal Reform Bill" (change keyed by the paragraph beginning "The destructive part . . .," 303). Signed "A." Not republished. Identified in Mill's bibliography as "The article entitled 'Parliamentary Proceedings of the Session' in the same number of the same work"; i.e., as "Tennyson's Poems" (MacMinn, 45). There are no corrections or emendations in the copy (tear-sheets) in Somerville College.

Parliamentary Proceedings of the Session

IN THE POSTSCRIPT to the first Number of this Review,[*] published while the Melbourne Ministry was in the process of formation, we explained why that portion of the House of Commons, who are entitled to the appellation of thorough reformers, ought not to connect themselves officially with any ministry which could be composed from the materials now existing in public life; and we described the attitude of support, but of qualified and distrustful support, which it appeared to us most consistent with the principles of the thorough reformers, and most conducive to their usefulness, that they should maintain towards the new administration. We believed that the Whigs would propose, on one or two important questions, measures considerably more extensive, and better calculated to facilitate further improvements, than would be proposed by any Tory ministry. On this ground, we wished that the Whigs should remain in office. That they were prepared to concede any improvements but those so urgently demanded by the public, that no government, raised to power by the public will, could refuse them without the immediate loss of office, we did not believe; nor, with regard to the greatest part of the evils which affect our social state, did we believe that the Whigs were, less than the Tories, attached to the evils, or less terrified at the remedies.

The course which we recommended has been that which the thorough reformers, both in the press and the House of Commons, have adopted. And that it was the advisable course, the conduct of the ministry has ever since been affording fresh proofs. To say nothing of minor matters, the Ministers have afforded us an opportunity of judging of them in regard to four great questions: the Corporations, and the Irish Church, the Ballot, and the Taxes on Knowledge. On the first two subjects their conduct has given ample reason why the complete reformers should support them; on the two latter, ample reason why that support should be, as we have already expressed ourselves, qualified and distrustful.

We are more desirous, on the present occasion, to dwell upon the favourable, than upon the unfavourable side. Yet, before we enter into an examination of the two measures which constitute the claim of the present Cabinet to the support of Reformers, we must make a few observations on the two other great questions just

[*John Stuart Mill, "Postscript," *London Review*, I (*L&WR*, XXX) (Apr., 1835), 256; i.e., the essay printed at pp. 289–93 above.]

alluded to; because we deem it important that the Reformers should be under no mistake concerning the probable duration and limits of the co-operation which is practicable between themselves and the Whig Cabinet.

We shall begin with the Taxes on Knowledge,[*] because it is the subject on which all we have to say will be soonest said.

This great question the former Melbourne Government left as a kind of legacy to the present. It was understood, and, by a distinguished member of that Government, proclaimed on more than one public occasion, that the ministry intended to take off the newspaper stamps.[†] The subject has been strongly pressed upon the present ministers since their appointment; numerous petitions against these taxes have latterly been presented to parliament; but, to all interrogations on the subject, ministers have returned evasive answers.[‡] The people ought to make them understand, that by their conduct on this question they will in a great measure be judged, and that the sentence is only suspended until their budget is produced. The language which they have as yet held on the subject is little honourable either to their sincerity as reformers, or to their discernment as statesmen. They are told that these taxes are the grand hindrance to what no one will look his fellow-creatures in the face and deny to be the very most important end which any persons in public trust can aim at—the instruction of the people. They are told that, by reason of these taxes, the people, who are willing to be instructed, cannot get instruction, and those who are willing and desirous to instruct the people are debarred the means of giving them instruction. Now, to such a proposition placed before them upon such grounds there are several answers which they might have returned. One was, "It is right; let us do it:" and this would have been the wisest and most virtuous answer. Another was, "It is not right; let us not do it:" and this might have been an honest, and would not have been an absolutely silly answer. Our ministers have contrived to find a third, different from either: "It is right; but we do not know whether we will do it or not." Mr. Spring Rice expressed his agreement in all the doctrines of those who object to the tax; but the glass-manufacturers also wanted to get *their* tax taken off, whereby we may drive a thriving trade in glass with all Europe; and the question must lie over until Mr. Spring Rice can decide which is best, an export of glass, or an instructed people.

What kind of statesmanship is this? The taxes on the diffusion of knowledge are either a positive good, or their existence is a violation of the first duty of a government; the most sacred claim of a people. Satisfy yourselves which of the two it is, and act accordingly; but for very shame, give over treating the question of

[*See 10 Anne, c. 19 (1711).]

[†See, e.g., John Russell, "Address to the Electors of the Southern Division of the County of Devon," *The Times*, 20 Apr., 1835, p. 1.]

[‡See John Charles Spencer, Speech on Stamps on Newspapers (22 May, 1834), *PD*, 3rd ser., Vol. 23, cols. 1210–13.]

the civilization of your people as a question of revenue—a question where the government is to find 400,000*l.* And this when, in four years, five millions of far less objectionable taxes have been taken off.

Before our next publication, ministers will have been forced to explain themselves categorically on this subject. For the present, we shall say no more upon it.

Ministers have declared their unabated determination to resist the Ballot. We view this declaration in a very serious light; and we think the importance of it will manifest itself more and more to all eyes.

A government which is determined to oppose the ballot must end by a coalition with the Tories. Without the ballot there will, in two or three years more, be a Tory parliament. We are unable to conceive how the evidence of this can be resisted. The majority of the electors, both in the old and in the new constituencies, are in a state of complete dependence upon the wealthy persons of their neighbourhood. Of these wealthy persons, a vast majority are Tories. The Reform Act did not change human nature. It did two things: it introduced into the constituency a large body of new electors, not yet corrupted by the foul influences; and it inspired the electors with an enthusiasm, which induced them very generally to brave those influences, and disregard the mandate of those who could do them good or ill. So stood the case in 1832: but in 1834? In two years, this effect of the Reform Bill had so spent itself, that the Tories, and those who were willing to act with the Tories, obtained within thirty of a majority of the Reformed House. The elections of Devonshire, Staffordshire, and Inverness-shire, were subsequent to that time. This the Tories call re-action. We call it the natural working of the constitution established by the Reform Bill; a constitution, which enables the people to carry all before them when driven by any violent excitement; but compels them, through the publicity of the suffrage, to exercise that power under pains and penalties, which prevent it from being ever exerted on common occasions, or in quiet times.

What did Lord John Russell and Lord Howick, the two ministers who made themselves spokesmen against the ballot, say to this?[*] They said, it was true there had been intimidation, gross intimidation, and, in the election which had just taken place, that of Lord John himself, intimidation beyond all former precedent; if it were let alone, however, perhaps it would cease of itself! Public opinion, and the growth of intelligence, would in time restrain, nay, according to Lord Howick, had already restrained, and were restraining, the intimidation, every day more and more. A hopeful and cheering view of human affairs, truly; but, like most of the maxims of the Whigs when they are talking like Tories, they have been somewhat late in finding it out. Why abolish the rotten boroughs? Why not trust to the growth of intelligence, and the power of public opinion, which were acting upon the

[*Russell and Henry George Grey, Speeches on the Ballot (2 June, 1835), *ibid.*, Vol. 28, cols. 447–52 and 427, respectively.]

boroughmongers, every day more and more? Why turn out Sir Robert Peel? Would public opinion, and the progress of intelligence, have been without effect upon that minister? What need of a police? What need of laws, and courts of justice? Cannot you rely upon the growth of intelligence, and the influence of public opinion upon the thieves? What need of an army or navy? Why not disband our forces, and trust for our protection to the public opinion of Europe?

It is time to have done with these propositions for giving uncontrolled mastery over the people to an irresponsible few, and trusting to public opinion to prevent them from abusing it; these fond anticipations, that men will not do what is in accordance with their interest, and with the opinion of all those whom they care for, out of deference to the opinion of those for whom they do not care. Intimidation in elections will increase, not diminish. It will be greater in the next general election than in the last, as it was greater in the last than in any preceding. Not the intimidation, but the feelings which make men resist intimidation, will diminish. He who has once voted against his conscience, will have less and less sense of degradation in so voting, every successive time. There are persons who believe that a great and salutary effect will be produced upon the parliamentary elections by Corporation Reform. We believe that it will produce some, but nothing like a decisive effect. Though the corruption and intimidation, hitherto exercised by corporations, were to cease, there are ample means both of corruption and intimidation in other hands, and by these the municipal elections themselves may be perverted, and through them the corporation property again brought into corrupt hands. If Corporation Reform strengthen the ministry at elections, it will be chiefly by rekindling some sparks of the expiring enthusiasm; an effect which is in its nature evanescent, and cannot be reproduced. No ministry can continue exciting the people to a fresh fit of enthusiasm every year.

We repeat, then, that without the ballot we shall speedily have a Tory parliament; and that the present ministers will have to decide, whether they will support the ballot, or abandon office to the Tories, or coalesce with the Tories on their own terms. The exact time when this decision must be made it is impossible to foresee, but by no power can it be postponed for more than a year or two. When it comes, which course will the ministers choose? Probably they will not all of them make the same choice. The problem will then be reduced to its simplest terms: Who is for the aristocracy and who for the people, will be the plain question. Ought the government, or ought it not, to be under the complete control of the possessors of large property? Those of the ministers who think that it ought, with nearly the whole of the Whig aristocracy, will combine with the Tories in a determined resistance to all further extension of popular influences. Those who think that it ought not, together with two-thirds of those members of the House of Commons who now support the ministry, will form a powerful Opposition party, resting upon the people. The contest will then be short and sharp, between the two principles which divide the world, the aristocratic principle and the democratic;

and in such a "stand-up fight," he is an indifferent prophet who cannot foresee that the victory will be with the side where the strength is growing, not with that where it is waning.

In the debate on Mr. Grote's motion,[*] the complete reformers made an exhibition of boldness, concert, and parliamentary talent, which greatly raised their character in the House, and ought to convince them what a power they might wield, if they, who are the most instructed portion of the House, were not, unhappily, (with some meritorious exceptions,) the least enterprising and energetic. The votes showed a considerable increase in the number of the avowed supporters of the ballot, since the last division two years ago. But a still more encouraging symptom, to those who were present, was the temper of the House: the manifest favour with which the proposition was received, by all except the Tories and the immediate adherents of ministers; and the tone of confidence in their strength, we might almost say of triumph, assumed by its supporters. Though the question was lost, it might have been supposed that they knew it was about to be carried, so completely were all the signs of conscious superiority on their side.

We shall now state, as briefly as possible, our sentiments on the two great measures of reform to which the ministry have, in our opinion rightly, postponed for the present session all minor questions. We mean, of course, the Municipal Corporation Bill,[†] and the Bill for reforming the Irish Church.[‡]

We regard both these measures as, in point of principle, of the very highest moment; and from one of them we expect important practical benefit. The importance of the other consists chiefly in the principle which it recognises.

We regard the Irish Church Bill as the final blow to the superstition (once so strong, but which has of late been so rapidly wearing out) of the inalienable character of endowments, and, in particular, of ecclesiastical endowments. For the first time, the popular branch of the legislature has sanctioned the principle, that, saving all existing life-interests, Parliament has the right, paying a reasonable, and no more than a reasonable, regard to the original purposes of endowments, to deal with the surplus as it deems most expedient. The House of Commons have once deliberately announced this principle in a solemn resolution,[§] and are about to pass a bill in which the power so claimed by them is actually exercised.

Considered with regard to its direct object, as a measure for reducing the sinecure church establishment of Ireland, the bill has two great defects. The first is, that it *is* a bill for the reduction of the sinecure church, and not for its total

[*_Ibid._, cols. 369–471 (2 June, 1835).]
[†Enacted as 5 & 6 William IV, c. 76 (1835).]
[‡"A Bill for the Better Regulation of Ecclesiastical Revenues, and the Promotion of Religious and Moral Instruction in Ireland," 6 William IV (7 July, 1835), *PP*, 1835, II, 379–427 (not enacted).]
[§Russell, Resolution on the Church of Ireland (7 Apr., 1835), *PD*, 3rd ser., Vol. 27, cols. 880–3.]

extinction. A measure of that extent, we believe, would not have been in advance of the public mind. No rational supporter of a church establishment now attempts to justify an inconsiderable minority in imposing their church upon the majority, or one nation in imposing theirs upon another nation. Even to attempt it is such an act of tyranny, as no nation ever submitted to but from the fear of the bayonet. Nothing can justify retaining the Irish Church, even on the most moderate scale, unless all other sects are to be established and endowed likewise.

From the present ministers, however, we looked for no measure beyond a diminution of the monstrous establishment: nor do we blame them for not proposing what the House of Commons probably would not have passed. But the bill they have proposed curtails only one part, and that the least overgrown part of the establishment: it reduces the number and emoluments of the parochial clergy, but leaves the bishops and the deans and chapters untouched. Ten bishops and two archbishops seem rather a costly instrument of superintendence for the religious instruction of eight hundred thousand persons. Several English bishops, a body whom few persons consider to be either overworked or underpaid, have singly the charge of dioceses containing much more than that number of communicants. If there is to be an endowed Church of Ireland, one bishop, with a fitting number of archdeacons, would be an amply sufficient allowance of superior clergy for such an establishment.

If, however, to make the reduction include the hierarchy as well as the parochial clergy, would have endangered the success of the bill in the House of Commons, ministers are not to be blamed for stopping short where they did. The contest at present is not for the details, but for the principle. The battle is to be fought with the House of Lords, and any ground, if it be but of tolerable width, will do well enough to fight that battle upon. The Bill is a challenge of the House of Lords to mortal combat. We believe that the challenge will be accepted, and that, though the struggle may be protracted, this victory will be the final one.

On the Bill for the reform of Municipal Corporations our remarks will extend to greater length, because the subject is of greater complexity, and is one of those on which details are all-important. In dealing with the Irish Church, or with the taxes on knowledge, there is a straight path before us: only deal destruction sufficiently wide, and you cannot be wrong: there is a simple test to judge what measure is the best; it is that which destroys the most. But on the subject to which we are now about to advert, Parliament have not only to destroy, but to rebuild: they have to construct a local government: a task the execution of which involves most of the leading principles of the art of politics—a work not very dissimilar in its nature, and only second in its importance, to that of framing the constitution of a state.

It has fared, however, with ministers in this instance, as it usually fares with the statesmen of this generation when they attempt to be reformers. The destructive part of their measures is almost always good, but the constructive part bad. This has been the remark made by the best judges on most of the Whig reforms. It is remarkably applicable to the Reform Bill itself; and it is applicable to the Slave Bill; to the East-India Bill, to the Bankruptcy Bill,[*] and in general to all Lord Brougham's law reforms,[†] which have swept away much that is bad, but substituted nothing which, in the opinion of those most competent to judge, is fit to stand as part of an improved system. The reason is obvious. Public men have now a work to perform, requiring far greater study and preparation than the works which devolved upon their predecessors, and this study and preparation they have not bestowed. They come to their task with minds not properly furnished. They can destroy, because to destroy is easy; even to perceive what deserves to be destroyed is generally not difficult; though this they seldom see until all the world is crying shame upon them for not seeing it. But to rebuild is a work of science; it demands a comprehensive survey and philosophical analysis of ends and means; and as they never have made any such survey, or performed any such analysis, they have no rule to go by but the rule of all unscientific craftsmen, the rule of thumb. By that, accordingly, they regulate themselves, and do, with as little alteration as possible, what others have done before them.

The destructive part of the Municipal Corporation Bill is of signal excellence. It tears down, with no unsparing hand, the old abomination. In the constructive part there is also one point of great merit—the liberal measure which has been dealt out of popular privilege. The ministry have shown no foolish distrust of the people. For the extension of the suffrage to all householders they are entitled to great praise; and if to this had been added the ballot, the responsibility of the town-councils to those whose interests are committed to their charge would have been nearly as complete as could be desired.

While, too, the town-councils are chosen by, and amenable to, the community, all other town-officers, except those intrusted with the administration of justice, are chosen by the town-councils.* This is judicious. In local, as in general government, we are of opinion that the people should elect the body which is to control the executive, but should not elect the executive functionaries themselves; for all executive duties require some peculiar capacity (appropriate aptitude, as Mr. Bentham was accustomed to style it),[‡] of which the people cannot judge

[*2 & 3 William IV, c. 45 (1832); 3 & 4 William IV, cc. 73, 85 (1833); and 1 & 2 William IV, c. 56 (1831).]

[†Including 1 & 2 William IV, c. 35 (1831); 2 William IV, cc. 34, 39 (1832); 2 & 3 William IV, cc. 51, 62, 110, 116, 122, 123 (1832); 3 & 4 William IV, cc. 41, 44, 67, 84 (1833); and 4 & 5 William IV, c. 36 (1834).]

*The only other exception is the auditors, who of course could not be chosen by those whose accounts they are appointed to check.

[‡Bentham used the phrase, for example, to describe Mill as fit for the House of Commons at the age of eighteen; see John M. Robson, "John Stuart Mill and Jeremy Bentham, with Some Observations on James Mill," in *Essays in English Literature*, ed. M. Maclure and F. W. Watt (Toronto: University of Toronto Press, 1964), p. 254 (citing Bentham Papers, University College London, xxxiv, 303).]

previously to trial; and the fittest person may possibly not present himself, unless it is the special duty of somebody to search him out.

We have now mentioned the principal points which appear to us worthy of commendation, in the municipal constitution provided by the Bill. We proceed to the less pleasant duty of pointing out the cases in which, for want of accurate and comprehensive principles, previously known, and well-digested in their heads, ministers have only been the servile copyists of the errors of their predecessors.

Local government consists of two parts—administration and judicature. There must be a provision for the management of the collective interests of the local community, and there must be a provision for the administration of justice. The provision made in this Bill for local administration consists of the mayor, the town-clerk, and the town-council; the provision for justice consists of the mayor, the magistrates, and the recorder.

To begin with the administrative body—the first thing that strikes us is, that instead of a committee for the dispatch of business, ministers are creating in every considerable town a debating club. Such is the necessary effect of making the council so numerous—reaching from sixteen to (in the case of Liverpool) the number of ninety members. This is courting the very mischief which the greatest pains should have been exerted to keep out. In parliament, the evil of long speeches must be submitted to; for this reason among others, that it is part of the office of parliament to be an arena for the promulgation and mutual collision of political opinions. But the town-council-room is meant to be a place of mere business, and business of a very commonplace kind: the members therefore should not exceed the number who can discuss and transact business by conversation round a table. We think they ought never to exceed thirty.* If the body is much more numerous, non-attendance will be the general rule, and the most important business will often be left in the hands of the few whose assiduity is stimulated by some private interest; while, on any occasion which brings the whole body together, its time will be wasted in declamation, and the real business of the town will be done carelessly, or not done at all.

We should have preferred that the election by wards had been universal. Requiring the electors to vote for the whole body at once, almost ensures their adopting the list tendered to them by some active and stirring junto in the town; or if they attempt to choose for themselves, they will choose carelessly, and give a vote to any one who asks for it: for men will take the trouble to make a conscientious selection of one or two persons, but not of twenty or fifty. Another consequence, which has been pointed out by several members of the House,[*] is, that when there

---

*In the French town-councils the usual number is fifteen; but the French councils have little to do except to vote money. They have not, properly speaking, the administration of the affairs of the town: that is reserved to the *maire*, an officer selected from the municipal council by the Crown, and responsible to the Crown for his acts.

[*See, e.g., Edward George Stanley, Speech on the Municipal Corporation Bill (15 June, 1835), *PD*, 3rd ser., Vol. 28, col. 823.]

are two parties, the weaker of the two will be deprived of all influence in the formation of the town-council. And an additional inconvenience, incident to this, is, that if, in the interval between one election and another, the stronger party becomes the weaker—a revolution which parliamentary elections prove to be of frequent occurrence—there will be a sudden and abrupt change of the whole body, to the interruption, so far as they are concerned, of all public business. It is, probably, to avoid this evil, that the plan has been hit upon, of partial renewals, one-third of the council going out every year—a most infelicitous *juste milieu*, which unites the inconveniences of a long and those of a short period—annual elections, and only triennial responsibility.

The mayor is not to be the mere chairman of the town-council, but has important administrative (not to mention judicial) duties devolving upon himself. If this be right (and, with respect to the administrative duties, we do not say that it is not right), it appears to us most injudicious that the mayor should be changed every year. This is blind imitation of the corporation of London, and most of the old corporations. It is a contrivance for having the chief administrative officer always in leading-strings, never out of his apprenticeship. As soon as he begins to understand his business you dismiss him, and bring in another who is still raw, and fit to be a screen for the town-clerk: who, on this system, will pull the strings of the puppet, who is to be called the mayor, but whose sole office will generally be to shelter the town-clerk from responsibility.

The provision made for the administration of justice is more faulty still. It is a considerable improvement, doubtless, on the old system; but it has most of the defects which we are accustomed to see in the judicial institutions of our country, and it has them for no reason that can be perceived, except that we are accustomed to them.

What is wanted for purposes of judicature, is a local judge, transacting (under appeal to a properly-constituted tribunal in the metropolis) *all* the judicial business of the district, and *no* part of the administrative business. Judicial and administrative duties should never be united in the same hands; for they are different sorts of business: they require different qualities, different kinds of men: the mode of choice suitable to the two kinds of officers is different—so are the checks, and the kind of responsibility; and the experience of all nations testifies to the importance of keeping those to whom the business of judicature is intrusted free from intermixture in the other affairs of the world, that the administration of justice may be pure, not only from the reality, but even from the suspicion, of partiality.

The principle of the separation of judicial from administrative duties is adopted in part by the Bill, but in so limited and inconsistent a manner as shows that the framers have no due sense of its importance. And the provision for judicature is altogether insufficient.

There is to be a local judge, under the name of a Recorder, wherever the town-council express their desire for one, and their willingnes to pay him a sufficient salary. This is so far good. What did the ministers next? They looked round, to see what provision for local judicature had been made by the wisdom of our ancestors; and they found, that it consisted of a court, which decided no civil, and only some classes of criminal cases, including neither the greatest nor the smallest, and which sat only once a quarter. Without looking any farther, our ministers determined that the local judge whom they are about to create shall decide only these same sorts of criminal cases, and that he also shall only sit once a quarter. But why, if a local tribunal be useful in one sort of criminal cases, will it not be useful in another? and if useful in criminal cases, why not also in civil? and if it be good that justice should be accessible once in three months, why not on every day of the year? Why must the redress of wrongs be delayed, and why must innocent people linger in prison, while the Recorder who is to try them at the next sessions is practising as a barrister in London? These are questions which the framers of the Bill have not asked themselves. They would have found them not only asked, but answered, in the writings of Mr. Bentham, the great teacher in this department of practical politics. There are many branches of the art of government on which sufficient light has not yet been thrown; there are others, on which the best ideas which exist are scattered through a hundred writers: but procedure, and judicial establishment, are subjects of which the alpha and omega are to be found in Mr. Bentham; and it is perfectly disgraceful to any one who, in this age, attempts to legislate on those subjects, not to be familiar with his views on a branch of politics, the philosophy of which he may be said to have created.

So far as respects civil justice, and the higher criminal cases, the Bill leaves matters as it found them, and recourse must still be had to the courts in London, or to the judges of assize. For those cases, again, which are considered too small to be tried by the Recorder, the Bill provides a class of judges called magistrates, who are to have the powers of justices of peace, except those usually exercised by the quarter sessions. These magistrates are to be selected by the Crown, from a number of persons to be recommended by the town-councils. We would suggest a more distinct explanation in the Bill of the cases in which magistrates are to be liable to removal. They should be removable by the Crown, on an address from the town-council.

The powers of these magistrates, like those of all persons who, in England, are called by that name, or by the equivalent one of justices of the peace, are a monstrous jumble of adminstrative and judicial functions. They have summary jurisdiction in small cases. They have the power of committing prisoners to take their trial at the Sessions or the Assizes; a function, stupidly classed in common language under the head of Police, but which is strictly judicial. It is a preliminary trial of the prisoner, for the purpose of ascertaining, not whether he is guilty, but whether there is sufficient presumption of his guilt to require that he be put upon a more formal trial. And the consequence of an unfavourable verdict, on this preliminary investigation, may be the infliction of a severer sentence, in the form of imprisonment previous to trial, than would be inflicted on proof of guilt, for some serious offences. These preliminary investigations are, therefore, acts of judicature, in the strictest sense. They require judicial qualities, as exalted as any other kind of judicial business, and ought always to be performed by a person called a judge. The only functions which are really of police are the simply executive ones, the enforcement of the laws by interposing *before* an offence is committed, and the apprehension of the offender *afterwards*. Of the heterogeneous functions of the magistrates, these are the only ones which require a distinct set of functionaries. The judicial business of the magistrates, whether of conviction or of committal, should be turned over to the Recorder, converted into a local judge always resident on the spot. It is a rule of the utmost importance, that no one is fit to try the smallest cases who is not fit for the greatest; for the small cases are quite as difficult, concern a much larger portion of the community, and are far more liable to be neglected, or slurred over, because they attract so much less of the attention of any but the parties immediately concerned.

The proposal, that the mayor should be *ex officio* a magistrate, and that he should be the local judge in the absence of the Recorder, is so monstrous, that we cannot believe it will be persevered in. It is a complete departure from the principle which the Bill to a certain extent adopts, that of withdrawing all judicial powers from the functionaries who carry on the local administration. The mayor is the very head and front[*] of the administration: in all the business of the town-council he is a principal party, and he has many administrative duties peculiar to himself. To crown all, this union of public functions of the most difficult and important kind is delegated to an officer who is to be changed every year; and in the smaller towns, to which the Crown is not to give magistrates except on special application, the mayor will often be the sole magistrate. We cannot easily conceive a worse. It will be, in reality, some mitigation of the mischief, that a permanent officer, the town-clerk, will generally dictate to the mayor all his acts, himself screened from being answerable for them.

The above are, we conceive, the principal objections to the detailed provisions of the Bill.* Amendments have been placed on the order-book of the House of Commons, calculated to force the discussion of almost all these points; and we trust that the complete reformers, many of whom are well acquainted with the

[*Cf. Shakespeare, *Othello*, I, iii, 80.]

*In the above strictures, many unavoidable coincidences of sentiment will be found with one of Mr. Roebuck's Pamphlets, which is dedicated to this subject, and with some excellent articles in the *Globe*. Both writers have done great service, and it is gratifying to us that our opinions are confirmed by such competent authority. [John Arthur Roebuck, *A Letter to the Electors of Bath on the Municipal Corporation Reform Bill*, in *Pamphlets for the People*, 2 vols., ed. J. A. Roebuck (London: Ely, 1835), Vol. I, 2nd pamphlet; Leading Articles, *Globe*, 22 June, 1835, pp. 2–3, 25 June, 1835, p. 4.]

subject, will not let slip such an occasion for impressing upon the public many of the most important principles of organic legislation. That there are those among them who will not neglect the opportunity, we have reason to be assured.*

But, after every abatement which the above considerations call upon us to make, from an estimate of the merits of this measure, it is still entitled to the character of being one of the greatest steps in improvement ever made by peaceable legislation in the internal government of a country. And we would rather waive the assertion of any or all of the objections to which it is liable, than expose the Bill itself to any jeopardy. But we fear no such result. On the contrary, we are convinced, that the more decidedly the reformers show that this Bill is not their ultimatum, and does not come up to all their wishes, the safer it will prove from mischievous defacement in the Tories' House. Were the Reformers to let the Tories believe that with the present measure they are fully satisfied, it might tempt them to try whether we may not be satisfied with less. It is the safest, as well as the most direct and plainest course, to evince to the enemy that the improvement this Bill gives us is barely enough, and that there is not a particle to spare.

*Since the observations in the text were written, some of the amendments have come on for discussion, but have been negatived, we regret to observe, without a division. This is a grievous mistake on the part of the reformers. Their object was, not to carry their propositions, but to force public attention to the subject; and this is only effectually done when motions are pressed to a division. It was thus only that Mr. Hume succeeded in making the impression upon the public mind which so wonderfully accelerated parliamentary reform. We regret that Sir John Hobhouse should have lent himself to the vulgar misrepresentation to which we are so much accustomed from the Whigs, that to propose improvements in a measure is to endanger or obstruct its passing. [Speech on Corporation Reform (1 July, 1835), *PD*, 3rd ser., Vol. 29, col. 162.]

POSTSCRIPT: THE CLOSE OF THE SESSION

1835

EDITOR'S NOTE

London Review, II (equivalent to *London and Westminster*, XXXI) (Oct., 1835), 270–7. Headed: "*POSTSCRIPT.* / THE CLOSE OF THE SESSION." Running titles: "Close of the Session." Signed "A." Not republished. Identified in Mill's bibliography as "The article entitled 'Close of the Session' in the same number of the same work"; i.e., as "De Tocqueville on Democracy in America [I]" (MacMinn, 45). There are no corrections or emendations in the copy (tear-sheets) in Somerville College.

Postscript:
The Close of the Session

THE TRANSACTIONS of which human life is made up, fall mostly into natural cycles or revolutions, which are commenced and completed within the compass of a year. The return of most periodical events, which are important or interesting to man, accompanies the return of the seasons.

In each of these cycles there is some one point at which, rather than at any other, it is natural to pause, and survey the course which has been run since the corresponding period of the preceding year. In the circle of agricultural operations, this point is the close of the harvest. The labours of the year have then been brought to their natural conclusion: the ground has been ploughed, the seed sown, all the chances of destruction or damage have been more or less victoriously left behind, and the fruits of the toil and anxiety of the past year have been, in a more or less perfect condition, gathered in and stored up to supply the wants of that which is to come.

What the close of the harvest is in the agricultural year, the close of the session is in the political. It is then that we are most inclined to look about us and observe what has been gained in the year previous. We are then entering into a period of comparative quiet, during which the laws of nature are working for us as surely as before, but are now working chiefly below the surface.

At this period of annual retrospection, a period at which our estimate of what has been, and of what is still going on, is likely to be more comprehensive, and less disturbed by passing influences, than at any other, there are two things which, for several years past, have struck upon us yearly with increasing force, and which are in every respect the most remarkable among the political features of the present time.

One is, the unexampled and almost miraculous rapidity of the march of public opinion. The movement of the public mind is no longer like that of the hour-hand of a clock, invisible to the passing eye, and making itself known only by its effects at long intervals. We may now almost be said to see it move. For however short a time we lose sight of it, when we next turn to it we find it farther on; and for some years past it has made annual strides, each of which distanced all anterior calculation, only to be itself surpassed by the next which followed it.

When they who are now thirty years of age were just old enough to take interest in public affairs, the adoration of everything which existed in England—church, law, judges, commercial and colonial monopolies, rotten boroughs and all—was, to appearance, as deeply rooted in the national mind, as at any former period of history. This degrading superstition must even then have been secretly much weakened; no outward sign, however, had yet betrayed its inward decay. Within a few years afterwards, the first deadly wound was given to the sordid sinister interests, of which this country had been till then the unresisting prey. The cause of Free Trade became a gained cause, little as had then or has even yet been done to give practical effect to it in our legislation. The irrevocable triumph of freedom of trade dates from the failure of the attempts to overset the Huskisson policy after the panic of 1826. At that time, the spirit of Law Reform had also had a beginning; and in 1827 Mr. Brougham's celebrated speech[*] gave it an impulse which has carried it onward ever since, even during the temporary suspension of the public interest in it, from the more exciting subjects with which the general attention has been engrossed. But in 1827 the principle of religious tests was still the recognized doctrine of the constitution, and it was part of the established laudation of Mr. Canning that he had given the death-blow to Radicalism. The year 1828 saw the disabilities of the Dissenters, and the year 1829 those of the Catholics, disappear, in law and in fact. The eyes of the nation were then instantly unsealed on the subject of political religion; and those who had predicted that these great measures would bring up the rear-guard of civilization, and awaken the inert mass who had slept since the accession of the House of Hanover (disturbed only by bad dreams during the era of Pitt) to the change of times and circumstances—these prophets saw their predictions fulfilled, in a shorter time than they had even dared to anticipate. In the summer of 1830, it just began to be remarked, that the majority was diminishing against giving representatives to Birmingham and Manchester. On the 25th of July, the man whom of all now alive Toryism has most reason to curse, issued the famous Ordinances:[†] and in the November following, Toryism in England had ceased to reign.

It is not necessary to trace minutely the subsequent progress. No one need be reminded what was the magnitude of the next step. That step gave us an instrument of government, which wanted only two things to make it adequate to most of the purposes for which Reform in Parliament was sought: the protection of the ballot, for electors in dependant circumstances; and to be freed from a House of Lords, determined to render the Reform of the House of Commons a nullity. The meeting of the first Reformed Parliament found a ministry in office, of whom it was the collective determination to make their policy subservient to the prevention of these two things. The first session which followed lost to this ministry the people's

---

[*Henry Brougham's Speech on the State of the Courts of Common Law was actually given on 7 Feb., 1828; see *PD*, n.s., Vol. 18, cols. 127–247.]

[†Charles X, of France. See Ordonnances nos. 15135-8 (25 juillet, 1830), *Bulletin des lois du royaume de France*, 8me sér., Tome XII, Bulletin 367, pp. 33–40.]

hearts, the second flung them out of office. We are now at the conclusion of the third.

Not for the sake of counting minor gains, but to see how much further we are advanced in the great movement, let us consider what this third year has done for us.

A last desperate attempt of the Tories to creep back into power as semi-reformers, despairing of it as anti-reformers, has been promptly crushed: and has had for its principal result, to lay bare to the people's eyes the extent of the aristocratic influence which can still be exercised over the composition of the House of Commons under the present mode of voting; and to place us at one stroke several years nearer to the ballot, than if that blunder of the king, or of the king's secret advisers, had not been committed.

This was visible to all eyes in June last, when Mr. Grote brought forward his motion.[*] That question, which has since slept, will, when it awakens, be found where it was then left; or rather, it will have moved noiselessly still further forward, for the silent progress of opinion is not less remarkable in the present times, than the changes which loudly proclaim themselves. Meanwhile, the current has made a bend in its course, and is now beating against the opposite side of the channel, preparing to carry away the other of the two great obstacles which resist its peaceful progress towards calmer seas. The great question of the approaching year will be the reconstitution of the House of Lords.

And now, whoever would seek for a test by which to estimate the present rate of the progress of public opinion, let him look at this. The first shock to the traditional attachment to the existing constitution of the House of Lords was given by their conduct on the Reform Bill. When that measure became law, it was thought that all was gained; and those who talked of reforming the House of Lords preached to deaf ears. This state of feeling had much altered two years ago; every reformer was then anxious for a creation of peers. Now, observe the difference. Not a voice is raised to suggest such an insignificant measure. The House of Lords is given up, as too bad to mend. No infusion of new blood would now save it. An entire change in its constitution is cried out for from the remotest corner of the three kingdoms; and few would be satisfied with any change short of abolishing the hereditary principle.

We said that two things appeared to us chiefly deserving of remark in the present condition of this country; and that the unexampled rapidity now apparent in the advance of public opinion was one of these. We have next to mention the other; which, in its way, is equally remarkable. This is, the insignificance of the men who are the visible instruments and the only apparent agents in this great change.

The revolution, for such it is, although pacific, which is marching onward with

[*George Grote, Motion on the Ballot (2 June, 1835), *PD*, 3rd ser., Vol. 28, cols. 369-95.]

such velocity among us, is a revolution without leaders. Not only has it no leaders in the cabinet, but it has none in Parliament. Not only has it no leaders in Parliament, but it has none in the popular press. Scarcely a person can be found who has done, or is doing, or is so much as attempting to do any thing more, either towards accelerating it or towards guiding it, than any other person.

If there is something elevating in the conception of the great results, which are daily shaping themselves forth under the plastic power of that irresistible Necessity, wrought by the natural laws of human civilization; and if there is much that is both gratifying and encouraging in that high average of comparative improvement among the people at large, evidenced by the gentleness and steadiness with which the mighty movement is thus far going on, without the application of one superior mind in any commanding station to prepare the way for it, or to guide it into the salutary course; there is, it must be confessed, something at once humiliating and disheartening in the individual insignificance of the men, who are in the positions which would enable them to modify the general tendency by some idea or impulse of their own, but who universally content themselves with yielding to the force by which they are pressed on from behind. For the first time in the recorded history of great political changes, not one man of commanding talents, not one *homme à grand caractère*, has shewn himself in any conspicuous part of the field of action. Those among our conspicuous public men or influential writers who have the head to conceive any thing better to be done, than to let the current of events float them down and land them wherever it will, are few indeed; and of those few, it seems that there is not one who, with the head to conceive, has also the heart to execute it.*

When we look around us, the only figure which stands erect and prominent, the only man who himself weighs for something in the balance of events, is Mr. O'Connell; and his influence, though it could not have been acquired but by a man of talents, and, above all, of activity, does not belong to him so much in himself, as because he embodies in his single person all Ireland. Mr. O'Connell does nothing whatever to guide the movement, but he does something to accelerate it; and accordingly we have lately seen him, with all his disadvantages, carrying off the undivided harvest of that popular favour, of which any one member of the now

---

*There are a few individual exceptions, of great merit; but they do not materially affect the statements in the text, because either their principal sphere of usefulness is, like that of Mr. Hume, a confined one, or their age and standing has not yet permitted them to give more than hopes of their hereafter effecting something worthy of remembrance. Even such exceptions as these are contemptibly few.

Perhaps the editor of the *Examiner,* as far as circumstances have permitted the development of a fine capacity, under the guidance of no ordinary degree of public virtue, approaches nearer than any other public man who can yet be named, to a complete exception.

Why does not Mr. Grote exert himself? There is not a man in parliament who *could* do so much, or who is more thoroughly the people's friend.

numerous radical party in the House of Commons, having the acquirements, abilities, character, and station in society which belong to many of them, might have reaped, by very ordinary exertion, a far larger share than he.

These are melancholy facts. Circumstances cannot always continue to do what men will not, or are not capable of. Circumstances are blind guides. The use of intellect is never with impunity abandoned in the affairs of nations. We imagine it is hardly supposed that things will always continue to go perfectly right of themselves; that the people will always, without being taught, know and demand of their own accord whatever is best for them; that they will never fall into any errors requiring to be corrected; that cultivated wisdom can suggest nothing more perfect, in reorganizing the whole social condition of a people, than is struck out spontaneously by the collective intellect of the uninstructed. It cannot be supposed, in short, that there are no longer any great things to be performed for mankind: we are reduced, therefore, to the necessity of concluding that no one of the present generation, who has yet met with the opportunity, esteems himself capable of performing them.

The causes of this absence of greatness, this small intellectual and moral stature of the men of the present day who have it most in their power to render their mental endowments serviceable to their fellow-creatures, must be sought in considerations more remote from common observation than would admit of being satisfactorily entered into in this place. They would be found, no doubt, to be partly connected with our social arrangements, and partly with the peculiarities which mark the present stage in the progressive advancement of the human mind.

Without looking any further into the subject at present, one or two observations remain to be made, more peculiarly applicable to the passing moment.

A compromise appears to have tacitly established itself, between the ministry, and the thorough reformers in parliament and in the press. What has been given up on both sides for the sake of the alliance, we can only infer from what we see. The concession made by the ministry seems to be, that instead of shaping their conduct so as to avert public indignation from the Lords, by never giving those careful guardians of the public weal any good measures to reject, they shall occasionally bring forward propositions acceptable to the people, allow the Lords to do their worst in spoiling them, and content themselves with splitting differences afterwards; thus taking upon themselves a part only, and not the whole, of the discredit attached to niggardly measures of reform. This seems to be the price which the ministers, placed as they are in a state of absolute dependence upon the support of the Radicals, are willing to pay for it. What they get in return is, that no measure is to be proposed which they do not like, no principle enunciated which may, even indirectly, reflect upon their conduct; and that any one who dislikes anything which they say or do, is to keep his disapprobation confined within his own breast. We think the ministers have the best of the bargain.

We do not wish the Radicals to attack the Ministry; we are anxious that they should co-operate with them. But we think they might co-operate without yoking themselves to the ministerial car, abdicating all independent action, and leaving nothing to distinguish them from the mere Whig coterie, except the memory of their former professions. As little do we see why the liberal press—not content with bedaubing the Ministry with fulsome adulation for all they do, whether it be what those papers have been just before recommending, or the very opposite—should be so tremblingly afraid of giving insertion to a single line which may lead a chance reader to think they have an opinion of their own—should seem to think all lost if their columns contain anything but a probable anticipation of what the Ministry will next day propose. It is a fact that it was far more usual, before there was a reform ministry, to see reform opinions, of a stronger kind than were held by the Whig leaders, advocated in the liberal newspapers, than now when circumstances are so much more propitious to liberal ideas. To give one specimen among hundreds: we remember no period for the last ten years, when such an exposure as our last Number contained of the jobbing in the English army for the benefit of the great families—of the manner in which our military establishment is systematically made an engine for extracting large annual sums from the people under false pretences, to give to the sons of the rich—would not have been laid hold of by nearly the whole liberal press, and beaten into the people's minds by successive blows, until they all rose up as one man, and demanded that the iniquity should cease. In the year of our Lord one thousand eight hundred and thirty-five, for the first time since the word *Reform* ceased to be opprobrious, not one of the daily papers professing liberal principles *dared* say a word in condemnation of one of the grossest, most palpable, and most costly abuses remaining in our public expenditure. They knew not how their masters would relish the exposure.

If their object be to benefit the Ministry, this is not the way to do it; and stone-blind with self-conceit must the Ministry be if they fancy it is. One journal which, while it generally supports a ministry, occasionally condemns some of its words or actions, is worth more to it than a hundred which dare not call their columns their own, nor give currency to an opinion or a sentiment which they do not believe to be acceptable to the givers of good things. When the *Times* supported, first the Wellington and then the Grey ministry, its support carried authority; not because any one believed in the honesty of the *Times* then more than now, but because it was known to have an independent judgment. It had not wedded itself to any ministry for better for worse. It did not commit the tasteless blunder of praising all they did. When it supported them, therefore, there was a concurrence of two opinions; the *Times* coinciding with the Ministry—not the voice of the ministry merely echoed back, by people who only struck into the same tune because their prompters had commenced it.

It is the daily press chiefly which has laid itself open to these strictures: the *Examiner,* the *Spectator,* and others, though perhaps of late rather more panegyrical than necessary, cannot be accused of having compromised their pristine independence. But the daily press, unfortunately, is exactly six times as powerful as the weekly press; for the power of all newspapers consists in repetition, and a daily paper can repeat the same thing six times as often as a weekly one. It is therefore in the same proportion more important that the power it wields should be usefully directed; and, by the course now spoken of, that power is at the best wholly thrown away.

One important function the liberal newspapers are now executing; and it is of such magnitude, that, in its behalf, we willingly, for the time, forgive them their shortcomings in all other matters. They are serving as instruments to collect and concentrate the public indignation, and direct it in one jet against the House of Lords. They have, with some spirit, placed themselves at their proper post in the front rank of that battle. This is, we trust, significant of the inclination of the Ministry. That, however, is of trifling importance: where the public voice is strong and unanimous, the Ministry must now go along with it. If the Tories imagine, from the truckling of the Ministry and of the majority of the Radicals on the Corporation Bill, that their tampering with that measure was a *coup de force*, and a victory, they will find to their cost that it is the last triumph they are destined to enjoy. It is the last straw on the back of a patient people. They are at present in a happy unconsciousness of the mischief to themselves which they have set a-going; but their state is one of somnambulism, and the shock which will awaken them will be the apparition of the HOUSE OF LORDS AMENDMENT BILL.

STATE OF POLITICS IN 1836

1836

EDITOR'S NOTE

London and Westminster Review, III & XXV (Apr., 1836), 271-8. Headed: "ART. XII. / STATE OF POLITICS IN 1836." Running titles: 271, 272, 274, 276, 278, "Commencement of the Session"; 273, 275, 277, "Progress of Reform." Signed "A." Not republished. Identified in Mill's bibliography as "An article entitled 'State of Politics in 1836,' and headed 'Commencement of the Session'—'Progress of Reform,' in the same number of the same review", i.e., as "Civilization" (MacMinn, 47). There are no corrections or emendations in the copy (tear-sheets) in Somerville College.

State of Politics in 1836

THE OPENING of the Session has been auspicious. The year 1836 promises to be not unfruitful of important improvements in the details of our laws, while it has already afforded new and hopeful indications not only of the rapidity, but of the tranquillity with which the nation is travelling towards the attainment of the best government to which in its present state of civilization it can aspire.

The advantages are generally much overrated, which this country has derived from her possession of the forms of popular government, for a long period, during which the other nations of Europe were more destitute of the forms than even of the substance. But among these otherwise overrated advantages, is one which it is hardly possible to overrate: public opinion has acquired, has irrevocably acquired, the means of expressing itself peacefully. Whether the nation is of one opinion or another, does not, as in all other European countries, remain questionable until the sword decides it. A country in which there were no public meetings, no liberty of association, and, except at Paris, practically no liberty of the press, had to fight for three days before it could get rid of a dynasty which had scarcely an adherent left; and the world cried wonder at so great a revolution accomplished with so little bloodshed. The English effected a much greater change—gave the mortal stroke to one of the most powerful aristocracies in existence—accomplished a revolution equal to those for which, in former days or in other countries, generations of human beings have been swept away—overcame (we take from the lips of the Tories the catalogue of their forces) the King, the Lords, the Church, and the Land; and accomplished this, merely by assuming so imposing an attitude, that the warrior of Torres Vedras and Waterloo was either not bold enough, or not remorseless enough, to lead the charge against them.

The passing of the Reform Bill was our taking of the Bastille; it was the first act of our great political change; and like its precursor, it is a sample of the character of all that will follow. As the one was bloody, and the beginning of a bloody revolution, so does the pacific character of the other almost guarantee the peacefulness of the changes yet to come.

This reflection, which must have occurred to many at that remarkable period whose spirit-stirring events gave occasion to it, has been, perhaps, too much lost sight of in the succeeding four years. The resistance which the course of reform has since encountered, created an exaggerated impression of the difficulties which still remained for it to overcome. It was to be expected, that the defeated army would rally after the first overthrow; that they would mistake the fatigue of their victorious adversaries, and the momentary hesitation what point next to attack, for a reaction in their own favour; would indulge hopes that the strength which levelled them to the ground was the result of a temporary exaltation, and that when it subsided, things would quietly return to their former course. Defeated aristocracies have always been prone to such vain hopes. The royalists, during the first French Revolution, were in weekly expectation of some change which was to restore their ascendancy; nay, the Carlists of France indulge such expectations even now. But the English aristocracy is preserved from the fate which usually attends on such illusions, by causes with which their own discernment has little to do: they cannot *fore*see, but it is not possible for any one, living in this country, not to *see*. They *fore*saw nothing during the two years' discussion of the Reform Bill; but when the moment came, they saw their weakness and quailed. They foresaw not, when Sir Robert Peel came in, nor even when he was turned out, that their attempt to maintain a Tory ministry with a reformed Parliament must, for the time at least, be unsuccessful. But their demeanour in the present session proves that they see it now. If they did not, would they have abstained, as they have done, from opposing Ministers in the House of Commons in almost any one of their measures? or would the implacable Orangemen have been driven to disband themselves by a word?

The spirit of the Tory party is broken. They will rally again; and the power which, with the present constitution of society in England, so long as the protection of the ballot is refused, they can always, except in times of universal enthusiasm, exercise over the elections, may enable them more than once to rally in considerable strength. But all is in vain; for it is becoming obvious to everybody else, and at each defeat it will become so to more and more among themselves, that if the time comes when their defeat cannot be accomplished *without* the ballot, it will be accomplished *by* the ballot.

Meanwhile, the strong minority which the Tories for a time possess, has produced for the present a closer union, and a consequent increase of moral strength, among the opposite ranks. And this result, in itself so desirable, has not been effected, as we feared it would be, by compromises of principle on the part of the thorough Reformers. The thorough Reformers have met the Whigs half way; but it is only half way. The Ministers have, this session, evinced an activity in the work of reform, and a disposition to make its spirit penetrate into various branches of our institutions yet unvisited by it, which prove that they are, in some measure, awakened to the necessities of their position; and entitle them, while such conduct continues, to the strenuous support of the more vigorous Reformers—though not to the kind of support which ministries are most prone to demand, and, we grieve to say it, most accustomed to receive—the suppression of the utterance of any opinion which it is not convenient to them to go along with.

Among the measures, either introduced into Parliament, or promised to be introduced, for which commendation cannot be refused to Ministers, we will enumerate the following.

First, the Marriage Bill.[*] This is entitled to a praise which can rarely be bestowed upon the attempts of English statesmen in the character of Reformers. Though it deals with only one branch of an extensive subject, it is, within the limits of that branch, a complete measure; it leaves no relic of the grievance which it professes to remedy. All former bills for the same ostensible purpose had one of two grievous defects; they either exacted, as the condition of the validity of a civil contract, the performance of a religious ceremony, or they made a distinction between the clergy of the established and those of the dissenting sects, degrading to the latter.[†] By the present bill, nothing, in the ceremony of marriage, is required by the State, but that with which alone the State is concerned, the due execution and registration of the civil contract; while, at the same time, the religious ceremony, though legally imposed upon no one, is allowed, at the option of those who prefer it, to have, when duly registered, the force of a civil contract; and this equally, with whatever formalities, and by a clergyman of whatever persuasion, the ceremony is performed.

With this measure is combined a plan for supplying one of the innumerable *desiderata* in our legal arrangements, a registration of births and deaths.[‡] The application of the machinery of the Poor Law Unions to this purpose, is a striking example of the manner in which one well-considered reform facilitates others. Having now, by the effect of Poor Law Reform, rural districts of the convenient size for municipal purposes, and local representative bodies of a tolerably popular character (the Boards of Guardians), we trust that we shall gradually see the whole of the local business (the *administrative* business we mean, not the *judicial*) turned over to these representative bodies. But a distinction must be made, which the framers of this measure have overlooked. The Boards of Guardians are fit bodies to

---

[*"A Bill for Marriages in England," 6 William IV (17 Feb., 1836), *PP*, 1836, I, 393–401 (subsequently enacted as 6 & 7 William IV, c. 85).]

[†See, e.g., "A Bill to Relieve Certain Persons Dissenting from the Church of England, from Some Parts of the Ceremony Required by Law in the Celebration of Marriages," 59 George III (28 June, 1819), *PP*, 1819, I, 357–8; "A Bill to Alter and Amend Certain Parts of an Act of His Late Majesty King George the Second, Commonly Called The Marriage Act, Affecting Certain Dissenters," 3 George IV (22 Apr., 1822), *ibid.*, 1822, II, 987–9; "A Bill for Granting Relief in Relation to the Celebration of Marriages to Certain Persons Dissenting from the United Church of England and Ireland," 4 William IV (10 Mar., 1834), *ibid.*, 1834, II, 147–59; and "A Bill Concerning the Marriages of Persons Not Being Members of the United Church of England and Ireland, and Objecting to Be Married According to the Rite Thereof," 5 William IV (30 Mar., 1835), *ibid.*, 1835, III, 413–21 (none of these enacted).]

[‡"A Bill for Registering Births, Deaths and Marriages in England," 6 William IV (17 Feb., 1836), *ibid.*, 1836, I, 309–26 (subsequently enacted as 6 & 7 William IV, c. 86).]

conduct all, or almost all, the business of local administration, but the Central Board is not the proper body to superintend it all. The Central Board has quite as much as it can do in superintending the administration of the Poor Laws. To watch over other local business, other central boards, or central single functionaries, are requisite; the Boards of Guardians corresponding with each on the business of its own department. If everything which the local boards might conveniently do, were to be done by them under the control of the Commissioners of the Poor Laws, those Commissioners would become the Home Minister. There should be a controlling board, or a controlling officer, for every leading department of local administration, and a home minister, besides, to appoint these various officers, and hold them to a proper responsibility.

Next comes, as bearing some relation to the subject last noticed, the bill introduced to consolidate the Turnpike Trusts, and place them under a central board.[*] No reform is more urgently required, and the principle of the measure is excellent; but its details are ill-considered. The roads are not placed, as they might advantageously be, under the superintendence of the Boards of Guardians; and the Central Board almost seems constituted in imitation of that prodigy of imbecility and jobbery the Record Commission, upon the incompetency and abuses of which, the exertions of Mr. Charles Buller and other meritorious persons are now throwing so much light.[†] A board composed of numerous members, some of them persons of too many occupations or of too much dignity to attend to the business, becomes a mere screen[‡] for the misconduct of the one, or the two or three, individuals, into whose hands the management really falls.

We shall next advert to the Irish Corporation Reform Bill;[§] and most satisfactory it is, that the destructive part of the bill, which in this, as in most of the reforming measures of our Ministers, is the most important part, even the House of Lords will not venture to deny to us. Not a Tory has dared to say a word in vindication of the existing corporations; and those nests of all that is sordid in jobbing, and odious in sectarian animosity, will be swept without further delay from that earth which they contaminate. We go the full length with those who assert the claim of the Irish to popular local institutions, as the most efficient of all instruments for training the people in the proper use of representative government.

[*"A Bill to Authorize the Consolidation of the Trusts of Turnpike Roads in That Part of Great Britain Called England," 6 William IV (9 Feb., 1836), *PP*, 1836, VI, 427–39 (not enacted).]

[†"Report from the Select Committee on the Record Commission," *ibid.*, XVI; see also Charles Buller's motion on the Record Commission (18 Feb., 1836), *PD*, 3rd ser., Vol. 31, cols. 551–9.]

[‡Cf. Bentham, *Letters to Lord Grenville*, in *Works*, ed. Bowring, Vol. V, p. 17.]

[§"A Bill for the Regulation of Municipal Corporations and Borough Towns in Ireland," 6 William IV (16 Feb., 1836), *PP*, 1836, II, 549–627 (not enacted).]

But this benefit ought to be afforded to the whole kingdom, and not merely to the inhabitants of a few towns. Whether or not the constructive parts of the present measure be rejected by the House of Lords, the Ministers should give notice, for next session, of a general measure for the creation of provincial representative assemblies throughout Ireland.

The Church Reform which is announced, (for the recommendations of the Church Commissioners may be considered as those of the Ministry,) has one point of excellence, and it is a considerable one.[*] By diminishing the number of sinecures, and increasing the restrictions on pluralities and non-residence, it renders the good things of the Church by so much less valuable to the aristocracy, and so far tends to deprive the institution of what principally upholds it in its iniquities. Other merit than this the measure has none; for the endowment of the clergy of a particular sect with national property, and with civil or political privileges denied to other sects, is intrinsically a mischief, which may be extirpated, but can scarcely be palliated; and the only inducement by which any person worthy of the name of a statesman in these times, could be induced to uphold the Church, would be the hope of unsectarianizing it. With this view the elevation of one man to a post of dignity in the Church, who was the friend and not the enemy of free inquiry, and who was known to estimate others according to the *spirit* of their religion, more than according to its dogmas, would be better entitled to the name of Church Reform than a hundred measures like the present. But this road will not be tried till it is too late.

The Tithe Bill,[†] though liable to serious objections, which have been very forcibly stated in the *Morning Chronicle*,[‡] is deserving of praise as an honest attempt to settle an important and most difficult practical question. In the adjustment it seems impossible to avoid doing injustice to somebody, and all that can be hoped is to render the injustice as little as possible. The average for a certain period of years, should obviously be the measure of what existing incumbents, at least, should hereafter receive. For apportioning the payment among the different estates of the parish, there are but two principles which seem possible: to assess each estate in proportion to its value, or according to the amount hitherto paid by each. Either system requires that there be somewhere a power to relieve extreme cases; and if we are not ripe for making this relief a charge prospectively upon the

---

[*"A Bill for Carrying into Effect the Fourth Report of the Commissioners Appointed to Consider the State of the Established Church in England and Wales," 7 William IV (8 July, 1836), *ibid.*, I, 621–31 (enacted as 6 & 7 William IV, c. 77). See also "Fourth Report from His Majesty's Commissioners Appointed to Consider the State of the Established Church," *PP*, 1836, XXXVI, 65–78 ("First Report," *ibid.*, 1835, XXII, 1–14; "Second Report," *ibid.*, 1836, XXXVI, 1–44; and "Third Report," *ibid.*, 47–60).]

[†"A Bill for the Commutation of Tithes in England," 6 William IV (11 Feb., 1836), *ibid.*, VI, 125–44 (enacted as 6 & 7 William IV, c. 71).]

[‡Leading Article, *Morning Chronicle*, 21 Mar., 1836, p. 2.]

Church property itself, the best mode of affording it would, perhaps, be a *pro rata* assessment upon all the other estates.

Lastly, we must not overlook, among the beneficial measures in progress, (notwithstanding the niggardly half-measure with which it is attempted to satisfy us on the important subject of the newspaper stamp,)[*] the improvements announced in our system of Taxation.[†] Much gross inequality of pressure, bearing, as is invariably the case, hardest upon those who can least afford it, will be remedied or greatly alleviated by the general revision of the stamp laws; and some partial relief from one of the most burthensome of our monopolies, that which taxes us from a million to a million and a half a-year for the privilege of buying bad timber from Canada instead of good from the Baltic, has been declared to be in immediate contemplation.

There are not wanting, to set against these subjects of commendation, serious grounds of complaint. The discreditable exhibition of Sir George Grey on Mr. Roebuck's motion respecting the Mauritius;[‡] the navy increased, on pretexts such as can never be wanting, and which were triumphantly exposed by Mr. Hume,[§] (the real cause being, according to general belief, that Ministers are smitten with the epidemic disease of Russo-phobia;) the reduction of the army (and the abolition of the privileges of the Guards, so obnoxious to the army itself) resisted, in the exact tone and spirit in which all reforms used to be resisted in the old Tory times, namely, not by argument, but by insolent assumption, and denial of facts generally notorious, or resting upon official evidence. We receive these and similar things, as a salutary warning how much of the old leaven still remains in the present Cabinet, and how little can be trusted to their own inclination towards good, when not acted upon by a little friendly compulsion. That compulsion must be applied, and, moreover, must be yielded to, if they would hope to retain the support of the real reformers beyond the present session. For by the measures now in progress the budget of Whig reforms is almost exhausted; and they must either join with the Tories in resisting, or with the Radicals in carrying, improvements of a more fundamental kind than any but the latter have yet ventured to identify themselves with. Fortunately for Ministers, they have the immense field of Law Reform from which to gather a harvest of popularity; and they have had the good sense to provide for themselves, in the present Master of the Rolls,[¶] a

---

[*"A Bill to Reduce the Stamp Duties Payable on Newspapers," *PP*, 1836, V, 821–53 (enacted as 6 & 7 William IV, c. 54).]

[†Richard George Robinson, Speech on the Taxation of the Country (24 Mar., 1836), *PD*, 3rd ser., Vol. 32, cols. 552–62.]

[‡George Grey, Speech on the State of the Mauritius (15 Feb., 1836), *ibid.*, Vol. 31, cols. 401–20; John Arthur Roebuck, Motion on the State of the Mauritius, *ibid.*, cols. 390–401.]

[§Joseph Hume, Speech on Spain (5 Feb., 1836), *ibid.*, col. 127.]

[¶Henry Bickersteth.]

coadjutor, whose zeal in the work will need no quickener, but will be a most salutary quickener to theirs, and of whose capacity it is sufficient here to say, that no man living is so thoroughly acquainted at once with the ends to be aimed at, and the means of attaining those ends with the least possible inconvenience.

The Radical party in Parliament has, with few exceptions, preserved its accustomed torpidity. Those who had formerly done something, have done more than usual; but those who were accustomed to do nothing, have done it still. Among the meritorious few, Mr. Hume may, as usual, be numbered; and it may be permitted to this Review to commemorate the fact, that several younger members, in whom it can claim a peculiar interest, have been active in asserting in Parliament the principles which they promulgate here.[*] This is not, we know, anything to boast of; but were the fact otherwise, there would be disgrace.

Among the features in the present session, which ought not to be passed without notice, is the great multitude of Private Bills—bills for authorizing the expenditure of capital on public undertakings of all sorts, but especially on internal communication. The rage for projects has taken that direction more decidedly than any other, and has reached a height which the famous bubble year, 1825, scarcely surpassed. It seems only needful for a surveyor and a parliamentary agent to lay their heads together and invent a new line of railroad, and their share list is almost immediately filled. This subject well deserves that the attention of the legislature should be bestowed upon it, more comprehensively and systematically than it has yet been.

There is no one but must wish for means of cheap and rapid conveyance from one of the great centres of commercial operations to another; and all must be satisfied that such means will, in no long period, be had. But no one can wish that lines of railroad should be more numerous than necessary; because, in the first place, it is far from desirable that this island, the most beautiful portion perhaps of the earth's surface for its size, should be levelled and torn up in a hundred unnecessary directions by those deformities; and next, because the test, the unerring test, of the usefulness of a railroad is its yielding a profit to the subscribers; a result which the undue multitude of railroads must necessarily frustrate, as to most, if not as to all of them. For example—we do not ground our opinion on any peculiar knowledge—on the face of the matter it seems absurd to suppose that both the Great Western Railway, and the London and Southampton, can pay; though it is just possible that either of them might, if the other did not exist. Nor is it desirable that the choice of a line should be determined by no better test than the judgment of an irresponsible engineer, and the parliamentary influence happened to be possessed by the private interests which expect to be

[*Contributors to the *London and Westminster* who were also members of parliament were Charles Buller, William Molesworth (proprietor of the review), and John Arthur Roebuck.]

benefited or injured by it. No railroad schemes ought to receive the sanction of Parliament, until, by a general survey of the country, it shall have been ascertained what are the shortest and most convenient lines for a general system of railway communication, to connect all the important points. If this were done, all railways on those lines would, sooner or later, be profitable, and their construction ought to be permitted on those lines only; the nation stipulating for as large a share of the profits as the competition of rival companies might assign to it. Then might we hope for some, though but a distant approximation to the good fortune of the States of Pennsylvania and New York, each of which will speedily defray the whole expenses of its internal government from the profits of railroads constructed at the public expense.

We must add one other consideration. In the choice of a line it is disgraceful that not one thought should be bestowed upon the character of the natural scenery which is threatened with destruction. It is highly desirable that there should be a railway to Brighton; scarcely any one which could be constructed would be convenient to such a multitude of persons, or is likely to be so profitable to the subscribers. But of the five rival lines which have been proposed, two, if not three, and particularly Stephenson's, would, to a great degree, annihilate the peculiar beauty of a spot unrivalled in the world for the exquisiteness, combined with the accessibility, of its natural scenery: the vale of Norbury, at the foot of Box Hill. Yet into the head of hardly one Member of Parliament does it appear to have come, that this consideration ought to weigh one feather, even on the question of preference among a variety of lines, in other respects probably about equal in their advantages. Yet these men have voted £11,000 of the people's money for two Correggios, and many thousands more for a building to put them in,[*] and will hold forth by the hour about encouraging the fine arts, and refining the minds of the people by the pleasures of imagination. We see, by this contrast, what amount of real taste, real wish to cultivate in the people the capacity of enjoying beauty, or real capacity for enjoying it themselves, is concerned in this profuse expenditure of public money; although two-thirds of these men would shout in chorus against "political economists" and "utilitarians" for having no imagination, and despising that faculty in others. The truth is, that in this country the sense of beauty, as a national characteristic, scarcely exists. What is mistaken for it is the taste for costliness, and for whatever has a costly appearance. If the Correggios could have been had for as many pence as they cost pounds, our precious aristocracy would have scoffed at the idea of their being worth purchasing.

[*By 4 & 5 William IV, c. 84 (1834), §17, which covers both the acquisition of the paintings and a grant towards the construction of the building (the National Gallery).]

WALSH'S CONTEMPORARY HISTORY

1836

EDITOR'S NOTE

London and Westminster Review, III & XXV (July, 1836), 281–300. Headed: "ART. I. / SIR JOHN WALSH'S CONTEMPORARY HISTORY. / *Chapters of Contemporary History*. By Sir John Walsh, Bart. / Second Edition. [London:] Murray, 1836." Running titles: left-hand, "Sir John Walsh's Contemporary History"; right-hand, "Tories, Whigs, and Radicals." Signed "A." Not republished. Identified in Mill's bibliography as "An article headed 'Tories, Whigs, and Radicals' being a Review of Sir John Walsh's 'Chapters of Contemporary History,' in the London and Westminster Review for July 1836 (No 6 and 49)" (MacMinn, 47). There are no corrections or emendations in the copy (tear-sheets) in Somerville College.

Walsh's Contemporary History

SIR JOHN WALSH sat in one short Parliament, as the representative, we believe, of one of the rotten boroughs which the Reform Bill has spared. In his legislative career we have not heard of his signalizing himself by anything remarkable; but the general verdict of the Tory press has assigned to him the character of the first pamphleteer of their party. For this reason, together with some others to be hereafter noticed, we have chosen his latest production as a text for some remarks which we desire to promulgate respecting the same circle of topics. We could have wished for another kind of antagonist; for it is more agreeable to us to cope with the rational arguments, than with the vulgar fallacies, of our opponents. We can discern in the pamphlet nothing of the ability which has been attributed to the writer; but, on the contrary, a remarkable incapacity both for thinking and for the expression of thoughts. We are willing to rest this opinion upon a single specimen; being able to produce one which, by exhibiting *multum in parvo* of the character of Sir John Walsh's mind, will enable us to be content with such further exemplification of it as may arise incidentally from our own course of remark.

> I have always thought, [says Sir John,] that, in answer to the sophistries of those who so perpetually confound innovation and improvement, there is a very natural and obvious view of the subject which has not been frequently brought forward. It is common to say that innovation is not improvement; but we may carry out the position farther, and assert that innovation is always in its nature opposed to improvement. (P. 73.)

Sir John's is not, as he flatters himself, a new view of this matter. He will find it in the celebrated Noodle's Oration;[*] and there is not a noodle of his acquaintance who will not tell him that *innovation* and *improvement* are the most opposite things in nature; *improvement* the best, and *innovation* the worst thing conceivable. And why not? They are as contrary as praise and blame; as a good and a bad name for the same thing. What is the meaning of Innovation? Something new. And Improvement? Something new likewise. What then is the difference between Improvement and Innovation? Improvement means, "something new, which I like;" Innovation means, "something new, which I *do not* like." Sir John Walsh's discovery, put into plain English, reads thus: "It is common to say that [a new thing which I do not like] is not [a new thing which I do like]; but we may carry out the

[*"Noodle's Oration" appears on pp. 386–8 of Sydney Smith, "Bentham's *Book of Fallacies*," *Edinburgh Review*, XLII (Aug., 1825), 367–89.]

position farther, and assert that [a new thing which I do not like] is always in its nature opposed to [a new thing which I do like]."

We had not thought that the murkiest corner of Noodledom could still send forth a person capable of delivering this truth as a profound maxim of political wisdom, now first promulgated by himself to an admiring world.

Sir John has been misled into thinking himself the author of the maxim, by being really the author of a remarkably silly commentary upon it.

He shall have the advantage, if it be an advantage, of stating his meaning in his own words.

Innovation—I mean the substitution of a new and untried system for an old one—must generally be advocated upon the ground that we have been long in error,—that we have made many steps in a false direction, that we have blindly wasted and misapplied our time and efforts. Should the error be proved, it must be corrected; when we are convinced that our course is a mistaken one, we must retrace our path, but the necessity is dispiriting. The very conviction that we have been deceived when we believed that we were right, the very proof of our fallibility, is of itself a discouragement to attempts in a new track. We feel that we have wasted time and power, that we were buoyed up by a delusive belief that we were advancing; and we have at last to learn that we have lost our labour. We have been wrong, therefore we may be wrong again. What better security have we now than we had before? The improvement obtained by the mere rectification of error is of a negative and unsatisfactory nature. Substantial improvement, real progress, is gained by adding truth to truth, and building on the foundation which is already laid. If the foundation should prove unsound, or the plan defective, all may have to be begun again; but we do not commonly call this advancing. Apply this reasoning to some other science than politics. Let us take the discoveries of Newton for example, which shed undying glory on the country which gave him birth, and which raise human nature itself to a higher scale in the creation, to a more intimate knowledge of the scheme and the attributes of its mighty Author. When, by the great law of gravity, the immortal philosopher explained all the wonderful mechanism of planetary motion, certain slight irregularities caught his attention, trifling vacillations which he was unable to account for upon his system, and which he was disposed to consider as exceptions attributable to the little caprices of nature.

The later observations of the eminent French mathematicians, and their use of new and refined methods of calculation, proved those apparent deviations to be strict results of an extended application of his principles. They discovered that these disturbances, as they are called, were the effects of the reciprocal action of the gravity of the different planetary bodies upon each other, and farther, that by a beautiful nicety in the adjustment, they balanced each other, so as never to introduce any permanent irregularity into the system. Here, then, is progress, wholesome, sound, indisputable progress—a principle satisfactorily explaining new facts, and the new facts corroborating the truth of the principle. Suppose now that we had found in La Place or La Grange a radical reformer in astronomical science—that their ingenuity had detected a flaw in the reasoning of the *Principia*[*]—that the immortal discoveries of Newton had been reduced to the level of the whirlpools of Des Cartes,[†] or any other fanciful and exploded theory, would this have been advance? How we

---

[*Isaac Newton, *Philosophiae naturalis principia mathematica*, in *Opera quae exstant omnia*, ed. Samuel Horsley, 5 vols. (London: Nichols, 1779–85), Vols. II–III.]

[†René Descartes, *Principia philosophiae*, in *Opera philosophica*, 4th ed. (Amsterdam: Elzevir, 1664), pp. 51, 61 ff. (III, xxx and liii ff.).]

should have regretted the overthrow of that noble and lucid system—how we should have mourned that our mental vision, which had been extended almost to embrace infinity, should have again been contracted to a narrow span![*] How painfully and reluctantly should we have surrendered the high and pure thoughts, the splendid prospect of the economy of the universe, which this proudest achievement of human intellect had spread before us! and with what a cold scepticism as to the reality of truth in anything—with what a mortified sense of the fallibility of our powers should we have recalled our absolute belief in a theory, which, while it enables the imagination to wing its loftiest flight, rests upon reason's firmest basis. (Pp. 74–6.)

Here is, at last, something like a meaning, gradually evolving itself: and we need nothing more to justify the opinion we have declared of Sir John Walsh's intellect, than this meaning, together with the manner in which it is expressed.

For, first, as to his power of expressing his own meaning; look at his attempt to compress it into a logical definition. "Innovation—I mean the substitution of a new and untried system for an old one." Would this enable any one even to guess what distinction the writer is about to draw? A person whose ideas are clear, uses words which make them sink into the mind, instead of letting them slide off it on the well-worn surface of a rhetorician's stock phrases. What Sir John would say, as we gather from the remainder of the passage, is this: "Innovation is something new, which, if right, implies the supposition that something old was wrong; Improvement is something new which does not imply that supposition." These two, he says, are contrary; and the former a direct, and the greatest possible, hinderance to the latter.

Now, admitting that it is one thing to change from wrong to right, and another thing to do something right which does not imply that we had previously done wrong, is it not in either case equally our business to do right now? And is there not something inconceivably pitiful in the attempt to insinuate that it is not quite so good a thing to do right in the one case as in the other? It deserves notice, moreover, that although in speculative inquiries (from which, with great inappropriateness, Sir John's illustration is taken) we may sometimes add truth to truth without finding ourselves out in any error; in practical matters we hardly ever adopt anything new, without giving up something old which is superseded by it. By an invention in machinery, an article can be produced at half the cost: if you purchase the new machine, and use it together with the old, it is improvement; if you discard the worthless instrument, then, according to Sir John Walsh, it is innovation. Your servant is lazy, dishonest, and a drunkard: you hire a new one; if you also retain the rascal, it is improvement; if you dismiss him, the benefit is "negative and unsatisfactory," and the change no better than an innovation. You inherit a fine estate, but in so unwholesome a situation that you cannot live in it: if you can afford to buy another estate, retaining the old one, according to Sir John

---

[*See George Herbert, "The Pulley," in *The Temple: Sacred Poems and Private Ejaculations* (Cambridge: Buck and Daniel, 1633), p. 153.]

Walsh you may; but if you *sell* the old estate to buy another, you do that which is not only not improvement, but "is always in its nature opposed to improvement, and of which the single tendency is always to suspend, often to retard it." If we had time for verbal criticism, we might ask how that which is *suspended* can fail to be *retarded*?

Even after allowing himself so wide a scope for the choice of his illustration, he cannot use it without its recoiling upon himself. He tells us, with that inflation of language by which writers of no imagination fancy they give additional dignity to the great results of science, that La Place's discoveries would have given him less pleasure if they had proved Newton to be wrong; but that proving him as they did to be right, here was "progress—wholesome, sound, indisputable progress." What, then, thinks Sir John of Newton himself? Did *he* not prove his predecessors to have been in the wrong? Or were his discoveries no "progress;" and will Sir John Walsh say of them too, "we do not commonly call this advancing?" Are they not, on the contrary, the era from which alone any real advance became possible?

Sir John, with a candour which is no very arduous virtue while confined to generals, acknowledges that "should the error be proved, it must be corrected." Then why profess so much dislike to correcting it? Men do not usually harp so much upon the painfulness of an operation which they are very sincerely desirous of seeing performed. "The necessity," it seems, "is dispiriting," and "the proof of our fallibility" (we quote his very words) "is a discouragement to attempts in a new track." This, then, is the objection to innovation—that it is an acknowledgment of our fallibility. Sir John undertakes to prove that "innovation is always in its nature opposed to improvement." And how does he substantiate the assertion? By saying that he dislikes to correct an error,—can the reader imagine why? because it proves to him that he is capable of committing one! a fact which, apparently, he would not otherwise have entertained a suspicion of.

We must tell Sir John Walsh, that when he says that detecting ourselves in an error disturbs our confidence in our own infallibility, he ascribes to it an effect which, by the consent of moralists, philosophers, Christians, and persons of common sense in all ages, is so far from being undesirable, that until it is accomplished neither wise thinking nor wise conduct is so much as possible; and that the discovery, instead of being one which ought to plunge us into dismay, is a necessary condition of all rational confidence in our own strength, or in the soundness of our own opinions. If Sir John Walsh were right, the discoveries of Bacon and Newton, instead of being the periods from which we reckon the improvement of physical science, should have struck a sudden damp into it, and chilled the heart of every scientific man with a "cold scepticism as to the reality of truth in anything." Is such the historical fact? Speak, O contemporary historian!

If this writer had not been held up by the Tory critics as one of the great rising ornaments of their party, we should not have thrown away time and space upon a controversy in which we are neither called upon to say, nor to answer, anything requiring thought, anything not absolutely trite. But the character of Toryism is better seen in Sir John Walsh and his class, than in men of some originality and power of mind. Nothing has given us a lower opinion of the Tories as a body, than to observe on what class of their advocates it is that their applause is lavished. Let the young and ambitious adventurer, who would rise by Toryism notwithstanding the disadvantage of a clear head, observe whether what we say is not true. The man whom they recognise as their champion is never he who gives to Toryism (what can be given to it, though not to Whiggism) something like a philosophic basis; who finds for their opinions the soundest, the most ingenious, or the most moral arguments by which they can be supported; but invariably the man who, with greater fluency or a more daring manner than ordinary, gets up and vents their most shattered and worn-out absurdities. There is another cause for this besides the greater adaptation of the latter class of arguments to the general calibre of their understanding. No one can make speculative Toryism a thing that will bear the light, without cutting off many of the most lucrative parts of practical Toryism. We never knew a Tory of any power of mind, who did not, either secretly or openly, give up the Irish Church. But the Tories in general deem this too high a price for a small improvement in their argument, and a great one in their character for honesty. Sir John Walsh for them. He throws his mantle over all. Even Irish Toryism is not too shocking a thing for him.*

*Sir John Walsh's last chapter [pp. 114–40] is on "The State of Ireland," and contains what he deems an idea of surpassing originality. This idea is ushered in by some remarks on the superficiality of the "boasted diffusion of knowledge," [p. 114,] the shallowness of the ordinary run of minds, and the little progress which has been made towards understanding the subjects with which we are most occupied, and particularly Ireland. Having lamented the obscurity which still involves this subject, and given it to be understood who is the person destined to convert that obscurity into the clearest light, he proceeds to state, as follows, the current misconceptions:

"The popular, current, superficial view of the state of Ireland is this, that it is a country containing an immense Catholic population, and a very small proportion of Protestants of the Church of England,—that the Protestants of the Church of England, supported by the power of the Tory Administrations at home, have established a monopoly of offices, places of trust and consideration, dignity and emolument, and have held their Catholic fellow-countrymen in a state of civil bondage,—that they have been governed by a narrow, bigoted, tyrannical spirit, making a different religious belief operate as a disqualification in every profession, a bar across every path which led to distinction or to fortune,—that the Established Church of Ireland being, as it is, the Church of a small minority of the people, is one great overgrown abuse,—that the English Cabinets have been contented to rule the country for years through the instrumentality of this faction, thereby perpetuating and exasperating religious differences, and sustaining through force the system of a sort of religious oligarchy, oppressive and unjust to the body of the nation,—that a wise and generous policy now dictates a conduct diametrically opposed in all respects to this harsh and exclusive system,—that the first object and care of the Executive in Ireland must be to obliterate every trace of those unjust preferences on the score of religion which have so long been the watchword of our Government. Protestant ascendency must no longer be the

Having now assigned the class of writers to which Sir John Walsh belongs, it is but just to add that he is one of the best of the class. His language is not only decorous, but respectful to his opponents. They are not all of them, in his eyes, demons, or profligate adventurers, or sciolists and coxcombs. At least, he does not call them so; though he affirms of them things hardly reconcilable with any other supposition. But we are not to look for consistency in a partisan's description of the opposite party. There is no want of candour in Sir John Walsh. He always states

principle on which power is to be exercised, honours or emoluments conferred—the interests of the great Catholic body must be duly considered, and equal eligibility of the two religious persuasions to all civil appointments practically acted upon,—that the domineering and tyrannical spirit of Orangeism must be crushed and discountenanced in every possible manner,—that the Irish Church Establishment, being unnecessary to the Protestants, and both oppressive and insulting to the Catholics, must be reduced or abolished,—that, in fine, Ireland has hitherto been treated as a conquered Catholic country under a garrison of Orangemen, backed by English power; that she is now to be governed as a free Catholic nation, in which the interests of the Protestants are to be reduced to their proper proportion." [Pp. 116–18.]

This really does seem to be no very incorrect picture of the real state of matters as to Ireland. But hear Sir John Walsh: "Now I assert, that whatever Minister were to form his opinions, or to mould his system of policy, upon these statements, would do so upon the most superficial grounds—upon views either wholly erroneous, or partial, confined, and limited. I contend that the most material circumstances, whether as regards the internal state of Ireland, or her peculiar relations with this country, are entirely lost sight of, or indeed never seem to have been noticed, in these loose, commonplace representations of her condition." [P. 118.] These material circumstances, which every one except Sir John Walsh has overlooked, are, that the Protestants are the rich, and the Catholics are the poor; that the Protestants are the descendants of foreigners, who seven hundred years ago conquered the country, possessed themselves of all the property, and have since remained a "garrison in an enemy's country;" that it was, therefore, natural that they should engross all the power, and that in the exercise of this power they should be "overbearing and arrogant." [Pp. 125, 123.]

"Six hundred and fifty years have been unable to produce a kindly and thorough fusion between the conquerors and the conquered, to efface the distinguishing marks of a different origin, or to heal those rankling animosities which still fester in their hearts." . . . "The citizen of Perronne occupies his thoughts little with the memory of Charles the Bold. The native of Alsace or of Lorraine deems himself just as good and complete a Frenchman as the inhabitant of Paris. The Catalonian and Castilian are both Spaniards. But the Celtic Irish peasant, divided from his Protestant countrymen by the two great barriers of language and religion, still cherishes the obscure traditions of a remote age; and, as the Protestant landowner or substantial tradesman passes him on the road, he throws a scowl over his shoulder, and in his deep gutteral Gaelic he curses them as Saxon invaders, usurpers, and heretics." [Pp. 121–2.]

If ever the argument of an unskilful advocate recoiled fatally upon its author, this does. The fact which Sir John, in his ignorance of history, imagines to be peculiar to Ireland, is common to all Europe. Seven hundred years ago, every country in Christendom was in the possession of a set of foreign invaders, who, having possessed themselves of the soil, and reduced the inhabitants to bondage, were masters (as Sir John says of the Protestants of Ireland) of all the property and intelligence in the country. The Commons of every nation in

fairly the principles and arguments of opponents, so far as he knows them; but what he knows is very small. Almost the only authorities he cites are the *Morning Chronicle* and the *Globe*; and these only since they became slavishly ministerial. He has, nevertheless, the modesty to conclude, that because he knows no more of the sentiments of the Reformers than these sources supply, there is therefore nothing further to be known. He charges the Reformers in good set terms with having no purposes of their own, and says roundly, that their only principle is to follow the popular cry; though in the very next page (p. 103) he says that this popular cry is a creation of theirs, artfully got up by them for their own purposes. It puzzles us to think how these two assertions can both be true: that they may both be false, we assure him that on proper inquiry he would find. He calls upon them to state the ends they propose, and the evils they desire to remedy (p. 110); and seems to be sincerely persuaded that these are matters which have not yet been disclosed. A person who undertakes to answer others should be better instructed in what they say. Cicero tells us that he always studied his adversary's side of the question, if possible more intensely than even his own.[*] We will not require so much from Sir John Walsh: to discover all that his opponents *might* say would be a task beyond his capacity; let him only make himself acquainted with what they *have* said. There are some parts of it, not unworthy of a politician's attention in these days. Meanwhile, we must allow Sir John Walsh the credit of having made one or two admissions, of which we intend availing ourselves, and of having told about an equal number of wholesome truths to the Parliamentary and ostensible leaders of our own party. These are merits; and they are the only ones which we have been able to discover in the pamphlet.

Europe are the descendants of men somewhat less barbarous, perhaps, but otherwise exactly in the situation of the aboriginal Irish. Serfs who ran away from their masters, or whom their masters allowed to purchase their freedom, were the origin of the *tiers-état*. How then happens it, that in every other country this oppressed class gradually emerged from insignificance; acquired freedom, wealth, and intelligence; obtained substantial, and at last even nominal equality of political privileges—until the very memory of their past injuries became obliterated, and no distinction remained between the children of the conquerors and the children of the conquered; while in Ireland alone no similar improvement took place, and the original relation between the two races remains, according to Sir J. Walsh, substantially the same as at the first conquest? There is but one explanation:—all other governments, though the fruits of conquest and spoliation, were not thoroughly bad, were not hopelessly incompatible with the improvement of the conquered; the Irish alone were under a government which would not let them improve—which would not let them become rich and intelligent—which rendered it *impossible* for them, like the servile population of other countries, to recover by industry what they had lost by conquest. And that such was the fact, is stamped, in characters of blood, on every page of Irish history.

[*See Cicero, *De oratore* (Latin and English), trans. E. W. Sutton and H. Rackham, 2 vols. (London: Heinemann; Cambridge, Mass.: Harvard University Press, 1942), Vol. I, pp. 108 (I, xxxiv), 272 (II, xxiv), and 304 (II, xxxiv). Cicero does not appear to have made explicitly the comparison with one's own case.]

In what follows we shall regard Sir John Walsh, not as Sir John Walsh, but as what he evidently desires to be considered, the representative of the opinions of his party; namely, that of which Sir Robert Peel is the head, and which may be defined as the more worldly-wise portion of the Tory faction. There need be no hesitation in admitting him as their organ, as we have not discovered one opinion, one sentiment, or one expression in the pamphlet, which might not just as well have been uttered by any other individual of the set.

The book professes to contain the Tory view of contemporary history. Sir John begins his history with the Reform Bill. As might be expected, his view of that measure differs considerably from that entertained by Reformers. Let us look at it. The time is never lost which is employed in understanding the state of mind of our opponents.

According to Sir John, the cry for reform was not produced by any real or supposed grievances; the people had no complaint against their governors, nor even thought they had. Complaints, though of the vaguest possible description, had indeed been made, and even, it would seem, believed. "We have heard, till reiterated assertion is taken for proof, of a century of misgovernment, a long monopoly of power, the perpetration of abuses, the rankness of corruption, the venality, extravagance, and incapacity of former ministries." (P. 31.)

Sir John, however, attributes the demand for the Reform Bill to no such cause, but either to "the appetite for speculative innovation" (p. 3), or to "the desires of the body of the people for a more active and direct participation in political power" (p. 2). We say *either*, because Sir John does not always adhere to the same theory. Whichever of these views, however, he adopts (and he seems to adopt them alternately), in one point he is consistent: in affirming that the increased power which the Reform Bill gave to the democracy, was desired not as a means, but as an end; that this great constitutional change was effected, and the further organic changes of the Ballot, Triennial Parliaments, Reform of the House of Lords, &c., are now sought, for their own sake, and not for the sake of any improvement to be thereby wrought in the actual management of public affairs. It was the love of meddling in their own government, not the desire of being better governed, that actuated the people. The class of persons who were eager for "practical reform" (by which he means improvement in the actual working of the government, as distinguished from changes in the constitution of the governing body) were those whom the Reform Bill found in power, and displaced; namely, the Tory aristocracy, whom Sir John compliments with the appelation of "the educated classes" (p. 76). These, indeed, were actuated by a burning zeal for all improvement. "Every enlarged view of political economy, every judicious mode of retrenchment, every practical reform" (p. 77), found in them zealous advocates. A body possessed by such an ardour of reformation, and which had so long held in their hands full power to give effect to their wishes, naturally left nothing to reform. Accordingly, Sir John Walsh triumphantly announces that no abuses have been detected or remedied since the Reform Bill passed. To have justified the expectation of its supporters, it ought, he thinks, to have been the means of bringing to light some undiscovered mystery of iniquity. This, indeed, would have appalled Sir John.

Had the recent changes drawn the curtain aside which veiled political profligacy and corruption, I should have experienced the mortification of discovering myself the most egregious of dupes; I should have felt the most depressing of all sensations, that of discovering the worthlessness and deceit of what had been the cherished object of my earliest veneration, which had long commanded the homage rendered to excellence and virtue. (Pp. 33–4.)

A person who so candidly confesses the extreme mortification with which he abandons any idea which has been instilled into him by his nurse, is not exactly fitted for a public teacher in an age of revolutions. Sir John, however, did not experience this humiliation.

Let it be remembered that Lord Grey and his colleagues held office four years—that, after having triumphantly carried the Reform Bill, they still, at the head of an overwhelming majority in the House of Commons, conducted affairs during two parliamentary sessions, and brought forward two ministerial batches of measures. Where were the corruptions detected—where were the abuses exposed—where was the prodigality checked? What materials of power and popularity would they not have acquired, if they could have denounced and held up their predecessors as political delinquents? (P. 31.)

If the Constitution under which we were born, and the system under which we have passed the larger portion of our lives, were in reality but one mass of abuses, but one vast conspiracy against the interest and happiness of the community, how does it arise that so complete a reform, that so entire a change of men, has thrown no light upon the concealed iniquities? (P. 33.)

Such is the Tory statement of the origin, progress, and character of the spirit of reform. And we have been thus explicit in setting it forth, for the purpose of giving to it, in behalf of our countrymen, a solemn, absolute, and indignant denial. It is not true that the demand for parliamentary reform had anything to do either with any general theory of government (which would have been no imputation) or, which would have been a great imputation, with the mere passion for the exercise of power. So far from having no connexion with practical grievances, it was and is directed solely against practical grievances. There is no passion in England for forms of government, considered in themselves. Nothing could be more inconsistent with the exclusively practical spirit of the English people. There is no hostility to aristocracy in England; the people would far rather be governed by their superiors than by their equals. Like all other nations, they had the partiality of habit for the institutions under which they had grown up; and the artifices of a whole century had wrought up this partiality into one of the most obstinate of prejudices. Of this prejudice the majority of the Reformers have had their full share; and it only yielded to a long and bitter experience of practical grievances, combined with irresistible evidence, which forced itself upon the most unreflecting among them, of the connexion between every one of those grievances and the sinister interest of some portion of those whom Grattan emphatically called "the proprietors of Parliament."[*]

Had we not repeatedly been startled by the shortness of men's memories as to the events of their own time, it would astonish us that even a Tory should have forgotten what was the main occupation of the public mind during the ten years preceding the Reform Bill. It was, to a degree unparalleled in our history, and with constantly increasing intensity, engrossed, not with theories of government, but with the exposure and denunciation of practical abuses. Before that time the assailants of the existing constitution of Parliament had had the weakness to rest their case mainly upon generalities; upon the received theory of the House of Commons; upon history, and the ancient practice of the Constitution. Accordingly they preached to deaf ears, until the Cartwright school of reformers died out, and others of a more "practical" kind succeeded, who bade adieu to abstractions, and insisted upon judging the tree by its fruits. The movement which gave existence to the Reform Bill, dates in reality from the period when Mr. Hume commenced his memorable exposures of the almost inconceivable profligacies of our public expenditure.[*] He was soon aided by writers (among whom Mr. Black, of the *Morning Chronicle*, and Mr. Fonblanque, of the *Examiner*, were the most conspicuous) who, by their repeated exposures, made the people sensible of the enormities in the administration of justice, especially those of the unpaid magistracy. Was there not during all the same period a growing disapprobation of the corn-laws? of the game-laws? of slavery? of the restrictions on industry? of tithes? of corporation abuses? of the vices of the law? of the inefficiency and extravagance of the Church Establishment? of the atrocious principle of holding Ireland in subjection by foreign bayonets to the most profligately tyrannical of native oligarchies? Sir John Walsh should have carried his readings of the *Morning Chronicle* further back. A Contemporary Historian should know something of contemporary history.

From the eager zeal for the redress of all grievances, which, according to Sir John, animated the whole of the ruling classes previously to the Reform Bill, joined to the fact that none of the evils which we have enumerated were redressed, or had any prospect of being so, during the continuance of their ascendency, we can only infer that these, in the opinion of Sir John, were not grievances. And this, indeed, is no unlikely opinion to be held by Sir John; but we cannot quite reconcile it with the credit he takes to the Conservatives for concurring in the reform of some of these very grievances *since* the Reform Act, and for their readiness to reform

---

[*Cf. Henry Grattan, Speech on Parliamentary Reform (15 May, 1797; Irish Commons), in *The Speeches of the Right Honourable Henry Grattan*, ed. Henry Grattan, 4 vols. (London: Longman, Hurst, Rees, Orme, and Brown; Dublin: Milliken, 1822), Vol. III, p. 334.]

[†For his first attack, see Joseph Hume, Speech in Introducing a Motion for Economy and Retrenchment (27 June, 1821), *PD*, n.s., Vol. 5, cols. 1345–1417.]

others which are yet uncorrected. This readiness, according to him, is no new quality of theirs. They were as eager to make these improvements formerly, when they had the power and did not, as now, when it no longer depends upon them:

> We are no reluctant, tardy, insincere converts to the cause of practical reform. We do not yield a constrained and interested acquiescence to an overpowering necessity. We are not inconsistent with ourselves. The great body of the Conservatives in the empire would have supported as heartily all Sir Robert Peel's proposed measures of last session ten years ago as they would now. (Pp. 78-9.)

Indeed! But Sir Robert Peel, if we mistake not, was in office ten years ago: if "the great body of the Conservatives" were all eagerness to have these measures proposed, why did not that recognised leader of the party, and Sir John Walsh's model of a statesman, propose them? And when, for instance, the Unitarian Marriage Bill,[*] which gave to one particular class of Dissenters a partial and scanty relief from that burden on their consciences which Sir Robert Peel last year proposed to take off entirely—when this Bill was thrown out by the House of Lords at the instigation of Lord Eldon[†] and the Bishops, the motive was doubtless an impatient frenzy of reformation, which would take no "instalment," and regarded anything but the removal of the entire grievance as a compromise with iniquity. Or is Sir John's statement (for it is ambiguously worded) satire in disguise; and does his assertion that the Tories would have supported the measures of Sir Robert Peel as heartily ten years ago as they would now, mean that they would give no more support to those measures now than they would have given formerly?

Sir John is more rational when he begins to treat not of past things, but of present. In this part of his discourse we are sometimes able to concur in his sentiments, and even to adopt his language.

For example, we agree with him when he says that the nation is rapidly arranging itself into the two divisions of Reformers and Anti-reformers, or, as he proposes to call them, Conservatives and Radicals: that these two parties (though the latter, as far as organization is concerned, is not a party) are both of them gaining strength, at the expense not of each other, but of the Indifferents and the *juste milieu*: and that there will soon be no middle party, as indeed what seemed such had long been rather an appearance than a reality.

"I believe," says Sir John—and this is one of the admissions, of which, to employ a French phrase, *nous prenons acte*—

> That, of what may be strictly called reaction, there has not been a particle. We have been strengthened by the accession of many neutrals, by the awakened energy of the timid and the

---

[*"A Bill for Granting Relief to Certain Persons Dissenting from the Church of England," 8 George IV (14 May, 1827), *PP*, 1826-27, II, 21-4 (not enacted).]

[†John Scott, Speech on Dissenters' Marriages Bill (26 June, 1827), *PD*, n.s., Vol. 17, cols. 1411-17.]

careless, by the discovery of many in the ranks of our opponents that their position was a false one. We have not yet gained one inch upon the democratic spirit; on the contrary, the very same causes which have strengthened us, have strengthened it in a nearly similar ratio. ... As the struggle becomes closer, and the objects less disguised and more apparent, each party will receive additions to its numbers up to a certain point; but a period may shortly arrive when almost every individual will have made his election between the two principles, and when these fluctuations will be rarer. (Pp. 83-5.)

Sir John is equally right in his character of the Whigs, which has excited such a storm of indignation from the *Edinburgh Review*.[*] They were, and are, a *coterie*, not a party; a *set*, confined to London and Edinburgh, who commanded a certain number of seats in Parliament, and a certain portion of the press, and were accepted by the Reformers as leaders, because they offered themselves, and because there was nobody else. When any man appeared in Parliament (they were too ignorant of their age ever to look beyond) whose talents qualified him to act a conspicuous part, they courted him, and if he was willing to become one of them, admitted him into the circle. They thus adopted Horner, and Romilly, and Brougham. By this means they always kept themselves apparently at the head of all that part of the public who professed liberal opinions. But their leadership was ostensible only. Since the questions arising out of the Hanoverian succession had been set at rest, the term Whig had never been the symbol of any principles. So long as popular dissatisfaction was directed against men, not things—against the particular acts of particular ministers—the Whigs, as being the men who were to replace those ministers if the people succeeded in turning them out, continued to be an essential element in the contest. Not so when the questions which divided the public came to be those which related to the reform of our institutions. The Whigs, who were a portion of the privileged class, and were under the full influence both of the interests and of the prejudices of that class, at once took up a position hostile to any thorough reform. This position the Liberals of the empire have never chosen to participate. They did not repudiate the Whigs; but as little did they repudiate what the Whigs repudiated. They were neither Whigs nor Radicals; they were Reformers. They had not predetermined how far parliamentary reform should go; but they were disposed to carry it as far as, on trial, should be found necessary for obtaining good government. They were not for the ballot, or annual parliaments, because the opinion did not generally prevail among them that nothing less would suffice; but they had no prejudice against either, if an extension of the suffrage, with septennial or triennial parliaments, should fail to give them a government of which the pervading spirit should be a regard to the public good.

This was the state of mind of the body of Reformers, down to the passing of the Reform Act; and for them it was essentially a sound and wholesome state. Those only who have qualified themselves by a greater degree of study and experience

---

[*William Empson, "Sir John Walsh's *Contemporary History*," *Edinburgh Review*, LXIII (Apr., 1836), 239-70.]

than has fallen to the lot of most, are entitled to have a confident opinion on the extent to which it may be necessary to carry a political change, previously to trial. The people, however, not having made up their minds, when the Reform Bill passed, whether any further constitutional change would be requisite or not, they naturally, where they were free to choose, chose mostly, as their first representatives, men whose minds were no more made up than theirs were: and hence that absence of any marked character or tendency, which our author notices in the new men who were then first introduced into public life (pp. 38-41). Sir John even states this less emphatically than it might be stated. He mistakes when he says (p. 10), "the elections of December 1832 returned two-thirds of the whole number decided Whigs." They were neither Whigs, nor decided; they were the essence of everything that is undecided. They were that *parti du ventre* (as it was styled in the French Convention) which has existed in most countries, at most critical periods; men who have no principle of guidance but the fear of extremes; who are constantly "betwixt two minds," and when they have made a step one way, make a step the contrary way for the sake of compensation; who have no confidence in any leaders, but having still less in themselves, are swayed by every breath, and may be driven even into the things they are most terrified at, by "pressure from without."[*]

It was by practising upon the weakness of such men, that the Stanley Cabinet (for the conduct of that ministry took its character from its worst member) was enabled for a session and a half to carry on the system which one of its members has since avowed that it deliberately pursued—that of proposing nothing in the Reformed House of Commons but what was agreeable to the Tories. This system could not last. The people became alienated, not because the Whigs did not propose further organic changes, for the experiment had only just commenced which was to convince the people that such were necessary; but because their "practical reforms," their "course of improvement in details,"[†] were shaped to the taste of those who were of Sir John Walsh's opinion, that no abuses existed previously to the Reform Bill. The Whigs became unpopular, not because they *wished* the Reform Bill to be a "final measure,"[‡] but because, rather than risk a "collision"[§] which might prevent that wish from being realized, they were willing to abandon all the ends to which the Reform Bill was intended as a means.

This it was that ruined the Whig Ministry, and for ever extinguished the policy of which they were the representatives. "When the Ministry," says Sir John, and

---

[*Walsh, p. 32. For the concluding phrase, see Charles Grey, Letter to Lord Ebrington (31 May, 1834), in *Examiner*, 8 June, 1834, p. 355.]

[†Walsh, pp. 77, 11.]

[‡Cf. Walsh, p. 111. For the origin of the phrase, see John Charles Spencer, Speech on the Ministerial Plan of Parliamentary Reform (1 Mar., 1831), *PD*, 3rd ser., Vol. 2, cols. 1139-44.]

[§Walsh, p. 19.]

we fully concur in the assertion—"when the Ministry of Lord Grey was broken up, first by the secession of Lord Stanley and his friends,[*] and subsequently by the Premier's own resignation, it was not a cabinet which was dissolved, it was a system of government which was overturned."(P. 1.)

The Grey Ministry represented one system of government, and fell because they would not abandon it. The Melbourne Ministry are the representatives of another system of government, one remove only from the former: and they too must soon make their election, to abandon it, or to fall.

The Grey Cabinet, as a body (though against the wishes of some of its individual members), acted on the principle not only of resisting any further Parliamentary Reform, but of not originating or supporting reforms of any kind, which, by producing a "collision," might possibly lead to that result. The Melbourne Ministry, as a body (also, it is believed, against the wishes of several of its members), has abandoned only one-half of this policy, retaining the other. It resists, with as much obstinacy as its predecessors, not only any proposition for a further increase of the popular control over the legislature, but the bare idea that such can be rendered necessary by any conceivable prolongation of the struggle against good government. The difference between the policy of the Grey and that of the Melbourne Ministry is, that the latter, though they deprecate "organic change,"[†] do not, as the former did, make the prevention of it the grand business of their government. To save the Lords from themselves is still their object, but no longer their sole object. They do not shield the Lords from the odium of rejecting good measures, by taking that odium upon themselves; they propose what they think good, and what is acceptable to the House of Commons, and let the Peers reject it at their peril.

Such a policy does not preclude, in the same manner as Lord Grey's did, the possibility of a co-operation between the Ministry and the more decided Reformers. But it limited greatly the class from which Lord Melbourne could recruit for his Ministry. In a cabinet constituted on such a principle, no Reformer could be included, whose convictions would not allow him to join in a determined resistance to all further organic changes. And this category now included every man of rising talent among the Reformers, except Lord Howick and perhaps one or two other scions of the great Whig families. Lord Melbourne was thus compelled to fall back upon those families, and upon the obscurer members of the old *coterie*; for all who were conspicuous by talents or reputation had been taken off, either by death or the progress of events. And hence that absence of individual weight of character and talent, which enemies and friends equally remark in the Melbourne Ministry. For it deserves notice as one of the signs of the times, that the Whig

[*James Robert George Graham, Charles Gordon Lennox, and Frederick Robinson.]
[†Walsh, p. 3.]

coterie is not renewed. There are no young Whigs. The vacancies which death makes in their ranks are not filled; and their ministry must henceforth be recruited from persons not of the clique.

Another effect of the adherence of the Whigs to that part of Lord Grey's policy which consists of resistance to further organic change, is, that they are now the weakest of the three parties in Parliament. Without the systematic support of the Radicals, they could not exist for a day. Of that great numerical majority in the country who were undecided as to the sufficiency of the Reform Bill to produce good government, a preponderating portion have now made up their minds. Since the last election, the Radicals in the House of Commons exceed the combined strength of the personal adherents of Ministers and the *parti du ventre*. Nor does any one doubt that were a general election to take place just now, whether the Tories were reduced in number or not, the Radicals would gain still further upon the Whigs.

A momentous question follows. Thus undisputedly the predominant section of the party in power—holding the fate of the ministry in their hands, and being the body to which apparently the country must look for the men who are hereafter to direct its counsels—why are the Parliamentary Radicals making no exertions to prove themselves worthy of this exalted destiny? Instead of taking the lead, as belongs in all combinations to those who hold the most decided opinions, why have they sunk into a mere section of the supporters of the Whig ministry? Why is all their Parliamentary conduct passive, not active? Except an occasional motion, to which the reputation of some individual among them is pledged, and which he could not without disgrace abandon, why do they originate nothing, but content themselves with supporting what the Ministers originate? Why do they not bring forward a succession of matured and well-digested reforms, which, being sent to the House of Lords, might compel that body to choose between the adoption of them and its own ruin? Why do they let slip every opportunity not only for acting, but even for speaking, like men in earnest about their opinions?

It is painful that some of the severest things said by Sir John Walsh of the Parliamentary Radicals are those which can least be gainsaid by their friends and supporters.

How much has the strength of this party been increased! It now numbers from 160 to 170 members; and if it is not in office, it holds the fate of a weak Ministry at its disposal. All this, however, has been accomplished *for* the parliamentary party, and not *by* them. The power of the press and the instincts of the democracy have shoved these 160 members into the House, but they seem to have arrived there merely because they were nearest the door when it was opened. (P. 60.)

There was abundant encouragement for all the more ardent and adventurous spirits to flock to their ranks. Their side was evidently the rising one. Its places of distinction were as yet unoccupied. Their designation was no longer a nickname associated with the ideas of the

Rotunda and Orator Hunt's blacking van. The weight they had acquired in the scale, and the prospect of power, had given respectability to the term of Radical. And yet, with all these inducements, with so fair a field, no new candidate appeared qualified for the post of leader of the English Movement.

It is a favourite theory with political philosophers, and one which is entitled to consideration, that the occasion creates the man—that as, if a gentleman wants a butler or a bailiff, he advertises for one and finds him, so that, when society and the circumstances of the times require a Cromwell or a Napoleon, the Cromwell or Napoleon is forthcoming. If this be true, certainly English society had no need just then of a Radical statesman, for no democratic Pitt or Fox started forth, a ready-made head of the Movement. Mr. O'Connell was the only person qualified, by his talents for debate and his general ability, to perform the part; but the English members were reluctant to enrol themselves in the list of his followers, and he restricted himself to his peculiar province. Had the metropolitan boroughs or the Scotch constituencies been able to lay their hand upon a Mirabeau, I do not know where he might have carried us; but no such Coryphæus appeared, and the chords which might have responded to his touch remained mute. (Pp. 56–7.)

In the following passage Sir John Walsh hits the nail on the head:

It may be that what the Movement party had gained in the respectability of its more prominent supporters, it had lost in the power derived from congeniality of feeling and active sympathy with the masses without, who are the sources of its strength.... That party which enumerated among its adherents the varied information of Mr. Warburton, the ingenious philosophy of Mr. Grote, or the high literary talent of Mr. E. Lytton Bulwer, could not be stigmatized with coarseness or vulgarity. But if it was less displeasing in these respects to the fastidious, *it was deficient in the enthusiasm, in the impetuosity which would have developed its full power, in vigour and earnestness of purpose.* A man armed with a club may put himself into all the graceful positions of a fencing-master, but, if he desires to make the most of his weapon, he must grasp it in both hands, and lay about him without regard to rule. (Pp. 58–9.)

That any one of the three gentlemen who are here mentioned, or of several others who might be added to them, could singly have accomplished in the last four years more than has been done in that time by the whole body of Parliamentary Radicals, no one who knows them can doubt. If any one of them had put forth his whole strength, in how different a position would he have now stood! What corresponding energy he would have called forth in many who now have been quiescent! and how different a place would the Parliamentary Radicals have by this time occupied in the public eye! Why have these men not shown themselves equal to the emergency? Why are they allowing the destinies of the country to slip through their hands? Because "*they are deficient in the enthusiasm, in the impetuosity which would have developed their full power, in vigour and earnestness of purpose.*"

There never were men purer in intention than the more influential of the Parliamentary Radicals. The opinions of most of them are in opposition to their private interests. Personal ambition they have none—would that they had! In *passive* virtue—in determination to sully their hands with no iniquity—in resistance to all propositions, from whatever quarter coming, inconsistent with the most rigid justice—no body of politicians ever were so exemplary. Of the three parties in Parliament they are beyond question the party of the most scrupulous conscience. Sir John Walsh helps to swell the vulgar cry that property is in danger from them. Whenever, on the contrary, property is endangered, it is on them chiefly that reliance is to be placed for its security. Sir John is miserably mistaken when he says that Lord Grey at the meeting of the first Reformed Parliament could have "paid the fundholders 7s. in the pound" (p. 10). Had no one else resisted such an iniquity, it would have raised such a spirit among the Radicals as would have ignominiously hurled its author from power. It is by the opposition of the Radicals, that measures inconsistent with the legal rights or just expectations of individuals are usually defeated. Sir John seems to take credit to the Tories for compelling the relinquishment of the clause in the Irish Church Temporalities' Bill which imposed a tax on existing incumbents.[*] That clause was abandoned in consequence of the general opposition of the Radicals. They had their full share in defeating the proposition of the Whigs in 1831 for taxing the transfer of stock, in violation of the express conditions on which every loan was concluded.[†]

How comes it that with so much passive integrity, there is in these men so little active energy? Why is it that men whom no consideration would bribe to do anything *against* their consciences, cannot be urged by any strength of motives to do anything *for* them? Because this is not an age of heroism, or of disinterested exertion, or of vigour of purpose; because the institutions which Sir John Walsh venerates, and the men whom he eulogizes, have actually extinguished activity of intellect and energy of character among our higher classes; because our church, our schools, and our universities, will not suffer great minds to grow up among us—minds fitted to accomplish great things, and to make their spirit pervade and elevate the smaller minds around them. It is because this people is becoming more and more a people of mere Mammon-worshippers—and will soon be irretrievably sunk into that worst degradation, unless our institutions of education, from Lambeth and Christchurch to the lowest charity school, shall be radically reformed,—unless a spirit in every respect the opposite of that which now prevails, shall penetrate into every nook and cranny of them, and give the dead carcasses a new life.

We offer this to Sir John Walsh as what he so earnestly demands, a categorical declaration of the principles and purposes of the Movement party. We hope he is

[*Clause 14 of "A Bill to Alter and Amend the Laws Relating to the Temporalities of the Church in Ireland," 3 William IV (11 Mar., 1833), *PP*, 1833, I, 345 (the bill was enacted as 3 & 4 William IV, c. 37).]

[†Proposed by Spencer in his Speech on the Budget (11 Feb., 1831), *PD*, 3rd ser., Vol. 2, cols. 416–18; the proposition, after opposition led by Henry Goulburn and Robert Peel, was withdrawn by Spencer in his Report on the Budget (14 Feb., 1831), *ibid.*, cols. 491–3.]

satisfied. *These* are our purposes. We have others; but these being the greatest, the most distant, and the most difficult of accomplishment, may be considered our ultimate objects. When this point is reached, we will not say that we shall stop, for it would be absurd to set limits to improvement: but it is not probable that, these things being attained, anything very important will remain to be struggled for.

When therefore Sir John demands to be told how far we desire to go in constitutional change, we answer, that this depends mainly upon Sir John's friends. We desire no constitutional changes, except as means; and necessary means we believe them to be, because the opinion we entertain of Sir John and his associates does not suffer us to believe that they will give us our ends without them. If we are wrong in this, the men whom Sir John celebrates have it in their power to undeceive us. They have only to *be* what Sir John says they already *are*. When they have given us a good code, a cheap procedure, courts which bring justice home to the people's doors; when they have abrogated the corn laws, corrected all partial taxation, abolished all useless expenditure, and taken off all restrictions upon industry; when they have made Ireland what it is fitted to be, the garden, not the Golgotha of Europe; when they have given us (what most civilized countries possess) an organized system of administration, in which every public function has somebody trained to it, somebody responsible for its performance, regularly watched and systematically instructed by superior authority; when they have done all this, and last and greatest of all, when, in the place of a church and universities which are a disgrace to reason, and a laughing-stock to Europe, they have given us such places and such methods of education, both for young and old, as are suited to the wants, and therefore in some important respects opposed to the spirit, of the age;—when these things shall have been done, and done without organic changes, then let Sir John Walsh repeat his question, and he shall receive an answer to his heart's desire.

FONBLANQUE'S ENGLAND UNDER SEVEN ADMINISTRATIONS

1837

EDITOR'S NOTE

London and Westminster Review, V & XXVII (Apr., 1837), 65–98. Headed: "ART. IV. / *England under Seven Administrations*. By Albany Fonblanque, Esq. 3 vols. [London:] Bentley: 1837." Running titles: "Fonblanque's England / Under Seven Administrations." Signed "A." Not republished. Identified in Mill's bibliography as "A review of Fonblanque's 'England under seven Administrations' in the London and Westminster Review for April 1837 (No 9 and 52)" (MacMinn, 48). In the Somerville College copy (tear-sheets) there are three corrections that have been adopted in the present edition: "on" is changed to "no" (351.18); "not all" is altered to "not at all" (359.27); and "writer panegyrist" is altered to "writer and panegyrist" (379.39–40).

Fonblanque's England under Seven Administrations

THESE THREE VOLUMES contain, not the best, (for they have left many of their equals behind them,) but a few of the best, as well as most permanently interesting, among the papers published in the *Examiner* by its present editor: a man, of whom it is saying little, to say, that he is *facile princeps* among English journalists; since it is doing infinitely too much honour to English journalists as a body, to speak of him as belonging to their craft. Mr. Fonblanque is something far higher than a great journalist; he is a great writer, who happens accidentally to be a journalist. Of the innumerable newspaper writers in this age of newspapers, his writings alone will take a place among English classics. In a generation whose bulkiest volumes are meant only for the day, his ephemeral productions, by the carefulnesss of their composition, and the lavish expenditure of mental resources upon their substance, might seem to be designed for immortality.

As mere writers for the day, there have been several journalists of our time as effective as Mr. Fonblanque; and (if we consider only immediate effect) even upon a wider scale, because upon a more ordinary class of minds. The most valuable of all talents for one who would be a successful journalist, is that of being skilfully common-place: and the writer who has received one-half of this gift from nature may add to it the other half with no greater degree of diligence and practice than are necessary to success in any other laborious profession. The influence of most journalists may be explained as Mr. Fonblanque himself explained Sir James Scarlett's extraordinary success with juries: "there are twelve Scarletts in the jury-box." Even when pursued with higher objects, newspaper writing is subject to the same condition as popular speaking—it must produce its impression at once, or not at all; and he is the most effective newspaper writer, as he is the most effective speaker, who can, without being tiresome or offensive, declaim upon one idea long enough to make it sink into the mind. Such was the secret of the good writers in the *Times*, when the *Times* had good writers.

But in advancing to this pitch of excellence, a person who has a multitude of ideas is apt to find them very much in his way. Seeing, as he does, the bearings of a hundred different things upon his subject, he knows not how to confine himself to one simple, broad, direct, common-place view of it. He neglects the feebler but more obvious reason, for the stronger one, but which is farther from the surface. He surrounds his leading idea with allusions and illustrations, which impress it more vividly upon the intelligent, but which call off the vulgar reader—demand from him a separate effort of attention, and so prevent him from being hurried away by the main stream of the thought.

We think Mr. Fonblanque is chargeable with these faults, in a degree highly creditable to his mental endowments. His eminence as a newspaper writer has been attained in spite of the higher qualities of his mind: and great must be his talents for popularity, when so great talents for something better than popularity have not prevented him from attaining it. If his unusual dialectic powers, his inexhaustible wit, and his perpetual play of fancy, have rendered the *Examiner* popular as a newspaper among the educated classes of almost all shades of opinion, a still higher degree of success may be anticipated for the present publication, since the very defects of his articles, as articles, arise from their excellencies as permanent literary productions.

Nothing, certainly, can more strikingly exemplify, than these three volumes, the difference between the treatment of a subject by a man of genius, and by the most judicious thinker or ablest writer who is without genius. Every one knows the insupportable tediousness of gone-by politics. The Spartan in the story, who, for the crime of using two words where one would have sufficed, was sentenced to read from beginning to end the history of Guicciardini, and at the end of a few pages begged to commute his punishment for the galleys,[*] would have prayed to exchange it for death if he had been condemned to read a file of English newspapers five years old. But with Mr. Fonblanque, the farther we go back, and the more completely his articles are reduced to their own intrinsic sources of interest, the more delightful they become. If the interest anywhere flags, it is towards the end of the last volume, where the contents are recent, and we come in contact with the exhausted controversies of the present day and hour. But the politics of Mr. Canning's time and of the Duke of Wellington's are fresh in Mr. Fonblanque's page, and we have accompanied him through them with as much of the excitement of novelty as if we had never heard of either of those personages before: for it was not in what the writer drew *from* his subject, but in what he brought *to* his subject that the interest resided. The matter immediately in hand might be local and temporary, but the whole universe was the source whence he drew parallel cases for its illustration; and the aptest and most felicitous analogies to enforce his own view of it, or confute his adversary's. Such, once more, is the prerogative of genius. To the ablest mechanical man of talent a subject is illuminated only by its own light: a man of genius will often see into its darkest corners by a spark struck from some familiar object, apparently altogether remote from it.

[*The story is found in Trajano Boccalini, *Advices from Parnassus*, revised and corrected by Mr. Hughes (London: Brown, *et al.*, 1706), p. 14 (VI), with reference to Francesco Guicciardini, *L'historia d'Italia* (Florence: Torret, 1561).]

Mr. Fonblanque's opinions, it need scarcely be said, are those of the philosophic radicals. That it may be more clear what we mean, we will state whom we term the philosophic radicals, and why we so denominate them. There are divers schools of radicals. There are the historical radicals, who demand popular institutions as the inheritance of Englishmen, transmitted to us from the Saxons or the barons of Runnymede. There are the metaphysical radicals, who hold the principles of democracy not as means to good government, but as corollaries from some unreal abstraction—from "natural liberty," or "natural rights." There are the radicals of occasion and circumstance, who are radicals because they disapprove the measures of the government for the time being. There are, lastly, the radicals of position, who are radicals, as somebody said, because they are not lords.[*] Those whom, in contradistinction to all these, we call philosophic radicals, are those who in politics observe the common practice of philosophers— that is, who, when they are discussing means, begin by considering the end, and when they desire to produce effects, think of causes. These persons became radicals, because they saw immense practical evils existing in the government and social condition of this country; and because the same examination which showed them the evils, showed also that the cause of those evils was the aristocratic principle in our government—the subjection of the many to the control of a comparatively few, who had an interest, or who fancied they had an interest, in perpetuating those evils. These inquirers looked still farther, and saw, that in the present imperfect condition of human nature, nothing better than this self-preference was ever to be expected from a dominant few; that the interests of the many were sure to be in their eyes a secondary consideration to their own ease or emolument. Perceiving, therefore, that we were ill-governed, and perceiving that so long as the aristocratic principle continued predominant in our government we could not expect to be otherwise, these persons became radicals, and the motto of their radicalism was, enmity to the Aristocratical principle.

Mr. Fonblanque's career as a public writer is coeval with the birth of this party. He was the first journalist who unfurled their banner: he has borne it bravely and steadily through all fortunes, during ten years of perpetual combat, and few men will have contributed more to its final triumph.

Mr. Fonblanque began his labours in the cause of radicalism in unpropitious times. The days of active persecution, indeed, were past; but Reform principles were discountenanced by all persons in authority, as much as their extreme contempt for those principles would suffer them to consider necessary. There was no apparent Reform party among people of property or education, and the demand for reform was believed to have been effectually put down. In this state of affairs,

[*Edward Barrington de Fonblanque, in *The Life and Labours of Albany Fonblanque* (London: Bentley, 1874), p. 6, attributes the maxim to Mill, who, he says, used it in a letter (now lost) to Albany Fonblanque.]

Mr. Fonblanque took up the cause; and was distinguished from almost all others who were at that time serving it by this honourable characteristic,—that he never in any single instance equivocated or temporized for the sake of an immediate purpose, nor ever concealed one particle of his ultimate designs. From the beginning, he scouted the notion that the possession of large property qualified men for power, or rendered it unnecessary to subject them to responsibility for the exercise of it. From the beginning, he avowed that the House of Lords, as it now exists, could never co-exist with a reformed House of Commons. From the beginning, he treated the political Church of England as a mere pretence for the misappropriation of a large portion of national wealth to sordid purposes. From the beginning, he invariably represented the Ballot as a *sine qua non* of good government, and universal suffrage as necessary to its perfection, though demanding, as a preliminary requisite, a degree of education and intelligence which was not yet, and would not soon be, reached. In this straightforward and open course of proceeding, we know not if Mr. Fonblanque had at the time of his commencement any associates, except the early writers in the *Westminster Review*, among whom, also, he himself was numbered. And now, when doctrines which were at that time so universally obnoxious have gone far towards becoming, and every discerning person sees that they must ultimately become, the general opinions of the community,—those who first descended into the arena and did battle for those principles, and by so doing raised them from being objects of the unaffected contempt of all persons of station or influence, to their present importance and honour, are entitled to turn round upon those who are applauding spectators of results they never hazarded anything to forward, and ask, by what other course, profitable as it might have been to themselves, they could so well have served their country and their opinions? and whether, if *they* too had equivocated, and compromised, and enunciated their opinions by halves, and kept the great questions out of sight for fear of damaging the small ones, and on the whole trimmed and truckled and played fast and loose with their convictions, as many would have had them, as many are even now counselling them, their opinions would have been now, or probably at any time during their lives, in the state of triumphant progress and prosperity in which they now behold them? At all times, and in all circumstances, has this truth been found invariable: whoever, having adopted his opinions on mature consideration, openly avows and publishes the full extent of those opinions (such things only excepted as, if unseasonably declared, might deprive him of a hearing altogether)—whoever, we say, does this, will lose many a point which, by compromising some portion of his opinions, he might have carried; but he will carry more points in the long run than the dissembler. He will not always have done well for his own reputation, for he will often be so far before his contemporaries as to be (in the words of Coleridge) dwarfed in the distance:[*] he

[*Samuel Taylor Coleridge, *Biographia Literaria*, 2 vols. in 1 (London: Rest Fenner, 1817), Vol. I, p. 35.]

will often not have done well for the interest of this or that particular truth; but (so far as it is possible for human wisdom to affirm anything universally of the variable course of human affairs) he will in all cases have done well for the interests of truth on the whole.

In characterizing Mr. Fonblanque's mind, most persons, we think, will agree, that it belongs to the *observing* class rather than to the *ratiocinative*. The two characters indeed are not inconsistent: a mind of the ratiocinative order may be skilful in observing, and Mr. Fonblanque, who is characteristically an observer, is also a good reasoner. It is nevertheless true, that some minds are most given to arguing downwards from principles to facts, and others upwards from facts to principles. Some minds form their opinion of a case by closely examining the case itself; others by applying to it some general law of nature, or of the human mind, within the scope of which it seems to come. Mr. Fonblanque is of the former kind. His radicalism is the result of no *à priori* principle. His distinctive and pre-eminent merit as a thinker is (as it seems to us), a keen eye for seeing and comprehending things as they are—for taking a just view of the existing influences in society, as they actually operate. His reflections on the ultimate causes of these phenomena seem to have been prompted by a previous thorough insight into the phenomena themselves; what he thought has been forced upon him by what he saw.

He saw the whole machinery of the government of this country systematically perverted, to the gain or supposed gain of the few; every object which only concerned the minds, bodies, or fortunes of the many treated with neglect or contempt; the many treated as having nothing to do with the laws but to obey them,[*] and seldom meddled with by their governors but for some purpose of vexation and annoyance. All this he found going on under cover of the most pharisaical professions, and the most pharisaical observances, religious, patriotic, and moral. The whole of the class intermediate between the many and the few he found grovelling in the most sordid worship of what he terms the two idols, Mammon and Fashion; thirsting insatiably for two things—the means of being admitted among the few, and the reputation of resembling them. Seeing all this, he looked out for the cause of it; and this he found to be, the constitution of the government of this country—which placed irresponsible power in the hands of a small class, made wealth the key to that power, and hereditary rank the symbol of the long possession of wealth. He saw that to destroy the mischief, it was necessary to dry up its source; and he declared war against the aristocratical principle.

The following passage, written in 1829, exemplifies those views of the state of English society which have made our author a radical.

After quoting an opinion of the *Morning Chronicle*,[†] that to raise the

---

[*See Samuel Horsley, Speech on the Treasonable Practices Bill (11 Nov., 1795), in Cobbett, ed., *Parliamentary History of England*, Vol. XXXII, col. 258.]

[†Unheaded Leader, *Morning Chronicle*, 16 Oct., 1829, p. 2.]

qualification of electors would destroy the influence of the landed aristocracy, Mr. Fonblanque says,

In this view we cannot concur. Our own observation has led us to the contrary conclusion, that the smaller gentry are for the most part sycophantically subservient to the great. They do not make their stand upon their own titles to consideration (either belonging to wealth or moral worth), but rely for consequence on the mere countenance of the class above them. The common ambition of the English gentry, and superior trading men, is to be known and noticed by persons of a rank above their own. For this pitiful object there are thousands ready to waive their independence. It is, indeed, an especial misfortune of England that the *New Rich* do not conceive the high point of pride of constituting in themselves a new power; but, on the contrary, are content to seek consequence by swimming in shoals, in the wake of the Aristocracy, and rejoice in the poor crumbs of courtesy which are cast to them, sometimes for policy, and sometimes for the sport of exposing their active littleness in the gambols of sycophancy. The two idolatries which corrupt us, morally and politically, in all ranks between luxury and labour, are Mammon-Worship, and Fashion-Worship. These *cults* are generally to be found in the same house: the man of business sets up a temple to Riches in his own breast; and his wife, his daughters, his sons, prostrate to Fashion, and compel his conformity, though the pride of Mammon, which is great, should resist the propitiatory sacrifices to the other idol.

We remember to have heard an experienced party politician number Lady Castlereagh's influence at Almack's, and the fashion of her suppers after the Opera, among the Parliamentary powers of her husband the Minister. Opposition was marked as unfashionable by these tests of ton, and men's wives, sons, and daughters, became active missionaries of the Ministry, and perpetual exhorters to a new birth unto Toryism. Almost every Liberal Member's family was against his politics, and the waverers gave way. In the inferior classes the same folly is observable in other instances. The grand society of a neighbourhood must be had at any price. Countenance and civil speech alone, indeed, are mighty things: witness certain of the radical Common Councilmen of the City, who have become hotly ministerial by virtue of discourse with the Duke of Wellington on the subject of the new bridge. Some of these worthies, to whom the Duke has affably said, "Good morning," are now surprised that they ever found anything amiss in his politics.

The excessive reverence for property, which the *Chronicle* attributes to the lower orders, is not to be denied; but we believe they do but share in a common sentiment from which none of us are entirely free. We all, Liberals and Serviles, Philosophers and Sentimentalists, are touched in some degree by this prevalent taint in the moral atmosphere. The best is he who is least affected by it. And when we examine the foible, it is one which under other forms has been cultivated by the arts, and by the imagination. What is property but power? Carry back the Yorkshire buckskinned 'Squires of the *Chronicle's* instance a few ages, and you have "the bold Barons," admirable in poetry, Waverley novels, and paintings, with their castles of strength, their steel-clad knights, and men-at-arms. Power in this form was picturesque, and power kept at a banker's shop has none of the show of martial array; but the power is the substantial matter at the root of admiration in either instance. On the other hand, a disposition to despise weakness seems to be a law of nature, which humanity prevails against with effort, by urging the sympathies, and stimulating them by the imagination. If one animal meets with misfortune, the others of his kind fall upon and destroy him. In the "Library of Entertaining Knowledge" this characteristic circumstance is noted:

"In the kennels of fox-hounds the following barbarous custom of the dogs towards one another has been sometimes observed. If a hound gets down *of his own accord* from the bench on which he is lying, no notice of it is taken by the others. But if a hapless hound fall off the bench *from awkwardness*, his companions fly at him, and bite him to death."[*]

Marmontel describes a practice of men strikingly similar to that of the hounds; for, says he, "All things are crimes in the unfortunate, and we treat a fallen man as mothers do fallen children, namely, chastise them for the mishap." (Vol. I, pp. 237–41.)[†]

The following article on the House of Lords appeared as early as 1827.

If the late political changes should be attended with no other advantage, they have yet effected a great good in the discovery they have brought about of the true character of the House of Lords. To thinking men, indeed, the character of this assembly could be no secret at any time,—it was argued *à priori* from its constitution—it was seen that wherever power is lodged without responsibility, the power is given for the benefit of those who hold it. But the world is not filled with thinking men; the majority take their opinions without examination from current authorities. To persons of this stamp, the late pranks of the House of Lords have proved extremely instructive.

A child treats its doll as a living creature, dandles and fondles it, gives it the air, dresses and undresses it, and puts it to bed. Some unlucky day it espies a little of the bran oozing out of its valued form; curiosity is set at work—how is it made, is the question—research begins—the opening in the seam of the puppet is increased, the stuffing pours out, and the plump and specious form of the idol is reduced to a trumpery piece of sewn leather, turned inside out, and cast with contempt away. Our grand State Puppet has been provoking this process of investigation; it has been letting its bran out, and the minds even of the little children of society have been set to work to see whether there is anything better in it. The stuffing of self-interest has escaped in a most unequivocal way, and the idea occurs to the simplest understanding, that by that substance only it is shaped. It is then seen that this boasted body, the Hereditary Legislature, is entirely insulated in power, and free even from the shadow of responsibility. The Commons are in some slight degree responsible to the people; and the name, the mere name, the *name* still, of responsibility, hangs over the servants of the Crown, the King's Ministers; but the Lords are untroubled with responsibility, in substance, shadow, or name. They have power on the most golden terms,—power without the necessity of qualification for the use, or responsibility for the abuse of it. Such a body, standing alone as it does, answerable in no quarter for its conduct, not only unrestrained by any substantial check, but not even reminded of its possible fallibility by any nominal one, must, according to the nature of things, prefer its own interests when occasions arise, with an audacity and contemptuous disregard to the sentiment of society, which can be hazarded in no other branch of the state. Its members are independent of the people, and independent of the King, who can make but not unmake them; and consequently they can at pleasure set both the people and the King at defiance. Nor can this surprise us: if we confer power without responsibility, we cannot be astonished to see it exercised without justice. Despots, little and great, many and few, will of course consult their own pleasure; and sometimes that pleasure happens to be good, sometimes bad; the good and the bad are matter of chance, of lottery, from which hap-hazard work a wisely-constituted government rescues society. When their individual interests are not concerned, it is the nature of men to be just; but our House of Lords, our Peers, are deeply interested in the perpetuity of most of the abuses which the people are interested in abating. Many men there are undoubtedly among them proof against narrow sinister influences, who

[*Charles Knight, *The Menageries*, 3 vols. (London: Knight, 1829–40), Vol. I, p. 54.]
[†Jean François Marmontel, *Mémoires d'un père*, 4 vols. (London: Peltier, 1805), Vol. II, pp. 179–80.]

pursue the good of their fellow-creatures as their sole object, and earn in the respect and love of mankind their meet reward: such, however, are those superior natures—the moral like the physical perfections—whose number in every class we know from experience to be extremely small. We may calculate on their presence, not on their preponderance. (Vol. I, pp. 35–8.)

After some other illustrations of the hereditary principle as judged by its fruits, he continues—

In the Duke, who has married an elderly lady of great fortune for *love*, we have the living evidence of that disdain of vile, sordid, pecuniary interest, which may be expected in men of this noble class! Without meaning anything unkind to the Duke, we must say that we wish, from the bottom of our hearts, that a liberal Earl of high political influence had married the rich elderly lady, instead of wedding himself to the Corn Amendment.[*] Perhaps it would have been the same thing to his Lordship, and certainly better for the country. We would, in truth, much rather find the whole House in rich, crummy widows, than let them meddle with our bread. The wisest thing that the Commons could do, would be to send up to the Lords, with the next year's Corn Bill, a vote of rich widows to the holders of mortgaged or impoverished estates. (Vol. I, p. 40.)

This idea is improved upon in the following felicitous mixture of solid truth and genuine wit. Mr. Fonblanque's titles and mottoes are often eminently happy. The passage we are about to quote is from an article on the Corn question, appropriately headed "The way to keep 'em."

Mr. Peel—it is useful to keep the public eternally reminded of what stuff this leader of the British aristocracy is made—had said in defence of the Corn Laws, that "it was the constitutional policy of the country to maintain the aristocracy and magistracy as essential parts of the community."[†] Mr. Fonblanque closes with the proposition, and proceeds in the following manner to point out the best and cheapest mode of doing it.

This is plain speaking. If however it be the constitutional policy of this country to maintain the Aristocracy and Magistracy, it is also the policy of this country to maintain them in the manner least onerous or detrimental to itself. The end being avowed and agreed on, the directest means will be the best, and it will be wiser to vote a yearly supply in pounds, shillings, and pence, for the maintenance of the Aristocracy and Magistracy of these realms, than to keep them by means of a tax on bread, which cramps the industry of the country. Let the Aristocracy and Magistracy take their place in the estimates with the Army and Navy; let money be voted for so many Lords and so many Squires a year, and country houses be built, repaired, or fitted and found, like ships. No one surely will grudge a few millions for the support of the wooden heads of Old England! If it be declared that we must take our Masters into keeping, in God's name let us do it openly and directly, and maintain them according to their wants. Mr. Goulburn, in this case, will come down to the House,

[*Presumably, in 1827, Fonblanque was referring to the measures in 7 & 8 George IV, c. 57 (1827).]

[†Robert Peel, Speech on the Corn Bill (29 Apr., 1828), *PD*, n.s., Vol. 19, cols. 227–8; quoted by Fonblanque, Vol. I, p. 164.]

and show that Squire Western[*] is so reduced in his fortunes as to be unable to afford a pack of hounds; whereupon the Commons will vote him the dogs necessary to the Constitution, inasmuch as they are necessary to the Squire's credit. Or he will set forth, that Lord Squander cannot keep a mistress, as he greatly desires to do, and as his ancestors have done before him; whereupon Parliament will vote him the wherewith for a concubine. One man cannot drink claret, another is sunk below champagne: various are the dilapidations in the estate of the Aristocracy and Magistracy, and the country must repair them, according to the Ministers, but not, we say, by a tax on bread:—substitute, in the place of it, the immediate process of a demand on the public purse. Let the wants of Lords and Squires be spread before us, hounds, horses, concubines, claret, champagne, &c., and the estimates to supply them shall be regularly discussed and voted, like those, as we have before said, of the Army and Navy. The advantage of this mode over the present method of maintaining the Aristocracy or Magistracy, or, in other words, of keeping our Masters, is manifest. By way of illustration—George Barnwell perceived it to be necessary to his constitution to keep a mistress, but for lack of a direct supply from his old-fashioned uncle for so requisite and respectable an appurtenance, he robbed the shop, and ultimately cut his kinsman's throat, just as the man killed the goose to get the golden eggs, or as the squires kill this country to keep up the price of their corn. If Barnwell's uncle had been distinctly told by a neighbourly Mr. Peel that it was absolutely necessary that his nephew should maintain Millwood, none of this mischief would have happened.[†] The robbery would have been avoided; also the personal inconvenience of assassination to the sufferer. What was requisite for Millwood's "dresses and decorations," as the play-bills have it, would have been considered, and the damage would not have exceeded the occasion. The present method of keeping our Millwood is attended with this obvious mischief, that the cost of the maintenance of the hussy is more than proportioned to her wants. Our Constitution requires that squires and lords should be supported; but squires and lords need support in different degrees: some need it very little; some very much; and some again not at all. How stupid it is then to give to these various claims and conditions one measure of supply! What a manifest offence against economy! As Lord Eldon would say, "God forbid" that we should dispute with Mr. Peel the propriety, fitness, and constitutional policy of starving the people for the good of the Aristocracy and Magistracy; all that we contend is, that they should be pinched with discretion, and that a judicious manner of picking pockets should be substituted for the practice of taking the bread out of their mouths. (Vol. I, pp. 164–7.)

On other occasions, he pursues the squirearchy with still more poignant raillery; as thus—

MAGISTRACIES TO BE SOLD

We would particularly refer the admirers of "things as they are"[‡] to an auction advertisement, in the *Courier, Globe*, and others papers, setting forth that on Tuesday the 16th of September, Mr. Driver will sell by order of his Majesty's Commissioners of Woods and Forests a Crown estate in Essex, stocked with game, &c., and conveying many most valuable privileges; "amongst others," says the affiche,

[*A character in Fielding's *The History of Tom Jones*.]
[†The references are to characters in George Lillo's *The London Merchant; or, The History of George Barnwell* (London: Gray, 1731).]
[‡Fonblanque presumably has in mind William Godwin's *Things As They Are; or, The Adventures of Caleb Williams*, 3 vols. (London: Crosby, 1794).]

"The owner of this manor and lordship (Havering atte Bower) *has the sole nomination and appointment of two of the Magistrates*, the tenants and inhabitants within the manor and lordship appointing the third, *who exercise an exclusive jurisdiction, the Magistrates for the county at large being prohibited from acting within this lordship.*"[*]

It seems to us that Mr. Driver has scarcely laid sufficient stress on this advantage. What an opportunity is here presented to Sporting Gentlemen who have the preservation of game at heart! The purchaser of the property may, if he please, make his keeper and helper Justices of the Peace as well as Guardians of the Birds,—an union of functions as rare as it is obviously desirable. The convenience of giving to the apprehender of poachers the magisterial power also of committing them, is indeed so manifest, that we are confident it is unnecessary to dilate further on the topic; and then how great the advantage of the exclusive jurisdiction,"the Magistrates of the County being prohibited from acting within this lordship!" How delightfully snug! Game and Justice within a ring fence! Everything done at home! Here the Squire may kill his own mutton, brew his own beer, and make his own law; ay, and his own law-expounder too. Nothing is wanting but a gaol on the estate, with a tread-mill, that he might have it to say that he ground his own prisoners also.

There is one benefit which Mr. Driver has omitted to recite, perhaps from some little delicacy—we too scarcely know how to name it—we would spare blushes, and it may be guessed what we would inquire—is there no * * * * on the property? You know what we mean; do not compel us to speak out, we really wish to be delicate—is there no "Justice Juice?" Is there no "Cat and Bagpipes," or "George and Dragon," within the snug jurisdiction; or, in plain terms, is there no licensing business? Say that there is, and we will dream the rest. What game is to the sportsman, public-houses are to the speculating Justice; and surely when two Magistracies are put up for sale, by order of his Majesty's Commissioners of Woods and Forests, it is strange that the mention of this important particular should have been altogether omitted. *Præfulgebat quod non visebatur*[†] may however have been the effect intended.

When Magistracies of exclusive jurisdiction are on sale, going by auction with arable and meadow, out-houses and barns, sheep and oxen, pots and pans, the imagination fills the territory with the advantages accruing from every conceivable abuse. Sentimental ladies may sing Mr. Bayley's choice of bliss,"I'd be a butterfly;"[‡] but for good, substantial, dishonest profits and enjoyment, we should chaunt,

"I'd be a Justice of Hav'ring atte Bower."

(Vol. I, pp. 192–4.)

One of the most honourable characteristics of Mr. Fonblanque is the ardour of his sympathy with the hard-handed many, and the indignant scorn with which he visits the indifference to their feelings, and positive hostility to their pleasures, so general among those who lay claim to the title of their betters. This spirit rouses, in

---

[*See, e.g. *Courier*, 3 and 10 Sept., 1828, p. [1]; *Globe and Traveller*, 15 Sept., 1828, p. [1]. The sale was held on the 23rd, not the 16th of September.]

[†Cf. Tacitus, *The Annals*, in *The Histories and The Annals* (Latin and English), trans. Clifford Moore and John Jackson, 4 vols. (London: Heinemann; New York: Putnam's Sons, 1925–37), Vol. II, p. 642 (III, 76, 11–13).]

[‡Nathaniel Thomas Bayly, *Psychae; or, Songs on Butterflies*, &c. (Malton: printed for private distribution, 1828), p. 2.]

addition, another of Mr. Fonblanque's strongest feelings—his profound abhorrence of cant.

Take the following on stopping up footpaths:

Let it be stated that a Prince or Princess has been pitiably straitened on an allowance of 12,000*l*. a-year, and Member after Member—yea, patriot after patriot—will spring up, with his heart in his mouth and his hand in our pockets, confess the hardship of the case, and his joyful readiness to concur in the required grant, vouching, at the same time, for the pleasure with which the public will defray this pleasing addition to its charges. How different is the reception of any representation of the privations, vexations, or sufferings, of the humble and labouring classes! We hear nothing then of liberality, or generosity, or the claims of justice, or the regards due to the comforts of the deserving.

Those who make light of provocations of this character are miserably ignorant of man. It is not always the greatest political wrong which has the greatest effect on men's minds; and we firmly believe that more of bitterness, more of fierce vindictive sentiment, towards the rich, has been produced by the path-stopping act, wheresoever it has been enforced, than by any other of the many bad acts that have been spawned by Parliament within the present century. The invasion of right and convenience is in this case so palpable, so obvious to every understanding, and so kept alive in the recollection by the daily consequent discomfort; and the motive is also so exasperatingly conspicuous in the improved domains of the rich and powerful, that it is not in the very large patience of the persons concerned to become reconciled to the wrong.

And who are the men who have authority to rob the labourer of the sweat of his brow, to deprive him of the short and pleasant path to his labour, and to add to the toil of him who lives by toil? The unpaid Magistrates—men notoriously appointed without regard to any judicial qualification, and who are as notoriously continued in the commission of the peace after the most decisive proofs of unfitness—to such as these the rights of the humble and industrious, in their paths to labour or recreation, are entrusted. When a canal or road, most essential to public convenience, is carried through the domain of a man of wealth, an Act of Parliament is necessary, and compensation is had; but when the way is to be stopped up, which has been of pleasure or convenience to the men of labour, nothing more is necessary than the consent of two Magistrates, and nothing more is given than notice of prosecution, with the utmost rigour of the law, to trespassers. And ours is the aristocracy which is declared not oppressive, and not to be likened to the French aristocracy, before the Revolution. (Vol. II, pp. 168–71.)

If space permitted, we would subjoin several passages from the striking articles on that topic so fertile in cant, the beer-houses.

Mr. Fonblanque never flattered the prejudices or passions of the more ignorant portion of the Radical Reformers. The doctrine of pledges, or instructions by the constituents to the representative,—a doctrine first taught to the people by the Tories, and which has recoiled upon themselves, Mr. Fonblanque has always treated as destructive of the very idea of a representative government. See for instance an excellent paper published in 1829 (Vol. I, pp. 234–5). He assailed with his most forcible weapons of argument, and ridicule, the outcry against the New Police.* The paper in Vol. II (pp. 299–308) on the "Equitable Adjust-

*For example, in the paper headed "The Ancient Watch and New Police," with the appropriate motto "Charley is my darling." (Vol. I, pp. 265–72.)

ment"[*] is one of the best denunciations ever written of that scheme of fraud. The commencement is an excellent specimen of Mr. Fonblanque's happiest manner; the simple statement of an argument has the effect of the most consummate, because apparently unstudied and unconscious wit:

> The idea of "Equitable Adjustment" is, probably, of as high antiquity as robbery, and in the felonious mind of all climes and ages, has been "often thought, though ne'er so well expressed."[†] The man in need, who supplied his wants by seizing on his neighbour's stores, doubtless regarded the action as an "Equitable Adjustment," and plumed himself on redressing the wrongs of fortune. The first rude intent of an "Equitable Adjustment" may, indeed, be traced in the history of Cain, who, seeing that his offering was less acceptable than Abel's, thought to relieve himself of the inequitable depression by slaying his brother.[‡] The needy soon began to contrast the abundance of others with their privations, and to perceive an equity giving them a decree, according to the power of their arms, or the nimbleness of their fingers, to share with the provident and thrifty. Each of these men sat as chancellor in his own Court of Equity, and adjusted to the uttermost of his opportunities and capacity. There is in the mind of man so natural and strong a disposition to Equitable Adjustment, that it may seem wonderful how law could ever prevail against it; but Equitable Adjustment was, at all times, and in all circumstances, attended with this great inconvenience, that there was no limiting its operation,—no security against its recurrence oftener than was desirable. The adjuster of one day might be subjected to adjustment the next, and the equity he had exercised upon one might be exercised on him by another, more needy and more potent. Hence, from no higher motive than convenience, law seems to have been generally preferred, and the institution of property secured. From the period when, all things considered, men thought it, on the whole, better not to be thieves, the names of purposes, actions, and actors, have been bestowed by the greater number, who have stickled for the distinction between *meum* and *tuum*: hence, the ancient practice of Equitable Adjustment has passed under the various descriptions of highway robbery, house-breaking, felony, larceny, or the yet larger terms of rapine, spoliation, &c. At no time, indeed, have the adjusters ceased to exist, and to cherish in their minds the principle of equity, as consecrating their method of settling the differences of fortune, or redressing the fluctuations of property; and it is remarkable, that their administration of equity has been as summary as that of the Court for the same object, having so many other points and practices in common with them, has been dilatory; yet, the identical motive which induces the speed of the one, explains the delay of the other, and we find the closest affinity between the working of the High Court of Chancery and the works of the unlicensed apostles of equity on the highway. Thus much we have said, to show, that the name of "Equitable Adjustment" is not so inappropriate to the design of those who have advocated it, as may at first appear, and that it is the proper clothing of the sentiment of those who yet hold to the

---

[*The phrase "equitable adjustment" seems to have originated with William Cobbett; see the fifth measure proposed in "The Petition of the Nobility, Gentry, and Others of the County of Norfolk," *Cobbett's Weekly Register*, XLV (11 Jan., 1823), 80.]

[†Alexander Pope, *An Essay on Criticism*, in *Works*, new ed., ed. Joseph Warton, *et al.*, 9 vols. (London: Priestley, 1822), Vol. I, p. 267 (II, 298).]

[‡Genesis, 4:3–8.]

"Good old rule, the simple plan,
That they should take, who have the power,
And they should keep, who can."[*]

(Vol. II, pp. 299–301.)

We subjoin a few extracts of a more miscellaneous character, for the more varied illustration of our author's manner. Our last quotation exemplified the wit of logic; in the following, on the old style of pamphleteering, we have the wit of fancy.

A pamphlet of the old-fashioned style is a composition of much circumlocution, and a sort of stuff which is best known by the name of *palaver*. It is a thing of stateliness and decorum, and two or three ideas pass slowly and solemnly along in a procession of winding phrases. The author dances a literary minuet, as it were, before the public; leading out his subject, bowing to it, putting on and taking off his hat, flourishing now a leg, now an arm, and moving over a very small space of ground with a very vast ceremony and parade of action—all wonderfully imposing, and unspeakably tedious to behold. (Vol. I, p. 68.)

The following is the introduction to an article on the unequal measure with which immoralities are visited upon "somebodies" and "nobodies:"

A striking inconsistency of judgment is the result of the very active state of the moral feelings in England, together with the general ignorance of moral principles. Every Briton makes it a point of conscience to keep a moral sentiment, and the more fierce its character, the greater he believes its virtue, or rather his own virtue in possessing it; but of any principle for the exercise of it he is commonly barren. His morality is chained up in his breast as the mastiff is chained up in his court-yard, and like the dog, it has generally a proneness to bark at beggars and vagabonds. (Vol. I, p. 206.)

No one excels our author in the happy application of a trait of comedy, or a nursery tale. The following was written during the No-Popery clamour against the Duke of Wellington:

The passing action (the removal of the Catholic disabilities)[†] great and laudable as it is in our eyes, will hardly be appreciated in history, for the ridicule attaching to the No-Popery panic will detract from the merit of having defied it, and compelled submission to the terms of reason and justice. The man who, a century ago, marched up to a hobgoblin, breathing fire and smoke, was only too hardy a hero in the eyes of the trembling beholders; but when the spectre was familiarly known to be a pumpkin with a candle in its sconce, the act of daring it sunk to a level with the absurd occasion. The superiority to a once pervading superstition is forgotten, and it is only remembered that the man was bold enough to brave a pumpkin and a rushlight. . . . It is all very fine in newspaper writers to talk of the estimate after-ages will form of his action, but the truth is, that its merit can only be understood by ourselves, who know the obstacles he encountered and overcame. There are certain conquests which, like the best witticisms, seem perfectly easy when they are made, and that

---

[*William Wordsworth, "Rob Roy's Grave," in *Poetical Works*, Vol. III, p. 26 (37–40).]

[†10 George IV, c. 7 (1829).]

under consideration is of the number. The Duke's task has been similar to the adventure we read of in the *Arabian Nights*, of the Prince who climbed the mountain for the singing tree and golden water.[*] He is stunned by a thousand Stentorian voices threatening resistance, and perplexed by unseen hands opposing his advances, but with high constancy and fortitude he makes good his way, and escapes the fate of those who look back when their objects are forward, that of being turned into stones. (Vol. I, pp. 216–17.)

On the quiet submission of mankind to political evils so long as they are not utterly unbearable:

John Bull is like the gentleman who occupied one of the Alpha cottages, when the neighbouring high-ways and bye-ways were not so good and safe as they now are, and who observed to a friend, that he had resolved to change his quarters, for, said he, "I have given it a fair trial; I have been knocked down and robbed regularly every night for the last three years, and I can bear it no longer."

Blessed are the knaves! for they are the only effective Reformers, and, thanks be to Providence! we rejoice in a goodly number of them. But for the hints they furnish in the way of practical demonstration, John Bull would never be convinced of the flaws in his jurisprudential policy. Until the steed is stolen, it is vain to attempt to persuade the honest gentleman of the theoretical convenience of bolts and bars.

Who has not read with delight Mrs. Hamilton's *Cottagers of Glenburnie*,[†] in which the dogged constancy of the Scotch to their habits of dirt and carelessness is so humorously described? *Mutato nomine de te fabula narratur*,[‡] O Bull. You are a man neat in your house and habits; you wash your hands twice and your face once a day; your corduroys are not greatly stained with beer, and your waistcoat is inconsiderably snuffy; you do not wear your stockings more than a week, and your shirt has knowledge of the laundry; there is no dunghill before your door, your barns and outhouses are in repair, your roads are excellent, and you hold the golden maxim, that "one stitch in time saves nine:"—but there is foulness, and slovenliness, and carelessness, beyond the house, the farm, and the person. What the Scotch of Mrs. Hamilton were in their domestic concerns, you, oh John, are in your political. There is a dung-hill before your door of justice, bigger and fouler than all the middensteads that ever stunk in Scotland—it is the Law, man. See in your public estate too the havoc the pigs make, against whom you have no fences, and who consequently devour your cabbages, grub up your carrots and turnips, stye in your house, and grunt in your Parliament—they are your Oligarchs—wilful creatures, vehement in filling themselves, inordinate in craving, and resolute in procuring their foul self-satisfaction.

It is with Mr. Bull as it was with Mr. Sawney in the less concern—"damned custom" renders him callous to the perception of the nuisances. "It's just vary weel,"—"it has always been that gait,"—or he "canna be fashed" to change. For this evil content there is no cure but in the consequently-growing enormity of inconvenience. Mischiefs are like jokes, laughed at till they are practical.... The sign of the fool with his finger in his mouth, and the sentiment, "Who'd have thought it?" is the precise emblem of English jurisprudence. (Vol. I, pp. 281–4.)

We cannot resist quoting an article in our author's happiest vein. It was written

---

[*"The Story of the Two Sisters, Who Were Jealous of Their Younger Sister," *Arabian Nights*, trans. Edward Forster, 5 vols. (London: Miller, 1802), Vol. V, pp. 420–42.]

[†Elizabeth Hamilton, *The Cottagers of Glenburnie* (Edinburgh: Manners and Miller, and Cheyne, 1808).]

[‡Horace, *Satires*, pp. 8–10 (I, i, 69–70).]

during the struggle for the Reform Bill, and is aimed equally at the Tories, and at the Whigs who truckled to them:

Æsop tells us that, once on a time, a fox wheedled a crow out of a piece of cheese;[*] but we have never heard that any arts of persuasion or cajolery redeemed anything from the jaws of the fox. It is clear that we have not had a crow to do with. For months every tongue was employed in assuring it how much it was respected and valued, what a sweet pretty creature it was, and ever would be reputed to be, if it would only open its mouth and drop the morsel to which it had no right. It turned its tail, however, most uncivilly upon all solicitations, and showed itself a sort of animal that thought a good bit in the mouth better than any quantity of fair words in the ear. Our Ministers have obviously great reliance on their powers of persuasion. Of Lord Althorp it may be said, as Mrs. Hardcastle remarked of Tony Lumpkin, "He would wile the bird from the tree:"[†] but ah! not the fox from the goose. If he has not the blandishment of oratory, he has the oratory of blandishment: but beasts of prey have no ear for civilities. We fear, we greatly fear, that wolves will never answer to the call of "Dilly, dilly, dilly, come and be killed,"[‡] however sweet may be the accent, or urgent the propriety.

When children commit errors, the parent's consolation is, "They will have more sense when they get older." This seems to have been the calculation with respect to the Peers. Though already the wickedest old body in the world, it is supposed they will know better in three or four months. When the sight of a venerable Bencher of the Temple failed, at the age of ninety, notwithstanding all the resources of art, he tranquilly remarked, that he believed he must leave it to time. We fear that time will not do more for the sight of the Peers than it did for our aged friend. They have had all encouragement in their obstinacy. Before they proved malcontent, they were assailed with flattery on the one hand, and menaces of destruction and creation on the other. They have proceeded to the extremity; they have insulted and defied the nation, denied its rights, and spurned its claims, and they have experienced none of the menaced consequences. The worst that is to happen to them is to be tried again. Can we wonder should they begin to be of opinion that threatened men live long. Great escapes give cowards confidence. The cry of "wolf"[§] has proved a false alarm, and the proverbial false security will follow on it; all warning will now be laughed at till the terrible reality appears.

Our contemporaries are beginning to have their doubts, whether Ministers can catch Peers by salting their tails. There is but one example in point of their practice, and the success of it is uncertain—it is that of a Frenchman who advertised a powder for killing fleas. A gentleman, troubled with a large majority of these tormentors, having in vain spread the bait, reproached the quack for his deception. The man coolly asked how the specific had been applied? and having heard, answered, "O Sare, but dat is quite wrong—first you catch de leetal flea, den you take him and hold him by the nape of his neck till he gape; den you put a grain of de powder down his trote—an den you let him run, and perhaps he bite you no more."

Ministers have had the flea by the nape of the neck, gaping, aye, and with the whole country open-mouthed too, and they put a grain of love-powder down the throat, and let it

[*Aesop, "The Fox and the Crow," in *Aesop's Fables*, trans. Vernon Stanley Vernon Jones (London: Heinemann; New York: Doubleday, Page, 1912), p. 6.]

[†Oliver Goldsmith, *She Stoops to Conquer* (London: Newbery, 1773), p. 86 (IV).]

[‡For this traditional nursery rhyme, see Iona and Peter Opie, comps., *The Oxford Nursery Rhyme Book* (Oxford: Clarendon Press, 1957), p. 171.]

[§"The Shepherd's Boy and the Wolf," *Aesop's Fables*, p. 41.]

run, and perhaps it will bite them no more—but perhaps it will. Our adversaries have natural allies in all the calamities that can visit mankind. On war they have always fondly reckoned. Pestilence they hailed as "*a diversion:*" and cholera seems to have landed, as if by friendly invitation, almost on Lord Londonderry's threshold. There is nothing to the minds of these men comparable in horror to honesty. The fabled shriek of *Mandrakes* torn out of the ground, expresses their supernatural agonies at being torn from the pockets of the people. Their attachment to plunder has absolutely something of the romance of passion in it, and when the struggle is over, we shall expect to see it illustrated in acts of *felo de se*, or deaths by melancholy; and celebrated in tales and tragedies. Goethe has made a most affecting story of one man's love for another man's wife;[*] and we really do not see why as much may not be made of one man's love for another man's money. This is a passion which we know never cloys, but grows with what it feeds on, and the disappointment will not be the less bitter after possession. As all the pernicious desires in their wildest indulgences are celebrated by poets and novelists, we think that the avarice of Boroughmongers, which has had such tremendous effects on the state of a great people, is well worthy of a tale, an epic, or a tragedy. We, as yet, want examples of the appropriate manner of catastrophe; but, as these worthies boast to be more of antique Romans than of Danes, we shall expect soon to read in the *Morning Post*, that, "yesterday a large party took poison with Sir Robert Peel;" that the Duke of Newcastle has thrown himself on his sword at Clumber; that the Duke of Wellington is pining with a green and yellow melancholy; and that his Grace of Cumberland has taken to his bed, and died. These things, seasoned with sentiment, the distress kept well in view, and the character of its causes artfully suppressed, may be worked into as moving a story as the *Sorrows of Werter*. The *Sorrows of Newcastle*!—how well it would sound, opening with a bread-and-butter description of a Borough, and ending with the loss of all fat things! But having thrown out the idea, we leave it to be worked out by persons who have the befitting genius for the pathetic. (Vol. II, pp. 106–10.)

Its length alone deters us from quoting the whole of the admirable article intituled "The Soothing System Illustrated." We shall cite the beginning and the ending:

It is well known to all the world (which means ourselves and friends), that Ministers are the best men breathing; having, however, this one fault (all the best people have some great *one*, by-the-by), that they are too good—to their enemies. A very melancholy instance of this propensity has just transpired. Poor Lord Althorp has been shockingly used by a Lancashire Tory, to whom he tendered some appeasing civility.[†] He did but open a friendly communication, as a man might do with a mad bull, asking him what had so transported him, and wherein he was displeased? when the savage tossed, tore, and gored and pinned him, and left him speechless!

The merchant in the *Arabian Nights*, who was eating nuts and throwing away the husks, was terrified by the sudden appearance of a raging giant—a sort of Lancashire gentleman—who desired him to prepare for instant death. The poor man comported himself like Lord Althorp, spoke most civilly, disavowed intention of offence, and begged to know wherein he had displeased? "Wretch!" cried the giant,—"you have dashed out the brains of my beloved son with your accursed nut-shells."[‡] The merchant was as much at a loss to

---

[*Johann Wolfgang von Goethe, *Die Leiden des jungen Werthers*, in *Werke*, 55 vols. (Stuttgart and Tübingen: Cotta'schen Buchhandlung, 1828–33), Vol. I, pp. 1–192.]

[†See William Hulton, "Correspondence with Lord Althorp," and John Charles Spencer, "Correspondence with William Hulton," both in *The Times*, 20 Dec., 1831, p. 3.]

[‡"The Story of the Merchant and the Genius," *Arabian Nights*, Vol. I, pp. 38–9.]

understand the connexion between the husks of nuts and the destruction of a giant's son, as was Lord Althorp to comprehend the relation of Mr. Hulton's displeasure to the words he had dropped; and his pain was the greater, as he knew, that, though he renounced nuts, he never could be secure against killing giants' sons, whose forms were so fine as to be imperceptible to the eye, and destructible by husks. The giant, as every one knows, proved in the end more placable than Mr. Hulton of Hulton Park—perhaps because the giant was not great man enough to have a park—perhaps because he had never been in the Commission of the Peace, which makes a gentleman understand his right to be angry. This story illustrates self-love, that vast passion, whose objects of affection are so small— against the wounds of whose minute and fragile offspring we can never be secure. The sons of giant pride are about in all directions; and although Lord Althorp be not husky in his speech, though his words fall soft as flakes of snow, yet shall he brain the first-born, the joy, the pride of the Gogs,[*] and be stunned with their complaints of wrong and threats of vengeance. Throw but the stone, however, and the giant dies—aye, were he ten times as big as Hulton of Hulton Park. Giantship, whatever it was formerly, when beasts could speak, is now conventional; if we allow men to lay down their own proprieties of consequence, they will fill them with insolence. By taking their just measure, we bring them down to their modesties or properties. We have not a doubt, that had our aforesaid merchant filliped a nut sharply against his bullying giant, instead of begging and praying, he would have knocked him down to insignificance, for the chip showed the softness of the block. (*Ibid.*, pp. 145–6, 154–5.)

There is an intermediate passage which we cannot omit. Lord Althorp had euphonically described the Manchester Massacre, as "the unfortunate transaction at Manchester."[†] Hereupon our author says,

It is one of the greatest discoveries of modern times, that when any considerable public mischief happens, nobody is to blame. The stars formerly had to answer for all crimes and miscarriages; but since the improvements in astronomy, they have been found innocent, and are no longer responsible for our calamities—had they not been timely set right in public opinion, the Georgium Sidus would have borne the blame of all the ills that have afflicted the country. Now, however, the stars and garters of the Peers are the only ones apostrophised as malignant causes of mischief. The instigations of the Devil succeeded; but, like an overworked advocate, he sunk under excess of business, and died of fatigue in the American war. Refinement then struck out the grand discovery, that the force of circumstances had to answer for all courses of action, and that events could be untoward, and transactions unfortunate, without any fault attaching to the persons ostensibly acting in them. This philosophy, which so wonderfully advances the cause of charity, has not yet obtained footing in our courts of justice; but, we foresee, and so doubtless do the lawyers, that their business will be utterly at an end whenever it is acknowledged there. Murder has not yet got the name of an "unfortunate transaction;" but when it does so, it is clear that humanity will have greatly gained, for the indictments will be laid for "unfortunate transactions," without any personality or occasion for a prisoner at the bar; and thus the odious character of the murderer will cease to exist—the thing, to be sure, may still happen untowardly; but what is a thing to a name? and words, indeed, are things, the representatives of things, and as much superior in consequence and power to them, as a Member of Parliament is of greater authority than his constituency. Had an earlier improvement of phraseology given to the Massacre of St. Bartholomew the name of the Transactions of St.

[*See Ezekiel, 38–9.]
[†Spencer, "Correspondence with William Hulton," p. 3.]

Bartholomew, that action would doubtless have been regarded with more indulgence. As for the atrocities of the French Revolution, adopting the nomenclature of Lord Althorp, may we not soften them under the description of the Philosophical Transactions? (*Ibid.*, pp. 147–9.)

An Edinburgh Reviewer (reported to be Lord Brougham) had broached the doctrine so grateful to the smatterers, that statesmanship is not a business requiring apprenticeship or study. "There is no such craft recognized in this state," said his Lordship, "as a professional statesman. All our institutions are ignorant of it; all our habits averse to it; nor is there one of a British statesman's functions which may not be conjoined with the cares of an industrious life."[*]

On this our author remarks—

This last sentence contains the very essence of quackery. It may be sold with the stamp of the *Edinburgh Review* on it, as "The Dunce's Cordial, or a Real Comfort to the Idle and Ignorant of both Houses of Parliament." The corollary is, that there is no political science; that the conduct of the affairs of a nation is a mere elegant pastime to a gentleman of a certain station in life, who has more profitable or personally agreeable pursuits for the occupation of his more valued hours. The idler, after having bent all the powers of his mighty mind to the reduction of a milliner's citadel of virtue, may apply with sufficient success the residue of the day to the toils of the Statesman in the House of Peers. The merchant, whose brain has been addled with the business of his counting-house, has merely to rise from his desk and to pass to St. Stephen's, *au fait* of the most complicated questions that can be submitted to the consideration of the legislator. The lawyer has only to close his briefs, and to be at once ready for the budget.

When we can do just as much as suits our convenience, duties are seldom onerous; and when they are utterly undefined, we may take credit for their exact performance, and marvel at their exceeding easiness—that is, if the simplicity and credulity of the world be at all proportioned to our impudent assurance.

If a cobbler were dubbed an Esculapius, we can imagine Dr. Last, who, from a long course of drenching and bleeding, had contracted an opinion that the skill accompanied the practice, *naively* saying, "Such a one (Dr. Baillie) was a physician by trade, a professional person. There is no such craft recognized in this country; all our hospitals are ignorant of it—all our habits averse to it; nor is there one of a British Physician's functions which may not be conjoined with the toils of a cobbler's life." Gentlemen, indeed, of a certain order are all Heaven-born Statesmen. No devotion of time or labour is necessary for their qualifications. Senators, they are *de facto* Statesmen. Had *Caleb Quotem*, the renowned Factotum, added M.P. to his various more useful callings, he would doubtless, after his painting, glazing, auctioneering, speechifying, almanacking, and essay-writing on hydrostatics, have found sufficient leisure for the wise direction of the affairs of the country.[†]

The proposition that the craft of a politican by trade, a professional statesman, is not recognized in this state, is partly true and partly false. We have an abundance of adventurous gentlemen who meddle in politics as a trade, but few indeed who are skilled in them as one. If we had the science together with the venal purpose, we should not complain;

[*Henry Brougham, "Mr. Burke—Dr. Laurence," *Edinburgh Review*, XLVI (Oct., 1827), 303.]

[†See Henry Lee, *Caleb Quotem and his Wife!* (London: Roach, 1809).]

but our fine folks have, it would seem, no idea of the occasion for political science, or even of the existence of political science. Arguing from their own ignorance, they infer that there is no knowledge; admiring the ease with which they conjoin doing nothing for the public with doing much for themselves, they suppose that the functions of a Statesman are comprehended in their miserable barren practices of aying, noing, inveighing, and declaiming; and judging of what they ought to be from what they are, they exclaim with a ludicrous and impudent self-complacency, like the dung in the fable, "How fine we apples swim!" (Vol. I, pp. 169–73.)[*]

Having illustrated our author's powers of combining pleasantry with argument, we will refresh the recollection of our readers with a few specimens of his success in a mere squib.

The following was written when the Duke of Wellington after being appointed Prime Minister, held along with that office his former one of Commander-in-Chief. If the paragraph alluded to ever really "appeared in the *Herald*," the coincidence not unnaturally suggested the idea of this *jeu d'esprit*.

The following paragraph has appeared in the *Herald*: "Some alarm was excited in the Palace of the Archbishop of Canterbury, at Lambeth, on Tuesday morning, at one o'clock, by the arrival of a dispatch from the Duke of Wellington, with the word 'Immediate' superscribed on the envelope. In consequence of this intimation, his Grace was awakened; the Archbishop immediately arose, and read the dispatch. The rumours on this unusual occurrence were various; but nothing has transpired from which any conjecture can be drawn as to the purport of the communication."

It is confidently rumoured that the purport of the communication was this: His Grace of Wellington notified in the most friendly terms to his Grace of Canterbury,[†] that the interests of the empire imperatively required that he, the Duke, should put himself at the head of the Protestant Church, and that it was therefore desired that his Grace of Canterbury should forthwith vacate his See to allow of the necessary arrangements—his Grace of Canterbury taking in exchange the cannonical office of Master-General of the Ordnance. Anticipating a possible but frivolous objection, the Duke explained that though he was not in Holy Orders, he would put his appointment in General Orders, which was nearly the same thing, orders being orders all the world over, and the distinction one merely of quality and not of a substantive character. The Duke ended, it is reported, by declaring that the Archbishop's exchange and his own consequent promotion *vice* Sutton should be gazetted next Tuesday, and read at the head of every regiment in his Majesty's service. The Archbishop, we hear, is resigned to the necessity, for there is no disputing the will of a man at the head of the Army and the head of the State, and comforts himself, on the score of pride, by dwelling on the precedent of Mr. Herries's descent from the Exchequer to the Mint; and on the score of fitness for his new office, by Mr. Goulburn's appointment to the Finance Department.

When this arrangement is completed, we understand that it is the intention of his Grace of Wellington to have some serious conversation with Lord Lyndhurst. There seems no reason why a Lawyer should be Chancellor. The delays of the Court have been a long complaint;

[*For "the fable," see James Gillray's cartoon, *The Apples and the Horse-Turds; or, Buonaparte among the Golden Pippins* (24 Feb., 1800), reproduced in Draper Hill, *Mr. Gillray the Caricaturist* (London: Phaidon Press, 1965), illustration no. 118.]

[†William Howley.]

and the Duke observes that the rapidity of his motions and the decision of his character cannot be questioned even by his enemies and detractors. In case of the event at which we are glancing, the Duke will be his own Vice, and Mr. Shadwell will be appointed to the command of a frigate. (Vol. I, pp. 146–8.)

We shall next quote a paper "written," says Mr. Fonblanque, "in ridicule of some very circumstantial and absurd accounts of the Duke of Wellington's habits, which appeared in the newspapers upon his Grace's accession to power in 1828."

The Duke of Wellington generally rises at about eight. Before he gets out of bed, he commonly pulls off his nightcap; and while he is dressing he sometimes whistles a tune, and occasionally damns his valet. The Duke of Wellington uses warm water in shaving, and lays on a greater quantity of lather than ordinary men. While shaving he chiefly breathes through his nose, with a view, as is conceived, of keeping the suds out of his mouth; and sometimes he blows out one cheek, sometimes the other, to present a better surface to the razor. When he is dressed he goes down to breakfast; and while descending the stairs he commonly takes occasion to blow his nose, which he does rather rapidly, following it up with three hasty wipes of his handkerchief, which he instantly afterwards deposits in his right-hand coat pocket. The Duke of Wellington's pockets are in the skirts of his coat, and the holes perpendicular. He wears false horizontal flaps, which have given the world an erroneous opinion of their position. The Duke of Wellington drinks tea for breakfast, which he sweetens with white sugar, and corrects with cream. He commonly stirs the fluid two or three times with a spoon before he raises it to his lips. The Duke of Wellington eats toast and butter, cold ham, tongue, fowls, beef, or eggs, and sometimes both meat and eggs; the eggs are generally those of the common domestic fowl. During breakfast the Duke of Wellington has a newspaper either in his hand, or else on the table, or in his lap. The Duke of Wellington's favourite paper is the *Examiner*. After breakfast the Duke of Wellington stretches himself out and yawns. He then pokes the fire and whistles. If there is no fire, he goes to the window and looks out. At about ten o'clock the General Post letters arrive. The Duke of Wellington seldom or never inspects the superscription, but at once breaks the seal and applies himself to the contents. The Duke of Wellington appears sometimes displeased with his correspondents, and says *pshaw*, in a clear, loud voice. About this time the Duke of Wellington retires for a few minutes, during which it is impossible to account for his motions with the desirable precision. At eleven o'clock, if the weather is fine, the Duke's horse is brought to the door. The Duke's horse on these occasions is always saddled and bridled. The Duke's horse is ordinarily the same white horse he rode at Waterloo, and which was eaten by the hounds at Strathfieldsaye. His hair is of a chestnut colour. Before the Duke goes out, he has his hat and gloves brought him by a servant. The Duke of Wellington always puts the hat on his head, and the gloves on his hands. The Duke's daily manner of mounting his horse is the same that it was on the morning of the glorious battle of Waterloo. His Grace first takes the rein in his left hand, which he lays on the horse's mane; he then puts his left foot in the stirrup, and with a spring brings his body up, and his right leg over the body of the animal by the way of the tail, and thus places himself in the saddle; he then drops his right foot into the stirrup, puts his horse to a walk, and seldom falls off, being an admirable equestrian. When acquaintances and friends salute the Duke in the streets, such is his affability that he either bows, touches his hat, or recognizes their civility in some way or other. The Duke of Wellington very commonly says, "How are you?"—"It's a fine day"—"How d'ye do?"—and makes frequent and various remarks on the weather, and the dust or the mud, as it may be. At twelve o'clock on Mondays, Wednesdays, and Fridays, the Duke's Master comes to teach him his Political Economy. The Duke makes wonderful progress in his studies, and his intructor is used pleasantly to observe, that "the Duke gets on like a house on fire." At the Treasury the Duke of Wellington does nothing but think. He sits on a leathern library chair, with his heels and a good part of his legs on the table. When thus in profound thought, he very frequently closes his eyes for hours together, and makes an extraordinary and rather appalling noise through his nose. Such is the Duke of Wellington's devotion to business, that he eats no luncheon. In the House of Lords the Duke's manner of proceeding is this—he walks up to the fire-place, turns his back to it, separates the skirts of his coat, tossing them over the dexter and sinister arms, thrusts his hands in his breeches' pockets, and so stands at ease. The characteristic of the Duke's oratory is a brevity the next thing to silence. As brevity is the soul of wit, it may confidently be affirmed that in this quality Lord North and Sheridan were fools compared with him. (Vol. I, pp. 160–3.)

When the late Mr. Henry Hunt appeared in Parliament, Mr. Fonblanque produced, under the title of "Biography à la Mode," a pretended sketch of his life, from which we quote the following passage: it was preceded by a flaming account of Mr. Hunt's ancestorial honours:

The present Mr. Hunt, member for Preston, was the second son of Everard Hunt, by Margaret Tollemash, a delicate shoot of one of the noblest families in the land.[*] His elder brother dying of the rickets, at the early age of three years, ten months, and eleven days, as we learn from the tablet to his memory in Stoke d'Auvely churchyard, Henry was educated as heir and hope of the noble house, nor did his youthful promise disappoint the fond hope of his parents. Loyalty seems to have been the instinct of his nature. His mother was used pleasantly to relate that, when the child was seven years of age, she chanced on approaching the nursery to hear a sound resembling that which an active full-grown bee of the bumble kind makes in the interior of an empty full-bellied pitcher, and, being naturally curious at hearing so remarkable and singular a noise, she stepped gently on her tiptoes to the door, and on listening attentively, ascertained that it was young master Harry warbling from his infant lips "God save great George our King." If a piece of money was given to him, the bent of his affections would appear in the delight with which he gazed at the head, and he would ask whether the King at London was made of gold or of silver?—for the child could not imagine royalty of the same substance as other folks. As Henry advanced from childhood to youth, these feelings of loyalty, directed by reason, settled down into a constitutional affection to the throne—that throne, we may add, which stands a bulwark of safety between the nobility and the people, protecting the latter, while its splendour reflects dignity and lustre upon the former. At eighteen, the young Hunt had the misfortune of losing his affectionate mother, in whom the pride of a noble descent was so blended with natural sweetness, that she moved through life with a dignified gentleness, that won all hearts and well-nigh broke them upon her ever lamentable demise, which took place on the 2nd of October, 1773. To dissipate the youth's grief, his father sent him to the University of Oxford, where he formed those connexions with the Whig Aristocracy which have been strengthened by time, intercourse, and the sympathy of feeling on political subjects.

After leaving Christchurch he entered into high life, and attracted the attention of the Prince of Wales, afterwards George IV, with whom a private friendship subsisted up to the demise of that ever-to-be-lamented, and ever-virtuous, monarch. Soon after his introduction in the Court circles, Mr. Hunt's father dying, he became the representative of his noble house: but the seductions of favour and fashion never warped the mind of our hero, who found time, amidst the riot of the gay world, for the studies of the philosopher, and the

[*Fonblanque invents, as a *jeu d'esprit*, the account of Hunt's family.]

writings of the moralist and the poet. To the blandishments of verse Mr. Hunt was no stranger, as an anecdote, not generally known, will show. Shakspeare says—

> The evil that men do lives after them:
> The good is oft interred with their bones.[*]

So it was with our late monarch, and hero's patron, George IV. It is not known that the last George was the inventor of the artful stitch called fine-drawing. Mr. Hunt, who happened to be acquainted with the fact that the honour of the invention belonged to the monarch, wrote upon the occasion a popular song, beginning

> Our King is a true British Tailor![†]

which became a great favourite with the trade, and has indeed been parodied in a song in honour of his present Majesty. As a proof of the value in which the late King held Mr. Hunt may be instanced the lodgings at Ilchester he gave him, in one of those houses the doors of which our sovereigns never shut against their people. Here Mr. Hunt resided two or three years, which he has often declared were the best spent and happiest of his life. Here he enjoyed the conversation of a benignant governor; and received the visits of the neighbouring magistracy, whose especial regards he had fixed. From this period up to the late election for Preston, Mr. Hunt's life has flowed in an even tide, his happiness only disturbed by the event which plunged the whole empire into a grief unparalleled in the history of affliction—we mean the deplored demise of his late Majesty, and some time father of his people, and friend, and protector, George IV. (Vol. II, pp. 182–5.)

The following, on "The General Hypocrisy," as our author justly denominates the general fast, ordained by Parliament at the suggestion of Mr. Perceval, shall be our last quotation in this vein:

That precious pot of ointment, that godly gentleman, Mr. Perceval, has at last had his pious will of us, and obtained from Ministers a promise of a General Fast,[‡] or rather of the order for one,—for as it is true that any man may take a horse to the water, but no one can make him drink,—so also it is certain that any rulers may direct a general fast, but no power can prevent men who have the means from ministering to the carnal cravings of their stomachs. The only effect will be to put the nation for one day through a grand ceremony of hypocrisy. In addition to the customary dinner, people will eat salt fish with egg sauce, which is a very good thing now and then for the palate, but decidedly dyspeptic, and apt for cholera, and should by no means be eaten where the disease exists.

How is the world changed! Time was, when contrition showed itself in beating the breast, tearing the hair, rending the garments, and screaming with energy. Now, the most pious man of the age proposes to settle the nation's long score of sins with one day of salt fish and egg sauce! What penitence! See twenty millions of sinners expiating their sins with fine large flakes of Newfoundland cod, smothered in an egg sauce, rich with cream, and stimulant with mustard, every glutton, as he gobbles it down, only remarking what a fine vehicle egg sauce is for mustard,—and certainly it is so. If we ever write a tragedy it shall be called "Contrition;" and the hero, after a tissue of enormities, shall, by way of

---

[**Julius Caesar*, III, ii, 85–6.]

[†Fonblanque is playing on the refrain of Thomas Williams' song in honour of the "Sailor King," William IV, *Our King!—a True British Sailor!* (London: Williams, [1830]).]

[‡See Spencer, Speech on the General Fast (26 Jan., 1832), *PD*, 3rd ser., Vol. 9, col. 902.]

catastrophe in the fifth act, order salt fish and egg sauce in addition to his customary meal.

A contemporary truly remarks that good Mr. Perceval has superseded the Bishops, nay, the Archbishops, who have not said a word about the necessity for this General Fast, perhaps because those worldly divines well know that it will only prove a General *Break-fast*. Mr. Perceval indeed explains, that he is the Member for Heaven; but we think we see signs of his differing with his constituency. For instance, he rather ungraciously flings in the teeth of the country the shameful prodigality of bounty shown to him and his.

"I was *taken up*," said the Hon. Member, "on the death of my father, by the nation, which abundantly provided for me and mine; and it is in gratitude for that kindness that I call on the house to address the Crown to issue a proclamation for a fast."[*]

Were he "taken up" by a mad doctor, it would be more becoming his peculiar claims to care. It is the "taking up" of him, and such as he, which constitutes the crying sin of the nation,—its endurance of abuse to absolute baseness. That is the true national humiliation. And this pot of godliness coolly talks of the abundant provision made for him. Why does he not look to be fed, according to Scripture, as the young ravens?[†] What does he do with that kitchen? What mean those fat partridges at the fire? What is the purpose of that vast cook? Is that simmering and bubbling from stew-pans, flesh-pots of abomination, devices of carnal cookery? And lo! there we spy a haunch of mutton hanging up to be dressed ten days hence, when tender,—perhaps on the general fast day, after the fish and the eggs, and the mustard! What providence is this—what thought of the morrow,[‡] and not the morrow of all souls,—aye, and of ten days after the morrow! Is this in any degree like the manners and customs of young ravens? Whoever saw a raven, young or old, with a cook and a kitchen range, and a larder, and a carnal joint hanging upon a devil's hook? Does Mr. Perceval (we will not call him *good* after such doings) suppose that the devil has never been in his kitchen?—aye, has he, and perhaps kissed his cook too, and looked with a leer into his stew-pans, and thought what a sop in the pan he would make of his miserable little soul, tricked out with all its earthly gauds and hypocrisies. Where is his treasure laid up?—at Ransom's;—aye, that will be no ransom for him from the pickle of Dives.[§] Again: What sort of tabernacle is that he tarries in? Is it in the least like a raven's nest? No, no; his nest has been very differently feathered, and it is lined most abundantly, as he truly says, with the golden fleece, from this most patient and most pillaged people of all on the face of the earth. He is like to the raven in nothing but blackness, and the dismalness of his croak.

It is curious, that in a squib called the "Unreported Meeting," in the *New Monthly Magazine* of April last,[¶] Mr. Perceval's argument, as to the absence of any mention of responsibility to the people, in scripture, is anticipated in the speech attributed to him:

"Mr. P—— could not agree with the last speaker, that it was vain to cast about for safety, in the sad strait to which they had been reduced. He thought prayer could not fail to procure their deliverance. While there was heaven there was hope. Many causes had conduced to their present condition of danger. The devil had not been inactive,—when, indeed, was he? The people were too well off; they waxed fat and kicked.[||] Fasts should be frequently enforced to keep down their pride. The visitations which formerly softened men's hearts are now unknown—as if Providence had deserted this guilty world, famines and pestilences

[*Spencer Perceval, Speech on the General Fast (26 Jan., 1832), *ibid.*, col. 900.]
[†See Job, 38:41–3.]
[‡See Matthew, 6:34.]
[§See Luke, 16:19–31.]
[¶Albany Fonblanque, "The Unreported Meeting," *New Monthly Magazine and Literary Journal*, XXXI (Apr., 1831), 337–46.]
[||See Deuteronomy, 32:15.]

have ceased. What was the consequence? the people became stiff-necked and puffed up with pride, and their hearts rose against their rulers. But this was not all. They were tasting of fruit of the tree of knowledge in its accursed ripeness. Man in his innocence was ignorant—he tasted of knowledge and he became a creature of sin.[*] The apples, sweet to the taste, and bitter in the belly, were now his daily food; the atrocious newspapers,—those deadly poisons to the soul, were gathered twice a day. Knowledge had never been designed for man, and yet he saw well-meaning persons engaged in promoting education, which was the ladder to sin. He was rejoiced to see that the Church was setting the example of neglecting learning in its own body. The vanity of acquirements, merely human, was properly renounced by guides to a heavenly destination. In a worldly and politic view, knowledge was an evil. Men who knew nothing beyond their own circumstances, were content and happy—with comparisons came discontent, and restlessness, and envy, and misery. Would we give knowledge to dogs and horses? No. Suppose horses could read and reason, what a clamour would be raised at every coach-stand, and what coachman would be able to manage his steeds? They would want Representation, forsooth!—they would want a horse on the box—they would want horses to measure out the corn, and keep the bins! Nothing could be more idle than the demand for Representation. *Had there been any virtue in Representation, would it not have been recommended in Scripture? But in the sacred books is there a word of a Representative Government? Providence would have given the Jewish people a Representative Government if it had been an advisable institution. It was, in his mind, a convincing argument against Representation, that it was not spoken of in Scripture.* It might be objected that boroughs were also unnamed; but the payment of taxes was especially recommended, and boroughs conduced to the exercise of that divinely enjoined duty. Our Constitution was matchless and faultless, and constructed on a model that could not fail. It was of three estates, King, Lords, and Commons, and though three, it was one. This perfection was argued to be a fault by the Reformers, who absurdly objected that one power ruled in all these forms. Because they cannot understand this merit, is its being to be denied? But with infidels in religion, or in politics, he would hold no argument. The honourable gentleman concluded with a Resolution, 'That a prayer should be composed for the preservation of Boroughs, and that frequent fasting was a discipline of the body and soul, essential to the good conduct of the people.'" (Vol. II, pp. 244–52.)

The squib here referred to, is well known to have been let off by Mr. Fonblanque himself. Indeed these volumes, selected from the *Examiner*, might easily be equalled, both in extent and in merit, by a selection from Mr. Fonblanque's writings not in the *Examiner*. The "Unreported Meeting," is one of those *jeux d'esprit* which would not willingly be let die. It contains several speeches, which we think are no way inferior to the oration of Mr. Perceval.

We quote as specially memorable, part of the speeches ascribed to Lord Monson (the proprietor of Gatton), and to the somewhat more celebrated Lord Huntingtower.

After a resolution in favour of potwallopers, moved by Sir Robert Peel, Lord Monson rose and expressed his dissent:

"Potwallopers were very likely the best class of electors; he did not dispute their merits; he believed their superiority; but, after all, they were but the best of the fallible. Say what we may, the men are but men, the best of whom stumbles six times a day. Now, bricks or stones

[*See Genesis, 2:17 and 3:4–6.]

never stumble, they are always to be reckoned upon. He had the happiness of possessing a borough on his lawn—this was a thing as near perfection as it was possible to be . . . . It was nonsense to suppose any virtue in popular election—the choice of the many, forsooth! Does not the proverb say, that too many cooks spoil the broth? One man was as likely to be right as a thousand. It was proper that the aristocracy should choose members for the people. What would become of the sheep if they chose their own dogs?—no, their shepherd chooses them . . . . Pursuing this sentiment, he must declare himself a parliamentary reformer . . . . He should propose, that sixty decayed towns be enfranchised. Places having twenty, or more than twenty inhabitants, to have the electoral right conveyed to the possession of the nearest ruin. The remains of ancient castles, religious buildings, and Roman camps, might be usefully represented. He should like to see members for Kenilworth, Glastonbury, St. George's Hill, &c. Thus, he would meet the revolutionary reform scheme, by a plan of constitutional reform . . . . It was truly said by some writer, who was a lord, and therefore of some authority, that Time is the great reformer; and how had Time reformed boroughs, but by depopulating them, by thinning away the rank abundance of the electoral bodies? The same lord, whose name he now remembered to be Bacon, observed that we should imitate Time in our reforms;[*] and how then could we better do that than by producing rottenness in the constituency? Time has decayed boroughs, and reformers should decay boroughs after its example. He disliked large towns; they were squalid, smoky, unairy, unhealthy. Who would compare Bramber with Brighton? The representation of decay was the representation of the condition of mortality. Out of corruption Nature reproduces life; and the life of the constitution, in like manner, springs from corruption. But the radicals would rail against the corruption of nature, and stop by bill, the progress of re-creation. From the disgustful worm comes the butterfly, with wings powdered with gold—from the rotten borough comes the member, bright with parliamentary honours. Like the butterfly, he might be called a pensioner; but such vulgar slang was to be despised. What he takes from the world he renders back in decoration." (*Incessant cheering*, and loud cries of *hear, hear, hear*, from Lord E——.)[†]

This really is very fair parliamentary argument, and the drollest part of it not more ludicrous than (for instance) Mr. Spring Rice's argument against the ballot "that it is absurd to expect moral effects from mechanical means."[‡] (What does Mr. Spring Rice think of the press?) But Mr. Rice never yet made so clever a speech. Our author's facility in giving the forms of logic and the colours of rhetoric to the absurdest trains of thought, is such as the rightful owners of the absurdities may well envy.

Let us now listen to Lord Huntingtower:

"Lord H. declared that these palliatives were idle—he cared not a rush who took offence at the term—he had tried more expedients than most men, but ingenuity could not make everything of insufficient means. Nothing would do but a return to the old feudal right of the gallows. When lords could hang, they were respected. The lenity of certain persons who should know better, was the great fault. He laughed at such petty doings as those that had caused so much talk at Stamford and Newark. His people had offended him at Grantham,

[*Both references are to Bacon, "Of Innovation," in *The Essays or Counsels, Civill and Morall* (1625), in *Works*, Vol. VI, p. 433.]

[†Fonblanque, "The Unreported Meeting," pp. 339-40.]

[‡Thomas Spring-Rice, Speech on the Ballot (7 Mar., 1837), *PD*, 3rd ser., Vol. 37, col. 64.]

and what did he do? Why, he made a fish-pond in the place of houses, and worried the dogs into meekness. The law had hitherto been their only instrument of power, but that was about to be withdrawn from them; or at least, it was to be shared with the people, which was as bad. If there were a club for every one's use, so heavy that none but giants could lift it, it was clear that the giants would be able to arm with it, while the people of common stature would only be controlled by it; but reduce the club to a size that may be wielded by the ordinary run of people, and the great lose their peculiar advantage. So it was with the law; by cheapening it, the poor would be enabled to beard the rich in court, and their insolence would be encouraged . . . . He had used the power of the purse on the law, but never abused it; he had used it regularly, but always in moderation. He had given notice to his attorney that he would never allow himself more than two hundred a year, in what were called vexatious proceedings, and that if more was charged in his bill it would be disallowed . . . . He had compelled obedience to his wishes by various means, but chiefly by nuisances which were of great convenience. He had employed many expedients in his private way, vicious bulls, indelicate operations before the windows of disagreeable people, and many more than he had patience to recite; if these things promoted prosecution, why then he had the parties in a court, with a hole in their pockets, and an attorney's bill on their shoulders. Law Reform, as it is called—Law Deform, as he would style it—would however take all power out of their hands, and strip them of any authority superior to the vulgar. Unless we can have some instrument of force which the people have not, how can we maintain our respect? Wrongs are complained of, but why? Because the resistance of obstinate people to some necessary command has provoked punishment. If the people were completely submissive to us, they would be kindly treated. Are we cruel to our cows, and our sheep, our dogs and our horses?—No; because they are ours, and we hurt not our own—they are obedient, and offer no provocation. So it would be with the people, were they what they were in the good old times, and should ever have remained, *adscripti glebæ*, serfs, and villains. But now they must have the protection of law! (his lordship emphatically added). I wonder they are not ashamed to hold the protection of law in common with the beasts of the field; is it not degrading, that Englishmen will consent to have the same shield over them which the legislature has flung over horses, and oxen, and jackasses?" (*Hear, hear, hear.*)[*]

This parody on the declamation against the ballot will not have escaped the reader: and as for the argument for absolute power, in the sentences immediately preceding, the Carlton Club should vote Mr. Fonblanque a thousand pounds for it. It is the best thing ever said in favour of Toryism.

One more quotation, and we have done. It has been seen that our author's wit is often not the mere ornament and garnishing of his argument, but the solid reasoning itself, playfully expressed. At other times, when the occasion demands a seriousness of feeling inconsistent with pleasantry, the following article, written at the end of 1830, shows with what lofty earnestness he can write. We quote it partly for this purpose, and partly for the intrinsic value of the lesson of encouragement which it so nobly conveys.

We have closed the year ONE of the People's Cause. We have closed a year that has teemed with events of a grandeur and importance to mankind, unparalleled in the history of the world. We have closed a year in which Justice has wielded the sword of Victory, and Fortune lent her wheel to Truth. We have closed a year which has carried the mind of Europe

[*Fonblanque, "The Unreported Meeting," pp. 342–3.]

forward an interval of ages beyond its antiquated trammels and thraldoms. We have closed a year which has dated the decrepitude of despotism, and the Herculean infancy of the democratic power; and must not our recollections swell with pride, and our expectations be full of confidence? The past indicates the future. Abroad we have the example of France, both for imitation and for warning. Her people have set before us the great lesson of virtue—her Government of error.

It cannot be denied, that for the last ten years, step after step has been won by the liberal party, and not one inch of ground anywhere lost. We have experienced no defeats—we have been stayed, indeed, but never thrust back; and, despite of obstinate opposition, object after object has been attained. The Liberals struggled long for Catholic Emancipation. Catholic Emancipation was declared the destruction of Religion, the delivery of society to all the powers of evil, the unloosing of Anti-Christ and Satan. It was carried;[*] and all the world perceived that the Liberals had been right. Nearly the same history applies to the Test Laws.[†] The alteration of the Commercial System was demanded: the Economists were forthwith declared visionaries, and their doctrines were condemned, under the all-convincing description of "new-fangled,"—one of the most potent phrases in the English language. With the success of the experiments came the late acknowledgment, that the economists were not such fools as the ignoramuses had thought them.

Reformers complained of the abuses, defects, and vices of the laws. "The law is perfection," was the first defence; and the objectors were denounced as false preachers of discontent, the inveterate enemies of all the excellences in our unrivalled institutions; and yet Law Reform is now the great business of the day; and judges claim, and merit praise, for their application to the purifying of the Augean stable. Thus again, after all, the Reformers were right. Lastly, we come to the grand question.

Who were they who have for years past denounced the corruption of the Lower House, called for its re-constitution, and insisted on the people's right to representation as the only security against the abuse of power? Radicals, clamourers without cause, it was said; men void of truth and justice, who slandered an institution as perfect as the wit of man could make it, and which, whatever theoretical flaws might be objected by visionaries, worked excellently well in practice. Two years ago the Honourable House declared, upon a division, that there was no rotten representation. Less than two months ago, a Minister fell because he offered the same impudent outrage to truth. Now, the vast majority of society, Whig, Tory, and Moderates, acknowledge the necessity of Parliamentary Reform. So again the Reformers, after all, were right. Two years back, when Sir Robert Peel uttered a scoff at the Ballot,[‡] the collective wisdom received it with shouts of applause. Six months ago, Mr. Brougham railed against secret voting at popular meetings, without provoking signs of displeasure or retort;[§] but now the judgment of the country is for the Ballot. Men of all classes and denominations, not interested in the foul influences, are convinced that the protection of the voter is necessary to the freedom of the suffrage. So here again, it will soon be seen, that the Reformers were right, after all. Where are they yet said to be wrong? Only, we reply, upon the ground where the battles are not yet fought out. They are said to be wrong, or wicked, or mischievous, for demanding that the franchise shall be co-extensive with the education and property of the country, and descending to the people as information

[*10 George IV, c. 7 (1829).]
[†13 Charles II, second session, c. 1 (1661), and 25 Charles II, c. 2 (1672), repealed by 9 George IV, c. 17 (1828).]
[‡Robert Peel, Speech on the Penryn Disfranchisement Bill (28 Mar., 1828), *PD*, n.s., Vol. 18, col. 1360.]
[§See *Examiner*, 8 Aug., 1830, p. 449.]

is spreading among them. They are said to be wrong for objecting to an expensive Church Establishment, and for thinking that the wealth of the Priesthood is not apostolic or conducive to religion. They are said to be wrong, or wicked, or mischievous, because they think it unjust, and impolitic, to cramp the industry of a nation by Corn Laws for the supposed advantage of the landed proprietors. They are said to be wrong, or disloyal, and seditious, for supposing that the dignity of the Crown can be maintained without extravagant ostentation, and that the conduct of the chief magistrate is a better security for it than his cost.

They are said to be wrong, or to betray an ignorant impatience of taxation, for contending that it is the duty of a Government to raise the moral character of the people by knowledge, and that it is barbarous impolicy to place out of their reach, by stamp duties, the information which would teach them prudence and conduct. They are said to be wrong for arguing that it is cheaper and better to direct men with books, than to control them with bayonets, and that letters are more explanatory missives than bullets.

Under these, and a very few other imputations of error, the Reformers may be cheered by reflecting that such opposition has been offered, for a season, to every measure (without any single exception) they have carried; and in relation to those objects we have recited, as well as to those already won, it will be confessed, at no distant day, that, after all, the Radicals were right.

We ask of our opponents to reflect on the many questions which the voice of society, and the acts of the State, have determined in our favour; and to consider whether it is not probable that we are as right, in the doctrines which remain unsettled, as in those now sanctioned and established? Have they not as much cause for self-distrust as the Reformers have for confidence?

Against what combined forces of sinister interest, custom and prejudice, have the Liberals made their impressions, and achieved their victories, by the vast power of truth alone! To the conviction of society, and to nothing else, do we owe our proud successes. (Vol. II, pp. 78–83.)

This eloquent and impressive passage will afford an appropriate transition to a few remarks which appear to us to be called for, as to the present political position of the *Examiner,* and the temporary, and in a great measure only apparent, separation which has taken place between Mr. Fonblanque, and that more active and vigorous section of the thorough reformers, of which he was for some years perhaps the most important, and certainly the most conspicuous representative.

We have delayed to the conclusion of our article, our observations on this topic, because we were desirous of considering the writer of the *Examiner* in his permanent, rather than in what we cannot but regard as his temporary character. The position which Mr. Fonblanque has established for himself in the history of our time, as not only one of the most powerful but one of the most uncompromising asserters of the doctrines of enlightened radicalism, in season and out of season, through good and ill report, deserved that the tribute of admiration and gratitude which we have endeavoured to render, should be undisturbed by the intrusion of any of the differences of opinion which exist between him and those whom we hope we may call his political friends, respecting the exigencies of the present moment, and the attitude which, at a single point in the varying course of passing politics, it becomes the enlightened radicals to assume. We confess, however, it was an unpleasant surprise to us, that a writer who, in the judgment of most of those entertaining the same opinions, occasionally outran the bounds of justice and discretion in his onslaughts upon Lord Grey's ministry, both collectively and individually, should depart still more widely from the same line in the contrary direction, when Lord Melbourne's ministry are concerned. We did not expect that he would so soon fall behind those whom he formerly ran so far before. The change is not in *them*, it is in *him*. We acknowledge, as we have always acknowledged, that Lord Melbourne's ministry is, in its spirit and general policy, several degrees in advance of Lord Grey's; and is entitled, against the Tories, to as much support from radicals as can be reconciled with the unqualified and energetic pursuit of their separate objects *as* radicals. And we may appeal to the whole conduct of the active section of the radicals since the commencement of the session (honour be to them, they have given us much to appeal to) and ask whether any support consistent with this object has been denied? rather, whether it has not been afforded more conspicuously and zealously, as well as more powerfully, than at any former time? The conduct of the radicals in this respect has left to Mr. Fonblanque no subject of complaint; but *they* have no small subject of complaint against *him*. They complain that while they have thought it incumbent on them to make the promulgation of their own principles their primary object, and support to the ministry altogether secondary to that; he, on the contrary, has, almost from the first coming in of the present ministry in 1835, acted as if his first object was to support and glorify the ministers, and the assertion of his own political doctrines only the second.

To Mr. Fonblanque, our description of that part of his conduct which we complain of, will probably appear an over-statement, and we shall be sorry if it does not. To many of those whose exertions have most effectively served radical opinions, we know that it will appear an understatement. Whatever course of conduct Mr. Fonblanque may think fit to adopt, that he is sincere in it there can be no manner of doubt, and as little in our minds of the unabated strength of his attachment to all the principles and all the political objects which he has hitherto pursued. Our difference with him is on a point of expediency, but it is on one of those points of expediency which involve principles. That it is possible to assert, when occasion arises, some of the most important doctrines of radicalism, and yet to maintain a general tone of systematic subserviency to ministers, as fulsome and undiscriminating as that of the most sordid place-hunter or parasite, we have examples in many members of parliament, and in the *Morning Chronicle*. That Journal advocates the ballot and the repeal of the corn laws; but who knows, or who thinks of it, in any other light than that of a mere ministerial hack writer and panegyrist? Far be it from our thoughts to insinuate the slightest vestige of a comparison between the *Examiner* and the *Morning Chronicle*. Mr. Fonblanque could not, if he would, and would not, if he could, be made a "utensil" of by any ministry: he has compromised no principle; there is no opinion he ever held, which he does not at times continue to advocate; nor does he spare individual members of the ministry, when they lay themselves open to radical attack. It is not any specific act, either of omission or commission, then, which we complain of, so much as a general lowering of the tone of political morality which formerly distinguished the *Examiner*. He no longer studies to keep a high standard of the duty of ministers and parliament perpetually in view, and to rebuke (with more or less severity, according to circumstances) every instance of deviation from it: he expends all his strength and his space in fighting for the ministers and their measures against the Tories (and occasionally against the radicals): while the advocacy of those broader and bolder views, to the fearless promulgation of which we owe that the Tories are not still in power, has become almost a subordinate feature in his Journal; and it is only his past reputation for radicalism which prevents him from being mistaken for a ministerialist with radical inclinations, rather than a radical who, without relaxing one iota in the pursuit of radical objects, consents to support the ministry. It was not thus that Mr. Fonblanque attained his proud eminence among English journalists; it was not thus that the only newspaper writer with whom he can be compared, the unapproachable Armand Carrel, made himself, without a seat in the legislature or any public station beyond the editorship of his journal, the most powerful political leader of his age and country.*

For us, in the way in which all radical battles have hitherto been fought and won, in that way we mean to persevere; not withholding, for the sake of any ministry or party, or from regard to the immediate fate of any party question, one particle of useful truth, for which we believe that in the present state of the public mind we can find audience. And as one of our chief examples and encouragements in this course is to be found in the past career of Mr. Fonblanque, so are we satisfied that we shall not long have to pursue it without his sympathy and assistance; that the distance which, in appearance more than in reality, divides that portion of the thorough reformers whom this Review more especially represents, from him who was so long their *decus et tutamen*,[*] will gradually diminish, and that before eighteen months have elapsed, the difference will have ceased to exist, except in memory.

*We are happy to learn that a memoir of the life of this extraordinary man will shortly appear in Paris, from the accomplished pen of his friend M. Désiré Nisard. [Jean Marie Napoléon Désiré Nisard, "Armand Carrel," *Revue des Deux Mondes*, XII (Oct., 1837), 5–54.]

[*Virgil, *Aeneid*, Vol. I, p. 462 (V, 262).]

PARTIES AND THE MINISTRY

1837

EDITOR'S NOTE

London and Westminster Review, VI & XXVIII (Oct., 1837), 1-26. Headed: "ART. I.—1.[Anon.] *Domestic Prospects of the Country under the New Parliament*. Third edition, revised. [London:] Ridgway. 1837. / 2. *Corrected Report of the Speech of Lord John Russell, at the Dinner given on his Election for Stroud, on Friday, July 28, 1837, and an Account of the Proceedings*. [London:] Knight. 1837. / 3. [George Pryme.] *A Letter to the Electors of Cambridge, touching Mr. Knight, Mr. Sutton, and the Poor-Laws*. By a Member of the University. Cambridge[: Johnson], 1837. / 4. [Thomas Perronet Thompson.] *Second Series—Letters of a Representative to his Constituents during the Session of 1837*. With Additions and Corrections. [London:] Effingham Wilson. 1837." Running titles as title. Signed "A." Not republished. Identified in Mill's bibliography as "An article entitled 'Parties and the Ministry', in the London and Westminster Review for October, 1837 (No 11 and 54)" (MacMinn, 49). The Somerville College copy (tear-sheets) has one emendation (adopted in the present edition): "do speak" is corrected to "do not speak" (389.13-14).

Parties and the Ministry

THE NEW PARLIAMENT is about to meet; and it is desirable to consider what is to be feared, and what is to be hoped, from the approaching trial of the strength of parties.

The Tories have made the public fully aware of their intentions and their anticipations. According to them, they are on the eve of coming again into place. They have reduced the already small ministerial majority. By pitting their long purses against the short purses of their opponents before the most disgracefully expensive of all judicial tribunals, Committees of the House of Commons, they hope to convert that majority into a minority; and they are assured of doing so at the next general election. And then, like Mrs. Partington, they will flourish their mop, and set the Atlantic at defiance.[*]

We cannot tell that these hopes may not be realised. We cannot tell that the Tories may not be permitted to succeed in making the counties, the small boroughs, and the freemen, under the Reform Act, what the counties, the small boroughs, and the freemen, were before. What then? Is it for us to blush, and hang our heads, and give up all for lost, and think ourselves beaten, and disgraced, and driven from the field? No, truly. They may do so, if they please, who prophesied of a millennium, in which the tiger was to grow ashamed of his claws, and the serpent of his venom,—who dreamed that bribery and intimidation would grow less as the temptation to them grew greater, and as the consciences of their unhappy victims grew more seared,—who believed that the Reform Act had been a mandate of reform in men's hearts, as well as in their outward institutions, and that there was to be no need henceforth of laws to protect us against the misuse of power, for that the powerful would stand so much in awe of the weak, would be so humble before them, would have so much respect for their "opinion," that they would let the government of this country pass out of their hands without an effort to retain it, without a fiercer word than "Good people, for charity's sake, your vote!" We, the visionaries, the Utopians, the Radicals, had none of these visions. We left them to the "practical men." *We* never bade the people trust to what the *Examiner* calls the "O fie" check. We never pretended that the Reform Bill, with its present

[*A character evidently invented by Sydney Smith in a speech at Taunton, reported in the Taunton *Courier*, 12 Oct., 1831, p. 3; see *The Works of the Rev. Sydney Smith*, 4 vols. (London: Longman, Orme, Brown, Green, and Longmans, 1840), Vol. IV, pp. 392–3.]

machinery, would be any better as a permanent constitution than the government by rotten boroughs. We had faith in the Ballot, even without the Reform Bill. We had no faith in the Reform Bill without the Ballot. The foundation of our hope in the Reform Bill was that it would bring the Ballot. We never believed that it would do so until the last moment. The last moment has arrived.

We are not accusing the Ministers. We never felt so little disposed to accuse them. We know all the allowances which are to be made for them. And if we did not, we agree with those who say that this is not a time when Reformers should turn against each other. Neither, we must add, is it a time when we believe they *could* do so with success. We are sensible how much the cause of Reform has lost by the *inertia* of Ministers. They have allowed the enthusiasm to go down, by giving it nothing to keep it up. But what is left of it still follows in their train, because it can do no otherwise, until a bolder party shall furnish leaders equally known and better trusted: they are still at the head of the Reform party, and the crowd behind them is striving to push them on, not to push them aside. We wish as heartily as any one that this were not so. But neither are we entitled to forget that its being so is the fault of no one so much as of our own party. Some of the best Radicals in Parliament were members of the House of Commons long before the Reform Bill. For the last five years we have never had fewer than seventy or eighty English and Scotch Radicals in Parliament, without counting the Irish; and in the last Parliament we had nearly double the number. If, with all this Parliamentary strength, and the country ready to respond to their call, our leaders have not yet succeeded in making themselves the leaders of the country; if some have been too old, others too young, some too impracticable, others too timid; if the ablest among them have been indolent, or dispirited, or frivolous, or, as in the one case of Mr. Roebuck, have not yet had time completely to conquer, even by the most valiant efforts, a prejudice against them which they took no pains to mollify; if they have never known how to strike the chord which was prepared to vibrate; if, with talents inferior to no party in the House—if with acquirements superior to any, they have not known how to make those talents and those acquirements recognised, and available for the common cause; if they have made their virtues and their faults equally an obstacle to their influence; if they have come forward with their accustomed honour, to take the lion's share of all unpopularity, and allowed the Whigs to carry off the credit of everything popular which has been effected by their joint strength; our party must resign itself for some time longer to the consequences of its past inefficiency. The body of Reformers throughout the country, in all walks of life, who have no means of judging political men but from what they read in the newspapers, will continue, until the contrary is proved to them, to believe that the Radicals in Parliament have shown all they can do, and that those Radicals are a sample of the best whom Radicalism can furnish. A vigorous, and, as far as it went, highly successful effort, was made by a few of the Radicals in the early part of the last session, to take a higher ground. We encouraged them to the effort, and we applaud them for it. But years of lost time cannot be made up in a few months; men's minds had settled into other channels; the post of honour which our friends had left so long unclaimed, they could not assume at a moment's warning; and the attacks of some of them on the Whigs, before they had shown themselves qualified to succeed the Whigs, were but partially responded to, because they appeared ill-timed to a large majority even of those who thought them true, and because numbers of those who go much further than the Whigs see no chance of resisting the Tories but by their aid, and, in proportion as they despair of the Whigs, despair of Reform.

We can see, as well as some of our friends, one not inconsiderable advantage, which might result from a Tory ministry, or a mixed ministry of Whigs and moderate Tories. There might be a far more efficient Radical party. There would be an end to the parrot cry of "Do not endanger the Ministry." We should be fighting for a cause, *then*, and not for a set of men. We should no longer be under leaders whose opinions, or whose fears, or the necessities of whose position, make them rather desirous to damp than to inflame the enthusiasm of their own supporters. We should be delivered from the anomalous state, in which we have neither the benefits of a liberal government, nor those of a liberal opposition; in which we can carry nothing through the two Houses, but what would be given by a Tory ministry, and yet are not able to make that vigorous appeal to the people out of doors, which under the Tories could be made and would be eagerly responded to. These are considerations which cannot but act strongly upon men who feel that they could play a part in this more energetic action upon the public mind. It is natural that men who think the cause in danger of being lost by timidity and lukewarmness— who think that all depends upon speaking out, upon aiming at great things, upon offering to the people objects worth fighting for, and a banner worth upholding—it is natural that they should sigh for a time when to raise this banner, when to proclaim these objects, will not be the way to be looked shily on by their own party, and called marplots, and impracticable men, and Tory-Radicals. We, too, differ in some things from Mr. Roebuck, and our able and upright friend the *Spectator*; but the want of literal conformity, which, as Colonel Thompson says in his admirable *Letters of a Representative*, "is always the excuse of feeble people,"[*] shall not be ours. If we differ from them somewhat, we agree with them in more. We sympathize cordially in the feelings which are now actuating them. We doubt if they feel more indignant than we do at the sort of reception which their manifestation of these feelings has met with; at the sort of interpretation which has been put upon it by some who ought to have known better. They have a right to deem it monstrous that there should be any man, calling himself a Radical Reformer, who cannot see how much justice there is in the feelings, how much far-sightedness in the views, which separate them from those

[*Thompson, *Letters*, p. 1.]

who are now attacking them; who cannot perceive, that the portion of the truth which they see, is that which the Whigs, and a number of the moderate Radicals, are losing themselves and their cause by not seeing. We should go much farther than they do, we should invite a Tory Ministry, we should hail its advent with delight, if we were as certain that the other Radicals would make a vigorous use of the opportunities it would give them, as we are that Mr. Roebuck would. But can Mr. Roebuck himself expect it? Alas! it is not, it never has been in our time, opportunities that were wanting to the men, but men to the opportunities.

It is supposed that those who are inert and tame on one side of the House would be impassioned and laborious on the other? For many years there never has been a time when great things might not have been done, if there had been anybody to do them; there never has been a turn in affairs which might not have been improved into some decided advantage for the popular cause, if there had been men in Parliament on the look-out to seize what opportunities it afforded, and to profit by them. The longer we live, and the more we extend our experience of human affairs, the less disposed are we to impute to accident any great thing which ever was accomplished on this earth. Those lucky accidents, to which men appear to owe their success, hardly ever occur but to persons who have cultivated the faculty of availing themselves of accidents; and for every one such man, there are a hundred or a thousand others, who, if they had made as good use of their opportunities and chances as he did of his, would have effected greater things. But there is a truth which the popular party during the last seven years has never ceased proving to us—that for men who have not the qualities which *command* success, the chapter of accidents can do little. If a man waits for circumstances, instead of making the most of those he has, it is likely he will make no better use of better circumstances; any conceivable amount of good fortune will be thrown away upon him.

We ask those Reformers who, because Ministers are ruining us, would drive the Reform party into opposition, how will that ensure us against being ruined in the same way, and even by the same men? If the Radicals, as a body, act as they have hitherto done, they will let the leadership of the party slip through their fingers in opposition as they did in power, and we shall have as tame an Opposition as we now have a tame Ministry. Some individual Radicals have distinguished themselves in debate, and will do so every year more and more; they have most of the rising men in the House, but they have no men who have as yet shewn themselves capable either of leading and keeping together a party, or (unless Mr. Roebuck or Colonel Thompson be an exception) of speaking to the masses in a language which they can understand and sympathize with. There is, in a few of the Radicals in Parliament, and in a greater number of those out of Parliament, talent and energy which may in time qualify them to play a distinguished part either as a Ministry or as an Opposition. Even now they would make as creditable a figure in office as the present holders, or any other set of men before the public. But the old established parties make up for their want of intrinsic superiority by their capacity of co-operation. We have not yet seen in any individual Radical even the promise of qualities by which he could lead a party single-handed; and without such a man, or the habit of organized concert, they will be feeble, on either side of the House, except as appendages to a party who have served a longer apprenticeship to the art of acting together.

For the popular party must have leaders: no party can hope to direct the public mind unless it has its cabinet ready made; no principles, be they even the truest, can rally a nation round them until they are personified in a set of men, whose cause is their cause, and whose banner presents one undivided object to the public eye; a symbol, representing to each man *that* in the common cause for the sake of which he loves it, and which he could not prevail upon so many to agree in fighting for, under its own separate standard. One man wishes more especially to reform one thing, one another: as, on the other side, one man is interested in preserving one abuse, another in preserving another; and as these are only able to make head by banding themselves together to bring men into power who though willing to abandon any particular abuse, make it their general effort to preserve abuses, so, on our side, each rests his hope of carrying his favourite reform, upon making sure, in the first instance, that some *men* who stand upon the general principle of Reform, shall be in a situation where any reform which they support will be supported by the whole body of Reformers: which being attained, all particular reforms become questions to be debated and determined among themselves by Reformers alone. This place may be filled by an Opposition party as well as by a Ministry, but it must be filled somehow: and it is already a sufficient misfortune to want confidence in our leaders, without struggling to put them aside when we cannot as yet succeed in putting ourselves into their place.

With these feelings we address ourselves to the present Ministry. We are willing to accept them as leaders until we can produce others, or until they leave us and join the enemy. We are willing to support them as Ministers, however little they may do to deserve support, if they will but be the enemies of the Tories. If we cannot do without their votes, they cannot do without our principles; they could not stand three days if the people took them at their word—if there were not men beside them and behind them to tell the country that the miserable Municipal Bills and Appropriation Clauses, which they affirm to be all that the people are fighting for, are not all, and that there is within these so diminutive bodies a strong spirit, which, because it will *not* thus be satisfied, because it will *not* stop where they say it will, is worth fighting for, *although* the immediate prize which seems to be contended about is so infinitesimally insignificant. We are willing to continue rendering them this service, which is essential to their existence. What we require of them, and we do not require it as a condition, but as a return, is: That they will consent to be kept in place, by consenting to do the things, without which it is not in human power to keep them there; and that they will fulfil the part which is incumbent upon those who are elected as leaders less from their personal influence than by the result of a compromise: namely, that they shall represent (we do not ask for more) the *average* opinion of their supporters.

There are many of our objects which, on these principles, we cannot expect them to support. But there is one which can be no longer trifled with. If they can *now* persist in refusing the Ballot, they are not worth supporting any longer; they will fall, and fall unregretted.

"All parties," says the pamphlet first on our list, and which is said to be from an official source—

> all parties, those for the Ballot, those for extended Suffrage, those for the abolition of Church Rates, those for grand plans of Public Education, those for the Appropriation Clause, those for Municipal Institutions in Ireland, those for yielding to Canada a more democratic form of Government than at present exists there, should one and all enter the new session with this conviction thoroughly impressed upon their minds, that there is not one of these questions, no, not one, which is not secondary to the great object of maintaining Lord Melbourne's Cabinet as the great agent of future improvement, free from every species of present embarrassment.[*]

The proposition is more confident than modest: but, permit us to ask, is that to be secondary to keeping in Lord Melbourne, which is the only possible means of keeping him in? He has still a majority: but on a most careful calculation of all the changes in the representation, giving each party the benefit of every seat in which it has substituted a sure man for a trimmer, we find the Tories gainers of a balance of seven seats, equivalent to fourteen on a division. The calculations which give Ministers a majority of thirty-seven are palpably absurd. They had not that in the last Parliament, and nobody denies that they have lost by the general election. Considering the certain majority for Ministers at the close of the Session as twenty-six, which was the majority at the last division on the Appropriation Clause, and the last on Church Rates,[†] it has been reduced to twelve: six Reformers turned out on petition would annihilate this; and when we consider the open profligacy of Election Committees, and the inferior means of the Reformers throughout the country either to prosecute their own petitions or to resist those of their opponents, such a result cannot be deemed improbable: nor, in so undecided a state of affairs, can the Ministry expect the accession of many trimmers. If we escape this peril, for how long do we escape it? At every vacancy, except in a few large towns, the Tories will oppose us, and defeat us: they always carried the partial elections, even during the enthusiasm of the Reform Bill; and now their purses and their coercion will on every occasion be strained to the very utmost. The casualties among three hundred and fifty men, a large proportion of them old, must

---

[*Anon., *Domestic Prospects*, p. 41.]

[†See *PD*, 3rd ser., Vol. 34, cols. 1259–64 (4 July, 1836), and *ibid*., Vol. 37, cols. 549–54 (15 Mar., 1837). There was no division on the Appropriation Clause in 1837, so Mill must have had the division of 1836 in mind, when the majority was twenty-six. On the Church Rates, the majority is given as twenty-three, not twenty-six.]

be of frequent occurrence: casualties in the Peerage too, and acceptances of office, must create some vacancies. We have already had all that the Queen's name could do for us; and those who expected wonders from it have been wofully disappointed. How, then, we implore Ministers to consider, can they hope to remain in office above a year or so at furthest, without something to protect the electors from the foul influences?

If the inducements derived from their own position are so strong, those derived from the opinions of their supporters are no less so. One of the Polignac Ministry, M. Guernon-Ranville, in the hour of sober reflection which preceded their act of madness, said of the French people in reference to the different parties in the chamber, *La France est centre gauche*. The result of the late elections enables us in like manner to say, England is moderate-Radical. Of the different shades of opinion composing the majority (those who are returned under Tory colours we do not speak of) the Whigs are considerably reduced in strength, and we have lost a few of the more decided Radicals; among whom it will be discreditable to the nation if Mr. Roebuck at least does not immediately find another seat. But the moderate Radicals have even increased in numbers. Several adherents of the Ministry have made a move towards Radicalism, and of the new Liberal members (very numerous in this Parliament), the moderate Radicals form a large proportion. Such persons compose the great majority of the Reform party in the higher and middle classes. They consist chiefly of men who have not till lately been active politicians, or whose opinions have advanced with events. They have hitherto not approved, or not responded to, any attacks on the Ministers; and, in all their movements, they are anxious to carry the Ministers with them. They are decidedly for King, Lords, and Commons. They have generally not yet made up their minds to the necessity of any organic change in the House of Lords. They are not for Universal Suffrage. Many of them are for the Church; not such as the Tories have made it, but yet the Church, such a Church in reality as we already have in pretence; far less radically altered in its constitution than *we* deem necessary, both for religion and for good government. But these men, so little inclined to extreme opinions, are universally for the Ballot. They are for shortening the duration of Parliaments. They are for abridging the expenses of elections; simplifying the qualification of voters; abolishing the rate-paying clauses. They are for abolishing, or consolidating into districts like those of Wales and Scotland, the small borough constituencies. They are for abrogating the Corn Laws. Friends as many of them are to the principle of a Church Establishment conformable to what they conceive to be the theory of the Church of England, they recognize none of the conditions which render such an institution legitimate in the monstrous anomaly calling itself the Irish Church; a Church forced upon a conquered people by a handful of foreigners, who confiscated their land, and for ages hunted them down like beasts of prey.

We affirm, and if the Ministers do not know it the first few divisions will teach it them, that these are the opinions generally prevailing among the new liberal

English members. These men represent the average strength of the Reform spirit; those who go further being in number and weight a full set-off against those who do not go so far. If additional proof be wanted, look to the Liberal newspapers in London and in the country. Those newspapers are adapted, by persons who have full opportunity of observation, to what they deem the prevailing sentiments of the public whom they address. A certain degree of attention to this is essential to the existence of every newspaper, not (like the *Examiner* and *Spectator,*) so superior in talent as to force itself into circulation without reference to its opinions. What then are the indications afforded by the Liberal press? Almost universally it supports the Ministers, and with a fulness and vehemence which shews that in doing so it conforms to the general feeling of the Reform party all over the country. But while thus supporting Ministers, and we must say it of some journals, with a slavishness and sycophancy which is neither honourable to them nor useful to those whom it is intended to serve; how many are there, even of the most Ministerial papers, which stop short in the expression of opinion where the Ministers stop, and do not find it necessary to go the length at least of the Ballot, to say nothing of other opinions greatly in advance of the Ministry? Let Ministers remember, that no party ever for long together recognized its hindmost men as its chiefs: the leaders are always either those who precede the rest in making up their minds and pointing out the course to be followed, or those who can at least be counted upon for adopting and giving effect to the opinion of the majority.

The Ballot is necessary to their continuance in power; it is demanded by the almost unanimous opinion of their supporters; and the country is now aware that they themselves have no rooted aversion to it, no objection but such as these considerations ought to remove. We have hitherto regarded Lord John Russell as its chief opponent. We should never think of addressing a man of Lord John Russell's character with any argument appealing solely to his interest; but from the revelations in his speech at Stroud (which have raised him in the opinion of all reasonable men much more than his previous opposition to the Ballot had lowered him) we now know that his objection was never one of principle. He concurred in proposing the Ballot when there was every objection to it that there can be now, and when facts had not so strikingly corroborated the *à priori* demonstration of its necessity.[*] Why, then, has he since opposed it? For a reason not necessarily disparaging to him: he thought that a statesman, who has to consider not only his own conviction, but the rules according to which *masses* of men may most wisely regulate their collective conduct, should give a fair trial to one great change, and allow its full effects to unfold themselves before beginning another. To this we cannot object: but what is to be considered a fair trial? The majority for the Reformers has dwindled from three hundred to twenty-six, and at last to twelve: is it necessary to the sufficiency of the trial, that this last remnant should disappear?

[*Russell, *Corrected Report of the Speech* (28 July, 1837), pp. 10–11.]

Must the patient die before it is right to apply the remedy? Will nothing satisfy you of the necessity of taking arms against the evil, but having those arms wrenched from you?

You *have* the power; you have it perhaps for the first time; certainly for the last. You have it, if what your adherents say be true—if you hold the option of dissolving the Parliament. With the knowledge that you have that power, together with that of creating Peers, you might perhaps carry the question even in this Parliament. But if it fail, throw yourselves once more upon the electors. It is the only question for which they would again renew their sacrifices. If there is a spark of generosity or humanity in your breasts, it is the only one for which you will henceforth demand them. We are unable to imagine how men with the feelings of human beings can say, year after year, to large masses of their dependent fellow countrymen, "Suffer for us, make yourselves martyrs for us, be beggars, you and your families, for our sake; to keep us in office, be ruined every three or four years, for, though we can carry no measures, we can appoint Bishops and Judges, and you ought to consider that sufficient. But we cannot do such an un-English thing as to protect you—be not you such cowards as to ask it; we cannot give you the Ballot, *that* is good for *us*, we require it in our clubs and societies to save us from frowns and harsh looks; *you* ought to be above such disguises; *you* ought not to need a screen; *you* ought to stand unmoved in the midst of ruin, to look tyranny in the face without trembling; wait a little, and perhaps your persecutors will cease to persecute, your landlords will send to implore your pardon, your customers will return to you: at all events *we* shall be Ministers"—and Ministers at what a cost! Not to sit on all the thrones in Europe would we have at our door all the evil now consequent upon any one general election—would we feel that we had blasted so many fair prospects, flung back so many brave men to the bottom of the hill which they had been climbing for half their lives by patient industry; that honest, upright, religious men, placed in *our* cause between the preservation of their self-respect, and distress to themselves and their families more dreadful than they could bear, gave way, and have ever since been making atonement in sackcloth and ashes; remorse-stricken, spirit-broken! We know single instances which, if published, as we trust they are destined to be, will fully justify these expressions. He must be insensible equally to shame and to humanity, who would again call on men to pass through this fiery furnace, except for one last struggle, to end in their being free.

In this cause, the personal cause of every elector, except the corrupt few who bring their votes to market, we might hope for an election like that of 1831, when in all the English counties but six Tories could find a seat. Now, too, Ministers might come forward with the best grace, and without even the semblance of inconsistency. For years they have said that they only waited further experience: they have now surely had enough of it. The very accusations against themselves, of undue influence, are an additional inducement: there cannot be a more effectual means of meeting those accusations than to propose the Ballot; and if their accusers be sincere they will have an opportunity of voting for it, as every *honest* Tory ought, who believes, as they all profess to do, that the country is with them. But if Ministers lose this opportunity, and let office slip from their hands inch by inch, their majority dying of a consumption before their eyes; with what face can they present themselves to the country, and ask the continuance in a defeated cause, of sacrifices which a good use of the hour of success would have rendered unnecessary? "You *were* in power," it will be answered—"you *could* have given us the means of good government, and did not: you had fair warning, and ample time and opportunity. Think you that we will toil and suffer again for men who have shewn themselves so little capable of appreciating or making use of our toils and sufferings? Retire into obscurity; there is no place for you among men who know what they would have, and who, when they will the end, will the means: for you the hindmost rank, if any rank at all; the post of honour is for braver men."

Thus much on the only question of immediate urgency. A few words now on general policy, and the means of advancing the Reform interest.

We are about to talk to Ministers in the language of expediency only: we assume that it is there they differ from us. We assume that they are sincere Reformers: that whatever is evil, they see to be evil, and would remedy; though, to do so, we, in many cases, should think it necessary to cut deep, where they would only pare the surface. We are safe in assuming, as between us and them, that there are not one or two things to be remedied, but many; and that it is a question only of prudence, whether we shall attempt several together, or endeavour to finish one before we begin another.

A timid policy says, "Encumber yourselves only with one question at a time: endeavour to have to deal in each conjuncture with only one set of enemies: nothing brings you sooner to a halt than going too fast: slow and sure." We leave it to others to say, that this is a timid policy; *we* say that it is a dangerous policy. We object to it, not for being too prudent, but for being too imprudent. The fault with which we charge the system of Ministers is rashness. We say that, by dint of wishing to fight their battle with the Tories on the narrowest ground possible, they have fought it on the worst ground possible; and that, to consider them as mere tacticians, they have shown as bad generalship as ever lost a campaign.

They were placed at the head of a nation divided into two parts, which have never been properly fused together; each part accustomed to consider itself distinct from the other, to feel its interests separate, and the affairs of the other to a certain extent foreign affairs, as much so as those of India, or Canada. Of these two sections, it was on the larger and more powerful—on England and Scotland—that their strength ultimately depended: it was on the strength of the interest they could excite *there*, that they had in the end to rely; and they are fighting all their battles, except one, on Irish questions. Again, they had to make themselves followed by a nation *practical* even to ridiculousness; which hardly ever attaches itself to a principle, or can see the value of one, further than the direct practical effects of any law, existing or proposed, in which the principle happens to be for the time embodied:—a nation given to distrust and dislike all that there is in principles beyond this, and whose first movement would be to fight against, rather than for, any one who has nothing but a principle to hold out. And Ministers are fighting all their battles, except one, on points on which the net practical result of victory would be zero, and all the value of the contest is in the principle it involves. But, again, this national indifference to principles considered in themselves, has one exception. There is a case, in which, instead of seeing in a principle only the practical result, this nation sees in every practical result only a principle, and goes to an excess one way equal to its excess the other—will not listen to consequences—is afraid to let itself be influenced by any consideration but the principle: this case is that of religion. And Ministers have contrived that in every one of their battles a religious principle should be capable of being appealed to against them; while, in several, they have but a principle of temporal interest, barren of temporal results, to oppose to a (mistaken) religious principle. They had nothing but a principle to offer, and they so contrived that the only principle which is potent merely as a principle, should appear to be against them.

Do we blame them, then, that they brought forward these questions? Do we advise them to a more ignoble truckling than they have ever yet been accused of? Far from it. They were bound by every honest motive to propose everything that they have proposed. What we assert is, that the proposing of these things should have been regarded by them as a matter of duty: the strength, which was to enable them to perform that duty, they should have looked for elsewhere. With such powerful antagonists, and nothing but the people's feelings for their support, it will not do to render the strongest feelings the people have, indifferent or hostile. A man with the talents of a great Reformer, knows how to make friends by one good deed and use them for another. The way to carry, without hindrance from the practical or from the religious feeling, the measures which you have proposed, is to flank those measures with other measures which will put those feelings on your side.

For instance, the measures now in dispute, all but the Municipal Bill,[*] and even that indirectly, relate to the temporalities of the clergy: those temporalities are not religion, but are capable of being confounded with it. The cry is raised, "Danger to the Church! Enemies to the Church! Papist and Infidel Alliance! Robbery of the Church! Religious Instruction denied to the Poor!" What is the mode of meeting this cry? By boldly throwing themselves upon the religious feeling itself. Let them propose, on high religious grounds, a radical Church Reform. Let it be such as to destroy the Church for ever as the patrimony of the

[*"A Bill for the Regulation of Municipal Corporations and Borough Towns in Ireland," 7 William IV (8 Feb., 1837), *PP*, 1837, II, 333-418.]

aristocracy, as a family provision for the stupidest son; and to appropriate its funds to training and paying real religious teachers, such men as raised the Scotch people from savages to their present civilization. How such a measure would winnow the chaff from the corn of their opponents! How it would declare who of those who cry out "Danger to the Church" are the religious men, and who are the Pharisees and sinners! How it would show who are the real robbers of the Church; who are they that deny religious instruction to the poor! A cry of "Church in Danger" from the bishops and rectors, against a measure supported by the curates, would be well received, would it not? How would those tremble who are now canting about the "two millions of destitute souls," if their religion could be brought to the test in a moment by the question—"Are you for the Church Reform Bill?" It would scatter them, as the profligate adventurers who tried to catch stray votes in popular constituencies by philo-pauperism and the cry of "No new Poor Law," were scattered when they were asked on the hustings, what they thought of the Corn Laws!

How, too, such a policy would annihilate the obstacles (the number of petitions in favour of Church-rates shows them to be far from inconsiderable) which the feeling for the Church now raises against measures intended to relieve the Church from the odium of being unjust to the Dissenters. Such measures, when they stand alone—when they are not part of a more enlarged scheme to make the state of the Church more satisfactory to sincere Churchmen—are liable (especially when proposed by a ministry whom the Catholics and the Dissenters support) to the imputation of being mere concessions to the Catholics and the Dissenters. A measure is not dangerous to the Church because those parties approve of it; but it is very naturally presumed that those parties would still approve of it, although it were dangerous to the Church. The effect of their support is, on the whole, to alienate the more ignorant class of Churchmen. Give a pledge, then, to all sincere Churchmen, that you are ready and anxious to strengthen everything in the Church which conduces to its professed ends—everything for the sake of which they value it; and give the Dissenters and the Catholics an opportunity of showing that they are ready to do the same.

The effect, in regard to the objects now contended about, would be, in accordance with the admirably conceived maxim of Mr. Henry Taylor (author of the *Statesman*), to "merge particular objections which are unanswerable in general ones which may be met."[*] They should drop their Appropriation Clause, appropriative of a surplus *in nubibus*; not foolish when first proposed—foolish to be now persevered in. Instead of it, let them tack to their Tithe Bill[†] a measure for reforming the Irish Church, and reducing it to the modest dimensions of a national

[*Henry Taylor, *The Statesman* (London: Longman, Rees, Orme, Brown, Green, and Longman, 1836), p. 159.]
[†"A Bill to Abolish Compositions for Tithes in Ireland, and to Substitute Rent-Charges in Lieu Thereof," 1 Victoria (13 June, 1838), *PP*, 1837–38, VI, 443–66.]

endowment suitable to a small minority. As for the surplus, let it vest in Commissioners and accumulate; we will engage to find a use for it when the time comes. What the Irish people want is not to save the few hundred thousands a year expended on the enormity, but to abate the nuisance and insult of the thing itself. Similarly would a Church Reform smooth all difficulties respecting Church rates. Let no portion of the endowments go to anything whatever but providing efficient religious teachers for the people, at the smallest expense that would be adequate; and let such teachers be provided for all who are willing to be taught by them. This done, the difficulty is reduced to a question of arithmetic: the funds being so much, the charges so much, is there a residue sufficient to build the necessary number of churches, and keep them in repair? We suspect very much the sincerity of any man who professes to doubt it. But if the fact turn out otherwise, then make up the deficiency from the Consolidated fund; granting from the same fund a duly proportionate amount to every Dissenting body which can appoint an appropriate organ for administering it.

It is thus that a Reform Ministry makes itself strong; not by splitting down the point in contention to a hair, and for fear of one enemy losing two friends; the enemies being enemies still—for, they are either interested, and then they know that whatever wears Reform colours is dangerous to them, and are all the more eager to slay the lion while he is afraid to bite; or they are sincere, and if so, they are your enemies because your designs are misunderstood, and the way to prevent them from being misunderstood is to show more of them. We do not say, propose measures for which the nation is not ripe; far from that; what the nation is not ripe for, is to a ministry, *quâ* ministry, as if it did not exist. The business of a Reform Ministry in its legislatorial capacity, is to seize the first moment when the public mind is ripe for a good measure, and propose it; and the more such measures they propose at once, the more they will carry; for, in the first place, the enthusiasm will be greater; and, in the next, one measure will explain the motives and correct the misrepresentations of another.

The same advice which we give to the Ministers, we give, *mutatis mutandis*, to the more advanced and more enlightened section of the Radicals. To them, as to the others, we offer one rule, which, being fully acted upon, includes all they stand in need of—"Attempt much." If they attempt much, chusing, as they are likely to do, the right objects, failures are of no consequence. If you attempt little, and fail in that little, you are ruined. In politics, as in war, every one makes mistakes, and the only persons who succeed are those who, by the number and character of their enterprises, establish a system of insurance against their own blunders, and draw upon the surplus popularity accumulated by successes, to indemnify them for failures. But our friends in the House of Commons are in need of a stock in hand, sufficient to cover their losses by honesty as well as their losses by unskilfulness: they are troubled with a conscience, and it requires a constant outlay of popularity to keep it up. If a conscience altogether has been described as an expensive article, a conscience like theirs—a purely negative conscience, which never bids them *do* anything, but only *not do*—is the most expensive of all; for, while it is making continual drafts upon their popularity, it never brings anything in.

Whatever inconveniences are necessarily attendant on honesty, a politician who lays claim to the character must submit to. He is bound to resist those who would be his most ardent supporters, when what they demand is unjust, or founded in ignorance. But he is not bound to neglect any honest means by which he may retain the confidence of his supporters even while he opposes their wishes: he is not doing his duty if his best friends are only made aware of his existence when something which they, or a portion of them, are eager for, requires to be opposed. The Radicals in Parliament are committing the same blunder as the Whigs: they are not performing those of their duties, the performance of which would make the others easy. They are wanting to the first obligation as well as the strongest interest of persons in their position—they are not putting themselves at the head of the working classes. A Radical party which does not rest upon the masses, is no better than a nonentity.

It used to be said in behalf of Whigs and Tories, by people who wished to stand well with both, that the former supported the principle of liberty in the constitution, and the latter that of authority, not that they did not equally agree in reverencing both principles, but that each party took under its more peculiar protection that one of the two elements which it conceived to be more especially in need of support. On this principle the Radicals may claim to themselves, as their peculiar office, a function in politics which stands more in need of them than any other: this is, the protection of the poor. This devolves upon the Radicals as their especial duty. No other political duty is so important. It is, God wot, left to them to perform. Let them show that the protection of the poor from the poor is not the only part of this duty which they are competent to. To serve the people is not the same thing as to please the people; but those who neglect the services which please, will find themselves disqualified from rendering those which displease. Do we find that the working classes—that large body of them who take interest in politics—look to the Parliamentary Radicals for any good; regard them with one spark of hope or confidence? Is there one Radical of mark in Parliament, or recently in it, except Mr. Roebuck, and in mere justice it must be added Colonel Thompson, who even aims at inspiring such confidence? No: they leave it to the patrons and champions of the corrupt freemen to claim the title of "tribunes of the poor." Hence it is that the poor do not love them, do not rally round them. They *must* be tribunes of the poor, and to some purpose too, if they mean to be anything. Those who will not flatter the people must make it doubly obvious that they are willing to serve them. It behoves them to earn two blessings for every single malediction. If it be their duty, as it is liable to be every man's duty, to oppose themselves upon occasion to the sentiments of large bodies of their countrymen, let them endeavour to have still larger bodies helping them, and sympathizing with them, and urging them on. They are willing to make bitter enemies; we implore them not to forget that they have need of warm friends.

On the other hand, let the working classes learn to know the Parliamentary Radicals, and to do them justice. They are the only party in politics who have, to any great degree, common objects with the working classes. They are the only party who are not overflowing with groundless dread, and jealousy, and suspicion of them. They are the only party who do not in their hearts condemn the whole of their operative fellow-citizens to perpetual helotage, to a state of exclusion from all direct influence on national affairs. The Radical party have other feelings. They look forward to a time, most of them think it is not yet come, when the whole adult population shall be qualified to give an equal voice in the election of members of Parliament. Others believe this and tremble; *they* believe it, and rejoice; and instead of wishing to retard, they anxiously desire, by national education and the action of the press, to advance this period, to hasten this progress. In the mean time, they are to a man determined enemies of every robbery, every unjust exclusion, every uncalled-for restraint which the people suffer. We know not a man among them who does not detest the Corn Laws. We know not one to whom high wages, and a condition of the labouring classes similar to that in the United States, is not the one thing needful, the polar star to direct all those of their exertions which have reference to the economical condition of the country. They demand, and they are the only party who demand, that all national property shall be applied to national purposes, and that the Church Establishment shall either cease to exist, or become what the Scottish Church was—the People's Church. They are the only party who will never be satisfied without cheap justice, justice brought home to every man's door, justice without cost to him, and giving him a prompt remedy for every wrong. They detest the insolent interferences with the ways, the pleasures, the amusements of the people. They wish to emancipate the poor from the impertinent meddling of men who do not know them and do not sympathize with them. With them, gentlemen and noblemen only count as so many men, except so far as they make themselves useful to others than themselves. Their principle of government is, until Universal Suffrage shall be possible, to do everything for the good of the working classes, which it would be necessary to do if there were Universal Suffrage.

These are the principles of the Radical party in Parliament, and no one who watches their conduct will fail to see it. Their fault is not want of attachment to the principles, but want of doing enough for them. It is time they bethought themselves that they are not there to bear witness passively for the truth, but to act for it; that they are not there to do something for their cause, but to do the most that can be done. If they do not the duties of leaders, the Radicals will find others who will, and whom *they* must be content to follow. The time is not now when feelings which are burning in the hearts of millions, will want tongues for utterance in high places. And there is a vitality in the principles, there is that in them both of absolute truth and of adaptation to the particular wants of the time, which will not suffer that in Parliament two or three shall be gathered together in their name,[*] proclaiming the purpose to stand or fall by them, and to go to what lengths soever they may lead, and that those two or three shall not soon wield a force before which ministries and aristocracies shall quail. We pity the men to whom there is given such a golden harvest, and who leave it to be reaped by others. The men are honest; what, if done, they would be the first to applaud, let them have the spirit to do.

While, however, they ought to rest upon the operative, and generally upon the productive classes, as their main stay, and as those whose just claims and legitimate interests it is especially theirs to defend, let them study not less to make manifest to the people of property the truth, for a truth it is, that even *their* interests, so far as conformable and not contrary to the ends for which society and government exist, are safer in the keeping of the Radicals than anywhere else. We know how strange this assertion will be likely to appear to a majority of the people of property, but we doubt if their present leaders, the profligate part of the Tory faction, will think it so: for we find them, fond as they are of representing the Radicals as enemies of property, to be at bottom so well convinced of their inviolable attachment to it, that they are at times well content to leave to them alone the burthen of defending it. We need not go farther for an instance than the late elections, and the conduct of the Tories in relation to the new Poor Law.

An immense majority of all parties in Parliament concurred in passing the new Poor Law, and so far the position of all was alike. At the late election all were under an equal temptation to bid high for the few votes which, if added to either side, would have given it a decided majority. But to the Radicals the difficulty was greater of withstanding the cry, because it proceeded from their own supporters; and the infamy of yielding to it would have been less, because the protection of the poor is their peculiar office. It would have been comparatively excusable in them, had they carried that principle to excess. It would but have been an over-zealous performance of their proper duty. It was not the Radicals, however, who, in almost every constituency where anything was to be gained by it, abandoned their principles for the sake of their party objects, and appeared as the enemies of the Poor Law. Every man of the Radicals remained faithful. Those who had always opposed the measure still opposed it, but of the others we are not aware of one who flinched. It was the Radicals who had to fight the battle of the people of property at a hundred hustings, against candidates put up by the party of the people of property, as a last chance of tricking a few pauper electors into voting for the supporters of low wages and dear bread.

We may be told that this was only the scum of the party; and people may talk to us of the Duke of Wellington, and his declaration on the Poor Law just before the dissolution of Parliament.[†] To the Duke of Wellington, and to that over-praised

[*Cf. Matthew, 18:20.]

[†Arthur Wellesley, Speech on the Poor-Law Amendment Act (7 Apr., 1837), *PD*, 3rd ser., Vol. 37, cols. 851–2.]

declaration, we are willing, we hope, to render as much honour as is due. We will thank him for it, when we find that we have derived any good from it. We did not want his assurances that the Tories do not mean to abrogate the law; we never imagined they did. It is no more the interest of the Tories to abrogate the new Poor Law than to confiscate the land, which the continuance of the old law for a generation longer would have done. What would have been really meritorious and honourable in the Duke of Wellington, would have been to have dissuaded his party, and his own son, from rolling themselves in the dirt from which his own hands were kept so studiously clean. As it was, his prudery was necessary to their prostitution. The electioneering cry of "No new Poor Law" was for the wretched electors whom it duped. The counter-declaration of the Duke of Wellington was for the people of property throughout the country, that they might not fancy that the electioneering cry meant anything, or that the leaders of the party would keep the promises their tools were allowed to make. It would have been fatal to the Tories at the late election if their anti-Poor-Law professions had been generally credited. The Duke may have meant honestly; but he by his honesty, and other men by their knavery, have played marvellously into each other's hands.

It is for the people of property, the quiet rich people throughout the country who are unconnected with office and with the seekers of office, and who adopt and value only the fair side of Tory principles, to declare whether this is the policy which is fitted to succeed with them; whether these are arts which they are inclined to encourage, and whether they will permit the authors of them to arrogate to themselves the name of Conservatives. We tell them that the Radicals are the only true Conservatives; the only persons who disdain to tamper with doctrines subversive of society—who make a stand for the fundamental principles of the social union whenever and wherever they see them endangered, even by those who are the enemies of *their* enemies, even by persons whom a different conduct would enlist among their most active adherents.

Consider, for instance, this matter of the Poor Law. The Tories have been in the habit of saying that the quarrel of Radicalism with Toryism is that of the house of Want against the house of Have; to which Colonel Thompson once very happily answered, that it is the house of Have against the house of Take.[*] But what was said of Radicalism as mere vulgar abuse, is true of the opposition to the new Poor Law. *That* is really the house of Want against the house of Have. On one side are all who *have*, including all who have laboured for what they have; on the other, are those who *want*, and who desire to satisfy their want by taking from those who have, without equivalent. On the one side is the principle of protection to property, protection to the produce of industry in the hands of the industrious; on the other side are the Have-nothings, who seek, not liberty to earn, not power to sell their labour in the dearest market and buy food in the cheapest; but to be maintained by

---

[*Thomas Perronet Thompson, "Parliamentary Reform," *Westminster Review*, XIV (Apr., 1831), 450.]

the people of property, to eat unearned bread at their expense. We do not mean that this is the light in which the question appears to *all* the enemies of the Poor Law; we know the contrary: but it is its true character, and if any one is in a mistake about the matter, it is not the Tories. The agitators against that law are attempting what the Radicals are vulgarly accused of aiming at; they are attacking the security of property, encouraging the indigent to prey upon the rest of society. They are proposing the very worst sort of agrarian law. And this is what the party supported by the landed aristocracy, and standing up for all the noxious privileges of the wealthy, are willing for personal gain to promise to support. Why did they dare do this? Why did they not recoil from the advocacy of that which no one would more dread to see carried? Because they knew that they could trust to the conservative principles of the Radicals: they knew that if *they* chose to abandon the first foundations of society and civilization, the Radicals would not, but would allow their enemies to gain whatever was to be gained by the fraud, and step in to save them from the fatal consequences.

It is not in this instance alone that the Radicals have had to defend really conservative principles against the pretended Conservatives. Who have stood up for the fund-holder? Who have placed themselves between him and the confiscation which was meditated against him by the agricultural party, by the authors of the Corn Laws, in common with Mr. Cobbett? Was it the Tories? The *Quarterly Review*, the organ of the Tory party, a year or two before the Reform Bill, distinctly and avowedly advocated what was called the "equitable adjustment."[*] Was it a Radical who wrote a pamphlet to prove that 33 per cent should be struck off from the National Debt, and from all the private debts of the landed interest? It was Sir James Graham.[†] Was it a Radical who pronounced in the House of Lords the famous *Nemo tenetur ad impossibile*? It was the aristocratic Whig, Earl Grey.[‡] But it was a Radical, the late Mr. Mill, who, with all his vehemence of character and force of reason, protested against the doctrines of them both, in the *Westminster* and *Parliamentary Reviews*.[§] It was a Radical, Colonel Thompson, who, in his *Catechism on the Corn Laws*, argued the cause of the fundholder in the fewest and most pregnant words in which we ever saw it put.[¶] When the right of property had ever to be vindicated in the person of the public creditor, it was to the *Examiner*, or *Tait's Magazine*, or the *Westminster Review*, that the task was abandoned.

[*See Edward Edwards, "Currency," *Quarterly Review*, XXXIX (Apr., 1829), 456–62. For the phrase "equitable adjustment" see pp. 361–2 above.]

[†Graham, *Corn and Currency* (1826).]

[‡Charles Grey, Speech on the Corn Laws (1 May, 1826), *PD*, n.s., Vol. 15, cols. 754–8.]

[§James Mill, "State of the Nation," *Westminster Review*, VI (Oct., 1826), 249–78; and "Summary Review of the Conduct and Measures of the Imperial Parliament," *PR*, 1826, pp. 793–7.]

[¶Thomas Perronet Thompson, *A Catechism on the Corn Laws* (1827), 17th ed. (London: Westminster Review, 1833), pp. 40–1.]

Property has scarcely ever, in any country, been in danger from the poor. Those who have always lived by industry respect the produce of industry, and have never yet been disposed to tear it away. In the very height of the French Revolution no private property was touched, except that of men who were in arms against their country; the Convention, during the Reign of Terror, rejected all propositions of an anti-property character, and such doctrines never appear practically in the history of the Revolution, but in the persons of Babœuf and his fellow-conspirators.[*] What the Radicals want, is protection to the property of the poor against the worst class of poor, the needy rich. Those, in whatever rank or party they are found, are the real enemies of property, the real Destructives. They are willing enough to invoke the sacredness of property in favour of what is not property,—the abuses by which they themselves profit. They are willing enough to give the name of enemies of property to the enemies of those abuses. But when property is really in danger, it is on those enemies that it leans for support, and its pretended friends, for the slightest personal gain, are ready to throw it overboard.

As for the organic changes which the Radicals are supposed to meditate, and which haunt the imaginations of rich and timid people with nameless fears, we have already* had occasion to say on that subject what we now repeat: It is utterly false that the Radicals desire organic changes as ends; they desire them as means to other ends, and will be satisfied to renounce them if those ends can be obtained otherwise. To stickle for words and forms instead of substances, is in no case the practice of the English Radicals. But a government of which the moving principle shall be the general interest, a government which shall be just to the working classes, we will not consent to be without; and whatever insists upon standing between us and that, let it call itself Church, or House of Lords, or by what other name soever, we will by God's help sweep from our path. There is a sufficient number of determined men in these islands, bent upon this, and resolute in the pursuit of it, to render these no idle words. It will not be the work of a year, or, possibly, of many years; but those are now alive who will see it done. Let it be the care of those who ought to be our leaders in this great enterprise, that they be not wanting to it.

Let them learn confidence in their own strength. The power of the Radical Reformers in this country is immense. The Tories have been fond of repeating, as if it were something wonderfully complimentary to them, a saying of Lord Brougham in the *Edinburgh Review*, that a great majority of the persons with more than five hundred a year are for the established order of things;[†] as if the same

---

[*Among François Noël Babeuf's fellow-conspirators in the Société des Egaux were Jean Baptiste Amar, Philippe Buonarroti, Augustin Alexandre Darthé, Jean Baptiste Drouet, Robert Lindet, and Marc Guillaume Vadier.]

*[John Stuart Mill,] Review of Sir John Walsh's *Chapters of Contemporary History*, in the *London and Westminster Review* [III & XXV] for July, 1836 [, 299]. [P. 348 above.]

[†Henry Brougham, "Last Session of Parliament—House of Lords," *Edinburgh Review*, LXII (Oct., 1835), 201.]

might not be said of every established order of things whatever,—as if those who are best off were ever the most disposed to change, or as if the rich were likely to be dissatisfied with the privileges of riches. But if Radicalism has not the men with the five hundreds a year, it has those with the fifties, who are in a way to become the more influential body of the two. It has the middle classes of the towns, and as many of those of the country as take any interest in politics. The middle classes have twenty times the aggregate amount of property of the higher classes. As for the men of thews and sinews,[*] the labouring multitude, it will not, we imagine, be disputed that they are Radicals. Among the young men of practical talent (the old will soon be off the stage) the Radicals are the growing power. Among those of speculative ability, a considerable number are theoretically Tories; for it is easy to a person of imagination to frame (like Mr. Coleridge) a theory of Toryism, finding a good use for everything that the Tories put to a bad one, and to dream pleasantly enough of a Church and an Aristocracy such as might be had in Utopia, but which the partisans of the Church and the Aristocracy as they now are would be the last to stir a finger for. Men of practical sagacity, who look abroad into the world, and judge of men and institutions as they find them there, and not as they read of them in books, are hardly ever Tories but from interested motives. Those who are looking forward to being counted among the aristocracy are Tories. The bar is Tory, because every young barrister intends to die a wealthy man and a peer. The Church is Tory, for reasons unnecessary to specify. Many who are not Tories are sceptical as to the importance of forms of government, and, in preference to changing them, endeavour to work those which exist to the best ends they can be turned to. But among the *working* part even of the aristocracy, the younger sons, and among that part of the legal profession who are rising but have not yet risen, not a few, and those generally the ablest and most efficient, are Radicals. They are showing it in every field of fair and open competition; and will show it more and more. Take, for example, the most important commissions appointed by the present Government,—the Corporation Commission, selected indiscriminately from Whigs and Radicals, or the two Commissions of Poor Law Inquiry for Ireland and England, from Whigs, Radicals, and Tories.[†] See how large a proportion of those who were thought worthy to be selected, and how decided a majority of those who justified their appointment by making any figure in it, were decided Radicals. If this be true even in the classes from which the aristrocracy is recruited, what must it be in others? There is a class, now greatly multiplying in this country, and generally overlooked by politicians in their calculations; those men of talent and

[*The phrase "thews and sinews" appears to have originated with Walter Scott; see *Rob Roy*, 3 vols. (Edinburgh: Constable, 1818), Vol. I, p. 60 (iii).]

[†For the report of the Commissioners on Municipal Corporations, see *PP*, 1835, XXIII–XXVI; for the reports of the Commissioners on the condition of the poorer classes in Ireland, see *ibid.*, 1835, XXXII; 1836, XXX; 1837, XXXI, 587–94; and for England, see the reports of the Select Committee on the Poor Law Amendment Act, *ibid.*, 1837, XVII.]

instruction, who are just below the rank in society which would of itself entitle them to associate with gentlemen. Persons of this class have the activity and energy which the higher classes in our state of civilization and education almost universally want. They have hitherto exerted that activity in other spheres. It is but of yesterday that they have begun to read and to think. They have now many of the advantages for mental cultivation which were so long confined to the higher classes, and they are using them. There are more hard students, more vigorous seekers of knowledge, in this class than there are at present in any other, and out of all proportion more who study the art of turning their knowledge to practical ends. They are, as it is natural they should be, Radicals to a man, and Radicals generally of a deep shade. They are the natural enemies of an order of things in which they are not in their proper place. We could name several men of this class, of whom it is as certain as any prediction in human affairs can be, that they will emerge into light, and make a figure in the world. We could name a still greater number who want only some slight turn in outward circumstances, to enable them to do the same. Many of these will abandon Radicalism as they rise in the world; but many will not; and for those who do there will be successors still pressing forward. It is among them that men fit to head a Radical party will be found, if they cannot be found among the Radicals of the higher classes. These are the men who will know how to speak to the people. They are above them in knowledge, in calmness, and in freedom from prejudice, and not so far above them in rank as to be incapable of understanding them and of being understood by them.

These elements of almost boundless power are ill marshalled and directed, we know. But they will not always be so; nor can any defect of organization prevent our strength from showing itself. We are felt to be the growing power; that which even the ambitious, who can afford to wait for their gratification, would do wisely to ally themselves with. Not one inch of ground, once gained, do we ever lose; and we carry every point we attack. We are foiled and driven back nine times; the tenth we succeed. What we accomplish is but a trifle, indeed, to what might be accomplished: let it be our study to accomplish more.

To our leaders, two things are especially to be recommended: activity, above all; and activity directed to the practical points. We have already exhorted them to apply themselves to those topics which speak strongest to popular feeling, which come home to men's lives and pursuits, to interests already felt. Let them also seize the occasions which will strengthen, and make manifest, their own capacity for practice and business. Let them not allow it to be thought that they can make speeches on a few great questions, and that this is all. Let them take the part their acquirements entitle them to in all the general business of the House. Let them show that they are not men of one subject, or of two or three subjects, but men equal to all the questions, versed in all the interests, which a Ministry and a Parliament have to decide upon. What gives Sir Robert Peel his personal influence? What makes so many adhere to him? The opinion, a greatly exaggerated one, entertained of his capacity for business. In moments of general enthusiasm it is enough that a party carries the favourite banner; but in the intervals between those moments, its importance depends upon the confidence inspired by its *personnel*: in such times as we ought always to be prepared for, times of momentary misgiving respecting the truth or applicability of principles, the prize rests with that party which can present the nation with the ablest practical man. If Radicalism had its Sir Robert Peel, he would be at the head of an administration within two years; and Radicalism must be a barren soil if it cannot rival so sorry a growth as that; if it cannot produce a match for perhaps the least gifted man that ever headed a powerful party in this country. Without one idea beyond common-place, Sir Robert Peel owes his success to his having been cast upon times which not only have not produced a statesman of the first rank, a William the Silent, a Gustavus Adolphus, a Jefferson, a Turgot; but not one even of the second-rate men who fill up the long interval between Richelieu and William Pitt; and not so much as a single third-rate man, except himself. He does not know his age; he has always blundered miserably in his estimate of it. But he knows the House of Commons, and the sort of men of whom it is composed. He knows what will act upon their minds, and is able to strike the right chord upon that instrument. He has, besides, all that the mere routine of office-experience can give, to a man who brought to it no principles drawn from a higher philosophy, and no desire for any. These qualifications are Sir Robert Peel's stock in trade as a practical statesman. Is it not a dire disgrace to the Radical leaders to be left behind by such a man? But then, he is always *using* his slender faculties; they, except a few young and still inexperienced men, let theirs slumber.

This is for the leaders. To the people, at the present moment, we have but one exhortation to give: let them hold themselves in readiness. No one knows what times may be coming: no one knows how soon, or in what cause his most strenuous exertions may be required. Ireland is already organized. Let England and Scotland be prepared at the first summons to start into Political Unions. Let the House of Commons be inundated with petitions on every subject on which Reformers are able to agree. Let Reformers meet, combine, and above all, register. The time may be close at hand, when the man who has lost a vote, which he might have given for the Ballot or for some other question of the first magnitude, will have cause bitterly to repent the negligence and supineness which has deprived him of his part in the struggle. All else may be left till the hour of need, but to secure a vote is a duty for which there is no postponement. This let the Reformers do; and let them then stand at their arms and wait their opportunity.

RADICAL PARTY AND CANADA:
LORD DURHAM AND THE CANADIANS

1838

EDITOR'S NOTE

London and Westminster Review, VI & XXVIII (Jan., 1838), 502–33. Headed: "ART. VIII.—1. *The Canadian Portfolio.* Conducted by John Arthur Roebuck, Esq., and other friends of Canada. Nos. 1 to 4. 1838. [London:] Charles Fox. / 2. [Thomas Frederick Elliot.] *The Canadian Controversy: Its Origin, Nature, and Merits.* 1838. [London:] Longman [, Orme, Brown, Green, and Longmans]. / 3. [Charles Neate.] *A Plain Statement of the Quarrel with Canada; in Which Is Considered, Who First Infringed the Constitution of the Colony.* 1838. [London:] Ridgway. / 4. [Anon.] *Hints on the Case of Canada, for the Consideration of Members of Parliament.* 1838. [London:] Murray. / 5. *Reports of Commissioners on Grievances Complained of in Lower Canada.* Ordered by the House of Commons to be printed, 20th February, 1837. [In *Parliamentary Papers,* 1837, XXIV, 3–416.] / 6. [Charles Edward Grey.] *Remarks on the Proceedings in Canada, in the Present Session of Parliament.* By one of the Commissioners. 10th April, 1837. [London:] Ridgway. / 7. *Papers Relative to the Affairs of Lower Canada.* Ordered by the House of Commons to be printed, 20th February, 1837. [In *Parliamentary Papers,* 1837, XLII, 413–56.] / 8. *Copies or Extracts of Correspondence Relative to the Affairs of Lower Canada.* Ordered by the House of Commons to be printed, 23rd December, 1837. [In *Parliamentary Papers,* 1837–38, XXXIX, 317–432.] / 9. *Copies or Extracts of Correspondence Relative to the Affairs of Lower Canada, Upper Canada, Nova Scotia, and New Brunswick.* Ordered by the House of Commons to be printed, 10th January, 1838. (In continuation of No. 8.) [*Ibid.,* pp. 433–52.] / 10. *A Bill to Make Temporary Provision for the Government of Lower Canada.* 17th January, 1838. [*Ibid.,* Vol. I, pp. 253–6. Enacted as 1 Victoria, c. 9 (1838).]" Running titles: 502–9, "Radical Party and Canada" (in some copies, "Radical Party in Canada"); 510–33, "Lord Durham and the Canadians" (the change is keyed by the paragraph, on 413, beginning, "The name of CANADA . . ."). In table of contents of *L&WR,* Vol. VI, "Lord Durham and the Canadians." Signed "A." Not republished. Identified in Mill's bibliography as "An article entitled 'Lord Durham and the Canadians' in the same number of the same review"; i.e., as "Ware's Letters from Palmyra" (MacMinn, 50). In the Somerville College copy (tear-sheets) there are two emendations (both of which are adopted in this edition): "Whigs to" is corrected to "Whigs would have to" (412.23–4); and "for—displaying" to "for displaying" (434.19). For comment on the essay, see xlii–xlvi and lix above.

Radical Party and Canada:
Lord Durham and the Canadians

WE HAD INTENDED, on the present occasion, to review and characterize the various divisions of the multitudinous and widely scattered Radical party: to show to each of the diversified bodies of men who compose it, what the others are, and are doing—by learning which it can alone know what itself is; to enable them to look at themselves, and at each other, in the light most calculated to allay unreasonable distrusts and awaken sympathies; to point out to them the common ground on which they may meet and co-operate, the common objects in the attainment whereof each would find the realization of his separate aims; the points, therefore, to which the efforts of all should converge, and the organization and marshalling, by which those efforts may be brought most vigorously to bear upon those points. By doing this, we should be, at the same time, placing before the well intentioned part of those who have not hitherto been in sympathy with us, a view of what Radicalism is. We should show them that the demons and spectres which frighten them from their propriety are not Radicalism, have no natural connection with Radicalism: That the essentials of it are not only reconcileable, but naturally allied, with all that ever was venerable or deserving of attachment in the doctrines and practices handed down to us from those ancestors, and those great teachers, whom they delight to honour: That it is the pretended apostles of those traditional opinions and institutions who dishonour them: That the low objects to which they prostitute them, and the low grounds on which they defend them, are loosening the hold which those old ideas had on the intellects and on the affections of mankind, and sinking what is good and noble in them, along with what is effete or despicable, into a common contempt: That it is the Radical view of them alone which can save them: That to be ever again objects of veneration in this New World, these Old Things must be seen with the eyes of Radicals: That they must reconcile themselves with Radicalism, must fill themselves to overflowing with its spirit: That Conservatives must adopt the Radical creed into their own creed —must discard all with which that creed is essentially incompatible, if they would save that in their own which is true and precious, from being lost to the world, overwhelmed in an unequal contest. For Radicalism is a thing which must prevail. It is a thing which the better and the worse influences of advancing civilization equally conspire to promote; and this age has no other power over it but that of deciding what *sort* of Radicalism shall, in the first instance, predominate. *That* mainly depends upon the attitude which those classes, on whom society has lavished its means of instruction and cultivation, may, ere it be too late, be wise enough to assume towards the remainder.

These were the topics to which we had destined the present article; but these things must now wait for our next publication.[*] A question has arisen which, for the present, places these great principles in abeyance; which suspends all united action among Radicals, which sets one portion of the friends of popular institutions at variance with another, and by rivetting all attention upon events of immediate urgency and of melancholy interest, interrupts for the time all movements and all discussions tending to the great objects of domestic policy. We need scarcely say that we allude to Canada. On this most grievous subject we shall, in the course of this article, declare our whole opinion. But as Canada will not occupy the whole session, and as the interval afforded by Lord Durham's mission will allow the public mind to revert to what was so strongly occupying it before, we are anxious in the first place to say something on the duties devolving upon the Radical party, in the position in which it is placed by Lord John Russell's declaration of hostilities on the first night of the session.[†]

It would be wasting time to expend any in discussing now, what Reformers ought to think of this ministerial declaration, or what feelings they ought to bestow in return for it. On that subject the mind of the country is made up. The Ministers are now understood. The alliance between them and the Radicals is broken, never more to be re-united. The late splendid demonstrations of Reform feeling, in all parts of the island, and the declarations of want of confidence in the Ministry, which have been carried by immense majorities at the greater part even of the meetings which were called by their friends—these facts, however attempted to be stifled by that systematic suppression of intelligence which the Whig and Tory newspapers have practised on this occasion to an extent unexampled in our remembrance, and which constitutes a distinct pecuniary fraud upon their subscribers—are nevertheless known and appreciated. They are a proof that the Ministry have been taken at their word: that their camp and that of the Radicals are now separated: that the Radicals are organizing themselves as a separate party; that the spirit of reform is no longer obedient to Lord John Russell's curb; and that, in determining what proceedings are fittest for promoting the rapid success of the cause of popular institutions, counsel will no longer be taken with its avowed enemies.

We can understand the terror of the mere place-holding portion of the Whigs, at demonstrations which so manifestly endanger their continuance in place; and the

[*See "Reorganization of the Reform Party," pp. 465–95 below, which did not appear in the *London and Westminster* until Apr., 1839.]

[†John Russell, Speech on the Address in Answer to the Queen's Speech (20 Nov., 1837), *PD*, 3rd ser., Vol. 39, cols. 65–73.]

consternation of those Radical writers, and local or sectional leaders of Radicals, who having for the first time in their lives known what it is to be courted by a Ministry, would gladly go on uniting the credit of being for the people, with the vanity and the more substantial advantages of being on the side of power. What we cannot so well understand is, why some sincere Radicals should behave as if they thought that the disclosure which has been made to us of the real purposes of the Ministry, and the knowledge which we have thence derived of what we have to expect from them, and of what we need not expect, is an evil: and so great an evil as to justify resentment; so great, that the man who has brought it upon us by his "untimely" questions to Lord John Russell,[*] should be treated as if he had inflicted on us a deadly injury. Mr. Wakley has had the usual fate of the messenger of ill news. He has roused the lethargic, and compelled the sleepy to open their eyes, and anger at being disturbed is their first feeling and his reward. If Mr. Wakley's silence could have made any difference in Lord John Russell's sentiments, no one would have regretted more than we, that the silence was ever broken; but since Mr. Wakley could only compel him to *say* what he already intended to *do*, is there any Reformer who wishes that it had remained unsaid? If the Ministerial mind had been undecided—had been gradually and insensibly coming round to us, it might have been wrong to break in upon that process, and force Ministers to a premature declaration when they were but half prepared to express the opinion which was desired; but since their minds were made up, and to an opinion the reverse of what was wished for, could this be too soon known? Is there not a lurking regret that we cannot longer enjoy the pleasure of being cheated, a pleasure rated so highly by the greatest judges of human nature, and which may be defined, the pleasure of not being called upon for any activity, for any foresight, for any exercise of our own judgment as to our duties, for any exertion to help ourselves or others? To have got rid of a delusion which made us torpid and cowardly, and to have acquired a self reliance which makes us vigorous and awake, is a gain, in our circumstances, inappreciable; and to whomsoever we owe it, that man has conferred a benefit, not inflicted an injury, and should be thanked, not snarled at.

The question of most pressing interest for the moment is, what ought now to be done by the Parliamentary Radicals. And by Radicals we here mean, those who believe in the absolute necessity of what Lord John Russell says he will never consent to—the Ballot, with or without an extension of the suffrage.*

[*See Thomas Wakley, Motion on the Address in Answer to the Queen's Speech (20 Nov., 1837), *ibid.*, cols. 37–48.]

*[Russell, speech of 20 Nov., 1837, cols. 68–9.] We observe there are persons who now begin to say, they are for the Ballot, but are not Radicals. We remember the time when to support the Ballot was considered the distinctive mark of Radicalism, the test which distinguished a Radical from a Whig. We expect to see the day when men will be found supporting universal suffrage, and yet disclaiming Radicalism. So much more afraid are mankind of words than of things.

On this point we can but refer to the opinions and sentiments of which we gave so full an exposition in the first article of our last Number.[*] It will scarcely be said that in that article we manifested any hostility to the Ministry, any unwillingness to be just to them, any indisposition to court their alliance. We went as far to meet them, we gave up as much to act in concert with them, as was possible without betraying our cause and degrading our character. We asked them for nothing but to serve themselves. We asked no more in return for their being supported in office, than that they would consent to be kept in it. We asked only that they would propose the Ballot, in the last Parliament in which they can remain Ministers without the Ballot. Though not for the sake of any of their measures, of which they can carry none without the consent of the Tories, yet for the sake of Ireland—to which the English and Scotch Radicals, though accused of being indifferent to it, have in reality postponed every other interest of their country—they have supported Ministers till the time when the Ballot became a vital question to their remaining Ministers on the principles they have hitherto professed. This exact time Ministers have chosen for declaring a degree of enmity to the Ballot, which they have never before expressed: and here, therefore, it is necessary that our support should terminate. For this is no *single* question: it is not one particular point on which the Ministers have gone back; it is the indication, or rather the avowal, of a change of policy. There is no mistake in the matter. The Ministers know as well as we do, that to remain in office they must either carry the Ballot or become Tories. The meaning of Lord John Russell's declaration is to apprise the world which side of the alternative they have chosen. Lord John Russell may talk of an engagement with his late colleagues, and a feeling of personal honour involved in not consenting to what is for his country's good. His country does not believe him. He states what is not the fact: he has no such feeling, he is conscious of no such obligation. To believe his assertion would be the insult; not to disbelieve it. If it be true now, was it not true at Stroud,[†] and in Devonshire,[‡] and on all the innumerable occasions on which he has declared, in a key ever rising higher and higher, that if intimidation and bribery continued, and could not otherwise be prevented, he might be compelled, although unwillingly, to support the Ballot? Did he say this, while in his heart, and as a man of honour, he felt for ever precluded from supporting it? And to this avowal of three years' systematic duplicity it is that some men have given the epithets candid and manly. The Reformers do not believe Lord John Russell to be so bad a man, as for his present convenience he gives himself out to be. They believe that he was sincere formerly, and that his present story of having his hands tied is an afterthought. They do not believe that he feels himself under any restraint as to his political course, or that

[*John Stuart Mill, "Parties and the Ministry," *London and Westminster Review*, VI & XXVIII (Oct., 1837), 1–26 (pp. 381–404 above).]
[†See Russell, *Corrected Report of the Speech*, pp. 10–11.]
[‡See Russell, Speech at Torquay (18 Sept., 1832), *The Times*, 21 Sept., 1832, pp. 3–4.]

his political opinions at any time sit so tightly on him as not to admit of being shaken off on a change of seasons. They are well assured that this very conduct of his is an example, not of the obstinacy which (judging from his demeanour this session) he seems to consider as one of his qualities, but of the pliability by which his political career has really been characterised. As on all former occasions, so now, he is yielding to the signs of the times; only his misfortune is that he reads them the backward way. There are always two contrary readings of a historical fact. It seemed to Reformers to be the true reading of the late general election, that unless the shield of the Ballot were thrown over the electors, or something given them that they should think worth fighting for, they would not longer persevere in their sacrifices and sufferings, merely to keep the Tories out and the Ministers in. But the Ministers have construed the same fact in another sense. Their reading is, that the country is becoming Conservative, and that they must become Conservative too: and the first fruit of this is Lord John's declaration.

On the mental hallucination which confounds the apathy arising from hopes gradually withered, and the growing reluctance to brave ruin and penury for no adequate national object, with a reaction in the public mind against those national objects which have never been so much as offered to it, we shall for the present spare our comments. It is enough that the Ministry intend to be Conservatives; that they look henceforth to the support of the Conservatives; and that the Tory leaders are looking towards the same object, and are studiously preparing the way for a coalition. They are throwing the Orangemen overboard. They are paying compliments to Lord Mulgrave. They are making signals of compromise on most of the little questions, which have been exaggerated into great ones because the Whigs were committed to them. The present session will be employed in getting rid of these stumbling-blocks. If after that time we do not see Peel and Wellington in office, it will be because they think it more for their interest to remain out of it, getting their work done for them by the present Ministers. If things continue as they are, we shall behold in another session, if not Sir Robert Peel and Lord John Russell, Sir Robert Peel's and Lord John Russell's followers, seated on the same benches, and enthusiastically supporting the same Ministry; while the opposition benches will be occupied by the Radical party, and by thirty or forty rabid Orangemen, the offscouring of the House.

It is a foresight of these things, we must tell Mr. O'Connell, and not insensibility to the interests of Ireland, that makes the bolder part of the English Radicals disapprove and resist his reckless partisanship of the Ministry. The charge of insensibility to Ireland we indignantly deny. Mr. O'Connell may be sincere in accusing us of it; for with him nobody cares for Ireland who cares for anything else. But it is unworthy of Mr. O'Connell's discernment not to perceive, that the good of Ireland, no less than of England and Scotland, depends upon maintaining the popular influence in the House of Commons, and that when this is in jeopardy, all minor risks must be cheerfully run, rather than lose a moment in taking up the necessary ground for covering our place of strength. When the time comes, and it has now come, at which a further perfecting of the representative system without delay is necessary not only to our advancing, but to our holding what we have already gained, including an honest executive in Ireland—from that time, open opposition, to any and every government which refuses those further improvements, is the only position which befits any Radical. And it remains to be shown in what manner this opposition can be carried on without playing into the hands of the Tories, and without exposing our Irish brethren to any risk which can be avoided,—we do not say of an Orange Government, which we consider impossible,—but of losing the Government which they love.

Let the Radicals, then, assume the precise position towards Lord Melbourne which they occupied in the first Reformed Parliament towards Lord Grey. Let them separate from the Ministry and go into declared opposition. Let their opposition not be factious; let them vote with the Whigs as they would with the Tories, in favour of whatever they propose worthy of support. But if the Tories should move a vote of want of confidence in Ministers, let the Radicals vote for it. At first it might appear that this would bring in the Tories, which it is our object to avoid, although even that would be amply compensated if it procured for us the only thing we at present care much about, a compact and vigorous Radical Opposition. But a very little consideration will show that a Tory Ministry need not, and would not, be the consequence. The necessary condition of a Ministry is to possess a majority, that majority could not be made up by Tories alone. It must be formed either of Whigs and Tories, or of Whigs and Radicals; and the Whigs would have to determine which. If they chose the Tories, it would then, we imagine, be tolerably obvious what way their disposition lay, and whether we had lost anything by exchanging a Ministry of concealed Tories for one of declared ones. But they would not; they are too honourable men to do it without making, at least, such conditions in favour of Ireland, as should guarantee Lord Mulgrave's generous and liberal system of government against any infringement; and the Duke of Wellington's compliments, so direct a rebuke to his own party, are, and we have no doubt were meant to be, a sufficient token that no difficulty of this kind shall stand in the way of a junction when otherwise attainable.[*]

If the Whigs did *not* choose a coalition with the Tories, they would, no doubt, retaliate by moving a vote of want of confidence in a Tory Ministry: and here the Radicals might, and in common honesty must, join with them. By ordinary good management on the part of the Radicals, both these motions would be carried; and the only Ministry which could then be formed, would be one in the formation of which the Whigs and the Radicals would have an equal voice. The Radicals ought not to drive the Whigs into the arms of the Tories by making hard terms with them.

[*See Arthur Wellesley, Speech on the State of Ireland (27 Nov., 1837), *PD*, 3rd ser., Vol. 39, col. 264.]

They might be satisfied with the remodelling of the present Ministry, leaving out Lord John Russell and any others who may consider themselves pledged against the Ballot. But the Radicals would have gained a victory. They would have asserted their share of influence, as a portion, and at least an equal portion, of the majority. They would have shaken off the character of a mere *tail*. They would have restored the drooping spirits and decaying hopes of the liberal party throughout the country. They would have taught the reformers to look to them not merely for an occasional speech, but for the attainment of important practical objects. They would rally public confidence round them, and round the Ministry which they had called into existence. That Ministry, too, would be altered in spirit, far more than it need be altered in the *personnel*. There would be no necessity to require that it should propose the Ballot, because it would be so situated that it could not long go on without proposing it. Such a Ministry would either itself be, or would prepare the way for, that of which the time will soon come, a Ministry of moderate Radicals, a Ministry which will take for its device the BALLOT, JUSTICE TO IRELAND, and JUSTICE TO CANADA.

The name of CANADA recals us to the more immediate object of this article. To that object we now turn: hoping, we trust not vainly, that now when, according to general opinion, the insurrection is quelled, and when the fate of an unfortunate people is in our hands, it may be possible to obtain for their case an impartial hearing. We know how strongly the tide has set in against them. We are painfully sensible that considerate and unprejudiced views of the occasion of the quarrel, are but beginning to find acceptance with the public mind; and that among a large portion even of those who form the effective strength of the popular party, the opinions which we feel bound to avow and justify on this unhappy contest will meet as yet with only partial sympathy. While, both for the sake of this cause and of all the other noble principles which are involved with it, and which must suffer when it suffers, we feel keenly the disadvantages under which it must for the present be advocated; yet this situation has nothing discouraging to us, for it is neither new nor unexpected. The friends of liberal opinions need never flatter themselves that on any new question the public mind will be with them at first. Not one victory has ever been gained by liberal opinions but after a protracted contest; on no one question are the people of England wiser than their grandfathers, but on those which have been much, and long, and well discussed. When we recollect that Ireland is at our doors, that Ireland has above a hundred representatives in the British Parliament, and that with these favourable circumstances it has required fifty years to procure even such imperfect justice to Ireland as we now see, can we wonder that Canada, which has none of these advantages, Canada, to which the attention of England has never once till this very occasion been seriously directed, should not obtain justice, and that her cause is yet only in the first stages of an uphill fight? It must be so; this is among the thousand and one mortifications which in all states of society, and under all governments, those who stand up for principles, or invoke justice from the strong for the weak, must lay their account with enduring. Mortifying enough it truly is, when, instead of having only to bear the defeat of an improvement, and the protraction for some time longer of an evil already in existence, they are condemned to witness their country rushing in blind ignorance, and under interested guidance, into positive wrong and injustice. But no generation that we remember has yet escaped a similar infliction: our grandfathers witnessed the American war, our fathers the crusade in behalf of despotism in France. We, of this generation, have now to bear our share of the common liability, and considering what an easy matter it has been found to bring it upon us, may be thankful that we have escaped so long.

In commenting on these unhappy transactions it is not our wish to enter into any retrospective crimination. A new state of things now exists in Canada, and the past has ceased to be of importance, save for the guidance of the future. But with a view to that future, and to the measures on which Lord Durham first, and afterwards the British Parliament, will have to deliberate, some reference to the past is indispensable.

Let us first get rid of the language of mere abuse, which men so inflamed by passion as to be lost to all perception of the most recognised moral distinctions, have heaped upon the insurgents to render them odious. They are styled rebels and traitors. The words are totally inapplicable to them. Take the matter on the testimony of their bitterest enemies, and what do those very enemies impute to them? Simply this, that it is a contest of races; that being a conquered people, they cherish the feelings of a conquered people, and have made an attempt to shake off their conquerors; is this treason? Is not this the conduct with which, when other parties were concerned, Englishmen have been called upon to sympathize, and to subscribe their money, and to proclaim their admiration of the sufferers and their abhorrence of the conqueror to every region on the earth? On the showing of their enemies, what have the Canadians done other than the Poles? We do not compare Lords Dalhousie and Aylmer to the Grand Duke Constantine, or the administration of our colonial office to that of Nicholas, although even of Nicholas it must be remembered that we have not *his* story; we have but that of the "rebels" and "traitors," as they are called in his vocabulary;[*] and does any one think that Mr. Papineau or Mr. Morin would have any difficulty in making out a case against us, to the satisfaction of a sympathizing audience in a rival nation, without our being heard, or having any opportunity of contradiction? Of the injuries inflicted by a foreign government, the people that suffers them, not the people that inflicts them, is the proper judge; and when such a people revolts, even improperly, against the foreign yoke, its conduct is not treason or rebellion, but war.

From this view of the case, which, as we infer from his language, has

[*See Nicholas I, "Proclamation of the Emperor of Russia" (17 Dec., 1830), *The Times*, 6 Jan., 1831, p. 2.]

commended itself to the vigorous and unsophisticated understanding of the Duke of Wellington,[*] and which has been forcibly argued in one of the anti-Canadian pamphlets* at the head of our article, what follows? That the Canadian contest not being rebellion, but war, the insurgents who fall into our hands are not criminals, who can be tried by a court of justice, but prisoners of war; and that not only that indiscriminate judicial massacre, at the prospect of which the ascendancy party in the colony are expressing so much delight, but any severities beyond what are implied in the precautions necessary against a second outbreak, would be as disgraceful, as much to be abhorred by all who make any pretension to civilization or humanity, as would similar treatment of any captives taken in honourable warfare. Unless there be among the insurgents men who, without justification from the laws of war, have been found wanting in similar forbearance towards *their* prisoners, banishment from the colony, or imprisonment for safe custody, and only while safe custody is required, must be the severest punishment inflicted even upon the chiefs. To shed blood, anywhere but in the field, in such a quarrel, would stamp indelible infamy on the perpetrators; and would meet with its

[*Wellesley, Speech on the Affairs of Canada (16 Jan., 1838), *PD*, 3rd ser., Vol. 40, cols. 3–4.]

*[Charles Neate,] *A Plain Statement of the Quarrel with Canada*. "Too much, by far," says this candid and liberal writer [pp. 15–18], "has been said of treason in this case, and that by men who should think less of antiquated laws, and more of modern rights. Once, indeed, rebellion against the Sovereign, under any circumstances, and by whatever authority, was called treason, and it is still so written in our law books [25 Edward III, stat. 5, c. 2 (1350)]: but the only sort of resistance which, in a representative government, justice and common sense will allow to be so called, and so punished, is the resistance of individuals to an united legislature. It will not be said that, in this sense of the word, the Canadian insurgents are committing treason against the Constitution of Canada; for their legislature is broken up, and in the dismemberment of that body, to which, when united, they owe their allegiance, each party is but clinging to the part which he most loves. It makes little difference to the justice of the case, that the executive of the colony, backed as it is by the resources of this country, has the power of crushing all opposition in its subjects. If the Canadian rebels are to be judged by their obligations to their own country, and to their own constitution, there would be no more justice in hanging Mr. Papineau, than there would have been some two hundred years ago in the execution of Hampden or of Essex, had it been their fate to fall into the hands of the royalists. Their case, too, was undoubtedly one of treason; but are there any Englishmen who think that their punishment would not have been murder? Unless we renounce the doctrine, that a people is represented by a majority of its citizens, we shall be compelled to admit, that the case of the Canadian insurgents, be it right or wrong, be it hopeless or triumphant, is the cause of the Canadian people. If, then, the acts of these men be not treason against Canada, it is hard to say that they are treason against us; for whatever subjection the collective body may be under to this country, the first duty of the individual colonist is to his own legislature, the first claim upon his allegiance is that of his own people.

"That people, it is true, have been guilty of an offence against us; but the offence of one people against another is not treason, and, whatever it be called, it should be punished only as the offences of nations are punished, by war. Experience will soon teach the Canadians, that they were too few to be enemies; let not passion make us forget, that they are too many

just punishment in another insurrection, ten times more difficult to quell than the present. A cause, generally, for the first time acquires a real hold upon the feelings of large masses, when martyrs have been made for it. A little will make men talk, but for making them take to their muskets and fight, there is nothing like having to avenge the blood of those whom they love and honour.

But the question is not to rest here. If we are to keep Canada, and if we are to keep her by any other means than tyranny; if Lord Durham's mission is to lead to anything but setting up a government of brute force, to be maintained at boundless expense to this country, until some embarrassment in our foreign affairs enable the oppressed majority to set themselves free; if this is not to be the end of it, the character of the Canadian insurrection must be thoroughly understood, and we are prepared thoroughly to discuss it. We are prepared to assert to the utmost, without restriction or qualification, the justice and holiness of the cause in which these men have taken arms. We are not prepared to vindicate the wisdom of their conduct. There go other things to warrant an insurrection, besides a just cause, and the principal of them is, a reasonable prospect of success. Where that is wanting, the temerity of the attempt, on the part of the leaders at least, cannot be justified—can at most admit of excuse. But it does not require victory to constitute success. If theirs is the just cause we affirm it to be, and if the English are a just people, is it not success to have drawn so much of their attention to it, when the most stirring appeals from the most patriotic voices in Parliament failed last year to interrupt that slumber which the din of arms has at last broken? Mr. Papineau—a man whom Mr. Edward Ellice, from personal knowledge, describes as "blameless in character, and of high talent and worth"[*]—Mr. Papineau ought, we are told, to

---

to be traitors. The ordinary incidents of the conflict, the usual consequences of a defeat, ending, as it probably will, if not in partial confiscation of their land, and in taxation of their products, yet, at least, in abridgment of their liberties, are enough surely for their punishment, and our security. Let us not, in the meantime, debase even the nature of civil war into the likeness of reciprocal murder. The usual arguments for the cutting off even of their leaders apply not to this case; for if we did visit upon their heads the offences of their followers, with what colour of truth could we pretend, that we did so for the sake of their countrymen whom they had deluded to their ruin? Would not the world see it was the sacrifice of the chiefs of one people to the interests of another; should not we feel, that it was vengeance we were inflicting, under the name and with the forms of justice? It is not thus, whatever we choose to make the issue of this contest, that it behoves us either to vindicate our quarrel, or to re-assert our rights. If Canada is to return to her subjection, let us remember that the blood of thousands slain in the field is more easily forgiven than that of one who dies on the scaffold; and if, which *is possible*, we should find it expedient to yield up to our colonists a dearly bought independence, let not the last memento we leave them of our rule be the gibbet of those men who, whatever *we* may think of their character, will be ever regarded by their countrymen as the authors of their nationality, the first assertors of their freedom."

[*Edward Ellice, Speech on the Affairs of Canada (25 Jan., 1838), *PD*, 3rd ser., Vol. 40, col. 491; in *The Times*, 26 Jan., 1838, p. 3.]

have followed the example of Mr. O'Connell: but is Mr. Papineau in Parliament, with seventy followers at his back, his country's affairs the turning point of all British politics, and a Ministry existing at his will? To their brethren and countrymen who have been ruined, and to the families of those who have been slain, the authors of this revolt have an account to render, which we pray that they may come well out of. But against us they are altogether in the right. The people of Canada had against the people of England legitimate cause of war. They had the provocation which, on every received principle of public law, is a breach of the conditions of allegiance. Their provocation was the open violation of their constitution, in the most fundamental of its provisions, by the passing of Resolutions through Parliament, for taking their money from their exchequer without their consent.[*]

We must dwell a little on this topic; for there is something very alarming to us in the nonchalance with which Englishmen treat so grave a matter as the infraction of a constitution. A Resolution taking away representative government from Lower Canada passes the Commons' House with about fifty dissentients,[†] and (except from the brave Working Men) hardly a whisper of public disapprobation. And there are liberal men who consider this a trifling matter, a thing which may be softly remonstrated against, but which is no "practical grievance;"[‡] and there are writers, and able writers too, who compare it to levying a rate for paving and lighting a corporate town when the corporation has refused to do it: we ask those writers if Parliament ever, by formal enactment, gave up the right to tax the corporate towns; or ever, by another act, placed all the taxes raised within one of them at the absolute disposal of the Town Council? If so, the cases of the municipality and of the colony would be *primâ facie* parallel. If not, the one act is an ordinary exercise of legitimate power, the other is breaking faith with a people; taking away from them the right which constitutes them members of a free state, and the violation of which, by the sense of all ages and nations, forms the *casus belli* between a people and their government. It is inflicting on them that injury which Hampden resisted, and for which Washington raised the standard of "treason and rebellion," and rung the knell of aristocratic government over the face of the earth. For it was not the twenty shillings of ship-money that Hampden was solicitous about, nor did the Americans make their Revolution for the sake of the penny a pound in the price of their tea, which was the ostensible matter in issue when the war began. They fought for the *securities* for good government, and to be willing to do so is one of the tests of a nation's fitness to enjoy them.

[*See Russell, Resolutions on the Affairs of Canada (6 Mar., 1837), *PD*, 3rd ser., Vol. 36, cols. 1304–6.]

[†See the Division on the Eighth Canada Resolution (24 Apr., 1837), *ibid.*, Vol. 38, cols. 248–9, where the negative vote is given as thirty-two.]

[‡See, e.g., John Arthur Roebuck, *et al.*, "To the People of England," *The Canadian Portfolio*, No. 1 (4 Jan., 1838), p. 29.]

And on what pretence have we done what even the Colonial Secretary* admits to be "violating one of the great principles of the Canadian constitution?" It is because they have refused the supplies. It is because they have used a right, which we gave them, but which we never intended they should use; or if we did, we intended that we, against whom they used it, were to be the judges whether they used it properly. By this impartial tribunal it has been decided that they have made a bad use of it, and that it is therefore to be taken away. Permit us to ask, since when has this discovery been adopted into English morals, that a constitution is a gift resumable at the discretion of the giver? We thought this doctrine had been confined to Charles X, and Ernest King of Hanover, on whom a great load of obloquy has been heaped very undeservedly, if the grant of a constitution implies a tacit condition that the powers it gives shall be forfeited on their being exercised disagreeably to the donor. That the power of despotic government, once parted with, may be re-assumed at pleasure, is a maxim we little thought to hear from the lips of Englishmen; or that political rights once bestowed upon a people are to be exercised according to the judgment of somebody who happens to be stronger. A constitution once conferred is sacred, and to revoke it or to infringe it ("a constitution which is violated is destroyed,") is a breach of the most solemn compact which man can make with man, or people with people, and to be justified only by those emergencies which justify anything—when society is threatened with dissolution—when anarchy or civil war is impending, and all laws and institutions, and all compacts to maintain laws and institutions, must give way before the terrible alternative.

Now let us see what would have been the evil incurred, supposing Parliament had still respected the Canadian constitution, and left to the Assembly the control over their own money. Much use has been made of the phrase "stopping the supplies,"[*] and it has been attempted to attach to it the ideas belonging to what is known by the same name in this country, viz., a complete annihilation of all government. It however turns out that the only supplies which the Assembly has power over (except those for bridges, roads, schools, and the Legislature itself) are the salaries of the Judges, of the Governor and his Council, and of a certain number of subordinate executive officers. These salaries have been suspended for three years, and we have had a most piteous tale of the hardships, and we do not question

---

*Lord Glenelg's despatch to Lord Gosford, dated 22nd May, 1837, in the first Canada papers of this Session, p. 11. [*PP*, 1837–38, XXXIX, 327; the despatch is part of the *Copies or Extracts of Correspondence Relative to the Affairs of Lower Canada* (23 Dec., 1837), pp. 317–432.]

[*The discussion derived from a passage in Russell's Speech on the Affairs of Canada (16 Jan., 1838), *PD*, 3rd ser., Vol. 40, col. 25, in *The Times*, 17 Jan., 1838, p. 3. The phrase was used with reference to Newfoundland by John Temple Leader, Speech on the Affairs of Canada (22 Dec., 1837), *PD*, 3rd ser., Vol. 39, col. 1437, in *The Times*, 23 Dec., 1837, p. 2.]

their truth, which have been suffered by some of the unpaid officers of Government. Now, suppose Parliament, which professes so much compassion for these people, instead of violating the Canadian constitution to pay them, had resolved to pay them itself, what would have been the cost to this country? The arrear for the whole three years is 127,744*l*.,* from which subtracting about 23,000*l*. drawn from the hereditary revenues of the Crown in Canada not given up to the Assembly, there remain 104,000*l*.—rather more than a year's income of Adelaide, the Queen Dowager. The Parliament of Canada, then, have in the last resort a power of fining this country about 35,000*l*. a year for maintaining a bad government in Canada, or, to say no worse, a government unacceptable to the majority of the Canadian people; and the stoppage of the wheels of government, the subversion of civilized society, and all that mountain of evil which we have heard so much about, resolves itself on examination into the incovenience of paying that sum.

We may ask, is this too great a power to be possessed by the people of a province, over rulers living at the other side of the globe, who appoint all their judicial and administrative officers, whose sanction is necessary to all their laws, and over whom they hold no other check, direct or indirect, to secure any the smallest consideration of their interests or their opinions? Is the power of making us pay 35,000*l*. a year, in addition to the fifty millions of taxes we pay already, when we who *can* control their government, although they cannot, suffer it to govern them in a manner odious to the majority—is this more than enough to secure a little attention to the interests of the Canadian people, from a public who allowed a Resolution for destroying the Canadian constitution to pass both Houses with scarcely more general interest or inquiry than happens on many a private Bill? Canada cannot invade us; she cannot interrupt our trade; she cannot cut off our revenue; she cannot touch any one of our national interests—only one thing she could do; she could tell us, that if she did not like the men we sent to govern her, we might pay them ourselves; that if we chose to offend her, our fault, or if you like it better, her misfortune, should cost us 35,000*l*. It is for the sake of taking away this power, that the national honour has been stained with breach of faith, and an English Parliament has followed the example of Polignac and King Ernest, in treating a constitutional charter as waste paper; it is to save this penalty of a third part of Queen Adelaide's income, contingent upon making the Canadians discontented with their government, that a brave and kind-hearted people have been goaded into insurrection, and unknown multitudes of them given over to slaughter and misery!

---

*142,160*l*. 14*s*. 6*d*. was the sum voted by Parliament; but the real amount, as appears from Lord Gosford's statement in p. 75 of the Parliamentary papers already referred to, was that mentioned in the text. ["Copy of a Despatch from the Earl of Gosford to Lord Glenelg," *PP*, 1837–38, XXXIX, 391.]

It has been seen that we have argued this question without reference to the original justice or reasonableness of the claims of the Canadians, because we maintain (woe the day when it is necessary to stand up for such a proposition!) that even if they were wrong, and the grounds on which they refused the supplies wholly indefensible, they were in the right from the moment when their representative institutions were invaded, and an outrage practised upon them which no brave people ever did, nor ever will, tamely submit to. But we go vastly farther. We assert, that their demands were right; that they were right on the whole, and right for the most part in the particulars. And this is the most important question of all at the present moment. For according as just concessions do or do not accompany the coercive proceedings about to be authorized by Parliament, will Canada either be reconciled to us, or continue during a few years of compulsory subjection to regard us with detestation, which as soon as she succeeds in throwing us off will be exchanged for contempt.

On this subject it is a source of gratifying reflection to us that this Review cannot charge any part of the ignorance which universally prevails as to the Canadian grievances, upon its own neglect. As long ago as 1827 the *Westminster Review* demanded the attention of the English public to the vices of the administration of Canada, and traced those vices expressly to the irresponsible constitution of the Legislative Council.[*] That article, as well as one in the second number of the *London Review*,[†] was written by Mr. Roebuck; which may serve as an answer to two assailants: to those who assert that the objection to the Legislative Council is a new complaint only four years old, made because a grievance was wanted, after all real grievances had been redressed; and to the hired advocate of the Canadian loyalists in the *Morning Chronicle*, who calls Mr. Roebuck the hired advocate of the Assembly,[‡] as if Mr. Roebuck, who was bred though not born in Canada, and spent the greater part of his youth there, had not been the champion of its people many years before he either was, or could look to be, their *hired* champion—and as if Mr. Roebuck's *hire*, as well as that of Lord Gosford and his subordinates, were not suspended by the unhappy differences which he is accused, by implication, of fomenting for his own advantage.

As, however, the undaunted struggles of Mr. Roebuck in a cause with which every principle of his political life is identified, and which had few friends in this country until *his* unwearied activity *obtruded* the case of the Canadians upon an inattentive public—as these exertions are called "a wonderful display of public opinion, produced by throwing backwards and forwards the voice of two or three

---

[*Roebuck, "Canada," *Westminster Review*, VIII (July, 1827), 1–31.]

[†Roebuck, "The Canadas and Their Grievances," *London Review*, I (*L&WR*, XXX) (July, 1835), 444–76.]

[‡Leading Article on Canadian Affairs, *Morning Chronicle*, 12 Jan., 1838, p. 2.]

individuals,"* it may be well to state that Mr. Roebuck is an entire stranger to the present article. The writer of it has never before publicly expressed any opinion on the claims of the Canadians, and he draws his facts not from Mr. Roebuck, or from any of the partisans of the Assembly, but from the Reports of Lord Gosford and the two other Government Commissioners[*]—of the men who advised the violation of the Canadian constitution—of the authors of Lord John Russell's policy—the men who told him all he knows of the colony—who furnished him with his brief, of which brief, however, a great part of his speech on the re-assembling of Parliament is in downright contradiction. If anything can excuse the Canadian people for having believed that less than drawing the sword would not procure them a hearing in the mother country, it is the inattention which has been the fate of the statements in these Reports.[†] There is not an imputation on the objects of the Canadian party which these documents do not refute; there is not a misrepresentation against the popular cause which they do not deny, not by implication or inference, but positively and in express terms. The Resolutions of last year never could have been passed, or if passed, never would have been acted upon, if the Members of the House of Commons had performed the duty of reading the Reports, and had thought that they would be read by their constituents.

The Reports bear marks, it is but justice to say, of good intention, and even of candour. The Commissioners appear to have gone out, Lord Gosford especially, with the ordinary Whig aversion to strong opinions on either side. All former Governors had been blind followers of the dominant, or, as it calls itself, the English party; we perceive no marks of this influence over Lord Gosford, and that party detests him as much as it applauded his predecessors. The Reports which he signed put that party altogether in the wrong, and the popular party generally in the right. But although the Commissioners carried out with them no unfair intention, they carried out a feeling which seems ineradicable in every official breast, namely, that when anything amounting to a quarrel has once arisen between subjects and a Government, no matter though the Government was first to blame, no matter though the demands of the subjects were just, and ought to be conceded, and never ought to have been refused; before any such concession can now be made, they must be punished for the course of energetic remonstrance by which they sought it; "the authority of Government must be asserted,"[‡] of the

*[Elliot,] *The Canadian Controversy*, p. 52.
[*"Reports of the Gosford Commission," *PP*, 1837, XXIV, 1–408. The other two commissioners were George Gipps and Charles Grey.]
[†"First Report of the Commissioners Appointed to Inquire into the Grievances Complained of in Lower Canada," *ibid.*, pp. 3–83; "Second Report," *ibid.*, pp. 85–104; "Third Report," *ibid.*, pp. 105–36; "Fourth Report," *ibid.*, pp. 137–9; "Fifth Report," *ibid.*, pp. 141–80; "General Report," *ibid.*, pp. 183–416.]
[‡Cf. Russell, speech of 16 Jan., 1838, col. 8.]

Government who are admitted to have been in the wrong, against the people who were in the right. And hence there is in the Reports of the Commissioners, what the House of Assembly noticed in their address to Lord Gosford on the 25th of August last,

> one essential and paramount contradiction, which pervades every part of them and forms their essence. It is, that while they admit the reality of the greater portion of the abuses and grievances of which we have complained, the Commissioners do not recommend their removal,* and the destruction of the causes which had produced them, but an act of aggression against this House which has denounced them, and the absolute destruction of the Representative Government in this province, by the illegal and violent spoliation of the public monies of the people by the Ministers or by the Parliament.†

Lord John Russell, in the speech[*] in which he introduced to Parliament the measures now in progress, drew a most charming picture of the generosity of the British Government towards the conquered Canadians, and a most hideous one of the ingratitude with which so much liberality had been requited, and said what used to be said to himself on the subject of the Catholics of Ireland, that our whole government of Canada has been one course of concession. It *has* been one course of concession, and so, thank God, bad government everywhere, in the present age, must be. But if he means that any one concession was made willingly, or till after protracted refusal, or in consequence of anything but the "factious violence," as it was then considered, of the House of Assembly, "working upon the prudence," or, if Lord John Russell prefers it, upon the good intentions of the English Government, then Lord John Russell says one thing, and Lord John Russell's commissioners and informants say the direct opposite. Let us hear them:

> The House of Assembly was not slow to perceive the importance of the functions which had been consigned to it by the Constitution; the Government alone was slow to perceive it, or if perceiving, to acknowledge it, and to provide with prudence for the consequences. Instead of shaping its policy so as to gain the confidence of that House, it adopted the unfortunate course of resting for support exclusively on the Legislative Council. The existence of a majority of French Canadians in the Assembly, seems to have been thought a sufficient reason that there should be a majority of English in the Council; for the principle observed in the first nominations, of making it of equal numbers, French and English, was early departed from, and thus the Council and Assembly were constituted on antagonist principles almost from the commencement.
>
> For a number of years the Council, keeping as it did, in close union with the Executive, prevailed; but in process of time the inherent force of a popular Assembly developed itself, and in the great contest which ensued about money matters, the Assembly came out completely successful. During this financial struggle, continued as it was for more than a

---

*This is an over-statement. The Commissioners do recommend that, *some* time or other, *some* of the grievances be removed.

†*PP, ut supra*, p. 39. ["Copy of a Despatch from the Earl of Gosford to Lord Glenelg" (including Louis Joseph Papineau's "House of Assembly's Address to Lord Gosford, 25 Aug., 1837"), *ibid.*, 1837–38, XXXIX, 355.]

[*Speech of 16 Jan., 1838, cols. 7–42.]

quarter of a century, it was only natural that other collateral causes of difference should arise, and if we were to examine into these, we believe we should also find that in every one of them the Assembly has carried its point. As a few instances, we will mention the right of the House to accuse and bring to trial public officers; their right to appoint an agent in England, and their right to control their own contingent expenses; their demand for a withdrawal of the judges from political affairs, or from seats in the legislative bodies, or the executive councils, and for the surrender of the proceeds of the Jesuits' estates. All these are points on which contests have taken place between the two Houses, and in every one of them the popular branch has prevailed, and the Council been successively driven from every position it had attempted to maintain. The Assembly, at the same time, by attacking abuses in the Administration, and bringing charges against numerous officers of the Executive, succeeded scarcely less in exposing the weakness of the Government, than that of the Council. Both the Council and the Government have been worsted in many a struggle that they never ought to have engaged in, and if the Assembly has, in consequence, grown presumptuous, we apprehend that such is only the ordinary effect of an unchecked course of success.

In the course of these protracted disputes, too, it has happened that the Assembly, composed almost exclusively of French Canadians, have constantly figured as the assertors of popular rights, and as the advocates of liberal institutions, whilst the Council, in which the English interest prevails, have, on the other hand, been made to appear as the supporters of arbitrary power, and of antiquated political doctrines; and to this alone we are persuaded the fact is to be attributed, that the majority of settlers from the United States have hitherto sided with the French, rather than the English party. The respesentatives of the counties of Stanstead and Missisquoi have not been sent to Parliament to defend the feudal system, to protect the French language, or to oppose a system of registration. They have been sent to lend their aid to the assertors of popular rights, and to oppose a government by which, in their opinion, settlers from the United States have been neglected or regarded with disfavour. Even during our own residence in the province, we have seen the Council continue to act in the same spirit, and discard what we believe would have proved a most salutary measure, in a manner which can hardly be taken otherwise than to indicate at least a coldness towards the establishment of customs, calculated to exercise the judgment and promote the general improvement of the people. We allude to a bill for enabling parishes and townships to elect local officers, and assess themselves for local purposes, which measure, though not absolutely rejected, was suffered to fail in a way that showed no friendliness to the principle.*

This is rather a different picture from the paternal Government so charmingly delineated by Lord John; and in this picture it will be remarked that the Legislative Council figures as the author of the grievances, and the Executive as its subservient tool. We find that every one of the improvements for which Lord John Russell takes credit, have been extorted from the perservering opposition of the Legislative Council. We find the prayers of the people stopped in that intermediate stage, and

---

*"General Report," pp. 5-8. [*PP*, 1837, XXIV, 187-8. The concluding reference is to "A Bill to Provide for the Nomination and Appointment of Parish and Township Officers, 5 & 6 William IV (Lower Canada), passed by the House of Assembly of Lower Canada on 14 Dec., 1835, but rejected by the Legislative Council. See *Journals of the House of Assembly of Lower Canada*, 1835-36, p. 277, and *Journals of the Legislative Council of the Province of Lower Canada*, 1835-36, pp. 114, 123, 232, 269.]

the representative of the Crown of England prevented from granting them, or shielded from the responsibility of refusing them. We find all the abuses in the Executive Government, which were not acknowledged then though they are acknowledged now, sheltered from reformation by the Council, as might well be the case, since it was the Council and their connexions who profited by them. We find the Council engrossing the patronage of Government, exercising, under the mask of the Governor, all his power, and forming the prop on which, by acknowledgment, the Government "rested exclusively for support." We find, according to the Commissioners, that this "tendency to lean for support rather on the Legislative Council than on the representatives of the people," has lasted "in an undiminished degree to the most recent times."* We find this body still unaltered in its constitution; altered indeed somewhat in its *personnel*, but almost solely by the introduction of some men considered renegades from the popular party, and of others too insignificant to be of any party at all; and we find it still displaying the same spirit, by throwing out, even during Lord Gosford's Administration, a bill for municipal institutions,[*] which the generally enlightened author of *The Canadian Controversy* [p. 41] thinks is the very thing Canada most requires, and which Lord Gosford considered "a most salutary measure."† We see all this; and will it be affirmed, in the face of this, that the Council must be maintained as the representative of the mother country? If it represented the mother country, would it reject measures of important reform, which the real representative of the mother country strenuously supports? Do we not see broadly apparent, what has always been asserted by the advocates of the Canadians, that the Council represents nobody; not the colony, for that is represented by the House of Assembly; not the aristocracy of the colony, for there is no such thing; not the mother country, for that is represented by the Governor and the Executive Council? That it is the organ of

---

*"Reports," p. 108. ["Third Report," *ibid.*, p. 106.]

[*"An Act to Incorporate the City of Quebec," 1 William IV, c. 52 (Lower Canada), and "An Act to Incorporate the City of Montreal," 1 William IV, c. 54 (Lower Canada) (both 12 Apr., 1832); on 7 Mar., 1836, the House of Assembly of Lower Canada passed two bills to extend the powers of the incorporated cities. These were rejected by the Legislative Council, whereupon the House of Assembly, on 12 Mar., 1836, passed "An Act to Continue for a Limited Time the Acts Relating to the Incorporations of the Cities of Quebec and Montreal" (*Journals of the House of Assembly of Lower Canada*, 1835–36, p. 691); this too was rejected by the Legislative Council (*Journals of the Legislative Council of the Province of Lower Canada*, 1835–36, p. 357).]

†They have done this, not once, but frequently. The Commissioners say, "In the present particular, at least, the leaders of the popular body have shown a laudable desire to get out of what has been called the French system, a system which made the Government everything, the people nothing; and their opponents have laboured, and are still labouring, to perpetuate the vices of a condition, the evils of which, as far as they hurt themselves, they are ever loud in denouncing. We need scarcely say that we allude to the frequent failure of bills for the election of township and parish officers, and for the management of other matters of local concernment." (P. 45.) ["General Report," p. 227.]

no interests but those of a jobbing local oligarchy; that the mother country is making itself odious by upholding a body which maintains grievances that itself would be willing to redress, and that there will be no good government for Canada until the complaints of the people go straight to the Governor, instead of being intercepted by a body pretending to be a part of themselves, and prevented, to use the Assembly's words, "from reaching the foot of the Throne."[*]

But of the spirit still pervading the Council no adequate conception can be formed from the single instance mentioned by the Commissioners. The reader may consult with advantage the descriptive list in the third number of the *Canadian Portfolio*, of *forty-two* bills, embracing all the most important matters of internal government, which were sent up by the Assembly to the Council in the single session of 1835-36, and either rejected, suffered to drop, or returned with amendments considered inadmissible.[†] Many of these are alleged to have been sent up too late in the session; and this is true of a proportion, but, as appears from the dates on which they passed the Assembly, and which are given in the *Portfolio*, not of a majority. But we wish here to take nothing upon the authority of the Canadian party. We will content ourselves with one fact, which will be disputed by no party, and which will give quite a sufficient idea of the spirit of the Legislative Council.

By the Jury Law of Canada, juries are summoned by the sheriff; an officer appointed for life, but removable at the will of the Crown. This officer, who, like all others named by the Executive, generally belongs to the local oligarchy, and never to the party opposed to them, determines by his will alone the mode of selecting jurors: he has the power, and, it is alleged on the Canadian side, unscrupulously exercises it, of packing juries so as to obtain any verdict he pleases. In 1832, however, a provincial act was passed, extending to Canada the principles of Sir Robert Peel's Jury Act.[‡] This bill gave satisfaction to the people, and put an end for a time to the very worst of the existing abuses; but unfortunately it expired in 1835. The Legislative Council refused to renew it. The old packing system was therefore re-introduced, and flourishes at this moment.[§] The Canadian leaders, if tried for treason or sedition before the Canadian courts, will be tried by judges whom they have kept without their salaries for three years, and one of whom, in the hearing of a friend of ours, declared several years ago that "the

[*Papineau, "House of Assembly's Address to Lord Gosford, 30 Sept., 1836," *PP*, 1837, XLII, 450.]

[†Roebuck, *et al.*, "The Want of an Elective Legislative Council No Grievance!" *The Canadian Portfolio*, No. 3 (12 Jan., 1838), pp. 65-104. Here Roebuck lists (pp. 102-3) not forty-two but forty-nine bills (thirty-four rejected and fifteen amended).]

[‡2 William IV, c. 22 (Lower Canada) (1832), in *The Provincial Statutes of Lower Canada*, Vol. 14, pp. 408-28, extending to Lower Canada the provisions of 6 George IV, c. 50 (1825).]

[§For corroboration of Mill's account, see "Report on the Affairs of British North America, from the Earl of Durham," *PP*, 1839, XVII, 45-7.]

hanging of Papineau would settle all disputes;" and juries packed by a sheriff to whom they have also refused his salary; both judges and sheriff belonging to the party which in the two Montreal papers, the *Herald* and *Courier*, is clamouring for a *special commission to try the traitors, as it would be absurd to fatten them all the winter for the gallows*.[*]

Have we made out our case? or does the reader still think that the Legislative Council is "no practical grievance," and that the Canadians ought to be robbed of their Constitution because they sought the removal of that grievance by exercising to the utmost all their constitutional privileges, that utmost power (so far as money was concerned) amounting to involving this country in a responsibility of thirty-five thousand pounds? Will Lord Durham's mission, of coercion and conciliation, produce the tranquillity which the Ministers themselves do not hope for more earnestly than we do, unless the measures of redress, to be embodied in the new Constitution, include the abrogation of this mischievous body?

The Commissioners (two out of three at least) approve, in principle, the demand for an Elective Council. "Under more favourable circumstances, at an earlier time, or had less animosity been excited, we can conceive" (they say) "that good might have resulted from the introduction of a principle of election." But they "cannot advise the experiment now," for the avowed reason, that "the concession of it, in the present excited state of public feeling, would afford a triumph to one portion of the population which would be fraught with danger."[†] Heaven knows it would afford no triumph to anybody now. The "danger" which was anticipated is explained in another place, by the Commissioners,* to be a civil war between the two races, in which the English party would be the aggressors. We direct attention to the circumstance, that the fear lest the loyal party should rebel is advanced as the chief reason for rejecting demands which, if there had been no such probability, would have been deemed fit to be granted. Since, then, not justice, but the apprehension of rebellion, and that from the loyal party, was to decide the case, the *reality* of rebellion ought, we think, to go for something on the other side. Or is it only unreasonable dissatisfaction, dissatisfaction *acknowledged* to be unreasonable, which has the privilege of expressing itself in that way?

The Council, it will be said, protects the English settlers: were it not for the Council, they would not think their lives and properties secure. And what is a Governor for? of what use is the whole machinery of the Executive, and why has the Governor power to reject every bill passed by the Legislature, if he cannot prevent one part of the community from tyrannizing over another? The only

---

[*A leading article on the Canadian rebellion in the *Spectator*, 13 Jan., 1838, pp. 30–1, quotes the Montreal *Courier* as saying "it would be ridiculous to fatten fellows all winter for the gallows." See also p. 455n below. The sheriff was Louis Gugy.]

[†"General Report," p. 189.]

*"Reports," p. 90. ["Second Report," p. 88.]

mischief the House of Assembly could do to the English, unless the Governor were a party to it, they can do as long as there is a House of Assembly: they can refuse any new enactments, which the interests or opinions of the English part of the population may call for. And upon this Lord Glenelg appears to take his stand in behalf of the Council. In his late speech in the House of Lords he claims the Council as the liberal party. He calls the Asssembly "those who were against improvement—attached to the obsolete notions of former times—unfriendly to commerce, to the spread of intelligence, to the diffusion of education"[*]—for which last great object, by the bye, they made one of the most munificent provisions, in proportion to their resources, ever made by any country[†]—the renewal of which has been lately refused by the Legislative Council on the express ground of its being too munificent. Let this be a sample of Lord Glenelg's accuracy when he gives the following history of the contests between the two bodies:

Thus it happened, on the one hand, that those who were the supporters of an oligarchy hostile to improvement made use of the rights and privileges of popular institutions, and pushed them to an extreme; and on the other, privileges not generally used to promote improvements and support free institutions, were pushed to an extreme for the purpose of supporting them.[‡]

Let us hear the Commissioners, and learn what good the improvements which the Council advocated have ever got by the support of such a body.

If we were to inquire, [say they,] in what degree the demands of the English have been advanced by its means, we doubt whether we should not find that the advocacy of the Council has tended rather to defeat, than to promote, the measures which the commercial classes have demanded, and continue to demand, with the greatest earnestness; for instance, the commutation of tenures, the establishment of registry offices, the settlement of the wild lands, and the facilitating of commercial intercourse.*

All this cry of a hostility to the English race, and a disposition on the part of the Assembly to tyrannize over them, is a mere work of art. Hear Sir George Gipps, one of the Commissioners. He says, explicitly, that the contest is not one of races, but of principles.

So long as the contest can be made to appear as one not of nationality but of political principle, the Americans, and a portion even of the British, will be on the democratic side. It is the policy of the leaders of the majority in the Assembly to give the dispute the character of a contest between the aristocratic and the democratic principle rather than one of nationality, and they have succeeded to a great extent; for, of the members from the townships, where there are no persons of French, but numbers of American origin, nearly as

[*Charles Grant, Speech on the Affairs of Canada (18 Jan., 1838), *PD*, 3rd ser., Vol. 40, cols. 162–77, in *Morning Chronicle*, 19 Jan., 1838, p. 2.]
[†See 6 William IV, c. 30 (Lower Canada), in *Provincial Statutes of Lower Canada*, Vol. 15, pp. 244–54.]
[‡Grant, speech of 18 Jan., 1838, p. 2.]
*"General Report," p. 7. [*PP*, 1837, XXIV, 189.]

many vote with the French party in the Assembly as against them; and if to the persons thus returned by the American or democratic interest be added the Englishmen who are sent to the Assembly by French constituencies, we shall find that of the twenty-two individuals with English names, or of English origin, who have seats in the Assembly, thirteen generally vote with the French party, and only nine against them. It is, I believe, [continues Sir George Gipps,] the apprehension that their democratic allies of British origin would change sides, should the dispute become one purely of nationality, that renders the leaders of the French party desirous of remaining for the present under the protection of Great Britain.*

Jealousies between the two races do, doubtless, exist; the late events have administered fresh fuel to them, and they are at this moment the greatest difficulty in the good government of the colony. But who is the cause of these jealousies? Who fostered them? We need only quote Lord Glenelg. More ingenuous than Lord John Russell, to whom the conduct of the English Government, from the first conquest, presented itself throughout in so amiable a light, the Colonial Secretary says (we quote from the daily papers)—

The Constitution of 1791, from the earlier years at least in the history of Canada, might be said not to be administered. It might have been very advantageous for the people of Canada if it had been so; but the *Executive Government took part with one race, against the other—it took part with the English race*, instead of being the umpire and arbitrator between both. All the honours and emoluments flowed in the same channel, and thus the popular institutions were severed, for the Canadians, from the Government, and they obtained no advantage through them. This was done while the Government usurped practically the funds of the State. Those funds were in the hands of the Governors—abuses crept in, and at length they prevailed to such an extent that many of the English united with the French race to obtain a redress of grievances.[*]

Remembering all this; remembering that it is but of yesterday that the French Canadians have been admitted to any share of the honours and offices of their native country; remembering that the local oligarchy, represented by the Council, have done their utmost to inflame those national differences which enable them to identify *their* cause with that of the British settlers and even of the mother country; is it to be wondered at that such animosities should exist? But will any one believe that they are the cause of the discontents, or that the Council have made themselves obnoxious to the French by upholding the English, when the party which is opposed to the Council is a mixed party of French and English, and when, "of the members from the townships, where there are no persons of French origin, nearly as many vote with the French party in the Assembly as against them?" The assertion is one of the misrepresentations, calumnies we may venture to call them, of which, from their distance and the popular ignorance on the subject, the Canadians

*"Reports," pp. 88–9. [George Gipps, "Extract of Minute of Proceedings on Monday, 14 March 1836," *ibid.*, pp. 96–7.]
[*Grant, speech of 18 Jan., 1838, p. 2.]

are liable to far more than we can at present meet; and of many others of which, the refutation, from the Commissioners' Reports, might be made fully as conclusive.*

To this people, thus calumniated, it will now be for Lord Durham to do justice. He has the power. A more enviable position than he now enjoys, if his soul is on a level with his opportunities, has been filled by no statesman of our era. The whole institutions of two great provinces are prostrate before him. Canada is a *tabula*

---

*We hear it, for instance, in every speech, and read it in every newspaper, that the Canadians are an ignorant peasantry, who, being hoodwinked by their *seigneurs*, and by their lawyers, are fighting to preserve the feudal system. Some scribes have actually dropped the expression, "heritable jurisdictions," as if any such thing existed in Canada. More discreet advocates have urged the hostility of the party to the Canada Tenures Act [6 George IV, c. 59 (1825)]: a law enacted by Parliament to facilitate the conversion of the feudal tenures into the tenure of free and common socage, under the English law. Now the Commissioners expressly declare that this pretended attachment to the bad parts of the old French law of landed property does not exist. "We believe," say they (General Report, p. 34 [*PP*, 1837, XXIV, 216]), "that the injurious tendency of heavy fines on the transfer of property, as well as of other obstacles to its free transmission, are beginning to be generally acknowledged, and that in reality there is less difference on this point than might at first sight appear; so that if the evils of the feudal tenure had not unfortunately been seized as topics for political declamation, and thrown into the general mass of subjects of party contest, they would probably receive an early remedy by common consent. In the views now expressed by leading Canadians of French origin, there is no desire whatever to perpetuate the onerous parts of the tenure, and the people have been moved, in some cases, to represent the inconvenience." After citing instances, the Commissioners say that a Committee of Assembly in 1834 "exhibited a feeling very favourable to the extinction, on reasonable terms, of the burthens of the seigneurial tenure;" that on the other great point, the inconveniences of the French law of mortgage, the House of Assembly expressed "just and liberal views more than ten years ago," [p. 224,] and that the distracted state of the province, and not any desire "to adhere to institutions no longer fitted to the intelligence of the age," is the cause why a remedy has not yet been applied. The objections of the Assembly to the Canada Tenures Act are stated by the Commissioners; they are numerous and weighty: we mention two of them; that, being framed in ignorance of the pre-existing law, it unsettled titles and destroyed existing rights, and also, "that it was far too favourable to the seigneur." [Pp. 216–17.] If this complaint proceeded from a people hoodwinked by their seigneurs, it says much for the public spirit and honourable feeling of the seigneurs. The Commissioners, after a full examination, declare all the objections to be valid; and recommend (what Parliament has since voted) that as soon as the question of compensation can be adjusted with the colony for the rights created under the Tenures Act, the Act shall be repealed, and the reform of the law of landed tenures left to the Provincial Parliament. [Pp. 217–20.] The fault which the Canadians find with the English tenures, is not the feudal customs which they are intended to replace, but those which they introduce. According to the usual custom of men who despise "theory," English legislators could hit upon no other means of getting rid of institutions which were supposed to be bad, than by transplanting their own, bodily. They could not manage to introduce, in place of the feudal tenures, the full and absolute property in land, which is common under English law, without introducing along with it the complicated and expensive English modes of conveyance (those which existed under the French customs being, according to the Commissioners, "simple, expeditious, and cheap,"

rasa[*] upon which it rests with him to inscribe what characters he pleases. The immediate pacification of the colony depends upon him alone; the institutions by which it is to be hereafter governed, upon Parliament, guided, as there is every appearance that the present Ministry at least are willing to be, almost implicitly by his advice.

He has, in the first place, what was the most necessary of all, and the investing him with which is an earnest of the good disposition of Ministers: he has powers for a general amnesty. We trust those powers are not granted to him in vain. If, when he arrives, the finds the insurrection at an end, or if the promise of oblivion can prevail upon any who still remain in arms to lay them down, great will be the responsibility of refusing it. It is not yet proved that there was any preconcerted insurrection. There was preconcerted arming and drilling; there were violent public meetings and political associations; but these may have been for passive resistance, and a display of force, like the measures of intimidation which carried the Reform Bill. There was nothing, about the final outbreak, which bore any marks of concert. Had insurrection been planned, it would have been better organized, and would not have been so soon begun. The people seem to have flown to arms for the rescue of their leaders, who were torn from them, or on the point of being so, to be immured in gaol, and tried by juries of their enemies; and some of whom were paraded with every mark of ignominy, by armed bodies of those enemies, through the very heart of the disaffected districts. But if they have been guilty, to the utmost extent, of whatever is included in a deliberate and concerted insurrection, they are not rebels, nor traitors; they are, we repeat, captives taken in war; who went to war with us, justly or unjustly, wisely or unwisely, but who have a claim to the rights of honourable warfare, and such treatment as a generous nation bestows on a vanquished enemy.

But while we do not fear that spirit of sanguinary vengeance, happily confined to the rabid party calling themselves Loyalists, and to the Orange newspaper writers, who long to be doing in Ireland what they instigate in Canada; it will not be a less

---

[p. 214,]) and without introducing the feudal institution of primogeniture. Now it is one of the properties of this favourite institution of aristocracy, that no people who have ever lived under anything else can bear it. "The people of all origins on this continent," say the Commissioners, "greatly prefer the equal division, which existed under the French law;" and the feeling is nowhere stronger, they say, than in the townships where there is not a single French inhabitant. [Pp. 214–15.] Accordingly the Commissioners recommend that the French methods of conveyance be restored, and the English tenures divested of the incident of primogeniture. Will the English public learn from this how grossly the dislike of the French Canadians to innovations in their social arrangements has been exaggerated, and how little credit is due, not merely to the ministerial press, but to Lord Glenelg, when he accuses the popular party of being the illiberal party, an "oligarchy hostile to improvement—unfriendly to commerce—attached to the obsolete notions of former times?"

[*Robert Smith appears to have originated the term in *A Sermon Preached at the Cathedral Church of St. Paul, Nov. 9, 1662* (Oxford: Robinson, 1663), p. 10.]

fatal mistake, nor in the end less productive of human suffering, if in the new arrangement of the government, the French Canadians are treated as a defeated party, the English as a victorious one; if the former are now to be considered as the ruled, the latter as the rulers. At the pass to which Ministers had brought matters by their first act of injustice, we do not quarrel with them for the course they have now adopted; it would be over-nice to make any mouths at the suspension of what remains of the Canadian constitution, after the only provision in it which renders the rest of any value has been despotically overruled and made a nullity. When a country is in a state of civil war it is hardly possible to execute a constitution. When a country is divided into two parties, exasperated, by the taste of each other's blood, beyond the possibility of a peaceful accommodation, an armed umpire with strength to make himself obeyed by both, is a blessing beyond all price, and such a mediator it behoves the mother country to be. In itself, therefore, the dictatorship which has been assumed, and of which Lord Durham is the immediate depositary, admits of justification. But if it shall prove to have been assumed only to remove the obstacles which the constitution of the House of Assembly has of late years opposed to the previously uncontrolled sway of a rapacious faction; if because the majority of the people, when they had the power over the Assembly, did not use it to our liking, we mean to remedy this inconvenience by taking the power from them and giving it to a minority; if we have set aside their constitution in order to confiscate the privileges of the old inhabitants for the benefiit of a small proportion of foreigners and new settlers; then will a stain rest upon the British name, to be effaced only on the day when all that is now done shall be undone; and the name of a Whig will be as infamous in American annals as is the name of a Tory in those of Ireland.

If the English and the French inhabitants of Canada cannot live under each other's government, which ought to give way? The whole numbers of the British race in Lower Canada do not even, on their own computation, amount to a third of the whole; and of these, that large portion who consist of emigrants or descendants of emigrants from the United States, and a part even of those of British origin, as the Commissioners acknowledge, side with the French party;[*] it cannot be they who think themselves in danger from the French, and demand protection. The remainder, Sir George Gipps distinctly asserts, are "for the most part the natives of our own isles."* Here, then, is a body of men, positively not of American birth, strangers, mere new-comers, and a portion of them, particularly the trading classes, not even perhaps intending to remain permanently in the colony—who have actually the presumption (or somebody has it for them) to expect that the political constitution of a long-settled country is to be shaped to suit their convenience. Not content with having what, under such circumstances, they

[*"Second Report," pp. 96–7.]
*"Reports," p. 99. [*Ibid.*, p. 97.]

would have in no country of the old world, the privileges of citizenship, and influence in public affairs proportional to their numbers, they must be the masters, and the old inhabitants of the country must be under their rule. They went to Canada, save the mark! under the faith of the British Parliament. Did Parliament promise them that because they went to Canada, the institutions necessary to protect or to satisfy the old inhabitants of the country should be denied to those inhabitants? Did Parliament promise them a veto on every act of the Legislature of the country? Let them wait till they are a majority. If they are, as they represent, the active, enterprising, and industrious part of the people, and the others are the ignorant and indolent portion, they will not have long to wait. Till that time, let them be satisfied if they have a share of representation proportional to their numbers, and if the Governor applies his veto to all laws which aim at preventing those numbers from increasing. If they ask aught beyond this, let them be told, and told in plain and unequivocating language, that Parliament does not intend that their presence there is to be an impediment to any settlement which is for the good of the colony or of the empire; that they went there under liability to all changes of institutions which the general interests of the population of the colony might require; that they went there subject to the certainty of a separation, sooner or later, and to the contingency of its happening in their time, a possibility which, while the United States exist, it would be rather bold to expect us to believe they had not fair warning of.

What *may* be done for the less numerous race, if it is found impossible that both should live harmoniously under one government, is to give them separate Legislatures. This has been done once, by separating Canada into two parts, the Upper and the Lower province. Sir Charles Grey, the least liberal of the three Commissioners, proposes that it should be done again; to which, according to him, local circumstances oppose no insuperable obstacle. Sir Charles Grey's plan is to divide Canada into three districts, with separate provincial parliaments, to each of which, the separation of the races being thus effected, he would have no objection to give an elective Upper House.* On this system neither of the races would be legislated for by the other: and a federal Legislature would be created, of delegates from the local Legislatures, to which the matters of common concernment to the three provinces would be exclusively referred. In this federation, Upper Canada, and the other North American colonies, might, he suggested, be ultimately included.

Of all changes in the political organization of Canada which there would be any chance of carrying through Parliament, none has occurred to us which appears liable to so little objection as this, or attended with more probabilities of good. The principle of separating the internal legislation and administration of each colony

---

*Pp. 64–5 of the "General Report." ["A Minute Delivered to the Secretary by Sir Charles Grey," *ibid.*, pp. 246–7.]

from the control of the interests common to the different colonies, has received the sanction of the highest authorities on both sides. It was one of Mr. Roebuck's propositions, in his statesman-like speech last year on conciliation with Canada, a speech which he has republished in the fourth number of the *Portfolio*, and to which we invite the attention of all who may still mistake his occasional violence of language, and the strength with which he expresses his speculative convictions, for impracticability in action, or incapacity for temperate views when the occasion calls for them.[*] Lord John Russell at the time expressed no other objection to Mr. Roebuck's propositions than that he feared they were too moderate to satisfy the Canadians.[†] Lord Glenelg, too, in his late speech, declared himself prepared, if Upper Canada should consent, to sanction a "federal union" between the two Canadas, and he enumerated among the objects which would be within the competence of the federal legislature, "the navigation of the St. Lawrence, the duties by which their commerce is to be regulated, their railroads, their bridges, their internal communications, and their monetary system."[‡]

It was part of Mr. Roebuck's proposition, that the federal legislature should be that tribunal for the impeachment of public functionaries,[§] the absence of which is the only objection the House of Assembly made to a permanent appropriation for the salaries of the judges,[¶] over whom, in the absence of such a tribunal, they did not choose to divest themselves of the degree of control implied in an annual vote. In answer to the demand for such a tribunal, Lord Gosford offered them the Legislative Council! and it is pretended to be wondered at, that they regarded the offer as a mockery.

We entreat Lord Durham, as he values the successful issue of the solemn trust he has, as he assures us, so reluctantly undertaken—and (we may say without disparagement to his feelings of honour and patriotism) as he values also that high reputation to which the applause of all parties on his nomination is so glorious a tribute, and those prospects of a brilliant career as a British statesman, which he will most assuredly either make or mar by his conduct in this emergency; by all these considerations we entreat him so to act upon his declared resolution of knowing no distinctions of opinion, party, or race, as to provide, if provision be needful, for the interests of a minority,—not by putting them over the heads of the majority, or by any legerdemain contrivance to give them a power in the

[*Roebuck, Speech on Canada (14 Apr., 1837), *PD*, 3rd ser., Vol. 37, cols. 1209–29, specifically cols. 1220–1, reprinted in Letter III, "What Ought to Be Done?" *The Canadian Portfolio*, No. 4 (16 Jan., 1838), pp. 106–19.]
[†Russell, Speech on Canada (14 Apr., 1837), *PD*, 3rd ser., Vol. 37, cols. 1239–40.]
[‡Grant, speech of 18 Jan., 1838, p. 2.]
[§Roebuck, speech of 14 Apr., 1837, col. 1220.]
[¶See 7 George IV, "An Act to Secure the Independence of the Judges in This Province [Lower Canada], and for Other Purposes Therein Mentioned" (20 Mar., 1826), *PP*, 1830, XXI, 79–81; rejected by the Legislative Council.]

Legislature beyond what their numbers entitle them to,—but either by the rigid exercise, for their protection against any meditated injustice, of the veto of the mother country, through its responsible representative, and not through an irresponsible council; or if that will not content them, by separating the two races, and giving to each of them a legislature apart. No other plan will render Canada, from this moment, other than a disgrace and a weakness to the British empire; by no other plan, when a separation comes, shall we have entitled ourselves to the kindly remembrances and friendly attachment of the Canadian people; by no other can we be saved from the disgrace of having first broken their constitution, and then used the insurrection that act of tyranny provoked, as an excuse for confiscating the rights of the native majority in favour of a handful of strangers.

Our subject draws to a conclusion. But we cannot leave it without awarding, so far as our words can have any influence, the just honour to that small, but even because of its smallness, that glorious minority, who, with a talent and energy as conspicuous as their intrepidity, have now and last year stood up for everlasting justice against temporary clamour; and afforded in the cause of the injured and calumniated, at the further side of the globe, an imperishable example of that constancy and resolution, and that defiance of unmerited unpopularity, which we find men every day claiming credit to themselves for displaying in defence of their own pockets, or of the selfish prerogatives of their "order." The conduct of Mr. Grote, Mr. Warburton, and Mr. Hume will live in history.[*] Nor ought we to omit Lord Brougham, who has shown by his conduct in this Parliament, that *he* at least perceives the time to be come when a practical statesman can best serve both the interests of his country and his own glory, by putting himself at the head of the moderate Radicals.[†] We have reserved Sir William Molesworth and Mr. Leader for the last place, because to them is due, not only honour for what they have done,[‡] but vindication against the accusations it has exposed them to. If, by the warmth of expression natural to men deeply penetrated with the truth of their principles, they exposed themselves to misconstructions of which a most ungenerous advantage was taken by their ministerial opponent, it is not upon their sentiments, but upon the reproaches which were heaped on those sentiments, that the condemnation not only of every high-minded person, but we will be bold to add, of every Christian, will rest. What was the feeling they expressed? That they

---

[*See Speeches on the Affairs of Canada, by George Grote (16 Jan., 1838), *PD*, 3rd ser., Vol. 40, cols. 59–65, and (23 Jan., 1838), cols. 399–406; by Henry Warburton (17 Jan., 1838), *ibid.*, cols. 102–9; and by Joseph Hume (16 Jan., 1838), *ibid.*, cols. 42–55, and (17 Jan., 1838), cols. 129–43.]

[†Henry Brougham, Speech on the Affairs of Canada (18 Jan., 1838), *ibid.*, cols. 177–217.]

[‡William Molesworth, Speech on the Affairs of Canada (23 Jan., 1838), *ibid.*, cols. 358–87; and Leader, Speech on the Affairs of Canada (22 Jan., 1838), *ibid.*, cols. 329–44.]

would learn with less regret, the defeat of the British troops in this war, than their success. Will their assailant be pleased to remember, that according to *their* view of the matter it is an *unjust* war? At what time since Christianity existed has it been held, that success in injustice was a lot which patriots ought to desire for their country? That to prosper in evil courses was not a far worse evil than to fail in them—was not the strongest mark of divine displeasure,—permitted only that the example of the subsequent chastisement and humiliation might be more memorable? Lord John Russell would bring us back to heathenism. That love of country, which would rather see the success of our country than that of the right, is an essentially Pagan sentiment, and even as such, repudiated by all the great philosophers and moralists of the Pagan world. If there is any one thing which we would hold up to especial honour in the conduct of Mr. Leader or of Sir William Molesworth (for we know not which of them it was) on this occasion, it is that they dared, in the face of a hostile assembly, and without the support of a favouring public, to declare the sentiment, which Lord John Russell has not thought it unworthy of him, strong in his majority, to hold up to obloquy and insult.

LORD DURHAM AND HIS ASSAILANTS

1838

EDITOR'S NOTE

London and Westminster, VII & XXIX (Aug., 1838), 507–12 (2nd ed. only). Headed: "ART. XII. [John George Lambton.] *An Ordinance to Provide for the Security of the Province of Lower Canada.* Passed by the Governor-General of Canada in Special Council the 28th day of June, 1838. [*Parliamentary Papers,* 1837–38, XXXIX, 914–16.]" Running titles as title. Signed "A." Not republished. Identified in Mill's bibliography as "An article headed 'Lord Durham and his Assailants' in the second edition of the same number of the same review"; i.e., as "Penal Code for India" (MacMinn, 51). There are no corrections or emendations in the copy (tear-sheets) in Somerville College. For comment on the essay, see xlii–xlvi above.

Lord Durham and His Assailants

WE AVAIL OURSELVES of a demand for a second edition of this number of our Review, to offer a few brief comments on the factious, unseemly, and in every way discreditable war of words which has been going on in the Houses of Lords and Commons respecting Lord Durham's ordinances.[*]

There are two modes of canvassing an act of any public functionary. The question may turn either upon the merits, or the technicalities. The point in issue may be, whether the act be right in itself—the most eligible means for attaining the acknowledged ends—and which therefore either *is* legal, or if it be not, *ought* to be legal, and should be made so with the least possible delay; or the objection may turn upon the words of the public officer's commission—the limitations to which his powers have been subjected, the forms and precautions with which he has been surrounded, not in order to weaken his authority for a good purpose (though that may be the incidental effect), but to prevent him from aiming at bad ones.

Now, when a man has been selected to fill a new office; to do a new thing, in new circumstances—circumstances which you in whose behalf he acts do not know, cannot know, do not pretend to know, still less could pretend to foreknow;—when this new thing, which he is sent to the other side of the globe to do, is considered to be so difficult, so delicate, so likely to be frustrated if at all opposed, that to enable him to do it every other constituted authority in the country must be suppressed, every place of public discussion shut up, every possibility of counteraction from every quarter precluded, at any cost, even that of the representative constitution of a free people; in which of the two lights of which we have spoken is it fit that the measures of this officer should first be viewed? *Even then*, undoubtedly, their substantial merits should not be the *only* consideration; even then, besides considering whether what he has done is right, it is necessary to consider also whether he had power to do it. But are any words adequate to express the contempt due to a mode of treating matters of high public concernment, which makes the last the *sole* consideration? which merges the former in it? which passes over the question whether what Lord Durham did be a thing which ought to be done—whether some such thing be not, in circumstances such as he was appointed to deal

[*See *PD*, 3rd ser., Vol. 44, cols. 1019–35 (7 Aug., 1838), 1056–1102 (9 Aug., 1838), 1127–46 (10 Aug., 1838), 1211–92 (14 Aug., 1838), 1296–1310 (15 Aug., 1838).]

with, the very thing which he ought to have been empowered to do, which he ought to have been expected to do, which he ought to have been encouraged to do—and makes the preservation of the Canadas and the reconciliation of two embittered parties lately engaged in shedding each other's blood, subordinate to the grave consideration whether what Lord Durham could lawfully punish, he could lawfully punish *as treason*, and whether men whom he could lawfully banish, he could lawfully banish *to Bermuda*?

With men meaning honestly, and having the intellects of statesmen instead of fribbles or legal pedants, the matter would in the first instance have been debated solely on the grounds of substantial justice and policy. The question would afterwards have been conscientiously examined, whether Lord Durham had gone beyond his powers, in order that if he had done so, and his acts were therefore wanting in legal validity, legal validity might be given to them; and the object for which his powers were created might not be defeated either by any technical error of his own, or by a blunder in the terms in which those powers were conferred upon him. For if, under the pressure of alleged necessity, you have confiscated the free constitution of a people and thrust aside all the acknowledged principles of a constitutional government, in order to enable Lord Durham to accomplish certain important ends, and if it should turn out that by this costly sacrifice you did not accomplish the ends, did not enable Lord Durham to adopt the means most conducive to the ends, what will it please your wisdom to do next? To submit, and leave the ends unaccomplished? Or may it perchance occur to you, that if the dearest privileges of a million of free-born human beings have been made perforce to give way to the exigency of the case, some nice scruples about encroachment on the authority of Parliament may do so too? It is becoming, is it not, to be so chary of your own "little brief authority,"[*] when you have made so light, in the very same case, of the most sacred constitutional rights of every one else?

Dismissing this pettifogging mode of dealing with the subject, let us turn to the really important view of it. What has Lord Durham really done? And was it a thing fit to be done, or which may be presumed fit to be done, under the circumstances?

Among so many flights of oratory about the mere *form* of Lord Durham's proceedings, about the enormity of his alleged infringement of his powers, by one solitary figure of rhetoric alone was any imputation cast upon the substance of the ordinance; the appeal *ad invidiam* rested entirely upon a misdescription. It was called an ordinance for putting men to death without trial.

But without trial! Was it not, on the contrary, distinctly stated in the ordinance, that there *should* be a trial? Not, indeed, for rebellion; the ordinance is one of *amnesty* for rebellion; amnesty to the men whom it banishes, as much as to those whom it sets free altogether. Not being to be punished for rebellion, it is rather unnecessary that they should be tried for it. The punishment denounced by the

[*Shakespeare, *Measure for Measure*, II, ii, 118.]

ordinance, is punishment for the violation of the ordinance; it is the *sanction* with which every prohibitive enactment must be accompanied. The ordinance is not a judicial act, it is a legislative act; it is not to punish men for their past conduct, it is to restrain their future conduct; it imputes to them no guilt; it has nothing to do with their guilt, it has to do only with the consequences of their being at large in the colony.

Now we affirm, without fear of contradiction from any one who has even the most elementary notions of human affairs, that if a man be appointed to restore tranquillity in a country after a civil war, and if that person have not the power to command that any twenty-three men, let them be the most virtuous citizens in the country, shall absent themselves from it until their return shall be judged consistent with safety, and not likely to disturb men's minds—then the appointment of that person is a mockery; and if he be a sane man, he has only been induced to undertake the office by a disgraceful fraud.

We are curious to know what idea the assailants of Lord Durham have formed of the state of a country in which a general insurrection has just been put down by the sword; or of the nature of the work of bringing such a country into a state of pacification. It is very well known what our opinion is of the conduct by which that insurrection was provoked; most unquestionably our own sympathies are not with the victors, but with the vanquished, in that melancholy struggle. However, they were vanquished; upon provocation, either sufficient or insufficient, they threw themselves upon the chances of war, and failed. Lord Durham was then sent out to heal the wound. We presume it was not to be expected that he should begin this task by exactly reversing the state of things which he found on his arrival; by making the vanquished victors and the victors vanquished; by exciting the feelings of triumph in the defeated party, of bitter indignation and resentment in that which is at present predominant. His part was not to excite, but to calm all feelings either of triumph or of mortification. His office was that of a peacemaker—of a mediator. It was no business of his who was right, or who most wrong, in the conflict which preceded; but how to prevent any future conflict. It was his duty to avoid irritating any party; to do nothing which could be construed by either side as a declaration in its favour; to shape every one of his proceedings so as in no way to impede the return of both parties to that tranquil state of mind, in which it might be possible to satisfy both by conceding what is really just in the demands of each, and nothing but what is just.

Now, without pretending to discuss the actual state of feeling in Canada, which, like most of our readers, we are much too far off to judge of; we pronounce it abstractedly impossible, that in any country whatever, the leaders of a popular party which has just attempted an insurrection could be at large in the country without retarding the progress of the public mind to this calm and reasonable state. Mr. Papineau and some others named in the ordinance may not have participated in the insurrection; or they may have participated in it, and may nevertheless be the most upright and purest patriots to be found in the colony. All this is really nothing to the point; they are the leaders of an insurgent party, and, as such, their absence is necessary, so long as their presence would be a hindrance to that reconciliation of parties, which, now that their party has been beaten, is the most desirable thing remaining, even for themselves. The measure is an ostracism, not a punishment: they are banished because they are dangerous, not because they are criminal. But if they are to be banished, there must be a penalty for returning from banishment; and the penalty is capital, because that is the usual penalty of state offences; and properly so, since any inferior punishment might be a premium on the offence, while, by denouncing the highest penalty of all, no necessity is incurred of actually inflicting it.

If indeed there were the slightest colour for the supposition that even *one* of these twenty-three men were banished *for ever*; if it were not obvious from the whole tenor of the ordinance, as well as from all which is known of Lord Durham, his advisers, and his purposes, that the sole object of it is, as the ordinance itself declares, "to provide for the *present* security of this province" [p. 914]; if the door were not studiously and widely opened to let in even Mr. Papineau himself to-morrow, if he should be able to satisfy Lord Durham that his influence would be used to restore peace to the public mind instead of disturbing it; we could then understand the passionate invectives of Mr. Leader, which are at present as unintelligible to us as they are, for his own sake, lamentable.[*]

Mr. Leader cannot so far mistake our feelings towards him as to suppose that we entertain any sentiment inconsistent with the most entire respect for his principles and intentions, and the warmest good wishes for his future political career, which it would grieve us to see compromised. Almost alone in the periodical press we stood by him,[†] when to do so might be deemed an act of courage on our part, when at least it would have been much more to our interest to do otherwise. We were not bound to identify ourselves with the opponents of the Canada Act;[‡] we never opposed it; we declared it to be right or wrong according as it should be executed. Our practical views differed as widely from Mr. Leader's as our language did, and most persons in our situation would have taken as much pains to separate their cause from his, as we took to avoid all semblance of separation. For great is the virtue of a passing word in reproof of "extreme views" and "intemperate language" on one's own side, for giving an air of moderation to one's sentiments: to say a little on one side and a little on the other is the only way to present an appearance of impartiality to vulgar eyes. We spurned the unworthy advantage. And the justice which we then claimed for Mr. Leader, we now owe to those whom

[*John Temple Leader, Speech on Canada (14 Aug., 1838), *PD*, 3rd ser., Vol. 44, cols. 1242-50.]
[†See John Stuart Mill, "Radical Party and Canada," pp. 434-5 above.]
[‡1 Victoria, c. 9 (1838).]

he has attacked, and to whom we much mistake his character if he do not soon feel that ample reparation is due from him.

If Lord Durham and his official advisers are the men Mr. Leader represents them, he may rely on it they will soon give him fairer cause of attack. The test of what they are, will be their plan for the permanent settlement of Canada; let us wait to see what that is—whether its basis be the predominance of an oligarchical party, or the removal of whatever is justly obnoxious to either party. If the former be the result, we shall deal the same measure to Lord Durham which we should have dealt to any other man through whose instrumentality a similar act of tyrannical injustice had been committed by a Whig or a Tory Ministry—and shall lament the failure of the hopes which we have built upon him, not only for justice to Canada, but for benefits to the empire and to reform, of which this is not the place to speak. But if Lord Durham fail us, have we anything better to expect from his successor? Is it imagined, for instance, that if he could be sufficiently damaged, the government of Canada would fall into the hands of Lord Brougham? For our part, deeming such a *dénouement* not particularly probable, and having no very great confidence that the change would be an improvement, we do not see the wisdom of declaring war against the only man who has it in his power to do what we wish done, in order to put in his place somebody who would almost certainly do the exact opposite. It is intelligible that the Tories, factious and envenomed beyond all recent precedent as a large portion of them have shown themselves during the last half-year, should strive, *per fas et nefas*, to lower the public estimation of the only man in the ranks of their enemies whom they really fear. But what is gain to them is bitter loss to the people; and Lord Durham is the very last man upon whom any one in earnest for Reform should permit himself, at the present time, to be betrayed into any act of hostility not called for by an imperious duty.

LORD DURHAM'S RETURN

1838

EDITOR'S NOTE

London and Westminster Review, XXXII (Dec., 1838), 241–60. Headed: "ART. VIII.— 1. [Anon.,] *The Preamble*. No. VII. Lord Durham's Return. November, 1838. / 2. *The Quebec Gazette of the 9th October*, 1838." Running titles: left-hand, "Lord Durham's Return:"; right-hand (page and line equivalents from this edition), "His Position" (448.15–449.8), "His Difficulties" (450.2–36), "The Political Prisoners" (451.32–452.17 and 453.17–454.11), "His Appointments" (455.7–456.12), "His Measures" (457.24–458.21), "His Resignation" (459.24–460.20), "The Proclamation" (461.16–462.11), and "His Success" (463.7–464.3). Signed "A." Not republished. Identified in Mill's bibliography as "An article entitled 'Lord Durham's Return' in the London and Westminster Review for December 1838 (No 62)" (MacMinn, 51). In the Somerville College copy (tear-sheets) there is one emendation (which is adopted in this edition): "this country" is corrected to "his country" (456n.7). For comment on the essay, see xlii–xlvi above.

Lord Durham's Return

THERE WERE CONSEQUENCES dependent upon Lord Durham's mission to Canada, calculated to make it the turning point of English politics for years to come, and to raise every incident connected with it, however secondary in appearance, to the character of an event in history. It was not merely because the interests consigned to his charge, to be rescued from a state of peril and difficulty without any recent example, were the lives and fortunes of a million of British subjects, and the British dominion over possessions among the most intrinsically valuable, however hitherto mismanaged, of that vast empire on which "the sun never sets."[*] In addition to so large a portion of the territory, there was delivered into his keeping the character also of England; her reputation in the eyes of all nations for wisdom and foresight, for justice, clemency, and magnanimity; at one of those critical instants when Europe, Asia, and America were looking on, to watch how England would act under this trial—whether like an irritated despot, or a serious and thoughtful ruler, intent upon profiting by experience, and gathering from her failures the most valuable kind of knowledge, that of her own mistakes. And along with interests of this importance to the physical resources and to the honour of England, there hung also upon Lord Durham's measures the contingency of a war: war with men of our own race and language—war with the great customer of our foreign trade—war with the only power by which that of England has ever yet been baffled—a war of opinion, and a war *against* liberty, in which the sympathy of all Europe would have been with our enemies; the only war which could bring us into conflict with the free nations of the world and with the despots at once. All this was involved in the result of Lord Durham's mission; and something greater still than all this, because involving, in its remoter consequences, these and all other national interests: the prospects of the popular cause in England; the possibility of an effective popular party, and of a Liberal Ministry worthy of the name.

What was the situation of politics? On one side, the great aristocratic party, recovered from the sudden shock which laid it prostrate in 1832, was progressively and rapidly reasserting its ascendancy; the illegitimate influences of property, the

[*The phrase seems originally to have been applied to the Spanish Empire; for example, see John Smith, in *Advertisements for the Unexperienced Planter of New England, or Anywhere* (London: Haviland, 1631), p. 37, where he says it should become equally applicable to the British Empire.]

power to bribe and the power to starve, slowly but surely resuming the dominion which belongs to them—under our present electoral system—at all seasons except those of temporary popular excitement. To this natural progress what was there to be opposed? A body, consisting indeed of half the nation on the showing of their enemies, five-sixths of it on their own showing, and who, under all disadvantages and abatements, still possessed between two and three hundred voices in Parliament; but whose objects and opinions were ostentatiously repudiated by their ostensible chiefs—standing actually paralyzed for want of a common banner—for want of a bond of union, and leaders. There was one man to whom this party might look, to whom it had for years looked, as the man who might supply this want; the one person of his rank and influence who was identified with their opinions, the one person identified with their opinions who might be thought of, who *had* been thought of, as the head of a future Administration. Lord Durham was this man. Of no other man was there the same reason to hope both that he might be *willing* to put himself at the head of the Liberals, and that he would be *able* by doing so to render them the predominant party. And he alone was so marked out for the position, by every consideration of character, station, and past services, that if he chose to assume it he could do so without rivalry or dispute; that all the best heads and hands which the party could produce would flock round him with their services and their counsels; and the whole of its effective strength would come forth at his voice, and give him that decisive majority in the House of Commons, with which he might again break the power of the aristocratic faction, and this time provide more effectually that the dead might not be able to revive.

Such was Lord Durham's position; such the consequences depending upon his qualifications for government. And these qualifications were now to be tried by a most unexpected, a most severe, but at the same time a most appropriate test. Severe, because the difficulties were arduous, and the file of precedents contained no case in point; but appropriate, because such circumstances are those which test the possession of the very qualities that are required.

Nations are not governed nor saved by fine sentiments, or clever personalities, or dialectical acuteness, or book-knowledge, or general theories. If they could, the Liberal party would not now be in search of a leader. A true politican knows how to put all these things to their proper use. But the man we want is the one who can recommend himself not solely by the ability to talk, nor even merely to think, but by the ability to *do*. We want a man who can wrestle with actual difficulties and subdue them; who can read "the aim of selfish natures hard to be spelled," can bend men's stubborn minds to things against which their passions rise in arms; who needs not sacrifice justice to policy, or policy to justice, but knows how to do justice, and attain the ends of policy by it. We want a man who can sustain himself where the consequences of every error he commits, instead of being left to accumulate for posterity, come back to him the next week or the next month, and throw themselves in his path; where no voting of bystanders can make that success, which is, in truth, failure; where there is a real thing to be done, a positive result to be brought about, to have accomplished which is success—not to have accomplished it, defeat.

The world has a memorable example of such a man in Washington, and an inferior, but still a great one, within his sphere, in the Duke of Wellington. Such a man as the first, or even as the last, we cannot look to have; but a much inferior degree of the same qualities would suffice us. Even these could not have accomplished what they did, had they not been well helped and counselled. We do not need a man who can be sufficient without help, but a man who can avail himself of help; who knows where to find help; who can either do or get done what the situation requires, by the best means it affords. We need a man who can seize the *great* circumstances of his political position; who can see where his objects lie, and what things stand between him and them; can conceive the outline of a policy by which they may be attained; and find men competent to assist him in filling up the details.

The popular party will soon be either the ascendant power in this country, or a thin, feeble, and divided opposition to the Tory ascendancy, according as they are or are not supposed to possess, or to be capable of producing, such men. It is what the world, at present, by no means gives them credit for. The world never gives credit to anybody for good qualities till it is compelled to do so. It denied them honesty, it denied them learning, literary accomplishments, philosophy, oratory, while it could: it now denies them capacity for action. They are considered essentially unpractical. Can they wonder at it? In the first place, this is a charge always made in politics against honest men. Next, it is a charge always made against men who stand up for general principles, or distant objects. But, above all, it is always made against men who are untried, and who there is no desire should be tried. They are untried. They have to prove that they can be men of action. They have their spurs yet to win.

Lord Durham, then, the man marked out as a leader for this party—as, for the present, almost its only possible leader—was suddenly in a position in which he would be obliged to show whether he was a man of action, or could become one. This was a conjuncture of the deepest import to all Liberals. And it was a conjuncture to try the quality, not of Lord Durham only, but of many persons besides. It was an occasion for sifting the really practical part of the great Liberal body from the unpractical. According to the disposition they manifested to aid or to obstruct Lord Durham in a business so vital to Liberal objects; according to the manner in which they judged him, or rather to the principles which they brought with them to judge him by, they would afford decisive evidence to which of those two sections of Liberals they belonged.

Now, then, what circumstances had Lord Durham to deal with? A country, the two divisions of whose inhabitants had just been cutting each other's throats, and in which the majority openly sympathised with an insurrection just suppressed, and suppressed only by a military force which they were physically unable to resist; one party still crying loudly for the blood of the other, which in its turn was muttering vengeance for the blood already shed. With one of these parties, the more numerous though momentarily the weaker, the public opinion of a neighbouring country, where public opinion is omnipotent, was urged by every motive of political sympathy and national aggrandizement to fraternize; the violent *acts* of the Loyalists of Upper Canada, and the violent *words* of a Lieutenant-Governor, had added to these incitements of ambition and sympathy the incitements of resentment; and if the storm burst which was manifestly gathering, a hundred thousand men would have been across the frontier before the news could reach England; four-fifths of the population of the Canadas would have risen to join them; and, in a fortnight, the fifteen thousand troops that garrison British America would have been shut up in the fortress of Quebec, or driven into the sea. The opposite party was comparatively weak on the American continent; but it was the energetic party; and made ample amends for its inferiority there, by its preponderance here. It had the whole of the aristocratic party enthusiastically in its interest. It had alone the ear of the English public. It was called the British party. All that was known of it by ninety-nine men out of a hundred was that it was the "loyal" party—the party of British connection. It had all the Tory and almost the whole of the Liberal press for its organs. In this dilemma was Lord Durham. One step too much towards the French side, and he might expect to be recalled, and to have all his projects for the good of Canada defeated, all his measures reversed. One step too much to the English side, and the empire was involved in the most ruinous, the most dishonourable, and the most fratricidal of wars.

Here were real difficulties: here was an emergency not to be conjured away by phrases: here was the occasion for a Governor-General, let him be Conservative or Liberal, to show whether he was a pedant and a formalist, or a man of action and reality; whether the Shibboleth of his party governed him, or he it; whether the attainment of his end, or the rules which he had learnt by heart, were dearest to him; whether he was a man bent upon succeeding in his object, or a man like the old Austrian tacticians opposed to Napoleon,[*] or the physician in Molière, who would rather kill his patient by rule than save him contrary to it.[†]

What indication would Lord Durham have given of himself—to which of the classes above characterized would he have proved himself to belong, if he had proposed to himself to cope with such a combination of circumstances as we have described, by the mere common-places of Liberalism? Could he have been fit for his post if he had looked into a book of rules or a catechism of doctrines for his conduct, and not at his position, and the ends and means which it dictated?

[*Including Michael von Kienmayer, Johann Joseph von Liechtenstein, and Franz von Weyrother.]

[†Jean Baptiste Poquelin Molière, *L'amour médecin* (Paris: Le Gras, 1666), pp. 39–40 (II, iii).]

We claim for Lord Durham, from dispassionate men of all parties, the recognition that he *did* apply his mind to those ends and means; that he took, in every essential particular, a just and a comprehensive view of them; that the scheme of policy which he conceived, and began to execute, contained within itself every element of success; that he has even already, to a very great extent, succeeded; and would have succeeded altogether if he had met with no obstacles but those which he could calculate upon, none but what were inherent in his situation; if each of his measures had been opposed by those only to whose principles it was adverse; if Conservatives had not rushed in to destroy a Conservative measure, Radicals to denounce the act which saved the lives of Radical leaders: both forgetting the essentials of their political creed in the common-places of it, and doing thereby as much as one act could do towards proving themselves the pedants and formalists which the latter are called, but which is now proved to be a character fully as applicable to the former. We leave the Tories in the hands of the *Standard*, a journal whose superiority to its party in real *understanding* of the principles they profess, never more strikingly asserted itself—and which on this occasion has merged the party passions it so strongly participates, in the sympathy of talent for talent and vigour for vigour, and given the candid construction at all times, and the support in time of need, due from consistent Tories to an officer of the Crown, engaged in an enterprise not of party but of national concernment, amidst difficulties over which only the honourable forbearance of the disinterested of all parties could enable him to triumph.

When Lord Durham landed in Canada the insurrection was already suppressed; the work of the sword was done, and what remained was to heal its wounds, and obviate the necessity of again drawing it. Lord Durham saw that the *sine quâ non* of success in this was a reconciliation of parties. Without it he might, indeed, have kept Canada by force, if the United States would have let him; but only by making the yoke of the mother country a tyranny; only by making her an object of detestation, of imprecation, to her subjects; never under such a government could Canada have been a safe place for Englishmen to dwell in; never could she have been anything but a drain upon our finances in peace, upon our military resources during actual or apprehended war. To restore a free constitution, and to restore it at the earliest period possible, was the only means of governing Canada which Parliament had contemplated, the only one which Lord Durham either could, or, we may presume to say, would, be a party to.

But the constitution being supposed re-established, was the struggle of the majority and minority to be renewed, which was all the fruit it had yet borne, and the sole justification, if justification there was, of its suspension? We waive all the matters of principle and of policy involved in the question whether the restoration of a constitution, without a previous reconciliation of parties, would have been desirable; but would it, we ask, have been *possible*? If a House of Representatives must be an instrument of one exasperated party or of the other, could Lord Durham expect the Lords and Commons of Great Britain to put that instrument into the hands of the party whom they considered disaffected? and could it, without the grossest injustice, and without consequences in the end still more fatal, have been put into the hands of the other?

To heal, therefore, the breach between the two parties; to avoid, so far as possible, whatever would either put in evidence the extent of the animosity which already existed, or give fresh occasion to it; to make it apparent that if there ever had been, there no longer was, any quarrel between the *races*, and that representative institutions might be restored without giving rise to a permanent conflict between the English and the French population—was the one condition of success in Lord Durham's enterprise; and to attain this, we challenge controversy when we assert, that his whole series of measures was admirably calculated.

The first thing to be disposed of, was the traces of the past insurrection, the political prisoners. We are not going to argue over again the worn-out topic of the ordinance.[*] We said enough on that manner in the second edition of our last number.* We have nothing to add to our defence of it; we have only to point out its relation to that comprehensive scheme for a reconciliation of parties which Lord

[*John George Lambton, "An Ordinance to Provide for the Security of the Province of Lower Canada," *PP*, 1837–38, XXXIX, 914–16; reviewed by Mill, "Radical Party and Canada," *London and Westminster Review*, VI & XXVIII (Jan., 1838), 2nd ed., 502–33 (pp. 405–35 above).]

*We will only, since we have been accused [by John Arthur Roebuck, in "Lord Durham's Administration in Canada: Letter I," *Spectator*, 3 Nov., 1838, pp. 1039–40] of setting up a defence for the Ordinance at variance with Lord Durham's own, point to the fact that Lord Durham's statement, now when we have it, exactly tallies with ours. We said, that the banishment of certain persons from the colony, during the Governor-General's pleasure, was not punishment without trial; not punishment at all, but a measure of *precaution*, removing from the province those whose presence in it would for the time be injurious; not a judicial, but a legislative act—a *privilegium*, in the language of the Roman law; an ostracism, not a punishment. What says Lord Durham? "As it was essential to my plans for the *future tranquillity* and improvement of the colony, that I should commence by *allaying actual irritation*, I had in the first place to determine the fate of those who were under prosecution, and to provide for the *present security* of the province, by *removing the most dangerous disturbers of its peace*. . . . I could not, without trial and conviction, take any measures of a purely penal character. But I thought myself justified in availing myself of an acknowledgment of guilt, and adopting *measures of precaution* against a small number of the most culpable *or most dangerous* of the accused." [Lambton, "A Proclamation," *The Times*, 7 Nov., 1838, p. 3.]

Mr. Roebuck, who is the party alleging that the despatch to Lord Glenelg described the Ordinance as a measure not of precaution, but of punishment [in "Lord Durham's Administration in Canada: Letter I," pp. 1039–40], must have in view the following passage: "I next applied myself, by answers to addresses and private applications, to the discouragement of any notion of the possibility of a general amnesty, and announced that my determination was to *punish the guilty*, and to extend mercy to the misguided." So far Mr. Roebuck's assertion is apparently justified; but what follows? "for which purpose *I*

Durham had conceived, and which we assert that he has in every respect acted up to. Had he granted an unconditional amnesty, he would have set the leaders of the French Canadians, including all who had been prominent in the insurrection, at large among their countrymen, to resume all their former influence, before he could form the slightest judgment whether that influence would be used for him or against him, to calm the irritation of the people or to exasperate it. He well knew that in the latter event they could do in the one way what would be far more than a match for all he could do in the other. We speak not of the irreconcilable offence which would have been given to the party so lately fighting with the insurgents, as it believed for life or death, and whose cries for the blood its fears demanded (cries not wholly unsupported, if report speak true, by the Lieutenant-Governor of Upper Canada)[*] could only have been kept in check by something which would carry with it the wiser heads of the Loyalist party itself. On the other hand, if he had tried these men by an unpacked jury, that is to say, a jury of their own party, the result would equally have been their liberation, with the character of persecuted men, and with the whole train of consequences flowing from the animosities engendered by the trial.* And was he to pack a jury? or to try them by the judges, by the men most odious to their party, without a jury? or was a court-martial to be the

---

issued a special commission for the trial of the prisoners, and sent the Attorney-General [Charles Richard Ogden] with it to Montreal." [Lambton, "Extract of a Despatch from the Earl of Durham to Lord Glenelg," *PP*, 1837–38, XXXIX, 913.] The men whom he intended to punish he intended to try; and the trial only did not take place because they pleaded guilty. There is not a single expression suggesting the most remote idea of punishment, which can fairly be applied to M. Papineau and those who had fled.

We cannot so completely exculpate the despatch from another of Mr. Roebuck's accusations. We regret that Lord Durham should, by implication, have called M. Papineau and the others the chief leaders and instigators of the revolt [*ibid*.], when he had no evidence against them but depositions *ex parte*, and when some of them, and M. Papineau in particular, positively deny the charge. But though we cannot think this justifiable, we see a wide difference between using these unguarded expressions in a confidential despatch which he could not foresee would be called for by Parliament, and what Mr. Roebuck terms "denouncing" M. Papineau "as a traitor," with "much emphasis," and "with all the formality of law." [Roebuck, "Lord Durham's Administration in Canada: Letter II," *Spectator*, 10 Nov., 1838, p. 1061.]

[*Francis Bond Head.]

*Our case, in this part of it, has been much strengthened since we formerly wrote, by the publication of the letter in which the prisoners in confinement petitioned to be disposed of without trial. As this important document has not attracted the degree of attention it merits, we reprint it.

"Montreal Gaol, June 25, 1838.

"My Lord,—We have some reason to apprehend that the expressions used by us in a letter addressed to your Lordship on the 18th instant may appear vague and ambiguous.

"Our intention, my Lord, was distinctly to avow that in pursuit of objects dear to the great mass of our population, we took a part that has eventuated in a charge of high treason.

"We professed our willingness to plead guilty, *whereby to avoid the necessity of a trial*,

resource? or a special commission appointed for the nonce? Imagine them so tried, imagine them found guilty by any of these tribunals, and of course sentenced to death, and the sentences commuted for transportation to Bermuda! What those in England, who are so bitter against Lord Durham now, would have said of him then, we know not; but when he, by what the French Canadians would have deemed a violation of all law, had procured a sentence which they would have considered to be in defiance of all justice, what chance would the persecutor of their leaders have had of gaining their confidence, what chance of winning back their affections to British rule?

Lord Durham disposed of the prisoners in the only way compatible with his policy, a policy not of *talking* about conciliation, but of *aiming* at it; and never in a similar situation did any government that we know of act with a happier union of vigour and lenity. And so it has been pronounced by as good judges of the principles of liberty as any English democrats, the people of the United States; whom this act above all others contributed to detach from the cause of Canadian separation; and (together with the assiduous cultivation of every opportunity of counteracting, by the expression of sentiments of good-will, the impression which some of his predecessors had made by the ostentatious avowal of opposite ones) has restored that peace and friendship between two great nations, which, so long as Lord Durham's policy is followed up, as the spirit of his administration shall rule in Canada, there is no danger that we should again see broken.

---

and to give, as far as in our power, tranquillity to the country; but whilst we were thus disposed to contribute to the happiness of others, we could not condescend to shield ourselves under the provisions of an ordinance passed by the late special council of the province. (Sir John Colborne's. [*Mill's identifying footnote.*]) [See "An Ordinance to Provide for the More Speedy Attainder of Persons Indicted for High Treason, Who Have Fled from the Province, or Remained Concealed Therein to Escape from Justice," *PP*, 1837-38, XXXIX, 553-4.]

"Permit us then, my Lord, to perform this great duty, to mark our entire confidence in your Lordship, to place ourselves at your disposal, without availing ourselves of provisions which would degrade us in our own eyes, by marking an unworthy distrust on both sides.

"With this short explanation of our feelings, we again place ourselves at your Lordship's discretion, and *pray that the peace of the country may not be endangered by a trial.*

"We have the honour to be, my Lord, with unfeigned respect, your Lordship's most obedient humble servants,

"R. S. M. Bouchette,   H. A. Gauvin,
Wolfred Nelson,   S. Marchesseau,
R. Des Rivières,   T. H. Goddu,
L. H. Masson,   B. Viger.

"The Right Hon. the Earl of Durham, Governor-General, &c."

Thus, then, if Lord Durham thought that the trial of the prisoners would be a public evil, by impeding the return of tranquillity, he did not stand alone in the opinion; authorities, which the friends at least of the popular party in Canada cannot reject, fully bore him out in it.

In every other act from which the spirit of his policy could be seen, the same general view of his position is apparent. His first act on entering the country, the composition of his two councils, was a declaration that he would put himself into the hands of neither party. But while he kept himself independent of both, he did not exclude either, from a share in his deliberations or in his favours. He gave, or offered, appointments to influential men on both sides,* and availed himself of the opinions of the moderate men of both, so far as they were willing to communicate them. It has been stated in print that he endeavoured, through the medium of Mr.

*Unfortunately, while his offers to influential British Canadians were commonly accepted, those to French Canadians were rejected. When Adam Thom, formerly editor of the *Montreal Herald*, was appointed an Assistant Commissioner of the Municipal Inquiry, Lord Durham made overtures of a similar nature to M. Taché, the fittest Frenchman for the purpose to be found in all Canada; but that gentleman refused, because he would not serve in the same Commission with Mr. Thom.

This appointment has been made a ground of bitter reproach against Lord Durham; and it has been asserted that Mr. Thom (though not editor at the time) was the author of the brutal paragraphs in the *Montreal Herald*, about "fattening people for the gallows." [See Roebuck, "Lord Durham's Administration in Canada: Letter III," *Spectator*, 17 Nov., 1838, pp. 1084–5. A leading article in the *Morning Chronicle*, 30 July, 1838, p. 2, also attributed the passage to the *Herald*; but see p. 426 above.] But Mr. Thom positively denies this, and we have evidence that Lord Durham disbelieved it. He found in Thom a man whom he deemed fit for his purpose, and finding few such men, it was his resolution not to pass them over. His predecessors, proceeding on a *false* notion of conciliation as he did on the true one, *excluded* the able men of each party, for fear of offending the other; and the result was that the men elevated to office were the least marked and influential men of each party—the insignificant, and the incompetent—those who, because they had done nothing, had afforded to the other party no particular ground of attack. Lord Durham has said, "I will not follow this rule. I will take into office the ablest men of each party. I will take men whom their own party confides in, never caring how obnoxious they are to their opponents. I will please the latter by taking their best men in their turn."

On the same principle he has just appointed James Stuart, one of the ablest leaders of the British party, to be Chief Justice at the King's Bench, although removed from the Attorney-Generalship by Lord Aylmer, in consequence of charges preferred against him by the Assembly. But his professional qualifications were pre-eminent; and it is not the interest even of the French, if they are to have opponents in high office, to have the feeblest and most insignificant of them, and have to struggle against hostility and imbecility combined. A stupid enemy is more to be desired than an able one, because less likely to acquire the power of doing harm; but give them the power, and it is from the stupid one that we pray heaven to defend us!

One appointment of Lord Durham's ought to be specially agreeable to those who condemn the last-mentioned:—those who, in the case of James Stuart, think the most eminent superiority of legal attainments no recommendation to a man implicated with party, ought not in the case of Mr. Arthur Buller to adopt a contrary standard, and represent legal experience as the grand consideration and impartiality as altogether secondary. Lord Durham, we have little doubt, did the best he could in both instances: he appointed Mr. Stuart for his law, Mr. Arthur Buller for his freedom from party; *both* for their ability. Those who know Mr. Arthur Buller, either privately or in his late capacity of a Charity Commissioner, are of opinion that sarcasms against frivolity and want of talent seldom were less appropriately employed.

Wakefield, to open a communication even with M. Papineau;[*] but we are informed that this is incorrect, and that Mr. Wakefield acted solely on his own prompting;[†] affording, however, by what he did, an opening to M. Papineau for fair and honourable explanation, which that gentleman, we will venture to say with more passion than judgment, rejected.* But the institutions which he was about to bestow on the colony, are what exhibit above all the superiority of his conceptions, and those of his advisers, over the peddling expedients of common-place politics. It is there that we can estimate the difference between a policy of conciliation and one of compromise; between the vulgar *juste-milieu* of mere time-servers, and that which aims at contenting all parties by being just to all. There are few statesmen in our days, who may not take a lesson from the means which Lord Durham chose for carrying with him the opinion of the majority of both races; from the system of healing measures which he devised, to detach the reasonable and disinterested portion of both parties from the unreasonable.

Though the leaders of parties have generally unworthy objects in view, their followers, as it has been often said, have almost always honest ones. Canada is no exception to this rule. Both the English and the French have grievances, which each believes that the other will not suffer to be removed. Among the demands of the French have long figured, in the most prominent place, free municipal institutions and a general system of education; and these they complain that the English will not let them have. The English want a system of registration, the commutation of feudal tenures, internal improvements, and facilities for coloniza-

[*Roebuck, "Lord Durham's Administration in Canada: Letter II," p. 1062.]
[†See Edward Gibbon Wakefield, "The French Canadians," *Spectator*, 24 Nov., 1838, p. 1109.]
*It is singular that the same persons, who attack Lord Durham for courting, as they think, the extreme loyalist party, by giving appointments to members of it, are no less bitter against him for what, on the same principle, they should approve—for endeavouring to come to some arrangement with M. Papineau, which might recal him to his country, with a prospect of his aiding instead of impeding the measures in progress towards good government and tranquillity. We must express our unaffected astonishment that any man not a rabid Ultra-Tory—much more that Mr. Roebuck [in his "Lord Durham's Administration in Canada: Letter II"]—should use language of the severest moral condemnation against Lord Durham on the imputation that, after holding forth M. Papineau to the world (say rather to Lord Glenelg) as a "leader and instigator of revolt" [Lambton, "Extract," p. 913], he sent an agent to treat with him. Is an instigator of revolt a person beyond the pale of human intercourse? and is this the new doctrine of the friends of liberty? If Lord Durham did think M. Papineau a man who rebelled against an established government, is it not a recognised fact that such may be men of the purest intentions and of the most unblemished honour? Could Lord Durham have given stronger evidence of his anxiety to be just to the French Canadians than by seeking to enter into communication with the man who best understood and had most faithfully served their objects, and whose mistrust of the English government nothing but the most straightforward dealing could give him a chance to remove?

tion; and complain that they could not get these from the French when the latter were masters of the Assembly.

We are not going to discuss the justice of these complaints; how greatly exaggerated the last are, we showed in a former article, from the evidence of Lord Gosford and his Commissioners.* But there must be some colour for them. They must have some appearance of truth, by which they are rendered credible, or they would not be serviceable even as pretexts. It is evident that disinterested English Canadians believe the one set of assertions, disinterested French Canadians the other. It is evident that the English and French generally, and not merely factious leaders on either side, see in each other the hindrance to their obtaining those improvements which impartial third parties would bestow upon them. The course, then, for Lord Durham was to seize the golden opportunity of giving to both what they were entitled to; of removing all that had occasioned heart-burning between the honest of the two parties, all that had afforded the dishonest of either a handle for misrepresentation. This was Lord Durham's duty; and to his honour be it said, this he would have done, this lesson he leaves for his successor.

The measures which were on the point of completion when his career was cut short, were four in number: all of first-rate importance, all such as ought to have been given, even though not asked for: two of them had been long demanded by the popular party, two by the English population. The first was, free municipal institutions: not only the grand instrument of honest local management, but the great "normal school" to fit a people for representative government, and which have never yet existed in Canada.[*] The preparation of this law was undertaken by Mr. Charles Buller, whose admirable speech in the House of Commons on that very subject no one can have forgotten.[†] The second measure was a comprehensive scheme of general education. The third was a Registry Act, for titles to landed property. The fourth was for the commutation of feudal tenures in Montreal, where they are peculiar, and peculiarly obnoxious to the English population.[‡] These were to be followed by others, among which the Proclamation enumerates "large and solid schemes of colonization and internal improvement," a "revision of the defective laws which regulate real property and commerce," the introduction of "a pure and competent administration of justice," the "eradication of the manifold abuses engendered by the negligence and corruption of former times, and so lamentably fostered by civil disunions."[§] These are the projects in the midst of

*See [Mill, "Radical Party and Canada,"] *London and Westminster Review* for January last, pp. 518, 524–5, and the note to p. 526. [Pp. 421, 426–8, and 429n–30n above.]

[*See "Report on the Affairs of British North America, from the Earl of Durham," *PP*, 1839, XVII, 411–68 (App. C).]

[†See Charles Buller, Speech on Municipal Corporations (Ireland) (20 Feb., 1837), *PD*, 3rd ser., Vol. 36, cols. 698–701.]

[‡See, for the "second measure," "Report," pp. 475–658 (App. D); for the third, pp. 676–90 (in App. E); for the fourth, pp. 660–73 (in App. E).]

[§Lambton, "Proclamation," p. 3.]

which Lord Durham has been interrupted; these the services, which Parliament thought fit to take from him the power of rendering. We know it is one thing to aim at these noble objects, another thing to accomplish them; we cannot tell with what degree of skill he, or his advisers, would have performed a task, difficult, without much trial and experience, even to the ablest men. But how many English statesmen can be named, capable of rising to the conception of such objects? Is there one other who, in Lord Durham's situation, would have had the public spirit and courage even to attempt the realization of them?

Passing now from what is known of Lord Durham's projects to what is only believed, to the scheme, so far as yet matured, which he is understood to have had in view for the future constitution of the colony;[*] this, too, so far as anything is known of it, is constructed upon the same great principle of impartial justice; the removal of all real evils; the satisfaction of the just demands of either side. The French sought to be freed from the *incubus* of a Legislative Council, a second chamber, representing neither the English nor the French population, neither the colony nor the mother country, but possessing a veto on every proposal emanating from either, and which it actually exercised against measures equally desired by both.[†] From this grievance it is understood that Lord Durham was prepared to relieve them.* The English complained that the French of Lower Canada, by their majority in the House of Assembly, possessed a veto on all measures which concerned the five colonies collectively; that the navigation of the St. Lawrence, the roads and canals, the post office and custom regulations, of all British America, were under the control of a portion of the people of one colony, who had no good-will, it was affirmed, either to commerce or colonization, and who, aiming at a separate nationality, were rather hostile than friendly to the improvement of the purely British provinces. Lord Durham's plan took such affairs entirely out of their cognizance, and placed them and all matters of common concernment under a federal body, to be chosen by all the provinces, and subject, in the same manner with the local legislatures, to the veto of the mother country. This project, the principle of which so exactly met the difficulties of the case, that every one who has sincerely applied his mind to an amicable adjustment, has hit upon it—that for a moment it united the suffrages of Mr. Roebuck and of Lord John Russell[‡]—had the further advantage, that it was the only legitimate means

[*See "Report," pp. 110–16.]

[†Cf. *ibid.*, pp. 116–17.]

*It has been recently asserted that this part of Lord Durham's plan has been given up. [See Roebuck, "Lord Durham's Administration in Canada: Letter III," pp. 1084–5, quoting a published letter by Adam Thom.] We should most deeply lament such an abandonment, and are convinced that it could only have been thought of, if at all, as a concession to some imaginary necessity. But the statement does not rest upon sufficient authority to entitle it to credence.

[‡See Roebuck, Speech on the Affairs of Canada (5 Feb., 1838), *PD*, 3rd ser., Vol. 40, col. 770; and John Russell, Speech on the Affairs of Canada (16 Jan., 1838), *ibid.*, col. 11.]

of destroying the so-much-talked-of nationality of the French Canadians. It would compel them to consider themselves, not as a separate family, but an integral portion of a larger body; it would merge their nationality of race in a nationality of country; instead of French Canadians it would make them British Americans; and this without bringing into their house and home, into their social and domestic relations, the customs of another people (which, whether practised on all of them or on a part, would be one of the last excesses of despotism), or establishing, as hitherto, over not only their necks but those of the English population, a petty oligarchy of the latter.

The mode in which the suffrage was to be regulated under the proposed constitution has not yet transpired, and we cannot, for this and other reasons, at present pronounce an opinion upon the scheme as a whole. There will be time enough and materials enough for discussing what must be the principal topic of the approaching session of Parliament. In the mean time let us come to the questions—was Lord Durham justified in resigning? and, if he resigned, can the manner be defended in which he published to the colony the reasons of his resignation?[*]

We think that he was justified. When a man has had grievous cause given him for resentment it is easy to accuse him of being actuated by it. But we see no ground for any such imputation. We see nothing in his conduct which is not defensible on public grounds. He declares that the moral force and consideration of his government were gone. What else was to be expected? The attacks in Parliament, the mere vituperation of his enemies, he could have stood; but to have the first and only completed act of his government annulled, was to strike with impotence all that he could thereafter do. If men at the distance of half the globe, in utter ignorance of the facts of the case and the situation of the colony, at the dictation of personal enmity and party spite, were suffered to overset one of his acts, his friends not merely looking on tamely, but, after a few deprecatory words, actually turning round to aid in the deed, and themselves giving the mortal blow—what better fate could he expect for any other of his proceedings? If the Conservative House so treated his Conservative measure, what hope was there for his Radical ones? Facts, which he did not then know, have justified his anticipations. On the very day preceding that which brought the news of his retirement, the chief newspaper organ at once of the Ministry and of the English Canadian party, fulminated an anathema against his plan of a federal legislature;[†] and it is some consolation for the abrupt close of his government, when we see that, however wisely his plans might have been formed, he would not have been suffered to carry them. The coalition between the Tory party at home, and those who are Liberals at home and Tories in the colonies—between the enemies of a representative constitution altogether, and the enemies of any which does not make the minority preponder-

[*See Lambton, "Proclamation," p. 3.]
[†Leading Article on Canada, *Morning Chronicle*, 17 Oct., 1838, p. 2.]

ant—would have been too strong for Lord Durham at the distance of half the globe; and the battle for good government in Canada, as well as for reform in Great Britain, will have to be fought here. Add, too, that Parliament, while showing so patriotic a zeal for keeping him within his powers, declined to render those powers sufficient; the ground assigned for the refusal being expressly the *unfitness* of Lord Durham to have that extension of power which Lord Melbourne at first solicited, but meekly withdrew his prayer without waiting for its rejection.

Lord Durham saw that he could do no good in Canada if the every-day weapon of a faction for making war upon another, its engine for working its adversaries out and itself in, was to be a presumptuous interference with his administration; and he felt that if his friends were not prepared to back him better, they should have looked out for a man who had no enemies.

Such measures as those which he had in view required, as he truly says, "all the strength which the cordial and stedfast support of the authorities at home can alone give to their distant authorities; all the moral force" that could be derived by a government

from the assurance that its acts would be final, and its engagements religiously observed . . . . Of what avail are the purposes and promises of a delegated power, whose acts are not respected by the authority from which it proceeds? With what confidence can I invite co-operation, or impose forbearance, whilst I touch ancient laws and habits, as well as deep-rooted abuses, with the weakened hands that have ineffectually essayed but a little more than the ordinary vigour of the police of troubled times?[*]

But the Proclamation! We are not surprised at the cry which has been raised against this noble and plain-spoken document. We can conceive what gall and wormwood,[†] to a certain class of official men, a state paper must be, so "remarkable" (it has been well said) "for its disregard of conventional usages, and its contemptuous treatment of the mysteries of state-craft."[‡] To speak so much truth to the governed concerning their government, has been not unnaturally reprobated, as contrary to all rule—as an embarrassment wantonly thrown in the path of his successor—an appeal to the public of the colony from the government at home—a sacrifice of the tranquillity of the province to childish pique.

We wonder that those who are in so much haste to call the Proclamation inflammatory, do not ask themselves what there was for it to inflame? Whether all upon whom the topics introduced into it could have any inflammatory effect, were not already roused to such a pitch of indignation, that the calm though feeling manner in which their sentiments were responded to by the Governor-General, was more calculated to temper than to add fuel to the fire? It can hardly be supposed that those who hanged Lords Brougham and Melbourne in effigy, and who voted

[*Lambton, "Proclamation," p. 3.]
[†Cf. Lamentations, 3:19.]
[‡Leading Article on Lord Durham, *Spectator*, 10 Nov., 1838, p. 1053.]

the addresses and passed the resolutions of which such multitudes have reached us, waited to form their opinion on the affront to Lord Durham until he told them that it was one. His address was no "appeal" to them; their sentence was already pronounced. The whole scope and object of the Proclamation has been carelessly misapprehended. It was not a complaint; there was no more complaint in it than was unavoidable. Its purpose, its declared purpose, was to explain the reasons of his retirement. All the addresses, all the resolutions, were solicitations to him to retain the government: the Proclamation was his answer.

If the only use of making this explanation had been to gratify personal feelings, by guarding his motives from misconstruction, then, as there would have been no public good to be attained, private sentiments, however creditable, might have found a more appropriate expression through private channels. But it was not as a mere matter of individual feeling that it was important for him to retain the confidence of all among the Canadian people who had bestowed it upon him. Though no longer their Governor, his connexion with them was not to cease; upon him it was to devolve to watch over their interests in England; he was the only man in the kingdom of first-rate political influence, the only man ever thought of as minister, or as a party leader, who did not at that moment stand convicted, in the minds of those whom he was addressing, of the grossest ignorance of all the circumstances of the colony, and the most presumptuous incapacity in legislating for it. When this last specimen of presumption and incapacity was making the whole British population of both the Canadas join with the French Canadians in denouncing the principle of distant colonial government, and the very officials talk familiarly of a separation, was it nothing to show to Canada that there was one British statesman who could understand her wants and feel for her grievances —that from any councils in the mother country in which *he* had influence she might expect justice—and that the man, on whose constancy and magnanimity so much depended, was not throwing up his mission from personal disgust, but returning to England because the manœuvres of his enemies had changed the place where he could serve them from Quebec to the House of Lords?

Viewed in this light, it seems to us that the Proclamation, with all in it that has been inveighed against—the ungrudging acknowledgment of past misgovernment and present abuses—the disclosure of his generous schemes for the improvement of the laws and administration, and for conferring "on an united people," not a restricted, but "a more extensive enjoyment of free and responsible government"[*]—so far from needing an apology, points out Lord Durham, beyond almost anything else which he has done, as the fit leader for the great Reform party of the empire. The proclamation was the necessary complement and winding up of his short administration—the explanation which was due to the people of Canada for the past, and the best legacy which he could leave to them for the future. So far

[*Lambton, "Proclamation," p. 3.]

from being inflammatory, it was in all probability the only kind of address to the people, which, in the then state of men's minds, could have had any healing effect.

As we have said all along, the main end of his administration was the reconciliation of the two parties, by exhibiting to both, embodied in a series of measures, a policy which, by satisfying the just claims of both, should convince them that there was no necessity for their being enemies—that both might hope for justice under a government knowing no distinction between them. If this, the one thing needful, was now debarred him by the mother country, was it not the next best thing, since he could not leave healing *measures*, to leave healing *principles* behind him? Next to *doing* the noble things spoken of in the proclamation, to point them out as fit to be done, was the thing most calculated—was the one thing calculated—to restore harmony in the colony. If the policy there chalked out is that on which alone a reconciliation of parties and races can be founded; then, since he could not give them the policy itself, he has done well and wisely in giving them the hope of such a policy; in giving them the idea of it, as a possible thing, as the thing which they should strive for, instead of separation, or the mere predominance of their own side; and which, as far as his influence reaches, he will yet help them to obtain.

These considerations are still further strengthened if we reflect in what position the disallowance of the ordinance found Lord Durham with respect to the French Canadians. He had as yet done nothing to redress what they deemed their grievances. His plans for their benefit, like all his other plans of general improvement, were yet unfinished; and they were a people too little accustomed to good treatment from their rulers to give their confidence until earned by actual benefits. Lord Durham had done enough to convince the more intelligent and experienced people of the United States—not enough to convince the French Canadians. Of the amnesty, qualified by the ordinance, they knew not at first what to think; but when they learnt from the despatch laid before Parliament that "Sir John Colborne and the heads of what is called the British party"[*] had approved of it, from that moment (we know the fact) the French, though previously undecided, deemed it their part to disapprove of it. This was mere prejudice in them; if Lord Durham could carry the British party with him in clemency to the French, the greater was the credit due to him; and having to give an account of his measure in a quarter where lenity was more likely to be imputed to it than severity, he naturally availed himself of the fact that it had obtained the acquiescence of those whose error was not likely to be on the lenient side. But when we consider how the French Canadians have seen governor after governor become the tool of the officials, and how seldom the two parties have concurred in approving of the same measures, we cannot wonder that a governor who had done but one great act, and that act in

[*Lambton, "Extract of a Despatch," p. 913.]

concert, as it now appeared, with the dominant faction, should not yet have made much progress in attaching the other party to his government.

If, then, Lord Durham had left matters in this state; if he had departed leaving no explanation to the Canadians of his principles and of his ulterior purposes, he would have gone away without doing a single act which could prove to the French population that there existed a British statesman willing to redress their grievances, and without giving a single lesson to the English party of what was due to the French. We maintain that, surrounded as he was at the last by the English inhabitants—leaving the country amidst the mingled sound of their plaudits and their lamentations, while the bulk of the French Canadians kept sullenly aloof—he had, from all these causes, an appearance of being the man of a party, of giving his countenance to the exclusive principles of a class, which appearance he was bound to throw off—from which it would have been criminal in him not to have taken the most direct means of freeing himself. And we foretel that his having done so will yet be found to be the greatest thing yet done to facilitate the settlement of Canada on a basis just, and therefore capable of being permanent. The whole English population are now committed, as far as the strongest public demonstrations can commit them, to the policy of a man, who has told them unambiguously and minutely, and in a manner admitting of no misunderstanding, that his plans involve full justice to the French Canadians. They have invested with their confidence, they have acknowledged as their virtual representative, the man who is identified with the principle of conciliation instead of coercion, of equal justice to all instead of the predominance of the few over the many. The English population has stood up openly as a distinct body from the jobbing official *clique* which has hitherto assumed to be its representative; and it may be hoped that the settlement of Canada which they will now exert themselves for, will be conceived under the inspiration of Lord Durham rather than that of the late legislative council.

It is time to conclude. We have attempted to do justice to the absent—to show that, instead of having done anything to justify the clamour which has been raised from so many discordant quarters against them, Lord Durham and his advisers, so far as their conduct can yet be judged of, have displayed qualities among the rarest to be found in English politicians, and which, wheresoever found, conspicuously mark out the possessors for that station at the head of the Reform party which the present Ministers have thought fit to abandon. But their defence is now in their own hands. They will soon be here, not only to combat their enemies, but to perform the more important duty of expounding their own views; and we shall not be long without full opportunity of judging whether Lord Durham is equal to the great destiny to which he is called (and which is not a destiny for any man who cannot give active guidance), or is wanting in the courage to claim it, or the energy and skill for its achievement.

Meanwhile, he has been thwarted, but he has not failed. He has shown how Canada ought to be governed; and if anything can allay her dissensions, and again attach her to the mother country, this will. He has at the critical moment taken the initiative of a healing policy; that which seeks popularity, not by courting it, but by deserving it, and conciliation, not by compromise, but by justice—by giving to everybody, not the half of what he asks, but the whole of what he ought to have. If this example had not been set at that juncture, the colony was lost; having been set, it may be followed, and the colony may be saved. He has disposed of the great immediate embarrassment, the political offenders. He has shown to the well-intentioned of both sides an honourable basis on which they may accommodate their differences. He has detached from the unreasonable of one party their chief support, the sympathy of the United States; and it is reserved for him to detach from the unreasonable of the other the sympathy of the people of England. He comes home master of the details of those abuses which he has recognized as the original causes of the disaffection; prepared to expose these as they have never before been exposed, and to submit to Parliament, after the most comprehensive inquiry which has ever taken place, the system on which the North American Colonies may be preserved and well governed hereafter.

If this be failure, failure is but the second degree of success; the first and highest degree may be yet to come.

REORGANIZATION OF THE REFORM PARTY

1839

EDITOR'S NOTE

London and Westminster Review, XXXII (Apr., 1839), 475–508. Headed: "ART. VIII.—["Marvell Redivivus."] *A Letter to the Earl of Durham on Reform in Parliament, by Paying the Elected*. London: [Sherwood, Gilbert, and Piper,] 1839." Running titles: left-hand, as title; right-hand (page and line equivalents in this edition), "Conservatives and Radicals" (468.20–469.13), "The Landholders" (470.8–471.5), "Small Proprietors" (471.41–472.36), "The Great Capitalists" (473.29–474.23), "The Middle Classes" (475.17–476.12), "Dissenters and Church Reformers" (477.6–40), "The Durham Policy" (478.33–479.25), "Divisions of Reformers" (480.19–481.12), "Universal Suffrage" (482.6–41), "Grievances of the Working Classes" (483.34–484.29 and 487.17–488.14), "Opinions of the Working Classes" (485.23–486.22), "Catholics and Voluntaries" (489.9–490.6), "Church Reformers" (490.41–491.34), "The Voluntaries" (492.31–493.27), and "Church Reform" (494.22–495.18). Signed "A." Not republished. Identified in Mill's bibliography as "An article headed 'Reorganization of the Radical [*sic*] Party' in the London and Westminister Review for April 1839 (No 63)" (MacMinn, 51). In the Somerville College copy (tear-sheets) there are four emendations (which are adopted in this edition): "modern" changed to "moderate" (467.10); "trio" changed to "threefold" (493.22); "principles" altered to "principle" (493.40); and "compound" corrected to "confound" (494.11). For comment on the essay, see xlvi and lx above.

Reorganization of the Reform Party

THE RADICALS have hitherto exhibited the spectacle of a great body of men without policy, leader, organization, concert, or simultaneous efforts. They must be mere material to make tools of, if they continue in this position one moment after they can get out of it. Their whole strength in the country has never been called forth, because no immediate purpose has ever been presented to them in which they all felt an equal interest—for which they were all equally impelled to exert themselves.

When we call the party which we desire to see formed, a Radical party, we mean not to circumscribe it by any partial or sectional limitation. We call it Radical because the moderate Radicals are in possession of a part of the ground on which it is necessary that the combination should be built; because the measures with which they, and we may add, with which any leader they may select, must be identified—the Ballot and Household Suffrage, or something equivalent to it, are a portion of those which must be comprehended in the practical policy of such a party. But we well know that the Reform party of the empire ought not to be, cannot be, Radical in any narrow or sectarian sense. There may be many *coteries* in a country, but there can be only two parties. What we must have to oppose to the great Conservative party is the whole Liberal party, not some mere section of it,—a combination which shall exclude no shade of opinion in which one sober or practicable man can be found,—one man capable of adapting rational means to honest ends; a phalanx, stretching from the Whig-Radicals at one extremity (if we may so term those among the persons calling themselves Whigs who are real Liberals) to the Ultra-Radicals and the Working Classes on the other.

Such a phalanx has existed; and by its support the Grey Ministry was enabled to carry the Reform Bill. We wish to see this great party reconstructed. We are persuaded that it can be, and that to accomplish this it only requires a popular leader. People are ready to cry out that it is impossible, because it is indeed no longer possible *by the same means*; but is not this what every rational view of politics would prepare us for? Was it ever known in history that the same thing took place twice in exactly the same manner? To find the means of accomplishing what *borné* politicians pronounce impracticable, is the test of statesmanship: we do not even think that the difficulties to be overcome in this instance are a very severe trial of it. It is a case for moral qualities, fully as much as for intellectual. A Lafayette will find his way to the object sooner than a Talleyrand. Straightforwardness and singleness of purpose, and the energy of a strong will, aided by sufficient knowledge of the state of opinions in Great Britain and Ireland, and of the peculiarities of the different classes of society, are the main requisites. And a very moderate degree of that knowledge is sufficient to point out, that it is not time to declare the object impracticable, since the means which are alone proper for attaining it have not yet been tried. What those means are, it is the purpose of the present article to investigate.

Our aim in this inquiry is altogether practical. We intend no doctrinal discussion. That a reform in many of the institutions of this country is needful, that the pursuit of such reform is a laudable undertaking, that there will never more be peace or content in this country without it, are propositions which we shall allow to rest upon their own evidence: we are not now addressing ourselves to any persons by whom they are denied, nor is this the time for stating how far, in our own opinion, the changes in the existing order of things ought to go. The question is not now about particular reforms, but how to carry on the Reform movement; not whose are the best ideas of reform, but how to plant the firmest footing for reform in general. Radicalism has done enough in speculation; its business now is to make itself practical. Most reformers are tolerably well aware of their ends; let them turn to what they have hitherto far less attended to—how to attain them. No reformer can hope to realize any reforms of importance but by means of a strong and united Reform party. To form this, must be an object paramount in the mind of each to the pursuit of his particular aims, because it is a condition precedent to them all; and we are either much mistaken, or this object will exact from every class of Reformers far less sacrifice or even postponement of their particular aims than is commonly thought, and that what is required from each is a better knowledge and juster appreciation of the opinions and feelings of his allies, rather than any compromise of his own.

Let us examine, then, what is the available strength of the Reform party; what proportion it collectively bears to that of our adversaries; and of what component parts that strength is made up; that we may have a clear view of the elements to be combined, and of the nature of the hindrances to their combining; and may know what are the obstacles to be overcome, in order to the organization of the party for powerful and systematic action on a combined plan.

Who, then, are the natural Radicals of the country, and who are the natural opponents of Radicalism? We use the words "natural Radicals," and "natural opponents of Radicalism," as an index to our whole mode of looking at this subject. One is constantly hearing of "reaction," or of "the progress of opinion;" of the growth, or spread, one day of Radicalism, another day of Conservatism; and newspapers are perpetually comparing notes about registrations, and municipal elections, to ascertain which of the two principles is gaining upon the other. How inconclusive such evidences are, has been very often pointed out. For our part we have hardly any belief in reactions, and but little in any growth of political opinion, whether Radical or Conservative, but the growth in numbers, intelligence, and wealth, of the classes who are already, and from the circumstances of their position, Radicals or Conservatives. Men change sides on particular questions, as their views change as to the point at which they can, or should, make their stand for their party; as the Duke of Wellington changed his opinion on the Catholic claims. But we know of no instances in our time, and have read of few in history (except in seasons of panic, which in this as in other respects produce strange phenomena) where a great and sudden movement took place in the feelings of a people, either towards Radicalism or Conservatism. We have known, it is true, many instances, and in these times can seldom be long without them, when circumstances have suddenly called out masses of Conservative or Radical feeling which already existed, from a passive state into an active. The real amount of either feeling which exists in our own country, at least, we believe to be at all periods much the same; saving the gradual changes, which the natural laws of the progress of society bring about.

In order to estimate the strength of the two parties, we must consider the permanent causes which are operating upon each of the separate divisions that compose the nation, and determining it towards the one party or the other: and these permanent causes (speaking as we are of bodies of men, and not of remarkable individuals) are for the most part to be looked for in their personal interests, or in their class feelings. We are the last persons to undervalue the power of moral convictions. But the convictions of the mass of mankind run hand in hand with their interests or with their class feelings. We have a strong faith, stronger than either politicians or philosophers generally have, in the influence of reason and virtue over men's minds; but it is in that of the reason and virtue on their own side of the question; in the ascendancy which may be exercised over them for their good, by the best and wisest persons of their own creed. We expect few conversions by the mere force of reason, from one creed to the other. Men's intellects and hearts have a large share in determining what *sort* of Conservatives or Liberals they will be; but it is their position (saving individual exceptions) which makes them Conservatives or Liberals.

If we would find, then, the line of distinction between the two parties, we must look out for another line of demarcation; we must find out who are the Privileged Classes, and who are the Disqualified. The former are the natural Conservatives of the country; the latter are the natural Radicals.

The Privileged Classes are all those who are contented with their position; who think that the institutions of the country work well for them; who feel that they have all the influence, or more than the influence, in the present order of things, which they could expect under any other; who enjoy a degree of consideration in society which satisfies their ambition, and find the legislature prompt to lend an ear to their complaints, and if they feel anything as an inconvenience to endeavour to devise a remedy for it. All, in short, who feel secure that their interests will not be postponed to those of other people, and still more all who feel secure that the interests of other people will be postponed to theirs, compose the Conservative body. Those who feel and think the reverse of all this are the Disqualified Classes. All who feel oppressed, or unjustly dealt with, by any of the institutions of the country; who are taxed more heavily than other people, or for other people's benefit; who have, or consider themselves to have, the field of employment for their pecuniary means or their bodily or mental faculties unjustly narrowed; who are denied the importance in society, or the influence in public affairs, which they consider due to them as a class, or who feel debarred as individuals from a fair chance of rising in the world; especially if others, in whom they do not recognize any superiority of merit, are artificially exalted above their heads: these compose the natural Radicals; to whom must be added a large proportion of those who, from whatever cause, are habitually ill at ease in their pecuniary circumstances; the sufferers from low wages, low profits, or want of employment: for even if they do not impute their situation to the government, they almost always think that the government could, if it chose, do something to relieve them; and, at all events, finding themselves ill off as they are, think they should not fare worse and would stand a chance of faring better under a change.

Let us proceed to make an inventory of these several classes, and begin with the Conservatives.

At the head of the Privileged, or in other words, the Satisfied Classes, must be placed the landed interest. They have the strongest reason possible for being satisfied with the government; they *are* the government. It was said without exaggeration before the Reform Bill, it may be repeated with very little exaggeration even yet, that the English Government is an oligarchy of landholders. They compose the House of Lords exclusively. In the House of Commons they possess the representation of the counties, and of most of the small towns. On all questions which interest them as landholders, and on which the Whig and Tory portion of them are united, their majority in the House of Commons is irresistible. That this power does not lie idle in their hands, the Corn Laws are an instance, intelligible to every capacity. And never was the fact more signally illustrated than in the last session of Parliament, on the occasion which Mr. Charles Villiers termed, in a spirited speech, the East Retford of the Corn Laws.[*] On the eve of the most decided scarcity of the last twenty years, a majority refused, not the admission of foreign corn to the home market, but the paltry permission to grind it here for re-exportation: a trifle, which did not even, to the extent of a trifle, infringe upon their monopoly, which did not encroach one hair's-breadth upon the right

[*Charles Pelham Villiers, Speech on Bonded Corn (9 May, 1838), *PD*, 3rd ser., Vol. 42, col. 1042.]

they arrogate to make their countrymen eat dear bread for their benefit: but against which the objection urged was, that in some case which was just conceivable, some remote or possible danger might chance to accrue, of an encroachment in some other way upon that insulting claim. Their fancies go before all other people's most substantial interests. If we desire other examples, the embarrassment is solely in the choice. The whole course of legislation has ever, and does now, run wholly in their favour. Not content with selling dear, they must borrow cheap; and in that hope—a fallacious one after all—the usury laws, abolished for the trading classes, are still kept up for the benefit of the landholders. Their land descends without probate or legacy duty, and is very incompletely liable to the claims of their creditors. When it comes to their turn to be creditors, they have secured to themselves the preference over all others (except the tax-gatherer) by the power of distraining for rent: all other people must first go to law—they may come at once on the premises and take. As the owners of advowsons, the endowments of the church of England are in reality theirs; they it is who, by converting the cure of souls into a family property, have made the Christian ministry the provision for the fool or profligate of a family,—for those who, being too stupid, or too idle, or too vicious to work, are fit only for an "easy life." The abuses of the church are the patrimony of the younger children of the landowners. Again, the government of the rural districts is altogether in their hands; as justices in quarter sessions they vote the taxes, control all the expenditure, decide without appeal a majority of all the causes, civil and criminal, which are tried in this country. As magistrates sitting singly or in petty sessions, not a police officer can move but by their warrant, not an act of administration can be done of which they have not the direct control. Accordingly they enjoy all the importance which appertains everywhere to the class that wields the powers of government. What the noble is in Austria, and the placeman in France, the landed proprietor is in England. A landowner and a man of consequence are synonymous. To become a landowner is what every one is looking to who desires to rise—is the test of having risen. It is the boast of America to be "a fine country for poor people;" if England cannot say as much, she may pride herself, however, on being the paradise of country gentlemen: they, with a luxury and comfort enjoyed by their class in no other country, combine a personal importance comparable only to that of the high nobility elsewhere, and the richest of them are from time to time aggregated to the nobility of their own country.

That the body for whose interest the present order of things is all contrived, should be Conservative of that order of things, can surprise nobody. The landholders, as a class, are generally unqualified Tories; those who are not so, mostly belong to the Conservative Whigs, differing from Tories in little but in hereditary personal connexions and in name. Neither among the landholders, nor among those whom the landholders can influence, could the party which we desire to see constituted, hope to find any great portion of its strength. These classes constitute, on the contrary, and will continue to constitute, the main body of the force which that party has to contend against.

Yet even on this, their weakest point, the Reformers are not altogether unsupported; nor need they, even on the present system of open voting, give up all the county elections for lost. First, it is only the *great* landed proprietors that are hostile. The small proprietors are on our side. On the Corn Laws indeed, but on the Corn Laws only, they have a common interest with the great landholders. In every other respect they belong to the natural Radicals. They are not rich, and derive no benefit from the privileges of riches; while they are more independent than any other persons can possibly be who are not rich, in a country where all power goes along with wealth. Wherever any considerable number remain of what were once the pride of England,—her yeomanry; wherever the multiplication of large fortunes, and the eagerness of men of fortune to buy land, has not yet extinguished the class of small proprietors, there the county elections return Liberals. It was this class which gave Sir James Graham so disagreeable a lesson in Cumberland. It is a similar class, in the part of Yorkshire nearest to Cumberland, that gives Mr. Cayley his majority; and in West Kent, that, in spite of the strongest influences, succeeds in returning Mr. Hodges. He is a shallow politician who imagines that the mere possession of land makes men Conservative. In France the Liberal deputies are mostly sent by the small proprietors of the agricultural departments, while the great manufacturers and merchants form the Conservative party. In every country in which landed property is much divided, the land will be on the side of democracy; as they well know who fight for primogeniture and entail as the bulwarks of Toryism, the main stay of an aristocratic constitution.

In addition to the small proprietors, the Reformers may claim another class connected with the land, who bear a strong affinity to small proprietors, the class of prosperous farmers with long leases. This class, rare in the south of England, where most of the farmers are tenants-at-will, is more frequent in the north, and in Scotland almost universal. Nearly every farmer in Scotland holds his land on lease, and feels himself almost as independent of his landlord as his landlord is of him. Accordingly, even under the unexciting circumstances of the last general election, full half the Members returned for the Scotch counties were Liberals. Such facts show the real value of the assertion one often hears, that the agricultural constituencies are at heart Tories, and would, even under the protection of the Ballot, send Tories to Parliament. Wherever the electors are in a position to declare their real sentiments we find them Liberals. The yeomanry are Liberals; and so are the farmers, in the country of long leases; and it is well known that everywhere in Scotland, except at Edinburgh, a Liberal and a Radical are synonymous. The tenants-at-will are not made of different stuff from the tenants for a term, or the small proprietors. The Ballot might not at first produce upon them its full effect, for habitual servitude leaves its traces on the mind as fetters do on the limbs; but a few years would make them feel their freedom as those feel it who have always enjoyed it. The slavish deference for their landlord, the notion that their vote goes with their rent, and is to be exercised at the landlord's pleasure, has sustained far too many shocks of late years, to have much strength left; and the English farmer will not, when no longer in the alternative of servility or ruin, be long found on a different side from the Scotch farmer and the English yeoman.

We have mentioned two classes connected with the land, whose co-operation a real Liberal party might even now count upon for giving it a majority in a general election. There is a third class, which, in a muster of our strength, is by no means to be neglected—the owners and occupiers of land connected with towns, or in the manufacturing or mining districts equivalent to towns. The number of persons thus situated who are county electors, though much reduced by the Reform Bill, is still considerable, and the rapid growth of the towns and of manufacturers makes the class an increasing one. The numerous small manufacturing towns not enfranchised by the Reform Bill furnish many of them; the potteries, and the mining districts, many more; and the class includes those who raise garden produce and other articles for the markets of the towns, and whose interest is not identical with that of the agriculturists generally, but with that of the town population. The body thus composed has even now a preponderant influence in not a few county elections. It returns both members for the West Riding of Yorkshire; and it still gives to the Liberals three of the four members for Cornwall, three of the four members for Durham. It will give us the members for Middlesex and Surrey, for South Lancashire, Glamorganshire, Warwickshire, Somersetshire, whenever the electors are appealed to at a critical moment, in a cause worthy of their efforts.

Besides these various classes, there are among the landowners many individuals of fortune and consequence, who though belonging by their interests to the Conservative side, are attached by their sentiments to Liberalism. In all privileged classes there are individuals whom some circumstance of a personal nature has alienated from their class, while there are others sufficiently generous and enlightened to see the interest of their class in the promotion of the general interest, and to desire it by no other means. Such were the glorious minority of the French *noblesse* in the States General of 1789; forty-five names, almost every one of which has made itself remembered for some personal merit. There are men of a similar description in this country, some of them possessing sufficient influence of wealth, and weight of character, to decide many a wavering vote in the House of Commons, and turn the balance of many an election. Lord Durham is such a man. Lord Fitzwilliam, Lord Radnor, are such men. Among the most valued adherents of the present Ministry some such are to be found, in whose sentiments, so far as known to the public, there is nothing to preclude them from bearing a part in the formation of a Liberal party such as we hope to see. Lord Spencer, for instance,

Lord Normanby,—may we not add, Lord Howick?—are far too precious to such a party not to be cordially welcomed to it, and if it be such as we wish it to be, it will be one to which they may honestly belong.

On the whole, although a large majority of the county members will remain Conservatives, at least during the continuance of open voting, we cannot, even after allowing for the presumable defection of the Conservative Whigs, reckon the minority that might be obtained in the English and Welsh counties by the Liberal party, at a general election held under circumstances of excitement, at fewer than forty-five or fifty, which is about the number that after an election held without any excitement at all, support the present Ministry.

To return to the Conservatives. The landowners, as we have already said, form their main strength. To the landowners, however, must be added (saving, as before, individual exceptions) nearly the whole class of very rich men. It is true, no other class of rich men find the legislature ever at their back, ready to make all its powers instrumental to the promotion of their class interests: no other class has the same actual participation in the direct business of government: nor has the man of great monied or mercantile wealth quite so much political influence or consideration in society as the great landowner has. But every rich man may be a landowner if he please; he expects, and intends, if not a landholder himself, to be the founder of a family of landholders; he looks upon himself as already belonging to the class, and cherishes its privileges, as he does those of the Peerage—as of personal interest to him, since they may one day be his own. A similar observation applies to the professions which partake of aristocracy,—the army, the navy, the bar. The heads of all the three professions rank with the aristocracy; the two former consist originally of the sons and brothers of the landowners. All these professions have moreover a direct interest adverse to the spirit of Reform. The army and navy fear retrenchment and injury to their prospects; and dislike generally the new ideas of the times; for this reason, among others, that the tendency of the new ideas is hostile to war. The lawyers fear law reform, which would render much of their hardly-acquired learning valueless, and though it would greatly add to the general amount of business of the profession, would, at least they think so, diminish the value of the great prizes. The army and navy therefore, with nearly all the leaders and a numerical majority of the bar, are generally Conservatives. To these it is scarcely necessary to add, the beneficed clergy of the Church of England, both in possession and in expectancy. They have been told, as everybody else is told, that the Church is part and parcel of the Constitution; and it is so much the most peccant part, that reform, they needs must feel, cannot creep into any other part and pass by this. Accordingly no other of the privileged classes is so intensely Tory, upon the whole, as the beneficed clergy. There *are* indeed in the Church, and even in the highest ranks of it, men to whom the labour is more precious than the reward, and who would care little for any risk which the temporalities of the Church might run in the attempt to make it spiritually what it professes to be. But of these hereafter: of these a large proportion may be claimed for the Reformers.

We are not aware of having omitted any important element of the Conservative strength; unless, indeed, it be the protected trades, those who share with the landowner the privilege of taxing the community to keep up their own prices; the shipping interest, the timber interest, the West India interest. These three in particular have long been the main pillars of Toryism among the commercial classes; for, like the Church of England clergy, they have been so long attacked, and with so much effect, as to feel that if the time ever comes for a general yielding up of exclusive privileges, theirs must be among the first to go.

Against these various denominations of Privileged Classes, of people who thrive under existing institutions better than they would hope to thrive under any probable change, and who are, therefore, the natural Conservatives of the country, we are now to set in array the classes who are dissatisfied with their position, and who compose the natural Radicals.

To begin with the middle classes. In almost every division of them the majority are on the side of change. The same cause which makes the landlords Conservatives, makes the bulk of the manufacturing and mercantile classes Reformers. The chief exceptions are the protected trades, and, as already mentioned, the very rich manufacturers and merchants of all denominations; though even these have sources of dissatisfaction in common with the rest. The class, as a class, feel that they have not justice done them by existing institutions. Their most essential interests are made to give way to the idlest fears, the most silly prejudices of the landowners. To keep up rents, and under a mistaken notion too of their being in reality much kept up, the profits of capital are brought down by the Corn Laws to the lowest scale; foreign nations whose produce we will not take, are unable to take our manufactures, and those who can, are provoked to enact retaliatory laws against us, and to establish manufactures which are treading upon the heels of ours. We are driven, or in yearly apprehension of being driven, out of one market after another. Our small capitalists are emigrating in numbers, because they can no longer live upon their profits. The difficulty of subsisting on the proceeds of a moderate capital, whether in business or at interest, continually increases. The field of employment becomes more and more crowded; contracted artificially by the Corn Laws. And this is not a casual evil, the result of a passing error, which can be remedied by the mere progress of discussion. Discussion has done its work; the obstacle lies deeper than it can reach. The landlords are masters of the legislature. They know their power; they have the manufacturers down, and they mean to keep them down. The heads of the agricultural party boast of the working of the Corn Laws. They triumph in having secured to themselves by these laws the full profit of a season of scarcity. They have their hands upon the loaf on every man's table, and will not let it go; and their organs load with abuse the "grasping capitalists," because they had rather not be ruined to fatten the landowners. The Corn Laws may be got rid of; but it can only be through a further Parliamentary Reform. The last reform left almost unabated the master-evil, the preponderance of the Corn Law interest. And the manufacturers and merchants will have to learn what the working classes have already learnt—that they must combine to agitate, not against the Corn Laws, but against the source of the Corn Laws, as well as of every other grievance—the vicious constitution of the legislature.

The bulk of the middle classes of the towns, the ten-pound electors, are still more universally Reformers. They are the greatest sufferers of all by low profits, and an overcrowded field of employment. They belong almost universally to the "uneasy classes." They are nearly all of them struggling either against the difficulty of subsisting, or against that of providing for their sons and daughters. They have no common interest or fellow feeling with the aristocracy; under no circumstances can they hope to be participators of aristocratic privileges; and they are accustomed to conjunct action, to meet in Corporations, form associations and hold public meetings, without waiting for a lord or the owner of ten thousand acres to put himself at their head. The new municipal bodies have been already of admirable use towards the political education of this class. Those assemblies are normal schools of real public business; and are forming, in all the considerable towns, able and experienced local leaders for the Reform party. Reform has another and a still stronger hold upon many of the class; upon many of those among them who are most prosperous in their circumstances, and least under the influence of the causes of dissatisfaction which act upon the trading classes through their pecuniary means. A great part of the most thriving and influential of the town electors are Dissenters; and as such, are in open opposition to one of the great aristocratic institutions, one with which all the rest are inseparably interwoven. No part of the Reform body, for constancy in their political conduct, are more entirely to be depended upon than these. Between them and the aristocracy, there is a deeper gulph fixed than can be said of any other portion of the middle class; and when men's consciences, and their interests, draw in the same direction, no wonder that they are irresistible.

Almost all the skilled employments, those which require talent and education but confer no rank,—what may be called the non-aristocratic professions—are to a great degree in the hands of Dissenters, and those professions may, in any case, be numbered among the natural Radicals. If the great landowners are mostly Tories, it would surprise some persons to know how many of the men who manage their affairs, how many of the stewards, and attorneys of men of fortune, are Dissenters and Liberals; and where the landlord does not take a very active part in politics, the influence of his agent in an election often goes as far as his. The men of active and aspiring talent, indeed, in all classes except the highest, are Radicals everywhere; for what is Radicalism, but the claim of pre-eminence for personal qualities above conventional or accidental advantages? And what more certain than that a man of talent, compelled to serve men of no talent, and taught by daily experience that, even if fortune favours him he can scarcely by the labours of a life raise his head to a level with their feet, will be, by a natural tendency, something of a leveller?

There is another body besides the Dissenters, whom their religious sentiments place among the natural Radicals, among those who either are Radicals already, or are ripe for being so as soon as they awaken to their position; we mean the Church Reformers, a growing body among the laity and even among the clergy of the Church of England. They are, more than can be said perhaps of any other class, determined to the Reform side by a sense of duty only, without the additional stimulus of a personal injury. They are not, like the Dissenters, taxed for the support of a worship which is not theirs; but they see the religion which is theirs, corrupted in the way in which every religion has been corrupted, by the secular interests of its ministers; and this because those ministers spring from the aristocracy, and are part and parcel of the aristocracy; because the class that predominate in the legislature present to livings, and by being the makers of ministries, are the dispensers of ecclesiastical dignities; because the proprietors of the land are the proprietors of the Church too, and their interest is that its much pay be burthened with little work. The Church Reformers will never attain their object while the House of Commons is under the influence of those for whose benefit Church abuses exist. They must be Radicals if they would be successful Church Reformers. Every doctrine and practice, which either in present times, or in times past, has tended to corrupt the Church, every claim which has been advanced to spiritual despotism, or countenance given to worldly sycophancy, has emanated from the Tory part of the body, and has been dictated by the desire to make the Church a political engine. For any aid in chasing such doctrines and practices out of the sanctuary, the Church Reformers can look to the Liberals alone.

In addition to all these classes must be included among the natural Radicals nearly all Scotland and all Ireland. Since the Church of John Knox followed the example of its richer sister, and from the People's Church made itself the Laird's Church, one half of the people of Scotland have become Voluntaries; most of the remainder are Church Reformers, enemies to the great abuse of both Churches' individual patronage. Half the members for the Scotch counties, and all the members for the boroughs, except one, are even now Liberals, most of them Radicals; and nearly all the places which now return Whigs will return Radicals when the present equivocal position of parties is ended, and the question is distinctly put between Radicalism and Conservatism. Of the Irish little need here be said. It would be strange, indeed, if a people who have never known any thing but oppression from their government, oppression slowly and reluctantly relaxed under the compulsion of their growing force; a people who have been for centuries, and are still, the most wronged and the most suffering in Europe—were not numbered among the Disqualified Classes; if they were not eager to ally themselves with anybody who will be, or who will but seem, the enemy of their enemies. And they well know, that where there is such a mass of mischief to be cleared away, where it is necessary to cut so deep, they will find no real fellow feeling but in the Radicals; that from them alone have they any chance of complete redress; and that their only policy is an alliance with the other Disqualified Classes, to give the ascendancy to the Radical interest in the empire.

Last, but not the least formidable part of the Radical body, comes the whole effective political strength of the working classes: classes deeply and increasingly discontented, and whose discontent now speaks out in a voice which will not be unheard; all whose movements are now made with an organization and concert of which those classes were never, at any former period, capable, and with a comprehension of political tactics, and of the necessity of postponing all subordinate ends to the main end, not yet reached by any other class of Reformers. As to this point, indeed, the whole Reform party has much to learn from their example. There are as many conflicting opinions, as much diversity of ultimate objects, among the Chartists themselves, as between the Chartists and the Moderate Radicals. But they have agreed for the present to let all disputed questions alone, and to pursue exclusively those changes in the representation, about the expediency of which they all are agreed, and through which alone they hope to obtain a legislature from whom they can look for a just adjudication of their points of difference. Much less mutual concession than this would make the Radicals complete masters of the next House of Commons.

These, then, are the Disqualified Classes; those who in addition to their share of the general interest, have a particular interest in opposition to things as they are; who either have special grievances, or upon whom the general grievances bear with peculiar weight. In calling upon all these sections to knit themselves together into one compact body, we are not seeking to build a party on a mere combination of classes for the promotion of separate interests, however legitimate. We are appealing in behalf of the general interest of all, to those whose particular interests have opened their eyes. It is not for themselves, it is for a principle, that we would summon them into the field. Instead of calling upon all sorts of men to seek redress for their particular wrongs by an alteration in the distribution of political power, we should beseech them to bear those private grievances patiently, and trust for relief to the progress of opinion among the ruling classes themselves, did we see in those classes any of the qualifications which entitle a government to the respect and attachment of the governed. We would bear many injuries rather than stir up discontent against institutions and rulers that we deemed, on the whole, beneficent. But before we accord any such forbearance, we demand that they make out their title to it. We do not acknowledge that any such right is conferred by the mere *possession* of power. As whatever is noble or disinterested in Toryism is founded upon a recognition of the moral duty of submission to rightful authority, so the moral basis of Radicalism is the refusal to pay that submission to an authority which is usurped, or to which the accidents of birth or fortune are the only title. The Tory acknowledges, along with the right to obedience, a correlative obligation to govern for the good of the ruled: the Radical requires the performance of that obligation as the condition of his obedience. He acknowledges no call upon him to pause in the pursuit of his just claims, rather than endanger institutions which he believes never were intended for his good. Believing the government of this country to be in the main a selfish oligarchy, carried on for the personal benefit of the ruling classes, he is not Utopian enough to address himself to the reason of his rulers, he endeavours to attain his object by taking away their power. One Radical differs from another as to the *amount* of change which he deems necessary for setting what is wrong right: but as to the *kind* of change there is no disagreement: it must be by diminishing the power of those who are unjustly favoured, and giving more to those who are unjustly depressed: it must be by adding weight in the scale to the two elements of Numbers and Intelligence, and taking it from that of Privilege. To do this, is the object of all Radicals: to do it cautiously and tentatively, but to go on doing it till it is done effectually, is the policy of Moderate Radicalism; it is the Durham policy, and under its banner we hope to see gathered together the whole Movement party of the empire.

It is not to be dissembled, however, that to form a united Movement party is not so easy as to form a compact Conservative one. Conservatives may differ on policy, but their end is the same, to keep the great institutions of the country as they are. Reformers differ not only about the means of effecting changes, but about the changes themselves. We have among us men who are terrified at Universal Suffrage, and men who hold that any thing short of Universal Suffrage would be a mischief and a delusion: we have men who cherish the principles of a Church Establishment, and men to whom the compulsory support of a State religion appears not only a tyranny but a sin. There are religious differences in our ranks, which of all differences of opinion set men most at variance with one another; and there is an opposition of interest, which gives birth, it would seem, to the most deep-rooted distrusts and aversions which exist in society—the opposition between capitalists and labourers. On these differences our adversaries rely. They know that they have nothing to fear if the physical strength of the Reform party can be set in array against the education and property of it, or if the latter can be divided against itself. They flatter themselves that the middle and the working classes, that the Catholics, the liberal Churchmen, and the Dissenters, can never act cordially together. And they hope that large bodies of the natural Radicals may be frightened into the arms of the Conservatives, by dread of Mr. O'Connell and of the Voluntaries, or of Mr. Stephens and Mr. Feargus O'Connor.

There is much plausibility in these hopes; nevertheless, the enemy may be reminded, that they counted upon exactly the same thing on the eve of the Reform

Bill. Then too they thought that the Reformers could never agree, could never join in asking for the same measure. The topic came round with the regularity of clock-work in every juvenile Tory's maiden speech against Reform. A month before Lord Grey came into office—the very day after the Duke of Wellington's famous declaration[*]—Sir Robert Peel said, "that although the Reformers might have a majority on the whole, there would be more voices for keeping the representation as it was, than there would be for any one mode of changing it." The event proved, however, that the Tory leader had made a false calculation. He had omitted to consider, that persons who were not agreed about their ultimate destination might be agreed about the next step; might have sufficient common sense to perceive, that they could not expect to accomplish more than one step at a time; and that they might as well make use of one another's assistance in taking that step, each being at liberty to go forward afterwards in his own peculiar track. What has been done once, may be done again, provided it can be well understood among us what *is* to be the next step, and that it be one which by those who wish to go farther shall still be deemed a good in itself, and not calculated to impede subsequent steps, unless indeed it should work so well as to satisfy those, by whom ulterior progress is desired. It is enough if we can agree about the things which it is possible to do just now. If Reform is to be deferred until Mr. Lovett and Mr. Cleave contend for it by the same arguments as Mr. Ward and Sir Lytton Bulwer, or until Dr. Wardlaw and Dr. Pye Smith talk exactly the same language in Church matters as Mr. Baptist Noel, we concede that it is not likely to be obtained in our time. But it is quite another thing, to believe that every one of these personages retaining his own sentiments and opinions, Dr. Wardlaw and Mr. Baptist Noel might consider one another as allies, not adversaries, a mutual help instead of a hindrance; and even that Mr. Lovett might be led to see in a policy which Mr. Ward would approve, advantage, and not injury, to the cause which he himself defends.

A great part of the difficulty arises from the mistaken, and, in reality, unpractical idea, that in order to help one another it is necessary that Reformers should be silent on their points of difference. So far from this, one Reformer often gives a more effectual support to another by demanding more than he, than by demanding only as much. We would have them aid one another not by leaving their opinions and feelings unspoken, but by speaking them. We would have every man loudly cry out for what he deems most important, for whatever he is most in earnest in desiring to see carried. Men are sure to be more stirring and active for all that they want, than for a part only of what they want: while, the more deeply-seated the dissatisfaction is seen to be, and the more it seems to require to satisfy it, the greater is the intimidation of the enemy. It is not those who ask for all, but those who reject less than all, that render union impossible. Men may combine in supporting a good thing which is to be had now, and continue to do all they can

[*Arthur Wellesley, Speech on the Address in Answer to the King's Speech (2 Nov., 1830), *PD*, 3rd ser., Vol. 1, cols. 52–3.]

by speech and writing for something they think better, which the time is not yet come for putting into a practical shape and carrying through Parliament. Each may drive at his separate and remote object in addition to, and not to the exclusion of, the immediate and practicable one. Voluntaries and Church Reformers, may mutually support one another at elections, without its being an understood condition that either, when elected, shall restrain the expression of any of his opinions on the Church question; and a man may join in agitating for Universal Suffrage with those who agree with him, and yet co-operate on other occasions with men who go no further than Household Suffrage.

A still greater obstacle has been the want of a directing head, the only possible bond of union of a body consisting of many scattered parts. In this respect, as in so many others, that becomes possible, as soon as we have a recognized leader, which was impracticable before. All ranks and shades of Reformers would not have rallied round "the Bill, the whole Bill, and nothing but the Bill," if it had been only the speculative project of an individual Member of Parliament: they took it because it was the thing offered to them by men who had a prospect of carrying a measure when they made it their own; and was distinguished from all other schemes of Reform by this, that it was actually to be had. It is as true now as then, that the different denominations of Reformers will not find out by themselves what it is that they can agree in supporting, what it is that would content all of them, at least as a step. There is no probability of their arranging among themselves how they may all join in agitating for the same thing. Some one in a sufficiently commanding position must give the word; some minister, or some one who may be made a minister, must declare the thing that is wanting; must announce it as the object of any administration which he will consent to form. The leader must not wait to receive his measures from his supporters. It is his business to know, better than they know themselves, not only what is in itself right, but what they are prepared to support. The leader of the Reform party, must be a leader who will lead. He must do like Lord Durham in Canada, "take the initiative." And it is because Lord Durham is almost the only man in the first rank of public life, and on the popular side, who has shown in practice that he both *can* do this and *dares* do it, that we believe him to be the man most fitted to be the popular leader, but we are far from thinking him the only man who would be able to make himself followed as such.

And let there be no misunderstanding. It is no single measure; it is a whole system of policy that the leader, whoever he is, will have to proclaim. It is not for the Ballot, nor even for the Ballot accompanied by Household Suffrage, that the whole force of the Movement party will ever again take the field. The Ballot is a necessary *part* of what must be contended for, and so is an extension of the Suffrage, corresponding to what is meant by Household Suffrage. But the present body of electors, even with any reinforcement that might be made to them from a class similar to their own, would still, in the estimation of the active Radicals among the working classes, be a mere oligarchy. It is the opinion of the

Operatives, that unless the Suffrage comes down to their own level, anything which enables it to be exercised more independently does them harm. The men of thews and sinews will never give their confidence to a party recommended only by willingness to take from the aristocracy and give to the shopocracy. On the other hand, to propose Universal Suffrage would be to bid adieu to all support from the middle class. Most of the Reformers who belong to that class at present, deem Universal Suffrage objectionable in principle: to no sober man among them does the time appear to be come for it; and if they were obliged to choose between the principles of the Whigs or even the moderate Tories, and those of the Chartists, very few of them would prefer the latter. A practical statesman must look farther and use other means, to induce the middle and the working classes to act in harmony.

No practical and judicious statesman could, even on the very unlikely supposition of his being so inclined, take his stand anywhere but on the middle class. He must necessarily rest, not on those who have no votes, but on those who have, and who can give him a majority in Parliament. It does not follow, that he is obliged to take their policy; it follows only, that he must be able to make them take his: that he must carry them with him in all he does, and need not attempt anything which there is no chance whatever of prevailing on them to support. He cannot therefore, attempt Universal Suffrage. To extend the franchise to the whole middle class, to equalize its distribution among that class, to enable that class to exercise it freely, all this he can and ought to aim at. He might even possibly propose some means of tempering the government of the middle classes with a partial admixture of representatives elected chiefly by the working men: for in such an amount of concession it would not be hopeless that the middle classes might be made to see both justice, and an increase of their own security. But it would be idle to expect that they could be induced to swamp themselves, and hand over to unskilled manual labour the entire powers of the government. Do we regret this? No: let Universal Suffrage be ever so desirable, let it even be ever so practicable when the minds of the other classes have been for some time gradually prepared for it by intermediate measures, it cannot be either good or practicable now. One great experiment in government is as much as a nation can safely make at a time. From the government of the higher to that of the middle classes is already a mighty change, and it is rather soon to begin making a second before we have more than half accomplished that. Let us have full experience of what that does for us before we try another. The French Revolution is an example of how little is ultimately gained by attempting greater changes than the general state of opinion is prepared for. After going the round for a whole generation of every form of government, from democracy to military despotism, what did the French at last sit down contented with? Exactly the same thing, neither more nor less, which they were ripe for when the revolution began.

What, then, has a liberal statesman to offer to the working classes? The greatest thing of all; and a thing which must precede Universal Suffrage—if Universal Suffrage is ever to come without a civil war. *He must redress the practical grievances of the working classes.* They are now the Parias of society; not a voice is ever raised in the legislature for their good, except it be for some restraint upon their liberty, or curtailment of their pleasures: an end must be put to this. The motto of a Radical politician should be, Government *by means of* the middle for the working classes. One of the most original and powerful of recent political writers,* has expressed the principle with admirable aptness and force:—Until Universal Suffrage be possible,—to govern the country as it would be necessary to govern it, if there were Universal Suffrage and the people were well educated and intelligent.

Is it conceivable, for instance, that in a country where there was Universal Suffrage, and where the people were intelligent, the labouring classes would suffer themselves to be taxed on the bread they eat, to the verge of starvation, avowedly to keep up the rents of the landlords? That the importation of almost all other kinds of provisions would be absolutely prohibited? That two-thirds of the whole revenue of the country would consist of taxes on the articles of their consumption? That even of those articles, the inferior qualities, which alone they consume, would be taxed three or four times higher in proportion to their value, than the finer qualities which are used by the richer classes? Is this a system of revenue and commerce which could ever co-exist with Universal Suffrage and an intelligent people?

Is it credible, again, that with such a Suffrage and such a people the exhibitions would be afforded us, which we now see every time that a man with a good coat and a man with a shabby coat come into collision before any of the petty courts of justice? Should we find police magistrates, when a nobleman's son has beaten somebody to death's door, or another has fired air-guns from a coach window, or a wretch of "respectable appearance" has grossly insulted a woman in the streets, almost apologizing to the culprits for fining them five pounds and dismissing them,—while a poor man on some trifling accusation has every presumption strained against him, the magistrates descant in set terms on the imperious demands of public justice and the enormity of his offence, and his family are left to starve or come upon the parish, while he is lying in prison for want of bail? Would it be the common practice of the legislature to fix as the minimum of penalty sums which amount to several weeks' wages of a working man, and as the maximum in exactly the same case, what to a man of fortune falls short of the average expenditure of half-a-day? Would there be vagrant laws which make poverty punishable—laws by which any magistrate may put any poor person into gaol? Would there be more persons in prison for offences against the game laws than for

---

*Mr. [Edward Gibbon] Wakefield, in his *England and America* [2 vols. (London: Bentley, 1833), Vol. I, p. 200].

all other offences together, and would gamekeepers be sent out in bands of a dozen at a time to wage mortal combat against men on account of the life of a pheasant?

Again, if the class that supplies the men who fight the battles of their country and man her ships, had any voice in making the laws of that country, is it likely that they would reserve the stripes for themselves, and leave the commissions and the honours for those who can pay for them? Would they suffer themselves to be impressed into the navy by force, because we will not make their portion in it such as any one will accept by choice; because we will neither give them the wages which they can earn in open market, nor leave an opening for them to rise so much as to the rank of a midshipman, in all the long years between the press-gang and Greenwich Hospital?

Again, if the people who walk in footpaths made the law, could a single magistrate, with the assistance of any other justice of peace who is dining at his house, shut up a path, aye, or a road, which existed before his park was made—by which for centuries the labourer had shortened his way to his work, and tasted the breath of free air—a path not even passing near his windows or intruding upon his privacy, but crossing some bye-corner of his domain, and exposing to some constructive jeopardy his hares and partridges? Would there be whole counties of England where the gentlemen have abolished every field path, where the foot passenger has nothing but a dusty road to travel on? Would the bit of grass by the side even of that road be enclosed to give an additional rood of ground to the Squirearchy of the adjoining fields? Would the commons on which the whole inhabitants of a village once enjoyed pure air and sunshine, and athletic amusements, be seized and ploughed up in one district after another; and would it have been laid down by the Court of King's Bench that compensation in any such case is due only to the neighbouring *landholders*, who alone had right of common, while those who have erected cottages and subsisted by the bit of ground they took in, and the cow or pig they turned out, may be ejected from their holding without equivalent? Could these things be if the working classes had a voice in the state?

And, more even than this, if the working classes had power to make their well-being a matter of concern to those who rule, if they had even power enough to make the ruling classes uneasy as to the consequences of their ignorance, could this government absolutely neglect one of its highest duties, one which not only republican America but nearly all the despotic governments of the Continent studiously and conscientiously execute—the duty of seeing the people taught? Could it continue neither to provide the teaching, nor to hold out any inducements to the people to find it for themselves? While it leaves all secular instruction, not only to the voluntary principle, but to the voluntary principle unaided by any of those facilities and encouragements which are quite compatible with the principle, would it maintain the most costly of all Church Establishments on pretence of religious instruction, while the real religious teaching of the poorer classes, such teaching as they receive, they owe after all to the voluntary principle? If the working classes had votes, would not everybody be anxious for their instruction, for their intellectual improvement? Would not every one be eager to establish, not bad, but good schools for them; to write books for them on the most important subjects, to make the best ideas of the best minds accessible to them, to present the grounds of every public measure, the justification of every institution of the state, in such a form as should convince them? And would not this necessity, even of itself, tend to make our institutions and measures much more generally such as *can* be so defended?

But we have not yet touched the core of the question. Such grievances as those we have mentioned have ceased to hold more than a secondary place in the estimation of the working classes themselves. Even the Corn Laws are now no longer capable of interesting them strongly. Their minds are engrossed with one subject—the relation between labourers and employers. It is for the sake of benefitting themselves in that relation, that they desire Universal Suffrage. They believe that they have not a just share of the fruits of their industry. They impute this to the large portion which is taken by the capitalist. They are persuaded that were there a reduction of taxation, or even a repeal of the Corn Laws, and all other things remained the same, not they but their masters would reap the benefit; and they care little for any changes in government, or even in society, that would not enable them to make their contract for wages on more advantageous terms. No political party will carry the working classes along with it unless it have something to propose which will be deemed by the more reasonable part of the working classes an evidence of good intentions on this point. But there is a much larger portion of them who are reasonable, and they would be much more easily satisfied than is supposed by those who are unacquainted with the state of their minds.

There is an enormous amount of misunderstanding among the other ranks of society as to the opinions of the working classes, and a degree of distrust and terror of their supposed projects, greatly beyond the cause for it. The quarrels between trades unions and capitalists, the cry for the "rights of labour"[*] against the "claims of capital,"[†] do not mean spoliation; nor is the Chartist agitation, as an able man among the Moderate Radicals has called it, "the anti-Poor-Law movement in disguise."[‡] The Oastlers and Stephenses represent only the worst portion of the Operative Radicals, almost confined, moreover, to a narrow district in the North. If we would know the sentiments of the intelligent leaders of the working classes, we must look to the Working Men's Association in London; who framed the People's Charter; who originated the agitation for it; who have some of their members present at every meeting which is held for it in any part of the

[*See, e.g., Leading Article on labour and capital, *Poor Man's Guardian*, II (3 Aug., 1833), 245.]

[†See Thomas Hodgskin, *Labour Defended against the Claims of Capital* (London: Knight and Lacey, 1825).]

[‡Edward Bulwer, "The People's Charter," *Monthly Chronicle*, II (Oct., 1838), 297.]

country; and who represent the best and most enlightened aspect of working-class Radicalism.

There is much error afloat even about the character, as men, of the politically active part of the Operative body. There is a notion abroad that they are the ill-conditioned and ill-conducted portion—the desperadoes of the class. The very contrary is the fact. Hardly any drunken or profligate working man is a politician. Such men do not read newspapers, or interest themselves in public measures; they take part in strikes, but not in Political Unions. The politicians of the class are almost universally its most respectable and well-conducted men. They are the heroes of their class; men respected and looked up to by the rest. We have been credibly informed that even the Glasgow convicts were sober domestic men, of unexceptionable habits in all relations between individual and individual, where their class feelings did not interfere;[*] and it is but in a small part that the class feelings take so terrible a shape. In London the political leaders of the working classes are not only some of their best men, but are also, to a great extent, instructed and cultivated men; they are, moreover, growing every day in instruction and intelligence; they have shaken off, within the last few years, many crude notions, and have made quite progress enough not to see any benefit to their class in a general conflagration, nor look to agrarian laws, or taxes on machinery, or a compulsory minimum of wages, as the means of improving its condition.

We do not dissemble that many even of the very best of these men entertain notions in political economy with which we by no means coincide. There is in fact no essential difference between their ideas as to the general circumstances which determine the condition of the labourer, and those common among their class. They believe that they are ground down by the capitalist. They believe that his superiority of means, and power of holding out longer than they can, enables him virtually to fix their wages. They ascribe the lowness of those wages, not, as is the truth, to the *over*-competition produced by their own excessive numbers, but to competition itself; and deem that state of things inevitable so long as the two classes exist separate—so long as the distinction is kept up between Capitalist and Labourer. These notions are in fact Owenism; and Owenism, as those are aware who habitually watch the progress of opinion, is at present in one form or other the actual creed of a great proportion of the working classes. But Owenism does not necessarily, it does not in the mind of its benevolent founder, imply any war against property. What is hoped for is, not violently to subvert, but quietly to supersede the present arrangements for the employment of capital and labour. The labourers wish to become their own capitalists; they have funds for the purpose, since they have funds for strikes, and Trade Societies, and Benefit Clubs. These funds they desire to employ as capitals of their own, administering them on their

[*Mill may have been informed about the Glasgow convicts (James Gibb, Peter Hacket, Thomas Hunter, William McLean, and Richard McNeil) by Francis Place; see his "Historical Narrative 1838," Place Papers, BL Add. MS 27,820, ff. 151–3.]

common account, and dividing the whole produce among the labourers. And what, it may be asked, prevents them from setting about this whenever they please? The defects of the law; which, on the subject of partnership, and especially of numerous partnerships, is one of the most imperfect in Europe: under which it is almost impossible for a numerous body to invest their joint savings in a productive employment, and to maintain any effectual control over the managers to whom the immediate direction must be entrusted.[*]

We believe few people have any idea of the amount of good will which might be gained from the working classes, and of the genuinely healing effect which would be produced upon their minds, by so apparently small a thing as the removal of this one grievance. A small thing to do, but a great thing to leave undone; a thing which would make the Operatives feel that they have fair play given them; that they have an opportunity of trying to improve their condition in the way by which they think it is to be improved—of trying, at their own risk, an experiment which nobody has the smallest right to prevent them from trying, and which, whether it succeed or fail, can do harm to nobody. On the contrary, either its success or failure would do good to everybody. If it succeeded—if the Co-operatives could contrive to carry on the great operations of industry independently of individual capitalists, independently of inequality of wealth and the irritating sense of contrariety of interest—where is the good man, of whatever political opinion, who would not hail their success? If they failed, would not this be an instruction to them in political economy, worth a thousand treatises? Would it not be the very lesson they need to learn, the very experience they require? Would it not teach them that the present arrangements respecting property and production, though they may not be the best conceivable, are the best practicable, and that the only real means of raising their condition are the correction of the abuses of government, the improvement of their own habits, and a due proportioning of their numbers to the field of employment, either by taking off the superfluous hands through systematic colonization, or by forbearing to call them into existence?

Such, then, are some of the duties of the government of the Middle Classes towards the working class: duties which those classes cannot leave unperformed, without drawing upon themselves the retribution which sooner or later awaits all classes or bodies of men who seize the powers of government, and emancipate themselves from its obligations. Suppose now that a leader could be found, that a party could be formed in public life, which stood upon the recognition of these duties as the ground of its existence, and while it upheld the government of the Middle Classes, used whatever influence it could acquire over those classes for the purpose of getting those duties performed,—would it be no advantage to the working classes that the middle classes should acknowledge such men as its

[*See 7 George IV, c. 46 (1826), 1 Victoria, c. 10 (1838), and 1 & 2 Victoria, c. 96 (1838).]

leaders, and engage itself in the support of their policy? Would it not be worth while for the working classes to lend a helping hand towards bringing about such a result—towards placing a party entertaining these sentiments in that commanding position? Without suspending the agitation for Universal Suffrage—for we desire to stifle no man's sincere opinion, least of all that of the most numerous and ill-used class—would they not find their account in showing that they seek it only as a means to a just and reasonable end, and that men who will the same end may have their support in endeavouring to work towards it by the existing means? As Mr. O'Connell agitates for Repeal *or* Justice to Ireland, why should not they, too, admit the alternative of Universal Suffrage *or* Equal Justice to the Working Classes? The degree of support which this would give to the attempt to obtain for them that equal justice, would lend a strength to their friends among the middle classes which would in time suffice to carry almost every thing which is desirable. Will they attain Universal Suffrage sooner by appearing to seek not merely justice but predominance? Will they arrive at it sooner by confirming the middle classes in the idea that not redress of wrong, but nothing less than the power of inflicting it, will satisfy them? If ever democratic institutions are to be obtained quietly, a great change in the sentiments of the two great classes towards one another must precede the concession; at present there is hardly a person possessed of the smallest property (and they are strong enough in this country, even in numbers, to make a desperate defence) who would not prefer almost any evils to those which they would expect from the political ascendancy of the working classes.

More than this; are the great and intelligent portion of the Operative classes of whom the London Working Men's Association is the representative, are even they themselves free from apprehension of the mass of brutish ignorance which is behind them? of the barbarians whom Universal Suffrage would let in, although at present caring nothing about it, and unable to do anything towards gaining it until the affair becomes one of brute force? Do they never think of the state of the agricultural labourers? of the depraved habits of a large proportion of the well-paid artisans? Do they forget Sir William Courtenay?[*] do they forget Swing? do they forget that in a great city like Glasgow it has been recently ascertained that every tenth house is a spirit shop? have they forgotten the secret murders, the throwing of sulphuric acid? Can they wonder that the middle classes, who know all these things, and who do not know *them*, should tremble at the idea of entrusting political power to such hands? Cannot the intelligent working classes be persuaded, that even for themselves it is better that Universal Suffrage should come gradually? that it should be approached by steps bearing some relation to the progressive extension of intelligence and morality, from the higher to the lower regions of their own manifold domain? Lord Durham's advice to them in one of his Newcastle speeches was the true one: to seek political power by one road, the only

[*Alias of John Nichols Tom (or Thom).]

safe, the only practicable one, by showing more and more that they are worthy of it.[*] The strongest prejudices exist, not inexcusably, in the minds of the best men among the middle classes, against them and their claims; let it be their effort to overcome those prejudices; let the Associations continue, as we are happy to say they do already, to inculcate temperance, economy, kindness, every household virtue, and every rational and intellectual pursuit, among their members. Let them systematically discountenance all appeals to violence, and let those who really disapprove of the destructive schemes propounded by some of the talkers, take fit opportunities of making known their disapprobation. Discussion is rapidly doing its work in cultivating the intelligence of the working classes; the appreciation of that intelligence will necessarily follow. Every year we expect to see an advancement both in their real good sense and good conduct, and in the recognition of it by other people.

We think it desirable even now that the suffrage should be such as to let in some members returned chiefly by the working classes. We think it of importance that Mr. Lovett and Mr. Vincent should make themselves heard in St. Stephen's as well as in Palace yard, and that the legislature should not have to learn the sentiments of the working classes at second-hand. We believe these and some others we could name, to be men who, to say the least, would do no discredit to the House of Commons. We desire, too, that a sufficient number of the respectable working men should have votes, for their influence to be felt in many elections in which they have not the preponderance. We would give them power, but not all power. We wish them to be strong enough to keep the middle classes in that salutary awe, without which, no doubt, those classes would be just like any other oligarchy; sufficiently strong for making it necessary to listen to their complaints, and for giving weight to the counsels of those who press their just claims upon the attention of the legislature. What precise extension of the suffrage would best do this, we cannot now undertake to decide: but there is evidently no particular difficulty in discovering it.

Next to the division between the middle and the working classes, the only other great discordance among Reformers relates to Church affairs. There, indeed, the dissonance by no means amounts to a rupture. The Dissenters, the Roman Catholics, and the liberal Churchmen, are far from being on the terms on which the Chartists and the middle classes are. All the efforts of the Tories to make a quarrel between them have not hitherto prevented them from being allies; but they are not, by any means, such close allies as they might be; nor is the full force of any of the three bodies, the Irish Catholics excepted, drawn forth to take part in the contest.

[*Lambton, Speech on the Suffrage (19 Oct., 1834), in *Speeches of the Earl of Durham Delivered at Public Meetings in Scotland and Newcastle* (London: Ridgway, 1835), pp. 96–7.]

Many a sincere reformer of the Church of England stands aloof, or leans to the Conservatives, from fear of the Voluntaries or of the Catholics, who at present may be regarded as Voluntaries; and many a Dissenter, even many a Voluntary, abstains from mixing actively in politics, because he does not like the Papists and Socinians with whom he is told that he would have to identify himself. A still greater number in all these classes confine their exertions in the cause to Ecclesiastical matters, and take little part in the general movement of political affairs; because they do not yet see, in any set of men who are competitors for office, any guarantee for the Ecclesiastical changes which they are desirous of; and being made Reformers chiefly by their religious sentiments, if they entered into political combinations it could only be for the sake of bringing men into power by whose elevation they would expect to forward their religious views: which views being different, cannot, it would at first sight appear, be all promoted by supporting the same men.

The latter difficulty, however, is more in appearance than in reality. The religious questions are no exceptions to the general rule, that all sections of Reformers are each other's best friends, and have, for immediate purposes, one common interest. The Voluntaries and the Church Reformers have different ultimate aims, it is true. But each of these parties ought not the less to see in the other its best ally. The Voluntary is not the foe of the Liberal Churchman, but his auxiliary; the thunderer without the gate, who is ever the main strength of the Reformer within. The Liberal Churchman is not the antagonist of the Voluntary, but his next of kin; they have the same enemies, and partially at least the same objects; they both recognize and deplore in the Church as it is, the predominance of the worldly character over the spiritual; the one holds this vice to be inherent in the very nature of a Church Establishment, the other hopes that the Church of England may be purged of it; but the former does not the less acknowledge that a reformed Church is a more spiritual thing than an unreformed one; and would not the less welcome the growing strength in the Church itself of those who wish to spiritualize it. Both are driving at the same end, by different means; but every step made by the one is so much gained for the other.

There are in the Established Church men who value, and even profess to value the Church, we will not say more than the Bible, but equally with it, and hold the one as much an essential part of Christianity as the other. And there are men who prize the Bible infinitely above the Church, and would regard with horror any imputation of putting the two on a level. To the former, the High Church party, we need not address ourselves. We wish to do them all justice. They have much to say for themselves. Many of them are sincerely religious men; and much of the best spirit of religion dwells even in those who have carried the High Church principle to the greatest pitch of exaggeration—the new school of Oxford Theology. It is not impossible that such men may even desire to see the Church more spiritualized, to see it purged of its abuses. But, believing as they do, that mankind in general are to take their religion not from private judgment but from an appointed authority, and that the Church of England, as by law established,[*] is that authority, to maintain that Church as a recognized national institution is naturally the first object, and anything else can only be secondary. It is to the Low Church party that we are now addressing ourselves, to those members of the Church with whom its spirituality passes before its political privileges; who are already in the habit of combining, for missionary objects, with persons beyond its pale; who desire to see it established, but would rather it were not established than not reformed. We speak to those who believe that the Church, as a national institution, has neglected its duties, has sacrificed the welfare of the flock to the luxury and ease of the shepherd; and who, if they were compelled to choose, would prefer the risks of the Voluntary system to the certain evils of a professedly Christian ministry sunk in indolence, and thinking more of its enjoyments than of its responsibility.

To such men we say, fear not the Voluntaries. It is true they would divest the Church of all existence as a political body; but what do you yourselves seek to do? To induce the Church to reform itself: but did any political body, whether hierarchy or aristocracy ever reform itself, until it trembled for its existence? Did it ever listen to the warning voice of the friend within the walls, save from terror of the enemy without? Take any of the great historical examples, the Reformation for instance. What has been the great purifier of the Roman Catholic Church? Is it not, confessedly Protestantism? Do not all enlightened Roman Catholics agree that the abuses with which they acknowledge that their church swarmed before the Reformation, were far too dear to the potentates of that church ever to have been yielded up to the mere remonstrances of good men within her pale, but for the imminent necessity of strengthening her against the assaults of the great Reformers? Turn, again, to the improvement, a real improvement as far as it goes, which the greatest adversaries of the Church of England admit to have taken place within the last fifty years in the character and conduct of her clergy: is not the beginning of this improvement, by universal admission, coeval with the rise of Methodism? The best reformers of the Church of England are those whom the authors and protectors of her abuses stand most in fear of, those who make her feel that "if she do not work, neither shall she eat."[†] The real Church Reformer ought to cherish the Voluntaries. They are not yet half strong enough for his purpose. The enemy are not yet by any means sufficiently alarmed.

The Voluntaries ought no less to cherish the Church Reformers. Are they not, if not as politicians, yet as religious men, aiming at the same end? Are not the Church Reformers endeavouring to make the Church what the Voluntaries say it can only be made by separating it from the State? If so, are they not the very persons from among whom a sincere Voluntary ought to look for converts to Voluntaryism? For

[*See, e.g., 5 & 6 Anne, c. 5, An Act for Securing the Church of England as by Law Established (1706).]
[†Cf. II Thessalonians, 3:10.]

men convinced as the Voluntaries are that a religious body cannot be both an established church and an apostolical one, but who find others (vainly, as they think) flattering themselves that it is possible to unite the two, what can be a more natural wish than this, "Let them try?" These are no idle speculations. There is already a numerous body of some of the most religious men in the Church (Mr. Charles Lushington in a recent pamphlet has spoken their sentiments)[*] who are hovering on the very verge of separation from her, in consequence of the abuses in her discipline, and the unprotestant and unchristian doctrines (as they deem them) which are extensively professed and highly patronized within her communion. Do not the Voluntaries, again, believe that not only what upholds the abuses of the Church, but what keeps the Church connected with the State, is secular interest? Let them, then, lay it well to heart, that every point which the Church Reformers carry, diminishes by so much the interested motives for supporting the Establishment: every sinecure abolished cuts off one possessor and fifty expectants from the supporters of things as they are; every step gained towards reducing the emoluments of dignitaries or equalizing those of incumbents, every iota of progress made in attaching duties to remuneration, and making it necessary for the clergy to lead laborious lives, diminishes the value of the Church to the self-interest of the aristocracy. Nay more, reform in the Church cannot be complete (and it is to the honour of Mr. Baptist Noel that he has proclaimed the fact) without cutting down to the ground the great principle of all abuse, the nomination of parochial ministers by irresponsible individuals. But when the system of advowsons is gone, all is gone that gives the gentry at large a personal interest in the Establishment. The Church would thenceforth stand as an institution, upon her spiritual merits alone; and the stanchest Voluntary need not fear to submit the question between the two principles, the voluntary and the compulsory, to that test. If the Church could be spiritualized, remaining an Established Church, it is his belief that she would at once, and of herself, renounce her endowments.

We cannot doubt, then, that the Dissenters and the Church Reformers will recognize that they have reason to link themselves together in strict alliance, and rejoice in the progress and strength of each other, almost as if it were their own. But there is also another feeling from which it is equally necessary for them to free themselves. As religious men, many of them feel a disinclination to associate for a common object with any but religious men. This reluctance stands greatly in the way of their attaining those of their religious objects to which the road lies through political ones; for no politician can afford to reject assistance because it is tendered to him by men whose religion is different from his, or who may appear to him not to be sufficiently under the influence of any religion. Having chosen his objects

[*Charles Lushington, *Dilemmas of a Churchman* (London: Ridgway, 1838).]

according to his own view of right, he must avail himself of any aid which circumstances render accessible to him, and must consider those who are best qualified for aiding him effectually as his most desirable allies. What, indeed, is this, but the very principle which religious men themselves follow, in associating for religious objects? Men of many different religious denominations co-operate in Bible Societies, Missionary Societies, Societies for the Propagation of the Gospel; they do not inquire if those with whom they associate agree with them in all respects, but only if they have the one religious requisite of a desire to promote the religious purpose for which they are joined together. Why should they not carry the same principle into politics, and be ready to ally themselves there also, as far as the immediate purpose requires, with those persons, whatever be their creed or sentiments, who possess the one *political* requisite of practical efficiency in the promotion of those political ends, in which their convictions as religious men, as well as their rights as citizens, are so directly interested?

But the appeals of the Tories to religious antipathies are intended to take effect, not so much upon the Dissenters or the real Church Reformers, as upon a numerous body of Churchmen who do not reflect much upon Ecclesiastical matters, nor have any very decided opinion on the debateable points, but who have a habitual dislike of Dissent and attachment to the Church, and are capable of being acted upon by vague fears for its safety. To these the Tories preach of an alliance of Papists, Dissenters, and Infidels, to destroy the Church: taking care to add, that this threefold conspiracy against the Church is at the bottom of all Radicalism; that the Constitution is attacked chiefly to get at the Church, and that those who wish to pull down the Church, as many of them as are not Papists or Dissenters, are enemies of all religion: from whence it is left to be inferred that the chosen seat and main stronghold of Christianity is the English aristocracy.

With regard to the assertion, that the infidels of the present day hate the Church as the great bulwark of Christianity, and the aristocracy as the bulwark of the Church, we could produce on the subject of it such an array of facts and considerations bearing on the character of modern infidelity, as would greatly disconcert those by whom the parrot cry is mechanically repeated, and prove how utterly ignorant those who give any credit to it must be of the march of European opinion, and the differences between the present age and that of Voltaire and Diderot. But to confine ourselves to the remark which lies nearest the surface, we do not believe that the generality of English infidels are hostile to the Church; we believe, on the contrary, that both infidels and indifferents very generally prefer the Church of England to the other forms of English Protestantism, as being more comprehensive, and allowing far greater divergence of opinion without exclusion from its communion. Both infidels and indifferents, too, are mostly, if we are not mistaken, rather favourable than otherwise to the principle of a Church Establishment. The famous argument of Hume, that an Established Church is the best security against fanaticism, expresses their real sentiments.[*] In a clergy voluntarily supported, they dread what they would probably call excess of zeal and lack of discretion. We believe that almost all persons, who are not much in earnest about religion, would prefer, for the sake of their own ease and quiet, an endowed to an unendowed clergy, although doubtless such of them as are Radicals desire for political and not religious reasons, that the Church should put off the character of an engine of state; an object which the religious reformers have in common with them, and which the difference of their religious sentiments constitutes no reason why they should not jointly pursue.

With respect to Papists, the accusation of hostile designs against the Church of England is a pure fiction, a paltry attempt to confound with the English Church Establishment the monstrous anomaly known as the Church of Ireland; a disgrace to the name of Church; a thing for which the very attempt to set up a defence is itself an insult, and against which, indeed, there is a perpetual alliance among all persons deserving the name of Reformers. The thing is open, undisguised tyranny, and admits of no compromise; nothing but unconditional surrender. Such a thing as a Church imposed by conquest, and upheld by means of foreign force, against the will of thirteen-fourteenths of the inhabitants, never would be submitted to by any people except at the point of the bayonet; and no Radical Ministry can make itself any party to the longer continuance of the enormity. We do not say that a bill ought to be brought in for its total extinction the moment a Ministry of Moderate Radicals comes into power; a government must consider times and circumstances, and not march too far in advance of the general sentiment. It ought to begin at once preparing the public mind for this act of justice. It should not hesitate to declare openly from the first to what point it hopes to come: and it should begin immediately to cut down the endowments to a modest provision for the religious instruction of a small minority.

The Church of England is a totally different thing from the Church of Ireland: against the one, war to the knife; in the other, the programme of the Moderate Radicals should be a thorough and comprehensive Reform. Not a Reform stopping at the dignitaries, and leaving untouched the parochial clergy; it is of more consequence to a nation to have good parish priests than good prelates: the Rector of Stanhope must be no more spared than the Bishop of Durham. Abuse for abuse, a better case may be made out for the salaries of the bishops than for the gross inequalities of livings; and nothing can better show how the subject of Church Reform has been trifled with, than that in none of the plans hitherto patronized by politicians has any provision been made for this branch of it. Difficulties would arise with respect to the owners of advowsons, to whose claims, although a property in the cure of souls is itself an abuse and the parent of all other abuses, an equitable consideration is nevertheless due. An approach, however, to equiliza-

[*Hume, *History of England*, Vol. IV, p. 31.]

tion in the emoluments and duties of the working clergy is indispensable. By throwing adjacent small parishes into one (the county of Norfolk contains, we believe, as many parishes as all Scotland), by subdividing large and populous town-parishes, and by compelling every clergyman hereafter presented to a rich living, to maintain a clergyman for some other place where he is wanted, the desirable end might be attained with little disturbance.

A party, whether in office or not, which announced the principles of such a plan; which, if in office, did as much as circumstances would admit towards immediately realizing it, lost no opportunity of approaching even a step nearer to it, and brought forward into the places of dignity and power in the Church the numerous worthy and able men who are favourable to these principles—would have the support of every liberal man among the lay members of the Church, that of the poorer clergy generally, and nearly the whole body of the curates! They would have the support of all the Dissenters, of all Scotland, as well as of all the Catholics of Ireland. Whenever, indeed, a Radical party shall form itself, the leaders of the Irish Catholics *must* take their place in it; Mr. O'Connell knows this perfectly well, whatever sparring may occasionally pass between him and some of the body; and with that quick feeling of the immediate interest of his country, which has never yet been at fault, he would be one of the foremost to give in his adhesion to any leader who would pledge himself to such a course of policy as we have been advocating.

To the formation of such a party we now look forward with considerable hope. All things are ripe for it. The ground is unoccupied; the man, in a suitable station, who "goes a-head" with a policy adapted for uniting the Reformers, will find all things prepared for him, and is sure of everything, to the Premiership inclusive, which their support can give. The policy we have outlined is the only policy by which the Reformers would be enabled to face the constituencies. If the trial of strength at the next general election were between Sir Robert Peel and Lord Melbourne, we do not believe the Whigs themselves think they would have any chance; but if it were between Sir Robert Peel and the leader of the party we have sketched; between the representatives of the two great principles,—not between two men whose politics differ from one another only by the shadow of a shade,—we should look with confident hopes to a very different result.

WHAT IS TO BE DONE WITH IRELAND?

1848?

EDITOR'S NOTE

Holograph MS, Walpole Collection, King's School, Canterbury. Not signed, but in Mill's hand. Not published, and therefore not listed in Mill's bibliography of his published writings. Dated on internal evidence. For a description of the MS, and comment on it, see lx–lxi and lxiii above.

Harriet Taylor's suggested revisions are indicated in pencil on the MS; these are given in footnotes, keyed by superscript letters, and identified as hers by the initials "HTM" (though, if the dating is correct, she was not yet married to Mill; this use conforms to that in other volumes of the *Collected Works*, and distinguishes her from her daughter, Helen Taylor). Where Mill's cancellations (made currently, before HTM's revisions were indicated) relate to her suggestions, these are indicated and identified as his by "JSM."

What Is to Be Done with Ireland?

THERE ARE ADVISERS who have a ready answer. *^a*You have*^a* conquered; they say *^b*to the Government*^b*. There is nothing to resist *^c*you. Your*^c* power has been tried, and found adequate. *^d*You*^d* are strong enough to tyrannize: *^e*therefore tyrannize*^e*. Make no pretence of a free press, or public meetings, or jury trial, or regular courts of justice. Govern by the sword. Trample out the last spark of freedom in the country. Place Ireland permanently in a "state of siege".[*] Agitation, demagoguism, is the real evil of Ireland. Put an end to it. Moral force is as bad as physical. Let neither of them any longer be tolerated. Stop the mouth of Ireland as well as tie her hands.

These *^f*suggestions*^f* are worth *^g*listening to,*^g* as an instance *^h*how far the force of impudence can go*^h*. It would be unjust either to the present ministers or to any who *ⁱ*are*ⁱ* likely to succeed them, to suppose them capable of acting on advice of this complexion. Yet this is at least a plan, though a detestable one. It is true, there is no great expenditure of ingenuity in it. Simple, straightforward military despotism is the vulgarest and least recondite of political conceptions. Still, those who recoil from this expedient ought to *^j*have*^j* some other. The condition of Ireland is not a thing which can be dealt with by people who do not know what ends they are aiming at.

Open, armed resistance to government has been suppressed. It would *^k* be more correct to say, that none has been attempted. There has been abundance of talking about an insurrection, but none of the reality. The military operations of Mr. Smith

[*Cf. Louis Blanc, *The History of Ten Years, 1830–1840*, trans. Walter K. Kelly, 2 vols. (Philadelphia: Lea and Blanchard, 1848), Vol. II, p. 415.]

*^{a–a}*Government has [*substituted by HTM*]
^{b–b}[*deleted by HTM*]
*^{c–c}*it. Its [*substituted by HTM*]
*^{d–d}*it [*incomplete revision by HTM*]
^{e–e}[*probably deleted by HTM*]
*^{f–f}*counsels [*substituted by HTM; JSM first wrote and then cancelled* counsels]
*^{g–g}*noticing only [*substituted by HTM; JSM first wrote and cancelled* attending *before writing* listening]
*^{h–h}*how much of the worst spirit of Toryism is still extant [*substituted by HTM*]
*^{i–i}*would be [*substituted by HTM*]
*^{j–j}*be able to suggest [*substituted by HTM*]
*^k*perhaps [*added by HTM*]

Folio 1r of "What Is to Be Done with Ireland?"
MS The King's School, Canterbury

O'Brien have been about as much a rebellion as the Boulogne expedition of Louis Napoleon was an invasion. There has been all possible inclination to rise, but no rising. And most of the individuals who attempted a rising, or who called on the people to rise, having fallen into the hands of the authorities, there will be no great difficulty in preventing any such attempts or instigations for some time to come. If that be the sole end of government, it is for the present attained. A people, in the utmost state of exasperation against the government short of that which would make them rush upon fixed bayonets, will be prevented, by those bayonets, for an indefinite period, from forcibly expelling or overthrowing the rulers whom they detest.

But this is not what will satisfy anybody as a permanent state. To get rid of the exasperation, by some means, must be the intention of everybody. Will it be enough, for this purpose, to repress by violence the outward signs of the feeling? or is it desired to get rid of the cause?

The cause of Irish disaffection is not demagogism. It is no creation of Mr. O'Connell or of Mr. Mitchell. These, and such as these, are the more or less able and active, and skilful *organs* of dissatisfaction, who by giving energetic expression to the general feeling, stimulate it into activity, and make it outwardly powerful, but do not create it where it is not. The causes of Irish disaffection are many and various; the greatest of them being, that several millions of the Irish people having nothing to support them but potatoes and for two or three months of every year not enough of those, even when the crop has not failed; all the remainder of what the land produces, be that remainder great or small, being taken, under the name of rent, by about eight thousand persons. If these several millions of Irish are dissatisfied under this kind of arrangement, it must be acknowledged that they have something to be dissatisfied with.

We shall be told, of course, that this is no fault of the government or of the English nation, and no just ground of outcry against them. And those who say this, will mostly say it *in all* sincerity. Conscious that they themselves have no wish and that most people whom they know have no wish, that the Irish should be starved or tyrannized over for any English purposes, but would even give something in a time of famine to keep them from starving, and have done so, *very* largely and liberally less than two years ago, for which bounty they have *by no means* received the thanks which their intentions deserved, they think it mere calumny to impute, in any degree, Ireland's poverty and wretchedness to any fault of theirs. But what avails it that England now no longer grinds down the Irish from religious bigotry or manufacturing jealousy; that Ireland's wretchedness and degradation are not the work, in the present generation at least, of England's

---

l-l[*underscored by HTM*]
m-m[*probably deleted by HTM*]
*n-n*not [*substituted by HTM*]

tyranny? They are the work of England's ignorance, *of England's* prejudice, *of England's* indifference; they are the effect of a vicious social system, upheld by England. They result from a radically wrong state of the most important social relation which exists in the country, that between the cultivators of the soil and the owners of it; that vicious state having been protected and perpetuated by a wrong and superstitious English notion of property in land.

It is *of no use saying,* that the fault is not in the laws of property or the customs relating to landed tenure, but in the people's own laziness, their recklessness, their improvident multiplication, which would keep them in the same state of semi-starvation, under any laws or customs whatever. This laziness, this recklessness, *this improvident multiplication,* are themselves part and parcel of the evil of a bad social system; *s* are a principal portion of the case against it. A people may be lazy and improvident under any system, but they *must* be so under the customs as to occupation of land, which exist in Ireland. When land is let by competition, it may almost be said by auction to peasants cultivating for food and not for profit, then if those peasants are superabundant in numbers, their competition makes them engage for rents impossible to be paid; and the utmost that can be paid becomes the landlord's by right, leaving the tenant still in debt to him. From that time no industry, temperance, or prudence can make the peasant better off; the landlord takes all. If here and there a peasant saves anything, he takes care that his farm shall shew no traces of it; he invests it in a distant savings bank, or hides it in the thatch of his cabin. On the other hand, no indolence, or improvident increase of numbers, makes him poorer: he and all his family are sure of potatoes while there are any on the farm, and if there is nothing left, it is the landlord's loss, not his.

But what, it will be said, is the remedy? What, against such an evil, can the government do? Is the legislature to set aside the proprietary rights of the Irish landlords? By what means can those rights be respected, and yet a larger portion of the produce of the soil, and a more secure tenure, be bestowed on the cultivators?—The thing is not easy. Nobody pretends that it is. To extinguish a system by which, under the name of sanctions of property, the land with all that it produces exists for the sole benefit, it may fairly be said, of a handful of persons who neither by their labour, their skill, nor their accumulations contribute in any way to its productiveness, is difficult, consistently not merely with the *claims* of property, but without some infringement of its acknowledged *rights*. Two things however are certain: first, that the thing, although difficult, is not impossible: and

---

o-o[*underscored by HTM*]
p-p[*underscored by HTM*]
*q-q*vain to say [*substituted by HTM*]
r-r[*evidently deleted by HTM*]
*s*and [*added by HTM*]

secondly, that difficult or not, it *must* be done. "If it cannot, government altogether, in Ireland, *is a failure*, and its foundations require to be broken up, and laid anew on some different plan. The social condition of Ireland, *once for all, cannot be tolerated; it is an abomination in the sight of mankind.*" It must be further said, that the more difficult any one declares it to effect this indispensable transformation of the state of society in Ireland the further he goes towards excusing, at least as to intention, the Irish revolutionary party. The great and salutary change the accomplishment of which by regular legislation is found so arduous, the French Revolution actually accomplished. Before 1789 the peasantry of most of the provinces of France were even more destitute and miserable than Irish cottiers. By the revolution and its consequences, the property of a great part of the soil of France passed into the hands of the peasantry; and the result was the greatest change for the better in their condition, both physical and moral, of which, within a single generation, there is any record. The Irish leaders believed, that ^{x} of such a change, or anything equivalent to it under English government, ^{y}there was no chance^y. They thought probably, that an Irish government might effect it, or at all events that an Irish revolution would: and that the value of the object was worth the risks of such a revolution. And who ^{z}will^z presume to say ^{a}that they were wrong in any of these anticipations? or^a that they miscalculated anything except their chances of success?

$^{t-t}$ought to [*substituted by HTM*]
$^{u-u}$[*vertical line, perhaps indicating cancellation, drawn down the centre of the page by HTM*]
$^{v-v}$[*circled by HTM*]
$^{w-w}$[*circled by HTM*]
^{x}there was no chance [*added by HTM; JSM first wrote and then cancelled* doubtless were convinced *for* believed *in the previous clause*]
$^{y-y}$[*deleted by HTM*]
$^{z-z}$shall [*substituted by HTM; JSM first wrote and then cancelled* undertake *for the next word,* presume]
$^{a-a}$[*put in parentheses by HTM, probably indicating deletion*]

ENGLAND AND IRELAND

1868

EDITOR'S NOTE

5th ed. London: Longmans, Green, Reader, and Dyer, 1869. Reprinted from the 4th, 3rd, 2nd, and 1st eds., all of which were issued in 1868 by Longmans, Green, Reader, and Dyer. Identified in Mill's bibliography as "A pamphlet entitled 'England and Ireland' published in February 1868" (MacMinn, 98). There are no copies in Somerville College; Mill's copy of the 2nd ed. is in the Goldsmith's Library, University of London Library, without correction or emendation. For comment on the work, see xlix–liii, lx–lxii, and lxiii–lxiv above.

The copy-text is the 5th edition (the last in Mill's lifetime), which has been collated with the four earlier editions and the surviving portions of the MS of the first draft (part of which is in the Harvard University Library, and part in the Yale University Library). The substantive variants among the printed editions are given in footnotes, in which the editions are signified by the last two digits of the year of publication, with superscripts when more than one edition appeared in the same year: i.e., "68^1" = 1st ed., "68^2" = 2nd ed., "68^3" = 3rd ed., "68^4" = 4th ed., and "69" = 5th ed.; these variants are keyed by superscript italic letters in the text. Superscript Greek letters in the text are keyed to the equivalent passages in the first draft, which is printed in App. A below; editorial notes (in square brackets and italics) indicate the relation between the printed text and the MS.

England and Ireland

ONCE AT LEAST in every generation the question, "What is to be done with Ireland?"[*] rises again to perplex the councils and trouble the conscience of the British nation. It has now risen more formidable than ever, and with the further aggravation, that it was unexpected. Irish disaffection, assuredly, is a familiar fact; and there have always been those among us who liked to explain it by a special taint or infirmity in the Irish character. But Liberal Englishmen had always attributed it to the multitude of unredressed wrongs. England had for ages, from motives of different degrees of unworthiness, made her yoke heavy upon Ireland. According to a well known computation, the whole land of the island had been confiscated three times over. Part had been taken to enrich powerful Englishmen and their Irish adherents; part to form the endowment of a hostile hierarchy; the rest had been given away to English and Scotch colonists, who held, and were intended to hold it as a garrison against the Irish. The manufactures of Ireland, except the linen manufacture, which was chiefly carried on by these colonists, were deliberately crushed for the avowed purpose of making more room for those of England. The vast majority of the native Irish, all who professed the Roman Catholic religion, were, in violation of the faith pledged to the Catholic army at Limerick, despoiled of all their political and most of their civil rights, and were left in existence only to plough or dig the ground, and pay rent to their task-masters. A nation which treats its subjects in this fashion cannot well expect to be loved by them. It is not necessary to discuss the circumstances of extenuation which an advocate might more or less justly urge to excuse these iniquities to the English conscience. Whatever might be their value in our own eyes, in those of the Irish they had not, and could not have, any extenuating virtue. Short of actual depopulation and desolation, or the direct personal enslaving of the inhabitants, little was omitted which could give a people cause to execrate its conquerors. But these just causes of disloyalty, it was at last thought, had been removed. The jealousy of Irish industry and enterprise has long ceased, and all inequality of commercial advantages between the two countries has been done away with. The civil rights of the Catholic population have been restored to them, and (with one or two trifling exceptions) their political disabilities have been taken off. The prizes

[*Cf. pp. 497–503 above.]

of professsional and of political life, in Ireland, England, and every British dependency, have been thrown open, in law and in fact, to Catholic as well as Protestant Irish. The alien Church indeed remains, but is no longer supported by a levy from the Catholic tillers of the soil; it has become a charge on the rent paid by them, mostly to Protestant landlords. The confiscations have not been reversed; but the hand of time has passed over them: they have reached the stage at which, in the opinion of reasonable men, the reversal of an injustice is but an injustice the more. The representatives of the Irish Catholics are a power in the House of Commons, sufficient at times to hold the balance of parties. Irish complaints, great and small, are listened to with patience, if not always with respect; and when they admit of a remedy which seems reasonable to English minds, there is no longer any reluctance to apply it. What, then, it is thought even by Liberal Englishmen, has Ireland to resent? What, indeed, remains from which resentment could arise? By dint of believing that disaffection had ceased to be reasonable, they came to think that it had ceased to be possible. All grievances, of a kind to exasperate the ruled against the rulers, had, they thought, disappeared. Nature, too, not in her kinder, but in one of her cruellest moods, had made it her study to relieve the conscience of the English rulers of Ireland. A people of whom, according to the Report of a Royal Commission, two millions and a half were for many weeks of each year in a state of chronic starvation,[*] were a sight which might cause some misgiving in a nation that had absolute power over them. But the Angel of Death had stepped in, and removed that spectre from before our gate. An appalling famine, followed by an unexampled and continuous emigration, had, by thinning the labour market, alleviated that extreme indigence which, by making the people desperate, might embitter them, we thought, even against a mild and just Government. Ireland was now not only well governed, but prosperous and improving. Surely the troubles of the British nation about Ireland were now at an end.

It is upon a people, or at least upon upper and middle classes, basking in this fool's paradise, that Fenianism has burst, like a clap of thunder in a clear sky, unlooked for and unintelligible, and has found them utterly unprepared to meet it and to deal with it. The disaffection which they flattered themselves had been cured, suddenly shows itself more intense, more violent, more unscrupulous, and more universal than ever. The population is divided between those who wish success to Fenianism, and those who, though disapproving its means and perhaps its ends, sympathize in its embittered feelings. Repressed by force in Ireland itself, the rebellion visits us in our own homes, scattering death among those who have given no provocation but that of being English-born. So deadly is the hatred, that it will run all risks merely to do us harm, with little or no prospect of any consequent good to itself. Our rulers are helpless to deal with this new outburst of enmity,

[*"Third Report of the Commissioners for Inquiring into the Condition of the Poorer Classes in Ireland," *PP*, 1836, XXX, 5.]

because they are unable to see that anything on their part has given cause for it. They are brought face to face with a spirit which will as little tolerate what we think our good government as our bad, and they have not been trained to manage problems of that difficulty. But though their statesmanship is at fault, their conscience is at ease, because the rebellion, they think, is not one of grievance or suffering; it is a rebellion for an idea—the idea of nationality. Alas for the self-complacent ignorance of irresponsible rulers, be they monarchs, classes, or nations! If there is anything sadder than the calamity itself, it is the unmistakeable sincerity and good faith with which numbers of Englishmen confess themselves incapable of comprehending it. They know not that the disaffection which neither has nor needs any other motive than aversion to the rulers, is the climax to a long growth of disaffection arising from causes that might have been removed. What seems to them the causelessness of the Irish repugnance to our rule, is the proof that they have almost let pass the last opportunity they are ever likely to have of setting it right. They have allowed what once was indignation against particular wrongs, to harden into a passionate determination to be no longer ruled on any terms by those to whom they ascribe all their evils. Rebellions are never really unconquerable until they have become rebellions for an idea. Revolt against practical ill-usage may be quelled by concessions; but wait till all practical grievances have merged in the demand for independence, and there is no knowing that any concession, short of independence, will appease the quarrel.

But what, it will be asked, is the provocation that England is giving to Ireland, now that she has left off crushing her commerce and persecuting her religion? What harm to Ireland does England intend, or knowingly inflict? What good, that she knows how to give her, would she not willingly bestow? Unhappily, her offence is precisely that she does not know; and is so well contented with not knowing, that Irishmen who are not hostile to her are coming to believe that she will not and cannot learn. Calm men, like the clerical authors of the Limerick declaration,[*] who disapprove of Fenianism and of all that the Fenians are doing, and who have no preference for separation in itself, are expressing a deliberate conviction that the English nation *cannot* see or understand what laws and institutions are necessary for a state of society and civilization like that of Ireland. The English people ought to ask themselves, seriously and without prejudice, what it is that gives sober men this opinion of them; and endeavour to remove it, or humbly confess that it is true, and fulfil the only duty which remains performable by them on that supposition, that of withdrawing from the attempt.

That this desperate form of disaffection, which does not demand to be better governed, which asks us for no benefit, no redress of grievances, not even any reparation for injuries, but simply to take ourselves off and rid the country of our

---

[*Richard Baptist O'Brien, "Limerick Declaration" (23 Dec., 1867), in *The Times*, 2 Jan., 1868, pp. 8–9.]

Folio 3r of draft of *England and Ireland*
MS Houghton Library, Harvard University

presence—that this revolt of mere nationality *a*has been so long in coming, proves that it might have been prevented from coming at all. More than a generation has elapsed since we renounced the desire to govern Ireland for the English: if at that epoch we had begun to know how to govern her for herself, the two nations would by this time have been one. But we neither knew, nor knew that we did not know. We had got a set of institutions of our own, which we thought suited us—whose imperfections we were, at any rate, used to: we, or our ruling classes, thought, that there could be no boon to any country equal to that of imparting *a*these*a* institutions to her, and as none of their benefits were any longer withheld from Ireland, Ireland, it seemed, could have nothing more to desire. What was not too bad for us, must be good enough for Ireland, or if not, Ireland or the nature of things was alone in fault.*a* *β*

*γ*It is always a most difficult task which a people assumes when it attempts to govern, either in the way of incorporation or as a dependency, another people very unlike itself. But whoever reflects on the constitution of society in these two countries, with any sufficient knowledge of the states of society which exist elsewhere, will be driven, however unwillingly, to the conclusion, that there is probably no other nation of the civilized world, which, if the task of governing Ireland had happened to devolve on it, would not have shown itself more capable of that work than England has hitherto done. The reasons are these: First, there is no other civilized nation which is so conceited of its own institutions, and of all its modes of public action, as England is; and secondly, there is no other civilized nation which is so far apart from Ireland in the character of its history, or so unlike it in the whole constitution of its social economy; and none, therefore, which if it applies to Ireland the modes of thinking and maxims of government which have grown up within itself, is so certain to go wrong.*γ*

The first indeed of our disqualifications, our conceit of ourselves, is certainly diminishing. Our governing classes are now quite accustomed to be told that the institutions which they thought must suit all mankind since they suited us, require far greater alteration than they dream of to be fit even for ourselves. When they were told this, they have long been in the habit of answering, that whatever defects these institutions may have in theory, they are suited to the opinions, the feelings, and the historical antecedents of the English people. But mark how little they really mean by this vindication. If suitability to the opinions, feelings, and historical antecedents of those who live under them is the best recommendation of institutions, it ought to have been remembered, that the opinions, feelings, and historical antecedents of the Irish people are totally different from, and in many respects contrary to those of the English; and that things which in England find

---

a-a[*cf.* App. A, 535]
*a-a*68¹ those
β[*two sentences deleted; see* App. A, 535–6]
γ-γ[*cf.* App. A, 536]

their chief justification in their being liked, cannot admit of the same justification in a country where they are detested. But the reason which recommends institutions to their own supporters, and that which is used to stop the mouths of opponents, are far from being always one and the same.

Let us take as an example, that one of our institutions which has the most direct connexion with the worst practical grievances of Ireland; absolute property in land, the land being engrossed by a comparatively small number of families. I am not going to discuss this institution, or to express, on the present occasion, any opinion about its abstract merits. Let these, if we will, be transcendant—let it be the best and highest form of agricultural and social economy, for anything I mean to say to the contrary. But I do say that this is not self-evident. It is not one of the truths which shine so brilliantly by their own light, that they are assented to by every sane man the moment he understands the words in which they are conveyed. On the contrary, what present themselves the most obviously at the first aspect of this institution are the objections to it. That a man should have absolute control over what his own labour and skill have created, and even over what he has received by gift or bequest from those who created it, is recommended by reasons of a very obvious character, and does not shock any natural feeling. Moveable property can be produced in indefinite quantity, and he who disposes as he likes of anything which, it can fairly be argued, would not have existed but for him, does no wrong to any one. It is otherwise with regard to land, a thing which no man made,[*] which exists in limited quantity, which was the original inheritance of all mankind, and which whoever appropriates, keeps others out of its possession. Such appropriation, when there is not enough left for all, is at the first aspect, an usurpation on the rights of other people. And though it is manifestly just that he who sows should be allowed to reap, this justice, which is the true moral foundation of property in land, avails little in favour of proprietors who reap but do not sow, and who assume the right of ejecting those who do. When the general condition of the land of a country is such as this, its title to the submission and attachment of those whom it seems to disinherit, is by no means obvious. It is a state of things which has great need of extrinsic recommendations. It requires to be rooted in the traditions and oldest recollections of the people; the landed families must be identified with the religion of the country, with its nationality, with its ancient rulers, leaders, defenders, teachers, and other objects of gratitude and veneration, or at least of ungrudging obedience.

These conditions have been found, in some considerable measure, or at all events, nothing contrary to them has been found, for many centuries, in England. All that is most opposite to them has at all times existed in Ireland. The traditions

[*Cf. Mill, *Principles of Political Economy, CW*, Vol. II, p. 230 (II, ii, 6), and his Speech on Mr. Chichester Fortescue's Land Bill (17 May, 1866) in *Chapters and Speeches on the Irish Land Question*, p. 104 (where he refers to the passage in his *Principles*).]

and recollections of native Irish society are wholly the contrary way. Before the Conquest, the Irish people knew nothing of absolute property in land. The land virtually belonged to the entire sept; the chief was little more than the managing member of the association. The feudal idea, which views all rights as emanating from a head landlord, came in with the conquest, was associated with foreign dominion, and has never to this day been recognised by the moral sentiments of the people. Originally the offspring not of industry but of spoliation, the right has not been allowed to purify itself by protracted possession, but has passed from the original spoliators to others by a series of fresh spoliations, so as to be always connected with the latest and most odious oppressions of foreign invaders. In the moral feelings of the Irish people, the right to hold the land goes, as it did in the beginning, with the right to till it. Since the last confiscations,[*] nearly all the land has been owned from generation to generation with a more absolute ownership than exists in almost any other country (except England), by landlords (mostly foreigners, and nearly all of a foreign religion) who had less to do with tilling it, who had less connexion with it of any useful kind—or indeed of any kind, for a large proportion did not even reside on it—than the landowners of any other known country. There are parts of Europe, such as East Prussia, where the land is chiefly owned in large estates, but where almost every landowner farms his own land. In Ireland, until a recent period, any one who knew the country might almost have counted those who did anything for their estate but consume its produce. The landlords were a mere burthen on the land. The whole rental of the country was wasted in maintaining, often in reckless extravagance, people who were not nearly as useful to the hive as the drones are, and were entitled to less respect. These are the antecedents of Irish history in respect to property in land. Let any Englishman put himself in the position of an Irish peasant, and ask himself whether, if the case were his own, the landed property of the country would have any sacredness to his feelings. Even the Whiteboy and the Rockite, in their outrages against the landlord, fought for, not against, the sacredness of what was property in their eyes; for it is not the right of the rent-receiver, but the right of the cultivator, with which the idea of property is connected in the Irish popular mind.

These facts being notorious, and the feelings engendered by them being, in part at least, perfectly reasonable in the eyes of every civilized people in the world except England, it is a characteristic specimen of the practical good sense by which England is supposed to be distinguished, that she should persist to this hour in forcing upon a people with such feelings, and such antecedents, her own idea of absolute property in land. If those who created English manufactures, commerce, navigation, and dominion, to say nothing of English literature and science, had gone to work in this style—had shown this amount of judgment in the adaptation

[*See 11 & 12 William III, c. 2 (1700).]

of means to ends—England would at the present time have been in something like the condition of the Papal territory, or of Spain.

Thus much as to the harmony of certain English institutions with the feelings and prepossessions of the Irish people, which, according to the received doctrine of our historical Conservatives, is the first point to be considered in either retaining old institutions or introducing new. But now, apart from the question of acceptability to Ireland, let us consider whether our own laws and usages, at least in relation to land, are the model we should even desire to follow in governing Ireland; whether the circumstances of the two countries are sufficiently similar, to warrant the belief, that things which may work well, or may not be fatally destructive to prosperity, in England, will be useful or innocuous, even if voluntarily accepted by the people of the neighbouring island.

*What are the main features in the social economy of Ireland? First, it is a country wholly agricultural. The entire population, with some not very important exceptions, cultivates the soil, or depends for its subsistence on cultivation. In this respect, if all the countries of Europe except Russia were arranged in a scale, Ireland would be at one extremity of the scale, England and Scotland at the other. In Great Britain, not more than a third of the population subsists by agriculture. In most countries of the Continent a great majority do so, though in no country but Russia so great a majority as in Ireland. Ireland, therefore, in this essential particular, bears more resemblance to almost any other country in Europe than she does to Great Britain.

When the agricultural population are but a fraction of the entire people; when the commercial and manufacturing development of the country leaves a large opening for the children of the agriculturists to seek and find subsistence elsewhere than on the soil; a bad tenure of land, though always mischievous, can in some measure be borne with. But when a people have no means of sustenance but the land, the conditions on which the land can be occupied, and support derived from it, are all in all. Now, under an apparent resemblance, those conditions are radically different in Ireland and in England. In England the land is rented and cultivated by capitalist farmers; in Ireland, except in the grazing districts, principally by manual labourers, or small farmers in nearly the same condition in life. The multitude of other differences which flow from this one difference, it would be too prolix to detail. But (what is still more important), in Ireland, where the well-being of the whole population depends on the terms on which they are permitted to occupy the land, those terms are the very worst* in Europe. There are many other countries in which the land is owned principally in large masses, and farmed in great part by manual labourers. But I doubt if there be now any other part of Europe where, as a general rule, these farm-labourers are entirely without a permanent interest in the soil. The serfs certainly were not; they could not be turned out of their holdings.

−[cf. App. A, 536]

The *métayers* in France, before the Revolution, could; and their wretchedness, accordingly, was the bye-word of Europe. There are still métayers in France, but those of them who have not, as many have, other land of their own in full property, are still the disturbing element of rural society. The departments which returned Socialist deputies to the Assemblies of 1848 and 1849 were chiefly those in which métayerism still lingered. The métayers of Italy are, by a custom, as binding as law, irremovable so long as they fulfil their contract. The Prussian peasants, even before the beneficent enfranchising legislation of Stein and Hardenberg,[*] had positive rights in the soil which they could not be deprived of. It is only in parts of Belgium that it is a frequent practice for small farmers to hold from large proprietors, with no other legal protection than the stipulations of a short lease: but their truly admirable industry owes its vigour to the fact that small landed properties are always to be had for money, at prices which they can hope to save. They, moreover, live in the midst of a large and thriving manufacturing industry, which takes off the hands that might otherwise compete unduly for the soil. In Ireland alone the whole agricultural population can be evicted by the mere will of the landlord, either at the expiration of a lease, or, in the far commoner case of their having no lease, at six months' notice. In Ireland alone the bulk of a population dependent wholly on the land, cannot look forward with confidence to a single year's occupation of it: while the sole outlet for the dispossessed cultivators, or for those whose competition raises the rents against the cultivators, is expatriation. So long as they remain in the country of their birth, their support must be drawn from a source for the permanence of which they have no guarantee, and the failure of which leaves them nothing to depend on but the poor-house.

In one circumstance alone England and Ireland are alike: the cultivated area of both countries is owned in large estates by a small class of great landlords. In the opinion of great landlords, and of the admirers of the state of society which produces them, this is enough: the interest and the wisdom of the landlords may be implicitly relied on for making everybody comfortable. Great landlords can do as they like with their estates, on this side of St. George's Channel; English landlords are absolute masters of the conditions on which they will let their land; and why should not Irish landlords be so? But in the first place, English landlords do not let their land to a labourer, but to a capitalist farmer, who is able to take care of his own interest. The capitalist has not to choose between the possession of a farm and destitution; the labourer has. This element subverts the whole basis on which the letting of farms, as a business transaction, and the foundation of a national economy, requires to rest. The capitalist farmer will beware of offering a rent that will leave him no profit; the peasant farmer will promise any amount of rent,

[*For reforms in Prussia initiated by Heinrich Friedrich Karl von Stein, and continued by Karl August von Hardenberg, see Ernst Rudolph Huber, ed., *Documente zur deutschen Verfassungsgeschichte*, 3 vols. (Stuttgart: Kohlhammer, 1961–65), Vol. I, pp. 38–47.]

whether he can pay it or not. England, moreover, not being a purely agricultural, but a commercial country, even great landlords learn to look at the management of estates in a somewhat commercial spirit, and can see their own advantage (where the love of political influence does not *b*interfere*b*) in making it the interest of the tenant to improve the land; or, if they can afford to do so, will often improve it for him. An average Irish landlord, instead of improving his estate, does not even put up the fences and farm-buildings which everywhere else it is the landlord's business to provide; they are left to be erected by the labourer-tenant for himself, and are such as a labourer-tenant is able to erect. If a tenant here and there is able and willing to make them a little better than ordinary, or to add in any other manner to the productiveness and value of the farm, there is nothing to prevent the landlord from waiting till it is done, and then seizing on the result, or requiring from the tenant additional rent for the use of the fruits of his own labour; and so many landlords even of high rank are not ashamed to do this, that it is evident their compeers do not think it at all disgraceful. It is usual to impute the worst abuses of Irish landlordism to middlemen. Middlemen are rapidly dying out, but there was lately a middleman[*] in the county of Clare, under whose landlordship Irish peasants, by their labour and their scanty means, reclaimed a considerable tract on the sea-coast, and founded thereon the flourishing watering-place of Kilkee. The middleman died, his lease fell in, and the tenants fancied that they should now be still better off; but the head landlord, the Marquis *c*of*c* Conyngham, at once put on rents equal to the full value of the improvements* (in some instances an increase of 700 per cent), and not content with this, pulled down a considerable portion of the

[*Mr. Studdert.]

*[68³] Replies have been made to this statement, by the Marquis of Conyngham in the *Times*, and by Lord Lifford in the House of Lords. [Francis Nathaniel Conyngham, "To the Editor of the Times" (24 Feb., 1868), *The Times*, 26 Feb., 1868, p. 10; and James Hewitt, Speech on the Tenure (Ireland) Bill (12 Mar., 1868), *PD*, 3rd ser., Vol. 190, cols. 1440–3.] But their replies do not contradict the statement on any essential point. They deny nothing which I had alleged, except that the rents were raised "to the full value of the improvements." In support of this denial, they state that after some portions of the estate had been sold, the tenants of the remainder presented a memorial to Lord Conyngham, praying that he would not sell their holdings, but that they might still continue his tenants. Now it is possible that the increased rents, enormous as they were, did not come up to the entire value which had been given to the holdings by the labour and capital of the tenants. But it is no proof of this, that the tenants were willing to pay the rents rather than be ejected; or that they preferred to remain under their old landlord, on whom they had some sort of moral claim, however imperfect might be his sense of it, rather than be transferred to a stranger, whose first act, like that of some other purchasers in the Encumbered Estates and Landed Estates Courts, might be to "clear the estate."

Lord Lifford, in the House of Lords, added another piece of evidence to prove that Lord Conyngham's rents were not excessive. It is, that the purchasers of the portions of his estate which he lately sold, immediately raised the rents 50 per cent. A more damaging fact for

*b-b*68¹, 68² prevent
c-c+68³, 68⁴, 69

town, reduced its population from 1879 to 950, and drove out the remainder to wander about Ireland, or to England or America, and swell the ranks of the bitter enemies of Great Britain.* Did the interest, any more than the good feelings, of this landlord, prevent him from destroying this remarkable creation of industry, and giving its creators cause bitterly to repent that they had ever made it? What might not be hoped from a people who had the energy and enterprise to create a flourishing town under liability to be robbed? And to what sympathy or consideration are those entitled who avail themselves of a bad law to perpetrate what is morally robbery?

When Irishmen ask to be protected against deeds of this description, they are told that the law they complain of is the same which exists in England. What signifies it that the law is the same, if opinion and the social circumstances of the country are better than the law, and prevent the oppression which the law permits? It is bad that one *can* be robbed in due course of law, but it is greatly worse when one actually is. England, with her capitalist farmers and her powerful public opinion, can afford to leave improper power in the hands of her great landlords—not, indeed, without serious evil to her agricultural population, the state of ^{d}whom^d is generally felt to be the most peccant part of her social condition; not without evil to all over whom power is exercised through the votes of that population; but yet without hindrance to the attainment, by the nation as a whole, of great wealth and prosperity. Ireland is very differently circumstanced. When, as a general rule, the land of a country is farmed by the very hands that till it, the social economy resulting is intolerable, unless either by law or custom the tenant is protected against arbitrary eviction, or arbitrary increase of rent. Nor is there any country of Western Europe save England (unless Spain be an exception) which, if Ireland had belonged to it, would not before this time have seen and acted on that principle; because there is not one which is not familiar with the principle and its bearings, from ample experience. England alone is without such experience of its own, and knows and cares too little about foreign countries to benefit by theirs.

Lord Conyngham could scarcely have been brought to light: for, had his own rents been ever so moderate, selling the land as he did by public competition, he sold for his own benefit, and doubtless for its full value, the power of exacting rents 50 per cent higher: taking thus for his own pocket the principal of which those rents are the interest, and which is the result of the labour of his tenants. Let me add, though it is not essential to the question, that, if I am rightly informed, the purchasers were Lord Conyngham's bailiff, and the brother of a clerk of his agent; and that the purchases were made over the heads of the unfortunate tenants, who strained their pecuniary means to the uttermost to enable themselves to buy back the property they had themselves created, but who were outbid and disappointed.

*The outline of these facts is matter of public notoriety. For details, far more impressive than I have ventured to quote, the reader may refer to the pamphlet of the Rev. Sylvester Malone, *Tenant-Wrong Illustrated in a Nutshell; or, A History of Kilkee in Relation to Landlordism during the Last Seven Years* [Dublin: Kelly, 1867].

$^{d-d}$68^1, 68^2 which

At a particular moment of the revolutionary war, a French armament, led by the illustrious Hoche, was only prevented by stress of weather from effecting a landing in Ireland. At that moment it was on the cards whether Ireland should not belong to France, or at least be organized as an independent country under French protection. Had this happened, does any one believe that the Irish peasant would not have become even as the French peasant? When the great landowners had fled, as they would have fled, to England, every farm on their estates would have become the property of the occupant, subject to some fixed payment ᵉto the State. Ireland would then have been in the condition in which small farming, and tenancy by manual labourers, are consistent with good agriculture and public prosperity. The small holder would have laboured for himself and not for others, and his interest would have coincided with the interest of the country in making every plot of land produce its utmost. What Hoche would have done for the Irish peasant, or its equivalent, has still to be done; and any government which will not do it does not fulfil the rational and moral conditions of a government. There is no necessity that it should be done as Hoche would most likely have done it, without indemnity to the losers. A few years ago it might not have been necessary to do as much as he would have done. The distribution of the waste land in peasant properties might then have sufficed. Perhaps even such small measures as that of securing to tenants a moderate compensation, in money or by length of lease, for improvements actually made, and abolishing the unjust privilege of distraining for rent, might have appeased or postponed disaffection, and given to great-landlordism a fresh term of existence. But such reforms as these, granted at the last moment, would hardly give a week's respite from active disaffection. The Irish are no longer reduced to take anything they can get. They have acquired the sense of being supported by prosperous multitudes of their countrymen on the opposite side of the Atlantic. These it is who will furnish the leaders, the pecuniary resources, the skill, the military discipline, and a great part of the effective force, in any future Irish rebellion: and it is the interest of these auxiliaries to refuse to listen to any form of compromise, since no share of its benefits would be for them, while they would lose the dream of a place in the world's eye as chiefs of an independent republic. With these for leaders, and a people like the Irish, always ready to trust implicitly those whom they think hearty in their cause, no accommodation is henceforth possible which does not give the Irish peasant all that he could gain by a revolution—permanent possession of the land, subject to fixed burthens. Such a change may be revolutionary; but revolutionary measures are the thing now required. It is not necessary that the revolution should be violent, still less that it should be unjust. It may and it ought to respect existing pecuniary interests which have the sanction of law. An equivalent ought to be given for the bare pecuniary value of all mischievous rights which landlords or any others are required to part

---

ᵉ⁻ᵉ[*cf.* App. A, 536–7]

with. But no mercy ought to be shown to the mischievous rights themselves; no scruples of purely English birth ought to stay our hands from effecting, since it has come to that, a real revolution in the economical and social constitution of Ireland. In the completeness of the revolution will lie its safety. Anything less than complete, unless as a step to completion, will give no help. There has been a time for proposals to effect this change by a gradual process, by encouragement of voluntary arrangements; but the volume of the Sibyl's books which contained them has been burned. If ever, in our time, Ireland is to be a consenting party to her union with England, the changes must be so made that the existing generation of Irish farmers shall at once enter upon their benefits. The rule of Ireland now rightfully belongs to those who, by means consistent with justice, will make the cultivators of the soil of Ireland the owners of it; and the English nation has got to decide whether it will be that just ruler or not.

Englishmen are not always incapable of shaking off insular prejudices, and governing another country according to its wants, and not according to common English habits and notions. It is what they have had to do in India; and those Englishmen who know something of India, are even now those who understand Ireland best. Persons who know both countries, have remarked many points of resemblance between the Irish and the Hindoo character; there certainly are many between the agricultural economy of Ireland and that of India. But, by a fortunate accident, the business of ruling India in the name of England did not rest with the Houses of Parliament or the offices at Westminster; it devolved on men who passed their lives in India, and made Indian interests their professional occupation. There was also the advantage, that the task was laid upon England after nations had begun to have a conscience, and not while they were sunk in the reckless savagery of the middle ages. The English rulers, accordingly, reconciled themselves to the idea that their business was not to sweep away the rights they found established, or wrench and compress them into the similitude of something English, but to ascertain what they were; having ascertained them, to abolish those only which were absolutely mischievous; otherwise to protect them, and use them as a starting point for further steps in improvement. This work of stripping off their preconceived English ideas was at first done clumsily and imperfectly, and at the cost of many mistakes; but as they honestly meant to do it, they in time succeeded, and India is now governed, if with a large share of the ordinary imperfections of rulers, yet with a full perception and recognition of its differences from England. What has been done for India has now to be done for Ireland; and as we should have deserved to be turned out of the one, had we not proved equal to the need, so shall we to lose the other.[e]

It is not consistent with self-respect, in a nation any more than in an individual, to wait till it is compelled by uncontrollable circumstances to resign that which it cannot in conscience hold. Before allowing its government to involve it in another repetition of the attempt to maintain English dominion over Ireland by brute force, the English nation ought to commune with its conscience, and solemnly reconsider its position. ⸢If England is unable to learn what has to be learnt, and unlearn what has to be unlearnt, in order to make her rule willingly accepted by the Irish people; or, to look at the hypothesis on its other side, if the Irish are incapable of being taught the superiority of English notions about the way in which they ought to be governed, and obstinately persist in preferring their own; if this supposition, whichever way we choose to turn it, is true, are we the power which, according to the general fitness of things and the rules of morality, ought to govern Ireland? If so, what are we dreaming of, when we give our sympathy to the Poles, the Italians, the Hungarians, the Servians, the Greeks, and I know not how many other oppressed nationalities? On what principle did we act when we renounced the government of the Ionian Islands?[*]

It is not to fear of consequences, but to a sense of right, that one would wish to appeal on this most momentous question. Yet it is not impertinent to say, that to hold Ireland permanently by the old bad means is simply impossible. Neither Europe nor America would now bear the sight of a Poland across the Irish Channel. Were we to attempt it, and a rebellion, so provoked, could hold its ground but for a few weeks, there would be an explosion of indignation all over the civilized world; on this single occasion Liberals and Catholics would be unanimous; Papal volunteeers and Garibaldians would fight side by side against us for the independence of Ireland, until the many enemies of British prosperity had time to complicate the situation by a foreign war. Were we even able to prevent a rebellion, or suppress it the moment it broke out, the holding down by military violence of a people in desperation, constantly struggling to break their fetters, is a spectacle which Russia is still able to give to mankind, because Russia is almost inaccessible to a foreign enemy; but the attempt could not long succeed with a country so vulnerable as England, having territories to defend in every part of the globe, and half her population dependent on foreign commerce. Neither do I believe that the mass of the British people, those who are not yet corrupted by power, would permit the attempt. The prophets who, judging, I presume, from themselves, always augur the worst of the moral sentiments of their countrymen, are already asseverating that, whether right or wrong, the British people would rather devastate Ireland from end to end and root out its inhabitants, than consent to its separation from England. If we believe them, the people of England are a kind of bloodhounds, always ready to break loose and perpetrate Jamaica horrors, unless they, and their like, are there to temper and restrain British brutality. This representation does not accord with my experience. I believe that these prophecies proceed from men who seek to make their countrymen responsible for what they themselves are burning to commit; and that the rising power in our affairs, the

[*See 27 & 28 Victoria, c. 77 (1864).]

⸢-⸢[cf. App. A, 537–8, *considerably rewritten in places*]

democracy of Great Britain, is opposed, on principle, to holding any people in subjection against their will. The question was put, some six months ago, to one of the largest and most enthusiastic public meetings ever assembled in London under one roof—"Do you think that England has a right to rule over Ireland if she cannot make the Irish people content with her rule?" and the shouts of "No!" which burst from every part of that great assemblage, will not soon be forgotten by those who heard them.[*] An age when delegates of working men meet in European Congresses to concert united action for the interests of labour, is not one in which labourers will cut down labourers at other people's bidding. The time is come when the democracy of one country will join hands with the democracy of another, rather than back their own ruling authorities in putting it down. I shall not believe, until I see it proved, that the English and Scotch people are capable of the folly and wickedness of carrying fire and sword over Ireland in order that their rulers may govern Ireland contrary to the will of the Irish people. That they would put down a partial outbreak, in order to get a fair trial for a system of government beneficent and generally acceptable to the people, I readily believe; nor should I in any way blame them for so doing.

$^\eta$Let it not, however, be supposed that I should regard either an absolute or a qualified separation of the two countries, otherwise than as a dishonour to one, and a serious misfortune to both. It would be a deep disgrace to us, that having the choice of, on the one hand, a peaceful legislative revolution in the laws and rules affecting the relation of the inhabitants to the soil, or on the other, of abandoning a task beyond our skill, and leaving Ireland to rule herself, incapacity for the better of the two courses should drive us to the worse. For that it would be greatly the worse even for Ireland, many Irishmen, even Irish Catholics, are probably still calm enough to perceive, if but good government can be had without it.$^\eta$

$^\theta$The mere geographical situation of the two countries makes them far more fit to exist as one nation than as two. Not only are they more powerful for defence against a foreign enemy combined than separate, but, if separate, they would be a standing menace to one another. Parted at the present time and with their present feelings, the two islands would be, of all countries in Europe, those which would have the most hostile disposition towards one another. Too much bitter feeling still remains between England and the United States, more than eighty years after separation; and Ireland has suffered from England, for many centuries, evils compared with which the greatest grievances of the Americans were, in all but their principle, insignificant. The persevering reciprocation of insults between English and American newspapers and public speakers has, before now, brought

[*John Stuart Mill, Speech to the National Reform Union Meeting at St. James's Hall (25 May, 1867), *Daily News*, 27 May, 1867, p. 2.]

$^{\eta-\eta}$[*completely rewritten; cf.* App. A, 538]
$^{\theta-\theta}$[*cf.* App. A, 538–9]

those two countries to the verge of a war; would there not be even more of this between countries still nearer neighbours, on the morrow of an unfriendly separation? In the perpetual state of irritated feeling thus kept up, trifles would become causes of quarrel. Disputes more or less serious, even collisions, would be for ever liable to occur. Ireland, therefore, besides having to defend herself against all other enemies, internal and external, without English help, would feel obliged to keep herself always armed and in readiness to fight England.[θ] 'An Irishman must have a very lofty idea of the resources of his country who thinks that this load upon the Irish taxpayer would be easily borne. A war-tax assessed upon the soil, for want of other taxable material, would be no small set-off against what the peasant would gain even by the entire cessation of rent. The burthen of the necessity of being always prepared for war, was no unimportant part of the motive which made the Northern States of America prefer a war at once to allowing the South to secede from the Union. Yet the necessity would not have weighed so heavily on them as it would on Ireland, because they were both the most powerful half of the American Union and the richest. To England, the necessity of being always in a state of preparation against Ireland would be comparatively a less inconvenience, because she already has to maintain, for defence against foreigners, a force that would in general suffice for both purposes. But Ireland would have to create both a fleet and an army; and, after all that could be done, so oppressive would be her sense of insecurity, that she would probably be driven to compromise her newly acquired independence, and seek the protection of alliances with Continental powers.'[κ]From that moment she would, in addition to her own wars, be dragged into a participation in theirs. Were she to choose the smaller evil, and remain free from any permanent entanglement, all enemies of Great Britain would not the less confidently look forward to an Irish alliance, and to being allowed to use Ireland as a basis of attack against Great Britain. Ireland would probably become, like Belgium formerly, one of the battle-fields of European war: while she would be in not unreasonable fear lest England should anticipate the danger, by herself occupying Ireland with a military force at every commencement of hostilities. On the part of England, the pacific character which English policy has assumed precludes any probability of aggressive war; but the ejected Irish higher classes (for ejected they could scarcely fail to be) would form an element hostile to Ireland on this side of the Irish Sea, which would be to the Irish Republic what the *émigrés* at Coblentz were to revolutionary France. In all this I am supposing that Ireland would succeed in establishing a regular and orderly government: but suppose that she failed? Suppose that she had to pass through an interval of partial anarchy first? What if there were a civil war between the Protestant and Catholic Irish, or between Ulster and the other provinces? Is it in human nature that the sympathies of England should not be principally with the

ι–ι[*cf. one sentence in* App. A, 539]
κ–κ[*cf.* App. A, 539]

English Protestant colony, and would not she either help that side, or be constantly believed to be on the point of helping it? For generations it is to be feared that the two nations would be either at war, or in a chronic state of precarious and armed peace, each constantly watching a probable enemy so near at hand that in an instant they might be at each other's throat.*ᵏ ᴧ*By this state of their relations it is almost superfluous to say that the poorer of the two countries would suffer most. To England it would be an inconvenience; to Ireland a public calamity, not only in the way of direct burthen, but by the paralyzing effect of a general feeling of insecurity upon industrial energy and enterprise.

But there is a contingency beyond all this, from the possibility of which we ought not to avert our eyes. Ireland might be invaded and conquered by a great military power. She might become a province of France. This is not the least likely thing to befal her, if her independence of England should be followed by protracted disorders, such as to make peaceably disposed persons welcome an armed pacificator capable of imposing on the conflicting parties a common servitude. How bitter such a result of all their struggles ought to be to patriotic Irishmen, I will not stop to show. But I ask any patriotic Englishman what he would think of such a prospect; and whether he is disposed to run the risk of it, in order that a few hundred families of the upper classes may continue to possess the land of Ireland, instead of its pecuniary value.$^\lambda$

$^\mu$All this evil, it may be thought, could be prevented by agreeing beforehand upon a close alliance and perpetual confederacy between the two nations. But is it likely that the party which had effected a separation in home affairs, would desire or consent to unity in foreign relations? A confederacy is an agreement to have the same friends and enemies, and can only subsist between peoples who have the same interests and feelings, and who, if they fight at all, would wish to fight on the same side. Great Britain and Ireland, if all community of interest between them were cut off, would generally prefer to be on contrary sides. In any Continental complications, the sympathies of England would be with Liberalism; while those of Ireland are sure to be on the same side as the Pope[*]—that is, on the side opposed to modern civilization and progress, and to the freedom of all except Catholic populations held in subjection by non-Catholic rulers. Besides, America is the country with which we are at present in most danger of having serious difficulties; and Ireland would be far more likely to confederate with America against us, than with us against America.$^\mu$ $^\nu$Some may say that this difference of national feeling, if an obstacle to alliance, is, *à fortiori*, a condemnation of union. But even the most Catholic of Irishmen may reasonably consider that Irish influence in the British Parliament is a great mitigator of British hostility to things with which Ireland

[*Pius IX.]

$^{\lambda-\lambda}$[*not in first draft*]
$^{\mu-\mu}$[*cf.* App. A, 539]
$^{\nu-\nu}$[*not in first draft*]

sympathizes; that a Pro-Catholic element in the House of Commons, which no English Government can venture to despise, helps to prevent the whole power of Great Britain from being in the hands of the Anti-Catholic element still so strong in England and Scotland. If there is any party in Great Britain which would not have cause to regret the separation of Ireland, it is the fanatical Protestant party. It may well be doubted if an independent Ireland could in any way give such effective support to any cause to which Ireland is attached, as by the forbearance and moderation which her presence in British councils imposes upon the power which would be likeliest, in case of conflict, to lead the van of the contrary side.*ᵛ*

*ᵍ*I see nothing that Ireland could gain by separation which might not be obtained by union, except the satisfaction, which she is thought to prize, of being governed solely by Irishmen—that is, almost always by men with a strong party animosity against some part of her population: unless indeed the stronger party began its career of freedom by driving the whole of the weaker party beyond the seas. In return, Irishmen would be shut out from all positions in Great Britain, except those which can be held by foreigners. There would be no more Irish prime-ministers, Irish commanders-in-chief, Irish generals and admirals in the British army and fleet. Not in Britain only, but in all Britain's dependencies—in India and the Colonies, Irishmen would *ᵉ*thenceforth*ᵉ* be on the footing of strangers. The loss would exceed the gain, not only by calculation, but in feeling. The first man in a small country would often gladly exchange positions with the fourth or fifth in a great one.

But why, it may be asked, cannot Ireland remain united with the British Crown by a mere personal tie, having the management of her own affairs, as Canada has, though a part of the same empire?[*] Or why may not Great Britain and Ireland be joined as Austria and Hungary are, each with its own separate administration and legislature, and an equal voice in the joint concerns of both?[†] I answer: The former of these relations would be to Ireland a derogation, a descent from even her present position. She is now at least a part of the governing country. She has something to say in the general affairs of the empire. Canada is but a dependency, with a provincial government, allowed to make its own laws and impose its taxes, but subject to the veto of the mother-country and not consulted at all about alliances or wars, in which it is nevertheless compelled to join. An union such as this can only exist as a temporary expedient, between countries which look forward to separation as soon as the weaker is able to stand alone, and which care not much how soon it comes. This mode of union, moreover, is still recent; it has stood no trials; it has not yet been exposed to the greatest trial—that of war. Let

[*By 30 Victoria, c. 3 (1867).]

[†See Gesetzartikel XII v.J.1867, in Samuel Radó-Rothfeld, *Die ungarische Verfassung geschichtlich dargestellt* (Berlin: Puttkammer and Mühlbrecht, 1898), pp. 190–203.]

ᵍ⁻ᵍ[*cf.* App. A, 539–40]
*ᵉ⁻ᵉ*68¹, 68² henceforth

war come, by an act of the British Government in which Canada is not represented, and from a motive in which Canada is not concerned, and how long will Canada be content to share the burthens and the dangers? Even in home affairs, Ireland would not relish the position of Canada. The veto of the Crown is virtually that of the British Parliament; and though it might, as in the case of Canada, be discreetly confined to what were considered imperial questions, the decision what questions were imperial would rest with the country in whose councils Ireland would no longer have a voice. It is very improbable that the veto would stop at things which, in the opinion of the subordinate country, were proper subjects for it. Canada is a great way off, and British rulers can tolerate much in a place from which they are not afraid that the contagion may spread to England. But Ireland is marked out for union with England, if only by this, that nothing important can take place in the one without making its effects felt in the other. If the British Parliament could sufficiently shake off its prejudices to use the veto on Irish legislation rightly, it could shake them off sufficiently to legislate for Ireland rightly, or to allow the Irish, as it already allows the Scotch members, to transact the business of their own country mainly by themselves.

These objections would not apply to an equal union, like that which has recently been agreed upon between Austria and Hungary. In that there is nothing humiliating to the pride of either country. But if the Canadian system has had but a short trial, the dual system of Austria and Hungary has had none. It has existed only a bare twelvemonth.$^{\xi}$ ^{o}Hungary, it is true, has been much longer attached by a personal bond to the reigning family of Austria, and Hungary had a Constitution, with some of the elements of freedom; but Austria had not. The difficulty of keeping two countries together without uniting them, begins with constitutional liberty. Countries very dissimilar in character, and even with some internal freedom, may be governed as England and Scotland were by the Stuarts, so long as the people have only certain limited rights, and the government of the two countries practically resides in a single will above them both. The difficulty arises when the unforced concurrence of both nations is required for the principal acts of their government. This relation, between Austria and Hungary, never existed till now.^{o} $^{\pi}$If an arrangement so untried and so unexampled be happily permanent—if it resist the chances of incurable difference of opinion on the subjects reserved for joint deliberation, foreign relations, finances, and war—its success will be owing to circumstances almost peculiar to the particular case, and which certainly do not exist between Great Britain and Ireland. In the first place, the two countries are nearly equal in military resources and prowess. They have fairly tried themselves against one another in open war, and know that neither can conquer the other without foreign aid. In the next place, while each is equally formidable to the other, each stands in need of the other for its own safety; neither is sufficient to

$^{o-o}$[*not in first draft*]
$^{\pi-\pi}$[*cf.* App. A, 540]

itself for maintaining its independence against powerful and encroaching neighbours. Lastly, they do not start with hostile feelings in the masses of either country towards the other. Hungary has not the wrongs of centuries to revenge; her direct injuries from Austria never reached the labouring classes, but were confined to portions of society whose conduct is directed more by political interest than by vindictive feeling. The reverse of all this is true between Great Britain and Ireland. The most favourable of all combinations of circumstances for the success and permanence of an equal alliance between independent nations under the same crown, exists between Hungary and Austria, the least favourable between England and Ireland.$^\pi$ ^{p}Nor let it be said that these reasons against an equal alliance are reasons *à fortiori* against union. The only one of them of which this could be said is the alienation of feeling, and this, if the real grounds of bitterness were removed, the close intercourse and community of interest engendered by union would more and more tend to heal: while the natural tendency of separation, either complete or only partial, would be to estrange the countries from each other more and more.^{p} $^\sigma$It may be added, that the Hungarian population, which has so nobly achieved its independence, has been trained from of old in the management of the details of its affairs, and has shown, in very trying circumstances, a measure of the qualities which fit a people for self-government, greater than has yet been evinced by Continental nations in many other respects far more advanced. The democracy of Ireland, and those who are likely to be its first leaders, have, at all events, yet to prove their possession of qualities at all similar.

For these reasons it is my conviction that the separation of Ireland from Great Britain would be most undesirable for both, and that the attempt to hold them together by any form of federal union would be unsatisfactory while it lasted, and would end either in reconquest or in complete separation. But in however many respects Ireland might be a loser, she would be a gainer in one. Let separation be ever so complete a failure, one thing it would do: it would convert the peasant farmers into peasant proprietors: and this one thing would be more than an equivalent for all that she would lose. The worst government that would give her this, would be more acceptable, and more deservedly acceptable, to the mass of the Irish people, than the best that withheld it; if goodness of any kind can be predicated of a Government that refuses the first and greatest benefit that can be conferred on such a country. This benefit, however, she can receive from the Government of the United Kingdom, if those who compose that government can be made to perceive that it is necessary and right.$^\sigma$ $^\tau$This duty once admitted and acted on, the difficulties of centuries in governing Ireland would disappear.

What the case requires is simply this. We have had commissions, under the authority of Parliament, to commute for an annual payment the burthen of tithe,

$^{p-p}$[*not in first draft*]
$^{\sigma-\sigma}$[*cf.* App. A, 540–1]
$^{\tau-\tau}$[*completely rewritten; cf.* App. A, 541]

and the variable obligations of copyholders.[*] What is wanted in Ireland is a commission of a similar kind to examine every farm which is let to a tenant, and commute the present variable for a fixed rent. But this great undertaking must not drag its slow length through generations, like the work of those other commissions. The time is passed for a mere amicable mediation of the State between the landlord and the tenant. There must be compulsory powers, and a strictly judicial inquiry. It must be ascertained in each case, as promptly as is consistent with due investigation, what annual payment would be an equivalent to the landlord for the rent he now receives (provided that rent be not excessive) and for the present value of whatever prospect there may be of an increase, from any other source than the peasant's own exertions.*ᵛ*This annual sum should be secured to the landlord under the guarantee of *ᶠ*law*ᶠ*. He should have the option of receiving it directly from the national treasury, by being inscribed as the owner of Consols sufficient to yield the amount. Those landlords who are the least useful in Ireland, and on the worst terms with their tenantry, would probably accept this opportunity of severing altogether their connexion with the Irish soil. Whether this was the case or not, every farm not farmed by the proprietor would become the permanent holding of the existing tenant, who would pay either to the landlord or to the State the fixed rent which had been decided upon; or less, if the income which it was thought just that the landlord should receive were more than the tenant could reasonably be required to pay.*ᵛ ᵠ ˣ*The benefit, to the cultivator, of a permanent property in the soil, does not depend on paying nothing for it, but on the certainty that the payment cannot be increased; and it is not even desirable that, in the first instance, the payment should be less than a fair rent.*ˣ ᵠ*If the land were let below its value, to this new kind of copyholder, he might be tempted to sublet it at a higher rent, and live on the difference, becoming a parasite supported in idleness on land which would still be farmed at a rackrent. He should therefore pay the full rent which was adjudged to the former proprietor, unless special circumstances made it unjust to require so much.* When such circumstances existed, the State must lose the difference; or if the Church property, after its resumption by the State, yielded a surplus beyond what is required for the secular education of the

―――
[*See 6 & 7 William IV, c. 71 (1836).]

*This same provision meets the objection sometimes made, that the worst farmers at present are those who hold on long leases or in perpetuity. Such farmers would not long stand the test of being held strictly to payment of the full amount of what is now a fair rent. They would soon either change their habits or give place to others.

ᵛ⁻ᵛ[cf. App. A, 541]

ᶠ⁻ᶠ68¹, 68² the State

ᵠ[MS sentence incorporated in ˣ⁻ˣbelow; see App. A, 541]

ˣ⁻ˣ[cf. App. A, 541–2; JSM reordered by taking from the MS the first part of this sentence (to increased) and, omitting the rest of the sentence and the paragraph, adding to the retained part the MS sentence in ᵠ, and placing them before a rewritten version of ᵠ⁻ᵠbelow]

ᵠ⁻ᵠ[cf. App. A, 541; see ˣ⁻ˣ above]

people, the remainder could not be better applied to the benefit of Ireland than in this manner.$^\psi$

$^\omega$We are told by many (I am sorry that Lord Stanley is one of them)[*] that in a generation after such a change, the land of Ireland would be overcrowded by the growth of population, would be sublet and subdivided, and things would be as bad as before the famine. Just in the same manner we were told that after a generation or two of peasant proprietorship, the whole rural territory of France would be a pauper warren, and its inhabitants would be engaged in "dividing, by logarithms, infinitesimal inheritances."[†] How have these predictions been fulfilled? The complaint now is that the population of France scarcely increases at all, and the rural population diminishes. And, in spite of the compulsory division of inheritances by the Code Civil,[‡] the reunions of small properties by marriage and inheritance fully balance the subdivisions. The obsolete school of English political economists, whom I may call the Tory school, because they were the friends of entail, primogeniture, high rents, great landed properties, and aristocratic institutions generally, predicted that peasant proprietorships would lead not only to excessive population, but to the wretchedest possible agriculture. What has the fact proved? I will not refer to the standard work on this subject, Mr. W. T. Thornton's *Plea for Peasant Proprietors*, or to Mr. Kay's *Social Condition of the People in England and Europe*, or to the multitude of authorities cited in my own *Political Economy*, or to the more recent careful and thoughtful researches of M. Emile de Laveleye.[§] I will quote from M. Léonce de Lavergne, at present the stock authority of the opponents of small landed properties. What says M. de Lavergne in his latest production, an article in the *Revue des Deux Mondes* of the 1st of December last? "As a general rule, the lands held in small properties are twice as productive as the others, so that if this element were to fail us, our agricultural produce would be considerably diminished."[¶] Those who still believe that small peasant properties are either detrimental to agriculture or con-

[*Edward Henry Stanley, Speech at Brighton (22 Jan., 1868), *The Times*, 23 Jan., 1868, p. 6.]

[†John Wilson Croker, "Agriculture in France—Division of Property," *Quarterly Review*, LXXIX (Dec., 1846), 217 (cf. John Stuart Mill, *Principles of Political Economy*, *CW*, Vols. II & III (Toronto: University of Toronto Press, 1965), Vol. II, p. 433.]

[‡See *Code civil des Français* (Paris: l'Imprimerie de la République, 1804), p. 136 (Livre III, Titre I, Chap. iii, Art. 745), and pp. 149, 152 (*ibid*., Chap. vi, Arts. 815, 832).]

[§William Thomas Thornton, *A Plea for Peasant Proprietors* (London: Murray, 1848); Joseph Kay, *The Social Condition and Education of the People in England and Europe*, 2 vols. (London: Longman, Brown, Green, and Longmans, 1850); Mill, *Principles* (1848; most recent ed., 6th, 1865), *CW*, esp. Vol. II, pp. 252–96 (II, vi-vii); Emile Louis Victor de Laveleye, *Etudes d'économie rurale* (Paris: Lacroix, Verboeckhoven, 1865).]

[¶Louis Gabriel Léonce Guilhaud de Lavergne, "L'Irlande en 1867," *Revue des Deux Mondes*, LXXII (Dec., 1867), 757.]

$^{\omega-\omega}$[*cf*. App. A, 542]

ducive to overpopulation, are discreditably behind the state of knowledge on the subject. There is no condition of landed property which excites such intense exertions for its improvement, as that in which all that can be added to the produce belongs to him who produces it. Nor does any condition afford so strong a motive against overpopulation; because it is much more obvious how many mouths can be supported by a piece of land, than how many hands can find employment in the general labour market.$^\omega$ $^\alpha$The danger of subletting is equally visionary. In the first place, subletting might be prohibited; but on the plan I propose there is no necessity for prohibiting it. If the holder, by his labour or outlay, adds to the value of the farm, he is well entitled to sublet it if he pleases. If its value augments from any other cause than his exertions, it will generally be from the increased prosperity of the country, which will be a proof that the new system is successful, and that he may sublet without inconvenience. Only one precaution is necessary. For years, perhaps for generations, he should not be allowed to let the land by competition, or for a variable rent. His lessee must acquire it as he himself did, on a permanent tenure, at an unchangeable rent, fixed by public authority; that the substituted, like the original, holder may have the full interest of a proprietor in making the most of the soil.$^\alpha$

$^\beta$All prognostics of failure drawn from the state of things preceding the famine are simply futile. The farmer, previous to the famine, was not proprietor of his bit of land; he was a cottier, at a nominal rent, puffed up by competition to a height far above what could, even under the most favourable circumstances, be paid, and the effect of which was that whether he gained much or little, beyond the daily potatoes of which his family could not be deprived, all was swept off for arrears of rent. Alone of all working people, the Irish cottier neither gained anything by industry and frugality, nor lost anything by idleness and reckless multiplication. That because he was not industrious and frugal without a motive, he will not be industrious and frugal when he has the strongest motive, is not a very plausible excuse for refusing him the chance. There is also another great change in his circumstances since the famine: the bridge to$^\beta$ $^\gamma$America has been built. If a population should grow up on the small estates more numerous than their produce can comfortably support, what is to prevent that surplus population from going the way of the millions who have already found in another continent the field for their labour which was not open to them at home?$^\gamma$ $^\delta$And the new emigrants, there would then be reason to hope, would not, as now, depart in bitterness, nor return in enmity.

The difficulty of governing Ireland lies entirely in our own minds; it is an incapability of understanding. When able to understand what justice requires,

$^{\alpha-\alpha}$[*not in first draft*]
$^{\beta-\beta}$[*cf.* App. A, 542; *Harvard fragment ends here*]
$^{\gamma-\gamma}$[*cf.* App. A, 542; *Yale fragment begins here*]
$^{\delta-\delta}$[*not in first draft, except for* $^{\epsilon-\epsilon}$]

liberal Englishmen do not refuse to do it. They understood the injustice of the political disabilities of Catholics, and they removed them.[*] They understand the injustice of endowing an alien Church, and they have made up their minds that the endowment shall no longer continue.[†] Foreign nations and posterity will judge England's capacity for government, by the ability she now shows to overcome the difficulty of seeing what justice requires in the matter of Irish landed tenure. To her it is a difficulty. Other nations see no difficulty in it. To the Prussian Conservative, Von Raumer, and the French Liberal, Gustave de Beaumont, it was already, thirty years ago, the most obvious thing in the world.[‡] It will seem so to future generations. Posterity will hardly be just to the men of our time. The superstitions of landlordism once cast off, it will be difficult to imagine what real and deep-rooted superstitions they once were, and how much of the best moral and even intellectual attributes was compatible with them. But not the less is he in whom any principle or feeling has become a superstition, convulsively clung to where the reasons fail, unfit to have the power of imposing his superstition on people who do not share it. If we cannot distinguish the essentials from the accidents of landed property; if it is and must remain to us the Ark of the Covenant which must be neither touched nor looked into,[§] for however indispensable a need, it is our duty to retire from a country where a modification of the constitution of landed property is the primary necessity of social life. ᵉIt may be that there is not wisdom or courage in English statesmen to look the idol in the face. We may be put off with some insignificant attempt to give tenants the hope of compensation for "unexhausted improvements"[¶]—something which, ten years, or even two years ago, would have been valuable as a pledge of good will, a sign of just purposes, and a ground of hope that more would be done when experience had proved this to be insufficient;ᵉ but which would not even then have been accepted as payment in full, and is now scarcely worth offering as an instalment. Even this, if proposed, ought to be voted for in preference to nothing. If a debtor acknowledges only sixpence when he owes a pound, he should be allowed to pay that sixpence; but let us not for a moment intermit the demand, that the remaining balance be paid up before the otherwise inevitable hour of bankruptcy arrives.ᵟ

ᶨFor let no one suppose that while this question remains as it is, the sum of all

[*10 George IV, c. 7 (1829).]
[†Enacted in 32 & 33 Victoria, c. 42 (1869).]
[‡Friedrich Ludwig Georg von Raumer, *England in 1835*, trans. Sarah Austin and H. E. Lloyd, 3 vols. (London: Murray, 1836); Gustave de Beaumont, *L'Irlande sociale, politique et religieuse*, 2 vols. (Paris: Gosselin, 1839).]
[§See II Samuel, 6:6–7, and I Kings, 8:6–8.]
[¶See "Minutes of Evidence Taken by the Select Committee on Tenure and Improvement of Land (Ireland) Act," *PP*, 1865, XI, 518.]

ᵉ⁻ᵉ[*cf*. App. A, 543; *incorporated from later part of MS*]
ᶨ⁻ᶨ[*cf*. App. A, 542–3; *see previous and succeeding variants*]

other things that could be done for Ireland would at all alleviate our difficulties there. Abundance of other things, indeed, require to be done. There are not only the religious endowments to be resumed, but their proceeds have to be applied, in the most effectual way possible, to the promotion of Irish improvement. The Church lands and tithes, augmented by the Maynooth endowment[*] and the *regium donum*,[†] would be more than enough, with the sums already appropriated to the purpose, to afford a complete unsectarian education to the entire people, including primary schools, middle schools, high schools, and universities, each grade to be open free of cost to the pupils who had most distinguished themselves in the grade below it. The administration of local justice, of local finance, and other local affairs, requires the hand of the reformer even more urgently than in England. Such minor matters as, though of small account in themselves, would help to conciliate Irish feeling, ought not to be neglected. Those are not wrong who have urged that, with parity of qualifications, Irishmen (when not partisans) should have the preference for Irish appointments; and there is no good reason why the heir to the throne should not, during part of every year, reside and hold a Court at Dublin. Those purely material improvements to which voluntary enterprise is not adequate, should, with due consideration and proper precautions, receive help from the State. The possible consolidation of Irish railways under State management, or under a single company by concession from the State, is already engaging the attention of our public men;[‡] and advances for drainage, and other improvements on a large scale, are, in a country so poor and backward as Ireland, economically admissible: only not on the plan hitherto adopted, of lending to the landlords, that the entire benefit of the improvement may accrue to their rents. It is scarcely credible that a large extension of *such* advances has within the last few weeks been publicly propounded as a remedy for Fenianism and all other Irish ills, and that a bill for that purpose, promoted by the Government, is actually before Parliament.[§] We have heard of people who would have cried fire during the Deluge: these people, if they had lived at the time of the Deluge, would have proposed to stop it by turning on a little more water.

But none of these things—not even the cashiering of the Irish Protestant Church—nor all these things taken together, could avail to stop the progress of

[*See 8 & 9 Victoria, c. 25 (1845).]

[†For its initiation, see "Out Letters (Ireland)" (10 Apr., 1691), VI, 85–6, in *Calendar of the Treasury Books, 1689–92*, Vol. IX, Pt. III, pp. 1258–9.]

[‡See "Report of the Commissioners Appointed to Inspect the Accounts and Examine the Works of Railways in Ireland," *PP*, 1867–68, XXXII, 469–646; and "Second Report," *ibid.*, 1868–69, XVII, 459–528.]

[§"A Bill to Confirm a Provisional Order under 'The Drainage and Improvements of Lands (Ireland) Act, 1863,' and the Acts Amending the Same," 31 Victoria (22 Nov., 1867), *ibid.*, 1867–68, II, 193–7; enacted as 31 Victoria, c. 3 (1867).]

Irish disaffection, because not one of them comes near its real cause.$^\zeta$ $^\eta$Matters of affronted feeling, and of minor or distant pecuniary interest, will occupy men's minds when the primary interests of subsistence and security have been cared for, and not before.$^\eta$ $^\theta$Let our statesmen be assured that now, when the long deferred day of Fenianism has come, nothing which is not accepted by the Irish tenantry as a permanent solution of the land difficulty, will prevent Fenianism, or something equivalent to it, from being the standing torment of the English Government and people. If without removing this difficulty, we attempt to hold Ireland by force, it will be at the expense of all the character we possess as lovers and maintainers of free government, or respecters of any rights except our own; it will most dangerously aggravate all our chances of misunderstandings with any of the great$^\theta$ powers of the world, culminating in war; we shall be in a state of open revolt against the universal conscience of Europe and Christendom, and more and more against our own. And we shall in the end be shamed, or, if not shamed, coerced, into releasing Ireland from the connexion; or we shall avert the necessity only by conceding with the worst grace, and when it will not prevent some generations of ill blood, that which if done at present may still be in time permanently to reconcile the two countries.

$^{\eta-\eta}$[*not in first draft*]
$^{\theta-\theta}$[*cf.* App. A, 543; *Yale fragment ends at bottom of the second folio of sheet 12*]

APPENDICES

Appendix A

England and Ireland
First Draft (Dec., 1867-Jan., 1868)

MS IN TWO PARTS, ff. 3, 6-11 in the Harvard University Library, f. 12 in the Yale University Library (other ff. lost). The full text of the surviving part of the MS is presented here, keyed to the text of the 5th ed. (505-32 above) by superscript page numbers and Greek letters. E.g., the first passage below begins "511$^{\alpha\text{-}\alpha}$", meaning that the equivalent passage in the 5th ed. appears on 511 and is enclosed in that version by superscript alphas. "H" and "Y" are used to indicate the sections in Harvard and Yale. The breaks between the entries are, of course, not found in the MS, but are introduced here to facilitate comparison. The sequence of Greek letters is established in the apparatus to the 5th ed.; therefore some letters do not appear here (because Mill expanded the text in rewriting; see, e.g., 523$^{\lambda\text{-}\lambda}$), and in two cases the sequence is broken (because Mill reordered part of the text; see 527$^{\chi\text{-}\chi}$, $^{\psi\text{-}\psi}$). Editorial notes (in square brackets and italics) indicate when necessary the relations between the MS and the printed versions. For a descriptive account of the MS, see lxi–lxii and lxiii–lxiv above.

511$^{\alpha\text{-}\alpha}$H [*the extant MS begins on the folio numbered 3 by JSM*] has been so long in coming, proves that it might have been prevented from coming at all. A whole generation has elapsed since we began to wish to govern Ireland for her own good & not for ours. If at that epoch we had begun to know how so to govern her the two nations would by this time have been one. But we neither knew, nor knew that we did not know: we had got a set of institutions of our own, which we thought suited us, & whose defects we were at any rate used to: & our wise ruling classes never suspected that when they ceased to withhold from Ireland the benefit of these, Ireland could need or desire anything more. What was not too bad for us, must be good for Ireland, or if not, Ireland or the nature of things was alone in fault.

511$^{\beta}$H [*not in printed versions*] Yet when they were told by thinking persons that the institutions which they thought must suit all mankind since they suited us, were not so perfect as they supposed, & that there was much in them, which even among ourselves needed great improvement, they were in the habit of answering that whatever defects these institutions might possess in theory, they were suited to the opinions, the feelings, & the historical antecedents of the English people. They well knew that the opinions, feelings, & historical antecedents of the Irish people were totally different from & in many things contrary to those of the English, but it never occurred to them that institutions which in England could only be justified by their being liked, did not admit of the same justification in a country where they were detested.

511γ-γH [*paragraph*] It is always a most difficult task which a people assumes when it attempts to govern, either by incorporation with itself or as a dependency, another people very unlike itself. But whoever reflects on the constitution of Irish society with any adequate knowledge of the states of society which exist in the world, must come however unwillingly, to the conclusion that there is probably no other civilised nation which if the task of governing Ireland had by chance devolved on it, would not have shewn itself more capable of that task than England has hitherto been. The reason is twofold; 1st: there is no other civilised nation which is so conceited of its institutions & its modes of public proceeding as England is, & so well satisfied of their sufficiency for all purposes. 2dly. there is no other civilised nation which is so extremely unlike Ireland not only in its antecedents but in the whole constitution of its social economy & which therefore if it applies its own modes of thinking & legislating to Ireland, is so sure to be in the wrong.

514δ-δH [*paragraph*] Let us consider the principal features in the social economy of Ireland. First, it is a country wholly agricultural. The entire population, with exceptions too insignificant for notice, cultivates the soil, & depends for its subsistence upon the cultivation. In this respect, if all the countries of Europe except Russia, were arranged in a scale, Ireland would be at one extremity of the scale, England & Scotland at the other. In Great Britain not more than a third of the population lives by agriculture: in most countries of the Continent a great majority does so, though in no country but Russia so great a majority as in Ireland.

When a people has no other means of support than the land the conditions on which support can be derived from the land are the fundamental question on which everything depends. With an apparent resemblance, those conditions are radically different in Ireland & in England. In England the land is rented & cultivated by capitalist farmers, in Ireland principally by manual labourers, holding directly either from the great landlords, or from sub-landlords. How infinite a quantity of other differences must flow from this one difference it is superfluous to detail. But it is of still greater importance to remark that in Ireland where the well being of the whole population depends on the conditions of occupancy of land, those conditions are the very worst [*ff. 4-5 missing from MS*]

518ϵ-ϵH to the State. Ireland would then have been in the condition in which small farms & tenancy by manual labourers of the bulk of the soil are consistent with good agriculture & national prosperity: the small holder would have cultivated for himself & not for others & his interest would have coincided with the interest of the country in making every piece of land produce its utmost. What Hoche would have done for the Irish peasant, or something equivalent in effect, still remains to be done, & any government which will not do it is guilty of a crime in holding possession & keeping out those who would. It is not necessary that it should be done as Hoche would have done it, without compensation to the losers: It would not perhaps have even been necessary, a few years ago, to do all that Hoche would have done. It may be that even so small a measure as that of securing to the tenant, when ejected, compensation for improvements, either in money or by a long lease & abolishing the unjust privilege of distraining for rent might often have sufficed to appease or adjourn disaffection & give great-landlordism a fresh term of rule. There needs but little power of appreciating circumstances to see that these things if tried at present would be scarcely a drop in the cup; would not give one week's intermission of active disaffection. The Irish are not now reduced to take anything they can get. They are not likely to lose, the sense of being backed by the multitudes of their prosperous countrymen on the other side of the Atlantic. They it is, who will furnish the leaders, the skill, & a great part of the effective strength in any future Irish rebellion; & it is the interest of these leaders to resist to the utmost any compromise since whatever the resident Irish might gain by it, they who do not live in Ireland, would gain nothing, but would lose the dream of a place in the world's eye as chiefs of an independent republic. With a people like the Irish always ready to trust implicitly those whom they believe to be thoroughly in their interest, no accommodation is henceforth practicable which does not give them all that they could gain by a revolution, permanent possession of the land, subject only to fixed burthens. Such a change may be called revolutionary; but revolutionary measures are what are now required. It is not necessary that the revolution should be violent, nor that it should be unjust. It may & it ought to respect all existing pecuniary interests which have the sanction of law. An equivalent ought to be given for the mere pecuniary value of all mischievous rights which either landlords or others are required to give up. But no mercy ought to be shewn to the mischievous rights themselves; no scruple of purely English birth ought to hold our hands from effecting since it has come to that, an actual revolution in the economical & social condition of Ireland. Only in the completeness of the revolution lies its safety. Anything less than complete, unless as a step to completion, will give us no help. The time is gone by when it can even be done gradually by cooperating with natural tendencies. If Ireland is ever in our time to be a consenting party to union with England, the changes must be so made that the present race of Irish farmers shall at once experience their benefits. The rule of Ireland now rightfully belongs to those who will by just means, make the cultivators of the soil of Ireland the owners of it; & the English nation has got to decide, whether it will be this just ruler or not.

English rulers have not always been incapable of shaking off insular prejudices, & ruling another country according to its wants & not according to English habits & notions. It is what they have had to do in India. Persons who know both, have remarked that there are many points of resemblance between the Irish & the Hindu character, there certainly are many between the agricultural economy of Ireland & that of India. But the business of ruling India for England did not devolve upon the Houses of Parliament, or the offices at Westminster; it fell to the lot of men who passed their lives in India & made Indian interests their sole occupation. Accordingly, having acquired India at a time when nations had begun to have a conscience, they reconciled themselves from the beginning to the idea that their business there was not to wrench & compress all rights into the similitude of what exists in England, but to find out what rights were recognised by the customs & ideas of India; to abolish them only when absolutely mischievous, in all other cases to protect them, & use them as a starting point for further steps in improvement. This work of stripping off their English ideas was at first done clumsily & imperfectly & at the cost of many mistakes. But as they sincerely meant to do it, they at last succeeded & India is now governed with a full perception & recognition of its differences from England. What has been done in India has yet to be done in Ireland; & as we should have deserved to be turned out of the one, had we not been equal to the need, so shall we of the other.

⁵²⁰ζ-ζH [*paragraph*] If England proves incapable of learning & of unlearning what has to be learnt & unlearnt in order to make her rule in Ireland willingly submitted to by the Irish people, she has but two courses to choose between. The first, is, to suspend indefinitely the

constitutional liberties of Ireland, & keep the country in subjection by fire & sword, as has so often been done in the bad old time. The second is, to withdraw entirely & leave Ireland to itself, united by a merely personal tie, like Hanover formerly, with the British crown, or separated from it altogether.

The first of these it is not risking much to say, is simply impossible. Neither Europe nor America would now tolerate a Poland across the Irish Channel. If an Irish rebellion could hold its ground but a few weeks, an universal explosion of opinion all over the civilised world would enable the many enemies of English prosperity to complicate the situation by a foreign war. Were we even able to prevent a rebellion or suppress it as soon as it broke out, the holding down by mere brute force, of a people in desperation, constantly struggling to break their fetters, is a spectacle which Russia can still give to the world because Russia is almost inaccessible to a foreign enemy, but the attempt would not long succeed with a country so vulnerable as England with territories to defend in every part of the globe & half her population dependent upon foreign commerce. Nor even if it could be done, do I believe that the body of the British people, who are not yet corrupted by power, have the will to do it. The kind of prophets who always augur the worst of the moral dispositions of their countrymen, are already asseverating that, whether right or wrong, the British people would rather desolate Ireland from end to end & exterminate the inhabitants than consent to her separation from England. I believe better things. I believe that the rising power in our government, the democracy of Great Britain, is opposed in principle to holding any people in subjection against their will. The question was put not much more than six months ago to one of the largest & most enthusiastic meetings ever assembled in London under one roof. "Do you think that England has any right to rule over Ireland if she cannot make the Irish people content with her rule?" & the shouts of "No!" which burst from every part of that great assembly will not easily be forgotten by any who heard them. A time when delegates of working men meet in European Congresses to concert united action for the interests of labour, is a time when the democracy of one country will join hands with the democracy of another rather than join with their own ruling authorities in keeping it down. However this may be, I shall not believe, until I see it proved, that the people of England & Scotland are capable of the atrocious wickedness of carrying fire & sword over Ireland in order to maintain there a social system equally pernicious & odious to the Irish people. That they would put down any partial outbreak in order to get a fair trial for the attempt to establish a system of government beneficent & acceptable to the people, I believe; nor should I in any way blame them for so doing.

$^{521\eta\text{-}\eta}$H [*paragraph*] A permanent military despotism over Ireland being, then, out of the question, we have to choose between a peaceful legislative revolution in the laws & rules which affect the relation of the inhabitants to the land, & a separation between the two countries. If either in our ignorance we cannot or in our perversity we will not accomplish the first; it remains to accommodate ourselves to the last. Which is the most desirable?

It is not necessary to say much of the evil consequences to England of the loss of Ireland. Both English & Irish are aware of them, & are more disposed to exaggerate than to extenuate them. In my opinion they are commonly much exaggerated, & should be ranked among inconveniences, rather than national calamities. I need speak only of the consequences to Ireland, & of those which are common to both, & I hold these sufficient to make the maintenance of union between the two countries eminently desirable, provided it is with the willing consent of both.

$^{521\theta\text{-}\theta}$H [*paragraph*] The mere geographical situation of the two countries makes them far more fitted to exist as one nation than as two. Not only are they stronger for defence against a foreign enemy combined than separate, but if separate they would be a standing menace to one another. Separated at this time & with their present feelings, Ireland & Great Britain would be, of all countries in Europe, those which would have the most hostile feeling towards one another. Hostile feeling, too much of it, still remains between England & the United States, more than eighty years after separation; & Ireland has actually suffered from England for many centuries, evils compared with which the greatest grievances of the Americans were a mere fleabite. Between two populations so close together & one at least habitually embittered against the other, mere trifles would become causes of quarrel. Disputes more or less serious, even collisions, would be ever liable to occur, & Ireland besides having to defend herself against all other external & internal enemies without help from England, would feel obliged to keep up an army always ready to fight England.

522ι-ιH   As far indeed as regards aggressive war against England, she would probably be forced by her weakness to wait for what is even now "Ireland's opportunity."

522κ-κH   But let England once be at war with any other country, especially France or America, & it would be difficult for Ireland to hold her hand from joining with our enemies. Those enemies moreover would look forward to such a junction, & to being allowed to use Ireland as a basis of attack on Great Britain: & Ireland would be in constant fear lest England, should anticipate such a result by herself occupying Ireland with a military force at the commencement of any war. Even when there was peace with foreign countries Ireland would never feel secure: England it is true has become so pacific in her policy that aggression from her might be little to be feared; but the ejected Irish higher classes—for the Irish higher classes would be ejected—would be a new element hostile to Ireland on the English side of St. George's Channel, & would be to the Irish Republic what the emigrés at Coblenz were to Revolutionary France. In all this I am supposing that Ireland succeeds in establishing a regular & orderly government. But what if she has to pass through an era of partial anarchy first? What if there were a civil war between the Protestants & Catholic Irish, or between Ulster & the other three provinces? Would not the sympathies of England be all with the English Protestant Colony, & would not England either help that side or be constantly believed to be on the point of helping it? For generations it is to be feared that the two nations would be either at war or in a chronic state of precarious & armed peace: each constantly watching a possible enemy who in an instant might be at his throat.

523μ-μH   [*paragraph*] These evils, it may perhaps be thought, might be provided against by a close alliance & perpetual confederation between the two countries. Never was there a vainer imagination. A confederation, that is, an agreement to have the same friends & the same enemies, can only subsist between peoples who have the same interests & feelings, & who if they fight at all, will wish to fight on the same side. Great Britain & Ireland would generally wish to fight on opposite sides. In any Continental complications, the sympathies of Ireland are sure to be on the same side with the Pope, that is, on the side opposed to the ideas of modern civilisation; & to all, except the Catholic Poles, who might be contending for freedom—those of England would be on the opposite side. The most Catholic power would always be the one which Ireland would wish to prevail. America is the country with which we are in most danger of having serious differences, & if Ireland had the choice she is more likely to confederate with America against us, than with us against America.

524ξ-ξH   [*paragraph*] Ireland, it is true, would have the satisfaction such as it is of being governed solely by Irishmen, that is, almost always by men with a strong party animosity to some part of the population: unless indeed, she expelled the Protestant part of her population entirely, & with it the greater part of her skill, industry, & enterprise. But in return Irishmen would be excluded from all positions in England, but those which can be held by foreigners: there would be no more Irish prime ministers, Irish lord chancellors, Irish generals & admirals in the British army & navy; & not in England only but in all England's dependencies in India & the colonies, Irishmen would henceforth be in the position of strangers. I think the loss would much outweigh the gain.

But it will be asked, cannot Ireland remain united with the British Crown by a merely personal tie, & retain the full management of her own affairs as Canada does, though a part of the same empire? or why should not England & Ireland be allied under one crown as Austria & Hungary are, with separate administrations & legislatures? I answer, the first of these relations would never satisfy Ireland. It would be a derogation or descent from even her present position into an inferior one. At present Ireland is part of the governing country. She has a voice in the general affairs of the Empire. Canada is a dependency, with a merely provincial government, allowed to make its own laws & levy its own taxes, but subject to the veto of the mother country, & having no voice at all in alliances or wars in which nevertheless it is forced to join. A union like this could only exist as a temporary expedient between countries which look forward to a separation, & do not much care how soon it comes. The union, besides, is still recent; it has stood no trials, & especially not the greatest trial, that of war. Let war come & by an act of the British Govt. in which Canada is not represented, will Canada be content to be involved in the war without having been consulted before engaging in it? Even in home affairs Ireland would not relish the position of Canada. The veto of the British Crown would be in fact the veto of the British Parlt. on even purely Irish legislation, & though it might as in the case of Canada be exercised with discretion & confined to what were considered imperial questions, the decision what questions were imperial would always rest with the more powerful country & the weaker would feel that having no voice in imperial questions it was more completely under foreign subjection than it is now. These objections would not in the same degree apply to the more equal union which has recently been established between Austria & Hungary. This union has nothing humiliating to the pride of either country. But if the Canadian system has had but a short trial, the dual system of Austria & Hungary has had none. It has not yet existed a whole twelvemonth.

$^{525\pi\text{-}\pi}$H If a system so untried & unexampled can possibly be permanent, this will be owing to circumstances which are almost peculiar to the particular case, & which certainly do not exist between G B & Ireland. In the first place, the two countries are nearly equal in military power; they have fully & fairly tried their strength against one another & they know that neither of them can conquer the other, without the aid of a foreign force. Not only is each of them equally formidable to the other, but each stands in need of the other for its own security: neither can trust to itself alone for maintaining its independence against powerful encroaching neighbours. Lastly, there was no hostility to begin with in the mass of either community towards the other: Hungary had not the carnage of centuries to avenge; & her wrongs from Austria never reached the labouring classes, but were chiefly confined to those portions of society whose conduct is governed more by political interest than by vindictive feeling. The contrary of all this is true between Gr. Britain & Ireland. The most favorable conjunction of circumstances that could possibly exist any where for the permanence of an equal alliance under the same crown but with different legislatures & executives, exists between Hungary & Austria, the least favorable possible between England & Ireland.

$^{526\sigma\text{-}\sigma}$H Add to this that the Hungarian population which has achieved its independence has been trained from of old in the habit of managing its own affairs in detail, & has shewn in very trying circumstances the possession of a larger measure of the qualities which fit a nation for self-government than has ever yet been shewn by Continental nations in many other respects much more advanced. The democracy of Ireland, & those who are likely to be its leaders, have, at all events, yet to shew their possession of qualities at all similar to these.

For these reasons I hold that the separation of Ireland from G. Britain whether as an independent nation or as a separate kingdom under the British Crown, is most undesirable for Ireland. But undesirable as it is, it would be vastly preferable to the continuance of her present state. Let separation be ever so complete a failure there is one thing which it would certainly do; it would convert the peasants into landed proprietors. The worst government that would do this, would be more acceptable to the mass of the Irish population, & would deserve to be more acceptable, than the best that left it undone, if goodness of any kind can be predicated of a government that refused this first & greatest of benefits. This benefit however it can receive from the government of the United Kingdom if those who compose that government once recognise it as necessary & right.

$^{526\tau\text{-}\tau}$H It remains to consider how this ought to be done, & how it can be so done as to be consistent with substantial justice.

The first step would be to ascertain the present rent of all the land in Ireland: not the rent engaged for, but that actually paid, in an average of a small number of years. This ought to be secured to every landlord, & he ought to have the opportunity of proving that he had ground for expecting an increase, from outlay already made by himself (not by the tenant) or from some cause actually in operation.

$^{527\upsilon\text{-}\upsilon}$H The existing rent with such moderate increase as he could prove himself entitled to, should be assured to him under the guarantee of the State. He should have the option of receiving it directly from the nation by being inscribed as the owner of Consols sufficient to yield the amount. Those landlords who are of the least use in Ireland & on the worst terms with their tenantry would probably accept this opportunity of dissolving altogether their connexion with Irish land. Those who did not, would continue to receive it as a fixed payment from the new proprietors.

Every farm would then become the permanent holding of the existing tenant, who would pay either to the former landlord or to the State the fixed quitrent which had been decided upon, or less if the income which it was thought just that the landlord should receive were more than the tenant could fairly be required to pay.

$^{527\phi}$H We must remember that it is not desirable, in the first instance, that the fixed payment should be less than a fair rent.

$^{527\psi\text{-}\psi}$H If the land were underlet, (as it were) to this new kind of copyholder, he might be tempted to sublet it at a higher rate & live upon the difference, becoming a mere parasite supported on the land which would still be farmed at a rackrent. If the receipts from the new proprietor did not cover the payments to the former landlord the State must lose the difference: or if the resumption of the Church property yielded any surplus beyond what is required for the secular education of the entire people, that surplus could not be better applied to the benefit of Ireland than in this manner.

$^{527\chi\text{-}\chi}$H [*paragraph*] The benefit to the cultivator, of a permanent property in the soil does not depend on paying no rent for it, but on the certainty that the rent cannot be increased, & that whatever he can do either by his labour or his outlay to make the land more productive or more valuable will belong to him & his children without any one's having the power to intercept it from them. If he saves anything he would probably find a more profitable application of his savings by employing them in improving the farm than in redeeming the quit rent. If by his own labour & exertions he adds to the value of the farm, he is well entitled to sublet it if he pleases. If its value rises from the general prosperity of the country, that will be a proof of the success of the new system & he may sublet it without inconvenience. But for many years, & perhaps generations, he must not be allowed to let it by competition, or for a variable rent, but his lessee must acquire it as he did, in a valuation by a public authority, & on a permanent tenure, so that the cultivator may have the full interest of a proprietor in making the most of the soil. [*only the equivalent of the first thirty-one words (to* increased*) survived in the printed text*]

528ω-ωH [*paragraph*] We are told, indeed, that in a single generation after the change, the land would be overcrowded by excess of population & subdivided & things would be as they were before the famine. So we were told that in a generation or two the rural territory of France under peasant proprietorship would be a "pauper-warren." What has the fact proved? The complaint now is that the rural population of France is not increasing at all, but actually decreasing. The gone-by school of English political economists whom I will call the Tory school, because they were the partisans of entail, primogeniture, high rents, great landed properties, & aristocratic institutions in general, predicted that peasant properties would lead to excessive population, & also to the wretchedest possible agriculture. What says M. Léonce de Lavergne, who is now the favourite authority of the opponents, not the friends, of small properties? In an article in the Revue des Deux Mondes published as lately as the 1st of December last, he says "As a general rule the lands held in small properties are twice as productive as the others so that if this element were to fail us our agricultural produce would be considerably diminished." Those who still believe that small peasant properties are either detrimental to agriculture or conducive to overpopulation really should be sent to school. They are discreditably behind the present state of knowledge on the subject. There is no condition of landed property which affords so strong a motive to the improvement of the land, as that in which the whole of the fruits belong to the person who tills it. There is no condition which affords so strong a motive against overpopulation, because it is much more obvious how many mouths can be supported by a piece of land, than how many people can find employment in the labour market.

529β-βH No argument at all can be drawn from the state of things which preceded the famine. The farmer was not then proprietor of his bit of land, he was a cottier, at a nominal rent raised by competition beyond what could ever be paid or which made it certain therefore that there would never be anything for the family but their meal of potatoes. Alone of all working people the cottier could neither gain anything by industry & frugality nor lose anything by their opposites. As peasant proprietors, or permanent holders at a moderate fixed rent, the whole benefit of their labour & abstinence is reaped by themselves, & they themselves suffer the penalty of indolence or imprudence. But in addition to this, there is another great change in their circumstances. The way to [*Harvard fragment ends on* f. 11]

529γ-γY [*Yale fragment begins on* f. 12] America is now open. If a population grow up on the small copyhold estates more numerous than their produce could support, what is there to prevent that surplus population from going the way of the millions who have already sought in another Continent the field for their labour which was not open to them in this.

530ζ-ζY [*paragraph*] The first & greatest difficulty of governing Ireland being thus got rid of, all minor difficulties would be as nothing. Of the Church grievance it is superfluous to speak, as England has apparently made up its mind that the only admissible course on this subject is the impartial disendowment of all religions. Life interests being of course respected, & the funds being applied exclusively to Irish purposes. The churchlands & tithes together with the Maynooth endowment & the *regium donum* would be more than enough (with the sums already appropriated to the purpose) to afford a complete unsectarian education, to the whole population including primary schools, middle schools, high schools, & universities, each grade of which should be open free of cost to the pupils who had distinguished themselves most in the grade below it. Such minor matters as though of small importance in themselves, would help to conciliate Irish feeling, ought not to be neglected; with parity of qualifications, Irishmen who are not partisans should have the preference over Englishmen & Scotchmen for posts in the government of Ireland; & there is no good reason why the heir to the throne should not, during a part of every year, reside & hold a Court in Dublin. For those purely material improvements to which voluntary enterprise is not adequate, should, with due consideration, receive help from the State. The project of consolidating Irish railways under State management, or under a single company by concession from the State, is already engaging the attention of British Statesmen: & advances for drainage & other improvements of land on a large scale, are, in a country so poor & so backward as Ireland, economically admissable, only not on the plan hitherto pursued of lending to the great landlords in order that their rents may reap the entire benefit of the improvement. It is scarcely credible that a large extension of *such* advances has within a very few weeks past been publicly propounded as the remedy for Fenianism & all other Irish ills! We have heard of people who would have cried fire at the time of the deluge: these people if they had lived at the time of the deluge would have proposed to cure it by turning on a little more water.

But none of these things, not even the cashiering of the Irish Protestant church, nor all these things taken together, will avail for a day to stay the progress of Irish disaffection or to advance the prosperity of Ireland, without the one thing needful, the assurance of the great instrument of production, the land, as a permanent possession in the hands of those who are to work it.

530ε-εY There probably is not wisdom or courage enough in English statesmen to venture on so great a change. Instead of it we shall have some insignificant attempt to give tenants the hope of some compensation for "unexhausted improvements" which might have been welcomed ten years or even two years ago as a sign of good will, & a ground of hope, that more would be done when experience had proved that this did not suffice.

532θ-θY But let our statesmen be assured that nothing which is not accepted by Ireland as a permanent solution of the land difficulty, will prevent Fenianism or something equivalent to Fenianism from being the standing torment of the English government & people; that if without overcoming this difficulty we attempt to hold Ireland by force, it will be at the expense of all our character in the world as the lovers and maintainers of free government, & will most dangerously aggravate all the chances of a misunderstanding with any of the great

[*Yale fragment ends at bottom of* f. 13]

Appendix B

List of Titles of "Notes on the Newspapers" (1834)

TO FACILITATE REFERENCE to the separate "Notes," this list supplies for each the page references in this edition, the date Mill gives (where no date appears, the preceding one applies), and the title.

No. I, March, 1834, pp. 151-68

Pp. 151-5. 2 Feb. The King's Speech
Pp. 155-7. 6 Feb. Mr. Shiel and Lord Althorp
Pp. 157-8. 7 Feb. Monopoly of the Post Office Clerks
Pp. 158-60. 12 Feb. Attendance in the House
Pp. 160-3. Lord Althorp's Budget
Pp. 163-4. 17 Feb. The Leeds Election
Pp. 165-8. Mr. O'Connell's Bill for the Liberty of the Press

No. II, April, 1834, pp. 168-96

Pp. 168-70. 21 Feb. The Ministerial Resolutions on Irish Tithe
Pp. 170-2. 22 Feb. The Debate on Agricultural Distress
Pp. 172-8. Mr. O'Connell's Declaration for the Pillage of the National Creditor
Pp. 178-81. 5 Mar. Mr. Buckingham's Motion on Impressment
Pp. 181-3. 1 Mar. The Dudley Election
Pp. 183-6. 8 Mar. The Debate on the Corn Laws
Pp. 186-8. 12 Mar. Political Oaths
Pp. 188-91. 15 Mar. The Trades' Unions
Pp. 191-3. 19 Mar. The Solicitor General's Motion on the Law of Libel
Pp. 193-4. 20 Mar. Sir Robert Peel on the Corn Laws
Pp. 194-6. 26 Mar. The Ministry and the Dissenters

No. III, May, 1834, pp. 196-218

Pp. 196-9. 16 Apr. The Tithe Bill
Pp. 199-202. 17 Apr. National Education
Pp. 202-3. 18 Apr. Mr. Roebuck and The Times
Pp. 203-6. The Proposed Reform of the Poor Laws
Pp. 206-11. 19 Apr. Government by Brute Force
Pp. 211-12. 22 Apr. The Church-Rate Abortion

TITLES OF NOTES ON THE NEWSPAPERS 545

Pp. 212-14. 24 Apr. The Beer-Houses
Pp. 214-18. 25 Apr. Repeal of the Union

No. IV, June, 1834, pp. 218-44

Pp. 218-21. 1 May. The Press and the Trades' Unions
Pp. 221-2. 2 May. Sir Robert Heron's Motion, and Mr. Bulwer's Amendment
Pp. 222-5. 8 May. Loss of the Registration Bills
Pp. 225-30. 13 May. Lord Brougham's Defence of the Church Establishment
Pp. 231-3. 14 May. Mr. William Brougham's Bills for a Registry of Births, Deaths, and Marriages
Pp. 233-5. 17 May. Sir Edward Knatchbull's Beer Bill
P. 235. 19 May. My Grandmother's Journal
Pp. 235-7. 22 May. Death of Lafayette
Pp. 237-8. 23 May. Lord Althorp and the Taxes on Knowledge
Pp. 238-41. 24 May. Progress of the Poor Law Bill
Pp. 241-3. 25 May. Honours to Science!
Pp. 243-4. 28 May. The Change in the Ministry

No. V, July, 1834, pp. 244-55

Pp. 244-5. 2 June. Abolition of Patronage in the Church of Scotland
Pp. 245-7. 4 June. Mr. Rawlinson and the Man of No Religion
Pp. 247-50. 6 June. Business of the House of Commons
P. 250. 14 June. The Tom-foolery at Oxford
Pp. 251-2. 17 June. Parliamentary Monstrosities
Pp. 252-4. The Ministry
P. 254. 20 June. The Beer Bill

No. VI, August, 1834, pp. 255-70

Pp. 255-8. 21 June. The Alleged Increase of Crime
Pp. 259-61. Debate on the Universities Admission Bill
Pp. 261-2. 4 July. The Chancellor's Declaration against the Taxes on Political Information
Pp. 262-3. 5 July. The Irish Tithe Bill
Pp. 263-5. 18 July. The Ministerial Changes
Pp. 265-6. 23 July. Lord Brougham's Speech on the Poor Law Amendment Bill
Pp. 267-8. The Rich and the Poor
Pp. 268-70. 27 July. Flogging in the Army

No. VII, September, 1834, pp. 270-80

Pp. 270-1. 2 Aug. Lord Melbourne's Reason for His Religion
Pp. 271-2. Lord Althorp and the Beer Bill
Pp. 272-3. 9 Aug. Major Pitman's Dismissal
Pp. 273-6. 10 Aug. The Government of Departments
Pp. 276-7. 12 Aug. Defeat of the Irish Tithe Bill
Pp. 277-9. 15 Aug. The Chancellor's Doctrine of Appeals
Pp. 279-80. 16 Aug. The Prorogation

Appendix C

Textual Emendations

IN THIS LIST, following the page and line numbers, the reading of the copy-text is given first, and then the emended reading in square brackets, with explanation if required. "SC" indicates Mill's library, Somerville College, Oxford. Typographical errors in versions earlier than the copy-text are ignored. In the two cases when manuscripts are the copy-texts, end-of-line punctuation, which Mill frequently omits, has been silently supplied.

5.25   written,some [written, some]
22.16   f Hume [of Hume]
22.17   blameable.' [blameable."]
23.7   Thsee [These]
24.21   state, [state;]
30.24   support. [support?]
32.22   superior. [superior?]
33n.5   proceedure [procedure]
35.9   occasions, [occasions] [*for sense*]
40.11   the ["the]
41.33   word." [word?"]
42n.6   "To . . . Israel;" ['To . . . Israel;'] [*no quotation marks in* Source]
44.21   service. [service?] [*for sense*]
45n.9   on [in]
52.20   to day [to-day] [*as in* Source]
56.2   his [this] [*as in* Source]
56.9   sup [sup-] [*end-of-line; setting altered in this ed.*]
64.21   Protestant" [Protestant,"]
71.11   *imperio*: [*imperio*;]
71.15   thatit [that it]
74.13   he [the]
74.13   imprope [improper]
75.16   ill blood [ill-blood] [*as in preceding quotation*]
77.33   easonings [reasonings]
78.18   &c. [&c.,] [*for sense*]
78n.3   Peel [Peel,]
78.21   This ["This]

TEXTUAL EMENDATIONS 547

78.25   Rights†? [Rights?†]
84.4   *equivoques* [*équivoques*]
86n.12 Solicitor-General [Solicitor General] [*for consistency*]
87.3   being [been]
87.9   think [thing]
88.15   than [that]
89n.7   p 81. [p. 81.]
91.26   measure,' [measure,"] [*restyled in this ed.*]
93n.3   pp. 375-7) [(pp. 375-7)]
93n.3   Committees [Committee]
93.7   which [which,] [*as in* Source; *dropped character*]
95n.14 p. 128 [p. 128.]
95.17   landords [landlords]
96.21   Wilcocks [Willcocks] [*as above,* 87n.4]
96.22   Mr Leslie [Mr. Leslie]
96.24   332.] [332].]
97.12   rise [rise.]
97.21   union: [union.]
103n.1 [p. 22] [[pp. 22-3],] [*restyled and corrected in this ed.*]
103n.2 [p. 6] [[p. 6],] [*restyled in this ed.*]
104.31 [p. 26] [pp. 26-7],] [*restyled and corrected in this ed.*]
105.3   one [one,]
106.6   answered; [answered:]
110.5   of [Of]
110.35 transactions. [transactions?]
111n.3 L.M., porter at an inn [I.K., poultry salesman] [*as in* Source; *presumably slip of the pen, as previous footnote concerns the evidence of* "L.M., porter at an inn" *who is, however, identified in the text as a poulterer*]
115.8   those," . . . "who [those,' . . . 'who] [*restyled in this ed.*]
116.16 start [state]
135.6   perfec [perfect]
144.18 act [Act] [*as elsewhere in passage*]
145.11 act [Act] [*as elsewhere in passage*]
151.14 Session [session] [*corrected by JSM in quotation at* 284.32]
151.14-15 Reformed Ministry [Reform Ministry] [*corrected by JSM in SC, and in quotation at* 284.33]
151.18 consequences: [consequences;] [*altered by JSM in quotation at* 284.36]
153n.5 Courts [Courts'] [*as in text and* Parliamentary Debates]
155.32 *necessité* [*nécessité*]
157.21 Vandalism [vandalism]
167.8   *préstige* [*prestige*]
167.10 conseqnences [consequences]
167.38 christian [Christian]
173n.20 Alliance [Affiance] [*as in* Source; *corrected in SC, perhaps not by JSM*]
174.34 him, [him;] [*to conform to rest of sentence*]
176.1   renewed [resumed] [*as in* Source (JSM)]
176.29 borrow [borrowed] [*as in* Source (JSM)]
177.46 fund [fund-] [*setting altered in this ed.*]
184.8   twentyp cent. [twenty per cent.]
184.16 ac [ac-] [*setting altered in this ed.*]

548   APPENDIX C

188n.5   com [com-] [*setting altered in this ed.*]
200.1   worse [worse.]
201.29   earn [learn]
201.30   country [country,] [*for sense*]
211.4   Times, ['Times,'] [*restyled in this ed.*]
213.35   not [but] [*corrected by JSM in SC copy*]
221.1   pre [pre-] [*setting altered in this ed.*]
221.30   members [members.]
224.7   Pedrillo [Pedro Garcias] [*corrected to* Source *reading in SC copy, though perhaps not by JSM*]
229.33   hem [them]
231.27   *régistres* [*registres*]
232.35   jun, [jun.,]
235.10   *Journal*— [*Journal.*—] [*restyled in this ed.*]
237.15   governmen titself [government itself]
238.22   1834 [1835] [*slip of the pen?*]
243.26   base [lease] [*corrected by JSM in SC copy*]
250.34   become [becomes]
251.13   suchat [such at]
262.17   acts [arts] [*corrected by JSM in SC copy*]
273.31   Guardian!' [Guardian'!] [*restyled in this ed.*]
275.5   fact [act]
278.10   involved. [involved?]
343.10   says (p. 10) [says (p. 10),]
351.18   on greater [no greater] [*corrected by JSM in SC copy*]
359.27   not all [not at all] [*as in* Source; *corrected by JSM in SC copy*]
361n.1   "the ["The]
364.32   yoar [your]
367.16   proportions [proprieties] [*as in* Source]
375.22-3   against corruption [against the corruption] [*as in* Source]
379.39   writer panegyrist [writer and panegyrist] [*corrected by JSM in SC copy*]
382.6   *the New Poor Law* [*the Poor-Laws*] [*as in* Source]
389.13-14   do speak [do not speak] [*corrected by JSM in SC copy*]
400.30   of [on]
407.19   them; [them:] [*as elsewhere in sentence*]
407.25   Radicals; that [Radicals: That] [*as elsewhere in sentence*]
412.24   Whigs to [Whigs would have to] [*corrected by JSM in SC copy*]
416n.14   is [*is*] [*as in* Source]
419.7-8   104,000*l*. rather more . . . Adelaide—the [104,000*l*.—rather more . . . Adelaide, the] [*for sense*]
424n.11   say (p. 45) [say (p. 45),] [*reference altered and moved in this ed.*]
430n.5   townships, [townships] [*for sense*]
434.19   for—displaying [for displaying] [*corrected by JSM in SC copy*]
443.16   denoûement [*dénouement*]
454n.18   J. H. Goddu [T. H. Goddu] [*as in* Source *and fact*]
454n.19   L. X. Masson [L. H. Masson] [*as in* Source *and fact*]
456n.7   this country [his country] [*corrected by JSM in SC copy*]
467.10   modern [moderate] [*corrected by JSM in SC copy*]
467.12   identified the [identified—the] [*for sense*]
474.39   *are*indeed [*are* indeed]

477.22 church [Church] [*as elsewhere in paragraph*]
481.12 become [becomes]
481.30 the almost [almost the] [*for sense*]
491.25 heragainst [her against]
493.22 trio [threefold] [*corrected by JSM in SC copy*]
493.40 principles [principle] [*corrected by JSM in SC copy*]
494.11 compound [confound] [*corrected by JSM in SC copy*]
501.20 That [that] [*slip of the pen?*]
502.5   state been [state having been] [*slip of the pen?*]
535.3   ours, [ours.] [*incomplete revision*]
537.6   Atlantic, [Atlantic.] [*incomplete revision*]
537.15 what are, [what are] [*incomplete revision*]
537.22 safety: [safety.]
537.25 changes this must [changes must] [*incomplete revision*]
537.26 once—experience [once experience]
538.14 commerce: [commerce.]
538.25 them [them.]
538.42 them [them.]
540.36 power strength [power;] [*treated as incomplete revision*]
541.25 amount, [amount.] [*incomplete revision*]
542.15 rural rural [rural] [*mistake in revision*]
543.13 For Those [For those] [*incomplete revision*]
543.15 of a [a] [*incomplete revision*]

Appendix D

Bibliographic Index of Persons and Works Cited, with Variants and Notes

LIKE MOST NINETEENTH-CENTURY AUTHORS, Mill is cavalier in his approach to sources, sometimes identifying them with insufficient care, and occasionally quoting them inaccurately. This Appendix is intended to help correct these deficiencies, and to serve as an index of names and titles (which are consequently omitted in the Index proper). Included here also are (at the end of the appendix) references to parliamentary documents of various kinds, entered in order of date under the heading "Parliamentary Papers and Petitions," and references to British, American, Austro-Hungarian, Canadian, French, and Scottish statute law, entered by country in order of date under the heading "Statutes." The material otherwise is arranged in alphabetical order, with an entry for each person or work quoted or referred to. Anonymous articles in newspapers are entered in order of date under the title of the particular newspaper. References to mythical and fictional characters are excluded. The following abbreviations are used: *PD* for Hansard's *Parliamentary Debates*, *PH* for *Parliamentary History and Review*, *PP* for *Parliamentary Papers*, and *PR* for *Parliamentary Review*.

The entries take the following form:
1. Identification: author, title, etc. in the usual bibliographic form. When only a surname is given, no other identification has been found.
2. Notes (if required) giving information about JSM's use of the source, indication if the work is in his library, Somerville College, Oxford (referred to simply as SC), and any other relevant information.
3. Lists of the pages where works are reviewed, quoted, and referred to.
4. In the case of quotations, a list of substantive variants between Mill's text and his source, in this form: Page and line reference to the present text. Reading in the present text] Reading in the source (page reference in the source).

The list of substantive variants also attempts to place quoted passages in their contexts by giving the beginnings and endings of sentences. The original wording is supplied where Mill has omitted two sentences or less; only the length of other omissions is given. There being uncertainty about the actual Classical texts used by Mill, the Loeb editions are cited when possible.

ABBOT, GEORGE. Referred to: 16

ABBOTT, JOSEPH. "Evidence Taken before the Select Committee of the House of Lords Appointed to Inquire into the State of Ireland, More Particularly with Reference to the

Circumstances Which May Have Led to Disturbances in That Part of the United Kingdom," *PP*, 1825, IX, 195-206.
REFERRED TO: 96

ABERCROMBY, JAMES. Referred to: 243, 252, 254

——— Speech on the Edinburgh City Election (16 June, 1834), *Morning Chronicle*, 17 June, 1834, 2.
NOTE: the quotation is from a reporter's summary.
QUOTED: 254
254.7 "he] He (2)
254.10 more completely] more immediately and more completely (2)

ACHESON, ARCHIBALD (Lord Gosford).
NOTE: the references at 421-2 and 432 are to the Canada Commissioners of whom Acheson, as Lord Gosford, was one; the references at 425 and 433 are to Gosford's actions as Governor General of Canada (1835-37). See also, under Parliamentary Papers, the various Reports of the Canada Commissioners.
REFERRED TO: 421-2, 425, 432, 433, 457

——— "Copy of a Despatch from the Earl of Gosford to Lord Glenelg, Dated Castle St. Lewis, Quebec, 26 Aug., 1837," *PP*, 1837-38, XXXIX, 353-7.
NOTE: the quotation is from an address of the Lower Canadian House of Assembly, prepared by Papineau, which Acheson, as Lord Gosford, enclosed in his despatch. The "Copy" forms part of the "Correspondence Relative to the Affairs of Lower Canada," *PP*, 1837-38, XXXIX, 317-430.
QUOTED: 422
422.5 one] We are found especially to notice in the reports in question, as far as they have come to our knowledge, one (355)
422.11 Parliament.] Parliament; whereas it was the duty of the commission, and of the mother country, to assist this House in the entire removal of these evils, and in rendering their recurrence impossible, by re-constituting the second branch of the Legislature by means of the elective principle, by repealing all laws and privileges unjustly obtained, and by ensuring the exercise of the powers and legitimate control of this House over the internal affairs of the province, and over all matters relative to its territory and the wants of its inhabitants, and more especially over the public revenue raised in it. (355)

——— "Copy of a Despatch from the Earl of Gosford to Lord Glenelg, Dated Castle St. Lewis, Quebec, 25 Oct., 1837," *PP*, 1837-38, XXXIX, 389-97.
NOTE: forms part of the "Correspondence Relative to the Affairs of Lower Canada," *PP*, 1837-38, XXXIX, 317-430.
REFERRED TO: 419n

——— "Reports of the Gosford Commission," *PP*, 1837, XXIV, 1-408.
REFERRED TO: 421, 429n

ADDISON, JOSEPH. *The Spectator*. 8 vols. London: Buckley, and Tonson, 1712-15.
REFERRED TO: 93

ADELAIDE (Queen Dowager of England). Referred to: 419

AESOP. *Aesop's Fables*. Trans. Vernon Stanley Vernon Jones. London: Heinemann; New York: Doubleday, Page, 1912.
NOTE: both references (the first to "The Fox and the Crow" and the second to "The Shepherd's Boy and the Wolf") are in quotations from Fonblanque. *Aesopi Phrygis fabulae graeca et latine* (Basel: Heruagis, 1544), the first Greek book JSM read, is in SC.
REFERRED TO: 365

ALCUIN. Letter to Charlemagne. In *Opera omnia*. Vols. C-CI of *Patrologiae cursus completus, series latina*. Ed. Jacques Paul Migne. Paris: Migne, 1851, C, col. 438.
QUOTED: 80
80.11-12 (*vox . . . Dei*)] Nec audiendi qui solent dicere: vox . . . Dei. (C, col. 438)

ALEXANDER THE GREAT.
NOTE: the reference at 173 is in a quotation from Livy.
REFERRED TO: 77, 173

ALLEGRI, ANTONIO.
NOTE: the references are to Correggio, the name by which the artist was generally known.
REFERRED TO: 249, 328

ALLEN.
NOTE: the reference is to a poacher, in a quotation from John Stafford's evidence, given before a Select Committee of the House of Commons.
REFERRED TO: 106

ALTHORP, LORD. See John Charles Spencer.

AMAR, JEAN BAPTISTE ANDRÉ.
NOTE: one of Babeuf's "fellow conspirators" in the Société des Egaux.
REFERRED TO: 401

ANNESLEY, FRANCIS (Baron Mountnorris).
NOTE: the reference is in a quotation from Hume; we have been unable to identify Annesley's two relatives.
REFERRED TO: 32

ANON.
NOTE: anonymous newspaper articles are listed, in chronological order, under the title of the newspaper. See *Examiner, Globe, Morning Chronicle, Morning Herald, Morning Post, Nottingham Review, Poor Man's Guardian, The Times.*

ANON. *Domestic Prospects of the Country under the New Parliament.* 3rd ed. rev. London: Ridgway, 1837.
REVIEWED: 381-404
QUOTED: 388
388.7-9 "All parties," . . . all parties, those] All parties, those (41)
388.12 enter the] enter upon the (41)

ANON. "Foreign Dependencies, Colonial Trade Bill," *PR*, 1825, 630-40.
REFERRED TO: 142

ANON. *Hints on the Case of Canada, for the Consideration of Members of Parliament.* London: Murray, 1838.
REVIEWED: 407-35

ANON. *A Letter on the Game Laws.* See John Weyland.

ANON. "Lord Durham's Return," *The Preamble*, No. VII (Nov., 1838), 200-21.
NOTE: this anti-Durham article (which contains the full text of Durham's "Proclamation" of 9 Oct., 1838, with critical notes) is not actually mentioned by JSM in his ostensible review of it.
REVIEWED: 445-64

ANON. *A Second Letter on the Game Laws.* See John Weyland.

APPERLEY, CHARLES JAMES. "Of the Game Laws; the Preservation of Game, and the Non-preservation of Foxes," *Sporting Magazine*, n.s., XVI (Aug., 1825), 295-308.
NOTE: Apperley wrote under the pseudonym "Nimrod."
QUOTED: 115, 116, 120
115.5 "A] [*paragraph*] Unwilling to trust to my own view of the proposed alterations in the game laws, I resolved upon consulting an old friend of mine on the subject; who, though no fox-hunter, is a good sportsman, a (307)
115.6-7 game" . . . "and] game and of foxes, and (307)
115.8 I] [*no paragraph*] I (307)
115.8 those, [says this preserver of game,] who] those who (307)
115.10 and contempt] and a contempt (308)

115.15   employer's] employers' (308)
116.11   "a] There is a (308)
116.13-14   country" . . . "but] country; but (308)
116.14   succeed:"] succeed. (308)
120n.8   *I had good reason to suspect*] [*not in italics*] (306)
120n.11   *shot him on the spot*] [*not in italics*] (306)

APPIUS CLAUDIUS.
   NOTE: the quotation derives from Livy (*q.v.* for the collation).
   QUOTED: 213

The Arabian Nights. Trans. Edward Forster. 5 vols. London: Miller, 1802.
   NOTE: this ed. (minus vol. IV) in SC. The references are in quotations from Fonblanque; that at 364 is to "The Story of the Two Sisters, Who Were Jealous of Their Younger Sister," V, 391-474; that at 366 is to "The Story of the Merchant and the Genius," I, 37-45.
   REFERRED TO: 364, 366

ARGYLE, EARL OF. See Archibald Campbell.

ARNDT, ERNST MORITZ. *Der Geist der Zeit*. See William Hazlitt.

AUGUSTUS. See Caesar Augustus.

AURANGZEB.
   NOTE: JSM uses the spelling Aurungzebe.
   REFERRED TO: 77

AYLMER, LORD. See Matthew Whitworth-Aylmer.

BABEUF, FRANÇOIS NOËL.
   NOTE: JSM uses the spelling Baboeuf.
   REFERRED TO: 401

BACON, FRANCIS. Referred to: 334

—— "Of Innovation." In *The Essayes or Counsels, Civill and Morall* (1625). In *The Works of Francis Bacon*. Ed. James Spedding, Robert Leslie Ellis, and Douglas Denon Heath. 14 vols. London: Longman, *et al.*, 1857-74, VI, 433.
   NOTE: the indirect quotations are in a quotation from Fonblanque. This ed. (which postdates the citations) used for ease of reference; in SC.
   QUOTED: 375

—— *Novum organum*. In *Works*, I, 119-365.
   REFERRED TO: 251

BAILLIE, MATTHEW.
   NOTE: the reference is in a quotation from Fonblanque.
   REFERRED TO: 368

BAINES, EDWARD. Referred to: 163, 164

BALFOUR, WILLIAM. Referred to: 39

BALL, ALEXANDER JOHN. Referred to: 269

BALMERINO, BARON. See John Elphinstone.

BANKES, GEORGE. *Reconsiderations on Certain Proposed Alterations in the Game Laws*. London: Hatchard, 1825.
   REVIEWED: 99-120
   QUOTED: 109-10, 111, 112
109.32   I must] [*paragraph*] I do not quarrel with this argument, although I must be allowed to doubt how far it will be substantiated by the experiment, but it does not interfere at all with the view which I take of the question: the poacher, I will admit, shall receive no more for the same quantity of game which he shall supply, when the sale is legalized, than he receives at this moment; he cannot well

receive less, since it appears that already he receives for pheasants, sometimes no more than one shilling a head; and, whilst I am on the subject of prices, I must (7)
 109.32 allowed, [says Mr. Bankes,] to] allowed to (7)
 109.33 pamphlet. "Few] pamphlet:—*[paragraph]* Few (7)
 109.37 I suggest, then, [continues Mr. Bankes,] that] *[paragraph]* I suggest then, that (7)
 109.39 poacher, viz. for pheasants, sometimes no more than one shilling a head, he] poacher, he (7)
 110.5 material! of] material!* *[5-line footnote omitted]* of (8)
 111.22 "even] *[paragraph]* It is not pretended that the destruction of game to which I am now adverting, is occasioned with a view of keeping up its price, which is said to be the case as to the supply of marine fish, and is a practical illustration of the benefit derived by the public from tradesmen who live in clusters; but in respect of fish, the monopoly is sustained, not by law, but by wealth in spite of the law; marine fish, can only be supplied by persons of considerable opulence, they must have vessels, nets, and other expensive implements, therefore contracts can be made in the certainty that there will be no interference on the part of poorer men who might be content with smaller profit; and above all, there is no apprehension of interference on the part of the thief, to whom even (5)
 112.9 saleable, [says Mr. Bankes (p. 26),] it] saleable, it (26)
 112.10 which makes] which shall make (26)
 112.14 uncontrolled; consequently] uncontrolled;* *[9-line footnote omitted]* consequently (26)
 112.21 discharged. With] discharged: with (27)
 112.27 said—Oh!] said? Oh! (27)

BANKES, HENRY. Speech on the Elective Franchise in Ireland (26 Apr., 1825; Commons), *PH*, 1825, 200.
REFERRED TO: 90-1

BANKES, WILLIAM JOHN. Speech on the Roman Catholic Clergy (29 Apr., 1825; Commons), *PH*, 1825, 205.
REFERRED TO: 86

BARING, FRANCIS THORNHILL. Statement on Criminal Prosecutions (4 Aug., 1834; Commons), *PD*, 3rd ser., Vol. 25, col. 929.
REFERRED TO: 275

BARRINGTON, MATTHEW. "Evidence Taken before the Select Committee Appointed to Inquire into the State of Ireland, More Particularly with Reference to the Circumstances Which May Have Led to Disturbances in That Part of the United Kingdom," *PP*, 1825, VIII, 573-84.
REFERRED TO: 88n, 96

——— "Evidence Taken before the Select Committee of the House of Lords Appointed to Inquire into the State of Ireland, More Particularly with Reference to the Circumstances Which May Have Led to Disturbances in That Part of the United Kingdom," *PP*, 1825, IX, 302-6.
REFERRED TO: 96

BASTWICK, JOHN. Referred to: 22, 29

——— *Flagellum pontificis et episcoporum latialium.* [Holland:] n.p., 1633.
REFERRED TO: 22

——— *The Letany of John Bastwick, Doctor of Phisicke, Being Now Full of Devotion, As Well As in Respect of the Common Calamities of Plague and Pestilence; As Also of His Owne Particular Miserie: Lying at This Instant in Limbo Patrum.* [London:] n.p., 1637.
REFERRED TO: 22

——— πράξεις τὸν ἐπισκόπων, *sive Apologeticus ad praesules anglicanos criminum ecclesiasticorum in curia celsae commissionis.* [London:] n.p., 1636.
REFERRED TO: 22

BAYLY, NATHANIEL THOMAS HAYNES. *Psychae; or, Songs on Butterflies, &c.* Malton: printed for private distribution, 1828.
NOTE: the quotation, in a quotation from Fonblanque (who uses the spelling "Bayley"), is from the first line of the first song on the second page of this collection.
QUOTED: 360
360.31 "I'd be a butterfly:"] I'd be a Butterfly born in a bower,/ Where roses and lilies and violets meet;/ Roving for ever from flower to flower,/ And kissing all buds that are pretty and sweet! (2, 1-4)

BEAUCLERK, AUBREY WILLIAM. Speech in Presentation of a Petition on the Dorsetshire Labourers (18 Apr., 1834; Commons), *PD*, 3rd ser., Vol. 22, col. 938.
NOTE: the reference is to the member who had "alluded to the melancholy conflict at Lyons."
REFERRED TO: 207-8

BEAUMONT, GUSTAVE DE LA BONNINIÈRE DE. *L'Irlande sociale, politique et religieuse.* 2 vols. Paris: Gosselin, 1839.
REFERRED TO: 530

BECHER, WILLIAM WRIXON. "Evidence Taken before the Select Committee Appointed to Inquire into the Disturbances in Ireland, *PP*, 1825, VII, 178-89.
REFERRED TO: 96

——— "Evidence Taken before the Select Committee of the House of Lords Appointed to Examine into the Nature and Extent of the Disturbances Which Have Prevailed in Those Districts of Ireland Which Are Now Subject to the Provisions of the Insurrection Act," *PP*, 1825, VII, 633-47.
REFERRED TO: 96

BEER BILL (Act). See 4 & 5 William IV, c. 85.

BELLASIS, HENRY.
NOTE: the reference is to him as one of three members of Parliament imprisoned in the Tower.
REFERRED TO: 28

BENTHAM, JEREMY.
NOTE: the quotation is of a term, "appropriate aptitude," frequently used by Bentham.
QUOTED: 303
REFERRED TO: 306

——— *A Fragment on Government: Being an Examination of What Is Delivered on the Subject of Government in General in the Introduction to Sir William Blackstone's Commentaries; with a Preface, in Which Is Given a Critique on the Work at Large.* In *The Works of Jeremy Bentham.* Ed. John Bowring. 11 vols. Edinburgh: Tait; London: Simpkin, Marshall; Dublin: Cumming, 1843, I.
NOTE: this ed. used for ease of reference. The first ed. (London: Payne, 1776) is in SC. Though the phrase comes from William Blackstone (*Commentaries*, IV, 49), JSM is undoubtedly quoting it from Bentham (who uses it in several places).
QUOTED: 72
72.25-6 "every thing is as . . . be."] [*paragraph*] Nor is a disposition to find "every thing as . . . be," less at variance with itself, than with reason and utility. (I, 230)

——— *Letters to Lord Grenville on the Proposed Reform in the Administration of Civil Justice in Scotland.* In *Works*, V, 1-53.
NOTE: the quotation is indirect.
QUOTED: 324
324.20-2 A board . . . becomes a mere screen] A *board*, my Lord, is a *screen*. (17)

——— *Plan of Parliamentary Reform, in the Form of a Catechism: with an Introduction, Showing the Necessity of Radical, and the Inadequacy of Moderate Reform.* In *Works*, III, 433-557.
REFERRED TO: 3

────── *Rationale of Judicial Evidence, Specially Applied to English Practice.* In *Works*, VI, 188-585, and VII.
NOTE: this ed. used for ease of reference; the ed. edited by JSM, 5 vols. (London: Hunt and Clarke, 1827) is in SC. The quotation reflects the sense, not the exact wording of the passages, and so is not collated.
QUOTED: 278

────── *The Rationale of Punishment.* London: Heward, 1830.
NOTE: translated by Richard Smith from *Théorie des peines et des récompenses*, ed. Pierre Etienne Louis Dumont, 2 vols. (London: Dulau, 1811).
REFERRED TO: 258

BERKELEY, ROBERT.
NOTE: the reference is to him as one of the judges impeached by Parliament in 1640.
REFERRED TO: 29

BEST, WILLIAM DRAPER (Lord Wynford).
NOTE: the first reference is to his Sabbath-day Bill; the third is in a quotation from JSM that includes the second.
REFERRED TO: 235, 250, 255n

BIBLE. Referred to: 490

────── Deuteronomy.
NOTE: the indirect quotation is in a quotation from Fonblanque.
QUOTED: 373
373.40 they waxed fat and kicked.] But Jeshurun waxed fat, and kicked: thou art waxen fat, thou art grown thick, thou are covered with fatness; then he forsook God which made him, and lightly esteemed the Rock of his salvation. (32:15)

────── Ezekiel.
NOTE: the reference is in a quotation from Fonblanque.
REFERRED TO: 367

────── Genesis.
NOTE: the references at 362 and 374 are in quotations from Fonblanque.
REFERRED TO: 362, 374, 531

────── Job.
NOTE: the reference is in a quotation from Fonblanque.
REFERRED TO: 373

────── I Kings.
NOTE: the quotation is in a quotation from Hume.
QUOTED: 42
REFERRED TO: 530
42n.6 'To your tents, O Israel;'] So when all Israel saw that the king hearkened not unto them, the people answered the king, saying, What portion have we in David? neither have we inheritance in the house of Jesse: to your tents, O Israel: now see to thine own house, David. (12:16)

────── Lamentations.
NOTE: the quotation is indirect.
QUOTED: 460
460.24-5 gall and wormwood] And I said, My strength and my hope is perished from the Lord:/ Remembering mine affliction and my misery, the wormwood and the gall. (3:18-19)

────── Luke.
NOTE: the quotation is indirect; the reference is in a quotation from Fonblanque.
QUOTED: 73
REFERRED TO: 373
73.22-3 love their enemies, turn the left cheek to those that smite them on the right, and do good to those that hate them, and despitefully use them.] But I say unto you which hear, Love your enemies, do good to them which hate you,/ Bless them that curse you, and pray for them which despitefully use

you./ And unto him that smiteth thee on the one cheek offer also the other; and him that taketh away thy cloke forbid not to take thy coat also. (6:27-9)

———— Matthew.
NOTE: the quotation at 398 is indirect.
QUOTED: 167, 398
REFERRED TO: 152, 373
167.38 "Judge not!"] Judge not, that ye be not judged. (7:1)
398.2 two or three shall be gathered together in their name] For where two or three are gathered together in my name, there am I in the midst of them. (18:20)

———— Proverbs.
NOTE: the quotation is indirect.
QUOTED: 165
165.10 a lion in the path.] The slothful man saith, There is a lion in the way; a lion is in the streets. (26:13)

———— II Samuel. Referred to: 530

———— II Thessalonians.
NOTE: the quotation is not exact.
QUOTED: 491
491.32 "if she do not work, neither shall she eat."] For even when we were with you, this we commanded you, that if any would not work, neither should he eat. (3:10)

BICKERSTETH, HENRY (Baron Langdale).
NOTE: the reference is to the Master of the Rolls.
REFERRED TO: 326-7

BINGHAM, PEREGRINE. "Prefatory Treatise on Political Fallacies," *PR*, 1825, 1-28.
NOTE: this is "a condensation and new arrangement of the matter" of Jeremy Bentham's *Book of Fallacies*, ed. Bingham (London: Hunt, 1824), in which the comparable passages to those here cited (in the order in which they occur) from the "Prefatory Treatise" may be found at 421 (fallacy of distrust), 401-8 (irrevocable laws), 440-8 (vague generalities), and 398-401 (wisdom of ancestors). The "Fallacy of Vows" JSM refers to is in the section on fallacies of authority.
REFERRED TO: 78-9, 80, 84n

BISHOP, DANIEL.
NOTE: the reference is to an officer of the law, in a quotation from John Stafford's evidence, given before a Select Committee of the House of Commons.
REFERRED TO: 105

———— "Evidence Taken before the Select Committee on the Laws Relating to Game," *PP*, 1823, IV, 135-9.
QUOTED: 105-6
REFERRED TO: 104n
105.33 "I] Yes [responding to question]; I (138)
105.37 miles, the] miles. The (137)
106.3 go on and] go and (136)

BLACK, JOHN. Referred to: 163, 273, 340

BLACKER, MAXWELL. "Evidence Taken before the Select Committee Appointed to Inquire into the Disturbances in Ireland," *PP*, 1825, VII, 47-80.
REFERRED TO: 89n, 93n, 96

BLAKE, ANTHONY RICHARD. "Evidence Taken before the Select Committee Appointed to Inquire into the State of Ireland, More Particularly with Reference to the Circumstances Which May Have Led to Disturbances in That Part of the United Kingdom," *PP*, 1825, VIII, 35-48, 742-5.
REFERRED TO: 87n, 88n

———— "Evidence Taken before the Select Committee of the House of Lords Appointed to

Inquire into the State of Ireland, More Particularly with Reference to the Circumstances Which May Have Led to Disturbances in That Part of the United Kingdom," *PP*, 1825, IX, 96-114.
REFERRED TO: 88n

BLAKE, WILLIAM. *Observations on the Principles Which Regulate the Course of Exchange; and on the Present Depreciated State of the Currency*. London: Lloyd, 1810.
NOTE: the reference is in a quotation from JSM's "The Currency Juggle."
REFERRED TO: 176

BLANC, LOUIS. *The History of Ten Years, 1830-1840; or, France under Louis Philippe*. Trans. Walter K. Kelly. 2 vols. Philadelphia: Lea and Blanchard, 1848.
NOTE: this is the earliest instance found of the use of the term.
QUOTED: 499
499.6 "state of siege"] The president [of the court trying the assassin Alibaud] having asked him [Alibaud] how long since he had entertained his deplorable design [to assassinate Louis Philippe], he replied: "Since the king declared Paris in a state of siege, since he sought to govern instead of reigning: since he caused the citizens to be massacred in the streets of Lyons and in the Cloitre St. Mery. (II, 415)

BLOMFIELD, CHARLES JAMES (Bishop of Chester). Speech on Roman Catholic Claims (29 Mar., 1825; Lords), *PH*, 1825, 167-8.
QUOTED: 81
81.33-5 "the petitioners belonged . . . contumely."] They held their seats in that house by a tenure which was both legally and morally not less strong than that by which the noble lords opposite held theirs; and they belonged . . . contumely (hear, hear). (168)

——— Speech on Roman Catholic Relief (17 May, 1825; Lords), *PH*, 1825, 237-41.
QUOTED: 67, 93
67.12 "purer . . . justice,"] Such a state of society could be improved by no such remedy as the present bill; it would require measures of a stronger and more efficacious character; it would require the introduction of a better religion, a purer . . . justice, a revision of the revenue laws, a general system of education; and last, though not least, a return of the proprietary of the country to the estates which they possessed within it (hear, hear). (239)
93.5-7 "a priesthood," . . . "which] Yet this was the same church which had produced a priesthood, to whose zeal, activity, and forbearance, every witness who had been examined before the committee had borne testimony—a priesthood which (240)

BLOUNT, CHARLES. Letter to the Editor of the *Sussex Advertiser* (30 July, 1834), *The Times*, 7 Aug., 1834, 1.
NOTE: the letter is signed Charles Blunt.
QUOTED: 274, 274n
REFERRED TO: 274
274.29-31 "the magistrates . . . that no . . . newspaper."] The resolution, I conclude, was made known to the committee, and Mr. Mabbott received instructions to return information to the Home-office, that all the magistrates, with the exception of one (Mr. Gear), had no doubt about the jury, and he concludes the communication by observing that the magistrates . . . that "no . . . *Guardian* newspaper." (1)
274n.7 a jail] the gaol (1)

BLOUNT, MOUNTJOY (Earl of Newport). Referred to: 39

BLUNT. See Charles Blount.

BOCCALINI, TRAJANO. *Advices from Parnassus, in Two Centuries, with the Political Touchstone, and an Appendix to It* (Italian, 1612). Revised and corrected by Mr. Hughes. London: Brown, *et al.*, 1706.
REFERRED TO: 352

BONAPARTE. See Napoleon I.

BONIFACE VIII (Pope). Referred to: 82

The Book of Common Prayer.
NOTE: the indirect quotations at 182 and 192 are from the General Confession, and the reference at 271 is to the Thirty-Nine Articles; both are found in *The Book of Common Prayer.* See *The Annotated Book of Common Prayer, Being an Historical, Ritual, and Theological Commentary on the Devotional System of the Church of England,* ed. John Henry Blunt (London: Rivington, 1866). See also next entry.
REFERRED TO: 182, 192, 271

The Booke of Common Prayer and Administration of the Sacraments. And Other Parts of Divine Service for the Use of the Church of Scotland. Edinburgh: printed by Young, 1637.
NOTE: the reference at 25 is to a new liturgy. See also the previous entry.
REFERRED TO: 25, 26

BOUCHETTE, ROBERT SHORE MILNES. Letter to Lord Durham (25 June, 1838), *Morning Chronicle,* 31 Oct., 1838, 2.
NOTE: Bouchette was one of eight prisoners who signed the letter, printed in the *Montreal Courier,* and later reprinted in the *Morning Chronicle,* which presumably served as JSM's source. The eight prisoners were Bouchette, Wolfred Nelson, R. Des Rivières, L.H. Masson, H.A. Gauvin, S. Marchesseau, T.H. Goddu, and B. Viger.
QUOTED: 453n-4n
453n.27   *whereby . . . trial*] [*not in italics*] (2)
454n.1   *and to*] and that to (2)
454n.1   *give . . . country*] [*not in italics*] (2)
454n.18   J.H.] T.H. (2) [*treated as typographical error in this ed.*]
454n.19   L.X.] L.H. (2) [*treated as typographical error in this ed.*]

BOURKE, RICHARD. "Evidence Taken before the Select Committee Appointed to Inquire into the State of Ireland, More Particularly with Reference to the Circumstances Which May Have Led to Disturbances in That Part of the United Kingdom," *PP,* 1825, VIII, 313-20, 324-41.
REFERRED TO: 89n, 96

——— "Evidence Taken before the Select Committee of the House of Lords Appointed to Inquire into the State of Ireland, More Particularly with Reference to the Circumstances Which May Have Led to Disturbances in That Part of the United Kingdom," *PP,* 1825, IX, 172-84.
REFERRED TO: 96

BOUVERIE, WILLIAM PLEYDELL (Lord Radnor). Referred to: 473

BOWRING, JOHN.
NOTE: the reference is to him as a Commissioner to France in 1834; see also George William Frederick Villiers.
REFERRED TO: 157

BRADLEY, CHARLES.
NOTE: the reference is in a quotation from the *Nottingham Review, q.v.*
REFERRED TO: 232

BRADLEY, MARY LOUISA.
NOTE: the reference is in a quotation from the *Nottingham Review, q.v.*
REFERRED TO: 232-3

BRAMSTON, JOHN.
NOTE: the reference is to him as one of the judges charged with offences by Parliament in 1640.
REFERRED TO: 29

BRAY, WILLIAM, ed. "Private Correspondence between King Charles I and His Secretary of State, Sir Edward Nicholas While His Majesty Was in Scotland, 1641 and at Other Times

during the Civil War." In *Memoirs, Illustrative of the Life and Writings of John Evelyn, Esq. F.R.S.* 2 vols. London: Colburn, 1818, II, 1-171.
NOTE: the correspondence is separately paginated.
REFERRED TO: 5n, 40

Brighton Guardian.
NOTE: the references at 274 and 274n are in quotations from Blount.
REFERRED TO: 273-4, 274n

BRINE, JAMES.
NOTE: the reference is to the sentencing of the six Dorsetshire labourers.
REFERRED TO: 207

BRODIE, GEORGE. *A History of the British Empire, from the Accession of Charles I, to the Restoration; with an Introduction, Tracing the Progress of Society, and the Constitution, from the Feudal Times, to the Opening of the History; and Including a Particular Examination of Mr. Hume's Statements, Relative to the Character of the English Government.* 4 vols. Edinburgh: Bell and Bradfute; London: Longman, Hurst, Rees, Orme, and Brown, 1822.
NOTE: the quotations at 10n and 20 are indirect.
REVIEWED: 1-58
QUOTED: 10n, 11, 20, 21, 22, 32n, 41, 42, 44, 45n, 47, 48, 52

10n.2   parliament he acknowledged the] Parliament, James had the imprudence to acknowledge the (I, 336n)
10n.3   impurities; he declared that he] impurities. He declared that his mind was ever free from thoughts of persecution, as he hopes those *of that religion* have proved since his accession. He expressed pity for the laity amongst them, and said he (I, 336n)
10n.5   to grant dispensation for] to dispense with (I, 336n)
10n.5   kings; if] kings. He wished he might be the means of uniting the two religions, for, if (I, 336n)
10n.6   half way;] half-way. [*the rest of the sentence is JSM's*] (I, 336n)
10.22   "declaring] The Scotch Clergy, full of the highest ambition, had converted the pulpit into a theatre for political declamation; and James had imbibed the bitterest hostility to every thing which approached to the Presbyterian form of ecclesiastical establishment, declaring (I, 333)
11.1-2   "The . . . kings," . . . "was] In 1610 he summoned Parliament, then busy with an inquiry into grievances, to Whitehall, and told them that "he did not intend to govern by the absolute power of a king, though he well knew the . . . kings was (I, 350)
11.4   none. As it was blasphemy," . . . "to] none; they can exalt and abase, and, like men at chess, make a pawn take a bishop or a knight: But that all kings, who are not tyrants or perjured, will bound themselves within the limits of their laws, and that those who persuade them to the contrary are vipers and pests, both against them and the commonwealth. Yet that as it is blasphemy to (I, 350-1)
11.7   In] [*no paragraph*] In (I, 351)
11.7   and struck] and he struck (I, 351)
11.9   star-chamber] Star-Chamber* [*footnote:*] *Howell's State Trials, vol. ii. p. 524. et seq. (I, 352)
11.18   revived.] revived: But though severities were practised to force men to contribute, such as ordering one Barnes a citizen of London, to carry a dispatch to Ireland, the scheme was very unsuccessful, as the people supported each other's resolution to resist it.† [*footnote omitted*] (I, 352)
20.9-10   the merchants . . . Turkey,] "the merchants . . . Turkey" [*Brodie is quoting Chambers*] (II, 275)
21.16   "after] They referred him, however, to the High Commission, that he might be degraded, and ordained that, after (II, 313)
21.21   slit: after] slit. After (II, 313)
22.21   "Sir] [*paragraph*] Sir (II, 319)
22.28   peace; his] peace. His (II, 319)
22.28   500*l*."] £500*. [*footnote:*] *Rush. vol. ii. p. 215. State Trials, vol. iii. p. 586. (II, 319)
32n.6   September] December (III, 83)

32n.7   that he] that "he [*Brodie is quoting from a letter of the Earl of Northumberland*] (III, 83)
32n.8   Strafforde."] *Strafforde**." [*footnote:*] *Sidney Papers, vol. ii. p. 665. (III, 83)
41.33-6   "When . . . word." . . . "questionless . . . and cut] That, besides this, they assaulted the servants of the members, and, with many oaths, expressed their regret at the absence of the accused members; nay, that some of them cried, "when . . . word;" and that when asked the meaning of that expression, they answered, that "questionless ... and have cut [*Brodie is quoting evidence given before a committee of the Commons*] (III, 268)
42.7-10   "with . . . gentlemen," . . . "*whereof* . . . place, which," . . . "must have had a wonderful effect."] He tells us that the members had nothing to apprehend, and merely feigned terror out of policy; yet, in the same breath, he informs us, that Lord Digby, whom he alleges, with what truth we shall examine by and bye, to have been the sole adviser of this breach of all faith and privilege, himself proposed to go into the city, "with . . . gentlemen, *whereof* . . . place; but the king liked not such enterprises." When the king had gone so far by this person's counsel, would it have been strange had he gone a little farther? and will it then be said that there was no ground for apprehension? The same writer says elsewhere, (Supplement to third volume of State Papers, p. 66, Character of Digby,) that when Digby perceived the consequences of his advice, "his great spirit was so far from failing, that when he saw the whole city upon the matter in arms to defend them, knowing in what house they were together, he offered the king, *with a select number of a dozen gentlemen*," (what! encounter the whole city, whose trained-bands were commanded by a very able and experienced officer, with only a dozen?) "who he presumed would stick to him, to seize upon their persons dead or alive, and without doubt he would have done it, *which must likewise have had a wonderful effect*." [*Brodie is quoting Clarendon's* History (I, iv, 283) *as well as the* State Papers] (III, 263n-4n)
44.19-20   "*many soldiers and commanders*"] "In this short journey," says he, "*many soldiers and commanders*, (who had assembled themselves jointly to solicit payment of their arrears for the late northern expedition *from the two houses of* Parliament,) waited on their majesties, and, leaving them at Hampton Court, provided their own accommodation at Kingston, the next place of receipt, and still so used for the overplus of company which the court itself could not entertain. [*Brodie is quoting from Lord Digby*] (III, 289n)
45n.12   "poor artificers and tradesmen."] This is an odd statement, because the petition bears, *in graemio*, to be from poor artificers and tradesmen, who attributed a decay of trade to the impolicy of the government. (III, 306n)
47.1   "the promise to the queen having shut] For long after this, he not only continued to negotiate, but solemnly denied—calling God Almighty to witness his sincerity—that he had any intention of war; though war that precluded accommodation, had then been resolved upon, and the same apologetical historian, whose office as councillor, &c. prevented the possibility of mistake, informs us that "the concert with the queen shut [*Brodie is quoting Hyde's* Life, *q.v.*] (III , 316)
48.11-13   "that . . . held:"] Now we have given our dates from the Journals, which prove beyond all doubt that . . . held. (III, 552n)
52.19   "To deal fairly with you, the] "To deal freely with you," he says in one of his letters to Hopkins, "the [*Brodie is quoting a letter of Charles's in Wagstaff's* Vindication, *q.v.*] (IV, 144)

BROUGHAM, HENRY PETER (Lord Brougham).
NOTE: the reference at 377, to a speech against secret voting, is in a quotation from Fonblanque.
REFERRED TO: 163, 196, 258, 265-6, 272-3, 277-9, 342, 377, 434, 443, 460

———   "Evidence Taken before the Select Committee of the House of Commons Appointed to Consider the Present State of the Law as Regards Libel and Slander, and to Report Their Observations Thereupon to the House [1834]." In "Report from the Select Committee of the House of Lords Appointed to Consider the Law of Defamation and Libel, and to Report Thereon to the House; with the Minutes of Evidence Taken before the Committee, and an Index," *PP*, 1843, V, 259-458.
NOTE: the Commons' Select Committee of 1834, referred to by JSM, met and took evidence, but did not issue a Report; the 1843 Lords' Committee, cited above, includes, as Appendix A (277-96), Brougham's testimony before the 1834 Committee; a summary of that testimony appeared in the *Spectator*, 5 July, 1834, 633 (reprinted in *The Times*, 7 July, 1834, 6), which is presumably the source upon which JSM based his remarks.
REFERRED TO: 261

——— "Last Session of Parliament—House of Lords," *Edinburgh Review*, LXII (Oct., 1835), 185-204.
REFERRED TO: 401

——— "Mr. Burke—Dr. Laurence," *Edinburgh Review*, XLVI (Oct., 1827), 269-303.
QUOTED: 368
REFERRED TO: 368
368.7-8 "There . . . state," . . . "as a professional statesman. All] He [Burke] was a politician by trade; a professional statesman. There . . . state; all (303)

——— Speech on Unlawful Societies in Ireland (15 Feb., 1825; Commons), *PH*, 1825, 102-7.
REFERRED TO: 73n, 75

——— Speech on Unlawful Societies in Ireland (18 Feb., 1825; Commons), *PH*, 1825, 118-21.
REFERRED TO: 74

——— Speech on Roman Catholic Claims (1 Mar., 1825; Commons), *PH*, 1825, 163-5.
REFERRED TO: 79

——— Speech on the Elective Franchise in Ireland (26 Apr., 1825; Commons), *PH*, 1825, 192-8.
QUOTED: 91
REFERRED TO: 91-2
91.16 "natural influence of property,"] The cause of this was the natural influence of property, of which he did not complain (hear). (193)
91.27 measure," &c &c.] measure for the purpose of checking that redundant population which he was ready to admit was a great evil in Ireland. (193)

——— Speech on the Catholic Clergy of Ireland (29 Apr., 1825; Commons), *PH*, 1825, 207-8.
QUOTED: 79n
79n.8 us."] us (hear, hear). (208)

——— Speech on the Established Church in Ireland (14 June, 1825; Commons), *PH*, 1825, 271-3.
REFERRED TO: 98

——— Speech on the Address on the King's Speech (29 Jan., 1828; Commons), *PD*, n.s., Vol. 18, cols. 49-58.
NOTE: this speech contains Brougham's famous declaration that "The schoolmaster was abroad."
REFERRED TO: 247-8

——— Speech on the State of the Courts of Common Law (7 Feb., 1828; Commons), *PD*, n.s., Vol. 18, cols. 127-247.
NOTE: the reference at 214 is to Brougham's six-hour speech; that at 312 is to his "celebrated speech" on law reform, the year of which JSM erroneously gives as 1827.
REFERRED TO: 214, 312

——— Speech in Introducing a Motion on Education (14 Mar., 1833; Lords), *PD*, 3rd ser., Vol. 16, cols. 632-8.
REFERRED TO: 200, 226

——— Speech on Jewish Disabilities (3 Mar., 1834; Lords), *PD*, 3rd ser., Vol. 21, col. 991.
REFERRED TO: 192

——— Speech on the Sale of Beer Bill (1834) (15 Apr., 1834; Lords), *PD*, 3rd ser., Vol. 22, cols. 762-4.
REFERRED TO: 213-14

BIBLIOGRAPHIC INDEX OF PERSONS AND WORKS CITED 563

——— Speech on the Progress of Education (16 Apr., 1834; Lords), *PD*, 3rd ser., Vol. 22, cols. 843-52.
REFERRED TO: 199, 200, 201, 225

——— Speech on Dissenters—Glasgow Petition (12 May, 1834; Lords), *Morning Chronicle*, 13 May, 1834, 1.
NOTE: the quotation derives from the *Morning Chronicle* report. The speech is in *PD*, 3rd ser., Vol. 23, cols. 843-8.
QUOTED: 225
REFERRED TO: 225, 227, 230
225.21 There] He had not concealed his alarm from the Deputation who had waited on him to place the Petition in his hands; he felt it to be his duty to let them know his sentiments on the subject [hear, hear, hear!]; it was because there (1)

——— Speech on the Church of Ireland—Commission (6 June, 1834; Lords), *PD*, 3rd ser., Vol. 24, cols. 298-306.
REFERRED TO: 253

——— Speech on Prison Discipline (20 June, 1834; Lords), *PD*, 3rd ser., Vol. 24, cols. 616-24.
REFERRED TO: 258

——— Speech in Introducing Petition on Stamp Duties (3 July, 1834; Lords), *Morning Chronicle*, 4 July, 1834, 2.
NOTE: *PD* gives no speech for Brougham or any other member of the House of Lords for 3 July, but does mention the Lord Chancellor's presentation on this day of a petition for repeal of the Stamp Duties (3rd ser., Vol. 24, col. 1095). It is, presumably, to the *Morning Chronicle* report of Brougham's speech that JSM is responding.
REFERRED TO: 261

——— Speech on Poor Laws' Amendment (21 July, 1834; Lords), *PD*, 3rd ser., Vol. 25, cols. 211-51.
REFERRED TO: 265-6

——— Speech on Appellate Jurisdiction (14 Aug., 1834; Lords), *PD*, 3rd ser., Vol. 25, cols. 1255-60.
REFERRED TO: 278

——— Speech on the Affairs of Canada (18 Jan., 1838; Lords), *PD*, 3rd ser., Vol. 40, cols. 177-217.
REFERRED TO: 434

BROUGHAM, WILLIAM. Referred to: 196, 231, 232

——— Notice of a Motion (7 Mar., 1834; Commons) to bring in a bill for the registry of births, marriages, and deaths, *The Times*, 8 Mar., 1834, 3.
NOTE: not reported in *PD*. See his Speech in Introducing a Bill (13 May, 1834).
REFERRED TO: 196

——— Speech in Introducing a Bill for a Registry of Births, Deaths and Marriages (13 May, 1834; Commons), *PD*, 3rd ser., Vol. 23, cols. 940-9.
NOTE: not enacted. Brougham gave notice of motion of his bill (see "A Bill to Establish a General Register of Births, Deaths and Marriages," 4 William IV [14 May, 1834]) on 7 Mar., 1834, in a speech not reported in *PD*; see his Notice of a Motion. In his speech of 13 May, he announced that, if the Registry Bill passed, he would introduce a Marriage Bill; but the Registry Bill failed, and so the other was not introduced by him.
REFERRED TO: 196

BROWNE, DENNIS. "Evidence Taken before the Select Committee Appointed to Inquire into the State of Ireland, More Particularly with Reference to the Circumstances Which May

Have Led to Disturbances in That Part of the United Kingdom," *PP*, 1825, VIII, 28-35.
NOTE: the quotation is indirect.
QUOTED: 85n

BROWNE, DOMINICK. "Evidence Taken before the Select Committee of the House of Lords Appointed to Inquire into the State of Ireland, More Particularly with Reference to the Circumstances Which May Have Led to Disturbances in That Part of the United Kingdom," *PP*, 1825, IX, 585-9.
REFERRED TO: 88n, 96

BROWNLOW, CHARLES. Speech on Unlawful Societies in Ireland (14 Feb., 1825; Commons), *PH*, 1825, 81-2.
QUOTED: 95
95.18-19 FOLLOWED . . . CHARGE] [*not in small caps*] (81)
95.19 by a] by any (81)

——— Speech on Catholic Relief (19 Apr., 1825; Commons), *PH*, 1825, 174-5.
REFERRED TO: 81-2

BRUTUS, MARCUS JUNIUS. Referred to: 187

BUCKINGHAM, DUKE OF. See George Villiers.

BUCKINGHAM, JAMES SILK. Speech in Introducing a Motion on Impressment of Seamen (4 Mar., 1834; Commons), *PD*, 3rd ser., Vol. 21, cols. 1063-79.
REFERRED TO: 178

——— Speech on the Sale of Beer Act (16 May, 1834; Commons), *PD*, 3rd ser., Vol. 23, cols. 1124-7.
REFERRED TO: 234

BULLER, ARTHUR. Referred to: 455n

BULLER, CHARLES.
NOTE: the reference at 327 is to him as one of the younger radical members of Parliament who also contributed to the *London and Westminster Review*; those at 443 and 463 are to Durham's advisers, of whom Buller was one.
REFERRED TO: 324, 327, 443, 457, 463

——— Motion on the Record Commission (18 Feb., 1836; Commons), *PD*, 3rd ser., Vol. 31, cols. 551-9.
NOTE: the reference is to Buller's disclosure of the incompetence and abuses of the Commissioners of Public Records; Buller on this occasion successfully moved for the appointment of a Select Committee, on which he served as chairman, to inquire into the Record Commission. See also under Parliamentary Papers, "Report from the Select Committee on the Record Commission" (1836).
REFERRED TO: 324

——— Speech on Municipal Corporations (Ireland) (20 Feb., 1837; Commons), *PD*, 3rd ser., Vol. 36, cols. 697-708.
NOTE: JSM must have had this speech in mind, for in it Buller includes a general theoretical consideration of the importance of municipal institutions.
REFERRED TO: 457

BULWER (later BULWER-LYTTON), EDWARD GEORGE EARLE LYTTON.
NOTE: the reference at 346 is in a quotation from Walsh.
REFERRED TO: 346, 480

——— "The People's Charter," *Monthly Chronicle*, II (Oct., 1838), 297-304.
QUOTED: 485
485.31-2 "the anti-Poor-Law movement in disguise."] [*paragraph*] The real fact is, that with nine tenths of the advocates of this new fanaticism, *the People's Charter is but the Anti-Poor Law agitation in disguise!* (297)

———— Speech in Moving an Amendment on Vacation of Seats on Acceptance of Office (1 May, 1834; Commons), *PD*, 3rd ser., Vol. 23, cols. 386-91.
REFERRED TO: 221

———— Speech in Introducing a Motion on Stamps on Newspapers (22 May, 1834; Commons), *PD*, 3rd ser., Vol. 23, cols. 1193-1206.
REFERRED TO: 237

BUONARROTI, PHILIPPE.
NOTE: one of Babeuf's "fellow conspirators" in the Société des Egaux.
REFERRED TO: 401

BURDETT, FRANCIS. Speech in Presenting a Petition on Catholic Claims (1 Mar., 1825; Commons), *PH*, 1825, 150-3.
QUOTED: 76
REFERRED TO: 77

76.22-7   "A more enlightened and liberal . . . men" . . . "did . . . country. The Church . . . adopt," . . . "bred up" . . . "as . . . religion."] [*JSM has altered the order of the extracts*] At the same time, for himself, he had no hesitation in saying, that, having been bred up in the religion of the Church of England, that alone, in his mind, would be a good reason to give for his preferring it, and as . . . religion (hear, hear). Farther, he certainly, upon reflection, did think, that if he had to choose his religion again, the Church . . . adopt. When he said this, he by no means meant to assert that objections might not be taken to parts of that system: many points in it, no doubt, might be altered and modified with great advantage; but his opinion applied to the system as a whole; and with respect to the clergy of the Church of England, take away only the ecclesiastical corporations, which like all other corporations, showed generally a narrow-minded, intolerant disposition, and for the clergy of the Church of England he had no hesitation in declaring, as far as his judgment went—a more enlightened liberal . . . men did . . . country. (151)

76.28-30   "There did . . . men." . . . "unfortunate . . . domination;" . . . "unwillingness . . . exercise;" a "right] [*JSM has altered the order of the extracts*] There was but one small faction in Ireland which opposed this liberal policy: and that opposition arose from their unwillingness . . . exercise. [*3-sentence omission*] There might be a few low pettifoggers hanging about the existing system, who might deserve this character [of being the worst of landlords and neighbours]; but he believed that, take the mass, there did . . . men than the Orangemen of Ireland. This, however, was apart from their unfortunate . . . domination, and from the right (152)

———— Speech on the Established Church in Ireland (14 June, 1825; Commons), *PH*, 1825, 271.
REFERRED TO: 97

———— Speech (10 Feb., 1834; Commons), *The Times*, 11 Feb., 1834, 2.
NOTE: this speech, in which Burdett offered a justification of hypocrisy on the part of members of the House, does not appear in *PD*.
REFERRED TO: 157

BURNET, GILBERT. *The Memoires of the Lives and Actions of James and William Dukes of Hamilton and Castleherald, &c.* London: Royston, 1677.
NOTE: the quotation is indirect.
QUOTED: 26
REFERRED TO: 5n, 26, 26n

26.14-15   *flatter the covenanters . . . pleases, . . . his chief end is, to win time*] And to this end I give you leave to flatter them . . . please, so you engage not me against my Grounds, (and in particular that you consent neither to the calling of Parliament nor General Assembly, untill the Covenant be disavowed and given up;) your chief end being now to win time, that they may not commit publick Follies untill I be ready to suppress them: and since it is (as you well observe) my own People, which by this means will be for a time ruined, so that the loss must be inevitably mine; and this if I could eschew, (were it not with a greater) were well. (55)

26.16   till the royal fleet shall have set sail.] As for the dividing of my Declaration, I find it most fit (in that way you have resolved it;) to which I shall adde, that I am content to forbear the latter part thereof, until you hear my Fleet hath set sail for Scotland. (55)

BURTON, HENRY. Referred to: 29

—————— *For God, and the King: The Summe of Two Sermons, Preached on the Fifth of November Last in St. Matthewes Friday-Streete.* [London:] n.p., 1636.
REFERRED TO: 22

BUSHE, CHARLES KENDAL.
NOTE: the relevant views of Bushe are given in *The Times*, 2 Aug., 1823, 3, and 5 Aug., 1823, 2.
REFERRED TO: 95n

BUTLER, JAMES (Duke of Ormonde).
NOTE: see also Thomas Carte.
REFERRED TO: 48-9, 52n

BYNG, JOHN.
NOTE: the source of the quotation has not been located.
QUOTED: 161

BYRON, JOHN. Referred to: 39, 40, 44

C.D. "Evidence Taken before the Select Committee on the Laws Relating to Game," *PP*, 1823, IV, 118-21, 134-5.
NOTE: C.D. is the first poulterer referred to at 110, the second referred to at 113; the quotations are indirect.
QUOTED: 110, 113

CAERNARVON, LORD. See Henry John George Herbert.

CAESAR AUGUSTUS. Referred to: 77

CAMPBELL, ARCHIBALD (Earl of Argyll).
NOTE: JSM uses the spelling Argyle. One of the references at 36 is in a quotation from Hume.
REFERRED TO: 36, 52, 53

CAMPBELL, JOHN (Earl of Loudon). Referred to: 28

CAMPBELL, JOHN.
NOTE: the reference at 182 and the reference at 274, both to the Attorney General, are in quotations from the *Examiner*; the reference at 248n is to the Attorney General.
REFERRED TO: 181-2, 224, 248n, 274

—————— Speech in Introducing a Motion on Law of Libel (18 Mar., 1834; Commons), *PD*, 3rd ser., Vol. 22, cols. 410-18.
NOTE: the reference at 191 is to the Solicitor General; that at 192 is to the government's response to O'Connell's initiative.
REFERRED TO: 191, 192

The Canadian Portfolio. See John Arthur Roebuck.

CANNING, GEORGE. Referred to: 123, 312, 352

—————— "Correspondence between Great Britain and the United States, Relative to Commercial Intercourse between America and the British West Indies," *PP*, 1826-27, XXV, 27-32, 38-41, 48-51.
QUOTED: 126, 129, 144
REFERRED TO: 123-47 *passim*
126.32 Since] [*no paragraph*] Since (31)
129.18 compacts; nor] compacts. Nor (51)
129.20-1 sacrifices. [*paragraph*] The] sacrifices. [*paragraph*] Between two Nations, as between two Individuals, most friendly to each other, there may sometimes happen, unfortunately, to exist some known subject of incurable difference of opinion. In any such case it is perhaps most advisable to keep

that subject as much as possible out of sight, and to take care that it shall not interfere with the tenour of their general intercourse and of their habitual relations. [*paragraph*] The (51)
144.33-4 "incurable difference of opinion,"] [*see* 129.20-1 *above*]

———— Speech on the Address from the Throne (3 Feb., 1825; Commons), *PH*, 1825, 38-40.
QUOTED: 70
70.19 "goaded"] Had the learned gent. [Brougham] forgotten how ministers were then goaded to stifle the restless spirit which was then said to prevail? (38)

———— Speech on Unlawful Societies in Ireland (15 Feb., 1825; Commons), *PH*, 1825, 97-102.
REFERRED TO: 73

———— Speech on the State of Ireland (26 May, 1825; Commons), *PH*, 1825, 260-1.
QUOTED: 84
84.3 "the . . . coronation oath,"] Who, among all the persons who had spoken on the subject, had disposed so unceremoniously, yet so satisfactorily, of the . . . coronation-oath to the removal of civil disabilities, as this very nobleman, who was represented as imitating the tone of a speech in which the objection of that coronation-oath formed the chief feature? (261)

———— Speech on the Established Church in Ireland (14 June, 1825; Commons), *PH*, 1825, 270-1.
QUOTED: 97
REFERRED TO: 98
97.24-5 "he had . . . House."] He had . . . house; and he believed that the hon. member [Hume] would find few supporters, either in that house, or in the country (hear, hear). (270-1)

Canons and Constitutions Ecclesiastical Gathered and Put in Forme for the Government of the Church of Scotland. Ratified and Approved by His Majesties Royall Warrand and Ordained to Be Observed by the Clergie and Others Whom They Concerne. Aberdeen: printed by Raban, 1636.
REFERRED TO: 25, 26

CANTERBURY, ARCHBISHOP OF (in 1834). See William Howley.

CARBERY, LORD. See John Evans-Freke.

CAREW, RANDOLPH. See Randolph Crewe.

CAREY, WILLIAM (Bishop of Exeter). Speech on Catholic Claims (13 Apr., 1825; Lords), *PH*, 1825, 169.
NOTE: the quotation is indirect.
QUOTED: 81
81.31 They called the clergy a *proscribed* body.] The fourth petition he had to present was the only one concerning which he expected to hear a dissentient voice, as it was from that proscribed body, the clergy. (169)

CARLYLE, THOMAS. "Signs of the Times," *Edinburgh Review*, XLIX (June, 1829), 439-59.
NOTE: the reference, to "the profoundest observer and critic on the spirit of the times whom we ever knew," is probably to Carlyle, who frequently calls journalists the new priesthood (for example, see also *Sartor Resartus*, I, vi, and III, vii).
REFERRED TO: 164

CARREL, ARMAND. Referred to: 380

CARTE, THOMAS. *An History of the Life of James, Duke of Ormonde, from His Birth in 1610, to His Death in 1688.* 3 vols. London: Knapton, Strahan, *et al.*, 1735-36.
REFERRED TO: 5n, 7, 48n, 49n, 52n

CARTWRIGHT, JOHN.
NOTE: the reference is to "the Cartwright school of reformers."
REFERRED TO: 340

CARY, LUCIUS (Viscount Falkland). Referred to: 46

CASTLEREAGH, LADY. See Emily Anne Stewart.

CASTLEREAGH, LORD. See Robert Stewart.

CATILINE (Lucius Sergius Catilina). Referred to: 185

CATOR, JOHN. Referred to: 249

CAVENDISH, WILLIAM (Earl of Newcastle). Referred to: 44

CAYLEY, EDWARD STILLINGFLEET. Referred to: 472

CECIL, WILLIAM (2nd Earl of Salisbury).
NOTE: the reference is to him as one of the Parliamentary commissioners.
REFERRED TO: 52n

CHADWICK, EDWIN. "Preventive Police," *London Review*, I (1829), 252-308.
QUOTED: 257
REFERRED TO: 257n
257.3 Some] [*no paragraph*] Some (260)
257.8 alone"... "as] alone, as (260)

CHALMERS, THOMAS. *Considerations on the System of Parochial Schools in Scotland, and on the Advantage of Establishing Them in Large Towns.* Glasgow: Hedderwick, 1819.
REFERRED TO: 259

CHAMBERS, RICHARD. Referred to: 20

CHANDOS, LORD. See Richard Plantagenet Temple Nugent Brydges Chandos Grenville.

CHAPMAN, HENRY SAMUEL. See Roebuck, *The Canadian Portfolio*.

CHARLES I (of England).
NOTE: the quotation is indirect; most of the references derive from Hume and Brodie. For Charles's correspondence, see Bray, Burnet, Carte, Collins, and Wentworth.
QUOTED: 26
REFERRED TO: 3-56 *passim*

CHARLES II (of England). Referred to: 23n, 58, 255-6

CHARLES X (of France).
NOTE: the reference at 312 is to the issuing of the "famous Ordinances" of 25 July, 1830.
REFERRED TO: 312, 418

CHARLES THE BOLD (Duke of Burgundy).
NOTE: the reference is in a quotation from Walsh.
REFERRED TO: 336n

CHATHAM, LORD. See William Pitt (the elder).

CHESTER, BISHOP OF (in 1825). See Charles James Blomfield.

CHILD, JOSIAH. Referred to: 130

CHOUNEUS, THOMAS. *Collectiones theologicarum quarundam conclusionum, ex diversis authorum sententiis . . . excerptae.* London: Seyle, 1635.
REFERRED TO: 21

CHOWNEY. See Thomas Chouneus.

CHURCH, JOHN. "Evidence Taken before the Select Committee Appointed to Inquire into the Disturbances in Ireland," *PP*, 1825, VII, 419-38, 449-58.
REFERRED TO: 89n, 96

CICERO, MARCUS TULLIUS. *De oratore* (Latin and English). Trans. E. W. Sutton and H. Rackham. 2 vols. London: Heinemann; Cambridge, Mass.: Harvard University Press, 1942.
NOTE: this ed. cited for ease of reference.
REFERRED TO: 337

CLARENDON, EARL OF. See Edward Hyde.

CLAY, HENRY. "Extract of Instructions to Albert Gallatin" (19 June, 1826), *Niles' Weekly Register*, XXXI, or 3rd ser., VII (23 Dec., 1826), 266-8.
NOTE: JSM incorrectly cites 23 June, 1826, as the date of this extract's appearance in *Niles' Weekly Register*.
REFERRED TO: 144, 146

CLEAVE, JOHN. Referred to: 480

CLINTON, HENRY PELHAM FIENNES PELHAM (4th Duke of Newcastle).
NOTE: the reference is in a quotation from Fonblanque.
REFERRED TO: 366

CLOTWORTHY, JOHN.
NOTE: the references are to him as one of eleven members excluded from Parliament.
REFERRED TO: 50, 52

COBBETT, WILLIAM.
NOTE: the reference at 95 is in a quotation from John North; that at 274 is in a quotation from the *Examiner*.
REFERRED TO: 95, 274, 400

———— "The Petition of the Nobility, Gentry, and Others of the County of Norfolk, in County Meeting Assembled, This 3d Day of January, 1823." In *Cobbett's Weekly Register*, XLV (11 Jan., 1823), 76-82.
NOTE: Cobbett claims the authorship of the Petition.
QUOTED: 361-2, 400
361.44-362.1 "equitable adjustment."] [*paragraph*] Your Petitioners, therefore, most humbly pray, that your Honourable House will be pleased to pass an Act for causing an efficient Reform in the Commons' House of Parliament, in order that such Parliament may adopt the measures necessary to effect the following purposes:— . . . [*paragraph*] 5. An equitable adjustment with regard to the Public Debt, and also with regard to all debts and contracts between Man and Man. (80)

———— and JOHN WRIGHT, eds. *The Parliamentary History of England, from the Norman Conquest, in 1066, to the Year 1803*. 36 vols. London: Bagshaw, Longmans, 1806-20.
REFERRED TO: 10n, 12n, 13n, 14n, 15n, 16n, 17n, 18n, 28n, 29n, 33n, 35n, 38n, 39n, 44n, 45n, 47n, 50n, 51n, 355n

COCHRANE, JOHN. Referred to: 37

Code civil des Français. Paris: l'Imprimerie de la République, 1804.
REFERRED TO: 528

COHEN, LEVY EMANUEL.
NOTE: the first reference at 274 and that at 276 are in quotations from the *Examiner*; that at 274n is in a quotation from Charles Blount.
REFERRED TO: 274, 274n, 276

COKE, EDWARD.
NOTE: the reference is to him as one of several popular leaders made sheriffs of counties to prevent their returning to Parliament in 1626.
REFERRED TO: 14

COKE, GEORGE (Bishop of Hereford).
NOTE: the reference is to him as one of twelve bishops impeached and subsequently imprisoned in 1641.
REFERRED TO: 39

COLBORNE, JOHN.
NOTE: the references are in quotations from a dispatch written by Lord Durham.
REFERRED TO: 454n, 462

———— "An Ordinance to Provide for the More Speedy Attainder of Persons Indicted for

High Treason, Who Have Fled from the Province, or Remained Concealed Therein to Escape from Justice," *PP*, 1837-38, XXXIX, 553-4.
NOTE: enacted as 1 Victoria, c. 19 (Lower Canada) (4 May, 1838), in *Ordinances Made and Passed by the Administrator of the Government, and Special Council for the Affairs of Lower Canada*, I (Quebec: Fisher and Kemble, 1838), 100-4.
REFERRED TO: 454n

COLERIDGE, SAMUEL TAYLOR. Referred to: 402

―――― *Biographia Literaria; or, Biographical Sketches of My Literary Life and Opinions*. 2 vols. in 1. London: Rest Fenner, 1817.
NOTE: in SC. The quotation is indirect.
QUOTED: 354
354.40 dwarfed in the distance] My mind is not capable of forming a more august conception, than arises from the contemplation of this great man in his latter days: poor, sick, old, blind, slandered, persecuted,/ "Darkness before, and danger's voice behind,"/ in an age in which he was as little understood by the party, *for* whom, as by that, *against* whom he had contended; and among men before whom he strode so far as to dwarf himself by the distance; yet still listening to the music of his own thoughts, or if additionally cheered, yet cheered only by the prophetic faith of two or three solitary individuals, he did nevertheless / —"Argue not / Against Heaven's hand or will, nor bate a jot / Of heart or hope; but still bore up and steer'd / Right onward." (I, 35)

―――― *Second Lay Sermon* ["*Blessed are ye that sow beside all waters*"] (1817). 2nd ed. In *On the Constitution of Church and State, and Lay Sermons*. London: Pickering, 1839.
NOTE: in SC. The quotation is indirect.
QUOTED: 283
283.12-13 If reforms were not to be weighed but counted] Men, I still think, ought to be weighed not counted. Their worth ought to be the final estimate of their value. (409)

COLLINGWOOD, CUTHBERT (Lord). Referred to: 269

COLLINS, ARTHUR, ed. *Letters and Memorials of State, in the Reigns of Queen Mary, Queen Elizabeth, King James, King Charles the First, Part of the Reign of King Charles the Second, and Oliver's Usurpation*. 2 vols. London: Osborne, 1746.
NOTE: this collection is known as the Sidney Papers. The reference at 32n is to a letter from the Earl of Northumberland to the Earl of Leicester; that at 46n, in a quotation from Brodie, is to letters of Lord Spencer to his wife.
REFERRED TO: 5n, 32n, 46n

COLLINS, MICHAEL. "Evidence Taken before the Select Committee Appointed to Inquire into the Disturbances in Ireland," *PP*, 1825, VII, 334-79.
REFERRED TO: 93, 96

The Complete Ready Reckoner, or Trader's Companion; Shewing . . . the Value of Any Quantity of Goods from One to One Thousand at Any Price from One Farthing to One Pound. London: Tallis, 1822.
NOTE: cited as representative of "Ready Reckoners."
REFERRED TO: 106n

CONSTANTINE PAVLOVICH (Grand Duke of Russia). Referred to: 414

CONTE, ANTOINE.
NOTE: the reference is to him as French Postmaster General in 1834.
REFERRED TO: 157

CONWAY, EDWARD (Lord). Referred to: 28

CONYNGHAM, FRANCIS NATHANIEL (Marquis of Conyngham). Referred to: 516-17

―――― "To the Editor of The Times" (24 Feb., 1868), *The Times*, 26 Feb., 1868, 10.
REFERRED TO: 516n-17n

COOKE, HENRY. "Evidence Taken before the Select Committee Appointed to Inquire into the State of Ireland, More Particularly with Reference to the Circumstances Which May Have Led to Disturbances in That Part of the United Kingdom," *PP*, 1825, VIII, 341-80.
REFERRED TO: 88n

——— "Evidence Taken before the Select Committee of the House of Lords Appointed to Inquire into the State of Ireland, More Particularly with Reference to the Circumstances Which May Have Led to Disturbances in That Part of the United Kingdom," *PP*, 1825, IX, 206-21, 268-71.
REFERRED TO: 96

COPLEY, JOHN SINGLETON (Lord Lyndhurst).
NOTE: the second reference is in a quotation from JSM that includes the first; the third is in a quotation from Fonblanque.
REFERRED TO: 250, 255, 369

CORBET, JOHN.
NOTE: the reference is to the five knights who tested the legality of their imprisonment.
REFERRED TO: 16

CORN LAWS. Most of the references are generally to "the Corn Laws"; references are given to the most recent Act (or Acts) at the time. See 55 George III, c. 26; 3 George IV, c. 60; 7 & 8 George IV, c. 57; and 9 George IV, c. 60.

CORREGGIO. See Antonio Allegri.

CORYTON, WILLIAM.
NOTE: the reference is to the leading members of Parliament imprisoned in 1629.
REFERRED TO: 19

COSIN, JOHN.
NOTE: the reference is to him as an ecclesiastic impeached by Parliament after the fall of Laud and Strafford.
REFERRED TO: 29

COSTELLO, THOMAS. "Evidence Taken before the Select Committee Appointed to Inquire into the State of Ireland, More Particularly with Reference to the Circumstances Which May Have Led to Disturbances in That Part of the United Kingdom," *PP*, 1825, VIII, 412-30.
REFERRED TO: 88n, 96

The Courier.
NOTE: the quotation, in a quotation from Fonblanque, is from an advertisement of 3 and 10 Sept., 1838, [1], for the sale by auction of "An Important Crown Estate.—The Manor and Lordship of Havering Atte Bower." The sale was to be held on the 23rd, not, as Fonblanque says, on the 16th Sept., 1828. For the collation, see the *Globe and Traveller*, 15 Sept., 1828; there are accidental, but no substantive differences between the two advertisements.
QUOTED: 359-60

COURTENAY, THOMAS PEREGRINE. Speech on the Roman Catholic Clergy (29 Apr., 1825; Commons), *PH*, 1825, 205-6.
REFERRED TO: 86

"COURTENAY, WILLIAM." See John Nichols Tom.

COUSIN, VICTOR. *Report on the State of Public Instruction in Prussia*. Trans. Sarah Austin. London: Wilson, 1834.
REFERRED TO: 229n

CRAWFORD, EARL OF. See Ludovic Lindsay.

CRAWLEY, FRANCIS.
NOTE: the reference is to him as one of the judges impeached by Parliament after the fall of Laud and Strafford.
REFERRED TO: 29

CREEVEY, THOMAS. Speech on the Roman Catholic Clergy (29 Apr., 1825; Commons), *PH*, 1825, 207.
REFERRED TO: 86

CREW, JOHN.
NOTE: the reference at 28 is to him as one of three members of Parliament imprisoned in the Tower; that at 52n is to him as one of the Parliamentary commissioners.
REFERRED TO: 28, 52n

CREWE, RANDOLPH.
NOTE: JSM, following Brodie, spells the name "Carew."
REFERRED TO: 16

CROKER, JOHN WILSON. "Agriculture in France—Division of Property," *Quarterly Review*, LXXIX (Dec., 1846), 202-38.
NOTE: in an Appendix to Vol. I of his *Principles of Political Economy* (all Library eds.), JSM quotes the same passage in the paragraph introducing his reprinting of three articles on French agriculture from the *Morning Chronicle*, 11, 13, and 16 Jan., 1847; see *CW*, II, 433.
QUOTED: 528
528.8 "dividing, by] The law has no limits—though the land has; and in a few years the Code Napoleon—still in all its power and vigour—will be employed in dividing fractions of square inches of land, and deciding by (217)

CROMWELL, OLIVER.
NOTE: the reference at 56 is in a quotation from Hume; that at 346 is in a quotation from Walsh.
REFERRED TO: 47, 48n, 49, 54, 56, 57, 346

CUMBERLAND, DUKE OF. See Ernest Augustus.

CURREY, WILLIAM SAMUEL. "Evidence Taken before the Select Committee Appointed to Inquire into the State of Ireland, More Particularly with Reference to the Circumstances Which May Have Led to Disturbances in That Part of the United Kingdom," *PP*, 1825, VIII, 293-313.
REFERRED TO: 88n, 89n, 96

CURRIE, JOHN. "Evidence Taken before the Select Committee Appointed to Inquire into the State of Ireland, More Particularly with Reference to the Circumstances Which May Have Led to Disturbances in That Part of the United Kingdom," *PP*, 1825, VIII, 619-36.
REFERRED TO: 96

DALHOUSIE, LORD. See James Andrew Broun Ramsay.

DALTON, JOHN. Referred to: 241

DARNELL, THOMAS.
NOTE: the reference is to the five knights who tested the legality of their imprisonment.
REFERRED TO: 16

DARTHÉ, AUGUSTIN ALEXANDRE.
NOTE: one of Babeuf's "fellow conspirators" in the Société des Egaux.
REFERRED TO: 401

DAVENPORT, HUMPHREY.
NOTE: the reference is to him as one of the judges impeached by Parliament after the fall of Laud and Strafford.
REFERRED TO: 29

DAWSON, GEORGE. Speech on Roman Catholic Relief (19 Apr., 1825; Commons), *PH*, 1825, 175-6.
REFERRED TO: 83

DAY, ROBERT. "Evidence Taken before the Select Committee Appointed to Inquire into the Disturbances in Ireland," *PP*, 1825, VII, 246-66.
REFERRED TO: 88n, 89n, 96

——— "Evidence Taken before the Select Committee of the House of Lords Appointed to Inquire into the State of Ireland, More Particularly with Reference to the Circumstances Which May Have Led to Disturbances in That Part of the United Kingdom," *PP*, 1825, IX, 522-34.
REFERRED TO: 85n, 88n, 96

DENMAN, THOMAS. Speech on Prison Discipline (20 June, 1834; Lords), *PD*, 3rd ser., Vol. 24, cols. 628-31.
REFERRED TO: 258

DERRY, BISHOP OF. See William Knox.

DESCARTES, RENÉ. *Principia philosophiae*. In *Opera philosophica*. 4th ed. Amsterdam: Elzevir, 1664.
NOTE: this ed. (works separately paged) in SC. The reference is in a quotation from Walsh.
REFERRED TO: 332

DES RIVIÈRES, RODOLPHE. See Robert Shore Milnes Bouchette.

DEVEREUX, ROBERT (Earl of Essex).
NOTE: the reference at 415n is in a quotation from Neate.
REFERRED TO: 38, 40, 48, 415n

DIDEROT, DENIS. Referred to: 493

DIGBY, GEORGE.
NOTE: one of the references at 44 is in a quotation from Hume; another is in a quotation from Brodie.
REFERRED TO: 42, 44

——— *The Lord Digby's Apology*. In John Nalson, *An Impartial Collection* (*q.v.*), II, 863-8.
QUOTED: 44
44.19-20 *"many soldiers and commanders"*] In this short Journey many Soldiers and Commanders (who had Assembled themselves, joyntly to solicite the Payment of their Arrears for the late Northern Expedition, from the two Houses of Parliament) waited on their Majesties, and leaving them at *Hampton-Court*, provided their own Accommodations at *Kingston*, the next Place of Receipt, and stil so used for the over-plus of company, which the Court it self could not entertain. (II, 865)

DIGGES, DUDLEY.
NOTE: the reference is to his being sent to the Tower as one of the principal managers of Buckingham's impeachment.
REFERRED TO: 15

D'ISRAELI, ISAAC. "The Royal Society." In *Quarrels of Authors; or, Some Memoirs for Our Literary History, Including Specimens of Controversy to the Reign of Elizabeth*. 3 vols. London: Murray, 1814, II, 3-77.
NOTE: the anecdote referred to reads: "When Charles II dined with the Members on the occasion of constituting them a Royal Society, towards the close of the evening, he expressed his satisfaction in being the first English Monarch who had laid a foundation for a Society who proposed that their sole studies should be directed to the investigation of the arcana of Nature; and added, with that peculiar gravity of countenance he usually wore on such occasions, that among such learned men he now hoped for a solution to a question which had long perplexed him. The case he thus stated: 'Suppose two pails of water were fixed in two different scales that were equally poised, and which weighed equally alike,

and that two live bream, or small fish, were put into either of these pails, he wanted to know the reason why that pail, with such addition, should not weigh more than the other pail which stood against it.'—Every one was ready to set at quiet the Royal curiosity; but it appeared that every one was giving a different opinion. One, at length, offered so ridiculous a solution, that another of the members could not refrain from a loud laugh; when the King, turning to him, insisted, that he should give his sentiments as well as the rest. This he did without hesitation; and told his Majesty, in plain terms, that he denied the fact!—On which the King, in high mirth, exclaimed, 'Odds fish, brother, you are in the right!'—The jest was not ill designed. The story was often useful, to cool the enthusiasm of the scientific visionary, who is apt often to account for what never has existed." (II, 19n-21n)
REFERRED TO: 255-6

DOHERTY, JOHN. "Evidence Taken before the Select Committee of the House of Lords Appointed to Inquire into the State of Ireland, More Particularly with Reference to the Circumstances Which May Have Led to Disturbances in That Part of the United Kingdom," *PP*, 1825, IX, 87-95.
REFERRED TO: 96

——— Speech on Unlawful Societies in Ireland (11 Feb., 1825; Commons), *PH*, 1825, 66-8.
NOTE: see also Thomas Spring-Rice.
QUOTED: 94
94.21-5 "Frequent allusions . . . THE . . . POOR . . . sentiments."] He proceeded to say, that frequent allusions . . . the . . . poor . . . sentiments (hear, hear). (67)

——— Speech on Unlawful Societies in Ireland (25 Feb., 1825; Commons), *PH*, 1825, 127-8.
NOTE: see also Thomas Spring-Rice.
QUOTED: 94
94.27-30 "As far . . . circuit . . . THE ADMINISTRATION . . . PURE . . . THE RIGHTS . . . RICH] He maintained, that as far . . . circuits . . . the administration . . . pure . . . the rights . . . rich (127)

DORISLAUS, ISAAC. Referred to: 57n

DOYLE, JAMES WARREN. "Evidence Taken before the Select Committee Appointed to Inquire into the State of Ireland, More Particularly with Reference to the Circumstances Which May Have Led to Disturbances in That Part of the United Kingdom," *PP*, 1825, VIII, 173-222, and IX, 223-48, 308-17.
REFERRED TO: 82, 83, 85n

DOYLEY. Referred to: 273

DRIVER.
NOTE: the references, to an auctioneer, are in a quotation from Fonblanque.
REFERRED TO: 359-60

DROUET, JEAN BAPTISTE.
NOTE: one of Babeuf's "fellow conspirators" in the Société des Egaux.
REFERRED TO: 401

DUGDALE, WILLIAM. *A Short View of the Late Troubles in England. . . . To which is added A Perfect Narrative of the Treaty at Uxbridge in an. 1644*. Oxford: printed at the Theater, 1681.
NOTE: the quotation is that on which Hume's account is based.
QUOTED: 45n
45n.12 "poor artificers and tradesmen."] [*paragraph*] But, within two days following, a Petition being brought into the House from *Suffolk*, calling upon them *to put the Kingdom into a* Posture: and another from many thousands of poor Tradesmen in London (as they stiled it) urging the like; alledging *a great decay of Trade, whereby they wanted Bread; and that they believed not any cause thereof to be in the House of Commons, but by reason of the Bishops and Popish-Lords, voting in the House of Peers:*

it was earnestly moved at a Conference (by Mr. *Hollies*) *that the Lords would no longer delay, but now joyn with them, to petition his Majesty that the Kingdom might be put into a Posture.* (87)

DUGGAN, MALACHI. "Evidence Taken before the Select Committee Appointed to Inquire into the Disturbances in Ireland," *PP*, 1825, VII, 207-24.
REFERRED TO: 85n

DUNFERMLINE, EARL OF. See Charles Seton.

DUNMORE [DUNMURE], JOHN.
NOTE: the reference is to his having been shown a petition by his friend, Baron Balmerino (Elphinstone).
REFERRED TO: 25

DURHAM, LORD. See John George Lambton.

DURHAM REPORT. See under Parliamentary Papers, "Report on the Affairs of British North America" (1839).

EARLE, WALTER.
NOTE: the reference is to the five knights who tested the legality of their imprisonment.
REFERRED TO: 16

EBRINGTON, LORD. See Hugh Fortescue.

EDINBURGH, BISHOP OF. See David Lindsay.

Edinburgh Review.
NOTE: the reference is in a quotation from Fonblanque.
REFERRED TO: 368

EDWARDS, EDWARD. "Currency," *Quarterly Review*, XXXIX (Apr., 1829), 451-75.
REFERRED TO: 400

ELDON, LORD. See John Scott.

ELIOT, JOHN.
NOTE: JSM uses the spelling Elliot. The reference at 15 is to his being sent to the Tower as one of the principal managers of Buckingham's impeachment; that at 18 is to him as one of the leading members imprisoned in 1629.
REFERRED TO: 15, 18

ELIZABETH I (of England).
NOTE: the reference derives from Brodie.
REFERRED TO: 9

ELLICE, EDWARD.
NOTE: the reference is to Ellice's vote in March of 1834 on Hume's motion on the Corn Laws; Ellice did not participate in the debate.
REFERRED TO: 186

——— Speech on Military Flogging—Case of Hutchinson (21 July, 1834; Commons), *PD*, 3rd ser., Vol. 25, cols. 279-83.
REFERRED TO: 268, 270

——— Speech on the Affairs of Canada (25 Jan., 1838; Commons), *PD*, 3rd ser., Vol. 40, cols. 484-501.
NOTE: JSM probably used the report in *The Times*, 26 Jan., 1838, 3, from which the collation is taken.
QUOTED: 416
416.24-5 "blameless . . . worth"] In speaking of Mr. Papineau, he wished to speak of him with truth and candour: he was a man whom he had known to be blameless . . . worth; but he was a man of strong passions, and supposing that he had taken no direct part in the insurrection, it would have been very difficult, he admitted, to acquit him of blame for affording it any encouragement. (3)

ELLIOT, JOHN. See John Eliot.

ELLIOT, THOMAS FREDERICK. *The Canadian Controversy: Its Origin, Nature, and Merits.* London: Longman, Orme, Brown, Green, and Longmans, 1838.
NOTE: the pamphlet is ostensibly reviewed, but is quoted only once and specifically referred to only once; the reference at 415 is to "the anti-Canadian pamphlets at the head of our article," of which this was one.
REVIEWED: 405-35
QUOTED: 420-1
REFERRED TO: 415, 424
420.35 "a wonderful] Seeing, however, how active are the gentlemen who have assumed to themselves the title of "Friends of Canada;"—how ubiquitous; how they are ever appearing in some new character on this side of the water or that,—at one moment correspondents in their own papers, at another holding the editor's pen in papers which are not their own;—considering the wonderful (51-2)
420.36 opinion, produced] opinion which is thus produced (52)
421.1 individuals,"] individuals: /"Alp answers alp; each mountain has its brother:"/ it is perhaps a proper tribute to so much industry not to pass over in silence the work which has come forth by the name of the "Canadian Portfolio." (52)

ELMORE, JOHN RICHARD. "Evidence Taken before the Select Committee Appointed to Inquire into the Disturbances in Ireland," *PP*, 1825, VII, 406-19.
REFERRED TO: 96

ELPHINSTONE, JOHN (2nd Baron Balmerino). Referred to: 25

EMPSON, WILLIAM. "Sir John Walsh's *Contemporary History*," *Edinburgh Review*, LXIII (Apr., 1836), 239-70.
REFERRED TO: 342

ENCOMBE, LORD. See John Scott.

ERNEST AUGUSTUS (Duke of Cumberland and King of Hanover).
NOTE: the reference at 366 is in a quotation from Fonblanque.
REFERRED TO: 366, 418, 419

ESSEX, EARL OF. See Robert Devereux.

ESTCOURT, THOMAS GRIMSTON BUCKNALL. Speech on Admission of the Dissenters to the Universities (20 June, 1834; Commons), *PD*, 3rd ser., Vol. 24, cols. 632-40.
NOTE: the quotation derives from the *Morning Chronicle* report, 21 June, 1834, 2.
QUOTED: 260
260.32-3 Do not] "don't (2)
260.34 life."] life" [hear!]. (2)

EVANS-FREKE, JOHN (Lord Carbery). "Evidence Taken before the Select Committee Appointed to Inquire into the State of Ireland, More Particularly with Reference to the Circumstances Which May Have Led to Disturbances in That Part of the United Kingdom," *PP*, 1825, VIII, 600-19.
REFERRED TO: 93n, 96

EWART, WILLIAM. Speech in Presenting a Petition on Free Trade—Corn Laws (19 Mar., 1834; Commons), *PD*, 3rd ser., Vol. 22, cols. 433-6.
REFERRED TO: 193

——— Speech on Admission of the Dissenters to the Universities (20 June, 1834; Commons), *PD*, 3rd ser., Vol. 24, cols. 651-3.
REFERRED TO: 260

An Exact Collection of All Remonstrances, Declarations, Votes, Orders, Ordinances, Proclamations, Petitions, Messages, Answers, and Other Remarkable Passages betweene the Kings Most Excellent Majesty, and His High Court of Parliament Beginning at His Majesties Return from Scotland, Being in December 1641, and

Continued untill March the 21, 1643. London: Husbands, Warren, and Best, 1643.
NOTE: this work is known as "Husbands' Collection."
REFERRED TO: 34n, 39n, 41n, 42n

The Examiner.
NOTE: anonymous articles follow, listed chronologically. The reference at 252 is inferential; that at 370 is in a quotation from Fonblanque. See also Fonblanque.
REFERRED TO: 174, 241, 252, 314n, 316, 340, 351, 352, 370, 374, 378, 379, 380, 390, 400

——— "The Inquisition," 16 Feb., 1834, 97-8.
NOTE: see also "The Acquittal" in the *Examiner* of the same day, 98-9.
REFERRED TO: 157

——— "The Spoiled Cabinet," 9 Mar., 1834, 146.
QUOTED: 182
182.24   indulgence? Apply] indulgence; apply (146)
182.41   slough.] slough: Miserable counsellors! (146)

——— "Tithe Commutation," 20 Apr., 1834, 242.
REFERRED TO: 197

——— "Much Ado about Nothing," 25 May, 1834, 323-4.
REFERRED TO: 241

——— "The Government and the Peers," 15 June, 1834, 369-70.
REFERRED TO: 252

——— "Public Money Applied to Private Prosecution," 20 July, 1834, 452-3.
QUOTED: 274
274.3   In] [*no paragraph*] In (452)
274.3-4   Government. . . . Who] Government. [*ellipsis indicates 4-sentence omission*] And who (452)
274.26   for libel; but] for libels. But (452)

——— "Military Misrule," 27 July, 1834, 467.
QUOTED: 268-9
268.17   We] Further, we (467)
268.29   road side?—And] road-side?—and (467)

——— Leading Article on the Prosecution of the *Brighton Guardian*, 10 Aug., 1834, 505.
QUOTED: 275-6
275.27   fact, Lord] fact that Government had undertaken to pay the expenses of the prosecution of the *Brighton Guardian* by some Sussex magistrates, honest Lord (505)

EXETER, BISHOP OF (in 1825). See William Carey.

FAIRFAX, THOMAS.
NOTE: the first reference at 55-6 is in a quotation from Hume.
REFERRED TO: 48, 55-6

FALCONER, THOMAS. See Roebuck, *The Canadian Portfolio.*

FALKLAND, VISCOUNT. See Lucius Cary.

FENWICK, JOHN. Referred to: 33n

FIELDING, HENRY. *The History of Tom Jones a Foundling* (1749). In *The Works of Henry Fielding, with Life.* 12 vols. London: Otridge and Rackham, *et al.*, 1824, VII-X.
NOTE: in SC. The reference at 155 is to Lady Bellaston, of questionable character; that at 359, in a quotation from Fonblanque, is to Squire Western.
REFERRED TO: 155, 359

FINCH, JOHN. Referred to: 29

FITZGERALD, AUGUSTUS FREDERICK (3rd Duke of Leinster). "Evidence Taken before the Select Committee of the House of Lords Appointed to Examine into the Nature and

Extent of the Disturbances Which Have Prevailed in Those Districts of Ireland Which Are Now Subject to the Provisions of the Insurrection Act," *PP*, 1825, VII, 700-5.
REFERRED TO: 96-7

FITZGERALD, WILLIAM VESEY. Speech on the Elective Franchise in Ireland (9 May, 1825; Commons), *PH*, 1825, 212-13.
REFERRED TO: 89

FITZWILLIAM, CHARLES WILLIAM WENTWORTH (Lord Milton, later 3rd Earl Fitzwilliam). Referred to: 473

———— Speech on the Game Laws Amendment Bill (31 May, 1824; Commons), *PD*, n.s., Vol. 11, cols. 958-9.
QUOTED: 108
108.8 thought] [*paragraph*] Lord *Milton* thought [*beginning of speech*] (col. 958)
108.10 amusement] amusements (col. 958)

———— Speech on the Elective Franchise in Ireland (9 May, 1825; Commons), *PH*, 1825, 214.
REFERRED TO: 88

FONBLANQUE, ALBANY.
NOTE: the reference at 314n is to the editor of the *Examiner*; the anonymous articles entered under *Examiner* were probably written by Fonblanque.
REFERRED TO: 314n, 340, 351-80 *passim*

———— *England under Seven Administrations*. 3 vols. London: Bentley, 1837.
REVIEWED: 351-80
QUOTED: 356-7, 357-8, 358, 358-9, 359-60, 361, 362-3, 363, 363-4, 364, 365-6, 366-7, 367-8, 368-9, 369-70, 370-1, 371-2, 372-4, 376-8
356.31-2 politics. [*paragraph*] The] politics! [*1-paragraph omission*] The (I, 239-40)
357.13 authorities.] authorities, and unfortunately from Blackstone more frequently than from Bentham. (I, 35)
357.14-15 instructive. [*paragraph*] A] instructive; they have made the most careless and thoughtless inquire [*sic*] into the utility of one of the three estates, and it is one of those inquiries which once instituted can only be attended with one conclusion. [*5-sentence omission*] [*paragraph*] A (I, 35-6)
358.8 In] [*no paragraph*] Then in (I, 40)
358.24-5 "it . . . community."] It . . . community. [*Fonblanque is quoting Peel*] (I, 164)
359.27 not all] not at all [*printer's error*] (I, 166)
361.4 Let] [*no paragraph*] Let (II, 168)
361.11-12 deserving. [*paragraph*] Those] deserving. [*8-sentence omission*] [*paragraph*] Those (II, 169-70)
363.36 rushlight. . . . It] rushlight. [*ellipsis indicates 5-sentence omission*] It (I, 216-17)
364.9 John] [*no paragraph*] John (I, 281)
364.13-14 longer." [*paragraph*] Blessed] longer." [*paragraph*] [*3-sentence omission*] Blessed (I, 282)
364.18-19 bars. [*paragraph*] Who] bars. [*1-paragraph omission*] Who (I, 282-3)
364.21 described?] described. (I, 283)
364.39 practical. . . . The] practical. The day furnishes an instance in point. Heaven knows how long the law has given every rogue power over our liberties, or the privilege of merely going to an office, taking an oath, and procuring the arrest of any individual whose temporary confinement may be agreeable to his malice or his schemes of knavery; the defect has been pointed out and neglected, but a case occurs, and the Magistrates are in wonderment at the negligence of the law, and the vicious opportunity to vexation afforded by it. The (I, 284)
364.40 it?"] it!" (I, 284)
365.17 have more] have a little more (II, 107)
365.19 they will know better] "they will know better" (II, 107)

BIBLIOGRAPHIC INDEX OF PERSONS AND WORKS CITED 579

365.29 "wolf"] wolf (II, 108)
366.21 his bed] his (*own*) bed (II, 110)
366.30 The] [*no paragraph*] The (II, 154)
367.18 properties] proprieties [*treated as typographical error in this ed.*] (II, 155)
368.12 very] every [*printer's error in* Source] (I, 169)
368.23-4 budget. [*paragraph*] When] budget. [*5-sentence omission*] [*paragraph*] When (I, 170)
368.27-8 assurance. [*paragraph*] If] assurance. [*paragraph*] We can easily imagine, however, that there really is much more simplicity than impudence, more delusion than imposture, in the notable doctrine above quoted. If (I, 171)
368.33 life." Gentlemen] life." Ne sutor ultra crepidam is indeed a proverb which will exclude the cobbler from physic; but it should receive a qualification from the oracle of the Edinburgh Review, and hold good with the single exception of public affairs, which it is argued may be directed by men of all denominations of occupation. Gentlemen (I, 171-2)
368.35 qualifications] qualification (I, 172)
368.39-40 country. [*paragraph*] The] country. [*4-sentence omission*] [*paragraph*] The (I, 172-3)
369.16 The] [*paragraph*] Since we wrote the above observations respecting the Duke of Wellington's expected assumption of the Episcopal character, the (I, 146)
369.16 "Some] [*paragraph*] "Some (I, 146)
369.17 at] about (I, 146)
369.21 occurrence] arrival (I, 147)
370.5-7 "written," . . . "in . . . 1828."] [*paragraph*] [The following paper was written in . . . 1828.] (I, 160)
370.45 you?"] you" (I, 162)
370.46 do?"] do" (I, 162)
373.16-17 cook? Is] cook? is (II, 246)
373.32-3 croak. [*paragraph*] It] croak. [*2-page omission*] [*paragraph*] It (II, 247-9)
374.25 King] Kings (II, 252)
377.6-7 error. [*paragraph*] It] error. [*9-sentence omission*] [*paragraph*] It (II, 79)

——— "The Unreported Meeting," *New Monthly Magazine and Literary Journal*, XXXI (Apr., 1831), 337-46.
NOTE: part quoted by Fonblanque in *England under Seven Administrations*.
QUOTED: 373-4, 374-5, 375-6
374.5 those] these (344)
374.17-22 *Had . . . Scripture*] [*not in italics*] (344)
374.29 That] [*paragraph*] That (344)
374.43 Potwallopers] [*no paragraph*] Potwallopers (339)
375.1 upon. He] upon; we know where to have and where to find them, and the ripeness of a borough is the rot of all the people out of it. He (339)
375.2 be. . . . It] [*ellipsis indicates 4-sentence omission*] (339)
375.4 broth? One] broth? and sure he was that too many cooks would spoil the Parliamentary porridge. He had heard a good rule—"One Church, one Physician and one Cook," to which he would add, one Nominator at Elections. One (339)
375.6-7 them. . . . Pursuing] [*ellipsis indicates 4-sentence omission*] (339-40)
375.7 reformer. . . . He] Reformer (disapprobation)—he felt the necessity of Parliamentary Reform, and he should move the disfranchisement of all boroughs and cities, in which the population pressed upon the patronage, or the means of management. He (340)
375.8 should propose] should also propose (340)
375.13 reform. . . . It] reform. [*paragraph*] It (340)
375.22-3 against corruption] against the corruption (340) [*treated as printer's error in this ed.*]
375.38 the old feudal] the feudal (342)
376.7 lose] lost (342)
376.9 encouraged. . . . He] [*ellipsis indicates 3-sentence omission*] (342)
376.11 hundred] hundreds (342)
376.12 disallowed. . . . He] disallowed. Such luxuries were to be indulged in temperately. He (342)

580   APPENDIX D

376.14 convenience. He] convenience. He liked the House of Commons, as it could be made a nuisance of, and thus an instrument of coercion. He (342)
376.17 shoulders. Law] shoulders. There was an end of them: they ran to seed—ran to costs. He was beaten in a prosecution the other day—what of that?—as the soldiers say, "Bad luck this day, better another time." (342)
376.19 we can have] we have (342)
376.22 submissive] submitted (342)
376.26 times] time (343)

FONBLANQUE, EDWARD BARRINGTON DE. *The Life and Labours of Albany Fonblanque.* London: Bentley, 1874.
NOTE: the reference arises from a phrase JSM attributes to "somebody," and Fonblanque attributes to JSM.
REFERRED TO: 353

FORTESCUE, HUGH (Lord Ebrington). Referred to: 252

FOSTER, JOHN LESLIE. "Evidence Taken before the Select Committee Appointed to Inquire into the Disturbances in Ireland," *PP*, 1825, VII, 241-6.
REFERRED TO: 96

——— "Evidence Taken before the Select Committee of the House of Lords Appointed to Inquire into the State of Ireland, More Particularly with Reference to the Circumstances Which May Have Led to Disturbances in That Part of the United Kingdom," *PP*, 1825, IX, 48-86, 498-504.
QUOTED: 85n, 88n
REFERRED TO: 88n, 89n, 96

——— Speech on Roman Catholic Claims (1 Mar., 1825; Commons), *PH*, 1825, 154.
REFERRED TO: 78

——— Speech on the Elective Franchise in Ireland (9 May, 1825; Commons), *PH*, 1825, 213.
REFERRED TO: 89

FOULIS, DAVID.
NOTE: the reference is in a quotation from Brodie.
REFERRED TO: 22

FOULIS, HENRY.
NOTE: the reference is in a quotation from Brodie.
REFERRED TO: 22

FOX, CHARLES JAMES.
NOTE: the reference at 346 is in a quotation from Walsh.
REFERRED TO: 135, 346

FOX, WILLIAM JOHNSON.
NOTE: the references are to the editor of the *Monthly Repository*.
REFERRED TO: 227n, 255n

FREDERICK AUGUSTUS (Duke of York). Speech on Roman Catholic Claims (25 Apr., 1825; Lords), *PH*, 1825, 187-8.
REFERRED TO: 83-4

FREDERICK WILLIAM II (of Prussia).
NOTE: referred to as "an infuriated despot."
REFERRED TO: 236

G. H. "Evidence Taken before the Select Committee on the Laws Relating to Game," *PP*, 1823, IV, 125-7.
NOTE: G. H. is the first poulterer referred to at 113; the quotation is indirect.
QUOTED: 113

BIBLIOGRAPHIC INDEX OF PERSONS AND WORKS CITED 581

GALLATIN, ALBERT. Referred to: 123, 144-5, 146
——— Correspondence between Great Britain and the United States, Relative to Commercial Intercourse between America and the British West Indies, *PP*, 1826-27, XXV, 25-7, 33-8, 42-7.
REFERRED TO: 123-47 *passim*
——— "Extract of Despatch to Henry Clay" (27 Oct., 1826), *Niles' Weekly Register*, XXXI, or 3rd ser., VII (6 Jan., 1827), 300.
REFERRED TO: 144, 146
GAME LAWS. See 22 & 23 Charles II, c. 25, and 57 George III, c. 90.
GARIBALDI, GIUSEPPE.
NOTE: the reference is to Garibaldians.
REFERRED TO: 520
GAUVIN, HENRI ALPHONSE. See Robert Shore Milnes Bouchette.
GEORGE III (of England).
NOTE: the reference is in a quotation from Fonblanque.
REFERRED TO: 371
GEORGE IV (of England).
NOTE: the references are in a quotation from Fonblanque.
REFERRED TO: 371, 372
——— Speech from the Throne (3 Feb., 1825), *PH*, 1825, 29-30.
QUOTED: 70
REFERRED TO: 71
70.26-8 "adopted . . . constitution," . . . "calculated . . . and exasperating] It is, therefore, the more to be regretted, that associations should exist in Ireland, which have adopted . . . Constitution, and calculated . . . and by exasperating (29)
GIBB, JAMES.
NOTE: the reference is to the Glasgow convicts, of whom Gibb was one.
REFERRED TO: 486
GILLRAY, JAMES. *The Apples and the Horse-Turds; or, Buonaparte among the Golden Pippins* (cartoon), 24 Feb., 1800.
NOTE: the quotation (from "the fable") is in a quotation from Fonblanque. The cartoon is reproduced as illustration no. 118 in Draper Hill, *Mr. Gillray the Caricaturist* (London: Phaidon Press, 1965).
QUOTED: 369
369.7-8 "How fine we apples swim!"] Explanation.—Some Horse-Turds being washed by the Current from a neighbouring Dunghill, espied a number of fair Apples swimming up the Stream, when, wishing to be thought of consequence, the Horse-Turds would every Moment be bawling out,—"Lack-a-day, how We Apples swim!" (In the cartoon, surrounded by floating symbols of monarchy and horse turds, Napoleon, also afloat, says, "A ha! par ma foi—how We Apples swim!")
GIPPS, GEORGE.
NOTE: the references are to the Canada Commissioners, of whom Gipps was one. See also, under Parliamentary Papers, the various Reports of the Canada Commissioners.
REFERRED TO: 421-2, 425, 432
——— "Extract of Minute of Proceedings [of Canada Commissioners] on Monday, 14 March 1836," *PP*, 1837, XXIV, 95-9.
NOTE: this formed part of the "Second Report of the Commissioners Appointed to Inquire into the Grievances Complained of in Lower Canada," *PP*, 1837, XXIV, 85-104.
QUOTED: 427-8, 428, 431
427.31 So] 9. [9th paragraph of Gipps's remarks in Second Report] And so in Lower Canada, should a contest ever arise (as but for the presence of the English authorities and English troops I believe it would) between the French Canadians and the English, I believe that all parties speaking English including settlers from the United States, would unite with the latter, and probably in the end prevail; but so (96)

428.5-6 believe,". . . "the] believe, the (97)
431.33 "for] 11. [11th paragraph of Gipps's remarks in Second Report] A withdrawal of the protection of England would, I believe, lead to an immediate struggle between the two races, and indeed I can scarcely doubt that, but for the presence of an overwhelming force, the same consequences would ensue were even the present demands of the Assembly complied with; and, as in this case, the English party would probably be the aggressors, the power of the Government would have in the first instance to be directed against men who are not only our fellow subjects, but for (97)

GISBORNE, THOMAS. Referred to: 212

——— Speech on Church Rates (21 Apr., 1834; Commons), *PD*, 3rd ser., Vol. 22, cols. 1022-4.
REFERRED TO: 212

GLAMORGAN, EARL OF. See Edward Somerset.

GLENELG, LORD. See Charles Grant.

The Globe.
NOTE: anonymous articles follow.
REFERRED TO: 337

——— Leading Articles on the Municipal Corporations Bill, 22 June, 1835, 2-3; 25 June, 1835, 4.
REFERRED TO: 307n

The Globe and Traveller.
NOTE: the quotation, in a quotation from Fonblanque, is from an advertisement of 15 Sept., 1828, [1], for the sale by auction of "An Important Crown Estate.—The Manor and Lordship of Havering Atte Bower." The sale was to be held on the 23rd, not, as Fonblanque says, the 16th of September, 1828.
QUOTED: 359-60
359.41-360.1 "amongst others," . . . "The owner . . . lordship (Havering atte Bower) has] Likewise the very valuable and important Manor and Lordship of Havering Atte Bower, extending over 15,000 Acres, including Romford and Hornchurch, and which extensive district possesses many most valuable privileges; amongst others, the owner . . . lordship has ([1])
360.1-2 has . . . two] [*not in italics*] ([1])
360.2 *two of the Magistrates*] two magistrates ([1])
360.3-4 who . . . lordship."] [*not in italics*] ([1])

GLOUCESTER, HENRY (Duke of).
NOTE: JSM uses the spelling "Glocester."
REFERRED TO: 55

GLYNNE, JOHN.
NOTE: the references are to him as one of eleven members excluded from Parliament.
REFERRED TO: 50, 52

GODDU, TOUSSAINT H. See Robert Shore Milnes Bouchette.

GODLEY, JOHN. "Evidence Taken before the Select Committee Appointed to Inquire into the State of Ireland, More Particularly with Reference to the Circumstances Which May Have Led to Disturbances in That Part of the United Kingdom," *PP*, 1825, VIII, 720-42.
REFERRED TO: 96

GODWIN, WILLIAM. *Things As They Are; or, The Adventures of Caleb Williams.* 3 vols. London: Crosby, 1794.
NOTE: the quotation, which is in a quotation from Fonblanque, is presumably from the title of Godwin's work; the phrase was popular in an ironic sense, occurring, for example, as a heading in James Mill's Commonplace Book (London Library), Vol. III, f. 145r.
QUOTED: 359

GOETHE, JOHANN WOLFGANG VON. *Die Leiden des jungen Werthers.* In *Werke.* 55 vols. Stuttgart and Tübingen: Cotta'schen Buchhandlung, 1828-33, I, 1-192.

NOTE: in SC. The reference is in a quotation from Fonblanque.
REFERRED TO: 366

GOLDSMITH, OLIVER. *She Stoops to Conquer; or, The Mistakes of a Night.* London: Newbery, 1773.
NOTE: the quotation is in a quotation from Fonblanque.
QUOTED: 365
365.12 "He would wile . . . tree:"] Ah he would charm . . . tree. (86)

GOODMAN, GODFREY (Bishop of Gloucester).
NOTE: the reference is to him as one of twelve bishops impeached and subsequently imprisoned in 1641.
REFERRED TO: 39

GORING, GEORGE.
NOTE: the reference derives from Hyde.
REFERRED TO: 44

GOSFORD, LORD. See Archibald Acheson.

GOULBURN, HENRY.
NOTE: the references are in quotations from Fonblanque.
REFERRED TO: 358, 369

———— Speech on Unlawful Societies in Ireland (10 Feb., 1825; Commons), *PH*, 1825, 51-4.
NOTE: at 71 and 73 JSM quotes the same passage from Goulburn's quotation from "Address of the Catholic Association to the People of Ireland."
QUOTED: 71, 73, 74
REFERRED TO: 73
71.14 "by the hatred they bore to Orangemen"] "In the name of foolish resources; by the hate you bear the Orangemen, your natural enemies (cheers from the Ministerial benches, re-echoed from the Opposition); by the confidence you repose in the Catholic Association, your natural and zealous friends; by the respect and affection you entertain for your clergy; by the affectionate reverence you bear for the gracious Monarch, who deigns to think of your sufferings with a view to your relief; and, above all, in the name of religion, and of the living God, we conjure you to abstain from all secret and illegal societies, and Whiteboy outrages" (hear, hear). (53)

———— Speech on Unlawful Societies in Ireland (25 Feb., 1825; Commons), *PH*, 1825, 128-9.
QUOTED: 95
95.8-11 *If . . . Man*, HE . . . FACT. With . . . THERE . . . AMONG . . . BRIBES] If . . . man, he . . . fact; but if it meant only that great inconvenience was felt by a poor man in prosecuting a suit at law, it was no more than was felt in this country, and was incidental to the condition of the poor in every state. With . . . there . . . amongst . . . bribes (128)

———— Speech on Roman Catholic Relief (19 and 21 Apr., 1825; Commons), *PH*, 1825, 178-80.
REFERRED TO: 83

———— Speech on the Elective Franchise in Ireland (26 Apr., 1825; Commons), *PH*, 1825, 202.
REFERRED TO: 90

———— Speech on the Roman Catholic Clergy (29 Apr., 1825; Commons), *PH*, 1825, 207.
REFERRED TO: 86

———— Speech on Admission of the Dissenters to the Universities (20 June, 1834; Commons), *PD*, 3rd ser., Vol. 24, cols. 670-82.
NOTE: the quotation derives from the *Morning Chronicle* report, 21 June, 1834, 3.
QUOTED: 260-1
260.35 "reflect] Let him reflect (3)
261.1 he (the son) might] he might (3)

261.2 devotion.] devotion; how he might have wandered from that path in which he was then safely walking;—let him reflect on this, and then let him vote for a measure that would involve the evils to which he had alluded, and render religious instruction impossible [hear, hear, hear!]. (3)

GOWER, FRANCIS LEVESON. Speech on the Roman Catholic Clergy (29 Apr., 1825; Commons), *PH*, 1825, 204-5.
REFERRED TO: 86

GRAHAM, JAMES (Earl of Montrose). Referred to: 36, 37, 57n

GRAHAM, JAMES ROBERT GEORGE.
NOTE: the reference at 344, in a quotation from Walsh, is to the resignation from Lord Grey's government of "Lord Stanley and his friends," one of whom was Graham.
REFERRED TO: 179, 185, 243, 344, 472

―――― *Corn and Currency; in an Address to the Land Owners*. London: Ridgway, 1826.
REFERRED TO: 174, 184, 400

―――― Speech on Impressment (15 Aug., 1833; Commons), *PD*, 3rd ser., Vol. 20, cols. 676-84.
NOTE: the reference is in a quotation from JSM.
REFERRED TO: 178

―――― Speech in Moving an Amendment on Impressment of Seamen (4 Mar., 1834; Commons), *PD*, 3rd ser., Vol. 21, cols. 1080-90.
REFERRED TO: 179, 180

―――― Speech on the Corn Laws (6 Mar., 1834; Commons), *PD*, 3rd ser., Vol. 21, cols. 1223-46.
REFERRED TO: 184, 223

―――― Speech on the Trade of Coopers (13 Mar., 1834; Commons), *PD*, 3rd ser., Vol. 22, cols. 161-6.
REFERRED TO: 207

GRANT, CHARLES (Lord Glenelg). Referred to: 452n-3n, 456n

―――― "Copy of a Despatch from Lord Glenelg to the Earl of Gosford, Dated Downing-street, 22 May 1837," *PP*, 1837-38, XXXIX, 326-8.
NOTE: this forms part of the "Correspondence Relative to the Affairs of Lower Canada," *PP*, 1837-38, XXXIX, 317-430.
QUOTED: 418
418.2 "violating . . . constitution?"] To avoid the necessity of violating . . . constitution, we have been willing to make every sacrifice excepting that of the honour of the Crown and the integrity of the Empire; and even now we are anxious that the experiment should be tried, whether yet a possibility remains of reconciling the assertion of those permanent interests with the maintenance of the principles of the Parliamentary Charter of 1791. (327)

―――― Speech on Roman Catholic Relief (10 May, 1825; Commons), *PH*, 1825, 221-2.
REFERRED TO: 92

―――― Speech on the Affairs of Canada (18 Jan., 1838; Lords), *PD*, 3rd ser., Vol. 40, cols. 162-77.
NOTE: the quotations derive from the *Morning Chronicle*, 19 Jan., 1838, 2.
QUOTED: 427, 428, 430n, 433
427.6-8 "those . . . improvement—attached . . . times—unfriendly . . . education"] Those who were returned by a numerical majority, comprising, it may be said, the whole of the Assembly, were those attached . . . times. They were unfriendly . . . education; and therefore not very friendly to the prevailing characteristics of the English race. [*4-sentence omission*] Those . . . improvement had the support and aid of popular institutions; while those who were really favourable to improvement, and had wealth and intelligence upon their side, were compelled to resort to the aristocratic party. (2)
427.18 of supporting them.] of enforcing them [hear, hear!]. (2)
428.19-20 *Executive . . . race*] [*not in italics*] (2)

430n.11-12   "oligarchy . . . times?" [*see entry for* 427.6-8 *above*]
433.11   "federal union"] A better prospect [than legislative union] might be obtained by a federal union; this would have a very considerable effect in adjusting the disputes between the provinces. (2)
433.13   "the] Amongst others [questions affecting the two provinces] there are the (2)
433.15   communications] communication (2)

GRATTAN, HENRY. Speech on Parliamentary Reform (15 May, 1797; Irish Commons). In *The Speeches of the Right Honourable Henry Grattan, in the Irish, and in the Imperial Parliament.* Ed. Henry Grattan (his son). 4 vols. London: Longman, Hurst, Rees, Orme, and Brown; Dublin: Milliken, 1822, III, 333-43.
QUOTED: 340
340.2-3   "the proprietors of Parliament."] The proprietors of boroughs have taken that right [of cities and towns to return members to Parliament] away; they have made public right private property; they have left indeed to the town the name of the return, and have imposed on the town the hardship and insult of their own nomination. (III, 334)

GRAY, THOMAS. "The Bard." In *The Works of Thomas Gray, with Memoirs of His Life and Writings by William Mason.* Ed. Thomas James Mathias. 2 vols. London: Porter, 1814, I, 25-32.
NOTE: in SC.
QUOTED: 257
257.1   "ample room and verge enough"] Weave the warp, and weave the woof,/ The winding-sheet of Edward's race:/ Give ample room, and verge enough / The characters of hell to trace. (I, 27; 49-52)

GREGORY VII (Pope). Referred to: 82

GRENVILLE, RICHARD PLANTAGENET TEMPLE NUGENT BRYDGES CHANDOS (Lord Chandos). Speech in Introducing a Motion on Agricultural Distress (21 Feb., 1834; Commons), *PD*, 3rd ser., Vol. 21, cols. 649-59.
REFERRED TO: 171

GREY, CHARLES (Lord).
NOTE: the reference at 251 is to the "Prime Minister"; the other references are to Lord Grey; that at 274 is in a quotation from the *Examiner*; those at 292, 316, 344, and 467 are to the Grey ministry; that at 339 and the first at 344 are in quotations from Walsh.
REFERRED TO: 221, 224, 251, 252, 263-5, 274, 285, 292, 316, 339, 344, 345, 347, 379, 412, 467, 480

———— Letter to Lord Ebrington (31 May, 1834), *Examiner*, 8 June, 1834, 355.
QUOTED: 252, 343
252.18   "constant . . . without."] But in pursuing a course of salutary improvement, I feel it indispensible [*sic*] that we shall be allowed to proceed with deliberation and caution; and, above all, that we should not be urged by a constant . . . without, to the adoption of any measures, the necessity of which has not been fully proved, and which are not strictly regulated by a careful attention to the settled institutions of the country, both in Church and State. (355)
343.18-19   "pressure from without." [*see collation for* 252.18]

———— "Secondary Punishments—Transportation," *Edinburgh Review*, LVIII (Jan., 1834), 336-62.
REFERRED TO: 258

———— Speech on the Corn Laws—Distress of the Manufacturing Districts (1 May, 1826; Lords), *PD*, n.s., Vol. 15, cols. 754-8.
NOTE: the same passage is quoted in both places.
QUOTED: 174, 400
174.36   *nemo tenetur ad impossibile*] Faith must be kept with the public creditor; but it was a sound maxim of law, that "nemo tenetur ad impossibilia." (col. 757)

———— Speech on the Dissenters (3 Mar., 1834; Lords), *PD*, 3rd ser., Vol. 21, cols. 922-3.
REFERRED TO: 195

——— Speech in Presenting the Cambridge University Petition (21 Mar., 1834; Lords), *PD*, 3rd ser., Vol. 22, cols. 497-508.
NOTE: the reference is to "the Premier."
REFERRED TO: 196

——— Speech on the Church of Ireland—Commission (6 June, 1834; Lords), *PD*, 3rd ser., Vol. 24, cols. 250-60.
NOTE: reported in *Morning Chronicle*, 7 June, 1834, 2, from which JSM presumably derives his quotation of Grey's citing of Napoleon.
QUOTED: 264
REFERRED TO: 252-3

264.22 "the spirit of the age;"] In that case [the removal of Grey's administration] my only prayer will be, that the Government may be placed in the hands that will conduct it on sound and safe principles; but I tell your Lordships again, that the principles on which it is conducted must be in conformity with the spirit of the age, in order that progress may be made in those further salutary improvements which necessarily grow out of the great measure of Reform. (2)

——— Speech on Suppression of Disturbances (Ireland) (4 July, 1834; Lords), *PD*, 3rd ser., Vol. 24, cols. 1127-30.
REFERRED TO: 262

GREY, CHARLES EDWARD.
NOTE: the references are to the Canada Commissioners, of whom Grey was one. See also, under Parliamentary Papers, the various Reports of the Canada Commissioners.
REFERRED TO: 421-2, 425

——— "A Minute Delivered to the Secretary by Sir Charles Grey, upon Signing the Sixth or General Report of the [Canada] Commissioners, on Thursday the 17th of November 1836," *PP*, 1837, XXIV, 232-48.
NOTE: this formed part of the "General Report of the Commissioners Appointed to Inquire into the Grievances Complained of in Lower Canada," *PP*, 1837, XXIV, 183-416.
REFERRED TO: 432

——— *Remarks on the Proceedings as to Canada, in the Present Session of Parliament.* By one of the Commissioners. London: Ridgway, 1837.
NOTE: JSM has, in his title, *Proceedings in Canada*.
REVIEWED: 405-35

GREY, EDWARD (Bishop of Hereford). Speech on Jewish Civil Disabilities (9 June, 1834; Lords), *The Times*, 10 June, 1834, 3.
NOTE: not in *PD*.
QUOTED: 251
REFERRED TO: 251

251.16 otherwise:"] otherwise; but at the same time, with reference to their doctrines on the subject of the Saviour, he thought it would be found, that while the Socinians disbelieved the Saviour's divinity, they admitted him to be "the Christ," whilst the Jews held the Lord Jesus to be an imposter. (3)

GREY, GEORGE. Speech on the State of the Mauritius (15 Feb., 1836; Commons), *PD*, 3rd ser., Vol. 31, cols. 401-20.
REFERRED TO: 326

GREY, HENRY GEORGE (Lord Howick). Referred to: 207, 209-10, 344, 474

——— Speech on the Corn Laws (7 Mar., 1834; Commons), *PD*, 3rd ser., Vol. 21, col. 1340.
REFERRED TO: 186

——— Speech on the Dorsetshire Labourers (18 Apr., 1834; Commons), *PD*, 3rd ser., Vol. 22, cols. 940-4.
REFERRED TO: 207-8, 209-10, 212

————— Speech on Sale of Beer (23 Apr., 1834; Commons), *PD*, 3rd ser., Vol. 22, cols. 1159-61.
REFERRED TO: 212-13

————— Speech in Moving an Amendment to the Sale of Beer Act (16 May, 1834; Commons), *PD*, 3rd ser., Vol. 23, cols. 1115-20.
REFERRED TO: 233

————— Speech on the Ballot (2 June, 1835; Commons), *PD*, 3rd ser., Vol. 28, cols. 425-9.
REFERRED TO: 299

GREY, LORD. See Charles Grey.

GROSVENOR, RICHARD (Marquis of Westminster). Speech on Jewish Civil Disabilities (9 June, 1834; Lords), *The Times*, 10 June, 1834, 3.
NOTE: not in *PD*.
REFERRED TO: 251

GROTE, GEORGE.
NOTE: the reference at 346 is in a quotation from Walsh.
REFERRED TO: 314n, 346, 434

————— Motion on the Ballot (2 June, 1835; Commons), *PD*, 3rd ser., Vol. 28, cols. 369-95.
NOTE: the references pertain to the debate (cols. 369-471) and division on Grote's motion.
REFERRED TO: 301, 313

————— Speech on the Affairs of Canada (16 Jan., 1838; Commons), *PD*, 3rd ser., Vol. 40, cols. 59-65.
REFERRED TO: 434

————— Speech on the Affairs of Canada (23 Jan., 1838; Commons), *PD*, 3rd ser., Vol. 40, cols. 399-406.
REFERRED TO: 434

GUERNON-RANVILLE, MARTIAL CÔME ANNIBAL PERPÉTUE MAGLOIRE, COMTE DE.
NOTE: the quotation has not been located.
QUOTED: 389

GUGY, LOUIS. Referred to: 426

GUICCIARDINI, FRANCESCO. *L'historia d'Italia*. Florence: Torret, 1561.
REFERRED TO: 352

GUSTAVUS ADOLPHUS (of Sweden). Referred to: 404

HACKET, PETER.
NOTE: the reference is to the Glasgow convicts, of whom Hacket was one.
REFERRED TO: 486

HALE, MATTHEW. *Historia placitorum coronae*. Ed. Sollom Emlyn. 2 vols. London: Gyles, *et al.*, 1736.
REFERRED TO: 33

HALL, JOSEPH (Bishop of Norwich).
NOTE: the reference is to him as one of twelve bishops impeached and subsequently imprisoned in 1641.
REFERRED TO: 39

HAMILTON, ELIZABETH. *The Cottagers of Glenburnie: A Tale for the Farmer's Ingle-nook*. Edinburgh: Manners and Miller, and Cheyne, 1808.
NOTE: the reference is in a quotation from Fonblanque.
REFERRED TO: 364

HAMILTON, JAMES (Marquis of).
NOTE: one of the references at 36 is in a quotation from Hume.
REFERRED TO: 26, 36, 53

HAMILTON, WILLIAM (Earl of Lanark, later Duke of Hamilton).
NOTE: JSM uses the spelling Laneric.
REFERRED TO: 36, 50, 51, 52

HAMMET, JAMES.
NOTE: the reference is to the sentencing of the six Dorsetshire labourers.
REFERRED TO: 207

HAMMOND, ROBERT. Referred to: 51

HAMPDEN, EDMUND.
NOTE: the reference is to him as one of five knights who tested the legality of their imprisonment.
REFERRED TO: 16

HAMPDEN, JOHN.
NOTE: the reference at 40 is in a quotation from Hume; that at 415n is in a quotation from Neate.
REFERRED TO: 23, 40-2, 47, 415n, 417

HANDLEY, BENJAMIN. Speech on Poor Laws' Amendment—Committee (16 June, 1834; Commons), *PD*, 3rd ser., Vol. 24, col. 475.
NOTE: the quotation presumably derives from the *Morning Chronicle* report of the debate, 17 June, 1834, 2.
QUOTED: 252
252.5-6 "ought . . . country."] If it would be as great an injury to the landed interest for the people, who ought . . . country, to go abroad and carry their capital with them, to grow food for themselves abroad, as it would be to let foreign corn come into the country, he hoped the Government would be upon its guard. (2)

HARBORD, EDWARD (Baron Suffield). *Considerations on the Game Laws*. London: Hatchard, 1825.
NOTE: the quotation at 109 is in a quotation from Bankes.
REVIEWED: 99-120
QUOTED: 103, 104, 109, 110
103.18 The] [*no paragraph*] The (22)
103.18 poacher, [says lord Suffield (p. 22)] will] poacher therefore will (22) [*restyled in this ed.*]
103.21-2 was seven or ten] was 7 or 10 (23)
103.25 hungry] hunger (23)
104.31 The] [*no paragraph*] The (26)
104.31 poachers, [says lord Suffield (p. 26)] united] poachers, united (26) [*restyled in this ed.*]
104.31 who become] who have become (26)
104.39 *get into trouble*] "get into trouble," (27)
110.18 I] [*no paragraph*] I (14)
110.18 heard, [says lord Suffield] from] heard from (14)
110.21 cash. From] cash.—From (14)
110.24 country] county (14)
110.25 game. . . . An] game. I have also the strongest reason to believe that young sportsmen very frequently pay for guns and shooting tackle by sending up game of all descriptions. If the cautious and irresponsible tone in which I have thought it right to speak respecting this description of law-breakers, should fail to make the proper impression, I have still another case to submit to the public, which will put beyond all question the probability of the poulterer's averment. An (14)
110.31 business. I] business. [*paragraph*] I (15)
110.35 transactions.] transactions? (15) [*treated as a typographical error in this ed.*]

——— Speech on the Game Laws (20 Feb., 1824; Lords), *PD*, n.s., Vol. 10, cols. 266-7.
QUOTED: 108
108.14 "so] He agreed in opinion with the noble earl [Grosvenor] who addressed their lordships yesterday, that the legalizing of the sale of game would not diminish it; but, so (col. 267)

HARDENBERG, KARL AUGUST VON. See Ernst Rudolph Huber.

HARLEY, EDWARD.
NOTE: the references are to him as one of eleven members excluded from Parliament.
REFERRED TO: 50, 52

HARRIS, EMMA.
NOTE: the reference is in a quotation from the anonymous article, "The Marriage Ceremony," in the *Nottingham Review*, q.v.
REFERRED TO: 232

HARRIS, JAMES EDWARD (Lord Malmesbury). Speech on the Progress of Education (16 Apr., 1834; Lords), *The Times*, 17 Apr., 1834, 3.
NOTE: JSM quotes a newspaper account (perhaps this one; see the collation), rather than the one subsequently published in *PD*, 3rd ser., Vol. 22, col. 852.
QUOTED: 201
201.37-9 "the founders of charity schools always take care to supply them with proper masters."] They were not necessary, because those who founded charity-schools always selected proper masters. (3)

HARRISON, THOMAS.
NOTE: the reference at 56 is in a quotation from Hume.
REFERRED TO: 8, 56, 57

HARROWBY, LORD. See Dudley Ryder.

HARVEY, DANIEL WHITTLE.
NOTE: the second reference is in a quotation from JSM that includes the first.
REFERRED TO: 250, 255

——— Speech on Church Rates (21 Apr., 1834; Commons), *PD*, 3rd ser., Vol. 22, cols. 1039-48.
REFERRED TO: 212

HASLERIG, ARTHUR.
NOTE: JSM uses the spelling Hazlerig.
REFERRED TO: 40-2, 47

HAZLITT, WILLIAM. *The Spirit of the Age; or, Contemporary Portraits.* London: Colburn, 1825.
NOTE: the quotations, which are indirect or at second- (or third-) hand, are of the term, "the spirit of the age," which probably derives from Ernst Moritz Arndt's *Der Geist der Zeit* (1805), referred to by Hazlitt in the *Examiner*, 1 Dec., 1816, 759. Hazlitt used the term in "The Drama. No. IV," *London Magazine* (Apr., 1820), 433, but JSM, who later used it as the title for a series of newspaper articles, probably was struck by the title of the work here cited (in which there is an account of Bentham).
QUOTED: 62, 250, 264

HEAD, FRANCIS BOND.
NOTE: the reference is to the Lieutenant-Governor of Upper Canada.
REFERRED TO: 453

HENRIETTA MARIA (of France, Queen of England).
NOTE: the reference at 11 is to the marriage of Charles I to "an avowed Catholic"; that at 21 is in a quotation from Hume; that at 44 derives from Hyde.
REFERRED TO: 11, 21, 44, 44-5, 45n, 46

HENRY VIII (of England).
NOTE: the reference at 9 derives from, and that at 11 is in a quotation from, Brodie.
REFERRED TO: 9, 11

The Herald.
NOTE: the reference is in a quotation from Fonblanque.
REFERRED TO: 369

HERBERT, GEORGE. "The Pulley." In *The Temple: Sacred Poems and Private Ejaculations*. Cambridge: Buck and Daniel, 1633, 153-4.
NOTE: the indirect quotation is in a quotation from Walsh.
QUOTED: 333

HERBERT, HENRY JOHN GEORGE (Lord Caernarvon). Speech on Admission to the Universities (1 Aug., 1834; Lords), *PD*, 3rd ser., Vol. 25, cols. 845-54.
NOTE: the name is generally spelled Carnarvon. He had earlier been Lord Porchester.
REFERRED TO: 271

HERBERT, PHILIP (4th Earl of Pembroke).
NOTE: the reference is to him as one of the Parliamentary commissioners.
REFERRED TO: 52n

HERBERT, THOMAS. *Memoirs of the Two Last Years of the Reign of That Unparallell'd Prince, of Ever Blessed Memory, King Charles I*. London: Clavell, 1702.
NOTE: the title page says by Herbert, Major Huntington, Col. Edward Coke, and Mr. Henry Firebrace.
REFERRED TO: 51, 52n-3n, 55, 56

HEREFORD, BISHOP OF. See Edward Grey.

HERON, ROBERT. Speech in Introducing a Motion on Vacation of Seats on Acceptance of Office (1 May, 1834; Commons), *PD*, 3rd ser., Vol. 23, cols. 382-6.
REFERRED TO: 221-2

HERRIES, JOHN CHARLES.
NOTE: the reference is in a quotation from Fonblanque.
REFERRED TO: 369

HERTFORD, MARQUIS OF. See William Seymour.

HEVENINGHAM, JOHN.
NOTE: the reference is to him as one of five knights who tested the legality of their imprisonment.
REFERRED TO: 16

HEWITT, JAMES (Lord Lifford). Speech on the Tenure (Ireland) Bill (1868) (12 Mar., 1868; Lords), *PD*, 3rd ser., Vol. 190, cols. 1439-47.
REFERRED TO: 516n

HEYMAN, PETER.
NOTE: the reference is to the leading members of Parliament imprisoned in 1629.
REFERRED TO: 16

HILL, MATTHEW DAVENPORT. Speech at Hull (22 Oct., 1833), *Examiner*, 10 Nov., 1833, 706.
NOTE: the reference concerns Hill's assertion that an Irish member (later identified as Sheil) had opposed the Irish Coercion Bill of 1833 in the House of Commons while privately expressing the opinion that such a measure was necessary.
REFERRED TO: 155

HILLYARD. Referred to: 20

HOBART, MILES.
NOTE: the reference is to the leading members of Parliament in 1629.
REFERRED TO: 16

HOBHOUSE, JOHN CAM. Speech on Corporation Reform (1 July, 1835; Commons), *PD*, 3rd ser., Vol. 29, col. 162.
REFERRED TO: 308n

HOCHE, LAZARE. Referred to: 518

HODGES, THOMAS LAW. Referred to: 472

BIBLIOGRAPHIC INDEX OF PERSONS AND WORKS CITED 591

HODGSKIN, THOMAS. *Labour Defended against the Claims of Capital.* London: Knight and Lacey, 1825.
NOTE: the quotation is from the title.
QUOTED: 485

HOLLES, DENZIL.
NOTE: JSM uses the spelling Hollis. The reference at 18 is to him as one of the leading members of Parliament imprisoned in 1629; that at 40 is in a quotation from Hume; those at 50 and 52 are to him as one of eleven members excluded from Parliament; that at 52n is to him as one of the Parliamentary commissioners.
REFERRED TO: 18, 40-2, 47, 49, 50, 52, 52n

HOLLINSWORTH, ROGER.
NOTE: the reference is in a quotation from the anonymous article, "The Marriage Ceremony," in the *Nottingham Review* (*q.v.*), which spells the name Holinsworth, but then refers to his wife as Mrs. Hollinsworth.
REFERRED TO: 232

HOLLIS. See Denzil Holles.

HOMER. *The Iliad.*
NOTE: as the reference is general, no edition is cited.
REFERRED TO: 194

HOPKINS, WILLIAM. Referred to: 52

HORACE (Quintus Horatius Flaccus). *Satires.* In *Satires, Epistles, and Ars poetica* (Latin and English). Trans. H. Rushton Fairclough. London: Heinemann; New York: Putnam's Sons, 1926, 4-244.
NOTE: this ed. used for ease of reference.
QUOTED: 261, 364
261.7 *Solvuntur risu tabulae.*] "Solventur risu tabulae, tu missus abibis." (132; II, i, 86)

HORNER, FRANCIS. Referred to: 342

HORSLEY, SAMUEL. Speech on the Treasonable Practices Bill (11 Nov., 1795; Lords). In Cobbett, ed., *The Parliamentary History of England* (*q.v.*), Vol. XXXII, cols. 257-8.
NOTE: the quotation is indirect.
QUOTED: 355

HOSKINS. Referred to: 245

HOTHAM, JOHN.
NOTE: the reference at 28 is to him as one of three members of Parliament imprisoned in the Tower.
REFERRED TO: 28, 44

HOWELL, THOMAS BAYLY, ed. *A Complete Collection of State Trials and Proceedings for High Treason and Other Crimes and Misdemeanours from the Earliest Period to the Year 1783, with Notes and Illustrations: Compiled by T.B. Howell, Esq. F.R.S., F.S.A., and Continued from the Year 1783 to the Present Time by Thomas Jones Howell, Esq.* 34 vols. London: Longman, *et al.*, 1809-28.
REFERRED TO: 11n, 16n, 17n, 20n, 21n, 22n, 23n, 25n, 29n, 30n, 39n, 40n

HOWICK, LORD. See Henry George Grey.

HOWLEY, WILLIAM (Archbishop of Canterbury).
NOTE: the reference at 369 is in a humorous quotation from Fonblanque.
REFERRED TO: 249-50, 369

——— *A Charge Delivered to the Clergy of the Diocese of London at the Primary Visitation of That Diocese in the Year 1814.* London: Payne and Foss, and Hatchard, 1814.
QUOTED: 249

249.29 "prostration . . . will,"] Its [Unitarianism's] influence has generally been confined to men of some education, whose thoughts have been little employed on the subject of religion; or who, loving rather to question than learn, have approached the oracles of divine truth without that humble docility, that prostration . . . will, which are indispensable to proficiency in Christian instruction. (16)

——— Speech on the Bill of Pains and Penalties against Her Majesty (7 Nov., 1820; Lords), *PD*, n.s., Vol. 3, col. 1711.
NOTE: Howley was then Bishop of London.
QUOTED: 249
249.30 "do] It was a maxim of the constitution of this country, that the King could do (col. 1711)

——— Speech on Dissenters—Glasgow Petition (12 May, 1834; Lords), *Morning Chronicle*, 13 May, 1834, 2.
NOTE: in *PD*, 3rd ser., Vol. 23, cols. 849-54, where the passages equivalent to those JSM is quoting (presumably) from the *Morning Chronicle* appear in cols. 853, 854.
QUOTED: 230
230.19-21 "while . . . friendly feeling . . . Churchmen."] It was grievous to think, that while . . . friendly feelings . . . Churchmen [hear, hear!]. (2)
230.24 "not" . . . "from] With respect to the Test and Corporation Acts, he and the majority of his Right Reverend brethren had resisted the Repeal of those Acts, not from (2)

HUBER, ERNST RUDOLPH, ed. *Dokumente zur deutschen Verfassungsgeschichte*. 3 vols. Stuttgart: Kohlhammer, 1961-65.
NOTE: reforms referred to, initiated by Stein and continued by Hardenberg, may be found in I, 38-47.
REFERRED TO: 515

HULTON, WILLIAM. "Correspondence with Lord Althorp," *The Times*, 20 Dec., 1831, 3.
NOTE: the reference, in a quotation from Fonblanque, is to a "Lancashire Tory." Hulton resigned his magistracy in Dec. of 1831 in response to a statement made by Althorp in the House of Commons, which Hulton understood to reflect unfavourably upon his conduct as a Manchester magistrate in the events of 1819 leading up to Peterloo.
REFERRED TO: 366-7

HUME, DAVID. Referred to: 3, 4

——— *The History of England from the Invasion of Julius Caesar to the Revolution in 1688*. 8 vols. London: Cadell, Rivington, *et al.*, 1823.
NOTE: as it is not known which ed. JSM used, reference is given to the one closest in date to his review of Brodie. One of the quotations at 14, one at 15, and that at 30, are indirect.
QUOTED: 12, 14, 15, 15-16, 16-17, 17, 18, 19n, 20, 20n, 21, 22, 23, 26, 27, 29n, 30, 31, 31-2, 33n, 35, 36, 37, 40, 41, 42n, 44, 45, 45n, 49, 52, 52n, 53, 54, 55, 55-6
REFERRED TO: 3, 5, 7-9, 13, 14, 25, 28, 32, 34, 34-5, 37, 38, 40, 43-4, 45n, 46, 48, 48n, 51, 52, 53-8, 57n, 493-4
12.3 "an] Animated with a warm regard to liberty, these generous patriots saw with regret an (VI, 204)
12.3 power was exercised] power exercised (VI, 204)
12.3 crown," . . . "it] crown, and were resolved to seize the opportunity which the King's necessities offered them, of reducing the prerogative within more reasonable compass. Though their ancestors had blindly given way to practices and precedents favourable to kingly power, and had been able, notwithstanding, to preserve some small remains of liberty; it would be impossible, they thought, when all these pretensions were methodized, and prosecuted by the increasing knowledge of the age, to maintain any shadow of popular government, in opposition to such unlimited authority in the sovereign. It (VI, 204)
12.32 "a] They attacked Montague, one of the King's chaplains, on account of a (VI, 210)
12.32 which] which he had lately published, and which (VI, 210)
12.33 torments:"] torments.^{e} [*footnote:*] ^{e}Parl. Hist. vol. vi. p. 353. Journ. 7 July, 1625. (VI, 210)
14.19 condition," . . . "was thus] condition was thereby (VI, 213)

14.25 undutiful."] undutiful.° [*footnote:*] °Parliamentary History, vol. vi. p. 449. Rushworth, vol. i. p. 224. (VI, 214)
15.33 Parliament," . . . "which] Parliament, which (VI, 223)
16.1 easier] more easy (VI, 223)
16.2 *agreeable . . . interest*] [*not in italics*] (VI, 223)
16.7-9 "Had . . . privileges."] Had . . . privileges: So high an idea had he received of kingly prerogative, and so contemptible a notion of the rights of those popular assemblies, from which he very naturally thought, he had met with such ill usage. (VI, 224)
16.28 foundation. Probity] foundation. On the contrary, if we consider the extreme difficulties to which he was so frequently reduced, and compare the sincerity of his professions and declarations; we shall avow, that probity (VII, 147)
16.32 "he] He had promised to the last house of commons a redress of this religious grievance: But he (VI, 220)
17.12-14 "forced . . . law"] Forced . . . law; these were the grievances complained of, and against these an eternal remedy was to be provided. (VI, 246)
18.3 "as this," : . . "was] And as it was (VI, 259)
18.4 he (Charles) met] he met (VI, 259)
18.6 great] just (VI, 259)
18.21-2 "an expedient," . . . "by] An expedient by (VI, 265)
18.23 pretensions."] pretensions, particularly with regard to the levying of tonnage and poundage. (VI, 265)
19n.4 "All] He was in this respect happy, that all (VI, 285)
19n.5-6 and every] and that every (VI, 285)
20.14-15 severities," . . . "were] severities were (VI, 306)
20.19-21 "the groundless charge" of popery against Laud, "was belied . . . conduct."] The groundless charge of popery, though belied . . . conduct, was continually urged against the prisoner; and every error rendered unpardonable by this imputation, which was supposed to imply the height of all enormities. (VII, 38)
20n.11 "the] But the grievances which tended chiefly to inflame the Parliament and nation, especially the latter, were the (VI, 388)
20n.14 these," . . . "were] these, were (VI, 388)
21.24 Leighton] [*no paragraph*] Leighton (VI, 295)
21.26 submission.] submission.¹ [*footnote:*] ¹Kennet's Complete Hist. (VI, 295)
22.16-17 "severity" . . . "perhaps . . . blameable."] The severity of the star-chamber, which was generally ascribed to Laud's passionate disposition, was, perhaps. . . blameable; but will naturally to us appear enormous, who enjoy, in the utmost latitude, that liberty of the press, which is esteemed so necessary in every monarchy confined by strict legal limitations. (VI, 307)
23.6 "every blessing . . . liberty"] All these were enjoyed by the people; and every other blessing . . . liberty, or rather the present exercise of liberty and its proper security.° [*footnote:*] °Clarendon, p. 74, 75. May, p. 18. Warwick, p. 62. (VI, 319-20)
23.8-9 "neither burthensome . . . properties, nor] [*paragraph*] The grievances under which the English laboured, when considered in themselves, without regard to the constitution, scarcely deserve the name; nor were they either burdensome . . . properties, or (VI, 319)
23.11-12 "enjoy . . . them!"] Eight ships, lying in the Thames, and ready to sail, were detained by order of the council; and in these were embarked Sir Arthur Hazelrig, John Hambden, John Pym, and Oliver Cromwell^y [*footnote omitted*] who had resolved for ever to abandon their native country, and fly to the other extremity of the globe; where they might enjoy . . . them. (VI, 309)
26.2-3 thought," . . . "that] He required the covenant to be renounced and recalled: And he thought, that (VI, 330)
26.6 subjects."] subjects.^m [*footnote:*] ^mRushworth, vol. ii, p. 754 &c. (VI, 330)
26.16-17 "was . . . history;"] In a word, the Parliament, after the commencement of their violences, and still more, after beginning the civil war, had reason for their scruples and jealousies, founded on the very nature of their situation, and on the general propensity of the human mind; not on any fault of the King's character; who was . . . history. (Note [F], VII, 526)

APPENDIX D

26.18-19 "it . . . particular;"] Perhaps it . . . particular. (Note [F], VII, 526)
26.19 "even] I shall first remark, that this imputation seems to be of a later growth than his own age; and that even (Note [F], VII, 523)
27.12-13 "retained . . . lost:"] He even secretly retained . . . lost.ᵐ [*footnote:*] ᵐBurnet's Memoirs, p. 154. Rush, vol. iii. p. 951. (VI, 343)
27.13 "in] In (VII, 147)
27.33 "The] [*paragraph*] The (VI, 345)
27.34 Traquaire," . . . "had] Traquaire had (VI, 345)
27.35 malcontents."] malcontents; and had conveyed this letter to the King. (VI, 345)
29n.16 "mild and prudent virtues"] The King gave his consent; and it is remarkable, that during all the severe inquiries carried on against the conduct of ministers and prelates, the mild and prudent virtues of this man, who bore both these invidious characters, remained unmolested.ᵏ [*footnote:*] ᵏWarwick, p. 95. (VI, 395)
30.4 "resolved] Finding, by experience, how unsuccessful those measures had proved, and observing the low condition to which he was now reduced, he resolved (VI, 391)
30.13-14 "with authority," . . . "to] These, joined to a small committee of lords, were vested with authority to (VI, 396)
30.16 conduct."] conduct.ᵐ [*footnote:*] ᵐClarendon, vol. i. p. 192. (VI, 396)
31.12 "innocent] but though four months were employed by all the managers in framing the accusation, and all Strafford's answers were extempory; it appears from comparison, not only that he was free from the crime of treason, of which there is not the least appearance, but that his conduct, making allowance for human infirmities, exposed to such severe scrutiny, was innocent (VI, 399)
31.18 "equally] [*paragraph*] In the government of Ireland, his administration had been equally (VI, 399)
31.19 interests] interest (VI, 399)
31.31 head.] head.ᵃ [*footnote:*] ᵃRushworth, vol. iv. p. 187. (VI, 401)
33n.15-16 "Such . . . genius, and presence . . . law] [*paragraph*] An accusation carried on by the united effort of three kingdoms against one man, unprotected by power, unassisted by counsel, discountenanced by authority, was likely to prove a very unequal contest: Yet such . . . genius, presence . . . law (VI, 398-9)
33n.19 *rigid law*] rigid law (VI, 400)
33n.20 and the] and to the (VI, 400)
33n.21 *necessity*] necessity (VI, 400)
35.21 uncontrollable.] uncontrollable.ᶻ [*footnote:*] ᶻClarendon, vol. i. p. 261, 262. Rushworth, vol. v. p. 264. (VI, 416)
35.21 with] of (VI, 416)
35.23 eyes."] eyes* [*footnote:*] *See note [BB] at the end of the volume. [*text:*] : A circumstance which, if it lessen our idea of his resolution or penetration, serves to prove the integrity of his heart, and the goodness of his disposition. (VI, 416)
36.6 "He arrived . . . in] [*paragraph*] Charles, despoiled in England of a considerable part of his authority, and dreading still farther encroachments upon him, arrived in (VI, 426)
36.7 there] *there* (VI, 426)
37.33-4 "All . . . return."] And, though all . . . return, the praise of these advantages was ascribed, not to the King, but to the Parliament who had extorted his consent to such salutary statutes. (VI, 449)
40.4 "egregious imprudence."] No man, in either house, ventured to speak a word in their vindication; so much displeased was every one at the egregious imprudence of which they had been guilty. (VI, 465)
40.11 after," . . . "the] after, the (VI, 465)
41.25 "accompanied," . . . "by] He was accompanied by (VI, 469)
41.27 staves] swords (VI, 469)
42n.5 populace," . . . "drew] populace, more insolent than the rest, drew (VI, 471)
42n.6 "To . . . Israel;"] *To . . . Israel!* (VI, 471)
42n.7 sovereign."] sovereign.ʷ [*footnote:*] ʷRushworth, vol. v. p. 479. Clarendon, vol. ii. p. 361. (VI, 471)
42.18 the king, . . . apprehensive] [*paragraph*] The King, apprehensive (VI, 472)
42.21 enemies. His] enemies: His (VI, 472)

BIBLIOGRAPHIC INDEX OF PERSONS AND WORKS CITED 595

44.18 kingdom."] kingdom.ᵃ [*footnote:*] ᵃClarendon. Rush. part iii. vol. i. chap. ii. p. 495. (VI, 484)

45n.10 "several . . . *beggars*,"] [*paragraph*] Another petition was presented by several poor people, or beggars, in the name of many thousands more; in which the petitioners proposed as a remedy for the public miseries, *That those noble worthies of the house of peers, who concur with the happy votes of the commons, may separate themselves from the rest, and sit and vote as one entire body.* (VI, 475)

45.12 "neither] Neither (Note [F], VII, 523)

49.17 friend."] friend, especially where that person must have had opportunities of knowing the truth. (VII, 517)

52.12-13 "Of . . . Parliament," . . . "Charles] [*paragraph*] Of . . . Parliament, Charles (VII, 124)

52n.12-13 commissioners," . . . "would] commissioners would (VII, 122)

52n.17 him."] him.ˢ [*footnote:*] ˢHerbert's Memoirs, p. 72. (VII, 122)

53.2 "Having] [*paragraph*] This measure being foreseen some time before, the King was exhorted to make his escape, which was conceived to be very easy: But having (VII, 130)

54.29 "The] [*no paragraph*] The (VII, 140)

54.30 justice. 'Poor souls,' said] justice: *Poor souls!* said (VII, 140)

54.31 '*for . . . commanders.*'] *for . . . commanders.*ᵗ [*footnote:*] ᵗRushworth, vol. viii. p. 1425. (VII, 140)

55.19 "the] [*paragraph*] Every night, during this interval, the (VII, 143)

55.20 forming] framing (VII, 143)

55.21 ears."] ears.ʸ [*footnote:*] ʸClement Walker's History of Independency. (VII, 143)

56.2 of his] of this (VII, 145) [*treated as typographical error in this ed.*]

56.7 struck; he] struck. He (VII, 145)

56.9 supplications."] supplications.ᶻ [*footnote:*] ᶻHerbert, p. 135. (VII, 145)

HUME, JOSEPH. Referred to: 159, 165, 308n, 314n, 326, 327, 340, 434

―――― Question on Criminal Prosecutions (4 Aug., 1834; Commons), *PD*, 3rd ser., Vol. 25, col. 929.
REFERRED TO: 275

―――― Speech in Introducing a Motion for Economy and Retrenchment (27 June, 1821; Commons), *PD*, n.s., Vol. 5, cols. 1345-1417.
REFERRED TO: 340

―――― Speech on the Roman Catholic Clergy (29 Apr., 1825; Commons), *PH*, 1825, 205.
REFERRED TO: 86

―――― Speech in Introducing a Motion on the Established Church in Ireland (14 June, 1825; Commons), *PH*, 1825, 267-70.
REFERRED TO: 97

―――― Speech on the Budget (14 Feb., 1834; Commons), *PD*, 3rd ser., Vol. 21, cols. 379-85.
NOTE: JSM's source for this speech and the House's reaction to it is the *Morning Chronicle*, 15 Feb., 1834, 3.
REFERRED TO: 162

―――― Speech in Introducing a Motion on the Corn Laws (6 Mar., 1834; Commons), *PD*, 3rd ser., Vol. 21, cols. 1197-1216.
REFERRED TO: 186

―――― Speech on Spain—Report on the Address (5 Feb., 1836; Commons), *PD*, 3rd ser., Vol. 31, cols. 126-9.
NOTE: the reference is to Hume's remarks on the navy estimates.
REFERRED TO: 326

―――― Speech on the Affairs of Canada (16 Jan., 1838; Commons), *PD*, 3rd ser., Vol. 40, cols. 42-55.
REFERRED TO: 434

——— Speech on the Affairs of Canada (17 Jan., 1838; Commons), *PD*, 3rd ser., Vol. 40, cols. 129-43.
REFERRED TO: 434

HUNT, HENRY.
NOTE: the references, except the first, are in a quotation from Fonblanque. Fonblanque invents the relatives of Hunt there mentioned as a *jeu d'esprit*.
REFERRED TO: 371-2

HUNTER, THOMAS.
NOTE: the reference is to the Glasgow convicts, of whom Hunter was one.
REFERRED TO: 486

HUNTINGTOWER, LORD. See William Manners.

HUSBANDS' COLLECTION. See *An Exact Collection*.

HUSKISSON, WILLIAM. Referred to: 140, 141, 312

——— *The Question Concerning the Depreciation of Our Currency Stated and Examined.* London: Murray, 1810.
NOTE: the reference is in a quotation from JSM's "The Currency Juggle," *q.v.*
REFERRED TO: 176

——— Speech on Colonial Trade (21 Mar., 1825; Commons), *PH*, 1825, 286-92.
NOTE: in *PD*, n.s., Vol.12, col. 1106.
QUOTED: 140
REFERRED TO: 141, 142, 143
140.13 The] [*no paragraph*] The (288)
140.24 America. Whatever] America. [*2-sentence omission*] Whatever (289)

HYDE, EDWARD. *The History of the Rebellion and Civil Wars in England, Begun in the Year 1641. With the Precedent Passages, and Actions, That Contributed Thereunto, and the Happy End, and Conclusion Thereof by the King's Blessed Restoration, and Return upon the 29th of May, in the Year 1660.* 3 vols. Oxford: printed at the Theater, 1702-04.
NOTE: the quotation at 42 is in a quotation from Brodie's *History* (*q.v.* for collation). One of the references at 45 is in a quotation from Hume.
QUOTED: 42, 45
REFERRED TO: 6, 34, 36, 37, 42n, 44, 45n, 46, 48, 50
42.7-9 "with ... gentlemen," ... "*whereof sir Thomas Lunsford was one* ... place,] And all this was done without the least communication with any body, but the Lord *Digby*, who advised it; and it is very true, was so willing to take the utmost hazard upon himself; that he did offer the King, when he knew in what house they were together, with ... Gentlemen, who would accompany him, whereof Sr *Thomas Lunsford* was one ... place; but the King liked no such Enterprizes. (I, 283)
42n.6 "To your tents, O Israel;"] And in his passage through the City, the Rude People flocked together, and cryed out, *Priviledge of Parliament, Priviledge of Parliament*; some of them pressing very near his own Coach, and amongst the rest one calling out with a very loud Voice, *To your Tents O Israel*. (I, 283)
45.16-17 "I ... these."] And I ... these: but it was an Erroneous and Unskilful suggestion; for an Act of Parliament, what circumstances soever concurred in the contriving and framing it, will be allways of too great reputation to be avoided, or to be declared void, by the sole Authority of any Private persons, or the Single power of the King Himself. (I, 335-6)

——— *The Life of Edward, Earl of Clarendon. Being a Continuation of the History of the Grand Rebellion from the Restoration to His Banishment in 1667.* 2 pts. in 1 vol. Oxford: Clarendon Printing House, 1759.
NOTE: JSM is quoting Brodie (*q.v.*), who quotes Hyde.
QUOTED: 47
REFERRED TO: 7

BIBLIOGRAPHIC INDEX OF PERSONS AND WORKS CITED 597

———— "Lord Digby." In Supplement to Vol. III of *State Papers Collected by Edward, Earl of Clarendon*. 3 vols. Vols. I and II ed. R. Scrope; Vol. III ed. T. Monkhouse. Oxford: Clarendon Printing House, 1767-86, li-lxxiv.
NOTE: JSM takes the quotation from Brodie (*q.v.* for the collation).
QUOTED: 42

HYDE, NICHOLAS. Referred to: 16

I.K. "Evidence Taken before the Select Committee on the Laws Relating to Game," *PP*, 1823, IV, 127-34.
NOTE: I.K. is the second poulterer referred to at 110; the third referred to at 113. The quotations at 110 and 113 are indirect; the quotation at 111n is from I.K., not L.M., to whom JSM mistakenly attributes it.
QUOTED: 110, 111n, 113
111n.4 *About . . . a-piece*] [*not in italics*] (129)
111n.5-6 *the prices . . . feeding*] [*not in italics*] (129)

INGLIS, ROBERT HARRY. Speech on Oaths of Catholic Members (11 Mar., 1834; Commons), *PD*, 3rd ser., Vol. 22, cols. 35-40.
REFERRED TO: 188

INGRAM, WILLIAM.
NOTE: the reference is to a gamekeeper, in a quotation from John Stafford's evidence, given before a Select Committee of the House of Commons.
REFERRED TO: 106

IRETON, HENRY.
NOTE: the reference at 56 is in a quotation from Hume.
REFERRED TO: 8, 49, 56, 57

JACOB, WILLIAM. "Funding System," *Quarterly Review*, XXXI (Mar., 1825), 311-27.
REFERRED TO: 174

JAMES I (of England).
NOTE: one of the references at 10 is in a quotation from Brodie; that at 16 is in a quotation from Hume.
REFERRED TO: 10-11, 12, 15, 16, 24

———— First Speech to Parliament. In Cobbett, *The Parliamentary History of England* (*q.v.*), Vol. I, cols. 977-88.
REFERRED TO: 10n

———— Speech of 14 Jan., 1604. In "Proceedings in a Conference at Hampton Court, Respecting Reformation of the Church: I Jac. A.D. 1604." In Howell, *State Trials* (*q.v.*), Vol. II, col. 35.
NOTE: the indirect quotation is in a quotation from Brodie.
QUOTED: 10, 11
10.22-3 "declaring that, under it, Jack, and Tom, and Dick, and Will, presumed to instruct him in affairs of state."] Then Jack, and Tom, and Will, and Dick, shall meet and censure me and my council. (II, 35) [*the quotation is from Brodie*, q.v.]

JAMES II (of England). Referred to: 78

JEFFERSON, THOMAS. Referred to: 404

JENKINSON, ROBERT BANKS (Lord Liverpool). Speech on Criminal Law (18 July, 1820; Lords), *PD*, n.s., Vol. 2, cols. 526-7.
REFERRED TO: 258

——— Speech on Unlawful Societies in Ireland (3 Mar., 1825; Lords), *PH*, 1825, 139-41.
REFERRED TO: 74n

——— Speech on Roman Catholic Relief (17 May, 1825; Lords), *PH*, 1825, 244-7.
QUOTED: 64
64.21-3 "The Protestant" . . . "gives an . . . is complete, of . . . qualified."] The difference was stated in a moment—the Protestant gave an . . . was complete; that of . . . qualified; and unless it could be proved that a half was equal to the whole, he could not yield to the Catholic claims. (244)

JESUS.
NOTE: the reference is in a quotation from Edward Grey, Bishop of Hereford.
REFERRED TO: 251

JOCELYN, ROBERT (Lord Roden). Speech on Unlawful Societies in Ireland (7 Mar., 1825; Lords), *PH*, 1825, 147.
QUOTED: 95
95.23-4 No . . . Ireland."] No . . . Ireland; nor was there any body of people more ready or anxious to acknowledge the boons they had received from Parliament, during the last two or three years, if they were permitted to do so by those persons who assumed an undue authority over them. (147)

JOHNSON, WILLIAM AUGUSTUS. Speech on the Elective Franchise in Ireland (9 May, 1825; Commons), *PH*, 1825, 213.
REFERRED TO: 88

JUXON, WILLIAM.
NOTE: the reference at 53n is to him as one of the King's advisers.
REFERRED TO: 29n, 53n

KAY, JOSEPH. *The Social Condition and Education of the People in England and Europe; Shewing the Results of the Primary Schools, and of the Division of Landed Property, in Foreign Countries.* 2 vols. London: Longman, Brown, Green, and Longmans, 1850.
REFERRED TO: 528

KEILY, JOHN. "Evidence Taken before the Select Committee Appointed to Inquire into the State of Ireland, More Particularly with Reference to the Circumstances Which May Have Led to Disturbances in That Part of the United Kingdom," *PP*, 1825, VIII, 393-412.
REFERRED TO: 96

KELLY, ARTHUR IRWIN. "Evidence Taken before the Select Committee Appointed to Inquire into the State of Ireland, More Particularly with Reference to the Circumstances Which May Have Led to Disturbances in That Part of the United Kingdom," *PP*, 1825, VIII, 504-27.
REFERRED TO: 96

——— "Evidence Taken before the Select Committee of the House of Lords Appointed to Inquire into the State of Ireland, More Particularly with Reference to the Circumstances Which May Have Led to Disturbances in That Part of the United Kingdom," *PP*, 1825, IX, 491-2.
REFERRED TO: 88n

KELLY, OLIVER. "Evidence Taken before the Select Committee Appointed to Inquire into the State of Ireland, More Particularly with Reference to the Circumstances Which May Have Led to Disturbances in That Part of the United Kingdom," *PP*, 1825, VIII, 239-64.
REFERRED TO: 87n, 88n

KIENMAYER, MICHAEL VON.
NOTE: the reference is to "the old Austrian tacticians" opposed to Napoleon.
REFERRED TO: 450

KIMBOLTON, LORD. See Edward Montagu.

KING.
   NOTE: the quotation is in a quotation from the anonymous leading article on Mr. Rawlinson in the *Morning Chronicle*, 4 June, 1834, 3.
   QUOTED: 245

KING, GEORGE (Earl of Kingston). "Evidence Taken before the Select Committee of the House of Lords Appointed to Inquire into the State of Ireland, More Particularly with Reference to the Circumstances Which May Have Led to Disturbances in That Part of the United Kingdom," *PP*, 1825, IX, 428-39.
   REFERRED TO: 96

——— Speech on Unlawful Societies in Ireland (3 Mar., 1825; Lords), *PH*, 1825, 143.
   REFERRED TO: 74n

KING, PETER (Lord King). Referred to: 81

——— *Speech of the Right Hon. Lord King, in the House of Lords, on Tuesday, July 2, 1811, upon the Second Reading of Earl Stanhope's Bill, Respecting Guineas and Bank Notes.* London: Ridgway, 1811.
   NOTE: the reference is in a quotation from JSM's "The Currency Juggle," *q.v.*
   REFERRED TO: 176

——— *Thoughts on the Restriction of Payments in Specie at the Banks of England and Ireland.* London: Cadell and Davies, 1803.
   NOTE: the reference is in a quotation from JSM's "The Currency Juggle," *q.v.*
   REFERRED TO: 176

KING'S SPEECH (Speech from the Throne). See George IV, William IV.

KINGSTON, EARL OF. See George King.

KNATCHBULL, EDWARD.
   NOTE: the references are to Knatchbull's 1834 Beer Bill.
   REFERRED TO: 233, 235, 271-2

KNIGHT, CHARLES. *The Menageries: Quadrupeds, Described and Drawn from Living Subjects.* 3 vols. London: Knight, 1829-40.
   NOTE: the quotation is in a quotation from Fonblanque.
   QUOTED: 356-7
   356.48 "In] [*no paragraph*] In (I, 54)
   356.48 kennels of fox-hounds] kennels of packs of fox-hounds (I, 54)
   356.49 *of his own accord*] [*not in italics*] (I, 54)
   357.1 fall] falls (I, 54)
   357.2 *from awkwardness*] [*not in italics*] (I, 54)

KNOX, JOHN. Referred to: 477

KNOX, WILLIAM (Bishop of Derry). "Evidence Taken before the Select Committee of the House of Lords Appointed to Inquire into the State of Ireland, More Particularly with Reference to the Circumstances Which May Have Led to Disturbances in That Part of the United Kingdom," *PP*, 1825, IX, 278-84.
   REFERRED TO: 88n

L.M. "Evidence Taken before the Select Committee on the Laws Relating to Game," *PP*, 1823, IV, 139-42.
   NOTE: L.M. is the third poulterer referred to at 110; the quotation there is indirect. At 111n.1 he is referred to as "porter at an inn"; at 111n.3 the quotation is mistakenly attributed to L.M., rather than I.K., *q.v.*
   QUOTED: 110
   REFERRED TO: 111n

LA FAYETTE, MARIE JOSEPH GILBERT DU MOTIER, MARQUIS DE.
NOTE: JSM uses the spelling Lafayette.
REFERRED TO: 235-7, 467-8

LAGRANGE, JOSEPH LOUIS.
NOTE: the reference is in a quotation from Walsh.
REFERRED TO: 332

LAING, MALCOLM. *The History of Scotland, from the Union of the Crowns on the Accession of James VI to the Throne of England, to the Union of the Kingdoms in the Reign of Queen Anne.* 2 vols. London: Cadell and Davies, 1800.
REFERRED TO: 37n, 58

LAMARQUE, JEAN MAXIMILIEN. See Joseph François Michaud.

LAMB, WILLIAM (Lord Melbourne).
NOTE: the references are to Lord Melbourne, those at 297, 298, 344, 379, and the first at 388 being to his ministry; the reference at 274 is in a quotation from the *Examiner*; that at 275 is to the "Home Minister"; the first at 388 is in a quotation from Anon., *Domestic Prospects of the Country under the New Parliament*.
REFERRED TO: 270-1, 274, 275, 297, 298, 344, 379, 388, 412, 460, 495

——— Speech on Unlawful Societies in Ireland (15 Feb., 1825; Commons), *PH*, 1825, 93.
QUOTED: 75
75.7 disposition," . . . "about] disposition about (93)

——— Speech on Admission of Dissenters to the Universities (1 Aug., 1834; Lords), *PD*, 3rd ser., Vol. 25, cols. 840-5.
NOTE: the quotation derives from the *Morning Chronicle*, 2 Aug., 1834, 2.
QUOTED: 270
REFERRED TO: 270-1

——— Speech at Derby (1 Dec., 1834), *The Times*, 5 Dec., 1834, 3.
NOTE: the reference is to Lord Melbourne's answer to the Derby address.
REFERRED TO: 292

LAMBERT, JOHN.
NOTE: the reference is to the general who was rival to George Monk.
REFERRED TO: 57

LAMBTON, JOHN GEORGE (Lord Durham).
REFERRED TO: 243, 408, 414, 416, 426, 429-30, 431, 433, 439-43, 447-64, 473, 479, 481

——— "Extract of a Despatch from the Earl of Durham to Lord Glenelg, Dated Castle of St. Lewis, Quebec, 29 June 1838," *PP*, 1837-38, XXXIX, 913-14.
NOTE: this forms part of "Papers Relating to Lower Canada," *PP*, 1837-38, XXXIX, 913-17.
QUOTED: 452n-3n, 456n, 462
REFERRED TO: 452n-3n
452n.27 *punish the guilty*] [*not in italics*] (913)
452n.27-8 misguided." . . . "for] misguided; for (913)
456n.13 "leader and instigator of revolt,"] [*paragraph*] The first step which I took on my arrival was to examine most carefully the list of prisoners and the depositions affecting each: in so doing, I discovered that against only eight or nine there existed any evidence which would warrant the application of great severity, the chief leaders and instigators of the revolt having fled from the province and being in safety in the United States. (913)
462.28 "Sir] [*paragraph*] These measures have met with the entire approbation of Sir (913)
462.29 party"] party: they declared they did not require any sanguinary punishment, but they desired security for the future, and the certainty that the returning tranquillity of the province should not be arrested by the machinations of these ringleaders of the rebellion, either here or in the United States. (913)

―――― "An Ordinance to Provide for the Security of the Province of Lower Canada," *PP*, 1837-38, XXXIX, 914-16.
NOTE: enacted as 2 Victoria, c. 1 (Lower Canada) (28 June, 1838), in *Ordinances Made and Passed by the Governor General and Special Council for the Affairs of the Province of Lower Canada*, II (Quebec: Fisher and Kemble, 1838), 6-12. Our usual method of collation has not been followed because the document is one long sentence.
REVIEWED: 439-43
QUOTED: 442
REFERRED TO: 452, 452n
442.16 *present*] [*not in italics*] (914)

―――― "A Proclamation," *The Times*, 7 Nov., 1838, 3.
NOTE: the Proclamation, occasioned by and giving the reasons for Durham's resignation and departure from Canada, was issued on 9 Oct., 1838; *The Times*, presumably the source used by JSM, reprinted the Proclamation from the *Quebec Gazette*.
QUOTED: 452n, 457, 460, 461
REFERRED TO: 459, 460-3
452n.13 "As] But, as (3)
452n.14 *future tranquillity*] [*not in italics*] (3)
452n.14-15 *allaying actual irritation*] [*not in italics*] (3)
452n.16 *present security*] [*not in italics*] (3)
452n.16-17 *removing . . . peace*] [*not in italics*] (3)
452n.17 *peace. . . . I*] [*not in italics; ellipsis indicates 4-sentence omission*] (3)
452n.18 *character*. But] character; but (3)
452n.19 *measures of precaution*] [*not in italics*] (3)
452n.20 *or most dangerous*] [*not in italics*] (3)
457.29-30 "large . . . improvement] Above all, I grieve to be thus forced to abandon the realization of such large . . . improvement as would connect the distant portions of these extensive colonies, and lay open the unwrought treasures of the wilderness to the wants of British industry and the energy of British enterprise. (3)
457.30-2 "revision of the . . . commerce," . . . "a . . . justice,"] I cannot but regret being obliged to renounce the still more glorious hope of employing unusual legislative powers in the endowment of that province [Lower Canada] with those free municipal institutions which are the only sure basis of local improvement and representative liberty, of establishing a system of general education, of revising the . . . commerce, and of introducing a . . . justice. (3)
457.32-4 "eradication of the manifold abuses engendered . . . civil disunions."] [*paragraph*] You will easily believe that, after all the exertions which I have made, it is with feelings of deep disappointment that I find myself thus suddenly deprived of the power of conferring great benefits on that province [Lower Canada] to which I have referred, of reforming the administrative system there, and eradicating the manifold abuses which had been engendered . . . civil dissensions. (3)
460.13 "all] I also trusted that I should enjoy throughout the course of my administration all (3)
460.15 distant authorities;] distant officers; and that even party feeling would refrain from molesting me whilst occupied in maintaining the integrity of the British empire. (3)
460.15-17 all . . . force" . . . "from] But in the present posture of your affairs, it was necessary that the most unusual confidence should accompany the delegation of a most unusual authority; and that, in addition to such great legal powers, the Government here should possess all . . . force that could be derived from (3)
460.18 observed. . . . Of] observed. [*ellipsis indicates 7½-paragraph omission*] Of (3)
461.34-6 "on . . . people," . . . "a . . . government"] I hoped to confer on . . . people a . . . government, and to merge the petty jealousies of a small community, and the odious animosities of origin, in the higher feelings of a nobler and more comprehensive nationality. (3)

―――― Speech on the Elective Franchise in Ireland (9 May, 1825; Commons), *PH*, 1825, 214.
REFERRED TO: 90

―――― Speech on the Suffrage (19 Oct., 1834). In *Speeches of the Earl of Durham Delivered at Public Meetings in Scotland and Newcastle*. London: Ridgway, 1835.
REFERRED TO: 488-9

LANERIC (LANARK), EARL OF. See William Hamilton.

LANSDOWNE, LORD. See Henry Petty-Fitzmaurice.

LAPLACE, PIERRE SIMON DE.
NOTE: the reference at 332 is in a quotation from Walsh.
REFERRED TO: 332, 334

LAUD, WILLIAM. Referred to: 8, 19, 19n, 20, 22-3, 29, 34

LAUDERDALE, DUKE OF. See John Maitland.

LAVELEYE, EMILE LOUIS VICTOR DE. *Etudes d'économie rurale. La Néerlande, par M. Emile de Laveleye. Précédé du rapport de M. Léonce de Lavergne sur l'économie rurale de la Belgique*. Paris: Lacroix, Verboeckhoven, 1865.
REFERRED TO: 528

LAVERGNE, LOUIS GABRIEL LÉONCE GUILHAUD DE. "L'Irlande en 1867," *Revue des Deux Mondes*, LXXII (Dec., 1867), 749-60.
QUOTED: 528
528.25-7 "As . . . diminished."] [*translated from:*] On peut affirmer qu'en règle générale les terres de la petite propriété sont deux fois plus productives que les autres, de sorte que, si cet élément venait à nous manquer, notre produit agricole baisserait sensiblement. (757)

LAWLER, JAMES. "Evidence Taken before the Select Committee Appointed to Inquire into the Disturbances in Ireland," *PP*, 1825, VII, 439-49.
REFERRED TO: 89n, 96

LEADER, JOHN TEMPLE. Referred to: 434, 435, 442-3

―――― Speech on the Affairs of Canada (22 Dec., 1837; Commons), *PD*, 3rd ser., Vol. 39, cols. 1431-45.
NOTE: reported in *The Times*, 23 Dec., 1837, 2; the quotation merely illustrates the use of this common phrase.
QUOTED: 418
418.26-7 "stopping the supplies"] Have they [the Ministers] heard nothing of the stopping the supplies in Newfoundland? (col. 1437)

―――― Speech on the Affairs of Canada (22 Jan., 1838; Commons), *PD*, 3rd ser., Vol. 40, cols. 329-44.
REFERRED TO: 434

―――― Speech on Canada—Declaratory and Indemnity Bill (1838) (14 Aug., 1838; Commons), *PD*, 3rd ser., Vol. 44, cols. 1242-50.
REFERRED TO: 442

LEE, HENRY. *Caleb Quotem and His Wife! or, Paint, Poetry, and Putty!* London: Roach, 1809.
NOTE: the reference is in a quotation from Fonblanque.
REFERRED TO: 368

LEICESTER, EARL OF. See Robert Sidney.

LEIGHTON, ALEXANDER.
NOTE: the references at 21 are in quotations from Brodie and Hume.
REFERRED TO: 13, 21

―――― *An Appeal to the Parliament; or, Sion's Plea against the Prelacie*. Amsterdam: successors of G. Thorp, 1629.
REFERRED TO: 21

LEINSTER, DUKE OF. See Augustus Frederick Fitzgerald.

LE MARCHANT, DENIS, ed. *The Reform Ministry, and the Reformed Parliament*. London: Ridgway, 1833.
NOTE: the reference is to the "ministerial manifesto"; put together by Le Marchant with the assistance of members of Grey's government, this pamphlet enjoyed an extraordinary success, nine editions being printed and sold within a matter of weeks.
REFERRED TO: 286

LENNOX, CHARLES GORDON (Duke of Richmond).
NOTE: the reference, in a quotation from Walsh, is to the resignation from Lord Grey's government of "Lord Stanley and his friends," one of whom was Lennox.
REFERRED TO: 344

——— Motion on Oaths (20 Mar., 1834; Lords), *Journals of the House of Lords*, LXVI, 81.
NOTE: there is no reference to the Duke of Richmond's motion in *Parliamentary Debates*.
REFERRED TO: 188

LENTHALL, WILLIAM.
NOTE: the reference is to him as one of the speakers of Parliament who joined with the army.
REFERRED TO: 50

LESAGE, ALAIN RENÉ. *Histoire de Gil Blas de Santillane*. 4 vols. Paris: Ribou, 1715-35.
REFERRED TO: 224

LESLIE, DAVID. Referred to: 36

A Letter to the Earl of Durham. See "Marvell Redivivus."

LEWIS, THOMAS FRANKLAND. "Evidence Taken before the Select Committee of the House of Lords Appointed to Inquire into the State of Ireland, More Particularly with Reference to the Circumstances Which May Have Led to Disturbances in That Part of the United Kingdom," *PP*, 1825, IX, 27-48.
QUOTED: 85n
85n.15-16 "I . . . marriages;"] The marriage fee is a large source of revenue to them [Irish priests]; and I . . . marriages. (41)

LEWIS, WILLIAM.
NOTE: the reference is to him as one of eleven members excluded from Parliament.
REFERRED TO: 50, 52

LIECHTENSTEIN, JOHANN JOSEPH VON (Prince).
NOTE: the reference is to "the old Austrian tacticians" opposed to Napoleon.
REFERRED TO: 450

LIFFORD, LORD. See James Hewitt.

LILLO, GEORGE. *The London Merchant; or, The History of George Barnwell*. London: Gray, 1731.
NOTE: the references, to Barnwell's uncle and to Millwood, are in a quotation from Fonblanque.
REFERRED TO: 359

LINDET, ROBERT.
NOTE: one of Babeuf's "fellow conspirators" in the Société des Egaux.
REFERRED TO: 401

LINDSAY, DAVID (Bishop of Edinburgh). Referred to: 25

LINDSAY, LUDOVIC (Earl of Crawford).
NOTE: the reference is in a quotation from Hume.
REFERRED TO: 36

LINDSEY, EARL OF. See Bertie Montague.

LITTLETON, EDWARD JOHN.
NOTE: the reference is to Littleton's vote in March of 1834 on Hume's motion on the Corn Laws; Littleton did not participate in the debate.
REFERRED TO: 186

——— Speech in Moving a Resolution on Tithes (Ireland) (20 Feb., 1834; Commons), *PD*, 3rd ser., Vol. 21, cols. 572-91.
NOTE: the reference is to the ministerial resolution on Irish Tithes, which was introduced by Littleton.
REFERRED TO: 168

LIVERPOOL, LORD. See Robert Banks Jenkinson.

LIVY (Titus Livius). *Livy* (Latin and English). 14 vols. Trans. B.O. Foster, *et al*. London: Heinemann; New York: Putnam's Sons; and (Vols. VI-XIV) Cambridge, Mass.: Harvard University Press, 1919-59.
NOTE: in the tag at 217, JSM is giving the sense rather than wording of the passage.
QUOTED: 173, 213, 217

173.9 *"qui bene est ausus vana contemnere;"*] Non cum Dareo rem esse dixisset, quem mulierum ac spadonum agmen trahentem, inter purpuram atque aurum oneratum fortunae apparatibus suae, praedam verius quam hostem, nihil aliud quam bene ausus vana contemnere incruentus devicit. (IV, 230; IX, 17, 16)

213.19 *domicilium plebis*;] Et illi carcerem aedificatum esse quod domicilium plebis Romanae vocare sit solitus. (II, 192; III, 57, 4)

217.39 *quâ nec mala nec remedia ferre potest*] Sed haec et his similia, utcumque animadversa aut existimata erunt, haud in magno equidem ponam discrimine: ad illa mihi pro se quisque acriter intendat animum, quae vita, qui mores fuerint, per quos viros quibusque artibus domi militaeque et partum et auctum imperium sit; labente deinde paulatim disciplina velut desidentis primo mores sequatur animo, deinde ut magis magisque lapsi sint, tum ire coeperint praecipites, donec ad haec tempora quibus nec vitia nostra nec remedia pati possumus perventum est. (I, 4-6; I, Praef., 9)

LLOYD, DAVID. *Memoires of the Lives, Actions, Sufferings and Deaths of Those Noble, Reverend, and Excellent Personages That Suffered by Death, Sequestration, Decimation or Otherwise for the Protestant Religion and the Great Principle Thereof, Allegiance to Their Soveraigne, in Our Late Intestine Wars, from 1637 to 1660, and from Thence Continued to 1666. With the Life and Martyrdom of King Charles I*. London: Speed, 1668.
NOTE: JSM, following Hume, uses the spelling Lloyde.
REFERRED TO: 55

LOCKE, JOHN. *Essay Concerning Human Understanding*. In *The Works of John Locke*. New ed. 10 vols. London: Tegg, Sharpe, Offor, Robinson, and Evans, 1823, I-III.
NOTE: in SC.
REFERRED TO: 228

——— *Two Treatises of Government*. In *Works*, V, 209-485.
NOTE: in SC. The indirect quotation is inferentially attributed to Locke; it is found elsewhere. JSM uses it in a letter, *EL*, *CW*, XII, 165.
QUOTED: 165

LOCKHART, JOHN INGRAM. Speech on Game Laws Amendment Bill (11 Mar., 1824; Commons), *PD*, n.s., Vol. 10, cols. 9-12.
QUOTED: 116
116.30 "qualifications] Those qualifications (col. 910)

LOFTUS, ADAM.
NOTE: the reference is in a quotation from Hume.
REFERRED TO: 31

London and Westminster Review. See *Westminster Review*.

London Gazette. Referred to: 184

London Review.
NOTE: the short-lived (1829) periodical of that name, not that edited later by JSM under the same title, for which see *Westminster Review.*
REFERRED TO: 257n

LONDONDERRY, LORD. See Charles William Stewart.

LONG, WALTER.
NOTE: the reference at 16 is to the leading members of Parliament imprisoned in 1629; those at 50 and 52 are to him as one of eleven members excluded from Parliament.
REFERRED TO: 16, 50, 52

LOUDON, EARL OF. See John Campbell.

LOUIS XIII (of France).
NOTE: the reference at 13 is to the "French king then at war with his protestant subjects at Rochelle"; that at 27, to "the king of France," is in a quotation from Hume.
REFERRED TO: 13, 27

LOUIS PHILIPPE (of France).
NOTE: the reference is to the king Lafayette gave "to his own country."
REFERRED TO: 236-7

LOVELACE, GEORGE.
NOTE: the reference is to the sentencing of the six Dorsetshire labourers.
REFERRED TO: 207

LOVELACE, JAMES.
NOTE: the reference is to the sentencing of the six Dorsetshire labourers.
REFERRED TO: 207

LOVETT, WILLIAM. Referred to: 480, 489

LUDLOW, EDMUND. *Memoirs.* 3 vols. Vivay: n.p., 1698-99.
REFERRED TO: 6, 45n

LUNSFORD, THOMAS.
NOTE: the reference at 42 is in a quotation from Hyde.
REFERRED TO: 39, 40, 42, 44

LUSHINGTON, CHARLES. *Dilemmas of a Churchman, Arising from the Discordant Doctrine and Political Practices of the Clergy of the Establishment.* London: Ridgway, 1838.
REFERRED TO: 492

LUSHINGTON, STEPHEN. Speech on Unlawful Societies in Ireland (14 Feb., 1825; Commons), *PH*, 1825, 88-9.
REFERRED TO: 73

——— Speech on Oaths of Catholic Members (11 Mar., 1834; Commons), *PD*, 3rd ser., Vol. 22, cols. 33-5.
REFERRED TO: 187

LYALL, GEORGE. Speech in Introducing a Motion on the Merchant Seamen's Widows' Bill (1834) (21 May, 1834; Commons), *PD*, 3rd ser., Vol. 23, cols. 1146-8.
NOTE: Lyall's Bill was enacted as 4 & 5 William IV, c. 34 (25 July, 1834).
REFERRED TO: 237

LYNDHURST, LORD. See John Singleton Copley.

MACARTY, JUSTIN. "Evidence Taken before the Select Committee Appointed to Inquire into the Disturbances in Ireland," *PP*, 1825, VII, 313-34.
REFERRED TO: 89n, 96

——— "Evidence Taken before the Select Committee of the House of Lords Appointed to Examine into the Nature and Extent of the Disturbances Which Have Prevailed in Those Districts of Ireland Which Are Now Subject to the Provisions of the Insurrection Act," *PP*, 1825, VII, 706-28.
REFERRED TO: 97

MACAULAY, CATHARINE. *The History of England, from the Accession of James I to That of the Brunswick Line.* 8 vols. London: Nourse, 1763-83.
NOTE: JSM uses the spelling Macauley.
REFERRED TO: 23n, 58

MACDONELL, RANDLE PATRICK. "Evidence Taken before the Select Committee Appointed to Inquire into the State of Ireland, More Particularly with Reference to the Circumstances Which May Have Led to Disturbances in That Part of the United Kingdom," *PP*, 1825, VIII, 745-67, 785-91.
REFERRED TO: 93n, 97

MACKINTOSH, JAMES. *Vindiciae gallicae: Defence of the French Revolution and Its English Admirers against the Accusations of the Right Hon. Edmund Burke; Including Some Strictures on the Late Production of Mons. de Calonne.* 2nd ed. London: Robinson, 1791.
QUOTED: 30
30.22 epithets."] *epithets.* (95)

MAITLAND, JOHN (Duke of Lauderdale). Referred to: 50, 51, 52

MALMESBURY, LORD. See James Edward Harris.

MALONE, SYLVESTER. *Tenant-Wrong Illustrated in a Nutshell; or, A History of Kilkee in Relation to Landlordism during the Last Seven Years, in a Letter to W.E. Gladstone.* Dublin: Kelly, 1867.
REFERRED TO: 517n

MALTHUS, THOMAS.
NOTE: the first reference is in a quotation from Brougham.
REFERRED TO: 91, 92

MANCHESTER, LORD. See Edward Montagu.

MANNERS, WILLIAM (Lord Huntingtower).
NOTE: the references are to a hypothetical speech ascribed by Fonblanque to Lord Huntingtower.
REFERRED TO: 374, 375

MANWARING. See Maynwaring.

MARCHESSEAU, SIMÉON. See Robert Shore Milnes Bouchette.

MARMONTEL, JEAN FRANÇOIS. *Mémoires d'un père.* 4 vols. London: Peltier, 1805.
NOTE: in SC. The quotation (a translation) is in a quotation from Fonblanque.
QUOTED: 357
357.4-5 "All . . . mishap."] [*translated from:*] Voilà comme on est: dès qu'un homme est dans le malheur, on l'accable, on lui fait des crimes de tout (et elle se mit à pleurer). [*3-sentence omission*] Chacun a sa façon d'aimer: la vôtre est de gronder vos amis du mal qu'ils se sont faits, comme une mère gronde son enfant lorsqu'il est tombé. (II, 179-80)

"MARVELL REDIVIVUS." *A Letter to the Earl of Durham on Reform in Parliament, by Paying the Elected.* London: Sherwood, Gilbert, and Piper, 1839.
NOTE: ostensibly reviewed, but not actually mentioned in the article.
REVIEWED: 465-95

MARY (of Scotland).
NOTE: the reference is to the mother of James I.
REFERRED TO: 10

MARY (Princess Royal of England and Princess of Orange).
NOTE: the reference is to the daughter of Charles I, wife of the son of the Prince of Orange and subsequently mother of William III.
REFERRED TO: 45

MASSEY, EDWARD.
NOTE: the references are to him as one of eleven members excluded from Parliament.
REFERRED TO: 50, 52

MASSON, LUC HYACINTHE. See Robert Shore Milnes Bouchette.

MAY, THOMAS. *The History of the Parliament of England, Which Began Nov. the Third, 1640.* London: Thomason, 1647.
REFERRED TO: 6

MAYNARD, JOHN.
NOTE: the references are to him as one of eleven members excluded from Parliament.
REFERRED TO: 50, 52

MAYNWARING, ROGER. Referred to: 17

—— *Religion and Allegiance: In Two Sermons Preached before the Kings Majestie.* London: Badger, 1627.
NOTE: JSM uses the spelling Manwaring.
REFERRED TO: 16, 17

MCLEAN, WILLIAM.
NOTE: one of the "Glasgow convicts."
REFERRED TO: 486

MCNEIL, RICHARD.
NOTE: one of the "Glasgow convicts."
REFERRED TO: 486

MELBOURNE, LORD. See William Lamb.

MÉRILHOU, JOSEPH. "Essai historique sur la vie et les ouvrages de Mirabeau." In *Oeuvres de Mirabeau*. 9 vols. Paris: Dupont and Brissot-Thivars, 1825-27, I, i-ccxix.
QUOTED: 172
172.35 *"Ma tête est aussi une puissance."*] [*paragraph*] Mirabeau avait la conscience de sa supériorité, et s'en expliquait avec naïveté; il disait à Suleau: "Lafayette a une armée, mais, croyez-moi, ma tête aussi est une puissance." (I, ccx-xi)

MICHAUD, JOSEPH FRANÇOIS AND LOUIS GABRIEL MICHAUD, eds. Biography of Jean Maximilien Lamarque. In *Biographie universelle ancienne et moderne*. 2nd ed. 45 vols. Paris: Desplaces and Michaud; Leipzig: Brockhaus, 1854-65, XXIII, 17-20.
NOTE: the quotation is of a comment by Lamarque.
QUOTED: 160
160.22 *"une halte dans la boue;"*] "Nous n'appelons pas cela du repos, c'est une halte dans la boue." (18)

MILL, JAMES. "Periodical Literature: *Edinburgh Review*," *Westminster Review*, I (Jan., 1824), 206-68.
REFERRED TO: 102

—— "State of the Nation," *Westminster Review*, VI (Oct., 1826), 249-78.
REFERRED TO: 400

—— "The State of the Nation," *London Review*, I (*L&WR*, XXX) (Apr., 1835), 1-24.
REFERRED TO: 291

—— "Summary Review of the Conduct and Measures of the Imperial Parliament," *PR*, 1826, 793-7.
REFERRED TO: 400

MILL, JOHN STUART. "The Currency Juggle," *Tait's Edinburgh Magazine*, II (Jan., 1833), 461-7. In *CW*, IV, 181-92.
QUOTED: 175-6
176.1   renewed] resumed (463) [*treated as a typographical error in this ed.*]
176.12 part] *part* (464)
176.16 that by far] that far (464)
176.26 remain.] remain? (464)
176.29 borrow] borrowed (464) [*treated as a typographical error in this ed.*]

—————— "Lord Durham and His Assailants," *London and Westminster Review*, VII & XXIX (Aug., 1838), 507-12.
NOTE: the essay printed at 437-43 above. It appeared (as JSM notes) only in the 2nd ed. of that number of the *L&WR*.
REFERRED TO: 452, 452n

—————— "Lord Durham and the Canadians." See "Radical Party and Canada."

—————— "The Ministerial Manifesto," *Examiner*, 22 Sept., 1833, 593-5.
REFERRED TO: 286

—————— "Notes on the Newspapers," *Monthly Repository*, n.s., VIII (Mar., 1834), 161-76.
NOTE: printed at 151-68 above.
QUOTED: 284
284.29 hands.—The] hands. [*paragraph*] In the first Session of the Reformed Parliament, many allowances were made, which will not be made again: the new legislative body had the full benefit of the reluctance to consider a first trial as final; and the novelty of the situation was such that the public were bewildered, and did not themselves see with sufficient clearness what ought to be done, to render them very severe judges of their representatives for what they left undone. The (161; 151 *above*)
284.33 Reform] Reformed (161; 151 *above*) [*printer's error; corrected by JSM in SC copy*]

—————— "Notes on the Newspapers," *Monthly Repository*, VIII (July, 1834), 521-8.
NOTE: printed at 244-55 above.
QUOTED: 255n
REFERRED TO: 256n

—————— "Parties and the Ministry," *London and Westminster Review*, VI & XXVIII (Oct., 1837), 1-26.
NOTE: printed at 381-404 above.
REFERRED TO: 410

—————— "Postscript," *London Review*, I (*L&WR*, XXX) (Apr., 1835), 254-6.
NOTE: printed at 289-93 above.
REFERRED TO: 297

—————— *The Principles of Political Economy, with Some of Their Applications to Social Philosophy. Collected Works*, II-III. Toronto: University of Toronto Press, 1965.
NOTE: 1st ed., 2 vols. (London: Parker, 1848). The quotation at 512 is indirect.
QUOTED: 512
REFERRED TO: 528n

—————— "Radical Party and Canada: Lord Durham and the Canadians," *London and Westminster Review*, VI & XXVIII, 2nd ed. (Jan., 1838), 502-33.
NOTE: printed at 405-35 above. In some copies of the number, the running title on the first eight pages is "Radical Party in Canada"; in all copies, the running title on the remaining pages, and the title in the Table of Contents of the *L&WR* is "Lord Durham and the Canadians."
REFERRED TO: 442, 452, 457, 457n

—————— "Reorganization of the Reform Party," *London and Westminster Review*, XXXII (Apr., 1839), 475-508.
NOTE: printed at 465-95 above. The reference is inferentially a forecast of the article.
REFERRED TO: 408

——— Review of Harriet Martineau's *A Tale of the Tyne*, *Examiner*, 27 Oct., 1833, 676-8.
QUOTED: 178-9
178.17 *the tyrant's plea*] [*not in italics*] (678)
178.24 must] *must* (678)

——— Speech on Mr. Chichester Fortescue's Land Bill (17 May, 1866). In *Chapters and Speeches on the Irish Land Question*. London: Longmans, Green, Reader, and Dyer, 1870, 97-107.
NOTE: the quotation, of a passage that originated in JSM's *Principles of Political Economy* (*q.v.*), is indirect.
QUOTED: 512

——— Speech to the National Reform Union Meeting at St. James's Hall (25 May, 1867), *Daily News*, 27 May, 1867, 2.
QUOTED: 521
521.4 Do you] I should like to know whether you (2)
521.4-5 that England has a right to rule over Ireland if she cannot make the Irish people content with her rule?] that we have any right to hold Ireland in subjection unless we can make Ireland contented with our government. (2)

——— "Walsh's *Contemporary History*," *London and Westminster Review*, III & XXV (July, 1836), 281-300.
NOTE: printed at 329-48 above.
REFERRED TO: 401

——— "What Is to Be Done with Ireland?" MS, King's School, Canterbury.
NOTE: printed at 497-503 above. The quotation, of the title, is inferentially related to JSM's MS.
QUOTED: 507

MILTON, LORD. See Charles William Wentworth Fitzwilliam.

MILTON, JOHN. *Eikonoclastes*. In *The Prose Works of John Milton*. Ed. Charles Symmons. 7 vols. London: Johnson, *et al.*, 1806, II, 383-472.
NOTE: in SC.
REFERRED TO: 45n

——— *Paradise Lost*. In *The Poetical Works of Mr. John Milton*. London: Tonson, 1695, 1-343.
NOTE: the same passage is quoted in both places. At 33n, JSM attributes it to William Pitt, speech of 18 Nov., 1783 (*q.v.*); Pitt was undoubtedly quoting Milton. The quotation at 178 is in a quotation from JSM's *Examiner* review of Harriet Martineau's *A Tale of the Tyne*.
QUOTED: 33n, 178
REFERRED TO: 186
178.17 "*the tyrant's plea*"] [*paragraph*] So spake the Fiend, and with necessity,/ The Tyrants plea, excus'd his devilish deeds. (97; IV, 393-4)

MIRABEAU, HONORÉ GABRIEL RIQUETI, COMTE DE.
NOTE: the reference is in a quotation from Walsh. See also Joseph Mérilhou.
REFERRED TO: 346

MITCHEL, JOHN.
NOTE: JSM uses the spelling Mitchell.
REFERRED TO: 501

MOLESWORTH, WILLIAM.
NOTE: the reference at 327 is to him as one of the younger Radical members of Parliament who also contributed to the *London and Westminster Review*.
REFERRED TO: 327, 434, 435

——— Speech on the Affairs of Canada (23 Jan., 1838; Commons), *PD*, 3rd ser., Vol. 40, cols. 358-87.
REFERRED TO: 434

MOLIÈRE, JEAN BAPTISTE POQUELIN. *L'amour médecin.* Paris: Le Gras, 1666.
REFERRED TO: 450

MONK, GEORGE.
NOTE: also spelled Monck.
REFERRED TO: 57-8

MONSON, FREDERICK JOHN (Lord).
NOTE: the reference is to a hypothetical speech ascribed by Fonblanque to Lord Monson.
REFERRED TO: 374-5

MONTAGU, EDWARD (Lord Kimbolton, later Earl of Manchester).
NOTE: JSM uses the spelling Montague. The references at 40-2 are to Lord Kimbolton as having been impeached with five other members of Parliament; that at 40 is in a quotation from Hume; that at 48 is to him as Earl of Manchester; that at 50 is to him as one of the speakers of Parliament who joined with the army.
REFERRED TO: 40-2, 48, 50

MONTAGU, RICHARD. *Appello Caesarem: A Just Appeale from Two Unjust Informers.* London: Lownes, 1625.
NOTE: JSM uses the spelling Montague.
REFERRED TO: 12

MONTAGUE, BERTIE (Earl of Lindsey).
NOTE: the reference at 53n is to him as one of the King's counsellors; that at 55 is to him as one of the four lords in Hume's "silly story" who offered themselves to suffer in place of Charles I.
REFERRED TO: 53n, 55

MONTROSE, EARL OF. See James Graham.

MORETON, THOMAS. See Morton.

MORIN, AUGUSTIN NORBERT. Referred to: 414

The Morning Chronicle.
NOTE: anonymous articles follow, listed chronologically.
REFERRED TO: 163, 182, 273, 337, 340, 379, 459

———— Unheaded Leader, 16 Oct., 1829, 2.
NOTE: the reference derives from Fonblanque.
REFERRED TO: 355-6

———— Leading Article on Attendance in the House of Commons, 12 Feb., 1834, 3.
REFERRED TO: 158

———— Report on the House of Commons Debate, 15 Feb., 1834, 2.
REFERRED TO: 162

———— Leading Article on the Leeds Election, 17 Feb., 1834, 2.
NOTE: the reference is to the liberal papers' exulting in the electoral success of Mr. Baines at Leeds.
REFERRED TO: 163

———— Leading Article on the Dudley Election, 1 Mar., 1834, 4.
REFERRED TO: 182

———— Leading Article on Mr. Rawlinson, 4 June, 1834, 3.
QUOTED: 245-6
245.35 admittance.] admittance? (3)

———— "An Old Tory Magistrate an Oppressor of the Poor," 23 July, 1834, 4.
QUOTED: 267
267.6 From] The Chairman then said, from (4)
267.8-9 *this case . . . proved*] [*not in italics*] (4)
267.9-10 *five pounds*] [*not in italics*] (4)

BIBLIOGRAPHIC INDEX OF PERSONS AND WORKS CITED 611

——— Leading Article on the Case of Major Pitman, 24 July, 1834, 4.
REFERRED TO: 267

——— Leading Article on Lord Brougham and Poor Laws, 25 July, 1834, 2-3.
REFERRED TO: 266

——— Leading Article on the Case of Major Pitman, 5 Aug., 1834, 3.
REFERRED TO: 273

——— Leading Article on the Tithes Bill, 21 Mar., 1836, 2.
REFERRED TO: 325

——— Leading Article on Canadian Affairs, 12 Jan., 1838, 2.
REFERRED TO: 420

——— Leading Article on Canadian Affairs, 30 July, 1838, 2.
REFERRED TO: 455n

——— Leading Article on Canada, 17 Oct., 1838, 2.
NOTE: the reference is to the newspaper that had "fulminated an anathema against" Durham's "plan of a federal legislature."
REFERRED TO: 459

The Morning Herald.
NOTE: anonymous articles follow, listed chronologically.
REFERRED TO: 235

——— Leading Article on the Beer-House Bill, 19 May, 1834, 2.
REFERRED TO: 235

——— Leading Article on the Established Church and Dissenters, 19 May, 1834, 2.
REFERRED TO: 235

——— Leading Article on Lord Wynford's Observance of Sabbath Bill, 19 May, 1834, 2.
REFERRED TO: 235

——— Leading Article on Omnibuses, 19 May, 1834, 2.
REFERRED TO: 235

——— Leading Article on the Poor Law Bill, 19 May, 1834, 2.
QUOTED: 235
235.17 "bashaws;"] The fact is, the expectant Bashaws are exceedingly impatient for their *places and salaries*, and they fear that the better the public become acquainted with the real nature of the Bill the less they will be disposed to tolerate a tyranny of Bashaws. (2)

The Morning Post.
NOTE: the reference is in a quotation from Fonblanque.
REFERRED TO: 366

——— Parliamentary Report, 20 Mar., 1834, 1.
REFERRED TO: 193

MORRITT, ROBERT. Referred to: 93

MORTON [MORETON], THOMAS (Bishop of Durham).
NOTE: the reference is to him as one of twelve bishops impeached and subsequently imprisoned in 1641.
REFERRED TO: 39

MORTON, THOMAS. *Speed the Plough: A Comedy in Five Acts.* London: Longman and Rees, 1800.
NOTE: not paged.
QUOTED: 158
158.7 "perhaps it would go out of itself."] Sir Abel Handy. "I say, Bob, I have it—perhaps it will go out of itself!" (V, ii, 34-5)

MOUNTNORRIS, BARON. See Francis Annesley.

MULGRAVE, LORD. See Constantine Henry Phipps.

MURRAY, DANIEL. Referred to: 82

——— "Evidence Taken before the Select Committee Appointed to Inquire into the State of Ireland, More Particularly with Reference to the Circumstances Which May Have Led to Disturbances in That Part of the United Kingdom," *PP*, 1825, VIII, 223-39, 646-72.
REFERRED TO: 87n

MURRAY, LINDLEY. *English Grammar, Adapted to the Different Classes of Learners. With an Appendix, Containing Rules and Observations for Promoting Perspicuity in Speaking and Writing.* York: Wilson, Spence, and Mawman, 1795.
REFERRED TO: 91

MURRAY, WILLIAM. Referred to: 37

NALSON, JOHN. *An Impartial Collection of the Great Affairs of State, from the Beginning of the Scotch Rebellion in the Year MDCXXXIX to the Murther of King Charles I. Wherein the First Occasions, and the Whole Series of the Late Troubles in England, Scotland, and Ireland, Are Faithfully Represented.* 2 vols. London: Mearne, *et al.*, 1682-83.
REFERRED TO: 28n; see also Digby, *The Lord Digby's Apology.*

NAPOLEON I (of France).
NOTE: the reference at 346 is in a quotation from Walsh.
REFERRED TO: 77, 232, 346, 450

NAPOLEON III (of France). Referred to: 501

NAVIGATION LAWS. See 12 Charles II, c. 18; 15 Charles II, c. 7; 6 George IV, c. 109.

NEATE, CHARLES. *A Plain Statement of the Quarrel with Canada; in Which Is Considered Who First Infringed the Constitution of the Colony.* London: Ridgway, 1838.
NOTE: though ostensibly reviewed, the pamphlet is referred to (and quoted) only once.
REVIEWED: 405-35
QUOTED: 415n-16n

415n.3-4   far," . . . "has] far has (15)

415n.10   legislature. It] Legislature, or in other words, treason of this kind is now in name only a crime against the Sovereign, but is, in reality, a crime against the Constitution. It (15)

415n.15-16   subjects. If the] subjects; it is not the less true, that no legitimate object of obedience is to be found complete and unimpaired within the limits of Canada; and if the (15-16)

415n.17   would be no] would no [*printer's error in* Source] (16)

415n.21   murder? Unless we] murder? It may be said, however, that the House of Assembly have not lent such authority as they might lend, to the acts of their countrymen. That Assembly is now prorogued, but if we look back upon their proceedings for the last three years, if we bear in mind that they have repudiated by a series of votes, and by overwhelming majorities, the constitution as it stood, we shall hardly be bold enough to deny, that the standard of rebellion is, in fact, their standard; and unless we (16)

416n.14   is] *is* (18) [*treated as printer's error in this ed.*]

NELSON, HORATIO (Lord). Referred to: 269

NELSON, WOLFRED. See Robert Shore Milnes Bouchette.

NEWCASTLE, DUKE OF. See Henry Pelham Fiennes Pelham Clinton.

NEWCASTLE, EARL OF. See William Cavendish.

NEWENHAM, WILLIAM HENRY WORTH. "Evidence Taken before the Select Committee Appointed to Inquire into the Disturbances in Ireland," *PP*, 1825, VII, 299-313.
REFERRED TO: 96

NEWPORT, EARL OF. See Mountjoy Blount.

NEWPORT, JOHN. "Evidence Taken before the Select Committee of the House of Lords Appointed to Inquire into the State of Ireland, More Particularly with Reference to the Circumstances Which May Have Led to Disturbances in That Part of the United Kingdom," *PP*, 1825, IX, 284-9.
REFERRED TO: 96

NEWTON, ISAAC.
NOTE: the references at 332 are in a quotation from Walsh.
REFERRED TO: 332, 334

——— *Philosophiae naturalis principia mathematica*. In *Opera quae exstant omnia*. Ed. Samuel Horsley. 5 vols. London: Nichols, 1779-85, II-III.
NOTE: this ed. used for ease of reference. The so-called "Jesuit's Edition" (Geneva: Barillot, 1739-42) is in SC. The reference is in a quotation from Walsh.
REFERRED TO: 332

NICHOLAS I (of Russia). "Proclamation of the Emperor of Russia" (17 Dec., 1830), *The Times*, 6 Jan., 1831, 2.
NOTE: there can be little doubt that JSM is referring to the "Proclamation," though the word "rebels" does not appear in this version.
QUOTED: 414

NICHOLAS, EDWARD.
NOTE: see also William Bray.
REFERRED TO: 5, 40

NICHOLS, ANTHONY.
NOTE: the references are to him as one of eleven members excluded from Parliament.
REFERRED TO: 50, 52

Niles' Register. See Henry Clay and Albert Gallatin.

NIMMO, ALEXANDER. "Evidence Taken before the Select Committee of the House of Lords Appointed to Examine into the Nature and Extent of the Disturbances Which Have Prevailed in Those Districts of Ireland Which Are Now Subject to the Provisions of the Insurrection Act," *PP*, 1825, VII, 630-2, 648-80.
REFERRED TO: 96

NIMROD. See Charles James Apperley.

NISARD, JEAN MARIE NAPOLÉON DÉSIRÉ. "Armand Carrel," *Revue des Deux Mondes*, XII (Oct., 1837), 5-54.
REFERRED TO: 380n

NOEL, BAPTIST WRIOTHESLEY.
NOTE: the reference at 492 is to a comment which has not been located.
REFERRED TO: 480, 492

NORMANBY, LORD. See Constantine Henry Phipps.

NORTH, FREDERICK (5th Earl of Guilford).
NOTE: the reference is in a quotation from Fonblanque.
REFERRED TO: 371

NORTH, JOHN. Speech on Unlawful Societies in Ireland (14 Feb., 1825; Commons), *PH*, 1825, 86-8.
QUOTED: 95
95.2-6 had desired . . . law. The . . . because . . . existing] had given them sound advice upon this subject. He had desired . . . law; and he had told them, with his usual good sense, that the people of England would pay more attention to such a list, with the names attached to it, than they would to all the declamation of their clubs. The . . . because . . . existing, (87)

NORTHUMBERLAND, EARL OF. See Algernon Percy.

Nottingham Review. "The Marriage Ceremony," 16 May, 1834, 4.
QUOTED: 232-3
    232.31 United Rights of Man and Woman,] 'UNITED RIGHTS OF MAN AND WOMAN,' (4)
    232.32 forward] henceforward (4)
    232.37 United Rights of Man and Woman,] [*see collation for* 232.31 *above*]
    233.3   1798. We] 1798; we (4)

NUGENT, GEORGE THOMAS JOHN (Marquis of Westmeath). "Evidence Taken before the Select Committee of the House of Lords Appointed to Examine into the Nature and Extent of the Disturbances Which Have Prevailed in Those Districts of Ireland Which Are Now Subject to the Provisions of the Insurrection Act," *PP*, 1825, VII, 728-31.
REFERRED TO: 96

OASTLER, RICHARD. Referred to: 485

O'BRIEN, RICHARD BAPTIST. "Limerick Declaration" (23 Dec., 1867), *The Times*, 2 Jan., 1868, 8-9.
NOTE: the reference is to the "clerical authors of the Limerick declaration"; although signed by nineteen clerics, the declaration was primarily the work of O'Brien, the militant Catholic Dean of Limerick.
REFERRED TO: 510

O'BRIEN, WILLIAM SMITH. Referred to: 500-1

———— "Evidence Taken before the Select Committee Appointed to Inquire into the State of Ireland, More Particularly with Reference to the Circumstances Which May Have Led to Disturbances in That Part of the United Kingdom," *PP*, 1825, VIII, 584-95.
REFERRED TO: 88n

O'CONNELL, DANIEL.
NOTE: the reference at 346 is in a quotation from Walsh.
REFERRED TO: 83, 153, 165, 172-4, 215, 262, 264-5, 314, 346, 411, 417, 479, 488, 495, 501

———— "Evidence Taken before the Select Committee Appointed to Inquire into the State of Ireland, More Particularly with Reference to the Circumstances Which May Have Led to Disturbances in That Part of the United Kingdom," *PP*, 1825, VIII, 48-85, 107-33.
REFERRED TO: 96

———— "Evidence Taken before the Select Committee of the House of Lords Appointed to Inquire into the State of Ireland, More Particularly with Reference to the Circumstances Which May Have Led to Disturbances in That Part of the United Kingdom," *PP*, 1825, IX, 123-71.
REFERRED TO: 96

———— Speech in Introducing a Bill on Libel Law (18 Feb., 1834; Commons), *PD*, 3rd ser., Vol. 21, cols. 468-78.
REFERRED TO: 165-6, 192, 261

———— Speech on Tithes (Ireland) (20 Feb., 1834; Commons), *PD*, 3rd ser., Vol. 21, cols. 591-8.
REFERRED TO: 169

———— Speech on Agricultural Distress (21 Feb., 1834; Commons), *PD*, 3rd ser., Vol. 21, cols. 684-6.
NOTE: the reference at 166n is to O'Connell's "profligate declaration in favour of the pillage of the widow and the orphan."
REFERRED TO: 166n, 172, 174-5

——— Speech on Oaths of Catholic Members (11 Mar., 1834; Commons), *PD*, 3rd ser., Vol. 22, cols. 15-24.
REFERRED TO: 186-7

——— Speech in Introducing a Motion on Repeal of the Union (22 Apr., 1834; Commons), *PD*, 3rd ser., Vol. 22, cols. 1092-1158.
REFERRED TO: 214-15

O'CONNOR, FEARGUS. Referred to: 479

O'DRISCOL, JOHN. "Evidence Taken before the Select Committee Appointed to Inquire into the Disturbances in Ireland," *PP*, 1825, VII, 379-402.
REFERRED TO: 96

——— "Evidence Taken before the Select Committee of the House of Lords Appointed to Examine into the Nature and Extent of the Disturbances Which Have Prevailed in Those Districts of Ireland Which Are Now Subject to the Provisions of the Insurrection Act," *PP*, 1825, VII, 732-9.
REFERRED TO: 93n, 97

OGDEN, CHARLES RICHARD.
NOTE: the reference, in a quotation from Lambton, is to the Attorney-General.
REFERRED TO: 453n

OPIE, IONA AND PETER, comps. *The Oxford Nursery Rhyme Book*. Oxford: Clarendon Press, 1957.
NOTE: the quotation of this traditional nursery rhyme is in a quotation from Fonblanque.
QUOTED: 365
365.15 "Dilly, dilly, dilly, come and be killed,"] Oh, what have you got for dinner, Mrs. Bond?/ There's beef in the larder, and ducks in the pond:/ Dilly, dilly, dilly, dilly, come to be killed,/ For you must be stuffed and my customers filled! (171)

ORDER IN COUNCIL ON COLONIAL TRADE, 3 May, 1826, *London Gazette*, 30 June, 1826, 1614.
REFERRED TO: 123-4, 125, 126, 127, 143, 144

ORMATHWAITE, LORD. See John Benn Walsh.

ORMONDE, EARL OF. See James Butler.

OWEN, JOHN (Bishop of St. Asaph).
NOTE: the reference is to him as one of twelve bishops impeached and subsequently imprisoned in 1641.
REFERRED TO: 39

OWEN, MORGAN (Bishop of Llandaff).
NOTE: the reference is to him as one of twelve bishops impeached and subsequently imprisoned in 1641.
REFERRED TO: 39

OWEN, ROBERT.
NOTE: the reference is to Owenism.
REFERRED TO: 486

——— Letter to the Editor of *The Times* (14 Apr., 1834), *The Times*, 15 Apr., 1834, 3.
NOTE: the reference is to Owen's denial of a charge made by *The Times* regarding the strike at Derby.
REFERRED TO: 210

——— Letter to the Editor of *The Times* (15 Apr., 1834), *The Times*, 18 Apr., 1834, 7.
NOTE: the reference is to the controversy between *The Times* and Owen regarding the strike at Derby.
REFERRED TO: 210

PAGE, THOMAS. "Evidence Taken before the Select Committee on the Laws Relating to Game," *PP*, 1823, IV, 149-53.
QUOTED: 107
107.8   also."] also; the difficulty is, to identify this sort of property; the fact of having possession of Game unlawfully, being punishable, enables us to bring them to conviction. (149)

PAPINEAU, LOUIS JOSEPH.
NOTE: the reference at 426 is in a quotation from a Canadian judge.
REFERRED TO: 414, 415n, 416-17, 426, 441, 453n, 456, 456n

——— "House of Assembly's Address to Lord Gosford, 30 Sept., 1836," *PP*, 1837, XLII, 450-3.
NOTE: appears in "Copy of a Despatch from the Earl of Gosford to Lord Glenelg, 3 Oct., 1836," which forms part of the *Papers Relative to the Affairs of Lower Canada*, Ordered by the House of Commons to Be Printed, 20 Feb., 1837, in *PP*, 1837, XLII, 413-56.
QUOTED: 425
425.6 "from reaching the foot of the Throne."] We trust that His Majesty's Government will not, after mature deliberation, entertain any doubt as to the correctness of our statements and assertions, particularly of the necessity of changing, conformably to the prayers of this House and of the people, a branch of the Legislature which has, with narrow and self-interested views, and moved by party spirit, interposed itself, of late more than ever, between the country and metropolitan state, and destroyed all our attempts to aid in the reparation of abuses, and by causing the result of our labours to reach the foot of the throne, to enable his Majesty's Government to confirm us in the belief of the sincerity of its intentions and promises. (450-1)

——— "House of Assembly's Address to Lord Gosford, 25 Aug., 1837," *PP*, 1837-38, XXXIX, 355.
NOTE: appears in "Copy of a Despatch from the Earl of Gosford to Lord Glenelg . . . 26 Aug., 1837" (*q.v.* under Acheson for the collation).
QUOTED: 422

The Parliamentary History and Review.
NOTE: this annual continued for only three years (actually, three issues, as the first two sets were both published in 1826, and the final volume in 1828); there were five volumes in all, the first two sets each consisting of one volume of *Parliamentary History*, and one of *Parliamentary Review*, and the last being only *Parliamentary Review* (an arrangement having been made with *Hansard's Debates* to use references to it, instead of publishing a "History"). The first issue is entitled *The Parliamentary History and Review; Containing Reports of the Proceedings of the Two Houses of Parliament during the Session of 1825:—6 Geo. IV. With Critical Remarks on the Principal Measures of the Session*, 2 vols. (London: Longman, Rees, Orme, Brown, and Green, 1826). The second issue has the same publishing data, date, and title, except for the identification of the session as that "*of 1826:—7 Geo. IV.*" The third is entitled *Parliamentary Review. Session of 1826-7:—7 & 8 Geo. IV* (London: Baldwin and Cradock, 1828).

Parliamentary Review. See *The Parliamentary History and Review*.

PARNELL, HENRY BROOKE. Referred to: 243

PEEL, ROBERT.
NOTE: the reference at 101 is to "a home secretary"; the first reference at 341 is in a quotation from Walsh; the references at 359 and 366 are in quotations from Fonblanque; that at 374 derives from an imaginary speech Fonblanque attributes to Peel; that at 425 is to Peel's Jury Act.
REFERRED TO: 101, 163, 171, 300, 322, 338, 341, 359, 366, 374, 403-4, 411, 425, 495

——— Speech on the Game Laws Amendment Bill (11 Mar., 1824; Commons), *PD*, n.s., Vol. 10, cols. 912-19.
NOTE: the quotation at 107 is indirect.
QUOTED: 102, 107, 113
REFERRED TO: 114

102.32 "second . . . of £20,000 per annum,"] Why, the second . . . of 20,000l. a year, is not by law qualified to kill game; the younger children of a man possessing the largest property in the kingdom, are not by law qualified to kill game on their father's own estates. (col. 913)
113.1 "Poachers," . . . "are much] Poachers, however, are much (col. 918)
113.19 laws," . . . "stand] laws stand (col. 914)
113.21 repeal—the constant] repeal. I will ask, whether these laws are not perfectly inoperative—whether they are not constantly, notoriously, and openly violated in every great town—and whether it is possible, in the present state of society, that it should be otherwise? The constant (col. 915)

———— Speech on the Address from the Throne (4 Feb., 1825; Commons), *PH*, 1825, 43-4.
QUOTED: 82n
82n.3 Chancellor, he] Chancellor, to whom the observations he alluded to were understood to apply, he (43)
82n.4 *consistent politician*] [*not in italics*] (43)

———— Speech on the Game Laws Amendment Bill (17 Feb., 1825; Commons), *PD*, n.s., Vol. 10, col. 528.
NOTE: see also Peel's speeches on 11 Mar., 1824, and 7 Mar., 1825.
REFERRED TO: 101

———— Speech on Unlawful Societies in Ireland (18 Feb., 1825; Commons), *PH*, 1825, 113-15.
REFERRED TO: 74

———— Speech on Roman Catholic Claims (1 Mar., 1825; Commons), *PH*, 1825, 160-3.
NOTE: the quotation is indirect, but so close to the original that it is collated below.
QUOTED: 79
REFERRED TO: 78
79.1-3 Retaining the . . . state, would it be . . . power?] Was he to be told, that, retaining the . . . state, it would be . . . power (hear, hear)? (162)

———— Speech on the Game Laws Amendment Bill (7 Mar., 1825; Commons), *PD*, n.s., Vol. 10, cols. 952-6.
NOTE: see also Peel's speeches on 11 Mar., 1824, and 17 Feb., 1825.
REFERRED TO: 101

———— Speech on Roman Catholic Relief (21 Apr., 1825; Commons), *PH*, 1825, 184-6.
REFERRED TO: 83

———— Speech on the Roman Catholic Clergy (29 Apr., 1825; Commons), *PH*, 1825, 206.
REFERRED TO: 86

———— Speech on the Established Church in Ireland (14 June, 1825; Commons), *PH*, 1825, 271.
REFERRED TO: 97, 98

———— Speech on the Penryn Disfranchisement Bill (1828) (28 Mar., 1828; Commons), *PD*, n.s., Vol. 18, col. 1360.
NOTE: the reference, to Peel's "scoff at the Ballot," is in a quotation from Fonblanque.
REFERRED TO: 377

———— Speech on the Corn Bill (1828) (29 Apr., 1828; Commons), *PD*, n.s., Vol. 19, cols. 225-8.
QUOTED: 358
358.24-5 "it was the constitutional policy of the country to maintain the aristocracy and magistracy as essential parts of the community."] That hon. Gentleman [William Bingham Baring] had confessed the constitutional policy, by which the aristocracy and magistracy of the country were maintained as essential parts of the community. (cols. 227-8)

———— Speech on Free Trade—Corn Laws (19 Mar., 1834; Commons), *PD*, 3rd ser., Vol. 22, cols. 442-9.
REFERRED TO: 193-4

——— Speech on Church Temporalities and Tithes (4 July, 1834; Commons), *Morning Chronicle*, 5 July, 1834, 3-4.
NOTE: the quotation presumably derives from the *Morning Chronicle* report; see *PD*, 3rd ser., Vol. 24, cols. 1188-98, esp. cols. 1189-90.
QUOTED: 262
262.17 government to which a Ministry can resort, the] Government, the (3)
262.18 hands] hand (3)
262.18 is] was (3)
262.18 vulgar."] vulgar [hear, hear, hear!]. (3)

PEEL, WILLIAM. Speech on the Game Laws Amendment Bill (11 Mar., 1824; Commons), *PD*, n.s., Vol. 10, cols. 905-7.
NOTE: the quotation at 107 is indirect.
QUOTED: 107, 108, 116, 117
REFERRED TO: 118
108.20 "Because if there] Some gentlemen would say indeed, that rather than have poachers they would have no game; but, because there (col. 906)
108.22 these] those (col. 906)
116.24-5 "great objection to] The great objection he had to (col. 906)
117.7 "was] He was (col. 905)

PEMBROKE, EARL OF. See Philip Herbert.

PENNY.
NOTE: the reference, to a poacher, is in a quotation from John Stafford's evidence, given before a Select Committee of the House of Commons.
REFERRED TO: 106

PERCEVAL, SPENCER. Speech on the General Fast—Exclusion of Strangers (26 Jan., 1832; Commons), *PD*, 3rd ser., Vol. 9, cols. 895-902.
NOTE: the eldest son of the former prime minister of the same name. The reference and quotation are in a quotation from Fonblanque.
QUOTED: 373
REFERRED TO: 373-4

PERCY, ALGERNON (Earl of Northumberland).
NOTE: the reference is to him as one of the parliamentary commissioners.
REFERRED TO: 52n

——— Letter to the Earl of Leicester (10 Dec., 1640). See Arthur Collins, ed., *Letters and Memorials*.

PERRINCHIEF, RICHARD. *The Royal Martyr; or, The Life and Death of King Charles I.* London: Royston, 1676.
NOTE: JSM, following Hume and Brodie, uses the spelling Perinchief.
REFERRED TO: 7, 54, 55, 56

PETTY, WILLIAM (Earl of Shelburne).
NOTE: the reference is to "the breaking up of the Shelburne Administration," an event which occurred in early 1783.
REFERRED TO: 135

PETTY-FITZMAURICE, HENRY (3rd Marquis of Lansdowne). Referred to: 265

——— Speech on the Church of Ireland—Commission (6 June, 1834; Lords), *PD*, 3rd ser., Vol. 24, cols. 290-3.
REFERRED TO: 253

PHELIPS, ROBERT.
NOTE: the reference is to him as one of several popular leaders made sheriffs of counties to prevent their returning to Parliament in 1626.
REFERRED TO: 14

PHIPPS, CONSTANTINE HENRY (Lord Mulgrave, later Lord Normanby).
NOTE: the references at 411 and 412 are to him as Lord Mulgrave; that at 474 as Lord Normanby. In 1831 Phipps, who had formerly held the courtesy title of Lord Normanby, succeeded his father to the earldom of Mulgrave; he was created Marquis of Normanby in 1838.
REFERRED TO: 411, 412, 474

PIERS, WILLIAM (Bishop of Bath and Wells).
NOTE: the reference at 29 is to him as an ecclesiastic who was impeached by Parliament after the fall of Laud and Strafford; that at 39 is to him as one of twelve bishops impeached and subsequently imprisoned in 1641.
REFERRED TO: 29, 39

PITMAN. Referred to: 267, 272-3

PITT, WILLIAM (the elder) (Lord Chatham).
NOTE: the reference is in a quotation from JSM's review of Harriet Martineau's *A Tale of the Tyne*, *q.v.*
REFERRED TO: 178

——— Speech (22 Nov., 1770; Lords). In John Almon, *Anecdotes of the Life of the Right Hon. William Pitt, Earl of Chatham. And of the Principal Events of His Time. With His Speeches in Parliament, from the Year 1736 to the Year 1778*. 3 vols. London: Longman, Hurst, Rees, and Orme, 1810, II, 179-211.
NOTE: the reference is in a quotation from JSM; it derives from James Graham's speech of 15 Aug., 1833, *q.v.*
REFERRED TO: 178

PITT, WILLIAM (the younger).
NOTE: the reference at 346 is in a quotation from Walsh.
REFERRED TO: 135, 312, 346, 404

——— Speech on Mr. Fox's Motion for Leave to Bring in His East India Bills (18 Nov., 1783; Commons). In Cobbett, *The Parliamentary History of England* (*q.v.*), Vol. XXIII, cols. 1208-11.
NOTE: the quotation is indirect.
QUOTED: 33n

PIUS IX (Pope).
NOTE: the reference, in 1868, is to "the Pope."
REFERRED TO: 523

PLACE, FRANCIS. "Historical Narrative 1838," Place Papers, British Library, Add. MS 27,820.
NOTE: the reference is to a credible informant respecting the Glasgow convicts. It is probable that Place, who in this MS gives an account of the strike in the Glasgow cotton mills, the ensuing violence, trial, and convictions on a charge of conspiracy, was the source of JSM's information.
REFERRED TO: 486

PLATO. *Gorgias*. In *Lysis, Symposium, Gorgias* (Greek and English). Trans. W.R.M. Lamb. London: Heinemann; Cambridge, Mass.: Harvard University Press, 1953, 158-532.
NOTE: JSM's partial translation of this dialogue was printed in *Monthly Repository*, VIII (Oct., Nov., and Dec., 1834), 691-710, 802-15, and 829-42; in *CW*, XI, 97-150.
REFERRED TO: 179

PLINY. *Natural History* (Latin and English). Trans. H. Rackham. 10 vols. London: Heinemann; Cambridge, Mass.: Harvard University Press, 1938-62.
NOTE: this ed. used for ease of reference. Pliny records a comment of Cicero's.
REFERRED TO: 194

PLUNKET, WILLIAM CONYNGHAM. Speech on Roman Catholic Claims (1 Mar., 1825; Commons), *PH*, 1825, 157-60.
NOTE: JSM's spelling, Plunkett, is that used in the *PH* and in Smith, *The Parliaments of England*.
REFERRED TO: 79

——— Speech on the Elective Franchise in Ireland (26 Apr., 1825; Commons), *PH*, 1825, 198-200.
NOTE: see preceding entry.
QUOTED: 89
89.20 "sturdy . . . yeomanry;"] It [the proposed measure] would operate gradually, and in the course of time a body of sturdy . . . yeomanry would supply the places of those in whose persons the elective franchise was now so much abused. (200)

PLUTARCH. *Life of Pompey*. In *Lives* (Greek and English). Trans. Bernadotte Perrin. 11 vols. London: Heinemann; Cambridge, Mass.: Harvard University Press, 1914-26, V, 116-324.
NOTE: this ed. cited for ease of reference.
REFERRED TO: 132

POLIGNAC, AUGUSTE JULES ARMAND MARIE, PRINCE DE.
NOTE: the reference at 389 is to the Polignac ministry.
REFERRED TO: 389, 419

POMPEY (Gnaeus Pompeius).
NOTE: see Plutarch, *Life of Pompey*.
REFERRED TO: 132

POOR LAW BILL (Act). See 4 & 5 William IV, c. 76.

The Poor Man's Guardian.
NOTE: anonymous articles follow, listed chronologically.

——— Leading Article on the Reform Bill, I (26 May, 1832), 401.
NOTE: the article is probably by Henry Hetherington, the editor. The reference is to the assertion of the "low Radicals" that the Reform Bill created an electorate dominated by the "shopocracy," a claim made in this article.
REFERRED TO: 161

——— Leading Article on Labour and Capital, II (3 Aug., 1833), 245.
NOTE: the article is probably by Henry Hetherington, the editor. Cited as an example of the use of the phrase "rights of labour."
QUOTED: 485
485.29 "rights of labour"] O'Connell may talk of repeal—Hume of economy—Attwood of currency—Cobbett of the stamp and auction duties—these gentlemen and their respective followers may talk themselves hoarse and blind on these or the like topics—but until the relative rights of labour and capital are understood and acted upon, their speechings will have no more effect on the country, than the chirpings of so many tom-tits. (245)

POPE, ALEXANDER. *An Essay on Criticism*. In *The Works of Alexander Pope: with Notes and Illustrations by Joseph Warton and Others*. New ed. Ed. Joseph Warton, *et al*. 9 vols. and Supplementary Vol. London: Priestley, 1822 (Supp. Vol., London: Hearne, 1825), I, 223-323.
NOTE: in SC. The quotation is in a quotation from Fonblanque.
QUOTED: 362
362.6-7 "often thought, though ne'er so well expressed."] True Wit is Nature to advantage dress'd;/ What oft was thought, but ne'er so well express'd;/ Something, whose truth convinc'd at sight we find,/ That gives us back the image of our mind. (I, 267; II, 297-300)

PORCHESTER, LORD. See Henry John George Herbert.

POWELL, THOMAS. "Evidence Taken before the Select Committee of the House of Lords Appointed to Examine into the Nature and Extent of the Disturbances Which Have

Prevailed in Those Districts of Ireland Which Are Now Subject to the Provisions of the Insurrection Act," *PP*, 1825, VII, 595-609.
REFERRED TO: 96

PRATT.
NOTE: the reference, to a poacher, is in a quotation from John Stafford's evidence, given before a Select Committee of the House of Commons.
REFERRED TO: 106

PRYME, GEORGE. *A Letter to the Electors of Cambridge, touching Mr. Knight, Mr. Sutton, and the Poor-Laws.* Cambridge: Johnson, 1837.
NOTE: though ostensibly reviewed, the pamphlet is not mentioned in the article.
REVIEWED: 381-404

PRYNNE, WILLIAM. Referred to: 13, 22, 29

——— *Histrio-Mastix: The Players Scourge, or Actors Tragoedie, Divided into Two Parts.* London: Sparke, 1633.
REFERRED TO: 22

——— *Newes from Ipswich. Discovering Certaine Late Detestable Practices of Some Domineering Lordly Prelates to Undermine the Established Doctrine and Discipline of Our Church, Extirpate All Orthodox Sincere Preachers and Preaching of Gods Word, Usher in Popery, Superstition and Idolatry; with Their Late Notorious Purgations of the New Fast-Booke, Contrary to His Majesties Proclamation, and Their Intolerable Affront Therein Offered to the Most Illustrious Lady Elizabeth the Kinge Onely Sister, and Her Children (Even Whiles They Are Now Royally Entertained at Court) in Blotting Them Out of the Collect; and to His Majesty, His Queene and Their Royall Progeny, in Blotting Them Out of the Number of Gods Elect.* Ipswich [Edinburgh: Anderson], 1636.
NOTE: published under the pseudonym "Matthew White."
REFERRED TO: 22

PYM, JOHN.
NOTE: the reference at 40 is in a quotation from Hume.
REFERRED TO: 23, 40-2, 47

The Quebec Gazette.
NOTE: in some periods, though not in 1838, known as the *Quebec Official Gazette*. The specific issue reviewed is that of 9 Oct., 1838.
REVIEWED: 445-64

RADCLIFFE, GEORGE.
NOTE: JSM refers to him as Ratcliffe.
REFERRED TO: 30

RADNOR, LORD. See William Pleydell Bouverie.

RAMSAY, JAMES ANDREW BROUN (Earl of Dalhousie). Referred to: 414

RATCLIFFE. See George Radcliffe.

RAUMER, FRIEDRICH LUDWIG GEORG VON. *England in 1835*. Trans. Sarah Austin and H.E. Lloyd. 3 vols. London: Murray, 1836.
NOTE: Sarah Austin translated the first two vols., H.E. Lloyd the third.
REFERRED TO: 530

RAWLINSON.
NOTE: the first reference and the quotation are in a quotation from the *Morning Chronicle*.
QUOTED: 245-6
REFERRED TO: 245-7

RAY, JOHN.
NOTE: JSM, following Brodie, uses the spelling Rea.
REFERRED TO: 20

REA. See John Ray.

REDESDALE, LORD. See John Freeman Mitford.

REFORM BILL (Act). See 2 & 3 William IV, c. 45.

REHOBOAM. Referred to: 42n

RICARDO, DAVID.
NOTE: the reference at 91 is in a quotation from Brougham.
REFERRED TO: 91, 130

——— *The High Price of Bullion, a Proof of the Depreciation of Bank Notes.* London: Murray, 1810.
NOTE: the reference is in a quotation from JSM'S "The Currency Juggle," *q.v.*
REFERRED TO: 176

——— *Observations on Some Passages in an Article in the Edinburgh Review, on the Depreciation of Paper Currency; also Suggestions for Securing to the Public a Currency As Invariable as Gold, with a Very Moderate Supply of That Metal. Being the Appendix, to the Fourth Edition of "The High Price of Bullion,"* &c. London: Murray, 1811.
NOTE: the reference is in a quotation from JSM's "The Currency Juggle," *q.v.*
REFERRED TO: 176

——— *Proposals for an Economical and Secure Currency; with Observations on the Profits of the Bank of England, as They Regard the Public and the Proprietors of Bank Stock.* London: Murray, 1816.
NOTE: the reference is in a quotation from JSM's "The Currency Juggle," *q.v.*
REFERRED TO: 176

——— *Reply to Mr. Bosanquet's Practical Observations on the Report of the Bullion Committee.* London: Murray, 1811.
NOTE: the reference is in a quotation from JSM's "The Currency Juggle," *q.v.*
REFERRED TO: 176

——— Speech on a Motion for a Committee on the Agricultural Distress (18 Feb., 1822; Commons), *PD*, n.s., Vol. 6, cols. 479-86.
NOTE: the reference is inferential; JSM may be referring to conversational remarks by Ricardo.
REFERRED TO: 131

RICHELIEU, ARMAND JEAN DU PLESSIS, CARDINAL DE. Referred to: 404

RICHMOND, DUKE OF (1st Duke of the third creation). See James Stuart.

RICHMOND, DUKE OF (1st Duke of the last creation). See Charles Gordon Lennox.

ROBINSON, FREDERICK (1st Earl of Ripon).
NOTE: the reference, in a quotation from Walsh, is to the resignation from Lord Grey's government of "Lord Stanley and his friends," one of whom was Robinson.
REFERRED TO: 344

ROBINSON, GEORGE RICHARD. Speech on the Taxation of the Country (24 Mar., 1836; Commons), *PD*, 3rd ser., Vol. 32, cols. 552-62.
REFERRED TO: 326

ROCHFORT, JOHN STAUNTON. "Evidence Taken before the Select Committee Appointed to Inquire into the State of Ireland, More Particularly with Reference to the Circumstances Which May Have Led to Disturbances in That Part of the United Kingdom," *PP*, 1825, VIII, 430-56.
REFERRED TO: 88n, 89n, 96

RODEN, LORD. See Robert Jocelyn.
ROEBUCK, JOHN ARTHUR.
NOTE: the reference at 327 is to him as one of the younger Radical members of Parliament who also contributed to the *London and Westminster Review*.
REFERRED TO: 191, 200-1, 202-3, 327, 384, 385, 386, 389, 396, 420-1

────── "Canada," *Westminster Review*, VIII (July, 1827), 1-31.
REFERRED TO: 420

────── "The Canadas and Their Grievances," *London Review*, I (*L&WR*, XXX) (July, 1835), 444-76.
REFERRED TO: 420

────── *A Letter to the Electors of Bath, on the Municipal Corporation Reform Bill; with a Postscript on the Conduct of Sir Robert Peel and Others, on the Discussion of the Question.* In *Pamphlets for the People*. 2 vols. Ed. J.A. Roebuck. London: Ely, 1835, I, 2nd pamphlet.
NOTE: each pamphlet is paginated separately.
REFERRED TO: 307n

────── "Lord Durham's Administration in Canada: Letter I," *Spectator*, 3 Nov., 1838, 1039-40.
REFERRED TO: 452n

────── "Lord Durham's Administration in Canada: Letter II," *Spectator*, 10 Nov., 1838, 1061-2.
QUOTED: 453n
REFERRED TO: 455-6, 456n
453n.14-15 "denouncing" M. Papineau "as a traitor," with "much emphasis," and "with all the formality of law."] To-day, with all the formality of law, with much emphasis and apparent sincerity M. Papineau is denounced as a traitor; he is banished his country, and he is threatened with death if he return without permission. (1061)

────── "Lord Durham's Administration in Canada: Letter III," *Spectator*, 17 Nov., 1838, 1084-5.
NOTE: the reference at 458n derives from Roebuck's quoting a published but unlocated letter of 29 Sept., 1838, by Adam Thom.
REFERRED TO: 455n, 458n

────── Motion on the State of the Mauritius (15 Feb., 1836; Commons), *PD*, 3rd ser., Vol. 31, cols. 390-401.
REFERRED TO: 326

────── Speech in Introducing a Motion on National Education (30 July, 1833; Commons), *PD*, 3rd ser., Vol. 20, cols. 139-66.
REFERRED TO: 200

────── Speech on Free Trade—Corn Laws (19 Mar., 1834; Commons), *PD*, 3rd ser., Vol. 22, cols. 439-42.
NOTE: JSM's source for this reference is the *Morning Post*, 20 Mar., 1834, 1.
REFERRED TO: 193

────── Speech in Introducing a Motion on the Canadas (15 Apr., 1834; Commons), *PD*, 3rd ser., Vol. 22, cols. 767-90.
NOTE: the reference is to Roebuck's "complete victory which . . . he has just obtained over the most redoubted debater [Stanley] in the House."
REFERRED TO: 202

────── Speech on Stamps on Newspapers (22 May, 1834; Commons), *PD*, 3rd ser., Vol. 23, cols. 1206-10.
REFERRED TO: 237

——— Speech in Introducing a Motion on National Education (3 June, 1834; Commons), *PD*, 3rd ser., Vol. 24, cols. 127-30.
NOTE: the reference at 200 is prospective.
REFERRED TO: 200, 254

——— Speech on Canada (14 Apr., 1837; Commons), *PD*, 3rd ser., Vol. 37, cols. 1209-29.
NOTE: reprinted as "Letter III. What Ought to Be Done?" in *The Canadian Portfolio*, No. IV, 16 Jan., 1838, 106-19.
REFERRED TO: 433

——— Speech on the Affairs of Canada (5 Feb., 1838; Lords), *PD*, 3rd ser., Vol. 40, cols. 735-71.
REFERRED TO: 458

———, et al. *The Canadian Portfolio. Conducted by John Arthur Roebuck, Esq., and Other Friends of Canada.* Nos. 1 to 4. London: Charles Fox, 1838.
NOTE: the "other friends of Canada" were Thomas Falconer and Henry Samuel Chapman. The quotation (which is repeated) is from No. 1, "To the People of England" (4 Jan., 1838); the reference is to No. 3, "The Want of an Elective Legislative Council No Grievance!" (12 Jan., 1838).
REVIEWED: 405-35
QUOTED: 417, 426
REFERRED TO: 425

417.19 "practical grievance;"] We are continually told that the Canadians have no practical grievances. (29)

ROMILLY, SAMUEL. Referred to: 342

RUSHWORTH, JOHN. *Historical Collections.* 7 vols. London: Thomason, Wright and Chiswell, *et al.*, 1659-1701.
REFERRED TO: 6, 7, 20n, 25n, 48

RUSSELL, JOHN (Lord). Referred to: 232, 390, 408, 409, 410, 411, 413, 421, 422-3, 428, 435

——— "Address to the Electors of the Southern Division of the County of Devon," *The Times*, 20 Apr., 1835, 1.
REFERRED TO: 298

——— *Corrected Report of the Speech of Lord John Russell, at the Dinner Given on His Election for Stroud, on Friday, July 28, 1837, and an Account of the Proceedings.* London: Knight, 1837.
NOTE: ostensibly reviewed by JSM in "Parties and the Ministry," but in fact referred to only once in that article, at 390.
REVIEWED: 381-404
REFERRED TO: 410

——— Resolution on the Church of Ireland (7 Apr., 1835; Commons), *PD*, 3rd ser., Vol. 27, cols. 880-3.
NOTE: the reference is to the discussion and passage of this resolution (see cols. 880-974).
REFERRED TO: 301

——— Resolutions on the Affairs of Canada (6 Mar., 1837; Commons), *PD*, 3rd ser., Vol. 36, cols. 1287-1306.
REFERRED TO: 417, 421

——— Speech at Torquay, 18 Sept., 1832, *The Times*, 21 Sept., 1832, 3-4.
REFERRED TO: 410

——— Speech on Dissenters' Marriages (10 Mar., 1834; Commons), *PD*, 3rd ser., Vol. 21, col. 1400.
REFERRED TO: 196

——— Speech at Totnes (Devonshire), 2 Dec., 1834, *The Times*, 8 Dec., 1834, 1.
REFERRED TO: 292

——— Speech on the Ballot (2 June, 1835; Commons), *PD*, 3rd ser., Vol. 28, cols. 447-52.
REFERRED TO: 299

——— Speech on Canada (14 Apr., 1837; Commons), *PD*, 3rd ser., Vol. 37, cols. 1234-49.
REFERRED TO: 433

——— Speech on the Address in Answer to the Queen's Speech (20 Nov., 1837; Commons), *PD*, 3rd ser., Vol. 39, cols. 65-73.
REFERRED TO: 408, 409-11

——— Speech on the Affairs of Canada (16 Jan., 1838; Commons), *PD*, 3rd ser., Vol. 40, cols. 7-42.
NOTE: the discussion of the phrase "stopping the supplies," to which JSM refers at 418, derived from a passage in this speech, which was reported in *The Times*, 17 Jan., 1838, 3; see also Leader, speech of 22 Dec., 1837. The sentiment quoted at 421, variously phrased, runs throughout the Canada debates in both the Lords and Commons.
QUOTED: 421
REFERRED TO: 418, 422, 428, 435, 458

421.33 "the authority of government must be asserted."] He felt it would not be safe if he were any longer to delay asking that house for powers to maintain the authority of Her Majesty in the province of Lower Canada, and that even on the score of humanity, instead of preventing bloodshed, he should only be giving the signal of civil war, if he were to obey the advice which had been given by withdrawing the troops of Her Majesty, and relinquishing the authority of the Crown over that province. (2)

RYDER, DUDLEY (Lord Harrowby). Speech on Roman Catholic Relief (17 May, 1825; Lords), *PH*, 1825, 247-8.
REFERRED TO: 92

ST. JOHN, OLIVER. Referred to: 47

SALISBURY, EARL OF. See William Cecil.

SANDERSON, ROBERT.
NOTE: the reference is to him as one of the king's advisers.
REFERRED TO: 53n

SAVILE, THOMAS (Earl of Sussex). Referred to: 46

SCARLETT, JAMES. Referred to: 351

SCOTT, JOHN (Lord Eldon).
NOTE: the references are in quotations from Peel and Fonblanque.
REFERRED TO: 82n, 359

——— Speech on Roman Catholic Relief (17 May, 1825; Lords), *PH*, 1825, 248-50.
REFERRED TO: 71

——— Speech on Dissenters' Marriages Bill (26 June, 1827; Lords), *PD*, n.s., Vol. 17, cols. 1411-17.
NOTE: the reference is to Lord Eldon's opposition to the Unitarian Marriage Bill.
REFERRED TO: 341

SCOTT, JOHN (Lord Encombe, later Lord Eldon).
NOTE: the grandson of John Scott (Lord Eldon).
REFERRED TO: 250

SCOTT, WALTER.
NOTE: the reference, in a quotation from Fonblanque, is to the Waverley novels.
REFERRED TO: 356

——— *Ivanhoe: A Romance*. Edinburgh: Constable, 1820.
REFERRED TO: 3

——— *Old Mortality*. In *Tales of My Landlord, Collected and Arranged by Jedediah Cleishbotham*. 4 vols. Edinburgh: Blackwood; London: Murray, 1816, II-IV.
NOTE: written under the pseudonym above.
REFERRED TO: 3

——— *Rob Roy*. 3 vols. Edinburgh: Constable, 1818.
NOTE: the quotation is indirect.
QUOTED: 402
402.8 thews and sinews,] With all these cares on his mind, my fellow traveller, to judge by his thewes and sinews, was a man who might have set danger at defiance with as much impunity as most men. (I, 60; 3)

SELDEN, JOHN.
NOTE: the reference is to him as one of the leading members of Parliament imprisoned in 1629.
REFERRED TO: 16

SETON, CHARLES (Earl of Dunfermline). Referred to: 28

SEYMOUR, FRANCIS.
NOTE: the reference is to him as one of several popular leaders made sheriffs of counties to prevent their returning to Parliament in 1626.
REFERRED TO: 14

SEYMOUR, WILLIAM (Marquis of Hertford).
NOTE: the reference at 53n is to him as one of the king's counsellors; that at 55 is to him as one of the four lords in Hume's "silly story" who offered themselves to suffer in place of Charles I.
REFERRED TO: 53n, 55

SHADWELL, LANCELOT.
NOTE: the reference is in a quotation from Fonblanque.
REFERRED TO: 370

SHAKESPEARE, WILLIAM. *Hamlet*. In *The Riverside Shakespeare*. Ed. G. Blakemore Evans. Boston: Houghton Mifflin, 1974, 1135-97.
NOTE: the quotation is indirect.
QUOTED: 111
111.31-2 Such a consummation, perhaps, is rather to be wished than dreaded;] To die, to sleep—/ No more, and by a sleep to say we end / The heart-ache and the thousand natural shocks / That flesh is heir to; 'tis a consummation / Devoutly to be wish'd. (1160; III, i, 59-63)

——— *Henry IV, Part II*. Ibid., 886-929.
QUOTED: 132
132.36 "appliances and means"] Canst thou, O partial sleep, give [then] repose / To the wet [sea-boy] in an hour so rude,/ And in the calmest and most stillest night,/ With all appliances and means to boot,/ Deny it to a king? (902; III, i, 26-30)

——— *Henry VIII*. Ibid., 976-1018.
QUOTED: 152
152.15-16 "*bold* bad man,"] Heaven will one day open / The King's eyes, that so long have slept upon / This bold bad man. (992; II, ii, 41-3)

——— *Julius Caesar*. Ibid., 1100-34.
NOTE: the quotation is in a quotation from Fonblanque.
QUOTED: 372
372.3-4 "The . . . bones."] The evil . . . bones;/ So let it be with Caesar. (1121; III, ii, 75-6)

——— *Macbeth*. Ibid., 1306-42.
QUOTED: 161
161.25-6 "keen . . . makes," . . . "peep through the dark and cry 'hold, hold.'"] Come, thick night,/ And pall thee in the dunnest smoke of hell,/ That my keen . . . makes,/ Nor heaven peep through the blanket of the dark / To cry, "Hold, hold!" (1316; I, v, 50-4)

────── *Measure for Measure. Ibid.*, 545-86.
QUOTED: 440

440.26 "little brief authority,"] Merciful heaven,/ Thou rather with thy sharp and sulphurous bolt / Splits the unwedgeable and gnarled oak / Than the soft myrtle; but man, proud man,/ Dress'd in a little brief authority,/ Most ignorant of what he's most assur'd / (His glassy essence), like an angry ape / Plays such fantastic tricks before high heaven / As makes the angels weep; who, with our spleens,/ Would all themselves laugh mortal. (561; II, ii, 114-23)

────── *Othello. Ibid.*, 1198-1248.
NOTE: the same passage is quoted in both places; the quotation at 307 is indirect.
QUOTED: 107, 307

107.29-30 "head and front of its offending;"] Most potent, grave, and reverend signiors,/ My very noble, and approv'd good masters:/ That I have ta'en away this old man's daughter,/ It is most true; true I have married her;/ The very head and front of my offending / Hath this extent, no more. (1208; I, iii, 76-81)

SHEIL, RICHARD LALOR.
NOTE: JSM spells his name Shiel.
REFERRED TO: 155-7

SHELBURNE, EARL OF. See William Petty.

SHELLEY, JOHN. Referred to: 117n-18n

────── Speech on the Game Laws Amendment Bill (11 Mar., 1824; Commons), *PD*, n.s., Vol. 10, cols. 903-5.
QUOTED: 117
REFERRED TO: 118
117.16 "Had not this country," asked Sir John Shelley, "Had] He would ask—had (col. 905)
117.17 these] those (col. 905)

SHERIDAN, RICHARD BRINSLEY.
NOTE: the reference is in a quotation from Fonblanque.
REFERRED TO: 371

SHIEL. See Sheil.

SIDNEY PAPERS. See Arthur Collins, ed., *Letters and Memorials*.

SIDNEY, ROBERT (Earl of Leicester).
NOTE: the reference is in a quotation from Brodie.
REFERRED TO: 32n

SIMPSON, RICHARD. "Evidence Taken before the Select Committee Appointed to Inquire into the Disturbances in Ireland," *PP*, 1825, VII, 402-6.
REFERRED TO: 89n

SKINNER, ROBERT (Bishop of Oxford).
NOTE: the reference is to him as one of twelve bishops impeached and subsequently imprisoned in 1641.
REFERRED TO: 39

SKIPPON, PHILIP. Referred to: 48

SMITH, ADAM. Referred to: 130

SMITH, JOHN. *Advertisements for the Unexperienced Planters of New England, or Anywhere*. London: Haviland, 1631.
QUOTED: 447

447.8 "the sun never sets."] I speake not this to discourage any with vaine feares, but could wish every English man to carry alwaies this Motto in his heart; Why should the brave Spanish Souldiers brag. The Sunne never sets in the Spanish dominions, but ever shineth on one part or other we have conquered for our King; who within these few hundred of yeares, was one of the least of most of his neighbours; but to animate us to do the like for yours, who is no way his inferior. . . . (37)

SMITH, JOHN PYE. Referred to: 480

SMITH, SYDNEY. "Bentham's *Book of Fallacies*," *Edinburgh Review*, XLII (Aug., 1825), 367-89.
NOTE: at the end of the article Smith illustrates Bentham's fallacies in a speech he calls the "Noodle's Oration."
REFERRED TO: 331

——— "The Game Laws," *Edinburgh Review*, XXXI (Mar., 1819), 295-309.
QUOTED: 112
112.3 "the very mention," . . . "of] The very mention of (301)

——— Speech at Taunton. In *The Works of the Rev. Sydney Smith*. 4 vols. London: Longman, Orme, Brown, Green, and Longmans, 1840, I, 392-5.
NOTE: the speech was reported in the *Taunton Courier*, 12 Oct., 1831, 3; the reference is to the spirited but vain attempt by Dame Partington of Sidmouth (apparently invented by Smith) to repel the stormy Atlantic with a mop, to which Smith compares the Lords' attempt to prevent a reform of Parliament. The edition cited postdates the reference, but the comparison was widely known in the 1830s.
REFERRED TO: 383

SMOLLETT, TOBIAS GEORGE. *The Adventures of Peregrine Pickle. In Which Are Included, Memoirs of a Lady of Quality*. 4 vols. London: Printed for the Author, 1751.
NOTE: the reference is to a vast machine for cutting cabbage.
REFERRED TO: 160

SOLON.
NOTE: the reference is to "our agricultural Solons."
REFERRED TO: 117n

SOMERSET, EDWARD (Earl of Glamorgan). Referred to: 49, 51

SOUTH, ROBERT. *A Sermon Preached at the Cathedral Church of St. Paul, Nov. 9, 1662*. London: J.G. for Robinson, Oxford, 1663.
NOTE: the first recorded use of the term *tabula rasa* (or *rasa tabula*). The sermon was reprinted as *A Sermon on Genesis 1.27*.
REFERRED TO: 430

SOUTHAMPTON, EARL OF. See Thomas Wriothesley.

The Spectator.
NOTE: anonymous articles follow, listed chronologically.
REFERRED TO: 316, 385, 390

——— Leading Article on the Canadian Rebellion, 13 Jan., 1838, 30-1.
REFERRED TO: 426

——— Leading Article on Lord Durham, 10 Nov., 1838, 1053.
QUOTED: 460
460.26-7 "remarkable" . . . "for . . . usages, and its . . . state-craft."] It is remarkable for . . . usages, its . . . state-craft, and the application of the worst names to bad things. (1053)

SPEECH FROM THE THRONE (4 Feb., 1834). See William IV.

SPENCER, HENRY. "Letters to His Lady, Dorothy" (21 Sept., and 13 Oct., 1642). See Arthur Collins, ed., *Letters and Memorials*.

SPENCER, JOHN CHARLES (Lord Althorp, later Lord Spencer).
NOTE: the reference at 203 is to the Poor Law Bill of Lord Althorp (Spencer's courtesy title); those at 365, 366, and 367 are in quotations from Fonblanque; that at 473 is to Lord Spencer, a title to which Althorp succeeded upon the death of his father.
REFERRED TO: 155, 203, 365, 366, 367, 473

——— "Correspondence with William Hulton," *The Times*, 20 Dec., 1831, 3.
NOTE: the reference is in a quotation from Fonblanque. See also William Hulton.
QUOTED: 367

REFERRED TO: 367

367.23-4 "the unfortunate transaction at Manchester."] Till I got Mr. [Francis] Philips's letter, I was not aware that I had even alluded to the unfortunate transactions at Manchester in 1819. (3)

———— Report on the Budget (14 Feb., 1831; Commons), *PD*, 3rd ser., Vol. 2, cols. 491-3.
REFERRED TO: 347

———— Speech on the Budget (11 Feb., 1831; Commons), *PD*, 3rd ser., Vol. 2, cols. 403-18.
REFERRED TO: 347

———— Speech on the Ministerial Plan of Parliamentary Reform (1 Mar., 1831; Commons), *PD*, 3rd ser., Vol. 2, cols. 1139-44.
NOTE: the quotation "final measure" from Walsh originates in public declarations by ministers in Lord Grey's government to the effect that the Reform Bill was intended as a "final settlement" of the issue; this speech of Lord Althorp's contained the first such declaration.
REFERRED TO: 343

———— Speech on the General Fast (26 Jan., 1832; Commons), *PD*, 3rd ser., Vol. 9, col. 902.
NOTE: the reference, in a quotation from Fonblanque, concerns the government's intention to appoint a day of fasting; Spencer, then Lord Althorp, spoke for the government on this occasion.
REFERRED TO: 372

———— Speech in Introducing a Motion on Supply—The Budget (19 Apr., 1833; Commons), *PD*, 3rd ser., Vol. 17, cols. 326-39.
NOTE: one of several speeches by Lord Althorp in 1833 in defence of the house tax.
REFERRED TO: 162

———— Speech in Introducing a Motion on House and Window Taxes (30 Apr., 1833; Commons), *PD*, 3rd ser., Vol. 17, cols. 769-76.
NOTE: one of several speeches by Lord Althorp in 1833 in defence of the house tax.
REFERRED TO: 162

———— Speech on the Inhabited House Duty (7 Aug., 1833; Commons), *PD*, 3rd ser., Vol. 20, cols. 421-5.
NOTE: one of several speeches by Lord Althorp in 1833 in defence of the house tax.
REFERRED TO: 162

———— Speech in Introducing a Motion on the Budget (14 Feb., 1834; Commons), *PD*, 3rd ser., Vol. 21, cols. 360-8.
QUOTED: 195
REFERRED TO: 160-1, 162

195.35 "call the attention"] In pursuance of the notice I gave on a former evening, it is now my duty to call the attention of the House to my view of the present state of the finances of the country. (col. 360)

———— Speech on Mr. Sheil—Character of Irish Members (14 Feb., 1834; Commons), *PD*, 3rd ser., Vol. 21, cols. 399-401.
REFERRED TO: 156

———— Speech on Agricultural Distress (21 Feb., 1834; Commons), *PD*, 3rd ser., Vol. 21, cols. 660-4.
NOTE: the reference is to the ministerial argument that "agriculturists must look for relief to a diminution of the poor rates."
REFERRED TO: 171-2

———— Speech on Timber Duties (4 Mar., 1834; Commons), *PD*, 3rd ser., Vol. 21, col. 1114.
NOTE: the reference is to the ministerial announcement respecting the Timber Duties.
REFERRED TO: 153n

——— Speech on the Corn Laws (7 Mar., 1834; Commons), *PD*, 3rd ser., Vol. 21, cols. 1328-9.
REFERRED TO: 186

——— Speech on Church Rates (18 Mar., 1834; Commons), *PD*, 3rd ser., Vol. 22, cols. 388-92.
REFERRED TO: 196

——— Speech in Introducing a Motion on Commutation of Tithes (England) (15 Apr., 1834; Commons), *PD*, 3rd ser., Vol. 22, cols. 818-28.
REFERRED TO: 197

——— Speech in Introducing a Motion on the Poor Laws (17 Apr., 1834; Commons), *PD*, 3rd ser., Vol. 22, cols. 874-89.
REFERRED TO: 203

——— Speech on Church Rates (21 Apr., 1834; Commons), *PD*, 3rd ser., Vol. 22, cols. 1057-9.
REFERRED TO: 211

——— Speech on Poor Laws Amendment (14 May, 1834; Commons), *PD*, 3rd ser., Vol. 23, cols. 971-3.
NOTE: the reference is to the ministry's announcement of its intention to modify the clause respecting the payment of wages out of rates.
REFERRED TO: 238

——— Speech on Danish Claims (16 May, 1834; Commons), *PD*, 3rd ser., Vol. 23, cols. 1138-9.
REFERRED TO: 237

——— Speech on Stamps on Newspapers (22 May, 1834; Commons), *PD*, 3rd ser., Vol. 23, cols. 1210-13.
NOTE: the reference at 298 is to "evasive answers" by the ministry concerning its avowed intention of removing the stamp tax.
REFERRED TO: 237, 298

——— Speech on the Beer-House Bill (1 Aug., 1834; Commons), *Morning Chronicle*, 2 Aug., 1834, 3.
NOTE: the statement quoted by JSM is not recorded in *PD*.
QUOTED: 272
272.10 "looked] Lord ALTHORP looked (3)
272.10 Court to be as] court as (3)
272.11 cases] causes (3)
272.13 country] county (3)

——— Statements on the Character of Irish Members (5 Feb., 1834; Commons), *PD*, 3rd ser., Vol. 21, cols. 121, 126.
REFERRED TO: 155

——— Statement on Local Courts—Judges' Rules (11 Feb., 1834; Commons), *PD*, 3rd ser., Vol. 21, col. 210.
NOTE: the reference is to the ministerial announcement concerning a Local Courts Bill.
REFERRED TO: 153n

——— Statement (23 May, 1834; Commons), *The Times*, 24 May, 1834, 4.
NOTE: the reference is to Althorp's expression of willingness "to limit the duration of the Central [Poor Law] Board to five years." Althorp's statement to this effect does not appear in *PD*.
REFERRED TO: 238

——— Statement on Criminal Prosecutions (4 Aug., 1834; Commons), *PD*, 3rd ser., Vol. 25, col. 929.
REFERRED TO: 275

——— Statement on Supply, &c. (5 Aug., 1834; Commons), *PD*, 3rd ser., Vol. 25, col. 993.
NOTE: the second reference is in a quotation from the *Examiner*.
REFERRED TO: 275

SPRING-RICE, THOMAS.
NOTE: the reference is to a speech which has not been located.
REFERRED TO: 298

——— Speech on Unlawful Societies in Ireland (25 Feb., 1825; Commons), *PH*, 1825, 126-7.
NOTE: Spring-Rice is quoting John Doherty.
QUOTED: 94n-5n
REFERRED TO: 95n

——— Speech in Presentation of a Petititon on Dissenters' Grievances—Cambridge Petition (24 Mar., 1834; Commons), *PD*, 3rd ser., Vol. 22, cols. 569-87.
NOTE: the reference is to the Secretary to the Treasury.
REFERRED TO: 196

——— Speech on Supply, &c. (14 Apr., 1834; Commons), *PD*, 3rd ser., Vol. 22, col. 761.
REFERRED TO: 199

——— Speech in Moving an Amendment on Repeal of the Union (23 Apr., 1834; Commons), *PD*, 3rd ser., Vol. 22, cols. 1164-1283.
REFERRED TO: 214-15

——— Speech on the Ballot (7 Mar., 1837; Commons), *PD*, 3rd ser., Vol. 37, cols. 61-6.
QUOTED: 375
375.31 "that it is absurd to expect moral effects from mechanical means."] He did not believe that it was in the power of any Act of Parliament to reach the evil; he did not believe they could arrive at moral results by mechanical means. (col. 64)

——— Statement on Criminal Prosecutions (4 Aug., 1834; Commons), *PD*, 3rd ser., Vol. 25, col. 929.
REFERRED TO: 274-5

STAFFORD, JOHN. "Evidence Taken before the Select Committee on the Laws Relating to Game," *PP*, 1823, IV, 143-8.
QUOTED: 106-7
106.7 "I] [*no paragraph*] I (143)
106.9 with] by (143)
106.10 castle. Vickery] castle; Vickery (143)
106.12 justice. It] justice; it (143)
106.14 murder. A] murder: A (143)
106.16 wounded. A] wounded; a (143)
106.21 life. And] life: And (144)
106.26 poaching. About] poaching; about (144)
106.30 shot. . . . Vickery] shot, and it was a considerable time after the offence was committed, before any trace could be obtained so as to discover the offenders; the fact was, the information that led to it was obtained from a convict who was on board one of the hulks; it was communicated to the office, and I rather think that I had an interview with the man myself; and from the information obtained from him, Vickery (144)
106.34 before. It] before; it (144)
106.36 thieves. . . . Both] thieves; there was hardly a granary in Bishop's Stortford or Hockerill, but these men had keys to open, and they used to steal the corn in a very particular way; when it was stored up stairs they used to get into a room below, bore a hole through the floor for the corn to run through, and when their sacks were full, they put a cork into the hole to fill it up, the persons would go into the granary next day and not know that any thing had been stolen; they stole besides, an immense

quantity of goods from the shop-keepers in the neighbourhood; these men were committed to Hertford, and there they were capitally convicted, but inasmuch as they were charged with the murder in Essex, they were removed to Chelmsford, and there tried again, both (144)
    106.45   these] those (144)
    106.45   poaching] poachers (144)
    107.4   them. I] them; I (144)

STAMP, MARY.
    NOTE: the reference is to a maidservant of Major Pitman.
    REFERRED TO: 267

The Standard. Referred to: 451

STANFIELD, JOHN.
    NOTE: the reference is to the sentencing of the six Dorsetshire labourers.
    REFERRED TO: 207

STANFIELD, THOMAS.
    NOTE: the reference is to the sentencing of the six Dorsetshire labourers.
    REFERRED TO: 207

STANLEY, EDWARD GEORGE GEOFFREY SMITH (Lord Stanley, later 14th Earl of Derby).
    NOTE: the reference at 344 is in a quotation from Walsh.
    REFERRED TO: 243, 343, 344

────── Speech on Arrears of Tithes (Ireland) (16 Apr., 1832; Commons), *PD*, 3rd ser., Vol. 12, cols. 593-5.
    NOTE: the reference is to Stanley's announcement of the extinction of Irish tithes.
    REFERRED TO: 153

────── Speech on Oaths of Catholic Members (11 Mar., 1834; Commons), *PD*, 3rd ser., Vol. 22, cols. 40-6.
    REFERRED TO: 187

────── Speech on the Canadas (15 Apr., 1834; Commons), *PD*, 3rd ser., Vol. 22, cols. 790-811.
    NOTE: the reference, to "the most redoubted debater in the House," concerns Roebuck's triumph over Stanley in the debate on Canada.
    REFERRED TO: 202

────── Speech on Church Rates (21 Apr., 1834; Commons), *PD*, 3rd ser., Vol. 22, cols. 1034-9.
    REFERRED TO: 211-12

────── Speech on the Municipal Corporation Bill (15 June, 1835; Commons), *PD*, 3rd ser., Vol. 28, cols. 822-7.
    REFERRED TO: 304-5

STANLEY, EDWARD HENRY (Lord Stanley, later 15th Earl of Derby). Speech at Brighton (22 Jan., 1868), *The Times*, 23 Jan., 1868, 6.
    REFERRED TO: 528

STAPLETON, PHILIP.
    NOTE: the references are to Stapleton as one of eleven members excluded from Parliament.
    REFERRED TO: 50, 52

STEIN, HEINRICH FREIDRICH KARL VON. See Ernst Rudolph Huber.

STEPHENS, JOSEPH RAYNER. Referred to: 479, 485

STEWART, CHARLES WILLIAM (Lord Londonderry).
    NOTE: the reference is in a quotation from Fonblanque.
    REFERRED TO: 366

STEWART, EMILY ANNE (née Hobart) (Lady Castlereagh).
NOTE: the reference is in a quotation from Fonblanque.
REFERRED TO: 356

STEWART, JOHN (Earl of Traquair).
NOTE: the third reference at 27 is in a quotation from Hume.
REFERRED TO: 27

STEWART, ROBERT (Lord Castlereagh).
NOTE: the reference at 135 is to "the Castlereagh ministry"; Castlereagh was considered to be the most prominent figure in an administration headed by Lord Liverpool. The reference at 356 is in a quotation from Fonblanque.
REFERRED TO: 135, 356

STRAFFORD, EARL OF. See Thomas Wentworth.

STRODE, WILLIAM.
NOTE: the reference at 16 is to the leading members of Parliament imprisoned in 1629; that at 40 is in a quotation from Hume.
REFERRED TO: 16, 40

STRUTT, EDWARD (Lord Belper).
NOTE: the identification is inferential.
REFERRED TO: 210-11

STUART, JAMES (Duke of Richmond).
NOTE: the reference at 53n is to him as one of the king's counsellors; that at 55 is to him as one of the four lords in Hume's "silly story" who offered themselves to suffer in place of Charles I.
REFERRED TO: 53n, 55

STUART, JAMES. Referred to: 455n

STUART-WORTLEY, JAMES ARCHIBALD.
NOTE: the references are to his Game Laws Bill; the first reference at 117, to the "member for Yorkshire," is in a quotation from William Peel.
REFERRED TO: 101, 102, 107-9, 116-17

——— Speech in Introducing the Game Laws Amendment Bill (17 Feb., 1825; Commons), *PD*, n.s., Vol. 10, cols. 187-9.
NOTE: see, under Parliamentary Papers, "A Bill to Amend the Laws for the Preservation of Game," 6 George IV (21 Mar., 1825).
REFERRED TO: 101

STUBBS, WILLIAM, ed. *Select Charters and Other Illustrations of English Constitutional History from the Earliest Times to the Reign of Edward the First*. Oxford: Clarendon Press, 1870.
NOTE: the reference is to the "Assize of the Forest" of Henry II.
REFERRED TO: 20n

STUDDERT.
NOTE: the reference is to a middleman in county Clare.
REFERRED TO: 516

SUFFIELD, BARON. See Edward Harbord.

SUSSEX, EARL OF. See Thomas Savile.

SUTTON, CHARLES.
NOTE: the reference is in a quotation from Fonblanque.
REFERRED TO: 369

TACHÉ, ETIENNE PASCHAL. Referred to: 455n

TACITUS. *The Annals*. In *The Histories and The Annals* (Latin and English). Trans. Clifford Moore and John Jackson. 4 vols. London: Heinemann; New York: Putnam's Sons, 1925-37, II-IV.
  NOTE: this ed. used for ease of reference. Two editions (Leyden: Elzevir, 1640; and Amsterdam: Elzevir, 1672-73) formerly in SC. The quotation (a modification of the tag) is in a quotation from Fonblanque.
  QUOTED: 360
  360.26 *Praefulgebat quod non visebatur*] sed praefulgebant Cassius atque Brutus eo ipso quod effigies eorum non visebantur. (II, 642; III, 76, 11-13)

Tait's Edinburgh Magazine. Referred to: 174, 400

TALLEYRAND-PÉRIGORD, CHARLES MAURICE DE. Referred to: 468

TAYLOR, HENRY. *The Statesman*. London: Longman, Rees, Orme, Brown, Green, and Longman, 1836.
  NOTE: reviewed by JSM and George Grote, *L&WR*, V & XXVII (Apr., 1837), 1-32; in *CW*, XIX, 617-47.
  QUOTED: 394
  394.34 "merge" He [a statesman] would find them [valuable legislative measures]—not certainly by shutting himself up in his closet and inventing what had not been thought of before—but by holding himself on the alert, by listening with all his ears (and he should have many ears abroad in the world) for the suggestions of circumstance, by catching the first moment of public complaint against real evil, encouraging it and turning it to account, by devising how to throw valuable measures that do not excite popular interest into one boat with those that do, by knowing (as a statesman who is competent to operations on a large scale may know) how to carry a measure by enlargement such as shall merge (158-9)
  394.34-5 particular objections which are unanswerable in general ones which may be met."] specific objections that would be insurmountable in general ones that can be met; in short by a thousand means and projects lying in the region between absolute spontaneous invention on the one hand and mere slavish adoption on the other,—such means and projects as will suggest themselves to one who meditates the good of mankind "sagacious of his quarry from afar," but not to a minister whose whole soul is and must be in the "notices of motions" and the order-book of the House of Commons, and who has no one behind to prompt him to other enterprise,—no closet or office-statesman for him to fall back upon as upon an inner mind. (159-60)

TENNENT, JAMES EMERSON. Speech on Repeal of the Union (24 Apr., 1834; Commons), *PD*, 3rd ser., Vol. 22, cols. 1288-1333.
  REFERRED TO: 215

THIRLWALL, CONNOP. Referred to: 260

—— *A Letter to Thomas Turton on the Admission of Dissenters to Academical Degrees*. Cambridge: Deighton, 1834.
  REFERRED TO: 260

THOM, ADAM.
  NOTE: the references at 443 and 463 are to Durham's advisers, of whom Thom was one. See also Roebuck, "Lord Durham's Administration in Canada: Letter III."
  REFERRED TO: 443, 455n, 463

THOM, JOHN NICHOLS. See Tom.

THOMPSON, THOMAS PERRONET. Referred to: 386, 396

—— *A Catechism on the Corn Laws: With a List of Fallacies and the Answers* (1827). 17th ed. London: Westminster Review, 1833.
  QUOTED: 177-8
  REFERRED TO: 400
  177.26 evil] *evil* (40)

177.38   itself. [*paragraph*] To] itself. [*3-sentence paragraph omitted*] [*paragraph*] To (41)
177.46-7   too. [*paragraph*] That] too. [*8-sentence paragraph omitted*] [*paragraph*] That (41)

────── *Letters of a Representative to His Constituents, During the Session of 1837.* [Second Series.] London: Wilson, 1837.
REVIEWED: 381-404
QUOTED: 385
385.31-3   but the want of literal conformity, . . . "is . . . people,"] The want of this literal conformity is . . . people. (1)

────── "Parliamentary Reform," *Westminster Review*, XIV (Apr., 1831), 440-56.
NOTE: the quotation is indirect.
QUOTED: 399
399.32   it is the house of Have against the house of Take.] The mistake is an easy one; it is not a "feud of the house of *Want* against the house of *Have*," but against the house of "*Take*." (450)

THOMSON, CHARLES EDWARD POULETT. Speech on the Corn Laws (7 Mar., 1834; Commons), *PD*, 3rd ser., Vol. 21, cols. 1276-1307.
REFERRED TO: 186

THORNTON, HENRY. *An Enquiry into the Nature and Effects of the Credit of Great Britain.* London: Hatchard, 1802.
NOTE: the reference is in a quotation from JSM's "The Currency Juggle," *q.v.*
REFERRED TO: 176

────── *Substance of Two Speeches in the Debate in the House of Commons, on the Report of the Bullion Committee, on the 7th and 14th of May, 1811.* London: Hatchard, 1811.
NOTE: the reference is in a quotation from JSM's "The Currency Juggle," *q.v.*
REFERRED TO: 176

THORNTON, WILLIAM THOMAS. *A Plea for Peasant Proprietors; with the Outlines of a Plan for Their Establishment in Ireland.* London: Murray, 1848.
REFERRED TO: 528

The Times.
NOTE: anonymous articles follow, listed chronologically. The reference at 224 is to *The Times'* hostility to the Poor Law Bill, a subject upon which the paper commented with great frequency during the spring of 1834; that at 252 is inferential.
REFERRED TO: 183, 202, 203, 224, 225, 252, 316, 351

────── Leading Article on British Foreign Policy, 17 Jan., 1834, 4.
NOTE: the quotation concerns the term "low Radicals" as used by *The Times*.
QUOTED: 161
161.12   "low Radicals,"] Yes, the Tories began the fight against reform by anticipating all manner of mischiefs as the result of it; and now that the battle has gone against them, they seek to realize their own predictions—or to throw upon them some varnish of credibility—by affirming of reform that it is actually as bad as they had foretold, or worse; that there is, as the Duke of Wellington asserted at the outset, an impossibility of carrying on the King's Government with an enlarged constituency and a reformed Parliament; that there is no sense of national dignity or honour left in the electors or their representatives; and that Russia and her retainers may insult, and outrage, and trample on this great nation as she likes; for that neither Parliament nor people will suffer the King of England to avenge indignity or to repel aggression; that peace on any terms will be insisted on; that no duty or principle of self-defence will be admitted; but that Mr. Joseph Hume and the low Radicals will strike the flag of England throughout the world, and let foreign tyrants ride rough-shod over us with impunity. (4)

────── Leading Article on the Post Office, 5 Feb., 1834, 4.
NOTE: the article announcing changes in the Post Office.
REFERRED TO: 157

────── Leading Article on the Post Office, 7 Feb., 1834, 2.
NOTE: the article proposing further reforms in the Post Office.
REFERRED TO: 158

——— Leading Article on the Poor Law Report, 25 Feb., 1834, 2.
REFERRED TO: 203, 204, 205

——— Leading Article on the Dudley Election, 1 Mar., 1834, 3.
REFERRED TO: 182

——— Leading Article on Trades Unions, 15 Mar., 1834, 5.
REFERRED TO: 188

——— Leading Article on Registration of Instruments Affecting Land, 2 Apr., 1834, 4.
REFERRED TO: 224

——— Leading Article on the Strike at Derby, 14 Apr., 1834, 4.
QUOTED: 210
210.24-5 body," . . . "of] body of (4)
210.25   *struck for wages*] [*not in italics*] (4)
210.28   *refused to take*] [*not in italics*] (4)

——— Leading Article on the Strike at Derby, 18 Apr., 1834, 5.
QUOTED: 211
REFERRED TO: 210-11
211.2 "printed . . . and list . . . conditions,"] Our firm impression was the former [refusal of Derby employees to work unless under conditions dictated by trades unions], and to confirm it we remember well that a letter from a Derby correspondent on the information of which our first of three or four articles was written, enclosed a printed . . . and a list . . . conditions which the workmen had adopted for the purpose of imposing on their Derby employers. (5)
211.5 "gave] The Derby masters, if we remember right, gave (5)
211.5 consider the] consider of the (5)
211.7 place."] place, so that nothing was done on their part with violence or precipitation. (5)

——— Leading Article on the Canadas, 19 Apr., 1834, 5.
NOTE: the reference is to *The Times*' criticism of Roebuck's speech of 15 Apr. on the Canadas, *q.v.*
REFERRED TO: 202

——— Leading Article on the Poor Laws, 19 Apr., 1834, 5.
REFERRED TO: 203

——— Leading Article on the Tailors' Strike, 1 May, 1834, 3.
REFERRED TO: 220

——— Leading Article on the Poor Law Bill, 14 May, 1834, 4-5.
QUOTED: 239
239.34 "protracted] There was a time when the inhabitants of these realms exerted, and not without success, all their energies and risked their very lives, in resisting the assumed prerogative of princes to levy money without the consent of Parliament, and to dispense with laws or the execution of laws: nor has it yet fallen out of fashion for writers upon English history, whether native or foreign, to point in terms of the highest panegyric to that protracted (5)

——— Leading Article on the Poor Law Bill, 20 May, 1834, 2.
NOTE: the article on the connection between support for the Poor Law Bill and republicanism.
REFERRED TO: 240

——— "Men of Science and Letters," 22 May, 1834, 3.
REFERRED TO: 241, 242

——— Leading Article on the Poor Law Bill, 23 May, 1834, 5.
NOTE: the article on the issue of responsibility with reference to the proposed board of Poor Law Commissioners.
REFERRED TO: 240

——— Leading Article on the Ministry, 9 June, 1834, 2.
REFERRED TO: 252

——— Leading Article on the Poor Law Bill, 23 July, 1834, 4.
REFERRED TO: 266

TIMOLEON. Referred to: 187

TOM [THOM], JOHN NICHOLS ("William Courtenay"). Referred to: 488

TRAQUAIR, EARL OF. See John Stewart.

TRENCH, CHARLES LE POER. Referred to: 93

——— "Evidence Taken before the Select Committee of the House of Lords Appointed to Inquire into the State of Ireland, More Particularly with Reference to the Circumstances Which May Have Led to Disturbances in That Part of the United Kingdom," *PP*, 1825, IX, 439-50.
REFERRED TO: 96

TRIGG.
NOTE: the reference, to a shoemaker, is in a quotation from John Stafford's evidence given before a Select Committee of the House of Commons.
REFERRED TO: 106

TURGOT, ANNE ROBERT JACQUES. Referred to: 404

TURNER.
NOTE: the reference, to a poacher, is in a quotation from John Stafford's evidence given before a Select Committee of the House of Commons.
REFERRED TO: 106

TURTON, THOMAS EDWARD MICHELL.
NOTE: the references are to Durham's advisers, of whom Turton was one.
REFERRED TO: 443, 463

TWISS, HORACE. Speech on Game Laws Amendment Bill (31 May, 1824; Commons), *PD*, n.s., Vol. 11, cols. 957-8.
QUOTED: 116-17
116.35 "its] Besides, if that provision [legalizing the sale of game] were more operative than he believed it would be, its (col. 957)
117.1 hucksters."] hucksters, and he was therefore sure that it would never be sanctioned by them in practice. (col. 957)

——— Speech on Roman Catholic Relief (10 May, 1825; Commons), *PH*, 1825, 216-21.
REFERRED TO: 92

USURY LAWS. See 12 Anne, second session, c. 16.

VADIER, MARC GUILLAUME ALEXIS.
NOTE: one of Babeuf's "fellow conspirators" in the Société des Egaux.
REFERRED TO: 401

VALENTINE, BENJAMIN.
NOTE: the reference is to one of the leading members of Parliament imprisoned in 1629.
REFERRED TO: 16

VANE, HENRY (the elder). Referred to: 39

VANE, HENRY (the younger). Referred to: 8, 47, 57

VICKERY.
NOTE: the reference, to an officer of the law, is in a quotation from John Stafford's evidence given before a Select Committee of the House of Commons.
REFERRED TO: 106

VICTORIA (of England). Referred to: 389

VIGER, BONAVENTURE. See Robert Shore Milnes Bouchette.

VILLIERS, CHARLES PELHAM. Speech on Bonded Corn (9 May, 1838; Commons), *PD*, 3rd ser., Vol. 42, cols. 1041-2.
NOTE: the quotation is indirect.
QUOTED: 470

VILLIERS, GEORGE (Duke of Buckingham). Referred to: 11, 12, 15, 18

——— Address to Both Houses of Parliament, 24 Feb., 1624. In *Journals of the House of Lords*, 27 Feb., 1624, III, 220.
NOTE: the reference is to his lies to Parliament on his and Charles's return from Spain.
REFERRED TO: 12

VILLIERS, GEORGE WILLIAM FREDERICK (4th Earl of Clarendon).
NOTE: the reference is to him as a Commissioner to France in 1834; see also John Bowring.
REFERRED TO: 157

VINCENT, HENRY. Referred to: 489

VIRGIL (Publius Virgilius Maro). *Aeneid*. In *Works*. Trans. H. Rushton Fairclough. 2 vols. London: Heinemann; New York: Putnam's Sons, 1916, I, 240-570; II, 2-364.
QUOTED: 279, 380

279.29 *Macte virtute, generose puer; sic itur ad astra.*] Aetheria tum forte plaga crinitus Apollo / desuper Ausonias acies urbemque videbat,/ nube sedens, atque his victorem adfatur Iulum:/ "macte nova virtute, puer: sic itur ad astra,/ dis genite et geniture deos. (II, 156; IX, 638-42)

380.31 *decus et tutamen*,] at qui deinde locum tenuit virtute secundum,/ levibus huic hamis consertam auroque trilicem / loricam, quam Demoleo detraxerat ipse / victor apud rapidum Simoenta sub Ilio alto,/ donat habere viro, decus et tutamen in armis. (I, 462; V, 258-62)

VOLTAIRE, FRANÇOIS MARIE AROUET. Referred to: 493

——— *Candide, ou l'optimisme*. In *Oeuvres complètes*. 66 vols. Paris: Renouard, 1817-25, XXXIX, 203-322.
NOTE: this ed. in SC.
QUOTED: 116

116.19 *pour encourager les autres*] Cela est incontestable, lui répliqua-t-on; mais dans ce pays-ci il est bon de tuer de temps en temps un amiral pour encourager les autres. (290)

WAGSTAFFE, THOMAS. *A Vindication of King Charles the Martyr: Proving That His Majesty Was the Author of Εἰκὼν Βασιλική*. 3rd ed. London: Wilkin, 1711.
NOTE: the quotation is in a quotation from Brodie (*q.v.* for collation).
QUOTED: 52
REFERRED TO: 5n

WAKEFIELD, EDWARD GIBBON.
NOTE: the references at 443 and 463 are to Durham's advisers, of whom Wakefield was one.
REFERRED TO: 443, 455-6, 463

——— *England and America; a Comparison of the Social and Political State of Both Nations*. 2 vols. London: Bentley, 1833.
NOTE: the quotation is indirect.
QUOTED: 483

——— "The French Canadians," *Spectator*, 24 Nov., 1838, 1109.
NOTE: a reply to Roebuck, "Lord Durham's Administration: Letter II," *q.v.*
REFERRED TO: 456

——— *The Hangman and the Judge; or, A Letter from Jack Ketch to Mr. Justice Alderson*. London: Wilson, 1833.
REFERRED TO: 258

WAKLEY, THOMAS.
   NOTE: the second reference is in a quotation from JSM that includes the first.
   REFERRED TO: 250, 255

——— Motion on the Address in Answer to the Queen's Speech (20 Nov., 1837; Commons), *PD*, 3rd ser., Vol. 39, cols. 37-48.
   REFERRED TO: 409

WALKER, CLEMENT. *The History of Independency, with the Rise, Growth, and Practice of That Powerfull and Restlesse Faction.* 2 pts. London: n.p., 1648-49.
   NOTE: published under the pseudonym of Theodorus Verax. Part II, separately paginated, has on its title page "*Anarchia Anglicana.*"
   REFERRED TO: 7, 54, 55

WALKER, HENRY.
   NOTE: the reference is to "one of the populace" who cast an insult at Charles I as he passed through London.
   REFERRED TO: 42n

WALLER, WILLIAM.
   NOTE: the references are to him as one of eleven members excluded from Parliament.
   REFERRED TO: 50, 52

WALSH, JOHN BENN (Lord Ormathwaite). Referred to: 329-48 *passim*

——— *Chapters of Contemporary History.* 2nd ed. London: Murray, 1836.
   NOTE: a copy of the 2nd ed. not being available, we have used the 1st (with which the 3rd agrees) for the references and collations. The quotations at 337 are indirect.
   REVIEWED: 329-48
   QUOTED: 331, 332-3, 333, 334, 335n, 335n-6n, 336n, 337, 338, 339, 341, 341-2, 343, 343-4, 345, 346, 347

   331.16 thought," . . . "that] thought that (73)
   331.20 improvement.] improvement; that its single tendency is always to suspend, often to retard it, and that it must be accompanied by great countervailing advantages, to overbalance this inclination. (73-4)
   335n.23 "boasted diffusion of knowledge,"] [*paragraph*] I have often been led to observe how very little the boasted diffusion of knowledge in these enlightened days seems, in fact, to promote its real increase—how few minds in this vast community appear to be stimulated, by the great facility of acquiring imperfect and superficial information upon every variety of subject, to push their own inquiries further, to investigate truths, and to detect and expose very flagrant errors. (114)
   335n.29 "The] [*no paragraph*] The (116)
   336n.28-9 "garrison . . . country;"] They [the Orangemen] have always felt themselves more or less a garrison . . . country,—preserving by union, by courage, and by the support of this nation, all that they had created of property and improvement. (125)
   336n.30 "overbearing and arrogant"] But it may be easily imagined that, placed in such a situation, their daring resolution was not always coupled with great mildness, and that they justly incurred the reproach of that overbearing and arrogant spirit of which we cannot conscientiously acquit the more violent Orangemen (123)
   336n.31 "Six] [*no paragraph*] Six (121)
   336n.33 hearts. . . . The] hearts. [*ellipsis indicates 3-sentence omission*] [*paragraph*] The (121)
   336n.39 passes] pass (122)
   338.16 "We] [*paragraph*] We (31)
   338.21 "the appetite . . . innovation"] Their object [that of Lord Grey and his colleagues] would be to arrest the progress of the movement against the national institutions, to curb the appetite . . . innovation, and to divert the restlessness and activity which late events had aroused in the public mind to the safe and useful channel of practical reform. (3)
   338.21-3 "the desires . . . power"] It was the declared purpose, and I have no doubt the sincere intention of Lord Grey's Government, to satisfy the desires . . . power, by the extensive changes introduced by the Reform Bill. (2)

338.37 "the educated classes"] The educated classes in England, ten years ago, joined to a real liberality of political opinion an intimate belief of the superiority and excellence of our constitution. (76)

338.39 reform"] reform, found in the great body of the educated and enlightened gentry of this country zealous and able advocates. (77)

339.5 "Had] [*no paragraph*] Had (33)
339.15 Let] [*no paragraph*] Let (31)
339.22 If] [*no paragraph*] If (33)
341.4 "We] [*no paragraph*] We (78)
341.4 reform. We] reform—we (78)
341.34-6 "I believe," . . . [*paragraph*] "That,] [*no paragraph*] I believe that (83)
341.37 timid] torpid (83)
342.3-4 ratio. . . . As] [*ellipsis indicates 1-page omission*] (84-5)
343.10 "the] The (10)

343.18-19 "pressure from without"] They dissolved at last, through internal disagreement and differences, indeed, but which were forced into notice and stimulated into action by the "pressure from without." (32)

343.28 "course of improvement in details,"] He recommended the course of practical improvement in details which, in fact, had been the policy of preceding Administrations ever since Mr. Canning's entrance into the Cabinet in 1822. (11)

343.31 "final measure,"] When the Reform Bill was brought forward, the Grey Ministry pledged themselves to regard it, as far as they were concerned, as a final settlement of the question. (111)

343.31 "collision"] They excited no party feeling, they involved no question which brought the principles of the contending parties into collision; they were not violently opposed by either of the great corporations primarily interested, and they created little sensation when compared with their magnitude. (19)

343.35-344.1 "When the Ministry," . . . "when] When (1)
345.33 "How] [*no paragraph*] And yet how (60)
345.34 disposal. All] disposal. [*paragraph*] All (60)
345.39 "There] [*no paragraph*] There (56)

346.20 strength. . . . That] strength. Its new advocates were either too much of speculative theorists, or young men whose habits and education identified them, perhaps in spite of themselves, with the upper classes, and who took up the cause of Radicalism a little from the desire of acquiring personal distinction by a new and short path. That (58)

346.24-5 it . . . *purpose*] [*not in italics*] (59)

347.8 "paid . . . pound"] He might have repealed twenty millions of taxes, and paid . . . pound. (10)

WARBURTON, GEORGE. "Evidence Taken before the Select Committee Appointed to Inquire into the Disturbances in Ireland," *PP*, 1825, VII, 124-45, 147-66.
REFERRED TO: 93n, 96

——— "Evidence Taken before the Select Committee of the House of Lords Appointed to Examine into the Nature and Extent of the Disturbances Which Have Prevailed in Those Districts of Ireland Which Are Now Subject to the Provisions of the Insurrection Act," *PP*, 1825, VII, 577-94, 609-10.
REFERRED TO: 96

WARBURTON, HENRY.
NOTE: the reference at 346 is in a quotation from Walsh.
REFERRED TO: 346, 434

——— Speech on the Repeal of the Malt Duty (27 Feb., 1834; Commons), *PD*, 3rd ser., Vol. 21, cols. 889-90.
REFERRED TO: 255

——— Speech on Supply, &c. (5 Aug., 1834; Commons), *PD*, 3rd ser., Vol. 25, cols. 993-4.
REFERRED TO: 275-6

——— Speech on the Affairs of Canada (17 Jan., 1838; Commons), *PD*, 3rd ser., Vol. 40, cols. 102-9.
REFERRED TO: 434

WARD, HENRY GEORGE. Referred to: 480

——— Speech in Introducing a Motion on the Record of Divisions in the House (11 Feb., 1834; Commons), *PD*, 3rd ser., Vol. 21, cols. 239-43.
REFERRED TO: 158

——— Speech in Introducing a Motion on the Church of Ireland (27 May, 1834; Commons), *PD*, 3rd ser., Vol. 23, cols. 1368-96.
REFERRED TO: 244, 252, 254

WARDLAW, RALPH. Referred to: 480

WARNER, JOHN (Bishop of Peterborough).
NOTE: the reference is to him as one of twelve bishops impeached and subsequently imprisoned in 1641.
REFERRED TO: 39

WARWICK, PHILIP. *Memoires of the Reigne of King Charles I with a Continuation to the Happy Restauration of King Charles II*. London: Chiswell, 1701.
REFERRED TO: 53n

WASHINGTON, GEORGE. Referred to: 417, 449

WELLESLEY, ARTHUR (1st Duke of Wellington).
NOTE: the references at 263 and 316 are to the Wellington ministry; those at 356, 364, 366, 369-70, and 370-1 are in quotations from Fonblanque.
REFERRED TO: 171, 250, 263, 316, 321, 352, 356, 363, 364, 366, 369, 369-70, 370, 370-1, 399, 411, 449, 469

——— Speech on the Address in Answer to the King's Speech (2 Nov., 1830; Lords), *PD*, 3rd ser., Vol. 1, cols. 44-53.
NOTE: the reference is to his declaration against reform.
REFERRED TO: 480

——— Speech on the Poor-Law Amendment Act (7 Apr., 1837; Lords), *PD*, 3rd ser., Vol. 37, cols. 851-2.
REFERRED TO: 398

——— Speech on the State of Ireland (27 Nov., 1837; Lords), *PD*, 3rd ser., Vol. 39, cols. 262-8.
NOTE: the reference is to Wellington's "compliments" to Mulgrave respecting the latter's administration in Ireland. JSM's observation, doubtless based on an *Examiner* report (3 Dec., 1837, 769, 770) of this speech, is rather misleading; whereas the *Examiner* focused on a single statement which might be taken as moderate praise of Mulgrave, the speech as a whole is not complimentary to the Irish Lord Lieutenant.
REFERRED TO: 412

——— Speech on the Affairs of Canada (16 Jan., 1838; Lords), *PD*, 3rd ser., Vol. 40, cols. 3-4.
REFERRED TO: 414-15

WELLESLEY, ARTHUR RICHARD (2nd Duke of Wellington). Referred to: 399

WELLINGTON, DUKE OF. See Arthur Wellesley.

WENTWORTH, THOMAS (Earl of Strafford).
NOTE: JSM spells the name Strafforde. The reference at 14 is to him as one of several popular leaders made sheriffs of counties to prevent their returning to Parliament in 1626; that at 22 is in a quotation from Brodie; two of the references at 31 and that at 35 are in quotations from Hume.
REFERRED TO: 5, 14, 19, 22, 29, 30-4, 32n, 33n, 35, 39

——— *The Earl of Strafforde's Letters and Despatches, with an Essay towards His Life by Sir George Radcliffe*. Ed. William Knowler. 2 vols. London: Bowyer, 1739.
REFERRED TO: 5, 28n, 31

WESTMEATH, MARQUIS OF. See George Thomas John Nugent.

WESTMINSTER, MARQUIS OF. See Richard Grosvenor.

The Westminster Review. Referred to: 174, 354, 400

WETHERELL, CHARLES. Speech on Unlawful Societies in Ireland (18 Feb., 1825; Commons), *PH*, 1825, 112-13.
NOTE: the reference is to the Solicitor-General.
REFERRED TO: 74, 74n

——— Speech on Roman Catholic Claims (1 Mar., 1825; Commons), *PH*, 1825, 155-6.
NOTE: JSM is in part quoting from the speech; quotation marks have been added as necessary.
QUOTED: 78
78.22 Constitution: Was] constitution. Was (156)
78.23 *state*] state (156)
78.25 and] And (156)

——— Speech on Roman Catholic Relief (10 May, 1825; Commons), *PH*, 1825, 222-4.
REFERRED TO: 86

[WEYLAND, JOHN.] *A Letter on the Game Laws. By a Country Gentleman, a Proprietor of Game*. London: Baldwin, Cradock, and Joy, 1815.
NOTE: we owe the attribution to Dr. Peter Munsche.
REVIEWED: 99-120
QUOTED: 103
103.29-30 evil," . . . "cannot] evil cannot (6)
103.35 enactments. This] enactments. [*paragraph*] This (7)
103.38 cause. The . . . it.] cause.* [*footnote:*] *The . . . it. (7)

——— *A Second Letter on the Game Laws. By a Country Gentleman, a Proprietor of Game*. London: Baldwin, and Hatchard, 1817.
NOTE: we owe the attribution to Dr. Peter Munsche.
REVIEWED: 99-120

WEYROTHER, FRANZ VON.
NOTE: the reference is to "the old Austrian tacticians" opposed to Napoleon.
REFERRED TO: 450

WHATELY, RICHARD. *Thoughts on Secondary Punishments in a Letter to Earl Grey . . . to Which Are Appended, Two Articles on Transportation to New South Wales and on Secondary Punishments; and Some Observations on Colonization*. London: Fellowes, 1832.
REFERRED TO: 258

Whig Club, Instituted in May, 1784, by John Bellamy, to Be Composed of Gentlemen, Who Solemnly Pledge Themselves to Support the Constitution of This Country, According to the Principles Established at the Glorious Revolution. [London: n.p., 1786.]
NOTE: this work, whose title uses one of the quoted phrases (both of which are commonplaces), lists the Whig toasts, one of which includes the other phrase.
QUOTED: 33n
33n.7-8 "glorious revolution,"] [*see title above*]
33n.8 "immortal memory."] The glorious and immortal memory of King William the Third. (1st Standing Toast, 15)

WHITELOCKE, BULSTRODE. *Memorials of the English Affairs; or, An Historical Account of*

What Passed from the Beginning of the Reign of King Charles the First, to King Charles the Second His Happy Restauration. London: Ponder, 1682.
REFERRED TO: 6, 7, 54

WHITMORE, WILLIAM WOLRYCHE. Speech in Introducing a Motion on Poor Laws' Amendment (16 June, 1834; Commons), *PD*, 3rd ser., Vol. 24, cols. 451-6.
REFERRED TO: 252

WHITWORTH-AYLMER, MATTHEW (Lord Aylmer). Referred to: 414, 455n

WIGNEY, ISAAC NEWTON. Speech in Introducing a Motion on the Case of the *Brighton Guardian* (4 Mar., 1834; Commons), *PD*, 3rd ser., Vol. 21, cols. 1115-17.
NOTE: the reference is to the Motion, which was introduced by Wigney, M.P. for Brighton.
REFERRED TO: 275

WILKS, JOHN. Speech on Parochial Registration (28 Mar., 1833; Commons), *PD*, 3rd ser., Vol. 16, cols. 1209-21.
REFERRED TO: 180

WILLCOCKS, RICHARD. "Evidence Taken before the Select Committee Appointed to Inquire into the Disturbances in Ireland," *PP*, 1825, VII, 96-123.
REFERRED TO: 87n, 96

——— "Evidence Taken before the Select Committee of the House of Lords Appointed to Examine into the Nature and Extent of the Disturbances Which Have Prevailed in Those Districts of Ireland Which Are Now Subject to the Provisions of the Insurrection Act," *PP*, 1825, VII, 544-60.
REFERRED TO: 96

WILLIAM III (of England). Referred to: 33n, 78

WILLIAM IV (of England).
NOTE: the reference at 372 is in a quotation from Fonblanque.
REFERRED TO: 221, 241, 313, 372

——— Speech from the Throne (4 Feb., 1834), *PD*, 3rd ser., Vol. 21, cols. 1-5.
QUOTED: 152-3
REFERRED TO: 151, 168, 171, 195, 264
152.33-4 "much . . . information," . . . "the] The reports which I will order to be laid before you from the Commissions appointed to inquire into the State of the Municipal Corporations, into the administration and effect of the Poor Laws, and into Ecclesiastical Revenues and Patronage in England and Wales, cannot fail to afford much . . . information, by which you will be enabled to judge of the (col. 12)
153.1-3 "final adjustment" . . . "without injury to . . . State;"] [*paragraph*] I recommend to you the early consideration of such a final adjustment of the tithes in that part of the United Kingdom [Ireland] as may extinguish all just causes of complaint, without injury to the rights and property of any class of my subjects, or to . . . State. (col. 4)

——— Prorogation of Parliament (15 Aug., 1834), *PD*, 3rd ser., Vol. 25, cols. 1266-9.
QUOTED: 279
279.33-4 "our jurisprudence," . . . "our municipal corporations."] [*paragraph*] To the important subject of our Jurisprudence and of our Municipal Corporations your attention will naturally be directed early in the next Session. (col. 1268)

WILLIAM (Prince of Orange).
NOTE: the reference is to Princess Mary's husband (later the father of William III).
REFERRED TO: 45

WILLIAM (the Silent) (Prince of Orange and Count of Nassau). Referred to: 404

WILLIAMS, JOHN (Bishop of Lincoln).
NOTE: the reference at 39 is to the twelve bishops impeached and subsequently imprisoned in 1641.
REFERRED TO: 22, 39

WILLIAMS, THOMAS. *Our King!—A True British Sailor!* London: Williams, [1830].
NOTE: the reference, in a quotation from Fonblanque, is to Fonblanque's parody of the refrain ("Our King is a True British Sailor") of this song in honour of the "Sailor King," King William IV. Williams is the composer; words anon.
REFERRED TO: 372

WILSON, DANIEL. Referred to: 74

WILSON, EFFINGHAM. Referred to: 258

WILSON, THOMAS MARYON. Referred to: 249

WINDEBANKE, FRANCIS.
NOTE: the reference is to him as one of those against whom Parliament prepared charges after the fall of Strafford and Laud.
REFERRED TO: 29

WINDHAM, WILLIAM HOWE. Speech on a New Military Plan (22 July, 1807; Commons), *PD*, 1st ser., Vol. 9, cols. 382-906.
QUOTED: 185
185.23 "a stake in the country"] With a view to police, a most important consideration in the establishment of the force in question, nothing could be more desirable than that those entrusted with arms and subject so little to any military control, should be persons of some substance and stake in the country. (col. 897)

WOOD, JOHN. Referred to: 156

WORDSWORTH, WILLIAM. *The Excursion, Being a Portion of The Recluse, a Poem.* In *Poetical Works.* 5 vols. London: Longman, Rees, Orme, Brown, and Green, 1827, V.
NOTE: in SC.
QUOTED: 173, 173n
173n.10 At] "Such timely warning," said the Wanderer, "gave / That visionary Voice; and, at (V, 143; IV, 294-5)

———— "Rob Roy's Grave." In *Poetical Works*, III, 24-30.
NOTE: the quotation is in a quotation from Fonblanque.
QUOTED: 363
363.1 "Good] For why?—because the good (III, 26; 37)
363.1 rule, the] Rule / Sufficeth them, the (III, 26; 37-8)

WORTLEY. See Stuart-Wortley.

WREN, MATTHEW (Bishop of Ely).
NOTE: the reference at 29 is to him as an ecclesiastic who was impeached by Parliament after the fall of Laud and Strafford; that at 39 is to him as one of twelve bishops impeached and subsequently imprisoned in 1641.
REFERRED TO: 29, 39

WRIGHT, ROBERT (Bishop of Coventry and Lichfield).
NOTE: the reference is to him as one of twelve bishops impeached and subsequently imprisoned in 1641.
REFERRED TO: 39

WRIOTHESLEY, THOMAS (Earl of Southampton).
NOTE: the reference at 53n is to him as one of the king's counsellors; that at 55 is to him as one of the four lords in Hume's "silly story" who offered themselves to suffer in place of Charles I.
REFERRED TO: 53n, 55

WYNFORD, LORD. See William Draper Best.

YORK, DUKE OF. See Frederick Augustus.

PARLIAMENTARY PAPERS, JOURNALS OF THE HOUSE OF LORDS, AND HOUSE OF LORDS SESSIONAL PAPERS

An Act for the More Speedy and Effectual Relief of Creditors (23 June, 1649). In *Journals of the House of Commons*, VI, 242.
NOTE: not enacted.
REFERRED TO: 56

An Act Touching Recording Conveyances and Incumbrances (7 Aug., 1649). In *Journals of the House of Commons*, VI, 275.
NOTE: not enacted.
REFERRED TO: 56

An Act for the Taking Away of Common Recoveries, and the Unnecessary Charge of Fines; and to Pass and Charge Lands, Intailed, as Lands in Fee (15 Apr., 1652). In *Journals of the House of Commons*, VII, 121.
NOTE: not enacted.
REFERRED TO: 56

"Out Letters (Ireland)" (10 Apr., 1691), VI, 85-6. In *Calendar of the Treasury Books, 1689-92*, IX, Pt. III, 1258-9.
NOTE: gives the initiation of the *regium donum*.
REFERRED TO: 531

"A Bill for the Provisional Establishment and Regulation of Trade and Intercourse between the Subjects of Great Britain and Those of the United States of North America," 23 George III (3 Mar., 1783), *House of Commons Sessional Papers of the Eighteenth Century*, XXXV (Bills 1782-84), 71-3.
NOTE: the Bill, introduced by Pitt, was not enacted.
REFERRED TO: 135

"Report from the Select Committee on the High Price of Gold Bullion," *PP*, 1810, III, 1-232.
NOTE: the reference is in a quotation from JSM's "The Currency Juggle," *q.v.*
REFERRED TO: 176

"Convention of Commerce, between Great Britain and the United States of America; Signed at London, 3rd July 1815," *PP*, 1816, XVII, 143-6.
REFERRED TO: 134-5, 138

"A Bill to Relieve Certain Persons Dissenting from the Church of England, from Some Parts of the Ceremony Required by Law in the Celebration of Marriages," 59 George III (28 June, 1819), *PP*, 1819, I, 357-8.
NOTE: the reference is to pre-1836 marriage bills, of which this was one; the Bill was not enacted.
REFERRED TO: 323

"A Bill to Alter and Amend Certain Parts of an Act of His Late Majesty King George the Second, Commonly Called The Marriage Act, Affecting Certain Dissenters," 3 George IV (22 Apr., 1822), *PP*, 1822, II, 987-9.
NOTE: the reference is to pre-1836 marriage bills, of which this was one; the Bill was not enacted.
REFERRED TO: 323

"Report from the Select Committee on the Laws Relating to Game," *PP*, 1823, IV, 107-53. See also Daniel Bishop, C.D., G.H., I.K., L.M., Thomas Page, John Stafford.
REVIEWED: 99-120

"A Bill to Amend the Laws for the Preservation of Game," 5 George IV (23 Feb., 1824), *PP*, 1824, I, 579-92.

NOTE: not enacted. JSM uses the debate on this Bill, rather than that on the Bill of 1825 with the same title (also introduced by Stuart Wortley) (*q.v.*), which was the occasion for "The Game Laws."
REFERRED TO: 101n, 113n

"Return of Persons Committed under the Vagrant Laws to the Respective Prisons and Houses of Correction in England and Wales, from the 1st January 1820 to the 1st January 1824, Specifying the Particular Act of Vagrancy," *PP*, 1824, XIX, 215-338.
REFERRED TO: 119

"A Bill to Amend the Laws for the Preservation of Game," 6 George IV (21 Mar., 1825), *PP*, 1825, II, 445-68.
NOTE: not enacted. As the debates on this Bill had not been published in "authoritative form" when JSM wrote "The Game Laws" (see 113n), he used the debates on the Bill with the same title of 1824, *q.v.*
REFERRED TO: 99-120 *passim*

"A Bill to Provide for the Removal of the Disqualifications under Which His Majesty's Roman Catholic Subjects Now Labour," 6 George IV (23 Mar., 1825), *PP*, 1825, III, 441-50.
NOTE: not enacted.
REFERRED TO: 76-84

"A Bill, Intitled, An Act to Declare Unlawful the Setting of Spring Guns, and Other Offensive Engines, Tending to the Destruction of Human Life, or Grievous Bodily Harm, in Woods and Plantations, or Elsewhere; and to Prevent the Same," 6 George IV (28 Mar., 1825), *PP*, 1825, III, 599-601.
NOTE: not enacted.
REFERRED TO: 117n-18n

"A Bill to Regulate the Exercise of the Elective Franchise in Counties at Large, in Ireland," 6 George IV (22 Apr., 1825), *PP*, 1825, III, 85-6.
NOTE: not enacted.
REFERRED TO: 84, 87-91

"Minutes of Evidence Taken before the Select Committee Appointed to Inquire into the Disturbances in Ireland," *PP*, 1825, VII, 1-499. See also William Wrixon Becher, Maxwell Blacker, John Church, Michael Collins, Robert Day, Malachi Duggan, John Richard Elmore, John Leslie Foster, James Lawler, Justin Macarty, William Henry Worth Newenham, John O'Driscol, Richard Simpson, George Warburton, Richard Willcocks.
NOTE: the evidence taken by this Committee was heard in 1824; referred to by JSM as the Commons' Committee of 1824.
REFERRED TO: 66, 82, 87

"Minutes of Evidence Taken before the Select Committee of the House of Lords Appointed to Examine into the Nature and Extent of the Disturbances Which Have Prevailed in Those Districts of Ireland Which Are Now Subject to the Provisions of the Insurrection Act," *PP*, 1825, VII, 501-802. See also William Wrixon Becher, Augustus Frederick Fitzgerald, Alexander Nimmo, Justin Macarty, George Thomas John Nugent, John O'Driscol, Thomas Powell, George Warburton, Richard Willcocks.
NOTE: the evidence taken by this Committee was heard in 1824; referred to by JSM as the Lords' Committee of 1824.
REFERRED TO: 66, 82, 87

"Report from the Select Committee Appointed to Inquire into the State of Ireland, More Particularly with Reference to the Circumstances Which May Have Led to Disturbances in That Part of the United Kingdom," *PP*, 1825, VIII, 4-172. See also Anthony Richard Blake, Dennis Browne, Daniel O'Connell.
NOTE: includes Minutes of Evidence.
REFERRED TO: 66, 82, 87

"Second Report from the Select Committee Appointed to Inquire into the State of Ireland, More Particularly with Reference to the Circumstances Which May Have Led to Disturbances in That Part of the United Kingdom," *PP*, 1825, VIII, 173-292. See also James Warren Doyle, Oliver Kelly, Daniel Murray.
NOTE: includes Minutes of Evidence.
REFERRED TO: 66, 82, 87

"Third Report from the Select Committee Appointed to Inquire into the State of Ireland, More Particularly with Reference to the Circumstances Which May Have Led to Disturbances in That Part of the United Kingdom," *PP*, 1825, VIII, 293-456. See also Richard Bourke, Henry Cooke, Thomas Costello, William Samuel Currey, John Keily, John Staunton Rochfort.
NOTE: includes Minutes of Evidence.
REFERRED TO: 66, 82, 87

"Fourth Report from the Select Committee Appointed to Inquire into the State of Ireland, More Particularly with Reference to the Circumstances Which May Have Led to Disturbances in That Part of the United Kingdom," *PP*, 1825, VIII, 457-855. See also Matthew Barrington, Anthony Richard Blake, John Currie, John Evans-Freke, John Godley, Arthur Irwin Kelly, Randle Patrick Macdonell, Daniel Murray, William O'Brien.
NOTE: includes Minutes of Evidence.
REFERRED TO: 66, 82, 87

"Minutes of Evidence Taken before the Select Committee Appointed to Inquire into the State of Ireland, More Particularly with Reference to the Circumstances Which May Have Led to Disturbances in That Part of the United Kingdom," *PP*, 1825, IX, 1-675. See also Joseph Abbott, Matthew Barrington, Anthony Richard Blake, Richard Bourke, Dominick Browne, Henry Cooke, Robert Day, John Doherty, James Warren Doyle, John Leslie Foster, Arthur Irwin Kelly, George King, William Knox, Thomas Frankland Lewis, John Newport, Daniel O'Connell, Charles Le Poer Trench.
REFERRED TO: 66, 82, 87

"Return of the Number of Persons Confined in the Different Gaols of Great Britain, for Offences against the Game Laws, Specifying Where Any of the Persons So Confined Have Been Put on the Tread Wheel, and by What Authority the Same Has Been Done," *PP*, 1825, XXIII, 565.
REFERRED TO: 107

"An Act to Secure the Independence of the Judges in This Province [Lower Canada], and for Other Purposes Therein Mentioned," 7 George IV (20 Mar., 1826), *PP*, 1830, XXI, 79-81.
NOTE: this bill was sent up to the Legislative Council by the House of Assembly on 20 Mar., 1826, and rejected by it, after a second reading, on 22 Mar., 1826.
REFERRED TO: 433

"A Bill for Granting Relief to Certain Persons Dissenting from the Church of England, in Respect of the Mode of Celebrating Marriage," 8 George IV (14 May, 1827), *PP*, 1826-27, II, 21-4.
NOTE: the reference is to the Unitarian Marriage Bill, which was not enacted.
REFERRED TO: 341

"Correspondence between Great Britain and the United States, Relative to Commercial Intercourse between America and the British West Indies," *PP*, 1826-27, XXV, 21-51.
REVIEWED: 123-47

"Copy of the First Report Made to His Majesty by the Commissioners Appointed to Inquire into the Law of England Respecting Real Property," *PP*, 1829, X, 1-671.
REFERRED TO: 224

"Copy of the Second Report Made to His Majesty by the Commissioners Appointed to Inquire into the Law of England Respecting Real Property," *PP*, 1830, XI, 1-627.
REFERRED TO: 224

"Copy of the Third Report made to His Majesty by the Commissioners Appointed to Inquire into the Law of England Respecting Real Property," *PP*, 1831-32, XXIII, 321-450.
REFERRED TO: 224

"A Bill to Alter and Amend the Laws Relating to the Temporalities of the Church in Ireland," 3 William IV (11 Mar., 1833), *PP*, 1833, I, 339-415.
NOTE: subsequently enacted as 3 & 4 William IV, c. 37 (1833).
REFERRED TO: 347

"A Bill Intituled an Act for Establishing Courts of Local Jurisdiction," 3 William IV (28 Mar., 1833), *House of Lords Sessional Papers*, 1833, CCCXIV, 205-38.
NOTE: not enacted.
REFERRED TO: 153, 153n

"A Bill for Establishing a General Register for All Deeds and Instruments Affecting Real Property in England and Wales," 3 William IV (13 May, 1833), *PP*, 1833, III, 489-540.
REFERRED TO: 180

"A Bill to Effect a Commutation of Tithes in England and Wales," 3 William IV (17 May, 1833), *PP*, 1833, IV, 431-73.
NOTE: not enacted.
REFERRED TO: 196-7

"Copy of the Fourth Report Made to His Majesty by the Commissioners Appointed to Inquire into the Law of England Respecting Real Property," *PP*, 1833, XXII, 1-194.
REFERRED TO: 224

"Petition from the Inhabitants of Liverpool for Repeal of the Corn Laws" (5 Feb., 1834). In "First Report of the Select Committee of the House of Commons on Public Petitions," *Reports of the Select Committee of the House of Commons on Public Petitions*, 1834, 4.
REFERRED TO: 193

"A Bill to Secure the Liberty of the Press," 4 William IV (25 Feb., 1834), *PP*, 1834, III, 449-53.
NOTE: not enacted.
REFERRED TO: 165, 166, 192

"A Bill to Abolish Compositions for Tithes in Ireland, and to Substitute in Lieu Thereof a Land Tax, and to Provide for the Redemption of the Same," 4 William IV (27 Feb., 1834), *PP*, 1834, IV, 241-303.
NOTE: not enacted.
REFERRED TO: 168-70, 188n, 262-3, 276-7

"A Bill for Granting Relief in Relation to the Celebration of Marriages to Certain Persons Dissenting from the United Church of England and Ireland," 4 William IV (10 Mar., 1834), *PP*, 1834, II, 147-59.
NOTE: the reference at 323 is to pre-1836 marriage bills, of which this was one; the Bill was not enacted.
REFERRED TO: 195, 232, 323

"A Bill for the Public Registering of All Deeds, Conveyances, Wills and Other Incumbrances That Shall Be Made of or That May Affect Any Honors, Manors, Lands, Tenements or Hereditaments within the Several Counties of England and Wales," 4 William IV (13 Mar., 1834), *PP*, 1834, III, 563-88.
NOTE: one of the two land registration bills referred to by JSM, neither of which was enacted.
REFERRED TO: 222-4

"A Bill for Establishing a General Register for All Deeds and Instruments Affecting Real Property in England and Wales," 4 William IV (14 Mar., 1834), *PP*, 1834, III, 591-639.
NOTE: one of the two land registration bills referred to by JSM, neither of which was enacted.
REFERRED TO: 222-4

"Petition from Resident Members of the Senate of the University of Cambridge to Open the University to Dissenters" (21 Mar., 1834), *Journals of the House of Lords*, LXVI, 88.
REFERRED TO: 196

"A Bill for the Commutation and Redemption of Tithes in England and Wales," 4 William IV (17 Apr., 1834), *PP*, 1834, IV, 193-234.
NOTE: not enacted.
REFERRED TO: 196-9

"A Bill to Remove Certain Disabilities Which Prevent Some Classes of His Majesty's Subjects from Resorting to the Universities of England, and Proceeding to Degrees Therein," 4 William IV (21 Apr., 1834), *PP*, 1834, IV, 515-17.
NOTE: not enacted.
REFERRED TO: 259-60, 276

"A Bill for the Relief of His Majesty's Subjects Professing the Jewish Religion," 4 William IV (25 Apr., 1834), *PP*, 1834, II, 587-8.
NOTE: not enacted.
REFERRED TO: 192, 276

"A Bill Intituled an Act for the Better Observance of the Lord's Day, and for the More Effectual Prevention of Drunkenness," 4 William IV (6 May, 1834), *House of Lords Sessional Papers*, 1834, [n.s.,] I, Pt. 1, 227-32.
NOTE: not enacted.
REFERRED TO: 235

"A Bill to Establish a General Register of Births, Deaths and Marriages in England," 4 William IV (14 May, 1834), *PP*, 1834, III, 459-77.
NOTE: introduced by William Brougham; not enacted. See also "A Bill for Registering Births, Deaths and Marriages in England," 6 William IV (17 Feb., 1836).
REFERRED TO: 196, 231, 232

"Petition of Persons of Christian Faith Resident in Edinburgh for Removal of Jewish Disabilities" (12 June, 1834), *Journals of the House of Lords*, LXVI, 580.
REFERRED TO: 251

"A Bill for the Abolition of Church Rates, and to Make Provision for the Necessary Repair of Parish Churches and Chapels, and for the Decent Performance of Divine Service Therein," 4 William IV (19 June, 1834), *PP*, 1834, I, 615-26.
NOTE: not enacted.
REFERRED TO: 211

"A Bill Intituled an Act to Alter and Amend the Appellate Jurisdiction of the House of Lords, and for Certain Other Purposes," 4 William IV (14 Aug., 1834), *House of Lords Sessional Papers*, 1834, [n.s.,] I, Pt. 2, 1265-70.
NOTE: not enacted.
REFERRED TO: 277-8

"Report from the Select Committee on the State of Education; with the Minutes of Evidence, and Index," *PP*, 1834, IX, 1-261.
REFERRED TO: 254

"Report from the Committee of Privileges," *PP*, 1834, XI, 313-16.
NOTE: the reference is to the Select Committee appointed to investigate Mr. Sheil (JSM spells the name "Shiel").
REFERRED TO: 156

"Second Report from the Select Committee on the Business of the House," *PP*, 1834, XI, 321-3.
QUOTED: 248

"Report from the Select Committee on Divisions of the House," *PP*, 1834, XI, 325-8.
REFERRED TO: 158

"Report from His Majesty's Commissioners for Inquiring into the Administration and Practical Operation of the Poor Laws," *PP*, 1834, XXVII; Appendix (A.), "Reports of Assistant Commissioners," XXVIII-XXIX; Appendix (B.1.), "Answers to Rural Queries," XXX-XXXIII; Appendix (B.2), "Answers to Town Queries," XXXIV-XXXVI; Appendix (C.), "Communications," XXXVII; Appendix (D.), "Labour Rate," XXXVIII, 1-221; Appendix (E.), "Vagrancy," XXXVIII, 223-319; Appendix (F.), "Foreign Communications," XXXVIII, 321-XXXIX, 862.
REFERRED TO: 172, 201, 203-5, 252

"A Bill Concerning the Marriages of Persons Not Being Members of the United Church of England and Ireland, and Objecting to Be Married According to the Rite Thereof," 5 William IV (30 Mar., 1835), *PP*, 1835, III, 413-21.
NOTE: the reference is to pre-1836 marriage bills, of which this was one; the Bill was not enacted.
REFERRED TO: 323

"A Bill for the Better Regulation of Ecclesiastical Revenues, and the Promotion of Religious and Moral Instruction in Ireland," 6 William IV (7 July, 1835), *PP*, 1835, II, 379-427.
NOTE: not enacted.
REFERRED TO: 301

"A Bill to Provide for the Nomination and Appointment of Parish and Township Officers, within the Seigniories and Townships of This Province" (14 Dec., 1835), *Journals of the House of Assembly of Lower Canada*, 1835-36, 277.
NOTE: the reference is in a quotation from *Parliamentary Papers*. Cf. Roebuck's account in *The Canadian Portfolio*, No. 3, 12 Jan., 1838, 72-3 and 102. The Bill was passed by the House of Assembly of Lower Canada on 14 Dec., 1835, but was rejected by the Legislative Council. See also *Journals of the Legislative Council of the Province of Lower Canada*, 1835-36, 114, 123, 232, 269.
REFERRED TO: 423

"First Report from the Select Committee of the House of Lords, Appointed to Inquire into the Expediency of Substituting Declarations in Lieu of Oaths; and to Whom Leave Was Given to Report from Time to Time to the House: Together with the Minutes of Evidence Taken before the Committee, and an Appendix and Index Thereto," *PP*, 1835, XIV, 399-520.
NOTE: the Committee met and heard evidence during the 1834 session but did not issue its Report until the following year.
REFERRED TO: 188n

"First Report from His Majesty's Commissioners Appointed to Consider the State of the Established Church with Reference to Ecclesiastical Duties and Revenues," *PP*, 1835, XXII, 1-14.
REFERRED TO: 325

"First Report of the Commissioners Appointed to Inquire into the Municipal Corporations in England and Wales," *PP*, 1835, XXIII-XXVI.
REFERRED TO: 402

"First Report from His Majesty's Commissioners for Inquiring into the Condition of the Poorer Classes in Ireland," *PP*, 1835, XXXII.
REFERRED TO: 402

"A Bill to Authorize the Consolidation of the Trusts of Turnpike Roads in That Part of Great Britain Called England," 6 William IV (9 Feb., 1836), *PP*, 1836, VI, 427-39.
NOTE: not enacted.
REFERRED TO: 324

"A Bill for the Commutation of Tithes in England," 6 William IV (11 Feb., 1836), *PP*, 1836, VI, 125-44.
NOTE: the reference is to the Tithe Bill, subsequently enacted as 6 & 7 William IV, c. 71 (1836).
REFERRED TO: 325

"A Bill for the Regulation of Municipal Corporations and Borough Towns in Ireland," 6 William IV (16 Feb., 1836), *PP*, 1836, II, 549-627.
NOTE: not enacted.
REFERRED TO: 324

"A Bill for Registering Births, Deaths and Marriages in England," 6 William IV (17 Feb., 1836), *PP*, 1836, I, 309-26.
NOTE: enacted as 6 & 7 William IV, c. 86 (1836).
REFERRED TO: 323

"A Bill for Marriages in England," 6 William IV (17 Feb., 1836), *PP*, 1836, I, 393-401.
NOTE: the reference is to the Marriage Bill, subsequently enacted as 6 & 7 William IV, c. 85 (1836).
REFERRED TO: 323

"An Act to Continue for a Limited Time the Acts Relating to the Incorporations of the Cities of Quebec and Montreal," 5 & 6 William IV (Lower Canada), (12 Mar., 1836), *Journals of the House of Assembly of Lower Canada*, 1835-36, 691.
NOTE: see under Statutes, Canadian, the note to 2 William IV, c. 52 (Lower Canada).
REFERRED TO: 424

"A Bill for Carrying into Effect the Fourth Report of the Commissioners Appointed to Consider the State of the Established Church in England and Wales, with Reference to Ecclesiastical Duties and Revenues," 7 William IV (8 July, 1836), *PP*, 1836, I, 621-31.
NOTE: the reference is to the Church Reform Bill, subsequently enacted as 6 & 7 William IV, c. 77 (1836).
REFERRED TO: 325

"A Bill to Reduce the Stamp Duties Payable on Newspapers, and to Consolidate and Amend the Laws Relating to the Duties on Newspapers and Advertisements Respectively," 7 William IV (19 July, 1836), *PP*, 1836, V, 821-53.
NOTE: the reference is to the Newspaper Stamp Bill, subsequently enacted as 6 & 7 William IV, c. 54 (1836).
REFERRED TO: 326

"Report from the Select Committee on the Record Commission; Together with the Minutes of Evidence, Appendix, and Index," *PP*, 1836, XVI.
NOTE: the reference is to Buller's disclosure of the incompetence and abuses of the Commissioners of Public Records; Buller moved the appointment of the Select Committee and acted as its chairman. See also Buller.
REFERRED TO: 324

"Third Report of the Commissioners for Inquiring into the Condition of the Poorer Classes in Ireland," *PP*, 1836, XXX.
NOTE: although the "Second Report" was written before the "Third," and printed in the same year, it did not appear in the *Parliamentary Papers* until 1837.
REFERRED TO: 402, 509

"Second Report from His Majesty's Commissioners Appointed to Consider the State of the Established Church with Reference to Ecclesiastical Duties and Revenues," *PP*, 1836, XXXVI, 1-44.
REFERRED TO: 325

"Third Report from His Majesty's Commissioners Appointed to Consider the State of the Established Church with Reference to Ecclesiastical Duties and Revenues," *PP*, 1836, XXXVI, 47-60.
REFERRED TO: 325

"Fourth Report from His Majesty's Commissioners Appointed to Consider the State of the Established Church with Reference to Ecclesiastical Duties and Revenues," *PP*, 1836, XXXVI, 65-78.
REFERRED TO: 325

"A Bill for the Regulation of Municipal Corporations and Borough Towns in Ireland," 7 William IV (8 Feb., 1837), *PP*, 1837, II, 333-418.
NOTE: not enacted.
REFERRED TO: 393

Papers Relative to the Affairs of Lower Canada. Ordered by the House of Commons to Be Printed, 20 Feb., 1837. In *PP*, 1837, XLII, 413-56.
REVIEWED: 405-35

Copies or Extracts of Correspondence Relative to the Affairs of Lower Canada. Ordered by the House of Commons to Be Printed, 23 Dec., 1837. In *PP*, 1837-38, XXXIX, 317-432.
NOTE: for the quotation at 418 see Charles Grant, "Copy of a Despatch"; for that at 422 see Archibald Acheson, "Copy of a Despatch."
REVIEWED: 405-35
QUOTED: 418, 422
REFERRED TO: 419n

"Reports from the Select Committee on the Poor Law Amendment Act," *PP*, 1837, XVII.
NOTE: there are twenty-two reports, all included in Vol. XVII. JSM's reference is to the "two Commissions of Poor Law Inquiry for Ireland and England"; the body examining the condition of the poor in Ireland was a Royal Commission; in England, the inquiry was conducted by this Select Committee, which JSM probably has in mind.
REFERRED TO: 402

"First Report of the Commissioners Appointed to Inquire into the Grievances Complained of in Lower Canada," *PP*, 1837, XXIV, 3-38.
NOTE: the references are to the Reports of the Canada Commissioners.
REFERRED TO: 421-2, 429, 457

"Second Report of the Commissioners Appointed to Inquire into the Grievances Complained of in Lower Canada," *PP*, 1837, XXIV, 85-104.
NOTE: the references at 421-2, 429, and 457 are to the Reports of the Canada Commissioners. For the quotations at 428 and 431, see George Gipps, "Extract."
QUOTED: 428, 431
REFERRED TO: 421-2, 426, 429, 431, 457

"Third Report of the Commissioners Appointed to Inquire into the Grievances Complained of in Lower Canada," *PP*, 1837, XXIV, 105-36.
NOTE: the references are to the Reports of the Canada Commissioners.
QUOTED: 424
REFERRED TO: 421-2, 429, 457

424.9 "tendency] In the first place, we think it much to be regretted that, at the time of conferring the Constitution on Canada, although the separation between the functions of the Legislative and Executive Council was duly recognised, yet the faulty practice of making them nearly identical, as to personal composition, was still adhered to; and that, whilst two-thirds of the Executive Council were selected from one branch of the Legislature, the expediency does not seem to have been felt of taking any members from the other, so that the Executive Authority thus early showed a tendency (106)

424.10-11 people," . . . "in . . . times."] people; a bias which, lasting, as it has done, in . . . times, cannot but have exercised a most unfavourable influence on the course of affairs. (106)

"Fourth Report of the Commissioners Appointed to Inquire into the Grievances Complained of in Lower Canada," *PP*, 1837, XXIV, 137-9.
NOTE: the references are to the Reports of the Canada Commissioners.
REFERRED TO: 421-2, 429, 457

"Fifth Report of the Commissioners Appointed to Inquire into the Grievances Complained of in Lower Canada," *PP*, 1837, XXIV, 141-80.
NOTE: the references are to the Reports of the Canada Commissioners.
REFERRED TO: 421-2, 429, 457

"General Report of the Commissioners Appointed to Inquire into the Grievances Complained of in Lower Canada," *PP*, 1837, XXIV, 183-416.
NOTE: the references at 421-2, 429, and 457 are to the Reports of the Canada Commissioners. See also Charles Edward Grey.
QUOTED: 422-3, 424, 424n, 426, 427, 429n-30n
REFERRED TO: 421-2, 429, 429n-30n, 432, 457
422.25   The] 9. [9th para. of Section I] The (187)
422.26   consigned] assigned (187)
422.35   For] 10. [10th para. of Section I] For (188)
422.37   which] that (188)
423.5   for a] for the (188)
423.17   In] 11. [11th para. of Section I] In (188)
424n.11 "In] We cannot help making these remarks, because we think that, in (227)
424n.13-14 everything, the] everything and the (227)
424n.14 and their] and that their (227)
426.16   "Under] We will even say, that under (189)
426.17   conceive" . . . "that] conceive that (189)
426.18-21 election." . . . "cannot . . . now," . . . "the concession . . . which would] election; by appointing a class of electors with a raised qualification, and also providing, in order to secure a due permanence of interest in the Province, that the individuals to be elected should be possessed of a substantial quantity of real estate; but we cannot . . . now. [*paragraph*] 16. [16th para. of Section I] The division of parties, confirmed as it is, and rendered conspicuous and more likely to last, by a difference of race, the violence that has been aroused, the almost uncontrollable power the measure would confer on the party which has lately risen into so great ascendancy, but has not yet, we fear, learned to enjoy its advantage with moderation; all are facts which combine to make us think it undesirable that an Elective Council should be bestowed upon Lower Canada. The concession . . . which, we have no hesitation in saying, would (189)
427.21   If we] If, on the other hand, we (189)
427.21   inquire," say they, "in] inquire in (189)
429n.9-10   "We believe," . . . "that] 5. [5th para. of Section IV] We believe, however, that (216)
429n.19 "exhibited] A Committee of Assembly, also, in 1834, in a Report to which we shall advert more particularly hereafter, exhibited (216)
429n.20 tenure;"] tenure. (216)
429n.21-3 "just . . . views more than ten years ago," . . . "to . . . age,"] 19. [19th para. of Section V] Seeing, then, the just . . . views expressed by the Assembly more than 10 years ago, we think it fair to presume that the want of any satisfactory provisions on this important subject should be attributed to the state of political dissension in which the Province has continued since 1823, and to the fact that the question has unfortunately always been considered one of party, rather than to a desire in any part of the Legislature to . . . age and the wants of the people. (224)
429n.27 "that . . . seigneur."] 3dly. [third complaint against Canada Tenures Act] That . . . seigneur, whilst it did very little for the censitaire, as the latter could not under it demand a commutation of tenure, except in cases where his seigneur had previously commuted with the Crown; also, that it went to deprive the censitaire of a right which he formerly possessed to claim any unconceded lands in a seigneury on the same terms as those on which lands had previously been conceded; and further, that in cases where the seigneury was held in mortmain, it afforded no hope to the censitaire of ever being able to obtain a commutation, for a surrender of the estate into the hands of the Crown being a necessary preliminary to its being regranted in free and common soccage, and the seigneurs holding in mortmain

being precluded from making such a surrender by their inability to alienate, they could never take advantage of the Act. (216-17)

429n.36   "simple, expeditious, and cheap,"] The modes of conveyance under the French customs are simple, expeditious and cheap, and if they were open to objection on the score of secrecy, that objection is removed in the townships by the establishment of a system of registry under the Provincial Act 10 & 11 Geo. 4, c. 8. (214)

430n.3-4   "The people . . . continent," . . . "greatly prefer the equal division, which existed under the French law;"] We may also state, that the French rules of descent are much preferred to the law of primogeniture by the people . . . Continent. (214)

"Second Report of the Commissioners for Inquiring into the Condition of the Poorer Classes in Ireland," *PP*, 1837, XXXI, 587-94.
NOTE: although written and printed in 1836, this report did not appear in the *Parliamentary Papers* until 1837, a year after the "Third Report."
REFERRED TO: 402

Copies or Extracts of Correspondence Relative to the Affairs of Lower Canada, Upper Canada, Nova Scotia, and New Brunswick. Ordered by the House of Commons to Be Printed, 10 Jan., 1838. In *PP*, 1837-38, XXXIX, 433-52.
REVIEWED: 405-35

"A Bill to Make Temporary Provision for the Government of Lower Canada" (17 Jan., 1838), *PP*, 1837-38, I, 253-6.
NOTE: enacted as 1 Victoria, c. 9 (10 Feb., 1838).
REVIEWED: 405-35

"A Bill to Abolish Compositions for Tithes in Ireland, and to Substitute Rent-Charges in Lieu Thereof," 1 Victoria (13 June, 1838), *PP*, 1837-38, VI, 443-66.
NOTE: the reference is to the government's expected Tithe Bill, which was subsequently enacted as 1 & 2 Victoria, c. 109.
REFERRED TO: 394

"Papers Relating to Lower Canada," *PP*, 1837-38, XXXIX, 913-17.
NOTE: see also John George Lambton.
QUOTED: 442
REFERRED TO: 439-42

"Report on the Affairs of British North America, from the Earl of Durham," *PP*, 1839, XVII, 1-690.
NOTE: the references are to the Report as a prospective document.
REFERRED TO: 425, 457-9

"Report from the Select Committee of the House of Lords Appointed to Consider the Law of Defamation and Libel, and to Report Thereon to the House; with the Minutes of Evidence Taken before the Committee, and an Index," *PP*, 1843, V, 259-458.
NOTE: the Commons Select Committee of 1834, referred to by JSM, met and took evidence, but did not issue a Report; the 1843 Lords' Committee, cited above, includes, as Appendix A (277-96), Brougham's testimony before the 1834 Committee, testimony which JSM presumably read in the Newspapers. See also Henry Peter Brougham.
REFERRED TO: 261

"Minutes of Evidence Taken by the Select Committee on Tenure and Improvement of Land (Ireland) Act," *PP*, 1865, XI, 353-573.
REFERRED TO: 530

"A Bill to Confirm a Provisional Order under 'The Drainage and Improvements of Lands (Ireland) Act, 1863,' and the Acts Amending the Same," 31 Victoria (22 Nov., 1867), *PP*, 1867-68, II, 193-7.
NOTE: enacted as 31 Victoria, c. 3 (7 Dec., 1867).
REFERRED TO: 531

BIBLIOGRAPHIC INDEX OF PERSONS AND WORKS CITED 655

"Report of the Commissioners Appointed to Inspect the Accounts and Examine the Works of Railways in Ireland, Made to the Lords Commissioners of Her Majesty's Treasury," *PP*, 1867-68, XXXII, 469-646.
REFERRED TO: 531

"Second Report of the Commissioners Appointed to Inspect the Accounts and Examine the Works of Railways in Ireland, Made to the Lords Commissioners of Her Majesty's Treasury," *PP*, 1868-69, XVII, 459-528.
REFERRED TO: 531

STATUTES

Following the British statutes, those of the United States, Austro-Hungary, Canada, France, and Scotland are listed; each list is chronological. In the British section information is taken from the *Statutes at Large*; where the *Statutes of the Realm*, which cover the period through Queen Anne's reign, do not corroborate such information, the difference is noted.

25 Edward III, Stat. 5, c. 2. An Act for Declaration of Treasons (1350).
NOTE: dated 1351-52 in *Statutes of the Realm*.
REFERRED TO: 415

4 Henry VII, c. 19. An Act for Maintenance of Husbandry (1487).
REFERRED TO: 19-20

35 Elizabeth, c. 6. An Act against Converting of Great Houses into Several Tenements, and for Restraint of Inmates and Inclosures, in and near about the City of London and Westminster (1593).
NOTE: dated 1592-93 in *Statutes of the Realm*.
REFERRED TO: 19-20

43 Elizabeth, c. 2. An Act for the Reliefe of the Poore (1601).
NOTE: see also 4 & 5 William IV, c. 76.
REFERRED TO: 257-8, 399

21 James I, c.3. An Act Concerning Monopolies and Dispensations with Penal Laws and the Forfeitures Thereof (1623).
NOTE: dated 1623-24 in *Statutes of the Realm*.
REFERRED TO: 11

21 James I, c. 34. An Act for Three Intire Subsidies, and Three Fifteens and Tenths Granted by the Temporalty (1623).
NOTE: listed as c. 33 and dated 1623-24 in *Statutes of the Realm*.
REFERRED TO: 12

1 Charles I, c. 6. An Act for Two Intire Subsidies Granted by the Temporalty (1625).
REFERRED TO: 12

3 Charles I, c. 1. The Petition Exhibited to His Majesty by the Lords Spiritual and Temporal and Commons in This Present Parliament Assembled, Concerning Divers Rights and Liberties of the Subjects (1627).
REFERRED TO: 17, 17-18, 38

3 Charles I, c. 7. An Act for Five Subsidies Granted by the Temporalty (1627).
NOTE: listed as c. 8 in *Statutes of the Realm*.
REFERRED TO: 17

16 Charles I, c. 1. An Act for the Preventing of Inconveniences Happening by the Long Intermission of Parliament (1640).
REFERRED TO: 30

16 Charles I, c. 7. An Act to Prevent Inconveniences by the Untimely Adjournment of Parliaments (1640).
REFERRED TO: 35

16 Charles I, c. 8. An Act for a Subsidy Granted to the King of Tonnage, Poundage and Other Sums Payable upon Merchandize Exported and Imported (1640).
REFERRED TO: 29

16 Charles I, c. 10. An Act for Regulating of the Privy Council, and for Taking Away the Court Commonly Called the Star-Chamber (1640).
REFERRED TO: 35

16 Charles I, c. 11. An Act for a Repeal of a Branch of a Statute Primo Elizabethae, Concerning Commissioners for Causes Ecclesiastical (1640).
REFERRED TO: 35

16 Charles I, c. 14. An Act for the Declaring Unlawful and Void the Late Proceedings Touching Ship-Money, and for the Vacating of All Records and Process Concerning the Same (1640).
REFERRED TO: 29

16 Charles I, c. 20. An Act for the Prevention of Vexatious Proceedings Touching the Order of Knighthood (1640).
REFERRED TO: 29

16 Charles I, c. 27. An Act for the Disinabling All Persons in Holy Orders to Exercise Any Temporal Jurisdiction or Authority (1640).
REFERRED TO: 45

16 Charles I, c. 28. An Act for the Raising of Soldiers for the Defence of England and Ireland (1640).
REFERRED TO: 38, 45

16 Charles I, Private Acts, c. 1. An Act for the Attainder of Thomas Earl of Strafford of High Treason (1640).
NOTE: listed as c. 38 in *Statutes of the Realm*.
REFERRED TO: 33, 33n, 34, 35

An Act for Abolishing the House of Peers (19 Mar., 1649). In *Acts and Ordinances of the Interregnum, 1642-1660*. Ed. Charles Harding Firth and Robert Sangster Rait. 3 vols. London: HMSO, 1911, II, 24.
REFERRED TO: 56

An Act for the Advancing and Regulating of the Trade of the Commonwealth (1 Aug., 1650). *Ibid.*, II, 403-6.
REFERRED TO: 56

An Act for Turning the Books of the Law, and All Proces and Proceedings in Courts of Justice, into English (22 Nov., 1650). *Ibid.*, II, 455-6.
REFERRED TO: 56

12 Charles II, c. 18. An Act for the Encouraging and Increasing of Shipping and Navigation (1660).
NOTE: the references are to the Navigation Laws.
REFERRED TO: 124, 138

13 Charles II, second session, c. 1. An Act for the Well-Governing and Regulating of Corporations (1661).
NOTE: the references, with the exception of that at 377 to the Test Acts, are to Catholic Disabilities.
REFERRED TO: 62-8, 377

15 Charles II, c. 7. An Act for the Encouragement of Trade (1663).
NOTE: the references are to the Navigation Laws.
REFERRED TO: 124, 138

22 & 23 Charles II, c. 25. An Act for the Better Preservation of the Game, and for Securing Warrens Not Inclosed, and the Several Fishings of This Realm (1670).
NOTE: the references are to the Game Laws.
REFERRED TO: 99-120, 213, 340, 483-4

25 Charles II, c. 2. An Act for Preventing Dangers Which May Happen from Popish Recusants (1672).
NOTE: the references, with the exception of that at 377 to the Test Laws, are to Catholic Disabilities.
REFERRED TO: 62-8, 377

30 Charles II, second session, c. 1. An Act for the More Effectual Preserving the King's Person and Government, by Disabling Papists from Sitting in Either House of Parliament (1677) [1678].
NOTE: the references are to Catholic Disabilities; the act is cited in *Statutes of the Realm* for the year 1678, the correct year of its enactment.
REFERRED TO: 62-8

1 William and Mary, second session, c. 2. An Act for Declaring the Rights and Liberties of the Subject, and Settling the Succession of the Crown (1688).
REFERRED TO: 78

7 & 8 William III, c. 27. An Act for the Better Security of His Majesty's Royal Person and Government (1696).
NOTE: the references are to Catholic Disabilities.
REFERRED TO: 62-8

8 William III, c. 4. An Act to Attaint Sir John Fenwick Baronet of High Treason (1696).
NOTE: listed as 8 & 9 William III, c. 4. (1696-97) in *Statutes of the Realm*.
REFERRED TO: 33n

11 & 12 William III, c. 2. An Act for Granting an Aid to His Majesty, by Sale of the Forfeited and Other Estates and Interests in Ireland, and by a Land Tax in England, for the Several Purposes Therein Mentioned (1700).
NOTE: the reference is to the "last confiscations" in Ireland; presumably JSM had in mind the Williamite confiscation, the key legislative enactment of which was this Act, generally known as the Act of Resumption. Cited in *Statutes of the Realm* as 11 William III, c. 2 (1698-99). The year of enactment was 1700.
REFERRED TO: 513

5 & 6 Anne, c. 5. An Act for Securing the Church of England as by Law Established (1706).
NOTE: the quotation, "religion by law established," derives from statutes such as this; cited in *Statutes of the Realm* as 6 Anne, c. 8 (1707). The quotation at 491 is indirect.
QUOTED: 271, 491

6 Anne, c. 6. An Act for Rendring the Union of the Two Kingdoms More Intire and Compleat (1707).
NOTE: the reference is to the Act of Union with Scotland; cited in *Statutes of the Realm* as 6 Anne, c. 40 (1707).
REFERRED TO: 78

9 Anne, c. 5. An Act for Securing the Freedom of Parliaments, by the Further Qualifying the Members to Sit in the House of Commons (1710).
NOTE: the reference is to the oath taken by members of Parliament that they possessed land worth a certain value per annum.
REFERRED TO: 184

10 Anne, c. 19. An Act for Laying Several Duties upon All Sope and Paper Made in Great Britain, or Imported into the Same; and upon Chequered or Striped Linens Imported; and

upon Certain Silks, Callicoes, Linens, and Stuffs, Printed, Painted, or Stained; and Several Kinds of Stampt Vellum, Parchment, and Paper; and upon Certain Printed Papers, Pamphlets, and Advertisements; for Raising the Sum of Eighteen Hundred Thousand Pounds by Way of Lottery towards Her Majesty's Supply; and for Licensing an Additional Number of Hackney Chairs; and for Charging Certain Stocks of Cards and Dice; and for Better Securing Her Majesty's Duties to Arise in the Office for the Stampt Duties by Licenses for Marriages and Otherwise; and for Relief of Persons Who Have Not Claimed Their Lottery Tickets in Due Time, or Have Lost Exchequer Bills, or Lottery Tickets; and for Borrowing Money upon Stock (Part of the Capital of the South Sea Company) for the Use of the Publick (1711).

NOTE: the references are to the "taxes on knowledge." Cited in *Statutes of the Realm* as 10 Anne, c. 19 (1711).

REFERRED TO: 261, 298

12 Anne, second session, c. 16. An Act to Reduce the Rate of Interest, Without Any Prejudice to Parliamentary Securities (1713).

NOTE: cited in *Statutes of the Realm* as 13 Anne, c. 15 (1714). The reference is to the Usury Laws, of which this was the most significant. 3 & 4 William IV, c. 98 (1833); 5 & 6 William IV, c. 41 (1835); and 1 Victoria, c. 80 (1837) substantially reduced the application of this statute, which was repealed, together with all other usury legislation, by 17 & 18 Victoria, c. 90 (1854).

REFERRED TO: 224, 471

5 George I, c. 27. An Act to Prevent the Inconveniences Arising from Seducing Artificers in the Manufactures of Great Britain into Foreign Parts (1718).

NOTE: in addition to providing penalties against those found guilty of enticing workmen abroad, this statute also imposed penalties, including loss of lands and citizenship, on any artificer "going into a foreign country, there to exercise his trade." Further legislation dealing with this question included 23 George II, c. 13 (1750); 22 George III, c. 60 (1782); and 25 George III, c. 67 (1785). All these statutes were repealed by 5 George IV, c. 97 (1824).

REFERRED TO: 219

37 George III, c. 45. An Act for Confirming and Continuing, for a Limited Time, the Restriction Contained in the Minute of Council of the 26th February, 1797, on Payments of Cash by the Bank (3 May, 1797).

NOTE: the reference is in a quotation from JSM's "The Currency Juggle" (*q.v.*); see also 37 George III, c. 91 (1797).

REFERRED TO: 175

37 George III, c. 91. An Act to Continue, for a Limited Time, an Act, Made in This Present Session of Parliament, Intituled, An Act for Confirming and Continuing, for a Limited Time, the Restriction Contained in the Minute of Council of the 26th February, 1797, on Payments of Cash by the Bank, under Certain Regulations and Restrictions (22 June, 1797).

NOTE: the reference is in a quotation from JSM's "The Currency Juggle," *q.v.*

REFERRED TO: 175

39 & 40 George III, c. 67. An Act for the Union of Great Britain and Ireland (2 July, 1800).

REFERRED TO: 97-8, 153, 214, 215

39 & 40 George III, c. 106. An Act to Repeal an Act Passed in the Last Session of Parliament, Intituled, An Act to Prevent Unlawful Combinations of Workmen; and to Substitute Other Provisions in Lieu Thereof (29 July, 1800).

NOTE: this was the most important Act to prevent combinations of workmen. It was repealed by 5 George IV, c. 95 (1824), and certain of its provisions were reintroduced by 6 George IV, c. 129 (1825).

REFERRED TO: 210

55 George III, c. 26. An Act to Amend the Laws Now in Force for Regulating the Importation of Corn (23 Mar., 1815).

NOTE: see also 3 George IV, c. 60 (1822); 7 & 8 George IV, c. 57 (1827); and 9 George IV, c. 60 (1828), all relevant to the period covered in the reference.
REFERRED TO: 340

57 George III, c. 19. An Act for the More Effectually Preventing Seditious Meetings and Assemblies (31 Mar., 1817).
NOTE: the references are to the statute under which the Dorsetshire labourers were charged; clause 25 deemed guilty of unlawful combination any society whose members took an oath "not required or authorized by Law."
REFERRED TO: 207, 209

57 George III, c. 90. An Act for the Prevention of Persons Going Armed by Night for the Destruction of Game; and for Repealing an Act, Made in the Last Session of Parliament, Relating to Rogues and Vagabonds (10 July, 1817).
NOTE: the references are to the Game Laws.
REFERRED TO: 101-20, 213, 340, 483

59 George III, c. 49. An Act to Continue the Restrictions Contained in Several Acts on Payments in Cash by the Bank of England until the 1st May 1823, and to Provide for the Gradual Resumption of Such Payments; and to Permit the Exportation of Gold and Silver (2 July, 1819).
NOTE: the reference is in a quotation from JSM's "The Currency Juggle," *q.v.*
REFERRED TO: 176

1 & 2 George IV, c. 37. An Act to Repeal the Duties of Customs on the Importation into Great Britain of Certain Sorts of Wood and Timber, and Certain Drawbacks or Allowances in Respect of Such Duties, and to Grant Other Duties and Drawbacks in Lieu Thereof (28 May, 1821).
NOTE: the reference is to the Timber Duties; this statute was completed and amended by 1 & 2 George IV, c. 84 (1821), *q.v.*
REFERRED TO: 153n

1 & 2 George IV, c. 84. An Act to Grant Duties of Customs on Certain Articles of Wood Imported into Great Britain, in Lieu of Former Duties; and to Amend an Act Made in the Fifty Ninth Year of His Late Majesty, for Granting Certain Duties of Customs in Great Britain (2 July, 1821).
NOTE: the reference is to the Timber Duties; this statute completed and amended 1 & 2 George IV, c. 37 (1821), *q.v.*
REFERRED TO: 153n

3 George IV, c. 1. An Act to Suppress Insurrections and Prevent Disturbance of the Public Peace in Ireland, until the First Day of August One Thousand Eight Hundred and Twenty Two (11 Feb., 1822).
NOTE: the reference is in a quotation from Doherty's address to the Jury in the Case of *Lawrence v. Dempster*. The Act was continued by 4 George IV, c. 58 (1823), and further continued (and amended) by 5 George IV, c. 105 (1824).
REFERRED TO: 94n-5n

3 George IV, c. 44. An Act to Regulate the Trade between His Majesty's Possessions in America and the West Indies, and Other Places in America and the West Indies (24 June, 1822).
NOTE: the reference at 140 is in a quotation from Huskisson.
REFERRED TO: 123-6, 140-6

3 George IV, c. 60. An Act to Amend the Laws Relating to the Importation of Corn (15 July, 1822).
NOTE: the reference at 178, in a quotation from T.P. Thompson, is to the Corn Laws; when Thompson first wrote (1827), this Act was presumably in his mind. For other Corn Laws, see 55

George III, c. 26 (1815); 7 & 8 George IV, c. 57 (1827); and 9 George IV, c. 60 (1828) (all included in the reference at 340).
REFERRED TO: 178, 340

4 George IV, c. 77. An Act to Authorize His Majesty, under Certain Circumstances, to Regulate the Duties and Drawbacks on Goods Imported or Exported in Foreign Vessels; and to Exempt Certain Foreign Vessels from Pilotage (18 July, 1823).
NOTE: the reference is to "several recent" reciprocity Acts.
REFERRED TO: 123

5 George IV, c. 1. An Act to Indemnify All Persons Concerned in Advising, Issuing or Acting under a Certain Order in Council, for Regulating the Tonnage Duties on Certain Foreign Vessels; and to Amend an Act of the Last Session of Parliament, for Authorizing His Majesty, under Certain Circumstances, to Regulate the Duties and Drawbacks on Goods Imported or Exported in Any Foreign Vessels (5 Mar., 1824).
NOTE: the reference is to "several recent" reciprocity Acts.
REFERRED TO: 123

5 George IV, c. 83. An Act for the Punishment of Idle and Disorderly Persons, and Rogues and Vagabonds, in That Part of Great Britain Called England (21 June, 1824).
REFERRED TO: 119

6 George IV, c. 4. An Act to Amend Certain Laws Relating to Unlawful Societies in Ireland (9 Mar., 1825).
NOTE: the reference is to the Act which suppressed the Catholic Association.
REFERRED TO: 70

6 George IV, c. 50. An Act for Consolidating and Amending the Laws Relative to Jurors and Juries (22 June, 1825).
REFERRED TO: 425

6 George IV, c. 59. An Act to Provide for the Extinction of Feudal and Seignioral Rights and Burthens on Lands Held *à Titre de Fief* and *à Titre de Cens*, in the Province of Lower Canada; and for the Gradual Conversion of Those Tenures into the Tenure of Free and Common Soccage; and for Other Purposes Relating to the Said Province (22 June, 1825).
REFERRED TO: 429n-30n

6 George IV, c. 109. An Act for the Encouragement of British Shipping and Navigation (5 July, 1825).
NOTE: replaced the Navigation Laws enacted during the reign of Charles II, which were repealed by 6 George IV, c. 105 (1825).
REFERRED TO: 138, 144

6 George IV, c. 114. An Act to Regulate the Trade of the British Possessions Abroad (5 July, 1825).
NOTE: the references are to the Reciprocity Act.
REFERRED TO: 123, 126, 128-9, 135-9, 144, 146

7 George IV, c. 46. An Act for the Better Regulating Copartnerships of Certain Bankers in England; and for Amending So Much of an Act of the Thirty Ninth and Fortieth Years of the Reign of His Late Majesty King George the Third, Intituled An Act for Establishing an Agreement with the Governor and Company of the Bank of England, for Advancing the Sum of Three Millions towards the Supply for the Service of the Year One Thousand Eight Hundred, as Relates to the Same (26 May, 1826).
NOTE: the reference is to the law of partnership, of which this formed a part.
REFERRED TO: 487

7 & 8 George IV, Private Acts, c. 35. An Act for Dividing, Allotting, Inclosing, and Exonerating from Tithes, Lands in the Hamlet of Penge, in the Parish of Battersea in the County of Surrey (14 June, 1827).

NOTE: the reference is to Cator's Penge-wood inclosure bill.
REFERRED TO: 249

7 & 8 George IV, c. 57. An Act to Permit, until 1st May, 1828, Certain Corn, Meal, and Flour to Be Entered for Home Consumption (2 July, 1827).
NOTE: the reference at 358, in a quotation from Fonblanque (writing in 1827), is presumably to this Act. For other Corn Laws, see 55 George III, c. 26 (1815); 3 George IV, c. 60 (1822); and 9 George IV, c. 60 (1828) (all included in the reference at 340).
REFERRED TO: 340, 358

9 George IV, c. 17. An Act for Repealing So Much of Several Acts as Imposes the Necessity of Receiving the Sacrament of the Lord's Supper as a Qualification for Certain Offices and Employments (9 May, 1828).
NOTE: the reference at 186-8 is to parliamentary oaths, one of which this Act provided for; those at 195, 230, and 377 are to the repeal of the Test Acts.
REFERRED TO: 186-8, 195, 230, 377

9 George IV, c. 60. An Act to Amend the Laws Relating to the Importation of Corn (15 July, 1828).
NOTE: the reference at 358 is in a quotation from Fonblanque. Most of the references are to the Corn Laws; this was in effect when most of the articles in this volume were written. For other Corn laws, see 55 George III, c. 26 (1815); 3 George IV, c. 60 (1822); and 7 & 8 George IV, c. 57 (1827).
REFERRED TO: 153, 183, 186, 193, 198, 199, 219, 224, 252, 340, 348, 358, 378, 389, 394, 397, 400, 470, 472, 475-6, 485

10 George IV, c. 7. An Act for the Relief of His Majesty's Roman Catholic Subjects (13 Apr., 1829).
NOTE: the reference at 186-8 is to parliamentary oaths, one of which this Act provided for; those at 363 and 377 are in quotations from Fonblanque.
REFERRED TO: 186-8, 195, 363, 377, 511, 530

1 William IV, c. 64. An Act to Permit the General Sale of Beer and Cyder by Retail in England (23 July, 1830).
REFERRED TO: 233

1 & 2 William IV, c. 35. An Act to Explain and Amend an Act for Regulating the Receipt and Future Appropriation of Fees and Emoluments Receivable by Officers of the Superior Courts of Common Law (15 Oct., 1831).
NOTE: one of Brougham's law reforms.
REFERRED TO: 303

1 & 2 William IV, c. 56. An Act to Establish a Court in Bankruptcy (20 Oct., 1831).
REFERRED TO: 303

2 William IV, c. 22 (1832). See under Statutes, Canada.

2 William IV, c. 34. An Act Consolidating and Amending the Laws against Offences Relating to the Coin (23 May, 1832).
NOTE: one of Brougham's law reforms.
REFERRED TO: 303

2 William IV, c. 39. An Act for Uniformity of Process in Personal Actions in His Majesty's Courts of Law at Westminster (23 May, 1832).
NOTE: one of Brougham's law reforms.
REFERRED TO: 303

2 & 3 William IV, c. 45. An Act to Amend the Representation of the People in England and Wales (7 June, 1832).
NOTE: the reference at 232 concerns the registration provisions of the Reform Act, clauses 37-60; that at 269 is in a quotation from the *Examiner*; that at 339 is in a quotation from Walsh.

REFERRED TO: 151, 152, 155, 161, 186, 191, 224, 232, 233, 250, 253, 263-4, 269, 283-6, 299, 303, 313, 321, 322, 331, 338, 339, 340, 343, 345, 365, 383-4, 388, 400, 430, 467, 470, 473, 479-80, 481

2 & 3 William IV, c. 51. An Act to Regulate the Practice and the Fees in the Vice Admiralty Courts Abroad, and to Obviate Doubts as to Their Jurisdiction (23 June, 1832).
NOTE: one of Brougham's law reforms.
REFERRED TO: 303

2 & 3 William IV, c. 62. An Act for Abolishing the Punishment of Death in Certain Cases, and Substituting a Lesser Punishment in Lieu Thereof (11 July, 1832).
NOTE: one of Brougham's law reforms.
REFERRED TO: 303

2 & 3 William IV, c. 110. An Act for the Better Regulation of the Duties to Be Performed by the Officers on the Plea or Common Law Side of the Court of Exchequer (15 Aug., 1832).
NOTE: one of Brougham's law reforms.
REFERRED TO: 303

2 & 3 William IV, c. 116. An Act to Provide for the Salaries of Certain High and Judicial Officers, and of Payments Heretofore Made out of the Civil List Revenues (16 Aug., 1832).
NOTE: one of Brougham's law reforms.
REFERRED TO: 303

2 & 3 William IV, c. 119. An Act to Amend Three Acts Passed Respectively in the Fourth, Fifth, and in the Seventh and Eighth Years of His Late Majesty King George the Fourth, Providing for the Establishing of Compositions for Tithes in Ireland; and to Make Such Compositions Permanent (16 Aug., 1832).
REFERRED TO: 169

2 & 3 William IV, c. 122. An Act for Making Provision for the Lord High Chancellor of England in Lieu of Fees Heretofore Received by Him (16 Aug., 1832).
NOTE: one of Brougham's law reforms.
REFERRED TO: 303

2 & 3 William IV, c. 123. An Act for Abolishing the Punishment of Death in Certain Cases of Forgery (16 Aug., 1832).
NOTE: one of Brougham's law reforms.
REFERRED TO: 303

3 William IV, c. 4. An Act for the More Effectual Suppression of Local Disturbances and Dangerous Associations in Ireland (2 Apr., 1833).
NOTE: the references at 254 and 264-5 are to the renewal of this Act by 4 & 5 William IV, c. 38 (1834).
REFERRED TO: 156, 254, 264-5

3 & 4 William IV, c. 27. An Act for the Limitation of Actions and Suits Relating to Real Property, and for Simplifying the Remedies for Trying the Rights Thereto (24 July, 1833).
NOTE: one of the reforms in property law carried through by Sir John Campbell.
REFERRED TO: 224

3 & 4 William IV, c. 37 (1833). See, under Parliamentary Papers, "A Bill to Alter and Amend the Laws" (11 Mar., 1833).

3 & 4 William IV, c. 41. An Act for the Better Administration of Justice in His Majesty's Privy Council (14 Aug., 1833).
NOTE: one of Brougham's law reforms.
REFERRED TO: 303

3 & 4 William IV, c. 42. An Act for the Further Amendment of the Law, and the Better Advancement of Justice (14 Aug., 1833).
NOTE: one of the reforms in property law carried through by Sir John Campbell.
REFERRED TO: 224

3 & 4 William IV, c. 44. An Act to Repeal so Much of Two Acts of the Seventh and Eighth Years and the Ninth Year of George the Fourth as Inflicts the Punishment of Death upon Persons Breaking, Entering, and Stealing in a Dwelling House; also for Giving Power to the Judges to Add to the Punishment of Transportation for Life in certain Cases of Forgery, and in Certain Other Cases (14 Aug., 1833).
NOTE: one of Brougham's law reforms.
REFERRED TO: 303

3 & 4 William IV, c. 67. An Act to Amend an Act of the Second Year of His Present Majesty, for the Uniformity of Process in Personal Actions in His Majesty's Courts of Law at Westminster (28 Aug., 1833).
NOTE: one of Brougham's law reforms.
REFERRED TO: 303

3 & 4 William IV, c. 73. An Act for the Abolition of Slavery Throughout the British Colonies; for Promoting the Industry of the Manumitted Slaves; and for Compensating the Persons Hitherto Entitled to the Services of Such Slaves (28 Aug., 1833).
NOTE: the reference at 179 is in a quotation from JSM; those at 283 and 303 are to the Slave Bill.
REFERRED TO: 179, 283, 303

3 & 4 William IV, c. 74. An Act for the Abolition of Fines and Recoveries, and for the Substitution of More Simple Modes of Assurance (28 Aug., 1833).
NOTE: one of the reforms in property law carried through by Sir John Campbell.
REFERRED TO: 224

3 & 4 William IV, c. 84. An Act to Provide for the Performance of the Duties of Certain Offices Connected with the Court of Chancery Which Have Been Abolished (28 Aug., 1833).
NOTE: one of Brougham's law reforms.
REFERRED TO: 303

3 & 4 William IV, c. 85. An Act for Effecting an Arrangement with the East India Company, and for the Better Government of His Majesty's Indian Territories, till the Thirtieth Day of April One Thousand Eight Hundred and Fifty-Four (28 Aug., 1833).
NOTE: the references are to the East India Bill.
REFERRED TO: 283, 303

3 & 4 William IV, c. 103. An Act to Regulate the Labour of Children and Young Persons in the Mills and Factories of the United Kingdom (29 Aug., 1833).
REFERRED TO: 232

3 & 4 William IV, c. 104. An Act to Render Freehold and Copyhold Estates Assets for the Payment of Simple and Contract Debts (29 Aug., 1833).
NOTE: one of the reforms in property law carried through by Sir John Campbell.
REFERRED TO: 224

3 & 4 William IV, c. 105. An Act for the Amendment of the Law Relating to Dower (29 Aug., 1833).
NOTE: one of the reforms in property law carried through by Sir John Campbell.
REFERRED TO: 224

3 & 4 William IV, c. 106. An Act for the Amendment of the Law of Inheritance (29 Aug., 1833).
NOTE: one of the reforms in property law carried through by Sir John Campbell.
REFERRED TO: 224

4 & 5 William IV, c. 36. An Act for Establishing a New Court for the Trial of Offences Committed in the Metropolis and Parts Adjoining (25 July, 1834).
NOTE: the reference at 279 is to the enlargement of "the jurisdiction of the Old Bailey"; that at 303 is to Brougham's law reforms.
REFERRED TO: 279, 303

4 & 5 William IV, c. 38. An Act to Continue, under Certain Modifications, to the First Day of August One Thousand Eight Hundred and Thirty-Five, an Act of the Third Year of His Present Majesty, for the More Effectual Suppression of Local Disturbances and Dangerous Associations in Ireland (30 July, 1834).
REFERRED TO: 254, 264-5

4 & 5 William IV, c. 41. An Act to Regulate the Appointment of Ministers to Churches in Scotland Erected by Voluntary Contribution (30 July, 1834).
NOTE: the reference is to a regulation adopted by the General Assembly of the Church of Scotland, a regulation upon which this statute was based.
REFERRED TO: 245

4 & 5 William IV, c. 76. An Act for the Amendment and Better Administration of the Laws Relating to the Poor in England and Wales (14 Aug., 1834).
NOTE: the references at 171-2, 201, 203-5, 213-14, 224, 235, 238-41, 252, 257-8, 265-6, 272, and 272n are to the Bill which, when enacted, became this statute; that at 485 is in a quotation from Bulwer. Some references involve matters going back to 43 Elizabeth, c. 2 (1601).
REFERRED TO: 171-2, 201, 203-5, 213-14, 224, 235, 238-41, 252, 257-8, 265-6, 272, 272n, 279, 283, 283n-4n, 285, 323-4, 394, 398, 399, 485

4 & 5 William IV, c. 84. An Act to Apply a Sum of Money out of the Consolidated Fund and the Surplus of Grants to the Service of the Year One Thousand Eight Hundred and Thirty-Four, and to Appropriate the Supplies Granted in This Session of Parliament (15 Aug., 1834).
NOTE: the references are to the purchase of two Correggio paintings by the British government and a grant towards the construction of the National Gallery, provided for by section 17 of this statute.
REFERRED TO: 249, 328

4 & 5 William IV, c. 85. An Act to Amend an Act Passed in the First Year of His Present Majesty, to Permit the General Sale of Beer and Cider by Retail in England (15 Aug., 1834).
NOTE: the references at 233-5, 255 and 271-2 are to the Bill that, when enacted, became this statute.
REFERRED TO: 233-5, 255, 271-2, 272n, 279

4 & 5 William IV, c. 94. An Act to Enable His Majesty to Invest Trading and Other Companies with the Powers Necessary for the Due Conduct of Their Affairs, and for the Security of the Rights and Interests of Their Creditors (15 Aug., 1834).
NOTE: the reference is to the Bill that, when enacted, became this statute.
REFERRED TO: 248n

5 & 6 William IV, c. 76. An Act to Provide for the Regulation of Municipal Corporations in England and Wales (9 Sept., 1835).
NOTE: the references are to the Bill that, when enacted, became this statute.
REFERRED TO: 301, 302-3, 317

6 & 7 William IV, c. 54 (1836). See, under Parliamentary Papers, "A Bill to Reduce the Stamp Duties" (19 July, 1836).

6 & 7 William IV, c. 71. An Act for the Commutation of Tithes in England and Wales (13 Aug., 1836).
NOTE: provided for the appointment of Tithe Commissioners to carry out the functions referred to by JSM.
REFERRED TO: 526-7

6 & 7 William IV, c. 77 (1836). See, under Parliamentary Papers, "A Bill for Carrying into Effect the Fourth Report" (8 July, 1836).

6 & 7 William IV, c. 85 (1836). See, under Parliamentary Papers, "A Bill for Marriages in England," 6 William IV (17 Feb., 1836).

6 & 7 William IV, c. 86 (1836). See, under Parliamentary Papers, "A Bill for Registering Births, Deaths and Marriages in England," 6 William IV (17 Feb., 1836).

1 Victoria, c. 9. An Act to Make Temporary Provision for the Government of Lower Canada (10 Feb., 1838).
NOTE: though ostensibly reviewed at 405-35, the Bill which led to the Act is not there specifically mentioned.
REVIEWED: 405-35
REFERRED TO: 442

1 Victoria, c. 10. An Act to Make Good Certain Contracts Which Have Been or May Be Entered into by Certain Banking and Other Copartnerships (20 Feb., 1838).
NOTE: the reference is to the law of partnership, of which this statute formed a part.
REFERRED TO: 487

1 & 2 Victoria, c. 96. An Act to Amend, until the End of the Next Session of Parliament, the Law Relative to Legal Proceedings by Certain Joint Stock Banking Companies Against Their Own Members, and by Such Members Against the Companies (14 Aug., 1838).
NOTE: the reference is to the law of partnership, of which this statute formed a part.
REFERRED TO: 487

8 & 9 Victoria, c. 25. An Act to Amend Two Acts Passed in Ireland for the Better Education of Persons Professing the Roman Catholic Religion, and for the Better Government of the College Established at Maynooth for the Education of Such Persons, and also an Act Passed in the Parliament of the United Kingdom for Amending the Said Two Acts (30 June, 1845).
REFERRED TO: 531

27 & 28 Victoria, c. 77. An Act to Repeal and in Part to Re-enact Certain Acts of Parliament Relating to the Ionian States, and to Establish the Validity of Certain Things Done in the Said States (29 July, 1864).
NOTE: the reference is to Britain's relinquishing rule of the Ionian Islands.
REFERRED TO: 520

30 Victoria, c. 3. An Act for the Union of Canada, Nova Scotia, and New Brunswick, and the Government Thereof; and for Purposes Connected Therewith (29 Mar., 1867).
NOTE: this indirect reference is to the British North America Act.
REFERRED TO: 524

31 Victoria, c. 3 (1867). See, under Parliamentary Papers, "A Bill to Confirm a Provisional Order" (22 Nov., 1867).

32 & 33 Victoria, c. 42. An Act to Put an End to the Establishment of the Church of Ireland, and to Make Provision in Respect of the Temporalities Thereof, and in Respect of the Royal College of Maynooth (26 July, 1869).
REFERRED TO: 530, 531

AMERICAN

1st Congress, Sess. II, c. 30. An Act Imposing Duties on the Tonnage of Ships or Vessels (20 July, 1790).
NOTE: the first of the Navigation Laws of the United States.
REFERRED TO: 138, 141, 142

14th Congress, Sess. II, c. 31. An Act Concerning the Navigation of the United States (1 Mar., 1817).
NOTE: one of the Navigation Laws of the United States.
REFERRED TO: 138, 141, 142

15th Congress, Sess. I, c. 70. An Act Concerning Navigation (18 Apr., 1818).
NOTE: this Act, together with 16th Congress, Sess. I, c. 122 (1820), prohibited "the circuitous intercourse" between Great Britain and her colonies through the United States referred to by JSM at 145-6; the references at 138-42 are to the Navigation Laws of the United States, of which this was one.
REFERRED TO: 128, 135, 138-42, 145-6

16th Congress, Sess. I, c. 122. An Act Supplementary to an Act, Entitled "An Act Concerning Navigation" (15 May, 1820).
NOTE: this Act, together with 15th Congress, Sess. I, c. 70 (1818), prohibited "the circuitous intercourse" between Great Britain and her colonies through the United States, referred to by JSM at 145-6; the references at 138-42 are to the Navigation Laws of the United States, of which this was one.
REFERRED TO: 128, 135, 138-42, 145-6

17th Congress, Sess. I, c. 56. An Act in Addition to the Act Concerning Navigation, also to Authorize the Appointment of Deputy Collectors (6 May, 1822).
NOTE: the temporary Act which authorized the President to open trade to British vessels on terms of reciprocity; replaced by 17th Congress, Sess. II, c. 22 (1823).
REFERRED TO: 141

17th Congress, Sess. II, c. 22. An Act to Regulate the Commercial Intercourse between the United States and Certain British Colonial Ports (1 Mar., 1823).
NOTE: referred to as the Alien Duty by JSM; the first reference at 126 is in a quotation from Canning; the second reference at 140 is in a quotation from Huskisson. This act replaced 17th Congress, Sess. I, c. 56 (1822).
REFERRED TO: 125-6, 127, 138-44, 145

18th Congress, Sess. I, c. 136. An Act to Amend the Several Acts Imposing Duties on Imports (22 May, 1824).
NOTE: the reference is to the United States' tariff law.
REFERRED TO: 139

AUSTRO-HUNGARIAN

Gesetzartikel XII v.J.1867, über die zwischen den Ländern der ungarischen Krone und den übrigen unter der Regierung Sr. Majestät stehenden Ländern obschwebenden gemeinsamen Angelegenheiten und über den Modus ihrer Behandlung. In Samuel Rado-Rothfeld, *Die ungarische Verfassung geschichtlich dargestellt mit einem Anhang: die wichtigsten Verfassungs-gesetze.* Berlin: Puttkammer and Mühlbrecht, 1898, 190-203.
REFERRED TO: 524, 525

CANADIAN

1 William IV, c. 52 (Lower Canada). An Act to Incorporate the City of Quebec (12 Apr., 1832).
NOTE: the municipal institutions acts were due for renewal on 1 May, 1836. The House of Assembly passed two bills on 7 Mar., 1836, that extended the powers of the incorporated cities. After the rejection of these bills by the Legislative Council, the House, on 12 Mar., 1836, passed a bill to continue the incorporation acts in their existing form. This too was rejected by the Council.
REFERRED TO: 424

1 William IV, c. 54 (Lower Canada). An Act to Incorporate the City of Montreal (12 Apr., 1832).
NOTE: see note to 1 William IV, c. 52 (Lower Canada).
REFERRED TO: 424

2 William IV, c. 22 (Lower Canada). An Act to Regulate the Qualification and Summoning of Jurors in Criminal and Civil Matters (25 Feb., 1832). In *The Provincial Statutes of Lower Canada*, Vol. 14. Quebec: Fisher and Kemble, 1832, 408-28.
REFERRED TO: 425

6 William IV, c. 30 (Lower Canada). An Act for the Encouragement of Education in This Province (21 Mar., 1836). In *The Provincial Statutes of Lower Canada*, Vol. 15. Quebec: Fisher and Kemble, 1835-36, 244-54.
REFERRED TO: 427

1 Victoria, c. 19 (Lower Canada) (4 May, 1838). See Colborne, "An Ordinance. . . ."

2 Victoria, c. 1 (Lower Canada) (28 June, 1838). See Lambton, "An Ordinance. . . ."

FRENCH

Ordonnance du roi qui suspend la liberté de la presse périodique et semi-périodique (no. 15135; 25 juillet, 1830). In *Bulletin des lois du royaume de France*, 8me sér., XII, Bulletin 367, 33-4.
REFERRED TO: 312

Ordonnance du roi qui dissout la chambre des députés des départemens (no. 15136; 25 juillet, 1830). *Ibid.*, 35.
REFERRED TO: 312

Ordonnance du roi qui réforme, selon les principes de la charte constitutionnelle, les règles d'élection, et prescrit l'exécution de l'article 46 de la charte (no. 15137; 25 juillet, 1830). *Ibid.*, 35-9.
REFERRED TO: 312

Ordonnance du roi qui convoque les colléges électoraux d'arrondissement pour le 6 septembre prochain, les colléges de département pour le 13, et la chambre des pairs et celle des députés pour le 28 du même mois (no. 15138; 25 juillet, 1830). *Ibid.*, 39-40.
REFERRED TO: 312

Loi sur les associations (no. 261; 10 avril, 1834). In *Bulletin*, 9me sér., 1re partie, VI, Bulletin 115, 25-6.
REFERRED TO: 208

SCOTTISH

(Includes non-statutory material printed in *The Acts of the Parliaments of Scotland*.)

James I, 1621, c. 1. "A Ratification of the Fyve Articles of the Generall Assemblie of the Kirk Holden at Pearthe in the Moneth of August 1618." In *The Acts of the Parliaments of Scotland*. Ed. T. Thomson and C. Innes. 12 vols. Edinburgh: "By Command," 1814-75, IV, 596-7.
REFERRED TO: 24, 26, 27

Charles I (1628-29). "Submissions and Surrenders of Teinds, &c. with His Majestie's Decreets Following Thereupon." *Ibid.*, V, 189-207.
NOTE: not an Act.
REFERRED TO: 24

Charles I (1630). "Ratification of the King's Decreets upon the Submissions." *Ibid.*, V, 209-26.
NOTE: not an Act.
REFERRED TO: 24

Charles I, 1633, c. 3. "Anent His Majesties Royall Prerogative and Apparell of Kirkmen." *Ibid.*, V, 20-1.
REFERRED TO: 24

Charles I, 1633, c. 9. "The Kings General Revocatione." *Ibid.*, V, 23.
NOTE: the revocation, of Oct., 1625, was confirmed during Charles I's visit to Scotland in 1633.
REFERRED TO: 24

Charles I (1633). "Domini electi ad articulos." *Ibid.*, V, 9-10.
NOTE: not an Act.
REFERRED TO: 24

Charles I (1639). "Minutes Done in the Articles, Sep. 16-19, A.D. 1639." *Ibid.*, V, 599.
NOTE: not an Act; the minutes provided that an act be drawn up.
REFERRED TO: 27

Charles I (1639). "Domini electi ad articulos." *Ibid.*, V, 253-4.
NOTE: not an Act.
REFERRED TO: 24

Charles I, 1640, c. 12. "Act Statuarie Appoynting Parliaments to Be Holden Once Everie Three Yeir." *Ibid.*, V, 268.
REFERRED TO: 27

Charles I, 1640, c. 18. "Act Anent the Ratification of the Covenant and of the Assemblies Supplication Act of Counsell and Act of Assemblie Concerning the Covenant." *Ibid.*, V, 270-6.
REFERRED TO: 25, 51

Charles I, 1640, c. 19. "Anent the Ratification of the Actes of the Assemblie." *Ibid.*, V, 276-7.
REFERRED TO: 27

Charles I, 1640, c. 21. "Act Anent the Choosing of Committies out of Everie Estate." *Ibid.*, V, 278-9.
REFERRED TO: 27

Charles I, 1641, c. 21. "Act Anente the Election of the Officers of Estate Counselloures and Sessionars." *Ibid.*, V, 354-5.
REFERRED TO: 38

Charles I, 1648, c. 94. "Act Anent Outreik of the Levie of Horse and Foote with the List of the Collonellis and Thair Proportiounes Thereof." *Ibid.*, VI, Pt. ii, 53-6.
REFERRED TO: 52

Index

References to *Parliamentary Papers* and statute law will be found in the Bibliographic Index (Appendix D above). The Appendices are not indexed, except for references (given in italics) in Appendix A that do not appear in *England and Ireland*.

ADMIRALTY, interference in coopers' strike by, 207
Agriculture, in Ireland, 514, 515
America. *See* United States
Aristocracy: in Scotland, 23, 244; and popular party of Presbyterians and Independents, 39, 47; in Ireland, 65, 67, 70, 88n, 89-90, 216; and Game Laws, 101-2; and reform, 151, 155, 474; and fundholders, 174; philosophy of, 184-5; as debtor, 185; and Church of England, 287, 325, 471, 474; and public opinion, 291; opposed to democratic principle, 300; and Reform Bill, 322; and taste, 328; Walsh on Tory, 338; English attitute to, 339, 358; Radicalism and, 353, 389, 402-3; Fonblanque on, 354, 355-6, 358-9; and Toryism, 402; power in House of Commons of, 447-8; professions associated with, 474; and middle classes, 476; and Christianity, 493; mentioned, 23, 102, 241, 277. *See also* Classes, upper
Army, discipline in, 268-70
Asia, 447
Atlantic, 383
Austria: union of with Hungary, 524-6; mentioned, 64, 471

BALLOT: need for in Ireland, 88-9; importance of, 299, 300-1; Tories and, 299, 322; Melbourne's government and, 299, 300, 303, 388, 390, 391-2, 409-ll, 413; Radicals and, 342, 383-4, 389, 390, 397, 409-11, 409n, 413, 467, 481; Fonblanque on, 354, 376; and tenants-at-will, 472-3; mentioned, 297, 313, 338, 375, 377, 379, 404, 472. *See also* Suffrage

Baltic, timber from, 326
Beer Houses, regulation of, 213-14, 233-5, 255, 271-2
Belgium, 515, 522
Bermuda, 440, 454
Bigotry: Hume on English, 13; Laud's, 19; Charles I's, 24; English religious, 501
Birmingham, 312
Bishop's Stortford, 105, 106
Brighton, 328

CAMBRIDGE UNIVERSITY: and Dissenters, 196; education at, 259; degrees from, 260; and Christianity, 260-1
Canada: trade of with British West Indies, 143, 143n, 144; bad timber from, 326; Radicals and, 413-14; insurrection in, 413-17, 415n-16n, 419, 425-6, 430-1, 441, 449-50; England and, 413-14, 415n-16n, 416-28, 429n-30n, 434-5, 525; Lord Durham and, 414, 416, 426, 429-30, 431, 433-4, 439-43, 447-64, 452n-4n, 455n, 456n, 458n, 481; *Westminster Review* and, 420; demands of, 420-1; English party in, 421, 426-8, 450, 462; government in, 422-34, 424n, 461; English and French in, 422-3, 426-32, 429n-30n, 450, 452, 454, 455n, 456-7, 456n, 458-9, 461; packing of juries in, 425; feudal tenure in, 429n-30n; Loyalists in, 430-1, 450, 453, 456n; mentioned, 388, 392, 408
Capital and labour, 131-2, 486
Catholic Association (Ireland): activities of, 68-9, 72; Protestant aristocracy and, 70; complaints against, 71, 73-5, 74n; inflammatory language of, 71, 72; levying money

670   INDEX

by, 73-4; and administration of justice, 75, 76; mentioned, 62, 82

Catholic claims and disabilities: justice of, 63; discussed in House of Commons, 76, 78-9; and treaty of Limerick, 77-8; and Church of England, 80-1; mentioned, 62, 469

Catholic emancipation (Ireland): arguments against, 63-5, 83; effects of, 66-7, 79n; discussed in House of Commons, 76, 78-9, 81-2, 90-1; mentioned, 63, 67, 68, 377

Catholics. *See* Roman Catholics

Cavaliers. *See* Royalists

Chartists, 478, 482, 489

Chelmsford, 106

Christ Church, Oxford, 347

Christianity: character of English, 246-7, 251, 260-1; aristocracy and, 493; Church of England as bulwark of, 493; mentioned, 435

Church of England: Laud's influence on, 19; and persecution, 20, 64; and Catholic claims, 80-1; and disestablishment, 153, 194-5, 212; political oaths and, 187-8; and State, 197, 211-12, 225-6, 230, 250, 286; and religious instruction, 226-8, 245, 484; as sectarian, 229-30; and Church of Scotland, 244-5; at Oxford, 250; reform of, 279, 325, 393-4, 494-5; aristocracy and, 287, 325, 471, 474; Walsh on, 335n; Fonblanque on, 354, 377-8; Radicals and, 389, 494; and Dissenters, 395; Toryism of, 402; Reformers in, 477, 489, 490, 491, 492; liberals in, 479, 490; and Voluntaries, 481, 490, 491-2; High Church party in, 490; Low Church party in, 491; as bulwark of Christianity, 493; preferred by infidels and indifferents, 493; mentioned, 21, 64, 86, 260, 270, 271, 286-7, 340, 477, 479

Church of Ireland: clergy of, 93; and tithes, 170, 262, 394-5; Grey on, 252; need for reform of, 301-2, 389, 394-5, 494; House of Lords and, 302; Tories and, 335; Walsh on, 335n-6n; moderate Radicals and, 494; mentioned, 63, 72, 97, 286, 297, 530, 531

Church of Scotland: history of, 244-5; and Church of England, 244-5; government of, 244; as People's Church, 397

Circumstances, and political leadership, 315, 386, 519

Clare, county of, 516

Classes, labouring: and upper classes, 153, 207, 214, 219, 220, 485; Trades' Unions and, 190; and law of property, 190-1; education of, 200; demoralization of, 203-4, 256; and government, 207, 233; morality of, 213-14; and Beer Houses, 234-5; and Parliamentary Radicals, 396; as Radicals, 467, 478; as Disqualified Classes, 470, 478; and Universal Suffrage, 481-3, 488-9; grievances of, 483-5, 489; and Political Unions, 486; Owenism of, 486; and Trade Societies, 486; and Benefit Clubs, 486; effect of Co-operatives on, 487; and middle classes, 487-8, 489; Lord Durham and, 488-9; mentioned, 479

Classes, middle: and house tax, 161, 162; press and, 218-19, 220; Fonblanque on, 355, 356-7; Radicals in, 389, 475, 476; and aristocracy, 475-6; and reform, 475-6; and Universal Suffrage, 482, 483, 485, 487-9; and government, 483, 487-8; and labouring classes, 487-8, 489; mentioned, 479, 508

Classes, upper: and reform, 151, 155, 389, 474; and labouring classes, 153, 207, 214, 220, 486; and house tax, 162; political truth and, 190; in House of Commons, 191; as privileged (or satisfied) classes, 469-70, 470-1, 473, 474; Liberalism of, 473-4; in Ireland, 522; mentioned, 509. *See also* Aristocracy

Commerce: nature and objects of, 129-31; consumer and, 130-2; principle of reciprocity in, 130, 133-4, 138-43; capital in, 132. *See also* Shipping, Trade

Conservative party: and Radicalism, 407, 467, 468, 469; and privileged classes, 469-70, 470-2, 474-5; and landowning, 472, 474, 475; common aim of, 479; and Ireland, 514; mentioned, 194, 285, 468. *See also* Tories

Conservatives. *See* Conservative party

Constitution, British: Walsh on, 339; mentioned, 95, 240, 340

Co-operation, and the production of wealth, 190-1

Co-operatives, effect of on labouring classes, 487

Corn Laws: Whig Ministry (Grey) and, 153, 224; Peel on, 193, 358; effects of, 198-9, 475; landlords and, 198-9, 470-1, 472; Fonblanque on, 378; moderate Radicals and, 389; mentioned, 178, 219, 252, 340, 348, 358, 379, 394. *See also* App. D, Statutes

Cornwall, 473

Council of York, 29, 32, 35

INDEX 671

Covenanters (Scotland): and Charles I, 26; and Argyle, 36; as bigotted Presbyterians, 47
Croyden, 250
Cumberland, 472

DANISH CLAIMS, 238
Derby: strike at, 210-11; mentioned, 292
Devonshire, 292, 299, 410
Dissenters: Whig promises to, 195; and tithes, 195-6, 211-12; and Church of England, 230, 394; and marriage ceremony, 232; and admission to universities, 259-61, 270; as natural Radicals, 477; and Church reform, 490, 493, 495; Tories and, 493; mentioned, 194, 279, 312, 341, 479. *See also* Voluntaries
Disqualified classes. *See* Classes, labouring
Divorce, 248
Dorchester, 209
Dorsetshire, 105, 113
Dorsetshire labourers, sentencing of, 207, 209
Dublin, 531

EDINBURGH, 254, 342, 472
Education: and individual's interests, 4; and normal schools, 199, 201; quality of English, 199-200; Brougham on national, 200, 225; need for public investigation of, 200-1; and State, 226-7; moral, 227-8; object of, 228-9; House of Commons and national, 254; at Oxford and Cambridge, 259
England: wealthy merchant class in, 23; popular party in (17th century), 38, 39; institutions in, 61-2; stage of moral improvement in, 62; misunderstanding of Ireland in, 88, 501-2, 508, 509, 511, 513, 514, 521, 529-30; electors in, 90; gaols in, 105, 107; offences against Game Laws in, 119; tithes in, 153, 170, 195-9, 213-14, 325-6, 340; newspapers in, 163-4; landlords in, 170-2, 470-2, 515-16; union of with Ireland, 215; government of Ireland by, 216-18, 499-503, 507, 508-12, 513, 514, 517, 519-21, 525, 529-30, 532; attitude to law in, 217; administration in, 231-2; and Church of Ireland, 262-3; character of people in, 267, 328, 339, 392-3; and reform, 312, 321-2, 340, 407; popular government in, 321; Fonblanque on morality in, 363, 364; political temper of, 389; and Canada, 413-14, 415n-16n, 416-28, 429n-30n, 434-5, 447, 450, 451-2, 454, 524-5; political situation (1838) in, 447-8; reaction to Lord Durham in, 454; Revolution of 1688 in, 462; sympathy for Canada in, 464; farmers in, 472; Catholics in, 507-8; attitude to institutions in, 511, 513, 517; economic conditions of, 514-17; and government of India, 519; sympathy in for repressed nationalities, 520; United States and, 521-2, 523; Liberalism in, 523; mentioned, 197, 215, 240, 252, 263, 265, 268, 275, 402, 404, 411, 450. *See also* Great Britain
Europe: and Ireland, 520; mentioned, 298, 321, 336n, 337n, 348, 391, 447, 487, 514, 515, 517, 532

FANATICISM, 8
Fear, effect of on reasoning, 62
Fenianism: nature of, 508-11; England and, 509-11; mentioned, 531, 532
France: Protestants in, 13; circulation of newspapers between England and, 157-8; centralization in, 206; Trades' Unions in, 207-8; government of, 221-2; *régistres de l'état civil* in, 231; army in, 269; 1789 Revolution in, 322, 401, 473, 482, 503; Fonblanque on 1789 Revolution in, 368; *métayers* in, 515; and Ireland, 518, 523; population of, 528; mentioned, 17, 64, 215, 260, 414, 471, 472, *539*
Fundholders: pillage of, 172-8; and landlords, 174-5; Radicals and, 175-6, 400; mentioned, 347

GAME LAWS: reform of, 101, 109, 111, 114; landlords and, 102, 114-16; and poaching, 103-13 *passim*; resident gentry and, 117-18; effects of, 213; mentioned, 340, 483-4
Genius, contrasted with talent, 352
Germany: Protestants in, 13; mentioned, 17, 260
Glamorganshire, 473
Glasgow, 488
Gloucestershire, 106
Government: resistance to, 9; James I and, 10-11; Charles I and, 11-15, 19-20; role of thinking in, 159; principle of good, 203; duty of, 207; and morals, 213-14, 229; principle of representative, 221; and science, 242-3; Fonblanque on ballot and good, 354; Fonblanque on duty of, 378; English an oligarchy of landlords, 470-1; experiment and, 482; rational and moral conditions of, 518
 local: and House of Commons, 249-50; analysis of, 302, 303, 304-6

672 INDEX

Great Britain: and international trade, 123-30, 132-8, 139n, 140-7; and United States, 126-9; reform in, 460; and Reform party, 468; agriculture in, 514, 515-16; and Ireland, 523-6; mentioned, 115, 260, 468, 517, 522. *See also* England, Scotland, Wales

Greek Orthodox Church, and persecution, 64

HANOVER, *538*

Hindus, character of, 519

History: Brodie on Hume's, 5, 55; sources for 17th-century, 5-7; use of sources in, 6; Brodie's, 9, 58

  Hume's: truth in, 3, 5, 12, 20n, 21, 28-9, 32, 36-7, 40, 42, 43-4, 45n, 49, 51, 52n, 57; as romance, 3-4, 34-5; treatment of sources in, 6-8, 43-6, 48-9, 53-5; arts in, 7-9, 14-15, 57n; defence of Charles I in, 8, 13, 16-18, 25-6, 30, 34, 46, 51, 52-4, 52n; inconsistency of, 14, 18, 33n; defence of Strafford in, 32-4

House of Commons: and Charles I, 12, 14-15, 17-19, 28, 38-9, 41-2, 44; and Popery, 13; Hume on, 13, 17; and Strafford, 29-34; moderation of, 29n; General Fast and, 48; and Catholic emancipation, 66-8, 76, 78-9, 84, 85-6, 523-4; rhetorical artifice in, 93-4; and Game Laws, 102, 104n, 107, 108n, 117-18; and poaching, 103-13 *passim*; and shipping, 123, 140; morality of, 155-7, 237-8; attendance in, 158-60; members' responsibilities in, 158-9, 248; vulgarity of, 162-3; Radicals in, 165-6, 297-8, 314-15, 345, 384, 385, 386-7, 395-6, 404, 448, 478; landlords and, 184, 470, 477; public opinion and, 185-6, 411; and reform, 191, 286-7; and Dissenters, 195-6, 211; and Poor Law Commission Report, 203-4; and local government, 249-50; and national education, 254; and Church of Ireland, 302; Tories and, 313, 322, 343, 383; Walsh on, 339; Whigs in, 344-5; Whig Ministry and, 344-5; Fonblanque on, 354, 357, 358, 368, 377; and Canada, 417-22, 452, 457-8; and Lord Durham, 439, 448; labouring classes and, 489; and Ireland, 508; mentioned, 43, 181, 193, 203, 215, 275, 279, 292, 301, 302, 304, 313, 340, 345, 473. *See also* Parliament

House of Lords: and Charles I, 18, 38-9; General Fast and, 48; and Catholic emancipation, 65, 67, 79; and Game Laws, 101, 108; landlords and, 170, 470; and Dissenters, 195-6; and national education, 201-2; religious prejudice in, 251; and Church of Ireland, 252-3, 302; and spirit of the age, 253; on crime, 256; and stamps on newspapers, 261; and Poor Law reform, 265; and Church of England, 270; and tithes, 276-7; appellate judicature of, 278; function of, 279; and reform, 286-7, 312, 313, 315, 324, 341; reform of, 313, 338; press and, 317; and Whig Ministry, 344; Radicals and, 345, 389; Fonblanque on, 354, 357-8, 365-6, 368; and Canada, 419, 427, 439, 452; and Lord Durham, 439, 460, 461; and Ireland, 516n; mentioned, 22, 116, 279, 292, 308, 385. *See also* Parliament

Hungary, union of with Austria, 524-6

IMPRESSMENT, 178, 180-1

Improvement, Walsh on innovation and, 332-3

Independents: and Presbyterians, 47, 49-51, 53-4; republican tenets of, 47; leaders of, 47, 57n; power of during Civil War, 48-50, 53; and Royalists, 50, 53-4; and Charles I, 51; mentioned, 48, 56, 57. *See also* Popular party (17th century)

India: English rule of, 216, 519; and Ireland, 217; mentioned, 392, 524

Institutions: and interests of public men, 61-2; effect of, 62, 227; Whig Ministry and, 241

Intellect: status of, 241-3; in affairs of nations, 315

Intelligence, nature of English, 154

Interest: general, 3, 72, 186, 190, 224, 250, 353, 355, 478; sinister, 53, 340; power of, 61, 64, 80, 81, 112, 214, 469, 476; of the few, 65, 68, 72, 101, 185, 186, 353, 355, 474-5; commercial, 130-1; government and, 207; Fonblanque on sinister, 357-8, 378

Inverness, 299

Ionian Islands, government of, 520

Ireland: Charles I and, 48-9, 50; 1825 parliamentary proceedings on, 61-98; Catholics in, 62, 95, 336n, 495, 507-9; Catholic emancipation and, 62, 95; poverty in, 66; landlords in, 66-7, 88-9, 168-70, 263, 501, 502, 507, 508, 512, 513, 515-17, 516n-17n, 518-19, 527; administration of justice in, 67, 94-5; magistracy of, 67, 79, 95n; division of rich and poor in, 67, 71, 94; tithes in, 67, 153, 168-70, 188n, 262-3, 276-7; aristocracy in, 67, 70, 88n, 89-90, 216; law in, 71, 79, 217, 517; Burdett on, 77; evils in, 79, 94n-5n, 502, 503; employment in, 84; elections in, 87-8; freeholders in, 90, 91; Protestant clergy in, 93,

INDEX

169, 277; Protestants in, 94-6, 253, 262, 336n; Union of with England, 153, 215; land tax in, 168-70; O'Connell and, 314; corporation reform in, 324-5; Walsh on, 335n-7n; subjection of, 340; Radicals and, 412, 413, 477-8; disqualified classes in, 477-8; just rule of, 488, 519-20; English government of, 499-503, 507, 508, 509-12, 513-14, 517, 519-21, 529-32; disaffection in, 501, 507, 508, 509-11, 532-3; condition of farmers in, 501, 502, 508, 514, 516, 517, 529; intolerable social system of, 502, 503; effect of 1789 French Revolution in, 503, 518; revolutionary party in, 503; manufactures in, 507; Fenians in, 508-11; 532; traditions of, 511-13; rights of property in, 512, 513; Whiteboys and Rockites in, 513; English Conservatives' view of, 514; social economy of, 514-16, 519; moral robbery in, 517; United States and, 518, 520, 523; India and, 519; question of separation of from England, 521-6; land rent revision in, 526-7; railways in, 531; mentioned, 28, 69, 279, 337n, 348, 388, 402, 410, 411, 413, 422, 431, 468
Irish Church. *See* Church of Ireland
Isle of Wight, 51, 54
Italy, *métayers* in, 515

JAMAICA, repression in, 520
Jewish emancipation, 322
Journalism: power of, 163-4; training for, 164; anonymity of, 183; Fonblanque's, 352, 353, 379-80; talents required for, 352. *See also* Newspapers, Press
Judicature: proper arrangements for, 278, 305-6, 307; local, 278, 305-6; Bentham as authority on, 306
Juries: English and Irish, 75; Canadian, 425-6
Justice: and Ireland, 66-7, 94-5, 254; and Catholic Association, 74-5; Quarter Sessions and, 272

KENT, 472

LABOUR. *See* Capital and labour
Lambeth Palace, 347
Lancashire, 366, 473
Landlords: in Ireland, 66-7, 89, 168-70, 263, 501, 502, 507, 508, 512, 513, 515-17, 516n-17n, 518-19, 527; and Game Laws, 102, 114; in England, 170-2, 470-2, 515-16; distress of, 170-2, 183-6; in Parliament, 170, 184-6; and Radicals, 174-5; and taxes, 184-5; mortgagees as real, 185; and tithes,

196-9; and Corn Laws, 198-9, 470, 472; power of, 219-20, 470-1, 473, 474, 475; and registration of property, 222-4. *See also* Aristocracy
Libel, law of, 166-7, 192-3, 261-2
Liberal party. *See* Liberals
Liberalism: Lord Durham and, 450; landlords and, 473; England and, 523. *See also* Liberals
Liberals, political: and reform, 342; Fonblanque on, 356, 377; as moderate Radicals, 389; effective popular party of, 448, 449, 467, 473; Lord Durham and, 448, 449; leadership of, 448-9; Whigs among, 467; county electors and, 473, 477; and labouring classes, 482-3; and Ireland, 520. *See also* Radicals, Reform party
Liberty: Hume on, 23; political forms and substance of, 87; English, 161, 206; of the press, 166, 192-3; Whigs and religious, 195-6
Limerick, 507
Liverpool, 304
London: 53, 118, 220, 246, 250, 305, 306, 327, 342, 390, 486; students of University of, 199, 250
London Working Men's Association, and labouring classes, 485, 488
Lords of Articles: James I and, 24; Scottish Parliament and, 27
Lyons, silk workers' strike at, 208

MAGISTRATES: in Ireland, 67, 79, 95n; power misused by, 118-20, 120n, 213, 233-4, 267-8, 272-3, 306-7; and beer houses, 234, 272; and administration of justice, 245-6, 272, 273-4; Marylebone, 245-7; Sussex, 276; Fonblanque on, 358-60, 361; mentioned, 358
Magna Carta, 353
Manchester, 312, 367
Marriage Law, 153
Mauritius, 326
Methodist Conference, 73
Middlesex, 473
Montreal, 426, 453n, 457
Morality, true end of, 4
Movement party: and Parliament, 191, 194-5, 284, 285; and *The Times*, 224-5; leadership of, 346; Walsh on, 346; principles and purposes of, 347, 481; and moderate Radicalism, 478; mentioned, 244, 276, 314, 340, 468, 479. *See also* Radicals, Reform party
Municipal corporations, 297, 301, 302-5. *See also* Government, local

NATIONALITY, in Ireland, 509
New South Wales, 107
Newspapers: circulation of, 157-8; free interchange of ideas in, 158; power of, 163-4; and Whig Ministry, 182-3, 273; personal enmity in, 202-3; and Poor Law reform, 204-5, 224-5, 240-1, 266; and Trades' Unions, 207, 210-11, 220; and registration, 224-5; stamp duty on, 237, 261-2, 297-9, 302, 326; and Church of Ireland, 252; liberal, 316, 317, 340, 390; Whig and Tory, 408; Canadian, 426, 430. *See also* Journalism, Press
New York State, 328
Norfolk, 113, 495

OATHS: political, 186-8; promissory, 188n
Operatives. *See* Classes, labouring
Orangemen: Christian principles of, 73; Burdett on, 76-7; power of, 76; Walsh on, 336n; mentioned, 71, 322, 411, 412, 430
Owenism, 486
Oxford Movement, 490
Oxford University: Toryism in, 250, 255n; education at, 259; degrees from, 260; and Christianity, 260-1

PAPISTS. *See* Roman Catholics
Paris, 208, 321, 336n
Parliament: Charles I and, 11-19, 28-30, 40, 53; Long, 28-36, 37-42, 44-9, 51-3, 56-7, 57n; factions in (17th century), 47; and Ireland, 61-98, 216; and Catholic emancipation, 65-6, 78-93; and Catholic Association, 68-9, 70, 74; great abuses escape notice in, 68; public opinion and, 80, 222-3; and elective franchise (Ireland), 87; convenience over truth in, 94; and Church of Ireland, 97-8; Reformed, 151-2, 162, 191, 233, 283, 284, 299, 312-13, 347; attendance in, 158-60; and the press, 163-4; landlords in, 184; need for reform of, 185-6, 191; and political oaths, 186-7; employers and, 189-90; mismanagement of public questions in, 222; and reform, 238-41, 313-14; and Radicals, 314-15, 315-16, 338, 384-5; and Tories, 322; and railways, 328; Whigs in, 342, 344-5; Fonblanque on, 361; and Canada, 413-14, 417-22, 430, 432, 434, 451, 459, 462, 525; authority of, 440; and Lord Durham, 457-8, 464; Irish influence in, 508, 523-4; and rule of India, 519; and tithes, 526; mentioned, 44, 50, 181, 202, 222, 260, 261, 277, 301, 302, 304, 323, 331, 340, 371, 386, 391, 398, 470, 481, 482
Pennsylvania, 328
Philosophic Radicals: in Parliament, 191, 212, 241; Fonblanque and, 353-4; definition of, 353. *See also* Radicals, Reform party
Poaching. *See* Game Laws
Poland: rebellion in, 414; and Ireland, 520
Political economy: attack on, 91, 328; capital and labour in, 131-2, 486; and Poor Laws, 266; Owenite of labouring classes, 486; Tory school of, 528; and small properties, 529
Political Unions, and labouring classes, 486
Politics: freedom of discussion in, 166; concessions in, 168; popular control of, 206
Poor Law: reform of, 171-2, 214, 238-40, 265-6, 283, 323; 1834 Commission on, 201, 203-6; effects of, 203-4, 213, 257-8, 265-6; administration of by Central Board, 205-6, 238-9; newspapers and, 224-5, 239-41, 266; House of Lords and, 265; local administration of, 324; Tories and, 398, 399-400; Radicals and, 398-400; mentioned, 152, 279, 394. *See also* App. D, Statutes
Popery: James I and, 10, 10n, 24; Parliament and, 12, 13; Charles I and, 13, 25; Hume on, 21; Scots' hostility to, 25. *See also* Roman Catholic Church
Popular party (17th century): Strafford and, 19; organization of, 25; in Scotland, 38; in England, 38, 39; and aristocracy, 39, 47; Hume on, 43. *See also* Presbyterians and Independents
Popular party (1830s). *See* Liberals, Movement party, Radicals, Reform party
Post Office, 157-8
Presbyterians: James I and church government of, 10; and Charles I, 24; and aristocratic party, 47; Independents and, 47, 49-51, 53-4; in Parliament, 51, 52-3; subjugation of, 57; and persecution, 64; mentioned, 83. *See also* Popular party (17th century)
Press: Parliament and, 163-4; liberty of, 165-8, 192-3, 321; Radical, 174-5, 297, 315, 400; and Whig Ministry, 182-3, 252; employers and, 189-90; middle classes and, 218; and reform, 314; liberal, 316, 317; and Whig Ministry, 316, 317; effect of, 316, 317; on House of Lords, 317; Tory, 331; Whigs and, 342; on Canada, 430n, 450. *See also* Journalism, Newspapers
Privileged classes. *See* Classes, upper
Production: labour and capital in, 131-2; object of, 131. *See also* Commerce, Shipping, Trade

INDEX 675

Property: and the general good, 108; inviolability of, 175; labouring classes and, 178-9, 190-1, 401; power of, 218-20; Radicals and, 218-19, 398, 400, 401, 402; registration of, 222-4; protection to, 258; Church of England and, 286; Fonblanque on, 354, 356; absolute right of in land, 502, 512, 513
Protestant Reformation, 23, 491
Protestants: and Catholics, 63-6, 83-4, 491; allegiance of, 64; in Ireland, 169, 508, 523, *540*; in England, 493, 524
Prussia: education in, 200; religion in, 229; army in, 269; landowners in, 513; mentioned, 37
Public opinion: and Reform Bill, 151; Whigs and, 181, 192, 299; and House of Commons, 185-6, 223; on Dorsetshire labourers, 207-8; on military flogging, 268-70; effect of, 299; resistance to, 300-1; rapid movement of, 311, 313; and House of Lords, 317; expression of, 321
Puritans: James I and, 10; Montague and, 13

QUEBEC, city of, 450

RADICAL PARTY: organization of, 165-6, 403, 408; character of, 327, 384-5, 395-6, 397, 407, 467; and universal suffrage, 397; duties of, 408; and Scotland, 495; and Catholics (Ireland), 495; mentioned, 315, 411. *See also* Reform party, Radicals
Radicalism. *See* Radicals
Radicals: and democracy, 154; and reform, 161, 291, 292, 308, 317, 342-3, 384-5, 468; attitude of to talent, 164, 476-7, 479; and fundholders, 174-6, 347, 400; and Church of England, 194-5, 489-90, 494; and property, 218-19, 399-401, 472; Walsh on, 337; and partiality for familiar institutions, 339; historical, 353; metaphysical, 353; of position, 353; and aristocratical principle, 353; Fonblanque and, 353-4, 361, 378-80; Fonblanque on, 361-2, 364, 377-8; and ballot, 383-4, 409-11, 409n, 467, 481; Tory, 385; leadership of, 386-7, 404, 451, 461, 463, 481, 487, 495; and labouring classes, 396-7, 402, 467; conservative principles of, 399, 400, 402, 407; power of, 401, 449; and middle classes, 402; and aristocracy, 402; and Ireland, 411-13, 494; and Canada, 413; Whig, 467; ultra, 467; diversity of, 478, 479, 481; and authority, 479; mentioned, 213, 243, 285, 312, 338, 341, 342, 469. *See also* Liberals, Movement party, Philosophic Radicals, Reform party
in Parliament during 1830s: and reform, 161, 291, 292, 308, 317, 412-13; organization of, 165-6, 467, 468, 481; faults of omission by, 191-2, 345, 384-5, 396; and Whig Ministries, 283, 297-8, 314-15, 322, 327, 345-6, 379, 383-4, 386-7, 389, 390, 408-13, 463; character of, 301, 385-6, 397-8; strength of, 384-5, 401; popular knowledge of, 384; advice to, 395, 403, 404, 468; and labouring classes, 396-7, 402, 482-3, 487-8; and Poor Law, 398-9; mentioned, 250, 468, 479
moderate: Fonblanque on, 377; character of, 389; and ballot, 413; and Ireland, 413; leadership of, 434; and Radical party, 467; policy of, 479; mentioned, 386
natural: disqualified classes as, 469-70, 478; yeomanry as, 472-3; middle classes as, 475-6; Dissenters as, 476-7; Church of England and, 477; labouring classes as, 478
Railways: and Parliament, 327-8; Irish, 531
Reason, in politics: and Whig Ministry, 154, 179; effect of, 469
Rebellions, when unconquerable, 509
Reform: aristocracy and, 151, 155, 474; Whig Ministries and, 154-5, 472; Radicals and, 161, 291, 292, 308, 317, 342-3, 383-5, 412-13, 468; political, 185-6, 191-2, 339; and Poor Law reform, 238-40; Lord Grey and, 263-5; religious, 279, 325-6, 393-4, 494-5; Lord Durham and, 443; middle classes and, 476
Reform Ministry. *See* Whig Ministry (Grey)
Reform party: JSM's idea of, 467-503; mentioned, 353, 385, 386, 389, 390, 461, 463. *See also* Liberals, Movement party, Philosophic Radicals, Radicals
Reformers. *See* Liberals, Movement party, Radicals, Reform party
Registration: of births, deaths, and marriages, 153, 180, 196, 231, 231n; of seamen, 180; expense of, 180; of property, 223-4; of voters, 232; of births and deaths, 323. *See also* App. D, Statutes
Religion: freedom of discussion in, 166; character of English, 227-8, 260-1, 270-1; state and, 227n; teaching of, 228-9; man of no, 245-7; among educated classes, 247; influence of, 247
Republicans, 241, 242
Restoration, the, 56, 58
Revolution, English, 56, 244
Roman Catholic Church: and arbitrary power, 10; James I and, 10n; Montague and, 12-13; and persecution, 20, 64; clergy of (in Ireland), 63-4, 73-4, 82-3, 84, 85-7, 85n, 88n; doctrines of, 82; mentioned, 491

Roman Catholics: in Ireland, 62, 67, 79, 169, 422, 495, 507-9, 521, 522, 530; hostility to, 63-4, 71, 78; allegiance of, 64; and Protestants, 65, 66, 83, 84; English, 77; and Church of England, 394; and Church reform, 489-90; Tories and, 493; in Parliament, 508, 523-4; on Ireland, 520; mentioned, 312, 479, 494
Romance, and history, 3
Royal Society of London, and Charles II, 255
Royalists: Scottish led by Montrose, 36; and Charles I, 46; insurrection of, 53; mentioned, 50, 54, 56
Runnymede. *See* Magna Carta
Russia: agriculture in, 514; mentioned, 326, 520

ST. BARTHOLOMEW, 136
St. Lawrence River, 433, 458
Saxons, 353
School societies, 200
Scotland: James I and, 10, 24; Charles I and, 24-8, 36-7, 50-2; Covenanters in, 25-6, 36, 47; Parliament in, 26, 27, 37n, 52; Trimmers in, 36; Royalists in, 36; and England, 52; Liberals and Radicals in, 472; natural Radicals in, 477; and Church reform, 495; anti-Catholic feeling in, 524; mentioned, 40, 43, 57, 215, 389, 392, 404, 411, 495, 525
Shipping: benefits of open, 131-4; and consumers, 132-3. *See also* Commerce, Great Britain, Trade, United States
Slavery: impressment as, 178-81; morality of, 180; mentioned, 340
Socinians, 490
Somersetshire, 473
Southampton, 327
Spain, 12, 15, 64, 514, 517
Spirit of the age: signs of, 82, 172-3, 311, 347, 348; and Whig Ministry, 243-4; and reform, 244, 263-4, 291; Tories and, 250; opposition to, 253, 259, 264; mentioned, 62
Staffordshire, 299
Statesmanship: principles of, 151-2, 160, 195-6, 292; of Whig Ministry, 298-9; Fonblanque on, 368-9; test of, 467-8; and religious belief, 492-3
Stroud, 390, 410
Stuart, House of, 9, 525. *See also* App. D under individual kings
Suffolk, 113
Suffrage: universal, 389, 397, 479, 481, 482, 483, 485, 488, 489; household, 467, 481

Surrey, 107, 473
Sussex, 113

TAXATION: 1834 budget and, 160-3; nature of, 161-2; on land (Ireland), 168-70, 277; landlords and, 170-1, 184-5; and national debt (England), 175; on food, 193-4; on newspapers, 237-8, 261-2, 297-9, 302, 326; on imports, 326. *See also* Tithes
Thought, necessity of for action, 69
Tithes: in Ireland, 67, 153, 168-70, 188n, 262-3, 276-7; in England, 153, 170, 195, 197-9, 211-12, 326, 340
Tolerance, religious, 13, 17, 62-3, 78
Tories: and Catholic emancipation, 68, 89, 90-1; in office, 181, 233, 275, 297, 300, 322, 385, 412; and Whigs, 182, 299, 412; philosophy of, 184-5, 335; consistency of, 225; and spirit of the age, 250; in House of Lords, 252; and reform, 291, 292-3, 324, 326, 338-41; public opinion and, 293; and ballot, 299, 301, 391-2; wealth and, 299; and Radicals, 308, 341, 345, 379, 385, 389, 398, 399-400, 401-2, 412, 489, 493; allies of, 321; party spirit of, 322; and Church of Ireland, 335, 335n; in House of Commons, 343, 345; Fonblanque on, 361, 364-6, 375-6, 377, 380; and Whig Ministry, 383, 387, 410-11; and Church of England, 389, 402; in 1831 election, 391; and authority, 396, 478; and Poor Law reform, 398, 400; and established order, 401; among aristocracy, 402, 472, 474; and Ireland, 431; and Lord Durham, 443, 451, 459-60; power of, 447-8; landlords as, 471-2, 476; moderate, 482; and Dissenters, 493; and Roman Catholics, 493; mentioned, 154, 202, 213, 231, 250, 262, 285, 313, 317, 389, 402, 443, 451. *See also* Conservative party
Torres Vedras, 321
Trade: colonial, 124-8, 135, 144-7; rights of, 124-5, 129-30; custom in, 127; triumph of free, 312. *See also* Commerce, Shipping
Trades' Unions: suppression of, 188-91; doctrine of, 189-90; interference with, 206-11; newspapers and, 207, 210-11, 220; in France, 208; precautions against offences from, 209; and oaths, 209-10; Derby manufacturers and, 210-11; and middle classes, 220
Treaty of Limerick, 77
Trimmers, in Scotland, 36
Truth: Hume and, 3; importance of, 93, 256, 354; facilities for diffusion of, 262

Tudors, 10
Tyranny, Charles I and religious, 8

ULSTER, 522
United States: and international trade, 123-9, 133-47; trade of with British West Indies, 125-6, 135, 137, 143-5; and Great Britain, 126-9, 134-47; independence of, 237; education in, 260, 484; War of Independence, 417; and Canada, 432, 451, 454, 462, 464; public opinion in, 450; and Ireland, 520, 523; and England, 521-2, 523; Civil War in, 522; mentioned, 216, 423, 431, 432, 447, 471, 517, 522, *539*
Universities: importance of, 259-60; reform of, 260. *See also* Cambridge, London, Oxford
Utilitarians, protests against, 328

VOLUNTARIES: in Scotland, 477; and Church Reformers, 477, 481, 490, 491-2; and natural Radicals, 479. *See also* Dissenters

WALES: offences against Game Laws in, 119; mentioned, 389, 474
Warwickshire, 473
Waterloo, 321
West Indies (British): trade of with United States, 125-6, 135, 137, 143-5; trade of with Canada, 143, 143n, 144
Whig Ministry (Grey): expectations of, 151-3; and Corn Laws, 153, 224; and reform, 154-5, 192-3, 283, 285, 286, 344; and budget, 160-2; and public opinion, 181, 182-3, 192-3, 221, 243-4; and Radicals, 191-2, 467; and tithes, 196-8; and Poor Law reform, 205, 238-9, 241; and Trades' Unions, 207-8; and stamps on newspapers, 237-8; vulgarity of, 262; changes in, 263-4; and Beer Bill, 271-2; isolation of departments in, 273-5; and Radicals, 283; Walsh on, 339; and Tories, 343; Fonblanque on, 379-80; mentioned, 312-13, 412. *See also* Whigs
Whig Ministry (Melbourne): House of Lords and, 292-3; Radicals and, 297, 315-16, 322, 326, 345, 379, 384-5, 386-9, 390, 407-8, 410-13, 463; and stamps on newspapers, 298-9; and ballot, 299, 300, 303, 388, 390, 391-2, 409-11, 413; and Church of Ireland, 302; and reform, 305-6, 317, 322, 324-5, 326, 344, 384, 392; newspapers and, 316, 390; Fonblanque and, 379-80; and Tories, 383, 410-11; advice to, 387-8, 391-5; and Lord Durham, 429-30; and Liberals, 473-4; mentioned, 298, 344. *See also* Whigs
Whigs: and Catholic emancipation, 68, 89, 90; and reform, 90, 291, 384, 385-6, 387-8, 408-9; philosophy of, 184-5, 335; conservative, 285; and Tories, 293, 297, 299, 412; Walsh on, 342, 343-4; and Liberals, 342; in House of Commons, 344; and Radicals, 347, 384-5, 387-9; Fonblanque on, 364-6, 377; and liberty, 396; and United States, 431; among landlords, 471; in Scotland, 477; mentioned, 202, 213, 262, 297, 308n, 402, 431, 443, 482, 495
  in office: policy of, 152-4; and reform, 154-5, 192, 194-5, 241, 257-8, 284, 285, 291; and Tories, 182; and tithes, 186-9; and Dissenters, 195-6, 211-12, 231; and education, 201-2, 254; and Trades' Unions, 207-8; and aristocracy, 300; mentioned, 238.
  See also Whig Ministry (Grey), Whig Ministry (Melbourne)
Working classes. *See* Classes, labouring

YORKSHIRE, 117, 216, 472, 473